W9-AQE-327

Thinking in Java

Third Edition

Bruce Eckel
President, MindView, Inc.

Comments from readers:

Much better than any other Java book I've seen. Make that "by an order of magnitude"... very complete, with excellent right-to-the-point examples and intelligent, not dumbed-down, explanations ... In contrast to many other Java books I found it to be unusually mature, consistent, intellectually honest, well-written and precise. IMHO, an ideal book for studying Java. **Anatoly Vorobey, Technion University, Haifa, Israel**

One of the absolutely best programming tutorials I've seen for any language. **Joakim Ziegler, FIX sysop**

Thank you for your wonderful, wonderful book on Java. **Dr. Gavin Pillay, Registrar, King Edward VIII Hospital, South Africa**

Thank you again for your awesome book. I was really floundering (being a non-C programmer), but your book has brought me up to speed as fast as I could read it. It's really cool to be able to understand the underlying principles and concepts from the start, rather than having to try to build that conceptual model through trial and error. Hopefully I will be able to attend your seminar in the not-too-distant future. **Randall R. Hawley, Automation Technician, Eli Lilly & Co.**

The best computer book writing I have seen. **Tom Holland**

This is one of the best books I've read about a programming language... The best book ever written on Java. **Ravindra Pai, Oracle Corporation, SUNOS product line**

This is the best book on Java that I have ever found! You have done a great job. Your depth is amazing. I will be purchasing the book when it is published. I have been learning Java since October 96. I have read a few books, and consider yours a "MUST READ." These past few months we have been focused on a product written entirely in Java. Your book has helped solidify topics I was shaky on and has expanded my knowledge base. I have even used some of your explanations as information in interviewing contractors to help our team. I have found how much Java knowledge they have by asking them about things I have learned from reading your book (e.g., the difference between arrays and Vectors). Your book is great! **Steve Wilkinson, Senior Staff Specialist, MCI Telecommunications**

Great book. Best book on Java I have seen so far. **Jeff Sinclair, Software Engineer, Kestral Computing**

Thank you for *Thinking in Java*. It's time someone went beyond mere language description to a thoughtful, penetrating analytic tutorial that doesn't kowtow to The Manufacturers. I've read almost all the others—only yours and Patrick Winston's have found a place in my heart. I'm already recommending it to customers. Thanks again. **Richard Brooks, Java Consultant, Sun Professional Services, Dallas**

Bruce, your book is wonderful! Your explanations are clear and direct. Through your fantastic book I have gained a tremendous amount of Java knowledge. The exercises are also FANTASTIC and do an excellent job reinforcing the ideas explained throughout the chapters. I look forward to reading more books written by you. Thank you for the tremendous service that you are providing by writing such great books. My code will be much better after reading Thinking in Java. I thank you and I'm sure any programmers who will have to maintain my code are also grateful to you. **Yvonne Watkins, Java Artisan, Discover Technologies, Inc.**

Other books cover the WHAT of Java (describing the syntax and the libraries) or the HOW of Java (practical programming examples). *Thinking in Java* is the only book I know that explains the WHY of Java; why it was designed the way it was, why it works the way it does, why it sometimes doesn't work, why it's better than C++, why it's not. Although it also does a good job of teaching the what and how of the language, *Thinking in Java* is definitely the thinking person's choice in a Java book. **Robert S. Stephenson**

Thanks for writing a great book. The more I read it the better I like it. My students like it, too. **Chuck Iverson**

I just want to commend you for your work on *Thinking in Java*. It is people like you that dignify the future of the Internet and I just want to thank you for your effort. It is very much appreciated. **Patrick Barrell, Network Officer Mamco, QAF Mfg. Inc.**

I really, really appreciate your enthusiasm and your work. I download every revision of your online books and am looking into languages and exploring what I would never have dared (C#, C++, Python, and Ruby, as a side effect) . I have at least 15 other Java books (I needed 3 to make both JavaScript and PHP viable!) and subscriptions to Dr. Dobbs, JavaPro, JDJ, JavaWorld, etc., as a result of my pursuit of Java (and Enterprise Java) and certification but I still keep your book in higher esteem. It truly is a thinking man's book. I subscribe to your newsletter and hope to one day sit down and solve some of the problems you extend for the solutions guides for you (I'll buy the guides!) in appreciation. But in the meantime, thanks a lot. **Joshua Long, www.starbuxman.com**

Most of the Java books out there are fine for a start, and most just have beginning stuff and a lot of the same examples. Yours is by far the best advanced thinking book I've seen. Please publish it soon! ... I also bought *Thinking in C++* just because I was so impressed with *Thinking in Java*. **George Laframboise, LightWorx Technology Consulting, Inc.**

I wrote to you earlier about my favorable impressions regarding your *Thinking in C++* (a book that stands prominently on my shelf here at work). And today I've been able to delve into Java with your e-book in my virtual hand, and I must say (in my best Chevy Chase from *Modern Problems*) "I like it!" Very informative and explanatory, without reading like a dry textbook. You cover the most important yet the least covered concepts of Java development: the whys. **Sean Brady**

I develop in both Java and C++, and both of your books have been lifesavers for me. If I am stumped about a particular concept, I know that I can count on your books to a) explain the thought to me clearly and b) have solid examples that pertain to what I am trying to accomplish. I have yet to find another author that I continually whole-heartedly recommend to anyone who is willing to listen. **Josh Asbury, A^3 Software Consulting, Cincinnati, OH**

Your examples are clear and easy to understand. You took care of many important details of Java that can't be found easily in the weak Java documentation. And you don't waste the reader's time with the basic facts a programmer already knows. **Kai Engert, Innovative Software, Germany**

I'm a great fan of your *Thinking in C++* and have recommended it to associates. As I go through the electronic version of your Java book, I'm finding that you've retained the same high level of writing. Thank you! **Peter R. Neuwald**

VERY well-written Java book...I think you've done a GREAT job on it. As the leader of a Chicago-area Java special interest group, I've favorably mentioned your book and Web site several times at our recent meetings. I would like to use *Thinking in Java* as the basis for a part of each monthly SIG meeting, in which we review and discuss each chapter in succession. **Mark Ertes**

By the way, printed TIJ2 in Russian is still selling great, and remains bestseller. Learning Java became synonym of reading TIJ2, isn't that nice? **Ivan Porty, translator and publisher of *Thinking In Java 2nd Edition* in Russian**

I really appreciate your work and your book is good. I recommend it here to our users and Ph.D. students. **Hugues Leroy // Irisa-Inria Rennes France, Head of Scientific Computing and Industrial Tranfert**

OK, I've only read about 40 pages of *Thinking in Java*, but I've already found it to be the most clearly written and presented programming book I've come across...and I'm a writer, myself, so I am probably a little critical. I have *Thinking in C++* on order and can't wait to crack it—I'm fairly new to programming and am hitting learning curves head-on everywhere. So this is just a quick note to say thanks for your excellent work. I had begun to burn a little low on enthusiasm from slogging through the mucky, murky prose of most computer books—even ones that came with glowing recommendations. I feel a whole lot better now. **Glenn Becker, Educational Theatre Association**

Thank you for making your wonderful book available. I have found it immensely useful in finally understanding what I experienced as confusing in Java and C++. Reading your book has been very satisfying. **Felix Bizaoui, Twin Oaks Industries, Louisa, Va.**

I must congratulate you on an excellent book. I decided to have a look at *Thinking in Java* based on my experience with *Thinking in C++*, and I was not disappointed. **Jaco van der Merwe, Software Specialist, DataFusion Systems Ltd, Stellenbosch, South Africa**

This has to be one of the best Java books I've seen. **E.F. Pritchard, Senior Software Engineer, Cambridge Animation Systems Ltd., United Kingdom**

Your book makes all the other Java books I've read or flipped through seem doubly useless and insulting. **Brett g Porter, Senior Programmer, Art & Logic**

I have been reading your book for a week or two and compared to the books I have read earlier on Java, your book seems to have given me a great start. I have recommended this book to a lot of my friends and they have rated it excellent. Please accept my congratulations for coming out with an excellent book. **Rama Krishna Bhupathi, Software Engineer, TCSI Corporation, San Jose**

Just wanted to say what a "brilliant" piece of work your book is. I've been using it as a major reference for in-house Java work. I find that the table of contents is just right for quickly locating the section that is required. It's also nice to see a book that is not just a rehash of the API nor treats the programmer like a dummy. **Grant Sayer, Java Components Group Leader, Ceedata Systems Pty Ltd, Australia**

Wow! A readable, in-depth Java book. There are a lot of poor (and admittedly a couple of good) Java books out there, but from what I've seen yours is definitely one of the best. **John Root, Web Developer, Department of Social Security, London**

I've *just* started *Thinking in Java*. I expect it to be very good because I really liked *Thinking in C++* (which I read as an experienced C++ programmer, trying to stay ahead of the curve). I'm somewhat less experienced in Java, but expect to be very satisfied. You are a wonderful author. **Kevin K. Lewis, Technologist, ObjectSpace, Inc.**

I think it's a great book. I learned all I know about Java from this book. Thank you for making it available for free over the Internet. If you wouldn't have I'd know nothing about Java at all. But the best thing is that your book isn't a commercial brochure for Java. It also shows the bad sides of Java. YOU have done a great job here. **Frederik Fix, Belgium**

I have been hooked to your books all the time. A couple of years ago, when I wanted to start with C++, it was *C++ Inside & Out* which took me around the fascinating world of C++. It helped me in getting better opportunities in life. Now, in pursuit of more knowledge and when I wanted to learn Java, I bumped into *Thinking in Java*—no doubts in my mind as to whether I need some other book. Just fantastic. It is more like rediscovering myself as I get along with the book. It is just a month since I started with Java, and heartfelt thanks to you, I am understanding it better now. **Anand Kumar S., Software Engineer, Computervision, India**

Your book stands out as an excellent general introduction. **Peter Robinson, University of Cambridge Computer Laboratory**

It's by far the best material I have come across to help me learn Java and I just want you to know how lucky I feel to have found it. THANKS! **Chuck Peterson, Product Leader, Internet Product Line, IVIS International**

The book is great. It's the third book on Java I've started and I'm about two-thirds of the way through it now. I plan to finish this one. I found out about it because it is used in some internal classes at Lucent Technologies and a friend told me the book was on the Net. Good work. **Jerry Nowlin, MTS, Lucent Technologies**

Of the six or so Java books I've accumulated to date, your *Thinking in Java* is by far the best and clearest. **Michael Van Waas, Ph.D., President, TMR Associates**

I just want to say thanks for *Thinking in Java*. What a wonderful book you've made here! Not to mention downloadable for free! As a student I find your books invaluable (I have a copy of *C++ Inside Out*, another great book about C++), because they not only teach me the how-to, but also the whys, which are of course very important in building a strong foundation in languages such as C++ or Java. I have quite a lot of friends here who love programming just as I do, and I've told them about your books. They think it's great! Thanks again! By the way, I'm Indonesian and I live in Java. **Ray Frederick Djajadinata, Student at Trisakti University, Jakarta**

The mere fact that you have made this work free over the Net puts me into shock. I thought I'd let you know how much I appreciate and respect what you're doing. **Shane LeBouthillier, Computer Engineering student, University of Alberta, Canada**

I have to tell you how much I look forward to reading your monthly column. As a newbie to the world of object oriented programming, I appreciate the time and thoughtfulness that you give to even the most elementary topic. I have downloaded your book, but you can bet that I will purchase the hard copy when it is published. Thanks for all of your help. **Dan Cashmer, B. C. Ziegler & Co.**

Just want to congratulate you on a job well done. First I stumbled upon the PDF version of *Thinking in Java*. Even before I finished reading it, I ran to the store and found *Thinking in C++*. Now, I have been in the computer business for over eight years, as a consultant, software engineer, teacher/trainer, and recently as self-employed, so I'd like to think that I have seen enough (not "have seen it all," mind you, but enough). However, these books cause my girlfriend to call me a "geek." Not that I have anything against the concept—it is just that I thought this phase was well beyond me. But I find myself truly enjoying both books, like no other computer book I have touched or bought so far. Excellent writing style, very nice introduction of every new topic, and lots of wisdom in the books. Well done. **Simon Goland, simonsez@smartt.com, Simon Says Consulting, Inc.**

I must say that your *Thinking in Java* is great! That is exactly the kind of documentation I was looking for. Especially the sections about good and poor software design using Java. **Dirk Duehr, Lexikon Verlag, Bertelsmann AG, Germany**

Thank you for writing two great books (*Thinking in C++*, *Thinking in Java*). You have helped me immensely in my progression to object oriented programming. **Donald Lawson, DCL Enterprises**

Thank you for taking the time to write a really helpful book on Java. If teaching makes you understand something, by now you must be pretty pleased with yourself. **Dominic Turner, GEAC Support**

It's the best Java book I have ever read—and I read some. **Jean-Yves MENGANT, Chief Software Architect NAT-SYSTEM, Paris, France**

Thinking in Java gives the best coverage and explanation. Very easy to read, and I mean the code fragments as well. **Ron Chan, Ph.D., Expert Choice, Inc., Pittsburgh PA**

Your book is great. I have read lots of programming books and your book still adds insights to programming in my mind. **Ningjian Wang, Information System Engineer, The Vanguard Group**

Thinking in Java is an excellent and readable book. I recommend it to all my students. **Dr. Paul Gorman, Department of Computer Science, University of Otago, Dunedin, New Zealand**

With your book, I have now understood what object oriented programming means. ... I believe that Java is much more straightforward and often even easier than Perl. **Torsten Römer, Orange Denmark**

You make it possible for the proverbial free lunch to exist, not just a soup kitchen type of lunch but a gourmet delight for those who appreciate good software and books about it. **Jose Suriol, Scylax Corporation**

Thanks for the opportunity of watching this book grow into a masterpiece! IT IS THE BEST book on the subject that I've read or browsed. **Jeff Lapchinsky, Programmer, Net Results Technologies**

Your book is concise, accessible and a joy to read. **Keith Ritchie, Java Research & Development Team, KL Group Inc.**

It truly is the best book I've read on Java! **Daniel Eng**

The best book I have seen on Java! **Rich Hoffarth, Senior Architect, West Group**

Thank you for a wonderful book. I'm having a lot of fun going through the chapters. **Fred Trimble, Actium Corporation**

You have mastered the art of slowly and successfully making us grasp the details. You make learning VERY easy and satisfying. Thank you for a truly wonderful tutorial. **Rajesh Rau, Software Consultant**

Thinking in Java rocks the free world! **Miko O'Sullivan, President, Idocs Inc.**

About *Thinking in C++*:

Best Book! Winner of the
1995 Software Development Magazine Jolt Award!

"This book is a tremendous achievement. You owe it to yourself to have a copy on your shelf. The chapter on iostreams is the most comprehensive and understandable treatment of that subject I've seen to date."

Al Stevens
Contributing Editor, *Doctor Dobbs Journal*

"Eckel's book is the only one to so clearly explain how to rethink program construction for object orientation. That the book is also an excellent tutorial on the ins and outs of C++ is an added bonus."

Andrew Binstock
Editor, *Unix Review*

"Bruce continues to amaze me with his insight into C++, and *Thinking in C++* is his best collection of ideas yet. If you want clear answers to difficult questions about C++, buy this outstanding book."

Gary Entsminger
Author, *The Tao of Objects*

"*Thinking in C++* patiently and methodically explores the issues of when and how to use inlines, references, operator overloading, inheritance, and dynamic objects, as well as advanced topics such as the proper use of templates, exceptions and multiple inheritance. The entire effort is woven in a fabric that includes Eckel's own philosophy of object and program design. A must for every C++ developer's bookshelf, *Thinking in C++* is the one C++ book you must have if you're doing serious development with C++."

Richard Hale Shaw
Contributing Editor, PC Magazine

Thinking in Java

Third Edition

Bruce Eckel
President, MindView, Inc.

PRENTICE HALL
Professional Technical Reference
Upper Saddle River, New Jersey 07458
www.phptr.com

Library of Congress Cataloging-in-Publication Data
Eckel, Bruce.
Thinking in Java / Bruce Eckel.--3rd ed.
p. cm.
Includes bibliographical references and index.
ISBN 0-13-100287-2
1. Java (Computer program language) I. Title.
QA76.73.J38 E25 2003
005.13'3--dc21 2002042490
CIP

Acquisitions Editor: Paul Petralia
Editorial/Production Supervision: Nicholas Radhuber
Manufacturing Manager: Maura Zaldivar
Marketing Manager: Bryan Gambrel
Cover Design: Daniel Will-Harris
Interior Design: Daniel Will-Harris, www.will-harris.com

Published by Pearson Education, Inc.
Publishing as Prentice Hall PTR
Upper Saddle River, NJ 07458

Prentice Hall books are widely used by corporations and government agencies for training, marketing, and resale. The publisher offers discounts on this book when ordered in bulk quantities. For more information, contact the Corporate Sales Department at 800-382-3419, fax: 201-236-7141, email: *corpsales@prenhall.com* or write: Corporate Sales Department, Prentice Hall PTR, One Lake Street, Upper Saddle River, New Jersey 07458.

Printed in the United States of America
10 9 8 7 6 5 4 3

ISBN 0-13-100287-2

Pearson Education LTD.
Pearson Education *Australia* PTY, Limited
Pearson Education *Singapore*, Pte. Ltd
Pearson Education *North Asia* Ltd
Pearson Education *Canada*, Ltd.
Pearson Educación de *Mexico*, S.A. de C.V.
Pearson Education-*Japan*
Pearson Education *Malaysia*, Pte. Ltd

Dedication

To the person who, even now,
is creating the next great computer language

Overview

What's Inside

3: Controlling Program Flow 107

4: Initialization & Cleanup 165

Preface

I suggested to my brother Todd, who is making the leap from hardware into programming, that the next big revolution will be in genetic engineering.

We'll have microbes designed to make food, fuel, and plastic; they'll clean up pollution and in general allow us to master the manipulation of the physical world for a fraction of what it costs now. I claimed that it would make the computer revolution look small in comparison.

Then I realized I was making a mistake common to science fiction writers: getting lost in the technology (which is of course easy to do in science fiction). An experienced writer knows that the story is never about the things; it's about the people. Genetics will have a very large impact on our lives, but I'm not so sure it will dwarf the computer revolution (which enables the genetic revolution)—or at least the information revolution. Information is about talking to each other: yes, cars and shoes and especially genetic cures are important, but in the end those are just trappings. What truly matters is how we relate to the world. And so much of that is about communication.

This book is a case in point. A majority of folks thought I was very bold or a little crazy to put the entire thing up on the Web. "Why would anyone buy it?" they asked. If I had been of a more conservative nature I wouldn't have done it, but I really didn't want to write another computer book in the same old way. I didn't know what would happen but it turned out to be the smartest thing I've ever done with a book.

For one thing, people started sending in corrections. This has been an amazing process, because folks have looked into every nook and cranny and caught both technical and grammatical errors, and I've been able to eliminate bugs of all sorts that I know would have otherwise slipped through. People have been simply terrific about this, very often saying "Now, I don't mean this in a critical way..." and then giving me a collection of errors I'm sure I never would have found. I feel like this has been a kind of group process and it has really made the book into something special. Because of the value of this feedback, I have created several incarnations of a system called "BackTalk" to collect and categorize comments.

But then I started hearing "OK, fine, it's nice you've put up an electronic version, but I want a printed and bound copy from a real publisher." I tried very hard to make it easy for everyone to print it out in a nice looking format but that didn't stem the demand for the published book. Most people don't want to read the entire book on screen, and hauling around a sheaf of papers, no matter how nicely printed, didn't appeal to them either. (Plus, I think it's not so cheap in terms of laser printer toner.) It seems that the computer revolution won't put publishers out of business, after all. However, one student suggested this may become a model for future publishing: books will be published on the Web first, and only if sufficient interest warrants it will the book be put on paper. Currently, the great majority of all books are financial failures, and perhaps this new approach could make the publishing industry more profitable.

This book became an enlightening experience for me in another way. I originally approached Java as "just another programming language," which in many senses it is. But as time passed and I studied it more deeply, I began to see that the fundamental intention of this language was different from other languages I had seen up to that point.

Programming is about managing complexity: the complexity of the problem you want to solve, laid upon the complexity of the machine in which it is solved. Because of this complexity, most of our programming projects fail. And yet, of all the programming languages of which I am aware, none of them have gone all-out and decided that their main design goal would be to conquer the complexity of developing and maintaining programs.[1] Of course, many language design decisions were made with complexity in mind, but at some point there were always some other issues that were considered essential to be added into the mix. Inevitably, those other issues are what cause programmers to eventually "hit the wall" with that language. For example, C++ had to be backwards-compatible with C (to allow easy migration for C programmers), as well as efficient. Those are both very useful goals and account for much of the success of C++, but they also expose extra

---

[1] I take this back on the 2nd edition: I believe that the Python language comes closest to doing exactly that. See www.Python.org.

complexity that prevents some projects from being finished (certainly, you can blame programmers and management, but if a language can help by catching your mistakes, why shouldn't it?). As another example, Visual BASIC (VB) was tied to BASIC, which wasn't really designed to be an extensible language, so all the extensions piled upon VB have produced some truly horrible and unmaintainable syntax. Perl is backwards-compatible with Awk, Sed, Grep, and other Unix tools it was meant to replace, and as a result is often accused of producing "write-only code" (that is, after a few months you can't read it). On the other hand, C++, VB, Perl, and other languages like Smalltalk had some of their design efforts focused on the issue of complexity and as a result are remarkably successful in solving certain types of problems.

What has impressed me most as I have come to understand Java is that somewhere in the mix of Sun's design objectives, it appears that there was the goal of reducing complexity *for the programmer*. As if to say "we care about reducing the time and difficulty of producing robust code." In the early days, this goal resulted in code that didn't run very fast (although there have been many promises made about how quickly Java will someday run) but it has indeed produced amazing reductions in development time; half or less of the time that it takes to create an equivalent C++ program. This result alone can save incredible amounts of time and money, but Java doesn't stop there. It goes on to wrap many of the complex tasks that have become important, such as multithreading and network programming, in language features or libraries that can at times make those tasks easy. And finally, it tackles some really big complexity problems: cross-platform programs, dynamic code changes, and even security, each of which can fit on your complexity spectrum anywhere from "impediment" to "show-stopper." So despite the performance problems we've seen, the promise of Java is tremendous: it can make us significantly more productive programmers.

One of the places I see the greatest impact for this is on the Web. Network programming has always been hard, and Java makes it easy (and the Java language designers are working on making it even easier). Network programming is how we talk to each other more effectively and cheaper than we ever have with telephones (email alone has revolutionized many businesses). As we talk to each other more, amazing things begin to happen, possibly more amazing even than the promise of genetic engineering.

In all ways—creating the programs, working in teams to create the programs, building user interfaces so the programs can communicate with the user, running the programs on different types of machines, and easily writing programs that communicate across the Internet—Java increases the communication bandwidth *between people*. I think that the results of the communication revolution may not be seen from the effects of moving large quantities of bits around; we shall see the true revolution because we will all be able to talk to each other more easily: one-on-one, but also in groups and, as a planet. I've heard it suggested that the next revolution is the formation of a kind of global mind that results from enough people and enough interconnectedness. Java may or may not be the tool that foments that revolution, but at least the possibility has made me feel like I'm doing something meaningful by attempting to teach the language.

Preface to the 3rd edition

Much of the motivation and effort for this edition is to bring the book up to date with the Java JDK 1.4 release of the language. However, it has also become clear that most readers use the book to get a solid grasp of the fundamentals so that they can move on to more complex topics. Because the language continues to grow, it became necessary—partly so that the book would not overstretch its bindings—to reevaluate the meaning of "fundamentals." This meant, for example, completely rewriting the "Concurrency" chapter (formerly called "Multithreading") so that it gives you a basic foundation in the core ideas of threading. Without that core, it's hard to understand more complex issues of threading.

I have also come to realize the importance of code testing. Without a built-in test framework with tests that are run every time you do a build of your system, you have no way of knowing if your code is reliable or not. To accomplish this in the book, a special unit testing framework was created to show and validate the output of each program. This was placed in Chapter 15, a new chapter, along with explanations of *ant* (the defacto standard Java build system, similar to *make*), JUnit (the defacto standard Java unit testing framework), and coverage of logging and assertions (new in JDK 1.4), along with an introduction to debugging and profiling. To encompass all these concepts, the new chapter is named "Discovering Problems," and it introduces what I now believe are fundamental skills that all Java programmers should have in their basic toolkit.

In addition, I've gone over every single example in the book and asked myself, "why did I do it this way?" In most cases I have done some modification and improvement, both to make the examples more consistent within themselves and also to demonstrate what I consider to be best practices in Java coding (at least, within the limitations of an introductory text). Examples that no longer made sense to me were removed, and new examples have been added. A number of the existing examples have had very significant redesign and reimplementation.

The 16 chapters in this book produce what I think is a fundamental introduction to the Java language. The book can feasibly be used as an introductory course. But what about the more advanced material?

The original plan for the book was to add a new section covering the fundamentals of the "Java 2 Enterprise Edition" (J2EE). Many of these chapters would be created by my friends and associates who work with me on seminars and other projects, such as Andrea Provaglio, Bill Venners, Chuck Allison, Dave Bartlett, and Jeremy Meyer. When I looked at the progress of these new chapters, and the book deadline I began to get a bit nervous. Then I noticed that the size of the first 16 chapters was effectively the same as the size of the second edition of the book. And people sometimes complain this is already too big.

Readers have made many, many wonderful comments about the first two editions of this book, which has naturally been very pleasant for me. However, every now and then, someone will have complaints, and for some reason one complaint that comes up periodically is "the book is too big." In my mind it is faint damnation indeed if "too many pages" is your only gripe. (One is reminded of the Emperor of Austria's complaint about Mozart's work: "Too many notes!" Not that I am in any way trying to compare myself to Mozart.) In addition, I can only assume that such a complaint comes from someone who is yet to be acquainted with the vastness of the Java language itself and has not seen the rest of the books on the subject. Despite this, one of the things I have attempted to do in this edition is trim out the portions that have become obsolete, or at least nonessential. In general, I've tried to go over everything, remove from the third edition what is no longer necessary, include changes, and improve everything I could. I feel comfortable removing portions because the original material remains on the Web site (*www.BruceEckel.com*) and the CD ROM that accompanies this book, in the form of the freely downloadable first and second editions of the book. If you want the old stuff, it's still available, and this is a wonderful relief for an author. For example, the "Design Patterns" chapter became too big and has been moved into a book of its own: *Thinking in Patterns (with Java)* (also downloadable at the Web site).

I had already decided that when the next version of Java (JDK 1.5) is released from Sun, which will presumably include a major new topic called *generics* (inspired by C++ templates), I would have to split the book in two in order to add that new chapter. A little voice said "why wait?" So, I decided to do it for this edition, and suddenly everything made sense. I *was* trying to cram too much into an introductory book.

The new book isn't a second volume, but rather a more advanced topic. It will be called *Thinking in Enterprise Java*, and it is currently available (in some form) as a free download from *www.BruceEckel.com*. Because it is a separate book, it can expand to fit the necessary topics. The goal, like *Thinking in Java*, is to produce a very understandable coverage of the basics of the J2EE technologies so that the reader is prepared for more advanced coverage of those topics. You can find more details in Appendix C.

For those of you who still can't stand the size of the book, I do apologize. Believe it or not, I have worked hard to keep it small. Despite the bulk, I feel like there may be enough alternatives to satisfy you. For one thing, the book is available electronically, so if you carry your laptop, you can put the book on that and add no extra weight to your daily commute. If you're really into slimming down, there are actually Palm Pilot versions of the book floating around. (One person told me he would read the book on his Palm in bed with the backlighting on to keep from annoying his wife. I can only hope that it helps send him to slumberland.) If you need it on paper, I know of people who print a chapter at a time and carry it in their briefcase to read on the train.

Java 2, JDK 1.4

The releases of the Java JDK are numbered 1.0, 1.1, 1.2, 1.3, and for this book, 1.4. Although these version numbers are still in the "ones," the standard way to refer to any version of the language that is JDK 1.2 or greater is to call it "Java 2." This indicates the very significant changes between "old Java"—which had many warts that I complained about in the first edition of this book—and this more modern and improved version of the language, which has far fewer warts and many additions and nice designs.

This book is written for Java 2, in particular JDK 1.4 (much of the code will not compile with earlier versions, and the build system will complain and stop if you try). I have the great luxury of getting rid of all the old stuff and writing to only the new, improved language, because the old information still exists in the earlier editions, on the Web, and on the CD ROM. Also, because anyone can freely download the JDK from java.sun.com, it means that by writing to JDK 1.4, I'm not imposing a financial hardship on anyone by forcing them to upgrade.

Previous versions of Java were slow in coming out for Linux (see *www.Linux.org*), but that seems to have been fixed, and new versions are released for Linux at the same time as for other platforms—now even the Macintosh is starting to keep up with more recent versions of Java. Linux is a very important development in conjunction with Java, because it is quickly becoming the most important server platform out there—fast, reliable, robust, secure, well-maintained, and free, it's a true revolution in the history of computing (I don't think we've ever seen all of those features in any tool before). And Java has found a very important niche in server-side programming in the form of *Servlets* and *JavaServer Pages* (JSPs), technologies that are huge improvements over the traditional *Common Gateway Interface* (CGI) programming (these and related topics are covered in *Thinking in Enterprise Java*).

Introduction

"He gave man speech, and speech created thought, Which is the measure of the Universe"—*Prometheus Unbound*, Shelley

> *Human beings ... are very much at the mercy of the particular language which has become the medium of expression for their society. It is quite an illusion to imagine that one adjusts to reality essentially without the use of language and that language is merely an incidental means of solving specific problems of communication and reflection. The fact of the matter is that the "real world" is to a large extent unconsciously built up on the language habits of the group.*
>
> *The Status Of Linguistics As A Science*, 1929, Edward Sapir

Like any human language, Java provides a way to express concepts. If successful, this medium of expression will be significantly easier and more flexible than the alternatives as problems grow larger and more complex.

You can't look at Java as just a collection of features—some of the features make no sense in isolation. You can use the sum of the parts only if you are thinking about *design*, not simply coding. And to understand Java in this way, you must understand the problems with it and with programming in general. This book discusses programming problems, why they are problems, and the approach Java has taken to solve them. Thus, the set of features that I explain in each chapter are based on the way I see a particular type of problem being solved with the language. In this way I hope to move you, a little at a time, to the point where the Java mindset becomes your native tongue.

Throughout, I'll be taking the attitude that you want to build a model in your head that allows you to develop a deep understanding of the language; if you encounter a puzzle, you'll be able to feed it to your model and deduce the answer.

Prerequisites

This book assumes that you have some programming familiarity: you understand that a program is a collection of statements, the idea of a subroutine/function/macro, control statements such as "if" and looping constructs such as "while," etc. However, you might have learned this in many places, such as programming with a macro language or working with a tool like Perl. As long as you've programmed to the point where you feel comfortable with the basic ideas of programming, you'll be able to work through this book. Of course, the book will be *easier* for the C programmers and more so for the C++ programmers, so don't count yourself out if you're not experienced with those languages—but come willing to work hard (also, the multimedia CD that accompanies this book will bring you up to speed in the fundamentals necessary to learn Java). However, I will be introducing the concepts of object-oriented programming (OOP) and Java's basic control mechanisms.

Although references will often be made to C and C++ language features, these are not intended to be insider comments, but instead to help all programmers put Java in perspective with those languages, from which, after all, Java is descended. I will attempt to make these references simple and to explain anything that I think a non- C/C++ programmer would not be familiar with.

Learning Java

At about the same time that my first book *Using C++* (Osborne/McGraw-Hill, 1989) came out, I began teaching that language. Teaching programming languages has become my profession; I've seen nodding heads, blank faces, and puzzled expressions in audiences all over the world since 1987. As I began giving in-house training with smaller groups of people, I discovered something during the exercises. Even those people who were smiling and nodding were confused about many issues. I found out, by creating and chairing the C++ track at the Software Development Conference for a number of years (and later creating and chairing the Java track), that I and other speakers tended to give the typical audience too many topics too quickly. So eventually, through both variety in the audience level and the way that I presented the material, I would end up losing some portion of the audience. Maybe it's asking too much, but because I am one of those people resistant to traditional lecturing (and for most people, I believe, such resistance results from boredom), I wanted to try to keep everyone up to speed.

For a time, I was creating a number of different presentations in fairly short order. Thus, I ended up learning by experiment and iteration (a technique that also works well in Java program design). Eventually, I developed a course using everything I had learned from my teaching experience. It tackles the learning problem in discrete, easy-to-digest steps, and in a hands-on seminar (the ideal learning situation), there are exercises following each of the short lessons. My company MindView, Inc. now gives this as the public and in-house *Thinking in Java* seminar; this is our main introductory seminar that provides the foundation for our more advanced seminars. You can find details at *www.MindView.net*. (The introductory seminar is also available as the *Hands-On Java* CD ROM. Information is available at the same Web site.)

The feedback that I get from each seminar helps me change and refocus the material until I think it works well as a teaching medium. But this book isn't just seminar notes; I tried to pack as much information as I could within these pages, and structured it to draw you through onto the next subject. More than anything, the book is designed to serve the solitary reader who is struggling with a new programming language.

Goals

Like my previous book *Thinking in C++*, this book has come to be structured around the process of teaching the language. In particular, my motivation is to create something that provides me with a way to teach the language in my own seminars. When I think of a chapter in the book, I think in terms of what makes a good lesson during a seminar. My goal is to get bite-sized pieces that can be taught in a reasonable amount of time, followed by exercises that are feasible to accomplish in a classroom situation.

My goals in this book are to:

1. Present the material one simple step at a time so that you can easily digest each concept before moving on.

2. Use examples that are as simple and short as possible. This sometimes prevents me from tackling "real world" problems, but I've found that beginners are usually happier when they can understand every detail of an example rather than being impressed by the scope of the problem it solves. Also, there's a severe limit to the amount of code that can be absorbed in a classroom situation. For this I will no doubt

receive criticism for using "toy examples," but I'm willing to accept that in favor of producing something pedagogically useful.

3. Carefully sequence the presentation of features so that you're exposed to a topic before you see it in use. Of course, this isn't always possible; in those situations, a brief introductory description is given.

4. Give you what I think is important for you to understand about the language, rather than everything I know. I believe there is an information importance hierarchy, and that there are some facts that 95 percent of programmers will never need to know—details that just confuse people and increase their perception of the complexity of the language. To take an example from C, if you memorize the operator precedence table (I never did), you can write clever code. But if you need to think about it, it will also confuse the reader/maintainer of that code. So forget about precedence, and use parentheses when things aren't clear.

5. Keep each section focused enough so that the lecture time—and the time between exercise periods—is small. Not only does this keep the audience's minds more active and involved during a hands-on seminar, but it gives the reader a greater sense of accomplishment.

6. Provide you with a solid foundation so that you can understand the issues well enough to move on to more difficult coursework and books.

JDK HTML documentation

The Java language and libraries from Sun Microsystems (a free download from *java.sun.com*) come with documentation in electronic form, readable using a Web browser, and virtually every third-party implementation of Java has this or an equivalent documentation system. Almost all the books published on Java have duplicated this documentation. So you either already have it or you can download it, and unless necessary, this book will not repeat that documentation, because it's usually much faster if you find the class descriptions with your Web browser than if you look them up in a book (and the on-line documentation is probably more up-to-date). You'll simply be referred to "the JDK documentation." This book will provide extra descriptions of the classes only when it's necessary to supplement that documentation so you can understand a particular example.

Chapters

This book was designed with one thing in mind: the way people learn the Java language. Seminar audience feedback helped me understand the difficult parts that needed illumination. In the areas where I got ambitious and included too many features all at once, I came to know—through the process of presenting the material—that if you include a lot of new features, you need to explain them all, and this easily compounds the student's confusion. As a result, I've taken a great deal of trouble to introduce the features as few at a time as possible.

The goal, then, is for each chapter to teach a single feature, or a small group of associated features, without relying on features that haven't been introduced yet. That way you can digest each piece in the context of your current knowledge before moving on.

Here is a brief description of the chapters contained in the book, that correspond to lectures and exercise periods in the *Thinking in Java* seminar.

Chapter 1: Introduction to Objects

(*Corresponding lecture on the CD ROM*). This chapter is an overview of what object-oriented programming is all about, including the answer to the basic question "What is an object?" It looks at interface versus implementation, abstraction and encapsulation, messages and methods, inheritance and composition, and the subtle concept of polymorphism. You'll also get an overview of issues of object creation such as constructors, where the objects live, where to put them once they're created, and the magical garbage collector that cleans up the objects that are no longer needed. Other issues will be introduced, including error handling with exceptions, multithreading for responsive user interfaces, and networking and the Internet. You'll learn what makes Java special and why it's been so successful.

Chapter 2: Everything is an Object

(*Corresponding lecture on the CD ROM*). This chapter moves you to the point where you can write your first Java program. It begins with an overview of the essentials: the concept of a *reference* to an object; how to create an object; an introduction to primitive types and arrays; scoping and the way objects are destroyed by the garbage collector; how everything in Java is a new data type (class); the basics of creating your own classes; methods, arguments, and return values; name visibility and using components from other libraries; the **static** keyword; and comments and embedded documentation.

Chapter 3: *Controlling Program Flow*

(*Corresponding set of lectures on the CD ROM: Thinking in C*). This chapter begins with all of the operators that come to Java from C and C++. In addition, you'll discover common operator pitfalls, casting, promotion, and precedence. This is followed by the basic control-flow and selection operations that you get with virtually any programming language: choice with **if-else**, looping with **for** and **while**, quitting a loop with **break** and **continue** as well as Java's labeled **break** and labeled **continue** (which account for the "missing goto" in Java), and selection using **switch**. Although much of this material has common threads with C and C++ code, there are some differences.

Chapter 4: *Initialization & Cleanup*

(*Corresponding lecture on the CD ROM*). This chapter begins by introducing the constructor, which guarantees proper initialization. The definition of the constructor leads into the concept of method overloading (since you might want several constructors). This is followed by a discussion of the process of cleanup, which is not always as simple as it seems. Normally, you just drop an object when you're done with it, and the garbage collector eventually comes along and releases the memory. This portion explores the garbage collector and some of its idiosyncrasies. The chapter concludes with a closer look at how things are initialized: automatic member initialization, specifying member initialization, the order of initialization, **static** initialization, and array initialization.

Chapter 5: *Hiding the Implementation*

(*Corresponding lecture on the CD ROM*). This chapter covers the way that code is packaged together, and why some parts of a library are exposed while other parts are hidden. It begins by looking at the **package** and **import** keywords, that perform file-level packaging and allow you to build libraries of classes. It then examines the subject of directory paths and file names. The remainder of the chapter looks at the **public**, **private,** and **protected** keywords, the concept of *package access*, and what the different levels of access control mean when used in various contexts.

Chapter 6: *Reusing Classes*

(*Corresponding lecture on the CD ROM*). The simplest way to reuse a class is to embed an object inside your new class with *composition*. However, composition isn't the only way to make new classes from existing ones. The concept of inheritance is standard in virtually all OOP languages. It's a way to take an existing class and add to its functionality (as well as change it—the subject of Chapter 7). Inheritance is often a way to reuse code by leaving the "base class" the same and just patching things here and there to produce what you want. In this chapter you'll learn how composition and inheritance reuse code in Java, and how to apply them.

Chapter 7: *Polymorphism*

(*Corresponding lecture on the CD ROM*). On your own, you might take nine months to discover and understand polymorphism, a cornerstone of OOP. Through small, simple examples, you'll see how to create a family of types with inheritance and manipulate objects in that family through their common base class. Java's polymorphism allows you to treat all objects in this family generically, which means that the bulk of your code doesn't rely on specific type information. This makes your code more flexible, so building programs and code maintenance is easier and cheaper.

Chapter 8: *Interfaces & Inner Classes*

Java provides special tool to set up design and reuse relationships: the *interface*, which is a pure abstraction of the interface of an object. The **interface** is more than just an abstract class taken to the extreme, since it allows you to perform a variation on C++'s "multiple inheritance" by creating a class that can be upcast to more than one base type.

At first, inner classes look like a simple code-hiding mechanism; you place classes inside other classes. You'll learn, however, that the inner class does more than that; it knows about and can communicate with the surrounding class. The kind of code you can write with inner classes is more elegant and clear. However, it is a new concept to most, and it takes some time to become comfortable with design using inner classes.

Chapter 9: Error Handling with Exceptions

The basic philosophy of Java is that badly-formed code will not be run. As much as possible, the compiler catches problems, but sometimes a problem—either a programmer error or a natural error condition that occurs as part of the normal execution of the program—can be detected and dealt with only at run time. Java has *exception handling* to deal with any problems that arise while the program is running. This chapter examines how the keywords **try**, **catch**, **throw**, **throws**, and **finally** work in Java, when you should throw exceptions, and what to do when you catch them. In addition, you'll see Java's standard exceptions, how to create your own, what happens with exceptions in constructors, and how exception handlers are discovered during an exception.

Chapter 10: Detecting Types

Java run-time type identification (RTTI) lets you find the exact type of an object when you have a reference to only the base type. Normally, you'll want to intentionally ignore the exact type and let Java's dynamic binding mechanism (polymorphism) implement the correct behavior for that type. But occasionally, it is very helpful to know the exact type of an object for which you have only a base reference. Often this information allows you to perform a special-case operation more efficiently. This chapter also introduces the Java *reflection* mechanism. You'll learn what RTTI and reflection are for and how to use them, and also how to get rid of RTTI when it doesn't belong there.

Chapter 11: Collections of Objects

It's a fairly simple program that has only a fixed quantity of objects with known lifetimes. In general, your programs will always be creating new objects at a variety of times that will be known only while the program is running. In addition, you won't know until run time the quantity or even the exact type of the objects you need. To solve the general programming problem, you need to create any number of objects anywhere, at any time. This chapter explores in depth the collections library that Java supplies to hold objects while you're working with them: the simple arrays and more sophisticated containers (data structures) such as **ArrayList** and **HashMap**.

Chapter 12: The Java I/O System

Theoretically, you can divide any program into three parts: input, process, and output. This implies that I/O (input/output) is an important part of the equation. In this chapter you'll learn about the different classes that Java provides for reading and writing files, blocks of memory, and the console. The evolution of the Java I/O framework and the JDK 1.4 "new" I/O (**nio**) will be examined. In addition, this chapter shows how you can take an object, "stream" it (so that it can be placed on disk or sent across a network), and then reconstruct it, which is handled for you with Java's *object serialization*. Java's compression libraries, which are used in the Java ARchive (JAR) file format, are examined. Finally, the new preferences application program interface (API) and regular expressions are explained.

Chapter 13: Concurrency

Java provides a built-in facility to support multiple concurrent subtasks, called *threads*, running within a single program. (Unless you have multiple processors on your machine, this is only the *appearance* of multiple subtasks.) Although these can be used anywhere, threads are most apparent when trying to create a responsive user interface so, for example, a user isn't prevented from pressing a button or entering data while some processing is going on. This chapter gives you a solid grounding in the fundamentals of concurrent programming.

Chapter 14: Creating Windows and Applets

Java comes with the Swing GUI library, which is a set of classes that handle windowing in a portable fashion. These windowed programs can either be World Wide Web applets or standalone applications. This chapter is an introduction to the creation of programs using Swing. Applet signing and *Java Web Start* are demonstrated. Also, the important *JavaBeans* technology is introduced, which is fundamental for the creation of Rapid Application Development (RAD) program-building tools.

Chapter 15: ***Discovering Problems***

Language-checking mechanisms can take us only so far in our quest to develop a correctly-working program. This chapter presents tools to solve the problems that the compiler doesn't. One of the biggest steps forward is the incorporation of *automated unit testing*. For this book, a custom testing system was developed to ensure the correctness of the program output, but the defacto standard **JUnit** testing system is also introduced. Automatic building is implemented with the open-source standard Ant tool, and for teamwork, the basics of CVS are explained. For problem reporting at run time, this chapter introduces the Java *assertion* mechanism (shown here used with *Design by Contract*), the logging API, debuggers, profilers, and even doclets (which can help discover problems in source code).

Chapter 16: ***Analysis & Design***

The object-oriented paradigm is a new and different way of thinking about programming, and many people have trouble at first knowing how to approach an OOP project. Once you understand the concept of an object, and as you learn to think more in an object-oriented style, you can begin to create "good" designs that take advantage of all the benefits that OOP has to offer. This chapter introduces the ideas of analysis, design, and some ways to approach the problems of developing good object-oriented programs in a reasonable amount of time. Topics include Unified Modeling Language (UML) diagrams and associated methodology, use cases, Class-Responsibility-Collaboration (CRC) cards, iterative development, *Extreme Programming* (XP), ways to develop and evolve reusable code, and strategies for transition to object-oriented programming.

Appendix A: ***Passing & Returning Objects***

Since the only way you talk to objects in Java is through references, the concepts of passing an object into a method and returning an object from a method have some interesting consequences. This appendix explains what you need to know to manage objects when you're moving in and out of methods, and also shows the **String** class, which uses a different approach to the problem.

Appendix B: Java Programming Guidelines

This appendix contains suggestions that I have discovered and collected over the years to help guide you while performing low-level program design and writing code.

Appendix C: Supplements

Descriptions of additional learning material available from MindView:

1. The CD ROM that's in the back of this book, which contains the *Foundations for Java* seminar-on-CD, to prepare you for this book.
2. The *Hands-On Java* CD ROM, 3rd Edition, available at *www.MindView.net*. A seminar-on-CD that's based on the material in this book.
3. The *Thinking in Java Seminar*. The MindView, Inc., main introductory seminar based on the material in this book. Schedule and registration pages can be found at *www.MindView.net*.
4. *Thinking in Enterprise Java*, a book that covers more advanced Java topics appropriate to enterprise programming. Available at *www.MindView.net*.
5. *The J2EE Seminar*. Introduces you to the practical development of real-world, Web-enabled, distributed applications with Java. See *www.MindView.net*.
6. Designing Objects & Systems Seminar. Object-oriented analysis, design, and implementation techniques. See *www.MindView.net*.
7. *Thinking in Patterns (with Java)*, which covers more advanced Java topics on design patterns and problem-solving techniques. Available at *www.MindView.net*.
8. *Thinking in Patterns Seminar*. A live seminar based on the above book. Schedule and registration pages can be found at *www.MindView.net*.
9. *Design Consulting and Reviews*. Assistance to help keep your project in good shape.

Appendix D: Resources

A list of some of the Java books I've found particularly useful.

Exercises

I've discovered that simple exercises are exceptionally useful to complete a student's understanding during a seminar, so you'll find a set at the end of each chapter.

Most exercises are designed to be easy enough that they can be finished in a reasonable amount of time in a classroom situation while the instructor observes, making sure that all the students are absorbing the material. Some are more challenging, but none present major challenges. (Presumably, you'll find those on your own—or more likely, they'll find you).

Solutions to selected exercises can be found in the electronic document *The Thinking in Java Annotated Solution Guide*, available for a small fee from *www.BruceEckel.com.*

The CD ROM

Another bonus with this edition is the CD ROM that is packaged in the back of the book. I've resisted putting CDs in the back of my books in the past because I felt the extra charge for a few kilobytes of source code on an enormous CD was not justified, preferring instead to allow people to download such things from my Web site. However, you'll soon see that this CD is different.

The CD doesn't contain the source code from the book, but instead has a link to the code at *www.MindView.net* (you don't need the link on the CD to get to the source code. You can just go to the site and find it that way). There are two reasons for this: the code was not complete at the time the CD had to be sent to the printer, and this approach allows the code to evolve and be corrected as any issues arise.

Because the book has changed significantly over the three editions, the CD contains the first and second editions of the book in HTML format, including sections that for aforementioned reasons were removed from later editions but which may in some cases be useful to you. In addition, you can download the HTML version of the current (third edition) book from *www.MindView.net*, and this will include corrections as they are discovered and fixed. One benefit of the HTML version is that the index is hyperlinked so navigating it is much simpler.

The bulk of the 400+ Megabytes of the CD, however, is a full multimedia course called *Foundations for Java*. This includes the *Thinking in C* seminar that gives you an introduction to the C syntax, operators, and functions that Java syntax is based upon. In addition, it includes the first seven lectures from the second edition of the *Hands-On Java* seminar-on-CD that I created and narrate. Although historically the entire *Hands-On Java* CD is only available for sale separately (this is also the case with the third edition of the *Hands-On Java* CD that may be available when you read this—see *www.MindView.net*), I decided to include the first seven lectures from the second edition because they will not have changed too much in relationship to the third edition of the book, so it will not only provide you (along with *Thinking in C*) with a foundation for this book, but in addition I hope it will give you a taste for the quality and value of the *Hands-On Java CD*, 3rd Edition.

I originally commissioned Chuck Allison to create the *Thinking in C* part of this seminar-on-CD ROM as a standalone product, but decided to include it with the second editions of both *Thinking in C++* and *Thinking in Java* because of the consistent experience of having people come to seminars without an adequate background in basic C syntax. The thinking apparently goes "I'm a smart programmer and I don't want to learn C, but rather C++ or Java, so I'll just skip C and go directly to C++/Java." After arriving at the seminar, it slowly dawns on folks that the prerequisite of understanding C syntax is there for a very good reason. By including the CD ROM with the book, we can ensure that everyone attends a seminar with adequate preparation.

The CD also allows the book to appeal to a wider audience. Even though Chapter 3 (Controlling Program Flow) does cover the fundamentals of the parts of Java that come from C, the CD is a gentler introduction, and assumes even less about the student's programming background than does the book. And being walked through the material in the first seven chapters via the corresponding lectures in the second edition of the *Hands-On Java* CD should help you get an even better foothold into Java. It is my hope that by including the CD, more people will be able to be brought into the fold of Java programming. The Hands-On Java CD ROM 3rd Edition is available only by ordering directly from the Web site *www.BruceEckel.com*.

Source code

All the source code for this book is available as copyrighted freeware, distributed as a single package, by visiting the Web site *www.BruceEckel.com*. To make sure that you get the most current version, this is the official site for distribution of the code and the electronic version of the book. You can find mirrored versions of the electronic book and the code on other sites (some of these sites are found at *www.BruceEckel.com*), but you should check the official site to ensure that the mirrored version is actually the most recent edition. You may distribute the code in classroom and other educational situations.

The primary goal of the copyright is to ensure that the source of the code is properly cited, and to prevent you from republishing the code in print media without permission. (As long as the source is cited, using examples from the book in most media is generally not a problem.)

In each source code file you will find a reference to the following copyright notice:

```
This computer source code is Copyright ©2003 MindView, Inc.
All Rights Reserved.

Permission to use, copy, modify, and distribute this
computer source code (Source Code) and its documentation
without fee and without a written agreement for the
purposes set forth below is hereby granted, provided that
the above copyright notice, this paragraph and the
following five numbered paragraphs appear in all copies.

1. Permission is granted to compile the Source Code and to
include the compiled code, in executable format only, in
personal and commercial software programs.

2. Permission is granted to use the Source Code without
modification in classroom situations, including in
presentation materials, provided that the book "Thinking in
Java" is cited as the origin.

3. Permission to incorporate the Source Code into printed
media may be obtained by contacting

MindView, Inc. 5343 Valle Vista La Mesa, California 91941
```

```
Wayne@MindView.net

4. The Source Code and documentation are copyrighted by
MindView, Inc. The Source code is provided without express
or implied warranty of any kind, including any implied
warranty of merchantability, fitness for a particular
purpose or non-infringement. MindView, Inc. does not
warrant that the operation of any program that includes the
Source Code will be uninterrupted or error- free. MindView,
Inc. makes no representation about the suitability of the
Source Code or of any software that includes the Source
Code for any purpose. The entire risk as to the quality
and performance of any program that includes the Source
code is with the user of the Source Code. The user
understands that the Source Code was developed for research
and instructional purposes and is advised not to rely
exclusively for any reason on the Source Code or any
program that includes the Source Code. Should the Source
Code or any resulting software prove defective, the user
assumes the cost of all necessary servicing, repair, or
correction.

5. IN NO EVENT SHALL MINDVIEW, INC., OR ITS PUBLISHER BE
LIABLE TO ANY PARTY UNDER ANY LEGAL THEORY FOR DIRECT,
INDIRECT, SPECIAL, INCIDENTAL, OR CONSEQUENTIAL DAMAGES,
INCLUDING LOST PROFITS, BUSINESS INTERRUPTION, LOSS OF
BUSINESS INFORMATION, OR ANY OTHER PECUNIARY LOSS, OR FOR
PERSONAL INJURIES, ARISING OUT OF THE USE OF THIS SOURCE
CODE AND ITS DOCUMENTATION, OR ARISING OUT OF THE INABILITY
TO USE ANY RESULTING PROGRAM, EVEN IF MINDVIEW, INC., OR
ITS PUBLISHER HAS BEEN ADVISED OF THE POSSIBILITY OF SUCH
DAMAGE. MINDVIEW, INC. SPECIFICALLY DISCLAIMS ANY
WARRANTIES, INCLUDING, BUT NOT LIMITED TO, THE IMPLIED
WARRANTIES OF MERCHANTABILITY AND FITNESS FOR A PARTICULAR
PURPOSE. THE SOURCE CODE AND DOCUMENTATION PROVIDED
HEREUNDER IS ON AN "AS IS" BASIS, WITHOUT ANY ACCOMPANYING
SERVICES FROM MINDVIEW, INC., AND MINDVIEW, INC. HAS NO
OBLIGATIONS TO PROVIDE MAINTENANCE, SUPPORT, UPDATES,
ENHANCEMENTS, OR MODIFICATIONS.

Please note that MindView, Inc. maintains a web site which
is the sole distribution point for electronic copies of the
Source Code, http://www.BruceEckel.com (and official mirror
sites), where it is freely available under the terms stated
```

```
above.

If you think you've found an error in the Source Code,
please submit a correction using the URL marked "feedback"
in the electronic version of the book, nearest the error
you've found.
```

You may use the code in your projects and in the classroom (including your presentation materials) as long as the copyright notice that appears in each source file is retained.

Coding standards

In the text of this book, identifiers (method, variable, and class names) are set in **bold**. Most keywords are also set in bold, except for those keywords that are used so much that the bolding can become tedious, such as "class."

I use a particular coding style for the examples in this book. This style follows the style that Sun itself uses in virtually all of the code you will find at its site (see *java.sun.com/docs/codeconv/index.html*), and seems to be supported by most Java development environments. If you've read my other works, you'll also notice that Sun's coding style coincides with mine—this pleases me, although I had nothing to do with it. The subject of formatting style is good for hours of hot debate, so I'll just say I'm not trying to dictate correct style via my examples; I have my own motivation for using the style that I do. Because Java is a free-form programming language, you can continue to use whatever style you're comfortable with.

The programs in this book are files that are included by the word processor in the text, directly from compiled files. Thus, the code files printed in the book should all work without compiler errors. The errors that *should* cause compile-time error messages are commented out with the comment **//!** so they can be easily discovered and tested using automatic means. Errors discovered and reported to the author will appear first in the distributed source code and later in updates of the book (which will also appear on the Web site *www.BruceEckel.com*).

Java versions

I generally rely on the Sun implementation of Java as a reference when determining whether behavior is correct.

This book focuses on and is tested with Java 2, JDK 1.4. If you need to learn about earlier releases of the language that are not covered in this edition, the first edition and second editions of the book are freely downloadable at *www.BruceEckel.com* and are also contained on the CD that is bound in with this book.

Errors

No matter how many tricks a writer uses to detect errors, some always creep in and these often leap off the page for a fresh reader.

Because the feedback provided by astute readers has been so valuable to me, I've developed several versions of a feedback system called *BackTalk* (conceived with the aid of Bill Venners, and implemented with the help of numerous others, using several different technologies). In the electronic version of this book, freely downloadable from *www.BruceEckel.com*, each paragraph in the text has its own unique URL that will produce an email that will register your comment in the BackTalk system, for that particular paragraph. This way it's very easy to track and update corrections. If you discover anything you believe to be an error, please use the BackTalk system to submit the error along with your suggested correction. Your help is appreciated.

Note on the cover design

The cover of *Thinking in Java* is inspired by the American Arts & Crafts Movement that began near the turn of the century and reached its zenith between 1900 and 1920. It began in England as a reaction to both the machine production of the Industrial Revolution and the highly ornamental style of the Victorian era. Arts & Crafts emphasized spare design, the forms of nature as seen in the art nouveau movement, hand-crafting, and the importance of the individual craftsperson, and yet it did not eschew the use of modern tools. There are many echoes with the situation we have today: the turn of the century, the evolution from the raw beginnings of the computer revolution to something more refined and meaningful to individual persons, and the emphasis on software craftsmanship rather than just manufacturing code.

I see Java in this same way: as an attempt to elevate the programmer away from an operating-system mechanic and toward being a "software craftsman."

Both the author and the book/cover designer (who have been friends since childhood) find inspiration in this movement, and both own furniture, lamps, and other pieces that are either original or inspired by this period.

The other theme in this cover suggests a collection box that a naturalist might use to display the insect specimens that he or she has preserved. These insects are objects that are placed within the box objects. The box objects are themselves placed within the "cover object," which illustrates the fundamental concept of aggregation in object-oriented programming. Of course, a programmer cannot help but make the association with "bugs," and here the bugs have been captured and presumably killed in a specimen jar, and finally confined within a small display box, as if to imply Java's ability to find, display, and subdue bugs (which is truly one of its most powerful attributes).

Acknowledgements

First, thanks to associates who have worked with me to give seminars, provide consulting, and develop teaching projects: Andrea Provaglio, Dave Bartlett, Bill Venners, Chuck Allison, Jeremy Meyer, and Larry O'Brien. I appreciate your patience as I continue to try to develop the best model for independent folks like us to work together.

Recently, no doubt because of the Internet, I have become associated with a surprisingly large number of people who assist me in my endeavors, usually working from their own home offices. In the past, I would have had to pay for a pretty big office space to accommodate all these folks, but because of the net and Fedex and occasionally the telephone, I'm able to benefit from their help without the extra costs. In my attempts to learn to better "play well with others," you have all been very helpful, and I hope to continue learning how to make my own work better through the efforts of others. Paula Steuer has been invaluable in taking over my haphazard business practices and making them sane (thanks for prodding me when I don't want to do something, Paula). Jonathan Wilcox, Esq., has sifted through my corporate structure and turned over every possible rock that might hide scorpions, and frog-marched us through the process of putting everything straight, legally. Thanks for your care and persistence. Sharlynn Cobaugh (who discovered Paula) has made herself an expert in sound processing and an essential part of creating the multimedia training CD ROMs, as well as tackling other problems. Thanks for your perseverance when faced with intractable computer problems. Evan Cofsky (Evan@TheUnixMan.com) has become an essential part of my development process, taking to the Python programming language like a duck (Hmm. Such a mixed metaphor could produce a fat Python) and solving all kinds of difficult problems, including the (final?) re-architecting of BackTalk into an email-driven XML database. The folks at Amaio in Prague have helped me out with several projects. Daniel Will-Harris was the original work-by-Internet inspiration, and he is of course fundamental to all my design solutions.

For this project, I took another step that had been fermenting in the back of my mind for awhile. For the summer of 2002, I created an internship program in Crested Butte, Colorado, initially looking for two interns and ending up with 5 (two volunteers). Not only did they contribute to the book but they helped keep me focused on the project. Thanks to JJ Badri, Ben Hindman, Mihajlo Jovanovic, Mark Welsh. Chintan Thakker was able to stay for a second internship through the end of the book process and beyond, and since I had to rent the intern condo in Mount Crested Butte anyway, we advertised for volunteers and got Mike Levin, Mike Shea, and Ian Phillips, who all made contributions. Someday I may do another internship program; visit www.MindView.net for news.

Thanks to the Doyle Street Cohousing Community for putting up with me for the two years that it took me to write the first edition of this book (and for putting up with me at all). Thanks very much to Kevin and Sonda Donovan for subletting their great place in gorgeous Crested Butte, Colorado for the summer while I worked on the first edition of the book (and to Kevin for all the great remodeling on my place in CB). Also thanks to the friendly residents of Crested Butte and the Rocky Mountain Biological Laboratory who make me feel so welcome. My yoga teachers in CB, Maria and Brenda, were instrumental in keeping me sane during the development of the 3rd edition.

Camp4 Coffee in Crested Butte, Colorado has become the standard hangout when teachers have come up to give seminars, and during seminar breaks it is the best and cheapest catering I've ever had. Thanks to my buddy Al Smith for creating it and making it such a great place, and for being such an interesting and entertaining part of the Crested Butte experience.

Thanks to Claudette Moore at Moore Literary Agency for her tremendous patience and perseverance in getting me exactly what I wanted. Thanks to Paul Petralia at Prentice Hall for continuing to *give* me what I want, and for going out of his way to make things run smoothly for me (and for putting up with all my special requirements).

My first two books were published with Jeff Pepper as editor at Osborne/McGraw-Hill. Jeff appeared at the right place and the right time at Prentice Hall to lay the original groundwork for these books, before passing the responsibility on to Paul. Thanks, Jeff.

Thanks to Rolf André Klaedtke (Switzerland); Martin Vlcek, Vlada & Pavel Lahoda, (Prague); and Marco Cantu (Italy) for hosting me on my first self-organized European seminar tour.

Thanks to Gen Kiyooka and his company Digigami, who graciously provided my Web server for the first several years of my presence on the Web. This was an invaluable learning aid.

Special thanks to Larry and Tina O'Brien, who helped turn my seminar into the first edition of the *Hands-On Java* CD ROM. (You can find out more at *www.BruceEckel.com.*)

Certain open-source tools have proved invaluable during my development process and I am very grateful to the creators every time I use these. Cygwin (*http://www.cygwin.com*) has solved innumerable problems for me that Windows can't/won't and I become more attached to it each day (if I only had this 15 years ago when my brain was still hard-wired with Gnu Emacs). CVS and Ant have become essential to my Java development process and I couldn't go back now. I've even become fond of JUnit (*http://www.junit.org*) now that they've *actually* made it "the simplest thing that could possibly work." IBM's Eclipse (*http://www.eclipse.org*) is a truly wonderful contribution to the development community, and I expect to see great things from it as it continues to evolve (how did IBM become hip? I must have missed a memo). Linux was used daily during the development process, especially by the interns. And of course, if I don't say it enough everywhere else, I use Python (www.Python.org) constantly to solve problems, the brainchild of my buddy Guido Van Rossum and the goofy geniuses at PythonLabs with whom I spent a few great days doing XP on Zope 3 (Tim, I've now framed that mouse you borrowed, officially named the

"TimMouse"). You guys need to find healthier places to eat lunch. (Also, thanks to the entire Python community, an amazing bunch of people).

Lots of people sent in corrections and I am indebted to them all, but particular thanks go to (for the first edition): Kevin Raulerson (found tons of great bugs), Bob Resendes (simply incredible), John Pinto, Joe Dante, Joe Sharp (all three were fabulous), David Combs (many grammar and clarification corrections), Dr. Robert Stephenson, John Cook, Franklin Chen, Zev Griner, David Karr, Leander A. Stroschein, Steve Clark, Charles A. Lee, Austin Maher, Dennis P. Roth, Roque Oliveira, Douglas Dunn, Dejan Ristic, Neil Galarneau, David B. Malkovsky, Steve Wilkinson, and a host of others. Prof. Ir. Marc Meurrens put in a great deal of effort to publicize and make the electronic version of the first edition of the book available in Europe.

Thanks to those who helped me rewrite the examples to use the Swing library (for the 2nd edition), and for other assistance: Jon Shvarts, Thomas Kirsch, Rahim Adatia, Rajesh Jain, Ravi Manthena, Banu Rajamani, Jens Brandt, Nitin Shivaram, Malcolm Davis, and everyone who expressed support.

There have been a spate of smart technical people in my life who have become friends and have also been both influential and unusual in that they do yoga and practice other forms of spiritual enhancement, which I find quite inspirational and instructional. They are Kraig Brockschmidt, Gen Kiyooka, and Andrea Provaglio (who helps in the understanding of Java and programming in general in Italy, and now in the United States as an associate of the MindView team).

It's not that much of a surprise to me that understanding Delphi helped me understand Java, since there are many concepts and language design decisions in common. My Delphi friends provided assistance by helping me gain insight into that marvelous programming environment. They are Marco Cantu (another Italian—perhaps being steeped in Latin gives one aptitude for programming languages?), Neil Rubenking (who used to do the yoga/vegetarian/Zen thing until he discovered computers), and of course Zack Urlocker (Delphi product manager), a long-time pal whom I've traveled the world with.

My friend Richard Hale Shaw's insights and support have been very helpful (and Kim's, too). Richard and I spent many months giving seminars together and trying to work out the perfect learning experience for the attendees.

The book design, cover design, and cover photo were created by my friend Daniel Will-Harris, noted author and designer (*www.Will-Harris.com*), who used to play with rub-on letters in junior high school while he awaited the invention of computers and desktop publishing, and complained of me mumbling over my algebra problems. However, I produced the camera-ready pages myself, so the typesetting errors are mine. Microsoft® Word XP for Windows was used to write the book and to create camera-ready pages in Adobe Acrobat; the book was created directly from the Acrobat PDF files. As a tribute to the electronic age, I happened to be overseas when the final version of the first and second editions of the book was produced—the first edition was sent from Capetown, South Africa and the second edition was posted from Prague. The third was from Crested Butte, Colorado. The body typeface is *Georgia* and the headlines are in *Verdana*. The cover typeface is *ITC Rennie Mackintosh.*

A special thanks to all my teachers and all my students (who are my teachers as well). The most fun writing teacher was Gabrielle Rico (author of *Writing the Natural Way*, Putnam, 1983). I'll always treasure the terrific week at Esalen.

My sweetie Dawn McGee took the back cover photo, and makes me smile that way.

The supporting cast of friends includes, but is not limited to: Andrew Binstock, Steve Sinofsky, JD Hildebrandt, Tom Keffer, Brian McElhinney, Brinkley Barr, Bill Gates at *Midnight Engineering Magazine*, Larry Constantine and Lucy Lockwood, Greg Perry, Dan Putterman, Christi Westphal, Gene Wang, Dave Mayer, David Intersimone, Andrea Rosenfield, Claire Sawyers, more Italians (Laura Fallai, Corrado, Ilsa, and Cristina Giustozzi), Chris and Laura Strand, the Almquists, Brad Jerbic, Marilyn Cvitanic, the Mabrys, the Haflingers, the Pollocks, Peter Vinci, the Robbins Families, the Moelter Families (and the McMillans), Michael Wilk, Dave Stoner, Laurie Adams, the Cranstons, Larry Fogg, Mike and Karen Sequeira, Gary Entsminger and Allison Brody, Kevin Donovan and Sonda Eastlack, Chester and Shannon Andersen, Joe Lordi, Dave and Brenda Bartlett, Patti Gast, the Rentschlers, the Sudeks, Dick, Patty, and Lee Eckel, Lynn and Todd, and their families. And of course, Mom and Dad.

1: Introduction to Objects

"We cut nature up, organize it into concepts, and ascribe significances as we do, largely because we are parties to an agreement that holds throughout our speech community and is codified in the patterns of our language ... we cannot talk at all except by subscribing to the organization and classification of data which the agreement decrees."
Benjamin Lee Whorf (1897-1941)

The genesis of the computer revolution was in a machine. The genesis of our programming languages thus tends to look like that machine.

But computers are not so much machines as they are mind amplification tools ("bicycles for the mind," as Steve Jobs is fond of saying) and a different kind of expressive medium. As a result, the tools are beginning to look less like machines and more like parts of our minds, and also like other forms of expression such as writing, painting, sculpture, animation, and filmmaking. Object-oriented programming (OOP) is part of this movement toward using the computer as an expressive medium.

This chapter will introduce you to the basic concepts of OOP, including an overview of development methods. This chapter, and this book, assume that you have had experience in a procedural programming language, although not necessarily C. If you think you need more preparation in programming and the syntax of C before tackling this book, you should work through the *Foundations for Java* training CD ROM, bound in the back of this book.

This chapter is background and supplementary material. Many people do not feel comfortable wading into object-oriented programming without understanding the big picture first. Thus, there are many concepts that are introduced here to give you a solid overview of OOP. However, other people may not get the big picture concepts until they've seen some of the mechanics first; these people may become bogged down and lost without some code to get their hands on. If you're part of this latter group and are eager to get to the specifics of the language, feel free to jump past this chapter—skipping it at this point will not prevent you from writing programs or learning the language. However, you will want to come back here eventually to fill in your knowledge so you can understand why objects are important and how to design with them.

The progress of abstraction

All programming languages provide abstractions. It can be argued that the complexity of the problems you're able to solve is directly related to the kind and quality of abstraction. By "kind" I mean, "What is it that you are abstracting?" Assembly language is a small abstraction of the underlying machine. Many so-called "imperative" languages that followed (such as FORTRAN, BASIC, and C) were abstractions of assembly language. These languages are big improvements over assembly language, but their primary abstraction still requires you to think in terms of the structure of the computer rather than the structure of the problem you are trying to solve. The programmer must establish the association between the machine model (in the "solution space," which is the place where you're modeling that problem, such as a computer) and the model of the problem that is actually being solved (in the "problem space," which is the place where the problem exists). The effort required to perform this mapping, and the fact that it is extrinsic to the programming language, produces programs that are difficult to write and expensive to maintain, and as a side effect created the entire "programming methods" industry.

The alternative to modeling the machine is to model the problem you're trying to solve. Early languages such as LISP and APL chose particular views of the world ("All problems are ultimately lists" or "All problems are algorithmic," respectively). PROLOG casts all problems into chains of decisions. Languages have been created for constraint-based programming and for programming exclusively by manipulating graphical symbols. (The latter proved to be too restrictive.) Each of these approaches is a good solution to the particular class of problem they're designed to solve, but when you step outside of that domain they become awkward.

The object-oriented approach goes a step further by providing tools for the programmer to represent elements in the problem space. This representation is general enough that the programmer is not constrained to any particular type of problem. We refer to the elements in the problem space and their representations in the solution space as "objects." (You will also need other objects that don't have problem-space analogs.) The idea is that the program is allowed to adapt itself to the lingo of the problem by adding new types of objects, so when you read the code describing the solution, you're reading words that also express the problem. This is a more flexible and powerful language abstraction than what we've had before.[1] Thus, OOP allows you to describe the problem in terms of the problem, rather than in terms of the computer where the solution will run. There's still a connection back to the computer: each object looks quite a bit like a little computer—it has a state, and it has operations that you can ask it to perform. However, this doesn't seem like such a bad analogy to objects in the real world—they all have characteristics and behaviors.

Alan Kay summarized five basic characteristics of Smalltalk, the first successful object-oriented language and one of the languages upon which Java is based. These characteristics represent a pure approach to object-oriented programming:

1. **Everything is an object.** Think of an object as a fancy variable; it stores data, but you can "make requests" to that object, asking it to perform operations on itself. In theory, you can take any conceptual component in the problem you're trying to solve (dogs, buildings, services, etc.) and represent it as an object in your program.

2. **A program is a bunch of objects telling each other what to do by sending messages**. To make a request of an object, you "send a message" to that object. More concretely, you can think of a message as a request to call a method that belongs to a particular object.

3. **Each object has its own memory made up of other objects**. Put another way, you create a new kind of object by making

---

[1] Some language designers have decided that object-oriented programming by itself is not adequate to easily solve all programming problems, and advocate the combination of various approaches into *multiparadigm* programming languages. See *Multiparadigm Programming in Leda* by Timothy Budd (Addison-Wesley 1995).

a package containing existing objects. Thus, you can build complexity into a program while hiding it behind the simplicity of objects.

4. **Every object has a type**. Using the parlance, each object is an *instance* of a *class*, in which "class" is synonymous with "type." The most important distinguishing characteristic of a class is "What messages can you send to it?"

5. **All objects of a particular type can receive the same messages**. This is actually a loaded statement, as you will see later. Because an object of type "circle" is also an object of type "shape," a circle is guaranteed to accept shape messages. This means you can write code that talks to shapes and automatically handle anything that fits the description of a shape. This *substitutability* is one of the powerful concepts in OOP.

Booch offers an even more succinct description of an object:

> *An object has state, behavior and identity.*

This means that an object can have internal data (which gives it state), methods (to produce behavior), and each object can be uniquely distinguished from every other object—to put this in a concrete sense, each object has a unique address in memory.[2]

An object has an interface

Aristotle was probably the first to begin a careful study of the concept of *type;* he spoke of "the class of fishes and the class of birds." The idea that all objects, while being unique, are also part of a class of objects that have characteristics and behaviors in common was used directly in the first object-oriented language, Simula-67, with its fundamental keyword **class** that introduces a new type into a program.

Simula, as its name implies, was created for developing simulations such as the classic "bank teller problem." In this, you have a bunch of tellers, customers, accounts, transactions, and units of money—a lot of "objects."

---

[2] This is actually a bit restrictive, since objects can conceivably exist in different machines and address spaces, and they can also be stored on disk. In these cases, the identity of the object must be determined by something other than memory address.

Objects that are identical except for their state during a program's execution are grouped together into "classes of objects" and that's where the keyword **class** came from. Creating abstract data types (classes) is a fundamental concept in object-oriented programming. Abstract data types work almost exactly like built-in types: You can create variables of a type (called *objects* or *instances* in object-oriented parlance) and manipulate those variables (called *sending messages* or *requests;* you send a message and the object figures out what to do with it). The members (elements) of each class share some commonality: every account has a balance, every teller can accept a deposit, etc. At the same time, each member has its own state: each account has a different balance, each teller has a name. Thus, the tellers, customers, accounts, transactions, etc., can each be represented with a unique entity in the computer program. This entity is the object, and each object belongs to a particular class that defines its characteristics and behaviors.

So, although what we really do in object-oriented programming is create new data types, virtually all object-oriented programming languages use the "class" keyword. When you see the word "type" think "class" and vice versa.[3]

Since a class describes a set of objects that have identical characteristics (data elements) and behaviors (functionality), a class is really a data type because a floating point number, for example, also has a set of characteristics and behaviors. The difference is that a programmer defines a class to fit a problem rather than being forced to use an existing data type that was designed to represent a unit of storage in a machine. You extend the programming language by adding new data types specific to your needs. The programming system welcomes the new classes and gives them all the care and type-checking that it gives to built-in types.

The object-oriented approach is not limited to building simulations. Whether or not you agree that any program is a simulation of the system you're designing, the use of OOP techniques can easily reduce a large set of problems to a simple solution.

Once a class is established, you can make as many objects of that class as you like, and then manipulate those objects as if they are the elements that exist in the problem you are trying to solve. Indeed, one of the challenges of object-

---

[3] Some people make a distinction, stating that type determines the interface while class is a particular implementation of that interface.

oriented programming is to create a one-to-one mapping between the elements in the problem space and objects in the solution space.

But how do you get an object to do useful work for you? There must be a way to make a request of the object so that it will do something, such as complete a transaction, draw something on the screen, or turn on a switch. And each object can satisfy only certain requests. The requests you can make of an object are defined by its *interface,* and the type is what determines the interface. A simple example might be a representation of a light bulb:

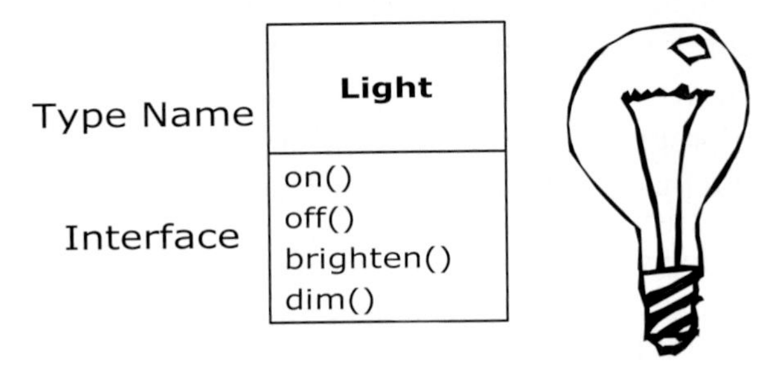


```
Light lt = new Light();
lt.on();
```

The interface establishes *what* requests you can make for a particular object. However, there must be code somewhere to satisfy that request. This, along with the hidden data, comprises the *implementation.* From a procedural programming standpoint, it's not that complicated. A type has a method associated with each possible request, and when you make a particular request to an object, that method is called. This process is usually summarized by saying that you "send a message" (make a request) to an object, and the object figures out what to do with that message (it executes code).

Here, the name of the type/class is **Light**, the name of this particular **Light** object is **lt**, and the requests that you can make of a **Light** object are to turn it on, turn it off, make it brighter, or make it dimmer. You create a **Light** object by defining a "reference" (**lt**) for that object and calling **new** to request a new object of that type. To send a message to the object, you state the name of the object and connect it to the message request with a period (dot). From the standpoint of the user of a predefined class, that's pretty much all there is to programming with objects.

The preceding diagram follows the format of the *Unified Modeling Language* (UML). Each class is represented by a box, with the type name in the top portion of the box, any data members that you care to describe in the middle portion of the box, and the *methods* (the functions that belong to this object, which receive any messages you send to that object) in the bottom portion of the box. Often, only the name of the class and the public methods are shown in UML design diagrams, so the middle portion is not shown. If you're interested only in the class name, then the bottom portion doesn't need to be shown, either.

An object provides services

While you're trying to develop or understand a program design, one of the best ways to think about objects is as "service providers." Your program itself will provide services to the user, and it will accomplish this by using the services offered by other objects. Your goal is to produce (or even better, locate in existing code libraries) a set of objects that provide the ideal services to solve your problem.

A way to start doing this is to ask "if I could magically pull them out of a hat, what objects would solve my problem right away?" For example, suppose you are creating a bookkeeping program. You might imagine some objects that contain pre-defined bookkeeping input screens, another set of objects that perform bookkeeping calculations, and an object that handles printing of checks and invoices on all different kinds of printers. Maybe some of these objects already exist, and for the ones that don't, what would they look like? What services would *those* objects provide, and what objects would *they* need to fulfill their obligations? If you keep doing this, you will eventually reach a point where you can say either "that object seems simple enough to sit down and write" or "I'm sure that object must exist already." This is a reasonable way to decompose a problem into a set of objects.

Thinking of an object as a service provider has an additional benefit: it helps to improve the cohesiveness of the object. *High cohesion* is a fundamental quality of software design: It means that the various aspects of a software component (such as an object, although this could also apply to a method or a library of objects) "fit together" well. One problem people have when designing objects is cramming too much functionality into one object. For example, in your check printing module, you may decide you need an object that knows all about formatting and printing. You'll probably discover that this is too much for one object, and that what you need is three or more objects. One object might be a catalog of all the possible check layouts, which can be queried for information about how to print a check. One object or set of objects could be a generic printing interface that knows all about different kinds of printers (but nothing about bookkeeping—this one is a candidate for buying rather than writing yourself). And a third object could use the services of the other two to accomplish the task. Thus, each object has a cohesive set of services it offers. In a good object-oriented design, each object does one thing well, but doesn't try to do too much. As seen here, this not only allows the discovery of objects that might be purchased (the printer interface object), but it also produces the possibility of an object that might be reused somewhere else (the catalog of check layouts).

Treating objects as service providers is a great simplifying tool, and it's very useful not only during the design process, but also when someone else is trying to understand your code or reuse an object—if they can see the value of the object based on what service it provides, it makes it much easier to fit it into the design.

The hidden implementation

It is helpful to break up the playing field into *class creators* (those who create new data types) and *client programmers*[4] (the class consumers who use the data types in their applications). The goal of the client programmer is to collect a toolbox full of classes to use for rapid application development. The goal of the class creator is to build a class that exposes only what's necessary to the client programmer and keeps everything else hidden. Why? Because if it's hidden, the client programmer can't access it, which means that the class creator can change the hidden portion at will without worrying about the impact on anyone else. The hidden portion usually represents the tender insides of an object that could easily be corrupted by a careless or uninformed client programmer, so hiding the implementation reduces program bugs.

The concept of implementation hiding cannot be overemphasized. In any relationship it's important to have boundaries that are respected by all parties involved. When you create a library, you establish a relationship with the client programmer, who is also a programmer, but one who is putting

---

[4] I'm indebted to my friend Scott Meyers for this term.

together an application by using your library, possibly to build a bigger library. If all the members of a class are available to everyone, then the client programmer can do anything with that class and there's no way to enforce rules. Even though you might really prefer that the client programmer not directly manipulate some of the members of your class, without access control there's no way to prevent it. Everything's naked to the world.

So the first reason for access control is to keep client programmers' hands off portions they shouldn't touch—parts that are necessary for the internal operation of the data type but not part of the interface that users need in order to solve their particular problems. This is actually a service to users because they can easily see what's important to them and what they can ignore.

The second reason for access control is to allow the library designer to change the internal workings of the class without worrying about how it will affect the client programmer. For example, you might implement a particular class in a simple fashion to ease development, and then later discover that you need to rewrite it in order to make it run faster. If the interface and implementation are clearly separated and protected, you can accomplish this easily.

Java uses three explicit keywords to set the boundaries in a class: **public**, **private**, and **protected**. Their use and meaning are quite straightforward. These *access specifiers* determine who can use the definitions that follow. **public** means the following element is available to everyone. The **private** keyword, on the other hand, means that no one can access that element except you, the creator of the type, inside methods of that type. **private** is a brick wall between you and the client programmer. Someone who tries to access a **private** member will get a compile-time error. The **protected** keyword acts like **private**, with the exception that an inheriting class has access to **protected** members, but not **private** members. Inheritance will be introduced shortly.

Java also has a "default" access, which comes into play if you don't use one of the aforementioned specifiers. This is usually called *package access* because classes can access the members of other classes in the same package, but outside of the package those same members appear to be **private**.

Reusing the implementation

Once a class has been created and tested, it should (ideally) represent a useful unit of code. It turns out that this reusability is not nearly so easy to achieve as many would hope; it takes experience and insight to produce a reusable object design. But once you have such a design, it begs to be reused. Code reuse is one of the greatest advantages that object-oriented programming languages provide.

The simplest way to reuse a class is to just use an object of that class directly, but you can also place an object of that class inside a new class. We call this "creating a member object." Your new class can be made up of any number and type of other objects, in any combination that you need to achieve the functionality desired in your new class. Because you are composing a new class from existing classes, this concept is called *composition* (if the composition happens dynamically, it's usually called *aggregation*). Composition is often referred to as a "has-a" relationship, as in "a car has an engine."

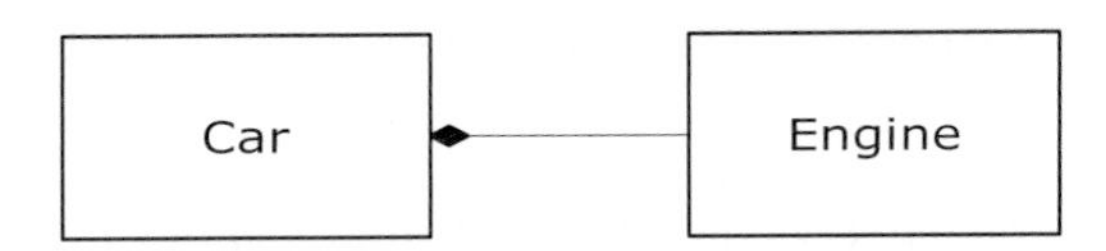

(This UML diagram indicates composition with the filled diamond, which states there is one car. I will typically use a simpler form: just a line, without the diamond, to indicate an association.[5])

Composition comes with a great deal of flexibility. The member objects of your new class are typically private, making them inaccessible to the client programmers who are using the class. This allows you to change those members without disturbing existing client code. You can also change the member objects at run time, to dynamically change the behavior of your program. Inheritance, which is described next, does not have this flexibility since the compiler must place compile-time restrictions on classes created with inheritance.

---

[5] This is usually enough detail for most diagrams, and you don't need to get specific about whether you're using aggregation or composition.

Because inheritance is so important in object-oriented programming it is often highly emphasized, and the new programmer can get the idea that inheritance should be used everywhere. This can result in awkward and overly complicated designs. Instead, you should first look to composition when creating new classes, since it is simpler and more flexible. If you take this approach, your designs will be cleaner. Once you've had some experience, it will be reasonably obvious when you need inheritance.

Inheritance: reusing the interface

By itself, the idea of an object is a convenient tool. It allows you to package data and functionality together by *concept*, so you can represent an appropriate problem-space idea rather than being forced to use the idioms of the underlying machine. These concepts are expressed as fundamental units in the programming language by using the **class** keyword.

It seems a pity, however, to go to all the trouble to create a class and then be forced to create a brand new one that might have similar functionality. It's nicer if we can take the existing class, clone it, and then make additions and modifications to the clone. This is effectively what you get with *inheritance,* with the exception that if the original class (called the *base class* or *superclass* or *parent class*) is changed, the modified "clone" (called the *derived class* or *inherited class* or *subclass* or *child class*) also reflects those changes.

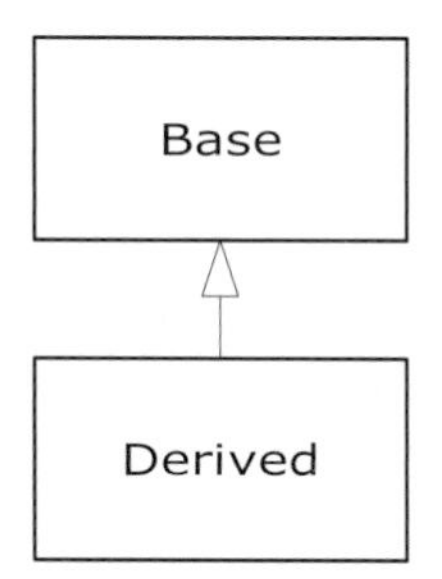

(The arrow in this UML diagram points from the derived class to the base class. As you will see, there is commonly more than one derived class.)

A type does more than describe the constraints on a set of objects; it also has a relationship with other types. Two types can have characteristics and behaviors in common, but one type may contain more characteristics than another and may also handle more messages (or handle them differently). Inheritance expresses this similarity between types by using the concept of base types and derived types. A base type contains all of the characteristics and behaviors that are shared among the types derived from it. You create a base type to represent the core of your ideas about some objects in your system. From the base type, you derive other types to express the different ways that this core can be realized.

For example, a trash-recycling machine sorts pieces of trash. The base type is "trash," and each piece of trash has a weight, a value, and so on, and can be shredded, melted, or decomposed. From this, more specific types of trash are derived that may have additional characteristics (a bottle has a color) or behaviors (an aluminum can may be crushed, a steel can is magnetic). In addition, some behaviors may be different (the value of paper depends on its type and condition). Using inheritance, you can build a type hierarchy that expresses the problem you're trying to solve in terms of its types.

A second example is the classic "shape" example, perhaps used in a computer-aided design system or game simulation. The base type is "shape," and each shape has a size, a color, a position, and so on. Each shape can be drawn, erased, moved, colored, etc. From this, specific types of shapes are derived (inherited)—circle, square, triangle, and so on — each of which may have additional characteristics and behaviors. Certain shapes can be flipped, for example. Some behaviors may be different, such as when you want to calculate the area of a shape. The type hierarchy embodies both the similarities and differences between the shapes.

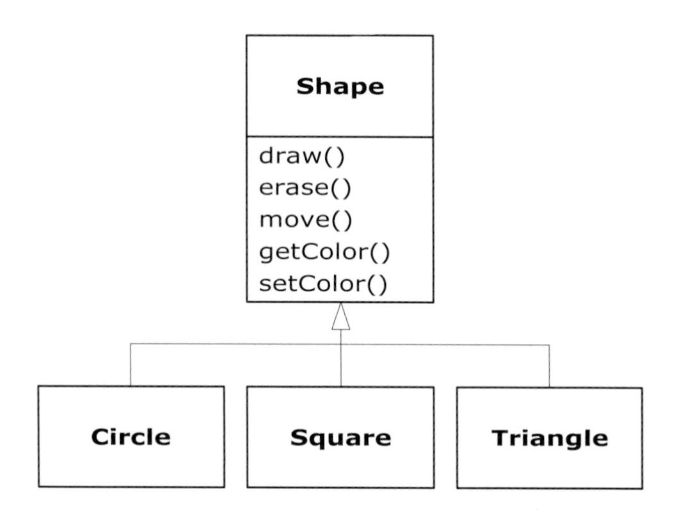

Casting the solution in the same terms as the problem is tremendously beneficial because you don't need a lot of intermediate models to get from a description of the problem to a description of the solution. With objects, the type hierarchy is the primary model, so you go directly from the description of the system in the real world to the description of the system in code. Indeed, one of the difficulties people have with object-oriented design is that it's too simple to get from the beginning to the end. A mind trained to look for complex solutions can initially be stumped by this simplicity.

When you inherit from an existing type, you create a new type. This new type contains not only all the members of the existing type (although the **private** ones are hidden away and inaccessible), but more importantly it duplicates the interface of the base class. That is, all the messages you can send to objects of the base class you can also send to objects of the derived class. Since we know the type of a class by the messages we can send to it, this means that the derived class *is the same type as the base class*. In the previous example, "a circle is a shape." This type equivalence via inheritance is one of the fundamental gateways in understanding the meaning of object-oriented programming.

Since both the base class and derived class have the same fundamental interface, there must be some implementation to go along with that interface. That is, there must be some code to execute when an object receives a particular message. If you simply inherit a class and don't do anything else, the methods from the base-class interface come right along into the derived class. That means objects of the derived class have not only the same type, they also have the same behavior, which isn't particularly interesting.

You have two ways to differentiate your new derived class from the original base class. The first is quite straightforward: You simply add brand new methods to the derived class. These new methods are not part of the base class interface. This means that the base class simply didn't do as much as you wanted it to, so you added more methods. This simple and primitive use for inheritance is, at times, the perfect solution to your problem. However, you should look closely for the possibility that your base class might also need these additional methods. This process of discovery and iteration of your design happens regularly in object-oriented programming.

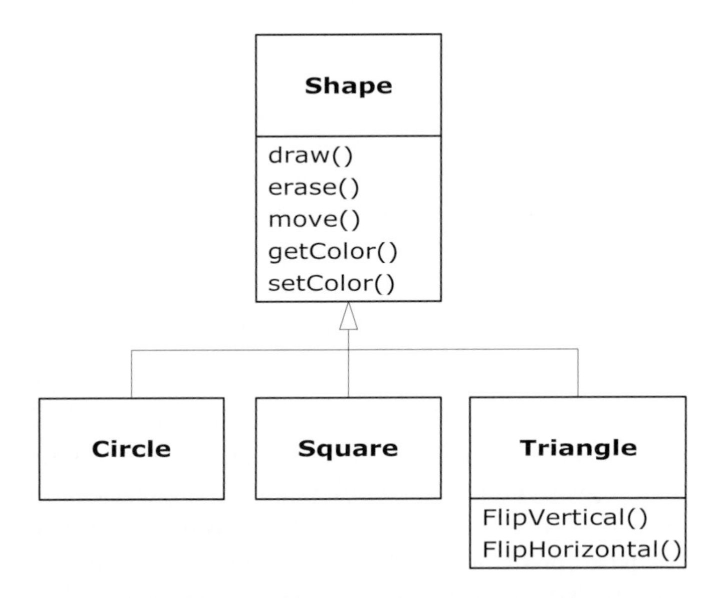

Although inheritance may sometimes imply (especially in Java, where the keyword for inheritance is **extends**) that you are going to add new methods to the interface, that's not necessarily true. The second and more important way to differentiate your new class is to *change* the behavior of an existing base-class method. This is referred to as *overriding* that method.

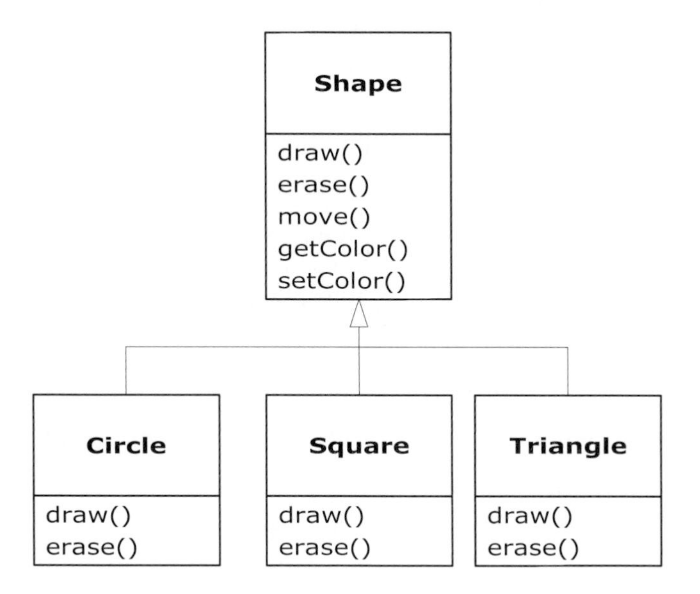

To override a method, you simply create a new definition for the method in the derived class. You're saying, "I'm using the same interface method here, but I want it to do something different for my new type."

Is-a vs. is-like-a relationships

There's a certain debate that can occur about inheritance: Should inheritance override *only* base-class methods (and not add new methods that aren't in the base class)? This would mean that the derived type is *exactly* the same type as the base class since it has exactly the same interface. As a result, you can exactly substitute an object of the derived class for an object of the base class. This can be thought of as *pure substitution*, and it's often referred to as the *substitution principle*. In a sense, this is the ideal way to treat inheritance. We often refer to the relationship between the base class and derived classes in this case as an *is-a* relationship, because you can say "a circle *is a* shape." A test for inheritance is to determine whether you can state the is-a relationship about the classes and have it make sense.

There are times when you must add new interface elements to a derived type, thus extending the interface and creating a new type. The new type can still be substituted for the base type, but the substitution isn't perfect because your new methods are not accessible from the base type. This can be described as an *is-like-a* relationship (my term). The new type has the interface of the old type but it also contains other methods, so you can't really say it's exactly the same. For example, consider an air conditioner. Suppose your house is wired with all the controls for cooling; that is, it has an interface that allows you to control cooling. Imagine that the air conditioner breaks down and you replace it with a heat pump, which can both heat and cool. The heat pump *is-like-an* air conditioner, but it can do more. Because the control system of your house is designed only to control cooling, it is restricted to communication with the cooling part of the new object. The interface of the new object has been extended, and the existing system doesn't know about anything except the original interface.

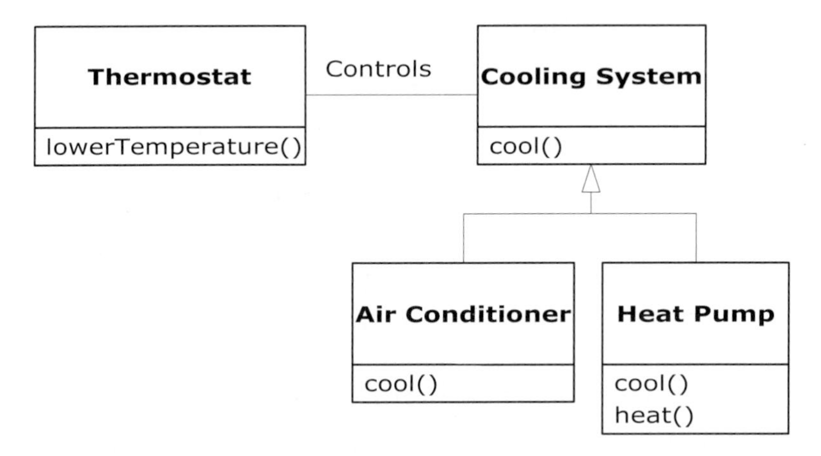

Of course, once you see this design it becomes clear that the base class "cooling system" is not general enough, and should be renamed to "temperature control system" so that it can also include heating—at which point the substitution principle will work. However, this diagram is an example of what can happen with design in the real world.

When you see the substitution principle it's easy to feel like this approach (pure substitution) is the only way to do things, and in fact it *is* nice if your design works out that way. But you'll find that there are times when it's equally clear that you must add new methods to the interface of a derived class. With inspection both cases should be reasonably obvious.

Interchangeable objects with polymorphism

When dealing with type hierarchies, you often want to treat an object not as the specific type that it is, but instead as its base type. This allows you to write code that doesn't depend on specific types. In the shape example, methods manipulate generic shapes without respect to whether they're circles, squares, triangles, or some shape that hasn't even been defined yet. All shapes can be drawn, erased, and moved, so these methods simply send a message to a shape object; they don't worry about how the object copes with the message.

Such code is unaffected by the addition of new types, and adding new types is the most common way to extend an object-oriented program to handle new situations. For example, you can derive a new subtype of shape called pentagon without modifying the methods that deal only with generic shapes. This ability to easily extend a design by deriving new subtypes is one of the essential ways to encapsulate change. This greatly improves designs while reducing the cost of software maintenance.

There's a problem, however, with attempting to treat derived-type objects as their generic base types (circles as shapes, bicycles as vehicles, cormorants as birds, etc.). If a method is going to tell a generic shape to draw itself, or a generic vehicle to steer, or a generic bird to move, the compiler cannot know at compile time precisely what piece of code will be executed. That's the whole point—when the message is sent, the programmer doesn't *want* to know what piece of code will be executed; the draw method can be applied equally to a circle, a square, or a triangle, and the object will execute the proper code depending on its specific type. If you don't have to know what piece of code will be executed, then when you add a new subtype, the code it executes can be different without requiring changes to the method call. Therefore, the compiler cannot know precisely what piece of code is executed, so what does it do? For example, in the following diagram the **BirdController** object just works with generic **Bird** objects and does not know what exact type they are. This is convenient from **BirdController**'s perspective because it doesn't have to write special code to determine the exact type of **Bird** it's working with or that **Bird**'s behavior. So how does it happen that, when **move( )** is called while ignoring the specific type of **Bird**, the right behavior will occur (a **Goose** runs, flies, or swims, and a **Penguin** runs or swims)?

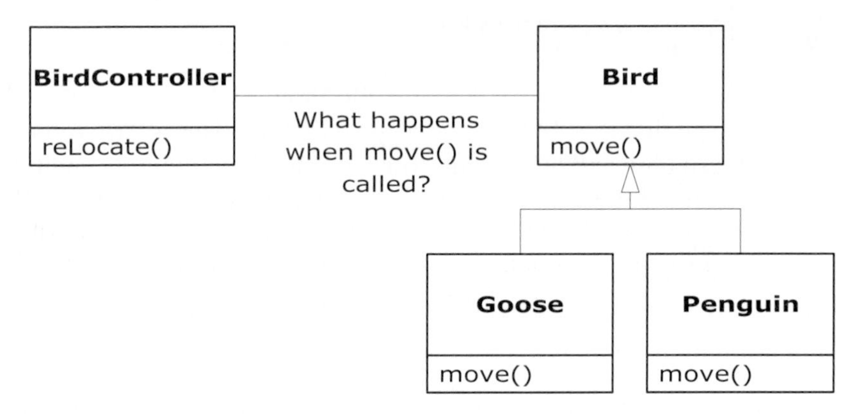

The answer is the primary twist in object-oriented programming: the compiler cannot make a function call in the traditional sense. The function call generated by a non-OOP compiler causes what is called *early binding*, a term you may not have heard before because you've never thought about it any other way. It means the compiler generates a call to a specific function name and the linker resolves this call to the absolute address of the code to be executed. In OOP, the program cannot determine the address of the code until run time, so some other scheme is necessary when a message is sent to a generic object.

To solve the problem, object-oriented languages use the concept of *late binding*. When you send a message to an object, the code being called isn't determined until run time. The compiler does ensure that the method exists and performs type checking on the arguments and return value (a language in which this isn't true is called *weakly typed*), but it doesn't know the exact code to execute.

To perform late binding, Java uses a special bit of code in lieu of the absolute call. This code calculates the address of the method body, using information stored in the object (this process is covered in great detail in Chapter 7). Thus, each object can behave differently according to the contents of that special bit of code. When you send a message to an object, the object actually does figure out what to do with that message.

In some languages you must explicitly state that you want a method to have the flexibility of late-binding properties (C++ uses the **virtual** keyword to do this). In these languages, by default, methods are *not* dynamically bound. In

Java, dynamic binding is the default behavior and you don't need to remember to add any extra keywords in order to get polymorphism.

Consider the shape example. The family of classes (all based on the same uniform interface) was diagrammed earlier in this chapter. To demonstrate polymorphism, we want to write a single piece of code that ignores the specific details of type and talks only to the base class. That code is *decoupled* from type-specific information and thus is simpler to write and easier to understand. And, if a new type—a **Hexagon**, for example—is added through inheritance, the code you write will work just as well for the new type of **Shape** as it did on the existing types. Thus, the program is *extensible*.

If you write a method in Java (as you will soon learn how to do):

```
void doStuff(Shape s) {
  s.erase();
  // ...
  s.draw();
}
```

This method speaks to any **Shape**, so it is independent of the specific type of object that it's drawing and erasing. If some other part of the program uses the **doStuff( )** method:

```
Circle c = new Circle();
Triangle t = new Triangle();
Line l = new Line();
doStuff(c);
doStuff(t);
doStuff(l);
```

the calls to **doStuff( )** automatically work correctly, regardless of the exact type of the object.

This is a rather amazing trick. Consider the line:

```
doStuff(c);
```

What's happening here is that a **Circle** is being passed into a method that's expecting a **Shape**. Since a **Circle** *is* a **Shape** it can be treated as one by **doStuff( )**. That is, any message that **doStuff( )** can send to a **Shape**, a **Circle** can accept. So it is a completely safe and logical thing to do.

We call this process of treating a derived type as though it were its base type *upcasting*. The name *cast* is used in the sense of casting into a mold and the *up* comes from the way the inheritance diagram is typically arranged, with the base type at the top and the derived classes fanning out downward. Thus, casting to a base type is moving up the inheritance diagram: "upcasting."

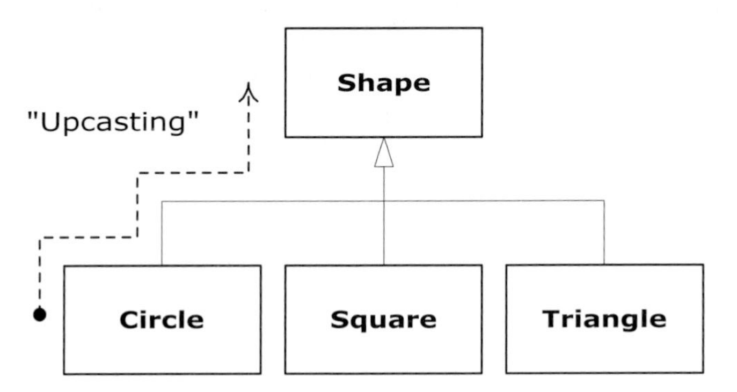

An object-oriented program contains some upcasting somewhere, because that's how you decouple yourself from knowing about the exact type you're working with. Look at the code in **doStuff( )**:

```
s.erase();
// ...
s.draw();
```

Notice that it doesn't say "If you're a **Circle**, do this, if you're a **Square**, do that, etc." If you write that kind of code, which checks for all the possible types that a **Shape** can actually be, it's messy and you need to change it every time you add a new kind of **Shape**. Here, you just say "You're a shape, I know you can **erase( )** and **draw( )** yourself, do it, and take care of the details correctly."

What's impressive about the code in **doStuff( )** is that, somehow, the right thing happens. Calling **draw( )** for **Circle** causes different code to be executed than when calling **draw( )** for a **Square** or a **Line**, but when the **draw( )** message is sent to an anonymous **Shape**, the correct behavior occurs based on the actual type of the **Shape**. This is amazing because, as mentioned earlier, when the Java compiler is compiling the code for **doStuff( )**, it cannot know exactly what types it is dealing with. So ordinarily, you'd expect it to end up calling the version of **erase( )** and **draw( )** for the base class **Shape**, and not for the specific **Circle**, **Square**, or **Line**. And yet the right thing happens because of polymorphism. The compiler and run-time system handle the details; all you need to know right now is that it does happen, and more importantly, how to design with it. When you send a message to an object, the object will do the right thing, even when upcasting is involved.

Abstract base classes and interfaces

Often in a design, you want the base class to present *only* an interface for its derived classes. That is, you don't want anyone to actually create an object of the base class, only to upcast to it so that its interface can be used. This is accomplished by making that class *abstract* by using the **abstract** keyword. If anyone tries to make an object of an **abstract** class, the compiler prevents it. This is a tool to enforce a particular design.

You can also use the **abstract** keyword to describe a method that hasn't been implemented yet—as a stub indicating "here is an interface method for all types inherited from this class, but at this point I don't have any implementation for it." An **abstract** method may be created only inside an **abstract** class. When the class is inherited, that method must be implemented, or the inheriting class becomes **abstract** as well. Creating an **abstract** method allows you to put a method in an interface without being forced to provide a possibly meaningless body of code for that method.

The **interface** keyword takes the concept of an **abstract** class one step further by preventing any method definitions at all. The **interface** is a very handy and commonly used tool, as it provides the perfect separation of interface and implementation. In addition, you can combine many interfaces together, if you wish, whereas inheriting from multiple regular classes or abstract classes is not possible.

Object creation, use & lifetimes

Technically, OOP is just about abstract data typing, inheritance, and polymorphism, but other issues can be at least as important. This section will cover these issues.

One of the most important factors of objects is the way they are created and destroyed. Where is the data for an object and how is the lifetime of the object controlled? There are different philosophies at work here. C++ takes the approach that control of efficiency is the most important issue, so it gives the programmer a choice. For maximum run-time speed, the storage and lifetime can be determined while the program is being written, by placing the objects on the stack (these are sometimes called *automatic* or *scoped* variables) or in the static storage area. This places a priority on the speed of storage allocation and release, and control of these can be very valuable in some situations. However, you sacrifice flexibility because you must know the exact quantity, lifetime, and type of objects while you're writing the program. If you are trying to solve a more general problem such as computer-aided design, warehouse management, or air-traffic control, this is too restrictive.

The second approach is to create objects dynamically in a pool of memory called the heap. In this approach, you don't know until run time how many objects you need, what their lifetime is, or what their exact type is. Those are determined at the spur of the moment while the program is running. If you need a new object, you simply make it on the heap at the point that you need it. Because the storage is managed dynamically, at run time, the amount of time required to allocate storage on the heap can be noticeably longer than the time to create storage on the stack. (Creating storage on the stack is often a single assembly instruction to move the stack pointer down and another to move it back up. The time to create heap storage depends on the design of the storage mechanism.) The dynamic approach makes the generally logical assumption that objects tend to be complicated, so the extra overhead of finding storage and releasing that storage will not have an important impact on the creation of an object. In addition, the greater flexibility is essential to solve the general programming problem.

Java uses the second approach, exclusively.[6] Every time you want to create an object, you use the **new** keyword to build a dynamic instance of that object.

There's another issue, however, and that's the lifetime of an object. With languages that allow objects to be created on the stack, the compiler determines how long the object lasts and can automatically destroy it. However, if you create it on the heap the compiler has no knowledge of its lifetime. In a language like C++, you must determine programmatically when to destroy the object, which can lead to memory leaks if you don't do it correctly (and this is a common problem in C++ programs). Java provides a feature called a *garbage collector* that automatically discovers when an object is no longer in use and destroys it. A garbage collector is much more

---

[6] Primitive types, which you'll learn about later, are a special case.

convenient because it reduces the number of issues that you must track and the code you must write. More important, the garbage collector provides a much higher level of insurance against the insidious problem of memory leaks (which has brought many a C++ project to its knees).

Collections and iterators

If you don't know how many objects you're going to need to solve a particular problem, or how long they will last, you also don't know how to store those objects. How can you know how much space to create for those objects? You can't, since that information isn't known until run time.

The solution to most problems in object-oriented design seems flippant: You create another type of object. The new type of object that solves this particular problem holds references to other objects. Of course, you can do the same thing with an array, which is available in most languages. But this new object, generally called a *container* (also called a *collection*, but the Java library uses that term in a different sense so this book will use "container"), will expand itself whenever necessary to accommodate everything you place inside it. So you don't need to know how many objects you're going to hold in a container. Just create a container object and let it take care of the details.

Fortunately, a good OOP language comes with a set of containers as part of the package. In C++, it's part of the Standard C++ Library and is sometimes called the Standard Template Library (STL). Object Pascal has containers in its Visual Component Library (VCL). Smalltalk has a very complete set of containers. Java also has containers in its standard library. In some libraries, a generic container is considered good enough for all needs, and in others (Java, for example) the library has different types of containers for different needs: several different kinds of **List** classes (to hold sequences), **Map** classes (also known as *associative arrays*, to associate objects with other objects), and **Set** classes (to hold one of each type of object). Container libraries may also include queues, trees, stacks, etc.

All containers have some way to put things in and get things out; there are usually methods to add elements to a container, and others to fetch those elements back out. But fetching elements can be more problematic, because a single-selection method is restrictive. What if you want to manipulate or compare a set of elements in the container instead of just one?

The solution is an *iterator*, which is an object whose job is to select the elements within a container and present them to the user of the iterator. As a class, it also provides a level of abstraction. This abstraction can be used to separate the details of the container from the code that's accessing that container. The container, via the iterator, is abstracted to be simply a sequence. The iterator allows you to traverse that sequence without worrying about the underlying structure—that is, whether it's an **ArrayList**, a **LinkedList**, a **Stack**, or something else. This gives you the flexibility to easily change the underlying data structure without disturbing the code in your program. Java began (in version 1.0 and 1.1) with a standard iterator, called **Enumeration**, for all of its container classes. Java 2 added a much more complete container library that contains an iterator called **Iterator** that does more than the older **Enumeration**.

From a design standpoint, all you really want is a sequence that can be manipulated to solve your problem. If a single type of sequence satisfied all of your needs, there'd be no reason to have different kinds. There are two reasons that you need a choice of containers. First, containers provide different types of interfaces and external behavior. A stack has a different interface and behavior than that of a queue, which is different from that of a set or a list. One of these might provide a more flexible solution to your problem than the other. Second, different containers have different efficiencies for certain operations. The best example compares two types of **List**: an **ArrayList** and a **LinkedList**. Both are simple sequences that can have identical interfaces and external behaviors. But certain operations can have radically different costs. Randomly accessing elements in an **ArrayList** is a constant-time operation; it takes the same amount of time regardless of the element you select. However, in a **LinkedList** it is expensive to move through the list to randomly select an element, and it takes longer to find an element that is farther down the list. On the other hand, if you want to insert an element in the middle of a sequence, it's cheaper in a **LinkedList** than in an **ArrayList**. These and other operations have different efficiencies depending on the underlying structure of the sequence. In the design phase, you might start with a **LinkedList** and, when tuning for performance, change to an **ArrayList**. Because of the abstraction via the base class **List** and via iterators, you can change from one to the other with minimal impact on your code.

The singly rooted hierarchy

One of the issues in OOP that has become especially prominent since the introduction of C++ is whether all classes should ultimately be inherited from a single base class. In Java (as with virtually all other OOP languages *except* for C++) the answer is yes, and the name of this ultimate base class is simply **Object**. It turns out that the benefits of the singly rooted hierarchy are many.

All objects in a singly rooted hierarchy have an interface in common, so they are all ultimately the same fundamental type. The alternative (provided by C++) is that you don't know that everything is the same basic type. From a backward-compatibility standpoint this fits the model of C better and can be thought of as less restrictive, but when you want to do full-on object-oriented programming you must then build your own hierarchy to provide the same convenience that's built into other OOP languages. And in any new class library you acquire, some other incompatible interface will be used. It requires effort (and possibly multiple inheritance) to work the new interface into your design. Is the extra "flexibility" of C++ worth it? If you need it—if you have a large investment in C—it's quite valuable. If you're starting from scratch, other alternatives such as Java can often be more productive.

All objects in a singly rooted hierarchy (such as Java provides) can be guaranteed to have certain functionality. You know you can perform certain basic operations on every object in your system. A singly rooted hierarchy, along with creating all objects on the heap, greatly simplifies argument passing (one of the more complex topics in C++).

A singly rooted hierarchy makes it much easier to implement a garbage collector (which is conveniently built into Java). The necessary support can be installed in the base class, and the garbage collector can thus send the appropriate messages to every object in the system. Without a singly rooted hierarchy and a system to manipulate an object via a reference, it is difficult to implement a garbage collector.

Since run time type information is guaranteed to be in all objects, you'll never end up with an object whose type you cannot determine. This is especially important with system-level operations, such as exception handling, and to allow greater flexibility in programming.

Downcasting vs. templates/generics

To make these containers reusable, they hold the one universal type in Java: **Object**. The singly rooted hierarchy means that everything is an **Object**, so a container that holds **Object**s can hold anything.[7] This makes containers easy to reuse.

To use such a container, you simply add object references to it and later ask for them back. But, since the container holds only **Object**s, when you add your object reference into the container it is upcast to **Object**, thus losing its identity. When you fetch it back, you get an **Object** reference, and not a reference to the type that you put in. So how do you turn it back into something that has the useful interface of the object that you put into the container?

Here, the cast is used again, but this time you're not casting up the inheritance hierarchy to a more general type. Instead, you cast down the hierarchy to a more specific type. This manner of casting is called *downcasting*. With upcasting, you know, for example, that a **Circle** is a type of **Shape** so it's safe to upcast, but you don't know that an **Object** is necessarily a **Circle** or a **Shape** so it's hardly safe to downcast unless you know exactly what you're dealing with.

It's not completely dangerous, however, because if you downcast to the wrong thing you'll get a run-time error called an *exception,* which will be described shortly. When you fetch object references from a container, though, you must have some way to remember exactly what they are so you can perform a proper downcast.

Downcasting and the run-time checks require extra time for the running program and extra effort from the programmer. Wouldn't it make sense to somehow create the container so that it knows the types that it holds, eliminating the need for the downcast and a possible mistake? The solution is called a *parameterized type* mechanism. A parameterized type is a class that the compiler can automatically customize to work with particular types. For example, with a parameterized container, the compiler could customize that container so that it would accept only **Shape**s and fetch only **Shape**s.

---

[7] Except, unfortunately, for primitives. This is discussed in detail later in the book.

Parameterized types are an important part of C++, partly because C++ has no singly rooted hierarchy. In C++, the keyword that implements parameterized types is "template." Java currently has no parameterized types since it is possible for it to get by—however awkwardly—using the singly rooted hierarchy. However, a current proposal for parameterized types uses a syntax that is strikingly similar to C++ templates, and we can expect to see parameterized types (which will be called *generics*) in the next version of Java.

Ensuring proper cleanup

Each object requires resources, most notably memory, in order to exist. When an object is no longer needed it must be cleaned up so that these resources are released for reuse. In simple programming situations the question of how an object is cleaned up doesn't seem too challenging: you create the object, use it for as long as it's needed, and then it should be destroyed. However, it's not hard to encounter situations that are more complex.

Suppose, for example, you are designing a system to manage air traffic for an airport. (The same model might also work for managing crates in a warehouse, or a video rental system, or a kennel for boarding pets.) At first it seems simple: Make a container to hold airplanes, then create a new airplane and place it in the container for each airplane that enters the air-traffic-control zone. For cleanup, simply delete the appropriate airplane object when a plane leaves the zone.

But perhaps you have some other system to record data about the planes; perhaps data that doesn't require such immediate attention as the main controller function. Maybe it's a record of the flight plans of all the small planes that leave the airport. So you have a second container of small planes, and whenever you create a plane object you also put it in this second container if it's a small plane. Then some background process performs operations on the objects in this container during idle moments.

Now the problem is more difficult: How can you possibly know when to destroy the objects? When you're done with the object, some other part of the system might not be. This same problem can arise in a number of other situations, and in programming systems (such as C++) in which you must explicitly delete an object when you're done with it this can become quite complex.

With Java, the garbage collector is designed to take care of the problem of releasing the memory (although this doesn't include other aspects of cleaning up an object). The garbage collector "knows" when an object is no longer in use, and it then automatically releases the memory for that object. This (combined with the fact that all objects are inherited from the single root class **Object** and that you can create objects only one way—on the heap) makes the process of programming in Java much simpler than programming in C++. You have far fewer decisions to make and hurdles to overcome.

Garbage collectors vs. efficiency and flexibility

If all this is such a good idea, why didn't they do the same thing in C++? Well of course there's a price you pay for all this programming convenience, and that price is run time overhead. As mentioned before, in C++ you can create objects on the stack, and in this case they're automatically cleaned up (but you don't have the flexibility of creating as many as you want at run time). Creating objects on the stack is the most efficient way to allocate storage for objects and to free that storage. Creating objects on the heap can be much more expensive. Always inheriting from a base class and making all method calls polymorphic also exacts a small toll. But the garbage collector is a particular problem because you never quite know when it's going to start up or how long it will take. This means that there's an inconsistency in the rate of execution of a Java program, so you can't use it in certain situations, such as when the rate of execution of a program is uniformly critical. (These are generally called real time programs, although not all real time programming problems are this stringent.)

The designers of the C++ language, trying to woo C programmers (and most successfully, at that), did not want to add any features to the language that would impact the speed or the use of C++ in any situation where programmers might otherwise choose C. This goal was realized, but at the price of greater complexity when programming in C++. Java is simpler than C++, but the trade-off is in efficiency and sometimes applicability. For a significant portion of programming problems, however, Java is the superior choice.

Exception handling: dealing with errors

Ever since the beginning of programming languages, error handling has been one of the most difficult issues. Because it's so hard to design a good error handling scheme, many languages simply ignore the issue, passing the problem on to library designers who come up with halfway measures that work in many situations but that can easily be circumvented, generally by just ignoring them. A major problem with most error handling schemes is that they rely on programmer vigilance in following an agreed-upon convention that is not enforced by the language. If the programmer is not vigilant—often the case if they are in a hurry—these schemes can easily be forgotten.

Exception handling wires error handling directly into the programming language and sometimes even the operating system. An exception is an object that is "thrown" from the site of the error and can be "caught" by an appropriate exception handler designed to handle that particular type of error. It's as if exception handling is a different, parallel path of execution that can be taken when things go wrong. And because it uses a separate execution path, it doesn't need to interfere with your normally executing code. This makes that code simpler to write because you aren't constantly forced to check for errors. In addition, a thrown exception is unlike an error value that's returned from a method or a flag that's set by a method in order to indicate an error condition—these can be ignored. An exception cannot be ignored, so it's guaranteed to be dealt with at some point. Finally, exceptions provide a way to reliably recover from a bad situation. Instead of just exiting the program, you are often able to set things right and restore execution, which produces much more robust programs.

Java's exception handling stands out among programming languages, because in Java, exception handling was wired in from the beginning and you're forced to use it. If you don't write your code to properly handle exceptions, you'll get a compile-time error message. This guaranteed consistency can sometimes make error handling much easier.

It's worth noting that exception handling isn't an object-oriented feature, although in object-oriented languages the exception is normally represented by an object. Exception handling existed before object-oriented languages.

Concurrency

A fundamental concept in computer programming is the idea of handling more than one task at a time. Many programming problems require that the program be able to stop what it's doing, deal with some other problem, and then return to the main process. The solution has been approached in many ways. Initially, programmers with low-level knowledge of the machine wrote interrupt service routines, and the suspension of the main process was initiated through a hardware interrupt. Although this worked well, it was difficult and nonportable, so it made moving a program to a new type of machine slow and expensive.

Sometimes, interrupts are necessary for handling time-critical tasks, but there's a large class of problems in which you're simply trying to partition the problem into separately running pieces so that the whole program can be more responsive. Within a program, these separately running pieces are called threads, and the general concept is called *concurrency* or *multithreading*. A common example of multithreading is the user interface. By using threads, a user can press a button and get a quick response rather than being forced to wait until the program finishes its current task.

Ordinarily, threads are just a way to allocate the time of a single processor. But if the operating system supports multiple processors, each thread can be assigned to a different processor, and they can truly run in parallel. One of the convenient features of multithreading at the language level is that the programmer doesn't need to worry about whether there are many processors or just one. The program is logically divided into threads and if the machine has more than one processor, then the program runs faster, without any special adjustments.

All this makes threading sound pretty simple. There is a catch: shared resources. If you have more than one thread running that's expecting to access the same resource, you have a problem. For example, two processes can't simultaneously send information to a printer. To solve the problem, resources that can be shared, such as the printer, must be locked while they are being used. So a thread locks a resource, completes its task, and then releases the lock so that someone else can use the resource.

Java's threading is built into the language, which makes a complicated subject much simpler. The threading is supported on an object level, so one thread of execution is represented by one object. Java also provides limited resource locking. It can lock the memory of any object (which is, after all, one kind of shared resource) so that only one thread can use it at a time. This is accomplished with the **synchronized** keyword. Other types of resources must be locked explicitly by the programmer, typically by creating an object to represent the lock that all threads must check before accessing that resource.

Persistence

When you create an object, it exists for as long as you need it, but under no circumstances does it exist when the program terminates. While this makes sense at first, there are situations in which it would be incredibly useful if an object could exist and hold its information even while the program wasn't running. Then the next time you started the program, the object would be there and it would have the same information it had the previous time the program was running. Of course, you can get a similar effect by writing the information to a file or to a database, but in the spirit of making everything an object, it would be quite convenient to be able to declare an object persistent and have all the details taken care of for you.

Java provides support for "lightweight persistence," which means that you can easily store objects on disk and later retrieve them. The reason it's "lightweight" is that you're still forced to make explicit calls to do the storage and retrieval. Lightweight persistence can be implemented both through *object serialization* (shown in Chapter 12) and *Java Data Objects* (JDO, shown in *Thinking in Enterprise Java*).

Java and the Internet

If Java is, in fact, yet another computer programming language, you may question why it is so important and why it is being promoted as a revolutionary step in computer programming. The answer isn't immediately obvious if you're coming from a traditional programming perspective. Although Java is very useful for solving traditional standalone programming problems, it is also important because it will solve programming problems on the World Wide Web.

What is the Web?

The Web can seem a bit of a mystery at first, with all this talk of "surfing," "presence," and "home pages." It's helpful to step back and see what it really is, but to do this you must understand client/server systems, another aspect of computing that's full of confusing issues.

Client/Server computing

The primary idea of a client/server system is that you have a central repository of information—some kind of data, often in a database—that you want to distribute on demand to some set of people or machines. A key to the client/server concept is that the repository of information is centrally located so that it can be changed and so that those changes will propagate out to the information consumers. Taken together, the information repository, the software that distributes the information, and the machine(s) where the information and software reside is called the server. The software that resides on the remote machine, communicates with the server, fetches the information, processes it, and then displays it on the remote machine is called the *client*.

The basic concept of client/server computing, then, is not so complicated. The problems arise because you have a single server trying to serve many clients at once. Generally, a database management system is involved, so the designer "balances" the layout of data into tables for optimal use. In addition, systems often allow a client to insert new information into a server. This means you must ensure that one client's new data doesn't walk over another client's new data, or that data isn't lost in the process of adding it to the database (this is called transaction processing). As client software changes, it must be built, debugged, and installed on the client machines, which turns out to be more complicated and expensive than you might think. It's especially problematic to support multiple types of computers and operating systems. Finally, there's the all-important performance issue: You might have hundreds of clients making requests of your server at any one time, so any small delay is crucial. To minimize latency, programmers work hard to offload processing tasks, often to the client machine, but sometimes to other machines at the server site, using so-called *middleware*. (Middleware is also used to improve maintainability.)

The simple idea of distributing information has so many layers of complexity that the whole problem can seem hopelessly enigmatic. And yet it's crucial: Client/server computing accounts for roughly half of all programming activities. It's responsible for everything from taking orders and credit-card transactions to the distribution of any kind of data—stock market, scientific, government, you name it. What we've come up with in the past is individual solutions to individual problems, inventing a new solution each time. These were hard to create and hard to use, and the user had to learn a new interface for each one. The entire client/server problem needs to be solved in a big way.

The Web as a giant server

The Web is actually one giant client/server system. It's a bit worse than that, since you have all the servers and clients coexisting on a single network at once. You don't need to know that, because all you care about is connecting to and interacting with one server at a time (even though you might be hopping around the world in your search for the correct server).

Initially it was a simple one-way process. You made a request of a server and it handed you a file, which your machine's browser software (i.e., the client) would interpret by formatting onto your local machine. But in short order people began wanting to do more than just deliver pages from a server. They wanted full client/server capability so that the client could feed information back to the server, for example, to do database lookups on the server, to add new information to the server, or to place an order (which required more security than the original systems offered). These are the changes we've been seeing in the development of the Web.

The Web browser was a big step forward: the concept that one piece of information could be displayed on any type of computer without change. However, browsers were still rather primitive and rapidly bogged down by the demands placed on them. They weren't particularly interactive, and tended to clog up both the server and the Internet because any time you needed to do something that required programming you had to send information back to the server to be processed. It could take many seconds or minutes to find out you had misspelled something in your request. Since the browser was just a viewer it couldn't perform even the simplest computing tasks. (On the other hand, it was safe, because it couldn't execute any programs on your local machine that might contain bugs or viruses.)

To solve this problem, different approaches have been taken. To begin with, graphics standards have been enhanced to allow better animation and video within browsers. The remainder of the problem can be solved only by incorporating the ability to run programs on the client end, under the browser. This is called client-side programming.

Client-side programming

The Web's initial server-browser design provided for interactive content, but the interactivity was completely provided by the server. The server produced static pages for the client browser, which would simply interpret and display them. Basic *HyperText Markup Language* (HTML) contains simple mechanisms for data gathering: text-entry boxes, check boxes, radio boxes, lists and drop-down lists, as well as a button that can only be programmed to reset the data on the form or "submit" the data on the form back to the server. This submission passes through the *Common Gateway Interface* (CGI) provided on all Web servers. The text within the submission tells CGI what to do with it. The most common action is to run a program located on the server in a directory that's typically called "cgi-bin." (If you watch the address window at the top of your browser when you push a button on a Web page, you can sometimes see "cgi-bin" within all the gobbledygook there.) These programs can be written in most languages. Perl has been a common choice because it is designed for text manipulation and is interpreted, so it can be installed on any server regardless of processor or operating system. However, Python (my favorite—see www.Python.org) has been making inroads because of its greater power and simplicity.

Many powerful Web sites today are built strictly on CGI, and you can in fact do nearly anything with CGI. However, Web sites built on CGI programs can rapidly become overly complicated to maintain, and there is also the problem of response time. The response of a CGI program depends on how much data must be sent, as well as the load on both the server and the Internet. (On top of this, starting a CGI program tends to be slow.) The initial designers of the Web did not foresee how rapidly this bandwidth would be exhausted for the kinds of applications people developed. For example, any sort of dynamic graphing is nearly impossible to perform with consistency because a *Graphics Interchange Format* (GIF) file must be created and moved from the server to the client for each version of the graph. And you've no doubt had direct experience with something as simple as validating the data on an input form. You press the submit button on a page; the data is shipped back to the server; the server starts a CGI program that discovers an error, formats an HTML page informing you of the error, and then sends the page back to you; you must then back up a page and try again. Not only is this slow, it's inelegant.

The solution is client-side programming. Most machines that run Web browsers are powerful engines capable of doing vast work, and with the original static HTML approach they are sitting there, just idly waiting for the server to dish up the next page. Client-side programming means that the Web browser is harnessed to do whatever work it can, and the result for the user is a much speedier and more interactive experience at your Web site.

The problem with discussions of client-side programming is that they aren't very different from discussions of programming in general. The parameters are almost the same, but the platform is different; a Web browser is like a limited operating system. In the end, you must still program, and this accounts for the dizzying array of problems and solutions produced by client-side programming. The rest of this section provides an overview of the issues and approaches in client-side programming.

Plug-ins

One of the most significant steps forward in client-side programming is the development of the plug-in. This is a way for a programmer to add new functionality to the browser by downloading a piece of code that plugs itself into the appropriate spot in the browser. It tells the browser "from now on you can perform this new activity." (You need to download the plug-in only once.) Some fast and powerful behavior is added to browsers via plug-ins, but writing a plug-in is not a trivial task, and isn't something you'd want to do as part of the process of building a particular site. The value of the plug-in for client-side programming is that it allows an expert programmer to develop a new language and add that language to a browser without the permission of the browser manufacturer. Thus, plug-ins provide a "back door" that allows the creation of new client-side programming languages (although not all languages are implemented as plug-ins).

Scripting languages

Plug-ins resulted in an explosion of scripting languages. With a scripting language, you embed the source code for your client-side program directly into the HTML page, and the plug-in that interprets that language is automatically activated while the HTML page is being displayed. Scripting languages tend to be reasonably easy to understand and, because they are simply text that is part of an HTML page, they load very quickly as part of the single server hit required to procure that page. The trade-off is that your code is exposed for everyone to see (and steal). Generally, however, you aren't doing amazingly sophisticated things with scripting languages, so this is not too much of a hardship.

This points out that the scripting languages used inside Web browsers are really intended to solve specific types of problems, primarily the creation of richer and more interactive graphical user interfaces (GUIs). However, a scripting language might solve 80 percent of the problems encountered in client-side programming. Your problems might very well fit completely within that 80 percent, and since scripting languages can allow easier and faster development, you should probably consider a scripting language before looking at a more involved solution such as Java or ActiveX programming.

The most commonly discussed browser scripting languages are JavaScript (which has nothing to do with Java; it's named that way just to grab some of Java's marketing momentum), VBScript (which looks like Visual BASIC), and Tcl/Tk, which comes from the popular cross-platform GUI-building language. There are others out there, and no doubt more in development.

JavaScript is probably the most commonly supported. It comes built into both Netscape Navigator and the Microsoft Internet Explorer (IE). Unfortunately, the flavor of JavaScript on the two browsers can vary widely (the Mozilla browser, freely downloadable from www.Mozilla.org, supports the ECMAScript standard, which may one day become universally supported). In addition, there are probably more JavaScript books available than there are for the other browser languages, and some tools automatically create pages using JavaScript. However, if you're already fluent in Visual BASIC or Tcl/Tk, you'll be more productive using those scripting languages rather than learning a new one. (You'll have your hands full dealing with the Web issues already.)

Java

If a scripting language can solve 80 percent of the client-side programming problems, what about the other 20 percent—the "really hard stuff?" Java is a popular solution for this. Not only is it a powerful programming language built to be secure, cross-platform, and international, but Java is being continually extended to provide language features and libraries that elegantly handle problems that are difficult in traditional programming languages, such as multithreading, database access, network programming, and distributed computing. Java allows client-side programming via the *applet* and with *Java Web Start*.

An applet is a mini-program that will run only under a Web browser. The applet is downloaded automatically as part of a Web page (just as, for example, a graphic is automatically downloaded). When the applet is activated, it executes a program. This is part of its beauty—it provides you with a way to automatically distribute the client software from the server at the time the user needs the client software, and no sooner. The user gets the latest version of the client software without fail and without difficult reinstallation. Because of the way Java is designed, the programmer needs to create only a single program, and that program automatically works with all computers that have browsers with built-in Java interpreters. (This safely includes the vast majority of machines.) Since Java is a full-fledged programming language, you can do as much work as possible on the client before and after making requests of the server. For example, you won't need to send a request form across the Internet to discover that you've gotten a date or some other parameter wrong, and your client computer can quickly do the work of plotting data instead of waiting for the server to make a plot and ship a graphic image back to you. Not only do you get the immediate win of speed and responsiveness, but the general network traffic and load on servers can be reduced, preventing the entire Internet from slowing down.

One advantage a Java applet has over a scripted program is that it's in compiled form, so the source code isn't available to the client. On the other hand, a Java applet can be decompiled without too much trouble, but hiding your code is often not an important issue. Two other factors can be important. As you will see later in this book, a compiled Java applet can require extra time to download, if it is large. A scripted program will just be integrated into the Web page as part of its text (and will generally be smaller and reduce server hits). This could be important to the responsiveness of your Web site. Another factor is the all-important learning curve. Regardless of what you've heard, Java is not a trivial language to learn. If you're a VISUAL BASIC programmer, moving to VBScript will be your fastest solution (assuming you can constrain your customers to Windows platforms), and since it will probably solve most typical client/server problems, you might be hard pressed to justify learning Java. If you're experienced with a scripting language you will certainly benefit from looking at JavaScript or VBScript before committing to Java, because they might fit your needs handily and you'll be more productive sooner.

.NET and C#

For awhile, the main competitor to Java applets was Microsoft's ActiveX, although it required that the client be running Windows. Since then, Microsoft has produced a full competitor to Java in the form of the **.NET** platform and the **C#** programming language. The **.NET** platform is roughly the same as the Java virtual machine and Java libraries, and **C#** bears unmistakable similarities to Java. This is certainly the best work that Microsoft has done in the arena of programming languages and programming environments. Of course, they had the considerable advantage of being able to see what worked well and what didn't work so well in Java, and build upon that, but build they have. This is the first time since its inception that Java has had any real competition, and if all goes well, the result will be that the Java designers at Sun will take a hard look at C# and why programmers might want to move to it, and will respond by making fundamental improvements to Java.

Currently, the main vulnerability and important question concerning **.NET** is whether Microsoft will allow it to be *completely* ported to other platforms. They claim there's no problem doing this, and the Mono project (www.go-mono.com) has a partial implementation of **.NET** working on Linux, but until the implementation is complete and Microsoft has not decided to squash any part of it, **.NET** as a cross-platform solution is still a risky bet.

To learn more about **.NET** and **C#**, see *Thinking in C#* by Larry O'Brien and Bruce Eckel, Prentice Hall 2003.

Security

Automatically downloading and running programs across the Internet can sound like a virus-builder's dream. If you click on a Web site, you might automatically download any number of things along with the HTML page: GIF files, script code, compiled Java code, and ActiveX components. Some of these are benign; GIF files can't do any harm, and scripting languages are generally limited in what they can do. Java was also designed to run its applets within a "sandbox" of safety, which prevents it from writing to disk or accessing memory outside the sandbox.

Microsoft's ActiveX is at the opposite end of the spectrum. Programming with ActiveX is like programming Windows—you can do anything you want. So if you click on a page that downloads an ActiveX component, that component might cause damage to the files on your disk. Of course, programs that you load onto your computer that are not restricted to running inside a Web browser can do the same thing. Viruses downloaded from Bulletin-Board Systems (BBSs) have long been a problem, but the speed of the Internet amplifies the difficulty.

The solution seems to be "digital signatures," whereby code is verified to show who the author is. This is based on the idea that a virus works because its creator can be anonymous, so if you remove the anonymity, individuals will be forced to be responsible for their actions. This seems like a good plan because it allows programs to be much more functional, and I suspect it will eliminate malicious mischief. If, however, a program has an unintentional destructive bug, it will still cause problems.

The Java approach is to prevent these problems from occurring, via the sandbox. The Java interpreter that lives on your local Web browser examines the applet for any untoward instructions as the applet is being loaded. In particular, the applet cannot write files to disk or erase files (one of the mainstays of viruses). Applets are generally considered to be safe, and since this is essential for reliable client/server systems, any bugs in the Java language that allow viruses are rapidly repaired. (It's worth noting that the browser software actually enforces these security restrictions, and some browsers allow you to select different security levels to provide varying degrees of access to your system.)

You might be skeptical of this rather draconian restriction against writing files to your local disk. For example, you may want to build a local database or save data for later use offline. The initial vision seemed to be that eventually everyone would get online to do anything important, but that was soon seen to be impractical (although low-cost "Internet appliances" might someday satisfy the needs of a significant segment of users). The solution is the "signed applet" that uses public-key encryption to verify that an applet does indeed come from where it claims it does. A signed applet can still trash your disk, but the theory is that since you can now hold the applet creators accountable, they won't do vicious things. Java provides a framework for digital signatures so that you will eventually be able to allow an applet to step outside the sandbox if necessary. Chapter 14 contains an example of how to sign an applet.

In addition, Java Web Start is a relatively new way to easily distribute standalone programs that don't need a web browser in which to run. This technology has the potential of solving many client side problems associated with running programs inside a browser. Web Start programs can either be signed, or they can ask the client for permission every time they are doing something potentially dangerous on the local system. Chapter 14 has a simple example and explanation of Java Web Start.

Digital signatures have missed an important issue, which is the speed that people move around on the Internet. If you download a buggy program and it does something untoward, how long will it be before you discover the damage? It could be days or even weeks. By then, how will you track down the program that's done it? And what good will it do you at that point?

Internet vs. intranet

The Web is the most general solution to the client/server problem, so it makes sense to use the same technology to solve a subset of the problem, in particular the classic client/server problem *within* a company. With traditional client/server approaches you have the problem of multiple types of client computers, as well as the difficulty of installing new client software, both of which are handily solved with Web browsers and client-side programming. When Web technology is used for an information network that is restricted to a particular company, it is referred to as an intranet. Intranets provide much greater security than the Internet, since you can physically control access to the servers within your company. In terms of training, it seems that once people understand the general concept of a browser it's much easier for them to deal with differences in the way pages and applets look, so the learning curve for new kinds of systems seems to be reduced.

The security problem brings us to one of the divisions that seems to be automatically forming in the world of client-side programming. If your program is running on the Internet, you don't know what platform it will be working under, and you want to be extra careful that you don't disseminate buggy code. You need something cross-platform and secure, like a scripting language or Java.

If you're running on an intranet, you might have a different set of constraints. It's not uncommon that your machines could all be Intel/Windows platforms. On an intranet, you're responsible for the quality of your own code and can repair bugs when they're discovered. In addition, you might already have a body of legacy code that you've been using in a more traditional client/server approach, whereby you must physically install client programs every time you do an upgrade. The time wasted in installing upgrades is the most compelling reason to move to browsers, because upgrades are invisible and automatic (Java Web Start is also a solution to this problem). If you are involved in such an intranet, the most sensible approach to take is the shortest path that allows you to use your existing code base, rather than trying to recode your programs in a new language.

When faced with this bewildering array of solutions to the client-side programming problem, the best plan of attack is a cost-benefit analysis. Consider the constraints of your problem and what would be the shortest path to your solution. Since client-side programming is still programming, it's always a good idea to take the fastest development approach for your particular situation. This is an aggressive stance to prepare for inevitable encounters with the problems of program development.

Server-side programming

This whole discussion has ignored the issue of server-side programming. What happens when you make a request of a server? Most of the time the request is simply "send me this file." Your browser then interprets the file in some appropriate fashion: as an HTML page, a graphic image, a Java applet, a script program, etc. A more complicated request to a server generally involves a database transaction. A common scenario involves a request for a complex database search, which the server then formats into an HTML page and sends to you as the result. (Of course, if the client has more intelligence via Java or a scripting language, the raw data can be sent and formatted at the client end, which will be faster and less load on the server.) Or you might want to register your name in a database when you join a group or place an order, which will involve changes to that database. These database requests must be processed via some code on the server side, which is generally referred to as server-side programming. Traditionally, server-side programming has been performed using Perl, Python, C++, or some other language, to create CGI programs, but more sophisticated systems have been appearing. These include Java-based Web servers that allow you to perform all your server-side programming in Java by writing what are called servlets. Servlets and their offspring, JSPs, are two of the most compelling reasons that companies who develop Web sites are moving to Java, especially because they eliminate the problems of dealing with differently-abled browsers (these topics are covered in *Thinking in Enterprise Java*).

Applications

Much of the brouhaha over Java has been over applets. Java is actually a general-purpose programming language that can solve the kinds of problems you can solve with other languages—at least in theory. And as pointed out previously, there might be more effective ways to solve most client/server problems. When you move out of the applet arena (and simultaneously release the restrictions, such as the one against writing to disk) you enter the world of general-purpose applications that run standalone, without a Web browser, just like any ordinary program does. Here, Java's strength is not only in its portability, but also its programmability. As you'll see throughout this book, Java has many features that allow you to create robust programs in a shorter period than with previous programming languages.

Be aware that this is a mixed blessing. You pay for the improvements through slower execution speed (although there is significant work going on in this area—in particular, the so-called "hotspot" performance improvements in recent versions of Java). Like any language, Java has built-in limitations that might make it inappropriate to solve certain types of programming problems. Java is a rapidly evolving language, however, and as each new release comes out it becomes more and more attractive for solving larger sets of problems.

Why Java succeeds

The reason Java has been so successful is that the goal was to solve many of the problems facing developers today. A fundamental goal of Java is improved productivity. This productivity comes in many ways, but the language is designed to be a significant improvement over its predecessors, and to provide important benefits to the programmer.

Systems are easier to express and understand

Classes designed to fit the problem tend to express it better. This means that when you write the code, you're describing your solution in the terms of the problem space ("Put the grommet in the bin") rather than the terms of the computer, which is the solution space ("Set the bit in the chip that means that the relay will close"). You deal with higher-level concepts and can do much more with a single line of code.

The other benefit of this ease of expression is maintenance, which (if reports can be believed) is a huge portion of the cost over a program's lifetime. If a program is easier to understand, then it's easier to maintain. This can also reduce the cost of creating and maintaining the documentation.

Maximal leverage with libraries

The fastest way to create a program is to use code that's already written: a library. A major goal in Java is to make library use easier. This is accomplished by casting libraries into new data types (classes), so that bringing in a library means adding new types to the language. Because the Java compiler takes care of how the library is used—guaranteeing proper initialization and cleanup, and ensuring that methods are called properly—you can focus on what you want the library to do, not how you have to do it.

Error handling

Error handling in C is a notorious problem, and one that is often ignored—finger-crossing is usually involved. If you're building a large, complex program, there's nothing worse than having an error buried somewhere with no clue as to where it came from. Java *exception handling* is a way to guarantee that an error is noticed, and that something happens as a result.

Programming in the large

Many traditional languages have built-in limitations to program size and complexity. BASIC, for example, can be great for pulling together quick solutions for certain classes of problems, but if the program gets more than a few pages long, or ventures out of the normal problem domain of that language, it's like trying to swim through an ever-more viscous fluid. There's no clear line that tells you when your language is failing you, and even if there were, you'd ignore it. You don't say, "My BASIC program just got too big; I'll have to rewrite it in C!" Instead, you try to shoehorn a few more lines in to add that one new feature. So the extra costs come creeping up on you.

Java is designed to aid *programming in the large*—that is, to erase those creeping-complexity boundaries between a small program and a large one. You certainly don't need to use OOP when you're writing a "hello, world" style utility program, but the features are there when you need them. And the compiler is aggressive about ferreting out bug-producing errors for small and large programs alike.

Java vs. C++?

Java looks a lot like C++, so naturally it would seem that C++ will be replaced by Java. But I'm starting to question this logic. For one thing, C++ still has some features that Java doesn't, and although there have been a lot of promises about Java someday being as fast or faster than C++, we've seen steady improvements but no dramatic breakthroughs. Also, there seems to be a continuing interest in C++, so I don't think that language is going away any time soon. Languages seem to hang around.

I'm beginning to think that the strength of Java lies in a slightly different arena than that of C++, which is a language that doesn't try to fit a mold. Certainly it has been adapted in a number of ways to solve particular problems. Some C++ tools combine libraries, component models, and code-generation tools to solve the problem of developing windowed end-user applications (for Microsoft Windows). And yet, what do the vast majority of Windows developers use? Microsoft's Visual BASIC (VB). This despite the fact that VB produces the kind of code that becomes unmanageable when the program is only a few pages long (and syntax that can be positively mystifying). As successful and popular as VB is, it's not a very good example of language design. It would be nice to have the ease and power of VB without the resulting unmanageable code. And that's where I think Java will shine: as the "next VB.[8]" You may or may not shudder to hear this, but think about it: so much of Java is intended to make it easy for the programmer to solve application-level problems like networking and cross-platform UI, and yet it has a language design that allows the creation of very large and flexible bodies of code. Add to this the fact that Java's type checking and error handling is a big improvement over most languages and you have the makings of a significant leap forward in programming productivity.

If you're developing all your code primarily from scratch, then the simplicity of Java over C++ will significantly shorten your development time—the anecdotal evidence (stories from C++ teams that I've talked to who have switched to Java) suggests a doubling of development speed over C++. If Java

---

[8] Microsoft is effectively saying "not so fast" with C# and .NET. Numerous people have raised the question of whether VB programmers want to change to *anything* else, whether that be Java, C#, or even VB.NET.

performance doesn't matter or you can somehow compensate for it, sheer time-to-market issues make it difficult to choose C++ over Java.

The biggest issue is performance. Interpreted Java has been slow, even 20 to 50 times slower than C in the original Java interpreters. This has improved greatly over time (especially with more recent versions of Java), but it will still remain an important number. Computers are about speed; if it wasn't significantly faster to do something on a computer then you'd do it by hand. (I've even heard it suggested that you start with Java, to gain the short development time, then use a tool and support libraries to translate your code to C++, if you need faster execution speed.)

The key to making Java feasible for many development projects is the appearance of speed improvements like so-called "just-in-time" (JIT) compilers, Sun's own "hotspot" technology, and even native code compilers. Of course, native code compilers will eliminate the touted cross-platform execution of the compiled programs, but they will also bring the speed of the executable closer to that of C and C++. And cross-compiling a program in Java should be a lot easier than doing so in C or C++. (In theory, you just recompile, but that promise has been made before for other languages.)

Summary

This chapter attempts to give you a feel for the broad issues of object-oriented programming and Java, including why OOP is different, and why Java in particular is different.

OOP and Java may not be for everyone. It's important to evaluate your own needs and decide whether Java will optimally satisfy those needs, or if you might be better off with another programming system (including the one you're currently using). If you know that your needs will be very specialized for the foreseeable future and if you have specific constraints that may not be satisfied by Java, then you owe it to yourself to investigate the alternatives (In particular, I recommend looking at Python; see www.Python.org). Even if you eventually choose Java as your language, you'll at least understand what the options were and have a clear vision of why you took that direction.

You know what a procedural program looks like: data definitions and function calls. To find the meaning of such a program, you have to work a little, looking through the function calls and low-level concepts to create a model in your mind. This is the reason we need intermediate representations when designing procedural programs—by themselves, these programs tend to be confusing because the terms of expression are oriented more toward the computer than to the problem you're solving.

Because Java adds many new concepts on top of what you find in a procedural language, your natural assumption may be that the **main( )** in a Java program will be far more complicated than for the equivalent C program. Here, you'll be pleasantly surprised: A well-written Java program is generally far simpler and much easier to understand than the equivalent C program. What you'll see are the definitions of the objects that represent concepts in your problem space (rather than the issues of the computer representation) and messages sent to those objects to represent the activities in that space. One of the delights of object-oriented programming is that, with a well-designed program, it's easy to understand the code by reading it. Usually, there's a lot less code as well, because many of your problems will be solved by reusing existing library code.

2: Everything is an Object

Although it is based on C++, Java is more of a "pure" object-oriented language.

Both C++ and Java are hybrid languages, but in Java the designers felt that the hybridization was not as important as it was in C++. A hybrid language allows multiple programming styles; the reason C++ is hybrid is to support backward compatibility with the C language. Because C++ is a superset of the C language, it includes many of that language's undesirable features, which can make some aspects of C++ overly complicated.

The Java language assumes that you want to do only object-oriented programming. This means that before you can begin you must shift your mindset into an object-oriented world (unless it's already there). The benefit of this initial effort is the ability to program in a language that is simpler to learn and to use than many other OOP languages. In this chapter we'll see the basic components of a Java program and we'll learn that everything in Java is an object, even a Java program.

You manipulate objects with references

Each programming language has its own means of manipulating data. Sometimes the programmer must be constantly aware of what type of manipulation is going on. Are you manipulating the object directly, or are you dealing with some kind of indirect representation (a pointer in C or C++) that must be treated with a special syntax?

All this is simplified in Java. You treat everything as an object, using a single consistent syntax. Although you *treat* everything as an object, the identifier you manipulate is actually a "reference" to an object.[1] You might imagine this scene as a television (the object) with your remote control (the reference). As long as you're holding this reference, you have a connection to the television, but when someone says "change the channel" or "lower the volume," what you're manipulating is the reference, which in turn modifies the object. If you want to move around the room and still control the television, you take the remote/reference with you, not the television.

Also, the remote control can stand on its own, with no television. That is, just because you have a reference doesn't mean there's necessarily an object connected to it. So if you want to hold a word or sentence, you create a **String** reference:

```
String s;
```

But here you've created *only* the reference, not an object. If you decided to send a message to **s** at this point, you'll get an error (at run time) because **s** isn't actually attached to anything (there's no television). A safer practice, then, is always to initialize a reference when you create it:

```
String s = "asdf";
```

However, this uses a special Java feature: strings can be initialized with quoted text. Normally, you must use a more general type of initialization for objects.

---

[1] This can be a flashpoint. There are those who say "clearly, it's a pointer," but this presumes an underlying implementation. Also, Java references are much more akin to C++ references than pointers in their syntax. In the first edition of this book, I chose to invent a new term, "handle," because C++ references and Java references have some important differences. I was coming out of C++ and did not want to confuse the C++ programmers whom I assumed would be the largest audience for Java. In the 2nd edition, I decided that "reference" was the more commonly used term, and that anyone changing from C++ would have a lot more to cope with than the terminology of references, so they might as well jump in with both feet. However, there are people who disagree even with the term "reference." I read in one book where it was "completely wrong to say that Java supports pass by reference," because Java object identifiers (according to that author) are *actually* "object references." And (he goes on) everything is *actually* pass by value. So you're not passing by reference, you're "passing an object reference by value." One could argue for the precision of such convoluted explanations, but I think my approach simplifies the understanding of the concept without hurting anything (well, the language lawyers may claim that I'm lying to you, but I'll say that I'm providing an appropriate abstraction.)

You must create all the objects

When you create a reference, you want to connect it with a new object. You do so, in general, with the **new** keyword. The keyword **new** says, "Make me a new one of these objects." So in the preceding example, you can say:

```
String s = new String("asdf");
```

Not only does this mean "Make me a new **String**," but it also gives information about *how* to make the **String** by supplying an initial character string.

Of course, **String** is not the only type that exists. Java comes with a plethora of ready-made types. What's more important is that you can create your own types. In fact, that's the fundamental activity in Java programming, and it's what you'll be learning about in the rest of this book.

Where storage lives

It's useful to visualize some aspects of how things are laid out while the program is running—in particular how memory is arranged. There are six different places to store data:

1. **Registers**. This is the fastest storage because it exists in a place different from that of other storage: inside the processor. However, the number of registers is severely limited, so registers are allocated by the compiler according to its needs. You don't have direct control, nor do you see any evidence in your programs that registers even exist.

2. **The stack**. This lives in the general random-access memory (RAM) area, but has direct support from the processor via its *stack pointer*. The stack pointer is moved down to create new memory and moved up to release that memory. This is an extremely fast and efficient way to allocate storage, second only to registers. The Java compiler must know, while it is creating the program, the exact size and lifetime of all the data that is stored on the stack, because it must generate the code to move the stack pointer up and down. This constraint places limits on the flexibility of your programs, so while some Java storage exists on the stack—in particular, object references—Java objects themselves are not placed on the stack.

3. **The heap**. This is a general-purpose pool of memory (also in the RAM area) where all Java objects live. The nice thing about the heap is that, unlike the stack, the compiler doesn't need to know how much storage it needs to allocate from the heap or how long that storage must stay on the heap. Thus, there's a great deal of flexibility in using storage on the heap. Whenever you need to create an object, you simply write the code to create it by using **new**, and the storage is allocated on the heap when that code is executed. Of course there's a price you pay for this flexibility. It takes more time to allocate heap storage than it does to allocate stack storage (if you even *could* create objects on the stack in Java, as you can in C++).

4. **Static storage**. "Static" is used here in the sense of "in a fixed location" (although it's also in RAM). Static storage contains data that is available for the entire time a program is running. You can use the **static** keyword to specify that a particular element of an object is static, but Java objects themselves are never placed in static storage.

5. **Constant storage**. Constant values are often placed directly in the program code, which is safe since they can never change. Sometimes constants are cordoned off by themselves so that they can be optionally placed in read-only memory (ROM), in embedded systems.

6. **Non-RAM storage**. If data lives completely outside a program, it can exist while the program is not running, outside the control of the program. The two primary examples of this are *streamed objects,* in which objects are turned into streams of bytes, generally to be sent to another machine, and *persistent objects,* in which the objects are placed on disk so they will hold their state even when the program is terminated. The trick with these types of storage is turning the objects into something that can exist on the other medium, and yet can be resurrected into a regular RAM-based object when necessary. Java provides support for *lightweight persistence*, and future versions of Java might provide more complete solutions for persistence.

Special case: primitive types

One group of types, which you'll use quite often in your programming, gets special treatment. You can think of these as "primitive" types. The reason for the special treatment is that to create an object with **new**—especially a small, simple variable—isn't very efficient, because **new** places objects on the heap.

For these types Java falls back on the approach taken by C and C++. That is, instead of creating the variable by using **new**, an "automatic" variable is created that is *not a reference*. The variable holds the value, and it's placed on the stack, so it's much more efficient.

Java determines the size of each primitive type. These sizes don't change from one machine architecture to another as they do in most languages. This size invariance is one reason Java programs are portable.

Primitive type	Size	Minimum	Maximum	Wrapper type
boolean	—	—	—	**Boolean**
char	16-bit	Unicode 0	Unicode 2^{16}- 1	**Character**
byte	8-bit	-128	+127	**Byte**
short	16-bit	-2^{15}	$+2^{15}-1$	**Short**
int	32-bit	-2^{31}	$+2^{31}-1$	**Integer**
long	64-bit	-2^{63}	$+2^{63}-1$	**Long**
float	32-bit	IEEE754	IEEE754	**Float**
double	64-bit	IEEE754	IEEE754	**Double**
void	—	—	—	**Void**

All numeric types are signed, so don't look for unsigned types.

The size of the **boolean** type is not explicitly specified; it is only defined to be able to take the literal values **true** or **false**.

The "wrapper" classes for the primitive data types allow you to make a nonprimitive object on the heap to represent that primitive type. For example:

```
char c = 'x';
Character C = new Character(c);
```

Or you could also use:

```
Character C = new Character('x');
```

The reasons for doing this will be shown in a later chapter.

High-precision numbers

Java includes two classes for performing high-precision arithmetic: **BigInteger** and **BigDecimal**. Although these approximately fit into the same category as the "wrapper" classes, neither one has a primitive analogue.

Both classes have methods that provide analogues for the operations that you perform on primitive types. That is, you can do anything with a **BigInteger** or **BigDecimal** that you can with an **int** or **float**, it's just that you must use method calls instead of operators. Also, since there's more involved, the operations will be slower. You're exchanging speed for accuracy.

BigInteger supports arbitrary-precision integers. This means that you can accurately represent integral values of any size without losing any information during operations.

BigDecimal is for arbitrary-precision fixed-point numbers; you can use these for accurate monetary calculations, for example.

Consult the JDK documentation for details about the constructors and methods you can call for these two classes.

Arrays in Java

Virtually all programming languages support arrays. Using arrays in C and C++ is perilous because those arrays are only blocks of memory. If a program accesses the array outside of its memory block or uses the memory before initialization (common programming errors), there will be unpredictable results.

One of the primary goals of Java is safety, so many of the problems that plague programmers in C and C++ are not repeated in Java. A Java array is guaranteed to be initialized and cannot be accessed outside of its range. The range checking comes at the price of having a small amount of memory overhead on each array as well as verifying the index at run time, but the assumption is that the safety and increased productivity is worth the expense.

When you create an array of objects, you are really creating an array of references, and each of those references is automatically initialized to a special value with its own keyword: **null**. When Java sees **null**, it recognizes that the reference in question isn't pointing to an object. You must assign an object to each reference before you use it, and if you try to use a reference that's still **null,** the problem will be reported at run time. Thus, typical array errors are prevented in Java.

You can also create an array of primitives. Again, the compiler guarantees initialization because it zeroes the memory for that array.

Arrays will be covered in detail in later chapters.

You never need to destroy an object

In most programming languages, the concept of the lifetime of a variable occupies a significant portion of the programming effort. How long does the variable last? If you are supposed to destroy it, when should you? Confusion over variable lifetimes can lead to a lot of bugs, and this section shows how Java greatly simplifies the issue by doing all the cleanup work for you.

Scoping

Most procedural languages have the concept of *scope*. This determines both the visibility and lifetime of the names defined within that scope. In C, C++, and Java, scope is determined by the placement of curly braces **{}**. So for example:

```
{
  int x = 12;
  // Only x available
  {
    int q = 96;
    // Both x & q available
  }
  // Only x available
  // q "out of scope"
}
```

A variable defined within a scope is available only to the end of that scope.

Any text after a '//' to the end of a line is a comment.

Indentation makes Java code easier to read. Since Java is a free-form language, the extra spaces, tabs, and carriage returns do not affect the resulting program.

Note that you *cannot* do the following, even though it is legal in C and C++:

```
{
  int x = 12;
  {
    int x = 96; // Illegal
  }
}
```

The compiler will announce that the variable **x** has already been defined. Thus the C and C++ ability to "hide" a variable in a larger scope is not allowed, because the Java designers thought that it led to confusing programs.

Scope of objects

Java objects do not have the same lifetimes as primitives. When you create a Java object using **new**, it hangs around past the end of the scope. Thus if you use:

```
{
  String s = new String("a string");
} // End of scope
```

the reference **s** vanishes at the end of the scope. However, the **String** object that **s** was pointing to is still occupying memory. In this bit of code, there is no way to access the object, because the only reference to it is out of scope. In later chapters you'll see how the reference to the object can be passed around and duplicated during the course of a program.

It turns out that because objects created with **new** stay around for as long as you want them, a whole slew of C++ programming problems simply vanish in Java. The hardest problems seem to occur in C++ because you don't get any help from the language in making sure that the objects are available when they're needed. And more important, in C++ you must make sure that you destroy the objects when you're done with them.

That brings up an interesting question. If Java leaves the objects lying around, what keeps them from filling up memory and halting your program? This is exactly the kind of problem that would occur in C++. This is where a bit of magic happens. Java has a *garbage collector*, which looks at all the objects that were created with **new** and figures out which ones are not being referenced anymore. Then it releases the memory for those objects, so the memory can be used for new objects. This means that you never need to worry about reclaiming memory yourself. You simply create objects, and when you no longer need them, they will go away by themselves. This eliminates a certain class of programming problem: the so-called "memory leak," in which a programmer forgets to release memory.

Creating new data types: class

If everything is an object, what determines how a particular class of object looks and behaves? Put another way, what establishes the *type* of an object? You might expect there to be a keyword called "type," and that certainly would have made sense. Historically, however, most object-oriented languages have used the keyword **class** to mean "I'm about to tell you what a new type of object looks like." The **class** keyword (which is so common that it will not be bold-faced throughout this book) is followed by the name of the new type. For example:

```
class ATypeName { /* Class body goes here */ }
```

This introduces a new type, although the class body consists only of a comment (the stars and slashes and what is inside, which will be discussed later in this chapter), so there is not too much that you can do with it. However, you can create an object of this type using **new**:

```
ATypeName a = new ATypeName();
```

But you cannot tell it to do much of anything (that is, you cannot send it any interesting messages) until you define some methods for it.

Fields and methods

When you define a class (and all you do in Java is define classes, make objects of those classes, and send messages to those objects), you can put two types of elements in your class: *fields* (sometimes called data members), and *methods* (sometimes called *member functions*). A field is an object of any type that you can communicate with via its reference. It can also be one of the primitive types (which isn't a reference). If it is a reference to an object, you must initialize that reference to connect it to an actual object (using **new**, as seen earlier) in a special method called a *constructor* (described fully in Chapter 4). If it is a primitive type, you can initialize it directly at the point of definition in the class. (As you'll see later, references can also be initialized at the point of definition.)

Each object keeps its own storage for its fields; the fields are not shared among objects. Here is an example of a class with some fields:

```
class DataOnly {
  int i;
  float f;
  boolean b;
}
```

This class doesn't *do* anything, but you can create an object:

```
DataOnly d = new DataOnly();
```

You can assign values to the fields, but you must first know how to refer to a member of an object. This is accomplished by stating the name of the object reference, followed by a period (dot), followed by the name of the member inside the object:

```
objectReference.member
```

For example:

```
d.i = 47;
d.f = 1.1f; // 'f' after number indicates float constant
d.b = false;
```

It is also possible that your object might contain other objects that contain data you'd like to modify. For this, you just keep "connecting the dots." For example:

```
myPlane.leftTank.capacity = 100;
```

The **DataOnly** class cannot do much of anything except hold data, because it has no methods. To understand how those work, you must first understand *arguments* and *return values*, which will be described shortly.

Default values for primitive members

When a primitive data type is a member of a class, it is guaranteed to get a default value if you do not initialize it:

Primitive type	Default
boolean	**false**
char	**'\u0000' (null)**
byte	**(byte)0**
short	**(short)0**
int	**0**
long	**0L**
float	**0.0f**
double	**0.0d**

Note carefully that the default values are what Java guarantees when the variable is used *as a member of a class*. This ensures that member variables of primitive types will always be initialized (something C++ doesn't do), reducing a source of bugs. However, this initial value may not be correct or even legal for the program you are writing. It's best to always explicitly initialize your variables.

This guarantee doesn't apply to "local" variables—those that are not fields of a class. Thus, if within a method definition you have:

```
int x;
```

Then **x** will get some arbitrary value (as in C and C++); it will not automatically be initialized to zero. You are responsible for assigning an appropriate value before you use **x**. If you forget, Java definitely improves on C++: you get a compile-time error telling you the variable might not have been initialized. (Many C++ compilers will warn you about uninitialized variables, but in Java these are errors.)

Methods, arguments, and return values

In many languages (like C and C++), the term *function* is used to describe a named subroutine. The term that is more commonly used in Java is *method,* as in "a way to do something." If you want, you can continue thinking in terms of functions. It's really only a syntactic difference, but this book follows the common Java usage of the term "method."

Methods in Java determine the messages an object can receive. In this section you will learn how simple it is to define a method.

The fundamental parts of a method are the name, the arguments, the return type, and the body. Here is the basic form:

```
returnType methodName( /* Argument list */ ) {
  /* Method body */
}
```

The return type is the type of the value that pops out of the method after you call it. The argument list gives the types and names for the information you want to pass into the method. The method name and argument list together uniquely identify the method.

Methods in Java can be created only as part of a class. A method can be called only for an object,[2] and that object must be able to perform that method call. If you try to call the wrong method for an object, you'll get an error message at compile time. You call a method for an object by naming the object followed by a period (dot), followed by the name of the method and its argument list, like this:

```
objectName.methodName(arg1, arg2, arg3);
```

For example, suppose you have a method **f( )** that takes no arguments and returns a value of type **int**. Then, if you have an object called **a** for which **f( )** can be called, you can say this:

```
int x = a.f();
```

The type of the return value must be compatible with the type of **x**.

This act of calling a method is commonly referred to as *sending a message to an object*. In the preceding example, the message is **f( )** and the object is **a**. Object-oriented programming is often summarized as simply "sending messages to objects."

---

[2] **static** methods, which you'll learn about soon, can be called *for the class*, without an object.

The argument list

The method argument list specifies what information you pass into the method. As you might guess, this information—like everything else in Java—takes the form of objects. So, what you must specify in the argument list are the types of the objects to pass in and the name to use for each one. As in any situation in Java where you seem to be handing objects around, you are actually passing references.[3] The type of the reference must be correct, however. If the argument is supposed to be a **String**, you must pass in a **String** or the compiler will give an error.

Consider a method that takes a **String** as its argument. Here is the definition, which must be placed within a class definition for it to be compiled:

```
int storage(String s) {
  return s.length() * 2;
}
```

This method tells you how many bytes are required to hold the information in a particular **String.** (Each **char** in a **String** is 16 bits, or two bytes, long, to support Unicode characters.) The argument is of type **String** and is called **s**. Once **s** is passed into the method, you can treat it just like any other object. (You can send messages to it.) Here, the **length( )** method is called, which is one of the methods for **String**s; it returns the number of characters in a string.

You can also see the use of the **return** keyword, which does two things. First, it means "leave the method, I'm done." Second, if the method produces a value, that value is placed right after the **return** statement. In this case, the return value is produced by evaluating the expression **s.length( ) * 2**.

You can return any type you want, but if you don't want to return anything at all, you do so by indicating that the method returns **void**. Here are some examples:

```
boolean flag() { return true; }
float naturalLogBase() { return 2.718f; }
void nothing() { return; }
```

---

[3] With the usual exception of the aforementioned "special" data types **boolean, char**, **byte**, **short**, **int**, **long**, **float,** and **double**. In general, though, you pass objects, which really means you pass references to objects.

```
void nothing2() {}
```

When the return type is **void**, then the **return** keyword is used only to exit the method, and is therefore unnecessary when you reach the end of the method. You can return from a method at any point, but if you've given a non-**void** return type, then the compiler will force you (with error messages) to return the appropriate type of value regardless of where you return.

At this point, it can look like a program is just a bunch of objects with methods that take other objects as arguments and send messages to those other objects. That is indeed much of what goes on, but in the following chapter you'll learn how to do the detailed low-level work by making decisions within a method. For this chapter, sending messages will suffice.

Building a Java program

There are several other issues you must understand before seeing your first Java program.

Name visibility

A problem in any programming language is the control of names. If you use a name in one module of the program, and another programmer uses the same name in another module, how do you distinguish one name from another and prevent the two names from "clashing?" In C this is a particular problem because a program is often an unmanageable sea of names. C++ classes (on which Java classes are based) nest functions within classes so they cannot clash with function names nested within other classes. However, C++ still allows global data and global functions, so clashing is still possible. To solve this problem, C++ introduced *namespaces* using additional keywords.

Java was able to avoid all of this by taking a fresh approach. To produce an unambiguous name for a library, the specifier used is not unlike an Internet domain name. In fact, the Java creators want you to use your Internet domain name in reverse since those are guaranteed to be unique. Since my domain name is **BruceEckel.com**, my utility library of foibles would be named **com.bruceeckel.utility.foibles**. After your reversed domain name, the dots are intended to represent subdirectories.

In Java 1.0 and Java 1.1 the domain extensions **com**, **edu**, **org**, **net**, etc., were capitalized by convention, so the library would appear: **COM.bruceeckel.utility.foibles**. Partway through the development of

Java 2, however, it was discovered that this caused problems, so now the entire package name is lowercase.

This mechanism means that all of your files automatically live in their own namespaces, and each class within a file must have a unique identifier. So you do not need to learn special language features to solve this problem—the language takes care of it for you.

Using other components

Whenever you want to use a predefined class in your program, the compiler must know how to locate it. Of course, the class might already exist in the same source code file that it's being called from. In that case, you simply use the class—even if the class doesn't get defined until later in the file (Java eliminates the "forward referencing" problem, so you don't need to think about it).

What about a class that exists in some other file? You might think that the compiler should be smart enough to simply go and find it, but there is a problem. Imagine that you want to use a class with a particular name, but more than one definition for that class exists (presumably these are different definitions). Or worse, imagine that you're writing a program, and as you're building it you add a new class to your library that conflicts with the name of an existing class.

To solve this problem, you must eliminate all potential ambiguities. This is accomplished by telling the Java compiler exactly what classes you want by using the **import** keyword. **import** tells the compiler to bring in a package, which is a library of classes. (In other languages, a library could consist of functions and data as well as classes, but remember that all code in Java must be written inside a class.)

Most of the time you'll be using components from the standard Java libraries that come with your compiler. With these, you don't need to worry about long, reversed domain names; you just say, for example:

```
import java.util.ArrayList;
```

to tell the compiler that you want to use Java's **ArrayList** class. However, **util** contains a number of classes and you might want to use several of them without declaring them all explicitly. This is easily accomplished by using '*' to indicate a wild card:

```java
import java.util.*;
```

It is more common to import a collection of classes in this manner than to import classes individually.

The **static** keyword

Ordinarily, when you create a class you are describing how objects of that class look and how they will behave. You don't actually get anything until you create an object of that class with **new**, and at that point data storage is created and methods become available.

But there are two situations in which this approach is not sufficient. One is if you want to have only one piece of storage for a particular piece of data, regardless of how many objects are created, or even if no objects are created. The other is if you need a method that isn't associated with any particular object of this class. That is, you need a method that you can call even if no objects are created. You can achieve both of these effects with the **static** keyword. When you say something is **static**, it means that data or method is not tied to any particular object instance of that class. So even if you've never created an object of that class you can call a **static** method or access a piece of **static** data. With ordinary, non-**static** data and methods, you must create an object and use that object to access the data or method, since non-**static** data and methods must know the particular object they are working with. Of course, since **static** methods don't need any objects to be created before they are used, they cannot *directly* access non-**static** members or methods by simply calling those other members without referring to a named object (since non-**static** members and methods must be tied to a particular object).

Some object-oriented languages use the terms *class data* and *class methods*, meaning that the data and methods exist only for the class as a whole, and not for any particular objects of the class. Sometimes the Java literature uses these terms too.

To make a field or method **static**, you simply place the keyword before the definition. For example, the following produces a **static** field and initializes it:

```java
class StaticTest {
  static int i = 47;
}
```

Now even if you make two **StaticTest** objects, there will still be only one piece of storage for **StaticTest.i.** Both objects will share the same **i**. Consider:

```
StaticTest st1 = new StaticTest();
StaticTest st2 = new StaticTest();
```

At this point, both **st1.i** and **st2.i** have the same value of 47 since they refer to the same piece of memory.

There are two ways to refer to a **static** variable. As the preceeding example indicates, you can name it via an object, by saying, for example, **st2.i**. You can also refer to it directly through its class name, something you cannot do with a non-static member. (This is the preferred way to refer to a **static** variable since it emphasizes that variable's **static** nature.)

```
StaticTest.i++;
```

The ++ operator increments the variable. At this point, both **st1.i** and **st2.i** will have the value 48.

Similar logic applies to static methods. You can refer to a static method either through an object as you can with any method, or with the special additional syntax **ClassName.method( )**. You define a static method in a similar way:

```
class StaticFun {
  static void incr() { StaticTest.i++; }
}
```

You can see that the **StaticFun** method **incr( )** increments the **static** data **i** using the ++ operator. You can call **incr( )** in the typical way, through an object:

```
StaticFun sf = new StaticFun();
sf.incr();
```

Or, because **incr( )** is a static method, you can call it directly through its class:

```
StaticFun.incr();
```

Although **static**, when applied to a field, definitely changes the way the data is created (one for each class versus the non-**static** one for each object), when applied to a method it's not so dramatic. An important use of **static** for methods is to allow you to call that method without creating an object. This is essential, as we will see, in defining the **main( )** method that is the entry point for running an application.

Like any method, a **static** method can create or use named objects of its type, so a **static** method is often used as a "shepherd" for a flock of instances of its own type.

Your first Java program

Finally, here's the first complete program. It starts by printing a string, and then the date, using the **Date** class from the Java standard library.

```
// HelloDate.java
import java.util.*;

public class HelloDate {
  public static void main(String[] args) {
    System.out.println("Hello, it's: ");
    System.out.println(new Date());
  }
}
```

At the beginning of each program file, you must place the **import** statement to bring in any extra classes you'll need for the code in that file. Note that I say "extra." That's because there's a certain library of classes that are automatically brought into every Java file: **java.lang**. Start up your Web browser and look at the documentation from Sun. (If you haven't downloaded the JDK documentation from *java.sun.com*, do so now[4]). If you look at the list of the packages, you'll see all the different class libraries that come with Java. Select **java.lang**. This will bring up a list of all the classes that are part of that library. Since **java.lang** is implicitly included in every Java code file, these classes are automatically available. There's no **Date** class listed in **java.lang**, which means you must import another library to use that. If you don't know the library where a particular class is, or if you want to see all of the classes, you can select "Tree" in the Java documentation. Now you can find every single class that comes with Java. Then you can use the browser's "find" function to find **Date**. When you do you'll see it listed as

---

[4] The Java compiler and documentation from Sun was not included on this book's CD because it tends to change regularly. By downloading it yourself, you will get the most recent version.

java.util.Date, which lets you know that it's in the **util** library and that you must **import java.util.*** in order to use **Date**.

If you go back to the beginning, select **java.lang** and then **System**, you'll see that the **System** class has several fields, and if you select **out**, you'll discover that it's a **static PrintStream** object. Since it's **static**, you don't need to create anything. The **out** object is always there, and you can just use it. What you can do with this **out** object is determined by the type it is: a **PrintStream**. Conveniently, **PrintStream** is shown in the description as a hyperlink, so if you click on that, you'll see a list of all the methods you can call for **PrintStream**. There are quite a few, and these will be covered later in this book. For now all we're interested in is **println( )**, which in effect means "print what I'm giving you out to the console and end with a newline." Thus, in any Java program you write you can say **System.out.println("things");** whenever you want to print something to the console.

The name of the class is the same as the name of the file. When you're creating a standalone program such as this one, one of the classes in the file must have the same name as the file. (The compiler complains if you don't do this.) That class must contain a method called **main( )** with this signature:

```
public static void main(String[] args) {
```

The **public** keyword means that the method is available to the outside world (described in detail in Chapter 5). The argument to **main( )** is an array of **String** objects. The **args** won't be used in this program, but the Java compiler insists that they be there because they hold the arguments from the command line.

The line that prints the date is quite interesting:

```
System.out.println(new Date());
```

The argument is a **Date** object that is being created just to send its value (which is automatically converted to a **String)** to **println( )**. As soon as this statement is finished, that **Date** is unnecessary, and the garbage collector can come along and get it anytime. We don't need to worry about cleaning it up.

Compiling and running

To compile and run this program, and all the other programs in this book, you must first have a Java programming environment. There are a number of third-party development environments, but in this book we will assume that you are using the Java Developer's Kit (JDK) from Sun, which is free. If you are using another development system,[5] you will need to look in the documentation for that system to determine how to compile and run programs.

Get on the Internet and go to *java.sun.com*. There you will find information and links that will lead you through the process of downloading and installing the JDK for your particular platform.

Once the JDK is installed, and you've set up your computer's path information so that it will find **javac** and **java**, download and unpack the source code for this book (you can find it at *www.BruceEckel.com*). This will create a subdirectory for each chapter in this book. Move to subdirectory **c02** and type:

```
javac HelloDate.java
```

This command should produce no response. If you get any kind of an error message, it means you haven't installed the JDK properly and you need to investigate those problems.

On the other hand, if you just get your command prompt back, you can type:

```
java HelloDate
```

and you'll get the message and the date as output.

This is the process you can use to compile and run each of the programs in this book. However, you will see that the source code for this book also has a file called **build.xml** in each chapter, and this contains "ant" commands for automatically building the files for that chapter. Buildfiles and Ant (including where to download it) are described more fully in Chapter 15, but once you have Ant installed (from *http://jakarta.apache.org/ant*) you can just type '**ant**' at the command prompt to compile and run the programs in each chapter. If you haven't installed Ant yet, you can just type the **javac** and **java** commands by hand.

---

[5] IBM's "jikes" compiler is a common alternative, as it is significantly faster than Sun's javac.

Comments and embedded documentation

There are two types of comments in Java. The first is the traditional C-style comment that was inherited by C++. These comments begin with a /* and continue, possibly across many lines, until a */. Note that many programmers will begin each line of a continued comment with a *, so you'll often see:

```
/* This is a comment
 * that continues
 * across lines
 */
```

Remember, however, that everything inside the /* and */ is ignored, so there's no difference in saying:

```
/* This is a comment that
continues across lines */
```

The second form of comment comes from C++. It is the single-line comment, which starts at a // and continues until the end of the line. This type of comment is convenient and commonly used because it's easy. You don't need to hunt on the keyboard to find / and then * (instead, you just press the same key twice), and you don't need to close the comment. So you will often see:

```
// This is a one-line comment
```

Comment documentation

One of the better ideas in Java is that writing code isn't the only important activity—documenting it is at least as important. Possibly the biggest problem with documenting code has been maintaining that documentation. If the documentation and the code are separate, it becomes a hassle to change the documentation every time you change the code. The solution seems simple: link the code to the documentation. The easiest way to do this is to put everything in the same file. To complete the picture, however, you need a special comment syntax to mark the documentation and a tool to extract those comments and put them in a useful form. This is what Java has done.

The tool to extract the comments is called *javadoc*, and it is part of the JDK installation. It uses some of the technology from the Java compiler to look for special comment tags that you put in your programs. It not only extracts the information marked by these tags, but it also pulls out the class name or method name that adjoins the comment. This way you can get away with the minimal amount of work to generate decent program documentation.

The output of javadoc is an HTML file that you can view with your Web browser. Thus, javadoc allows you to create and maintain a single source file and automatically generate useful documentation. Because of javadoc we have a standard for creating documentation, and it's easy enough that we can expect or even demand documentation with all Java libraries.

In addition, you can write your own javadoc handlers, called *doclets*, if you want to perform special operations on the information processed by javadoc (output in a different format, for example). Doclets are introduced in Chapter 15.

What follows is only an introduction and overview of the basics of javadoc. A thorough description can be found in the JDK documentation downloadable from *java.sun.com* (note that this documentation doesn't come packed with the JDK; you have to do a separate download to get it). When you unpack the documentation, look in the "tooldocs" subdirectory (or follow the "tooldocs" link).

Syntax

All of the javadoc commands occur only within /** comments. The comments end with */ as usual. There are two primary ways to use javadoc: embed HTML or use "doc tags." *Standalone doc tags* are commands that start with a '@' and are placed at the beginning of a comment line. (A leading '*', however, is ignored.) *Inline doc tags* can appear anywhere within a javadoc comment and also start with a '@' but are surrounded by curly braces.

There are three "types" of comment documentation, which correspond to the element the comment precedes: class, variable, or method. That is, a class comment appears right before the definition of a class; a variable comment appears right in front of the definition of a variable, and a method comment appears right in front of the definition of a method. As a simple example:

```
/** A class comment */
public class DocTest {
  /** A variable comment */
  public int i;
  /** A method comment */
```

```
  public void f() {}
}
```

Note that javadoc will process comment documentation for only **public** and **protected** members. Comments for **private** and package-access members (see Chapter 5) are ignored, and you'll see no output. (However, you can use the **-private** flag to include **private** members as well.) This makes sense, since only **public** and **protected** members are available outside the file, which is the client programmer's perspective. However, all **class** comments are included in the output.

The output for the preceding code is an HTML file that has the same standard format as all the rest of the Java documentation, so users will be comfortable with the format and can easily navigate your classes. It's worth entering the preceding code, sending it through javadoc, and viewing the resulting HTML file to see the results.

Embedded HTML

Javadoc passes HTML commands through to the generated HTML document. This allows you full use of HTML; however, the primary motive is to let you format code, such as:

```
/**
* <pre>
* System.out.println(new Date());
* </pre>
*/
```

You can also use HTML just as you would in any other Web document to format the regular text in your descriptions:

```
/**
* You can <em>even</em> insert a list:
* <ol>
* <li> Item one
* <li> Item two
* <li> Item three
* </ol>
*/
```

Note that within the documentation comment, asterisks at the beginning of a line are thrown away by javadoc, along with leading spaces. Javadoc reformats everything so that it conforms to the standard documentation appearance. Don't use headings such as **<h1>** or **<hr>** as embedded HTML, because javadoc inserts its own headings and yours will interfere with them.

All types of comment documentation—class, variable, and method—can support embedded HTML.

Some example tags

Here are some of the javadoc tags available for code documentation. Before trying to do anything serious using javadoc, you should consult the javadoc reference in the downloadable JDK documentation to get full coverage of the way to use javadoc.

@see: referring to other classes

The **@see** tag allows you to refer to the documentation in other classes. Javadoc will generate HTML with the **@see** tags hyperlinked to the other documentation. The forms are:

```
@see classname
@see fully-qualified-classname
@see fully-qualified-classname#method-name
```

Each one adds a hyperlinked "See Also" entry to the generated documentation. Javadoc will not check the hyperlinks you give it to make sure they are valid.

{@link *package.class#member label*}

Very similar to **@see**, except that it can be used inline and uses the *label* as the hyperlink text rather than "See Also."

{@docRoot}

Produces the relative path to the documentation root directory. Useful for explicit hyperlinking to pages in the documentation tree.

{@inheritDoc}

Inherits the documentation from the nearest base class of this class into the current doc comment.

@version

This is of the form:

```
@version version-information
```

in which **version-information** is any significant information you see fit to include. When the **-version** flag is placed on the javadoc command line, the version information will be called out specially in the generated HTML documentation.

@author

This is of the form:

```
@author author-information
```

in which **author-information** is, presumably, your name, but it could also include your email address or any other appropriate information. When the **-author** flag is placed on the javadoc command line, the author information will be called out specially in the generated HTML documentation.

You can have multiple author tags for a list of authors, but they must be placed consecutively. All the author information will be lumped together into a single paragraph in the generated HTML.

@since

This tag allows you to indicate the version of this code that began using a particular feature. You'll see it appearing in the HTML Java documentation to indicate what version of the JDK is used.

@param

This is used for method documentation, and is of the form:

```
@param parameter-name description
```

in which **parameter-name** is the identifier in the method parameter list, and **description** is text that can continue on subsequent lines. The description is considered finished when a new documentation tag is encountered. You can have any number of these, presumably one for each parameter.

@return

This is used for method documentation, and looks like this:

```
@return description
```

in which **description** gives you the meaning of the return value. It can continue on subsequent lines.

@throws

Exceptions will be demonstrated in Chapter 9. Briefly, they are objects that can be "thrown" out of a method if that method fails. Although only one exception object can emerge when you call a method, a particular method might produce any number of different types of exceptions, all of which need descriptions. So the form for the exception tag is:

```
@throws fully-qualified-class-name description
```

in which **fully-qualified-class-name** gives an unambiguous name of an exception class that's defined somewhere, and **description** (which can continue on subsequent lines) tells you why this particular type of exception can emerge from the method call.

@deprecated

This is used to indicate features that were superseded by an improved feature. The deprecated tag is a suggestion that you no longer use this particular feature, since sometime in the future it is likely to be removed. A method that is marked **@deprecated** causes the compiler to issue a warning if it is used.

Documentation example

Here is the first Java program again, this time with documentation comments added:

```
//: c02:HelloDate.java
import java.util.*;

/** The first Thinking in Java example program.
 * Displays a string and today's date.
 * @author Bruce Eckel
 * @author www.BruceEckel.com
 * @version 2.0
*/
public class HelloDate {
  /** Sole entry point to class & application
   * @param args array of string arguments
   * @return No return value
```

```
   * @exception exceptions No exceptions thrown
  */
  public static void main(String[] args) {
    System.out.println("Hello, it's: ");
    System.out.println(new Date());
  }
} ///:~
```

The first line of the file uses my own technique of putting a '**//:**' as a special marker for the comment line containing the source file name. That line contains the path information to the file (in this case, **c02** indicates Chapter 2) followed by the file name.[6] The last line also finishes with a comment, and this one ('**///:~**') indicates the end of the source code listing, which allows it to be automatically updated into the text of this book after being checked with a compiler and executed.

Coding style

The style described in the *Code Conventions for the Java Programming Language*[7] is to capitalize the first letter of a class name. If the class name consists of several words, they are run together (that is, you don't use underscores to separate the names), and the first letter of each embedded word is capitalized, such as:

```
class AllTheColorsOfTheRainbow { // ...
```

This is sometimes called "camel-casing." For almost everything else: methods, fields (member variables), and object reference names, the accepted style is just as it is for classes *except* that the first letter of the identifier is lowercase. For example:

```
class AllTheColorsOfTheRainbow {
  int anIntegerRepresentingColors;
```

---

[6] Originally, I created a tool using Python (see www.Python.org), which uses this information to extract the code files, put them in appropriate subdirectories, and create makefiles. In this edition, all the files are stored in Concurrent Versions System (CVS) and automatically incorporated into this book using a Visual BASIC for Applications (VBA) macro. This new approach seems to work much better in terms of code maintenance, mostly because of CVS.

[7] http://java.sun.com/docs/codeconv/index.html. To preserve space in this book and seminar presentations, not all of these guidelines could be followed.

```
  void changeTheHueOfTheColor(int newHue) {
    // ...
  }
  // ...
}
```

The user must also type all these long names, so be merciful.

The Java code you will see in the Sun libraries also follows the placement of open-and-close curly braces that you see used in this book.

Summary

The goal of this chapter is just enough Java to understand how to write a simple program. You've also gotten an overview of the language and some of its basic ideas. However, the examples so far have all been of the form "do this, then do that, then do something else." What if you want the program to make choices, such as "if the result of doing this is red, do that; if not, then do something else"? The support in Java for this fundamental programming activity will be covered in the next chapter.

Exercises

Solutions to selected exercises can be found in the electronic document *The Thinking in Java Annotated Solution Guide*, available for a small fee from *www.BruceEckel.com*.

1. Following the **HelloDate.java** example in this chapter, create a "hello, world" program that simply prints out that statement. You need only a single method in your class (the "main" one that gets executed when the program starts). Remember to make it **static** and to include the argument list, even though you don't use the argument list. Compile the program with **javac** and run it using **java**. If you are using a different development environment than the JDK, learn how to compile and run programs in that environment.

2. Find the code fragments involving **ATypeName** and turn them into a program that compiles and runs.

3. Turn the **DataOnly** code fragments into a program that compiles and runs.

4. Modify Exercise 3 so that the values of the data in **DataOnly** are assigned to and printed in **main( )**.

5. Write a program that includes and calls the **storage( )** method defined as a code fragment in this chapter.

6. Turn the **StaticFun** code fragments into a working program.

7. Write a program that prints three arguments taken from the command line. To do this, you'll need to index into the command-line array of **String**s.

8. Turn the **AllTheColorsOfTheRainbow** example into a program that compiles and runs.

9. Find the code for the second version of **HelloDate.java**, which is the simple comment documentation example. Execute **javadoc** on the file and view the results with your Web browser.

10. Turn **docTest** into a file that compiles, then run it through **javadoc**. Verify the resulting documentation with your Web browser.

11. Add an HTML list of items to the documentation in Exercise 10.

12. Take the program in Exercise 1 and add comment documentation to it. Extract this comment documentation into an HTML file using **javadoc** and view it with your Web browser.

13. In Chapter 4, locate the **Overloading.java** example and add javadoc documentation. Extract this comment documentation into an HTML file using **javadoc** and view it with your Web browser.

3: Controlling Program Flow

Like a sentient creature, a program must manipulate its world and make choices during execution.

In Java you manipulate data using operators, and you make choices with execution control statements. Java was inherited from C++, so most of these statements and operators will be familiar to C and C++ programmers. Java has also added some improvements and simplifications.

If you find yourself floundering a bit in this chapter, make sure you go through the multimedia CD ROM bound into this book: *Foundations for Java*. It contains audio lectures, slides, exercises, and solutions specifically designed to bring you up to speed with the fundamentals necessary to learn Java.

Using Java operators

An operator takes one or more arguments and produces a new value. The arguments are in a different form than ordinary method calls, but the effect is the same. Addition (+), subtraction and unary minus (-), multiplication (*), division (/), and assignment (=) all work much the same in any programming language.

All operators produce a value from their operands. In addition, an operator can change the value of an operand. This is called a *side effect*. The most common use for operators that modify their operands is to generate the side effect, but you should keep in mind that the value produced is available for your use, just as in operators without side effects.

Almost all operators work only with primitives. The exceptions are '=', '==' and '!=', which work with all objects (and are a point of confusion for objects). In addition, the **String** class supports '+' and '+='.

Precedence

Operator precedence defines how an expression evaluates when several operators are present. Java has specific rules that determine the order of evaluation. The easiest one to remember is that multiplication and division happen before addition and subtraction. Programmers often forget the other precedence rules, so you should use parentheses to make the order of evaluation explicit. For example:

```
a = x + y - 2/2 + z;
```

has a very different meaning from the same statement with a particular grouping of parentheses:

```
a = x + (y - 2)/(2 + z);
```

Assignment

Assignment is performed with the operator =. It means "take the value of the right-hand side (often called the *rvalue*) and copy it into the left-hand side (often called the *lvalue*)." An rvalue is any constant, variable, or expression that can produce a value, but an lvalue must be a distinct, named variable. (That is, there must be a physical space to store the value.) For instance, you can assign a constant value to a variable:

```
a = 4;
```

but you cannot assign anything to constant value—it cannot be an lvalue. (You can't say **4 = a;**.)

Assignment of primitives is quite straightforward. Since the primitive holds the actual value and not a reference to an object, when you assign primitives, you copy the contents from one place to another. For example, if you say **a = b** for primitives, then the contents of **b** are copied into **a**. If you then go on to modify **a**, **b** is naturally unaffected by this modification. As a programmer, this is what you've come to expect for most situations.

When you assign objects, however, things change. Whenever you manipulate an object, what you're manipulating is the reference, so when you assign "from one object to another," you're actually copying a reference from one place to another. This means that if you say **c = d** for objects, you end up with both **c** and **d** pointing to the object that, originally, only **d** pointed to. Here's an example that demonstrates this behavior:

```java
//: c03:Assignment.java
// Assignment with objects is a bit tricky.
import com.bruceeckel.simpletest.*;

class Number {
  int i;
}

public class Assignment {
  static Test monitor = new Test();
  public static void main(String[] args) {
    Number n1 = new Number();
    Number n2 = new Number();
    n1.i = 9;
    n2.i = 47;
    System.out.println("1: n1.i: " + n1.i +
      ", n2.i: " + n2.i);
    n1 = n2;
    System.out.println("2: n1.i: " + n1.i +
      ", n2.i: " + n2.i);
    n1.i = 27;
    System.out.println("3: n1.i: " + n1.i +
      ", n2.i: " + n2.i);
    monitor.expect(new String[] {
      "1: n1.i: 9, n2.i: 47",
      "2: n1.i: 47, n2.i: 47",
      "3: n1.i: 27, n2.i: 27"
    });
  }
} ///:~
```

First, notice that something new has been added. The line:

```java
import com.bruceeckel.simpletest.*;
```

imports the "**simpletest**" library that has been created to test the code in this book, and is explained in Chapter 15. At the beginning of the **Assignment** class, you see the line:

```java
  static Test monitor = new Test();
```

This creates an instance of the **simpletest** class **Test**, called **monitor**. Finally, at the end of **main( )**, you see the statement:

```java
    monitor.expect(new String[] {
      "1: n1.i: 9, n2.i: 47",
```

```
      "2: n1.i: 47, n2.i: 47",
      "3: n1.i: 27, n2.i: 27"
    });
```

This is the expected output of the program, expressed as an array of **String** objects. When the program is run, it not only prints out the output, but it compares it to this array to verify that the array is correct. Thus, when you see a program in this book that uses **simpletest**, you will also see an **expect( )** call that will show you what the output of the program is. This way, you see validated output from the program.

The **Number** class is simple, and two instances of it (**n1** and **n2**) are created within **main( )**. The **i** value within each **Number** is given a different value, and then **n2** is assigned to **n1**, and **n1** is changed. In many programming languages you would expect **n1** and **n2** to be independent at all times, but because you've assigned a reference, you'll see the output in the **expect( )** statement. Changing the **n1** object appears to change the **n2** object as well! This is because both **n1** and **n2** contain the same reference, which is pointing to the same object. (The original reference that was in **n1**, that pointed to the object holding a value of 9, was overwritten during the assignment and effectively lost; its object will be cleaned up by the garbage collector.)

This phenomenon is often called *aliasing*, and it's a fundamental way that Java works with objects. But what if you don't want aliasing to occur in this case? You could forego the assignment and say:

```
n1.i = n2.i;
```

This retains the two separate objects instead of tossing one and tying **n1** and **n2** to the same object, but you'll soon realize that manipulating the fields within objects is messy and goes against good object-oriented design principles. This is a nontrivial topic, so it is left for Appendix A, which is devoted to aliasing. In the meantime, you should keep in mind that assignment for objects can add surprises.

Aliasing during method calls

Aliasing will also occur when you pass an object into a method:

```
//: c03:PassObject.java
// Passing objects to methods may not be what
// you're used to.
import com.bruceeckel.simpletest.*;
```

```
class Letter {
  char c;
}

public class PassObject {
  static Test monitor = new Test();
  static void f(Letter y) {
    y.c = 'z';
  }
  public static void main(String[] args) {
    Letter x = new Letter();
    x.c = 'a';
    System.out.println("1: x.c: " + x.c);
    f(x);
    System.out.println("2: x.c: " + x.c);
    monitor.expect(new String[] {
      "1: x.c: a",
      "2: x.c: z"
    });
  }
} ///:~
```

In many programming languages, the method **f( )** would appear to be making a copy of its argument **Letter y** inside the scope of the method. But once again a reference is being passed, so the line

```
y.c = 'z';
```

is actually changing the object outside of **f( )**. The output in the **expect( )** statement shows this.

Aliasing and its solution is a complex issue and, although you must wait until Appendix A for all the answers, you should be aware of it at this point so you can watch for pitfalls.

Mathematical operators

The basic mathematical operators are the same as the ones available in most programming languages: addition (+), subtraction (-), division (/), multiplication (*) and modulus (%, which produces the remainder from integer division). Integer division truncates, rather than rounds, the result.

Java also uses a shorthand notation to perform an operation and an assignment at the same time. This is denoted by an operator followed by an equal sign, and is consistent with all the operators in the language (whenever it makes sense). For example, to add 4 to the variable **x** and assign the result to **x**, use: **x += 4**.

This example shows the use of the mathematical operators:

```
//: c03:MathOps.java
// Demonstrates the mathematical operators.
import com.bruceeckel.simpletest.*;
import java.util.*;

public class MathOps {
  static Test monitor = new Test();
  // Shorthand to print a string and an int:
  static void printInt(String s, int i) {
    System.out.println(s + " = " + i);
  }
  // Shorthand to print a string and a float:
  static void printFloat(String s, float f) {
    System.out.println(s + " = " + f);
  }
  public static void main(String[] args) {
    // Create a random number generator,
    // seeds with current time by default:
    Random rand = new Random();
    int i, j, k;
    // Choose value from 1 to 100:
    j = rand.nextInt(100) + 1;
    k = rand.nextInt(100) + 1;
    printInt("j", j);  printInt("k", k);
    i = j + k; printInt("j + k", i);
    i = j - k; printInt("j - k", i);
    i = k / j; printInt("k / j", i);
    i = k * j; printInt("k * j", i);
    i = k % j; printInt("k % j", i);
    j %= k; printInt("j %= k", j);
    // Floating-point number tests:
    float u,v,w;  // applies to doubles, too
    v = rand.nextFloat();
    w = rand.nextFloat();
    printFloat("v", v); printFloat("w", w);
    u = v + w; printFloat("v + w", u);
    u = v - w; printFloat("v - w", u);
    u = v * w; printFloat("v * w", u);
```

```
    u = v / w; printFloat("v / w", u);
    // the following also works for
    // char, byte, short, int, long,
    // and double:
    u += v; printFloat("u += v", u);
    u -= v; printFloat("u -= v", u);
    u *= v; printFloat("u *= v", u);
    u /= v; printFloat("u /= v", u);
    monitor.expect(new String[] {
      "%% j = -?\\d+",
      "%% k = -?\\d+",
      "%% j \\+ k = -?\\d+",
      "%% j - k = -?\\d+",
      "%% k / j = -?\\d+",
      "%% k \\* j = -?\\d+",
      "%% k % j = -?\\d+",
      "%% j %= k = -?\\d+",
      "%% v = -?\\d+\\.\\d+(E-?\\d)?",
      "%% w = -?\\d+\\.\\d+(E-?\\d)?",
      "%% v \\+ w = -?\\d+\\.\\d+(E-?\\d)??",
      "%% v - w = -?\\d+\\.\\d+(E-?\\d)??",
      "%% v \\* w = -?\\d+\\.\\d+(E-?\\d)??",
      "%% v / w = -?\\d+\\.\\d+(E-?\\d)??",
      "%% u \\+= v = -?\\d+\\.\\d+(E-?\\d)??",
      "%% u -= v = -?\\d+\\.\\d+(E-?\\d)??",
      "%% u \\*= v = -?\\d+\\.\\d+(E-?\\d)??",
      "%% u /= v = -?\\d+\\.\\d+(E-?\\d)??"
    });
  }
} ///:~
```

The first thing you will see are some shorthand methods for printing: the **printInt( )** prints a **String** followed by an **int** and the **printFloat( )** prints a **String** followed by a **float**.

To generate numbers, the program first creates a **Random** object. Because no arguments are passed during creation, Java uses the current time as a seed for the random number generator. The program generates a number of different types of random numbers with the **Random** object simply by calling the methods: **nextInt( )** and **nextFloat( )** (you can also call **nextLong( )** or **nextDouble( )**).

The modulus operator, when used with the result of the random number generator, limits the result to an upper bound of the operand minus 1 (99 in this case).

Regular expressions

Since random numbers are used to generate the output for this program, the **expect( )** statement can't just show literal output as it did before, since the output will vary from one run to the next. To solve this problem, *regular expressions*, a new feature introduced in Java JDK 1.4 (but an old feature in languages like Perl and Python) will be used inside the **expect( )** statement. Although coverage of this intensely powerful tool doesn't occur until Chapter 12, to understand these statements you'll need an introduction to regular expressions. Here, you'll learn just enough to read the **expect( )** statements, but if you want a full description, look up **java.util.regex.Pattern** in the downloadable JDK documentation.

A regular expression is a way to describe strings in general terms, so that you can say: "If a string has these things in it, then it matches what I'm looking for." For example, to say that a number might or might not be preceded by a minus sign, you put in the minus sign followed by a question mark, like this:

```
-?
```

To describe an integer, you say that it's one or more digits. In regular expressions, a digit is '**\d**', but in a Java **String** you have to "escape" the backslash by putting in a second backslash: '**\\d**'. To indicate "one or more of the preceding expression" in regular expressions, you use the '+'. So to say "possibly a minus sign, followed by one or more digits," you write:

```
-?\\d+
```

Which you can see in the first lines of the **expect( )** statement in the preceding code.

One thing that is *not* part of the regular expression syntax is the '**%%**' (note the space included for readability) at the beginning of the lines in the **expect( )** statement. This is a flag used by **simpletest** to indicate that the rest of the line is a regular expression. So you won't see it in normal regular expressions, only in **simpletest expect( )** statements.

Any other characters that are not special characters to regular expression searches are treated as exact matches. So in the first line:

```
%% j = -?\\d+
```

The 'j = ' is matched exactly. However, in the third line, the '+' in 'j + k' must be escaped because it is a special regular expression character, as is '*'. The rest of the lines should be understandable from this introduction. Later in the book, when additional features of regular expressions are used inside **expect( )** statements, they will be explained.

Unary minus and plus operators

The unary minus (-)and unary plus (+) are the same operators as binary minus and plus. The compiler figures out which use is intended by the way you write the expression. For instance, the statement

```
x = -a;
```

has an obvious meaning. The compiler is able to figure out:

```
x = a * -b;
```

but the reader might get confused, so it is clearer to say:

```
x = a * (-b);
```

Unary minus inverts the sign on the data. Unary plus provides symmetry with unary minus, although it doesn't have any effect.

Auto increment and decrement

Java, like C, is full of shortcuts. Shortcuts can make code much easier to type, and either easier or harder to read.

Two of the nicer shortcuts are the increment and decrement operators (often referred to as the auto-increment and auto-decrement operators). The decrement operator is -- and means "decrease by one unit." The increment operator is ++ and means "increase by one unit." If **a** is an **int**, for example, the expression ++**a** is equivalent to (**a** = **a** + **1**). Increment and decrement operators not only modify the variable, but also produce the value of the variable as a result.

There are two versions of each type of operator, often called the *prefix* and *postfix* versions. *Pre-increment* means the ++ operator appears before the variable or expression, and *post-increment* means the ++ operator appears after the variable or expression. Similarly, *pre-decrement* means the -- operator appears before the variable or expression, and *post-decrement* means the **--** operator appears after the variable or expression. For pre-increment and pre-decrement, (i.e., **++a** or **--a**), the operation is performed and the value is produced. For post-increment and post-decrement (i.e. **a++** or **a--**), the value is produced, then the operation is performed. As an example:

```
//: c03:AutoInc.java
// Demonstrates the ++ and -- operators.
import com.bruceeckel.simpletest.*;

public class AutoInc {
  static Test monitor = new Test();
  public static void main(String[] args) {
    int i = 1;
    System.out.println("i : " + i);
    System.out.println("++i : " + ++i); // Pre-increment
    System.out.println("i++ : " + i++); // Post-increment
    System.out.println("i : " + i);
    System.out.println("--i : " + --i); // Pre-decrement
    System.out.println("i-- : " + i--); // Post-decrement
    System.out.println("i : " + i);
    monitor.expect(new String[] {
      "i : 1",
      "++i : 2",
      "i++ : 2",
      "i : 3",
      "--i : 2",
      "i-- : 2",
      "i : 1"
    });
  }
} ///:~
```

You can see that for the prefix form, you get the value after the operation has been performed, but with the postfix form, you get the value before the operation is performed. These are the only operators (other than those involving assignment) that have side effects. (That is, they change the operand rather than using just its value.)

The increment operator is one explanation for the name C++, implying "one step beyond C." In an early Java speech, Bill Joy (one of the Java creators), said that "Java=C++--" (C plus plus minus minus), suggesting that Java is C++ with the unnecessary hard parts removed, and therefore a much simpler language. As you progress in this book, you'll see that many parts are simpler, and yet Java isn't *that* much easier than C++.

Relational operators

Relational operators generate a **boolean** result. They evaluate the relationship between the values of the operands. A relational expression produces **true** if the relationship is true, and **false** if the relationship is untrue. The relational operators are less than (<), greater than (>), less than or equal to (<=), greater than or equal to (>=), equivalent (==) and not equivalent (!=). Equivalence and nonequivalence work with all built-in data types, but the other comparisons won't work with type **boolean**.

Testing object equivalence

The relational operators == and **!=** also work with all objects, but their meaning often confuses the first-time Java programmer. Here's an example:

```
//: c03:Equivalence.java
import com.bruceeckel.simpletest.*;

public class Equivalence {
  static Test monitor = new Test();
  public static void main(String[] args) {
    Integer n1 = new Integer(47);
    Integer n2 = new Integer(47);
    System.out.println(n1 == n2);
    System.out.println(n1 != n2);
    monitor.expect(new String[] {
      "false",
      "true"
    });
  }
} ///:~
```

The expression **System.out.println(n1 == n2)** will print the result of the **boolean** comparison within it. Surely the output should be **true** and then **false**, since both **Integer** objects are the same. But while the *contents* of the objects are the same, the references are not the same and the operators == and **!=** compare object references. So the output is actually **false** and then **true**. Naturally, this surprises people at first.

What if you want to compare the actual contents of an object for equivalence? You must use the special method **equals( )** that exists for all objects (not primitives, which work fine with == and **!=**). Here's how it's used:

```
//: c03:EqualsMethod.java
import com.bruceeckel.simpletest.*;

public class EqualsMethod {
  static Test monitor = new Test();
  public static void main(String[] args) {
    Integer n1 = new Integer(47);
    Integer n2 = new Integer(47);
    System.out.println(n1.equals(n2));
    monitor.expect(new String[] {
      "true"
    });
  }
} ///:~
```

The result will be **true**, as you would expect. Ah, but it's not as simple as that. If you create your own class, like this:

```
//: c03:EqualsMethod2.java
import com.bruceeckel.simpletest.*;

class Value {
  int i;
}

public class EqualsMethod2 {
  static Test monitor = new Test();
  public static void main(String[] args) {
    Value v1 = new Value();
    Value v2 = new Value();
    v1.i = v2.i = 100;
    System.out.println(v1.equals(v2));
    monitor.expect(new String[] {
      "false"
    });
  }
} ///:~
```

you're back to square one: the result is **false**. This is because the default behavior of **equals( )** is to compare references. So unless you *override* **equals( )** in your new class you won't get the desired behavior.

Unfortunately, you won't learn about overriding until Chapter 7 and about the proper way to define **equals( )** until Chapter 11, but being aware of the way **equals( )** behaves might save you some grief in the meantime.

Most of the Java library classes implement **equals( )** so that it compares the contents of objects instead of their references.

Logical operators

Each of the logical operators AND (&&), OR (||) and NOT (!) produces a **boolean** value of **true** or **false** based on the logical relationship of its arguments. This example uses the relational and logical operators:

```
//: c03:Bool.java
// Relational and logical operators.
import com.bruceeckel.simpletest.*;
import java.util.*;

public class Bool {
  static Test monitor = new Test();
  public static void main(String[] args) {
    Random rand = new Random();
    int i = rand.nextInt(100);
    int j = rand.nextInt(100);
    System.out.println("i = " + i);
    System.out.println("j = " + j);
    System.out.println("i > j is " + (i > j));
    System.out.println("i < j is " + (i < j));
    System.out.println("i >= j is " + (i >= j));
    System.out.println("i <= j is " + (i <= j));
    System.out.println("i == j is " + (i == j));
    System.out.println("i != j is " + (i != j));
    // Treating an int as a boolean is not legal Java:
//! System.out.println("i && j is " + (i && j));
//! System.out.println("i || j is " + (i || j));
//! System.out.println("!i is " + !i);
    System.out.println("(i < 10) && (j < 10) is "
       + ((i < 10) && (j < 10)) );
    System.out.println("(i < 10) || (j < 10) is "
       + ((i < 10) || (j < 10)) );
    monitor.expect(new String[] {
      "%% i = -?\\d+",
      "%% j = -?\\d+",
      "%% i > j is (true|false)",
```

```
      "%% i < j is (true|false)",
      "%% i >= j is (true|false)",
      "%% i <= j is (true|false)",
      "%% i == j is (true|false)",
      "%% i != j is (true|false)",
      "%% \\(i < 10\\) && \\(j < 10\\) is (true|false)",
      "%% \\(i < 10\\) \\|\\| \\(j < 10\\) is (true|false)"
    });
  }
} ///:~
```

In the regular expressions in the **expect( )** statement, parentheses have the effect of grouping an expression, and the vertical bar '|' means OR. So:

```
(true|false)
```

Means that this part of the string may be either 'true' or 'false'. Because these characters are special in regular expressions, they must be escaped with a '\\' if you want them to appear as ordinary characters in the expression.

You can apply AND, OR, or NOT to **boolean** values only. You can't use a non-**boolean** as if it were a **boolean** in a logical expression as you can in C and C++. You can see the failed attempts at doing this commented out with a **//!** comment marker. The subsequent expressions, however, produce **boolean** values using relational comparisons, then use logical operations on the results.

Note that a **boolean** value is automatically converted to an appropriate text form if it's used where a **String** is expected.

You can replace the definition for **int** in the preceding program with any other primitive data type except **boolean**. Be aware, however, that the comparison of floating-point numbers is very strict. A number that is the tiniest fraction different from another number is still "not equal." A number that is the tiniest bit above zero is still nonzero.

Short-circuiting

When dealing with logical operators, you run into a phenomenon called "short circuiting." This means that the expression will be evaluated only *until* the truth or falsehood of the entire expression can be unambiguously determined. As a result, the latter parts of a logical expression might not be evaluated. Here's an example that demonstrates short-circuiting:

```java
//: c03:ShortCircuit.java
// Demonstrates short-circuiting behavior.
// with logical operators.
import com.bruceeckel.simpletest.*;

public class ShortCircuit {
  static Test monitor = new Test();
  static boolean test1(int val) {
    System.out.println("test1(" + val + ")");
    System.out.println("result: " + (val < 1));
    return val < 1;
  }
  static boolean test2(int val) {
    System.out.println("test2(" + val + ")");
    System.out.println("result: " + (val < 2));
    return val < 2;
  }
  static boolean test3(int val) {
    System.out.println("test3(" + val + ")");
    System.out.println("result: " + (val < 3));
    return val < 3;
  }
  public static void main(String[] args) {
    if(test1(0) && test2(2) && test3(2))
      System.out.println("expression is true");
    else
      System.out.println("expression is false");
    monitor.expect(new String[] {
      "test1(0)",
      "result: true",
      "test2(2)",
      "result: false",
      "expression is false"
    });
  }
} ///:~
```

Each test performs a comparison against the argument and returns true or false. It also prints information to show you that it's being called. The tests are used in the expression:

```java
if(test1(0) && test2(2) && test3(2))
```

You might naturally think that all three tests would be executed, but the output shows otherwise. The first test produced a **true** result, so the expression evaluation continues. However, the second test produced a **false** result. Since this means that the whole expression must be **false**, why continue evaluating the rest of the expression? It could be expensive. The reason for short-circuiting, in fact, is that you can get a potential performance increase if all the parts of a logical expression do not need to be evaluated.

Bitwise operators

The bitwise operators allow you to manipulate individual bits in an integral primitive data type. Bitwise operators perform Boolean algebra on the corresponding bits in the two arguments to produce the result.

The bitwise operators come from C's low-level orientation, where you often manipulate hardware directly and must set the bits in hardware registers. Java was originally designed to be embedded in TV set-top boxes, so this low-level orientation still made sense. However, you probably won't use the bitwise operators much.

The bitwise AND operator (**&**) produces a one in the output bit if both input bits are one, otherwise it produces a zero. The bitwise OR operator (**|**) produces a one in the output bit if either input bit is a one and produces a zero only if both input bits are zero. The bitwise EXCLUSIVE OR, or XOR (**^**), produces a one in the output bit if one or the other input bit is a one, but not both. The bitwise NOT (**~**, also called the *ones complement* operator) is a unary operator; it takes only one argument. (All other bitwise operators are binary operators.) Bitwise NOT produces the opposite of the input bit—a one if the input bit is zero, a zero if the input bit is one.

The bitwise operators and logical operators use the same characters, so it is helpful to have a mnemonic device to help you remember the meanings: because bits are "small," there is only one character in the bitwise operators.

Bitwise operators can be combined with the **=** sign to unite the operation and assignment: **&=**, **|=** and **^=** are all legitimate. (Since **~** is a unary operator, it cannot be combined with the **=** sign.)

The **boolean** type is treated as a one-bit value, so it is somewhat different. You can perform a bitwise AND, OR, and XOR, but you can't perform a bitwise NOT (presumably to prevent confusion with the logical NOT). For **boolean**s, the bitwise operators have the same effect as the logical operators except that they do not short circuit. Also, bitwise operations on **boolean**s include an XOR logical operator that is not included under the list of "logical" operators. You're prevented from using **boolean**s in shift expressions, which are described next.

Shift operators

The shift operators also manipulate bits. They can be used solely with primitive, integral types. The left-shift operator (<<) produces the operand to the left of the operator shifted to the left by the number of bits specified after the operator (inserting zeroes at the lower-order bits). The signed right-shift operator (>>) produces the operand to the left of the operator shifted to the right by the number of bits specified after the operator. The signed right shift >> uses *sign extension*: if the value is positive, zeroes are inserted at the higher-order bits; if the value is negative, ones are inserted at the higher-order bits. Java has also added the unsigned right shift >>>, which uses *zero extension*: regardless of the sign, zeroes are inserted at the higher-order bits. This operator does not exist in C or C++.

If you shift a **char**, **byte,** or **short**, it will be promoted to **int** before the shift takes place, and the result will be an **int**. Only the five low-order bits of the right-hand side will be used. This prevents you from shifting more than the number of bits in an **int**. If you're operating on a **long**, you'll get a **long** result. Only the six low-order bits of the right-hand side will be used, so you can't shift more than the number of bits in a **long**.

Shifts can be combined with the equal sign (<<= or >>= or >>>=). The lvalue is replaced by the lvalue shifted by the rvalue. There is a problem, however, with the unsigned right shift combined with assignment. If you use it with **byte** or **short**, you don't get the correct results. Instead, these are promoted to **int** and right shifted, but then truncated as they are assigned back into their variables, so you get **-1** in those cases. The following example demonstrates this:

```
//: c03:URShift.java
// Test of unsigned right shift.
import com.bruceeckel.simpletest.*;

public class URShift {
  static Test monitor = new Test();
  public static void main(String[] args) {
    int i = -1;
    System.out.println(i >>>= 10);
    long l = -1;
```

```
    System.out.println(l >>>= 10);
    short s = -1;
    System.out.println(s >>>= 10);
    byte b = -1;
    System.out.println(b >>>= 10);
    b = -1;
    System.out.println(b>>>10);
    monitor.expect(new String[] {
      "4194303",
      "18014398509481983",
      "-1",
      "-1",
      "4194303"
    });
  }
} ///:~
```

In the last shift, the resulting value is not assigned back into **b**, but is printed directly, so the correct behavior occurs.

Here's an example that demonstrates the use of all the operators involving bits:

```
//: c03:BitManipulation.java
// Using the bitwise operators.
import com.bruceeckel.simpletest.*;
import java.util.*;

public class BitManipulation {
  static Test monitor = new Test();
  public static void main(String[] args) {
    Random rand = new Random();
    int i = rand.nextInt();
    int j = rand.nextInt();
    printBinaryInt("-1", -1);
    printBinaryInt("+1", +1);
    int maxpos = 2147483647;
    printBinaryInt("maxpos", maxpos);
    int maxneg = -2147483648;
    printBinaryInt("maxneg", maxneg);
    printBinaryInt("i", i);
    printBinaryInt("~i", ~i);
    printBinaryInt("-i", -i);
    printBinaryInt("j", j);
    printBinaryInt("i & j", i & j);
```

```
    printBinaryInt("i | j", i | j);
    printBinaryInt("i ^ j", i ^ j);
    printBinaryInt("i << 5", i << 5);
    printBinaryInt("i >> 5", i >> 5);
    printBinaryInt("(~i) >> 5", (~i) >> 5);
    printBinaryInt("i >>> 5", i >>> 5);
    printBinaryInt("(~i) >>> 5", (~i) >>> 5);

    long l = rand.nextLong();
    long m = rand.nextLong();
    printBinaryLong("-1L", -1L);
    printBinaryLong("+1L", +1L);
    long ll = 9223372036854775807L;
    printBinaryLong("maxpos", ll);
    long lln = -9223372036854775808L;
    printBinaryLong("maxneg", lln);
    printBinaryLong("l", l);
    printBinaryLong("~l", ~l);
    printBinaryLong("-l", -l);
    printBinaryLong("m", m);
    printBinaryLong("l & m", l & m);
    printBinaryLong("l | m", l | m);
    printBinaryLong("l ^ m", l ^ m);
    printBinaryLong("l << 5", l << 5);
    printBinaryLong("l >> 5", l >> 5);
    printBinaryLong("(~l) >> 5", (~l) >> 5);
    printBinaryLong("l >>> 5", l >>> 5);
    printBinaryLong("(~l) >>> 5", (~l) >>> 5);
    monitor.expect("BitManipulation.out");
  }
  static void printBinaryInt(String s, int i) {
    System.out.println(
      s + ", int: " + i + ", binary: ");
    System.out.print("   ");
    for(int j = 31; j >= 0; j--)
      if(((1 << j) &  i) != 0)
        System.out.print("1");
      else
        System.out.print("0");
    System.out.println();
  }
  static void printBinaryLong(String s, long l) {
    System.out.println(
      s + ", long: " + l + ", binary: ");
```

```
    System.out.print("   ");
    for(int i = 63; i >= 0; i--)
      if(((1L << i) & l) != 0)
        System.out.print("1");
      else
        System.out.print("0");
    System.out.println();
  }
} ///:~
```

The two methods at the end, **printBinaryInt( )** and **printBinaryLong( )**, take an **int** or a **long**, respectively, and print it out in binary format along with a descriptive string. You can ignore the implementation of these for now.

You'll note the use of **System.out.print( )** instead of **System.out.println( )**. The **print( )** method does not emit a newline, so it allows you to output a line in pieces.

In this case, the **expect( )** statement takes a file name, from which it reads the expected lines (which may or may not include regular expressions). This is useful in situations where the output is too long or inappropriate to include in the book. The files ending with ".out" are part of the code distribution, available for download from *www.BruceEckel.com*, so you can open the file and look at it to see what the output should be (or simply run the program yourself).

As well as demonstrating the effect of all the bitwise operators for **int** and **long**, this example also shows the minimum, maximum, +1, and -1 values for **int** and **long** so you can see what they look like. Note that the high bit represents the sign: 0 means positive and 1 means negative. The output for the **int** portion looks like this:

```
-1, int: -1, binary:
   11111111111111111111111111111111
+1, int: 1, binary:
   00000000000000000000000000000001
maxpos, int: 2147483647, binary:
   01111111111111111111111111111111
maxneg, int: -2147483648, binary:
   10000000000000000000000000000000
i, int: 59081716, binary:
   00000011100001011000001111110100
~i, int: -59081717, binary:
   11111100011110100111110000001011
```

```
-i, int: -59081716, binary:
   11111100011110100111110000001100
j, int: 198850956, binary:
   00001011110110100011100110001100
i & j, int: 58720644, binary:
   00000011100000000000000110000100
i | j, int: 199212028, binary:
   00001011110111111011101111111100
i ^ j, int: 140491384, binary:
   00001000010111111011101001111000
i << 5, int: 1890614912, binary:
   01110000101100000111111010000000
i >> 5, int: 1846303, binary:
   00000000000111000010110000011111
(~i) >> 5, int: -1846304, binary:
   11111111111000111101001111100000
i >>> 5, int: 1846303, binary:
   00000000000111000010110000011111
(~i) >>> 5, int: 132371424, binary:
   00000111111000111101001111100000
```

The binary representation of the numbers is referred to as *signed two's complement*.

Ternary if-else operator

This operator is unusual because it has three operands. It is truly an operator because it produces a value, unlike the ordinary if-else statement that you'll see in the next section of this chapter. The expression is of the form:

```
boolean-exp ? value0 : value1
```

If *boolean-exp* evaluates to **true**, *value0* is evaluated, and its result becomes the value produced by the operator. If *boolean-exp* is **false**, *value1* is evaluated and its result becomes the value produced by the operator.

Of course, you could use an ordinary **if-else** statement (described later), but the ternary operator is much terser. Although C (where this operator originated) prides itself on being a terse language, and the ternary operator might have been introduced partly for efficiency, you should be somewhat wary of using it on an everyday basis—it's easy to produce unreadable code.

The conditional operator can be used for its side effects or for the value it produces, but in general you want the value, since that's what makes the operator distinct from the **if-else**. Here's an example:

```
static int ternary(int i) {
  return i < 10 ? i * 100 : i * 10;
}
```

You can see that this code is more compact than what you'd need to write without the ternary operator:

```
static int alternative(int i) {
  if (i < 10)
    return i * 100;
  else
    return i * 10;
}
```

The second form is easier to understand, and doesn't require a lot more typing. So be sure to ponder your reasons when choosing the ternary operator—it's generally warranted when you're setting a variable to one of two values.

The comma operator

The comma is used in C and C++ not only as a separator in function argument lists, but also as an operator for sequential evaluation. The sole place that the comma *operator* is used in Java is in **for** loops, which will be described later in this chapter.

String operator +

There's one special usage of an operator in Java: the + operator can be used to concatenate strings, as you've already seen. It seems a natural use of the + even though it doesn't fit with the traditional way that + is used. This capability seemed like a good idea in C++, so *operator overloading* was added to C++ to allow the C++ programmer to add meanings to almost any operator. Unfortunately, operator overloading combined with some of the other restrictions in C++ turns out to be a fairly complicated feature for programmers to design into their classes. Although operator overloading would have been much simpler to implement in Java than it was in C++, this feature was still considered too complex, so Java programmers cannot implement their own overloaded operators like C++ programmers can.

The use of the **String** + has some interesting behavior. If an expression begins with a **String**, then all operands that follow must be **String**s (remember that the compiler will turn a quoted sequence of characters into a **String**):

```
int x = 0, y = 1, z = 2;
String sString = "x, y, z ";
System.out.println(sString + x + y + z);
```

Here, the Java compiler will convert **x**, **y**, and **z** into their **String** representations instead of adding them together first. And if you say:

```
System.out.println(x + sString);
```

Java will turn **x** into a **String**.

Common pitfalls when using operators

One of the pitfalls when using operators is attempting to leave out the parentheses when you are even the least bit uncertain about how an expression will evaluate. This is still true in Java.

An extremely common error in C and C++ looks like this:

```
while(x = y) {
  // ....
}
```

The programmer was clearly trying to test for equivalence (==) rather than do an assignment. In C and C++ the result of this assignment will always be **true** if **y** is nonzero, and you'll probably get an infinite loop. In Java, the result of this expression is not a **boolean,** but the compiler expects a **boolean** and won't convert from an **int**, so it will conveniently give you a compile-time error and catch the problem before you ever try to run the program. So the pitfall never happens in Java. (The only time you won't get a compile-time error is when **x** and **y** are **boolean**, in which case **x** = **y** is a legal expression, and in the preceding example, probably an error.)

A similar problem in C and C++ is using bitwise AND and OR instead of the logical versions. Bitwise AND and OR use one of the characters (**&** or **|**) while logical AND and OR use two (**&&** and **||**). Just as with = and ==, it's easy to type just one character instead of two. In Java, the compiler again prevents this, because it won't let you cavalierly use one type where it doesn't belong.

Casting operators

The word *cast* is used in the sense of "casting into a mold." Java will automatically change one type of data into another when appropriate. For instance, if you assign an integral value to a floating-point variable, the compiler will automatically convert the **int** to a **float**. Casting allows you to make this type conversion explicit, or to force it when it wouldn't normally happen.

To perform a cast, put the desired data type (including all modifiers) inside parentheses to the left of any value. Here's an example:

```
void casts() {
  int i = 200;
  long l = (long)i;
  long l2 = (long)200;
}
```

As you can see, it's possible to perform a cast on a numeric value as well as on a variable. In both casts shown here, however, the cast is superfluous, since the compiler will automatically promote an **int** value to a **long** when necessary. However, you are allowed to use superfluous casts to make a point or to make your code more clear. In other situations, a cast may be essential just to get the code to compile.

In C and C++, casting can cause some headaches. In Java, casting is safe, with the exception that when you perform a so-called *narrowing conversion* (that is, when you go from a data type that can hold more information to one that doesn't hold as much), you run the risk of losing information. Here the compiler forces you to do a cast, in effect saying "this can be a dangerous thing to do—if you want me to do it anyway you must make the cast explicit." With a *widening conversion* an explicit cast is not needed, because the new type will more than hold the information from the old type so that no information is ever lost.

Java allows you to cast any primitive type to any other primitive type, except for **boolean,** which doesn't allow any casting at all. Class types do not allow casting. To convert one to the other, there must be special methods. (**String** is a special case, and you'll find out later in this book that objects can be cast within a *family* of types; an **Oak** can be cast to a **Tree** and vice-versa, but not to a foreign type such as a **Rock**.)

Literals

Ordinarily, when you insert a literal value into a program, the compiler knows exactly what type to make it. Sometimes, however, the type is ambiguous. When this happens, you must guide the compiler by adding some extra information in the form of characters associated with the literal value. The following code shows these characters:

```
//: c03:Literals.java

public class Literals {
  char c = 0xffff; // max char hex value
  byte b = 0x7f; // max byte hex value
  short s = 0x7fff; // max short hex value
  int i1 = 0x2f; // Hexadecimal (lowercase)
  int i2 = 0X2F; // Hexadecimal (uppercase)
  int i3 = 0177; // Octal (leading zero)
  // Hex and Oct also work with long.
  long n1 = 200L; // long suffix
  long n2 = 200l; // long suffix (but can be confusing)
  long n3 = 200;
  //! long l6(200); // not allowed
  float f1 = 1;
  float f2 = 1F; // float suffix
  float f3 = 1f; // float suffix
  float f4 = 1e-45f; // 10 to the power
  float f5 = 1e+9f; // float suffix
  double d1 = 1d; // double suffix
  double d2 = 1D; // double suffix
  double d3 = 47e47d; // 10 to the power
} ///:~
```

Hexadecimal (base 16), which works with all the integral data types, is denoted by a leading **0x** or **0X** followed by **0-9** or **a-f** either in uppercase or lowercase. If you try to initialize a variable with a value bigger than it can hold (regardless of the numerical form of the value), the compiler will give you an error message. Notice in the preceding code the maximum possible hexadecimal values for **char**, **byte,** and **short**. If you exceed these, the compiler will automatically make the value an **int** and tell you that you need a narrowing cast for the assignment. You'll know you've stepped over the line.

Octal (base 8) is denoted by a leading zero in the number and digits from 0-7. There is no literal representation for binary numbers in C, C++, or Java.

A trailing character after a literal value establishes its type. Uppercase or lowercase **L** means **long**, upper or lowercase **F** means **float** and uppercase or lowercase **D** means **double**.

Exponents use a notation that I've always found rather dismaying: **1.39 e-47f**. In science and engineering, 'e' refers to the base of natural logarithms, approximately 2.718. (A more precise **double** value is available in Java as **Math.E**.) This is used in exponentiation expressions such as $1.39 \times e^{-47}$, which means 1.39×2.718^{-47}. However, when FORTRAN was invented, they decided that **e** would naturally mean "ten to the power," which is an odd decision because FORTRAN was designed for science and engineering, and one would think its designers would be sensitive about introducing such an ambiguity.[1] At any rate, this custom was followed in C, C++ and now Java. So if you're used to thinking in terms of **e** as the base of natural logarithms, you must do a mental translation when you see an expression such as **1.39 e-47f** in Java; it means 1.39×10^{-47}.

Note that you don't need to use the trailing character when the compiler can figure out the appropriate type. With

```
long n3 = 200;
```

there's no ambiguity, so an **L** after the 200 would be superfluous. However, with

```
float f4 = 1e-47f; // 10 to the power
```

the compiler normally takes exponential numbers as doubles, so without the trailing **f**, it will give you an error telling you that you must use a cast to convert **double** to **float**.

---

[1] John Kirkham writes, "I started computing in 1962 using FORTRAN II on an IBM 1620. At that time, and throughout the 1960s and into the 1970s, FORTRAN was an all uppercase language. This probably started because many of the early input devices were old teletype units that used 5 bit Baudot code, which had no lowercase capability. The 'E' in the exponential notation was also always upper case and was never confused with the natural logarithm base 'e', which is always lowercase. The 'E' simply stood for exponential, which was for the base of the number system used—usually 10. At the time octal was also widely used by programmers. Although I never saw it used, if I had seen an octal number in exponential notation I would have considered it to be base 8. The first time I remember seeing an exponential using a lowercase 'e' was in the late 1970s and I also found it confusing. The problem arose as lowercase crept into FORTRAN, not at its beginning. We actually had functions to use if you really wanted to use the natural logarithm base, but they were all uppercase."

Promotion

You'll discover that if you perform any mathematical or bitwise operations on primitive data types that are smaller than an **int** (that is, **char**, **byte,** or **short**), those values will be promoted to **int** before performing the operations, and the resulting value will be of type **int**. So if you want to assign back into the smaller type, you must use a cast. (And, since you're assigning back into a smaller type, you might be losing information.) In general, the largest data type in an expression is the one that determines the size of the result of that expression; if you multiply a **float** and a **double**, the result will be **double**; if you add an **int** and a **long**, the result will be **long**.

Java has no "sizeof"

In C and C++, the **sizeof( )** operator satisfies a specific need: it tells you the number of bytes allocated for data items. The most compelling need for **sizeof( )** in C and C++ is portability. Different data types might be different sizes on different machines, so the programmer must find out how big those types are when performing operations that are sensitive to size. For example, one computer might store integers in 32 bits, whereas another might store integers as 16 bits. Programs could store larger values in integers on the first machine. As you might imagine, portability is a huge headache for C and C++ programmers.

Java does not need a **sizeof( )** operator for this purpose, because all the data types are the same size on all machines. You do not need to think about portability on this level—it is designed into the language.

Precedence revisited

Upon hearing me complain about the complexity of remembering operator precedence during one of my seminars, a student suggested a mnemonic that is simultaneously a commentary: "Ulcer Addicts Really Like C A lot."

Mnemonic	**Operator type**	**Operators**
Ulcer	Unary	+ - ++--
Addicts	Arithmetic (and shift)	* / % + - << >>
Really	Relational	> < >= <= == !=
Like	Logical (and bitwise)	**&& || & | ^**
C	Conditional (ternary)	**A > B ? X : Y**

A Lot	Assignment	= (and compound assignment like *=)

Of course, with the shift and bitwise operators distributed around the table it is not a perfect mnemonic, but for non-bit operations it works.

A compendium of operators

The following example shows which primitive data types can be used with particular operators. Basically, it is the same example repeated over and over, but using different primitive data types. The file will compile without error because the lines that would cause errors are commented out with a **//!**.

```
//: c03:AllOps.java
// Tests all the operators on all the primitive data types
// to show which ones are accepted by the Java compiler.

public class AllOps {
  // To accept the results of a boolean test:
  void f(boolean b) {}
  void boolTest(boolean x, boolean y) {
    // Arithmetic operators:
    //! x = x * y;
    //! x = x / y;
    //! x = x % y;
    //! x = x + y;
    //! x = x - y;
    //! x++;
    //! x--;
    //! x = +y;
    //! x = -y;
    // Relational and logical:
    //! f(x > y);
    //! f(x >= y);
    //! f(x < y);
    //! f(x <= y);
    f(x == y);
    f(x != y);
    f(!y);
    x = x && y;
    x = x || y;
    // Bitwise operators:
    //! x = ~y;
    x = x & y;
```

```
    x = x | y;
    x = x ^ y;
    //! x = x << 1;
    //! x = x >> 1;
    //! x = x >>> 1;
    // Compound assignment:
    //! x += y;
    //! x -= y;
    //! x *= y;
    //! x /= y;
    //! x %= y;
    //! x <<= 1;
    //! x >>= 1;
    //! x >>>= 1;
    x &= y;
    x ^= y;
    x |= y;
    // Casting:
    //! char c = (char)x;
    //! byte B = (byte)x;
    //! short s = (short)x;
    //! int i = (int)x;
    //! long l = (long)x;
    //! float f = (float)x;
    //! double d = (double)x;
  }
  void charTest(char x, char y) {
    // Arithmetic operators:
    x = (char)(x * y);
    x = (char)(x / y);
    x = (char)(x % y);
    x = (char)(x + y);
    x = (char)(x - y);
    x++;
    x--;
    x = (char)+y;
    x = (char)-y;
    // Relational and logical:
    f(x > y);
    f(x >= y);
    f(x < y);
    f(x <= y);
    f(x == y);
    f(x != y);
```

```
    //! f(!x);
    //! f(x && y);
    //! f(x || y);
    // Bitwise operators:
    x= (char)~y;
    x = (char)(x & y);
    x  = (char)(x | y);
    x = (char)(x ^ y);
    x = (char)(x << 1);
    x = (char)(x >> 1);
    x = (char)(x >>> 1);
    // Compound assignment:
    x += y;
    x -= y;
    x *= y;
    x /= y;
    x %= y;
    x <<= 1;
    x >>= 1;
    x >>>= 1;
    x &= y;
    x ^= y;
    x |= y;
    // Casting:
    //! boolean b = (boolean)x;
    byte B = (byte)x;
    short s = (short)x;
    int i = (int)x;
    long l = (long)x;
    float f = (float)x;
    double d = (double)x;
  }
  void byteTest(byte x, byte y) {
    // Arithmetic operators:
    x = (byte)(x* y);
    x = (byte)(x / y);
    x = (byte)(x % y);
    x = (byte)(x + y);
    x = (byte)(x - y);
    x++;
    x--;
    x = (byte)+ y;
    x = (byte)- y;
    // Relational and logical:
```

```
    f(x > y);
    f(x >= y);
    f(x < y);
    f(x <= y);
    f(x == y);
    f(x != y);
    //! f(!x);
    //! f(x && y);
    //! f(x || y);
    // Bitwise operators:
    x = (byte)~y;
    x = (byte)(x & y);
    x = (byte)(x | y);
    x = (byte)(x ^ y);
    x = (byte)(x << 1);
    x = (byte)(x >> 1);
    x = (byte)(x >>> 1);
    // Compound assignment:
    x += y;
    x -= y;
    x *= y;
    x /= y;
    x %= y;
    x <<= 1;
    x >>= 1;
    x >>>= 1;
    x &= y;
    x ^= y;
    x |= y;
    // Casting:
    //! boolean b = (boolean)x;
    char c = (char)x;
    short s = (short)x;
    int i = (int)x;
    long l = (long)x;
    float f = (float)x;
    double d = (double)x;
  }
  void shortTest(short x, short y) {
    // Arithmetic operators:
    x = (short)(x * y);
    x = (short)(x / y);
    x = (short)(x % y);
    x = (short)(x + y);
```

```
    x = (short)(x - y);
    x++;
    x--;
    x = (short)+y;
    x = (short)-y;
    // Relational and logical:
    f(x > y);
    f(x >= y);
    f(x < y);
    f(x <= y);
    f(x == y);
    f(x != y);
    //! f(!x);
    //! f(x && y);
    //! f(x || y);
    // Bitwise operators:
    x = (short)~y;
    x = (short)(x & y);
    x = (short)(x | y);
    x = (short)(x ^ y);
    x = (short)(x << 1);
    x = (short)(x >> 1);
    x = (short)(x >>> 1);
    // Compound assignment:
    x += y;
    x -= y;
    x *= y;
    x /= y;
    x %= y;
    x <<= 1;
    x >>= 1;
    x >>>= 1;
    x &= y;
    x ^= y;
    x |= y;
    // Casting:
    //! boolean b = (boolean)x;
    char c = (char)x;
    byte B = (byte)x;
    int i = (int)x;
    long l = (long)x;
    float f = (float)x;
    double d = (double)x;
  }
```

```
void intTest(int x, int y) {
  // Arithmetic operators:
  x = x * y;
  x = x / y;
  x = x % y;
  x = x + y;
  x = x - y;
  x++;
  x--;
  x = +y;
  x = -y;
  // Relational and logical:
  f(x > y);
  f(x >= y);
  f(x < y);
  f(x <= y);
  f(x == y);
  f(x != y);
  //! f(!x);
  //! f(x && y);
  //! f(x || y);
  // Bitwise operators:
  x = ~y;
  x = x & y;
  x = x | y;
  x = x ^ y;
  x = x << 1;
  x = x >> 1;
  x = x >>> 1;
  // Compound assignment:
  x += y;
  x -= y;
  x *= y;
  x /= y;
  x %= y;
  x <<= 1;
  x >>= 1;
  x >>>= 1;
  x &= y;
  x ^= y;
  x |= y;
  // Casting:
  //! boolean b = (boolean)x;
  char c = (char)x;
```

```
    byte B = (byte)x;
    short s = (short)x;
    long l = (long)x;
    float f = (float)x;
    double d = (double)x;
  }
  void longTest(long x, long y) {
    // Arithmetic operators:
    x = x * y;
    x = x / y;
    x = x % y;
    x = x + y;
    x = x - y;
    x++;
    x--;
    x = +y;
    x = -y;
    // Relational and logical:
    f(x > y);
    f(x >= y);
    f(x < y);
    f(x <= y);
    f(x == y);
    f(x != y);
    //! f(!x);
    //! f(x && y);
    //! f(x || y);
    // Bitwise operators:
    x = ~y;
    x = x & y;
    x = x | y;
    x = x ^ y;
    x = x << 1;
    x = x >> 1;
    x = x >>> 1;
    // Compound assignment:
    x += y;
    x -= y;
    x *= y;
    x /= y;
    x %= y;
    x <<= 1;
    x >>= 1;
    x >>>= 1;
```

```
    x &= y;
    x ^= y;
    x |= y;
    // Casting:
    //! boolean b = (boolean)x;
    char c = (char)x;
    byte B = (byte)x;
    short s = (short)x;
    int i = (int)x;
    float f = (float)x;
    double d = (double)x;
  }
  void floatTest(float x, float y) {
    // Arithmetic operators:
    x = x * y;
    x = x / y;
    x = x % y;
    x = x + y;
    x = x - y;
    x++;
    x--;
    x = +y;
    x = -y;
    // Relational and logical:
    f(x > y);
    f(x >= y);
    f(x < y);
    f(x <= y);
    f(x == y);
    f(x != y);
    //! f(!x);
    //! f(x && y);
    //! f(x || y);
    // Bitwise operators:
    //! x = ~y;
    //! x = x & y;
    //! x = x | y;
    //! x = x ^ y;
    //! x = x << 1;
    //! x = x >> 1;
    //! x = x >>> 1;
    // Compound assignment:
    x += y;
    x -= y;
```

```
    x *= y;
    x /= y;
    x %= y;
    //! x <<= 1;
    //! x >>= 1;
    //! x >>>= 1;
    //! x &= y;
    //! x ^= y;
    //! x |= y;
    // Casting:
    //! boolean b = (boolean)x;
    char c = (char)x;
    byte B = (byte)x;
    short s = (short)x;
    int i = (int)x;
    long l = (long)x;
    double d = (double)x;
  }
  void doubleTest(double x, double y) {
    // Arithmetic operators:
    x = x * y;
    x = x / y;
    x = x % y;
    x = x + y;
    x = x - y;
    x++;
    x--;
    x = +y;
    x = -y;
    // Relational and logical:
    f(x > y);
    f(x >= y);
    f(x < y);
    f(x <= y);
    f(x == y);
    f(x != y);
    //! f(!x);
    //! f(x && y);
    //! f(x || y);
    // Bitwise operators:
    //! x = ~y;
    //! x = x & y;
    //! x = x | y;
    //! x = x ^ y;
```

```
    //! x = x << 1;
    //! x = x >> 1;
    //! x = x >>> 1;
    // Compound assignment:
    x += y;
    x -= y;
    x *= y;
    x /= y;
    x %= y;
    //! x <<= 1;
    //! x >>= 1;
    //! x >>>= 1;
    //! x &= y;
    //! x ^= y;
    //! x |= y;
    // Casting:
    //! boolean b = (boolean)x;
    char c = (char)x;
    byte B = (byte)x;
    short s = (short)x;
    int i = (int)x;
    long l = (long)x;
    float f = (float)x;
  }
} ///:~
```

Note that **boolean** is quite limited. You can assign to it the values **true** and **false**, and you can test it for truth or falsehood, but you cannot add booleans or perform any other type of operation on them.

In **char**, **byte**, and **short**, you can see the effect of promotion with the arithmetic operators. Each arithmetic operation on any of those types produces an **int** result, which must be explicitly cast back to the original type (a narrowing conversion that might lose information) to assign back to that type. With **int** values, however, you do not need to cast, because everything is already an **int**. Don't be lulled into thinking everything is safe, though. If you multiply two **int**s that are big enough, you'll overflow the result. The following example demonstrates this:

```
//: c03:Overflow.java
// Surprise! Java lets you overflow.
import com.bruceeckel.simpletest.*;

public class Overflow {
```

```java
  static Test monitor = new Test();
  public static void main(String[] args) {
    int big = 0x7fffffff; // max int value
    System.out.println("big = " + big);
    int bigger = big * 4;
    System.out.println("bigger = " + bigger);
    monitor.expect(new String[] {
      "big = 2147483647",
      "bigger = -4"
    });
  }
} ///:~
```

You get no errors or warnings from the compiler, and no exceptions at run time. Java is good, but it's not *that* good.

Compound assignments do *not* require casts for **char**, **byte,** or **short**, even though they are performing promotions that have the same results as the direct arithmetic operations. On the other hand, the lack of the cast certainly simplifies the code.

You can see that, with the exception of **boolean**, any primitive type can be cast to any other primitive type. Again, you must be aware of the effect of a narrowing conversion when casting to a smaller type, otherwise you might unknowingly lose information during the cast.

Execution control

Java uses all of C's execution control statements, so if you've programmed with C or C++, then most of what you see will be familiar. Most procedural programming languages have some kind of control statements, and there is often overlap among languages. In Java, the keywords include **if-else**, **while**, **do-while**, **for**, and a selection statement called **switch**. Java does not, however, support the much-maligned **goto** (which can still be the most expedient way to solve certain types of problems). You can still do a goto-like jump, but it is much more constrained than a typical **goto**.

true and false

All conditional statements use the truth or falsehood of a conditional expression to determine the execution path. An example of a conditional expression is **A == B**. This uses the conditional operator == to see if the value of **A** is equivalent to the value of **B**. The expression returns **true** or

false. Any of the relational operators you've seen earlier in this chapter can be used to produce a conditional statement. Note that Java doesn't allow you to use a number as a **boolean**, even though it's allowed in C and C++ (where truth is nonzero and falsehood is zero). If you want to use a non-**boolean** in a **boolean** test, such as **if(a)**, you must first convert it to a **boolean** value by using a conditional expression, such as **if(a != 0)**.

if-else

The **if-else** statement is probably the most basic way to control program flow. The **else** is optional, so you can use **if** in two forms:

```
if(Boolean-expression)
  statement
```

or

```
if(Boolean-expression)
  statement
else
  statement
```

The conditional must produce a **boolean** result. The *statement* is either a simple statement terminated by a semicolon, or a compound statement, which is a group of simple statements enclosed in braces. Any time the word "*statement*" is used, it always implies that the statement can be simple or compound.

As an example of **if-else**, here is a **test( )** method that will tell you whether a guess is above, below, or equivalent to a target number:

```
//: c03:IfElse.java
import com.bruceeckel.simpletest.*;

public class IfElse {
  static Test monitor = new Test();
  static int test(int testval, int target) {
    int result = 0;
    if(testval > target)
      result = +1;
    else if(testval < target)
      result = -1;
    else
      result = 0; // Match
```

```
    return result;
  }
  public static void main(String[] args) {
    System.out.println(test(10, 5));
    System.out.println(test(5, 10));
    System.out.println(test(5, 5));
    monitor.expect(new String[] {
      "1",
      "-1",
      "0"
    });
  }
} ///:~
```

It is conventional to indent the body of a control flow statement so the reader can easily determine where it begins and ends.

return

The **return** keyword has two purposes: It specifies what value a method will return (if it doesn't have a **void** return value) and it causes that value to be returned immediately. The preceding **test( )** method can be rewritten to take advantage of this:

```
//: c03:IfElse2.java
import com.bruceeckel.simpletest.*;

public class IfElse2 {
  static Test monitor = new Test();
  static int test(int testval, int target) {
    if(testval > target)
      return +1;
    else if(testval < target)
      return -1;
    else
      return 0; // Match
  }
  public static void main(String[] args) {
    System.out.println(test(10, 5));
    System.out.println(test(5, 10));
    System.out.println(test(5, 5));
    monitor.expect(new String[] {
      "1",
      "-1",
```

```
        "0"
      });
  }
} ///:~
```

There's no need for **else**, because the method will not continue after executing a **return**.

Iteration

Looping is controlled by **while**, **do-while** and **for**, which are sometimes classified as *iteration statements*. A *statement* repeats until the controlling *Boolean-expression* evaluates to false. The form for a **while** loop is

```
while(Boolean-expression)
  statement
```

The *Boolean-expression* is evaluated once at the beginning of the loop and again before each further iteration of the *statement*.

Here's a simple example that generates random numbers until a particular condition is met:

```
//: c03:WhileTest.java
// Demonstrates the while loop.
import com.bruceeckel.simpletest.*;

public class WhileTest {
  static Test monitor = new Test();
  public static void main(String[] args) {
    double r = 0;
    while(r < 0.99d) {
      r = Math.random();
      System.out.println(r);
      monitor.expect(new String[] {
        "%% \\d\\.\\d+E?-?\\d*"
      }, Test.AT_LEAST);
    }
  }
} ///:~
```

This uses the **static** method **random( )** in the **Math** library, which generates a **double** value between 0 and 1. (It includes 0, but not 1.) The conditional expression for the **while** says "keep doing this loop until the number is 0.99 or greater." Each time you run this program, you'll get a different-sized list of numbers.

In the **expect( )** statement, you see the **Test.AT_LEAST** flag following the expected list of strings. The **expect( )** statement can include several different flags to modify its behavior; this one says that **expect( )** should see at least the lines shown, but others may also appear (which it ignores). Here, it says "you should see at least one double value."

do-while

The form for **do-while** is

```
do
  statement
while(Boolean-expression);
```

The sole difference between **while** and **do-while** is that the statement of the **do-while** always executes at least once, even if the expression evaluates to false the first time. In a **while**, if the conditional is false the first time the statement never executes. In practice, **do-while** is less common than **while**.

for

A **for** loop performs initialization before the first iteration. Then it performs conditional testing and, at the end of each iteration, some form of "stepping." The form of the **for** loop is:

```
for(initialization; Boolean-expression; step)
  statement
```

Any of the expressions *initialization*, *Boolean-expression* or *step* can be empty. The expression is tested before each iteration, and as soon as it evaluates to **false**, execution will continue at the line following the **for** statement. At the end of each loop, the *step* executes.

for loops are usually used for "counting" tasks:

```
//: c03:ListCharacters.java
// Demonstrates "for" loop by listing
// all the lowercase ASCII letters.
import com.bruceeckel.simpletest.*;

public class ListCharacters {
```

```
  static Test monitor = new Test();
  public static void main(String[] args) {
    for(int i = 0; i < 128; i++)
      if(Character.isLowerCase((char)i))
        System.out.println("value: " + i +
          " character: " + (char)i);
    monitor.expect(new String[] {
      "value: 97 character: a",
      "value: 98 character: b",
      "value: 99 character: c",
      "value: 100 character: d",
      "value: 101 character: e",
      "value: 102 character: f",
      "value: 103 character: g",
      "value: 104 character: h",
      "value: 105 character: i",
      "value: 106 character: j",
      "value: 107 character: k",
      "value: 108 character: l",
      "value: 109 character: m",
      "value: 110 character: n",
      "value: 111 character: o",
      "value: 112 character: p",
      "value: 113 character: q",
      "value: 114 character: r",
      "value: 115 character: s",
      "value: 116 character: t",
      "value: 117 character: u",
      "value: 118 character: v",
      "value: 119 character: w",
      "value: 120 character: x",
      "value: 121 character: y",
      "value: 122 character: z"
    });
  }
} ///:~
```

Note that the variable **i** is defined at the point where it is used, inside the control expression of the **for** loop, rather than at the beginning of the block denoted by the open curly brace. The scope of **i** is the expression controlled by the **for**.

This program also uses the **java.lang.Character** "wrapper" class, which not only wraps the primitive **char** type in an object, but also provides other utilities. Here, the **static isLowerCase( )** method is used to detect whether the character in question is a lower-case letter.

Traditional procedural languages like C require that all variables be defined at the beginning of a block so that when the compiler creates a block, it can allocate space for those variables. In Java and C++, you can spread your variable declarations throughout the block, defining them at the point that you need them. This allows a more natural coding style and makes code easier to understand.

You can define multiple variables within a **for** statement, but they must be of the same type:

```
for(int i = 0, j = 1; i < 10 && j != 11; i++, j++)
  // body of for loop
```

The **int** definition in the **for** statement covers both **i** and **j**. The ability to define variables in the control expression is limited to the **for** loop. You cannot use this approach with any of the other selection or iteration statements.

The comma operator

Earlier in this chapter I stated that the comma *operator* (not the comma *separator*, which is used to separate definitions and method arguments) has only one use in Java: in the control expression of a **for** loop. In both the initialization and step portions of the control expression, you can have a number of statements separated by commas, and those statements will be evaluated sequentially. The previous bit of code uses this ability. Here's another example:

```
//: c03:CommaOperator.java
import com.bruceeckel.simpletest.*;

public class CommaOperator {
  static Test monitor = new Test();
  public static void main(String[] args) {
    for(int i = 1, j = i + 10; i < 5;
        i++, j = i * 2) {
      System.out.println("i= " + i + " j= " + j);
    }
    monitor.expect(new String[] {
      "i= 1 j= 11",
      "i= 2 j= 4",
```

```
      "i= 3 j= 6",
      "i= 4 j= 8"
    });
  }
} ///:~
```

You can see that in both the initialization and step portions, the statements are evaluated in sequential order. Also, the initialization portion can have any number of definitions *of one type*.

break and continue

You can also control the flow of the loop inside the body of any of the iteration statements by using **break** and **continue**. **break** quits the loop without executing the rest of the statements in the loop. **continue** stops the execution of the current iteration and goes back to the beginning of the loop to begin the next iteration.

This program shows examples of **break** and **continue** within **for** and **while** loops:

```
//: c03:BreakAndContinue.java
// Demonstrates break and continue keywords.
import com.bruceeckel.simpletest.*;

public class BreakAndContinue {
  static Test monitor = new Test();
  public static void main(String[] args) {
    for(int i = 0; i < 100; i++) {
      if(i == 74) break; // Out of for loop
      if(i % 9 != 0) continue; // Next iteration
      System.out.println(i);
    }
    int i = 0;
    // An "infinite loop":
    while(true) {
      i++;
      int j = i * 27;
      if(j == 1269) break; // Out of loop
      if(i % 10 != 0) continue; // Top of loop
      System.out.println(i);
    }
    monitor.expect(new String[] {
      "0",
```

```
      "9",
      "18",
      "27",
      "36",
      "45",
      "54",
      "63",
      "72",
      "10",
      "20",
      "30",
      "40"
    });
  }
} ///:~
```

In the **for** loop, the value of **i** never gets to 100 because the **break** statement breaks out of the loop when **i** is 74. Normally, you'd use a **break** like this only if you didn't know when the terminating condition was going to occur. The **continue** statement causes execution to go back to the top of the iteration loop (thus incrementing **i**) whenever **i** is not evenly divisible by 9. When it is, the value is printed.

The second portion shows an "infinite loop" that would, in theory, continue forever. However, inside the loop there is a **break** statement that will break out of the loop. In addition, you'll see that the **continue** moves back to the top of the loop without completing the remainder. (Thus printing happens in the second loop only when the value of **i** is divisible by 10.) In the output, The value 0 is printed, because 0 % 9 produces 0.

A second form of the infinite loop is **for(;;)**. The compiler treats both **while(true)** and **for(;;)** in the same way, so whichever one you use is a matter of programming taste.

The infamous "goto"

The **goto** keyword has been present in programming languages from the beginning. Indeed, **goto** was the genesis of program control in assembly language: "If condition A, then jump here, otherwise jump there." If you read the assembly code that is ultimately generated by virtually any compiler, you'll see that program control contains many jumps (the Java compiler produces its own "assembly code," but this code is run by the Java Virtual Machine rather than directly on a hardware CPU).

A **goto** is a jump at the source-code level, and that's what brought it into disrepute. If a program will always jump from one point to another, isn't there some way to reorganize the code so the flow of control is not so jumpy? **goto** fell into true disfavor with the publication of the famous "Goto considered harmful" paper by Edsger Dijkstra, and since then goto-bashing has been a popular sport, with advocates of the cast-out keyword scurrying for cover.

As is typical in situations like this, the middle ground is the most fruitful. The problem is not the use of **goto**, but the overuse of **goto**; in rare situations **goto** is actually the best way to structure control flow.

Although **goto** is a reserved word in Java, it is not used in the language; Java has no **goto**. However, it does have something that looks a bit like a jump tied in with the **break** and **continue** keywords. It's not a jump but rather a way to break out of an iteration statement. The reason it's often thrown in with discussions of **goto** is because it uses the same mechanism: a label.

A label is an identifier followed by a colon, like this:

```
label1:
```

The *only* place a label is useful in Java is right before an iteration statement. And that means *right* before—it does no good to put any other statement between the label and the iteration. And the sole reason to put a label before an iteration is if you're going to nest another iteration or a switch inside it. That's because the **break** and **continue** keywords will normally interrupt only the current loop, but when used with a label, they'll interrupt the loops up to where the label exists:

```
label1:
outer-iteration {
  inner-iteration {
    //...
    break; // 1
    //...
    continue;  // 2
    //...
    continue label1; // 3
    //...
    break label1;  // 4
  }
}
```

In case 1, the **break** breaks out of the inner iteration and you end up in the outer iteration. In case 2, the **continue** moves back to the beginning of the inner iteration. But in case 3, the **continue label1** breaks out of the inner iteration *and* the outer iteration, all the way back to **label1**. Then it does in fact continue the iteration, but starting at the outer iteration. In case 4, the **break label1** also breaks all the way out to **label1**, but it does not reenter the iteration. It actually does break out of both iterations.

Here is an example using **for** loops:

```
//: c03:LabeledFor.java
// Java's "labeled for" loop.
import com.bruceeckel.simpletest.*;

public class LabeledFor {
  static Test monitor = new Test();
  public static void main(String[] args) {
    int i = 0;
    outer: // Can't have statements here
    for(; true ;) { // infinite loop
      inner: // Can't have statements here
      for(; i < 10; i++) {
        System.out.println("i = " + i);
        if(i == 2) {
          System.out.println("continue");
          continue;
        }
        if(i == 3) {
          System.out.println("break");
          i++; // Otherwise i never
               // gets incremented.
          break;
        }
        if(i == 7) {
          System.out.println("continue outer");
          i++; // Otherwise i never
               // gets incremented.
          continue outer;
        }
        if(i == 8) {
          System.out.println("break outer");
          break outer;
        }
        for(int k = 0; k < 5; k++) {
```

```
          if(k == 3) {
            System.out.println("continue inner");
            continue inner;
          }
        }
      }
    }
    // Can't break or continue to labels here
    monitor.expect(new String[] {
      "i = 0",
      "continue inner",
      "i = 1",
      "continue inner",
      "i = 2",
      "continue",
      "i = 3",
      "break",
      "i = 4",
      "continue inner",
      "i = 5",
      "continue inner",
      "i = 6",
      "continue inner",
      "i = 7",
      "continue outer",
      "i = 8",
      "break outer"
    });
  }
} ///:~
```

Note that **break** breaks out of the **for** loop, and that the increment-expression doesn't occur until the end of the pass through the **for** loop. Since **break** skips the increment expression, the increment is performed directly in the case of **i == 3**. The **continue outer** statement in the case of **i == 7** also goes to the top of the loop and also skips the increment, so it too is incremented directly.

If not for the **break outer** statement, there would be no way to get out of the outer loop from within an inner loop, since **break** by itself can break out of only the innermost loop. (The same is true for **continue**.)

Of course, in the cases where breaking out of a loop will also exit the method, you can simply use a **return**.

Here is a demonstration of labeled **break** and **continue** statements with **while** loops:

```
//: c03:LabeledWhile.java
// Java's "labeled while" loop.
import com.bruceeckel.simpletest.*;

public class LabeledWhile {
  static Test monitor = new Test();
  public static void main(String[] args) {
    int i = 0;
    outer:
    while(true) {
      System.out.println("Outer while loop");
      while(true) {
        i++;
        System.out.println("i = " + i);
        if(i == 1) {
          System.out.println("continue");
          continue;
        }
        if(i == 3) {
          System.out.println("continue outer");
          continue outer;
        }
        if(i == 5) {
          System.out.println("break");
          break;
        }
        if(i == 7) {
          System.out.println("break outer");
          break outer;
        }
      }
    }
    monitor.expect(new String[] {
      "Outer while loop",
      "i = 1",
      "continue",
      "i = 2",
      "i = 3",
      "continue outer",
      "Outer while loop",
      "i = 4",
```

```
      "i = 5",
      "break",
      "Outer while loop",
      "i = 6",
      "i = 7",
      "break outer"
    });
  }
} ///:~
```

The same rules hold true for **while**:

1. A plain **continue** goes to the top of the innermost loop and continues.

2. A labeled **continue** goes to the label and reenters the loop right after that label.

3. A **break** "drops out of the bottom" of the loop.

4. A labeled **break** drops out of the bottom of the end of the loop denoted by the label.

It's important to remember that the *only* reason to use labels in Java is when you have nested loops and you want to **break** or **continue** through more than one nested level.

In Dijkstra's "goto considered harmful" paper, what he specifically objected to was the labels, not the goto. He observed that the number of bugs seems to increase with the number of labels in a program. Labels and gotos make programs difficult to analyze statically, since it introduces cycles in the program execution graph. Note that Java labels don't suffer from this problem, since they are constrained in their placement and can't be used to transfer control in an ad hoc manner. It's also interesting to note that this is a case where a language feature is made more useful by restricting the power of the statement.

switch

The **switch** is sometimes classified as a *selection statement*. The **switch** statement selects from among pieces of code based on the value of an integral expression. Its form is:

```
switch(integral-selector) {
  case integral-value1 : statement; break;
```

```
  case integral-value2 : statement; break;
  case integral-value3 : statement; break;
  case integral-value4 : statement; break;
  case integral-value5 : statement; break;
  // ...
  default: statement;
}
```

Integral-selector is an expression that produces an integral value. The **switch** compares the result of *integral-selector* to each *integral-value*. If it finds a match, the corresponding *statement* (simple or compound) executes. If no match occurs, the **default** *statement* executes.

You will notice in the preceding definition that each **case** ends with a **break**, which causes execution to jump to the end of the **switch** body. This is the conventional way to build a **switch** statement, but the **break** is optional. If it is missing, the code for the following case statements execute until a **break** is encountered. Although you don't usually want this kind of behavior, it can be useful to an experienced programmer. Note that the last statement, following the **default**, doesn't have a **break** because the execution just falls through to where the **break** would have taken it anyway. You could put a **break** at the end of the **default** statement with no harm if you considered it important for style's sake.

The **switch** statement is a clean way to implement multiway selection (i.e., selecting from among a number of different execution paths), but it requires a selector that evaluates to an integral value, such as **int** or **char**. If you want to use, for example, a string or a floating-point number as a selector, it won't work in a **switch** statement. For non-integral types, you must use a series of **if** statements.

Here's an example that creates letters randomly and determines whether they're vowels or consonants:

```
//: c03:VowelsAndConsonants.java
// Demonstrates the switch statement.
import com.bruceeckel.simpletest.*;

public class VowelsAndConsonants {
  static Test monitor = new Test();
  public static void main(String[] args) {
    for(int i = 0; i < 100; i++) {
      char c = (char)(Math.random() * 26 + 'a');
```

```
        System.out.print(c + ": ");
        switch(c) {
          case 'a':
          case 'e':
          case 'i':
          case 'o':
          case 'u': System.out.println("vowel");
                    break;
          case 'y':
          case 'w': System.out.println("Sometimes a vowel");
                    break;
          default:  System.out.println("consonant");
        }
        monitor.expect(new String[] {
          "%% [aeiou]: vowel|[yw]: Sometimes a vowel|" +
            "[^aeiouyw]: consonant"
        }, Test.AT_LEAST);
      }
    }
} ///:~
```

Since **Math.random( )** generates a value between 0 and 1, you need only multiply it by the upper bound of the range of numbers you want to produce (26 for the letters in the alphabet) and add an offset to establish the lower bound.

Although it appears you're switching on a character here, the **switch** statement is actually using the integral value of the character. The single-quoted characters in the **case** statements also produce integral values that are used for comparison.

Notice how the **case**s can be "stacked" on top of each other to provide multiple matches for a particular piece of code. You should also be aware that it's essential to put the **break** statement at the end of a particular case; otherwise, control will simply drop through and continue processing on the next case.

In the regular expression in this **expect( )** statement, the '|' is used to indicate three different possibilities. The '**[]**' encloses a "set" of characters in a regular expression, so the first part says "one of a, e, i, o, or u, followed by a colon and the word 'vowel'." The second possibility indicates either y or w and: "Sometimes a vowel." The set in the third possibility begins with a '^', which means "*not* any of the characters in this set," so it indicates anything other than a vowel will match.

Calculation details

The statement:

```
char c = (char)(Math.random() * 26 + 'a');
```

deserves a closer look. **Math.random( )** produces a **double**, so the value 26 is converted to a **double** to perform the multiplication, which also produces a **double**. This means that **'a'** must be converted to a **double** to perform the addition. The **double** result is turned back into a **char** with a cast.

What does the cast to **char** do? That is, if you have the value 29.7 and you cast it to a **char**, is the resulting value 30 or 29? The answer to this can be seen in this example:

```
//: c03:CastingNumbers.java
// What happens when you cast a float
// or double to an integral value?
import com.bruceeckel.simpletest.*;

public class CastingNumbers {
  static Test monitor = new Test();
  public static void main(String[] args) {
    double
      above = 0.7,
      below = 0.4;
    System.out.println("above: " + above);
    System.out.println("below: " + below);
    System.out.println("(int)above: " + (int)above);
    System.out.println("(int)below: " + (int)below);
    System.out.println("(char)('a' + above): " +
      (char)('a' + above));
    System.out.println("(char)('a' + below): " +
      (char)('a' + below));
    monitor.expect(new String[] {
      "above: 0.7",
      "below: 0.4",
      "(int)above: 0",
      "(int)below: 0",
      "(char)('a' + above): a",
      "(char)('a' + below): a"
    });
```

```
  }
} ///:~
```

So the answer is that casting from a **float** or **double** to an integral value always truncates the number.

A second question concerns **Math.random( )**. Does it produce a value from zero to one, inclusive or exclusive of the value '1'? In math lingo, is it (0,1), or [0,1], or (0,1] or [0,1)? (The square bracket means "includes," whereas the parenthesis means "doesn't include.") Again, a test program *might* provide the answer:

```
//: c03:RandomBounds.java
// Does Math.random() produce 0.0 and 1.0?
// {RunByHand}

public class RandomBounds {
  static void usage() {
    System.out.println("Usage: \n\t" +
      "RandomBounds lower\n\tRandomBounds upper");
    System.exit(1);
  }
  public static void main(String[] args) {
    if(args.length != 1) usage();
    if(args[0].equals("lower")) {
      while(Math.random() != 0.0)
        ; // Keep trying
      System.out.println("Produced 0.0!");
    }
    else if(args[0].equals("upper")) {
      while(Math.random() != 1.0)
        ; // Keep trying
      System.out.println("Produced 1.0!");
    }
    else
      usage();
  }
} ///:~
```

To run the program, you type a command line of either:

```
java RandomBounds lower
```

or

```
java RandomBounds upper
```

In both cases you are forced to break out of the program manually, so it would *appear* that **Math.random( )** never produces either 0.0 or 1.0. But this is where such an experiment can be deceiving. If you consider[2] that there are about 2^{62} different double fractions between 0 and 1, the likelihood of reaching any one value experimentally might exceed the lifetime of one computer, or even one experimenter. It turns out that 0.0 *is* included in the output of **Math.random( )**. Or, in math lingo, it is [0,1).

Summary

This chapter concludes the study of fundamental features that appear in most programming languages: calculation, operator precedence, type casting, and selection and iteration. Now you're ready to begin taking steps that move you closer to the world of object-oriented programming. The next chapter will cover the important issues of initialization and cleanup of objects, followed in the subsequent chapter by the essential concept of implementation hiding.

Exercises

Solutions to selected exercises can be found in the electronic document *The Thinking in Java Annotated Solution Guide*, available for a small fee from *www.BruceEckel.com*.

1. There are two expressions in the section labeled "precedence" early in this chapter. Put these expressions into a program and demonstrate that they produce different results.

---

[2] Chuck Allison writes: The total number of numbers in a floating-point number system is
2(M-m+1)b^(p-1) + 1
where **b** is the base (usually 2), **p** is the precision (digits in the mantissa), **M** is the largest exponent, and **m** is the smallest exponent. IEEE 754 uses:
M = 1023, m = -1022, p = 53, b = 2
so the total number of numbers is
2(1023+1022+1)2^52
= 2((2^10-1) + (2^10-1))2^52
= (2^10-1)2^54
= 2^64 - 2^54
Half of these numbers (corresponding to exponents in the range [-1022, 0]) are less than 1 in magnitude (both positive and negative), so 1/4 of that expression, or 2^62 - 2^52 + 1 (approximately 2^62) is in the range [0,1). See my paper at http://www.freshsources.com/1995006a.htm (last of text).

2. Put the methods **ternary( )** and **alternative( )** into a working program.

3. From the sections labeled "if-else" and "return," modify the two **test( )** methods so that **testval** is tested to see if it is within the range between (and including) the arguments **begin** and **end**.

4. Write a program that prints values from 1 to 100.

5. Modify Exercise 4 so that the program exits by using the **break** keyword at value 47. Try using **return** instead.

6. Write a method that takes two **String** arguments and uses all the **boolean** comparisons to compare the two **Strings** and print the results. For the **==** and **!=**, also perform the **equals( )** test. In **main( )**, call your method with some different **String** objects.

7. Write a program that generates 25 random **int** values. For each value, use an **if-else** statement to classify it as greater than, less than, or equal to a second randomly-generated value.

8. Modify Exercise 7 so that your code is surrounded by an "infinite" **while** loop. It will then run until you interrupt it from the keyboard (typically by pressing Control-C).

9. Write a program that uses two nested **for** loops and the modulus operator (**%**) to detect and print prime numbers (integral numbers that are not evenly divisible by any other numbers except for themselves and 1).

10. Create a **switch** statement that prints a message for each **case**, and put the **switch** inside a **for** loop that tries each **case**. Put a **break** after each **case** and test it, then remove the **breaks** and see what happens.

4: Initialization & Cleanup

As the computer revolution progresses, "unsafe" programming has become one of the major culprits that makes programming expensive.

Two of these safety issues are *initialization* and *cleanup*. Many C bugs occur when the programmer forgets to initialize a variable. This is especially true with libraries when users don't know how to initialize a library component, or even that they must. Cleanup is a special problem because it's easy to forget about an element when you're done with it, since it no longer concerns you. Thus, the resources used by that element are retained and you can easily end up running out of resources (most notably, memory).

C++ introduced the concept of a *constructor*, a special method automatically called when an object is created. Java also adopted the constructor, and in addition has a garbage collector that automatically releases memory resources when they're no longer being used. This chapter examines the issues of initialization and cleanup, and their support in Java.

Guaranteed initialization with the constructor

You can imagine creating a method called **initialize( )** for every class you write. The name is a hint that it should be called before using the object. Unfortunately, this means the user must remember to call the method. In Java, the class designer can guarantee initialization of every object by providing a special method called a *constructor*. If a class has a constructor, Java automatically calls that constructor when an object is created, before users can even get their hands on it. So initialization is guaranteed.

The next challenge is what to name this method. There are two issues. The first is that any name you use could clash with a name you might like to use as a member in the class. The second is that because the compiler is responsible for calling the constructor, it must always know which method to call. The C++ solution seems the easiest and most logical, so it's also used in Java: The name of the constructor is the same as the name of the class. It makes sense that such a method will be called automatically on initialization.

Here's a simple class with a constructor:

```
//: c04:SimpleConstructor.java
// Demonstration of a simple constructor.
import com.bruceeckel.simpletest.*;

class Rock {
  Rock() { // This is the constructor
    System.out.println("Creating Rock");
  }
}

public class SimpleConstructor {
  static Test monitor = new Test();
  public static void main(String[] args) {
    for(int i = 0; i < 10; i++)
      new Rock();
    monitor.expect(new String[] {
      "Creating Rock",
      "Creating Rock",
      "Creating Rock",
      "Creating Rock",
      "Creating Rock",
      "Creating Rock",
      "Creating Rock",
      "Creating Rock",
      "Creating Rock",
      "Creating Rock"
    });
  }
} ///:~
```

Now, when an object is created:

```
new Rock();
```

storage is allocated and the constructor is called. It is guaranteed that the object will be properly initialized before you can get your hands on it.

Note that the coding style of making the first letter of all methods lowercase does not apply to constructors, since the name of the constructor must match the name of the class *exactly*.

Like any method, the constructor can have arguments to allow you to specify *how* an object is created. The preceding example can easily be changed so the constructor takes an argument:

```
//: c04:SimpleConstructor2.java
// Constructors can have arguments.
import com.bruceeckel.simpletest.*;

class Rock2 {
  Rock2(int i) {
    System.out.println("Creating Rock number " + i);
  }
}

public class SimpleConstructor2 {
  static Test monitor = new Test();
  public static void main(String[] args) {
    for(int i = 0; i < 10; i++)
      new Rock2(i);
    monitor.expect(new String[] {
      "Creating Rock number 0",
      "Creating Rock number 1",
      "Creating Rock number 2",
      "Creating Rock number 3",
      "Creating Rock number 4",
      "Creating Rock number 5",
      "Creating Rock number 6",
      "Creating Rock number 7",
      "Creating Rock number 8",
      "Creating Rock number 9"
    });
  }
} ///:~
```

Constructor arguments provide you with a way to provide parameters for the initialization of an object. For example, if the class **Tree** has a constructor that takes a single integer argument denoting the height of the tree, you would create a **Tree** object like this:

```
Tree t = new Tree(12);  // 12-foot tree
```

If **Tree(int)** is your only constructor, then the compiler won't let you create a **Tree** object any other way.

Constructors eliminate a large class of problems and make the code easier to read. In the preceding code fragment, for example, you don't see an explicit call to some **initialize( )** method that is conceptually separate from creation. In Java, creation and initialization are unified concepts—you can't have one without the other.

The constructor is an unusual type of method because it has no return value. This is distinctly different from a **void** return value, in which the method returns nothing but you still have the option to make it return something else. Constructors return nothing and you don't have an option (the **new** expression does return a reference to the newly-created object, but the constructor itself has no return value). If there were a return value, and if you could select your own, the compiler would somehow need to know what to do with that return value.

Method overloading

One of the important features in any programming language is the use of names. When you create an object, you give a name to a region of storage. A method is a name for an action. By using names to describe your system, you create a program that is easier for people to understand and change. It's a lot like writing prose—the goal is to communicate with your readers.

You refer to all objects and methods by using names. Well-chosen names make it easier for you and others to understand your code.

A problem arises when mapping the concept of nuance in human language onto a programming language. Often, the same word expresses a number of different meanings—it's *overloaded*. This is useful, especially when it comes to trivial differences. You say "wash the shirt," "wash the car," and "wash the dog." It would be silly to be forced to say, "shirtWash the shirt," "carWash the car," and "dogWash the dog" just so the listener doesn't need to make any distinction about the action performed. Most human languages are redundant, so even if you miss a few words, you can still determine the meaning. We don't need unique identifiers—we can deduce meaning from context.

Most programming languages (C in particular) require you to have a unique identifier for each function. So you could not have one function called **print( )** for printing integers and another called **print( )** for printing floats—each function requires a unique name.

In Java (and C++), another factor forces the overloading of method names: the constructor. Because the constructor's name is predetermined by the name of the class, there can be only one constructor name. But what if you want to create an object in more than one way? For example, suppose you build a class that can initialize itself in a standard way or by reading information from a file. You need two constructors, one that takes no arguments (the *default* constructor,[1] also called the *no-arg* constructor), and one that takes a **String** as an argument, which is the name of the file from which to initialize the object. Both are constructors, so they must have the same name—the name of the class. Thus, *method overloading* is essential to allow the same method name to be used with different argument types. And although method overloading is a must for constructors, it's a general convenience and can be used with any method.

Here's an example that shows both overloaded constructors and overloaded ordinary methods:

```
//: c04:Overloading.java
// Demonstration of both constructor
// and ordinary method overloading.
import com.bruceeckel.simpletest.*;
import java.util.*;

class Tree {
  int height;
  Tree() {
    System.out.println("Planting a seedling");
    height = 0;
  }
  Tree(int i) {
    System.out.println("Creating new Tree that is "
      + i + " feet tall");
```

[1] In some of the Java literature from Sun, they instead refer to these with the awkward but descriptive name "no-arg constructors." The term "default constructor" has been in use for many years, so I will use that.

```
    height = i;
  }
  void info() {
    System.out.println("Tree is " + height + " feet tall");
  }
  void info(String s) {
    System.out.println(s + ": Tree is "
      + height + " feet tall");
  }
}

public class Overloading {
  static Test monitor = new Test();
  public static void main(String[] args) {
    for(int i = 0; i < 5; i++) {
      Tree t = new Tree(i);
      t.info();
      t.info("overloaded method");
    }
    // Overloaded constructor:
    new Tree();
    monitor.expect(new String[] {
      "Creating new Tree that is 0 feet tall",
      "Tree is 0 feet tall",
      "overloaded method: Tree is 0 feet tall",
      "Creating new Tree that is 1 feet tall",
      "Tree is 1 feet tall",
      "overloaded method: Tree is 1 feet tall",
      "Creating new Tree that is 2 feet tall",
      "Tree is 2 feet tall",
      "overloaded method: Tree is 2 feet tall",
      "Creating new Tree that is 3 feet tall",
      "Tree is 3 feet tall",
      "overloaded method: Tree is 3 feet tall",
      "Creating new Tree that is 4 feet tall",
      "Tree is 4 feet tall",
      "overloaded method: Tree is 4 feet tall",
      "Planting a seedling"
    });
  }
} ///:~
```

A **Tree** object can be created either as a seedling, with no argument, or as a plant grown in a nursery, with an existing height. To support this, there is a default constructor, and one that takes the existing height.

You might also want to call the **info( )** method in more than one way. For example, if you have an extra message you want printed, you can use **info(String)**, and **info( )** if you have nothing more to say. It would seem strange to give two separate names to what is obviously the same concept. Fortunately, method overloading allows you to use the same name for both.

Distinguishing overloaded methods

If the methods have the same name, how can Java know which method you mean? There's a simple rule: each overloaded method must take a unique list of argument types.

If you think about this for a second, it makes sense. How else could a programmer tell the difference between two methods that have the same name, other than by the types of their arguments?

Even differences in the ordering of arguments are sufficient to distinguish two methods: (Although you don't normally want to take this approach, as it produces difficult-to-maintain code.)

```
//: c04:OverloadingOrder.java
// Overloading based on the order of the arguments.
import com.bruceeckel.simpletest.*;

public class OverloadingOrder {
  static Test monitor = new Test();
  static void print(String s, int i) {
    System.out.println("String: " + s + ", int: " + i);
  }
  static void print(int i, String s) {
    System.out.println("int: " + i + ", String: " + s);
  }
  public static void main(String[] args) {
    print("String first", 11);
    print(99, "Int first");
    monitor.expect(new String[] {
      "String: String first, int: 11",
      "int: 99, String: Int first"
    });
```

```
  }
} ///:~
```

The two **print( )** methods have identical arguments, but the order is different, and that's what makes them distinct.

Overloading with primitives

A primitive can be automatically promoted from a smaller type to a larger one, and this can be slightly confusing in combination with overloading. The following example demonstrates what happens when a primitive is handed to an overloaded method:

```
//: c04:PrimitiveOverloading.java
// Promotion of primitives and overloading.
import com.bruceeckel.simpletest.*;

public class PrimitiveOverloading {
  static Test monitor = new Test();
  void f1(char x) { System.out.println("f1(char)"); }
  void f1(byte x) { System.out.println("f1(byte)"); }
  void f1(short x) { System.out.println("f1(short)"); }
  void f1(int x) { System.out.println("f1(int)"); }
  void f1(long x) { System.out.println("f1(long)"); }
  void f1(float x) { System.out.println("f1(float)"); }
  void f1(double x) { System.out.println("f1(double)"); }

  void f2(byte x) { System.out.println("f2(byte)"); }
  void f2(short x) { System.out.println("f2(short)"); }
  void f2(int x) { System.out.println("f2(int)"); }
  void f2(long x) { System.out.println("f2(long)"); }
  void f2(float x) { System.out.println("f2(float)"); }
  void f2(double x) { System.out.println("f2(double)"); }

  void f3(short x) { System.out.println("f3(short)"); }
  void f3(int x) { System.out.println("f3(int)"); }
  void f3(long x) { System.out.println("f3(long)"); }
  void f3(float x) { System.out.println("f3(float)"); }
  void f3(double x) { System.out.println("f3(double)"); }

  void f4(int x) { System.out.println("f4(int)"); }
  void f4(long x) { System.out.println("f4(long)"); }
  void f4(float x) { System.out.println("f4(float)"); }
  void f4(double x) { System.out.println("f4(double)"); }
```

```java
  void f5(long x) { System.out.println("f5(long)"); }
  void f5(float x) { System.out.println("f5(float)"); }
  void f5(double x) { System.out.println("f5(double)"); }

  void f6(float x) { System.out.println("f6(float)"); }
  void f6(double x) { System.out.println("f6(double)"); }

  void f7(double x) { System.out.println("f7(double)"); }

  void testConstVal() {
    System.out.println("Testing with 5");
    f1(5);f2(5);f3(5);f4(5);f5(5);f6(5);f7(5);
  }
  void testChar() {
    char x = 'x';
    System.out.println("char argument:");
    f1(x);f2(x);f3(x);f4(x);f5(x);f6(x);f7(x);
  }
  void testByte() {
    byte x = 0;
    System.out.println("byte argument:");
    f1(x);f2(x);f3(x);f4(x);f5(x);f6(x);f7(x);
  }
  void testShort() {
    short x = 0;
    System.out.println("short argument:");
    f1(x);f2(x);f3(x);f4(x);f5(x);f6(x);f7(x);
  }
  void testInt() {
    int x = 0;
    System.out.println("int argument:");
    f1(x);f2(x);f3(x);f4(x);f5(x);f6(x);f7(x);
  }
  void testLong() {
    long x = 0;
    System.out.println("long argument:");
    f1(x);f2(x);f3(x);f4(x);f5(x);f6(x);f7(x);
  }
  void testFloat() {
    float x = 0;
    System.out.println("float argument:");
    f1(x);f2(x);f3(x);f4(x);f5(x);f6(x);f7(x);
  }
```

```java
  void testDouble() {
    double x = 0;
    System.out.println("double argument:");
    f1(x);f2(x);f3(x);f4(x);f5(x);f6(x);f7(x);
  }
  public static void main(String[] args) {
    PrimitiveOverloading p =
      new PrimitiveOverloading();
    p.testConstVal();
    p.testChar();
    p.testByte();
    p.testShort();
    p.testInt();
    p.testLong();
    p.testFloat();
    p.testDouble();
    monitor.expect(new String[] {
      "Testing with 5",
      "f1(int)",
      "f2(int)",
      "f3(int)",
      "f4(int)",
      "f5(long)",
      "f6(float)",
      "f7(double)",
      "char argument:",
      "f1(char)",
      "f2(int)",
      "f3(int)",
      "f4(int)",
      "f5(long)",
      "f6(float)",
      "f7(double)",
      "byte argument:",
      "f1(byte)",
      "f2(byte)",
      "f3(short)",
      "f4(int)",
      "f5(long)",
      "f6(float)",
      "f7(double)",
      "short argument:",
      "f1(short)",
      "f2(short)",
```

```
      "f3(short)",
      "f4(int)",
      "f5(long)",
      "f6(float)",
      "f7(double)",
      "int argument:",
      "f1(int)",
      "f2(int)",
      "f3(int)",
      "f4(int)",
      "f5(long)",
      "f6(float)",
      "f7(double)",
      "long argument:",
      "f1(long)",
      "f2(long)",
      "f3(long)",
      "f4(long)",
      "f5(long)",
      "f6(float)",
      "f7(double)",
      "float argument:",
      "f1(float)",
      "f2(float)",
      "f3(float)",
      "f4(float)",
      "f5(float)",
      "f6(float)",
      "f7(double)",
      "double argument:",
      "f1(double)",
      "f2(double)",
      "f3(double)",
      "f4(double)",
      "f5(double)",
      "f6(double)",
      "f7(double)"
    });
  }
} ///:~
```

You'll see that the constant value 5 is treated as an **int**, so if an overloaded method is available that takes an **int**, it is used. In all other cases, if you have a data type that is smaller than the argument in the method, that data type is promoted. **char** produces a slightly different effect, since if it doesn't find an exact **char** match, it is promoted to **int**.

What happens if your argument is *bigger* than the argument expected by the overloaded method? A modification of the preceding program gives the answer:

```
//: c04:Demotion.java
// Demotion of primitives and overloading.
import com.bruceeckel.simpletest.*;

public class Demotion {
  static Test monitor = new Test();
  void f1(char x) { System.out.println("f1(char)"); }
  void f1(byte x) { System.out.println("f1(byte)"); }
  void f1(short x) { System.out.println("f1(short)"); }
  void f1(int x) { System.out.println("f1(int)"); }
  void f1(long x) { System.out.println("f1(long)"); }
  void f1(float x) { System.out.println("f1(float)"); }
  void f1(double x) { System.out.println("f1(double)"); }

  void f2(char x) { System.out.println("f2(char)"); }
  void f2(byte x) { System.out.println("f2(byte)"); }
  void f2(short x) { System.out.println("f2(short)"); }
  void f2(int x) { System.out.println("f2(int)"); }
  void f2(long x) { System.out.println("f2(long)"); }
  void f2(float x) { System.out.println("f2(float)"); }

  void f3(char x) { System.out.println("f3(char)"); }
  void f3(byte x) { System.out.println("f3(byte)"); }
  void f3(short x) { System.out.println("f3(short)"); }
  void f3(int x) { System.out.println("f3(int)"); }
  void f3(long x) { System.out.println("f3(long)"); }

  void f4(char x) { System.out.println("f4(char)"); }
  void f4(byte x) { System.out.println("f4(byte)"); }
  void f4(short x) { System.out.println("f4(short)"); }
  void f4(int x) { System.out.println("f4(int)"); }

  void f5(char x) { System.out.println("f5(char)"); }
  void f5(byte x) { System.out.println("f5(byte)"); }
  void f5(short x) { System.out.println("f5(short)"); }

  void f6(char x) { System.out.println("f6(char)"); }
```

```
  void f6(byte x) { System.out.println("f6(byte)"); }

  void f7(char x) { System.out.println("f7(char)"); }

  void testDouble() {
    double x = 0;
    System.out.println("double argument:");
    f1(x);f2((float)x);f3((long)x);f4((int)x);
    f5((short)x);f6((byte)x);f7((char)x);
  }
  public static void main(String[] args) {
    Demotion p = new Demotion();
    p.testDouble();
    monitor.expect(new String[] {
      "double argument:",
      "f1(double)",
      "f2(float)",
      "f3(long)",
      "f4(int)",
      "f5(short)",
      "f6(byte)",
      "f7(char)"
    });
  }
} ///:~
```

Here, the methods take narrower primitive values. If your argument is wider, then you must *cast* to the necessary type by placing the type name inside parentheses. If you don't do this, the compiler will issue an error message.

You should be aware that this is a *narrowing conversion,* which means you might lose information during the cast. This is why the compiler forces you to do it—to flag the narrowing conversion.

Overloading on return values

It is common to wonder "Why only class names and method argument lists? Why not distinguish between methods based on their return values?" For example, these two methods, which have the same name and arguments, are easily distinguished from each other:

```
void f() {}
int f() {}
```

This works fine when the compiler can unequivocally determine the meaning from the context, as in **int x = f( )**. However, you can also call a method and ignore the return value. This is often referred to as *calling a method for its side effect*, since you don't care about the return value, but instead want the other effects of the method call. So if you call the method this way:

```
f();
```

how can Java determine which **f( )** should be called? And how could someone reading the code see it? Because of this sort of problem, you cannot use return value types to distinguish overloaded methods.

Default constructors

As mentioned previously, a default constructor (a.k.a. a "no-arg" constructor) is one without arguments that is used to create a "basic object." If you create a class that has no constructors, the compiler will automatically create a default constructor for you. For example:

```
//: c04:DefaultConstructor.java

class Bird {
  int i;
}

public class DefaultConstructor {
  public static void main(String[] args) {
    Bird nc = new Bird(); // Default!
  }
} ///:~
```

The line

```
new Bird();
```

creates a new object and calls the default constructor, even though one was not explicitly defined. Without it, we would have no method to call to build our object. However, if you define any constructors (with or without arguments), the compiler will *not* synthesize one for you:

```
class Hat {
  Hat(int i) {}
  Hat(double d) {}
}
```

Now if you say:

```
new Hat();
```

the compiler will complain that it cannot find a constructor that matches. It's as if when you don't put in any constructors, the compiler says "You are bound to need *some* constructor, so let me make one for you." But if you write a constructor, the compiler says "You've written a constructor so you know what you're doing; if you didn't put in a default it's because you meant to leave it out."

The **this** keyword

If you have two objects of the same type called **a** and **b**, you might wonder how it is that you can call a method **f( )** for both those objects:

```
class Banana { void f(int i) { /* ... */ } }
Banana a = new Banana(), b = new Banana();
a.f(1);
b.f(2);
```

If there's only one method called **f( )**, how can that method know whether it's being called for the object **a** or **b**?

To allow you to write the code in a convenient object-oriented syntax in which you "send a message to an object," the compiler does some undercover work for you. There's a secret first argument passed to the method **f( )**, and that argument is the reference to the object that's being manipulated. So the two method calls become something like:

```
Banana.f(a,1);
Banana.f(b,2);
```

This is internal and you can't write these expressions and get the compiler to accept them, but it gives you an idea of what's happening.

Suppose you're inside a method and you'd like to get the reference to the current object. Since that reference is passed *secretly* by the compiler, there's no identifier for it. However, for this purpose there's a keyword: **this**. The **this** keyword—which can be used only inside a method—produces the reference to the object the method has been called for. You can treat this reference just like any other object reference. Keep in mind that if you're calling a method of your class from within another method of your class, you don't need to use **this**. You simply call the method. The current **this** reference is automatically used for the other method. Thus you can say:

```
class Apricot {
  void pick() { /* ... */ }
  void pit() { pick(); /* ... */ }
}
```

Inside **pit( )**, you *could* say **this.pick( )** but there's no need to.[2] The compiler does it for you automatically. The **this** keyword is used only for those special cases in which you need to explicitly use the reference to the current object. For example, it's often used in **return** statements when you want to return the reference to the current object:

```
//: c04:Leaf.java
// Simple use of the "this" keyword.
import com.bruceeckel.simpletest.*;

public class Leaf {
  static Test monitor = new Test();
  int i = 0;
  Leaf increment() {
    i++;
    return this;
  }
  void print() {
    System.out.println("i = " + i);
  }
  public static void main(String[] args) {
    Leaf x = new Leaf();
    x.increment().increment().increment().print();
    monitor.expect(new String[] {
      "i = 3"
    });
  }
} ///:~
```

---

[2] Some people will obsessively put **this** in front of every method call and field reference, arguing that it makes it "clearer and more explicit." Don't do it. There's a reason that we use high-level languages: they do things for us. If you put **this** in when it's not necessary, you will confuse and annoy everyone who reads your code, since all the rest of the code they've read *won't* use **this** everywhere. Following a consistent and straightforward coding style saves time and money.

Because **increment( )** returns the reference to the current object via the **this** keyword, multiple operations can easily be performed on the same object.

Calling constructors from constructors

When you write several constructors for a class, there are times when you'd like to call one constructor from another to avoid duplicating code. You can make such a call by by using the **this** keyword.

Normally, when you say **this**, it is in the sense of "this object" or "the current object," and by itself it produces the reference to the current object. In a constructor, the **this** keyword takes on a different meaning when you give it an argument list. It makes an explicit call to the constructor that matches that argument list. Thus you have a straightforward way to call other constructors:

```
//: c04:Flower.java
// Calling constructors with "this."
import com.bruceeckel.simpletest.*;

public class Flower {
  static Test monitor = new Test();
  int petalCount = 0;
  String s = new String("null");
  Flower(int petals) {
    petalCount = petals;
    System.out.println(
      "Constructor w/ int arg only, petalCount= "
      + petalCount);
  }
  Flower(String ss) {
    System.out.println(
      "Constructor w/ String arg only, s=" + ss);
    s = ss;
  }
  Flower(String s, int petals) {
    this(petals);
//!    this(s); // Can't call two!
    this.s = s; // Another use of "this"
    System.out.println("String & int args");
  }
  Flower() {
    this("hi", 47);
    System.out.println("default constructor (no args)");
```

```
  }
  void print() {
//! this(11); // Not inside non-constructor!
    System.out.println(
      "petalCount = " + petalCount + " s = "+ s);
  }
  public static void main(String[] args) {
    Flower x = new Flower();
    x.print();
    monitor.expect(new String[] {
      "Constructor w/ int arg only, petalCount= 47",
      "String & int args",
      "default constructor (no args)",
      "petalCount = 47 s = hi"
    });
  }
} ///:~
```

The constructor **Flower(String s, int petals)** shows that, while you can call one constructor using **this**, you cannot call two. In addition, the constructor call must be the first thing you do, or you'll get a compiler error message.

This example also shows another way you'll see **this** used. Since the name of the argument **s** and the name of the member data **s** are the same, there's an ambiguity. You can resolve it using **this.s**, to say that you're referring to the member data. You'll often see this form used in Java code, and it's used in numerous places in this book.

In **print( )** you can see that the compiler won't let you call a constructor from inside any method other than a constructor.

The meaning of **static**

With the **this** keyword in mind, you can more fully understand what it means to make a method **static**. It means that there is no **this** for that particular method. You cannot call non-**static** methods from inside **static** methods[3] (although the reverse is possible), and you can call a **static** method for the

[3] The one case in which this is possible occurs if you pass a reference to an object into the **static** method. Then, via the reference (which is now effectively **this**), you can call non-**static** methods and access non-**static** fields. But typically, if you want to do something like this, you'll just make an ordinary, non-**static** method.

class itself, without any object. In fact, that's primarily what a **static** method is for. It's as if you're creating the equivalent of a global function (from C). However, global functions are not permitted in Java, and putting the **static** method inside a class allows it access to other **static** methods and to **static** fields.

Some people argue that **static** methods are not object-oriented, since they do have the semantics of a global function; with a **static** method, you don't send a message to an object, since there's no **this**. This is probably a fair argument, and if you find yourself using a *lot* of static methods, you should probably rethink your strategy. However, **static**s are pragmatic, and there are times when you genuinely need them, so whether or not they are "proper OOP" should be left to the theoreticians. Indeed, even Smalltalk has the equivalent in its "class methods."

Cleanup: finalization and garbage collection

Programmers know about the importance of initialization, but often forget the importance of cleanup. After all, who needs to clean up an **int**? But with libraries, simply "letting go" of an object once you're done with it is not always safe. Of course, Java has the garbage collector to reclaim the memory of objects that are no longer used. Now consider an unusual case: suppose your object allocates "special" memory without using **new**. The garbage collector only knows how to release memory allocated *with* **new**, so it won't know how to release the object's "special" memory. To handle this case, Java provides a method called **finalize( )** that you can define for your class. Here's how it's *supposed* to work. When the garbage collector is ready to release the storage used for your object, it will first call **finalize( )**, and only on the next garbage-collection pass will it reclaim the object's memory. So if you choose to use **finalize( )**, it gives you the ability to perform some important cleanup *at the time of garbage collection.*

This is a potential programming pitfall because some programmers, especially C++ programmers, might initially mistake **finalize( )** for the *destructor* in C++, which is a function that is always called when an object is destroyed. But it is important to distinguish between C++ and Java here, because in C++, *objects always get destroyed* (in a bug-free program), whereas in Java, objects do not always get garbage collected. Or, put another way:

> *1. Your objects might not get garbage collected.*
>
> *2. Garbage collection is not destruction.*

If you remember this, you will stay out of trouble. What it means is that if there is some activity that must be performed before you no longer need an object, you must perform that activity yourself. Java has no destructor or similar concept, so you must create an ordinary method to perform this cleanup. For example, suppose that in the process of creating your object, it draws itself on the screen. If you don't explicitly erase its image from the screen, it might never get cleaned up. If you put some kind of erasing functionality inside **finalize( )**, then if an object is garbage collected and **finalize( )** is called (there's no guarantee this will happen), then the image will first be removed from the screen, but if it isn't, the image will remain.

You might find that the storage for an object never gets released because your program never nears the point of running out of storage. If your program completes and the garbage collector never gets around to releasing the storage for any of your objects, that storage will be returned to the operating system *en masse* as the program exits. This is a good thing, because garbage collection has some overhead, and if you never do, it you never incur that expense.

What is **finalize( )** for?

So, if you should not use **finalize( )** as a general-purpose cleanup method, what good is it?

A third point to remember is:

> *3. Garbage collection is only about memory.*

That is, the sole reason for the existence of the garbage collector is to recover memory that your program is no longer using. So any activity that is associated with garbage collection, most notably your **finalize( )** method, must also be only about memory and its deallocation.

Does this mean that if your object contains other objects, **finalize( )** should explicitly release those objects? Well, no—the garbage collector takes care of the release of all object memory regardless of how the object is created. It turns out that the need for **finalize( )** is limited to special cases in which your object can allocate some storage in some way other than creating an object. But, you might observe, everything in Java is an object, so how can this be?

It would seem that **finalize( )** is in place because of the possibility that you'll do something C-like by allocating memory using a mechanism other than the normal one in Java. This can happen primarily through *native methods*, which are a way to call non-Java code from Java. (Native methods are covered in Appendix B in the electronic 2nd edition of this book, available on this book's CD ROM and at www.BruceEckel.com.) C and C++ are the only languages currently supported by native methods, but since they can call subprograms in other languages, you can effectively call anything. Inside the non-Java code, C's **malloc( )** family of functions might be called to allocate storage, and unless you call **free( )**, that storage will not be released, causing a memory leak. Of course, **free( )** is a C and C++ function, so you'd need to call it in a native method inside your **finalize( )**.

After reading this, you probably get the idea that you won't use **finalize( )** much.[4] You're correct; it is not the appropriate place for normal cleanup to occur. So where should normal cleanup be performed?

You must perform cleanup

To clean up an object, the user of that object must call a cleanup method at the point the cleanup is desired. This sounds pretty straightforward, but it collides a bit with the C++ concept of the destructor. In C++, all objects are destroyed. Or rather, all objects *should be* destroyed. If the C++ object is created as a local (i.e., on the stack—not possible in Java), then the destruction happens at the closing curly brace of the scope in which the object was created. If the object was created using **new** (like in Java), the destructor is called when the programmer calls the C++ operator **delete** (which doesn't exist in Java). If the C++ programmer forgets to call **delete**, the destructor is never called, and you have a memory leak, plus the other parts of the object

---

[4] Joshua Bloch goes further in his section titled "avoid finalizers": "Finalizers are unpredictable, often dangerous, and generally unnecessary." *Effective Java,* page 20 (Addison-Wesley 2001).

never get cleaned up. This kind of bug can be very difficult to track down, and is one of the compelling reasons to move from C++ to Java.

In contrast, Java doesn't allow you to create local objects—you must always use **new**. But in Java, there's no "delete" to call to release the object, because the garbage collector releases the storage for you. So from a simplistic standpoint, you could say that because of garbage collection, Java has no destructor. You'll see as this book progresses, however, that the presence of a garbage collector does not remove the need for or utility of destructors. (And you should never call **finalize( )** directly, so that's not an appropriate avenue for a solution.) If you want some kind of cleanup performed other than storage release, you must *still* explicitly call an appropriate method in Java, which is the equivalent of a C++ destructor without the convenience.

Remember that neither garbage collection nor finalization is guaranteed. If the JVM isn't close to running out of memory, then it might not waste time recovering memory through garbage collection.

The termination condition

In general, you can't rely on **finalize( )** being called, and you must create separate "cleanup" methods and call them explicitly. So it appears that **finalize( )** is only useful for obscure memory cleanup that most programmers will never use. However, there is a very interesting use of **finalize( )** that does not rely on it being called every time. This is the verification of the *termination condition*[5] of an object.

At the point that you're no longer interested in an object—when it's ready to be cleaned up—that object should be in a state whereby its memory can be safely released. For example, if the object represents an open file, that file should be closed by the programmer before the object is garbage collected. If any portions of the object are not properly cleaned up, then you have a bug in your program that could be very difficult to find. The value of **finalize( )** is that it can be used to eventually discover this condition, even if it isn't always called. If one of the finalizations happens to reveal the bug, then you discover the problem, which is all you really care about.

---

[5] A term coined by Bill Venners (www.artima.com) during a seminar that he and I were giving together.

Here's a simple example of how you might use it:

```
//: c04:TerminationCondition.java
// Using finalize() to detect an object that
// hasn't been properly cleaned up.
import com.bruceeckel.simpletest.*;

class Book {
  boolean checkedOut = false;
  Book(boolean checkOut) {
    checkedOut = checkOut;
  }
  void checkIn() {
    checkedOut = false;
  }
  public void finalize() {
    if(checkedOut)
      System.out.println("Error: checked out");
  }
}

public class TerminationCondition {
  static Test monitor = new Test();
  public static void main(String[] args) {
    Book novel = new Book(true);
    // Proper cleanup:
    novel.checkIn();
    // Drop the reference, forget to clean up:
    new Book(true);
    // Force garbage collection & finalization:
    System.gc();
    monitor.expect(new String[] {
      "Error: checked out"}, Test.WAIT);
  }
} ///:~
```

The termination condition is that all **Book** objects are supposed to be checked in before they are garbage collected, but in **main( )**, a programmer error doesn't check in one of the books. Without **finalize( )** to verify the termination condition, this could be a difficult bug to find.

Note that **System.gc( )** is used to force finalization (and you should do this during program development to speed debugging). But even if it isn't, it's highly probable that the errant **Book** will eventually be discovered through repeated executions of the program (assuming the program allocates enough storage to cause the garbage collector to execute).

How a garbage collector works

If you come from a programming language where allocating objects on the heap is expensive, you may naturally assume that Java's scheme of allocating everything (except primitives) on the heap is also expensive. However, it turns out that the garbage collector can have a significant impact on *increasing* the speed of object creation. This might sound a bit odd at first—that storage release affects storage allocation—but it's the way some JVMs work, and it means that allocating storage for heap objects in Java can be nearly as fast as creating storage on the stack in other languages.

For example, you can think of the C++ heap as a yard where each object stakes out its own piece of turf. This real estate can become abandoned sometime later and must be reused. In some JVMs, the Java heap is quite different; it's more like a conveyor belt that moves forward every time you allocate a new object. This means that object storage allocation is remarkably rapid. The "heap pointer" is simply moved forward into virgin territory, so it's effectively the same as C++'s stack allocation. (Of course, there's a little extra overhead for bookkeeping, but it's nothing like searching for storage.)

Now you might observe that the heap isn't in fact a conveyor belt, and if you treat it that way, you'll eventually start paging memory a lot (which is a big performance hit) and later run out. The trick is that the garbage collector steps in, and while it collects the garbage it compacts all the objects in the heap so that you've effectively moved the "heap pointer" closer to the beginning of the conveyor belt and farther away from a page fault. The garbage collector rearranges things and makes it possible for the high-speed, infinite-free-heap model to be used while allocating storage.

To understand how this works, you need to get a little better idea of the way different garbage collector (GC) schemes work. A simple but slow garbage collection technique is is called *reference counting*. This means that each object contains a reference counter, and every time a reference is attached to an object, the reference count is increased. Every time a reference goes out of scope or is set to **null**, the reference count is decreased. Thus, managing reference counts is a small but constant overhead that happens throughout the lifetime of your program. The garbage collector moves through the entire list of objects, and when it finds one with a reference count of zero it releases that storage. The one drawback is that if objects circularly refer to each other they can have nonzero reference counts while still being garbage. Locating such self-referential groups requires significant extra work for the garbage collector. Reference counting is commonly used to explain one kind of garbage collection, but it doesn't seem to be used in any JVM implementations.

In faster schemes, garbage collection is not based on reference counting. Instead, it is based on the idea that any nondead object must ultimately be traceable back to a reference that lives either on the stack or in static storage. The chain might go through several layers of objects. Thus, if you start in the stack and the static storage area and walk through all the references, you'll find all the live objects. For each reference that you find, you must trace into the object that it points to and then follow all the references in *that* object, tracing into the objects they point to, etc., until you've moved through the entire web that originated with the reference on the stack or in static storage. Each object that you move through must still be alive. Note that there is no problem with detached self-referential groups—these are simply not found, and are therefore automatically garbage.

In the approach described here, the JVM uses an *adaptive* garbage-collection scheme, and what it does with the live objects that it locates depends on the variant currently being used. One of these variants is *stop-and-copy*. This means that—for reasons that will become apparent—the program is first stopped (this is not a background collection scheme). Then, each live object that is found is copied from one heap to another, leaving behind all the garbage. In addition, as the objects are copied into the new heap, they are packed end-to-end, thus compacting the new heap (and allowing new storage to simply be reeled off the end as previously described).

Of course, when an object is moved from one place to another, all references that point at (i.e., that *reference*) the object must be changed. The reference that goes from the heap or the static storage area to the object can be changed right away, but there can be other references pointing to this object that will be encountered later during the "walk." These are fixed up as they are found (you could imagine a table that maps old addresses to new ones).

There are two issues that make these so-called "copy collectors" inefficient. The first is the idea that you have two heaps and you slosh all the memory back and forth between these two separate heaps, maintaining twice as much memory as you actually need. Some JVMs deal with this by allocating the heap in chunks as needed and simply copying from one chunk to another.

The second issue is the copying. Once your program becomes stable, it might be generating little or no garbage. Despite that, a copy collector will still copy all the memory from one place to another, which is wasteful. To prevent this, some JVMs detect that no new garbage is being generated and switch to a different scheme (this is the "adaptive" part). This other scheme is called *mark-and-sweep*, and it's what earlier versions of Sun's JVM used all the time. For general use, mark-and-sweep is fairly slow, but when you know you're generating little or no garbage, it's fast.

Mark-and-sweep follows the same logic of starting from the stack and static storage and tracing through all the references to find live objects. However, each time it finds a live object, that object is marked by setting a flag in it, but the object isn't collected yet. Only when the marking process is finished does the sweep occur. During the sweep, the dead objects are released. However, no copying happens, so if the collector chooses to compact a fragmented heap, it does so by shuffling objects around.

The "stop-and-copy" refers to the idea that this type of garbage collection is *not* done in the background; instead, the program is stopped while the garbage collection occurs. In the Sun literature you'll find many references to garbage collection as a low-priority background process, but it turns out that the garbage collection was not implemented that way, at least in earlier versions of the Sun JVM. Instead, the Sun garbage collector ran when memory got low. In addition, mark-and-sweep requires that the program be stopped.

As previously mentioned, in the JVM described here memory is allocated in big blocks. If you allocate a large object, it gets its own block. Strict stop-and-copy requires copying every live object from the source heap to a new heap before you could free the old one, which translates to lots of memory. With blocks, the garbage collection can typically copy objects to dead blocks as it collects. Each block has a *generation count* to keep track of whether it's alive. In the normal case, only the blocks created since the last garbage collection are compacted; all other blocks get their generation count bumped if they have been referenced from somewhere. This handles the normal case of lots of short-lived temporary objects. Periodically, a full sweep is made—large objects are still not copied (they just get their generation count bumped), and blocks containing small objects are copied and compacted. The JVM monitors the efficiency of garbage collection and if it becomes a waste of time because all objects are long-lived, then it switches to mark-and-sweep. Similarly, the JVM keeps track of how successful mark-and-sweep is, and if the heap starts to become fragmented, it switches back to stop-and-copy. This is where the "adaptive" part comes in, so you end up with a mouthful: "Adaptive generational stop-and-copy mark-and-sweep."

There are a number of additional speedups possible in a JVM. An especially important one involves the operation of the loader and what is called a *just-in-time* (JIT) compiler. A JIT compiler partially or fully converts a program into native machine code so that it doesn't need to be interpreted by the JVM and thus runs much faster. When a class must be loaded (typically, the first time you want to create an object of that class), the **.class** file is located, and the byte codes for that class are brought into memory. At this point, one approach is to simply JIT compile all the code, but this has two drawbacks: it takes a little more time, which, compounded throughout the life of the program, can add up; and it increases the size of the executable (byte codes are significantly more compact than expanded JIT code), and this might cause paging, which definitely slows down a program. An alternative approach is *lazy evaluation,* which means that the code is not JIT compiled until necessary. Thus, code that never gets executed might never be JIT compiled. The Java HotSpot technologies in recent JDKs take a similar approach by increasingly optimizing a piece of code each time it is executed, so the more the code is executed, the faster it gets.

Member initialization

Java goes out of its way to guarantee that variables are properly initialized before they are used. In the case of variables that are defined locally to a method, this guarantee comes in the form of a compile-time error. So if you say:

```
void f() {
  int i;
  i++; // Error -- i not initialized
}
```

you'll get an error message that says that **i** might not have been initialized. Of course, the compiler could have given **i** a default value, but it's more likely that this is a programmer error and a default value would have covered that up. Forcing the programmer to provide an initialization value is more likely to catch a bug.

If a primitive is a field in a class, however, things are a bit different. Since any method can initialize or use that data, it might not be practical to force the user to initialize it to its appropriate value before the data is used. However, it's unsafe to leave it with a garbage value, so each primitive field of a class is guaranteed to get an initial value. Those values can be seen here:

```
//: c04:InitialValues.java
// Shows default initial values.
import com.bruceeckel.simpletest.*;

public class InitialValues {
  static Test monitor = new Test();
  boolean t;
  char c;
  byte b;
  short s;
  int i;
  long l;
  float f;
  double d;
  void print(String s) { System.out.println(s); }
  void printInitialValues() {
    print("Data type      Initial value");
    print("boolean        " + t);
    print("char           [" + c + "]");
    print("byte           " + b);
    print("short          " + s);
    print("int            " + i);
    print("long           " + l);
    print("float          " + f);
    print("double         " + d);
  }
  public static void main(String[] args) {
    InitialValues iv = new InitialValues();
    iv.printInitialValues();
    /* You could also say:
    new InitialValues().printInitialValues();
    */
    monitor.expect(new String[] {
      "Data type      Initial value",
      "boolean        false",
```

```
      "char                  [" + (char)0 + "]",
      "byte                  0",
      "short                 0",
      "int                   0",
      "long                  0",
      "float                 0.0",
      "double                0.0"
    });
  }
} ///:~
```

You can see that even though the values are not specified, they automatically get initialized (The **char** value is a zero, which prints as a space). So at least there's no threat of working with uninitialized variables.

You'll see later that when you define an object reference inside a class without initializing it to a new object, that reference is given a special value of **null** (which is a Java keyword).

Specifying initialization

What happens if you want to give a variable an initial value? One direct way to do this is simply to assign the value at the point you define the variable in the class. (Notice you cannot do this in C++, although C++ novices always try.) Here the field definitions in class **InitialValues** are changed to provide initial values:

```
class InitialValues {
  boolean b = true;
  char c = 'x';
  byte B = 47;
  short s = 0xff;
  int i = 999;
  long l = 1;
  float f = 3.14f;
  double d = 3.14159;
  //. . .
```

You can also initialize nonprimitive objects in this same way. If **Depth** is a class, you can create a variable and initialize it like so:

```
class Measurement {
  Depth d = new Depth();
  // . . .
```

If you haven't given **d** an initial value and you try to use it anyway, you'll get a run-time error called an *exception* (covered in Chapter 9).

You can even call a method to provide an initialization value:

```
class CInit {
  int i = f();
  //...
}
```

This method can have arguments, of course, but those arguments cannot be other class members that haven't been initialized yet. Thus, you can do this:

```
class CInit {
  int i = f();
  int j = g(i);
  //...
}
```

But you cannot do this:

```
class CInit {
  int j = g(i);
  int i = f();
  //...
}
```

This is one place in which the compiler, appropriately, *does* complain about forward referencing, since this has to do with the order of initialization and not the way the program is compiled.

This approach to initialization is simple and straightforward. It has the limitation that *every* object of type **InitialValues** will get these same initialization values. Sometimes this is exactly what you need, but at other times you need more flexibility.

Constructor initialization

The constructor can be used to perform initialization, and this gives you greater flexibility in your programming because you can call methods and perform actions at run time to determine the initial values. There's one thing to keep in mind, however: You aren't precluding the automatic initialization, which happens before the constructor is entered. So, for example, if you say:

```
class Counter {
```

```
  int i;
  Counter() { i = 7; }
  // . . .
```

then **i** will first be initialized to 0, then to 7. This is true with all the primitive types and with object references, including those that are given explicit initialization at the point of definition. For this reason, the compiler doesn't try to force you to initialize elements in the constructor at any particular place, or before they are used—initialization is already guaranteed.[6]

Order of initialization

Within a class, the order of initialization is determined by the order that the variables are defined within the class. The variable definitions may be scattered throughout and in between method definitions, but the variables are initialized before any methods can be called—even the constructor. For example:

```
//: c04:OrderOfInitialization.java
// Demonstrates initialization order.
import com.bruceeckel.simpletest.*;

// When the constructor is called to create a
// Tag object, you'll see a message:
class Tag {
  Tag(int marker) {
    System.out.println("Tag(" + marker + ")");
  }
}

class Card {
  Tag t1 = new Tag(1); // Before constructor
  Card() {
    // Indicate we're in the constructor:
    System.out.println("Card()");
    t3 = new Tag(33); // Reinitialize t3
  }
  Tag t2 = new Tag(2); // After constructor
  void f() {
```

[6] In contrast, C++ has the *constructor initializer list* that causes initialization to occur before entering the constructor body, and is enforced for objects. See *Thinking in C++, 2nd edition* (available on this book's CD ROM and at *www.BruceEckel.com*).

```
    System.out.println("f()");
  }
  Tag t3 = new Tag(3); // At end
}

public class OrderOfInitialization {
  static Test monitor = new Test();
  public static void main(String[] args) {
    Card t = new Card();
    t.f(); // Shows that construction is done
    monitor.expect(new String[] {
      "Tag(1)",
      "Tag(2)",
      "Tag(3)",
      "Card()",
      "Tag(33)",
      "f()"
    });
  }
} ///:~
```

In **Card**, the definitions of the **Tag** objects are intentionally scattered about to prove that they'll all get initialized before the constructor is entered or anything else can happen. In addition, **t3** is reinitialized inside the constructor.

From the output, you can see that, the **t3** reference gets initialized twice: once before and once during the constructor call. (The first object is dropped, so it can be garbage collected later.) This might not seem efficient at first, but it guarantees proper initialization—what would happen if an overloaded constructor were defined that did *not* initialize **t3** and there wasn't a "default" initialization for **t3** in its definition?

Static data initialization

When the data is **static**, the same thing happens; if it's a primitive and you don't initialize it, it gets the standard primitive initial values. If it's a reference to an object, it's **null** unless you create a new object and attach your reference to it.

If you want to place initialization at the point of definition, it looks the same as for non-**static**s. There's only a single piece of storage for a **static**, regardless of how many objects are created. But the question arises of when the **static** storage gets initialized. An example makes this question clear:

```java
//: c04:StaticInitialization.java
// Specifying initial values in a class definition.
import com.bruceeckel.simpletest.*;

class Bowl {
  Bowl(int marker) {
    System.out.println("Bowl(" + marker + ")");
  }
  void f(int marker) {
    System.out.println("f(" + marker + ")");
  }
}

class Table {
  static Bowl b1 = new Bowl(1);
  Table() {
    System.out.println("Table()");
    b2.f(1);
  }
  void f2(int marker) {
    System.out.println("f2(" + marker + ")");
  }
  static Bowl b2 = new Bowl(2);
}

class Cupboard {
  Bowl b3 = new Bowl(3);
  static Bowl b4 = new Bowl(4);
  Cupboard() {
    System.out.println("Cupboard()");
    b4.f(2);
  }
  void f3(int marker) {
    System.out.println("f3(" + marker + ")");
  }
  static Bowl b5 = new Bowl(5);
}

public class StaticInitialization {
  static Test monitor = new Test();
  public static void main(String[] args) {
    System.out.println("Creating new Cupboard() in main");
    new Cupboard();
    System.out.println("Creating new Cupboard() in main");
```

```java
    new Cupboard();
    t2.f2(1);
    t3.f3(1);
    monitor.expect(new String[] {
      "Bowl(1)",
      "Bowl(2)",
      "Table()",
      "f(1)",
      "Bowl(4)",
      "Bowl(5)",
      "Bowl(3)",
      "Cupboard()",
      "f(2)",
      "Creating new Cupboard() in main",
      "Bowl(3)",
      "Cupboard()",
      "f(2)",
      "Creating new Cupboard() in main",
      "Bowl(3)",
      "Cupboard()",
      "f(2)",
      "f2(1)",
      "f3(1)"
    });
  }
  static Table t2 = new Table();
  static Cupboard t3 = new Cupboard();
} ///:~
```

Bowl allows you to view the creation of a class, and **Table** and **Cupboard** create **static** members of **Bowl** scattered through their class definitions. Note that **Cupboard** creates a non-**static Bowl b3** prior to the **static** definitions.

From the output, you can see that the **static** initialization occurs only if it's necessary. If you don't create a **Table** object and you never refer to **Table.b1** or **Table.b2**, the **static Bowl b1** and **b2** will never be created. They are initialized only when the *first* **Table** object is created (or the first **static** access occurs). After that, the **static** objects are not reinitialized.

The order of initialization is **static**s first, if they haven't already been initialized by a previous object creation, and then the non-**static** objects. You can see the evidence of this in the output.

It's helpful to summarize the process of creating an object. Consider a class called **Dog**:

1. The first time an object of type **Dog** is created (the constructor is actually a **static** method), *or* the first time a **static** method or **static** field of class **Dog** is accessed, the Java interpreter must locate **Dog.class**, which it does by searching through the classpath.

2. As **Dog.class** is loaded (creating a **Class** object, which you'll learn about later), all of its **static** initializers are run. Thus, **static** initialization takes place only once, as the **Class** object is loaded for the first time.

3. When you create a **new Dog( )**, the construction process for a **Dog** object first allocates enough storage for a **Dog** object on the heap.

4. This storage is wiped to zero, automatically setting all the primitives in that **Dog** object to their default values (zero for numbers and the equivalent for **boolean** and **char**) and the references to **null**.

5. Any initializations that occur at the point of field definition are executed.

6. Constructors are executed. As you shall see in Chapter 6, this might actually involve a fair amount of activity, especially when inheritance is involved.

Explicit static initialization

Java allows you to group other **static** initializations inside a special "**static** clause" (sometimes called a *static block*) in a class. It looks like this:

```
class Spoon {
  static int i;
  static {
    i = 47;
  }
  // . . .
```

It appears to be a method, but it's just the **static** keyword followed by a block of code. This code, like other **static** initializations, is executed only once: the first time you make an object of that class *or* the first time you access a **static** member of that class (even if you never make an object of that class). For example:

```java
//: c04:ExplicitStatic.java
// Explicit static initialization with the "static" clause.
import com.bruceeckel.simpletest.*;

class Cup {
  Cup(int marker) {
    System.out.println("Cup(" + marker + ")");
  }
  void f(int marker) {
    System.out.println("f(" + marker + ")");
  }
}

class Cups {
  static Cup c1;
  static Cup c2;
  static {
    c1 = new Cup(1);
    c2 = new Cup(2);
  }
  Cups() {
    System.out.println("Cups()");
  }
}

public class ExplicitStatic {
  static Test monitor = new Test();
  public static void main(String[] args) {
    System.out.println("Inside main()");
    Cups.c1.f(99);  // (1)
    monitor.expect(new String[] {
      "Inside main()",
      "Cup(1)",
      "Cup(2)",
      "f(99)"
    });
  }
  // static Cups x = new Cups();  // (2)
  // static Cups y = new Cups();  // (2)
} ///:~
```

The **static** initializers for **Cups** run when either the access of the **static** object **c1** occurs on the line marked (1), or if line (1) is commented out and the lines marked (2) are uncommented. If both (1) and (2) are commented out, the **static** initialization for **Cups** never occurs. Also, it doesn't matter if one or both of the lines marked (2) are uncommented; the static initialization only occurs once.

Non-static instance initialization

Java provides a similar syntax for initializing non-**static** variables for each object. Here's an example:

```
//: c04:Mugs.java
// Java "Instance Initialization."
import com.bruceeckel.simpletest.*;

class Mug {
  Mug(int marker) {
    System.out.println("Mug(" + marker + ")");
  }
  void f(int marker) {
    System.out.println("f(" + marker + ")");
  }
}

public class Mugs {
  static Test monitor = new Test();
  Mug c1;
  Mug c2;
  {
    c1 = new Mug(1);
    c2 = new Mug(2);
    System.out.println("c1 & c2 initialized");
  }
  Mugs() {
    System.out.println("Mugs()");
  }
  public static void main(String[] args) {
    System.out.println("Inside main()");
    Mugs x = new Mugs();
    monitor.expect(new String[] {
      "Inside main()",
      "Mug(1)",
      "Mug(2)",
      "c1 & c2 initialized",
      "Mugs()"
    });
  }
```

```
} ///:~
```

You can see that the instance initialization clause:

```
  {
    c1 = new Mug(1);
    c2 = new Mug(2);
    System.out.println("c1 & c2 initialized");
  }
```

looks exactly like the static initialization clause except for the missing **static** keyword. This syntax is necessary to support the initialization of *anonymous inner classes* (see Chapter 8).

Array initialization

Initializing arrays in C is error-prone and tedious. C++ uses *aggregate initialization* to make it much safer.[7] Java has no "aggregates" like C++ does, since everything is an object in Java. It does have arrays, and these are supported with array initialization.

An array is simply a sequence of either objects or primitives that are all the same type and packaged together under one identifier name. Arrays are defined and used with the square-brackets *indexing operator* **[ ]**. To define an array, you simply follow your type name with empty square brackets:

```
int[] a1;
```

You can also put the square brackets after the identifier to produce exactly the same meaning:

```
int a1[];
```

This conforms to expectations from C and C++ programmers. The former style, however, is probably a more sensible syntax, since it says that the type is "an **int** array." That style will be used in this book.

The compiler doesn't allow you to tell it how big the array is. This brings us back to that issue of "references." All that you have at this point is a reference to an array, and there's been no space allocated for the array. To create

---

[7] See *Thinking in C++, 2nd edition* for a complete description of C++ aggregate initialization.

storage for the array, you must write an initialization expression. For arrays, initialization can appear anywhere in your code, but you can also use a special kind of initialization expression that must occur at the point where the array is created. This special initialization is a set of values surrounded by curly braces. The storage allocation (the equivalent of using **new**) is taken care of by the compiler in this case. For example:

```
int[] a1 = { 1, 2, 3, 4, 5 };
```

So why would you ever define an array reference without an array?

```
int[] a2;
```

Well, it's possible to assign one array to another in Java, so you can say:

```
a2 = a1;
```

What you're really doing is copying a reference, as demonstrated here:

```
//: c04:Arrays.java
// Arrays of primitives.
import com.bruceeckel.simpletest.*;

public class Arrays {
  static Test monitor = new Test();
  public static void main(String[] args) {
    int[] a1 = { 1, 2, 3, 4, 5 };
    int[] a2;
    a2 = a1;
    for(int i = 0; i < a2.length; i++)
      a2[i]++;
    for(int i = 0; i < a1.length; i++)
      System.out.println(
        "a1[" + i + "] = " + a1[i]);
    monitor.expect(new String[] {
      "a1[0] = 2",
      "a1[1] = 3",
      "a1[2] = 4",
      "a1[3] = 5",
      "a1[4] = 6"
    });
  }
} ///:~
```

You can see that **a1** is given an initialization value but **a2** is not; **a2** is assigned later—in this case, to another array.

There's something new here: All arrays have an intrinsic member (whether they're arrays of objects or arrays of primitives) that you can query—but not change—to tell you how many elements there are in the array. This member is **length**. Since arrays in Java, like C and C++, start counting from element zero, the largest element you can index is **length - 1**. If you go out of bounds, C and C++ quietly accept this and allow you to stomp all over your memory, which is the source of many infamous bugs. However, Java protects you against such problems by causing a run-time error (an *exception*, the subject of Chapter 9) if you step out of bounds. Of course, checking every array access costs time and code and there's no way to turn it off, which means that array accesses might be a source of inefficiency in your program if they occur at a critical juncture. For Internet security and programmer productivity, the Java designers thought that this was a worthwhile trade-off.

What if you don't know how many elements you're going to need in your array while you're writing the program? You simply use **new** to create the elements in the array. Here, **new** works even though it's creating an array of primitives (**new** won't create a nonarray primitive):

```
//: c04:ArrayNew.java
// Creating arrays with new.
import com.bruceeckel.simpletest.*;
import java.util.*;

public class ArrayNew {
  static Test monitor = new Test();
  static Random rand = new Random();
  public static void main(String[] args) {
    int[] a;
    a = new int[rand.nextInt(20)];
    System.out.println("length of a = " + a.length);
    for(int i = 0; i < a.length; i++)
      System.out.println("a[" + i + "] = " + a[i]);
    monitor.expect(new Object[] {
      "%% length of a = \\d+",
      new TestExpression("%% a\\[\\d+\\] = 0", a.length)
    });
  }
} ///:~
```

The **expect( )** statement contains something new in this example: the **TestExpression** class. A **TestExpression** object takes an expression, either an ordinary string or a regular expression as shown here, and a second integer argument that indicates that the preceding expression will be repeated that many times. **TestExpression** not only prevents needless duplication in the code, but in this case, it allows the number of repetitions to be determined at run time.

The size of the array is chosen at random by using the **Random.nextInt( )** method, which produces a value from zero to that of its argument. Because of the randomness, it's clear that array creation is actually happening at run time. In addition, the output of this program shows that array elements of primitive types are automatically initialized to "empty" values. (For numerics and **char**, this is zero, and for **boolean**, it's **false**.)

Of course, the array could also have been defined and initialized in the same statement:

```
int[] a = new int[rand.nextInt(20)];
```

This is the preferred way to do it, if you can.

If you're dealing with an array of nonprimitive objects, you must always use **new**. Here, the reference issue comes up again, because what you create is an array of references. Consider the wrapper type **Integer,** which is a class and not a primitive:

```
//: c04:ArrayClassObj.java
// Creating an array of nonprimitive objects.
import com.bruceeckel.simpletest.*;
import java.util.*;

public class ArrayClassObj {
  static Test monitor = new Test();
  static Random rand = new Random();
  public static void main(String[] args) {
    Integer[] a = new Integer[rand.nextInt(20)];
    System.out.println("length of a = " + a.length);
    for(int i = 0; i < a.length; i++) {
      a[i] = new Integer(rand.nextInt(500));
      System.out.println("a[" + i + "] = " + a[i]);
    }
    monitor.expect(new Object[] {
      "%% length of a = \\d+",
      new TestExpression("%% a\\[\\d+\\] = \\d+", a.length)
    });
  }
```

```
} ///:~
```

Here, even after **new** is called to create the array:

```
Integer[] a = new Integer[rand.nextInt(20)];
```

it's only an array of references, and not until the reference itself is initialized by creating a new **Integer** object is the initialization complete:

```
a[i] = new Integer(rand.nextInt(500));
```

If you forget to create the object, however, you'll get an exception at run time when you try to use the empty array location.

Take a look at the formation of the **String** object inside the print statements. You can see that the reference to the **Integer** object is automatically converted to produce a **String** representing the value inside the object.

It's also possible to initialize arrays of objects by using the curly-brace-enclosed list. There are two forms:

```
//: c04:ArrayInit.java
// Array initialization.

public class ArrayInit {
  public static void main(String[] args) {
    Integer[] a = {
      new Integer(1),
      new Integer(2),
      new Integer(3),
    };
    Integer[] b = new Integer[] {
      new Integer(1),
      new Integer(2),
      new Integer(3),
    };
  }
} ///:~
```

The first form is useful at times, but it's more limited since the size of the array is determined at compile time. The final comma in the list of initializers is optional. (This feature makes for easier maintenance of long lists.)

The second form provides a convenient syntax to create and call methods that can produce the same effect as C's *variable argument lists* (known as "varargs" in C). These can include unknown quantities of arguments as well as unknown types. Since all classes are ultimately inherited from the common root class **Object** (a subject you will learn more about as this book progresses), you can create a method that takes an array of **Object** and call it like this:

```
//: c04:VarArgs.java
// Using array syntax to create variable argument lists.
import com.bruceeckel.simpletest.*;

class A { int i; }

public class VarArgs {
  static Test monitor = new Test();
  static void print(Object[] x) {
    for(int i = 0; i < x.length; i++)
      System.out.println(x[i]);
  }
  public static void main(String[] args) {
    print(new Object[] {
      new Integer(47), new VarArgs(),
      new Float(3.14), new Double(11.11)
    });
    print(new Object[] {"one", "two", "three" });
    print(new Object[] {new A(), new A(), new A()});
    monitor.expect(new Object[] {
      "47",
      "%% VarArgs@\\p{XDigit}+",
      "3.14",
      "11.11",
      "one",
      "two",
      "three",
      new TestExpression("%% A@\\p{XDigit}+", 3)
    });
  }
} ///:~
```

You can see that **print( )** takes an array of **Object**, then steps through the array and prints each one. The standard Java library classes produce sensible output, but the objects of the classes created here—**A** and **VarArgs**—print the class name, followed by an '@' sign, and yet another regular expression construct, **\p{XDigit}**, which indicates a hexadecimal digit. The trailing '+' means there will be one or more hexadecimal digits. Thus, the default behavior (if you don't define a **toString( )** method for your class, which will be described later in the book) is to print the class name and the address of the object.

Multidimensional arrays

Java allows you to easily create multidimensional arrays:

```
//: c04:MultiDimArray.java
// Creating multidimensional arrays.
import com.bruceeckel.simpletest.*;
import java.util.*;

public class MultiDimArray {
  static Test monitor = new Test();
  static Random rand = new Random();
  public static void main(String[] args) {
    int[][] a1 = {
      { 1, 2, 3, },
      { 4, 5, 6, },
    };
    for(int i = 0; i < a1.length; i++)
      for(int j = 0; j < a1[i].length; j++)
        System.out.println(
          "a1[" + i + "][" + j + "] = " + a1[i][j]);
    // 3-D array with fixed length:
    int[][][] a2 = new int[2][2][4];
    for(int i = 0; i < a2.length; i++)
      for(int j = 0; j < a2[i].length; j++)
        for(int k = 0; k < a2[i][j].length; k++)
          System.out.println("a2[" + i + "][" + j + "][" +
            k + "] = " + a2[i][j][k]);
    // 3-D array with varied-length vectors:
    int[][][] a3 = new int[rand.nextInt(7)][][];
    for(int i = 0; i < a3.length; i++) {
      a3[i] = new int[rand.nextInt(5)][];
      for(int j = 0; j < a3[i].length; j++)
        a3[i][j] = new int[rand.nextInt(5)];
    }
    for(int i = 0; i < a3.length; i++)
      for(int j = 0; j < a3[i].length; j++)
        for(int k = 0; k < a3[i][j].length; k++)
          System.out.println("a3[" + i + "][" + j + "][" +
            k + "] = " + a3[i][j][k]);
```

```
    // Array of nonprimitive objects:
    Integer[][] a4 = {
      { new Integer(1), new Integer(2)},
      { new Integer(3), new Integer(4)},
      { new Integer(5), new Integer(6)},
    };
    for(int i = 0; i < a4.length; i++)
      for(int j = 0; j < a4[i].length; j++)
        System.out.println("a4[" + i + "][" + j +
            "] = " + a4[i][j]);
    Integer[][] a5;
    a5 = new Integer[3][];
    for(int i = 0; i < a5.length; i++) {
      a5[i] = new Integer[3];
      for(int j = 0; j < a5[i].length; j++)
        a5[i][j] = new Integer(i * j);
    }
    for(int i = 0; i < a5.length; i++)
      for(int j = 0; j < a5[i].length; j++)
        System.out.println("a5[" + i + "][" + j +
            "] = " + a5[i][j]);
    // Output test
    int ln = 0;
    for(int i = 0; i < a3.length; i++)
      for(int j = 0; j < a3[i].length; j++)
        for(int k = 0; k < a3[i][j].length; k++)
          ln++;
    monitor.expect(new Object[] {
      "a1[0][0] = 1",
      "a1[0][1] = 2",
      "a1[0][2] = 3",
      "a1[1][0] = 4",
      "a1[1][1] = 5",
      "a1[1][2] = 6",
      new TestExpression(
        "%% a2\\[\\d\\]\\[\\d\\]\\[\\d\\] = 0", 16),
      new TestExpression(
        "%% a3\\[\\d\\]\\[\\d\\]\\[\\d\\] = 0", ln),
      "a4[0][0] = 1",
      "a4[0][1] = 2",
      "a4[1][0] = 3",
      "a4[1][1] = 4",
      "a4[2][0] = 5",
      "a4[2][1] = 6",
```

```
      "a5[0][0] = 0",
      "a5[0][1] = 0",
      "a5[0][2] = 0",
      "a5[1][0] = 0",
      "a5[1][1] = 1",
      "a5[1][2] = 2",
      "a5[2][0] = 0",
      "a5[2][1] = 2",
      "a5[2][2] = 4"
    });
  }
} ///:~
```

The code used for printing uses **length** so that it doesn't depend on fixed array sizes.

The first example shows a multidimensional array of primitives. You delimit each vector in the array by using curly braces:

```
int[][] a1 = {
  { 1, 2, 3, },
  { 4, 5, 6, },
};
```

Each set of square brackets moves you into the next level of the array.

The second example shows a three-dimensional array allocated with **new**. Here, the whole array is allocated at once:

```
int[][][] a2 = new int[2][2][4];
```

But the third example shows that each vector in the arrays that make up the matrix can be of any length:

```
int[][][] a3 = new int[rand.nextInt(7)][][];
for(int i = 0; i < a3.length; i++) {
  a3[i] = new int[rand.nextInt(5)][];
  for(int j = 0; j < a3[i].length; j++)
    a3[i][j] = new int[rand.nextInt(5)];
}
```

The first **new** creates an array with a random-length first element and the rest undetermined. The second **new** inside the **for** loop fills out the elements but leaves the third index undetermined until you hit the third **new**.

You will see from the output that array values are automatically initialized to zero if you don't give them an explicit initialization value.

You can deal with arrays of nonprimitive objects in a similar fashion, which is shown in the fourth example, demonstrating the ability to collect many **new** expressions with curly braces:

```
Integer[][] a4 = {
  { new Integer(1), new Integer(2)},
  { new Integer(3), new Integer(4)},
  { new Integer(5), new Integer(6)},
};
```

The fifth example shows how an array of nonprimitive objects can be built up piece by piece:

```
Integer[][] a5;
a5 = new Integer[3][];
for(int i = 0; i < a5.length; i++) {
  a5[i] = new Integer[3];
  for(int j = 0; j < a5[i].length; j++)
    a5[i][j] = new Integer(i*j);
}
```

The **i*j** is just to put an interesting value into the **Integer**.

Summary

This seemingly elaborate mechanism for initialization, the constructor, should give you a strong hint about the critical importance placed on initialization in the language. As Bjarne Stroustrup, the inventor of C++, was designing that language, one of the first observations he made about productivity in C was that improper initialization of variables causes a significant portion of programming problems. These kinds of bugs are hard to find, and similar issues apply to improper cleanup. Because constructors allow you to *guarantee* proper initialization and cleanup (the compiler will not allow an object to be created without the proper constructor calls), you get complete control and safety.

In C++, destruction is quite important because objects created with **new** must be explicitly destroyed. In Java, the garbage collector automatically releases the memory for all objects, so the equivalent cleanup method in Java isn't necessary much of the time (but when it is, as observed in this chapter, you must do it yourself). In cases where you don't need destructor-like behavior, Java's garbage collector greatly simplifies programming and adds much-needed safety in managing memory. Some garbage collectors can even clean up other resources like graphics and file handles. However, the garbage collector does add a run-time cost, the expense of which is difficult to put into perspective because of the historical slowness of Java interpreters. Although Java has had significant performance increases over time, the speed problem has taken its toll on the adoption of the language for certain types of programming problems.

Because of the guarantee that all objects will be constructed, there's actually more to the constructor than what is shown here. In particular, when you create new classes using either *composition* or *inheritance,* the guarantee of construction also holds, and some additional syntax is necessary to support this. You'll learn about composition, inheritance, and how they affect constructors in future chapters.

Exercises

Solutions to selected exercises can be found in the electronic document *The Thinking in Java Annotated Solution Guide*, available for a small fee from *www.BruceEckel.com.*

1. Create a class with a default constructor (one that takes no arguments) that prints a message. Create an object of this class.

2. Add an overloaded constructor to Exercise 1 that takes a **String** argument and prints it along with your message.

3. Create an array of object references of the class you created in Exercise 2, but don't actually create objects to assign into the array. When you run the program, notice whether the initialization messages from the constructor calls are printed.

4. Complete Exercise 3 by creating objects to attach to the array of references.

5. Create an array of **String** objects and assign a string to each element. Print the array by using a **for** loop.

6. Create a class called **Dog** with an overloaded **bark( )** method. This method should be overloaded based on various primitive data types, and print different types of barking, howling, etc., depending on

which overloaded version is called. Write a **main( )** that calls all the different versions.

7. Modify Exercise 6 so that two of the overloaded methods have two arguments (of two different types), but in reversed order relative to each other. Verify that this works.

8. Create a class without a constructor, and then create an object of that class in **main( )** to verify that the default constructor is automatically synthesized.

9. Create a class with two methods. Within the first method, call the second method twice: the first time without using **this**, and the second time using **this**.

10. Create a class with two (overloaded) constructors. Using **this**, call the second constructor inside the first one.

11. Create a class with a **finalize( )** method that prints a message. In **main( )**, create an object of your class. Explain the behavior of your program.

12. Modify Exercise 11 so that your **finalize( )** will always be called.

13. Create a class called **Tank** that can be filled and emptied, and has a *termination condition* that it must be empty when the object is cleaned up. Write a **finalize( )** that verifies this termination condition. In **main( )**, test the possible scenarios that can occur when your **Tank** is used.

14. Create a class containing an **int** and a **char** that are not initialized, and print their values to verify that Java performs default initialization.

15. Create a class containing an uninitialized **String** reference. Demonstrate that this reference is initialized by Java to **null**.

16. Create a class with a **String** field that is initialized at the point of definition, and another one that is initialized by the constructor. What is the difference between the two approaches?

17. Create a class with a **static String** field that is initialized at the point of definition, and another one that is initialized by the **static** block. Add a **static** method that prints both fields and demonstrates that they are both initialized before they are used.

18. Create a class with a **String** that is initialized using "instance initialization." Describe a use for this feature (other than the one specified in this book).

19. Write a method that creates and initializes a two-dimensional array of **double**. The size of the array is determined by the arguments of the method, and the initialization values are a range determined by beginning and ending values that are also arguments of the method. Create a second method that will print the array generated by the first method. In **main( )** test the methods by creating and printing several different sizes of arrays.

20. Repeat Exercise 19 for a three-dimensional array.

21. Comment the line marked (1) in **ExplicitStatic.java** and verify that the static initialization clause is not called. Now uncomment one of the lines marked (2) and verify that the static initialization clause *is* called. Now uncomment the other line marked (2) and verify that static initialization only occurs once.

5: Hiding the Implementation

A primary consideration in object-oriented design is "separating the things that change from the things that stay the same."

This is particularly important for libraries. Users (*client programmers*) of that library must be able to rely on the part they use, and know that they won't need to rewrite code if a new version of the library comes out. On the flip side, the library creator must have the freedom to make modifications and improvements with the certainty that the client code won't be affected by those changes.

This can be achieved through convention. For example, the library programmer must agree to not remove existing methods when modifying a class in the library, since that would break the client programmer's code. The reverse situation is thornier, however. In the case of a field, how can the library creator know which fields have been accessed by client programmers? This is also true with methods that are only part of the implementation of a class, and not meant to be used directly by the client programmer. But what if the library creator wants to rip out an old implementation and put in a new one? Changing any of those members might break a client programmer's code. Thus the library creator is in a strait jacket and can't change anything.

To solve this problem, Java provides *access specifiers* to allow the library creator to say what is available to the client programmer and what is not. The levels of access control from "most access" to "least access" are **public**, **protected**, package access (which has no keyword), and **private**. From the previous paragraph you might think that, as a library designer, you'll want to keep everything as "private" as possible, and expose only the methods that you want the client programmer to use. This is exactly right, even though it's often counterintuitive for people who program in other languages (especially C) and are used to accessing everything without restriction. By the end of this chapter you should be convinced of the value of access control in Java.

The concept of a library of components and the control over who can access the components of that library is not complete, however. There's still the question of how the components are bundled together into a cohesive library unit. This is controlled with the **package** keyword in Java, and the access specifiers are affected by whether a class is in the same package or in a separate package. So to begin this chapter, you'll learn how library components are placed into packages. Then you'll be able to understand the complete meaning of the access specifiers.

package: the library unit

A package is what becomes available when you use the **import** keyword to bring in an entire library, such as

```
import java.util.*;
```

This brings in the entire utility library that's part of the standard Java distribution. For instance, there's a class called **ArrayList** in **java.util**, so you can now either specify the full name **java.util.ArrayList** (which you can do without the **import** statement), or you can simply say **ArrayList** (because of the **import**).

If you want to bring in a single class, you can name that class in the **import** statement

```
import java.util.ArrayList;
```

Now you can use **ArrayList** with no qualification. However, none of the other classes in **java.util** are available.

The reason for all this importing is to provide a mechanism to manage *name spaces*. The names of all your class members are insulated from each other. A method **f( )** inside a class **A** will not clash with an **f( )** that has the same signature (argument list) in class **B**. But what about the class names? Suppose you create a **Stack** class that is installed on a machine that already has a **Stack** class that's written by someone else? This potential clashing of names is why it's important to have complete control over the name spaces in Java, and to be able to create a completely unique name regardless of the constraints of the Internet.

Most of the examples thus far in this book have existed in a single file and have been designed for local use, so they haven't bothered with package names. (In this case the class name is placed in the "default package.") This is certainly an option, and for simplicity's sake this approach will be used whenever possible throughout the rest of this book. However, if you're planning to create libraries or programs that are friendly to other Java programs on the same machine, you must think about preventing class name clashes.

When you create a source-code file for Java, it's commonly called a *compilation unit* (sometimes a *translation unit*). Each compilation unit must have a name ending in **.java**, and inside the compilation unit there can be a **public** class that must have the same name as the file (including capitalization, but excluding the **.java** filename extension). There can be only *one* **public** class in each compilation unit, otherwise the compiler will complain. If there are additional classes in that compilation unit, they are hidden from the world outside that package because they're *not* **public**, and they comprise "support" classes for the main **public** class.

When you compile a **.java** file, you get an output file *for each class in the* **.java** file. Each output file has the name of a class in the **.java** file, but with an extension of **.class**. Thus you can end up with quite a few **.class** files from a small number of **.java** files. If you've programmed with a compiled language, you might be used to the compiler spitting out an intermediate form (usually an "obj" file) that is then packaged together with others of its kind using a linker (to create an executable file) or a librarian (to create a library). That's not how Java works. A working program is a bunch of **.class** files, which can be packaged and compressed into a Java ARchive (JAR) file (using Java's **jar** archiver). The Java interpreter is responsible for finding, loading, and interpreting[1] these files.

A library is a group of these class files. Each file has one class that is **public** (you're not forced to have a **public** class, but it's typical), so there's one component for each file. If you want to say that all these components (each in their own separate **.java** and **.class** files) belong together, that's where the **package** keyword comes in.

When you say:

---

[1] There's nothing in Java that forces the use of an interpreter. There exist native-code Java compilers that generate a single executable file.

```
package mypackage;
```

at the beginning of a file (if you use a **package** statement, it *must* appear as the first noncomment in the file), you're stating that this compilation unit is part of a library named **mypackage**. Or, put another way, you're saying that the **public** class name within this compilation unit is under the umbrella of the name **mypackage**, and anyone who wants to use the name must either fully specify the name or use the **import** keyword in combination with **mypackage** (using the choices given previously). Note that the convention for Java package names is to use all lowercase letters, even for intermediate words.

For example, suppose the name of the file is **MyClass.java**. This means there can be one and only one **public** class in that file, and the name of that class must be **MyClass** (including the capitalization):

```
package mypackage;
public class MyClass {
  // . . .
```

Now, if someone wants to use **MyClass** or, for that matter, any of the other **public** classes in **mypackage**, they must use the **import** keyword to make the name or names in **mypackage** available. The alternative is to give the fully qualified name:

```
mypackage.MyClass m = new mypackage.MyClass();
```

The **import** keyword can make this much cleaner:

```
import mypackage.*;
// . . .
MyClass m = new MyClass();
```

It's worth keeping in mind that what the **package** and **import** keywords allow you to do, as a library designer, is to divide up the single global name space so you won't have clashing names, no matter how many people get on the Internet and start writing classes in Java.

Creating unique package names

You might observe that, since a package never really gets "packaged" into a single file, a package could be made up of many **.class** files, and things could get a bit cluttered. To prevent this, a logical thing to do is to place all the **.class** files for a particular package into a single directory; that is, use the hierarchical file structure of the operating system to your advantage. This is one way that Java references the problem of clutter; you'll see the other way later when the **jar** utility is introduced.

Collecting the package files into a single subdirectory solves two other problems: creating unique package names, and finding those classes that might be buried in a directory structure someplace. This is accomplished, as was introduced in Chapter 2, by encoding the path of the location of the **.class** file into the name of the **package**. By convention, the first part of the **package** name is the reversed Internet domain name of the creator of the class. Since Internet domain names are guaranteed to be unique, *if* you follow this convention, your **package** name will be unique and you'll never have a name clash. (That is, until you lose the domain name to someone else who starts writing Java code with the same path names as you did.) Of course, if you don't have your own domain name, then you must fabricate an unlikely combination (such as your first and last name) to create unique package names. If you've decided to start publishing Java code, it's worth the relatively small effort to get a domain name.

The second part of this trick is resolving the **package** name into a directory on your machine, so when the Java program runs and it needs to load the **.class** file (which it does dynamically, at the point in the program where it needs to create an object of that particular class, or the first time you access a **static** member of the class), it can locate the directory where the **.class** file resides.

The Java interpreter proceeds as follows. First, it finds the environment variable CLASSPATH[2] (set via the operating system, and sometimes by the installation program that installs Java or a Java-based tool on your machine). CLASSPATH contains one or more directories that are used as roots in a search for **.class** files. Starting at that root, the interpreter will take the package name and replace each dot with a slash to generate a path name from the CLASSPATH root (so **package foo.bar.baz** becomes **foo\bar\baz** or **foo/bar/baz** or possibly something else, depending on your operating system). This is then concatenated to the various entries in the CLASSPATH. That's where it looks for the **.class** file with the name corresponding to the

---

[2] When referring to the environment variable, capital letters will be used (CLASSPATH).

class you're trying to create. (It also searches some standard directories relative to where the Java interpreter resides).

To understand this, consider my domain name, which is **bruceeckel.com**. By reversing this, **com.bruceeckel** establishes my unique global name for my classes. (The com, edu, org, etc., extensions were formerly capitalized in Java packages, but this was changed in Java 2 so the entire package name is lowercase.) I can further subdivide this by deciding that I want to create a library named **simple**, so I'll end up with a package name:

```
package com.bruceeckel.simple;
```

Now this package name can be used as an umbrella name space for the following two files:

```
//: com:bruceeckel:simple:Vector.java
// Creating a package.
package com.bruceeckel.simple;

public class Vector {
  public Vector() {
    System.out.println("com.bruceeckel.simple.Vector");
  }
} ///:~
```

When you create your own packages, you'll discover that the **package** statement must be the first noncomment code in the file. The second file looks much the same:

```
//: com:bruceeckel:simple:List.java
// Creating a package.
package com.bruceeckel.simple;

public class List {
  public List() {
    System.out.println("com.bruceeckel.simple.List");
  }
} ///:~
```

Both of these files are placed in the subdirectory on my system:

```
C:\DOC\JavaT\com\bruceeckel\simple
```

If you walk back through this, you can see the package name **com.bruceeckel.simple**, but what about the first portion of the path?

That's taken care of in the CLASSPATH environment variable, which is, on my machine:

```
CLASSPATH=.;D:\JAVA\LIB;C:\DOC\JavaT
```

You can see that the CLASSPATH can contain a number of alternative search paths.

There's a variation when using JAR files, however. You must put the name of the JAR file in the classpath, not just the path where it's located. So for a JAR named **grape.jar** your classpath would include:

```
CLASSPATH=.;D:\JAVA\LIB;C:\flavors\grape.jar
```

Once the classpath is set up properly, the following file can be placed in any directory:

```
//: c05:LibTest.java
// Uses the library.
import com.bruceeckel.simpletest.*;
import com.bruceeckel.simple.*;

public class LibTest {
  static Test monitor = new Test();
  public static void main(String[] args) {
    Vector v = new Vector();
    List l = new List();
    monitor.expect(new String[] {
      "com.bruceeckel.simple.Vector",
      "com.bruceeckel.simple.List"
    });
  }
} ///:~
```

When the compiler encounters the **import** statement for the **simple** library, it begins searching at the directories specified by CLASSPATH, looking for subdirectory com\bruceeckel\simple, then seeking the compiled files of the appropriate names (**Vector.class** for **Vector**, and **List.class** for **List**). Note that both the classes and the desired methods in **Vector** and **List** must be **public**.

Setting the CLASSPATH has been such a trial for beginning Java users (it was for me, when I started) that Sun made the JDK in Java 2 a bit smarter. You'll find that when you install it, even if you don't set the CLASSPATH, you'll be able to compile and run basic Java programs. To compile and run the source-code package for this book (available at *www.BruceEckel.com*), however, you will need to add the base directory of the book's code tree to your CLASSPATH.

Collisions

What happens if two libraries are imported via '*' and they include the same names? For example, suppose a program does this:

```
import com.bruceeckel.simple.*;
import java.util.*;
```

Since **java.util.*** also contains a **Vector** class, this causes a potential collision. However, as long as you don't write the code that actually causes the collision, everything is OK—this is good, because otherwise you might end up doing a lot of typing to prevent collisions that would never happen.

The collision *does* occur if you now try to make a **Vector**:

```
Vector v = new Vector();
```

Which **Vector** class does this refer to? The compiler can't know, and the reader can't know either. So the compiler complains and forces you to be explicit. If I want the standard Java **Vector**, for example, I must say:

```
java.util.Vector v = new java.util.Vector();
```

Since this (along with the CLASSPATH) completely specifies the location of that **Vector**, there's no need for the **import java.util.*** statement unless I'm using something else from **java.util**.

A custom tool library

With this knowledge, you can now create your own libraries of tools to reduce or eliminate duplicate code. Consider, for example, creating an alias for **System.out.println( )** to reduce typing. This can be part of a package called **tools**:

```
//: com:bruceeckel:tools:P.java
// The P.rint & P.rintln shorthand.
package com.bruceeckel.tools;

public class P {
  public static void rint(String s) {
```

```
    System.out.print(s);
  }
  public static void rintln(String s) {
    System.out.println(s);
  }
} ///:~
```

You can use this shorthand to print a **String** either with a newline (**P.rintln( )**) or without a newline (**P.rint( )**).

You can guess that the location of this file must be in a directory that starts at one of the CLASSPATH locations, then continues **com/bruceeckel/tools**. After compiling, the **P.class** file can be used anywhere on your system with an **import** statement:

```
//: c05:ToolTest.java
// Uses the tools library.
import com.bruceeckel.tools.*;
import com.bruceeckel.simpletest.*;

public class ToolTest {
  static Test monitor = new Test();
  public static void main(String[] args) {
    P.rintln("Available from now on!");
    P.rintln("" + 100); // Force it to be a String
    P.rintln("" + 100L);
    P.rintln("" + 3.14159);
    monitor.expect(new String[] {
      "Available from now on!",
      "100",
      "100",
      "3.14159"
    });
  }
} ///:~
```

Notice that all objects can easily be forced into **String** representations by putting them in a **String** expression; in the preceding example, starting the expression with an empty **String** does the trick. But this brings up an interesting observation. If you call **System.out.println(100)**, it works without casting it to a **String**. With some extra overloading, you can get the **P** class to do this as well (this is an exercise at the end of this chapter).

So from now on, whenever you come up with a useful new utility, you can add it to your own **tools** or **util** directory.

Using imports to change behavior

A feature that is missing from Java is C's *conditional compilation*, which allows you to change a switch and get different behavior without changing any other code. The reason such a feature was left out of Java is probably because it is most often used in C to solve cross-platform issues: Different portions of the code are compiled depending on the platform that the code is being compiled for. Since Java is intended to be automatically cross-platform, such a feature should not be necessary.

However, there are other valuable uses for conditional compilation. A very common use is for debugging code. The debugging features are enabled during development and disabled in the shipping product. You can accomplish this by changing the **package** that's imported to change the code used in your program from the debug version to the production version. This technique can be used for any kind of conditional code.

Package caveat

It's worth remembering that anytime you create a package, you implicitly specify a directory structure when you give the package a name. The package *must* live in the directory indicated by its name, which must be a directory that is searchable starting from the CLASSPATH. Experimenting with the **package** keyword can be a bit frustrating at first, because unless you adhere to the package-name to directory-path rule, you'll get a lot of mysterious run-time messages about not being able to find a particular class, even if that class is sitting there in the same directory. If you get a message like this, try commenting out the **package** statement, and if it runs, you'll know where the problem lies.

Java access specifiers

When used, the Java access specifiers **public**, **protected,** and **private** are placed in front of each definition for each member in your class, whether it's a field or a method. Each access specifier controls the access for only that particular definition. This is a distinct contrast to C++, in which the access specifier controls all the definitions following it until another access specifier comes along.

One way or another, everything has some kind of access specified for it. In the following sections, you'll learn all about the various types of access, starting with the default access.

Package access

What if you give no access specifier at all, as in all the examples before this chapter? The default access has no keyword, but it is commonly referred to as *package access* (and sometimes "friendly"). It means that all the other classes in the current package have access to that member, but to all the classes outside of this package, the member appears to be **private**. Since a compilation unit—a file—can belong only to a single package, all the classes within a single compilation unit are automatically available each other via package access.

Package access allows you to group related classes together in a package so that they can easily interact with each other. When you put classes together in a package, thus granting mutual access to their package-access members, you "own" the code in that package. It makes sense that only code you own should have package access to other code you own. You could say that package access gives a meaning or a reason for grouping classes together in a package. In many languages the way you organize your definitions in files can be arbitrary, but in Java you're compelled to organize them in a sensible fashion. In addition, you'll probably want to exclude classes that shouldn't have access to the classes being defined in the current package.

The class controls which code has access to its members. There's no magic way to "break in." Code from another package can't show up and say, "Hi, I'm a friend of **Bob**'s!" and expect to see the **protected**, package-access, and **private** members of **Bob**. The only way to grant access to a member is to:

1. Make the member **public**. Then everybody, everywhere, can access it.

2. Give the member package access by leaving off any access specifier, and put the other classes in the same package. Then the other classes in that package can access the member.

3. As you'll see in Chapter 6, when inheritance is introduced, an inherited class can access a **protected** member as well as a **public** member (but not **private** members). It can access package-access members only if the two classes are in the same package. But don't worry about that now.

4. Provide "accessor/mutator" methods (also known as "get/set" methods) that read and change the value. This is the most civilized approach in terms of OOP, and it is fundamental to JavaBeans, as you'll see in Chapter 14.

public: interface access

When you use the **public** keyword, it means that the member declaration that immediately follows **public** is available to everyone, in particular to the client programmer who uses the library. Suppose you define a package **dessert** containing the following compilation unit:

```
//: c05:dessert:Cookie.java
// Creates a library.
package c05.dessert;

public class Cookie {
  public Cookie() {
   System.out.println("Cookie constructor");
  }
  void bite() { System.out.println("bite"); }
} ///:~
```

Remember, **Cookie.java** must reside in a subdirectory called **dessert**, in a directory under **c05** (indicating Chapter 5 of this book) that must be under one of the CLASSPATH directories. Don't make the mistake of thinking that Java will always look at the current directory as one of the starting points for searching. If you don't have a '**.**' as one of the paths in your CLASSPATH, Java won't look there.

Now if you create a program that uses **Cookie**:

```
//: c05:Dinner.java
// Uses the library.
import com.bruceeckel.simpletest.*;
import c05.dessert.*;

public class Dinner {
  static Test monitor = new Test();
  public Dinner() {
   System.out.println("Dinner constructor");
  }
  public static void main(String[] args) {
    Cookie x = new Cookie();
```

```
    //! x.bite(); // Can't access
    monitor.expect(new String[] {
      "Cookie constructor"
    });
  }
} ///:~
```

you can create a **Cookie** object, since its constructor is **public** and the class is **public**. (We'll look more at the concept of a **public** class later.) However, the **bite( )** member is inaccessible inside **Dinner.java** since **bite( )** provides access only within package **dessert**, so the compiler prevents you from using it.

The default package

You might be surprised to discover that the following code compiles, even though it would appear that it breaks the rules:

```
//: c05:Cake.java
// Accesses a class in a separate compilation unit.
import com.bruceeckel.simpletest.*;

class Cake {
  static Test monitor = new Test();
  public static void main(String[] args) {
    Pie x = new Pie();
    x.f();
    monitor.expect(new String[] {
      "Pie.f()"
    });
  }
} ///:~
```

In a second file in the same directory:

```
//: c05:Pie.java
// The other class.

class Pie {
  void f() { System.out.println("Pie.f()"); }
} ///:~
```

You might initially view these as completely foreign files, and yet **Cake** is able to create a **Pie** object and call its **f( )** method! (Note that you must have '.' in your CLASSPATH in order for the files to compile.) You'd typically think that

Pie and **f( )** have package access and therefore not available to **Cake**. They *do* have package access—that part is correct. The reason that they are available in **Cake.java** is because they are in the same directory and have no explicit package name. Java treats files like this as implicitly part of the "default package" for that directory, and thus they provide package access to all the other files in that directory.

private: you can't touch that!

The **private** keyword means that no one can access that member except the class that contains that member, inside methods of that class. Other classes in the same package cannot access **private** members, so it's as if you're even insulating the class against yourself. On the other hand, it's not unlikely that a package might be created by several people collaborating together, so **private** allows you to freely change that member without concern that it will affect another class in the same package.

The default package access often provides an adequate amount of hiding; remember, a package-access member is inaccessible to the client programmer using the class. This is nice, since the default access is the one that you normally use (and the one that you'll get if you forget to add any access control). Thus, you'll typically think about access for the members that you explicitly want to make **public** for the client programmer, and as a result, you might not initially think you'll use the **private** keyword often since it's tolerable to get away without it. (This is a distinct contrast with C++.) However, it turns out that the consistent use of **private** is very important, especially where multithreading is concerned. (As you'll see in Chapter 13.)

Here's an example of the use of **private**:

```
//: c05:IceCream.java
// Demonstrates "private" keyword.

class Sundae {
  private Sundae() {}
  static Sundae makeASundae() {
    return new Sundae();
  }
}

public class IceCream {
  public static void main(String[] args) {
```

```
    //! Sundae x = new Sundae();
    Sundae x = Sundae.makeASundae();
  }
} ///:~
```

This shows an example in which **private** comes in handy: you might want to control how an object is created and prevent someone from directly accessing a particular constructor (or all of them). In the preceding example, you cannot create a **Sundae** object via its constructor; instead, you must call the **makeASundae( )** method to do it for you.[3]

Any method that you're certain is only a "helper" method for that class can be made **private,** to ensure that you don't accidentally use it elsewhere in the package and thus prohibit yourself from changing or removing the method. Making a method **private** guarantees that you retain this option.

The same is true for a **private** field inside a class. Unless you must expose the underlying implementation (which is less likely than you might think), you should make all fields **private**. However, just because a reference to an object is **private** inside a class doesn't mean that some other object can't have a **public** reference to the same object. (See Appendix A for issues about aliasing.)

protected: inheritance access

Understanding the **protected** access specifier requires a jump ahead. First, you should be aware that you don't need to understand this section to continue through this book up through inheritance (Chapter 6). But for completeness, here is a brief description and example using **protected**.

The **protected** keyword deals with a concept called *inheritance*, which takes an existing class—which we refer to as the *base class*—and adds new members to that class without touching the existing class. You can also change the behavior of existing members of the class. To inherit from an existing class, you say that your new class **extends** an existing class, like this:

```
class Foo extends Bar {
```

[3] There's another effect in this case: Since the default constructor is the only one defined, and it's **private**, it will prevent inheritance of this class. (A subject that will be introduced in Chapter 6.)

The rest of the class definition looks the same.

If you create a new package and inherit from a class in another package, the only members you have access to are the **public** members of the original package. (Of course, if you perform the inheritance in the *same* package, you can manipulate all the members that have package access) Sometimes the creator of the base class would like to take a particular member and grant access to derived classes but not the world in general. That's what **protected** does. **protected** also gives package access—that is, other classes in the same package may access **protected** elements.

If you refer back to the file **Cookie.java**, the following class *cannot* call the package-access member **bite( )**:

```
//: c05:ChocolateChip.java
// Can't use package-access member from another package.
import com.bruceeckel.simpletest.*;
import c05.dessert.*;

public class ChocolateChip extends Cookie {
  private static Test monitor = new Test();
  public ChocolateChip() {
   System.out.println("ChocolateChip constructor");
  }
  public static void main(String[] args) {
    ChocolateChip x = new ChocolateChip();
    //! x.bite(); // Can't access bite
    monitor.expect(new String[] {
      "Cookie constructor",
      "ChocolateChip constructor"
    });
  }
} ///:~
```

One of the interesting things about inheritance is that if a method **bite( )** exists in class **Cookie**, then it also exists in any class inherited from **Cookie**. But since **bite( )** has package access and is in a foreign package, it's unavailable to us in this one. Of course, you could make it **public**, but then everyone would have access, and maybe that's not what you want. If we change the class **Cookie** as follows:

```
public class Cookie {
  public Cookie() {
    System.out.println("Cookie constructor");
```

```
  }
  protected void bite() {
    System.out.println("bite");
  }
}
```

then **bite( )** still has the equivalent of package access within package **dessert**, but it is also accessible to anyone inheriting from **Cookie**. However, it is *not* **public**.

Interface and implementation

Access control is often referred to as *implementation hiding*. Wrapping data and methods within classes in combination with implementation hiding is often called *encapsulation*.[4] The result is a data type with characteristics and behaviors.

Access control puts boundaries within a data type for two important reasons. The first is to establish what the client programmers can and can't use. You can build your internal mechanisms into the structure without worrying that the client programmers will accidentally treat the internals as part of the interface that they should be using.

This feeds directly into the second reason, which is to separate the interface from the implementation. If the structure is used in a set of programs, but client programmers can't do anything but send messages to the **public** interface, then you are free to change anything that's *not* **public** (e.g., package access, **protected**, or **private**) without breaking client code.

We're now in the world of object-oriented programming, where a **class** is actually describing "a class of objects," as you would describe a class of fishes or a class of birds. Any object belonging to this class will share these characteristics and behaviors. The class is a description of the way all objects of this type will look and act.

In the original OOP language, Simula-67, the keyword **class** was used to describe a new data type. The same keyword has been used for most object-oriented languages. This is the focal point of the whole language: the creation of new data types that are more than just boxes containing data and methods.

---

[4] However, people often refer to implementation hiding alone as encapsulation.

The class is the fundamental OOP concept in Java. It is one of the keywords that will *not* be set in bold in this book—it becomes annoying with a word repeated as often as "class."

For clarity, you might prefer a style of creating classes that puts the **public** members at the beginning, followed by the **protected**, package access, and **private** members. The advantage is that the user of the class can then read down from the top and see first what's important to them (the **public** members, because they can be accessed outside the file), and stop reading when they encounter the non-**public** members, which are part of the internal implementation:

```
public class X {
  public void pub1() { /* . . . */ }
  public void pub2() { /* . . . */ }
  public void pub3() { /* . . . */ }
  private void priv1() { /* . . . */ }
  private void priv2() { /* . . . */ }
  private void priv3() { /* . . . */ }
  private int i;
  // . . .
}
```

This will make it only partially easier to read, because the interface and implementation are still mixed together. That is, you still see the source code—the implementation—because it's right there in the class. In addition, the comment documentation supported by javadoc (described in Chapter 2) lessens the importance of code readability by the client programmer. Displaying the interface to the consumer of a class is really the job of the *class browser*, a tool whose job is to look at all the available classes and show you what you can do with them (i.e., what members are available) in a useful fashion. Class browsers have become an expected part of any good Java development tool.

Class access

In Java, the access specifiers can also be used to determine which classes *within* a library will be available to the users of that library. If you want a class to be available to a client programmer, you use the **public** keyword on the entire class definition. This controls whether the client programmer can even create an object of the class.

To control the access of a class, the specifier must appear before the keyword **class**. Thus you can say:

```
public class Widget {
```

Now if the name of your library is **mylib**, any client programmer can access **Widget** by saying

```
import mylib.Widget;
```

or

```
import mylib.*;
```

However, there's an extra set of constraints:

1. There can be only one **public** class per compilation unit (file). The idea is that each compilation unit has a single public interface represented by that **public** class. It can have as many supporting package-access classes as you want. If you have more than one **public** class inside a compilation unit, the compiler will give you an error message.

2. The name of the **public** class must exactly match the name of the file containing the compilation unit, including capitalization. So for **Widget**, the name of the file must be **Widget.java**, not **widget.java** or **WIDGET.java**. Again, you'll get a compile-time error if they don't agree.

3. It is possible, though not typical, to have a compilation unit with no **public** class at all. In this case, you can name the file whatever you like.

What if you've got a class inside **mylib** that you're just using to accomplish the tasks performed by **Widget** or some other **public** class in **mylib**? You don't want to go to the bother of creating documentation for the client programmer, and you think that sometime later you might want to completely change things and rip out your class altogether, substituting a different one. To give you this flexibility, you need to ensure that no client programmers become dependent on your particular implementation details hidden inside **mylib**. To accomplish this, you just leave the **public** keyword off the class, in which case it has package access. (That class can be used only within that package.)

When you create a package-access class, it still makes sense to make the fields of the class **private**—you should always make fields as private as possible—but it's generally reasonable to give the methods the same access as the class (package access). Since a package-access class is usually used only within the package, you only need to make the methods of such a class **public** if you're forced to, and in those cases, the compiler will tell you.

Note that a class cannot be **private** (that would make it accessible to no one but the class) or **protected**.[5] So you have only two choices for class access: package access or **public**. If you don't want anyone else to have access to that class, you can make all the constructors **private**, thereby preventing anyone but you, inside a **static** member of the class, from creating an object of that class. Here's an example:

```
//: c05:Lunch.java
// Demonstrates class access specifiers. Make a class
// effectively private with private constructors:

class Soup {
  private Soup() {}
  // (1) Allow creation via static method:
  public static Soup makeSoup() {
    return new Soup();
  }
  // (2) Create a static object and return a reference
  // upon request.(The "Singleton" pattern):
  private static Soup ps1 = new Soup();
  public static Soup access() {
    return ps1;
  }
  public void f() {}
}

class Sandwich { // Uses Lunch
  void f() { new Lunch(); }
}

// Only one public class allowed per file:
public class Lunch {
```

---

5 Actually, an *inner class* can be private or protected, but that's a special case. These will be introduced in Chapter 7.

```
  void test() {
    // Can't do this! Private constructor:
    //! Soup priv1 = new Soup();
    Soup priv2 = Soup.makeSoup();
    Sandwich f1 = new Sandwich();
    Soup.access().f();
  }
} ///:~
```

Up to now, most of the methods have been returning either **void** or a primitive type, so the definition:

```
  public static Soup access() {
    return ps1;
  }
```

might look a little confusing at first. The word before the method name (**access**) tells what the method returns. So far, this has most often been **void,** which means it returns nothing. But you can also return a reference to an object, which is what happens here. This method returns a reference to an object of class **Soup**.

The **class Soup** shows how to prevent direct creation of a class by making all the constructors **private**. Remember that if you don't explicitly create at least one constructor, the default constructor (a constructor with no arguments) will be created for you. By writing the default constructor, it won't be created automatically. By making it **private**, no one can create an object of that class. But now how does anyone use this class? The preceding example shows two options. First, a **static** method is created that creates a new **Soup** and returns a reference to it. This could be useful if you want to do some extra operations on the **Soup** before returning it, or if you want to keep count of how many **Soup** objects to create (perhaps to restrict their population).

The second option uses what's called a *design pattern*, which is covered in *Thinking in Patterns (with Java)* at *www.BruceEckel.com*. This particular pattern is called a "singleton" because it allows only a single object to ever be created. The object of class **Soup** is created as a **static private** member of **Soup**, so there's one and only one, and you can't get at it except through the **public** method **access( )**.

As previously mentioned, if you don't put an access specifier for class access, it defaults to package access. This means that an object of that class can be created by any other class in the package, but not outside the package.

(Remember, all the files within the same directory that don't have explicit **package** declarations are implicitly part of the default package for that directory.) However, if a **static** member of that class is **public**, the client programmer can still access that **static** member even though they cannot create an object of that class.

Summary

In any relationship it's important to have boundaries that are respected by all parties involved. When you create a library, you establish a relationship with the user of that library—the client programmer—who is another programmer, but one putting together an application or using your library to build a bigger library.

Without rules, client programmers can do anything they want with all the members of a class, even if you might prefer they don't directly manipulate some of the members. Everything's naked to the world.

This chapter looked at how classes are built to form libraries: first, the way a group of classes is packaged within a library, and second, the way the class controls access to its members.

It is estimated that a C programming project begins to break down somewhere between 50K and 100K lines of code because C has a single "name space": names begin to collide, causing an extra management overhead. In Java, the **package** keyword, the package naming scheme, and the **import** keyword give you complete control over names, so the issue of name collision is easily avoided.

There are two reasons for controlling access to members. The first is to keep users' hands off tools that they shouldn't touch: tools that are necessary for the internal operations of the data type, but not part of the interface that users need to solve their particular problems. So making methods and fields **private** is a service to users, because they can easily see what's important to them and what they can ignore. It simplifies their understanding of the class.

The second and most important reason for access control is to allow the library designer to change the internal workings of the class without worrying about how it will affect the client programmer. You might build a class one way at first, and then discover that restructuring your code will provide much greater speed. If the interface and implementation are clearly separated and protected, you can accomplish this without forcing users to rewrite their code.

Access specifiers in Java give valuable control to the creator of a class. The users of the class can clearly see exactly what they can use and what to ignore. More important, though, is the ability to ensure that no user becomes dependent on any part of the underlying implementation of a class. If you know this as the creator of the class, you can change the underlying implementation at will, because you know that no client programmer will be affected by the changes; they can't access that part of the class.

When you have the ability to change the underlying implementation, you can freely improve your design. You also have the freedom to make mistakes. No matter how carefully you plan and design, you'll make mistakes. Knowing that it's relatively safe to make these mistakes means you'll be more experimental, you'll learn more quickly, and you'll finish your project sooner.

The public interface to a class is what the user *does* see, so that is the most important part of the class to get "right" during analysis and design. Even that allows you some leeway for change. If you don't get the interface right the first time, you can *add* more methods, as long as you don't remove any that client programmers have already used in their code.

Exercises

Solutions to selected exercises can be found in the electronic document *The Thinking in Java Annotated Solution Guide*, available for a small fee from *www.BruceEckel.com*.

1. Write a program that creates an **ArrayList** object without explicitly importing **java.util.***.

2. In the section labeled "package: the library unit," turn the code fragments concerning **mypackage** into a compiling and running set of Java files.

3. In the section labeled "Collisions," take the code fragments and turn them into a program and verify that collisions do in fact occur.

4. Generalize the class **P** defined in this chapter by adding all the overloaded versions of **rint( )** and **rintln( )** necessary to handle all the different basic Java types.

5. Create a class with **public**, **private**, **protected,** and package-access fields and method members. Create an object of this class and see what kind of compiler messages you get when you try to access all the class members. Be aware that classes in the same directory are part of the "default" package.

6. Create a class with **protected** data. Create a second class in the same file with a method that manipulates the **protected** data in the first class.

7. Change the class **Cookie** as specified in the section labeled "protected: inheritance access." Verify that **bite( )** is not **public**.

8. In the section titled "Class access" you'll find code fragments describing **mylib** and **Widget**. Create this library, then create a **Widget** in a class that is not part of the **mylib** package.

9. Create a new directory and edit your CLASSPATH to include that new directory. Copy the **P.class** file (produced by compiling **com.bruceeckel.tools.P.java**) to your new directory and then change the names of the file, the **P** class inside, and the method names. (You might also want to add additional output to watch how it works.) Create another program in a different directory that uses your new class.

10. Following the form of the example **Lunch.java**, create a class called **ConnectionManager** that manages a fixed array of **Connection** objects. The client programmer must not be able to explicitly create **Connection** objects, but can only get them via a **static** method in **ConnectionManager**. When the **ConnectionManager** runs out of objects, it returns a **null** reference. Test the classes in **main( )**.

11. Create the following file in the c05/local directory (presumably in your CLASSPATH):

```
// c05:local:PackagedClass.java
package c05.local;
class PackagedClass {
  public PackagedClass() {
    System.out.println("Creating a packaged class");
  }
}
```

Then create the following file in a directory other than c05:

```
// c05:foreign:Foreign.java
package c05.foreign;
import c05.local.*;
public class Foreign {
   public static void main (String[] args) {
      PackagedClass pc = new PackagedClass();
   }
}
```

Explain why the compiler generates an error. Would making the **Foreign** class part of the **c05.local** package change anything?

6: Reusing Classes

One of the most compelling features about Java is code reuse. But to be revolutionary, you've got to be able to do a lot more than copy code and change it.

That's the approach used in procedural languages like C, and it hasn't worked very well. Like everything in Java, the solution revolves around the class. You reuse code by creating new classes, but instead of creating them from scratch, you use existing classes that someone has already built and debugged.

The trick is to use the classes without soiling the existing code. In this chapter you'll see two ways to accomplish this. The first is quite straightforward: you simply create objects of your existing class inside the new class. This is called *composition,* because the new class is composed of objects of existing classes. You're simply reusing the functionality of the code, not its form.

The second approach is more subtle. It creates a new class as a *type of* an existing class. You literally take the form of the existing class and add code to it without modifying the existing class. This magical act is called *inheritance*, and the compiler does most of the work. Inheritance is one of the cornerstones of object-oriented programming, and has additional implications that will be explored in Chapter 7.

It turns out that much of the syntax and behavior are similar for both composition and inheritance (which makes sense because they are both ways of making new types from existing types). In this chapter, you'll learn about these code reuse mechanisms.

Composition syntax

Until now, composition has been used quite frequently. You simply place object references inside new classes. For example, suppose you'd like an object that holds several **String** objects, a couple of primitives, and an object of another class. For the nonprimitive objects, you put references inside your new class, but you define the primitives directly:

```
//: c06:SprinklerSystem.java
```

```java
// Composition for code reuse.
import com.bruceeckel.simpletest.*;

class WaterSource {
  private String s;
  WaterSource() {
    System.out.println("WaterSource()");
    s = new String("Constructed");
  }
  public String toString() { return s; }
}

public class SprinklerSystem {
  private static Test monitor = new Test();
  private String valve1, valve2, valve3, valve4;
  private WaterSource source;
  private int i;
  private float f;
  public String toString() {
    return
      "valve1 = " + valve1 + "\n" +
      "valve2 = " + valve2 + "\n" +
      "valve3 = " + valve3 + "\n" +
      "valve4 = " + valve4 + "\n" +
      "i = " + i + "\n" +
      "f = " + f + "\n" +
      "source = " + source;
  }
  public static void main(String[] args) {
    SprinklerSystem sprinklers = new SprinklerSystem();
    System.out.println(sprinklers);
    monitor.expect(new String[] {
      "valve1 = null",
      "valve2 = null",
      "valve3 = null",
      "valve4 = null",
      "i = 0",
      "f = 0.0",
      "source = null"
    });
  }
} ///:~
```

One of the methods defined in both classes is special: **toString( )**. You will learn later that every nonprimitive object has a **toString( )** method, and it's called in special situations when the compiler wants a **String** but it has an object. So in the expression in **SprinklerSystem.toString( )**:

```
"source = " + source;
```

the compiler sees you trying to add a **String** object ("**source** = ") to a **WaterSource**. Because you can only "add" a **String** to another **String**, it says "I'll turn **source** into a **String** by calling **toString( )**!" After doing this it can combine the two **String**s and pass the resulting **String** to **System.out.println( )**. Any time you want to allow this behavior with a class you create, you need only write a **toString( )** method.

Primitives that are fields in a class are automatically initialized to zero, as noted in Chapter 2. But the object references are initialized to **null**, and if you try to call methods for any of them, you'll get an exception. It's actually good (and useful) that you can still print them out without throwing an exception.

It makes sense that the compiler doesn't just create a default object for every reference, because that would incur unnecessary overhead in many cases. If you want the references initialized, you can do it:

1. At the point the objects are defined. This means that they'll always be initialized before the constructor is called.
2. In the constructor for that class.
3. Right before you actually need to use the object. This is often called *lazy initialization*. It can reduce overhead in situations where object creation is expensive and the object doesn't need to be created every time.

All three approaches are shown here:

```
//: c06:Bath.java
// Constructor initialization with composition.
import com.bruceeckel.simpletest.*;

class Soap {
  private String s;
  Soap() {
    System.out.println("Soap()");
    s = new String("Constructed");
  }
  public String toString() { return s; }
```

```
}

public class Bath {
  private static Test monitor = new Test();
  private String // Initializing at point of definition:
    s1 = new String("Happy"),
    s2 = "Happy",
    s3, s4;
  private Soap castille;
  private int i;
  private float toy;
  public Bath() {
    System.out.println("Inside Bath()");
    s3 = new String("Joy");
    i = 47;
    toy = 3.14f;
    castille = new Soap();
  }
  public String toString() {
    if(s4 == null) // Delayed initialization:
      s4 = new String("Joy");
    return
      "s1 = " + s1 + "\n" +
      "s2 = " + s2 + "\n" +
      "s3 = " + s3 + "\n" +
      "s4 = " + s4 + "\n" +
      "i = " + i + "\n" +
      "toy = " + toy + "\n" +
      "castille = " + castille;
  }
  public static void main(String[] args) {
    Bath b = new Bath();
    System.out.println(b);
    monitor.expect(new String[] {
      "Inside Bath()",
      "Soap()",
      "s1 = Happy",
      "s2 = Happy",
      "s3 = Joy",
      "s4 = Joy",
      "i = 47",
      "toy = 3.14",
      "castille = Constructed"
    });
```

```
  }
} ///:~
```

Note that in the **Bath** constructor, a statement is executed before any of the initializations take place. When you don't initialize at the point of definition, there's still no guarantee that you'll perform any initialization before you send a message to an object reference—except for the inevitable run-time exception.

When **toString( )** is called it fills in **s4** so that all the fields are properly initialized by the time they are used.

Inheritance syntax

Inheritance is an integral part of Java (and all OOP languages). It turns out that you're always doing inheritance when you create a class, because unless you explicitly inherit from some other class, you implicitly inherit from Java's standard root class **Object**.

The syntax for composition is obvious, but to perform inheritance there's a distinctly different form. When you inherit, you say "This new class is like that old class." You state this in code by giving the name of the class as usual, but before the opening brace of the class body, put the keyword **extends** followed by the name of the *base class*. When you do this, you automatically get all the fields and methods in the base class. Here's an example:

```
//: c06:Detergent.java
// Inheritance syntax & properties.
import com.bruceeckel.simpletest.*;

class Cleanser {
  protected static Test monitor = new Test();
  private String s = new String("Cleanser");
  public void append(String a) { s += a; }
  public void dilute() { append(" dilute()"); }
  public void apply() { append(" apply()"); }
  public void scrub() { append(" scrub()"); }
  public String toString() { return s; }
  public static void main(String[] args) {
    Cleanser x = new Cleanser();
    x.dilute(); x.apply(); x.scrub();
    System.out.println(x);
    monitor.expect(new String[] {
```

```
      "Cleanser dilute() apply() scrub()"
    });
  }
}

public class Detergent extends Cleanser {
  // Change a method:
  public void scrub() {
    append(" Detergent.scrub()");
    super.scrub(); // Call base-class version
  }
  // Add methods to the interface:
  public void foam() { append(" foam()"); }
  // Test the new class:
  public static void main(String[] args) {
    Detergent x = new Detergent();
    x.dilute();
    x.apply();
    x.scrub();
    x.foam();
    System.out.println(x);
    System.out.println("Testing base class:");
    monitor.expect(new String[] {
      "Cleanser dilute() apply() " +
      "Detergent.scrub() scrub() foam()",
      "Testing base class:",
    });
    Cleanser.main(args);
  }
} ///:~
```

This demonstrates a number of features. First, in the **Cleanser append( )** method, **String**s are concatenated to **s** using the += operator, which is one of the operators (along with '+') that the Java designers "overloaded" to work with **String**s.

Second, both **Cleanser** and **Detergent** contain a **main( )** method. You can create a **main( )** for each one of your classes, and it's often recommended to code this way so that your test code is wrapped in with the class. Even if you have a lot of classes in a program, only the **main( )** for the class invoked on the command line will be called. (As long as **main( )** is **public**, it doesn't matter whether the class that it's part of is **public**.) So in this case, when you say **java Detergent**, **Detergent.main( )** will be called. But you can also say **java Cleanser** to invoke **Cleanser.main( )**, even though **Cleanser** is not a

public class. This technique of putting a **main( )** in each class allows easy unit testing for each class. And you don't need to remove the **main( )** when you're finished testing; you can leave it in for later testing.

Here, you can see that **Detergent.main( )** calls **Cleanser.main( )** explicitly, passing it the same arguments from the command line (however, you could pass it any **String** array).

It's important that all of the methods in **Cleanser** are **public**. Remember that if you leave off any access specifier, the member defaults to package access, which allows access only to package members. Thus, *within this package*, anyone could use those methods if there were no access specifier. **Detergent** would have no trouble, for example. However, if a class from some other package were to inherit from **Cleanser**, it could access only **public** members. So to plan for inheritance, as a general rule make all fields **private** and all methods **public**. (**protected** members also allow access by derived classes; you'll learn about this later.) Of course, in particular cases you must make adjustments, but this is a useful guideline.

Note that **Cleanser** has a set of methods in its interface: **append( )**, **dilute( )**, **apply( )**, **scrub( )**, and **toString( )**. Because **Detergent** is *derived from* **Cleanser** (via the **extends** keyword), it automatically gets all these methods in its interface, even though you don't see them all explicitly defined in **Detergent**. You can think of inheritance, then, as reusing the class.

As seen in **scrub( )**, it's possible to take a method that's been defined in the base class and modify it. In this case, you might want to call the method from the base class inside the new version. But inside **scrub( )**, you cannot simply call **scrub( )**, since that would produce a recursive call, which isn't what you want. To solve this problem, Java has the keyword **super** that refers to the "superclass" that the current class has been inherited from. Thus the expression **super.scrub( )** calls the base-class version of the method **scrub( )**.

When inheriting you're not restricted to using the methods of the base class. You can also add new methods to the derived class exactly the way you put any method in a class: just define it. The method **foam( )** is an example of this.

In **Detergent.main( )** you can see that for a **Detergent** object, you can call all the methods that are available in **Cleanser** as well as in **Detergent** (i.e., **foam( )**).

Initializing the base class

Since there are now two classes involved—the base class and the derived class—instead of just one, it can be a bit confusing to try to imagine the resulting object produced by a derived class. From the outside, it looks like the new class has the same interface as the base class and maybe some additional methods and fields. But inheritance doesn't just copy the interface of the base class. When you create an object of the derived class, it contains within it a *subobject* of the base class. This subobject is the same as if you had created an object of the base class by itself. It's just that from the outside, the subobject of the base class is wrapped within the derived-class object.

Of course, it's essential that the base-class subobject be initialized correctly, and there's only one way to guarantee this: perform the initialization in the constructor by calling the base-class constructor, which has all the appropriate knowledge and privileges to perform the base-class initialization. Java automatically inserts calls to the base-class constructor in the derived-class constructor. The following example shows this working with three levels of inheritance:

```
//: c06:Cartoon.java
// Constructor calls during inheritance.
import com.bruceeckel.simpletest.*;

class Art {
  Art() {
    System.out.println("Art constructor");
  }
}

class Drawing extends Art {
  Drawing() {
    System.out.println("Drawing constructor");
  }
}

public class Cartoon extends Drawing {
  private static Test monitor = new Test();
  public Cartoon() {
```

```
    System.out.println("Cartoon constructor");
  }
  public static void main(String[] args) {
    Cartoon x = new Cartoon();
    monitor.expect(new String[] {
      "Art constructor",
      "Drawing constructor",
      "Cartoon constructor"
    });
  }
} ///:~
```

You can see that the construction happens from the base "outward," so the base class is initialized before the derived-class constructors can access it. Even if you don't create a constructor for **Cartoon( )**, the compiler will synthesize a default constructor for you that calls the base class constructor.

Constructors with arguments

The preceding example has default constructors; that is, they don't have any arguments. It's easy for the compiler to call these because there's no question about what arguments to pass. If your class doesn't have default arguments, or if you want to call a base-class constructor that has an argument, you must explicitly write the calls to the base-class constructor using the **super** keyword and the appropriate argument list:

```
//: c06:Chess.java
// Inheritance, constructors and arguments.
import com.bruceeckel.simpletest.*;

class Game {
  Game(int i) {
    System.out.println("Game constructor");
  }
}

class BoardGame extends Game {
  BoardGame(int i) {
    super(i);
    System.out.println("BoardGame constructor");
  }
}

public class Chess extends BoardGame {
```

```
  private static Test monitor = new Test();
  Chess() {
    super(11);
    System.out.println("Chess constructor");
  }
  public static void main(String[] args) {
    Chess x = new Chess();
    monitor.expect(new String[] {
      "Game constructor",
      "BoardGame constructor",
      "Chess constructor"
    });
  }
} ///:~
```

If you don't call the base-class constructor in **BoardGame( )**, the compiler will complain that it can't find a constructor of the form **Game( )**. In addition, the call to the base-class constructor *must* be the first thing you do in the derived-class constructor. (The compiler will remind you if you get it wrong.)

Catching base constructor exceptions

As just noted, the compiler forces you to place the base-class constructor call first in the body of the derived-class constructor. This means nothing else can appear before it. As you'll see in Chapter 9, this also prevents a derived-class constructor from catching any exceptions that come from a base class. This can be inconvenient at times.

Combining composition and inheritance

It is very common to use composition and inheritance together. The following example shows the creation of a more complex class, using both inheritance and composition, along with the necessary constructor initialization:

```
//: c06:PlaceSetting.java
// Combining composition & inheritance.
import com.bruceeckel.simpletest.*;

class Plate {
  Plate(int i) {
    System.out.println("Plate constructor");
```

```
  }
}

class DinnerPlate extends Plate {
  DinnerPlate(int i) {
    super(i);
    System.out.println("DinnerPlate constructor");
  }
}

class Utensil {
  Utensil(int i) {
    System.out.println("Utensil constructor");
  }
}

class Spoon extends Utensil {
  Spoon(int i) {
    super(i);
    System.out.println("Spoon constructor");
  }
}

class Fork extends Utensil {
  Fork(int i) {
    super(i);
    System.out.println("Fork constructor");
  }
}

class Knife extends Utensil {
  Knife(int i) {
    super(i);
    System.out.println("Knife constructor");
  }
}

// A cultural way of doing something:
class Custom {
  Custom(int i) {
    System.out.println("Custom constructor");
  }
}
```

```
public class PlaceSetting extends Custom {
  private static Test monitor = new Test();
  private Spoon sp;
  private Fork frk;
  private Knife kn;
  private DinnerPlate pl;
  public PlaceSetting(int i) {
    super(i + 1);
    sp = new Spoon(i + 2);
    frk = new Fork(i + 3);
    kn = new Knife(i + 4);
    pl = new DinnerPlate(i + 5);
    System.out.println("PlaceSetting constructor");
  }
  public static void main(String[] args) {
    PlaceSetting x = new PlaceSetting(9);
    monitor.expect(new String[] {
      "Custom constructor",
      "Utensil constructor",
      "Spoon constructor",
      "Utensil constructor",
      "Fork constructor",
      "Utensil constructor",
      "Knife constructor",
      "Plate constructor",
      "DinnerPlate constructor",
      "PlaceSetting constructor"
    });
  }
} ///:~
```

Although the compiler forces you to initialize the base classes, and requires that you do it right at the beginning of the constructor, it doesn't watch over you to make sure that you initialize the member objects, so you must remember to pay attention to that.

Guaranteeing proper cleanup

Java doesn't have the C++ concept of a *destructor*, a method that is automatically called when an object is destroyed. The reason is probably that in Java, the practice is simply to forget about objects rather than to destroy them, allowing the garbage collector to reclaim the memory as necessary.

Often this is fine, but there are times when your class might perform some activities during its lifetime that require cleanup. As mentioned in Chapter 4, you can't know when the garbage collector will be called, or if it will be called. So if you want something cleaned up for a class, you must explicitly write a special method to do it, and make sure that the client programmer knows that they must call this method. On top of this—as described in Chapter 9 ("Error Handling with Exceptions")—you must guard against an exception by putting such cleanup in a **finally** clause.

Consider an example of a computer-aided design system that draws pictures on the screen:

```
//: c06:CADSystem.java
// Ensuring proper cleanup.
package c06;
import com.bruceeckel.simpletest.*;
import java.util.*;

class Shape {
  Shape(int i) {
    System.out.println("Shape constructor");
  }
  void dispose() {
    System.out.println("Shape dispose");
  }
}

class Circle extends Shape {
  Circle(int i) {
    super(i);
    System.out.println("Drawing Circle");
  }
  void dispose() {
    System.out.println("Erasing Circle");
    super.dispose();
  }
}

class Triangle extends Shape {
  Triangle(int i) {
    super(i);
    System.out.println("Drawing Triangle");
  }
  void dispose() {
```

```
    System.out.println("Erasing Triangle");
    super.dispose();
  }
}

class Line extends Shape {
  private int start, end;
  Line(int start, int end) {
    super(start);
    this.start = start;
    this.end = end;
    System.out.println("Drawing Line: "+ start+ ", "+ end);
  }
  void dispose() {
    System.out.println("Erasing Line: "+ start+ ", "+ end);
    super.dispose();
  }
}

public class CADSystem extends Shape {
  private static Test monitor = new Test();
  private Circle c;
  private Triangle t;
  private Line[] lines = new Line[5];
  public CADSystem(int i) {
    super(i + 1);
    for(int j = 0; j < lines.length; j++)
      lines[j] = new Line(j, j*j);
    c = new Circle(1);
    t = new Triangle(1);
    System.out.println("Combined constructor");
  }
  public void dispose() {
    System.out.println("CADSystem.dispose()");
    // The order of cleanup is the reverse
    // of the order of initialization
    t.dispose();
    c.dispose();
    for(int i = lines.length - 1; i >= 0; i--)
      lines[i].dispose();
    super.dispose();
  }
  public static void main(String[] args) {
    CADSystem x = new CADSystem(47);
```

```
      try {
        // Code and exception handling...
      } finally {
        x.dispose();
      }
      monitor.expect(new String[] {
        "Shape constructor",
        "Shape constructor",
        "Drawing Line: 0, 0",
        "Shape constructor",
        "Drawing Line: 1, 1",
        "Shape constructor",
        "Drawing Line: 2, 4",
        "Shape constructor",
        "Drawing Line: 3, 9",
        "Shape constructor",
        "Drawing Line: 4, 16",
        "Shape constructor",
        "Drawing Circle",
        "Shape constructor",
        "Drawing Triangle",
        "Combined constructor",
        "CADSystem.dispose()",
        "Erasing Triangle",
        "Shape dispose",
        "Erasing Circle",
        "Shape dispose",
        "Erasing Line: 4, 16",
        "Shape dispose",
        "Erasing Line: 3, 9",
        "Shape dispose",
        "Erasing Line: 2, 4",
        "Shape dispose",
        "Erasing Line: 1, 1",
        "Shape dispose",
        "Erasing Line: 0, 0",
        "Shape dispose",
        "Shape dispose"
      });
    }
  } ///:~
```

Everything in this system is some kind of **Shape** (which is itself a kind of **Object**, since it's implicitly inherited from the root class). Each class overrides **Shape**'s **dispose( )** method in addition to calling the base-class version of that method using **super**. The specific **Shape** classes—**Circle**, **Triangle**, and **Line**—all have constructors that "draw," although any method called during the lifetime of the object could be responsible for doing something that needs cleanup. Each class has its own **dispose( )** method to restore nonmemory things back to the way they were before the object existed.

In **main( )**, you can see two keywords that are new, and won't officially be introduced until Chapter 9: **try** and **finally**. The **try** keyword indicates that the block that follows (delimited by curly braces) is a *guarded region*, which means that it is given special treatment. One of these special treatments is that the code in the **finally** clause following this guarded region is *always* executed, no matter how the **try** block exits. (With exception handling, it's possible to leave a **try** block in a number of nonordinary ways.) Here, the **finally** clause is saying "always call **dispose( )** for **x**, no matter what happens." These keywords will be explained thoroughly in Chapter 9.

Note that in your cleanup method, you must also pay attention to the calling order for the base-class and member-object cleanup methods in case one subobject depends on another. In general, you should follow the same form that is imposed by a C++ compiler on its destructors: first perform all of the cleanup work specific to your class, in the reverse order of creation. (In general, this requires that base-class elements still be viable.) Then call the base-class cleanup method, as demonstrated here.

There can be many cases in which the cleanup issue is not a problem; you just let the garbage collector do the work. But when you must do it explicitly, diligence and attention are required, because there's not much you can rely on when it comes to garbage collection. The garbage collector might never be called. If it is, it can reclaim objects in any order it wants. It's best to not rely on garbage collection for anything but memory reclamation. If you want cleanup to take place, make your own cleanup methods and don't rely on **finalize( )**.

Name hiding

If a Java base class has a method name that's overloaded several times, redefining that method name in the derived class will *not* hide any of the base-class versions (unlike C++). Thus overloading works regardless of whether the method was defined at this level or in a base class:

```java
//: c06:Hide.java
// Overloading a base-class method name in a derived class
// does not hide the base-class versions.
import com.bruceeckel.simpletest.*;

class Homer {
  char doh(char c) {
    System.out.println("doh(char)");
    return 'd';
  }
  float doh(float f) {
    System.out.println("doh(float)");
    return 1.0f;
  }
}

class Milhouse {}

class Bart extends Homer {
  void doh(Milhouse m) {
    System.out.println("doh(Milhouse)");
  }
}

public class Hide {
  private static Test monitor = new Test();
  public static void main(String[] args) {
    Bart b = new Bart();
    b.doh(1);
    b.doh('x');
    b.doh(1.0f);
    b.doh(new Milhouse());
    monitor.expect(new String[] {
      "doh(float)",
      "doh(char)",
      "doh(float)",
      "doh(Milhouse)"
    });
  }
} ///:~
```

You can see that all the overloaded methods of **Homer** are available in **Bart**, even though **Bart** introduces a new overloaded method (in C++ doing this would hide the base-class methods). As you'll see in the next chapter, it's far more common to override methods of the same name, using exactly the same signature and return type as in the base class. It can be confusing otherwise (which is why C++ disallows it—to prevent you from making what is probably a mistake).

Choosing composition vs. inheritance

Both composition and inheritance allow you to place subobjects inside your new class (composition explicitly does this—with inheritance it's implicit). You might wonder about the difference between the two, and when to choose one over the other.

Composition is generally used when you want the features of an existing class inside your new class, but not its interface. That is, you embed an object so that you can use it to implement functionality in your new class, but the user of your new class sees the interface you've defined for the new class rather than the interface from the embedded object. For this effect, you embed **private** objects of existing classes inside your new class.

Sometimes it makes sense to allow the class user to directly access the composition of your new class; that is, to make the member objects **public**. The member objects use implementation hiding themselves, so this is a safe thing to do. When the user knows you're assembling a bunch of parts, it makes the interface easier to understand. A **car** object is a good example:

```
//: c06:Car.java
// Composition with public objects.

class Engine {
  public void start() {}
  public void rev() {}
  public void stop() {}
}

class Wheel {
  public void inflate(int psi) {}
}

class Window {
  public void rollup() {}
```

```java
  public void rolldown() {}
}

class Door {
  public Window window = new Window();
  public void open() {}
  public void close() {}
}

public class Car {
  public Engine engine = new Engine();
  public Wheel[] wheel = new Wheel[4];
  public Door
    left = new Door(),
    right = new Door(); // 2-door
  public Car() {
    for(int i = 0; i < 4; i++)
      wheel[i] = new Wheel();
  }
  public static void main(String[] args) {
    Car car = new Car();
    car.left.window.rollup();
    car.wheel[0].inflate(72);
  }
} ///:~
```

Because in this case the composition of a car is part of the analysis of the problem (and not simply part of the underlying design), making the members **public** assists the client programmer's understanding of how to use the class and requires less code complexity for the creator of the class. However, keep in mind that this is a special case, and that in general you should make fields **private**.

When you inherit, you take an existing class and make a special version of it. In general, this means that you're taking a general-purpose class and specializing it for a particular need. With a little thought, you'll see that it would make no sense to compose a car using a vehicle object—a car doesn't contain a vehicle, it *is* a vehicle. The *is-a* relationship is expressed with inheritance, and the *has-a* relationship is expressed with composition.

protected

Now that you've been introduced to inheritance, the keyword **protected** finally has meaning. In an ideal world, the **private** keyword would be enough. In real projects, there are times when you want to make something hidden from the world at large and yet allow access for members of derived classes. The **protected** keyword is a nod to pragmatism. It says "This is **private** as far as the class user is concerned, but available to anyone who inherits from this class or anyone else in the same **package**." (In Java, **protected** also provides package access.)

The best approach is to leave the fields **private**; you should always preserve your right to change the underlying implementation. You can then allow controlled access to inheritors of your class through **protected** methods:

```
//: c06:Orc.java
// The protected keyword.
import com.bruceeckel.simpletest.*;
import java.util.*;

class Villain {
  private String name;
  protected void set(String nm) { name = nm; }
  public Villain(String name) { this.name = name; }
  public String toString() {
    return "I'm a Villain and my name is " + name;
  }
}

public class Orc extends Villain {
  private static Test monitor = new Test();
  private int orcNumber;
  public Orc(String name, int orcNumber) {
    super(name);
    this.orcNumber = orcNumber;
  }
  public void change(String name, int orcNumber) {
    set(name); // Available because it's protected
    this.orcNumber = orcNumber;
  }
  public String toString() {
    return "Orc " + orcNumber + ": " + super.toString();
  }
```

```java
  public static void main(String[] args) {
    Orc orc = new Orc("Limburger", 12);
    System.out.println(orc);
    orc.change("Bob", 19);
    System.out.println(orc);
    monitor.expect(new String[] {
      "Orc 12: I'm a Villain and my name is Limburger",
      "Orc 19: I'm a Villain and my name is Bob"
    });
  }
} ///:~
```

You can see that **change( )** has access to **set( )** because it's **protected**. Also note the way that **Orc**'s **toString( )** method is defined in terms of the base-class version of **toString( )**.

Incremental development

One of the advantages of inheritance is that it supports *incremental development*. You can introduce new code without causing bugs in existing code; in fact, you isolate new bugs inside the new code. By inheriting from an existing, functional class and adding fields and methods (and redefining existing methods), you leave the existing code—that someone else might still be using—untouched and unbugged. If a bug happens, you know that it's in your new code, which is much shorter and easier to read than if you had modified the body of existing code.

It's rather amazing how cleanly the classes are separated. You don't even need the source code for the methods in order to reuse the code. At most, you just import a package. (This is true for both inheritance and composition.)

It's important to realize that program development is an incremental process, just like human learning. You can do as much analysis as you want, but you still won't know all the answers when you set out on a project. You'll have much more success—and more immediate feedback—if you start out to "grow" your project as an organic, evolutionary creature, rather than constructing it all at once like a glass-box skyscraper.

Although inheritance for experimentation can be a useful technique, at some point after things stabilize you need to take a new look at your class hierarchy with an eye to collapsing it into a sensible structure. Remember that underneath it all, inheritance is meant to express a relationship that says:

"This new class is a *type of* that old class." Your program should not be concerned with pushing bits around, but instead with creating and manipulating objects of various types to express a model in the terms that come from the problem space.

Upcasting

The most important aspect of inheritance is not that it provides methods for the new class. It's the relationship expressed between the new class and the base class. This relationship can be summarized by saying, "The new class *is a type of* the existing class."

This description is not just a fanciful way of explaining inheritance—it's supported directly by the language. As an example, consider a base class called **Instrument** that represents musical instruments, and a derived class called **Wind**. Because inheritance means that all of the methods in the base class are also available in the derived class, any message you can send to the base class can also be sent to the derived class. If the **Instrument** class has a **play( )** method, so will **Wind** instruments. This means we can accurately say that a **Wind** object is also a type of **Instrument**. The following example shows how the compiler supports this notion:

```
//: c06:Wind.java
// Inheritance & upcasting.
import java.util.*;

class Instrument {
  public void play() {}
  static void tune(Instrument i) {
    // ...
    i.play();
  }
}

// Wind objects are instruments
// because they have the same interface:
public class Wind extends Instrument {
  public static void main(String[] args) {
    Wind flute = new Wind();
    Instrument.tune(flute); // Upcasting
  }
} ///:~
```

What's interesting in this example is the **tune( )** method, which accepts an **Instrument** reference. However, in **Wind.main( )** the **tune( )** method is called by giving it a **Wind** reference. Given that Java is particular about type checking, it seems strange that a method that accepts one type will readily accept another type, until you realize that a **Wind** object is also an **Instrument** object, and there's no method that **tune( )** could call for an **Instrument** that isn't also in **Wind**. Inside **tune( )**, the code works for **Instrument** and anything derived from **Instrument**, and the act of converting a **Wind** reference into an **Instrument** reference is called *upcasting*.

Why "upcasting"?

The reason for the term is historical, and based on the way class inheritance diagrams have traditionally been drawn: with the root at the top of the page, growing downward. (Of course, you can draw your diagrams any way you find helpful.) The inheritance diagram for **Wind.java** is then:

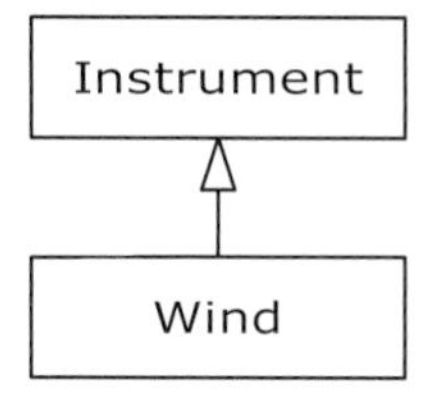

Casting from a derived type to a base type moves *up* on the inheritance diagram, so it's commonly referred to as *upcasting*. Upcasting is always safe because you're going from a more specific type to a more general type. That is, the derived class is a superset of the base class. It might contain more methods than the base class, but it must contain *at least* the methods in the base class. The only thing that can occur to the class interface during the upcast is that it can lose methods, not gain them. This is why the compiler allows upcasting without any explicit casts or other special notation.

You can also perform the reverse of upcasting, called *downcasting*, but this involves a dilemma that is the subject of Chapter 10.

Composition vs. inheritance revisited

In object-oriented programming, the most likely way that you'll create and use code is by simply packaging data and methods together into a class, and using objects of that class. You'll also use existing classes to build new classes with composition. Less frequently, you'll use inheritance. So although inheritance gets a lot of emphasis while learning OOP, it doesn't mean that you should use it everywhere you possibly can. On the contrary, you should use it sparingly, only when it's clear that inheritance is useful. One of the clearest ways to determine whether you should use composition or inheritance is to ask whether you'll ever need to upcast from your new class to the base class. If you must upcast, then inheritance is necessary, but if you don't need to upcast, then you should look closely at whether you need inheritance. The next chapter (on polymorphism) provides one of the most compelling reasons for upcasting, but if you remember to ask "Do I need to upcast?" you'll have a good tool for deciding between composition and inheritance.

The **final** keyword

Java's **final** keyword has slightly different meanings depending on the context, but in general it says "This cannot be changed." You might want to prevent changes for two reasons: design or efficiency. Because these two reasons are quite different, it's possible to misuse the **final** keyword.

The following sections discuss the three places where **final** can be used: for data, methods, and classes.

Final data

Many programming languages have a way to tell the compiler that a piece of data is "constant." A constant is useful for two reasons:

1. It can be a *compile-time constant* that won't ever change.

2. It can be a value initialized at run time that you don't want changed.

In the case of a compile-time constant, the compiler is allowed to "fold" the constant value into any calculations in which it's used; that is, the calculation can be performed at compile time, eliminating some run-time overhead. In Java, these sorts of constants must be primitives and are expressed with the **final** keyword. A value must be given at the time of definition of such a constant.

A field that is both **static** and **final** has only one piece of storage that cannot be changed.

When using **final** with object references rather than primitives, the meaning gets a bit confusing. With a primitive, **final** makes the *value* a constant, but with an object reference, **final** makes the *reference* a constant. Once the reference is initialized to an object, it can never be changed to point to another object. However, the object itself can be modified; Java does not provide a way to make any arbitrary object a constant. (You can, however, write your class so that objects have the effect of being constant.) This restriction includes arrays, which are also objects.

Here's an example that demonstrates **final** fields:

```
//: c06:FinalData.java
// The effect of final on fields.
import com.bruceeckel.simpletest.*;
import java.util.*;

class Value {
  int i; // Package access
  public Value(int i) { this.i = i; }
}

public class FinalData {
  private static Test monitor = new Test();
  private static Random rand = new Random();
  private String id;
  public FinalData(String id) { this.id = id; }
  // Can be compile-time constants:
  private final int VAL_ONE = 9;
  private static final int VAL_TWO = 99;
  // Typical public constant:
  public static final int VAL_THREE = 39;
  // Cannot be compile-time constants:
  private final int i4 = rand.nextInt(20);
  static final int i5 = rand.nextInt(20);
  private Value v1 = new Value(11);
  private final Value v2 = new Value(22);
  private static final Value v3 = new Value(33);
  // Arrays:
  private final int[] a = { 1, 2, 3, 4, 5, 6 };
  public String toString() {
    return id + ": " + "i4 = " + i4 + ", i5 = " + i5;
  }
  public static void main(String[] args) {
    FinalData fd1 = new FinalData("fd1");
```

```
    //! fd1.VAL_ONE++; // Error: can't change value
    fd1.v2.i++; // Object isn't constant!
    fd1.v1 = new Value(9); // OK -- not final
    for(int i = 0; i < fd1.a.length; i++)
      fd1.a[i]++; // Object isn't constant!
    //! fd1.v2 = new Value(0); // Error: Can't
    //! fd1.v3 = new Value(1); // change reference
    //! fd1.a = new int[3];
    System.out.println(fd1);
    System.out.println("Creating new FinalData");
    FinalData fd2 = new FinalData("fd2");
    System.out.println(fd1);
    System.out.println(fd2);
    monitor.expect(new String[] {
      "%% fd1: i4 = \\d+, i5 = \\d+",
      "Creating new FinalData",
      "%% fd1: i4 = \\d+, i5 = \\d+",
      "%% fd2: i4 = \\d+, i5 = \\d+"
    });
  }
} ///:~
```

Since **VAL_ONE** and **VAL_TWO** are **final** primitives with compile-time values, they can both be used as compile-time constants and are not different in any important way. **VAL_THREE** is the more typical way you'll see such constants defined: **public** so they're usable outside the package, **static** to emphasize that there's only one, and **final** to say that it's a constant. Note that **final static** primitives with constant initial values (that is, compile-time constants) are named with all capitals by convention, with words separated by underscores. (This is just like C constants, which is where the convention originated.) Also note that **i5** cannot be known at compile time, so it is not capitalized.

Just because something is **final** doesn't mean that its value is known at compile time. This is demonstrated by initializing **i4** and **i5** at run time using randomly generated numbers. This portion of the example also shows the difference between making a **final** value **static** or non-**static**. This difference shows up only when the values are initialized at run time, since the compile-time values are treated the same by the compiler. (And presumably optimized out of existence.) The difference is shown when you run the program. Note that the values of **i4** for **fd1** and **fd2** are unique, but the value for **i5** is not changed by creating the second **FinalData** object. That's because it's **static** and is initialized once upon loading and not each time a new object is created.

The variables **v1** through **v3** demonstrate the meaning of a **final** reference. As you can see in **main( )**, just because **v2** is **final** doesn't mean that you can't change its value. Because it's a reference, **final** means that you cannot rebind **v2** to a new object. You can also see that the same meaning holds true for an array, which is just another kind of reference. (There is no way that I know of to make the array references themselves **final**.) Making references **final** seems less useful than making primitives **final**.

Blank finals

Java allows the creation of *blank finals*, which are fields that are declared as **final** but are not given an initialization value. In all cases, the blank final *must* be initialized before it is used, and the compiler ensures this. However, blank finals provide much more flexibility in the use of the **final** keyword since, for example, a **final** field inside a class can now be different for each object, and yet it retains its immutable quality. Here's an example:

```
//: c06:BlankFinal.java
// "Blank" final fields.

class Poppet {
  private int i;
  Poppet(int ii) { i = ii; }
}

public class BlankFinal {
  private final int i = 0; // Initialized final
  private final int j; // Blank final
  private final Poppet p; // Blank final reference
  // Blank finals MUST be initialized in the constructor:
  public BlankFinal() {
    j = 1; // Initialize blank final
    p = new Poppet(1); // Initialize blank final reference
  }
  public BlankFinal(int x) {
    j = x; // Initialize blank final
    p = new Poppet(x); // Initialize blank final reference
  }
  public static void main(String[] args) {
    new BlankFinal();
    new BlankFinal(47);
```

```
  }
} ///:~
```

You're forced to perform assignments to **final**s either with an expression at the point of definition of the field or in every constructor. That way it's guaranteed that the **final** field is always initialized before use.

Final arguments

Java allows you to make arguments **final** by declaring them as such in the argument list. This means that inside the method you cannot change what the argument reference points to:

```
//: c06:FinalArguments.java
// Using "final" with method arguments.

class Gizmo {
  public void spin() {}
}

public class FinalArguments {
  void with(final Gizmo g) {
    //! g = new Gizmo(); // Illegal -- g is final
  }
  void without(Gizmo g) {
    g = new Gizmo(); // OK -- g not final
    g.spin();
  }
  // void f(final int i) { i++; } // Can't change
  // You can only read from a final primitive:
  int g(final int i) { return i + 1; }
  public static void main(String[] args) {
    FinalArguments bf = new FinalArguments();
    bf.without(null);
    bf.with(null);
  }
} ///:~
```

The methods **f( )** and **g( )** show what happens when primitive arguments are **final**: you can read the argument, but you can't change it. This feature seems only marginally useful, and is probably not something you'll use.

Final methods

There are two reasons for **final** methods. The first is to put a "lock" on the method to prevent any inheriting class from changing its meaning. This is done for design reasons when you want to make sure that a method's behavior is retained during inheritance and cannot be overridden.

The second reason for **final** methods is efficiency. If you make a method **final**, you are allowing the compiler to turn any calls to that method into *inline* calls. When the compiler sees a **final** method call, it can (at its discretion) skip the normal approach of inserting code to perform the method call mechanism (push arguments on the stack, hop over to the method code and execute it, hop back and clean off the stack arguments, and deal with the return value) and instead replace the method call with a copy of the actual code in the method body. This eliminates the overhead of the method call. Of course, if a method is big, then your code begins to bloat, and you probably won't see any performance gains from inlining, since any improvements will be dwarfed by the amount of time spent inside the method. It is implied that the Java compiler is able to detect these situations and choose wisely whether to inline a **final** method. However, it's best to let the compiler and JVM handle efficiency issues and make a method **final** only if you want to explicitly prevent overriding.[1]

final and private

Any **private** methods in a class are implicitly **final**. Because you can't access a **private** method, you can't override it. You can add the **final** specifier to a **private** method, but it doesn't give that method any extra meaning.

This issue can cause confusion, because if you try to override a **private** method (which is implicitly **final**), it seems to work, and the compiler doesn't give an error message:

```
//: c06:FinalOverridingIllusion.java
// It only looks like you can override
// a private or private final method.
import com.bruceeckel.simpletest.*;
```

---

[1] Don't fall prey to the urge to prematurely optimize. If you get your system working and it's too slow, it's doubtful that you can fix it with the **final** keyword. However, Chapter 15 has information about profiling, which *can* be helpful in speeding up your program.

```
class WithFinals {
  // Identical to "private" alone:
  private final void f() {
    System.out.println("WithFinals.f()");
  }
  // Also automatically "final":
  private void g() {
    System.out.println("WithFinals.g()");
  }
}

class OverridingPrivate extends WithFinals {
  private final void f() {
    System.out.println("OverridingPrivate.f()");
  }
  private void g() {
    System.out.println("OverridingPrivate.g()");
  }
}

class OverridingPrivate2 extends OverridingPrivate {
  public final void f() {
    System.out.println("OverridingPrivate2.f()");
  }
  public void g() {
    System.out.println("OverridingPrivate2.g()");
  }
}

public class FinalOverridingIllusion {
  private static Test monitor = new Test();
  public static void main(String[] args) {
    OverridingPrivate2 op2 = new OverridingPrivate2();
    op2.f();
    op2.g();
    // You can upcast:
    OverridingPrivate op = op2;
    // But you can't call the methods:
    //! op.f();
    //! op.g();
    // Same here:
    WithFinals wf = op2;
    //! wf.f();
```

```
    //! wf.g();
    monitor.expect(new String[] {
      "OverridingPrivate2.f()",
      "OverridingPrivate2.g()"
    });
  }
} ///:~
```

"Overriding" can only occur if something is part of the base-class interface. That is, you must be able to upcast an object to its base type and call the same method (the point of this will become clear in the next chapter). If a method is **private**, it isn't part of the base-class interface. It is just some code that's hidden away inside the class, and it just happens to have that name, but if you create a **public**, **protected**, or package-access method with the same name in the derived class, there's no connection to the method that might happen to have that name in the base class. You haven't overridden the method; you've just created a new method. Since a **private** method is unreachable and effectively invisible, it doesn't factor into anything except for the code organization of the class for which it was defined.

Final classes

When you say that an entire class is **final** (by preceding its definition with the **final** keyword), you state that you don't want to inherit from this class or allow anyone else to do so. In other words, for some reason the design of your class is such that there is never a need to make any changes, or for safety or security reasons you don't want subclassing.

```
//: c06:Jurassic.java
// Making an entire class final.

class SmallBrain {}

final class Dinosaur {
  int i = 7;
  int j = 1;
  SmallBrain x = new SmallBrain();
  void f() {}
}

//! class Further extends Dinosaur {}
// error: Cannot extend final class 'Dinosaur'
```

```
public class Jurassic {
  public static void main(String[] args) {
    Dinosaur n = new Dinosaur();
    n.f();
    n.i = 40;
    n.j++;
  }
} ///:~
```

Note that the fields of a **final** class can be **final** or not, as you choose. The same rules apply to **final** for fields regardless of whether the class is defined as **final**. However, because it prevents inheritance, all *methods* in a **final** class are implicitly **final**, since there's no way to override them. You can add the **final** specifier to a method in a **final** class, but it doesn't add any meaning.

Final caution

It can seem to be sensible to make a method **final** while you're designing a class. You might feel that no one could possibly want to override your methods. Sometimes this is true.

But be careful with your assumptions. In general, it's difficult to anticipate how a class can be reused, especially a general-purpose class. If you define a method as **final**, you might prevent the possibility of reusing your class through inheritance in some other programmer's project simply because you couldn't imagine it being used that way.

The standard Java library is a good example of this. In particular, the Java 1.0/1.1 **Vector** class was commonly used and might have been even more useful if, in the name of efficiency (which was almost certainly an illusion), all the methods hadn't been made **final**. It's easily conceivable that you might want to inherit and override with such a fundamentally useful class, but the designers somehow decided this wasn't appropriate. This is ironic for two reasons. First, **Stack** is inherited from **Vector**, which says that a **Stack** *is* a **Vector**, which isn't really true from a logical standpoint. Second, many of the most important methods of **Vector**, such as **addElement( )** and **elementAt( )**, are **synchronized**. As you will see in Chapter 11, this incurs a significant performance overhead that probably wipes out any gains provided by **final**. This lends credence to the theory that programmers are consistently bad at guessing where optimizations should occur. It's just too bad that such a clumsy design made it into the standard library, where everyone had to cope with it. (Fortunately, the Java 2 container library replaces **Vector** with **ArrayList**, which behaves much more civilly. Unfortunately, there's still new code being written that uses the old container library.)

It's also interesting to note that **Hashtable**, another important Java 1.0/1.1 standard library class, does *not* have any **final** methods. As mentioned elsewhere in this book, it's quite obvious that some classes were designed by completely different people than others. (You'll see that the method names in **Hashtable** are much briefer compared to those in **Vector**, another piece of evidence.) This is precisely the sort of thing that should *not* be obvious to consumers of a class library. When things are inconsistent, it just makes more work for the user—yet another paean to the value of design and code walkthroughs. (Note that the Java 2 container library replaces **Hashtable** with **HashMap**.)

Initialization and class loading

In more traditional languages, programs are loaded all at once as part of the startup process. This is followed by initialization, and then the program begins. The process of initialization in these languages must be carefully controlled so that the order of initialization of **static**s doesn't cause trouble. C++, for example, has problems if one **static** expects another **static** to be valid before the second one has been initialized.

Java doesn't have this problem because it takes a different approach to loading. Because everything in Java is an object, many activities become easier, and this is one of them. As you will learn more fully in the next chapter, the compiled code for each class exists in its own separate file. That file isn't loaded until the code is needed. In general, you can say that "class code is loaded at the point of first use." This is often not until the first object of that class is constructed, but loading also occurs when a **static** field or **static** method is accessed.

The point of first use is also where the **static** initialization takes place. All the **static** objects and the **static** code block will be initialized in textual order (that is, the order that you write them down in the class definition) at the point of loading. The **static**s, of course, are initialized only once.

Initialization with inheritance

It's helpful to look at the whole initialization process, including inheritance, to get a full picture of what happens. Consider the following example:

```
//: c06:Beetle.java
// The full process of initialization.
import com.bruceeckel.simpletest.*;

class Insect {
  protected static Test monitor = new Test();
  private int i = 9;
  protected int j;
  Insect() {
    System.out.println("i = " + i + ", j = " + j);
    j = 39;
  }
  private static int x1 =
    print("static Insect.x1 initialized");
  static int print(String s) {
    System.out.println(s);
    return 47;
  }
}

public class Beetle extends Insect {
  private int k = print("Beetle.k initialized");
  public Beetle() {
    System.out.println("k = " + k);
    System.out.println("j = " + j);
  }
  private static int x2 =
    print("static Beetle.x2 initialized");
  public static void main(String[] args) {
    System.out.println("Beetle constructor");
    Beetle b = new Beetle();
    monitor.expect(new String[] {
      "static Insect.x1 initialized",
      "static Beetle.x2 initialized",
      "Beetle constructor",
      "i = 9, j = 0",
      "Beetle.k initialized",
      "k = 47",
      "j = 39"
```

```
    });
  }
} ///:~
```

The first thing that happens when you run Java on **Beetle** is that you try to access **Beetle.main( )** (a **static** method), so the loader goes out and finds the compiled code for the **Beetle** class (this happens to be in a file called **Beetle.class**). In the process of loading it, the loader notices that it has a base class (that's what the **extends** keyword says), which it then loads. This will happen whether or not you're going to make an object of that base class. (Try commenting out the object creation to prove it to yourself.)

If the base class has a base class, that second base class would then be loaded, and so on. Next, the **static** initialization in the root base class (in this case, **Insect**) is performed, and then the next derived class, and so on. This is important because the derived-class static initialization might depend on the base class member being initialized properly.

At this point, the necessary classes have all been loaded so the object can be created. First, all the primitives in this object are set to their default values and the object references are set to **null**—this happens in one fell swoop by setting the memory in the object to binary zero. Then the base-class constructor will be called. In this case the call is automatic, but you can also specify the base-class constructor call (as the first operation in the **Beetle( )** constructor) by using **super**. The base class construction goes through the same process in the same order as the derived-class constructor. After the base-class constructor completes, the instance variables are initialized in textual order. Finally, the rest of the body of the constructor is executed.

Summary

Both inheritance and composition allow you to create a new type from existing types. Typically, however, composition reuses existing types as part of the underlying implementation of the new type, and inheritance reuses the interface. Since the derived class has the base-class interface, it can be *upcast* to the base, which is critical for polymorphism, as you'll see in the next chapter.

Despite the strong emphasis on inheritance in object-oriented programming, when you start a design you should generally prefer composition during the first cut and use inheritance only when it is clearly necessary. Composition tends to be more flexible. In addition, by using the added artifice of inheritance with your member type, you can change the exact type, and thus the behavior, of those member objects at run time. Therefore, you can change the behavior of the composed object at run time.

When designing a system, your goal is to find or create a set of classes in which each class has a specific use and is neither too big (encompassing so much functionality that it's unwieldy to reuse) nor annoyingly small (you can't use it by itself or without adding functionality).

Exercises

Solutions to selected exercises can be found in the electronic document *The Thinking in Java Annotated Solution Guide*, available for a small fee from *www.BruceEckel.com*.

1. Create two classes, **A** and **B**, with default constructors (empty argument lists) that announce themselves. Inherit a new class called **C** from **A**, and create a member of class **B** inside **C**. Do not create a constructor for **C**. Create an object of class **C** and observe the results.

2. Modify Exercise 1 so that **A** and **B** have constructors with arguments instead of default constructors. Write a constructor for **C** and perform all initialization within **C**'s constructor.

3. Create a simple class. Inside a second class, define a reference to an object of the first class. Use lazy initialization to instantiate this object.

4. Inherit a new class from class **Detergent**. Override **scrub( )** and add a new method called **sterilize( )**.

5. Take the file **Cartoon.java** and comment out the constructor for the **Cartoon** class. Explain what happens.

6. Take the file **Chess.java** and comment out the constructor for the **Chess** class. Explain what happens.

7. Prove that default constructors are created for you by the compiler.

8. Prove that the base-class constructors are (a) always called and (b) called before derived-class constructors.

9. Create a base class with only a nondefault constructor, and a derived class with both a default (no-arg) and nondefault constructor. In the derived-class constructors, call the base-class constructor.

10. Create a class called **Root** that contains an instance of each of the classes (that you also create) named **Component1**, **Component2**, and **Component3**. Derive a class **Stem** from **Root** that also contains an instance of each "component." All classes should have default constructors that print a message about that class.

11. Modify Exercise 10 so that each class only has nondefault constructors.

12. Add a proper hierarchy of **dispose( )** methods to all the classes in Exercise 11.

13. Create a class with a method that is overloaded three times. Inherit a new class, add a new overloading of the method, and show that all four methods are available in the derived class.

14. In **Car.java** add a **service( )** method to **Engine** and call this method in **main( )**.

15. Create a class inside a package. Your class should contain a **protected** method. Outside of the package, try to call the **protected** method and explain the results. Now inherit from your class and call the **protected** method from inside a method of your derived class.

16. Create a class called **Amphibian**. From this, inherit a class called **Frog**. Put appropriate methods in the base class. In **main( )**, create a **Frog** and upcast it to **Amphibian** and demonstrate that all the methods still work.

17. Modify Exercise 16 so that **Frog** overrides the method definitions from the base class (provides new definitions using the same method signatures). Note what happens in **main( )**.

18. Create a class with a **static final** field and a **final** field and demonstrate the difference between the two.

19. Create a class with a blank **final** reference to an object. Perform the initialization of the blank **final** inside all constructors. Demonstrate

the guarantee that the **final** must be initialized before use, and that it cannot be changed once initialized.

20. Create a class with a **final** method. Inherit from that class and attempt to override that method.

21. Create a **final** class and attempt to inherit from it.

22. Prove that class loading takes place only once. Prove that loading may be caused by either the creation of the first instance of that class or by the access of a **static** member.

23. In **Beetle.java**, inherit a specific type of beetle from class **Beetle**, following the same format as the existing classes. Trace and explain the output.

7: Polymorphism

Polymorphism is the third essential feature of an object-oriented programming language, after data abstraction and inheritance.

It provides another dimension of separation of interface from implementation, to decouple *what* from *how*. Polymorphism allows improved code organization and readability as well as the creation of *extensible* programs that can be "grown" not only during the original creation of the project, but also when new features are desired.

Encapsulation creates new data types by combining characteristics and behaviors. Implementation hiding separates the interface from the implementation by making the details **private**. This sort of mechanical organization makes ready sense to someone with a procedural programming background. But polymorphism deals with decoupling in terms of *types*. In the last chapter, you saw how inheritance allows the treatment of an object as its own type *or* its base type. This ability is critical because it allows many types (derived from the same base type) to be treated as if they were one type, and a single piece of code to work on all those different types equally. The polymorphic method call allows one type to express its distinction from another, similar type, as long as they're both derived from the same base type. This distinction is expressed through differences in behavior of the methods that you can call through the base class.

In this chapter, you'll learn about polymorphism (also called *dynamic binding* or *late binding* or *run-time binding*) starting from the basics, with simple examples that strip away everything but the polymorphic behavior of the program.

Upcasting revisited

In Chapter 6 you saw how an object can be used as its own type or as an object of its base type. Taking an object reference and treating it as a reference to its base type is called *upcasting* because of the way inheritance trees are drawn with the base class at the top.

You also saw a problem arise, which is embodied in the following example about musical instruments. Since several examples play **Notes**, we should create the **Note** class separately, in a package:

```
//: c07:music:Note.java
// Notes to play on musical instruments.
package c07.music;
import com.bruceeckel.simpletest.*;

public class Note {
  private String noteName;
  private Note(String noteName) {
    this.noteName = noteName;
  }
  public String toString() { return noteName; }
  public static final Note
    MIDDLE_C = new Note("Middle C"),
    C_SHARP  = new Note("C Sharp"),
    B_FLAT   = new Note("B Flat");
    // Etc.
} ///:~
```

This is an "enumeration" class, which has a fixed number of constant objects to choose from. You can't make additional objects because the constructor is private.

In the following example, **Wind** is a type of **Instrument**, therefore **Wind** is inherited from **Instrument**:

```
//: c07:music:Music.java
// Inheritance & upcasting.
package c07.music;
import com.bruceeckel.simpletest.*;

public class Music {
  private static Test monitor = new Test();
  public static void tune(Instrument i) {
    // ...
    i.play(Note.MIDDLE_C);
  }
  public static void main(String[] args) {
    Wind flute = new Wind();
    tune(flute); // Upcasting
    monitor.expect(new String[] {
      "Wind.play() Middle C"
```

```
    });
  }
} ///:~
```

```
//: c07:music:Wind.java
package c07.music;

// Wind objects are instruments
// because they have the same interface:
public class Wind extends Instrument {
  // Redefine interface method:
  public void play(Note n) {
    System.out.println("Wind.play() " + n);
  }
} ///:~
```

```
//: c07:music:Music.java
// Inheritance & upcasting.
package c07.music;
import com.bruceeckel.simpletest.*;

public class Music {
  private static Test monitor = new Test();
  public static void tune(Instrument i) {
    // ...
    i.play(Note.MIDDLE_C);
  }
  public static void main(String[] args) {
    Wind flute = new Wind();
    tune(flute); // Upcasting
    monitor.expect(new String[] {
      "Wind.play() Middle C"
    });
  }
} ///:~
```

The method **Music.tune( )** accepts an **Instrument** reference, but also anything derived from **Instrument**. In **main( )**, you can see this happening as a **Wind** reference is passed to **tune( )**, with no cast necessary. This is acceptable—the interface in **Instrument** must exist in **Wind**, because **Wind** is inherited from **Instrument**. Upcasting from **Wind** to **Instrument** may "narrow" that interface, but it cannot make it anything less than the full interface to **Instrument**.

Forgetting the object type

Music.java might seem strange to you. Why should anyone intentionally *forget* the type of an object? This is what happens when you upcast, and it seems like it could be much more straightforward if **tune( )** simply takes a **Wind** reference as its argument. This brings up an essential point: If you did that, you'd need to write a new **tune( )** for every type of **Instrument** in your system. Suppose we follow this reasoning and add **Stringed** and **Brass** instruments:

```
//: c07:music:Music2.java
// Overloading instead of upcasting.
package c07.music;
import com.bruceeckel.simpletest.*;

class Stringed extends Instrument {
  public void play(Note n) {
    System.out.println("Stringed.play() " + n);
  }
}

class Brass extends Instrument {
  public void play(Note n) {
    System.out.println("Brass.play() " + n);
  }
}

public class Music2 {
  private static Test monitor = new Test();
  public static void tune(Wind i) {
    i.play(Note.MIDDLE_C);
  }
  public static void tune(Stringed i) {
    i.play(Note.MIDDLE_C);
  }
  public static void tune(Brass i) {
    i.play(Note.MIDDLE_C);
  }
  public static void main(String[] args) {
    Wind flute = new Wind();
    Stringed violin = new Stringed();
    Brass frenchHorn = new Brass();
    tune(flute); // No upcasting
    tune(violin);
```

```
    tune(frenchHorn);
    monitor.expect(new String[] {
      "Wind.play() Middle C",
      "Stringed.play() Middle C",
      "Brass.play() Middle C"
    });
  }
} ///:~
```

This works, but there's a major drawback: you must write type-specific methods for each new **Instrument** class you add. This means more programming in the first place, but it also means that if you want to add a new method like **tune( )** or a new type of **Instrument**, you've got a lot of work to do. Add the fact that the compiler won't give you any error messages if you forget to overload one of your methods and the whole process of working with types becomes unmanageable.

Wouldn't it be much nicer if you could just write a single method that takes the base class as its argument, and not any of the specific derived classes? That is, wouldn't it be nice if you could forget that there are derived classes, and write your code to talk only to the base class?

That's exactly what polymorphism allows you to do. However, most programmers who come from a procedural programming background have a bit of trouble with the way polymorphism works.

The twist

The difficulty with **Music.java** can be seen by running the program. The output is **Wind.play( )**. This is clearly the desired output, but it doesn't seem to make sense that it would work that way. Look at the **tune( )** method:

```
public static void tune(Instrument i) {
  // ...
  i.play(Note.MIDDLE_C);
}
```

It receives an **Instrument** reference. So how can the compiler possibly know that this **Instrument** reference points to a **Wind** in this case and not a **Brass** or **Stringed**? The compiler can't. To get a deeper understanding of the issue, it's helpful to examine the subject of *binding*.

Method-call binding

Connecting a method call to a method body is called *binding*. When binding is performed before the program is run (by the compiler and linker, if there is one), it's called *early binding*. You might not have heard the term before because it has never been an option with procedural languages. C compilers have only one kind of method call, and that's early binding.

The confusing part of the preceding program revolves around early binding, because the compiler cannot know the correct method to call when it has only an **Instrument** reference.

The solution is called *late binding*, which means that the binding occurs at run time, based on the type of object. Late binding is also called *dynamic binding* or *run-time binding*. When a language implements late binding, there must be some mechanism to determine the type of the object at run time and to call the appropriate method. That is, the compiler still doesn't know the object type, but the method-call mechanism finds out and calls the correct method body. The late-binding mechanism varies from language to language, but you can imagine that some sort of type information must be installed in the objects.

All method binding in Java uses late binding unless the method is **static** or **final** (**private** methods are implicitly **final**). This means that ordinarily you don't need to make any decisions about whether late binding will occur—it happens automatically.

Why would you declare a method **final**? As noted in the last chapter, it prevents anyone from overriding that method. Perhaps more important, it effectively "turns off" dynamic binding, or rather it tells the compiler that dynamic binding isn't necessary. This allows the compiler to generate slightly more efficient code for **final** method calls. However, in most cases it won't make any overall performance difference in your program, so it's best to only use **final** as a design decision, and not as an attempt to improve performance.

Producing the right behavior

Once you know that all method binding in Java happens polymorphically via late binding, you can write your code to talk to the base class and know that all the derived-class cases will work correctly using the same code. Or to put it another way, you "send a message to an object and let the object figure out the right thing to do."

The classic example in OOP is the "shape" example. This is commonly used because it is easy to visualize, but unfortunately it can confuse novice programmers into thinking that OOP is just for graphics programming, which is of course not the case.

The shape example has a base class called **Shape** and various derived types: **Circle**, **Square**, **Triangle**, etc. The reason the example works so well is that it's easy to say "a circle is a type of shape" and be understood. The inheritance diagram shows the relationships:

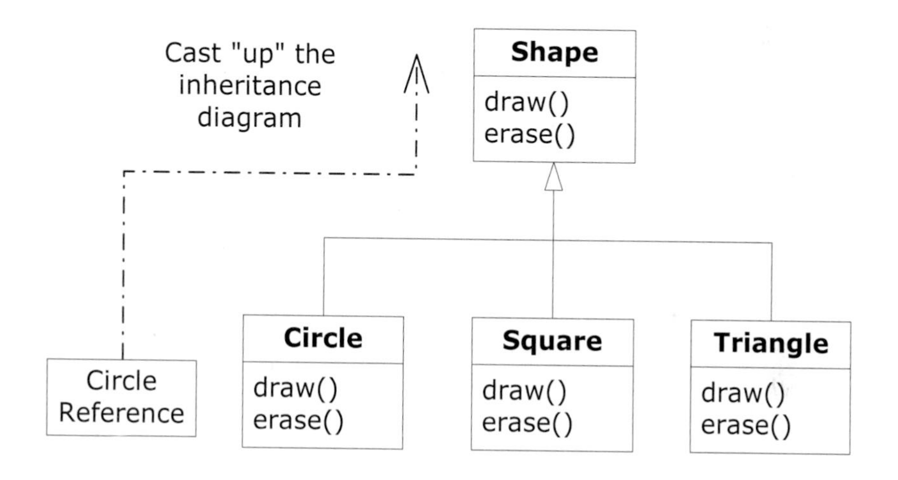

The upcast could occur in a statement as simple as:

```
Shape s = new Circle();
```

Here, a **Circle** object is created, and the resulting reference is immediately assigned to a **Shape**, which would seem to be an error (assigning one type to another); and yet it's fine because a **Circle** *is* a **Shape** by inheritance. So the compiler agrees with the statement and doesn't issue an error message.

Suppose you call one of the base-class methods (that have been overridden in the derived classes):

```
s.draw();
```

Again, you might expect that **Shape**'s **draw( )** is called because this is, after all, a **Shape** reference—so how could the compiler know to do anything else?

And yet the proper **Circle.draw( )** is called because of late binding (polymorphism).

The following example puts it a slightly different way:

```
//: c07:Shapes.java
// Polymorphism in Java.
import com.bruceeckel.simpletest.*;
import java.util.*;

class Shape {
  void draw() {}
  void erase() {}
}

class Circle extends Shape {
  void draw() {
    System.out.println("Circle.draw()");
  }
  void erase() {
    System.out.println("Circle.erase()");
  }
}

class Square extends Shape {
  void draw() {
    System.out.println("Square.draw()");
  }
  void erase() {
    System.out.println("Square.erase()");
  }
}

class Triangle extends Shape {
  void draw() {
    System.out.println("Triangle.draw()");
  }
  void erase() {
    System.out.println("Triangle.erase()");
  }
}

// A "factory" that randomly creates shapes:
class RandomShapeGenerator {
  private Random rand = new Random();
```

```java
  public Shape next() {
    switch(rand.nextInt(3)) {
      default:
      case 0: return new Circle();
      case 1: return new Square();
      case 2: return new Triangle();
    }
  }
}

public class Shapes {
  private static Test monitor = new Test();
  private static RandomShapeGenerator gen =
    new RandomShapeGenerator();
  public static void main(String[] args) {
    Shape[] s = new Shape[9];
    // Fill up the array with shapes:
    for(int i = 0; i < s.length; i++)
      s[i] = gen.next();
    // Make polymorphic method calls:
    for(int i = 0; i < s.length; i++)
      s[i].draw();
    monitor.expect(new Object[] {
      new TestExpression("%% (Circle|Square|Triangle)"
        + "\\.draw\\(\\)", s.length)
    });
  }
} ///:~
```

The base class **Shape** establishes the common interface to anything inherited from **Shape**—that is, all shapes can be drawn and erased. The derived classes override these definitions to provide unique behavior for each specific type of shape.

RandomShapeGenerator is a kind of "factory" that produces a reference to a randomly-selected **Shape** object each time you call its **next( )** method. Note that the upcasting happens in the **return** statements, each of which takes a reference to a **Circle**, **Square**, or **Triangle** and sends it out of **next( )** as the return type, **Shape**. So whenever you call **next( )**, you never get a chance to see what specific type it is, since you always get back a plain **Shape** reference.

main( ) contains an array of **Shape** references filled through calls to **RandomShapeGenerator.next( )**. At this point you know you have

Shapes, but you don't know anything more specific than that (and neither does the compiler). However, when you step through this array and call **draw( )** for each one, the correct type-specific behavior magically occurs, as you can see from the output when you run the program.

The point of choosing the shapes randomly is to drive home the understanding that the compiler can have no special knowledge that allows it to make the correct calls at compile time. All the calls to **draw( )** must be made through dynamic binding.

Extensibility

Now let's return to the musical instrument example. Because of polymorphism, you can add as many new types as you want to the system without changing the **tune( )** method. In a well-designed OOP program, most or all of your methods will follow the model of **tune( )** and communicate only with the base-class interface. Such a program is *extensible* because you can add new functionality by inheriting new data types from the common base class. The methods that manipulate the base-class interface will not need to be changed at all to accommodate the new classes.

Consider what happens if you take the instrument example and add more methods in the base class and a number of new classes. Here's the diagram:

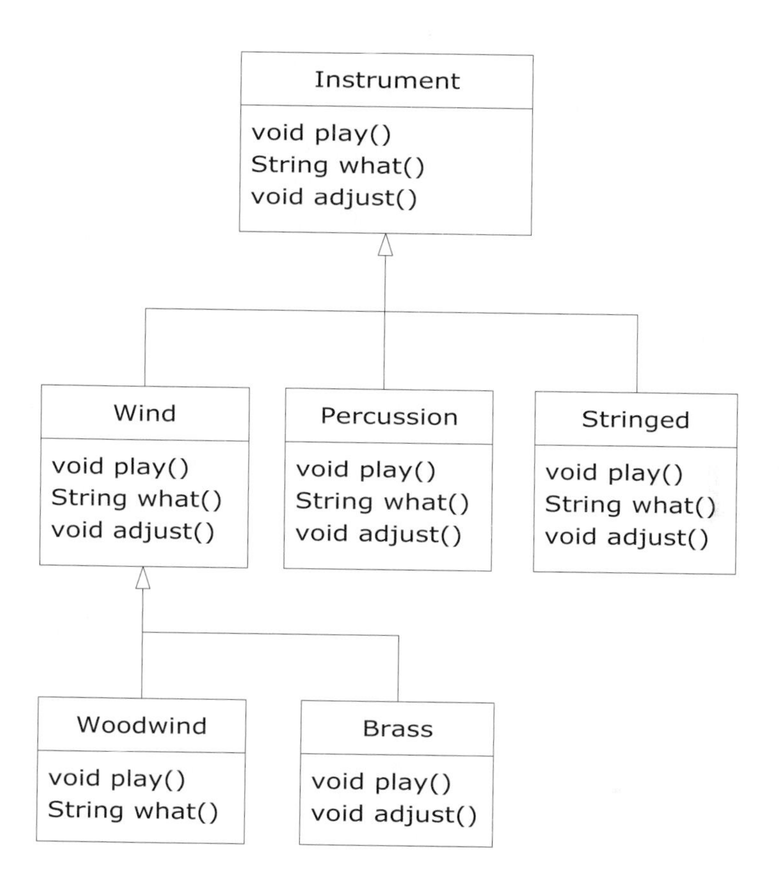

All these new classes work correctly with the old, unchanged **tune( )** method. Even if **tune( )** is in a separate file and new methods are added to the interface of **Instrument**, **tune( )** will still work correctly, even without recompiling it. Here is the implementation of the diagram:

```
//: c07:music3:Music3.java
// An extensible program.
package c07.music3;
import com.bruceeckel.simpletest.*;
import c07.music.Note;

class Instrument {
  void play(Note n) {
    System.out.println("Instrument.play() " + n);
  }
  String what() { return "Instrument"; }
  void adjust() {}
}
```

```
class Wind extends Instrument {
  void play(Note n) {
    System.out.println("Wind.play() " + n);
  }
  String what() { return "Wind"; }
  void adjust() {}
}

class Percussion extends Instrument {
  void play(Note n) {
    System.out.println("Percussion.play() " + n);
  }
  String what() { return "Percussion"; }
  void adjust() {}
}

class Stringed extends Instrument {
  void play(Note n) {
    System.out.println("Stringed.play() " + n);
  }
  String what() { return "Stringed"; }
  void adjust() {}
}

class Brass extends Wind {
  void play(Note n) {
    System.out.println("Brass.play() " + n);
  }
  void adjust() {
    System.out.println("Brass.adjust()");
  }
}

class Woodwind extends Wind {
  void play(Note n) {
    System.out.println("Woodwind.play() " + n);
  }
  String what() { return "Woodwind"; }
}

public class Music3 {
  private static Test monitor = new Test();
  // Doesn't care about type, so new types
```

```
  // added to the system still work right:
  public static void tune(Instrument i) {
    // ...
    i.play(Note.MIDDLE_C);
  }
  public static void tuneAll(Instrument[] e) {
    for(int i = 0; i < e.length; i++)
      tune(e[i]);
  }
  public static void main(String[] args) {
    // Upcasting during addition to the array:
    Instrument[] orchestra = {
      new Wind(),
      new Percussion(),
      new Stringed(),
      new Brass(),
      new Woodwind()
    };
    tuneAll(orchestra);
    monitor.expect(new String[] {
      "Wind.play() Middle C",
      "Percussion.play() Middle C",
      "Stringed.play() Middle C",
      "Brass.play() Middle C",
      "Woodwind.play() Middle C"
    });
  }
} ///:~
```

The new methods are **what( )**, which returns a **String** reference with a description of the class, and **adjust( )**, which provides some way to adjust each instrument.

In **main( )**, when you place something inside the **orchestra** array, you automatically upcast to **Instrument**.

You can see that the **tune( )** method is blissfully ignorant of all the code changes that have happened around it, and yet it works correctly. This is exactly what polymorphism is supposed to provide. Changes in your code don't cause damage to parts of the program that should not be affected. Put another way, polymorphism is an important technique for the programmer to "separate the things that change from the things that stay the same."

Pitfall: "overriding" private methods

Here's something you might innocently try to do:

```
//: c07:PrivateOverride.java
// Abstract classes and methods.
import com.bruceeckel.simpletest.*;

public class PrivateOverride {
  private static Test monitor = new Test();
  private void f() {
    System.out.println("private f()");
  }
  public static void main(String[] args) {
    PrivateOverride po = new Derived();
    po.f();
    monitor.expect(new String[] {
      "private f()"
    });
  }
}

class Derived extends PrivateOverride {
  public void f() {
    System.out.println("public f()");
  }
} ///:~
```

You might reasonably expect the output to be "**public f( )**", but a **private** method is automatically final, and is also hidden from the derived class. So **Derived**'s **f( )** in this case is a brand new method; it's not even overloaded, since the base-class version of **f( )** isn't visible in **Derived**.

The result of this is that only non-**private** methods may be overridden, but you should watch out for the appearance of overriding **private** methods, which generates no compiler warnings, but doesn't do what you might expect. To be clear, you should use a different name from a **private** base-class method in your derived class.

Abstract classes and methods

In all the instrument examples, the methods in the base class **Instrument** were always "dummy" methods. If these methods are ever called, you've done something wrong. That's because the intent of **Instrument** is to create a *common interface* for all the classes derived from it.

The only reason to establish this common interface is so it can be expressed differently for each different subtype. It establishes a basic form, so you can say what's in common with all the derived classes. Another way of saying this is to call **Instrument** an *abstract base class* (or simply an *abstract class*). You create an abstract class when you want to manipulate a set of classes through this common interface. All derived-class methods that match the signature of the base-class declaration will be called using the dynamic binding mechanism. (However, as seen in the last section, if the method's name is the same as the base class but the arguments are different, you've got overloading, which probably isn't what you want.)

If you have an abstract class like **Instrument**, objects of that class almost always have no meaning. That is, **Instrument** is meant to express only the interface, and not a particular implementation, so creating an **Instrument** object makes no sense, and you'll probably want to prevent the user from doing it. This can be accomplished by making all the methods in **Instrument** print error messages, but that delays the information until run time and requires reliable exhaustive testing on the user's part. It's better to catch problems at compile time.

Java provides a mechanism for doing this called the *abstract method*.[1] This is a method that is incomplete; it has only a declaration and no method body. Here is the syntax for an abstract method declaration:

```
abstract void f();
```

A class containing abstract methods is called an *abstract class*. If a class contains one or more abstract methods, the class itself must be qualified as **abstract**. (Otherwise, the compiler gives you an error message.)

---

[1] For C++ programmers, this is the analogue of C++'s *pure virtual function*.

If an abstract class is incomplete, what is the compiler supposed to do when someone tries to make an object of that class? It cannot safely create an object of an abstract class, so you get an error message from the compiler. This way, the compiler ensures the purity of the abstract class, and you don't need to worry about misusing it.

If you inherit from an abstract class and you want to make objects of the new type, you must provide method definitions for all the abstract methods in the base class. If you don't (and you may choose not to), then the derived class is also abstract, and the compiler will force you to qualify *that* class with the **abstract** keyword.

It's possible to create a class as **abstract** without including any **abstract** methods. This is useful when you've got a class in which it doesn't make sense to have any **abstract** methods, and yet you want to prevent any instances of that class.

The **Instrument** class can easily be turned into an **abstract** class. Only some of the methods will be **abstract**, since making a class abstract doesn't force you to make all the methods **abstract**. Here's what it looks like:

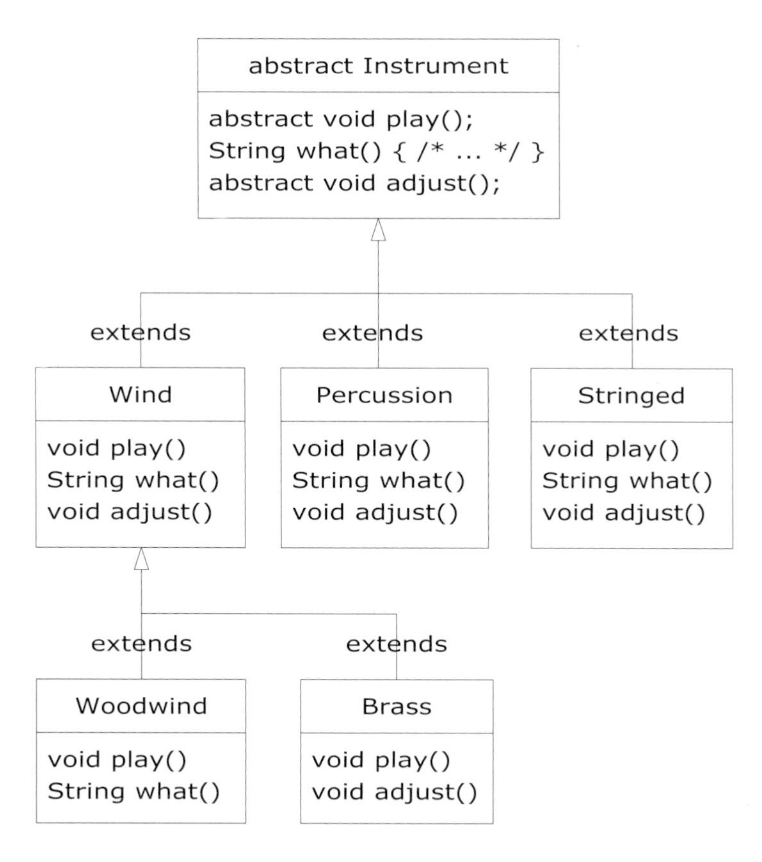

Here's the orchestra example modified to use **abstract** classes and methods:

```
//: c07:music4:Music4.java
// Abstract classes and methods.
package c07.music4;
import com.bruceeckel.simpletest.*;
import java.util.*;
import c07.music.Note;

abstract class Instrument {
  private int i; // Storage allocated for each
  public abstract void play(Note n);
  public String what() {
    return "Instrument";
  }
  public abstract void adjust();
}

class Wind extends Instrument {
```

```
  public void play(Note n) {
    System.out.println("Wind.play() " + n);
  }
  public String what() { return "Wind"; }
  public void adjust() {}
}

class Percussion extends Instrument {
  public void play(Note n) {
    System.out.println("Percussion.play() " + n);
  }
  public String what() { return "Percussion"; }
  public void adjust() {}
}

class Stringed extends Instrument {
  public void play(Note n) {
    System.out.println("Stringed.play() " + n);
  }
  public String what() { return "Stringed"; }
  public void adjust() {}
}

class Brass extends Wind {
  public void play(Note n) {
    System.out.println("Brass.play() " + n);
  }
  public void adjust() {
    System.out.println("Brass.adjust()");
  }
}

class Woodwind extends Wind {
  public void play(Note n) {
    System.out.println("Woodwind.play() " + n);
  }
  public String what() { return "Woodwind"; }
}

public class Music4 {
  private static Test monitor = new Test();
  // Doesn't care about type, so new types
  // added to the system still work right:
  static void tune(Instrument i) {
```

```
    // ...
    i.play(Note.MIDDLE_C);
  }
  static void tuneAll(Instrument[] e) {
    for(int i = 0; i < e.length; i++)
      tune(e[i]);
  }
  public static void main(String[] args) {
    // Upcasting during addition to the array:
    Instrument[] orchestra = {
      new Wind(),
      new Percussion(),
      new Stringed(),
      new Brass(),
      new Woodwind()
    };
    tuneAll(orchestra);
    monitor.expect(new String[] {
      "Wind.play() Middle C",
      "Percussion.play() Middle C",
      "Stringed.play() Middle C",
      "Brass.play() Middle C",
      "Woodwind.play() Middle C"
    });
  }
} ///:~
```

You can see that there's really no change except in the base class.

It's helpful to create **abstract** classes and methods because they make the abstractness of a class explicit, and tell both the user and the compiler how it was intended to be used.

Constructors and polymorphism

As usual, constructors are different from other kinds of methods. This is also true when polymorphism is involved. Even though constructors are not polymorphic (they're actually **static** methods, but the **static** declaration is implicit), it's important to understand the way constructors work in complex hierarchies and with polymorphism. This understanding will help you avoid unpleasant entanglements.

Order of constructor calls

The order of constructor calls was briefly discussed in Chapter 4 and again in Chapter 6, but that was before polymorphism was introduced.

A constructor for the base class is always called during the construction process for a derived class, chaining up the inheritance hierarchy so that a constructor for every base class is called. This makes sense because the constructor has a special job: to see that the object is built properly. A derived class has access to its own members only, and not to those of the base class (whose members are typically **private**). Only the base-class constructor has the proper knowledge and access to initialize its own elements. Therefore, it's essential that all constructors get called, otherwise the entire object wouldn't be constructed. That's why the compiler enforces a constructor call for every portion of a derived class. It will silently call the default constructor if you don't explicitly call a base-class constructor in the derived-class constructor body. If there is no default constructor, the compiler will complain. (In the case where a class has no constructors, the compiler will automatically synthesize a default constructor.)

Let's take a look at an example that shows the effects of composition, inheritance, and polymorphism on the order of construction:

```
//: c07:Sandwich.java
// Order of constructor calls.
package c07;
import com.bruceeckel.simpletest.*;

class Meal {
  Meal() { System.out.println("Meal()"); }
}

class Bread {
  Bread() { System.out.println("Bread()"); }
}

class Cheese {
  Cheese() { System.out.println("Cheese()"); }
}

class Lettuce {
  Lettuce() { System.out.println("Lettuce()"); }
}
```

```
class Lunch extends Meal {
  Lunch() { System.out.println("Lunch()"); }
}

class PortableLunch extends Lunch {
  PortableLunch() { System.out.println("PortableLunch()");}
}

public class Sandwich extends PortableLunch {
  private static Test monitor = new Test();
  private Bread b = new Bread();
  private Cheese c = new Cheese();
  private Lettuce l = new Lettuce();
  public Sandwich() {
    System.out.println("Sandwich()");
  }
  public static void main(String[] args) {
    new Sandwich();
    monitor.expect(new String[] {
      "Meal()",
      "Lunch()",
      "PortableLunch()",
      "Bread()",
      "Cheese()",
      "Lettuce()",
      "Sandwich()"
    });
  }
} ///:~
```

This example creates a complex class out of other classes, and each class has a constructor that announces itself. The important class is **Sandwich**, which reflects three levels of inheritance (four, if you count the implicit inheritance from **Object**) and three member objects. You can see the output when a **Sandwich** object is created in **main( )**. This means that the order of constructor calls for a complex object is as follows:

1. The base-class constructor is called. This step is repeated recursively such that the root of the hierarchy is constructed first, followed by the next-derived class, etc., until the most-derived class is reached.

2. Member initializers are called in the order of declaration.

3. The body of the derived-class constructor is called.

The order of the constructor calls is important. When you inherit, you know all about the base class and can access any **public** and **protected** members of the base class. This means that you must be able to assume that all the members of the base class are valid when you're in the derived class. In a normal method, construction has already taken place, so all the members of all parts of the object have been built. Inside the constructor, however, you must be able to assume that all members that you use have been built. The only way to guarantee this is for the base-class constructor to be called first. Then when you're in the derived-class constructor, all the members you can access in the base class have been initialized. Knowing that all members are valid inside the constructor is also the reason that, whenever possible, you should initialize all member objects (that is, objects placed in the class using composition) at their point of definition in the class (e.g., **b**, **c,** and **l** in the preceding example). If you follow this practice, you will help ensure that all base class members *and* member objects of the current object have been initialized. Unfortunately, this doesn't handle every case, as you will see in the next section.

Inheritance and cleanup

When using composition and inheritance to create a new class, most of the time you won't have to worry about cleaning up; subobjects can usually be left to the garbage collector. If you do have cleanup issues, you must be diligent and create a **dispose( )** method (the name I have chosen to use here; you may come up with something better) for your new class. And with inheritance, you must override **dispose( )** in the derived class if you have any special cleanup that must happen as part of garbage collection. When you override **dispose( )** in an inherited class, it's important to remember to call the base-class version of **dispose( )**, since otherwise the base-class cleanup will not happen. The following example demonstrates this:

```
//: c07:Frog.java
// Cleanup and inheritance.
import com.bruceeckel.simpletest.*;

class Characteristic {
  private String s;
  Characteristic(String s) {
    this.s = s;
    System.out.println("Creating Characteristic " + s);
```

```
  }
  protected void dispose() {
    System.out.println("finalizing Characteristic " + s);
  }
}

class Description {
  private String s;
  Description(String s) {
    this.s = s;
    System.out.println("Creating Description " + s);
  }
  protected void dispose() {
    System.out.println("finalizing Description " + s);
  }
}

class LivingCreature {
  private Characteristic p = new Characteristic("is
alive");
  private Description t =
    new Description("Basic Living Creature");
  LivingCreature() {
    System.out.println("LivingCreature()");
  }
  protected void dispose() {
    System.out.println("LivingCreature dispose");
    t.dispose();
    p.dispose();
  }
}

class Animal extends LivingCreature {
  private Characteristic p= new Characteristic("has
heart");
  private Description t =
    new Description("Animal not Vegetable");
  Animal() {
    System.out.println("Animal()");
  }
  protected void dispose() {
    System.out.println("Animal dispose");
    t.dispose();
    p.dispose();
```

```
    super.dispose();
  }
}

class Amphibian extends Animal {
  private Characteristic p =
    new Characteristic("can live in water");
  private Description t =
    new Description("Both water and land");
  Amphibian() {
    System.out.println("Amphibian()");
  }
  protected void dispose() {
    System.out.println("Amphibian dispose");
    t.dispose();
    p.dispose();
    super.dispose();
  }
}

public class Frog extends Amphibian {
  private static Test monitor = new Test();
  private Characteristic p = new Characteristic("Croaks");
  private Description t = new Description("Eats Bugs");
  public Frog() {
    System.out.println("Frog()");
  }
  protected void dispose() {
    System.out.println("Frog dispose");
    t.dispose();
    p.dispose();
    super.dispose();
  }
  public static void main(String[] args) {
    Frog frog = new Frog();
    System.out.println("Bye!");
    frog.dispose();
    monitor.expect(new String[] {
      "Creating Characteristic is alive",
      "Creating Description Basic Living Creature",
      "LivingCreature()",
      "Creating Characteristic has heart",
      "Creating Description Animal not Vegetable",
      "Animal()",
```

```
      "Creating Characteristic can live in water",
      "Creating Description Both water and land",
      "Amphibian()",
      "Creating Characteristic Croaks",
      "Creating Description Eats Bugs",
      "Frog()",
      "Bye!",
      "Frog dispose",
      "finalizing Description Eats Bugs",
      "finalizing Characteristic Croaks",
      "Amphibian dispose",
      "finalizing Description Both water and land",
      "finalizing Characteristic can live in water",
      "Animal dispose",
      "finalizing Description Animal not Vegetable",
      "finalizing Characteristic has heart",
      "LivingCreature dispose",
      "finalizing Description Basic Living Creature",
      "finalizing Characteristic is alive"
    });
  }
} ///:~
```

Each class in the hierarchy also contains a member objects of types **Characteristic** and **Description**, which must also be disposed. The order of disposal should be the reverse of the order of initialization, in case one subobject is dependent on another. For fields, this means the reverse of the order of declaration (since fields are initialized in declaration order). For base classes (following the form that's used in C++ for destructors), you should perform the derived-class cleanup first, then the base-class cleanup. That's because the derived-class cleanup could call some methods in the base class that require the base-class components to be alive, so you must not destroy them prematurely. From the output you can see that all parts of the **Frog** object are disposed in reverse order of creation.

From this example, you can see that although you don't always need to perform cleanup, when you do, the process requires care and awareness.

Behavior of polymorphic methods inside constructors

The hierarchy of constructor calls brings up an interesting dilemma. What happens if you're inside a constructor and you call a dynamically-bound method of the object being constructed? Inside an ordinary method, you can imagine what will happen: The dynamically-bound call is resolved at run time, because the object cannot know whether it belongs to the class that the method is in or some class derived from it. For consistency, you might think this is what should happen inside constructors.

This is not exactly the case. If you call a dynamically-bound method inside a constructor, the overridden definition for that method is used. However, the *effect* can be rather unexpected and can conceal some difficult-to-find bugs.

Conceptually, the constructor's job is to bring the object into existence (which is hardly an ordinary feat). Inside any constructor, the entire object might be only partially formed—you can know only that the base-class objects have been initialized, but you cannot know which classes are inherited from you. A dynamically bound method call, however, reaches "outward" into the inheritance hierarchy. It calls a method in a derived class. If you do this inside a constructor, you call a method that might manipulate members that haven't been initialized yet—a sure recipe for disaster.

You can see the problem in the following example:

```
//: c07:PolyConstructors.java
// Constructors and polymorphism
// don't produce what you might expect.
import com.bruceeckel.simpletest.*;

abstract class Glyph {
  abstract void draw();
  Glyph() {
    System.out.println("Glyph() before draw()");
    draw();
    System.out.println("Glyph() after draw()");
  }
}

class RoundGlyph extends Glyph {
  private int radius = 1;
  RoundGlyph(int r) {
    radius = r;
    System.out.println(
      "RoundGlyph.RoundGlyph(), radius = " + radius);
  }
  void draw() {
```

```
    System.out.println(
      "RoundGlyph.draw(), radius = " + radius);
  }
}

public class PolyConstructors {
  private static Test monitor = new Test();
  public static void main(String[] args) {
    new RoundGlyph(5);
    monitor.expect(new String[] {
      "Glyph() before draw()",
      "RoundGlyph.draw(), radius = 0",
      "Glyph() after draw()",
      "RoundGlyph.RoundGlyph(), radius = 5"
    });
  }
} ///:~
```

In **Glyph**, the **draw( )** method is **abstract**, so it is designed to be overridden. Indeed, you are forced to override it in **RoundGlyph**. But the **Glyph** constructor calls this method, and the call ends up in **RoundGlyph.draw( )**, which would seem to be the intent. But if you look at the output, you can see that when **Glyph**'s constructor calls **draw( )**, the value of **radius** isn't even the default initial value 1. It's 0. This would probably result in either a dot or nothing at all being drawn on the screen, and you'd be left staring, trying to figure out why the program won't work.

The order of initialization described in the earlier section isn't quite complete, and that's the key to solving the mystery. The actual process of initialization is:

1. The storage allocated for the object is initialized to binary zero before anything else happens.

2. The base-class constructors are called as described previously. At this point, the overridden **draw( )** method is called (yes, *before* the **RoundGlyph** constructor is called), which discovers a **radius** value of zero, due to Step 1.

3. Member initializers are called in the order of declaration.

4. The body of the derived-class constructor is called.

There's an upside to this, which is that everything is at least initialized to zero (or whatever zero means for that particular data type) and not just left as garbage. This includes object references that are embedded inside a class via composition, which become **null**. So if you forget to initialize that reference, you'll get an exception at run time. Everything else gets zero, which is usually a telltale value when looking at output.

On the other hand, you should be pretty horrified at the outcome of this program. You've done a perfectly logical thing, and yet the behavior is mysteriously wrong, with no complaints from the compiler. (C++ produces more rational behavior in this situation.) Bugs like this could easily be buried and take a long time to discover.

As a result, a good guideline for constructors is, "Do as little as possible to set the object into a good state, and if you can possibly avoid it, don't call any methods." The only safe methods to call inside a constructor are those that are **final** in the base class. (This also applies to **private** methods, which are automatically **final**.) These cannot be overridden and thus cannot produce this kind of surprise.

Designing with inheritance

Once you learn about polymorphism, it can seem that everything ought to be inherited, because polymorphism is such a clever tool. This can burden your designs; in fact, if you choose inheritance first when you're using an existing class to make a new class, things can become needlessly complicated.

A better approach is to choose composition first, especially when it's not obvious which one you should use. Composition does not force a design into an inheritance hierarchy. But composition is also more flexible since it's possible to dynamically choose a type (and thus behavior) when using composition, whereas inheritance requires an exact type to be known at compile time. The following example illustrates this:

```
//: c07:Transmogrify.java
// Dynamically changing the behavior of an object
// via composition (the "State" design pattern).
import com.bruceeckel.simpletest.*;

abstract class Actor {
  public abstract void act();
}
```

```java
class HappyActor extends Actor {
  public void act() {
    System.out.println("HappyActor");
  }
}

class SadActor extends Actor {
  public void act() {
    System.out.println("SadActor");
  }
}

class Stage {
  private Actor actor = new HappyActor();
  public void change() { actor = new SadActor(); }
  public void performPlay() { actor.act(); }
}

public class Transmogrify {
  private static Test monitor = new Test();
  public static void main(String[] args) {
    Stage stage = new Stage();
    stage.performPlay();
    stage.change();
    stage.performPlay();
    monitor.expect(new String[] {
      "HappyActor",
      "SadActor"
    });
  }
} ///:~
```

A **Stage** object contains a reference to an **Actor**, which is initialized to a **HappyActor** object. This means **performPlay( )** produces a particular behavior. But since a reference can be rebound to a different object at run time, a reference for a **SadActor** object can be substituted in **actor**, and then the behavior produced by **performPlay( )** changes. Thus you gain dynamic flexibility at run time. (This is also called the *State Pattern*. See *Thinking in Patterns (with Java)* at *www.BruceEckel.com*.) In contrast, you can't decide to inherit differently at run time; that must be completely determined at compile time.

A general guideline is "Use inheritance to express differences in behavior, and fields to express variations in state." In the preceding example, both are used; two different classes are inherited to express the difference in the **act( )** method, and **Stage** uses composition to allow its state to be changed. In this case, that change in state happens to produce a change in behavior.

Pure inheritance vs. extension

When studying inheritance, it would seem that the cleanest way to create an inheritance hierarchy is to take the "pure" approach. That is, only methods that have been established in the base class or **interface** are to be overridden in the derived class, as seen in this diagram:

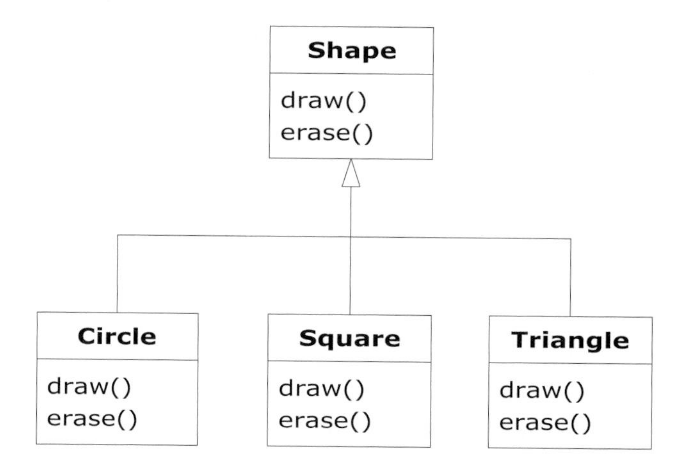

This can be called a pure "is-a" relationship because the interface of a class establishes what it is. Inheritance guarantees that any derived class will have the interface of the base class and nothing less. If you follow this diagram, derived classes will also have *no more* than the base-class interface.

This can be thought of as *pure substitution*, because derived class objects can be perfectly substituted for the base class, and you never need to know any extra information about the subclasses when you're using them:

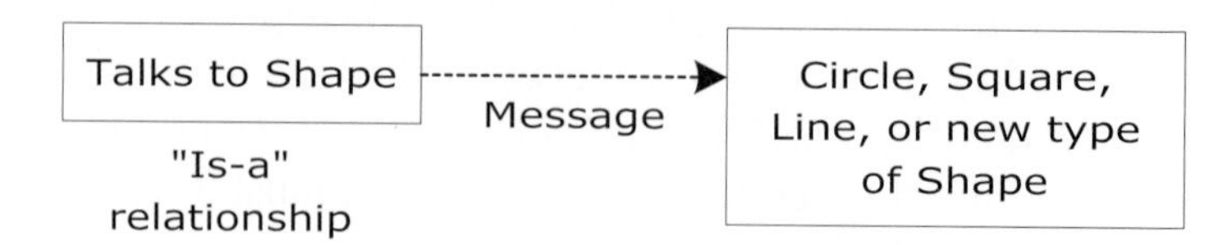

That is, the base class can receive any message you can send to the derived class because the two have exactly the same interface. All you need to do is upcast from the derived class and never look back to see what exact type of object you're dealing with. Everything is handled through polymorphism.

When you see it this way, it seems like a pure is-a relationship is the only sensible way to do things, and any other design indicates muddled thinking and is by definition broken. This too is a trap. As soon as you start thinking this way, you'll turn around and discover that extending the interface (which, unfortunately, the keyword **extends** seems to encourage) is the perfect solution to a particular problem. This could be termed an "is-like-a" relationship, because the derived class is *like* the base class—it has the same fundamental interface—but it has other features that require additional methods to implement:

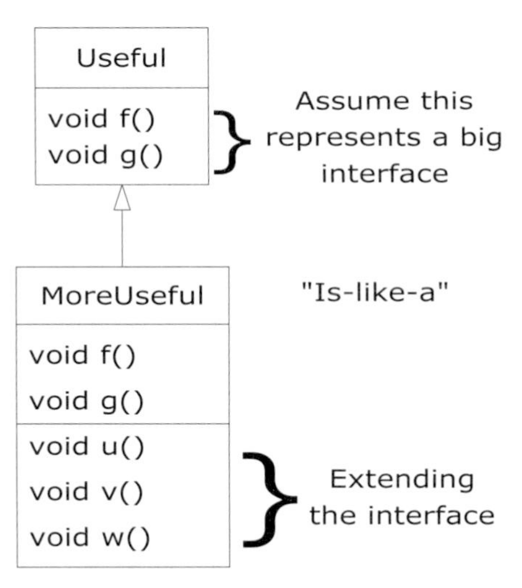

While this is also a useful and sensible approach (depending on the situation), it has a drawback. The extended part of the interface in the derived class is not available from the base class, so once you upcast, you can't call the new methods:

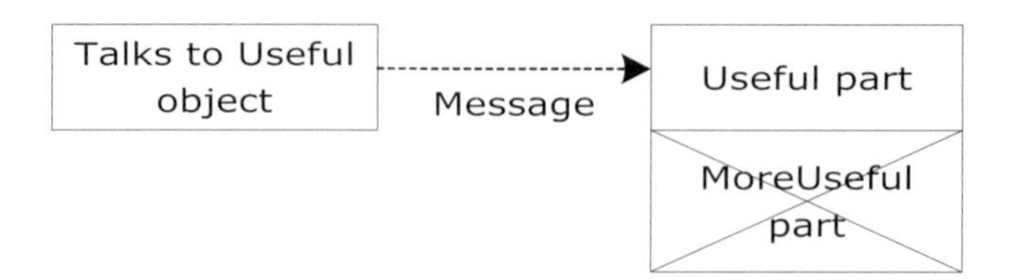

If you're not upcasting in this case, it won't bother you, but often you'll get into a situation in which you need to rediscover the exact type of the object so you can access the extended methods of that type. The following section shows how this is done.

Downcasting and run-time type identification

Since you lose the specific type information via an *upcast* (moving up the inheritance hierarchy), it makes sense that to retrieve the type information—that is, to move back down the inheritance hierarchy—you use a *downcast*. However, you know an upcast is always safe; the base class cannot have a bigger interface than the derived class. Therefore, every message you send through the base class interface is guaranteed to be accepted. But with a downcast, you don't really know that a shape (for example) is actually a circle. It could instead be a triangle or square or some other type.

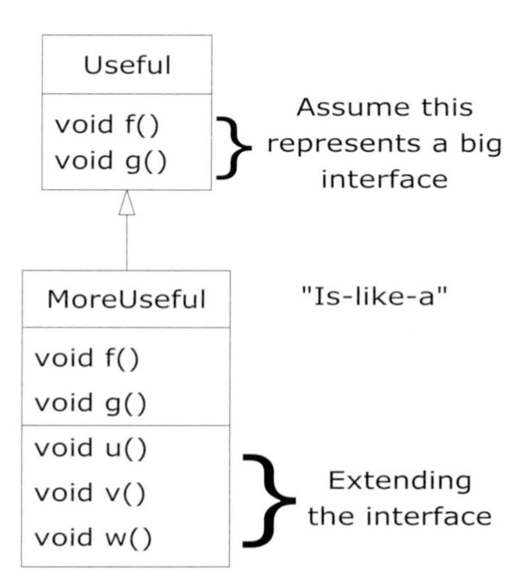

To solve this problem, there must be some way to guarantee that a downcast is correct, so that you won't accidentally cast to the wrong type and then send a message that the object can't accept. This would be quite unsafe.

In some languages (like C++) you must perform a special operation in order to get a type-safe downcast, but in Java, *every* cast is checked! So even though it looks like you're just performing an ordinary parenthesized cast, at run time this cast is checked to ensure that it is in fact the type you think it is. If it isn't, you get a **ClassCastException**. This act of checking types at run time is called *run-time type identification* (RTTI). The following example demonstrates the behavior of RTTI:

```
//: c07:RTTI.java
// Downcasting & Run-Time Type Identification (RTTI).
// {ThrowsException}

class Useful {
  public void f() {}
  public void g() {}
}

class MoreUseful extends Useful {
  public void f() {}
  public void g() {}
  public void u() {}
  public void v() {}
  public void w() {}
}

public class RTTI {
  public static void main(String[] args) {
    Useful[] x = {
      new Useful(),
      new MoreUseful()
    };
    x[0].f();
    x[1].g();
    // Compile time: method not found in Useful:
    //! x[1].u();
    ((MoreUseful)x[1]).u(); // Downcast/RTTI
    ((MoreUseful)x[0]).u(); // Exception thrown
  }
} ///:~
```

As in the diagram, **MoreUseful** extends the interface of **Useful**. But since it's inherited, it can also be upcast to a **Useful**. You can see this happening in the initialization of the array **x** in **main( )**. Since both objects in the array are of class **Useful**, you can send the **f( )** and **g( )** methods to both, and if you try to call **u( )** (which exists only in **MoreUseful**), you'll get a compile-time error message.

If you want to access the extended interface of a **MoreUseful** object, you can try to downcast. If it's the correct type, it will be successful. Otherwise, you'll get a **ClassCastException**. You don't need to write any special code for this exception, since it indicates a programmer error that could happen anywhere in a program.

There's more to RTTI than a simple cast. For example, there's a way to see what type you're dealing with *before* you try to downcast it. All of Chapter 10 is devoted to the study of different aspects of Java run-time type identification.

Summary

Polymorphism means "different forms." In object-oriented programming, you have the same face (the common interface in the base class) and different forms using that face: the different versions of the dynamically bound methods.

You've seen in this chapter that it's impossible to understand, or even create, an example of polymorphism without using data abstraction and inheritance. Polymorphism is a feature that cannot be viewed in isolation (like a **switch** statement can, for example), but instead works only in concert, as part of a "big picture" of class relationships. People are often confused by other, non-object-oriented features of Java, like method overloading, which are sometimes presented as object-oriented. Don't be fooled: If it isn't late binding, it isn't polymorphism.

To use polymorphism—and thus object-oriented techniques—effectively in your programs, you must expand your view of programming to include not just members and messages of an individual class, but also the commonality among classes and their relationships with each other. Although this requires significant effort, it's a worthy struggle, because the results are faster program development, better code organization, extensible programs, and easier code maintenance.

Exercises

Solutions to selected exercises can be found in the electronic document *The Thinking in Java Annotated Solution Guide*, available for a small fee from *www.BruceEckel.com*.

1. Add a new method in the base class of **Shapes.java** that prints a message, but don't override it in the derived classes. Explain what happens. Now override it in one of the derived classes but not the others, and see what happens. Finally, override it in all the derived classes.

2. Add a new type of **Shape** to **Shapes.java** and verify in **main( )** that polymorphism works for your new type as it does in the old types.

3. Change **Music3.java** so that **what( )** becomes the root **Object** method **toString( )**. Try printing the **Instrument** objects using **System.out.println( )** (without any casting).

4. Add a new type of **Instrument** to **Music3.java** and verify that polymorphism works for your new type.

5. Modify **Music3.java** so that it randomly creates **Instrument** objects the way **Shapes.java** does.

6. Create an inheritance hierarchy of **Rodent**: **Mouse**, **Gerbil**, **Hamster**, etc. In the base class, provide methods that are common to all **Rodent**s, and override these in the derived classes to perform different behaviors depending on the specific type of **Rodent**. Create an array of **Rodent**, fill it with different specific types of **Rodent**s, and call your base-class methods to see what happens.

7. Modify Exercise 6 so that **Rodent** is an **abstract** class. Make the methods of **Rodent** abstract whenever possible.

8. Create a class as **abstract** without including any **abstract** methods and verify that you cannot create any instances of that class.

9. Add class **Pickle** to **Sandwich.java**.

10. Modify Exercise 6 so that it demonstrates the order of initialization of the base classes and derived classes. Now add member objects to both the base and derived classes and show the order in which their initialization occurs during construction.

11. Create a base class with two methods. In the first method, call the second method. Inherit a class and override the second method. Create an object of the derived class, upcast it to the base type, and call the first method. Explain what happens.

12. Create a base class with an **abstract print( )** method that is overridden in a derived class. The overridden version of the method prints the value of an **int** variable defined in the derived class. At the point of definition of this variable, give it a nonzero value. In the base-class constructor, call this method. In **main( )**, create an object of the derived type, and then call its **print( )** method. Explain the results.

13. Following the example in **Transmogrify.java**, create a **Starship** class containing an **AlertStatus** reference that can indicate three different states. Include methods to change the states.

14. Create an **abstract** class with no methods. Derive a class and add a method. Create a **static** method that takes a reference to the base class, downcasts it to the derived class, and calls the method. In **main( )**, demonstrate that it works. Now put the **abstract** declaration for the method in the base class, thus eliminating the need for the downcast.

8: Interfaces & Inner Classes

Interfaces and inner classes provide more sophisticated ways to organize and control the objects in your system.

C++, for example, does not contain such mechanisms, although the clever programmer may simulate them. The fact that they exist in Java indicates that they were considered important enough to provide direct support through language keywords.

In Chapter 7 you learned about the **abstract** keyword, which allows you to create one or more methods in a class that have no definitions—you provide part of the interface without providing a corresponding implementation, which is created by inheritors. The **interface** keyword produces a completely abstract class, one that provides no implementation at all. You'll learn that the **interface** is more than just an abstract class taken to the extreme, since it allows you to perform a variation on C++'s "multiple inheritance" by creating a class that can be upcast to more than one base type.

At first, inner classes look like a simple code-hiding mechanism: you place classes inside other classes. You'll learn, however, that the inner class does more than that—it knows about and can communicate with the surrounding class—and that the kind of code you can write with inner classes is more elegant and clear, although it is a new concept to most. It takes some time to become comfortable with design using inner classes.

Interfaces

The **interface** keyword takes the **abstract** concept one step further. You could think of it as a "pure" **abstract** class. It allows the creator to establish the form for a class: method names, argument lists, and return types, but no method bodies. An **interface** can also contain fields, but these are implicitly **static** and **final**. An **interface** provides only a form, but no implementation.

An **interface** says, "This is what all classes that *implement* this particular interface will look like." Thus, any code that uses a particular **interface** knows what methods might be called for that **interface**, and that's all. So the **interface** is used to establish a "protocol" between classes. (Some object-oriented programming languages have a keyword called *protocol* to do the same thing.)

To create an **interface**, use the **interface** keyword instead of the **class** keyword. Like a class, you can add the **public** keyword before the **interface** keyword (but only if that **interface** is defined in a file of the same name) or leave it off to give package access, so that it is only usable within the same package.

To make a class that conforms to a particular **interface** (or group of **interfaces**), use the **implements** keyword, which says, "The **interface** is what it looks like, but now I'm going to say how it *works*." Other than that, it looks like inheritance. The diagram for the instrument example shows this:

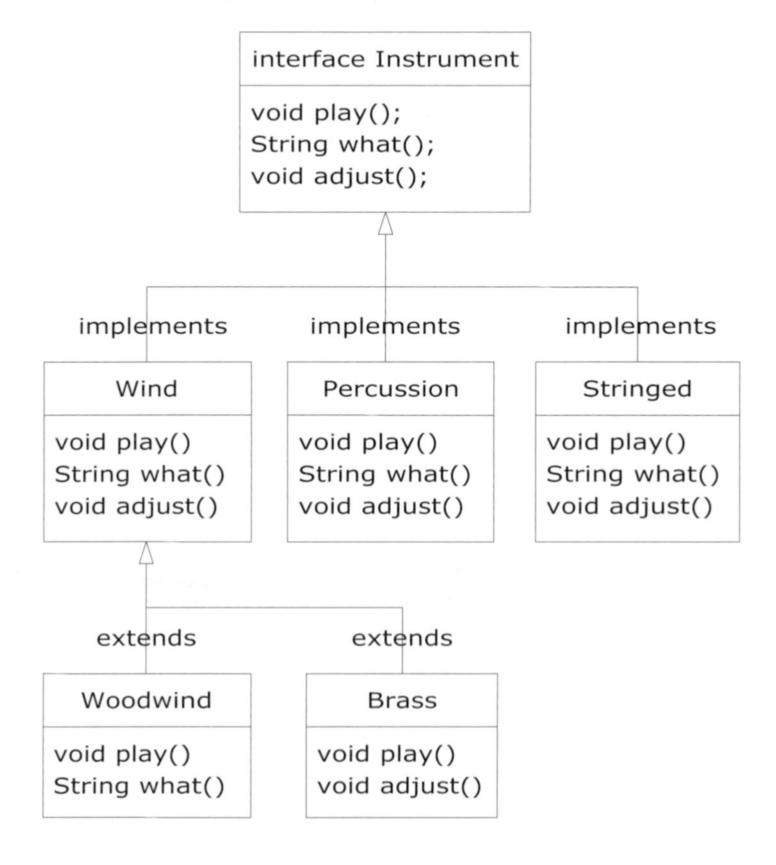

You can see from the **Woodwind** and **Brass** classes that once you've implemented an **interface**, that implementation becomes an ordinary class that can be extended in the regular way.

You can choose to explicitly declare the method declarations in an **interface** as **public**, but they are **public** even if you don't say it. So when you **implement** an **interface**, the methods from the **interface** must be defined as **public**. Otherwise, they would default to package access, and you'd be reducing the accessibility of a method during inheritance, which is not allowed by the Java compiler.

You can see this in the modified version of the **Instrument** example. Note that every method in the **interface** is strictly a declaration, which is the only thing the compiler allows. In addition, none of the methods in **Instrument** are declared as **public**, but they're automatically **public** anyway:

```
//: c08:music5:Music5.java
// Interfaces.
package c08.music5;
import com.bruceeckel.simpletest.*;
import c07.music.Note;

interface Instrument {
  // Compile-time constant:
  int I = 5; // static & final
  // Cannot have method definitions:
  void play(Note n); // Automatically public
  String what();
  void adjust();
}

class Wind implements Instrument {
  public void play(Note n) {
    System.out.println("Wind.play() " + n);
  }
  public String what() { return "Wind"; }
  public void adjust() {}
}

class Percussion implements Instrument {
  public void play(Note n) {
    System.out.println("Percussion.play() " + n);
  }
  public String what() { return "Percussion"; }
```

```
  public void adjust() {}
}

class Stringed implements Instrument {
  public void play(Note n) {
    System.out.println("Stringed.play() " + n);
  }
  public String what() { return "Stringed"; }
  public void adjust() {}
}

class Brass extends Wind {
  public void play(Note n) {
    System.out.println("Brass.play() " + n);
  }
  public void adjust() {
    System.out.println("Brass.adjust()");
  }
}

class Woodwind extends Wind {
  public void play(Note n) {
    System.out.println("Woodwind.play() " + n);
  }
  public String what() { return "Woodwind"; }
}

public class Music5 {
  private static Test monitor = new Test();
  // Doesn't care about type, so new types
  // added to the system still work right:
  static void tune(Instrument i) {
    // ...
    i.play(Note.MIDDLE_C);
  }
  static void tuneAll(Instrument[] e) {
    for(int i = 0; i < e.length; i++)
      tune(e[i]);
  }
  public static void main(String[] args) {
    // Upcasting during addition to the array:
    Instrument[] orchestra = {
      new Wind(),
      new Percussion(),
```

```
      new Stringed(),
      new Brass(),
      new Woodwind()
    };
    tuneAll(orchestra);
    monitor.expect(new String[] {
      "Wind.play() Middle C",
      "Percussion.play() Middle C",
      "Stringed.play() Middle C",
      "Brass.play() Middle C",
      "Woodwind.play() Middle C"
    });
  }
} ///:~
```

The rest of the code works the same. It doesn't matter if you are upcasting to a "regular" class called **Instrument**, an **abstract** class called **Instrument**, or to an **interface** called **Instrument**. The behavior is the same. In fact, you can see in the **tune( )** method that there isn't any evidence about whether **Instrument** is a "regular" class, an **abstract** class, or an **interface**. This is the intent: Each approach gives the programmer different control over the way objects are created and used.

"Multiple inheritance" in Java

The **interface** isn't simply a "more pure" form of **abstract** class. It has a higher purpose than that. Because an **interface** has no implementation at all—that is, there is no storage associated with an **interface**—there's nothing to prevent many **interfaces** from being combined. This is valuable because there are times when you need to say "An **x** is an **a** *and* a **b** *and* a **c**." In C++, this act of combining multiple class interfaces is called *multiple inheritance*, and it carries some rather sticky baggage because each class can have an implementation. In Java, you can perform the same act, but only one of the classes can have an implementation, so the problems seen in C++ do not occur with Java when combining multiple interfaces:

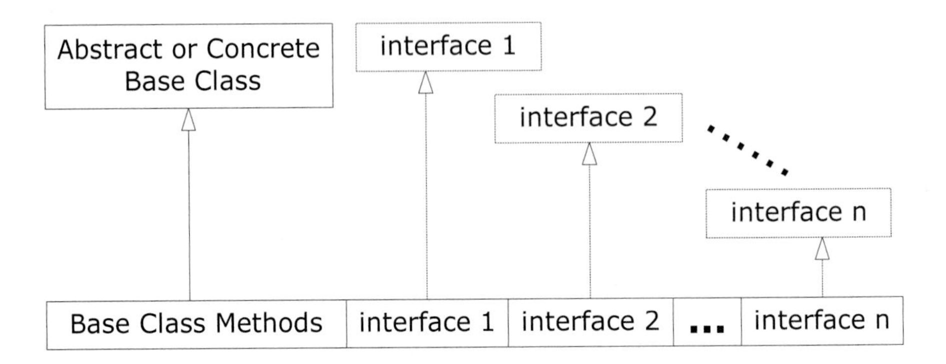

In a derived class, you aren't forced to have a base class that is either an **abstract** or "concrete" (one with no **abstract** methods). If you *do* inherit from a non-**interface**, you can inherit from only one. All the rest of the base elements must be **interface**s. You place all the interface names after the **implements** keyword and separate them with commas. You can have as many **interface**s as you want; each one becomes an independent type that you can upcast to. The following example shows a concrete class combined with several **interface**s to produce a new class:

```
//: c08:Adventure.java
// Multiple interfaces.

interface CanFight {
  void fight();
}

interface CanSwim {
  void swim();
}

interface CanFly {
  void fly();
}

class ActionCharacter {
  public void fight() {}
}

class Hero extends ActionCharacter
    implements CanFight, CanSwim, CanFly {
  public void swim() {}
  public void fly() {}
```

```
}

public class Adventure {
  public static void t(CanFight x) { x.fight(); }
  public static void u(CanSwim x) { x.swim(); }
  public static void v(CanFly x) { x.fly(); }
  public static void w(ActionCharacter x) { x.fight(); }
  public static void main(String[] args) {
    Hero h = new Hero();
    t(h); // Treat it as a CanFight
    u(h); // Treat it as a CanSwim
    v(h); // Treat it as a CanFly
    w(h); // Treat it as an ActionCharacter
  }
} ///:~
```

You can see that **Hero** combines the concrete class **ActionCharacter** with the interfaces **CanFight**, **CanSwim**, and **CanFly**. When you combine a concrete class with interfaces this way, the concrete class must come first, then the interfaces. (The compiler gives an error otherwise.)

Note that the signature for **fight( )** is the same in the **interface CanFight** and the class **ActionCharacter**, and that **fight( )** is *not* provided with a definition in **Hero**. The rule for an **interface** is that you can inherit from it (as you will see shortly), but then you've got another **interface**. If you want to create an object of the new type, it must be a class with all definitions provided. Even though **Hero** does not explicitly provide a definition for **fight( )**, the definition comes along with **ActionCharacter**, so it is automatically provided and it's possible to create objects of **Hero**.

In class **Adventure**, you can see that there are four methods that take as arguments the various interfaces and the concrete class. When a **Hero** object is created, it can be passed to any of these methods, which means it is being upcast to each **interface** in turn. Because of the way interfaces are designed in Java, this works without any particular effort on the part of the programmer.

Keep in mind that the core reason for interfaces is shown in the preceding example: to be able to upcast to more than one base type. However, a second reason for using interfaces is the same as using an **abstract** base class: to prevent the client programmer from making an object of this class and to establish that it is only an interface. This brings up a question: Should you use an **interface** or an **abstract** class? An **interface** gives you the benefits of an **abstract** class *and* the benefits of an **interface**, so if it's possible to create your base class without any method definitions or member variables, you should always prefer **interface**s to **abstract** classes. In fact, if you know something is going to be a base class, your first choice should be to make it an **interface**, and only if you're forced to have method definitions or member variables should you change to an **abstract** class, or if necessary a concrete class.

Name collisions when combining interfaces

You can encounter a small pitfall when implementing multiple interfaces. In the preceding example, both **CanFight** and **ActionCharacter** have an identical **void fight( )** method. This is not a problem, because the method is identical in both cases. But what if it isn't? Here's an example:

```
//: c08:InterfaceCollision.java

interface I1 { void f(); }
interface I2 { int f(int i); }
interface I3 { int f(); }
class C { public int f() { return 1; } }

class C2 implements I1, I2 {
  public void f() {}
  public int f(int i) { return 1; } // overloaded
}

class C3 extends C implements I2 {
  public int f(int i) { return 1; } // overloaded
}

class C4 extends C implements I3 {
  // Identical, no problem:
  public int f() { return 1; }
}

// Methods differ only by return type:
//! class C5 extends C implements I1 {}
//! interface I4 extends I1, I3 {} ///:~
```

The difficulty occurs because overriding, implementation, and overloading get unpleasantly mixed together, and overloaded methods cannot differ only by return type. When the last two lines are uncommented, the error messages say it all:

InterfaceCollision.java:23: f( ) in C cannot implement f( ) in I1; attempting to use incompatible return type
found : int
required: void
InterfaceCollision.java:24: interfaces I3 and I1 are incompatible; both define f( ), but with different return type

Using the same method names in different interfaces that are intended to be combined generally causes confusion in the readability of the code, as well. Strive to avoid it.

Extending an interface with inheritance

You can easily add new method declarations to an **interface** by using inheritance, and you can also combine several **interface**s into a new **interface** with inheritance. In both cases you get a new **interface**, as seen in this example:

```
//: c08:HorrorShow.java
// Extending an interface with inheritance.

interface Monster {
  void menace();
}

interface DangerousMonster extends Monster {
  void destroy();
}

interface Lethal {
  void kill();
}

class DragonZilla implements DangerousMonster {
  public void menace() {}
  public void destroy() {}
}

interface Vampire extends DangerousMonster, Lethal {
  void drinkBlood();
}
```

```java
class VeryBadVampire implements Vampire {
  public void menace() {}
  public void destroy() {}
  public void kill() {}
  public void drinkBlood() {}
}

public class HorrorShow {
  static void u(Monster b) { b.menace(); }
  static void v(DangerousMonster d) {
    d.menace();
    d.destroy();
  }
  static void w(Lethal l) { l.kill(); }
  public static void main(String[] args) {
    DangerousMonster barney = new DragonZilla();
    u(barney);
    v(barney);
    Vampire vlad = new VeryBadVampire();
    u(vlad);
    v(vlad);
    w(vlad);
  }
} ///:~
```

DangerousMonster is a simple extension to **Monster** that produces a new **interface**. This is implemented in **DragonZilla**.

The syntax used in **Vampire** works *only* when inheriting interfaces. Normally, you can use **extends** with only a single class, but since an **interface** can be made from multiple other interfaces, **extends** can refer to multiple base interfaces when building a new **interface**. As you can see, the **interface** names are simply separated with commas.

Grouping constants

Because any fields you put into an **interface** are automatically **static** and **final**, the **interface** is a convenient tool for creating groups of constant values, much as you would with an **enum** in C or C++. For example:

```java
//: c08:Months.java
// Using interfaces to create groups of constants.
package c08;
```

```
public interface Months {
  int
    JANUARY = 1, FEBRUARY = 2, MARCH = 3,
    APRIL = 4, MAY = 5, JUNE = 6, JULY = 7,
    AUGUST = 8, SEPTEMBER = 9, OCTOBER = 10,
    NOVEMBER = 11, DECEMBER = 12;
} ///:~
```

Notice the Java style of using all uppercase letters (with underscores to separate multiple words in a single identifier) for **static final**s that have constant initializers.

The fields in an **interface** are automatically **public**, so it's unnecessary to specify that.

You can use the constants from outside the package by importing **c08.*** or **c08.Months** just as you would with any other package, and referencing the values with expressions like **Months.JANUARY**. Of course, what you get is just an **int**, so there isn't the extra type safety that C++'s **enum** has, but this (commonly used) technique is certainly an improvement over hard coding numbers into your programs. (That approach is often referred to as using "magic numbers," and it produces very difficult-to-maintain code.)

If you do want extra type safety, you can build a class like this:[1]

```
//: c08:Month.java
// A more robust enumeration system.
package c08;
import com.bruceeckel.simpletest.*;

public final class Month {
  private static Test monitor = new Test();
  private String name;
  private Month(String nm) { name = nm; }
  public String toString() { return name; }
  public static final Month
    JAN = new Month("January"),
    FEB = new Month("February"),
    MAR = new Month("March"),
```

[1] This approach was inspired by an e-mail from Rich Hoffarth. Item 21 in Joshua Bloch's *Effective Java* (Addison-Wesley, 2001) covers the topic in much more detail.

```
    APR = new Month("April"),
    MAY = new Month("May"),
    JUN = new Month("June"),
    JUL = new Month("July"),
    AUG = new Month("August"),
    SEP = new Month("September"),
    OCT = new Month("October"),
    NOV = new Month("November"),
    DEC = new Month("December");
  public static final Month[] month =  {
    JAN, FEB, MAR, APR, MAY, JUN,
    JUL, AUG, SEP, OCT, NOV, DEC
  };
  public static final Month number(int ord) {
    return month[ord - 1];
  }
  public static void main(String[] args) {
    Month m = Month.JAN;
    System.out.println(m);
    m = Month.number(12);
    System.out.println(m);
    System.out.println(m == Month.DEC);
    System.out.println(m.equals(Month.DEC));
    System.out.println(Month.month[3]);
    monitor.expect(new String[] {
      "January",
      "December",
      "true",
      "true",
      "April"
    });
  }
} ///:~
```

Month is a **final** class with a **private** constructor, so no one can inherit from it or make any instances of it. The only instances are the **final static** ones created in the class itself: **JAN**, **FEB**, **MAR**, etc. These objects are also used in the array **month**, which lets you iterate through an array of **Month2** objects. The **number( )** method allows you to select a **Month** by giving its corresponding month number. In **main( )** you can see the type safety; **m** is a **Month** object so it can be assigned only to a **Month**. The previous example **Months.java** provided only **int** values, so an **int** variable intended to represent a month could actually be given any integer value, which wasn't very safe.

This approach also allows you to use == or **equals( )** interchangeably, as shown at the end of **main( )**. This works because there can be only one instance of each value of **Month**. In Chapter 11 you'll learn about another way to set up classes so the objects can be compared to each other.

There's also a month field in **java.util.Calendar**.

Apache's Jakarta Commons project contains tools to create enumerations similar to what's shown in the preceding example, but with less effort. See *http://jakarta.apache.org/commons*, under "lang," in the package **org.apache.commons.lang.enum**. This project also has many other potentially useful libraries.

Initializing fields in interfaces

Fields defined in interfaces are automatically **static** and **final**. These cannot be "blank finals," but they can be initialized with nonconstant expressions. For example:

```
//: c08:RandVals.java
// Initializing interface fields with
// non-constant initializers.
import java.util.*;

public interface RandVals {
  Random rand = new Random();
  int randomInt = rand.nextInt(10);
  long randomLong = rand.nextLong() * 10;
  float randomFloat = rand.nextLong() * 10;
  double randomDouble = rand.nextDouble() * 10;
} ///:~
```

Since the fields are **static**, they are initialized when the class is first loaded, which happens when any of the fields are accessed for the first time. Here's a simple test:

```
//: c08:TestRandVals.java
import com.bruceeckel.simpletest.*;

public class TestRandVals {
  private static Test monitor = new Test();
  public static void main(String[] args) {
    System.out.println(RandVals.randomInt);
    System.out.println(RandVals.randomLong);
```

```
    System.out.println(RandVals.randomFloat);
    System.out.println(RandVals.randomDouble);
    monitor.expect(new String[] {
      "%% -?\\d+",
      "%% -?\\d+",
      "%% -?\\d\\.\\d+E?-?\\d+",
      "%% -?\\d\\.\\d+E?-?\\d+"
    });
  }
} ///:~
```

The fields, of course, are not part of the interface but instead are stored in the static storage area for that interface.

Nesting interfaces

Interfaces may be nested within classes and within other interfaces.[2] This reveals a number of very interesting features:

```
//: c08:nesting:NestingInterfaces.java
package c08.nesting;

class A {
  interface B {
    void f();
  }
  public class BImp implements B {
    public void f() {}
  }
  private class BImp2 implements B {
    public void f() {}
  }
  public interface C {
    void f();
  }
  class CImp implements C {
    public void f() {}
  }
  private class CImp2 implements C {
    public void f() {}
  }
```

[2] Thanks to Martin Danner for asking this question during a seminar.

```
  private interface D {
    void f();
  }
  private class DImp implements D {
    public void f() {}
  }
  public class DImp2 implements D {
    public void f() {}
  }
  public D getD() { return new DImp2(); }
  private D dRef;
  public void receiveD(D d) {
    dRef = d;
    dRef.f();
  }
}

interface E {
  interface G {
    void f();
  }
  // Redundant "public":
  public interface H {
    void f();
  }
  void g();
  // Cannot be private within an interface:
  //! private interface I {}
}

public class NestingInterfaces {
  public class BImp implements A.B {
    public void f() {}
  }
  class CImp implements A.C {
    public void f() {}
  }
  // Cannot implement a private interface except
  // within that interface's defining class:
  //! class DImp implements A.D {
  //!  public void f() {}
  //! }
  class EImp implements E {
    public void g() {}
```

```
  }
  class EGImp implements E.G {
    public void f() {}
  }
  class EImp2 implements E {
    public void g() {}
    class EG implements E.G {
      public void f() {}
    }
  }
  public static void main(String[] args) {
    A a = new A();
    // Can't access A.D:
    //! A.D ad = a.getD();
    // Doesn't return anything but A.D:
    //! A.DImp2 di2 = a.getD();
    // Cannot access a member of the interface:
    //! a.getD().f();
    // Only another A can do anything with getD():
    A a2 = new A();
    a2.receiveD(a.getD());
  }
} ///:~
```

The syntax for nesting an interface within a class is reasonably obvious, and just like non-nested interfaces, these can have **public** or package-access visibility. You can also see that both **public** and package-access nested interfaces can be implemented as **public**, package-access, and **private** nested classes.

As a new twist, interfaces can also be **private**, as seen in **A.D** (the same qualification syntax is used for nested interfaces as for nested classes). What good is a **private** nested interface? You might guess that it can only be implemented as a **private** inner class as in **DImp**, but **A.DImp2** shows that it can also be implemented as a **public** class. However, **A.DImp2** can only be used as itself. You are not allowed to mention the fact that it implements the **private** interface, so implementing a **private** interface is a way to force the definition of the methods in that interface without adding any type information (that is, without allowing any upcasting).

The method **getD( )** produces a further quandary concerning the **private** interface: It's a **public** method that returns a reference to a **private** interface. What can you do with the return value of this method? In **main( )**, you can see several attempts to use the return value, all of which fail. The only thing that works is if the return value is handed to an object that has permission to use it—in this case, another **A**, via the **receiveD( )** method.

Interface **E** shows that interfaces can be nested within each other. However, the rules about interfaces—in particular, that all interface elements must be **public**—are strictly enforced here, so an interface nested within another interface is automatically **public** and cannot be made **private**.

NestingInterfaces shows the various ways that nested interfaces can be implemented. In particular, notice that when you implement an interface, you are not required to implement any interfaces nested within. Also, **private** interfaces cannot be implemented outside of their defining classes.

Initially, these features may seem like they are added strictly for syntactic consistency, but I generally find that once you know about a feature, you often discover places where it is useful.

Inner classes

It's possible to place a class definition within another class definition. This is called an *inner class*. The inner class is a valuable feature because it allows you to group classes that logically belong together and to control the visibility of one within the other. However, it's important to understand that inner classes are distinctly different from composition.

While you're learning about them, the need for inner classes isn't always obvious. At the end of this section, after all of the syntax and semantics of inner classes have been described, you'll find examples that should begin to make clear the benefits of inner classes.

You create an inner class just as you'd expect—by placing the class definition inside a surrounding class:

```
//: c08:Parcel1.java
// Creating inner classes.

public class Parcel1 {
  class Contents {
    private int i = 11;
    public int value() { return i; }
  }
  class Destination {
```

```
    private String label;
    Destination(String whereTo) {
      label = whereTo;
    }
    String readLabel() { return label; }
  }
  // Using inner classes looks just like
  // using any other class, within Parcel1:
  public void ship(String dest) {
    Contents c = new Contents();
    Destination d = new Destination(dest);
    System.out.println(d.readLabel());
  }
  public static void main(String[] args) {
    Parcel1 p = new Parcel1();
    p.ship("Tanzania");
  }
} ///:~
```

The inner classes, when used inside **ship( )**, look just like the use of any other classes. Here, the only practical difference is that the names are nested within **Parcel1**. You'll see in a while that this isn't the only difference.

More typically, an outer class will have a method that returns a reference to an inner class, like this:

```
//: c08:Parcel2.java
// Returning a reference to an inner class.

public class Parcel2 {
  class Contents {
    private int i = 11;
    public int value() { return i; }
  }
  class Destination {
    private String label;
    Destination(String whereTo) {
      label = whereTo;
    }
    String readLabel() { return label; }
  }
  public Destination to(String s) {
    return new Destination(s);
  }
  public Contents cont() {
```

```
    return new Contents();
  }
  public void ship(String dest) {
    Contents c = cont();
    Destination d = to(dest);
    System.out.println(d.readLabel());
  }
  public static void main(String[] args) {
    Parcel2 p = new Parcel2();
    p.ship("Tanzania");
    Parcel2 q = new Parcel2();
    // Defining references to inner classes:
    Parcel2.Contents c = q.cont();
    Parcel2.Destination d = q.to("Borneo");
  }
} ///:~
```

If you want to make an object of the inner class anywhere except from within a non-**static** method of the outer class, you must specify the type of that object as *OuterClassName.InnerClassName*, as seen in **main( )**.

Inner classes and upcasting

So far, inner classes don't seem that dramatic. After all, if it's hiding you're after, Java already has a perfectly good hiding mechanism—just give the class package access (visible only within a package) rather than creating it as an inner class.

However, inner classes really come into their own when you start upcasting to a base class, and in particular to an **interface**. (The effect of producing an interface reference from an object that implements it is essentially the same as upcasting to a base class.) That's because the inner class—the implementation of the **interface**—can then be completely unseen and unavailable to anyone, which is convenient for hiding the implementation. All you get back is a reference to the base class or the **interface**.

First, the common interfaces will be defined in their own files so they can be used in all the examples:

```
//: c08:Destination.java
public interface Destination {
  String readLabel();
} ///:~
```

```java
//: c08:Contents.java
public interface Contents {
  int value();
} ///:~
```

Now **Contents** and **Destination** represent interfaces available to the client programmer. (The **interface**, remember, automatically makes all of its members **public**.)

When you get back a reference to the base class or the **interface**, it's possible that you can't even find out the exact type, as shown here:

```java
//: c08:TestParcel.java
// Returning a reference to an inner class.

class Parcel3 {
  private class PContents implements Contents {
    private int i = 11;
    public int value() { return i; }
  }
  protected class PDestination implements Destination {
    private String label;
    private PDestination(String whereTo) {
      label = whereTo;
    }
    public String readLabel() { return label; }
  }
  public Destination dest(String s) {
    return new PDestination(s);
  }
  public Contents cont() {
    return new PContents();
  }
}

public class TestParcel {
  public static void main(String[] args) {
    Parcel3 p = new Parcel3();
    Contents c = p.cont();
    Destination d = p.dest("Tanzania");
    // Illegal -- can't access private class:
    //! Parcel3.PContents pc = p.new PContents();
  }
} ///:~
```

In the example, **main( )** must be in a separate class in order to demonstrate the privateness of the inner class **PContents**.

In **Parcel3**, something new has been added: The inner class **PContents** is **private**, so no one but **Parcel3** can access it. **PDestination** is **protected**, so no one but **Parcel3**, classes in the same package (since **protected** also gives package access), and the inheritors of **Parcel3** can access **PDestination**. This means that the client programmer has restricted knowledge and access to these members. In fact, you can't even downcast to a **private** inner class (or a **protected** inner class unless you're an inheritor), because you can't access the name, as you can see in **class TestParcel**. Thus, the **private** inner class provides a way for the class designer to completely prevent any type-coding dependencies and to completely hide details about implementation. In addition, extension of an **interface** is useless from the client programmer's perspective since the client programmer cannot access any additional methods that aren't part of the **public interface**. This also provides an opportunity for the Java compiler to generate more efficient code.

Normal (non-inner) classes cannot be made **private** or **protected**; they may only be given **public** or package access.

Inner classes in methods and scopes

What you've seen so far encompasses the typical use for inner classes. In general, the code that you'll write and read involving inner classes will be "plain" inner classes that are simple and easy to understand. However, the design for inner classes is quite complete, and there are a number of other, more obscure, ways that you can use them if you choose; inner classes can be created within a method or even an arbitrary scope. There are two reasons for doing this:

1. As shown previously, you're implementing an interface of some kind so that you can create and return a reference.

2. You're solving a complicated problem and you want to create a class to aid in your solution, but you don't want it publicly available.

In the following examples, the previous code will be modified to use:

1. A class defined within a method

2. A class defined within a scope inside a method

3. An anonymous class implementing an interface

4. An anonymous class extending a class that has a nondefault constructor

5. An anonymous class that performs field initialization

6. An anonymous class that performs construction using instance initialization (anonymous inner classes cannot have constructors)

Although it's an ordinary class with an implementation, **Wrapping** is also being used as a common "interface" to its derived classes:

```
//: c08:Wrapping.java
public class Wrapping {
  private int i;
  public Wrapping(int x) { i = x; }
  public int value() { return i; }
} ///:~
```

You'll notice that **Wrapping** has a constructor that requires an argument, to make things a bit more interesting.

The first example shows the creation of an entire class within the scope of a method (instead of the scope of another class). This is called a *local inner class*:

```
//: c08:Parcel4.java
// Nesting a class within a method.

public class Parcel4 {
  public Destination dest(String s) {
    class PDestination implements Destination {
      private String label;
      private PDestination(String whereTo) {
        label = whereTo;
      }
      public String readLabel() { return label; }
    }
    return new PDestination(s);
  }
```

```
  public static void main(String[] args) {
    Parcel4 p = new Parcel4();
    Destination d = p.dest("Tanzania");
  }
} ///:~
```

The class **PDestination** is part of **dest( )** rather than being part of **Parcel4**. (Also notice that you could use the class identifier **PDestination** for an inner class inside each class in the same subdirectory without a name clash.) Therefore, **PDestination** cannot be accessed outside of **dest( )**. Notice the upcasting that occurs in the return statement—nothing comes out of **dest( )** except a reference to **Destination**, the base class. Of course, the fact that the name of the class **PDestination** is placed inside **dest( )** doesn't mean that **PDestination** is not a valid object once **dest( )** returns.

The next example shows how you can nest an inner class within any arbitrary scope:

```
//: c08:Parcel5.java
// Nesting a class within a scope.

public class Parcel5 {
  private void internalTracking(boolean b) {
    if(b) {
      class TrackingSlip {
        private String id;
        TrackingSlip(String s) {
          id = s;
        }
        String getSlip() { return id; }
      }
      TrackingSlip ts = new TrackingSlip("slip");
      String s = ts.getSlip();
    }
    // Can't use it here! Out of scope:
    //! TrackingSlip ts = new TrackingSlip("x");
  }
  public void track() { internalTracking(true); }
  public static void main(String[] args) {
    Parcel5 p = new Parcel5();
    p.track();
  }
} ///:~
```

The class **TrackingSlip** is nested inside the scope of an **if** statement. This does not mean that the *class* is conditionally created—it gets compiled along with everything else. However, it's not available outside the scope in which it is defined. Other than that, it looks just like an ordinary class.

Anonymous inner classes

The next example looks a little strange:

```
//: c08:Parcel6.java
// A method that returns an anonymous inner class.

public class Parcel6 {
  public Contents cont() {
    return new Contents() {
      private int i = 11;
      public int value() { return i; }
    }; // Semicolon required in this case
  }
  public static void main(String[] args) {
    Parcel6 p = new Parcel6();
    Contents c = p.cont();
  }
} ///:~
```

The **cont( )** method combines the creation of the return value with the definition of the class that represents that return value! In addition, the class is anonymous; it has no name. To make matters a bit worse, it looks like you're starting out to create a **Contents** object:

```
return new Contents()
```

But then, before you get to the semicolon, you say, "But wait, I think I'll slip in a class definition":

```
return new Contents() {
  private int i = 11;
  public int value() { return i; }
};
```

What this strange syntax means is: "Create an object of an anonymous class that's inherited from **Contents**." The reference returned by the **new** expression is automatically upcast to a **Contents** reference. The anonymous inner-class syntax is a shorthand for:

```
class MyContents implements Contents {
  private int i = 11;
  public int value() { return i; }
}
return new MyContents();
```

In the anonymous inner class, **Contents** is created by using a default constructor. The following code shows what to do if your base class needs a constructor with an argument:

```
//: c08:Parcel7.java
// An anonymous inner class that calls
// the base-class constructor.

public class Parcel7 {
  public Wrapping wrap(int x) {
    // Base constructor call:
    return new Wrapping(x) { // Pass constructor argument.
      public int value() {
        return super.value() * 47;
      }
    }; // Semicolon required
  }
  public static void main(String[] args) {
    Parcel7 p = new Parcel7();
    Wrapping w = p.wrap(10);
  }
} ///:~
```

That is, you simply pass the appropriate argument to the base-class constructor, seen here as the **x** passed in **new Wrapping(x)**.

The semicolon at the end of the anonymous inner class doesn't mark the end of the class body (as it does in C++). Instead, it marks the end of the expression that happens to contain the anonymous class. Thus, it's identical to the use of the semicolon everywhere else.

You can also perform initialization when you define fields in an anonymous class:

```
//: c08:Parcel8.java
// An anonymous inner class that performs
// initialization. A briefer version of Parcel4.java.

public class Parcel8 {
```

```
    // Argument must be final to use inside
    // anonymous inner class:
    public Destination dest(final String dest) {
      return new Destination() {
        private String label = dest;
        public String readLabel() { return label; }
      };
    }
    public static void main(String[] args) {
      Parcel8 p = new Parcel8();
      Destination d = p.dest("Tanzania");
    }
  } ///:~
```

If you're defining an anonymous inner class and want to use an object that's defined outside the anonymous inner class, the compiler requires that the argument reference be **final**, like the argument to **dest( )**. If you forget, you'll get a compile-time error message.

As long as you're simply assigning a field, the approach in this example is fine. But what if you need to perform some constructor-like activity? You can't have a named constructor in an anonymous class (since there's no name!), but with *instance initialization*, you can, in effect, create a constructor for an anonymous inner class, like this:

```
//: c08:AnonymousConstructor.java
// Creating a constructor for an anonymous inner class.
import com.bruceeckel.simpletest.*;

abstract class Base {
  public Base(int i) {
    System.out.println("Base constructor, i = " + i);
  }
  public abstract void f();
}

public class AnonymousConstructor {
  private static Test monitor = new Test();
  public static Base getBase(int i) {
    return new Base(i) {
      {
        System.out.println("Inside instance initializer");
      }
      public void f() {
```

```
        System.out.println("In anonymous f()");
      }
    };
  }
  public static void main(String[] args) {
    Base base = getBase(47);
    base.f();
    monitor.expect(new String[] {
      "Base constructor, i = 47",
      "Inside instance initializer",
      "In anonymous f()"
    });
  }
} ///:~
```

In this case, the variable **i** did *not* have to be final. While **i** is passed to the base constructor of the anonymous class, it is never directly used *inside* the anonymous class.

Here's the "parcel" theme with instance initialization. Note that the arguments to **dest( )** must be final since they are used within the anonymous class:

```
//: c08:Parcel9.java
// Using "instance initialization" to perform
// construction on an anonymous inner class.
import com.bruceeckel.simpletest.*;

public class Parcel9 {
  private static Test monitor = new Test();
  public Destination
  dest(final String dest, final float price) {
    return new Destination() {
      private int cost;
      // Instance initialization for each object:
      {
        cost = Math.round(price);
        if(cost > 100)
          System.out.println("Over budget!");
      }
      private String label = dest;
      public String readLabel() { return label; }
    };
  }
  public static void main(String[] args) {
```

```
    Parcel9 p = new Parcel9();
    Destination d = p.dest("Tanzania", 101.395F);
    monitor.expect(new String[] {
      "Over budget!"
    });
  }
} ///:~
```

Inside the instance initializer you can see code that couldn't be executed as part of a field initializer (that is, the **if** statement). So in effect, an instance initializer is the constructor for an anonymous inner class. Of course, it's limited; you can't overload instance initializers, so you can have only one of these constructors.

The link to the outer class

So far, it appears that inner classes are just a name-hiding and code-organization scheme, which is helpful but not totally compelling. However, there's another twist. When you create an inner class, an object of that inner class has a link to the enclosing object that made it, and so it can access the members of that enclosing object—*without* any special qualifications. In addition, inner classes have access rights to all the elements in the enclosing class.[3] The following example demonstrates this:

```
//: c08:Sequence.java
// Holds a sequence of Objects.
import com.bruceeckel.simpletest.*;

interface Selector {
  boolean end();
  Object current();
  void next();
}

public class Sequence {
  private static Test monitor = new Test();
  private Object[] objects;
  private int next = 0;
```

[3] This is very different from the design of *nested classes* in C++, which is simply a name-hiding mechanism. There is no link to an enclosing object and no implied permissions in C++.

```
  public Sequence(int size) { objects = new Object[size]; }
  public void add(Object x) {
    if(next < objects.length)
      objects[next++] = x;
  }
  private class SSelector implements Selector {
    private int i = 0;
    public boolean end() { return i == objects.length; }
    public Object current() { return objects[i]; }
    public void next() { if(i < objects.length) i++; }
  }
  public Selector getSelector() { return new SSelector(); }
  public static void main(String[] args) {
    Sequence sequence = new Sequence(10);
    for(int i = 0; i < 10; i++)
      sequence.add(Integer.toString(i));
    Selector selector = sequence.getSelector();
    while(!selector.end()) {
      System.out.println(selector.current());
      selector.next();
    }
    monitor.expect(new String[] {
      "0",
      "1",
      "2",
      "3",
      "4",
      "5",
      "6",
      "7",
      "8",
      "9"
    });
  }
} ///:~
```

The **Sequence** is simply a fixed-sized array of **Object** with a class wrapped around it. You call **add( )** to add a new **Object** to the end of the sequence (if there's room left). To fetch each of the objects in a **Sequence**, there's an interface called **Selector**, which allows you to see if you're at the **end( )**, to look at the **current( ) Object**, and to move to the **next( ) Object** in the **Sequence**. Because **Selector** is an **interface**, many other classes can implement the **interface** in their own ways, and many methods can take the **interface** as an argument, in order to create generic code.

Here, the **SSelector** is a **private** class that provides **Selector** functionality. In **main( )**, you can see the creation of a **Sequence**, followed by the addition of a number of **String** objects. Then, a **Selector** is produced with a call to **getSelector( )**, and this is used to move through the **Sequence** and select each item.

At first, the creation of **SSelector** looks like just another inner class. But examine it closely. Note that each of the methods—**end( )**, **current( ),** and **next( )**—refer to **objects**, which is a reference that isn't part of **SSelector**, but is instead a **private** field in the enclosing class. However, the inner class can access methods and fields from the enclosing class as if it owned them. This turns out to be very convenient, as you can see in the preceding example.

So an inner class has automatic access to the members of the enclosing class. How can this happen? The inner class must keep a reference to the particular object of the enclosing class that was responsible for creating it. Then, when you refer to a member of the enclosing class, that (hidden) reference is used to select that member. Fortunately, the compiler takes care of all these details for you, but you can also understand now that an object of an inner class can be created only in association with an object of the enclosing class. Construction of the inner class object requires the reference to the object of the enclosing class, and the compiler will complain if it cannot access that reference. Most of the time this occurs without any intervention on the part of the programmer.

Nested classes

If you don't need a connection between the inner class object and the outer class object, then you can make the inner class **static**. This is commonly called a *nested class.*[4] To understand the meaning of **static** when applied to inner classes, you must remember that the object of an ordinary inner class implicitly keeps a reference to the object of the enclosing class that created it. This is not true, however, when you say an inner class is **static**. A nested class means:

1. You don't need an outer-class object in order to create an object of a nested class.

---

[4] Roughly similar to nested classes in C++, except that those classes cannot access private members as they can in Java.

2. You can't access a non-**static** outer-class object from an object of a nested class.

Nested classes are different from ordinary inner classes in another way, as well. Fields and methods in ordinary inner classes can only be at the outer level of a class, so ordinary inner classes cannot have **static** data, **static** fields, or nested classes. However, nested classes can have all of these:

```
//: c08:Parcel10.java
// Nested classes (static inner classes).

public class Parcel10 {
  private static class ParcelContents implements Contents {
    private int i = 11;
    public int value() { return i; }
  }
  protected static class ParcelDestination
  implements Destination {
    private String label;
    private ParcelDestination(String whereTo) {
      label = whereTo;
    }
    public String readLabel() { return label; }
    // Nested classes can contain other static elements:
    public static void f() {}
    static int x = 10;
    static class AnotherLevel {
      public static void f() {}
      static int x = 10;
    }
  }
  public static Destination dest(String s) {
    return new ParcelDestination(s);
  }
  public static Contents cont() {
    return new ParcelContents();
  }
  public static void main(String[] args) {
    Contents c = cont();
    Destination d = dest("Tanzania");
  }
} ///:~
```

In **main( )**, no object of **Parcel10** is necessary; instead, you use the normal syntax for selecting a **static** member to call the methods that return references to **Contents** and **Destination**.

As you will see shortly, in an ordinary (non-**static**) inner class, the link to the outer class object is achieved with a special **this** reference. A nested class does not have this special **this** reference, which makes it analogous to a **static** method.

Normally, you can't put any code inside an **interface**, but a nested class can be part of an **interface**. Since the class is **static**, it doesn't violate the rules for interfaces—the nested class is only placed inside the namespace of the interface:

```
//: c08:IInterface.java
// Nested classes inside interfaces.

public interface IInterface {
  static class Inner {
    int i, j, k;
    public Inner() {}
    void f() {}
  }
} ///:~
```

Earlier in this book I suggested putting a **main( )** in every class to act as a test bed for that class. One drawback to this is the amount of extra compiled code you must carry around. If this is a problem, you can use a nested class to hold your test code:

```
//: c08:TestBed.java
// Putting test code in a nested class.

public class TestBed {
  public TestBed() {}
  public void f() { System.out.println("f()"); }
  public static class Tester {
    public static void main(String[] args) {
      TestBed t = new TestBed();
      t.f();
    }
  }
} ///:~
```

This generates a separate class called **TestBed$Tester** (to run the program, you say **java TestBed$Tester**). You can use this class for testing, but you don't need to include it in your shipping product; you can simply delete **TestBed$Tester.class** before packaging things up.

Referring to the outer class object

If you need to produce the reference to the outer class object, you name the outer class followed by a dot and **this**. For example, in the class **Sequence.SSelector**, any of its methods can produce the stored reference to the outer class **Sequence** by saying **Sequence.this**. The resulting reference is automatically the correct type. (This is known and checked at compile time, so there is no run-time overhead.)

Sometimes you want to tell some other object to create an object of one of its inner classes. To do this you must provide a reference to the other outer class object in the **new** expression, like this:

```
//: c08:Parcel11.java
// Creating instances of inner classes.

public class Parcel11 {
  class Contents {
    private int i = 11;
    public int value() { return i; }
  }
  class Destination {
    private String label;
    Destination(String whereTo) { label = whereTo; }
    String readLabel() { return label; }
  }
  public static void main(String[] args) {
    Parcel11 p = new Parcel11();
    // Must use instance of outer class
    // to create an instances of the inner class:
    Parcel11.Contents c = p.new Contents();
    Parcel11.Destination d = p.new Destination("Tanzania");
  }
} ///:~
```

To create an object of the inner class directly, you don't follow the same form and refer to the outer class name **Parcel11** as you might expect, but instead you must use an *object* of the outer class to make an object of the inner class:

```
Parcel11.Contents c = p.new Contents();
```

Thus, it's not possible to create an object of the inner class unless you already have an object of the outer class. This is because the object of the inner class is quietly connected to the object of the outer class that it was made from. However, if you make a nested class (a **static** inner class), then it doesn't need a reference to the outer class object.

Reaching outward from a multiply-nested class

[5]It doesn't matter how deeply an inner class may be nested—it can transparently access all of the members of all the classes it is nested within, as seen here:

```
//: c08:MultiNestingAccess.java
// Nested classes can access all members of all
// levels of the classes they are nested within.

class MNA {
  private void f() {}
  class A {
    private void g() {}
    public class B {
      void h() {
        g();
        f();
      }
    }
  }
}

public class MultiNestingAccess {
  public static void main(String[] args) {
    MNA mna = new MNA();
    MNA.A mnaa = mna.new A();
    MNA.A.B mnaab = mnaa.new B();
    mnaab.h();
  }
} ///:~
```

[5] Thanks again to Martin Danner.

You can see that in **MNA.A.B**, the methods **g( )** and **f( )** are callable without any qualification (despite the fact that they are **private**). This example also demonstrates the syntax necessary to create objects of multiply-nested inner classes when you create the objects in a different class. The "**.new**" syntax produces the correct scope, so you do not have to qualify the class name in the constructor call.

Inheriting from inner classes

Because the inner class constructor must attach to a reference of the enclosing class object, things are slightly complicated when you inherit from an inner class. The problem is that the "secret" reference to the enclosing class object *must* be initialized, and yet in the derived class there's no longer a default object to attach to. The answer is to use a syntax provided to make the association explicit:

```
//: c08:InheritInner.java
// Inheriting an inner class.

class WithInner {
  class Inner {}
}

public class InheritInner extends WithInner.Inner {
  //! InheritInner() {} // Won't compile
  InheritInner(WithInner wi) {
    wi.super();
  }
  public static void main(String[] args) {
    WithInner wi = new WithInner();
    InheritInner ii = new InheritInner(wi);
  }
} ///:~
```

You can see that **InheritInner** is extending only the inner class, not the outer one. But when it comes time to create a constructor, the default one is no good, and you can't just pass a reference to an enclosing object. In addition, you must use the syntax

```
enclosingClassReference.super();
```

inside the constructor. This provides the necessary reference, and the program will then compile.

Can inner classes be overridden?

What happens when you create an inner class, then inherit from the enclosing class and redefine the inner class? That is, is it possible to override the entire inner class? This seems like it would be a powerful concept, but "overriding" an inner class as if it were another method of the outer class doesn't really do anything:

```
//: c08:BigEgg.java
// An inner class cannot be overriden like a method.
import com.bruceeckel.simpletest.*;

class Egg {
  private Yolk y;
  protected class Yolk {
    public Yolk() { System.out.println("Egg.Yolk()"); }
  }
  public Egg() {
    System.out.println("New Egg()");
    y = new Yolk();
  }
}

public class BigEgg extends Egg {
  private static Test monitor = new Test();
  public class Yolk {
    public Yolk() { System.out.println("BigEgg.Yolk()"); }
  }
  public static void main(String[] args) {
    new BigEgg();
    monitor.expect(new String[] {
      "New Egg()",
      "Egg.Yolk()"
    });
  }
} ///:~
```

The default constructor is synthesized automatically by the compiler, and this calls the base-class default constructor. You might think that since a **BigEgg** is being created, the "overridden" version of **Yolk** would be used, but this is not the case, as you can see from the output.

This example shows that there isn't any extra inner class magic going on when you inherit from the outer class. The two inner classes are completely separate entities, each in their own namespace. However, it's still possible to explicitly inherit from the inner class:

```
//: c08:BigEgg2.java
// Proper inheritance of an inner class.
import com.bruceeckel.simpletest.*;

class Egg2 {
  protected class Yolk {
    public Yolk() { System.out.println("Egg2.Yolk()"); }
    public void f() { System.out.println("Egg2.Yolk.f()");}
  }
  private Yolk y = new Yolk();
  public Egg2() { System.out.println("New Egg2()"); }
  public void insertYolk(Yolk yy) { y = yy; }
  public void g() { y.f(); }
}

public class BigEgg2 extends Egg2 {
  private static Test monitor = new Test();
  public class Yolk extends Egg2.Yolk {
    public Yolk() { System.out.println("BigEgg2.Yolk()"); }
    public void f() {
      System.out.println("BigEgg2.Yolk.f()");
    }
  }
  public BigEgg2() { insertYolk(new Yolk()); }
  public static void main(String[] args) {
    Egg2 e2 = new BigEgg2();
    e2.g();
    monitor.expect(new String[] {
      "Egg2.Yolk()",
      "New Egg2()",
      "Egg2.Yolk()",
      "BigEgg2.Yolk()",
      "BigEgg2.Yolk.f()"
    });
  }
} ///:~
```

Now **BigEgg2.Yolk** explicitly **extends Egg2.Yolk** and overrides its methods. The method **insertYolk( )** allows **BigEgg2** to upcast one of its own **Yolk** objects into the **y** reference in **Egg2**, so when **g( )** calls **y.f( )**, the overridden version of **f( )** is used. The second call to **Egg2.Yolk( )** is the base-class constructor call of the **BigEgg2.Yolk** constructor. You can see that the overridden version of **f( )** is used when **g( )** is called.

Local inner classes

As noted earlier, inner classes can also be created inside code blocks, typically inside the body of a method. A local inner class cannot have an access specifier because it isn't part of the outer class, but it does have access to the final variables in the current code block and all the members of the enclosing class. Here's an example comparing the creation of a local inner class with an anonymous inner class:

```
//: c08:LocalInnerClass.java
// Holds a sequence of Objects.
import com.bruceeckel.simpletest.*;

interface Counter {
  int next();
}

public class LocalInnerClass {
  private static Test monitor = new Test();
  private int count = 0;
  Counter getCounter(final String name) {
    // A local inner class:
    class LocalCounter implements Counter {
      public LocalCounter() {
        // Local inner class can have a constructor
        System.out.println("LocalCounter()");
      }
      public int next() {
        System.out.print(name); // Access local final
        return count++;
      }
    }
    return new LocalCounter();
  }
  // The same thing with an anonymous inner class:
  Counter getCounter2(final String name) {
    return new Counter() {
      // Anonymous inner class cannot have a named
      // constructor, only an instance initializer:
      {
        System.out.println("Counter()");
```

```
      }
      public int next() {
        System.out.print(name); // Access local final
        return count++;
      }
    };
  }
  public static void main(String[] args) {
    LocalInnerClass lic = new LocalInnerClass();
    Counter
      c1 = lic.getCounter("Local inner "),
      c2 = lic.getCounter2("Anonymous inner ");
    for(int i = 0; i < 5; i++)
      System.out.println(c1.next());
    for(int i = 0; i < 5; i++)
      System.out.println(c2.next());
    monitor.expect(new String[] {
      "LocalCounter()",
      "Counter()",
      "Local inner 0",
      "Local inner 1",
      "Local inner 2",
      "Local inner 3",
      "Local inner 4",
      "Anonymous inner 5",
      "Anonymous inner 6",
      "Anonymous inner 7",
      "Anonymous inner 8",
      "Anonymous inner 9"
    });
  }
} ///:~
```

Counter returns the next value in a sequence. It is implemented as both a local class and an anonymous inner class, both of which have the same behaviors and capabilities. Since the name of the local inner class is not accessible outside the method, the only justification for using a local inner class instead of an anonymous inner class is if you need a named constructor and/or overloaded constructor, since an anonymous inner class can only use instance initialization.

The only reason to make a local inner class rather than an anonymous inner class is if you need to make more than one object of that class.

Inner class identifiers

Since every class produces a **.class** file that holds all the information about how to create objects of this type (this information produces a "meta-class" called the **Class** object), you might guess that inner classes must also produce **.class** files to contain the information for *their* **Class** objects. The names of these files/classes have a strict formula: the name of the enclosing class, followed by a '**$**', followed by the name of the inner class. For example, the **.class** files created by **LocalInnerClass.java** include:

```
Counter.class
LocalInnerClass$2.class
LocalInnerClass$1LocalCounter.class
LocalInnerClass.class
```

If inner classes are anonymous, the compiler simply starts generating numbers as inner class identifiers. If inner classes are nested within inner classes, their names are simply appended after a '**$**' and the outer class identifier(s).

Although this scheme of generating internal names is simple and straightforward, it's also robust and handles most situations.[6] Since it is the standard naming scheme for Java, the generated files are automatically platform-independent. (Note that the Java compiler is changing your inner classes in all sorts of other ways in order to make them work.)

Why inner classes?

At this point you've seen a lot of syntax and semantics describing the way inner classes work, but this doesn't answer the question of why they exist. Why did Sun go to so much trouble to add this fundamental language feature?

Typically, the inner class inherits from a class or implements an **interface**, and the code in the inner class manipulates the outer class object that it was

---

[6] On the other hand, '$' is a meta-character to the Unix shell and so you'll sometimes have trouble when listing the **.class** files. This is a bit strange coming from Sun, a Unix-based company. My guess is that they weren't considering this issue, but instead thought you'd naturally focus on the source-code files.

created within. So you could say that an inner class provides a kind of window into the outer class.

A question that cuts to the heart of inner classes is this: If I just need a reference to an **interface**, why don't I just make the outer class implement that **interface**? The answer is "If that's all you need, then that's how you should do it." So what is it that distinguishes an inner class implementing an **interface** from an outer class implementing the same **interface**? The answer is that you can't always have the convenience of **interface**s—sometimes you're working with implementations. So the most compelling reason for inner classes is:

> *Each inner class can independently inherit from an implementation. Thus, the inner class is not limited by whether the outer class is already inheriting from an implementation.*

Without the ability that inner classes provide to inherit—in effect—from more than one concrete or **abstract** class, some design and programming problems would be intractable. So one way to look at the inner class is as the rest of the solution of the multiple-inheritance problem. Interfaces solve part of the problem, but inner classes effectively allow "multiple implementation inheritance." That is, inner classes effectively allow you to inherit from more than one non-**interface**.

To see this in more detail, consider a situation in which you have two interfaces that must somehow be implemented within a class. Because of the flexibility of interfaces, you have two choices: a single class or an inner class:

```
//: c08:MultiInterfaces.java
// Two ways that a class can implement multiple interfaces.

interface A {}
interface B {}

class X implements A, B {}

class Y implements A {
  B makeB() {
    // Anonymous inner class:
    return new B() {};
  }
}
```

```java
public class MultiInterfaces {
  static void takesA(A a) {}
  static void takesB(B b) {}
  public static void main(String[] args) {
    X x = new X();
    Y y = new Y();
    takesA(x);
    takesA(y);
    takesB(x);
    takesB(y.makeB());
  }
} ///:~
```

Of course, this assumes that the structure of your code makes logical sense either way. However, you'll ordinarily have some kind of guidance from the nature of the problem about whether to use a single class or an inner class. But without any other constraints, the approach in the preceding example doesn't really make much difference from an implementation standpoint. Both of them work.

However, if you have **abstract** or concrete classes instead of **interface**s, you are suddenly limited to using inner classes if your class must somehow implement both of the others:

```java
//: c08:MultiImplementation.java
// With concrete or abstract classes, inner
// classes are the only way to produce the effect
// of "multiple implementation inheritance."
package c08;

class D {}
abstract class E {}

class Z extends D {
  E makeE() { return new E() {}; }
}

public class MultiImplementation {
  static void takesD(D d) {}
  static void takesE(E e) {}
  public static void main(String[] args) {
    Z z = new Z();
    takesD(z);
    takesE(z.makeE());
```

```
    }
} ///:~
```

If you didn't need to solve the "multiple implementation inheritance" problem, you could conceivably code around everything else without the need for inner classes. But with inner classes you have these additional features:

1. The inner class can have multiple instances, each with its own state information that is independent of the information in the outer class object.

2. In a single outer class you can have several inner classes, each of which implement the same **interface** or inherit from the same class in a different way. An example of this will be shown shortly.

3. The point of creation of the inner class object is not tied to the creation of the outer class object.

4. There is no potentially confusing "is-a" relationship with the inner class; it's a separate entity.

As an example, if **Sequence.java** did not use inner classes, you'd have to say "a **Sequence** is a **Selector**," and you'd only be able to have one **Selector** in existence for a particular **Sequence**. You can easily have a second method, **getRSelector( )**, that produces a **Selector** that moves backward through the sequence. This kind of flexibility is only available with inner classes.

Closures & Callbacks

A *closure* is a callable object that retains information from the scope in which it was created. From this definition, you can see that an inner class is an object-oriented closure, because it doesn't just contain each piece of information from the outer class object ("the scope in which it was created"), but it automatically holds a reference back to the whole outer class object, where it has permission to manipulate all the members, even **private** ones.

One of the most compelling arguments made to include some kind of pointer mechanism in Java was to allow *callbacks*. With a callback, some other object is given a piece of information that allows it to call back into the originating object at some later point. This is a very powerful concept, as you will see later in the book. If a callback is implemented using a pointer, however, you must rely on the programmer to behave and not misuse the pointer. As you've seen by now, Java tends to be more careful than that, so pointers were not included in the language.

The closure provided by the inner class is a perfect solution—more flexible and far safer than a pointer. Here's an example:

```
//: c08:Callbacks.java
// Using inner classes for callbacks
import com.bruceeckel.simpletest.*;

interface Incrementable {
  void increment();
}

// Very simple to just implement the interface:
class Callee1 implements Incrementable {
  private int i = 0;
  public void increment() {
    i++;
    System.out.println(i);
  }
}

class MyIncrement {
  void increment() {
    System.out.println("Other operation");
  }
  static void f(MyIncrement mi) { mi.increment(); }
}

// If your class must implement increment() in
// some other way, you must use an inner class:
class Callee2 extends MyIncrement {
  private int i = 0;
  private void incr() {
    i++;
    System.out.println(i);
  }
  private class Closure implements Incrementable {
    public void increment() { incr(); }
  }
  Incrementable getCallbackReference() {
    return new Closure();
  }
```

```
}

class Caller {
  private Incrementable callbackReference;
  Caller(Incrementable cbh) { callbackReference = cbh; }
  void go() { callbackReference.increment(); }
}

public class Callbacks {
  private static Test monitor = new Test();
  public static void main(String[] args) {
    Callee1 c1 = new Callee1();
    Callee2 c2 = new Callee2();
    MyIncrement.f(c2);
    Caller caller1 = new Caller(c1);
    Caller caller2 = new Caller(c2.getCallbackReference());
    caller1.go();
    caller1.go();
    caller2.go();
    caller2.go();
    monitor.expect(new String[] {
      "Other operation",
      "1",
      "2",
      "1",
      "2"
    });
  }
} ///:~
```

This example also provides a further distinction between implementing an interface in an outer class versus doing so in an inner class. **Callee1** is clearly the simpler solution in terms of the code. **Callee2** inherits from **MyIncrement**, which already has a different **increment( )** method that does something unrelated to the one expected by the **Incrementable** interface. When **MyIncrement** is inherited into **Callee2**, **increment( )** can't be overridden for use by **Incrementable**, so you're forced to provide a separate implementation using an inner class. Also note that when you create an inner class, you do not add to or modify the interface of the outer class.

Notice that everything except **getCallbackReference( )** in **Callee2** is **private**. To allow *any* connection to the outside world, the **interface**

Incrementable is essential. Here you can see how **interface**s allow for a complete separation of interface from implementation.

The inner class **Closure** implements **Incrementable** to provide a hook back into **Callee2**—but a safe hook. Whoever gets the **Incrementable** reference can, of course, only call **increment( )** and has no other abilities (unlike a pointer, which would allow you to run wild).

Caller takes an **Incrementable** reference in its constructor (although the capturing of the callback reference could happen at any time) and then, sometime later, uses the reference to "call back" into the **Callee** class.

The value of the callback is in its flexibility; you can dynamically decide what methods will be called at run time. The benefit of this will become more evident in Chapter 14, where callbacks are used everywhere to implement GUI functionality.

Inner classes & control frameworks

A more concrete example of the use of inner classes can be found in something that I will refer to here as a *control framework*.

An *application framework* is a class or a set of classes that's designed to solve a particular type of problem. To apply an application framework, you typically inherit from one or more classes and override some of the methods. The code that you write in the overridden methods customizes the general solution provided by that application framework in order to solve your specific problem (this is an example of the *Template Method* design pattern; see *Thinking in Patterns (with Java)* at *www.BruceEckel.com*). The control framework is a particular type of application framework dominated by the need to respond to events; a system that primarily responds to events is called an *event-driven system*. One of the most important problems in application programming is the graphical user interface (GUI), which is almost entirely event-driven. As you will see in Chapter 14, the Java Swing library is a control framework that elegantly solves the GUI problem and that heavily uses inner classes.

To see how inner classes allow the simple creation and use of control frameworks, consider a control framework whose job is to execute events whenever those events are "ready." Although "ready" could mean anything, in this case the default will be based on clock time. What follows is a control framework that contains no specific information about what it's controlling.

That information is supplied during inheritance, when the "template method" is implemented.

First, here is the interface that describes any control event. It's an **abstract** class instead of an actual **interface** because the default behavior is to perform the control based on time. Thus, some of the implementation is included here:

```
//: c08:controller:Event.java
// The common methods for any control event.
package c08.controller;

public abstract class Event {
  private long eventTime;
  protected final long delayTime;
  public Event(long delayTime) {
    this.delayTime = delayTime;
    start();
  }
  public void start() { // Allows restarting
    eventTime = System.currentTimeMillis() + delayTime;
  }
  public boolean ready() {
    return System.currentTimeMillis() >= eventTime;
  }
  public abstract void action();
} ///:~
```

The constructor captures the time (from the time of creation of the object) when you want the **Event** to run and then calls **start( )**, which takes the current time and adds the delay time to produce the time when the event will occur. Rather than being included in the constructor, **start( )** is a separate method because this way, it allows you to restart the timer after the event has run out so the **Event** object can be reused. For example, if you want a repeating event, you can simply call **start( )** inside your **action( )** method.

ready( ) tells you when it's time to run the **action( )** method. Of course, **ready( )** could be overridden in a derived class to base the **Event** on something other than time.

The following file contains the actual control framework that manages and fires events. The **Event** objects are held inside a container object of type **ArrayList**, which you'll learn more about in Chapter 11. For now, all you need to know is that **add( )** will append an **Object** to the end of the **ArrayList**, **size( )** produces the number of entries in the **ArrayList**, **get( )** will fetch an element from the **ArrayList** at a particular index, and **remove( )** removes an element from the **ArrayList**, given the element number you want to remove.

```
//: c08:controller:Controller.java
// With Event, the generic framework for control systems.
package c08.controller;
import java.util.*;

public class Controller {
  // An object from java.util to hold Event objects:
  private List eventList = new ArrayList();
  public void addEvent(Event c) { eventList.add(c); }
  public void run() {
    while(eventList.size() > 0) {
      for(int i = 0; i < eventList.size(); i++) {
        Event e = (Event)eventList.get(i);
        if(e.ready()) {
          System.out.println(e);
          e.action();
          eventList.remove(i);
        }
      }
    }
  }
} ///:~
```

The **run( )** method loops through **eventList**, hunting for an **Event** object that's **ready( )** to run. For each one it finds **ready( )**, it prints information using the object's **toString( )** method, calls the **action( )** method**,** and then removes the **Event** from the list.

Note that so far in this design you know nothing about exactly *what* an **Event** does. And this is the crux of the design—how it "separates the things that change from the things that stay the same." Or, to use my term, the "vector of change" is the different actions of the various kinds of **Event** objects, and you express different actions by creating different **Event** subclasses.

This is where inner classes come into play. They allow two things:

1. To create the entire implementation of a control framework in a single class, thereby encapsulating everything that's unique about that implementation. Inner classes are used to express the many different kinds of **action( )** necessary to solve the problem.

2. Inner classes keep this implementation from becoming awkward, since you're able to easily access any of the members in the outer class. Without this ability the code might become unpleasant enough that you'd end up seeking an alternative.

Consider a particular implementation of the control framework designed to control greenhouse functions.[7] Each action is entirely different: turning lights, water, and thermostats on and off, ringing bells, and restarting the system. But the control framework is designed to easily isolate this different code. Inner classes allow you to have multiple derived versions of the same base class, **Event**, within a single class. For each type of action, you inherit a new **Event** inner class, and write the control code in the **action( )** implementation.

As is typical with an application framework, the class **GreenhouseControls** is inherited from **Controller**:

```
//: c08:GreenhouseControls.java
// This produces a specific application of the
// control system, all in a single class. Inner
// classes allow you to encapsulate different
// functionality for each type of event.
import com.bruceeckel.simpletest.*;
import c08.controller.*;

public class GreenhouseControls extends Controller {
  private static Test monitor = new Test();
  private boolean light = false;
  public class LightOn extends Event {
    public LightOn(long delayTime) { super(delayTime); }
    public void action() {
      // Put hardware control code here to
      // physically turn on the light.
      light = true;
```

[7] For some reason this has always been a pleasing problem for me to solve; it came from my earlier book *C++ Inside & Out*, but Java allows a much more elegant solution.

```
    }
    public String toString() { return "Light is on"; }
  }
  public class LightOff extends Event {
    public LightOff(long delayTime) { super(delayTime); }
    public void action() {
      // Put hardware control code here to
      // physically turn off the light.
      light = false;
    }
    public String toString() { return "Light is off"; }
  }
  private boolean water = false;
  public class WaterOn extends Event {
    public WaterOn(long delayTime) { super(delayTime); }
    public void action() {
      // Put hardware control code here.
      water = true;
    }
    public String toString() {
      return "Greenhouse water is on";
    }
  }
  public class WaterOff extends Event {
    public WaterOff(long delayTime) { super(delayTime); }
    public void action() {
      // Put hardware control code here.
      water = false;
    }
    public String toString() {
      return "Greenhouse water is off";
    }
  }
  private String thermostat = "Day";
  public class ThermostatNight extends Event {
    public ThermostatNight(long delayTime) {
      super(delayTime);
    }
    public void action() {
      // Put hardware control code here.
      thermostat = "Night";
    }
    public String toString() {
      return "Thermostat on night setting";
```

```
    }
  }
  public class ThermostatDay extends Event {
    public ThermostatDay(long delayTime) {
      super(delayTime);
    }
    public void action() {
      // Put hardware control code here.
      thermostat = "Day";
    }
    public String toString() {
      return "Thermostat on day setting";
    }
  }
  // An example of an action() that inserts a
  // new one of itself into the event list:
  public class Bell extends Event {
    public Bell(long delayTime) { super(delayTime); }
    public void action() {
      addEvent(new Bell(delayTime));
    }
    public String toString() { return "Bing!"; }
  }
  public class Restart extends Event {
    private Event[] eventList;
    public Restart(long delayTime, Event[] eventList) {
      super(delayTime);
      this.eventList = eventList;
      for(int i = 0; i < eventList.length; i++)
        addEvent(eventList[i]);
    }
    public void action() {
      for(int i = 0; i < eventList.length; i++) {
        eventList[i].start(); // Rerun each event
        addEvent(eventList[i]);
      }
      start(); // Rerun this Event
      addEvent(this);
    }
    public String toString() {
      return "Restarting system";
    }
  }
  public class Terminate extends Event {
```

```java
    public Terminate(long delayTime) { super(delayTime); }
    public void action() { System.exit(0); }
    public String toString() { return "Terminating";  }
  }
} ///:~
```

Note that **light**, **water**, and **thermostat** belong to the outer class **GreenhouseControls**, and yet the inner classes can access those fields without qualification or special permission. Also, most of the **action( )** methods involve some sort of hardware control.

Most of the **Event** classes look similar, but **Bell** and **Restart** are special. **Bell** rings and then adds a new **Bell** object to the event list, so it will ring again later. Notice how inner classes *almost* look like multiple inheritance: **Bell** and **Restart** have all the methods of **Event** and also appear to have all the methods of the outer class **GreenhouseControls**.

Restart is given an array of **Event** objects that it adds to the controller. Since **Restart( )** is just another **Event** object, you can also add a **Restart** object within **Restart.action( )** so that the system regularly restarts itself.

The following class configures the system by creating a **GreenhouseControls** object and adding various kinds of **Event** objects. This is an example of the *Command* design pattern:

```java
//: c08:GreenhouseController.java
// Configure and execute the greenhouse system.
// {Args: 5000}
import c08.controller.*;

public class GreenhouseController {
  public static void main(String[] args) {
    GreenhouseControls gc = new GreenhouseControls();
    // Instead of hard-wiring, you could parse
    // configuration information from a text file here:
    gc.addEvent(gc.new Bell(900));
    Event[] eventList = {
      gc.new ThermostatNight(0),
      gc.new LightOn(200),
      gc.new LightOff(400),
      gc.new WaterOn(600),
      gc.new WaterOff(800),
      gc.new ThermostatDay(1400)
    };
```

```
    gc.addEvent(gc.new Restart(2000, eventList));
    if(args.length == 1)
      gc.addEvent(
        gc.new Terminate(Integer.parseInt(args[0])));
    gc.run();
  }
} ///:~
```

This class initializes the system, so it adds all the appropriate events. Of course, a more flexible way to accomplish this is to avoid hard-coding the events and instead read them from a file. (An exercise in Chapter 12 asks you to modify this example to do just that.) If you provide a command-line argument, it uses this to terminate the program after that many milliseconds (this is used for testing).

This example should move you toward an appreciation of the value of inner classes, especially when used within a control framework. However, in Chapter 14 you'll see how elegantly inner classes are used to describe the actions of a graphical user interface. By the time you finish that chapter, you should be fully convinced.

Summary

Interfaces and inner classes are more sophisticated concepts than what you'll find in many OOP languages; for example, there's nothing like them in C++. Together, they solve the same problem that C++ attempts to solve with its multiple inheritance (MI) feature. However, MI in C++ turns out to be rather difficult to use, whereas Java interfaces and inner classes are, by comparison, much more accessible.

Although the features themselves are reasonably straightforward, the use of these features is a design issue, much the same as polymorphism. Over time, you'll become better at recognizing situations where you should use an interface, or an inner class, or both. But at this point in this book, you should at least be comfortable with the syntax and semantics. As you see these language features in use, you'll eventually internalize them.

Exercises

Solutions to selected exercises can be found in the electronic document *The Thinking in Java Annotated Solution Guide*, available for a small fee from *www.BruceEckel.com*.

1. Prove that the fields in an **interface** are implicitly **static** and **final**.

2. Create an **interface** containing three methods, in its own **package**. Implement the interface in a different **package**.

3. Prove that all the methods in an **interface** are automatically **public**.

4. In **c07:Sandwich.java**, create an interface called **FastFood** (with appropriate methods) and change **Sandwich** so that it also implements **FastFood**.

5. Create three **interfaces**, each with two methods. Inherit a new **interface** from the three, adding a new method. Create a class by implementing the new **interface** and also inheriting from a concrete class. Now write four methods, each of which takes one of the four **interfaces** as an argument. In **main( )**, create an object of your class and pass it to each of the methods.

6. Modify Exercise 5 by creating an **abstract** class and inheriting that into the derived class.

7. Modify **Music5.java** by adding a **Playable interface**. Move the **play( )** declaration from **Instrument** to **Playable**. Add **Playable** to the derived classes by including it in the **implements** list. Change **tune( )** so that it takes a **Playable** instead of an **Instrument**.

8. Change Exercise 6 in Chapter 7 so that **Rodent** is an **interface**.

9. In **Adventure.java**, add an **interface** called **CanClimb**, following the form of the other interfaces.

10. Write a program that imports and uses **Month.java**.

11. Following the example given in **Month.java**, create an enumeration of days of the week.

12. Create an **interface** with at least one method, in its own package. Create a class in a separate package. Add a **protected** inner class that implements the **interface**. In a third package, inherit from your class and, inside a method, return an object of the **protected** inner class, upcasting to the **interface** during the return.

13. Create an **interface** with at least one method, and implement that **interface** by defining an inner class within a method, which returns a reference to your **interface**.

14. Repeat Exercise 13 but define the inner class within a scope within a method.

15. Repeat Exercise 13 using an anonymous inner class.

16. Modify **HorrorShow.java** to implement **DangerousMonster** and **Vampire** using anonymous classes.

17. Create a **private** inner class that implements a **public interface**. Write a method that returns a reference to an instance of the **private** inner class, upcast to the **interface**. Show that the inner class is completely hidden by trying to downcast to it.

18. Create a class with a nondefault constructor (one with arguments) and no default constructor (no "no-arg" constructor). Create a second class that has a method that returns a reference to the first class. Create the object to return by making an anonymous inner class that inherits from the first class.

19. Create a class with a **private** field and a **private** method. Create an inner class with a method that modifies the outer class field and calls the outer class method. In a second outer class method, create an object of the inner class and call its method, then show the effect on the outer class object.

20. Repeat Exercise 19 using an anonymous inner class.

21. Create a class containing a nested class. In **main( )**, create an instance of the inner class.

22. Create an **interface** containing a nested class. Implement this **interface** and create an instance of the nested class.

23. Create a class containing an inner class that itself contains an inner class. Repeat this using nested classes. Note the names of the **.class** files produced by the compiler.

24. Create a class with an inner class. In a separate class, make an instance of the inner class.

25. Create a class with an inner class that has a nondefault constructor (one that takes arguments). Create a second class with an inner class that inherits from the first inner class.

26. Repair the problem in **WindError.java**.

27. Modify **Sequence.java** by adding a method **getRSelector( )** that produces a different implementation of the **Selector interface** that moves backward through the sequence from the end to the beginning.

28. Create an **interface U** with three methods. Create a class **A** with a method that produces a reference to a **U** by building an anonymous inner class. Create a second class **B** that contains an array of **U**. **B** should have one method that accepts and stores a reference to a **U** in the array, a second method that sets a reference in the array (specified by the method argument) to **null**, and a third method that moves through the array and calls the methods in **U**. In **main( )**, create a group of **A** objects and a single **B**. Fill the **B** with **U** references produced by the **A** objects. Use the **B** to call back into all the **A** objects. Remove some of the **U** references from the **B**.

29. In **GreenhouseControls.java**, add **Event** inner classes that turn fans on and off. Configure **GreenhouseController.java** to use these new **Event** objects.

30. Inherit from **GreenhouseControls** in **GreenhouseControls.java** to add **Event** inner classes that turn water mist generators on and off. Write a new version of **GreenhouseController.java** to use these new **Event** objects.

31. Show that an inner class has access to the **private** elements of its outer class. Determine whether the reverse is true.

9: Error Handling with Exceptions

The basic philosophy of Java is that "badly formed code will not be run."

The ideal time to catch an error is at compile time, before you even try to run the program. However, not all errors can be detected at compile time. The rest of the problems must be handled at run time through some formality that allows the originator of the error to pass appropriate information to a recipient who will know how to handle the difficulty properly.

C and other earlier languages often had multiple error-handling schemes, and these were generally established by convention and not as part of the programming language. Typically, you returned a special value or set a flag, and the recipient was supposed to look at the value or the flag and determine that something was amiss. However, as the years passed, it was discovered that programmers who use a library tend to think of themselves as invincible—as in, "Yes, errors might happen to others, but not in *my* code." So, not too surprisingly, they wouldn't check for the error conditions (and sometimes the error conditions were too silly to check for[1]). If you *were* thorough enough to check for an error every time you called a method, your code could turn into an unreadable nightmare. Because programmers could still coax systems out of these languages, they were resistant to admitting the truth: that this approach to handling errors was a major limitation to creating large, robust, maintainable programs.

The solution is to take the casual nature out of error handling and to enforce formality. This actually has a long history, because implementations of *exception handling* go back to operating systems in the 1960s, and even to BASIC's "**on error goto**." But C++ exception handling was based on Ada,

[1] The C programmer can look up the return value of **printf( )** for an example of this.

and Java's is based primarily on C++ (although it looks more like that in Object Pascal).

The word "exception" is meant in the sense of "I take exception to that." At the point where the problem occurs, you might not know what to do with it, but you do know that you can't just continue on merrily; you must stop, and somebody, somewhere, must figure out what to do. But you don't have enough information in the current context to fix the problem. So you hand the problem out to a higher context where someone is qualified to make the proper decision (much like a chain of command).

The other rather significant benefit of exceptions is that they clean up error handling code. Instead of checking for a particular error and dealing with it at multiple places in your program, you no longer need to check at the point of the method call (since the exception will guarantee that someone catches it). And, you need to handle the problem in only one place, the so-called *exception handler*. This saves you code, and it separates the code that describes what you want to do from the code that is executed when things go awry. In general, reading, writing, and debugging code becomes much clearer with exceptions than when using the old way of error handling.

Because exception handling is the only official way that Java reports errors, and it is enforced by the Java compiler, there are only so many examples that can be written in this book without learning about exception handling. This chapter introduces you to the code you need to write to properly handle exceptions, and the way you can generate your own exceptions if one of your methods gets into trouble.

Basic exceptions

An *exceptional condition* is a problem that prevents the continuation of the method or scope that you're in. It's important to distinguish an exceptional condition from a normal problem, in which you have enough information in the current context to somehow cope with the difficulty. With an exceptional condition, you cannot continue processing because you don't have the information necessary to deal with the problem *in the current context*. All you can do is jump out of the current context and relegate that problem to a higher context. This is what happens when you throw an exception.

Division is a simple example. If you're about to divide by zero, it's worth checking for that condition. But what does it mean that the denominator is zero? Maybe you know, in the context of the problem you're trying to solve in that particular method, how to deal with a zero denominator. But if it's an unexpected value, you can't deal with it and so must throw an exception rather than continuing along that execution path.

When you throw an exception, several things happen. First, the exception object is created in the same way that any Java object is created: on the heap, with **new**. Then the current path of execution (the one you couldn't continue) is stopped and the reference for the exception object is ejected from the current context. At this point the exception handling mechanism takes over and begins to look for an appropriate place to continue executing the program. This appropriate place is the *exception handler,* whose job is to recover from the problem so the program can either try another tack or just continue.

As a simple example of throwing an exception, consider an object reference called **t**. It's possible that you might be passed a reference that hasn't been initialized, so you might want to check before trying to call a method using that object reference. You can send information about the error into a larger context by creating an object representing your information and "throwing" it out of your current context. This is called *throwing an exception.* Here's what it looks like:

```
if(t == null)
  throw new NullPointerException();
```

This throws the exception, which allows you—in the current context—to abdicate responsibility for thinking about the issue further. It's just magically handled somewhere else. Precisely *where* will be shown shortly.

Exception arguments

Like any object in Java, you always create exceptions on the heap using **new**, which allocates storage and calls a constructor. There are two constructors in all standard exceptions; The first is the default constructor, and the second takes a string argument so you can place pertinent information in the exception:

```
  throw new NullPointerException("t = null");
```

This string can later be extracted using various methods, as you'll see.

The keyword **throw** causes a number of relatively magical things to happen. Typically, you'll first use **new** to create an object that represents the error condition. You give the resulting reference to **throw**. The object is, in effect, "returned" from the method, even though that object type isn't normally what the method is designed to return. A simplistic way to think about exception handling is as a different kind of return mechanism, although you get into trouble if you take that analogy too far. You can also exit from ordinary scopes by throwing an exception. But a value is returned, and the method or scope exits.

Any similarity to an ordinary return from a method ends here, because *where* you return is someplace completely different from where you return for a normal method call. (You end up in an appropriate exception handler that might be far—many levels away on the call stack—from where the exception was thrown.)

In addition, you can throw any type of **Throwable** (the exception root class) object that you want. Typically, you'll throw a different class of exception for each different type of error. The information about the error is represented both inside the exception object and implicitly in the name of the exception class, so someone in the bigger context can figure out what to do with your exception. (Often, the only information is the type of exception, and nothing meaningful is stored within the exception object.)

Catching an exception

If a method throws an exception, it must assume that exception will be "caught" and dealt with. One of the advantages of exception handling is that it allows you to concentrate on the problem you're trying to solve in one place, and then deal with the errors from that code in another place.

To see how an exception is caught, you must first understand the concept of a *guarded region*. This is a section of code that might produce exceptions and is followed by the code to handle those exceptions.

The **try** block

If you're inside a method and you throw an exception (or another method you call within this method throws an exception), that method will exit in the process of throwing. If you don't want a **throw** to exit the method, you can set up a special block within that method to capture the exception. This is called the *try block* because you "try" your various method calls there. The try block is an ordinary scope preceded by the keyword **try**:

```
try {
  // Code that might generate exceptions
}
```

If you were checking for errors carefully in a programming language that didn't support exception handling, you'd have to surround every method call with setup and error testing code, even if you call the same method several times. With exception handling, you put everything in a try block and capture all the exceptions in one place. This means your code is much easier to write and read because the goal of the code is not confused with the error checking.

Exception handlers

Of course, the thrown exception must end up someplace. This "place" is the *exception handler,* and there's one for every exception type you want to catch. Exception handlers immediately follow the try block and are denoted by the keyword **catch**:

```
try {
  // Code that might generate exceptions
} catch(Type1 id1) {
  // Handle exceptions of Type1
} catch(Type2 id2) {
  // Handle exceptions of Type2
} catch(Type3 id3) {
  // Handle exceptions of Type3
}

// etc...
```

Each catch clause (exception handler) is like a little method that takes one and only one argument of a particular type. The identifier (**id1**, **id2**, and so on) can be used inside the handler, just like a method argument. Sometimes you never use the identifier because the type of the exception gives you enough information to deal with the exception, but the identifier must still be there.

The handlers must appear directly after the try block. If an exception is thrown, the exception handling mechanism goes hunting for the first handler with an argument that matches the type of the exception. Then it enters that catch clause, and the exception is considered handled. The search for handlers stops once the catch clause is finished. Only the matching catch clause executes; it's not like a **switch** statement in which you need a **break** after each **case** to prevent the remaining ones from executing.

Note that within the try block, a number of different method calls might generate the same exception, but you need only one handler.

Termination vs. resumption

There are two basic models in exception handling theory. In *termination* (which is what Java and C++ support), you assume that the error is so critical that there's no way to get back to where the exception occurred. Whoever threw the exception decided that there was no way to salvage the situation, and they don't *want* to come back.

The alternative is called *resumption*. It means that the exception handler is expected to do something to rectify the situation, and then the faulting method is retried, presuming success the second time. If you want resumption, it means you still hope to continue execution after the exception is handled. In this case, your exception is more like a method call—which is how you should set up situations in Java in which you want resumption-like behavior. (That is, don't throw an exception; call a method that fixes the problem.) Alternatively, place your **try** block inside a **while** loop that keeps reentering the **try** block until the result is satisfactory.

Historically, programmers using operating systems that supported resumptive exception handling eventually ended up using termination-like code and skipping resumption. So although resumption sounds attractive at first, it isn't quite so useful in practice. The dominant reason is probably the *coupling* that results; your handler must often be aware of where the exception is thrown, and contain nongeneric code specific to the throwing location. This makes the code difficult to write and maintain, especially for large systems where the exception can be generated from many points.

Creating your own exceptions

You're not stuck using the existing Java exceptions. The JDK exception hierarchy can't foresee all the errors you might want to report, so you can create your own to denote a special problem that your library might encounter.

To create your own exception class, you must inherit from an existing exception class, preferably one that is close in meaning to your new exception (although this is often not possible). The most trivial way to create a new type of exception is just to let the compiler create the default constructor for you, so it requires almost no code at all:

```
//: c09:SimpleExceptionDemo.java
// Inheriting your own exceptions.
import com.bruceeckel.simpletest.*;

class SimpleException extends Exception {}

public class SimpleExceptionDemo {
  private static Test monitor = new Test();
  public void f() throws SimpleException {
    System.out.println("Throw SimpleException from f()");
    throw new SimpleException();
  }
  public static void main(String[] args) {
    SimpleExceptionDemo sed = new SimpleExceptionDemo();
    try {
      sed.f();
    } catch(SimpleException e) {
      System.err.println("Caught it!");
    }
    monitor.expect(new String[] {
      "Throw SimpleException from f()",
      "Caught it!"
    });
  }
} ///:~
```

The compiler creates a default constructor, which automatically (and invisibly) calls the base-class default constructor. Of course, in this case you don't get a **SimpleException(String)** constructor, but in practice that isn't used much. As you'll see, the most important thing about an exception is the class name, so most of the time an exception like the one shown here is satisfactory.

Here, the result is printed to the console *standard error* stream by writing to **System.err**. This is usually a better place to send error information than **System.out**, which may be redirected. If you send output to **System.err**, it will not be redirected along with **System.out** so the user is more likely to notice it.

You can also create an exception class that has a constructor with a **String** argument:

```
//: c09:FullConstructors.java
import com.bruceeckel.simpletest.*;

class MyException extends Exception {
  public MyException() {}
  public MyException(String msg) { super(msg); }
}

public class FullConstructors {
  private static Test monitor = new Test();
  public static void f() throws MyException {
    System.out.println("Throwing MyException from f()");
    throw new MyException();
  }
  public static void g() throws MyException {
    System.out.println("Throwing MyException from g()");
    throw new MyException("Originated in g()");
  }
  public static void main(String[] args) {
    try {
      f();
    } catch(MyException e) {
      e.printStackTrace();
    }
    try {
      g();
    } catch(MyException e) {
      e.printStackTrace();
    }
    monitor.expect(new String[] {
      "Throwing MyException from f()",
      "MyException",
      "%% \tat FullConstructors.f\\(.*\\)",
      "%% \tat FullConstructors.main\\(.*\\)",
      "Throwing MyException from g()",
      "MyException: Originated in g()",
      "%% \tat FullConstructors.g\\(.*\\)",
      "%% \tat FullConstructors.main\\(.*\\)"
```

```
    });
  }
} ///:~
```

The added code is small: two constructors that define the way **MyException** is created. In the second constructor, the base-class constructor with a **String** argument is explicitly invoked by using the **super** keyword.

In the handlers, one of the **Throwable** (from which **Exception** is inherited) methods is called: **printStackTrace( )**. This produces information about the sequence of methods that were called to get to the point where the exception happened. By default, the information goes to the standard error stream, but overloaded versions allow you to send the results to any other stream as well.

The process of creating your own exceptions can be taken further. You can add extra constructors and members:

```
//: c09:ExtraFeatures.java
// Further embellishment of exception classes.
import com.bruceeckel.simpletest.*;

class MyException2 extends Exception {
  private int x;
  public MyException2() {}
  public MyException2(String msg) { super(msg); }
  public MyException2(String msg, int x) {
    super(msg);
    this.x = x;
  }
  public int val() { return x; }
  public String getMessage() {
    return "Detail Message: "+ x + " "+ super.getMessage();
  }
}

public class ExtraFeatures {
  private static Test monitor = new Test();
  public static void f() throws MyException2 {
    System.out.println("Throwing MyException2 from f()");
    throw new MyException2();
  }
  public static void g() throws MyException2 {
    System.out.println("Throwing MyException2 from g()");
```

```
    throw new MyException2("Originated in g()");
  }
  public static void h() throws MyException2 {
    System.out.println("Throwing MyException2 from h()");
    throw new MyException2("Originated in h()", 47);
  }
  public static void main(String[] args) {
    try {
      f();
    } catch(MyException2 e) {
      e.printStackTrace();
    }
    try {
      g();
    } catch(MyException2 e) {
      e.printStackTrace();
    }
    try {
      h();
    } catch(MyException2 e) {
      e.printStackTrace();
      System.err.println("e.val() = " + e.val());
    }
    monitor.expect(new String[] {
      "Throwing MyException2 from f()",
      "MyException2: Detail Message: 0 null",
      "%% \tat ExtraFeatures.f\\(.*\\)",
      "%% \tat ExtraFeatures.main\\(.*\\)",
      "Throwing MyException2 from g()",
      "MyException2: Detail Message: 0 Originated in g()",
      "%% \tat ExtraFeatures.g\\(.*\\)",
      "%% \tat ExtraFeatures.main\\(.*\\)",
      "Throwing MyException2 from h()",
      "MyException2: Detail Message: 47 Originated in h()",
      "%% \tat ExtraFeatures.h\\(.*\\)",
      "%% \tat ExtraFeatures.main\\(.*\\)",
      "e.val() = 47"
    });
  }
} ///:~
```

A field **i** has been added, along with a method that reads that value and an additional constructor that sets it. In addition, **Throwable.getMessage( )**

has been overridden to produce a more interesting detail message. **getMessage( )** is something like **toString( )** for exception classes.

Since an exception is just another kind of object, you can continue this process of embellishing the power of your exception classes. Keep in mind, however, that all this dressing-up might be lost on the client programmers using your packages, since they might simply look for the exception to be thrown and nothing more. (That's the way most of the Java library exceptions are used.)

The exception specification

In Java, you're encouraged to inform the client programmer, who calls your method, of the exceptions that might be thrown from your method. This is civilized, because the caller can know exactly what code to write to catch all potential exceptions. Of course, if source code is available, the client programmer could hunt through and look for **throw** statements, but often a library doesn't come with sources. To prevent this from being a problem, Java provides syntax (and *forces* you to use that syntax) to allow you to politely tell the client programmer what exceptions this method throws, so the client programmer can handle them. This is the *exception specification* and it's part of the method declaration, appearing after the argument list.

The exception specification uses an additional keyword, **throws**, followed by a list of all the potential exception types. So your method definition might look like this:

```
void f() throws TooBig, TooSmall, DivZero { //...
```

If you say

```
void f() { // ...
```

it means that no exceptions are thrown from the method (*except* for the exceptions inherited from **RuntimeException**, which can be thrown anywhere without exception specifications—this will be described later).

You can't lie about an exception specification. If the code within your method causes exceptions, but your method doesn't handle them, the compiler will detect this and tell you that you must either handle the exception or indicate with an exception specification that it may be thrown from your method. By enforcing exception specifications from top to bottom, Java guarantees that a certain level of exception correctness can be ensured at compile time.

There is one place you can lie: You can claim to throw an exception that you really don't. The compiler takes your word for it, and forces the users of your method to treat it as if it really does throw that exception. This has the beneficial effect of being a placeholder for that exception, so you can actually start throwing the exception later without requiring changes to existing code. It's also important for creating **abstract** base classes and **interface**s whose derived classes or implementations may need to throw exceptions.

Exceptions that are checked and enforced at compile time are called *checked exceptions*.

Catching any exception

It is possible to create a handler that catches any type of exception. You do this by catching the base-class exception type **Exception** (there are other types of base exceptions, but **Exception** is the base that's pertinent to virtually all programming activities):

```
catch(Exception e) {
  System.err.println("Caught an exception");
}
```

This will catch any exception, so if you use it you'll want to put it at the *end* of your list of handlers to avoid preempting any exception handlers that might otherwise follow it.

Since the **Exception** class is the base of all the exception classes that are important to the programmer, you don't get much specific information about the exception, but you can call the methods that come from *its* base type **Throwable**:

String getMessage( )
String getLocalizedMessage( )
Gets the detail message, or a message adjusted for this particular locale.

String toString( )
Returns a short description of the Throwable, including the detail message if there is one.

void printStackTrace( )
void printStackTrace(PrintStream)
void printStackTrace(java.io.PrintWriter)
Prints the Throwable and the Throwable's call stack trace. The call stack shows the sequence of method calls that brought you to the point at which the exception was thrown. The first version prints to standard error, the second and third prints to a stream of your choice (in Chapter 12, you'll understand why there are two types of streams).

Throwable fillInStackTrace( )
Records information within this **Throwable** object about the current state of the stack frames. Useful when an application is rethrowing an error or exception (more about this shortly).

In addition, you get some other methods from **Throwable**'s base type **Object** (everybody's base type). The one that might come in handy for exceptions is **getClass( )**, which returns an object representing the class of this object. You can in turn query this **Class** object for its name with **getName( )**. You can also do more sophisticated things with **Class** objects that aren't necessary in exception handling.

Here's an example that shows the use of the basic **Exception** methods:

```
//: c09:ExceptionMethods.java
// Demonstrating the Exception Methods.
import com.bruceeckel.simpletest.*;

public class ExceptionMethods {
  private static Test monitor = new Test();
  public static void main(String[] args) {
    try {
      throw new Exception("My Exception");
    } catch(Exception e) {
      System.err.println("Caught Exception");
      System.err.println("getMessage():" + e.getMessage());
      System.err.println("getLocalizedMessage():" +
        e.getLocalizedMessage());
      System.err.println("toString():" + e);
      System.err.println("printStackTrace():");
      e.printStackTrace();
    }
    monitor.expect(new String[] {
      "Caught Exception",
```

```
      "getMessage():My Exception",
      "getLocalizedMessage():My Exception",
      "toString():java.lang.Exception: My Exception",
      "printStackTrace():",
      "java.lang.Exception: My Exception",
      "%% \tat ExceptionMethods.main\\(.*\\)"
    });
  }
} ///:~
```

You can see that the methods provide successively more information—each is effectively a superset of the previous one.

Rethrowing an exception

Sometimes you'll want to rethrow the exception that you just caught, particularly when you use **Exception** to catch any exception. Since you already have the reference to the current exception, you can simply rethrow that reference:

```
catch(Exception e) {
  System.err.println("An exception was thrown");
  throw e;
}
```

Rethrowing an exception causes it to go to the exception handlers in the next-higher context. Any further **catch** clauses for the same **try** block are still ignored. In addition, everything about the exception object is preserved, so the handler at the higher context that catches the specific exception type can extract all the information from that object.

If you simply rethrow the current exception, the information that you print about that exception in **printStackTrace( )** will pertain to the exception's origin, not the place where you rethrow it. If you want to install new stack trace information, you can do so by calling **fillInStackTrace( )**, which returns a **Throwable** object that it creates by stuffing the current stack information into the old exception object. Here's what it looks like:

```
//: c09:Rethrowing.java
// Demonstrating fillInStackTrace()
import com.bruceeckel.simpletest.*;

public class Rethrowing {
  private static Test monitor = new Test();
```

```
  public static void f() throws Exception {
    System.out.println("originating the exception in f()");
    throw new Exception("thrown from f()");
  }
  public static void g() throws Throwable {
    try {
      f();
    } catch(Exception e) {
      System.err.println("Inside g(),e.printStackTrace()");
      e.printStackTrace();
      throw e; // 17
      // throw e.fillInStackTrace(); // 18
    }
  }
  public static void
  main(String[] args) throws Throwable {
    try {
      g();
    } catch(Exception e) {
      System.err.println(
        "Caught in main, e.printStackTrace()");
      e.printStackTrace();
    }
    monitor.expect(new String[] {
      "originating the exception in f()",
      "Inside g(),e.printStackTrace()",
      "java.lang.Exception: thrown from f()",
      "%% \tat Rethrowing.f(.*?)",
      "%% \tat Rethrowing.g(.*?)",
      "%% \tat Rethrowing.main(.*?)",
      "Caught in main, e.printStackTrace()",
      "java.lang.Exception: thrown from f()",
      "%% \tat Rethrowing.f(.*?)",
      "%% \tat Rethrowing.g(.*?)",
      "%% \tat Rethrowing.main(.*?)"
    });
  }
} ///:~
```

The important line numbers are marked as comments. With line 17 uncommented (as shown), the output is as shown, so the exception stack trace always remembers its true point of origin no matter how many times it gets rethrown.

With line 17 commented and line 18 uncommented, **fillInStackTrace( )** is used instead, and the result is:

```
originating the exception in f()
Inside g(),e.printStackTrace()
java.lang.Exception: thrown from f()
        at Rethrowing.f(Rethrowing.java:9)
        at Rethrowing.g(Rethrowing.java:12)
        at Rethrowing.main(Rethrowing.java:23)
Caught in main, e.printStackTrace()
java.lang.Exception: thrown from f()
        at Rethrowing.g(Rethrowing.java:18)
        at Rethrowing.main(Rethrowing.java:23)
```

(Plus additional complaints from the **Test.expect( )** method.) Because of **fillInStackTrace( )**, line 18 becomes the new point of origin of the exception.

The class **Throwable** must appear in the exception specification for **g( )** and **main( )** because **fillInStackTrace( )** produces a reference to a **Throwable** object. Since **Throwable** is a base class of **Exception**, it's possible to get an object that's a **Throwable** but *not* an **Exception**, so the handler for **Exception** in **main( )** might miss it. To make sure everything is in order, the compiler forces an exception specification for **Throwable**. For example, the exception in the following program is *not* caught in **main( )**:

```
//: c09:ThrowOut.java
// {ThrowsException}
public class ThrowOut {
  public static void
  main(String[] args) throws Throwable {
    try {
      throw new Throwable();
    } catch(Exception e) {
      System.err.println("Caught in main()");
    }
  }
} ///:~
```

It's also possible to rethrow a different exception from the one you caught. If you do this, you get a similar effect as when you use **fillInStackTrace( )**—the information about the original site of the exception is lost, and what you're left with is the information pertaining to the new **throw**:

```java
//: c09:RethrowNew.java
// Rethrow a different object from the one that was caught.
// {ThrowsException}
import com.bruceeckel.simpletest.*;

class OneException extends Exception {
  public OneException(String s) { super(s); }
}

class TwoException extends Exception {
  public TwoException(String s) { super(s); }
}

public class RethrowNew {
  private static Test monitor = new Test();
  public static void f() throws OneException {
    System.out.println("originating the exception in f()");
    throw new OneException("thrown from f()");
  }
  public static void
  main(String[] args) throws TwoException {
    try {
      f();
    } catch(OneException e) {
      System.err.println(
        "Caught in main, e.printStackTrace()");
      e.printStackTrace();
      throw new TwoException("from main()");
    }
    monitor.expect(new String[] {
      "originating the exception in f()",
      "Caught in main, e.printStackTrace()",
      "OneException: thrown from f()",
      "\tat RethrowNew.f(RethrowNew.java:18)",
      "\tat RethrowNew.main(RethrowNew.java:22)",
      "Exception in thread \"main\" " +
      "TwoException: from main()",
      "\tat RethrowNew.main(RethrowNew.java:28)"
    });
  }
} ///:~
```

The final exception knows only that it came from **main( )** and not from **f( )**.

You never have to worry about cleaning up the previous exception, or any exceptions for that matter. They're all heap-based objects created with **new**, so the garbage collector automatically cleans them all up.

Exception chaining

Often you want to catch one exception and throw another, but still keep the information about the originating exception—this is called *exception chaining*. Prior to JDK 1.4, programmers had to write their own code to preserve the original exception information, but now all **Throwable** subclasses may take a *cause* object in their constructor. The *cause* is intended to be the originating exception, and by passing it in you maintain the stack trace back to its origin, even though you're creating and throwing a new exception at this point.

It's interesting to note that the only **Throwable** subclasses that provide the *cause* argument in the constructor are the three fundamental exception classes **Error** (used by the JVM to report system errors), **Exception**, and **RuntimeException**. If you want to chain any other exception types, you do it through the **initCause( )** method rather than the constructor.

Here's an example that allows you to dynamically add fields to a **DynamicFields** object at run time:

```
//: c09:DynamicFields.java
// A Class that dynamically adds fields to itself.
// Demonstrates exception chaining.
// {ThrowsException}
import com.bruceeckel.simpletest.*;

class DynamicFieldsException extends Exception {}

public class DynamicFields {
  private static Test monitor = new Test();
  private Object[][] fields;
  public DynamicFields(int initialSize) {
    fields = new Object[initialSize][2];
    for(int i = 0; i < initialSize; i++)
      fields[i] = new Object[] { null, null };
  }
  public String toString() {
    StringBuffer result = new StringBuffer();
    for(int i = 0; i < fields.length; i++) {
```

```
      result.append(fields[i][0]);
      result.append(": ");
      result.append(fields[i][1]);
      result.append("\n");
    }
    return result.toString();
  }
  private int hasField(String id) {
    for(int i = 0; i < fields.length; i++)
      if(id.equals(fields[i][0]))
        return i;
    return -1;
  }
  private int
  getFieldNumber(String id) throws NoSuchFieldException {
    int fieldNum = hasField(id);
    if(fieldNum == -1)
      throw new NoSuchFieldException();
    return fieldNum;
  }
  private int makeField(String id) {
    for(int i = 0; i < fields.length; i++)
      if(fields[i][0] == null) {
        fields[i][0] = id;
        return i;
      }
    // No empty fields. Add one:
    Object[][]tmp = new Object[fields.length + 1][2];
    for(int i = 0; i < fields.length; i++)
      tmp[i] = fields[i];
    for(int i = fields.length; i < tmp.length; i++)
      tmp[i] = new Object[] { null, null };
    fields = tmp;
    // Reursive call with expanded fields:
    return makeField(id);
  }
  public Object
  getField(String id) throws NoSuchFieldException {
    return fields[getFieldNumber(id)][1];
  }
  public Object setField(String id, Object value)
  throws DynamicFieldsException {
    if(value == null) {
      // Most exceptions don't have a "cause" constructor.
```

```
      // In these cases you must use initCause(),
      // available in all Throwable subclasses.
      DynamicFieldsException dfe =
        new DynamicFieldsException();
      dfe.initCause(new NullPointerException());
      throw dfe;
    }
    int fieldNumber = hasField(id);
    if(fieldNumber == -1)
      fieldNumber = makeField(id);
    Object result = null;
    try {
      result = getField(id); // Get old value
    } catch(NoSuchFieldException e) {
      // Use constructor that takes "cause":
      throw new RuntimeException(e);
    }
    fields[fieldNumber][1] = value;
    return result;
  }
  public static void main(String[] args) {
    DynamicFields df = new DynamicFields(3);
    System.out.println(df);
    try {
      df.setField("d", "A value for d");
      df.setField("number", new Integer(47));
      df.setField("number2", new Integer(48));
      System.out.println(df);
      df.setField("d", "A new value for d");
      df.setField("number3", new Integer(11));
      System.out.println(df);
      System.out.println(df.getField("d"));
      Object field = df.getField("a3"); // Exception
    } catch(NoSuchFieldException e) {
      throw new RuntimeException(e);
    } catch(DynamicFieldsException e) {
      throw new RuntimeException(e);
    }
    monitor.expect(new String[] {
      "null: null",
      "null: null",
      "null: null",
      "",
      "d: A value for d",
```

```
      "number: 47",
      "number2: 48",
      "",
      "d: A new value for d",
      "number: 47",
      "number2: 48",
      "number3: 11",
      "",
      "A value for d",
      "Exception in thread \"main\" " +
      "java.lang.RuntimeException: " +
      "java.lang.NoSuchFieldException",
      "\tat DynamicFields.main(DynamicFields.java:98)",
      "Caused by: java.lang.NoSuchFieldException",
      "\tat DynamicFields.getFieldNumber(" +
      "DynamicFields.java:37)",
      "\tat DynamicFields.getField(DynamicFields.java:58)",
      "\tat DynamicFields.main(DynamicFields.java:96)"
    });
  }
} ///:~
```

Each **DynamicFields** object contains an array of **Object-Object** pairs. The first object is the field identifier (a **String**), and the second is the field value, which can be any type except an unwrapped primitive. When you create the object, you make an educated guess about how many fields you need. When you call **setField( )**, it either finds the existing field by that name or creates a new one, and puts in your value. If it runs out of space, it adds new space by creating an array of length one longer and copying the old elements in. If you try to put in a **null** value, then it throws a **DynamicFieldsException** by creating one and using **initCause( )** to insert a **NullPointerException** as the cause.

As a return value, **setField( )** also fetches out the old value at that field location using **getField( )**, which could throw a **NoSuchFieldException**. If the client programmer calls **getField( )**, then they are responsible for handling **NoSuchFieldException**, but if this exception is thrown inside **setField( )**, it's a programming error, so the **NoSuchFieldException** is converted to a **RuntimeException** using the constructor that takes a *cause* argument.

Standard Java exceptions

The Java class **Throwable** describes anything that can be thrown as an exception. There are two general types of **Throwable** objects ("types of" = "inherited from"). **Error** represents compile-time and system errors that you don't worry about catching (except in special cases). **Exception** is the basic type that can be thrown from any of the standard Java library class methods and from your methods and run-time accidents. So the Java programmer's base type of interest is usually **Exception**.

The best way to get an overview of the exceptions is to browse the HTML Java documentation that you can download from *java.sun.com*. It's worth doing this once just to get a feel for the various exceptions, but you'll soon see that there isn't anything special between one exception and the next except for the name. Also, the number of exceptions in Java keeps expanding; basically, it's pointless to print them in a book. Any new library you get from a third-party vendor will probably have its own exceptions as well. The important thing to understand is the concept and what you should do with the exceptions.

The basic idea is that the name of the exception represents the problem that occurred, and the exception name is intended to be relatively self-explanatory. The exceptions are not all defined in **java.lang**; some are created to support other libraries such as **util**, **net,** and **io**, which you can see from their full class names or what they are inherited from. For example, all I/O exceptions are inherited from **java.io.IOException**.

The special case of **RuntimeException**

The first example in this chapter was

```
if(t == null)
  throw new NullPointerException();
```

It can be a bit horrifying to think that you must check for **null** on every reference that is passed into a method (since you can't know if the caller has passed you a valid reference). Fortunately, you don't—this is part of the standard run-time checking that Java performs for you, and if any call is made to a **null** reference, Java will automatically throw a **NullPointerException**. So the above bit of code is always superfluous.

There's a whole group of exception types that are in this category. They're always thrown automatically by Java and you don't need to include them in your exception specifications. Conveniently enough, they're all grouped together by putting them under a single base class called **RuntimeException**, which is a perfect example of inheritance; It establishes a family of types that have some characteristics and behaviors in common. Also, you never need to write an exception specification saying that a method might throw a **RuntimeException** (or any type inherited from **RuntimeException**), because they are *unchecked exceptions*. Because they indicate bugs, you don't usually catch a **RuntimeException**—it's dealt with automatically. If you were forced to check for **RuntimeException**s, your code could get too messy. Even though you don't typically catch **RuntimeExceptions**, in your own packages you might choose to throw some of the **RuntimeException**s.

What happens when you don't catch such exceptions? Since the compiler doesn't enforce exception specifications for these, it's quite plausible that a **RuntimeException** could percolate all the way out to your **main( )** method without being caught. To see what happens in this case, try the following example:

```
//: c09:NeverCaught.java
// Ignoring RuntimeExceptions.
// {ThrowsException}
import com.bruceeckel.simpletest.*;

public class NeverCaught {
  private static Test monitor = new Test();
  static void f() {
    throw new RuntimeException("From f()");
  }
  static void g() {
    f();
  }
  public static void main(String[] args) {
    g();
    monitor.expect(new String[] {
      "Exception in thread \"main\" " +
      "java.lang.RuntimeException: From f()",
      "        at NeverCaught.f(NeverCaught.java:7)",
      "        at NeverCaught.g(NeverCaught.java:10)",
      "        at NeverCaught.main(NeverCaught.java:13)"
    });
```

```
    }
} ///:~
```

You can already see that a **RuntimeException** (or anything inherited from it) is a special case, since the compiler doesn't require an exception specification for these types.

So the answer is: If a **RuntimeException** gets all the way out to **main( )** without being caught, **printStackTrace( )** is called for that exception as the program exits.

Keep in mind that you can only ignore exceptions of type **RuntimeException** (and subclasses) in your coding, since all other handling is carefully enforced by the compiler. The reasoning is that a **RuntimeException** represents a programming error:

1. An error you cannot anticipate. For example, a **null** reference that is outside of your control.

2. An error that you, as a programmer, should have checked for in your code (such as **ArrayIndexOutOfBoundsException** where you should have paid attention to the size of the array). An exception that happens from point #1 often becomes an issue for point #2.

You can see what a tremendous benefit it is to have exceptions in this case, since they help in the debugging process.

It's interesting to notice that you cannot classify Java exception handling as a single-purpose tool. Yes, it is designed to handle those pesky run-time errors that will occur because of forces outside your code's control, but it's also essential for certain types of programming bugs that the compiler cannot detect.

Performing cleanup with finally

There's often some piece of code that you want to execute whether or not an exception is thrown within a **try** block. This usually pertains to some operation other than memory recovery (since that's taken care of by the garbage collector). To achieve this effect, you use a **finally** clause[2] at the end of all the exception handlers. The full picture of an exception handling section is thus:

```
try {
  // The guarded region: Dangerous activities
  // that might throw A, B, or C
} catch(A a1) {
  // Handler for situation A
} catch(B b1) {
  // Handler for situation B
} catch(C c1) {
  // Handler for situation C
} finally {
  // Activities that happen every time
}
```

To demonstrate that the **finally** clause always runs, try this program:

```
//: c09:FinallyWorks.java
// The finally clause is always executed.
import com.bruceeckel.simpletest.*;

class ThreeException extends Exception {}

public class FinallyWorks {
  private static Test monitor = new Test();
  static int count = 0;
  public static void main(String[] args) {
    while(true) {
      try {
        // Post-increment is zero first time:
        if(count++ == 0)
          throw new ThreeException();
        System.out.println("No exception");
      } catch(ThreeException e) {
        System.err.println("ThreeException");
      } finally {
        System.err.println("In finally clause");
        if(count == 2) break; // out of "while"
```

---

[2] C++ exception handling does not have the **finally** clause because it relies on destructors to accomplish this sort of cleanup.

```
      }
    }
    monitor.expect(new String[] {
      "ThreeException",
      "In finally clause",
      "No exception",
      "In finally clause"
    });
  }
} ///:~
```

From the output, you can see that whether or not an exception is thrown, the **finally** clause is always executed.

This program also gives a hint for how you can deal with the fact that exceptions in Java (like exceptions in C++) do not allow you to resume back to where the exception was thrown, as discussed earlier. If you place your **try** block in a loop, you can establish a condition that must be met before you continue the program. You can also add a **static** counter or some other device to allow the loop to try several different approaches before giving up. This way you can build a greater level of robustness into your programs.

What's **finally** for?

In a language without garbage collection *and* without automatic destructor calls,[3] **finally** is important because it allows the programmer to guarantee the release of memory regardless of what happens in the **try** block. But Java has garbage collection, so releasing memory is virtually never a problem. Also, it has no destructors to call. So when do you need to use **finally** in Java?

The **finally** clause is necessary when you need to set something *other* than memory back to its original state. This is some kind of cleanup like an open file or network connection, something you've drawn on the screen, or even a switch in the outside world, as modeled in the following example:

```
//: c09:Switch.java
```

---

[3] A destructor is a function that's always called when an object becomes unused. You always know exactly where and when the destructor gets called. C++ has automatic destructor calls, and C# (which is much more like Java) has a way that automatic destruction can occur.

```
public class Switch {
  private boolean state = false;
  public boolean read() { return state; }
  public void on() { state = true; }
  public void off() { state = false; }
} ///:~
```

```
//: c09:OnOffException1.java
public class OnOffException1 extends Exception {} ///:~
```

```
//: c09:OnOffException2.java
public class OnOffException2 extends Exception {} ///:~
```

```
//: c09:OnOffSwitch.java
// Why use finally?

public class OnOffSwitch {
  private static Switch sw = new Switch();
  public static void f()
  throws OnOffException1,OnOffException2 {}
  public static void main(String[] args) {
    try {
      sw.on();
      // Code that can throw exceptions...
      f();
      sw.off();
    } catch(OnOffException1 e) {
      System.err.println("OnOffException1");
      sw.off();
    } catch(OnOffException2 e) {
      System.err.println("OnOffException2");
      sw.off();
    }
  }
} ///:~
```

The goal here is to make sure that the switch is off when **main( )** is completed, so **sw.off( )** is placed at the end of the try block and at the end of each exception handler. But it's possible that an exception could be thrown that isn't caught here, so **sw.off( )** would be missed. However, with **finally** you can place the cleanup code from a try block in just one place:

```
//: c09:WithFinally.java
// Finally Guarantees cleanup.

public class WithFinally {
```

```
  static Switch sw = new Switch();
  public static void main(String[] args) {
    try {
      sw.on();
      // Code that can throw exceptions...
      OnOffSwitch.f();
    } catch(OnOffException1 e) {
      System.err.println("OnOffException1");
    } catch(OnOffException2 e) {
      System.err.println("OnOffException2");
    } finally {
      sw.off();
    }
  }
} ///:~
```

Here the **sw.off( )** has been moved to just one place, where it's guaranteed to run no matter what happens.

Even in cases in which the exception is not caught in the current set of **catch** clauses, **finally** will be executed before the exception handling mechanism continues its search for a handler at the next higher level:

```
//: c09:AlwaysFinally.java
// Finally is always executed.
import com.bruceeckel.simpletest.*;

class FourException extends Exception {}

public class AlwaysFinally {
  private static Test monitor = new Test();
  public static void main(String[] args) {
    System.out.println("Entering first try block");
    try {
      System.out.println("Entering second try block");
      try {
        throw new FourException();
      } finally {
        System.out.println("finally in 2nd try block");
      }
    } catch(FourException e) {
      System.err.println(
        "Caught FourException in 1st try block");
    } finally {
      System.err.println("finally in 1st try block");
```

```
    }
    monitor.expect(new String[] {
      "Entering first try block",
      "Entering second try block",
      "finally in 2nd try block",
      "Caught FourException in 1st try block",
      "finally in 1st try block"
    });
  }
} ///:~
```

The **finally** statement will also be executed in situations in which **break** and **continue** statements are involved. Note that, along with the labeled **break** and labeled **continue**, **finally** eliminates the need for a **goto** statement in Java.

Pitfall: the lost exception

Unfortunately, there's a flaw in Java's exception implementation. Although exceptions are an indication of a crisis in your program and should never be ignored, it's possible for an exception to simply be lost. This happens with a particular configuration using a **finally** clause:

```
//: c09:LostMessage.java
// How an exception can be lost.
// {ThrowsException}
import com.bruceeckel.simpletest.*;

class VeryImportantException extends Exception {
  public String toString() {
    return "A very important exception!";
  }
}

class HoHumException extends Exception {
  public String toString() {
    return "A trivial exception";
  }
}

public class LostMessage {
  private static Test monitor = new Test();
  void f() throws VeryImportantException {
    throw new VeryImportantException();
```

```
  }
  void dispose() throws HoHumException {
    throw new HoHumException();
  }
  public static void main(String[] args) throws Exception {
    LostMessage lm = new LostMessage();
    try {
      lm.f();
    } finally {
      lm.dispose();
    }
    monitor.expect(new String[] {
      "Exception in thread \"main\" A trivial exception",
      "\tat LostMessage.dispose(LostMessage.java:24)",
      "\tat LostMessage.main(LostMessage.java:31)"
    });  }
} ///:~
```

You can see that there's no evidence of the **VeryImportantException**, which is simply replaced by the **HoHumException** in the **finally** clause. This is a rather serious pitfall, since it means that an exception can be completely lost, and in a far more subtle and difficult-to-detect fashion than the preceding example. In contrast, C++ treats the situation in which a second exception is thrown before the first one is handled as a dire programming error. Perhaps a future version of Java will repair this problem (on the other hand, you will typically wrap any method that throws an exception, such as **dispose( )**, inside a **try-catch** clause).

Exception restrictions

When you override a method, you can throw only the exceptions that have been specified in the base-class version of the method. This is a useful restriction, since it means that code that works with the base class will automatically work with any object derived from the base class (a fundamental OOP concept, of course), including exceptions.

This example demonstrates the kinds of restrictions imposed (at compile time) for exceptions:

```
//: c09:StormyInning.java
// Overridden methods may throw only the exceptions
// specified in their base-class versions, or exceptions
// derived from the base-class exceptions.
```

```
class BaseballException extends Exception {}
class Foul extends BaseballException {}
class Strike extends BaseballException {}

abstract class Inning {
  public Inning() throws BaseballException {}
  public void event() throws BaseballException {
    // Doesn't actually have to throw anything
  }
  public abstract void atBat() throws Strike, Foul;
  public void walk() {} // Throws no checked exceptions
}

class StormException extends Exception {}
class RainedOut extends StormException {}
class PopFoul extends Foul {}

interface Storm {
  public void event() throws RainedOut;
  public void rainHard() throws RainedOut;
}

public class StormyInning extends Inning implements Storm {
  // OK to add new exceptions for constructors, but you
  // must deal with the base constructor exceptions:
  public StormyInning()
    throws RainedOut, BaseballException {}
  public StormyInning(String s)
    throws Foul, BaseballException {}
  // Regular methods must conform to base class:
//! void walk() throws PopFoul {} //Compile error
  // Interface CANNOT add exceptions to existing
  // methods from the base class:
//! public void event() throws RainedOut {}
  // If the method doesn't already exist in the
  // base class, the exception is OK:
  public void rainHard() throws RainedOut {}
  // You can choose to not throw any exceptions,
  // even if the base version does:
  public void event() {}
  // Overridden methods can throw inherited exceptions:
  public void atBat() throws PopFoul {}
  public static void main(String[] args) {
```

```java
    try {
      StormyInning si = new StormyInning();
      si.atBat();
    } catch(PopFoul e) {
      System.err.println("Pop foul");
    } catch(RainedOut e) {
      System.err.println("Rained out");
    } catch(BaseballException e) {
      System.err.println("Generic baseball exception");
    }
    // Strike not thrown in derived version.
    try {
      // What happens if you upcast?
      Inning i = new StormyInning();
      i.atBat();
      // You must catch the exceptions from the
      // base-class version of the method:
    } catch(Strike e) {
      System.err.println("Strike");
    } catch(Foul e) {
      System.err.println("Foul");
    } catch(RainedOut e) {
      System.err.println("Rained out");
    } catch(BaseballException e) {
      System.err.println("Generic baseball exception");
    }
  }
} ///:~
```

In **Inning**, you can see that both the constructor and the **event( )** method say they will throw an exception, but they never do. This is legal because it allows you to force the user to catch any exceptions that might be added in overridden versions of **event( )**. The same idea holds for **abstract** methods, as seen in **atBat( )**.

The **interface Storm** is interesting because it contains one method (**event( )**) that is defined in **Inning**, and one method that isn't. Both methods throw a new type of exception, **RainedOut**. When **StormyInning extends Inning** and **implements Storm**, you'll see that the **event( )** method in **Storm** *cannot* change the exception interface of **event( )** in **Inning**. Again, this makes sense because otherwise you'd never know if you were catching the correct thing when working with the base class. Of course, if a method described in an **interface** is not in the base class, such as **rainHard( )**, then there's no problem if it throws exceptions.

The restriction on exceptions does not apply to constructors. You can see in **StormyInning** that a constructor can throw anything it wants, regardless of what the base-class constructor throws. However, since a base-class constructor must always be called one way or another (here, the default constructor is called automatically), the derived-class constructor must declare any base-class constructor exceptions in its exception specification. Note that a derived-class constructor cannot catch exceptions thrown by its base-class constructor.

The reason **StormyInning.walk( )** will not compile is that it throws an exception, but **Inning.walk( )** does not. If this were allowed, then you could write code that called **Inning.walk( )** and that didn't have to handle any exceptions, but then when you substituted an object of a class derived from **Inning**, exceptions would be thrown so your code would break. By forcing the derived-class methods to conform to the exception specifications of the base-class methods, substitutability of objects is maintained.

The overridden **event( )** method shows that a derived-class version of a method may choose not to throw any exceptions, even if the base-class version does. Again, this is fine since it doesn't break any code that is written—assuming the base-class version throws exceptions. Similar logic applies to **atBat( )**, which throws **PopFoul**, an exception that is derived from **Foul** thrown by the base-class version of **atBat( )**. This way, if you write code that works with **Inning** and calls **atBat( )**, you must catch the **Foul** exception. Since **PopFoul** is derived from **Foul**, the exception handler will also catch **PopFoul**.

The last point of interest is in **main( )**. Here, you can see that if you're dealing with exactly a **StormyInning** object, the compiler forces you to catch only the exceptions that are specific to that class, but if you upcast to the base type, then the compiler (correctly) forces you to catch the exceptions for the base type. All these constraints produce much more robust exception-handling code.[4]

---

[4] ISO C++ added similar constraints that require derived-method exceptions to be the same as, or derived from, the exceptions thrown by the base-class method. This is one case in which C++ is actually able to check exception specifications at compile time.

It's useful to realize that although exception specifications are enforced by the compiler during inheritance, the exception specifications are not part of the type of a method, which comprises only the method name and argument types. Therefore, you cannot overload methods based on exception specifications. In addition, just because an exception specification exists in a base-class version of a method doesn't mean that it must exist in the derived-class version of the method. This is quite different from inheritance rules, where a method in the base class must also exist in the derived class. Put another way, the "exception specification interface" for a particular method may narrow during inheritance and overriding, but it may not widen—this is precisely the opposite of the rule for the class interface during inheritance.

Constructors

When writing code with exceptions, it's particularly important that you always ask "If an exception occurs, will this be properly cleaned up?" Most of the time you're fairly safe, but in constructors there's a problem. The constructor puts the object into a safe starting state, but it might perform some operation—such as opening a file—that doesn't get cleaned up until the user is finished with the object and calls a special cleanup method. If you throw an exception from inside a constructor, these cleanup behaviors might not occur properly. This means that you must be especially diligent while you write your constructor.

Since you've just learned about **finally**, you might think that it is the correct solution. But it's not quite that simple, because **finally** performs the cleanup code *every time,* even in the situations in which you don't want the cleanup code executed until the cleanup method runs. Thus, if you do perform cleanup in **finally**, you must set some kind of flag when the constructor finishes normally so that you don't do anything in the **finally** block if the flag is set. Because this isn't particularly elegant (you are coupling your code from one place to another), it's best if you try to avoid performing this kind of cleanup in **finally** unless you are forced to.

In the following example, a class called **InputFile** is created that opens a file and allows you to read it one line (converted into a **String**) at a time. It uses the classes **FileReader** and **BufferedReader** from the Java standard I/O library that will be discussed in Chapter 12, but which are simple enough that you probably won't have any trouble understanding their basic use:

```
//: c09:Cleanup.java
```

```java
// Paying attention to exceptions in constructors.
import com.bruceeckel.simpletest.*;
import java.io.*;

class InputFile {
  private BufferedReader in;
  public InputFile(String fname) throws Exception {
    try {
      in = new BufferedReader(new FileReader(fname));
      // Other code that might throw exceptions
    } catch(FileNotFoundException e) {
      System.err.println("Could not open " + fname);
      // Wasn't open, so don't close it
      throw e;
    } catch(Exception e) {
      // All other exceptions must close it
      try {
        in.close();
      } catch(IOException e2) {
        System.err.println("in.close() unsuccessful");
      }
      throw e; // Rethrow
    } finally {
      // Don't close it here!!!
    }
  }
  public String getLine() {
    String s;
    try {
      s = in.readLine();
    } catch(IOException e) {
      throw new RuntimeException("readLine() failed");
    }
    return s;
  }
  public void dispose() {
    try {
      in.close();
      System.out.println("dispose() successful");
    } catch(IOException e2) {
      throw new RuntimeException("in.close() failed");
    }
  }
}
```

```
public class Cleanup {
  private static Test monitor = new Test();
  public static void main(String[] args) {
    try {
      InputFile in = new InputFile("Cleanup.java");
      String s;
      int i = 1;
      while((s = in.getLine()) != null)
        ; // Perform line-by-line processing here...
      in.dispose();
    } catch(Exception e) {
      System.err.println("Caught Exception in main");
      e.printStackTrace();
    }
    monitor.expect(new String[] {
      "dispose() successful"
    });
  }
} ///:~
```

The constructor for **InputFile** takes a **String** argument, which is the name of the file you want to open. Inside a **try** block, it creates a **FileReader** using the file name. A **FileReader** isn't particularly useful until you turn around and use it to create a **BufferedReader** that you can actually talk to—notice that one of the benefits of **InputFile** is that it combines these two actions.

If the **FileReader** constructor is unsuccessful, it throws a **FileNotFoundException**, which must be caught separately. This is the one case in which you don't want to close the file, because it wasn't successfully opened. Any *other* catch clauses must close the file because it *was* opened by the time those catch clauses are entered. (Of course, this is trickier if more than one method can throw a **FileNotFoundException**. In that case, you might want to break things into several **try** blocks.) The **close( )** method might throw an exception so it is tried and caught even though it's within the block of another **catch** clause—it's just another pair of curly braces to the Java compiler. After performing local operations, the exception is rethrown, which is appropriate because this constructor failed, and you wouldn't want the calling method to assume that the object had been properly created and was valid.

In this example, which doesn't use the aforementioned flagging technique, the **finally** clause is definitely *not* the place to **close( )** the file, since that would close it every time the constructor completed. Because we want the file to be open for the useful lifetime of the **InputFile** object, this would not be appropriate.

The **getLine( )** method returns a **String** containing the next line in the file. It calls **readLine( ),** which can throw an exception, but that exception is caught so **getLine( )** doesn't throw any exceptions. One of the design issues with exceptions is whether to handle an exception completely at this level, to handle it partially and pass the same exception (or a different one) on, or whether to simply pass it on. Passing it on, when appropriate, can certainly simplify coding. In this situation, the **getLine( )** method *converts* the exception to a **RuntimeException** to indicate a programming error.

The **dispose( )** method must be called by the user when finished using the **InputFile** object. This will release the system resources (such as file handles) that are used by the **BufferedReader** and/or **FileReader** objects. You don't want to do this until you're finished with the **InputFile** object, at the point you're going to let it go. You might think of putting such functionality into a **finalize( )** method, but as mentioned in Chapter 4, you can't always be sure that **finalize( )** will be called (even if you *can* be sure that it will be called, you don't know *when*). This is one of the downsides to Java; All cleanup—other than memory cleanup—doesn't happen automatically, so you must inform the client programmer that they are responsible, and possibly guarantee that cleanup occurs using **finalize( )**.

In **Cleanup.java** an **InputFile** is created to open the same source file that creates the program, the file is read in a line at a time, and line numbers are added. All exceptions are caught generically in **main( )**, although you could choose greater granularity.

One of the benefits of this example is to show you why exceptions are introduced at this point in the book—there are many libraries (like I/O, mentioned earlier) that you can't use without dealing with exceptions. Exceptions are so integral to programming in Java, especially because the compiler enforces them, that you can accomplish only so much without knowing how to work with them.

Exception matching

When an exception is thrown, the exception handling system looks through the "nearest" handlers in the order they are written. When it finds a match, the exception is considered handled, and no further searching occurs.

Matching an exception doesn't require a perfect match between the exception and its handler. A derived-class object will match a handler for the base class, as shown in this example:

```
//: c09:Human.java
// Catching exception hierarchies.
import com.bruceeckel.simpletest.*;

class Annoyance extends Exception {}
class Sneeze extends Annoyance {}

public class Human {
  private static Test monitor = new Test();
  public static void main(String[] args) {
    try {
      throw new Sneeze();
    } catch(Sneeze s) {
      System.err.println("Caught Sneeze");
    } catch(Annoyance a) {
      System.err.println("Caught Annoyance");
    }
    monitor.expect(new String[] {
      "Caught Sneeze"
    });
  }
} ///:~
```

The **Sneeze** exception will be caught by the first **catch** clause that it matches, which is the first one, of course. However, if you remove the first catch clause, leaving only:

```
    try {
      throw new Sneeze();
    } catch(Annoyance a) {
      System.err.println("Caught Annoyance");
    }
```

the code will still work because it's catching the base class of **Sneeze**. Put another way, **catch(Annoyance e)** will catch an **Annoyance** *or any class derived from it*. This is useful because if you decide to add more derived exceptions to a method, then the client programmer's code will not need changing as long as the client catches the base class exceptions.

If you try to "mask" the derived-class exceptions by putting the base-class catch clause first, like this:

```
try {
  throw new Sneeze();
} catch(Annoyance a) {
  System.err.println("Caught Annoyance");
} catch(Sneeze s) {
  System.err.println("Caught Sneeze");
}
```

the compiler will give you an error message, since it sees that the **Sneeze** catch-clause can never be reached.

Alternative approaches

An exception-handling system is a trap door that allows your program to abandon execution of the normal sequence of statements. The trap door is used when an "exceptional condition" occurs, such that normal execution is no longer possible or desirable. Exceptions represent conditions that the current method is unable to handle. The reason exception handling systems were developed is because the approach of dealing with each possible error condition produced by each function call was too onerous, and programmers simply weren't doing it. As a result, they were ignoring the errors. It's worth observing that the issue of programmer convenience in handling errors was a prime motivation for exceptions in the first place.

One of the important guidelines in exception handling is "don't catch an exception unless you know what to do with it." In fact, one of the important *goals* of exception handling is to move the error-handling code away from the point where the errors occur. This allows you to focus on what you want to accomplish in one section of your code, and how you're going to deal with problems in a distinct separate section of your code. As a result, your mainline code is not cluttered with error-handling logic, and it's much easier to understand and maintain.

Checked exceptions complicate this scenario a bit, because they force you to add catch clauses in places where you may not be ready to handle an error. This results in the "harmful if swallowed" problem:

```
try {
  // ... to do something useful
} catch(ObligatoryException e) {} // Gulp!
```

Programmers (myself included, in the first edition of this book) would just do the simplest thing, and swallow the exception—often unintentionally, but once you do it, the compiler has been satisfied, so unless you remember to revisit and correct the code, the exception will be lost. The exception happens, but it vanishes completely when swallowed. Because the compiler forces you to write code right away to handle the exception, this seems like the easiest solution even though it's probably the worst thing you can do.

Horrified upon realizing that I had done this, in the second edition I "fixed" the problem by printing the stack trace inside the handler (as is still seen—appropriately—in a number of examples in this chapter). While this is useful to trace the behavior of exceptions, it still indicates that you don't really know what to do with the exception at that point in your code. In this section we'll look at some of the issues and complications arising from checked exceptions, and options that you have when dealing with them.

This topic seems simple. But it is not only complicated, it is also an issue of some volatility. There are people who are staunchly rooted on either side of the fence and who feel that the correct answer (theirs) is blatantly obvious. I believe the reason for one of these positions is the distinct benefit seen in going from a poorly-typed language like pre-ANSI C to a strong, statically-typed language (that is, checked at compile-time) like C++ or Java. When you make that transition (as I did), the benefits are so dramatic that it can seem like strong static type checking is always the best answer to most problems. My hope is to relate a little bit of my own evolution, that has brought the *absolute* value of strong static type checking into question; clearly, it's very helpful much of the time, but there's a fuzzy line we cross when it begins to get in the way and become a hindrance (one of my favorite quotes is: "All models are wrong. Some are useful.").

History

Exception handling originated in systems like PL/1 and Mesa, and later appeared in CLU, Smalltalk, Modula-3, Ada, Eiffel, C++, Python, Java, and the post-Java languages Ruby and C#. The Java design is similar to C++, except in places where the Java designers felt that the C++ design caused problems.

To provide programmers with a framework that they were more likely to use for error handling and recovery, exception handling was added to C++ rather late in the standardization process, promoted by Bjarne Stroustrup, the language's original author. The model for C++ exceptions came primarily from CLU. However, other languages existed at that time that also supported exception handling: Ada, Smalltalk (both of which had exceptions but no exception specifications) and Modula-3 (which included both exceptions and specifications).

In their seminal paper[5] on the subject, Liskov and Snyder note that a major defect of languages like C that report errors in a transient fashion is that:

> *"...every invocation must be followed by a conditional test to determine what the outcome was. This requirement leads to programs that are difficult to read, and probably inefficient as well, thus discouraging programmers from signaling and handling exceptions."*

Note that one of the original motivations of exception handling was to prevent this requirement, but with checked exceptions in Java we commonly see exactly this kind of code. They go on to say:

> *"...requiring that the text of a handler be attached to the invocation that raises the exception would lead to unreadable programs in which expressions were broken up with handlers."*

Following the CLU approach when designing C++ exceptions, Stroustrup stated that the goal was to reduce the amount of code required to recover from errors. I believe that he was observing that programmers were typically not writing error-handling code in C because the amount and placement of such code was daunting and distracting. As a result, they were used to doing it the C way, ignoring errors in code and using debuggers to track down problems. To use exceptions, these C programmers had to be convinced to write "additional" code that they weren't normally writing. Thus, to draw

---

5 Barbara Liskov and Alan Snyder: *Exception Handling in CLU*, IEEE Transactions on Software Engineering, Vol. SE-5, No. 6, November 1979. This paper is not available on the Internet, only in print form so you'll have to contact a library to get a copy.

them into a better way of handling errors, the amount of code they would need to "add" must not be onerous. I think it's important to keep this goal in mind when looking at the effects of checked exceptions in Java.

C++ brought an additional idea over from CLU: the exception specification, to programmatically state in the method signature what exceptions may result from calling that method. The exception specification really has two purposes. It can say "I'm originating this exception in my code, you handle it." But it can also mean "I'm ignoring this exception that can occur as a result of my code, you handle it." We've been focusing on the "you handle it" part when looking at the mechanics and syntax of exceptions, but here I'm particularly interested in the fact that often we ignore exceptions and that's what the exception specification can state.

In C++ the exception specification is not part of the type information of a function. The only compile-time checking is to ensure that exception specifications are used consistently; for example, if a function or method throws exceptions, then the overloaded or derived versions must also throw those exceptions. Unlike Java, however, no compile-time checking occurs to determine whether or not the function or method will actually throw that exception, or whether the exception specification is complete (that is, whether it accurately describes all exceptions that may be thrown). That validation does happen, but only at run time. If an exception is thrown that violates the exception specification, the C++ program will call the standard library function **unexpected( )**.

It is interesting to note that, because of the use of templates, exception specifications are not used at all in the standard C++ library. Exception specifications, then, may have a significant impact on the design of Java *generics* (Java's version of C++ templates, expected to appear in JDK 1.5).

Perspectives

First, it's worth noting that Java effectively invented the checked exception (clearly inspired by C++ exception specifications and the fact that C++ programmers typically don't bother with them). It has been an experiment, which no language since has chosen to duplicate.

Secondly, checked exceptions appear to be an obvious good thing when seen in introductory examples and in small programs. It has been suggested that the subtle difficulties begin to appear when programs start to get large. Of course, largeness usually doesn't happen overnight; it creeps. Languages that may not be suited for large-scale projects are used for small projects that grow, and at some point we realize that things have gone from manageable to difficult. This is what I'm suggesting may be the case with too much type checking; in particular, with checked exceptions.

The scale of the program seems to be a significant issue. This is a problem because most discussions tend to use small programs as demonstrations. One of the C# designers observed that:

> *"Examination of small programs leads to the conclusion that requiring exception specifications could both enhance developer productivity and enhance code quality, but experience with large software projects suggests a different result—decreased productivity and little or no increase in code quality."*[6]

In reference to uncaught exceptions, the CLU creators stated:

> *"We felt it was unrealistic to require the programmer to provide handlers in situations where no meaningful action can be taken."*[7]

When explaining why a function declaration with no specification means that it can throw *any* exception, rather than *no* exceptions, Stroustrup states:

> *"However, that would require exception specifications for essentially every function, would be a significant cause for recompilation, and would inhibit cooperation with software written in other languages. This would encourage programmers to subvert the exception-handling mechanisms and to write spurious code to suppress exceptions. It would provide a false sense of security to people who failed to notice the exception."*[8]

We see this very behavior—subverting the exceptions—happening with checked exceptions in Java.

---

[6] http://discuss.develop.com/archives/wa.exe?A2=ind0011A&L=DOTNET&P=R32820

[7] ibid

[8] Bjarne Stroustrup, *The C++ Programming Language, 3rd edition, Addison-Wesley 1997,* pp 376.

Martin Fowler (author of *UML Distilled*, *Refactoring*, and *Analysis Patterns*) wrote the following to me:

> *"...on the whole I think that exceptions are good, but Java checked exceptions are more trouble than they are worth."*

I now think that Java's important step was to unify the error reporting model, so that all errors are *reported* using exceptions. This wasn't happening with C++, because for backward compatibility with C the old model of just ignoring errors was still available. But if you have consistent reporting with exceptions, then the exceptions can be used if desired, and if not, they will propagate out to the highest level (the console or other container program). When Java changed the C++ model so that exceptions were the only way to report errors, the extra enforcement of checked exceptions may have become less necessary.

In the past, I have been a strong believer that both checked exceptions and strong static type checking were essential to robust program development. However, both anecdotal and direct experience[9] with languages that are more dynamic than static have lead me to think that the great benefits actually come from:

1. A unified error-reporting model via exceptions, regardless of whether the programmer is forced by the compiler to handle them.

2. Type checking, regardless of *when* it takes place. That is, as long as proper use of a type is enforced, it doesn't matter if it happens at compile time or run time.

On top of this, there are very significant productivity benefits to reducing the compile-time constraints upon the programmer. Indeed, *reflection* (and eventually, *generics*) is required to compensate for the over-constraining nature of strong static typing, as you shall see in the next chapter and in a number of examples throughout the book.

I've already been told by some that what I say here constitutes blasphemy, and by uttering these words my reputation will be destroyed, civilizations will fall, and a higher percentage of programming projects will fail. The belief that

---

[9] Indirectly with Smalltalk via conversations with many experienced programmers in that language; directly with Python (*www.Python.org*).

the compiler can save your project by pointing out errors at compile time runs strong, but it's even more important to realize the limitation of what the compiler is able to do; in Chapter 15, I emphasize the value of an automated build process and unit testing, which give you far more leverage than you get by trying to turn everything into a syntax error. It's worth keeping in mind that:

> *A good programming language is one that helps programmers write good programs. No programming language will prevent its users from writing bad programs.*[10]

In any event, the likelihood of checked exceptions ever being removed from Java seems dim. It would be too radical of a language change, and proponents within Sun appear to be quite strong. Sun has a history and policy of absolute backwards compatibility—to give you a sense of this, virtually all Sun software runs on all Sun hardware, no matter how old. However, if you find that some checked exceptions are getting in your way, or especially if you find yourself being forced to catch exceptions, but you don't know what to do with them, there are some alternatives.

Passing exceptions to the console

In simple programs, like many of those in this book, the easiest way to preserve the exceptions without writing a lot of code is to pass them out of **main( )** to the console. For example, if you want to open a file for reading (something you'll learn about in detail in Chapter 12), you must open and close a **FileInputStream**, which throws exceptions. For a simple program, you can do this (you'll see this approach used in numerous places throughout this book):

```
//: c09:MainException.java
import java.io.*;

public class MainException {
  // Pass all exceptions to the console:
  public static void main(String[] args) throws Exception {
    // Open the file:
    FileInputStream file =
```

---

[10] *(Kees Koster, designer of the CDL language, as quoted by Bertrand Meyer, designer of the Eiffel Language).* http://www.elj.com/elj/v1/n1/bm/right/.

```java
      new FileInputStream("MainException.java");
    // Use the file ...
    // Close the file:
    file.close();
  }
} ///:~
```

Note that **main( )** is also a method that may have an exception specification, and here the type of exception is **Exception**, the root class of all checked exceptions. By passing it out to the console, you are relieved from writing try-catch clauses within the body of **main( )**. (Unfortunately, file I/O is significantly more complex than it would appear to be from this example, so don't get too excited until after you've read Chapter 12).

Converting checked to unchecked exceptions

Throwing an exception from **main( )** is convenient when you're writing a **main( )**, but not generally useful. The real problem is when you are writing an ordinary method body, and you call another method and realize "I have no idea what to do with this exception here, but I don't want to swallow it or print some banal message." With JDK 1.4 chained exceptions, a new and simple solution prevents itself. You simply "wrap" a checked exception inside a **RuntimeException**, like this:

```java
try {
  // ... to do something useful
} catch(IDontKnowWhatToDoWithThisCheckedException e) {
  throw new RuntimeException(e);
}
```

This seems to be an ideal solution if you want to "turn off" the checked exception—you don't swallow it, and you don't have to put it in your method's exception specification, but because of exception chaining you don't lose any information from the original exception.

This technique provides the option to ignore the exception and let it bubble up the call stack without being required to write **try-catch** clauses and/or exception specifications. However, you may still catch and handle the specific exception by using **getCause( )**, as seen here:

```java
//: c09:TurnOffChecking.java
// "Turning off" Checked exceptions.
```

```java
import com.bruceeckel.simpletest.*;
import java.io.*;

class WrapCheckedException {
  void throwRuntimeException(int type) {
    try {
      switch(type) {
        case 0: throw new FileNotFoundException();
        case 1: throw new IOException();
        case 2: throw new RuntimeException("Where am I?");
        default: return;
      }
    } catch(Exception e) { // Adapt to unchecked:
      throw new RuntimeException(e);
    }
  }
}

class SomeOtherException extends Exception {}

public class TurnOffChecking {
  private static Test monitor = new Test();
  public static void main(String[] args) {
    WrapCheckedException wce = new WrapCheckedException();
    // You can call f() without a try block, and let
    // RuntimeExceptions go out of the method:
    wce.throwRuntimeException(3);
    // Or you can choose to catch exceptions:
    for(int i = 0; i < 4; i++)
      try {
        if(i < 3)
          wce.throwRuntimeException(i);
        else
          throw new SomeOtherException();
      } catch(SomeOtherException e) {
          System.out.println("SomeOtherException: " + e);
      } catch(RuntimeException re) {
        try {
          throw re.getCause();
        } catch(FileNotFoundException e) {
          System.out.println(
            "FileNotFoundException: " + e);
        } catch(IOException e) {
          System.out.println("IOException: " + e);
```

```
            } catch(Throwable e) {
              System.out.println("Throwable: " + e);
            }
          }
        monitor.expect(new String[] {
          "FileNotFoundException: " +
          "java.io.FileNotFoundException",
          "IOException: java.io.IOException",
          "Throwable: java.lang.RuntimeException: Where am I?",
          "SomeOtherException: SomeOtherException"
        });
      }
    } ///:~
```

WrapCheckedException.throwRuntimeException( ) contains code that generates different types of exceptions. These are caught and wrapped inside **RuntimeException** objects, so they become the "cause" of those exceptions.

In **TurnOffChecking**, you can see that it's possible to call **throwRuntimeException( )** with no try block because the method does not throw any checked exceptions. However, when you're ready to catch exceptions, you still have the ability to catch any exception you want by putting your code inside a **try** block. You start by catching all the exceptions you explicitly know might emerge from the code in your **try** block—in this case, **SomeOtherException** is caught first. Lastly, you catch **RuntimeException** and **throw** the result of **getCause( )** (the wrapped exception). This extracts the originating exceptions, which can then be handled in their own **catch** clauses.

The technique of wrapping a checked exception in a **RuntimeException** will be used when appropriate throughout the rest of this book.

Exception guidelines

Use exceptions to:

1. Handle problems at the appropriate level. (Avoid catching exceptions unless you know what to do with them).

2. Fix the problem and call the method that caused the exception again.

3. Patch things up and continue without retrying the method.

4. Calculate some alternative result instead of what the method was supposed to produce.

5. Do whatever you can in the current context and rethrow the *same* exception to a higher context.

6. Do whatever you can in the current context and throw a *different* exception to a higher context.

7. Terminate the program.

8. Simplify. (If your exception scheme makes things more complicated, then it is painful and annoying to use.)

9. Make your library and program safer. (This is a short-term investment for debugging, and a long-term investment for application robustness.)

Summary

Improved error recovery is one of the most powerful ways that you can increase the robustness of your code. Error recovery is a fundamental concern for every program you write, but it's especially important in Java, where one of the primary goals is to create program components for others to use. *To create a robust system, each component must be robust.* By providing a consistent error-reporting model with exceptions, Java allows components to reliably communicate problems to client code.

The goals for exception handling in Java are to simplify the creation of large, reliable programs using less code than currently possible, and to do so with more confidence that your application doesn't have an unhandled error. Exceptions are not terribly difficult to learn, and are one of those features that provide immediate and significant benefits to your project.

Exercises

Solutions to selected exercises can be found in the electronic document *The Thinking in Java Annotated Solution Guide*, available for a small fee from *www.BruceEckel.com*.

1. Create a class with a **main( )** that throws an object of class **Exception** inside a **try** block. Give the constructor for **Exception** a **String** argument. Catch the exception inside a **catch** clause and

print the **String** argument. Add a **finally** clause and print a message to prove you were there.

2. Create your own exception class using the **extends** keyword. Write a constructor for this class that takes a **String** argument and stores it inside the object with a **String** reference. Write a method that prints out the stored **String**. Create a **try-catch** clause to exercise your new exception.

3. Write a class with a method that throws an exception of the type created in Exercise 2. Try compiling it without an exception specification to see what the compiler says. Add the appropriate exception specification. Try out your class and its exception inside a try-catch clause.

4. Define an object reference and initialize it to **null**. Try to call a method through this reference. Now wrap the code in a **try-catch** clause to catch the exception.

5. Create a class with two methods, **f( )** and **g( )**. In **g( )**, throw an exception of a new type that you define. In **f( )**, call **g( )**, catch its exception and, in the **catch** clause, throw a different exception (of a second type that you define). Test your code in **main( )**.

6. Repeat the previous exercise, but inside the **catch** clause, wrap **g( )**'s exception in a **RuntimeException**.

7. Create three new types of exceptions. Write a class with a method that throws all three. In **main( )**, call the method but only use a single **catch** clause that will catch all three types of exceptions.

8. Write code to generate and catch an **ArrayIndexOutOfBoundsException**.

9. Create your own resumption-like behavior by using a **while** loop that repeats until an exception is no longer thrown.

10. Create a three-level hierarchy of exceptions. Now create a base-class **A** with a method that throws an exception at the base of your hierarchy. Inherit **B** from **A** and override the method so it throws an exception at level two of your hierarchy. Repeat by inheriting class **C**

from **B**. In **main( )**, create a **C** and upcast it to **A**, then call the method.

11. Demonstrate that a derived-class constructor cannot catch exceptions thrown by its base-class constructor.

12. Show that **OnOffSwitch.java** can fail by throwing a **RuntimeException** inside the **try** block.

13. Show that **WithFinally.java** doesn't fail by throwing a **RuntimeException** inside the **try** block.

14. Modify Exercise 7 by adding a **finally** clause. Verify that your **finally** clause is executed, even if a **NullPointerException** is thrown.

15. Create an example where you use a flag to control whether cleanup code is called, as described in the second paragraph after the heading "Constructors."

16. Modify **StormyInning.java** by adding an **UmpireArgument** exception type and methods that throw this exception. Test the modified hierarchy.

17. Remove the first catch clause in **Human.java** and verify that the code still compiles and runs properly.

18. Add a second level of exception loss to **LostMessage.java** so that the **HoHumException** is itself replaced by a third exception.

19. Add an appropriate set of exceptions to **c08:GreenhouseControls.java**.

20. Add an appropriate set of exceptions to **c08:Sequence.java**.

21. Change the file name string in **MainException.java** to name a file that doesn't exist. Run the program and note the result.

10: Detecting Types

The idea of run-time type identification (RTTI) seems fairly simple at first: It lets you find the exact type of an object when you have only a reference to the base type.

However, the *need* for RTTI uncovers a whole plethora of interesting (and often perplexing) OO design issues, and raises fundamental questions of how you should structure your programs.

This chapter looks at the ways that Java allows you to discover information about objects and classes at run time. This takes two forms: "Traditional" RTTI, which assumes that you have all the types available at compile time and run time, and the "reflection" mechanism, which allows you to discover class information solely at run time. The "traditional" RTTI will be covered first, followed by a discussion of reflection.

The need for RTTI

Consider the now familiar example of a class hierarchy that uses polymorphism. The generic type is the base class **Shape**, and the specific derived types are **Circle**, **Square**, and **Triangle**:

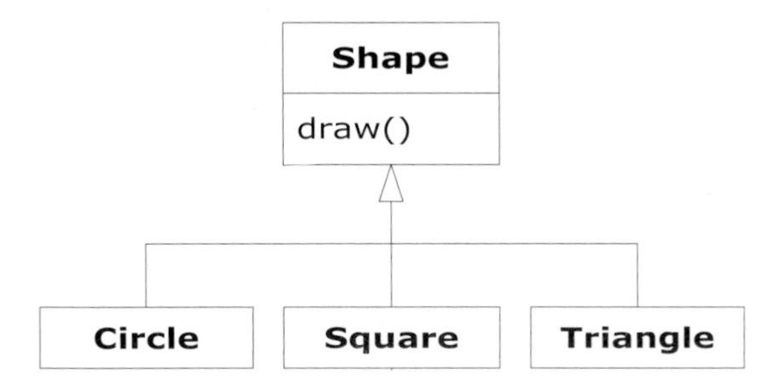

This is a typical class hierarchy diagram, with the base class at the top and the derived classes growing downward. The normal goal in object-oriented programming is for your code to manipulate references to the base type (**Shape**, in this case), so if you decide to extend the program by adding a new class (such as **Rhomboid**, derived from **Shape**), the bulk of the code is not affected. In this example, the dynamically bound method in the **Shape** interface is **draw( )**, so the intent is for the client programmer to call **draw( )** through a generic **Shape** reference. In all of the derived classes, **draw( )** is overridden, and because it is a dynamically bound method, the proper behavior will occur even though it is called through a generic **Shape** reference. That's polymorphism.

Thus, you generally create a specific object (**Circle**, **Square**, or **Triangle**), upcast it to a **Shape** (forgetting the specific type of the object), and use that anonymous **Shape** reference in the rest of the program.

As a brief review of polymorphism and upcasting, you might code the preceding example as follows:

```
//: c10:Shapes.java
import com.bruceeckel.simpletest.*;

class Shape {
  void draw() { System.out.println(this + ".draw()"); }
}

class Circle extends Shape {
  public String toString() { return "Circle"; }
}

class Square extends Shape {
  public String toString() { return "Square"; }
}

class Triangle extends Shape {
  public String toString() { return "Triangle"; }
}

public class Shapes {
  private static Test monitor = new Test();
  public static void main(String[] args) {
    // Array of Object, not Shape:
    Object[] shapeList = {
      new Circle(),
      new Square(),
```

```
      new Triangle()
    };
    for(int i = 0; i < shapeList.length; i++)
      ((Shape)shapeList[i]).draw(); // Must cast
    monitor.expect(new String[] {
      "Circle.draw()",
      "Square.draw()",
      "Triangle.draw()"
    });
  }
} ///:~
```

The base class contains a **draw( )** method that indirectly uses **toString( )** to print an identifier for the class by passing **this** to **System.out.println( )**. If that method sees an object, it automatically calls the **toString( )** method to produce a **String** representation. Each of the derived classes overrides the **toString( )** method (from **Object**) so that **draw( )** ends up (polymorphically) printing something different in each case.

In **main( )**, specific types of **Shape** are created and added to an array. This array is a bit odd because it isn't an array of **Shape** (although it could be), but instead an array of the root class **Object**. The reason for this is to start preparing you for Chapter 11, which presents tools called *collections* (also called *containers*), whose sole job is to hold and manage other objects for you. However, to be generally useful these collections need to hold anything. Therefore they hold **Object**s. So an array of **Object** will demonstrate an important issue that you will encounter in the Chapter 11 collections.

In this example, the upcast occurs when the shape is placed in the array of **Object**s. Since everything in Java (with the exception of primitives) is an **Object**, an array of **Object**s can also hold **Shape** objects. But during the upcast to **Object**, the fact is lost that the objects are **Shape**s. To the array, they are just **Object**s.

At the point that you fetch an element out of the array with the index operator, things get a little busy. Since the array holds only **Object**s, indexing naturally produces an **Object** reference. But we know it's really a **Shape** reference, and we want to send **Shape** messages to that object. So a cast to **Shape** is necessary using the traditional "**(Shape)**" cast. This is the most basic form of RTTI, because all casts are checked at run time for correctness. That's exactly what RTTI means: at run time, the type of an object is identified.

In this case, the RTTI cast is only partial: The **Object** is cast to a **Shape**, and not all the way to a **Circle**, **Square**, or **Triangle**. That's because the only thing we *know* at this point is that the array is full of **Shape**s. At compile time, this is enforced only by your own self-imposed rules, but at run time the cast ensures it.

Now polymorphism takes over and the exact code that's executed for the **Shape** is determined by whether the reference is for a **Circle**, **Square**, or **Triangle**. And in general, this is how it should be; you want the bulk of your code to know as little as possible about *specific* types of objects, and to just deal with the general representation of a family of objects (in this case, **Shape**). As a result, your code will be easier to write, read, and maintain, and your designs will be easier to implement, understand, and change. So polymorphism is a general goal in object-oriented programming.

But what if you have a special programming problem that's easiest to solve if you know the exact type of a generic reference? For example, suppose you want to allow your users to highlight all the shapes of any particular type by turning them purple. This way, they can find all the triangles on the screen by highlighting them. Or perhaps your method needs to "rotate" a list of shapes, but it makes no sense to rotate a circle so you'd like to skip only the circle, objects. With RTTI, you can ask a **Shape** reference the exact type that it's referring to, and thus select and isolate special cases.

The **Class** object

To understand how RTTI works in Java, you must first know how type information is represented at run time. This is accomplished through a special kind of object called the *Class object,* which contains information about the class. In fact, the **Class** object is used to create all of the "regular" objects of your class.

There's a **Class** object for each class that is part of your program. That is, each time you write and compile a new class, a single **Class** object is also created (and stored, appropriately enough, in an identically named **.class** file). At run time, when you want to make an object of that class, the Java Virtual Machine (JVM) that's executing your program first checks to see if the **Class** object for that type is loaded. If not, the JVM loads it by finding the **.class** file with that name. Thus, a Java program isn't completely loaded before it begins, which is different from many traditional languages.

Once the **Class** object for that type is in memory, it is used to create all objects of that type. If this seems shadowy or if you don't really believe it, here's a demonstration program to prove it:

```
//: c10:SweetShop.java
// Examination of the way the class loader works.
import com.bruceeckel.simpletest.*;

class Candy {
  static {
    System.out.println("Loading Candy");
  }
}

class Gum {
  static {
    System.out.println("Loading Gum");
  }
}

class Cookie {
  static {
    System.out.println("Loading Cookie");
  }
}

public class SweetShop {
  private static Test monitor = new Test();
  public static void main(String[] args) {
    System.out.println("inside main");
    new Candy();
    System.out.println("After creating Candy");
    try {
      Class.forName("Gum");
    } catch(ClassNotFoundException e) {
      System.out.println("Couldn't find Gum");
    }
    System.out.println("After Class.forName(\"Gum\")");
    new Cookie();
    System.out.println("After creating Cookie");
    monitor.expect(new String[] {
      "inside main",
      "Loading Candy",
      "After creating Candy",
```

```
      "Loading Gum",
      "After Class.forName(\"Gum\")",
      "Loading Cookie",
      "After creating Cookie"
    });
  }
} ///:~
```

Each of the classes **Candy**, **Gum**, and **Cookie** have a **static** clause that is executed as the class is loaded for the first time. Information will be printed to tell you when loading occurs for that class. In **main( )**, the object creations are spread out between print statements to help detect the time of loading.

You can see from the output that each **Class** object is loaded only when it's needed, and the **static** initialization is performed upon class loading.

A particularly interesting line is:

```
Class.forName("Gum");
```

This method is a **static** member of **Class** (to which all **Class** objects belong). A **Class** object is like any other object, so you can get and manipulate a reference to it (that's what the loader does). One of the ways to get a reference to the **Class** object is **forName( )**, which takes a **String** containing the textual name (watch the spelling and capitalization!) of the particular class you want a reference for. It returns a **Class** reference, which is being ignored here; the call to **forName( )** is being made for its side effect, which is to load the class **Gum** if it isn't already loaded. In the process of loading, **Gum**'s **static** clause is executed.

In the preceding example, if **Class.forName( )** fails because it can't find the class you're trying to load, it will throw a **ClassNotFoundException** (ideally, exception names tell you just about everything you need to know about the problem). Here, we simply report the problem and move on, but in more sophisticated programs, you might try to fix the problem inside the exception handler.

Class literals

Java provides a second way to produce the reference to the **Class** object: the *class literal*. In the preceding program this would look like:

```
Gum.class;
```

which is not only simpler, but also safer since it's checked at compile time. Because it eliminates the method call, it's also more efficient.

Class literals work with regular classes as well as interfaces, arrays, and primitive types. In addition, there's a standard field called **TYPE** that exists for each of the primitive wrapper classes. The **TYPE** field produces a reference to the **Class** object for the associated primitive type, such that:

... is equivalent to ...	
boolean.class	**Boolean.TYPE**
char.class	**Character.TYPE**
byte.class	**Byte.TYPE**
short.class	**Short.TYPE**
int.class	**Integer.TYPE**
long.class	**Long.TYPE**
float.class	**Float.TYPE**
double.class	**Double.TYPE**
void.class	**Void.TYPE**

My preference is to use the "**.class**" versions if you can, since they're more consistent with regular classes.

Checking before a cast

So far, you've seen RTTI forms including:

1. The classic cast; e.g., "**(Shape),**" which uses RTTI to make sure the cast is correct. This will throw a **ClassCastException** if you've performed a bad cast.

2. The **Class** object representing the type of your object. The **Class** object can be queried for useful run time information.

In C++, the classic cast "**(Shape)**" does *not* perform RTTI. It simply tells the compiler to treat the object as the new type. In Java, which does perform the type check, this cast is often called a "type safe downcast." The reason for the term "downcast" is the historical arrangement of the class hierarchy diagram. If casting a **Circle** to a **Shape** is an upcast, then casting a **Shape** to a **Circle** is a downcast. However, you know a **Circle** is also a **Shape**, and the compiler freely allows an upcast assignment, but you *don't* know that a **Shape** is necessarily a **Circle**, so the compiler doesn't allow you to perform a downcast assignment without using an explicit cast.

There's a third form of RTTI in Java. This is the keyword **instanceof**, which tells you if an object is an instance of a particular type. It returns a **boolean** so you use it in the form of a question, like this:

```
if(x instanceof Dog)
  ((Dog)x).bark();
```

The **if** statement checks to see if the object **x** belongs to the class **Dog** *before* casting **x** to a **Dog**. It's important to use **instanceof** before a downcast when you don't have other information that tells you the type of the object; otherwise, you'll end up with a **ClassCastException**.

Ordinarily, you might be hunting for one type (triangles to turn purple, for example), but you can easily tally *all* of the objects by using **instanceof**. Suppose you have a family of **Pet** classes:

```
//: c10:Pet.java
package c10;
public class Pet {} ///:~
```

```
//: c10:Dog.java
package c10;
public class Dog extends Pet {} ///:~
```

```
//: c10:Pug.java
package c10;
public class Pug extends Dog {} ///:~
```

```
//: c10:Cat.java
package c10;
public class Cat extends Pet {} ///:~
```

```
//: c10:Rodent.java
package c10;
public class Rodent extends Pet {} ///:~
```

```
//: c10:Gerbil.java
package c10;
```

```java
public class Gerbil extends Rodent {} ///:~
```

```java
//: c10:Hamster.java
package c10;
public class Hamster extends Rodent {} ///:~
```

In the coming example, we want to keep track of the number of any particular type of **Pet**, so we'll need a class that holds this number in an **int**. You can think of it as a modifiable **Integer**:

```java
//: c10:Counter.java
package c10;

public class Counter {
  int i;
  public String toString() { return Integer.toString(i); }
} ///:~
```

Next, we need a tool that holds two things together: an indicator of the **Pet** type and a **Counter** to hold the pet quantity. That is, we want to be able to say "how may **Gerbil** objects are there?" An ordinary array won't work here, because you refer to objects in an array by their index numbers. What we want to do here is refer to the objects in the array by their **Pet** type. We want to *associate* **Counter** objects with **Pet** objects. There is a standard data structure , called an *associative array*, for doing exactly this kind of thing. Here is an extremely simple version:

```java
//: c10:AssociativeArray.java
// Associates keys with values.
package c10;
import com.bruceeckel.simpletest.*;

public class AssociativeArray {
  private static Test monitor = new Test();
  private Object[][] pairs;
  private int index;
  public AssociativeArray(int length) {
    pairs = new Object[length][2];
  }
  public void put(Object key, Object value) {
    if(index >= pairs.length)
      throw new ArrayIndexOutOfBoundsException();
    pairs[index++] = new Object[] { key, value };
  }
  public Object get(Object key) {
```

```
    for(int i = 0; i < index; i++)
      if(key.equals(pairs[i][0]))
        return pairs[i][1];
    throw new RuntimeException("Failed to find key");
  }
  public String toString() {
    String result = "";
    for(int i = 0; i < index; i++) {
      result += pairs[i][0] + " : " + pairs[i][1];
      if(i < index - 1) result += "\n";
    }
    return result;
  }
  public static void main(String[] args) {
    AssociativeArray map = new AssociativeArray(6);
    map.put("sky", "blue");
    map.put("grass", "green");
    map.put("ocean", "dancing");
    map.put("tree", "tall");
    map.put("earth", "brown");
    map.put("sun", "warm");
    try {
      map.put("extra", "object"); // Past the end
    } catch(ArrayIndexOutOfBoundsException e) {
      System.out.println("Too many objects!");
    }
    System.out.println(map);
    System.out.println(map.get("ocean"));
    monitor.expect(new String[] {
      "Too many objects!",
      "sky : blue",
      "grass : green",
      "ocean : dancing",
      "tree : tall",
      "earth : brown",
      "sun : warm",
      "dancing"
    });
  }
} ///:~
```

Your first observation might be that this appears to be a general-purpose tool, so why not put it in a package like **com.bruceeckel.tools**? Well, it is indeed a general-purpose tool—so useful, in fact, that **java.util** contains a number of associative arrays (which are also called *maps*) that do a lot more than this one does, and do it a lot faster. A large portion of Chapter 11 is devoted to associative arrays, but they are significantly more complicated, so using this one will keep things simple and at the same time begin to familiarize you with the value of associative arrays.

In an associative array, the "indexer" is called a *key*, and the associated object is called a *value*. Here, we associate keys and values by putting them in an array of two-element arrays, which you see here as **pairs**. This will just be a fixed-length array that is created in the constructor, so we need **index** to make sure we don't run off the end. When you **put( )** in a new key-value pair, a new two-element array is created and inserted at the next available location in **pairs**. If **index** is greater than or equal to the length of **pairs**, then an exception is thrown.

To use the **get( )** method, you pass in the **key** that you want it to look up, and it produces the associated value as the result or throws an exception if it can't be found. The **get( )** method is using what is possibly the least efficient approach imaginable to locate the value: starting at the top of the array and using **equals( )** to compare keys. But the point here is simplicity, not efficiency, and the real maps in Chapter 11 have solved the performance problems, so we don't need to worry about it here.

The essential methods in an associative array are **put( )** and **get( )**, but for easy display, **toString( )** has been overridden to print the key-value pairs. To show that it works, **main( )** loads an **AssociativeArray** with pairs of strings and prints the resulting map, followed by a **get( )** of one of the values.

Now that all the tools are in place, we can use **instanceof** to count **Pet**s:

```
//: c10:PetCount.java
// Using instanceof.
package c10;
import com.bruceeckel.simpletest.*;
import java.util.*;

public class PetCount {
  private static Test monitor = new Test();
  private static Random rand = new Random();
  static String[] typenames = {
    "Pet", "Dog", "Pug", "Cat",
    "Rodent", "Gerbil", "Hamster",
  };
```

```
  // Exceptions thrown to console:
  public static void main(String[] args) {
    Object[] pets = new Object[15];
    try {
      Class[] petTypes = {
        Class.forName("c10.Dog"),
        Class.forName("c10.Pug"),
        Class.forName("c10.Cat"),
        Class.forName("c10.Rodent"),
        Class.forName("c10.Gerbil"),
        Class.forName("c10.Hamster"),
      };
      for(int i = 0; i < pets.length; i++)
        pets[i] = petTypes[rand.nextInt(petTypes.length)]
          .newInstance();
    } catch(InstantiationException e) {
      System.out.println("Cannot instantiate");
      System.exit(1);
    } catch(IllegalAccessException e) {
      System.out.println("Cannot access");
      System.exit(1);
    } catch(ClassNotFoundException e) {
      System.out.println("Cannot find class");
      System.exit(1);
    }
    AssociativeArray map =
      new AssociativeArray(typenames.length);
    for(int i = 0; i < typenames.length; i++)
      map.put(typenames[i], new Counter());
    for(int i = 0; i < pets.length; i++) {
      Object o = pets[i];
      if(o instanceof Pet)
        ((Counter)map.get("Pet")).i++;
      if(o instanceof Dog)
        ((Counter)map.get("Dog")).i++;
      if(o instanceof Pug)
        ((Counter)map.get("Pug")).i++;
      if(o instanceof Cat)
        ((Counter)map.get("Cat")).i++;
      if(o instanceof Rodent)
        ((Counter)map.get("Rodent")).i++;
      if(o instanceof Gerbil)
        ((Counter)map.get("Gerbil")).i++;
      if(o instanceof Hamster)
```

```
        ((Counter)map.get("Hamster")).i++;
    }
    // List each individual pet:
    for(int i = 0; i < pets.length; i++)
      System.out.println(pets[i].getClass());
    // Show the counts:
    System.out.println(map);
    monitor.expect(new Object[] {
      new TestExpression("%% class c10\\."+
        "(Dog|Pug|Cat|Rodent|Gerbil|Hamster)",
        pets.length),
      new TestExpression(
        "%% (Pet|Dog|Pug|Cat|Rodent|Gerbil|Hamster)" +
        " : \\d+", typenames.length)
    });
  }
} ///:~
```

In **main( )** an array **petTypes** of **Class** objects is created using **Class.forName( )**. Since the **Pet** objects are in package **c09**, the package name must be used when naming the classes.

Next, the **pets** array is filled by randomly indexing into **petTypes** and using the selected **Class** object to generate a new instance of that class with **Class.newInstance( )**, which uses the default (no-arg) class constructor to generate the new object.

Both **forName( )** and **newInstance( )** can generate exceptions, which you can see handled in the **catch** clauses following the **try** block. Again, the names of the exceptions are relatively useful explanations of what went wrong (**IllegalAccessException** relates to a violation of the Java security mechanism).

After creating the **AssociativeArray**, it is filled with key-value pairs of pet names and **Counter** objects. Then each **Pet** in the randomly-generated array is tested and counted using **instanceof**. The array and **AssociativeArray** are printed so you can compare the results.

There's a rather narrow restriction on **instanceof**: You can compare it to a named type only, and not to a **Class** object. In the preceding example you might feel that it's tedious to write out all of those **instanceof** expressions, and you're right. But there is no way to cleverly automate **instanceof** by creating an array of **Class** objects and comparing it to those instead (stay tuned—you'll see an alternative). This isn't as great a restriction as you might think, because you'll eventually understand that your design is probably flawed if you end up writing a lot of **instanceof** expressions.

Of course, this example is contrived—you'd probably put a **static** field in each type and increment it in the constructor to keep track of the counts. You would do something like that *if* you had control of the source code for the class and could change it. Since this is not always the case, RTTI can come in handy.

Using class literals

It's interesting to see how the **PetCount.java** example can be rewritten using class literals. The result is cleaner in many ways:

```
//: c10:PetCount2.java
// Using class literals.
package c10;
import com.bruceeckel.simpletest.*;
import java.util.*;

public class PetCount2 {
  private static Test monitor = new Test();
  private static Random rand = new Random();
  public static void main(String[] args) {
    Object[] pets = new Object[15];
    Class[] petTypes = {
      // Class literals:
      Pet.class,
      Dog.class,
      Pug.class,
      Cat.class,
      Rodent.class,
      Gerbil.class,
      Hamster.class,
    };
    try {
      for(int i = 0; i < pets.length; i++) {
        // Offset by one to eliminate Pet.class:
        int rnd = 1 + rand.nextInt(petTypes.length - 1);
        pets[i] = petTypes[rnd].newInstance();
      }
    } catch(InstantiationException e) {
      System.out.println("Cannot instantiate");
```

```
      System.exit(1);
    } catch(IllegalAccessException e) {
      System.out.println("Cannot access");
      System.exit(1);
    }
    AssociativeArray map =
      new AssociativeArray(petTypes.length);
    for(int i = 0; i < petTypes.length; i++)
      map.put(petTypes[i].toString(), new Counter());
    for(int i = 0; i < pets.length; i++) {
      Object o = pets[i];
      if(o instanceof Pet)
        ((Counter)map.get("class c10.Pet")).i++;
      if(o instanceof Dog)
        ((Counter)map.get("class c10.Dog")).i++;
      if(o instanceof Pug)
        ((Counter)map.get("class c10.Pug")).i++;
      if(o instanceof Cat)
        ((Counter)map.get("class c10.Cat")).i++;
      if(o instanceof Rodent)
        ((Counter)map.get("class c10.Rodent")).i++;
      if(o instanceof Gerbil)
        ((Counter)map.get("class c10.Gerbil")).i++;
      if(o instanceof Hamster)
        ((Counter)map.get("class c10.Hamster")).i++;
    }
    // List each individual pet:
    for(int i = 0; i < pets.length; i++)
      System.out.println(pets[i].getClass());
    // Show the counts:
    System.out.println(map);
    monitor.expect(new Object[] {
      new TestExpression("%% class c10\\." +
        "(Dog|Pug|Cat|Rodent|Gerbil|Hamster)",
        pets.length),
      new TestExpression("%% class c10\\." +
        "(Pet|Dog|Pug|Cat|Rodent|Gerbil|Hamster) : \\d+",
        petTypes.length)
    });
  }
} ///:~
```

Here, the **typenames** array has been removed in favor of getting the type name strings from the **Class** object. Notice that the system can distinguish between classes and interfaces.

You can also see that the creation of **petTypes** does not need to be surrounded by a **try** block since it's evaluated at compile time and thus won't throw any exceptions, unlike **Class.forName( )**.

When the **Pet** objects are dynamically created, you can see that the random number is restricted so it is between one and **petTypes.length** and does not include zero. That's because zero refers to **Pet.class**, and presumably a generic **Pet** object is not interesting. However, since **Pet.class** is part of **petTypes**, the result is that all of the pets get counted.

A dynamic **instanceof**

The **Class.isInstance** method provides a way to dynamically call the **instanceof** operator. Thus, all those tedious **instanceof** statements can be removed in the **PetCount** example:

```
//: c10:PetCount3.java
// Using isInstance()
package c10;
import com.bruceeckel.simpletest.*;
import java.util.*;

public class PetCount3 {
  private static Test monitor = new Test();
  private static Random rand = new Random();
  public static void main(String[] args) {
    Object[] pets = new Object[15];
    Class[] petTypes = {
      // Class literals:
      Pet.class,
      Dog.class,
      Pug.class,
      Cat.class,
      Rodent.class,
      Gerbil.class,
      Hamster.class,
    };
    try {
      for(int i = 0; i < pets.length; i++) {
        // Offset by one to eliminate Pet.class:
```

```
        int rnd = 1 + rand.nextInt(petTypes.length - 1);
        pets[i] = petTypes[rnd].newInstance();
      }
    } catch(InstantiationException e) {
      System.out.println("Cannot instantiate");
      System.exit(1);
    } catch(IllegalAccessException e) {
      System.out.println("Cannot access");
      System.exit(1);
    }
    AssociativeArray map =
      new AssociativeArray(petTypes.length);
    for(int i = 0; i < petTypes.length; i++)
      map.put(petTypes[i].toString(), new Counter());
    for(int i = 0; i < pets.length; i++) {
      Object o = pets[i];
      // Using Class.isInstance() to eliminate
      // individual instanceof expressions:
      for(int j = 0; j < petTypes.length; ++j)
        if(petTypes[j].isInstance(o))
          ((Counter)map.get(petTypes[j].toString())).i++;
    }
    // List each individual pet:
    for(int i = 0; i < pets.length; i++)
      System.out.println(pets[i].getClass());
    // Show the counts:
    System.out.println(map);
    monitor.expect(new Object[] {
      new TestExpression("%% class c10\\." +
        "(Dog|Pug|Cat|Rodent|Gerbil|Hamster)",
        pets.length),
      new TestExpression("%% class c10\\." +
        "(Pet|Dog|Pug|Cat|Rodent|Gerbil|Hamster) : \\d+",
        petTypes.length)
    });
  }
} ///:~
```

You can see that the **isInstance( )** method has eliminated the need for the **instanceof** expressions. In addition, this means that you can add new types of pets simply by changing the **petTypes** array; the rest of the program does not need modification (as it did when using the **instanceof** expressions).

instanceof vs. **Class** equivalence

When querying for type information, there's an important difference between either form of **instanceof** (that is, **instanceof** or **isInstance( )**, which produce equivalent results) and the direct comparison of the **Class** objects. Here's an example that demonstrates the difference:

```
//: c10:FamilyVsExactType.java
// The difference between instanceof and class
package c10;
import com.bruceeckel.simpletest.*;

class Base {}
class Derived extends Base {}

public class FamilyVsExactType {
  private static Test monitor = new Test();
  static void test(Object x) {
    System.out.println("Testing x of type " +
      x.getClass());
    System.out.println("x instanceof Base " +
      (x instanceof Base));
    System.out.println("x instanceof Derived " +
      (x instanceof Derived));
    System.out.println("Base.isInstance(x) " +
      Base.class.isInstance(x));
    System.out.println("Derived.isInstance(x) " +
      Derived.class.isInstance(x));
    System.out.println("x.getClass() == Base.class " +
      (x.getClass() == Base.class));
    System.out.println("x.getClass() == Derived.class " +
      (x.getClass() == Derived.class));
    System.out.println("x.getClass().equals(Base.class)) "+
      (x.getClass().equals(Base.class)));
    System.out.println(
      "x.getClass().equals(Derived.class)) " +
      (x.getClass().equals(Derived.class)));
  }
  public static void main(String[] args) {
    test(new Base());
    test(new Derived());
    monitor.expect(new String[] {
      "Testing x of type class c10.Base",
      "x instanceof Base true",
      "x instanceof Derived false",
```

```
      "Base.isInstance(x) true",
      "Derived.isInstance(x) false",
      "x.getClass() == Base.class true",
      "x.getClass() == Derived.class false",
      "x.getClass().equals(Base.class)) true",
      "x.getClass().equals(Derived.class)) false",
      "Testing x of type class c10.Derived",
      "x instanceof Base true",
      "x instanceof Derived true",
      "Base.isInstance(x) true",
      "Derived.isInstance(x) true",
      "x.getClass() == Base.class false",
      "x.getClass() == Derived.class true",
      "x.getClass().equals(Base.class)) false",
      "x.getClass().equals(Derived.class)) true"
    });
  }
} ///:~
```

The **test( )** method performs type checking with its argument using both forms of **instanceof**. It then gets the **Class** reference and uses == and **equals( )** to test for equality of the **Class** objects. Reassuringly, **instanceof** and **isInstance( )** produce exactly the same results, as do **equals( )** and ==. But the tests themselves draw different conclusions. In keeping with the concept of type, **instanceof** says "are you this class, or a class derived from this class?" On the other hand, if you compare the actual **Class** objects using ==, there is no concern with inheritance—it's either the exact type or it isn't.

RTTI syntax

Java performs its RTTI using the **Class** object, even if you're doing something like a cast. The class **Class** also has a number of other ways you can use RTTI.

First, you must get a reference to the appropriate **Class** object. One way to do this, as shown in the previous example, is to use a string and the **Class.forName( )** method. This is convenient because you don't need an object of that type in order to get the **Class** reference. However, if you do already have an object of the type you're interested in, you can fetch the **Class** reference by calling a method that's part of the **Object** root class: **getClass( )**. This returns the **Class** reference representing the actual type of the object. **Class** has many interesting methods demonstrated in the following example:

```
//: c10:ToyTest.java
// Testing class Class.
import com.bruceeckel.simpletest.*;

interface HasBatteries {}
interface Waterproof {}
interface Shoots {}
class Toy {
  // Comment out the following default constructor
  // to see NoSuchMethodError from (*1*)
  Toy() {}
  Toy(int i) {}
}

class FancyToy extends Toy
implements HasBatteries, Waterproof, Shoots {
  FancyToy() { super(1); }
}

public class ToyTest {
  private static Test monitor = new Test();
  static void printInfo(Class cc) {
    System.out.println("Class name: " + cc.getName() +
      " is interface? [" + cc.isInterface() + "]");
  }
  public static void main(String[] args) {
    Class c = null;
    try {
      c = Class.forName("FancyToy");
    } catch(ClassNotFoundException e) {
      System.out.println("Can't find FancyToy");
      System.exit(1);
    }
    printInfo(c);
    Class[] faces = c.getInterfaces();
    for(int i = 0; i < faces.length; i++)
      printInfo(faces[i]);
    Class cy = c.getSuperclass();
    Object o = null;
    try {
      // Requires default constructor:
```

```
      o = cy.newInstance(); // (*1*)
    } catch(InstantiationException e) {
      System.out.println("Cannot instantiate");
      System.exit(1);
    } catch(IllegalAccessException e) {
      System.out.println("Cannot access");
      System.exit(1);
    }
    printInfo(o.getClass());
    monitor.expect(new String[] {
      "Class name: FancyToy is interface? [false]",
      "Class name: HasBatteries is interface? [true]",
      "Class name: Waterproof is interface? [true]",
      "Class name: Shoots is interface? [true]",
      "Class name: Toy is interface? [false]"
    });
  }
} ///:~
```

You can see that **class FancyToy** is quite complicated, since it inherits from **Toy** and **implements** the **interface**s **HasBatteries**, **Waterproof**, and **Shoots**. In **main( )**, a **Class** reference is created and initialized to the **FancyToy Class** using **forName( )** inside an appropriate **try** block.

The **Class.getInterfaces( )** method returns an array of **Class** objects representing the interfaces that are contained in the **Class** object of interest.

If you have a **Class** object, you can also ask it for its direct base class using **getSuperclass( )**. This, of course, returns a **Class** reference that you can further query. This means that at run time, you can discover an object's entire class hierarchy.

The **newInstance( )** method of **Class** can, at first, seem like just another way to **clone( )** an object. However, you can create a new object with **newInstance( )** *without* an existing object, as seen here, because there is no **Toy** object—only **cy**, which is a reference to **y**'s **Class** object. This is a way to implement a "virtual constructor," which allows you to say "I don't know exactly what type you are, but create yourself properly anyway." In the preceding example, **cy** is just a **Class** reference with no further type information known at compile time. And when you create a new instance, you get back an **Object reference**. But that reference is pointing to a **Toy** object. Of course, before you can send any messages other than those accepted by **Object**, you have to investigate it a bit and do some casting. In addition, the class that's being created with **newInstance( )** must have a default constructor. In the next section, you'll see how to dynamically create objects of classes using any constructor, with the Java *reflection* API (Application Programmer Interface).

The final method in the listing is **printInfo( ),** which takes a **Class** reference and gets its name with **getName( ),** and finds out whether it's an interface with **isInterface( )**. Thus, with the **Class** object you can find out just about everything you want to know about an object.

Reflection: run time class information

If you don't know the precise type of an object, RTTI will tell you. However, there's a limitation: The type must be known at compile time in order for you to be able to detect it using RTTI and do something useful with the information. Put another way, the compiler must know about all the classes you're working with for RTTI.

This doesn't seem like that much of a limitation at first, but suppose you're given a reference to an object that's not in your program space. In fact, the class of the object isn't even available to your program at compile time. For example, suppose you get a bunch of bytes from a disk file or from a network connection, and you're told that those bytes represent a class. Since the compiler can't know about this class that shows up later while it's compiling the code for your program, how can you possibly use such a class?

In a traditional programming environment, this seems like a far-fetched scenario. But as we move into a larger programming world, there are important cases in which this happens. The first is component-based programming, in which you build projects using *Rapid Application Development* (RAD) in an application builder tool. This is a visual approach to creating a program (which you see on the screen as a "form") by moving icons that represent components onto the form. These components are then configured by setting some of their values at program time. This design-time configuration requires that any component be instantiable, that it exposes parts of itself, and that it allows its values to be read and set. In addition, components that handle GUI events must expose information about appropriate methods so that the RAD environment can assist the programmer in overriding these event-handling methods. Reflection provides the mechanism to detect the available methods and produce the method names. Java provides a structure for component-based programming through JavaBeans (described in Chapter 14).

Another compelling motivation for discovering class information at run time is to provide the ability to create and execute objects on remote platforms across a network. This is called *Remote Method Invocation* (RMI), and it allows a Java program to have objects distributed across many machines. This distribution can happen for a number of reasons. For example, perhaps you're doing a computation-intensive task, and in order to speed things up, you want to break it up and put pieces on machines that are idle. In other situations you might want to place code that handles particular types of tasks (e.g., "Business Rules" in a multitier client/server architecture) on a particular machine, so that machine becomes a common repository describing those actions, and it can be easily changed to affect everyone in the system. (This is an interesting development, since the machine exists solely to make software changes easy!) Along these lines, distributed computing also supports specialized hardware that might be good at a particular task—matrix inversions, for example—but inappropriate or too expensive for general-purpose programming.

The class **Class** (described previously in this chapter) supports the concept of *reflection*, and there's an additional library, **java.lang.reflect,** with classes **Field**, **Method**, and **Constructor** (each of which implement the **Member interface**). Objects of these types are created by the JVM at run time to represent the corresponding member in the unknown class. You can then use the **Constructor**s to create new objects, the **get( )** and **set( )** methods to read and modify the fields associated with **Field** objects, and the **invoke( )** method to call a method associated with a **Method** object. In addition, you can call the convenience methods **getFields( )**, **getMethods( )**, **getConstructors( )**, etc., to return arrays of the objects representing the fields, methods, and constructors. (You can find out more by looking up the class **Class** in the JDK documentation.) Thus, the class information for anonymous objects can be completely determined at run time, and nothing need be known at compile time.

It's important to realize that there's nothing magic about reflection. When you're using reflection to interact with an object of an unknown type, the JVM will simply look at the object and see that it belongs to a particular class (just like ordinary RTTI), but then, before it can do anything else, the **Class** object must be loaded. Thus, the **.class** file for that particular type must still be available to the JVM, either on the local machine or across the network. So the true difference between RTTI and reflection is that with RTTI, the compiler opens and examines the **.class** file at compile time. Put another way, you can call all the methods of an object in the "normal" way. With reflection, the **.class** file is unavailable at compile time; it is opened and examined by the run-time environment.

A class method extractor

You'll rarely need to use the reflection tools directly; they're in the language to support other Java features, such as object serialization (Chapter 12) and JavaBeans (Chapter 14). However, there are times when it's quite useful to be able to dynamically extract information about a class. One extremely useful tool is a class method extractor. As mentioned before, looking at a class definition source code or JDK documentation shows only the methods that are defined or overridden *within that class definition*. But there could be dozens more available to you that have come from base classes. To locate these is both tedious and time consuming.[1] Fortunately, reflection provides a way to write a simple tool that will automatically show you the entire interface. Here's the way it works:

```
//: c10:ShowMethods.java
// Using reflection to show all the methods of a class,
// even if the methods are defined in the base class.
// {Args: ShowMethods}
import java.lang.reflect.*;
import java.util.regex.*;

public class ShowMethods {
  private static final String usage =
    "usage: \n" +
    "ShowMethods qualified.class.name\n" +
    "To show all methods in class or: \n" +
    "ShowMethods qualified.class.name word\n" +
    "To search for methods involving 'word'";
  private static Pattern p = Pattern.compile("\\w+\\.");
  public static void main(String[] args) {
```

[1] Especially in the past. However, Sun has greatly improved its HTML Java documentation so that it's easier to see base-class methods.

```
      if(args.length < 1) {
        System.out.println(usage);
        System.exit(0);
      }
      int lines = 0;
      try {
        Class c = Class.forName(args[0]);
        Method[] m = c.getMethods();
        Constructor[] ctor = c.getConstructors();
        if(args.length == 1) {
          for(int i = 0; i < m.length; i++)
            System.out.println(
              p.matcher(m[i].toString()).replaceAll(""));
          for(int i = 0; i < ctor.length; i++)
            System.out.println(
              p.matcher(ctor[i].toString()).replaceAll(""));
          lines = m.length + ctor.length;
        } else {
          for(int i = 0; i < m.length; i++)
            if(m[i].toString().indexOf(args[1]) != -1) {
              System.out.println(
                p.matcher(m[i].toString()).replaceAll(""));
              lines++;
            }
          for(int i = 0; i < ctor.length; i++)
            if(ctor[i].toString().indexOf(args[1]) != -1) {
              System.out.println(p.matcher(
                ctor[i].toString()).replaceAll(""));
              lines++;
            }
        }
      } catch(ClassNotFoundException e) {
        System.out.println("No such class: " + e);
      }
    }
} ///:~
```

The **Class** methods **getMethods( )** and **getConstructors( )** return an array of **Method** and array of **Constructor**, respectively. Each of these classes has further methods to dissect the names, arguments, and return values of the methods they represent. But you can also just use **toString( )**, as is done here, to produce a **String** with the entire method signature. The rest of the code extracts the command line information, determines if a particular signature matches your target string (using **indexOf( )**), and strips off the name qualifiers.

To strip the name qualifiers like "**java.lang.**" from "**java.lang.String**," Java JDK 1.4 *regular expressions* offer a powerful and succinct tool that has been available in some languages for many years. You've already seen simple usage of regular expressions inside the **expect( )** statements of the **com.bruceeckel.simpletest.Test** class. In the preceding example, you can see the basic coding steps necessary to use regular expressions in your own programs.

After importing **java.util.regex**, you first compile the regular expression by using the **static Pattern.compile( )** method, which produces a **Pattern** object using the string argument. In this case, the argument is

```
"\\w+\\."
```

To understand this or any other regular expression, look at the JDK documentation under **java.util.regex.Pattern**. For this one, you'll find that '**\w**' means "a word character: [a-zA-Z_0-9]." The '+' means "one or more of the preceding expression"—so in this case, one or more word characters—and the '\.' produces a literal period (rather than the period operator, which means "any character" in a regular expression). So this expression will match any sequence of word characters followed by a period, which is exactly what we need to strip off the qualifiers.

After you have a compiled **Pattern** object, you use it by calling the **matcher( )** method, passing the string that you want to search. The **matcher( )** method produces a **Matcher** object, which has a set of operations to choose from (you can see all of these in the JDK documentation for **java.util.regex.Matcher**). Here, the **replaceAll( )** method is used to replace all the matches with empty strings—that is, to delete the matches.

As a more compact alternative, you can use the regular expressions built into the **String** class. For example, the last use of **replaceAll( )** in the preceding program could be rewritten from:

```
p.matcher(ctor[i].toString()).replaceAll("")
```

to

```
ctor[i].toString().replaceAll("\\w+\\.", "")
```

without precompiling the regular expression. This form is good for single-shot uses of regular expressions, but the precompiled form is significantly more efficient if you need to use the regular expression more than once, as is the case with this example.

This example shows reflection in action, since the result produced by **Class.forName( )** cannot be known at compile time, and therefore all the method signature information is being extracted at run time. If you investigate the JDK documentation on reflection, you'll see that there is enough support to actually set up and make a method call on an object that's totally unknown at compile time (there will be examples of this later in this book). Although initially this is something you may not think you'll ever need, the value of full reflection can be quite surprising.

An enlightening experiment is to run

```
java ShowMethods ShowMethods
```

This produces a listing that includes a **public** default constructor, even though you can see from the code that no constructor was defined. The constructor you see is the one that's automatically synthesized by the compiler. If you then make **ShowMethods** a non-**public** class (that is, package access), the synthesized default constructor no longer shows up in the output. The synthesized default constructor is automatically given the same access as the class.

Another interesting experiment is to invoke **java ShowMethods java.lang.String** with an extra argument of **char**, **int**, **String**, etc.

This tool can be a real time-saver while you're programming, when you can't remember if a class has a particular method and you don't want to go hunting through the index or class hierarchy in the JDK documentation, or if you don't know whether that class can do anything with, for example, **Color** objects.

Chapter 14 contains a GUI version of this program (customized to extract information for Swing components) so you can leave it running while you're writing code, to allow quick lookups.

Summary

RTTI allows you to discover type information from an anonymous base-class reference. Thus, it's ripe for misuse by the novice, since it might make sense before polymorphic method calls do. For many people coming from a procedural background, it's difficult not to organize their programs into sets of **switch** statements. They could accomplish this with RTTI and thus lose the important value of polymorphism in code development and maintenance. The intent of Java is that you use polymorphic method calls throughout your code, and you use RTTI only when you must.

However, using polymorphic method calls as they are intended requires that you have control of the base-class definition, because at some point in the extension of your program you might discover that the base class doesn't include the method you need. If the base class comes from a library or is otherwise controlled by someone else, one solution to the problem is RTTI: you can inherit a new type and add your extra method. Elsewhere in the code you can detect your particular type and call that special method. This doesn't destroy the polymorphism and extensibility of the program, because adding a new type will not require you to hunt for switch statements in your program. However, when you add new code in your main body that requires your new feature, you must use RTTI to detect your particular type.

Putting a feature in a base class might mean that, for the benefit of one particular class, all of the other classes derived from that base require some meaningless stub of a method. This makes the interface less clear and annoys those who must override abstract methods when they derive from that base class. For example, consider a class hierarchy representing musical instruments. Suppose you wanted to clear the spit valves of all the appropriate instruments in your orchestra. One option is to put a **clearSpitValve( )** method in the base class **Instrument**, but this is confusing because it implies that **Percussion** and **Electronic** instruments also have spit valves. RTTI provides a much more reasonable solution in this case because you can place the method in the specific class (**Wind** in this case), where it's appropriate. However, a more appropriate solution is to put a **prepareInstrument( )** method in the base class, but you might not see this when you're first solving the problem and could mistakenly assume that you must use RTTI.

Finally, RTTI will sometimes solve efficiency problems. Suppose your code nicely uses polymorphism, but it turns out that one of your objects reacts to this general purpose code in a horribly inefficient way. You can pick out that type using RTTI and write case-specific code to improve the efficiency. Be wary, however, of programming for efficiency too soon. It's a seductive trap. It's best to get the program working *first*, then decide if it's running fast enough, and only then should you attack efficiency issues—with a profiler (see Chapter 15).

Exercises

Solutions to selected exercises can be found in the electronic document *The Thinking in Java Annotated Solution Guide*, available for a small fee from *www.BruceEckel.com*.

1. Add **Rhomboid** to **Shapes.java**. Create a **Rhomboid**, upcast it to a **Shape**, then downcast it back to a **Rhomboid**. Try downcasting to a **Circle** and see what happens.

2. Modify Exercise 1 so that it uses **instanceof** to check the type before performing the downcast.

3. Modify **Shapes.java** so that it can "highlight" (set a flag) in all shapes of a particular type. The **toString( )** method for each derived **Shape** should indicate whether that **Shape** is "highlighted."

4. Modify **SweetShop.java** so that each type of object creation is controlled by a command-line argument. That is, if your command line is "**java SweetShop Candy**," then only the **Candy** object is created. Notice how you can control which **Class** objects are loaded via the command-line argument.

5. Add a new type of **Pet** to **PetCount3.java**. Verify that it is created and counted correctly in **main( )**.

6. Write a method that takes an object and recursively prints all the classes in that object's hierarchy.

7. Modify Exercise 6 so that it uses **Class. getDeclaredFields( )** to also display information about the fields in a class.

8. In **ToyTest.java**, comment out **Toy**'s default constructor and explain what happens.

9. Incorporate a new kind of **interface** into **ToyTest.java** and verify that it is detected and displayed properly.

10. Write a program to determine whether an array of **char** is a primitive type or a true object.

11. Implement **clearSpitValve( )** as described in the summary.

12. Implement the **rotate(Shape)** method described in this chapter, such that it checks to see if it is rotating a **Circle** (and, if so, doesn't perform the operation).

13. In **ToyTest.java**, use reflection to create a **Toy** object using the nondefault constructor.

14. Look up the interface for **java.lang.Class** in the JDK documentation from *java.sun.com*. Write a program that takes the name of a class as a command-line argument, then uses the **Class** methods to dump all the information available for that class. Test your program with a standard library class and a class you create.

15. Modify the regular expression in **ShowMethods.java** to additionally strip off the keywords **native** and **final** (hint: use the "or" operator '|').

11: Collections of Objects

It's a fairly simple program that has only a fixed quantity of objects with known lifetimes.

In general, your programs will always be creating new objects based on some criteria that will be known only at the time the program is running. You won't know until run time the quantity or even the exact type of the objects you need. To solve the general programming problem, you need to be able to create any number of objects, anytime, anywhere. So you can't rely on creating a named reference to hold each one of your objects:

```
MyObject myReference;
```

since you'll never know how many of these you'll actually need.

Most languages provide some way to solve this rather essential problem. Java has several ways to hold objects (or rather, references to objects). The built-in type is the array, which has been discussed before. Also, the Java utilities library has a reasonably complete set of *container classes* (also known as *collection classes*, but because the Java 2 libraries use the name **Collection** to refer to a particular subset of the library, I shall also use the more inclusive term "container"). Containers provide sophisticated ways to hold and even manipulate your objects.

Arrays

Most of the necessary introduction to arrays is in the last section of Chapter 4, which showed how you define and initialize an array. Holding objects is the focus of this chapter, and an array is just one way to hold objects. But there are a number of other ways to hold objects, so what makes an array special?

There are three issues that distinguish arrays from other types of containers: efficiency, type, and the ability to hold primitives. The array is the most efficient way that Java provides to store and randomly access a sequence of object references. The array is a simple linear sequence, which makes element access fast, but you pay for this speed; when you create an array object, its size is fixed and cannot be changed for the lifetime of that array object. You might suggest creating an array of a particular size and then, if you run out of space, creating a new one and moving all the references from the old one to the new one. This is the behavior of the **ArrayList** class, which will be studied later in this chapter. However, because of the overhead of this flexibility, an **ArrayList** is measurably less efficient than an array.

In C++, the **vector** container class *does* know the type of objects it holds, but it has a different drawback when compared with arrays in Java: The C++ **vector**'s **operator[]** doesn't do bounds checking, so you can run past the end.[1] In Java, you get bounds checking regardless of whether you're using an array or a container; you'll get a **RuntimeException** if you exceed the bounds. This type of exception indicates a programmer error, and thus you don't need to check for it in your code. As an aside, the reason the C++ **vector** doesn't check bounds with every access is speed; in Java, you have the constant performance overhead of bounds checking all the time for both arrays and containers.

The other generic container classes that will be studied in this chapter, **List**, **Set**, and **Map**, all deal with objects as if they had no specific type. That is, they treat them as type **Object**, the root class of all classes in Java. This works fine from one standpoint: You need to build only one container, and any Java object will go into that container. (Except for primitives, which can be placed in containers as constants using the Java primitive wrapper classes, or as changeable values by wrapping in your own class.) This is the second place where an array is superior to the generic containers: When you create an array, you create it to hold a specific type (which is related to the third factor—an array can hold primitives, whereas a container cannot). This means that you get compile-time type checking to prevent you from inserting the wrong type or mistaking the type that you're extracting. Of course, Java will prevent you from sending an inappropriate message to an object at either compile time or run time. So it's not riskier one way or the other, it's just nicer if the compiler points it out to you, faster at run time, and there's less likelihood that the end user will get surprised by an exception.

---

[1] It's possible, however, to ask how big the **vector** is, and the **at( )** method *does* perform bounds checking.

For efficiency and type checking, it's always worth trying to use an array. However, when you're solving a more general problem, arrays can be too restrictive. After looking at arrays, the rest of this chapter will be devoted to the container classes provided by Java.

Arrays are first-class objects

Regardless of what type of array you're working with, the array identifier is actually a reference to a true object that's created on the heap. This is the object that holds the references to the other objects, and it can be created either implicitly, as part of the array initialization syntax, or explicitly with a **new** expression. Part of the array object (in fact, the only field or method you can access) is the read-only **length** member that tells you how many elements can be stored in that array object. The '**[]**' syntax is the only other access that you have to the array object.

The following example shows the various ways that an array can be initialized, and how the array references can be assigned to different array objects. It also shows that arrays of objects and arrays of primitives are almost identical in their use. The only difference is that arrays of objects hold references, but arrays of primitives hold the primitive values directly.

```
//: c11:ArraySize.java
// Initialization & re-assignment of arrays.
import com.bruceeckel.simpletest.*;

class Weeble {} // A small mythical creature

public class ArraySize {
  private static Test monitor = new Test();
  public static void main(String[] args) {
    // Arrays of objects:
    Weeble[] a; // Local uninitialized variable
    Weeble[] b = new Weeble[5]; // Null references
    Weeble[] c = new Weeble[4];
    for(int i = 0; i < c.length; i++)
      if(c[i] == null) // Can test for null reference
        c[i] = new Weeble();
    // Aggregate initialization:
    Weeble[] d = {
      new Weeble(), new Weeble(), new Weeble()
    };
    // Dynamic aggregate initialization:
```

```
    a = new Weeble[] {
      new Weeble(), new Weeble()
    };
    System.out.println("a.length=" + a.length);
    System.out.println("b.length = " + b.length);
    // The references inside the array are
    // automatically initialized to null:
    for(int i = 0; i < b.length; i++)
      System.out.println("b[" + i + "]=" + b[i]);
    System.out.println("c.length = " + c.length);
    System.out.println("d.length = " + d.length);
    a = d;
    System.out.println("a.length = " + a.length);

    // Arrays of primitives:
    int[] e; // Null reference
    int[] f = new int[5];
    int[] g = new int[4];
    for(int i = 0; i < g.length; i++)
      g[i] = i*i;
    int[] h = { 11, 47, 93 };
    // Compile error: variable e not initialized:
    //!System.out.println("e.length=" + e.length);
    System.out.println("f.length = " + f.length);
    // The primitives inside the array are
    // automatically initialized to zero:
    for(int i = 0; i < f.length; i++)
      System.out.println("f[" + i + "]=" + f[i]);
    System.out.println("g.length = " + g.length);
    System.out.println("h.length = " + h.length);
    e = h;
    System.out.println("e.length = " + e.length);
    e = new int[] { 1, 2 };
    System.out.println("e.length = " + e.length);
    monitor.expect(new String[] {
      "a.length=2",
      "b.length = 5",
      "b[0]=null",
      "b[1]=null",
      "b[2]=null",
      "b[3]=null",
      "b[4]=null",
      "c.length = 4",
      "d.length = 3",
```

```
      "a.length = 3",
      "f.length = 5",
      "f[0]=0",
      "f[1]=0",
      "f[2]=0",
      "f[3]=0",
      "f[4]=0",
      "g.length = 4",
      "h.length = 3",
      "e.length = 3",
      "e.length = 2"
    });
  }
} ///:~
```

The array **a** is an uninitialized local variable, and the compiler prevents you from doing anything with this reference until you've properly initialized it. The array **b** is initialized to point to an array of **Weeble** references, but no actual **Weeble** objects are ever placed in that array. However, you can still ask what the size of the array is, since **b** is pointing to a legitimate object. This brings up a slight drawback: You can't find out how many elements are actually *in* the array, since **length** tells you only how many elements *can* be placed in the array; that is, the size of the array object, not the number of elements it actually holds. However, when an array object is created, its references are automatically initialized to **null**, so you can see whether a particular array slot has an object in it by checking to see whether it's **null**. Similarly, an array of primitives is automatically initialized to zero for numeric types, **(char)0** for **char**, and **false** for **boolean**.

Array **c** shows the creation of the array object followed by the assignment of **Weeble** objects to all the slots in the array. Array **d** shows the "aggregate initialization" syntax that causes the array object to be created (implicitly with **new** on the heap, just like for array **c**) *and* initialized with **Weeble** objects, all in one statement.

The next array initialization could be thought of as a "dynamic aggregate initialization." The aggregate initialization used by **d** must be used at the point of **d**'s definition, but with the second syntax you can create and initialize an array object anywhere. For example, suppose **hide( )** is a method that takes an array of **Weeble** objects. You could call it by saying:

```
hide(d);
```

but you can also dynamically create the array you want to pass as the argument:

```
hide(new Weeble[] { new Weeble(), new Weeble() });
```

In many situations this syntax provides a more convenient way to write code.

The expression:

```
a = d;
```

shows how you can take a reference that's attached to one array object and assign it to another array object, just as you can do with any other type of object reference. Now both **a** and **d** are pointing to the same array object on the heap.

The second part of **ArraySize.java** shows that primitive arrays work just like object arrays *except* that primitive arrays hold the primitive values directly.

Containers of primitives

Container classes can hold only references to **Object**s. An array, however, can be created to hold primitives directly, as well as references to **Object**s. It *is* possible to use the "wrapper" classes, such as **Integer**, **Double**, etc., to place primitive values inside a container, but the wrapper classes for primitives can be awkward to use. In addition, it's much more efficient to create and access an array of primitives than a container of wrapped primitives.

Of course, if you're using a primitive type and you need the flexibility of a container that automatically expands when more space is needed, the array won't work, and you're forced to use a container of wrapped primitives. You might think that there should be a specialized type of **ArrayList** for each of the primitive data types, but Java doesn't provide this for you.[2]

Returning an array

Suppose you're writing a method and you don't just want to return just one thing, but a whole bunch of things. Languages like C and C++ make this

---

[2] This is one of the places where C++ is distinctly superior to Java, since C++ supports *parameterized types* with the **template** keyword.

difficult because you can't just return an array, only a pointer to an array. This introduces problems because it becomes messy to control the lifetime of the array, which easily leads to memory leaks.

Java takes a similar approach, but you just "return an array." Unlike C++, with Java you never worry about responsibility for that array—it will be around as long as you need it, and the garbage collector will clean it up when you're done.

As an example, consider returning an array of **String**:

```
//: c11:IceCream.java
// Returning arrays from methods.
import com.bruceeckel.simpletest.*;
import java.util.*;

public class IceCream {
  private static Test monitor = new Test();
  private static Random rand = new Random();
  public static final String[] flavors = {
    "Chocolate", "Strawberry", "Vanilla Fudge Swirl",
    "Mint Chip", "Mocha Almond Fudge", "Rum Raisin",
    "Praline Cream", "Mud Pie"
  };
  public static String[] flavorSet(int n) {
    String[] results = new String[n];
    boolean[] picked = new boolean[flavors.length];
    for(int i = 0; i < n; i++) {
      int t;
      do
        t = rand.nextInt(flavors.length);
      while(picked[t]);
      results[i] = flavors[t];
      picked[t] = true;
    }
    return results;
  }
  public static void main(String[] args) {
    for(int i = 0; i < 20; i++) {
      System.out.println(
        "flavorSet(" + i + ") = ");
      String[] fl = flavorSet(flavors.length);
      for(int j = 0; j < fl.length; j++)
        System.out.println("\t" + fl[j]);
```

```
      monitor.expect(new Object[] {
        "%% flavorSet\\(\\d+\\) = ",
        new TestExpression("%% \\t(Chocolate|Strawberry|"
          + "Vanilla Fudge Swirl|Mint Chip|Mocha Almond "
          + "Fudge|Rum Raisin|Praline Cream|Mud Pie)", 8)
      });
    }
  }
} ///:~
```

The method **flavorSet( )** creates an array of **String** called **results**. The size of this array is **n**, determined by the argument that you pass into the method. Then it proceeds to choose flavors randomly from the array **flavors** and place them into **results**, which it finally returns. Returning an array is just like returning any other object—it's a reference. It's not important that the array was created within **flavorSet( )**, or that the array was created anyplace else, for that matter. The garbage collector takes care of cleaning up the array when you're done with it, and the array will persist for as long as you need it.

As an aside, notice that when **flavorSet( )** chooses flavors randomly, it ensures that a particular choice hasn't already been selected. This is performed in a **do** loop that keeps making random choices until it finds one not already in the **picked** array. (Of course, a **String** comparison also could have been performed to see if the random choice was already in the **results** array.) If it's successful, it adds the entry and finds the next one (**i** gets incremented).

main( ) prints out 20 full sets of flavors, so you can see that **flavorSet( )** chooses the flavors in a random order each time. It's easiest to see this if you redirect the output into a file. And while you're looking at the file, remember that you just *want* the ice cream, you don't *need* it.

The **Arrays** class

In **java.util**, you'll find the **Arrays** class, which holds a set of **static** methods that perform utility functions for arrays. There are four basic methods: **equals( )**, to compare two arrays for equality; **fill( )**, to fill an array with a value; **sort( )**, to sort the array; and **binarySearch( )**, to find an element in a sorted array. All of these methods are overloaded for all the primitive types and **Object**s. In addition, there's a single **asList( )** method that takes any array and turns it into a **List** container, which you'll learn about later in this chapter.

Although useful, the **Arrays** class stops short of being fully functional. For example, it would be nice to be able to easily print the elements of an array without having to code a **for** loop by hand every time. And as you'll see, the **fill( )** method only takes a single value and places it in the array, so if you wanted, for example, to fill an array with randomly generated numbers, **fill( )** is no help.

Thus it makes sense to supplement the **Arrays** class with some additional utilities, which will be placed in the **package com.bruceeckel.util** for convenience. These will print an array of any type and fill an array with values or objects that are created by an object called a *generator* that you can define.

Because code needs to be created for each primitive type as well as **Object**, there's a lot of nearly duplicated code.[3] For example, a "generator" interface is required for each type because the return type of **next( )** must be different in each case:

```
//: com:bruceeckel:util:Generator.java
package com.bruceeckel.util;
public interface Generator { Object next(); } ///:~
```

```
//: com:bruceeckel:util:BooleanGenerator.java
package com.bruceeckel.util;
public interface BooleanGenerator { boolean next(); } ///:~
```

```
//: com:bruceeckel:util:ByteGenerator.java
package com.bruceeckel.util;
public interface ByteGenerator { byte next(); } ///:~
```

```
//: com:bruceeckel:util:CharGenerator.java
package com.bruceeckel.util;
public interface CharGenerator { char next(); } ///:~
```

```
//: com:bruceeckel:util:ShortGenerator.java
package com.bruceeckel.util;
public interface ShortGenerator { short next(); } ///:~
```

```
//: com:bruceeckel:util:IntGenerator.java
package com.bruceeckel.util;
public interface IntGenerator { int next(); } ///:~
```

---

[3] The C++ programmer will note how much the code could be collapsed with the use of default arguments and templates. The Python programmer will note that this entire library would be largely unnecessary in that language.

```java
//: com:bruceeckel:util:LongGenerator.java
package com.bruceeckel.util;
public interface LongGenerator { long next(); } ///:~
```

```java
//: com:bruceeckel:util:FloatGenerator.java
package com.bruceeckel.util;
public interface FloatGenerator { float next(); } ///:~
```

```java
//: com:bruceeckel:util:DoubleGenerator.java
package com.bruceeckel.util;
public interface DoubleGenerator { double next(); } ///:~
```

Arrays2 contains a variety of **toString( )** methods, overloaded for each type. These methods allow you to easily print an array. The **toString( )** code introduces the use of **StringBuffer** instead of **String** objects. This is a nod to efficiency; when you're assembling a string in a method that might be called a lot, it's wiser to use the more efficient **StringBuffer** rather than the more convenient **String** operations. Here, the **StringBuffer** is created with an initial value, and **Strings** are appended. Finally, the **result** is converted to a **String** as the return value:

```java
//: com:bruceeckel:util:Arrays2.java
// A supplement to java.util.Arrays, to provide additional
// useful functionality when working with arrays. Allows
// any array to be converted to a String, and to be filled
// via a user-defined "generator" object.
package com.bruceeckel.util;
import java.util.*;

public class Arrays2 {
  public static String toString(boolean[] a) {
    StringBuffer result = new StringBuffer("[");
    for(int i = 0; i < a.length; i++) {
      result.append(a[i]);
      if(i < a.length - 1)
        result.append(", ");
    }
    result.append("]");
    return result.toString();
  }
  public static String toString(byte[] a) {
    StringBuffer result = new StringBuffer("[");
    for(int i = 0; i < a.length; i++) {
      result.append(a[i]);
```

```
      if(i < a.length - 1)
        result.append(", ");
    }
    result.append("]");
    return result.toString();
  }
  public static String toString(char[] a) {
    StringBuffer result = new StringBuffer("[");
    for(int i = 0; i < a.length; i++) {
      result.append(a[i]);
      if(i < a.length - 1)
        result.append(", ");
    }
    result.append("]");
    return result.toString();
  }
  public static String toString(short[] a) {
    StringBuffer result = new StringBuffer("[");
    for(int i = 0; i < a.length; i++) {
      result.append(a[i]);
      if(i < a.length - 1)
        result.append(", ");
    }
    result.append("]");
    return result.toString();
  }
  public static String toString(int[] a) {
    StringBuffer result = new StringBuffer("[");
    for(int i = 0; i < a.length; i++) {
      result.append(a[i]);
      if(i < a.length - 1)
        result.append(", ");
    }
    result.append("]");
    return result.toString();
  }
  public static String toString(long[] a) {
    StringBuffer result = new StringBuffer("[");
    for(int i = 0; i < a.length; i++) {
      result.append(a[i]);
      if(i < a.length - 1)
        result.append(", ");
    }
    result.append("]");
```

```
    return result.toString();
  }
  public static String toString(float[] a) {
    StringBuffer result = new StringBuffer("[");
    for(int i = 0; i < a.length; i++) {
      result.append(a[i]);
      if(i < a.length - 1)
        result.append(", ");
    }
    result.append("]");
    return result.toString();
  }
  public static String toString(double[] a) {
    StringBuffer result = new StringBuffer("[");
    for(int i = 0; i < a.length; i++) {
      result.append(a[i]);
      if(i < a.length - 1)
        result.append(", ");
    }
    result.append("]");
    return result.toString();
  }
  // Fill an array using a generator:
  public static void fill(Object[] a, Generator gen) {
    fill(a, 0, a.length, gen);
  }
  public static void
  fill(Object[] a, int from, int to, Generator gen) {
    for(int i = from; i < to; i++)
      a[i] = gen.next();
  }
  public static void
  fill(boolean[] a, BooleanGenerator gen) {
      fill(a, 0, a.length, gen);
  }
  public static void
  fill(boolean[] a, int from, int to,BooleanGenerator gen){
    for(int i = from; i < to; i++)
      a[i] = gen.next();
  }
  public static void fill(byte[] a, ByteGenerator gen) {
    fill(a, 0, a.length, gen);
  }
  public static void
```

```
fill(byte[] a, int from, int to, ByteGenerator gen) {
  for(int i = from; i < to; i++)
    a[i] = gen.next();
}
public static void fill(char[] a, CharGenerator gen) {
  fill(a, 0, a.length, gen);
}
public static void
fill(char[] a, int from, int to, CharGenerator gen) {
  for(int i = from; i < to; i++)
    a[i] = gen.next();
}
public static void fill(short[] a, ShortGenerator gen) {
  fill(a, 0, a.length, gen);
}
public static void
fill(short[] a, int from, int to, ShortGenerator gen) {
  for(int i = from; i < to; i++)
    a[i] = gen.next();
}
public static void fill(int[] a, IntGenerator gen) {
    fill(a, 0, a.length, gen);
}
public static void
fill(int[] a, int from, int to, IntGenerator gen) {
  for(int i = from; i < to; i++)
    a[i] = gen.next();
}
public static void fill(long[] a, LongGenerator gen) {
  fill(a, 0, a.length, gen);
}
public static void
fill(long[] a, int from, int to, LongGenerator gen) {
  for(int i = from; i < to; i++)
    a[i] = gen.next();
}
public static void fill(float[] a, FloatGenerator gen) {
  fill(a, 0, a.length, gen);
}
public static void
fill(float[] a, int from, int to, FloatGenerator gen) {
  for(int i = from; i < to; i++)
    a[i] = gen.next();
}
```

```
  public static void fill(double[] a, DoubleGenerator gen){
    fill(a, 0, a.length, gen);
  }
  public static void
  fill(double[] a, int from, int to, DoubleGenerator gen) {
    for(int i = from; i < to; i++)
      a[i] = gen.next();
  }
  private static Random r = new Random();
  public static class
  RandBooleanGenerator implements BooleanGenerator {
    public boolean next() { return r.nextBoolean(); }
  }
  public static class
  RandByteGenerator implements ByteGenerator {
    public byte next() { return (byte)r.nextInt(); }
  }
  private static String ssource =
    "ABCDEFGHIJKLMNOPQRSTUVWXYZabcdefghijklmnopqrstuvwxyz";
  private static char[] src = ssource.toCharArray();
  public static class
  RandCharGenerator implements CharGenerator {
    public char next() {
      return src[r.nextInt(src.length)];
    }
  }
  public static class
  RandStringGenerator implements Generator {
    private int len;
    private RandCharGenerator cg = new RandCharGenerator();
    public RandStringGenerator(int length) {
      len = length;
    }
    public Object next() {
      char[] buf = new char[len];
      for(int i = 0; i < len; i++)
        buf[i] = cg.next();
      return new String(buf);
    }
  }
  public static class
  RandShortGenerator implements ShortGenerator {
    public short next() { return (short)r.nextInt(); }
  }
```

```
  public static class
  RandIntGenerator implements IntGenerator {
    private int mod = 10000;
    public RandIntGenerator() {}
    public RandIntGenerator(int modulo) { mod = modulo; }
    public int next() { return r.nextInt(mod); }
  }
  public static class
  RandLongGenerator implements LongGenerator {
    public long next() { return r.nextLong(); }
  }
  public static class
  RandFloatGenerator implements FloatGenerator {
    public float next() { return r.nextFloat(); }
  }
  public static class
  RandDoubleGenerator implements DoubleGenerator {
    public double next() {return r.nextDouble();}
  }
} ///:~
```

To fill an array of elements using a generator, the **fill( )** method takes a reference to an appropriate generator **interface**, which has a **next( )** method that will somehow produce an object of the right type (depending on how the interface is implemented). The **fill( )** method simply calls **next( )** until the desired range has been filled. Now you can create any generator by implementing the appropriate **interface** and use your generator with **fill( )**.

Random data generators are useful for testing, so a set of inner classes is created to implement all the primitive generator interfaces, as well as a **String** generator to represent **Object**. You can see that **RandStringGenerator** uses **RandCharGenerator** to fill an array of characters, which is then turned into a **String**. The size of the array is determined by the constructor argument.

To generate numbers that aren't too large, **RandIntGenerator** defaults to a modulus of 10,000, but the overloaded constructor allows you to choose a smaller value.

Here's a program to test the library and demonstrate how it is used:

```
//: c11:TestArrays2.java
// Test and demonstrate Arrays2 utilities.
import com.bruceeckel.util.*;
```

```
public class TestArrays2 {
  public static void main(String[] args) {
    int size = 6;
    // Or get the size from the command line:
    if(args.length != 0) {
      size = Integer.parseInt(args[0]);
      if(size < 3) {
        System.out.println("arg must be >= 3");
        System.exit(1);
      }
    }
    boolean[] a1 = new boolean[size];
    byte[] a2 = new byte[size];
    char[] a3 = new char[size];
    short[] a4 = new short[size];
    int[] a5 = new int[size];
    long[] a6 = new long[size];
    float[] a7 = new float[size];
    double[] a8 = new double[size];
    Arrays2.fill(a1, new Arrays2.RandBooleanGenerator());
    System.out.println("a1 = " + Arrays2.toString(a1));
    Arrays2.fill(a2, new Arrays2.RandByteGenerator());
    System.out.println("a2 = " + Arrays2.toString(a2));
    Arrays2.fill(a3, new Arrays2.RandCharGenerator());
    System.out.println("a3 = " + Arrays2.toString(a3));
    Arrays2.fill(a4, new Arrays2.RandShortGenerator());
    System.out.println("a4 = " + Arrays2.toString(a4));
    Arrays2.fill(a5, new Arrays2.RandIntGenerator());
    System.out.println("a5 = " + Arrays2.toString(a5));
    Arrays2.fill(a6, new Arrays2.RandLongGenerator());
    System.out.println("a6 = " + Arrays2.toString(a6));
    Arrays2.fill(a7, new Arrays2.RandFloatGenerator());
    System.out.println("a7 = " + Arrays2.toString(a7));
    Arrays2.fill(a8, new Arrays2.RandDoubleGenerator());
    System.out.println("a8 = " + Arrays2.toString(a8));
  }
} ///:~
```

The **size** parameter has a default value, but you can also set it from the command line.

Filling an array

The Java standard library **Arrays** also has a **fill( )** method, but that is rather trivial; it only duplicates a single value into each location, or in the case of objects, copies the same reference into each location. Using **Arrays2.toString( )**, the **Arrays.fill( )** methods can be easily demonstrated:

```
//: c11:FillingArrays.java
// Using Arrays.fill()
import com.bruceeckel.simpletest.*;
import com.bruceeckel.util.*;
import java.util.*;

public class FillingArrays {
  private static Test monitor = new Test();
  public static void main(String[] args) {
    int size = 6;
    // Or get the size from the command line:
    if(args.length != 0)
      size = Integer.parseInt(args[0]);
    boolean[] a1 = new boolean[size];
    byte[] a2 = new byte[size];
    char[] a3 = new char[size];
    short[] a4 = new short[size];
    int[] a5 = new int[size];
    long[] a6 = new long[size];
    float[] a7 = new float[size];
    double[] a8 = new double[size];
    String[] a9 = new String[size];
    Arrays.fill(a1, true);
    System.out.println("a1 = " + Arrays2.toString(a1));
    Arrays.fill(a2, (byte)11);
    System.out.println("a2 = " + Arrays2.toString(a2));
    Arrays.fill(a3, 'x');
    System.out.println("a3 = " + Arrays2.toString(a3));
    Arrays.fill(a4, (short)17);
    System.out.println("a4 = " + Arrays2.toString(a4));
    Arrays.fill(a5, 19);
    System.out.println("a5 = " + Arrays2.toString(a5));
    Arrays.fill(a6, 23);
    System.out.println("a6 = " + Arrays2.toString(a6));
    Arrays.fill(a7, 29);
    System.out.println("a7 = " + Arrays2.toString(a7));
```

```
    Arrays.fill(a8, 47);
    System.out.println("a8 = " + Arrays2.toString(a8));
    Arrays.fill(a9, "Hello");
    System.out.println("a9 = " + Arrays.asList(a9));
    // Manipulating ranges:
    Arrays.fill(a9, 3, 5, "World");
    System.out.println("a9 = " + Arrays.asList(a9));
    monitor.expect(new String[] {
      "a1 = [true, true, true, true, true, true]",
      "a2 = [11, 11, 11, 11, 11, 11]",
      "a3 = [x, x, x, x, x, x]",
      "a4 = [17, 17, 17, 17, 17, 17]",
      "a5 = [19, 19, 19, 19, 19, 19]",
      "a6 = [23, 23, 23, 23, 23, 23]",
      "a7 = [29.0, 29.0, 29.0, 29.0, 29.0, 29.0]",
      "a8 = [47.0, 47.0, 47.0, 47.0, 47.0, 47.0]",
      "a9 = [Hello, Hello, Hello, Hello, Hello, Hello]",
      "a9 = [Hello, Hello, Hello, World, World, Hello]"
    });
  }
} ///:~
```

You can either fill the entire array or, as the last two statements show, a range of elements. But since you can only provide a single value to use for filling using **Arrays.fill( )**, the **Arrays2.fill( )** methods produce much more interesting results.

Copying an array

The Java standard library provides a **static** method, **System.arraycopy( )**, which can make much faster copies of an array than if you use a **for** loop to perform the copy by hand. **System.arraycopy( )** is overloaded to handle all types. Here's an example that manipulates arrays of **int**:

```
//: c11:CopyingArrays.java
// Using System.arraycopy()
import com.bruceeckel.simpletest.*;
import com.bruceeckel.util.*;
import java.util.*;

public class CopyingArrays {
  private static Test monitor = new Test();
  public static void main(String[] args) {
    int[] i = new int[7];
```

```
    int[] j = new int[10];
    Arrays.fill(i, 47);
    Arrays.fill(j, 99);
    System.out.println("i = " + Arrays2.toString(i));
    System.out.println("j = " + Arrays2.toString(j));
    System.arraycopy(i, 0, j, 0, i.length);
    System.out.println("j = " + Arrays2.toString(j));
    int[] k = new int[5];
    Arrays.fill(k, 103);
    System.arraycopy(i, 0, k, 0, k.length);
    System.out.println("k = " + Arrays2.toString(k));
    Arrays.fill(k, 103);
    System.arraycopy(k, 0, i, 0, k.length);
    System.out.println("i = " + Arrays2.toString(i));
    // Objects:
    Integer[] u = new Integer[10];
    Integer[] v = new Integer[5];
    Arrays.fill(u, new Integer(47));
    Arrays.fill(v, new Integer(99));
    System.out.println("u = " + Arrays.asList(u));
    System.out.println("v = " + Arrays.asList(v));
    System.arraycopy(v, 0, u, u.length/2, v.length);
    System.out.println("u = " + Arrays.asList(u));
    monitor.expect(new String[] {
      "i = [47, 47, 47, 47, 47, 47, 47]",
      "j = [99, 99, 99, 99, 99, 99, 99, 99, 99, 99]",
      "j = [47, 47, 47, 47, 47, 47, 47, 99, 99, 99]",
      "k = [47, 47, 47, 47, 47]",
      "i = [103, 103, 103, 103, 103, 47, 47]",
      "u = [47, 47, 47, 47, 47, 47, 47, 47, 47, 47]",
      "v = [99, 99, 99, 99, 99]",
      "u = [47, 47, 47, 47, 47, 99, 99, 99, 99, 99]"
    });
  }
} ///:~
```

The arguments to **arraycopy( )** are the source array, the offset into the source array from whence to start copying, the destination array, the offset into the destination array where the copying begins, and the number of elements to copy. Naturally, any violation of the array boundaries will cause an exception.

The example shows that both primitive arrays and object arrays can be copied. However, if you copy arrays of objects, then only the references get copied—there's no duplication of the objects themselves. This is called a *shallow copy* (see Appendix A).

Comparing arrays

Arrays provides the overloaded method **equals( )** to compare entire arrays for equality. Again, these are overloaded for all the primitives and for **Object**. To be equal, the arrays must have the same number of elements, and each element must be equivalent to each corresponding element in the other array, using the **equals( )** for each element. (For primitives, that primitive's wrapper class **equals( )** is used; for example, **Integer.equals( )** for **int**.) For example:

```
//: c11:ComparingArrays.java
// Using Arrays.equals()
import com.bruceeckel.simpletest.*;
import java.util.*;

public class ComparingArrays {
  private static Test monitor = new Test();
  public static void main(String[] args) {
    int[] a1 = new int[10];
    int[] a2 = new int[10];
    Arrays.fill(a1, 47);
    Arrays.fill(a2, 47);
    System.out.println(Arrays.equals(a1, a2));
    a2[3] = 11;
    System.out.println(Arrays.equals(a1, a2));
    String[] s1 = new String[5];
    Arrays.fill(s1, "Hi");
    String[] s2 = {"Hi", "Hi", "Hi", "Hi", "Hi"};
    System.out.println(Arrays.equals(s1, s2));
    monitor.expect(new String[] {
      "true",
      "false",
      "true"
    });
  }
} ///:~
```

Originally, **a1** and **a2** are exactly equal, so the output is "true," but then one of the elements is changed, which makes the result "false." In the last case, all the elements of **s1** point to the same object, but **s2** has five unique objects.

However, array equality is based on contents (via **Object.equals( )**) , so the result is "true."

Array element comparisons

One of the missing features in the Java 1.0 and 1.1 libraries was algorithmic operations—even simple sorting. This was a rather confusing situation to someone expecting an adequate standard library. Fortunately, Java 2 remedied the situation, at least for the sorting problem.

A problem with writing generic sorting code is that sorting must perform comparisons based on the actual type of the object. Of course, one approach is to write a different sorting method for every different type, but you should be able to recognize that this does not produce code that is easily reused for new types.

A primary goal of programming design is to "separate things that change from things that stay the same," and here, the code that stays the same is the general sort algorithm, but the thing that changes from one use to the next is the way objects are compared. So instead of placing the comparison code into many different sort routines, the technique of the *callback* is used. With a callback, the part of the code that varies from case to case is separated, and the part of the code that's always the same will call back to the code that changes.

Java has two ways to provide comparison functionality. The first is with the "natural" comparison method that is imparted to a class by implementing the **java.lang.Comparable** interface. This is a very simple interface with a single method, **compareTo( )**. This method takes another **Object** as an argument and produces a negative value if the current object is less than the argument, zero if the argument is equal, and a positive value if the current object is greater than the argument .

Here's a class that implements **Comparable** and demonstrates the comparability by using the Java standard library method **Arrays.sort( )**:

```
//: c11:CompType.java
// Implementing Comparable in a class.
import com.bruceeckel.util.*;
import java.util.*;

public class CompType implements Comparable {
```

```
  int i;
  int j;
  public CompType(int n1, int n2) {
    i = n1;
    j = n2;
  }
  public String toString() {
    return "[i = " + i + ", j = " + j + "]";
  }
  public int compareTo(Object rv) {
    int rvi = ((CompType)rv).i;
    return (i < rvi ? -1 : (i == rvi ? 0 : 1));
  }
  private static Random r = new Random();
  public static Generator generator() {
    return new Generator() {
      public Object next() {
        return new CompType(r.nextInt(100),r.nextInt(100));
      }
    };
  }
  public static void main(String[] args) {
    CompType[] a = new CompType[10];
    Arrays2.fill(a, generator());
    System.out.println(
      "before sorting, a = " + Arrays.asList(a));
    Arrays.sort(a);
    System.out.println(
      "after sorting, a = " + Arrays.asList(a));
  }
} ///:~
```

When you define the comparison method, you are responsible for deciding what it means to compare one of your objects to another. Here, only the **i** values are used in the comparison, and the **j** values are ignored.

The **static randInt( )** method produces positive values between zero and 100, and the **generator( )** method produces an object that implements the **Generator** interface by creating an anonymous inner class (see Chapter 8). This builds **CompType** objects by initializing them with random values. In **main( )**, the generator is used to fill an array of **CompType**, which is then sorted. If **Comparable** hadn't been implemented, then you'd get a **ClassCastException** at run time when you tried to call **sort( )**. This is because **sort( )** casts its argument to **Comparable**.

Now suppose someone hands you a class that doesn't implement **Comparable**, or hands you this class that *does* implement **Comparable**, but you decide you don't like the way it works and would rather have a different comparison method for the type. The solution is in contrast to hard-wiring the comparison code into each different object. Instead, the *strategy* design pattern[4] is used. With a strategy, the part of the code that varies is encapsulated inside its own class (the strategy object). You hand a strategy object to the code that's always the same, which uses the strategy to fulfill its algorithm. That way, you can make different objects to express different ways of comparison and feed them to the same sorting code. Here, you create a strategy by defining a separate class that implements an interface called **Comparator**. This has two methods, **compare( )** and **equals( )**. However, you don't have to implement **equals( )** except for special performance needs, because anytime you create a class, it is implicitly inherited from **Object**, which has an **equals( )**. So you can just use the default **Object equals( )** and satisfy the contract imposed by the interface.

The **Collections** class (which we'll look at more later) contains a single **Comparator** that reverses the natural sorting order. This can be applied easily to the **CompType**:

```
//: c11:Reverse.java
// The Collecions.reverseOrder() Comparator
import com.bruceeckel.util.*;
import java.util.*;

public class Reverse {
  public static void main(String[] args) {
    CompType[] a = new CompType[10];
    Arrays2.fill(a, CompType.generator());
    System.out.println(
      "before sorting, a = " + Arrays.asList(a));
    Arrays.sort(a, Collections.reverseOrder());
    System.out.println(
      "after sorting, a = " + Arrays.asList(a));
  }
} ///:~
```

---

4 *Design Patterns*, Erich Gamma *et al.*, Addison-Wesley 1995.

The call to **Collections.reverseOrder( )** produces the reference to the **Comparator**.

As a second example, the following **Comparator** compares **CompType** objects based on their **j** values rather than their **i** values:

```
//: c11:ComparatorTest.java
// Implementing a Comparator for a class.
import com.bruceeckel.util.*;
import java.util.*;

class CompTypeComparator implements Comparator {
  public int compare(Object o1, Object o2) {
    int j1 = ((CompType)o1).j;
    int j2 = ((CompType)o2).j;
    return (j1 < j2 ? -1 : (j1 == j2 ? 0 : 1));
  }
}

public class ComparatorTest {
  public static void main(String[] args) {
    CompType[] a = new CompType[10];
    Arrays2.fill(a, CompType.generator());
    System.out.println(
      "before sorting, a = " + Arrays.asList(a));
    Arrays.sort(a, new CompTypeComparator());
    System.out.println(
      "after sorting, a = " + Arrays.asList(a));
  }
} ///:~
```

The **compare( )** method must return a negative integer, zero, or positive integer if the first argument is less than, equal to, or greater than the second, respectively.

Sorting an array

With the built-in sorting methods, you can sort any array of primitives, or any array of objects that either implements **Comparable** or has an associated **Comparator**. This fills a big hole in the Java libraries; believe it or not, there was no support in Java 1.0 or 1.1 for sorting **Strings**! Here's an example that generates random **String** objects and sorts them:

```
//: c11:StringSorting.java
```

```
// Sorting an array of Strings.
import com.bruceeckel.util.*;
import java.util.*;

public class StringSorting {
  public static void main(String[] args) {
    String[] sa = new String[30];
    Arrays2.fill(sa, new Arrays2.RandStringGenerator(5));
    System.out.println(
      "Before sorting: " + Arrays.asList(sa));
    Arrays.sort(sa);
    System.out.println(
      "After sorting: " + Arrays.asList(sa));
  }
} ///:~
```

One thing you'll notice about the output in the **String** sorting algorithm is that it's *lexicographic*, so it puts all the words starting with uppercase letters first, followed by all the words starting with lowercase letters. (Telephone books are typically sorted this way.) You may also want to group the words together regardless of case, and you can do this by defining a **Comparator** class, thereby overriding the default **String Comparable** behavior. For reuse, this will be added to the "util" package:

```
//: com:bruceeckel:util:AlphabeticComparator.java
// Keeping upper and lowercase letters together.
package com.bruceeckel.util;
import java.util.*;

public class AlphabeticComparator implements Comparator {
  public int compare(Object o1, Object o2) {
    String s1 = (String)o1;
    String s2 = (String)o2;
    return s1.toLowerCase().compareTo(s2.toLowerCase());
  }
} ///:~
```

By casting to **String** at the beginning, you'll get an exception if you attempt to use this with the wrong type. Each **String** is converted to lowercase before the comparison. **String**'s built-in **compareTo( )** method provides the desired functionality.

Here's a test using **AlphabeticComparator**:

```java
//: c11:AlphabeticSorting.java
// Keeping upper and lowercase letters together.
import com.bruceeckel.util.*;
import java.util.*;

public class AlphabeticSorting {
  public static void main(String[] args) {
    String[] sa = new String[30];
    Arrays2.fill(sa, new Arrays2.RandStringGenerator(5));
    System.out.println(
      "Before sorting: " + Arrays.asList(sa));
    Arrays.sort(sa, new AlphabeticComparator());
    System.out.println(
      "After sorting: " + Arrays.asList(sa));
  }
} ///:~
```

The sorting algorithm that's used in the Java standard library is designed to be optimal for the particular type you're sorting—a Quicksort for primitives, and a stable merge sort for objects. So you shouldn't need to spend any time worrying about performance unless your profiler points you to the sorting process as a bottleneck.

Searching a sorted array

Once an array is sorted, you can perform a fast search for a particular item by using **Arrays.binarySearch( )**. However, it's very important that you do not try to use **binarySearch( )** on an unsorted array; the results will be unpredictable. The following example uses a **RandIntGenerator** to fill an array, and then uses the same generator to produce values to search for:

```java
//: c11:ArraySearching.java
// Using Arrays.binarySearch().
import com.bruceeckel.util.*;
import java.util.*;

public class ArraySearching {
  public static void main(String[] args) {
    int[] a = new int[100];
    Arrays2.RandIntGenerator gen =
      new Arrays2.RandIntGenerator(1000);
    Arrays2.fill(a, gen);
    Arrays.sort(a);
    System.out.println(
```

```
      "Sorted array: " + Arrays2.toString(a));
    while(true) {
      int r = gen.next();
      int location = Arrays.binarySearch(a, r);
      if(location >= 0) {
        System.out.println("Location of " + r +
          " is " + location + ", a[" +
          location + "] = " + a[location]);
        break; // Out of while loop
      }
    }
  }
} ///:~
```

In the **while** loop, random values are generated as search items until one of them is found.

Arrays.binarySearch( ) produces a value greater than or equal to zero if the search item is found. Otherwise, it produces a negative value representing the place that the element should be inserted if you are maintaining the sorted array by hand. The value produced is

```
-(insertion point) - 1
```

The insertion point is the index of the first element greater than the key, or **a.size( )**, if all elements in the array are less than the specified key.

If the array contains duplicate elements, there is no guarantee which one will be found. The algorithm is thus not really designed to support duplicate elements, but rather to tolerate them. If you need a sorted list of nonduplicated elements, use a **TreeSet** (to maintain sorted order) or **LinkedHashSet** (to maintain insertion order), which will be introduced later in this chapter. These classes take care of all the details for you automatically. Only in cases of performance bottlenecks should you replace one of these classes with a hand-maintained array.

If you have sorted an object array using a **Comparator** (primitive arrays do not allow sorting with a **Comparator**), you must include that same **Comparator** when you perform a **binarySearch( )** (using the overloaded version of the method that's provided). For example, the **AlphabeticSorting.java** program can be modified to perform a search:

```
//: c11:AlphabeticSearch.java
// Searching with a Comparator.
```

```
import com.bruceeckel.simpletest.*;
import com.bruceeckel.util.*;
import java.util.*;

public class AlphabeticSearch {
  private static Test monitor = new Test();
  public static void main(String[] args) {
    String[] sa = new String[30];
    Arrays2.fill(sa, new Arrays2.RandStringGenerator(5));
    AlphabeticComparator comp = new AlphabeticComparator();
    Arrays.sort(sa, comp);
    int index = Arrays.binarySearch(sa, sa[10], comp);
    System.out.println("Index = " + index);
    monitor.expect(new String[] {
      "Index = 10"
    });
  }
} ///:~
```

The **Comparator** must be passed to the overloaded **binarySearch( )** as the third argument. In this example, success is guaranteed because the search item is selected from the array itself.

Array summary

To summarize what you've seen so far, your first and most efficient choice to hold a group of objects should be an array, and you're forced into this choice if you want to hold a group of primitives. In the remainder of this chapter we'll look at the more general case, when you don't know at the time you're writing the program how many objects you're going to need, or if you need a more sophisticated way to store your objects. Java provides a library of *container classes* to solve this problem, the basic types of which are **List**, **Set**, and **Map**. You can solve a surprising number of problems by using these tools.

Among their other characteristics—**Set**, for example, holds only one object of each value, and **Map** is an *associative array* that lets you associate any object with any other object—the Java container classes will automatically resize themselves. So, unlike arrays, you can put in any number of objects and you don't need to worry about how big to make the container while you're writing the program.

Introduction to containers

To me, container classes are one of the most powerful tools for raw development because they significantly increase your programming muscle. The Java 2 containers represent a thorough redesign[5] of the rather poor showings in Java 1.0 and 1.1. Some of the redesign makes things tighter and more sensible. It also fills out the functionality of the containers library, providing the behavior of linked lists, queues, and deques (double-ended queues, pronounced "decks").

The design of a containers library is difficult (true of most library design problems). In C++, the container classes covered the bases with many different classes. This was better than what was available prior to the C++ container classes (nothing), but it didn't translate well into Java. At the other extreme, I've seen a containers library that consists of a single class, "container," which acts like both a linear sequence and an associative array at the same time. The Java 2 container library strikes a balance: the full functionality that you expect from a mature container library, but easier to learn and use than the C++ container classes and other similar container libraries. The result can seem a bit odd in places. Unlike some of the decisions made in the early Java libraries, these oddities were not accidents, but carefully considered decisions based on trade-offs in complexity. It might take you a little while to get comfortable with some aspects of the library, but I think you'll find yourself rapidly acquiring and using these new tools.

The Java 2 container library takes the issue of "holding your objects" and divides it into two distinct concepts:

1. **Collection**: a group of individual elements, often with some rule applied to them. A **List** must hold the elements in a particular sequence, and a **Set** cannot have any duplicate elements. (A *bag*, which is not implemented in the Java container library—since **List**s provide you with enough of that functionality—has no such rules.)

2. **Map**: a group of key-value object pairs. At first glance, this might seem like it ought to be a **Collection** of pairs, but when you try to implement it that way the design gets awkward, so it's clearer to make

---

[5] By Joshua Bloch at Sun.

it a separate concept. On the other hand, it's convenient to look at portions of a **Map** by creating a **Collection** to represent that portion. Thus, a **Map** can return a **Set** of its keys, a **Collection** of its values, or a **Set** of its pairs. **Map**s, like arrays, can easily be expanded to multiple dimensions without adding new concepts; you simply make a **Map** whose values are **Map**s (and the values of *those* **Map**s can be **Map**s, etc.).

We will first look at the general features of containers, then go into details, and finally learn why there are different versions of some containers and how to choose between them.

Printing containers

Unlike arrays, the containers print nicely without any help. Here's an example that also introduces you to the basic types of containers:

```
//: c11:PrintingContainers.java
// Containers print themselves automatically.
import com.bruceeckel.simpletest.*;
import java.util.*;

public class PrintingContainers {
  private static Test monitor = new Test();
  static Collection fill(Collection c) {
    c.add("dog");
    c.add("dog");
    c.add("cat");
    return c;
  }
  static Map fill(Map m) {
    m.put("dog", "Bosco");
    m.put("dog", "Spot");
    m.put("cat", "Rags");
    return m;
  }
  public static void main(String[] args) {
    System.out.println(fill(new ArrayList()));
    System.out.println(fill(new HashSet()));
    System.out.println(fill(new HashMap()));
    monitor.expect(new String[] {
      "[dog, dog, cat]",
      "[dog, cat]",
      "{dog=Spot, cat=Rags}"
```

```
        });
    }
} ///:~
```

As mentioned before, there are two basic categories in the Java container library. The distinction is based on the number of items that are held in each location of the container. The **Collection** category only holds one item in each location (the name is a bit misleading, because entire container libraries are often called "collections"). It includes the **List**, which holds a group of items in a specified sequence, and the **Set**, which only allows the addition of one item of each type. The **ArrayList** is a type of **List**, and **HashSet** is a type of **Set**. To add items to any **Collection**, there's an **add( )** method.

The **Map** holds key-value pairs, rather like a mini database. The preceding example uses one flavor of **Map**, the **HashMap**. If you have a **Map** that associates states with their capitals and you want to know the capital of Ohio, you look it up—almost as if you were indexing into an array. (Maps are also called *associative arrays*.) To add elements to a **Map**, there's a **put( )** method that takes a key and a value as arguments. The example only shows adding elements and does not look up the elements after they're added. That will be shown later.

The overloaded **fill( )** methods fill **Collection**s and **Map**s, respectively. If you look at the output, you can see that the default printing behavior (provided via the container's various **toString( )** methods) produces quite readable results, so no additional printing support is necessary as it was with arrays. A **Collection** is printed surrounded by square brackets, with each element separated by a comma. A **Map** is surrounded by curly braces, with each key and value associated with an equal sign (keys on the left, values on the right).

You can also immediately see the basic behavior of the different containers. The **List** holds the objects exactly as they are entered, without any reordering or editing. The **Set**, however, only accepts one of each object, and it uses its own internal ordering method (in general, you are only concerned with whether or not something is a member of the **Set**, not the order in which it appears—for that you'd use a **List**). And the **Map** also only accepts one of each type of item, based on the key, and it also has its own internal ordering and does not care about the order in which you enter the items. If maintaining the insertion sequence is important, you can use a **LinkedHashSet** or **LinkedHashMap**.

Filling containers

Although the problem of printing the containers is taken care of, filling containers suffers from the same deficiency as **java.util.Arrays**. Just like **Arrays**, there is a companion class called **Collections** containing **static** utility methods, including one called **fill( )**. This **fill( )** also just duplicates a single object reference throughout the container, and also only works for **List** objects and not **Set**s or **Map**s:

```
//: c11:FillingLists.java
// The Collections.fill() method.
import com.bruceeckel.simpletest.*;
import java.util.*;

public class FillingLists {
  private static Test monitor = new Test();
  public static void main(String[] args) {
    List list = new ArrayList();
    for(int i = 0; i < 10; i++)
      list.add("");
    Collections.fill(list, "Hello");
    System.out.println(list);
    monitor.expect(new String[] {
      "[Hello, Hello, Hello, Hello, Hello, " +
        "Hello, Hello, Hello, Hello, Hello]"
    });
  }
} ///:~
```

This method is made even less useful by the fact that it can only replace elements that are already in the **List** and will not add new elements.

To be able to create interesting examples, here is a complementary **Collections2** library (part of **com.bruceeckel.util** for convenience) with a **fill( )** method that uses a generator to add elements and allows you to specify the number of elements you want to **add( )**. The **Generator interface** defined previously will work for **Collection**s, but the **Map** requires its own generator **interface** since a pair of objects (one key and one value) must be produced by each call to **next( )**. Here is the **Pair** class:

```
//: com:bruceeckel:util:Pair.java
package com.bruceeckel.util;

public class Pair {
```

```
  public Object key, value;
  public Pair(Object k, Object v) {
    key = k;
    value = v;
  }
} ///:~
```

Next, the generator **interface** that produces the **Pair**:

```
//: com:bruceeckel:util:MapGenerator.java
package com.bruceeckel.util;
public interface MapGenerator { Pair next(); } ///:~
```

With these, a set of utilities for working with the container classes can be developed:

```
//: com:bruceeckel:util:Collections2.java
// To fill any type of container using a generator object.
package com.bruceeckel.util;
import java.util.*;

public class Collections2 {
  // Fill an array using a generator:
  public static void
  fill(Collection c, Generator gen, int count) {
    for(int i = 0; i < count; i++)
      c.add(gen.next());
  }
  public static void
  fill(Map m, MapGenerator gen, int count) {
    for(int i = 0; i < count; i++) {
      Pair p = gen.next();
      m.put(p.key, p.value);
    }
  }
  public static class
  RandStringPairGenerator implements MapGenerator {
    private Arrays2.RandStringGenerator gen;
    public RandStringPairGenerator(int len) {
      gen = new Arrays2.RandStringGenerator(len);
    }
    public Pair next() {
      return new Pair(gen.next(), gen.next());
    }
  }
```

```
  // Default object so you don't have to create your own:
  public static RandStringPairGenerator rsp =
    new RandStringPairGenerator(10);
  public static class
  StringPairGenerator implements MapGenerator {
    private int index = -1;
    private String[][] d;
    public StringPairGenerator(String[][] data) {
      d = data;
    }
    public Pair next() {
      // Force the index to wrap:
      index = (index + 1) % d.length;
      return new Pair(d[index][0], d[index][1]);
    }
    public StringPairGenerator reset() {
      index = -1;
      return this;
    }
  }
  // Use a predefined dataset:
  public static StringPairGenerator geography =
    new StringPairGenerator(CountryCapitals.pairs);
  // Produce a sequence from a 2D array:
  public static class StringGenerator implements Generator{
    private String[][] d;
    private int position;
    private int index = -1;
    public StringGenerator(String[][] data, int pos) {
      d = data;
      position = pos;
    }
    public Object next() {
      // Force the index to wrap:
      index = (index + 1) % d.length;
      return d[index][position];
    }
    public StringGenerator reset() {
      index = -1;
      return this;
    }
  }
  // Use a predefined dataset:
  public static StringGenerator countries =
```

```
    new StringGenerator(CountryCapitals.pairs, 0);
  public static StringGenerator capitals =
    new StringGenerator(CountryCapitals.pairs, 1);
} ///:~
```

Both versions of **fill( )** take an argument that determines the number of items to add to the container. In addition, there are two generators for the map: **RandStringPairGenerator**, which creates any number of pairs of gibberish **String**s with length determined by the constructor argument; and **StringPairGenerator**, which produces pairs of **String**s given a two-dimensional array of **String**. The **StringGenerator** also takes a two-dimensional array of **String** but generates single items rather than **Pair**s. The **static rsp**, **geography**, **countries**, and **capitals** objects provide prebuilt generators, the last three using all the countries of the world and their capitals. Note that if you try to create more pairs than are available, the generators will loop around to the beginning, and if you are putting the pairs into a **Map**, the duplicates will just be ignored.

Here is the predefined dataset, which consists of country names and their capitals:

```
//: com:bruceeckel:util:CountryCapitals.java
package com.bruceeckel.util;

public class CountryCapitals {
  public static final String[][] pairs = {
    // Africa
    {"ALGERIA","Algiers"}, {"ANGOLA","Luanda"},
    {"BENIN","Porto-Novo"}, {"BOTSWANA","Gaberone"},
    {"BURKINA FASO","Ouagadougou"},
    {"BURUNDI","Bujumbura"},
    {"CAMEROON","Yaounde"}, {"CAPE VERDE","Praia"},
    {"CENTRAL AFRICAN REPUBLIC","Bangui"},
    {"CHAD","N'djamena"},  {"COMOROS","Moroni"},
    {"CONGO","Brazzaville"}, {"DJIBOUTI","Dijibouti"},
    {"EGYPT","Cairo"}, {"EQUATORIAL GUINEA","Malabo"},
    {"ERITREA","Asmara"}, {"ETHIOPIA","Addis Ababa"},
    {"GABON","Libreville"}, {"THE GAMBIA","Banjul"},
    {"GHANA","Accra"}, {"GUINEA","Conakry"},
    {"GUINEA","-"}, {"BISSAU","Bissau"},
    {"COTE D'IVOIR (IVORY COAST)","Yamoussoukro"},
    {"KENYA","Nairobi"}, {"LESOTHO","Maseru"},
    {"LIBERIA","Monrovia"}, {"LIBYA","Tripoli"},
    {"MADAGASCAR","Antananarivo"}, {"MALAWI","Lilongwe"},
```

```
{"MALI","Bamako"}, {"MAURITANIA","Nouakchott"},
{"MAURITIUS","Port Louis"}, {"MOROCCO","Rabat"},
{"MOZAMBIQUE","Maputo"}, {"NAMIBIA","Windhoek"},
{"NIGER","Niamey"}, {"NIGERIA","Abuja"},
{"RWANDA","Kigali"},
{"SAO TOME E PRINCIPE","Sao Tome"},
{"SENEGAL","Dakar"}, {"SEYCHELLES","Victoria"},
{"SIERRA LEONE","Freetown"}, {"SOMALIA","Mogadishu"},
{"SOUTH AFRICA","Pretoria/Cape Town"},
{"SUDAN","Khartoum"},
{"SWAZILAND","Mbabane"}, {"TANZANIA","Dodoma"},
{"TOGO","Lome"}, {"TUNISIA","Tunis"},
{"UGANDA","Kampala"},
{"DEMOCRATIC REPUBLIC OF THE CONGO (ZAIRE)",
 "Kinshasa"},
{"ZAMBIA","Lusaka"}, {"ZIMBABWE","Harare"},
// Asia
{"AFGHANISTAN","Kabul"}, {"BAHRAIN","Manama"},
{"BANGLADESH","Dhaka"}, {"BHUTAN","Thimphu"},
{"BRUNEI","Bandar Seri Begawan"},
{"CAMBODIA","Phnom Penh"},
{"CHINA","Beijing"}, {"CYPRUS","Nicosia"},
{"INDIA","New Delhi"}, {"INDONESIA","Jakarta"},
{"IRAN","Tehran"}, {"IRAQ","Baghdad"},
{"ISRAEL","Tel Aviv"}, {"JAPAN","Tokyo"},
{"JORDAN","Amman"}, {"KUWAIT","Kuwait City"},
{"LAOS","Vientiane"}, {"LEBANON","Beirut"},
{"MALAYSIA","Kuala Lumpur"}, {"THE MALDIVES","Male"},
{"MONGOLIA","Ulan Bator"},
{"MYANMAR (BURMA)","Rangoon"},
{"NEPAL","Katmandu"}, {"NORTH KOREA","P'yongyang"},
{"OMAN","Muscat"}, {"PAKISTAN","Islamabad"},
{"PHILIPPINES","Manila"}, {"QATAR","Doha"},
{"SAUDI ARABIA","Riyadh"}, {"SINGAPORE","Singapore"},
{"SOUTH KOREA","Seoul"}, {"SRI LANKA","Colombo"},
{"SYRIA","Damascus"},
{"TAIWAN (REPUBLIC OF CHINA)","Taipei"},
{"THAILAND","Bangkok"}, {"TURKEY","Ankara"},
{"UNITED ARAB EMIRATES","Abu Dhabi"},
{"VIETNAM","Hanoi"}, {"YEMEN","Sana'a"},
// Australia and Oceania
{"AUSTRALIA","Canberra"}, {"FIJI","Suva"},
{"KIRIBATI","Bairiki"},
{"MARSHALL ISLANDS","Dalap-Uliga-Darrit"},
```

```
{"MICRONESIA","Palikir"}, {"NAURU","Yaren"},
{"NEW ZEALAND","Wellington"}, {"PALAU","Koror"},
{"PAPUA NEW GUINEA","Port Moresby"},
{"SOLOMON ISLANDS","Honaira"}, {"TONGA","Nuku'alofa"},
{"TUVALU","Fongafale"}, {"VANUATU","< Port-Vila"},
{"WESTERN SAMOA","Apia"},
// Eastern Europe and former USSR
{"ARMENIA","Yerevan"}, {"AZERBAIJAN","Baku"},
{"BELARUS (BYELORUSSIA)","Minsk"},
{"GEORGIA","Tbilisi"},
{"KAZAKSTAN","Almaty"}, {"KYRGYZSTAN","Alma-Ata"},
{"MOLDOVA","Chisinau"}, {"RUSSIA","Moscow"},
{"TAJIKISTAN","Dushanbe"}, {"TURKMENISTAN","Ashkabad"},
{"UKRAINE","Kyiv"}, {"UZBEKISTAN","Tashkent"},
// Europe
{"ALBANIA","Tirana"}, {"ANDORRA","Andorra la Vella"},
{"AUSTRIA","Vienna"}, {"BELGIUM","Brussels"},
{"BOSNIA","-"}, {"HERZEGOVINA","Sarajevo"},
{"CROATIA","Zagreb"}, {"CZECH REPUBLIC","Prague"},
{"DENMARK","Copenhagen"}, {"ESTONIA","Tallinn"},
{"FINLAND","Helsinki"}, {"FRANCE","Paris"},
{"GERMANY","Berlin"}, {"GREECE","Athens"},
{"HUNGARY","Budapest"}, {"ICELAND","Reykjavik"},
{"IRELAND","Dublin"}, {"ITALY","Rome"},
{"LATVIA","Riga"}, {"LIECHTENSTEIN","Vaduz"},
{"LITHUANIA","Vilnius"}, {"LUXEMBOURG","Luxembourg"},
{"MACEDONIA","Skopje"}, {"MALTA","Valletta"},
{"MONACO","Monaco"}, {"MONTENEGRO","Podgorica"},
{"THE NETHERLANDS","Amsterdam"}, {"NORWAY","Oslo"},
{"POLAND","Warsaw"}, {"PORTUGAL","Lisbon"},
{"ROMANIA","Bucharest"}, {"SAN MARINO","San Marino"},
{"SERBIA","Belgrade"}, {"SLOVAKIA","Bratislava"},
{"SLOVENIA","Ljujiana"}, {"SPAIN","Madrid"},
{"SWEDEN","Stockholm"}, {"SWITZERLAND","Berne"},
{"UNITED KINGDOM","London"}, {"VATICAN CITY","---"},
// North and Central America
{"ANTIGUA AND BARBUDA","Saint John's"},
{"BAHAMAS","Nassau"},
{"BARBADOS","Bridgetown"}, {"BELIZE","Belmopan"},
{"CANADA","Ottawa"}, {"COSTA RICA","San Jose"},
{"CUBA","Havana"}, {"DOMINICA","Roseau"},
{"DOMINICAN REPUBLIC","Santo Domingo"},
{"EL SALVADOR","San Salvador"},
{"GRENADA","Saint George's"},
```

```
    {"GUATEMALA","Guatemala City"},
    {"HAITI","Port-au-Prince"},
    {"HONDURAS","Tegucigalpa"}, {"JAMAICA","Kingston"},
    {"MEXICO","Mexico City"}, {"NICARAGUA","Managua"},
    {"PANAMA","Panama City"}, {"ST. KITTS","-"},
    {"NEVIS","Basseterre"}, {"ST. LUCIA","Castries"},
    {"ST. VINCENT AND THE GRENADINES","Kingstown"},
    {"UNITED STATES OF AMERICA","Washington, D.C."},
    // South America
    {"ARGENTINA","Buenos Aires"},
    {"BOLIVIA","Sucre (legal)/La Paz(administrative)"},
    {"BRAZIL","Brasilia"}, {"CHILE","Santiago"},
    {"COLOMBIA","Bogota"}, {"ECUADOR","Quito"},
    {"GUYANA","Georgetown"}, {"PARAGUAY","Asuncion"},
    {"PERU","Lima"}, {"SURINAME","Paramaribo"},
    {"TRINIDAD AND TOBAGO","Port of Spain"},
    {"URUGUAY","Montevideo"}, {"VENEZUELA","Caracas"},
  };
} ///:~
```

This is simply a two-dimensional array of **String** data.[6] Here's a simple test using the **fill( )** methods and generators:

```
//: c11:FillTest.java
import com.bruceeckel.util.*;
import java.util.*;

public class FillTest {
  private static Generator sg =
    new Arrays2.RandStringGenerator(7);
  public static void main(String[] args) {
    List list = new ArrayList();
    Collections2.fill(list, sg, 25);
    System.out.println(list + "\n");
    List list2 = new ArrayList();
    Collections2.fill(list2, Collections2.capitals, 25);
    System.out.println(list2 + "\n");
    Set set = new HashSet();
    Collections2.fill(set, sg, 25);
    System.out.println(set + "\n");
```

[6] This data was found on the Internet, then processed by creating a Python program (see *www.Python.org*).

```
    Map m = new HashMap();
    Collections2.fill(m, Collections2.rsp, 25);
    System.out.println(m + "\n");
    Map m2 = new HashMap();
    Collections2.fill(m2, Collections2.geography, 25);
    System.out.println(m2);
  }
} ///:~
```

With these tools you can easily test the various containers by filling them with interesting data.

Container disadvantage: unknown type

The "disadvantage" to using the Java containers is that you lose type information when you put an object into a container. This happens because the programmer of that container class had no idea what specific type you wanted to put in the container, and making the container hold only your type would prevent it from being a general-purpose tool. So instead, the container holds references to **Object**, which is the root of all the classes, so it holds any type. (Of course, this doesn't include primitive types, since they aren't real objects, and thus, are not inherited from anything.) This is a great solution, except:

1. Because the type information is thrown away when you put an object reference into a container, there's no restriction on the type of object that can be put into your container, even if you mean it to hold only, say, cats. Someone could just as easily put a dog into the container.

2. Because the type information is lost, the only thing the container knows that it holds is a reference to an object. You must perform a cast to the correct type before you use it.

On the up side, Java won't let you *misuse* the objects that you put into a container. If you throw a dog into a container of cats and then try to treat everything in the container as a cat, you'll get a **RuntimeException** when you pull the dog reference out of the cat container and try to cast it to a cat.

Here's an example using the basic workhorse container, **ArrayList**. For starters, you can think of **ArrayList** as "an array that automatically expands itself." Using an **ArrayList** is straightforward: create one, put objects in using **add( ),** and later get them out with **get( )** using an index—just like you would with an array, but without the square brackets.[7] **ArrayList** also has a method **size( )** to let you know how many elements have been added so you don't inadvertently run off the end and cause an exception.

First, **Cat** and **Dog** classes are created:

```
//: c11:Cat.java
package c11;

public class Cat {
  private int catNumber;
  public Cat(int i) { catNumber = i; }
  public void id() {
    System.out.println("Cat #" + catNumber);
  }
} ///:~
```

```
//: c11:Dog.java
package c11;

public class Dog {
  private int dogNumber;
  public Dog(int i) { dogNumber = i; }
  public void id() {
    System.out.println("Dog #" + dogNumber);
  }
} ///:~
```

Cats and **Dog**s are placed into the container, then pulled out:

```
//: c11:CatsAndDogs.java
// Simple container example.
// {ThrowsException}
package c11;
import java.util.*;

public class CatsAndDogs {
  public static void main(String[] args) {
    List cats = new ArrayList();
```

[7] This is a place where operator overloading would be nice.

```
    for(int i = 0; i < 7; i++)
      cats.add(new Cat(i));
    // Not a problem to add a dog to cats:
    cats.add(new Dog(7));
    for(int i = 0; i < cats.size(); i++)
      ((Cat)cats.get(i)).id();
      // Dog is detected only at run time
  }
} ///:~
```

The classes **Cat** and **Dog** are distinct; they have nothing in common except that they are **Object**s. (If you don't explicitly say what class you're inheriting from, you automatically inherit from **Object**.) Since **ArrayList** holds **Object**s, you can not only put **Cat** objects into this container using the **ArrayList** method **add( )**, but you can also add **Dog** objects without complaint at either compile time or run time. When you go to fetch out what you think are **Cat** objects using the **ArrayList** method **get( )**, you get back a reference to an object that you must cast to a **Cat**. Then you need to surround the entire expression with parentheses to force the evaluation of the cast before calling the **id( )** method for **Cat**; otherwise, you'll get a syntax error. Then, at run time, when you try to cast the **Dog** object to a **Cat**, you'll get an exception.

This is more than just an annoyance. It's something that can create difficult-to-find bugs. If one part (or several parts) of a program inserts objects into a container, and you discover only in a separate part of the program through an exception that a bad object was placed in the container, then you must find out where the bad insert occurred. Most of the time this isn't a problem, but you should be aware of the possibility.

Sometimes it works anyway

It turns out that in some cases things seem to work correctly without casting back to your original type. One case is quite special: The **String** class has some extra help from the compiler to make it work smoothly. Whenever the compiler expects a **String** object and it hasn't got one, it will automatically call the **toString( )** method that's defined in **Object** and can be overridden by any Java class. This method produces the desired **String** object, which is then used wherever it is wanted.

Thus, all you need to do to make objects of your class print is to override the **toString( )** method, as shown in the following example:

```java
//: c11:Mouse.java
// Overriding toString().

public class Mouse {
  private int mouseNumber;
  public Mouse(int i) { mouseNumber = i; }
  // Override Object.toString():
  public String toString() {
    return "This is Mouse #" + mouseNumber;
  }
  public int getNumber() { return mouseNumber; }
} ///:~
```

```java
//: c11:MouseTrap.java

public class MouseTrap {
  static void caughtYa(Object m) {
    Mouse mouse = (Mouse)m; // Cast from Object
    System.out.println("Mouse: " + mouse.getNumber());
  }
} ///:~
```

```java
//: c11:WorksAnyway.java
// In special cases, things just seem to work correctly.
import com.bruceeckel.simpletest.*;
import java.util.*;

public class WorksAnyway {
  private static Test monitor = new Test();
  public static void main(String[] args) {
    List mice = new ArrayList();
    for(int i = 0; i < 3; i++)
      mice.add(new Mouse(i));
    for(int i = 0; i < mice.size(); i++) {
      // No cast necessary, automatic
      // call to Object.toString():
      System.out.println("Free mouse: " + mice.get(i));
      MouseTrap.caughtYa(mice.get(i));
    }
    monitor.expect(new String[] {
      "Free mouse: This is Mouse #0",
      "Mouse: 0",
      "Free mouse: This is Mouse #1",
      "Mouse: 1",
      "Free mouse: This is Mouse #2",
```

```
      "Mouse: 2"
    });
  }
} ///:~
```

You can see **toString( )** overridden in **Mouse**. In the second **for** loop in **main( )** you find the statement:

```
System.out.println("Free mouse: " + mice.get(i));
```

After the '+' sign the compiler expects to see a **String** object. **get( )** produces an **Object**, so to get the desired **String**, the compiler implicitly calls **toString( )**. Unfortunately, you can work this kind of magic only with **String**; it isn't available for any other type.

A second approach to hiding the cast has been placed inside **MouseTrap**. The **caughtYa( )** method accepts not a **Mouse**, but an **Object,** which it then casts to a **Mouse**. This is quite presumptuous, of course, since by accepting an **Object**, anything could be passed to the method. However, if the cast is incorrect—if you passed the wrong type—you'll get an exception at run time. This is not as good as compile-time checking, but it's still robust. Note that in the use of this method:

```
MouseTrap.caughtYa(mice.get(i));
```

no cast is necessary.

Making a type-conscious **ArrayList**

You might not want to give up on this issue just yet. A more ironclad solution is to create a new class using the **ArrayList**, such that it will accept only your type and produce only your type:

```
//: c11:MouseList.java
// A type-conscious List.
import java.util.*;

public class MouseList {
  private List list = new ArrayList();
  public void add(Mouse m) { list.add(m); }
  public Mouse get(int index) {
    return (Mouse)list.get(index);
  }
  public int size() { return list.size(); }
} ///:~
```

Here's a test for the new container:

```
//: c11:MouseListTest.java
import com.bruceeckel.simpletest.*;

public class MouseListTest {
  private static Test monitor = new Test();
  public static void main(String[] args) {
    MouseList mice = new MouseList();
    for(int i = 0; i < 3; i++)
      mice.add(new Mouse(i));
    for(int i = 0; i < mice.size(); i++)
      MouseTrap.caughtYa(mice.get(i));
    monitor.expect(new String[] {
      "Mouse: 0",
      "Mouse: 1",
      "Mouse: 2"
    });
  }
} ///:~
```

This is similar to the previous example, except that the new **MouseList** class has a **private** member of type **ArrayList** and methods just like **ArrayList**. However, it doesn't accept and produce generic **Object**s, only **Mouse** objects.

Note that if **MouseList** had instead been *inherited* from **ArrayList**, the **add(Mouse)** method would simply overload the existing **add(Object)**, and there would still be no restriction on what type of objects could be added, and you wouldn't get the desired results. Using composition, the **MouseList** simply uses the **ArrayList**, performing some activities before passing the responsibility for the rest of the operation on to the **ArrayList**.

Because a **MouseList** will accept only a **Mouse**, if you say:

```
mice.add(new Pigeon());
```

you will get an error message *at compile time*. This approach, while more tedious from a coding standpoint, will tell you immediately if you're using a type improperly.

Note that no cast is necessary when using **get( )**; it's always a **Mouse**.

Parameterized types

This kind of problem isn't isolated. There are numerous cases in which you need to create new types based on other types, and in which it is useful to have specific type information at compile time. This is the concept of a *parameterized type*. In C++, this is directly supported by the language using *templates*. It is likely that Java JDK 1.5 will provide *generics*, the Java version of parameterized types.

Iterators

In any container class, you must have a way to put things in and a way to get things out. After all, that's the primary job of a container—to hold things. In the **ArrayList**, **add( )** is the way that you insert objects, and **get( )** is *one* way to get things out. **ArrayList** is quite flexible; you can select anything at any time, and select multiple elements at once using different indexes.

If you want to start thinking at a higher level, there's a drawback: You need to know the exact type of the container in order to use it. This might not seem bad at first, but what if you start out using an **ArrayList**, and later on you discover that because of the features you need in the container you actually need to use a **Set** instead? Or suppose you'd like to write a piece of generic code that doesn't know or care what type of container it's working with, so that it could be used on different types of containers without rewriting that code?

The concept of an *iterator* (yet another design pattern) can be used to achieve this abstraction. An iterator is an object whose job is to move through a sequence of objects and select each object in that sequence without the client programmer knowing or caring about the underlying structure of that sequence. In addition, an iterator is usually what's called a "light-weight" object: one that's cheap to create. For that reason, you'll often find seemingly strange constraints for iterators; for example, some iterators can move in only one direction.

The Java **Iterator** is an example of an iterator with these kinds of constraints. There's not much you can do with one except:

1. Ask a container to hand you an **Iterator** using a method called **iterator( )**. This **Iterator** will be ready to return the first element in the sequence on your first call to its **next( )** method.

2. Get the next object in the sequence with **next( )**.

3. See if there *are* any more objects in the sequence with **hasNext( )**.

4. Remove the last element returned by the iterator with **remove( )**.

That's all. It's a simple implementation of an iterator, but still powerful (and there's a more sophisticated **ListIterator** for **List**s). To see how it works, let's revisit the **CatsAndDogs.java** program from earlier in this chapter. In the original version, the method **get( )** was used to select each element, but in the following modified version, an **Iterator** is used:

```
//: c11:CatsAndDogs2.java
// Simple container with Iterator.
package c11;
import com.bruceeckel.simpletest.*;
import java.util.*;

public class CatsAndDogs2 {
  private static Test monitor = new Test();
  public static void main(String[] args) {
    List cats = new ArrayList();
    for(int i = 0; i < 7; i++)
      cats.add(new Cat(i));
    Iterator e = cats.iterator();
    while(e.hasNext())
      ((Cat)e.next()).id();
  }
} ///:~
```

You can see that the last few lines now use an **Iterator** to step through the sequence instead of a **for** loop. With the **Iterator**, you don't need to worry about the number of elements in the container. That's taken care of for you by **hasNext( )** and **next( )**.

As another example, consider the creation of a general-purpose printing method:

```
//: c11:Printer.java
// Using an Iterator.
import java.util.*;

public class Printer {
  static void printAll(Iterator e) {
    while(e.hasNext())
```

```
      System.out.println(e.next());
  }
} ///:~
```

Look closely at **printAll( )**. Note that there's no information about the type of sequence. All you have is an **Iterator**, and that's all you need to know about the sequence: that you can get the next object, and that you can know when you're at the end. This idea of taking a container of objects and passing through it to perform an operation on each one is powerful and will be seen throughout this book.

The example is even more generic, since it implicitly uses the **Object.toString( )** method. The **println( )** method is overloaded for all the primitive types as well as **Object**; in each case, a **String** is automatically produced by calling the appropriate **toString( )** method.

Although it's unnecessary, you can be more explicit using a cast, which has the effect of calling **toString( )**:

```
System.out.println((String)e.next());
```

In general, however, you'll want to do something more than call **Object** methods, so you'll run up against the type-casting issue again. You must assume you've gotten an **Iterator** to a sequence of the particular type you're interested in, and cast the resulting objects to that type (getting a run-time exception if you're wrong).

We can test it by printing **Hamster**s:

```
//: c11:Hamster.java

public class Hamster {
  private int hamsterNumber;
  public Hamster(int hamsterNumber) {
    this.hamsterNumber = hamsterNumber;
  }
  public String toString() {
    return "This is Hamster #" + hamsterNumber;
  }
} ///:~
```

```
//: c11:HamsterMaze.java
// Using an Iterator.
import com.bruceeckel.simpletest.*;
import java.util.*;
```

```
public class HamsterMaze {
  private static Test monitor = new Test();
  public static void main(String[] args) {
    List list = new ArrayList();
    for(int i = 0; i < 3; i++)
      list.add(new Hamster(i));
    Printer.printAll(list.iterator());
    monitor.expect(new String[] {
      "This is Hamster #0",
      "This is Hamster #1",
      "This is Hamster #2"
    });
  }
} ///:~
```

You could write **printAll( )** to accept a **Collection** object instead of an **Iterator**, but the latter provides better decoupling.

Unintended recursion

Because (like every other class) the Java standard containers are inherited from **Object**, they contain a **toString( )** method. This has been overridden so that they can produce a **String** representation of themselves, including the objects they hold. Inside **ArrayList**, for example, the **toString( )** steps through the elements of the **ArrayList** and calls **toString( )** for each one. Suppose you'd like to print the address of your class. It seems to make sense to simply refer to **this** (in particular, C++ programmers are prone to this approach):

```
//: c11:InfiniteRecursion.java
// Accidental recursion.
// {RunByHand}
import java.util.*;

public class InfiniteRecursion {
  public String toString() {
    return " InfiniteRecursion address: " + this + "\n";
  }
  public static void main(String[] args) {
    List v = new ArrayList();
    for(int i = 0; i < 10; i++)
      v.add(new InfiniteRecursion());
    System.out.println(v);
```

```
  }
} ///:~
```

If you simply create an **InfiniteRecursion** object and then print it, you'll get an endless sequence of exceptions. This is also true if you place the **InfiniteRecursion** objects in an **ArrayList** and print that **ArrayList** as shown here. What's happening is automatic type conversion for **String**s. When you say:

```
"InfiniteRecursion address: " + this
```

The compiler sees a **String** followed by a '+' and something that's not a **String**, so it tries to convert **this** to a **String**. It does this conversion by calling **toString( )**, which produces a recursive call.

If you really do want to print the address of the object in this case, the solution is to call the **Object toString( )** method, which does just that. So instead of saying **this**, you'd say **super.toString( )**.

Container taxonomy

Collections and **Map**s may be implemented in different ways according to your programming needs. It's helpful to look at a diagram of the Java containers (as of JDK 1.4):

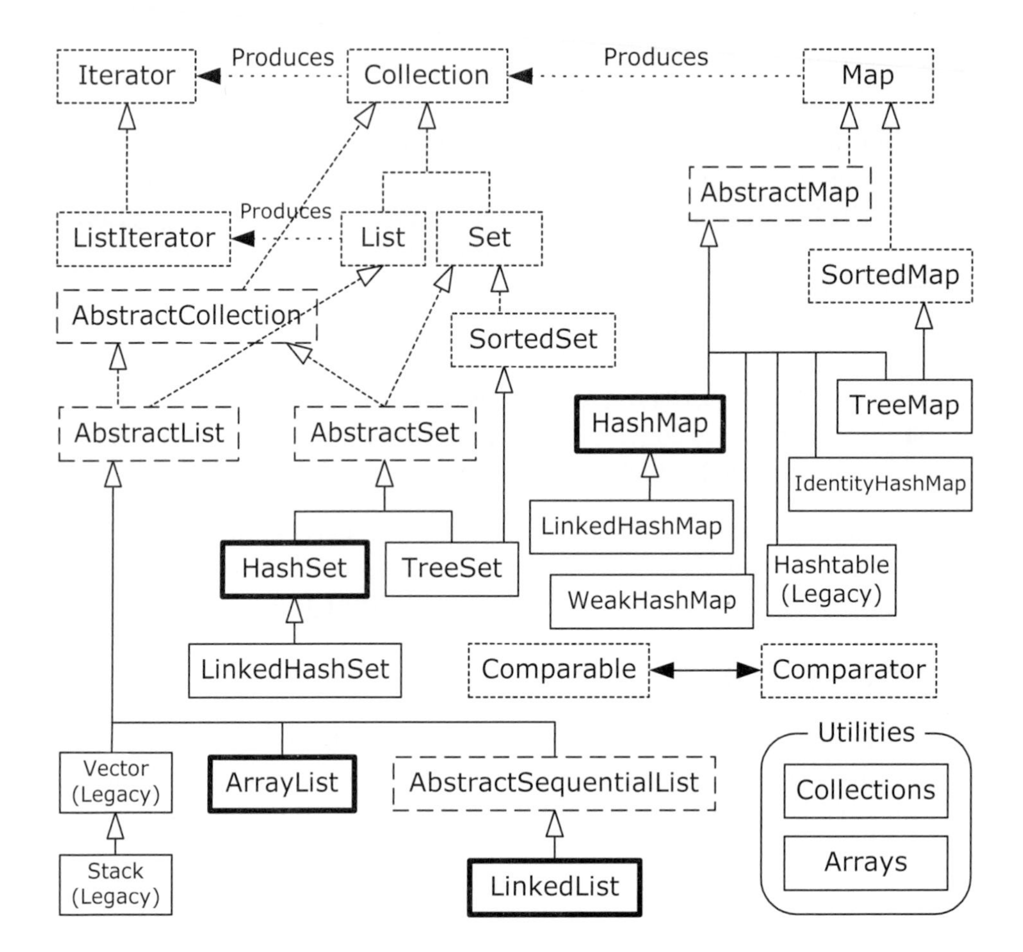

This diagram can be a bit overwhelming at first, but you'll see that there are really only three container components—**Map**, **List**, and **Set**—and only two or three implementations of each one. The containers that you will generally use most of the time have heavy black lines around them. When you see this, the containers are not so daunting.

The dotted boxes represent **interface**s, the dashed boxes represent **abstract** classes, and the solid boxes are regular (concrete) classes. The dotted-line arrows indicate that a particular class is implementing an **interface** (or in the case of an **abstract** class, partially implementing that **interface**). The solid arrows show that a class can produce objects of the class the arrow is pointing to. For example, any **Collection** can produce an **Iterator** and a **List** can produce a **ListIterator** (as well as an ordinary **Iterator**, since **List** is inherited from **Collection**).

The interfaces that are concerned with holding objects are **Collection**, **List**, **Set**, and **Map**. Ideally, you'll write most of your code to talk to these interfaces, and the only place where you'll specify the precise type you're using is at the point of creation. So you can create a **List** like this:

```
List x = new LinkedList();
```

Of course, you can also decide to make **x** a **LinkedList** (instead of a generic **List**) and carry the precise type information around with **x**. The beauty (and the intent) of using the **interface** is that if you decide you want to change your implementation, all you need to do is change it at the point of creation, like this:

```
List x = new ArrayList();
```

The rest of your code can remain untouched (some of this genericity can also be achieved with iterators).

In the class hierarchy, you can see a number of classes whose names begin with "**Abstract**," and these can seem a bit confusing at first. They are simply tools that partially implement a particular interface. If you were making your own **Set**, for example, you wouldn't start with the **Set** interface and implement all the methods; instead, you'd inherit from **AbstractSet** and do the minimal necessary work to make your new class. However, the containers library contains enough functionality to satisfy your needs virtually all the time. So for our purposes, you can ignore any class that begins with "**Abstract**."

Therefore, when you look at the diagram, you're really concerned with only those **interface**s at the top of the diagram and the concrete classes (those with solid boxes around them). You'll typically make an object of a concrete class, upcast it to the corresponding **interface**, and then use the **interface** throughout the rest of your code. In addition, you do not need to consider the legacy elements when writing new code. Therefore, the diagram can be greatly simplified to look like this:

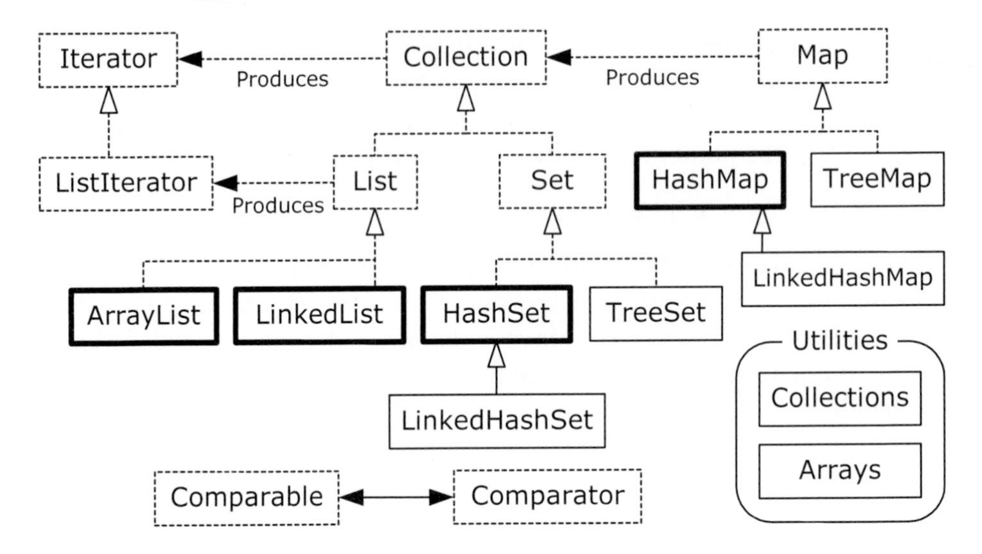

Now it only includes the interfaces and classes that you will encounter on a regular basis, and also the elements that we will focus on in this chapter. Note that the **WeakHashMap** and the JDK 1.4 **IdentityHashMap** are not included on this diagram, because they are special-purpose tools that you will rarely use.

Here's a simple example that fills a **Collection** (represented here with an **ArrayList**) with **String** objects and then prints each element in the **Collection**:

```
//: c11:SimpleCollection.java
// A simple example using Java 2 Collections.
import com.bruceeckel.simpletest.*;
import java.util.*;

public class SimpleCollection {
  private static Test monitor = new Test();
  public static void main(String[] args) {
    // Upcast because we just want to
    // work with Collection features
    Collection c = new ArrayList();
    for(int i = 0; i < 10; i++)
      c.add(Integer.toString(i));
    Iterator it = c.iterator();
    while(it.hasNext())
      System.out.println(it.next());
    monitor.expect(new String[] {
      "0",
```

```
            "1",
            "2",
            "3",
            "4",
            "5",
            "6",
            "7",
            "8",
            "9"
        });
    }
} ///:~
```

The first line in **main( )** creates an **ArrayList** object and then upcasts it to a **Collection**. Since this example uses only the **Collection** methods, any object of a class inherited from **Collection** would work, but **ArrayList** is the typical workhorse **Collection**.

The **add( )** method, as its name suggests, puts a new element in the **Collection**. However, the documentation carefully states that **add( )** "ensures that this Container contains the specified element." This is to allow for the meaning of **Set**, which adds the element only if it isn't already there. With an **ArrayList**, or any sort of **List**, **add( )** always means "put it in," because **List**s don't care if there are duplicates.

All **Collection**s can produce an **Iterator** via their **iterator( )** method. Here, an **Iterator** is created and used to traverse the **Collection**, printing each element.

Collection functionality

The following table shows everything you can do with a **Collection** (not including the methods that automatically come through with **Object**), and thus, everything you can do with a **Set** or a **List**. (**List** also has additional functionality.) **Map**s are not inherited from **Collection** and will be treated separately.

boolean add(Object)	Ensures that the container holds the argument. Returns false if it doesn't add the argument. (This is an "optional" method, described later in this chapter.)
boolean	Adds all the elements in the argument.

addAll(Collection)	Returns **true** if any elements were added. ("Optional.")
void clear( )	Removes all the elements in the container. ("Optional.")
boolean contains(Object)	**true** if the container holds the argument.
boolean containsAll(Collection)	**true** if the container holds all the elements in the argument.
boolean isEmpty( )	**true** if the container has no elements.
Iterator iterator( )	Returns an **Iterator** that you can use to move through the elements in the container.
boolean remove(Object)	If the argument is in the container, one instance of that element is removed. Returns **true** if a removal occurred. ("Optional.")
boolean removeAll(Collection)	Removes all the elements that are contained in the argument. Returns **true** if any removals occurred. ("Optional.")
boolean retainAll(Collection)	Retains only elements that are contained in the argument (an "intersection" from set theory). Returns **true** if any changes occurred. ("Optional.")
int size( )	Returns the number of elements in the container.
Object[] toArray( )	Returns an array containing all the elements in the container.
Object[] toArray(Object[] a)	Returns an array containing all the elements in the container, whose type is that of the array a rather than plain **Object** (you must cast the array to the right type).

Notice that there's no **get( )** method for random-access element selection. That's because **Collection** also includes **Set**, which maintains its own internal ordering (and thus makes random-access lookup meaningless). Thus, if you want to examine the elements of a **Collection**, you must use an iterator.

The following example demonstrates all of these methods. Again, these work with anything that implements **Collection**, but an **ArrayList** is used as a kind of "least-common denominator":

```
//: c11:Collection1.java
// Things you can do with all Collections.
import com.bruceeckel.simpletest.*;
import java.util.*;
import com.bruceeckel.util.*;

public class Collection1 {
  private static Test monitor = new Test();
  public static void main(String[] args) {
    Collection c = new ArrayList();
    Collections2.fill(c, Collections2.countries, 5);
    c.add("ten");
    c.add("eleven");
    System.out.println(c);
    // Make an array from the List:
    Object[] array = c.toArray();
    // Make a String array from the List:
    String[] str = (String[])c.toArray(new String[1]);
    // Find max and min elements; this means
    // different things depending on the way
    // the Comparable interface is implemented:
    System.out.println("Collections.max(c) = " +
      Collections.max(c));
    System.out.println("Collections.min(c) = " +
      Collections.min(c));
    // Add a Collection to another Collection
    Collection c2 = new ArrayList();
    Collections2.fill(c2, Collections2.countries, 5);
    c.addAll(c2);
    System.out.println(c);
    c.remove(CountryCapitals.pairs[0][0]);
    System.out.println(c);
    c.remove(CountryCapitals.pairs[1][0]);
    System.out.println(c);
    // Remove all components that are
    //  in the argument collection:
    c.removeAll(c2);
    System.out.println(c);
    c.addAll(c2);
    System.out.println(c);
```

```
    // Is an element in this Collection?
    String val = CountryCapitals.pairs[3][0];
    System.out.println("c.contains(" + val  + ") = "
      + c.contains(val));
    // Is a Collection in this Collection?
    System.out.println(
      "c.containsAll(c2) = " + c.containsAll(c2));
    Collection c3 = ((List)c).subList(3, 5);
    // Keep all the elements that are in both
    // c2 and c3 (an intersection of sets):
    c2.retainAll(c3);
    System.out.println(c);
    // Throw away all the elements
    // in c2 that also appear in c3:
    c2.removeAll(c3);
    System.out.println("c.isEmpty() = " +  c.isEmpty());
    c = new ArrayList();
    Collections2.fill(c, Collections2.countries, 5);
    System.out.println(c);
    c.clear(); // Remove all elements
    System.out.println("after c.clear():");
    System.out.println(c);
    monitor.expect(new String[] {
      "[ALGERIA, ANGOLA, BENIN, BOTSWANA, BURKINA FASO, " +
        "ten, eleven]",
      "Collections.max(c) = ten",
      "Collections.min(c) = ALGERIA",
      "[ALGERIA, ANGOLA, BENIN, BOTSWANA, BURKINA FASO, " +
      "ten, eleven, BURUNDI, CAMEROON, CAPE VERDE, " +
      "CENTRAL AFRICAN REPUBLIC, CHAD]",
      "[ANGOLA, BENIN, BOTSWANA, BURKINA FASO, ten, " +
      "eleven, BURUNDI, CAMEROON, CAPE VERDE, " +
      "CENTRAL AFRICAN REPUBLIC, CHAD]",
      "[BENIN, BOTSWANA, BURKINA FASO, ten, eleven, " +
      "BURUNDI, CAMEROON, CAPE VERDE, " +
      "CENTRAL AFRICAN REPUBLIC, CHAD]",
      "[BENIN, BOTSWANA, BURKINA FASO, ten, eleven]",
      "[BENIN, BOTSWANA, BURKINA FASO, ten, eleven, " +
      "BURUNDI, CAMEROON, CAPE VERDE, " +
      "CENTRAL AFRICAN REPUBLIC, CHAD]",
      "c.contains(BOTSWANA) = true",
      "c.containsAll(c2) = true",
      "[BENIN, BOTSWANA, BURKINA FASO, ten, eleven, " +
      "BURUNDI, CAMEROON, CAPE VERDE, " +
```

```
      "CENTRAL AFRICAN REPUBLIC, CHAD]",
      "c.isEmpty() = false",
      "[COMOROS, CONGO, DJIBOUTI, EGYPT, " +
      "EQUATORIAL GUINEA]",
      "after c.clear():",
      "[]"
    });
  }
} ///:~
```

ArrayLists are created containing different sets of data and upcast to **Collection** objects, so it's clear that nothing other than the **Collection** interface is being used. **main( )** uses simple exercises to show all of the methods in **Collection**.

The following sections describe the various implementations of **List**, **Set,** and **Map** and indicate in each case (with an asterisk) which one should be your default choice. You'll notice that the legacy classes **Vector**, **Stack**, and **Hashtable** are *not* included, because in all cases there are preferred classes within the Java 2 Containers.

List functionality

The basic **List** is quite simple to use, as you've seen so far with **ArrayList**. Although most of the time you'll just use **add( )** to insert objects, **get( )** to get them out one at a time, and **iterator( )** to get an **Iterator** for the sequence, there's also a set of other methods that can be useful.

In addition, there are actually two types of **List**: the basic **ArrayList**, which excels at randomly accessing elements, and the much more powerful **LinkedList**, which is not designed for fast random access, but has a much more general set of methods.

List (interface)	Order is the most important feature of a **List**; it promises to maintain elements in a particular sequence. **List** adds a number of methods to **Collection** that allow insertion and removal of elements in the middle of a **List**. (This is recommended only for a **LinkedList**.) A **List** will produce a **ListIterator**, and by using this you can traverse the **List** in both directions, as well as insert and remove elements in the middle of the **List**.

ArrayList*	A **List** implemented with an array. Allows rapid random access to elements, but is slow when inserting and removing elements from the middle of a list. **ListIterator** should be used only for back-and-forth traversal of an **ArrayList**, but not for inserting and removing elements, which is expensive compared to **LinkedList**.
LinkedList	Provides optimal sequential access, with inexpensive insertions and deletions from the middle of the **List**. Relatively slow for random access. (Use **ArrayList** instead.) Also has **addFirst( )**, **addLast( )**, **getFirst( )**, **getLast( )**, **removeFirst( )**, and **removeLast( )** (which are not defined in any interfaces or base classes) to allow it to be used as a stack, a queue, and a deque.

The methods in the following example each cover a different group of activities: things that every list can do (**basicTest( )**), moving around with an **Iterator** (**iterMotion( )**) versus changing things with an **Iterator** (**iterManipulation( )**), seeing the effects of **List** manipulation (**testVisual( )**), and operations available only to **LinkedList**s.

```
//: c11:List1.java
// Things you can do with Lists.
import java.util.*;
import com.bruceeckel.util.*;

public class List1 {
  public static List fill(List a) {
    Collections2.countries.reset();
    Collections2.fill(a, Collections2.countries, 10);
    return a;
  }
  private static boolean b;
  private static Object o;
  private static int i;
  private static Iterator it;
  private static ListIterator lit;
  public static void basicTest(List a) {
    a.add(1, "x"); // Add at location 1
    a.add("x"); // Add at end
    // Add a collection:
    a.addAll(fill(new ArrayList()));
```

```
    // Add a collection starting at location 3:
    a.addAll(3, fill(new ArrayList()));
    b = a.contains("1"); // Is it in there?
    // Is the entire collection in there?
    b = a.containsAll(fill(new ArrayList()));
    // Lists allow random access, which is cheap
    // for ArrayList, expensive for LinkedList:
    o = a.get(1); // Get object at location 1
    i = a.indexOf("1"); // Tell index of object
    b = a.isEmpty(); // Any elements inside?
    it = a.iterator(); // Ordinary Iterator
    lit = a.listIterator(); // ListIterator
    lit = a.listIterator(3); // Start at loc 3
    i = a.lastIndexOf("1"); // Last match
    a.remove(1); // Remove location 1
    a.remove("3"); // Remove this object
    a.set(1, "y"); // Set location 1 to "y"
    // Keep everything that's in the argument
    // (the intersection of the two sets):
    a.retainAll(fill(new ArrayList()));
    // Remove everything that's in the argument:
    a.removeAll(fill(new ArrayList()));
    i = a.size(); // How big is it?
    a.clear(); // Remove all elements
  }
  public static void iterMotion(List a) {
    ListIterator it = a.listIterator();
    b = it.hasNext();
    b = it.hasPrevious();
    o = it.next();
    i = it.nextIndex();
    o = it.previous();
    i = it.previousIndex();
  }
  public static void iterManipulation(List a) {
    ListIterator it = a.listIterator();
    it.add("47");
    // Must move to an element after add():
    it.next();
    // Remove the element that was just produced:
    it.remove();
    // Must move to an element after remove():
    it.next();
    // Change the element that was just produced:
```

```
    it.set("47");
  }
  public static void testVisual(List a) {
    System.out.println(a);
    List b = new ArrayList();
    fill(b);
    System.out.print("b = ");
    System.out.println(b);
    a.addAll(b);
    a.addAll(fill(new ArrayList()));
    System.out.println(a);
    // Insert, remove, and replace elements
    // using a ListIterator:
    ListIterator x = a.listIterator(a.size()/2);
    x.add("one");
    System.out.println(a);
    System.out.println(x.next());
    x.remove();
    System.out.println(x.next());
    x.set("47");
    System.out.println(a);
    // Traverse the list backwards:
    x = a.listIterator(a.size());
    while(x.hasPrevious())
      System.out.print(x.previous() + " ");
    System.out.println();
    System.out.println("testVisual finished");
  }
  // There are some things that only LinkedLists can do:
  public static void testLinkedList() {
    LinkedList ll = new LinkedList();
    fill(ll);
    System.out.println(ll);
    // Treat it like a stack, pushing:
    ll.addFirst("one");
    ll.addFirst("two");
    System.out.println(ll);
    // Like "peeking" at the top of a stack:
    System.out.println(ll.getFirst());
    // Like popping a stack:
    System.out.println(ll.removeFirst());
    System.out.println(ll.removeFirst());
    // Treat it like a queue, pulling elements
    // off the tail end:
```

```
    System.out.println(ll.removeLast());
    // With the above operations, it's a dequeue!
    System.out.println(ll);
  }
  public static void main(String[] args) {
    // Make and fill a new list each time:
    basicTest(fill(new LinkedList()));
    basicTest(fill(new ArrayList()));
    iterMotion(fill(new LinkedList()));
    iterMotion(fill(new ArrayList()));
    iterManipulation(fill(new LinkedList()));
    iterManipulation(fill(new ArrayList()));
    testVisual(fill(new LinkedList()));
    testLinkedList();
  }
} ///:~
```

In **basicTest( )** and **iterMotion( )** the calls are made in order to show the proper syntax, and although the return value is captured, it is not used. In some cases, the return value isn't captured at all. You should look up the full usage of each of these methods in the JDK documentation from *java.sun.com* before you use them.

Remember that a container is only a storage cabinet to hold objects. If that cabinet solves all of your needs, it doesn't really matter how it is implemented (a basic concept with most types of objects). If you're working in a programming environment that has built-in overhead due to other factors, then the cost difference between an **ArrayList** and a **LinkedList** might not matter. You might need only one type of sequence. You can even imagine the "perfect" container abstraction, which can automatically change its underlying implementation according to the way it is used.

Making a stack from a **LinkedList**

A stack is sometimes referred to as a "last-in, first-out" (LIFO) container. That is, whatever you "push" on the stack last is the first item you can "pop" out. Like all of the other containers in Java, what you push and pop are **Object**s, so you must cast what you pop, unless you're just using **Object** behavior.

The **LinkedList** has methods that directly implement stack functionality, so you can also just use a **LinkedList** rather than making a stack class. However, a stack class can sometimes tell the story better:

```java
//: c11:StackL.java
// Making a stack from a LinkedList.
import com.bruceeckel.simpletest.*;
import java.util.*;
import com.bruceeckel.util.*;

public class StackL {
  private static Test monitor = new Test();
  private LinkedList list = new LinkedList();
  public void push(Object v) { list.addFirst(v); }
  public Object top() { return list.getFirst(); }
  public Object pop() { return list.removeFirst(); }
  public static void main(String[] args) {
    StackL stack = new StackL();
    for(int i = 0; i < 10; i++)
      stack.push(Collections2.countries.next());
    System.out.println(stack.top());
    System.out.println(stack.top());
    System.out.println(stack.pop());
    System.out.println(stack.pop());
    System.out.println(stack.pop());
    monitor.expect(new String[] {
      "CHAD",
      "CHAD",
      "CHAD",
      "CENTRAL AFRICAN REPUBLIC",
      "CAPE VERDE"
    });
  }
} ///:~
```

If you want only stack behavior, inheritance is inappropriate here because it would produce a class with all the rest of the **LinkedList** methods (you'll see later that this very mistake was made by the Java 1.0 library designers with **Stack**).

Making a queue from a **LinkedList**

A *queue* is a "*first-in, first-out*" (FIFO) container. That is, you put things in at one end and pull them out at the other. So the order in which you put them in will be the same order that they come out. **LinkedList** has methods to support queue behavior, so these can be used in a **Queue** class:

```java
//: c11:Queue.java
```

```
// Making a queue from a LinkedList.
import com.bruceeckel.simpletest.*;
import java.util.*;

public class Queue {
  private static Test monitor = new Test();
  private LinkedList list = new LinkedList();
  public void put(Object v) { list.addFirst(v); }
  public Object get() { return list.removeLast(); }
  public boolean isEmpty() { return list.isEmpty(); }
  public static void main(String[] args) {
    Queue queue = new Queue();
    for(int i = 0; i < 10; i++)
      queue.put(Integer.toString(i));
    while(!queue.isEmpty())
      System.out.println(queue.get());
    monitor.expect(new String[] {
      "0",
      "1",
      "2",
      "3",
      "4",
      "5",
      "6",
      "7",
      "8",
      "9"
    });
  }
} ///:~
```

You can also easily create a *deque* (double-ended queue) from a **LinkedList**. This is like a queue, but you can add and remove elements from either end.

Set functionality

Set has exactly the same interface as **Collection**, so there isn't any extra functionality like there is with the two different **List**s. Instead, the **Set** is exactly a **Collection**—it just has different behavior. (This is the ideal use of inheritance and polymorphism: to express different behavior.) A **Set** refuses to hold more than one instance of each object value (what constitutes the "value" of an object is more complex, as you shall see).

Set (interface)	Each element that you add to the **Set** must be unique; otherwise, the **Set** doesn't add the duplicate element. **Object**s added to a **Set** must define **equals( )** to establish object uniqueness. **Set** has exactly the same interface as **Collection**. The **Set** interface does not guarantee that it will maintain its elements in any particular order.
HashSet*	For **Set**s where fast lookup time is important. **Object**s must also define **hashCode( )**.
TreeSet	An ordered **Set** backed by a tree. This way, you can extract an ordered sequence from a **Set**.
LinkedHashSet (JDK 1.4)	Has the lookup speed of a **HashSet**, but maintains the order in which you add the elements (the insertion order), internally using a linked list. Thus, when you iterate through the **Set**, the results appear in insertion order.

The following example does *not* show everything you can do with a **Set**, since the interface is the same as **Collection**, and so was exercised in the previous example. Instead, this demonstrates the behavior that makes a **Set** unique:

```
//: c11:Set1.java
// Things you can do with Sets.
import com.bruceeckel.simpletest.*;
import java.util.*;

public class Set1 {
  private static Test monitor = new Test();
  static void fill(Set s) {
    s.addAll(Arrays.asList(
      "one two three four five six seven".split(" ")));
  }
  public static void test(Set s) {
    // Strip qualifiers from class name:
    System.out.println(
      s.getClass().getName().replaceAll("\\w+\\.", ""));
    fill(s); fill(s); fill(s);
    System.out.println(s); // No duplicates!
    // Add another set to this one:
    s.addAll(s);
    s.add("one");
    s.add("one");
    s.add("one");
```

```
    System.out.println(s);
    // Look something up:
    System.out.println("s.contains(\"one\"): " +
      s.contains("one"));
  }
  public static void main(String[] args) {
    test(new HashSet());
    test(new TreeSet());
    test(new LinkedHashSet());
    monitor.expect(new String[] {
      "HashSet",
      "[one, two, five, four, three, seven, six]",
      "[one, two, five, four, three, seven, six]",
      "s.contains(\"one\"): true",
      "TreeSet",
      "[five, four, one, seven, six, three, two]",
      "[five, four, one, seven, six, three, two]",
      "s.contains(\"one\"): true",
      "LinkedHashSet",
      "[one, two, three, four, five, six, seven]",
      "[one, two, three, four, five, six, seven]",
      "s.contains(\"one\"): true"
    });
  }
} ///:~
```

Duplicate values are added to the **Set**, but when it is printed, you'll see that the **Set** has accepted only one instance of each value.

When you run this program, you'll notice that the order maintained by the **HashSet** is different from **TreeSet** and **LinkedHashSet**, since each has a different way of storing elements so they can be located later. (**TreeSet** keeps elements sorted into a red-black tree data structure, whereas **HashSet** uses a hashing function, which is designed specifically for rapid lookups. **LinkedHashSet** uses hashing internally for lookup speed, but *appears* to maintain elements in insertion order using a linked list.) When creating your own types, be aware that a **Set** needs a way to maintain a storage order, which means that you must implement the **Comparable** interface and define the **compareTo( )** method. Here's an example:

```
//: c11:Set2.java
// Putting your own type in a Set.
import com.bruceeckel.simpletest.*;
import java.util.*;
```

```
public class Set2 {
  private static Test monitor = new Test();
  public static Set fill(Set a, int size) {
    for(int i = 0; i < size; i++)
      a.add(new MyType(i));
    return a;
  }
  public static void test(Set a) {
    fill(a, 10);
    fill(a, 10); // Try to add duplicates
    fill(a, 10);
    a.addAll(fill(new TreeSet(), 10));
    System.out.println(a);
  }
  public static void main(String[] args) {
    test(new HashSet());
    test(new TreeSet());
    test(new LinkedHashSet());
    monitor.expect(new String[] {
      "[2 , 4 , 9 , 8 , 6 , 1 , 3 , 7 , 5 , 0 ]",
      "[9 , 8 , 7 , 6 , 5 , 4 , 3 , 2 , 1 , 0 ]",
      "[0 , 1 , 2 , 3 , 4 , 5 , 6 , 7 , 8 , 9 ]"
    });
  }
} ///:~
```

The form for the definitions for **equals( )** and **hashCode( )** will be described later in this chapter. You must define an **equals( )** in both cases, but the **hashCode( )** is absolutely necessary only if the class will be placed in a **HashSet** (which is likely, since that should generally be your first choice as a **Set** implementation). However, as a programming style, you should always override **hashCode( )** when you override **equals( )**. This process will be fully detailed later in this chapter.

In the **compareTo( )**, note that I did *not* use the "simple and obvious" form **return i-i2**. Although this is a common programming error, it would only work properly if **i** and **i2** were "unsigned" **int**s (if Java *had* an "unsigned" keyword, which it does not). It breaks for Java's signed **int**, which is not big enough to represent the difference of two signed **int**s. If **i** is a large positive integer and **j** is a large negative integer, **i-j** will overflow and return a negative value, which will not work.

SortedSet

If you have a **SortedSet** (of which **TreeSet** is the only one available), the elements are guaranteed to be in sorted order, which allows additional functionality to be provided with these methods in the **SortedSet** interface:

Comparator comparator( ): Produces the **Comparator** used for this **Set**, or **null** for natural ordering.

Object first( ): Produces the lowest element.

Object last( ): Produces the highest element.

SortedSet subSet(fromElement, toElement): Produces a view of this **Set** with elements from **fromElement**, inclusive, to **toElement**, exclusive.

SortedSet headSet(toElement): Produces a view of this **Set** with elements less than **toElement**.

SortedSet tailSet(fromElement): Produces a view of this **Set** with elements greater than or equal to **fromElement**.

Here's a simple demonstration:

```
//: c11:SortedSetDemo.java
// What you can do with a TreeSet.
import com.bruceeckel.simpletest.*;
import java.util.*;

public class SortedSetDemo {
  private static Test monitor = new Test();
  public static void main(String[] args) {
    SortedSet sortedSet = new TreeSet(Arrays.asList(
    "one two three four five six seven eight".split(" ")));
    System.out.println(sortedSet);
    Object
      low = sortedSet.first(),
      high = sortedSet.last();
    System.out.println(low);
    System.out.println(high);
    Iterator it = sortedSet.iterator();
    for(int i = 0; i <= 6; i++) {
      if(i == 3) low = it.next();
      if(i == 6) high = it.next();
      else it.next();
    }
```

```
    System.out.println(low);
    System.out.println(high);
    System.out.println(sortedSet.subSet(low, high));
    System.out.println(sortedSet.headSet(high));
    System.out.println(sortedSet.tailSet(low));
    monitor.expect(new String[] {
      "[eight, five, four, one, seven, six, three, two]",
      "eight",
      "two",
      "one",
      "two",
      "[one, seven, six, three]",
      "[eight, five, four, one, seven, six, three]",
      "[one, seven, six, three, two]"
    });
  }
} ///:~
```

Note that **SortedSet** means "sorted according to the comparison function of the object," not "insertion order."

Map functionality

An **ArrayList** allows you to select from a sequence of objects using a number, so in a sense it associates numbers to objects. But what if you'd like to select from a sequence of objects using some other criterion? A stack is an example. Its selection criterion is "the last thing pushed on the stack." A powerful twist on this idea of "selecting from a sequence" is termed a *map*, a *dictionary*, or an *associative array* (you saw a simple example of this in **AssociativeArray.java** in the previous chapter). Conceptually, it seems like an **ArrayList**, but instead of looking up objects using a number, you look them up using another object! This is a key technique in programming.

The concept shows up in Java as the **Map** interface. The **put(Object key, Object value)** method adds a value (the thing you want) and associates it with a key (the thing you look it up with). **get(Object key)** produces the value given the corresponding key. You can also test a **Map** to see if it contains a key or a value with **containsKey( )** and **containsValue( )**.

The standard Java library contains different types of **Map**s: **HashMap**, **TreeMap**, **LinkedHashMap**, **WeakHashMap**, and **IdentityHashMap**. The all have the same basic **Map** interface, but they differ in behaviors including efficiency, order in which the pairs are held and presented, how long the objects are held by the map, and how key equality is determined.

A big issue with maps is performance. If you look at what must be done for a **get( )**, it seems pretty slow to search through (for example) an **ArrayList** for the key. This is where **HashMap** speeds things up. Instead of a slow search for the key, it uses a special value called a *hash code*. The hash code is a way to take some information in the object in question and turn it into a "relatively unique" **int** for that object. All Java objects can produce a hash code, and **hashCode( )** is a method in the root class **Object**. A **HashMap** takes the **hashCode( )** of the object and uses it to quickly hunt for the key. This results in a dramatic performance improvement.[8]

Map (interface)	Maintains key-value associations (pairs) so you can look up a value using a key.
HashMap*	Implementation based on a hash table. (Use this instead of **Hashtable**.) Provides constant-time performance for inserting and locating pairs. Performance can be adjusted via constructors that allow you to set the *capacity* and *load factor* of the hash table.
LinkedHashMap (JDK 1.4)	Like a **HashMap**, but when you iterate through it, you get the pairs in insertion order, or in least-recently-used (LRU) order. Only slightly slower than a **HashMap**, except when iterating, where it is faster due to the linked list used to maintain the internal ordering.
TreeMap	Implementation based on a red-black tree. When you view the keys or the pairs, they will be in sorted order (determined by **Comparable** or **Comparator**, discussed later). The point of a **TreeMap** is that you

[8] If these speedups still don't meet your performance needs, you can further accelerate table lookup by writing your own **Map** and customizing it to your particular types to avoid delays due to casting to and from **Object**s. To reach even higher levels of performance, speed enthusiasts can use Donald Knuth's *The Art of Computer Programming, Volume 3: Sorting and Searching, Second Edition* to replace overflow bucket lists with arrays that have two additional benefits: they can be optimized for disk storage characteristics and they can save most of the time of creating and garbage collecting individual records.

	get the results in sorted order. **TreeMap** is the only **Map** with the **subMap( )** method, which allows you to return a portion of the tree.
WeakHashMap	A map of *weak keys* that allow objects referred to by the map to be released; designed to solve certain types of problems. If no references outside the map are held to a particular key, it may be garbage collected.
IdentityHashMap (JDK 1.4)	A hash map that uses == instead of **equals( )** to compare keys. Only for solving special types of problems; not for general use.

Hashing is the most commonly used way to store elements in a map. Sometimes you'll need to know the details of how hashing works, so we'll look at that a little later.

The following example uses the **Collections2.fill( )** method and the test data sets that were previously defined:

```
//: c11:Map1.java
// Things you can do with Maps.
import java.util.*;
import com.bruceeckel.util.*;

public class Map1 {
  private static Collections2.StringPairGenerator geo =
    Collections2.geography;
  private static Collections2.RandStringPairGenerator
    rsp = Collections2.rsp;
  // Producing a Set of the keys:
  public static void printKeys(Map map) {
    System.out.print("Size = " + map.size() + ", ");
    System.out.print("Keys: ");
    System.out.println(map.keySet());
  }
  public static void test(Map map) {
    // Strip qualifiers from class name:
    System.out.println(
      map.getClass().getName().replaceAll("\\w+\\.", ""));
    Collections2.fill(map, geo, 25);
    // Map has 'Set' behavior for keys:
    Collections2.fill(map, geo.reset(), 25);
```

```
    printKeys(map);
    // Producing a Collection of the values:
    System.out.print("Values: ");
    System.out.println(map.values());
    System.out.println(map);
    String key = CountryCapitals.pairs[4][0];
    String value = CountryCapitals.pairs[4][1];
    System.out.println("map.containsKey(\"" + key +
      "\"): " + map.containsKey(key));
    System.out.println("map.get(\"" + key + "\"): "
      + map.get(key));
    System.out.println("map.containsValue(\""
      + value + "\"): " + map.containsValue(value));
    Map map2 = new TreeMap();
    Collections2.fill(map2, rsp, 25);
    map.putAll(map2);
    printKeys(map);
    key = map.keySet().iterator().next().toString();
    System.out.println("First key in map: " + key);
    map.remove(key);
    printKeys(map);
    map.clear();
    System.out.println("map.isEmpty(): " + map.isEmpty());
    Collections2.fill(map, geo.reset(), 25);
    // Operations on the Set change the Map:
    map.keySet().removeAll(map.keySet());
    System.out.println("map.isEmpty(): " + map.isEmpty());
  }
  public static void main(String[] args) {
    test(new HashMap());
    test(new TreeMap());
    test(new LinkedHashMap());
    test(new IdentityHashMap());
    test(new WeakHashMap());
  }
} ///:~
```

The **printKeys( )** and **printValues( )** methods are not only useful utilities, they also demonstrate how to produce **Collection** views of a **Map**. The **keySet( )** method produces a **Set** backed by the keys in the **Map**. Similar treatment is given to **values( )**, which produces a **Collection** containing all the values in the **Map.** (Note that keys must be unique, but values may contain duplicates.) Since these **Collection**s are backed by the **Map**, any changes in a **Collection** will be reflected in the associated **Map**.

The rest of the program provides simple examples of each **Map** operation and tests each type of **Map**.

As an example of the use of a **HashMap**, consider a program to check the randomness of Java's **Random** class. Ideally, it would produce a perfect distribution of random numbers, but to test this you need to generate a bunch of random numbers and count the ones that fall in the various ranges. A **HashMap** is perfect for this, since it associates objects with objects (in this case, the value object contains the number produced by **Math.random( )** along with the number of times that number appears):

```
//: c11:Statistics.java
// Simple demonstration of HashMap.
import java.util.*;

class Counter {
  int i = 1;
  public String toString() { return Integer.toString(i); }
}

public class Statistics {
  private static Random rand = new Random();
  public static void main(String[] args) {
    Map hm = new HashMap();
    for(int i = 0; i < 10000; i++) {
      // Produce a number between 0 and 20:
      Integer r = new Integer(rand.nextInt(20));
      if(hm.containsKey(r))
        ((Counter)hm.get(r)).i++;
      else
        hm.put(r, new Counter());
    }
    System.out.println(hm);
  }
} ///:~
```

In **main( )**, each time a random number is generated it is wrapped inside an **Integer** object so that reference can be used with the **HashMap**. (You can't use a primitive with a container—only an object reference.) The **containsKey( )** method checks to see if this key is already in the container (that is, has the number been found already?). If so, the **get( )** method produces the associated value for the key, which in this case is a **Counter** object. The value **i** inside the counter is incremented to indicate that one more of this particular random number has been found.

If the key has not been found yet, the method **put( )** will place a new key-value pair into the **HashMap**. Since **Counter** automatically initializes its variable **i** to one when it's created, it indicates the first occurrence of this particular random number.

To display the **HashMap**, it is simply printed. The **HashMap toString( )** method moves through all the key-value pairs and calls the **toString( )** for each one. The **Integer.toString( )** is predefined, and you can see the **toString( )** for **Counter**. The output from one run (with some line breaks added) is:

```
{15=529, 4=488, 19=518, 8=487, 11=501, 16=487, 18=507,
3=524, 7=474, 12=485, 17=493, 2=490, 13=540, 9=453, 6=512,
1=466, 14=522, 10=471, 5=522, 0=531}
```

You might wonder at the necessity of the class **Counter,** which seems like it doesn't even have the functionality of the wrapper class **Integer**. Why not use **int** or **Integer**? Well, you can't use an **int** because all of the containers can hold only **Object** references. After you've seen containers, the wrapper classes might begin to make a little more sense to you, since you can't put any of the primitive types in containers. However, the only thing you *can* do with the Java wrappers is initialize them to a particular value and read that value. That is, there's no way to change a value once a wrapper object has been created. This makes the **Integer** wrapper immediately useless to solve the problem, so we're forced to create a new class that does satisfy the need.

SortedMap

If you have a **SortedMap** (of which **TreeMap** is the only one available), the keys are guaranteed to be in sorted order, which allows additional functionality to be provided with these methods in the **SortedMap** interface:

Comparator comparator( ): Produces the comparator used for this **Map**, or **null** for natural ordering.

Object firstKey( ): Produces the lowest key.

Object lastKey( ): Produces the highest key.

SortedMap subMap(fromKey, toKey): Produces a view of this **Map** with keys from **fromKey**, inclusive, to **toKey**, exclusive.

SortedMap headMap(toKey): Produces a view of this **Map** with keys less than **toKey**.

SortedMap tailMap(fromKey): Produces a view of this **Map** with keys greater than or equal to **fromKey**.

Here's an example that's similar to **SortedSetDemo.java** and shows this additional behavior of **TreeMaps**:

```
//: c11:SimplePairGenerator.java
import com.bruceeckel.util.*;
//import java.util.*;

public class SimplePairGenerator implements MapGenerator {
  public Pair[] items = {
    new Pair("one", "A"), new Pair("two", "B"),
    new Pair("three", "C"), new Pair("four", "D"),
    new Pair("five", "E"), new Pair("six", "F"),
    new Pair("seven", "G"), new Pair("eight", "H"),
    new Pair("nine", "I"), new Pair("ten", "J")
  };
  private int index = -1;
  public Pair next() {
    index = (index + 1) % items.length;
    return items[index];
  }
  public static SimplePairGenerator gen =
    new SimplePairGenerator();
} ///:~
```

```
//: c11:SortedMapDemo.java
// What you can do with a TreeMap.
import com.bruceeckel.simpletest.*;
import com.bruceeckel.util.*;
import java.util.*;

public class SortedMapDemo {
  private static Test monitor = new Test();
  public static void main(String[] args) {
    TreeMap sortedMap = new TreeMap();
    Collections2.fill(
      sortedMap, SimplePairGenerator.gen, 10);
    System.out.println(sortedMap);
    Object
      low = sortedMap.firstKey(),
```

```
      high = sortedMap.lastKey();
    System.out.println(low);
    System.out.println(high);
    Iterator it = sortedMap.keySet().iterator();
    for(int i = 0; i <= 6; i++) {
      if(i == 3) low = it.next();
      if(i == 6) high = it.next();
      else it.next();
    }
    System.out.println(low);
    System.out.println(high);
    System.out.println(sortedMap.subMap(low, high));
    System.out.println(sortedMap.headMap(high));
    System.out.println(sortedMap.tailMap(low));
    monitor.expect(new String[] {
      "{eight=H, five=E, four=D, nine=I, one=A, seven=G," +
      " six=F, ten=J, three=C, two=B}",
      "eight",
      "two",
      "nine",
      "ten",
      "{nine=I, one=A, seven=G, six=F}",
      "{eight=H, five=E, four=D, nine=I, " +
      "one=A, seven=G, six=F}",
      "{nine=I, one=A, seven=G, six=F, " +
      "ten=J, three=C, two=B}"
    });
  }
} ///:~
```

Here, the pairs are stored by key-sorted order. Because there is a sense of order in the **TreeMap**, the concept of "location" makes sense, so you can have first and last elements and submaps.

LinkedHashMap

The **LinkedHashMap** hashes everything for speed, but also produces the pairs in insertion order during a traversal (**println( )** iterates through the map, so you see the results of traversal). In addition, a **LinkedHashMap** can be configured in the constructor to use a *least-recently-used* (LRU) algorithm based on accesses, so elements that haven't been accessed (and thus are candidates for removal) appear at the front of the list. This allows easy creation of programs that do periodic cleanup in order to save space. Here's a simple example showing both features:

```java
//: c11:LinkedHashMapDemo.java
// What you can do with a LinkedHashMap.
import com.bruceeckel.simpletest.*;
import com.bruceeckel.util.*;
import java.util.*;

public class LinkedHashMapDemo {
  private static Test monitor = new Test();
  public static void main(String[] args) {
    LinkedHashMap linkedMap = new LinkedHashMap();
    Collections2.fill(
      linkedMap, SimplePairGenerator.gen, 10);
    System.out.println(linkedMap);
    // Least-recently used order:
    linkedMap = new LinkedHashMap(16, 0.75f, true);
    Collections2.fill(
      linkedMap, SimplePairGenerator.gen, 10);
    System.out.println(linkedMap);
    for(int i = 0; i < 7; i++) // Cause accesses:
      linkedMap.get(SimplePairGenerator.gen.items[i].key);
    System.out.println(linkedMap);
    linkedMap.get(SimplePairGenerator.gen.items[0].key);
    System.out.println(linkedMap);
    monitor.expect(new String[] {
      "{one=A, two=B, three=C, four=D, five=E, " +
       "six=F, seven=G, eight=H, nine=I, ten=J}",
      "{one=A, two=B, three=C, four=D, five=E, " +
       "six=F, seven=G, eight=H, nine=I, ten=J}",
      "{eight=H, nine=I, ten=J, one=A, two=B, " +
       "three=C, four=D, five=E, six=F, seven=G}",
      "{eight=H, nine=I, ten=J, two=B, three=C, " +
       "four=D, five=E, six=F, seven=G, one=A}"
    });
  }
} ///:~
```

You can see from the output that the pairs are indeed traversed in insertion order, even for the LRU version. However, after the first seven items (only) are accessed, the last three items move to the front of the list. Then, when "**one**" is accessed again, it moves to the back of the list.

Hashing and hash codes

In **Statistics.java**, a standard library class (**Integer**) was used as a key for the **HashMap**. It worked because it has all the necessary wiring to make it behave correctly as a key. But a common pitfall occurs with **HashMaps** when you create your own classes to be used as keys. For example, consider a weather predicting system that matches **Groundhog** objects to **Prediction** objects. It seems fairly straightforward—you create the two classes, and use **Groundhog** as the key and **Prediction** as the value:

```
//: c11:Groundhog.java
// Looks plausible, but doesn't work as a HashMap key.

public class Groundhog {
  protected int number;
  public Groundhog(int n) { number = n; }
  public String toString() {
    return "Groundhog #" + number;
  }
} ///:~
```

```
//: c11:Prediction.java
// Predicting the weather with groundhogs.

public class Prediction {
  private boolean shadow = Math.random() > 0.5;
  public String toString() {
    if(shadow)
      return "Six more weeks of Winter!";
    else
      return "Early Spring!";
  }
} ///:~
```

```
//: c11:SpringDetector.java
// What will the weather be?
import com.bruceeckel.simpletest.*;
import java.util.*;
import java.lang.reflect.*;

public class SpringDetector {
  private static Test monitor = new Test();
  // Uses a Groundhog or class derived from Groundhog:
  public static void
```

```
  detectSpring(Class groundHogClass) throws Exception {
    Constructor ghog = groundHogClass.getConstructor(
      new Class[] {int.class});
    Map map = new HashMap();
    for(int i = 0; i < 10; i++)
      map.put(ghog.newInstance(
        new Object[]{ new Integer(i) }), new Prediction());
    System.out.println("map = " + map + "\n");
    Groundhog gh = (Groundhog)
      ghog.newInstance(new Object[]{ new Integer(3) });
    System.out.println("Looking up prediction for " + gh);
    if(map.containsKey(gh))
      System.out.println((Prediction)map.get(gh));
    else
      System.out.println("Key not found: " + gh);
  }
  public static void main(String[] args) throws Exception {
    detectSpring(Groundhog.class);
    monitor.expect(new String[] {
      "%% map = \\{(Groundhog #\\d=" +
      "(Early Spring!|Six more weeks of Winter!)" +
      "(, )?){10}\\}",
      "",
      "Looking up prediction for Groundhog #3",
      "Key not found: Groundhog #3"
    });
  }
} ///:~
```

Each **Groundhog** is given an identity number, so you can look up a **Prediction** in the **HashMap** by saying, "Give me the **Prediction** associated with **Groundhog** #3." The **Prediction** class contains a **boolean** that is initialized using **Math.random( )** and a **toString( )** that interprets the result for you. The **detectSpring( )** method is created using reflection to instantiate and use the **Class Groundhog** or any derived class. This will come in handy when we inherit a new type of **Groundhog** to solve the problem demonstrated here. A **HashMap** is filled with **Groundhog**s and their associated **Prediction**s. The **HashMap** is printed so that you can see it has been filled. Then a **Groundhog** with an identity number of 3 is used as a key to look up the prediction for **Groundhog** #3 (which you can see must be in the **Map**).

It seems simple enough, but it doesn't work. The problem is that **Groundhog** is inherited from the common root class **Object** (which is what happens if you don't specify a base class, thus all classes are ultimately inherited from **Object**). It is **Object**'s **hashCode( )** method that is used to generate the hash code for each object, and by default it just uses the address of its object. Thus, the first instance of **Groundhog(3)** does *not* produce a hash code equal to the hash code for the second instance of **Groundhog(3)** that we tried to use as a lookup.

You might think that all you need to do is write an appropriate override for **hashCode( )**. But it still won't work until you've done one more thing: override the **equals( )** that is also part of **Object**. **equals( )** is used by the **HashMap** when trying to determine if your key is equal to any of the keys in the table.

A proper **equals( )** must satisfy the following five conditions:

1. Reflexive: For any **x**, **x.equals(x)** should return **true**.

2. Symmetric: For any **x** and **y**, **x.equals(y)** should return **true** if and only if **y.equals(x)** returns **true**.

3. Transitive: For any **x**, **y**, and **z**, if **x.equals(y)** returns **true** and **y.equals(z)** returns **true**, then **x.equals(z)** should return **true**.

4. Consistent: For any **x** and **y**, multiple invocations of **x.equals(y)** consistently return **true** or consistently return **false**, provided no information used in equals comparisons on the object is modified.

5. For any non-null **x**, **x.equals(null)** should return **false**.

Again, the default **Object.equals( )** simply compares object addresses, so one **Groundhog(3)** is not equal to another **Groundhog(3)**. Thus, to use your own classes as keys in a **HashMap**, you must override both **hashCode( )** and **equals( )**, as shown in the following solution to the groundhog problem:

```
//: c11:Groundhog2.java
// A class that's used as a key in a HashMap
// must override hashCode() and equals().

public class Groundhog2 extends Groundhog {
  public Groundhog2(int n) { super(n); }
```

```
  public int hashCode() { return number; }
  public boolean equals(Object o) {
    return (o instanceof Groundhog2)
      && (number == ((Groundhog2)o).number);
  }
} ///:~
```

```
//: c11:SpringDetector2.java
// A working key.
import com.bruceeckel.simpletest.*;
import java.util.*;

public class SpringDetector2 {
  private static Test monitor = new Test();
  public static void main(String[] args) throws Exception {
    SpringDetector.detectSpring(Groundhog2.class);
    monitor.expect(new String[] {
      "%% map = \\{(Groundhog #\\d=" +
      "(Early Spring!|Six more weeks of Winter!)" +
      "(, )?){10}\\}",
      "",
      "Looking up prediction for Groundhog #3",
      "%% Early Spring!|Six more weeks of Winter!"
    });
  }
} ///:~
```

Groundhog2.hashCode( ) returns the groundhog number as a hash value. In this example, the programmer is responsible for ensuring that no two groundhogs exist with the same ID number. The **hashCode( )** is not required to return a unique identifier (something you'll understand better later in this chapter), but the **equals( )** method must be able to strictly determine whether two objects are equivalent. Here, **equals( )** is based on the groundhog number, so if two **Groundhog2** objects exist as keys in the **HashMap** with the same groundhog number, it will fail.

Even though it appears that the **equals( )** method is only checking to see whether the argument is an instance of **Groundhog2** (using the **instanceof** keyword, which was explained in Chapter 10), the **instanceof** actually quietly does a second sanity check to see if the object is **null**, since **instanceof** produces **false** if the left-hand argument is **null**. Assuming it's the correct type and not **null**, the comparison is based on the actual **ghNumber**s. You can see from the output that the behavior is now correct.

When creating your own class to use in a **HashSet**, you must pay attention to the same issues as when it is used as a key in a **HashMap**.

Understanding **hashCode( )**

The preceding example is only a start toward solving the problem correctly. It shows that if you do not override **hashCode( )** and **equals( )** for your key, the hashed data structure (**HashSet**, **HashMap**, **LinkedHashSet**, or **LinkedHashMap**) will not be able to deal with your key properly. However, to get a good solution for the problem you need to understand what's going on inside the hashed data structure.

First, consider the motivation behind hashing: you want to look up an object using another object. But you can accomplish this with a **TreeSet** or **TreeMap**, too. It's also possible to implement your own **Map**. To do so, the **Map.entrySet( )** method must be supplied to produce a set of **Map.Entry** objects. **MPair** will be defined as the new type of **Map.Entry**. In order for it to be placed in a **TreeSet**, it must implement **equals( )** and be **Comparable**:

```
//: c11:MPair.java
// A new type of Map.Entry.
import java.util.*;

public class MPair implements Map.Entry, Comparable {
  private Object key, value;
  public MPair(Object k, Object v) {
    key = k;
    value = v;
  }
  public Object getKey() { return key; }
  public Object getValue() { return value; }
  public Object setValue(Object v) {
    Object result = value;
    value = v;
    return result;
  }
  public boolean equals(Object o) {
    return key.equals(((MPair)o).key);
  }
  public int compareTo(Object rv) {
    return ((Comparable)key).compareTo(((MPair)rv).key);
  }
} ///:~
```

Notice that the comparisons are only interested in the keys, so duplicate values are perfectly acceptable.

The following example implements a **Map** using a pair of **ArrayLists**:

```
//: c11:SlowMap.java
// A Map implemented with ArrayLists.
import com.bruceeckel.simpletest.*;
import java.util.*;
import com.bruceeckel.util.*;

public class SlowMap extends AbstractMap {
  private static Test monitor = new Test();
  private List
    keys = new ArrayList(),
    values = new ArrayList();
  public Object put(Object key, Object value) {
    Object result = get(key);
    if(!keys.contains(key)) {
      keys.add(key);
      values.add(value);
    } else
      values.set(keys.indexOf(key), value);
    return result;
  }
  public Object get(Object key) {
    if(!keys.contains(key))
      return null;
    return values.get(keys.indexOf(key));
  }
  public Set entrySet() {
    Set entries = new HashSet();
    Iterator
      ki = keys.iterator(),
      vi = values.iterator();
    while(ki.hasNext())
      entries.add(new MPair(ki.next(), vi.next()));
    return entries;
  }
  public String toString() {
    StringBuffer s = new StringBuffer("{");
    Iterator
      ki = keys.iterator(),
      vi = values.iterator();
```

```
    while(ki.hasNext()) {
      s.append(ki.next() + "=" + vi.next());
      if(ki.hasNext()) s.append(", ");
    }
    s.append("}");
    return s.toString();
  }
  public static void main(String[] args) {
    SlowMap m = new SlowMap();
    Collections2.fill(m, Collections2.geography, 15);
    System.out.println(m);
    monitor.expect(new String[] {
      "{ALGERIA=Algiers, ANGOLA=Luanda, BENIN=Porto-Novo,"+
      " BOTSWANA=Gaberone, BURKINA FASO=Ouagadougou, " +
      "BURUNDI=Bujumbura, CAMEROON=Yaounde, " +
      "CAPE VERDE=Praia, CENTRAL AFRICAN REPUBLIC=Bangui,"+
      " CHAD=N'djamena, COMOROS=Moroni, " +
      "CONGO=Brazzaville, DJIBOUTI=Dijibouti, " +
      "EGYPT=Cairo, EQUATORIAL GUINEA=Malabo}"
    });
  }
} ///:~
```

The **put( )** method simply places the keys and values in corresponding **ArrayList**s. In **main( )**, a **SlowMap** is loaded and then printed to show that it works.

This shows that it's not that hard to produce a new type of **Map**. But as the name suggests, a **SlowMap** isn't very fast, so you probably wouldn't use it if you had an alternative available. The problem is in the lookup of the key; there is no order, so a simple linear search is used, which is the slowest way to look something up.

The whole point of hashing is speed: Hashing allows the lookup to happen quickly. Since the bottleneck is in the speed of the key lookup, one of the solutions to the problem could be to keep the keys sorted and then use **Collections.binarySearch( )** to perform the lookup (an exercise at the end of this chapter will walk you through this process).

Hashing goes further by saying that all you want to do is to store the key *somewhere* so that it can be quickly found. As you've seen in this chapter, the fastest structure in which to store a group of elements is an array, so that will be used for representing the key information (note carefully that I said "key information," and not the key itself). Also seen in this chapter was the fact that an array, once allocated, cannot be resized, so we have a problem: We want to be able to store any number of values in the **Map**, but if the number of keys is fixed by the array size, how can this be?

The answer is that the array will not hold the keys. From the key object, a number will be derived that will index into the array. This number is the *hash code*, produced by the **hashCode( )** method (in computer science parlance, this is the *hash function*) defined in **Object** and presumably overridden by your class. To solve the problem of the fixed-size array, more than one key may produce the same index. That is, there may be *collisions*. Because of this, it doesn't matter how big the array is; each key object will land somewhere in that array.

So the process of looking up a value starts by computing the hash code and using it to index into the array. If you could guarantee that there were no collisions (which could be possible if you have a fixed number of values) then you'd have a *perfect hashing function*, but that's a special case. In all other cases, collisions are handled by *external chaining:* The array points not directly to a value, but instead to a list of values. These values are searched in a linear fashion using the **equals( )** method. Of course, this aspect of the search is much slower, but if the hash function is good, there will only be a few values in each slot. So instead of searching through the entire list, you quickly jump to a slot where you have to compare a few entries to find the value. This is much faster, which is why the **HashMap** is so quick.

Knowing the basics of hashing, it's possible to implement a simple hashed **Map**:

```
//: c11:SimpleHashMap.java
// A demonstration hashed Map.
import java.util.*;
import com.bruceeckel.util.*;

public class SimpleHashMap extends AbstractMap {
  // Choose a prime number for the hash table
  // size, to achieve a uniform distribution:
  private static final int SZ = 997;
  private LinkedList[] bucket = new LinkedList[SZ];
  public Object put(Object key, Object value) {
    Object result = null;
    int index = key.hashCode() % SZ;
```

```
    if(index < 0) index = -index;
    if(bucket[index] == null)
      bucket[index] = new LinkedList();
    LinkedList pairs = bucket[index];
    MPair pair = new MPair(key, value);
    ListIterator it = pairs.listIterator();
    boolean found = false;
    while(it.hasNext()) {
      Object iPair = it.next();
      if(iPair.equals(pair)) {
        result = ((MPair)iPair).getValue();
        it.set(pair); // Replace old with new
        found = true;
        break;
      }
    }
    if(!found)
      bucket[index].add(pair);
    return result;
  }
  public Object get(Object key) {
    int index = key.hashCode() % SZ;
    if(index < 0) index = -index;
    if(bucket[index] == null) return null;
    LinkedList pairs = bucket[index];
    MPair match = new MPair(key, null);
    ListIterator it = pairs.listIterator();
    while(it.hasNext()) {
      Object iPair = it.next();
      if(iPair.equals(match))
        return ((MPair)iPair).getValue();
    }
    return null;
  }
  public Set entrySet() {
    Set entries = new HashSet();
    for(int i = 0; i < bucket.length; i++) {
      if(bucket[i] == null) continue;
      Iterator it = bucket[i].iterator();
      while(it.hasNext())
        entries.add(it.next());
    }
    return entries;
  }
```

```
  public static void main(String[] args) {
    SimpleHashMap m = new SimpleHashMap();
    Collections2.fill(m, Collections2.geography, 25);
    System.out.println(m);
  }
} ///:~
```

Because the "slots" in a hash table are often referred to as *buckets,* the array that represents the actual table is called **bucket**. To promote even distribution, the number of buckets is typically a prime number.[9] Notice that it is an array of **LinkedList**, which automatically provides for collisions; each new item is simply added to the end of the list.

The return value of **put( )** is **null** or, if the key was already in the list, the old value associated with that key. The return value is **result**, which is initialized to **null**, but if a key is discovered in the list, then **result** is assigned to that key.

For both **put( )** and **get( )**, the first thing that happens is that the **hashCode( )** is called for the key, and the result is forced to a positive number. Then it is forced to fit into the **bucket** array using the modulus operator and the size of the array. If that location is **null**, it means there are no elements that hash to that location, so a new **LinkedList** is created to hold the object that just did. However, the normal process is to look through the list to see if there are duplicates, and if there are, the old value is put into **result** and the new value replaces the old. The **found** flag keeps track of whether an old key-value pair was found and, if not, the new pair is appended to the end of the list.

In **get( )**, you'll see very similar code as that contained in **put( )**, but simpler. The index is calculated into the **bucket** array, and if a **LinkedList** exists, it is searched for a match.

---

[9] As it turns out, a prime number is not actually the ideal size for hash buckets, and recent hashed implementations in Java uses a power of two size (after extensive testing). Division or remainder is the slowest operation on a modern processor. With a power-of-two hash table length, masking can be used instead of division. Since **get( )** is by far the most common operation, the % is a large part of the cost, and the power-of-two approach eliminates this (but may also affect some **hashCode( )** methods).

entrySet( ) must find and traverse all the lists, adding them to the result **Set**. Once this method has been created, the **Map** can be tested by filling it with values and then printing them.

HashMap performance factors

To understand the issues, some terminology is necessary:

> ***Capacity:*** The number of buckets in the table.
>
> ***Initial capacity:*** The number of buckets when the table is created. **HashMap** and **HashSet** have constructors that allow you to specify the initial capacity.
>
> ***Size:*** The number of entries currently in the table.
>
> ***Load factor:*** size/capacity. A load factor of 0 is an empty table, 0.5 is a half-full table, etc. A lightly loaded table will have few collisions and so is optimal for insertions and lookups (but will slow down the process of traversing with an iterator). **HashMap** and **HashSet** have constructors that allow you to specify the load factor, which means that when this load factor is reached, the container will automatically increase the capacity (the number of buckets) by roughly doubling it and will redistribute the existing objects into the new set of buckets (this is called *rehashing*).

The default load factor used by **HashMap** is 0.75 (it doesn't rehash until the table is ¾ full). This seems to be a good trade-off between time and space costs. A higher load factor decreases the space required by the table but increases the lookup cost, which is important because lookup is what you do most of the time (including both **get( )** and **put( )**).

If you know that you'll be storing many entries in a **HashMap**, creating it with an appropriately large initial capacity will prevent the overhead of automatic rehashing.[10]

---

[10] In a private message, Joshua Bloch wrote: "... I believe that we erred by allowing implementation details (such as hash table size and load factor) into our APIs. The client should perhaps tell us the maximum expected size of a collection, and we should take it from there. Clients can easily do more harm than good by choosing values for these parameters. As an extreme example, consider **Vector**'s capacityIncrement. No one should ever set this, and we shouldn't have provided it. If you set it to any non-zero value, the asymptotic cost of a sequence of appends goes from linear to quadratic. In other words, it destroys your performance. Over time, we're beginning to wise up about this sort of thing. If you look at **IdentityHashMap**, you'll see that it has no low-level tuning parameters."

Overriding **hashCode( )**

Now that you understand what's involved in the function of the **HashMap**, the issues involved in writing a **hashCode( )** will make more sense.

First of all, you don't have control of the creation of the actual value that's used to index into the array of buckets. That is dependent on the capacity of the particular **HashMap** object, and that capacity changes depending on how full the container is, and what the load factor is. The value produced by your **hashCode( )** will be further processed in order to create the bucket index (in **SimpleHashMap**, the calculation is just a modulo by the size of the bucket array).

The most important factor in creating a **hashCode( )** is that, regardless of when **hashCode( )** is called, it produces the same value for a particular object every time it is called. If you end up with an object that produces one **hashCode( )** value when it is **put( )** into a **HashMap** and another during a **get( )**, you won't be able to retrieve the objects. So if your **hashCode( )** depends on mutable data in the object, the user must be made aware that changing the data will effectively produce a different key by generating a different **hashCode( )**.

In addition, you will probably *not* want to generate a **hashCode( )** that is based on unique object information—in particular, the value of **this** makes a bad **hashCode( )** because then you can't generate a new identical key to the one used to **put( )** the original key-value pair. This was the problem that occurred in **SpringDetector.java**, because the default implementation of **hashCode( )** *does* use the object address. So you'll want to use information in the object that identifies the object in a meaningful way.

One example can be seen in the **String** class. **String**s have the special characteristic that if a program has several **String** objects that contain identical character sequences, then those **String** objects all map to the same memory (the mechanism for this is described in Appendix A). So it makes sense that the **hashCode( )** produced by two separate instances of **new String("hello")** should be identical. You can see this in the following program:

```
//: c11:StringHashCode.java
import com.bruceeckel.simpletest.*;

public class StringHashCode {
```

```
  private static Test monitor = new Test();
  public static void main(String[] args) {
    System.out.println("Hello".hashCode());
    System.out.println("Hello".hashCode());
    monitor.expect(new String[] {
      "69609650",
      "69609650"
    });
  }
} ///:~
```

The **hashCode( )** for **String** is clearly based on the contents of the **String**.

So for a **hashCode( )** to be effective, it must be fast and it must be meaningful; that is, it must generate a value based on the contents of the object. Remember that this value doesn't have to be unique—you should lean toward speed rather than uniqueness—but between **hashCode( )** and **equals( )**, the identity of the object must be completely resolved.

Because the **hashCode( )** is further processed before the bucket index is produced, the range of values is not important; it just needs to generate an **int**.

There's one other factor: A good **hashCode( )** should result in an even distribution of values. If the values tend to cluster, then the **HashMap** or **HashSet** will be more heavily loaded in some areas and will not be as fast as it could be with an evenly distributed hashing function.

In *Effective Java* (Addison-Wesley 2001), Joshua Bloch gives a basic recipe for generating a decent **hashCode( )**:

1. Store some constant nonzero value, say 17, in an **int** variable called **result**.

2. For each significant field **f** in your object (each field taken into account by the **equals( )**, that is), calculate an **int** hash code **c** for the field:

Field type	Calculation
boolean	**c = (f ? 0 : 1)**
byte, char, short, or **int**	**c = (int)f**

long	**c = (int)(f ^ (f >>>32))**
float	**c = Float.floatToIntBits(f);**
double	**long l = Double.doubleToLongBits(f);** **c = (int)(l ^ (l >>> 32))**
Object, where **equals( )** calls **equals( )** for this field	**c = f.hashCode( )**
Array	Apply above rules to each element

3. Combine the hash code(s) computed above:
   result = 37 * result + c;

4. Return **result**.

5. Look at the resulting **hashCode( )** and make sure that equal instances have equal hash codes.

Here's an example that follows these guidelines:

```
//: c11:CountedString.java
// Creating a good hashCode().
import com.bruceeckel.simpletest.*;
import java.util.*;

public class CountedString {
  private static Test monitor = new Test();
  private static List created = new ArrayList();
  private String s;
  private int id = 0;
  public CountedString(String str) {
    s = str;
    created.add(s);
    Iterator it = created.iterator();
    // Id is the total number of instances
    // of this string in use by CountedString:
    while(it.hasNext())
      if(it.next().equals(s))
        id++;
  }
```

```
  public String toString() {
    return "String: " + s + " id: " + id +
      " hashCode(): " + hashCode();
  }
  public int hashCode() {
    // Very simple approach:
    // return s.hashCode() * id;
    // Using Joshua Bloch's recipe:
    int result = 17;
    result = 37*result + s.hashCode();
    result = 37*result + id;
    return result;
  }
  public boolean equals(Object o) {
    return (o instanceof CountedString)
      && s.equals(((CountedString)o).s)
      && id == ((CountedString)o).id;
  }
  public static void main(String[] args) {
    Map map = new HashMap();
    CountedString[] cs = new CountedString[10];
    for(int i = 0; i < cs.length; i++) {
      cs[i] = new CountedString("hi");
      map.put(cs[i], new Integer(i));
    }
    System.out.println(map);
    for(int i = 0; i < cs.length; i++) {
      System.out.println("Looking up " + cs[i]);
      System.out.println(map.get(cs[i]));
    }
    monitor.expect(new String[] {
      "{String: hi id: 4 hashCode(): 146450=3," +
      " String: hi id: 10 hashCode(): 146456=9," +
      " String: hi id: 6 hashCode(): 146452=5," +
      " String: hi id: 1 hashCode(): 146447=0," +
      " String: hi id: 9 hashCode(): 146455=8," +
      " String: hi id: 8 hashCode(): 146454=7," +
      " String: hi id: 3 hashCode(): 146449=2," +
      " String: hi id: 5 hashCode(): 146451=4," +
      " String: hi id: 7 hashCode(): 146453=6," +
      " String: hi id: 2 hashCode(): 146448=1}",
      "Looking up String: hi id: 1 hashCode(): 146447",
      "0",
      "Looking up String: hi id: 2 hashCode(): 146448",
```

```
      "1",
      "Looking up String: hi id: 3 hashCode(): 146449",
      "2",
      "Looking up String: hi id: 4 hashCode(): 146450",
      "3",
      "Looking up String: hi id: 5 hashCode(): 146451",
      "4",
      "Looking up String: hi id: 6 hashCode(): 146452",
      "5",
      "Looking up String: hi id: 7 hashCode(): 146453",
      "6",
      "Looking up String: hi id: 8 hashCode(): 146454",
      "7",
      "Looking up String: hi id: 9 hashCode(): 146455",
      "8",
      "Looking up String: hi id: 10 hashCode(): 146456",
      "9"
    });
  }
} ///:~
```

CountedString includes a **String** and an **id** that represents the number of **CountedString** objects that contain an identical **String**. The counting is accomplished in the constructor by iterating through the **static ArrayList** where all the **String**s are stored.

Both **hashCode( )** and **equals( )** produce results based on both fields; if they were just based on the **String** alone or the **id** alone, there would be duplicate matches for distinct values.

In **main( )**, a bunch of **CountedString** objects are created, using the same **String** to show that the duplicates create unique values because of the count **id**. The **HashMap** is displayed so that you can see how it is stored internally (no discernible orders), and then each key is looked up individually to demonstrate that the lookup mechanism is working properly.

Writing a proper **hashCode( )** and **equals( )** for a new class can be tricky. You can find tools to help you do this in Apache's "Jakarta Commons" project at *jakarta.apache.org/commons*, under "lang" (this project also has many other potentially useful libraries, and appears to be the Java community's answer to the C++ community's *www.boost.org*).

Holding references

The **java.lang.ref** library contains a set of classes that allow greater flexibility in garbage collection. These classes are especially useful when you have large objects that may cause memory exhaustion. There are three classes inherited from the abstract class **Reference**: **SoftReference**, **WeakReference**, and **PhantomReference**. Each of these provides a different level of indirection for the garbage collector if the object in question is *only* reachable through one of these **Reference** objects.

If an object is *reachable*, it means that somewhere in your program the object can be found. This could mean that you have an ordinary reference on the stack that goes right to the object, but you might also have a reference to an object that has a reference to the object in question; there could be many intermediate links. If an object is reachable, the garbage collector cannot release it because it's still in use by your program. If an object isn't reachable, there's no way for your program to use it, so it's safe to garbage collect that object.

You use **Reference** objects when you want to continue to hold onto a reference to that object; you want to be able to reach that object, but you also want to allow the garbage collector to release that object. Thus, you have a way to go on using the object, but if memory exhaustion is imminent, you allow that object to be released.

You accomplish this by using a **Reference** object as an intermediary between you and the ordinary reference, *and* there must be no ordinary references to the object (ones that are not wrapped inside **Reference** objects). If the garbage collector discovers that an object is reachable through an ordinary reference, it will not release that object.

In the order of **SoftReference**, **WeakReference**, and **PhantomReference**, each one is "weaker" than the last and corresponds to a different level of reachability. Soft references are for implementing memory-sensitive caches. Weak references are for implementing "canonicalizing mappings"—where instances of objects can be simultaneously used in multiple places in a program, to save storage—that do not prevent their keys (or values) from being reclaimed. Phantom references are for scheduling premortem cleanup actions in a more flexible way than is possible with the Java finalization mechanism.

With **SoftReference**s and **WeakReference**s, you have a choice about whether to place them on a **ReferenceQueue** (the device used for premortem cleanup actions), but a **PhantomReference** can only be built on a **ReferenceQueue**. Here's a simple demonstration:

```
//: c11:References.java
// Demonstrates Reference objects
import java.lang.ref.*;

class VeryBig {
  private static final int SZ = 10000;
  private double[] d = new double[SZ];
  private String ident;
  public VeryBig(String id) { ident = id; }
  public String toString() { return ident; }
  public void finalize() {
    System.out.println("Finalizing " + ident);
  }
}

public class References {
  private static ReferenceQueue rq = new ReferenceQueue();
  public static void checkQueue() {
    Object inq = rq.poll();
    if(inq != null)
      System.out.println("In queue: " +
        (VeryBig)((Reference)inq).get());
  }
  public static void main(String[] args) {
    int size = 10;
    // Or, choose size via the command line:
    if(args.length > 0)
      size = Integer.parseInt(args[0]);
    SoftReference[] sa = new SoftReference[size];
    for(int i = 0; i < sa.length; i++) {
      sa[i] = new SoftReference(
        new VeryBig("Soft " + i), rq);
      System.out.println("Just created: " +
        (VeryBig)sa[i].get());
      checkQueue();
    }
    WeakReference[] wa = new WeakReference[size];
    for(int i = 0; i < wa.length; i++) {
      wa[i] = new WeakReference(
```

```
        new VeryBig("Weak " + i), rq);
      System.out.println("Just created: " +
        (VeryBig)wa[i].get());
      checkQueue();
    }
    SoftReference s =
      new SoftReference(new VeryBig("Soft"));
    WeakReference w =
      new WeakReference(new VeryBig("Weak"));
    System.gc();
    PhantomReference[] pa = new PhantomReference[size];
    for(int i = 0; i < pa.length; i++) {
      pa[i] = new PhantomReference(
        new VeryBig("Phantom " + i), rq);
      System.out.println("Just created: " +
        (VeryBig)pa[i].get());
      checkQueue();
    }
  }
} ///:~
```

When you run this program (you'll want to pipe the output through a "more" utility so that you can view the output in pages), you'll see that the objects are garbage collected, even though you still have access to them through the **Reference** object (to get the actual object reference, you use **get( )**). You'll also see that the **ReferenceQueue** always produces a **Reference** containing a **null** object. To make use of this, you can inherit from the particular **Reference** class you're interested in and add more useful methods to the new type of **Reference**.

The **WeakHashMap**

The containers library has a special **Map** to hold weak references: the **WeakHashMap**. This class is designed to make the creation of canonicalized mappings easier. In such a mapping, you are saving storage by making only one instance of a particular value. When the program needs that value, it looks up the existing object in the mapping and uses that (rather than creating one from scratch). The mapping may make the values as part of its initialization, but it's more likely that the values are made on demand.

Since this is a storage-saving technique, it's very convenient that the **WeakHashMap** allows the garbage collector to automatically clean up the keys and values. You don't have to do anything special to the keys and values you want to place in the **WeakHashMap**; these are automatically wrapped in **WeakReferences** by the map. The trigger to allow cleanup is if the key is no longer in use, as demonstrated here:

```
//: c11:CanonicalMapping.java
// Demonstrates WeakHashMap.
import java.util.*;
import java.lang.ref.*;

class Key {
  private String ident;
  public Key(String id) { ident = id; }
  public String toString() { return ident; }
  public int hashCode() { return ident.hashCode(); }
  public boolean equals(Object r) {
    return (r instanceof Key)
      && ident.equals(((Key)r).ident);
  }
  public void finalize() {
    System.out.println("Finalizing Key "+ ident);
  }
}

class Value {
  private String ident;
  public Value(String id) { ident = id; }
  public String toString() { return ident; }
  public void finalize() {
    System.out.println("Finalizing Value " + ident);
  }
}

public class CanonicalMapping {
  public static void main(String[] args) {
    int size = 1000;
    // Or, choose size via the command line:
    if(args.length > 0)
      size = Integer.parseInt(args[0]);
    Key[] keys = new Key[size];
    WeakHashMap map = new WeakHashMap();
    for(int i = 0; i < size; i++) {
      Key k = new Key(Integer.toString(i));
      Value v = new Value(Integer.toString(i));
      if(i % 3 == 0)
```

```
        keys[i] = k; // Save as "real" references
      map.put(k, v);
    }
    System.gc();
  }
} ///:~
```

The **Key** class must have a **hashCode( )** and an **equals( )** since it is being used as a key in a hashed data structure, as described previously in this chapter.

When you run the program, you'll see that the garbage collector will skip every third key, because an ordinary reference to that key has also been placed in the **keys** array, and thus those objects cannot be garbage collected.

Iterators revisited

We can now demonstrate the true power of the **Iterator**: the ability to separate the operation of traversing a sequence from the underlying structure of that sequence. The class **PrintData** (defined earlier in the chapter) uses an **Iterator** to move through a sequence and call the **toString( )** method for every object. In the following example, two different types of containers are created—an **ArrayList** and a **HashMap**—and they are each filled with, respectively, **Mouse** and **Hamster** objects. (These classes are defined earlier in this chapter.) Because an **Iterator** hides the structure of the underlying container, **Printer.printAll( )** doesn't know or care what kind of container the **Iterator** comes from:

```
//: c11:Iterators2.java
// Revisiting Iterators.
import com.bruceeckel.simpletest.*;
import java.util.*;

public class Iterators2 {
  private static Test monitor = new Test();
  public static void main(String[] args) {
    List list = new ArrayList();
    for(int i = 0; i < 5; i++)
      list.add(new Mouse(i));
    Map m = new HashMap();
    for(int i = 0; i < 5; i++)
      m.put(new Integer(i), new Hamster(i));
    System.out.println("List");
```

```
    Printer.printAll(list.iterator());
    System.out.println("Map");
    Printer.printAll(m.entrySet().iterator());
    monitor.expect(new String[] {
      "List",
      "This is Mouse #0",
      "This is Mouse #1",
      "This is Mouse #2",
      "This is Mouse #3",
      "This is Mouse #4",
      "Map",
      "4=This is Hamster #4",
      "3=This is Hamster #3",
      "2=This is Hamster #2",
      "1=This is Hamster #1",
      "0=This is Hamster #0"
    }, Test.IGNORE_ORDER);
  }
} ///:~
```

For the **HashMap**, the **entrySet( )** method produces a **Set** of **Map.entry** objects, which contain both the key and the value for each entry, so you see both of them printed.

Note that **PrintData.print( )** takes advantage of the fact that the objects in these containers are of class **Object** so the call **toString( )** by **System.out.println( )** is automatic. It's more likely that in your problem, you must make the assumption that your **Iterator** is walking through a container of some specific type. For example, you might assume that everything in the container is a **Shape** with a **draw( )** method. Then you must downcast from the **Object** that **Iterator.next( )** returns to produce a **Shape**.

Choosing an implementation

By now you should understand that there are really only three container components: **Map**, **List**, and **Set**, but more than one implementation of each interface. If you need to use the functionality offered by a particular interface, how do you decide which implementation to use?

To understand the answer, you must be aware that each different implementation has its own features, strengths, and weaknesses. For example, you can see in the diagram that the "feature" of **Hashtable**,

Vector, and **Stack** is that they are legacy classes, so that old code doesn't break. On the other hand, it's best if you don't use those for new code.

The distinction between the other containers often comes down to what they are "backed by"; that is, the data structures that physically implement your desired **interface**. This means that, for example, **ArrayList** and **LinkedList** implement the **List** interface, so the basic operations are the same regardless of which one you use. However, **ArrayList** is backed by an array, and **LinkedList** is implemented in the usual way for a doubly linked list, as individual objects each containing data along with references to the previous and next elements in the list. Because of this, if you want to do many insertions and removals in the middle of a list, a **LinkedList** is the appropriate choice. (**LinkedList** also has additional functionality that is established in **AbstractSequentialList**.) If not, an **ArrayList** is typically faster.

As another example, a **Set** can be implemented as either a **TreeSet**, a **HashSet**, or a **LinkedHashSet**. Each of these have different behaviors: **HashSet** is for typical use and provides raw speed on lookup, **LinkedHashSet** keeps pairs in insertion order, and **TreeSet** is backed by **TreeMap** and is designed to produce a constantly sorted set. The idea is that you can choose the implementation based on the behavior you need. Most of the time, the **HashSet** is all that's necessary and should be your default choice of **Set**.

Choosing between **Lists**

The most convincing way to see the differences between the implementations of **List** is with a performance test. The following code establishes an inner base class to use as a test framework, then creates an array of anonymous inner classes, one for each different test. Each of these inner classes is called by the **test( )** method. This approach allows you to easily add and remove new kinds of tests.

```
//: c11:ListPerformance.java
// Demonstrates performance differences in Lists.
// {Args: 500}
import java.util.*;
import com.bruceeckel.util.*;

public class ListPerformance {
  private static int reps = 10000;
```

```
  private static int quantity = reps / 10;
  private abstract static class Tester {
    private String name;
    Tester(String name) { this.name = name; }
    abstract void test(List a);
  }
  private static Tester[] tests = {
    new Tester("get") {
      void test(List a) {
        for(int i = 0; i < reps; i++) {
          for(int j = 0; j < quantity; j++)
            a.get(j);
        }
      }
    },
    new Tester("iteration") {
      void test(List a) {
        for(int i = 0; i < reps; i++) {
          Iterator it = a.iterator();
          while(it.hasNext())
            it.next();
        }
      }
    },
    new Tester("insert") {
      void test(List a) {
        int half = a.size()/2;
        String s = "test";
        ListIterator it = a.listIterator(half);
        for(int i = 0; i < reps * 10; i++)
          it.add(s);
      }
    },
    new Tester("remove") {
      void test(List a) {
        ListIterator it = a.listIterator(3);
        while(it.hasNext()) {
          it.next();
          it.remove();
        }
      }
    },
  };
  public static void test(List a) {
```

```
    // Strip qualifiers from class name:
    System.out.println("Testing " +
      a.getClass().getName().replaceAll("\\w+\\.", ""));
    for(int i = 0; i < tests.length; i++) {
      Collections2.fill(a, Collections2.countries.reset(),
        quantity);
      System.out.print(tests[i].name);
      long t1 = System.currentTimeMillis();
      tests[i].test(a);
      long t2 = System.currentTimeMillis();
      System.out.println(": " + (t2 - t1));
    }
  }
  public static void testArrayAsList(int reps) {
    System.out.println("Testing array as List");
    // Can only do first two tests on an array:
    for(int i = 0; i < 2; i++) {
      String[] sa = new String[quantity];
      Arrays2.fill(sa, Collections2.countries.reset());
      List a = Arrays.asList(sa);
      System.out.print(tests[i].name);
      long t1 = System.currentTimeMillis();
      tests[i].test(a);
      long t2 = System.currentTimeMillis();
      System.out.println(": " + (t2 - t1));
    }
  }
  public static void main(String[] args) {
    // Choose a different number of
    // repetitions via the command line:
    if(args.length > 0)
      reps = Integer.parseInt(args[0]);
    System.out.println(reps + " repetitions");
    testArrayAsList(reps);
    test(new ArrayList());
    test(new LinkedList());
    test(new Vector());
  }
} ///:~
```

To provide a base class for the specific tests, the inner class **Tester** is **abstract**. It contains a **String** to be printed when the test starts and an **abstract** method **test( )** that does the work. All the different types of tests are collected in one place, the array **tests**, which is initialized with different anonymous inner classes that inherit from **Tester**. To add or remove tests, simply add or remove an inner class definition from the array, and everything else happens automatically.

To compare array access to container access (primarily against **ArrayList**), a special test is created for arrays by wrapping one as a **List** using **Arrays.asList( )**. Note that only the first two tests can be performed in this case, because you cannot insert or remove elements from an array.

The **List** that's handed to **test( )** is first filled with elements, then each test in the **tests** array is timed. The results will vary from machine to machine; they are intended to give only an order of magnitude comparison between the performance of the different containers. Here is a summary of one run:

Type	Get	Iteration	Insert	Remove
array	172	516	na	na
ArrayList	281	1375	328	30484
LinkedList	5828	1047	109	16
Vector	422	1890	360	30781

As expected, arrays are faster than any container for random-access lookups and iteration. You can see that random accesses (**get( )**) are cheap for **ArrayList**s and expensive for **LinkedList**s. (Oddly, iteration is *faster* for a **LinkedList** than an **ArrayList**, which is a bit counterintuitive.) On the other hand, insertions and removals from the middle of a list are dramatically cheaper for a **LinkedList** than for an **ArrayList**—*especially* removals. **Vector** is generally not as fast as **ArrayList**, and it should be avoided; it's only in the library for legacy code support (the only reason it works in this program is because it was adapted to be a **List** in Java 2). The best approach is probably to choose an **ArrayList** as your default and to change to a **LinkedList** if you discover performance problems due to many insertions and removals from the middle of the list. And of course, if you are working with a fixed-sized group of elements, use an array.

Choosing between **Sets**

You can choose a **TreeSet**, a **HashSet**, or a **LinkedHashSet** depending on the behavior you desire. The following test program gives an indication of the performance trade-off between the implementations:

```
//: c11:SetPerformance.java
// {Args: 500}
import java.util.*;
import com.bruceeckel.util.*;

public class SetPerformance {
  private static int reps = 50000;
  private abstract static class Tester {
    String name;
    Tester(String name) { this.name = name; }
    abstract void test(Set s, int size);
  }
  private static Tester[] tests = {
    new Tester("add") {
      void test(Set s, int size) {
        for(int i = 0; i < reps; i++) {
          s.clear();
          Collections2.fill(s,
            Collections2.countries.reset(),size);
        }
      }
    },
    new Tester("contains") {
      void test(Set s, int size) {
        for(int i = 0; i < reps; i++)
          for(int j = 0; j < size; j++)
            s.contains(Integer.toString(j));
      }
    },
    new Tester("iteration") {
      void test(Set s, int size) {
        for(int i = 0; i < reps * 10; i++) {
          Iterator it = s.iterator();
          while(it.hasNext())
            it.next();
        }
      }
    },
  };
  public static void test(Set s, int size) {
    // Strip qualifiers from class name:
    System.out.println("Testing " +
      s.getClass().getName().replaceAll("\\w+\\.", "") +
      " size " + size);
```

```
    Collections2.fill(s,
      Collections2.countries.reset(), size);
    for(int i = 0; i < tests.length; i++) {
      System.out.print(tests[i].name);
      long t1 = System.currentTimeMillis();
      tests[i].test(s, size);
      long t2 = System.currentTimeMillis();
      System.out.println(": " +
        ((double)(t2 - t1)/(double)size));
    }
  }
  public static void main(String[] args) {
    // Choose a different number of
    // repetitions via the command line:
    if(args.length > 0)
      reps = Integer.parseInt(args[0]);
    System.out.println(reps + " repetitions");
    // Small:
    test(new TreeSet(), 10);
    test(new HashSet(), 10);
    test(new LinkedHashSet(), 10);
    // Medium:
    test(new TreeSet(), 100);
    test(new HashSet(), 100);
    test(new LinkedHashSet(), 100);
    // Large:
    test(new TreeSet(), 1000);
    test(new HashSet(), 1000);
    test(new LinkedHashSet(), 1000);
  }
} ///:~
```

The following table shows the results of one run. (Of course, this will be different according to the computer and JVM you are using; you should run the test yourself as well):

Type	Test size	Add	Contains	Iteration
TreeSet	10	25.0	23.4	39.1
	100	17.2	27.5	45.9
	1000	26.0	30.2	9.0
HashSet	10	18.7	17.2	64.1
	100	17.2	19.1	65.2

	1000	8.8	16.6	12.8
LinkedHashSet	10	20.3	18.7	64.1
	100	18.6	19.5	49.2
	1000	10.0	16.3	10.0

The performance of **HashSet** is generally superior to **TreeSet** for all operations (but in particular for addition and lookup, the two most important operations). The only reason **TreeSet** exists is because it maintains its elements in sorted order, so you use it only when you need a sorted **Set**.

Note that **LinkedHashSet** is slightly more expensive for insertions than **HashSet**; this is because of the extra cost of maintaining the linked list along with the hashed container. However, traversal is cheaper with **LinkedHashSet** because of the linked list.

Choosing between **Maps**

When choosing between implementations of **Map**, the size of the **Map** is what most strongly affects performance, and the following test program gives an indication of this trade-off:

```
//: c11:MapPerformance.java
// Demonstrates performance differences in Maps.
// {Args: 500}
import java.util.*;
import com.bruceeckel.util.*;

public class MapPerformance {
  private static int reps = 50000;
  private abstract static class Tester {
    String name;
    Tester(String name) { this.name = name; }
    abstract void test(Map m, int size);
  }
  private static Tester[] tests = {
    new Tester("put") {
      void test(Map m, int size) {
        for(int i = 0; i < reps; i++) {
          m.clear();
          Collections2.fill(m,
            Collections2.geography.reset(), size);
        }
```

```
      }
    },
    new Tester("get") {
      void test(Map m, int size) {
        for(int i = 0; i < reps; i++)
          for(int j = 0; j < size; j++)
            m.get(Integer.toString(j));
      }
    },
    new Tester("iteration") {
      void test(Map m, int size) {
        for(int i = 0; i < reps * 10; i++) {
          Iterator it = m.entrySet().iterator();
          while(it.hasNext())
            it.next();
        }
      }
    },
  };
  public static void test(Map m, int size) {
    // Strip qualifiers from class name:
    System.out.println("Testing " +
      m.getClass().getName().replaceAll("\\w+\\.", "") +
      " size " + size);
    Collections2.fill(m,
      Collections2.geography.reset(), size);
    for(int i = 0; i < tests.length; i++) {
      System.out.print(tests[i].name);
      long t1 = System.currentTimeMillis();
      tests[i].test(m, size);
      long t2 = System.currentTimeMillis();
      System.out.println(": " +
        ((double)(t2 - t1)/(double)size));
    }
  }
  public static void main(String[] args) {
    // Choose a different number of
    // repetitions via the command line:
    if(args.length > 0)
      reps = Integer.parseInt(args[0]);
    System.out.println(reps + " repetitions");
    // Small:
    test(new TreeMap(), 10);
    test(new HashMap(), 10);
```

```
    test(new LinkedHashMap(), 10);
    test(new IdentityHashMap(), 10);
    test(new WeakHashMap(), 10);
    test(new Hashtable(), 10);
    // Medium:
    test(new TreeMap(), 100);
    test(new HashMap(), 100);
    test(new LinkedHashMap(), 100);
    test(new IdentityHashMap(), 100);
    test(new WeakHashMap(), 100);
    test(new Hashtable(), 100);
    // Large:
    test(new TreeMap(), 1000);
    test(new HashMap(), 1000);
    test(new LinkedHashMap(), 1000);
    test(new IdentityHashMap(), 1000);
    test(new WeakHashMap(), 1000);
    test(new Hashtable(), 1000);
  }
} ///:~
```

Because the size of the map is the issue, you'll see that the timing tests divide the time by the size to normalize each measurement. Here is one set of results. (Yours will probably be different.)

Type	Test size	Put	Get	Iteration
TreeMap	10	26.6	20.3	43.7
	100	34.1	27.2	45.8
	1000	27.8	29.3	8.8
HashMap	10	21.9	18.8	60.9
	100	21.9	18.6	63.3
	1000	11.5	18.8	12.3
LinkedHashMap	10	23.4	18.8	59.4
	100	24.2	19.5	47.8
	1000	12.3	19.0	9.2
IdentityHashMap	10	20.3	25.0	71.9
	100	19.7	25.9	56.7
	1000	13.1	24.3	10.9

Type	Test size	Put	Get	Iteration
WeakHashMap	10	26.6	18.8	76.5
	100	26.1	21.6	64.4
	1000	14.7	19.2	12.4
Hashtable	10	18.8	18.7	65.7
	100	19.4	20.9	55.3
	1000	13.1	19.9	10.8

As you might expect, **Hashtable** performance is roughly equivalent to **HashMap**. (You can also see that **HashMap** is generally a bit faster; **HashMap** is intended to replace **Hashtable**.) The **TreeMap** is generally slower than the **HashMap**, so why would you use it? As a way to create an ordered list. The behavior of a tree is such that it's always in order and doesn't have to be specially sorted. Once you fill a **TreeMap**, you can call **keySet( )** to get a **Set** view of the keys, then **toArray( )** to produce an array of those keys. You can then use the **static** method **Arrays.binarySearch( )** (discussed later) to rapidly find objects in your sorted array. Of course, you would probably only do this if, for some reason, the behavior of a **HashMap** was unacceptable, since **HashMap** is designed to rapidly find things. Also, you can easily create a **HashMap** from a **TreeMap** with a single object creation. In the end, when you're using a **Map**, your first choice should be **HashMap**, and only if you need a constantly sorted **Map** will you need **TreeMap**.

LinkedHashMap is slightly slower than **HashMap** because it maintains the linked list in addition to the hashed data structure. **IdentityHashMap** has different performance because it uses == rather than **equals( )** for comparisons.

Sorting and searching **Lists**

Utilities to perform sorting and searching for **List**s have the same names and signatures as those for sorting arrays of objects, but are **static** methods of **Collections** instead of **Arrays**. Here's an example, modified from **ArraySearching.java**:

```
//: c11:ListSortSearch.java
// Sorting and searching Lists with 'Collections.'
```

```java
import com.bruceeckel.util.*;
import java.util.*;

public class ListSortSearch {
  public static void main(String[] args) {
    List list = new ArrayList();
    Collections2.fill(list, Collections2.capitals, 25);
    System.out.println(list + "\n");
    Collections.shuffle(list);
    System.out.println("After shuffling: " + list);
    Collections.sort(list);
    System.out.println(list + "\n");
    Object key = list.get(12);
    int index = Collections.binarySearch(list, key);
    System.out.println("Location of " + key +
      " is " + index + ", list.get(" +
      index + ") = " + list.get(index));
    AlphabeticComparator comp = new AlphabeticComparator();
    Collections.sort(list, comp);
    System.out.println(list + "\n");
    key = list.get(12);
    index = Collections.binarySearch(list, key, comp);
    System.out.println("Location of " + key +
      " is " + index + ", list.get(" +
      index + ") = " + list.get(index));
  }
} ///:~
```

The use of these methods is identical to the ones in **Arrays**, but you're using a **List** instead of an array. Just like searching and sorting with arrays, if you sort using a **Comparator**, you must **binarySearch( )** using the same **Comparator**.

This program also demonstrates the **shuffle( )** method in **Collections**, which randomizes the order of a **List**.

Utilities

There are a number of other useful utilities in the **Collections** class:

max(Collection) **min(Collection)**	Produces the maximum or minimum element in the argument using the natural comparison method of the objects in the

	Collection.
max(Collection, Comparator) **min(Collection, Comparator)**	Produces the maximum or minimum element in the **Collection** using the **Comparator**.
indexOfSubList(List source, List target)	Produces starting index of the *first* place where **target** appears inside **source**.
lastIndexOfSubList(List source, List target)	Produces starting index of the *last* place where **target** appears inside **source**.
replaceAll(List list, Object oldVal, Object newVal)	Replace all **oldVal** with **newVal**.
reverse( )	Reverses all the elements in place.
rotate(List list, int distance)	Moves all elements forward by **distance**, taking the ones off the end and placing them at the beginning.
copy(List dest, List src)	Copies elements from **src** to **dest**.
swap(List list, int i, int j)	Swaps elements at locations **i** and **j** in **list**. Probably faster than what you'd write by hand.
fill(List list, Object o)	Replaces all the elements of list with **o**.
nCopies(int n, Object o)	Returns an immutable **List** of size n whose references all point to **o**.
enumeration(Collection)	Produces an old-style **Enumeration** for the argument.
list(Enumeration e)	Returns an **ArrayList** generated using the **Enumeration**. For converting from legacy code.

Note that **min( )** and **max( )** work with **Collection** objects, not with **Lists**, so you don't need to worry about whether the **Collection** should be sorted or not. (As mentioned earlier, you *do* need to **sort( )** a **List** or an array before performing a **binarySearch( )**.)

```
//: c11:Utilities.java
// Simple demonstrations of the Collections utilities.
```

```java
import com.bruceeckel.simpletest.*;
import java.util.*;
import com.bruceeckel.util.*;

public class Utilities {
  private static Test monitor = new Test();
  public static void main(String[] args) {
    List list = Arrays.asList(
      "one Two three Four five six one".split(" "));
    System.out.println(list);
    System.out.println("max: " + Collections.max(list));
    System.out.println("min: " + Collections.min(list));
    AlphabeticComparator comp = new AlphabeticComparator();
    System.out.println("max w/ comparator: " +
      Collections.max(list, comp));
    System.out.println("min w/ comparator: " +
      Collections.min(list, comp));
    List sublist =
      Arrays.asList("Four five six".split(" "));
    System.out.println("indexOfSubList: " +
      Collections.indexOfSubList(list, sublist));
    System.out.println("lastIndexOfSubList: " +
      Collections.lastIndexOfSubList(list, sublist));
    Collections.replaceAll(list, "one", "Yo");
    System.out.println("replaceAll: " + list);
    Collections.reverse(list);
    System.out.println("reverse: " + list);
    Collections.rotate(list, 3);
    System.out.println("rotate: " + list);
    List source =
      Arrays.asList("in the matrix".split(" "));
    Collections.copy(list, source);
    System.out.println("copy: " + list);
    Collections.swap(list, 0, list.size() - 1);
    System.out.println("swap: " + list);
    Collections.fill(list, "pop");
    System.out.println("fill: " + list);
    List dups = Collections.nCopies(3, "snap");
    System.out.println("dups: " + dups);
    // Getting an old-style Enumeration:
    Enumeration e = Collections.enumeration(dups);
    Vector v = new Vector();
    while(e.hasMoreElements())
      v.addElement(e.nextElement());
```

```
    // Converting an old-style Vector
    // to a List via an Enumeration:
    ArrayList arrayList = Collections.list(v.elements());
    System.out.println("arrayList: " + arrayList);
    monitor.expect(new String[] {
      "[one, Two, three, Four, five, six, one]",
      "max: three",
      "min: Four",
      "max w/ comparator: Two",
      "min w/ comparator: five",
      "indexOfSubList: 3",
      "lastIndexOfSubList: 3",
      "replaceAll: [Yo, Two, three, Four, five, six, Yo]",
      "reverse: [Yo, six, five, Four, three, Two, Yo]",
      "rotate: [three, Two, Yo, Yo, six, five, Four]",
      "copy: [in, the, matrix, Yo, six, five, Four]",
      "swap: [Four, the, matrix, Yo, six, five, in]",
      "fill: [pop, pop, pop, pop, pop, pop, pop]",
      "dups: [snap, snap, snap]",
      "arrayList: [snap, snap, snap]"
    });
  }
} ///:~
```

The output explains the behavior of each utility method. Note the difference in **min( )** and **max( )** with the **AlphabeticComparator** because of capitalization.

Making a **Collection** or **Map** unmodifiable

Often it is convenient to create a read-only version of a **Collection** or **Map**. The **Collections** class allows you to do this by passing the original container into a method that hands back a read-only version. There are four variations on this method, one each for **Collection** (if you can't treat a **Collection** as a more specific type), **List**, **Set,** and **Map**. This example shows the proper way to build read-only versions of each:

```
//: c11:ReadOnly.java
// Using the Collections.unmodifiable methods.
import java.util.*;
import com.bruceeckel.util.*;
```

```java
public class ReadOnly {
  private static Collections2.StringGenerator gen =
    Collections2.countries;
  public static void main(String[] args) {
    Collection c = new ArrayList();
    Collections2.fill(c, gen, 25); // Insert data
    c = Collections.unmodifiableCollection(c);
    System.out.println(c); // Reading is OK
    //! c.add("one"); // Can't change it

    List a = new ArrayList();
    Collections2.fill(a, gen.reset(), 25);
    a = Collections.unmodifiableList(a);
    ListIterator lit = a.listIterator();
    System.out.println(lit.next()); // Reading is OK
    //! lit.add("one"); // Can't change it

    Set s = new HashSet();
    Collections2.fill(s, gen.reset(), 25);
    s = Collections.unmodifiableSet(s);
    System.out.println(s); // Reading is OK
    //! s.add("one"); // Can't change it

    Map m = new HashMap();
    Collections2.fill(m, Collections2.geography, 25);
    m = Collections.unmodifiableMap(m);
    System.out.println(m); // Reading is OK
    //! m.put("Ralph", "Howdy!");
  }
} ///:~
```

Calling the "unmodifiable" method for a particular type does not cause compile-time checking, but once the transformation has occurred, any calls to methods that modify the contents of a particular container will produce an **UnsupportedOperationException**.

In each case, you must fill the container with meaningful data *before* you make it read-only. Once it is loaded, the best approach is to replace the existing reference with the reference that is produced by the "unmodifiable" call. That way, you don't run the risk of accidentally trying to change the contents once you've made it unmodifiable. On the other hand, this tool also allows you to keep a modifiable container as **private** within a class and to return a read-only reference to that container from a method call. So, you can change it from within the class, but everyone else can only read it.

Synchronizing a **Collection** or **Map**

The **synchronized** keyword is an important part of the subject of *multithreading*, a more complicated topic that will not be introduced until Chapter 13. Here, I shall note only that the **Collections** class contains a way to automatically synchronize an entire container. The syntax is similar to the "unmodifiable" methods:

```
//: c11:Synchronization.java
// Using the Collections.synchronized methods.
import java.util.*;

public class Synchronization {
  public static void main(String[] args) {
    Collection c =
      Collections.synchronizedCollection(new ArrayList());
    List list =
      Collections.synchronizedList(new ArrayList());
    Set s = Collections.synchronizedSet(new HashSet());
    Map m = Collections.synchronizedMap(new HashMap());
  }
} ///:~
```

In this case, you immediately pass the new container through the appropriate "synchronized" method; that way, there's no chance of accidentally exposing the unsynchronized version.

Fail fast

The Java containers also have a mechanism to prevent more than one process from modifying the contents of a container. The problem occurs if you're iterating through a container, and some other process steps in and inserts, removes, or changes an object in that container. Maybe you've already passed that object, maybe it's ahead of you, maybe the size of the container shrinks after you call **size( )**—there are many scenarios for disaster. The Java containers library incorporates a *fail-fast* mechanism that looks for any changes to the container other than the ones your process is personally responsible for. If it detects that someone else is modifying the container, it immediately produces a **ConcurrentModificationException**. This is the "fail-fast" aspect—it doesn't try to detect a problem later on using a more complex algorithm.

It's quite easy to see the fail-fast mechanism in operation—all you have to do is create an iterator and then add something to the collection that the iterator is pointing to, like this:

```
//: c11:FailFast.java
// Demonstrates the "fail fast" behavior.
// {ThrowsException}
import java.util.*;

public class FailFast {
  public static void main(String[] args) {
    Collection c = new ArrayList();
    Iterator it = c.iterator();
    c.add("An object");
    // Causes an exception:
    String s = (String)it.next();
  }
} ///:~
```

The exception happens because something is placed in the container *after* the iterator is acquired from the container. The possibility that two parts of the program could be modifying the same container produces an uncertain state, so the exception notifies you that you should change your code—in this case, acquire the iterator *after* you have added all the elements to the container.

Note that you cannot benefit from this kind of monitoring when you're accessing the elements of a **List** using **get( )**.

Unsupported operations

It's possible to turn an array into a **List** with the **Arrays.asList( )** method:

```
//: c11:Unsupported.java
// Sometimes methods defined in the
// Collection interfaces don't work!
// {ThrowsException}
import java.util.*;

public class Unsupported {
  static List a = Arrays.asList(
    "one two three four five six seven eight".split(" "));
  static List a2 = a.subList(3, 6);
  public static void main(String[] args) {
    System.out.println(a);
```

```
    System.out.println(a2);
    System.out.println("a.contains(" + a.get(0) + ") = " +
      a.contains(a.get(0)));
    System.out.println("a.containsAll(a2) = " +
      a.containsAll(a2));
    System.out.println("a.isEmpty() = " + a.isEmpty());
    System.out.println("a.indexOf(" + a.get(5) + ") = " +
      a.indexOf(a.get(5)));
    // Traverse backwards:
    ListIterator lit = a.listIterator(a.size());
    while(lit.hasPrevious())
      System.out.print(lit.previous() + " ");
    System.out.println();
    // Set the elements to different values:
    for(int i = 0; i < a.size(); i++)
      a.set(i, "47");
    System.out.println(a);
    // Compiles, but won't run:
    lit.add("X"); // Unsupported operation
    a.clear(); // Unsupported
    a.add("eleven"); // Unsupported
    a.addAll(a2); // Unsupported
    a.retainAll(a2); // Unsupported
    a.remove(a.get(0)); // Unsupported
    a.removeAll(a2); // Unsupported
  }
} ///:~
```

You'll discover that only a portion of the **Collection** and **List** interfaces are actually implemented. The rest of the methods cause the unwelcome appearance of something called an **UnsupportedOperationException**. The **Collection interface**—as well as some of the other **interface**s in the Java containers library—contain "optional" methods, which might or might not be "supported" in the concrete class that **implements** that **interface**. Calling an unsupported method causes an **UnsupportedOperationException** to indicate a programming error.

"What?!?" you say, incredulous. "The whole point of **interface**s and base classes is that they promise these methods will do something meaningful! This breaks that promise; it says that not only will calling some methods *not* perform a meaningful behavior, but they will stop the program! Type safety was just thrown out the window!"

It's not quite that bad. With a **Collection**, **List**, **Set**, or **Map**, the compiler still restricts you to calling only the methods in that **interface**, so it's not like Smalltalk (in which you can call any method for any object, and find out only when you run the program whether your call does anything). In addition, most methods that take a **Collection** as an argument only read from that **Collection**—all the "read" methods of **Collection** are *not* optional.

This approach prevents an explosion of interfaces in the design. Other designs for container libraries always seem to end up with a confusing plethora of interfaces to describe each of the variations on the main theme, and are thus difficult to learn. It's not even possible to capture all of the special cases in **interface**s, because someone can always invent a new **interface**. The "unsupported operation" approach achieves an important goal of the Java containers library: The containers are simple to learn and use; unsupported operations are a special case that can be learned later. For this approach to work, however:

1. The **UnsupportedOperationException** must be a rare event. That is, for most classes all operations should work, and only in special cases should an operation be unsupported. This is true in the Java containers library, since the classes you'll use 99 percent of the time—**ArrayList**, **LinkedList**, **HashSet**, and **HashMap**, as well as the other concrete implementations—support all of the operations. The design does provide a "back door" if you want to create a new **Collection** without providing meaningful definitions for all the methods in the **Collection interface**, and yet still fit it into the existing library.

2. When an operation *is* unsupported, there should be reasonable likelihood that an **UnsupportedOperationException** will appear at implementation time, rather than after you've shipped the product to the customer. After all, it indicates a programming error: You've used an implementation incorrectly. This point is less certain and is where the experimental nature of this design comes into play. Only over time will we find out how well it works.

In the preceding example, **Arrays.asList( )** produces a **List** that is backed by a fixed-size array. Therefore, it makes sense that the only supported operations are the ones that don't change the size of the array. If, on the other hand, a new **interface** were required to express this different kind of behavior (called, perhaps, "**FixedSizeList**"), it would throw open the door to complexity, and soon you wouldn't know where to start when trying to use the library.

Note that you can always pass the result of **Arrays.asList( )** as a constructor argument to a **List** or **Set** in order to create a regular container that allows the use of all the methods.

The documentation for a method that takes a **Collection**, **List**, **Set**, or **Map** as an argument should specify which of the optional methods must be implemented. For example, sorting requires the **set( )** and **Iterator.set( )** methods, but not **add( )** and **remove( )**.

Java 1.0/1.1 containers

Unfortunately, a lot of code was written using the Java 1.0/1.1 containers, and even new code is sometimes written using these classes. So although you should never use the old containers when writing new code, you'll still need to be aware of them. However, the old containers were quite limited, so there's not that much to say about them. (Since they are in the past, I will try to refrain from overemphasizing some of the hideous design decisions.)

Vector & Enumeration

The only self-expanding sequence in Java 1.0/1.1 was the **Vector**, so it saw a lot of use. Its flaws are too numerous to describe here (see the first edition of this book, available as a free download from *www.BruceEckel.com*). Basically, you can think of it as an **ArrayList** with long, awkward method names. In the Java 2 container library, **Vector** was adapted so that it could fit as a **Collection** and a **List**, so in the following example, the **Collections2.fill( )** method is successfully used. This turns out to be a bit perverse, as it may confuse some people into thinking that **Vector** has gotten better, when it is actually included only to support pre-Java 2 code.

The Java 1.0/1.1 version of the iterator chose to invent a new name, "enumeration," instead of using a term that everyone was already familiar with. The **Enumeration** interface is smaller than **Iterator**, with only two methods, and it uses longer method names: **boolean hasMoreElements( )** produces **true** if this enumeration contains more elements, and **Object nextElement( )** returns the next element of this enumeration if there are any more (otherwise it throws an exception).

Enumeration is only an interface, not an implementation, and even new libraries sometimes still use the old **Enumeration**, which is unfortunate but generally harmless. Even though you should always use **Iterator** when you can in your own code, you must be prepared for libraries that want to hand you an **Enumeration**.

In addition, you can produce an **Enumeration** for any **Collection** by using the **Collections.enumeration( )** method, as seen in this example:

```
//: c11:Enumerations.java
// Java 1.0/1.1 Vector and Enumeration.
import java.util.*;
import com.bruceeckel.util.*;

public class Enumerations {
  public static void main(String[] args) {
    Vector v = new Vector();
    Collections2.fill(v, Collections2.countries, 100);
    Enumeration e = v.elements();
    while(e.hasMoreElements())
      System.out.println(e.nextElement());
    // Produce an Enumeration from a Collection:
    e = Collections.enumeration(new ArrayList());
  }
} ///:~
```

The Java 1.0/1.1 **Vector** has only an **addElement( )** method, but **fill( )** uses the **add( )** method that was pasted on while **Vector** was being turned into a **List**. To produce an **Enumeration**, you call **elements( )**, then you can use it to perform a forward iteration.

The last line creates an **ArrayList** and uses **enumeration( )** to adapt an **Enumeration** from the **ArrayList Iterator**. Thus, if you have old code that wants an **Enumeration**, you can still use the new containers.

Hashtable

As you've seen in the performance comparison in this chapter, the basic **Hashtable** is very similar to the **HashMap**, even down to the method names. There's no reason to use **Hashtable** instead of **HashMap** in new code.

Stack

The concept of the stack was introduced earlier, with the **LinkedList**. What's rather odd about the Java 1.0/1.1 **Stack** is that instead of using a **Vector** as a building block, **Stack** is *inherited* from **Vector**. So it has all of the characteristics and behaviors of a **Vector** plus some extra **Stack** behaviors. It's difficult to know whether the designers consciously thought that this was an especially useful way of doing things, or whether it was just a naïve design; in any event it was clearly not reviewed before it was rushed into distribution, so this bad design is *still* hanging around (but you should never use it).

Here's a simple demonstration of **Stack** that pushes each line from a **String** array:

```
//: c11:Stacks.java
// Demonstration of Stack Class.
import com.bruceeckel.simpletest.*;
import java.util.*;
import c08.Month;

public class Stacks {
  private static Test monitor = new Test();
  public static void main(String[] args) {
    Stack stack = new Stack();
    for(int i = 0; i < Month.month.length; i++)
      stack.push(Month.month[i] + " ");
    System.out.println("stack = " + stack);
    // Treating a stack as a Vector:
    stack.addElement("The last line");
    System.out.println("element 5 = " +
      stack.elementAt(5));
    System.out.println("popping elements:");
    while(!stack.empty())
      System.out.println(stack.pop());
    monitor.expect(new String[] {
      "stack = [January , February , March , April , May "+
        ", June , July , August , September , October , " +
        "November , December ]",
      "element 5 = June ",
      "popping elements:",
      "The last line",
      "December ",
      "November ",
      "October ",
```

```
      "September ",
      "August ",
      "July ",
      "June ",
      "May ",
      "April ",
      "March ",
      "February ",
      "January "
    });
  }
} ///:~
```

Each line in the **months** array is inserted into the **Stack** with **push( )**, and later fetched from the top of the stack with a **pop( )**. To make a point, **Vector** operations are also performed on the **Stack** object. This is possible because, by virtue of inheritance, a **Stack** *is* a **Vector**. Thus, all operations that can be performed on a **Vector** can also be performed on a **Stack**, such as **elementAt( )**.

As mentioned earlier, you should use a **LinkedList** when you want stack behavior.

BitSet

A **BitSet** is used if you want to efficiently store a lot of on-off information. It's efficient only from the standpoint of size; if you're looking for efficient access, it is slightly slower than using an array of some native type.

In addition, the minimum size of the **BitSet** is that of a **long**: 64 bits. This implies that if you're storing anything smaller, like 8 bits, a **BitSet** will be wasteful; you're better off creating your own class, or just an array, to hold your flags if size is an issue.

A normal container expands as you add more elements, and the **BitSet** does this as well. The following example shows how the **BitSet** works:

```
//: c11:Bits.java
// Demonstration of BitSet.
import java.util.*;

public class Bits {
  public static void printBitSet(BitSet b) {
    System.out.println("bits: " + b);
```

```
    String bbits = new String();
    for(int j = 0; j < b.size() ; j++)
      bbits += (b.get(j) ? "1" : "0");
    System.out.println("bit pattern: " + bbits);
  }
  public static void main(String[] args) {
    Random rand = new Random();
    // Take the LSB of nextInt():
    byte bt = (byte)rand.nextInt();
    BitSet bb = new BitSet();
    for(int i = 7; i >= 0; i--)
      if(((1 << i) &  bt) != 0)
        bb.set(i);
      else
        bb.clear(i);
    System.out.println("byte value: " + bt);
    printBitSet(bb);

    short st = (short)rand.nextInt();
    BitSet bs = new BitSet();
    for(int i = 15; i >= 0; i--)
      if(((1 << i) &  st) != 0)
        bs.set(i);
      else
        bs.clear(i);
    System.out.println("short value: " + st);
    printBitSet(bs);

    int it = rand.nextInt();
    BitSet bi = new BitSet();
    for(int i = 31; i >= 0; i--)
      if(((1 << i) &  it) != 0)
        bi.set(i);
      else
        bi.clear(i);
    System.out.println("int value: " + it);
    printBitSet(bi);

    // Test bitsets >= 64 bits:
    BitSet b127 = new BitSet();
    b127.set(127);
    System.out.println("set bit 127: " + b127);
    BitSet b255 = new BitSet(65);
    b255.set(255);
```

```
    System.out.println("set bit 255: " + b255);
    BitSet b1023 = new BitSet(512);
    b1023.set(1023);
    b1023.set(1024);
    System.out.println("set bit 1023: " + b1023);
  }
} ///:~
```

The random number generator is used to create a random **byte**, **short**, and **int**, and each one is transformed into a corresponding bit pattern in a **BitSet**. This works fine because a **BitSet** is 64 bits, so none of these cause it to increase in size. Then a **BitSet** of 512 bits is created. The constructor allocates storage for twice that number of bits. However, you can still set bit 1024 or greater.

Summary

To review the containers provided in the standard Java library:

1. An array associates numerical indices to objects. It holds objects of a known type so that you don't have to cast the result when you're looking up an object. It can be multidimensional, and it can hold primitives. However, its size cannot be changed once you create it.

2. A **Collection** holds single elements, and a **Map** holds associated pairs.

3. Like an array, a **List** also associates numerical indices to objects—you can think of arrays and **List**s as ordered containers. The **List** automatically resizes itself as you add more elements. But a **List** can hold only **Object reference**s, so it won't hold primitives, and you must always cast the result when you pull an **Object** reference out of a container.

4. Use an **ArrayList** if you're doing a lot of random accesses, but a **LinkedList** if you will be doing a lot of insertions and removals in the middle of the list.

5. The behavior of queues, deques, and stacks is provided via the **LinkedList**.

6. A **Map** is a way to associate not numbers, but *objects* with other objects. The design of a **HashMap** is focused on rapid access, whereas

a **TreeMap** keeps its keys in sorted order, and thus is not as fast as a **HashMap**. A **LinkedHashMap** keeps its elements in insertion order, but may also reorder them with its LRU algorithm.

7. A **Set** only accepts one of each type of object. **HashSet**s provide maximally fast lookups, whereas **TreeSet**s keep the elements in sorted order. **LinkedHashSet**s keep elements in insertion order.

8. There's no need to use the legacy classes **Vector**, **Hashtable**, and **Stack** in new code.

The containers are tools that you can use on a day-to-day basis to make your programs simpler, more powerful, and more effective.

Exercises

Solutions to selected exercises can be found in the electronic document *The Thinking in Java Annotated Solution Guide*, available for a small fee from *www.BruceEckel.com.*

1. Create an array of **double** and **fill( )** it using **RandDoubleGenerator**. Print the results.

2. Create a new class called **Gerbil** with an **int gerbilNumber** that's initialized in the constructor (similar to the **Mouse** example in this chapter). Give it a method called **hop( )** that prints out which gerbil number this is, and that it's hopping. Create an **ArrayList** and add a bunch of **Gerbil** objects to the **List**. Now use the **get( )** method to move through the **List** and call **hop( )** for each **Gerbil**.

3. Modify Exercise 2 so you use an **Iterator** to move through the **List** while calling **hop( )**.

4. Take the **Gerbil** class in Exercise 2 and put it into a **Map** instead, associating the name of the **Gerbil** as a **String** (the key) for each **Gerbil** (the value) you put in the table. Get an **Iterator** for the **keySet( )** and use it to move through the **Map**, looking up the **Gerbil** for each key and printing out the key and telling the **gerbil** to **hop( )**.

5. Create a **List** (try both **ArrayList** and **LinkedList**) and fill it using **Collections2.countries**. Sort the list and print it, then apply **Collections.shuffle( )** to the list repeatedly, printing it each time so

that you can see how the **shuffle( )** method randomizes the list differently each time.

6. Demonstrate that you can't add anything but a **Mouse** to a **MouseList**.

7. Modify **MouseList.java** so that it inherits from **ArrayList** instead of using composition. Demonstrate the problem with this approach.

8. Repair **CatsAndDogs.java** by creating a **Cats** container (utilizing **ArrayList**) that will only accept and retrieve **Cat** objects.

9. Fill a **HashMap** with key-value pairs. Print the results to show ordering by hash code. Extract the pairs, sort by key, and place the result into a **LinkedHashMap**. Show that the insertion order is maintained.

10. Repeat the previous example with a **HashSet** and **LinkedHashSet**.

11. Create a new type of container that uses a **private ArrayList** to hold the objects. Using a **Class** reference, capture the type of the first object you put in it, and then allow the user to insert objects of only that type from then on.

12. Create a container that encapsulates an array of **String**, and that only adds **String**s and gets **String**s, so that there are no casting issues during use. If the internal array isn't big enough for the next add, your container should automatically resize it. In **main( )**, compare the performance of your container with an **ArrayList** holding **String**s.

13. Repeat Exercise 12 for a container of **int**, and compare the performance to an **ArrayList** holding **Integer** objects. In your performance comparison, include the process of incrementing each object in the container.

14. Using the utilities in **com.bruceeckel.util**, create an array of each primitive type and of **String**, then fill each array by using an appropriate generator, and print each array using the appropriate **print( )** method.

15. Create a generator that produces character names from your favorite movies (you can use *Snow White* or *Star Wars* as a fallback) and loops around to the beginning when it runs out of names. Use the utilities in **com.bruceeckel.util** to fill an array, an **ArrayList**, a **LinkedList**, and both types of **Set**, then print each container.

16. Create a class containing two **String** objects and make it **Comparable** so that the comparison only cares about the first **String**. Fill an array and an **ArrayList** with objects of your class by using the **geography** generator. Demonstrate that sorting works properly. Now make a **Comparator** that only cares about the second **String** and demonstrate that sorting works properly. Also perform a binary search using your **Comparator**.

17. Modify Exercise 16 so that an alphabetic sort is used.

18. Use **Arrays2.RandStringGenerator** to fill a **TreeSet**, but by using alphabetic ordering. Print the **TreeSet** to verify the sort order.

19. Create both an **ArrayList** and a **LinkedList**, and fill each using the **Collections2.capitals** generator. Print each list using an ordinary **Iterator**, then insert one list into the other by using a **ListIterator**, inserting at every other location. Now perform the insertion starting at the end of the first list and moving backward.

20. Write a method that uses an **Iterator** to step through a **Collection** and print the **hashCode( )** of each object in the container. Fill all the different types of **Collection**s with objects and apply your method to each container.

21. Repair the problem in **InfiniteRecursion.java**.

22. Create a class, then make an initialized array of objects of your class. Fill a **List** from your array. Create a subset of your **List** by using **subList( )**, then remove this subset from your **List** by using **removeAll( )**.

23. Change Exercise 6 in Chapter 7 to use an **ArrayList** to hold the **Rodent**s and an **Iterator** to move through the sequence of **Rodent**s. Remember that an **ArrayList** holds only **Object**s, so you must use a cast when accessing individual **Rodent**s.

24. Following the **Queue.java** example, create a **Deque** class and test it.

25. Use a **TreeMap** in **Statistics.java**. Now add code that tests the performance difference between **HashMap** and **TreeMap** in that program.

26. Produce a **Map** and a **Set** containing all the countries that begin with "A."

27. Using **Collections2.countries**, fill a **Set** multiple times with the same data and verify that the **Set** ends up with only one of each instance. Try this with both kinds of **Set**.

28. Starting with **Statistics.java**, create a program that runs the test repeatedly and looks to see if any one number tends to appear more than the others in the results.

29. Rewrite **Statistics.java** using a **HashSet** of **Counter** objects (you'll have to modify **Counter** so that it will work in the **HashSet**). Which approach seems better?

30. Fill a **LinkedHashMap** with **String** keys and objects of your choice. Now extract the pairs, sort them based on the keys, and re-insert them into the **Map**.

31. Modify the class in Exercise 16 so that the class will work with **HashSet**s and as a key in **HashMap**s.

32. Using **SlowMap.java** for inspiration, create a **SlowSet**.

33. Create a **FastTraversalLinkedList** that internally uses a **LinkedList** for rapid insertions and removals, and an **ArrayList** for rapid traversals and **get( )** operations. Test it by modifying **ArrayPerformance.java**.

34. Apply the tests in **Map1.java** to **SlowMap** to verify that it works. Fix anything in **SlowMap** that doesn't work correctly.

35. Implement the rest of the **Map** interface for **SlowMap**.

36. Modify **MapPerformance.java** to include tests of **SlowMap**.

37. Modify **SlowMap** so that instead of two **ArrayList**s, it holds a single **ArrayList** of **MPair** objects. Verify that the modified version works correctly. Using **MapPerformance.java**, test the speed of your new **Map**. Now change the **put( )** method so that it performs a **sort( )** after each pair is entered, and modify **get( )** to use **Collections.binarySearch( )** to look up the key. Compare the performance of the new version with the old ones.

38. Add a **char** field to **CountedString** that is also initialized in the constructor, and modify the **hashCode( )** and **equals( )** methods to include the value of this **char**.

39. Modify **SimpleHashMap** so that it reports collisions, and test this by adding the same data set twice so that you see collisions.

40. Modify **SimpleHashMap** so that it reports the number of "probes" necessary when collisions occur. That is, how many calls to **next( )** must be made on the **Iterator**s that walk the **LinkedList**s looking for matches?

41. Implement the **clear( )** and **remove( )** methods for **SimpleHashMap**.

42. Implement the rest of the **Map** interface for **SimpleHashMap**.

43. Add a **private rehash( )** method to **SimpleHashMap** that is invoked when the load factor exceeds 0.75. During rehashing, double the number of buckets, then search for the first prime number greater than that to determine the new number of buckets.

44. Following the example in **SimpleHashMap.java**, create and test a **SimpleHashSet**.

45. Modify **SimpleHashMap** to use **ArrayList**s instead of **LinkedList**s. Modify **MapPerformance.java** to compare the performance of the two implementations.

46. Using the HTML documentation for the JDK (downloadable from *java.sun.com*), look up the **HashMap** class. Create a **HashMap**, fill it with elements, and determine the load factor. Test the lookup speed with this map, then attempt to increase the speed by making a new

HashMap with a larger initial capacity and copying the old map into the new one, then run your lookup speed test again on the new map.

47. In Chapter 8, locate the **GreenhouseController.java** example, which consists of four files. In **Controller.java**, the class **Controller** uses an **ArrayList**. Change the code to use a **LinkedList** instead, and use an **Iterator** to cycle through the set of events.

48. (Challenging). Write your own hashed map class, customized for a particular key type: **String** for this example. Do not inherit it from **Map**. Instead, duplicate the methods so that the **put( )** and **get( )** methods specifically take **String** objects, not **Object**s, as keys. Everything that involves keys should not use generic types; instead, work with **String**s to avoid the cost of upcasting and downcasting. Your goal is to make the fastest possible custom implementation. Modify **MapPerformance.java** to test your implementation versus a **HashMap**.

49. (Challenging). Find the source code for **List** in the Java source code library that comes with all Java distributions. Copy this code and make a special version called **intList** that holds only **int**s. Consider what it would take to make a special version of **List** for all the primitive types. Now consider what happens if you want to make a linked list class that works with all the primitive types.

50. Modify **c08:Month.java** to make it implement the **Comparable** interface.

51. Modify the **hashCode( )** in **CountedString.java** by removing the multiplication by **id**, and demonstrate that **CountedString** still works as a key. What is the problem with this approach?

12: The Java I/O System

Creating a good input/output (I/O) system is one of the more difficult tasks for the language designer.

This is evidenced by the number of different approaches. The challenge seems to be in covering all eventualities. Not only are there different sources and sinks of I/O that you want to communicate with (files, the console, network connections, etc.), but you need to talk to them in a wide variety of ways (sequential, random-access, buffered, binary, character, by lines, by words, etc.).

The Java library designers attacked this problem by creating lots of classes. In fact, there are so many classes for Java's I/O system that it can be intimidating at first (ironically, the Java I/O design actually prevents an explosion of classes). There was also a significant change in the I/O library after Java 1.0, when the original **byte**-oriented library was supplemented with **char**-oriented, Unicode-based I/O classes. In JDK 1.4, the **nio** classes (for "new I/O," a name we'll still be using years from now) were added for improved performance and functionality. As a result, there are a fair number of classes to learn before you understand enough of Java's I/O picture that you can use it properly. In addition, it's rather important to understand the evolution history of the I/O library, even if your first reaction is "don't bother me with history, just show me how to use it!" The problem is that without the historical perspective, you will rapidly become confused with some of the classes and when you should and shouldn't use them.

This chapter will give you an introduction to the variety of I/O classes in the standard Java library and how to use them.

The **File** class

Before getting into the classes that actually read and write data to streams, we'll look at a utility provided with the library to assist you in handling file directory issues.

The **File** class has a deceiving name; you might think it refers to a file, but it doesn't. It can represent either the *name* of a particular file or the *names* of a set of files in a directory. If it's a set of files, you can ask for that set using the **list( )** method, which returns an array of **String**. It makes sense to return an array rather than one of the flexible container classes, because the number of elements is fixed, and if you want a different directory listing, you just create a different **File** object. In fact, "FilePath" would have been a better name for the class. This section shows an example of the use of this class, including the associated **FilenameFilter interface**.

A directory lister

Suppose you'd like to see a directory listing. The **File** object can be listed in two ways. If you call **list( )** with no arguments, you'll get the full list that the **File** object contains. However, if you want a restricted list—for example, if you want all of the files with an extension of **.java**—then you use a "directory filter," which is a class that tells how to select the **File** objects for display.

Here's the code for the example. Note that the result has been effortlessly sorted (alphabetically) using the **java.utils.Arrays.sort( )** method and the **AlphabeticComparator** defined in Chapter 11:

```
//: c12:DirList.java
// Displays directory listing using regular expressions.
// {Args: "D.*\.java"}
import java.io.*;
import java.util.*;
import java.util.regex.*;
import com.bruceeckel.util.*;

public class DirList {
  public static void main(String[] args) {
    File path = new File(".");
    String[] list;
    if(args.length == 0)
      list = path.list();
```

```
    else
      list = path.list(new DirFilter(args[0]));
    Arrays.sort(list, new AlphabeticComparator());
    for(int i = 0; i < list.length; i++)
      System.out.println(list[i]);
  }
}

class DirFilter implements FilenameFilter {
  private Pattern pattern;
  public DirFilter(String regex) {
    pattern = Pattern.compile(regex);
  }
  public boolean accept(File dir, String name) {
    // Strip path information, search for regex:
    return pattern.matcher(
      new File(name).getName()).matches();
  }
} ///:~
```

The **DirFilter** class "implements" the **interface FilenameFilter**. It's useful to see how simple the **FilenameFilter interface** is:

```
public interface FilenameFilter {
  boolean accept(File dir, String name);
}
```

It says all that this type of object does is provide a method called **accept( )**. The whole reason behind the creation of this class is to provide the **accept( )** method to the **list( )** method so that **list( )** can "call back" **accept( )** to determine which file names should be included in the list. Thus, this structure is often referred to as a *callback*. More specifically, this is an example of the *Strategy Pattern*, because **list( )** implements basic functionality, and you provide the *Strategy* in the form of a **FilenameFilter** in order to complete the algorithm necessary for **list( )** to provide its service. Because **list( )** takes a **FilenameFilter** object as its argument, it means that you can pass an object of any class that implements **FilenameFilter** to choose (even at run time) how the **list( )** method will behave. The purpose of a callback is to provide flexibility in the behavior of code.

DirFilter shows that just because an **interface** contains only a set of methods, you're not restricted to writing only those methods. (You must at least provide definitions for all the methods in an interface, however.) In this case, the **DirFilter** constructor is also created.

The **accept( )** method must accept a **File** object representing the directory that a particular file is found in, and a **String** containing the name of that file. You might choose to use or ignore either of these arguments, but you will probably at least use the file name. Remember that the **list( )** method is calling **accept( )** for each of the file names in the directory object to see which one should be included; this is indicated by the **boolean** result returned by **accept( )**.

To make sure the element you're working with is only the file name and contains no path information, all you have to do is take the **String** object and create a **File** object out of it, then call **getName( )**, which strips away all the path information (in a platform-independent way). Then **accept( )** uses a regular expression **matcher** object to see if the regular expression **regex** matches the name of the file. Using **accept( )**, the **list( )** method returns an array.

Anonymous inner classes

This example is ideal for rewriting using an anonymous inner class (described in Chapter 8). As a first cut, a method **filter( )** is created that returns a reference to a **FilenameFilter**:

```
//: c12:DirList2.java
// Uses anonymous inner classes.
// {Args: "D.*\.java"}
import java.io.*;
import java.util.*;
import java.util.regex.*;
import com.bruceeckel.util.*;

public class DirList2 {
  public static FilenameFilter filter(final String regex) {
    // Creation of anonymous inner class:
    return new FilenameFilter() {
      private Pattern pattern = Pattern.compile(regex);
      public boolean accept(File dir, String name) {
        return pattern.matcher(
          new File(name).getName()).matches();
      }
    }; // End of anonymous inner class
```

```
  }
  public static void main(String[] args) {
    File path = new File(".");
    String[] list;
    if(args.length == 0)
      list = path.list();
    else
      list = path.list(filter(args[0]));
    Arrays.sort(list, new AlphabeticComparator());
    for(int i = 0; i < list.length; i++)
      System.out.println(list[i]);
  }
} ///:~
```

Note that the argument to **filter( )** must be **final**. This is required by the anonymous inner class so that it can use an object from outside its scope.

This design is an improvement because the **FilenameFilter** class is now tightly bound to **DirList2**. However, you can take this approach one step further and define the anonymous inner class as an argument to **list( )**, in which case it's even smaller:

```
//: c12:DirList3.java
// Building the anonymous inner class "in-place."
// {Args: "D.*\.java"}
import java.io.*;
import java.util.*;
import java.util.regex.*;
import com.bruceeckel.util.*;

public class DirList3 {
  public static void main(final String[] args) {
    File path = new File(".");
    String[] list;
    if(args.length == 0)
      list = path.list();
    else
      list = path.list(new FilenameFilter() {
        private Pattern pattern = Pattern.compile(args[0]);
        public boolean accept(File dir, String name) {
          return pattern.matcher(
            new File(name).getName()).matches();
        }
      });
    Arrays.sort(list, new AlphabeticComparator());
```

```
    for(int i = 0; i < list.length; i++)
      System.out.println(list[i]);
  }
} ///:~
```

The argument to **main( )** is now **final**, since the anonymous inner class uses **args[0]** directly.

This shows you how anonymous inner classes allow the creation of specific, one-off classes to solve problems. One benefit of this approach is that it keeps the code that solves a particular problem isolated together in one spot. On the other hand, it is not always as easy to read, so you must use it judiciously.

Checking for and creating directories

The **File** class is more than just a representation for an existing file or directory. You can also use a **File** object to create a new directory or an entire directory path if it doesn't exist. You can also look at the characteristics of files (size, last modification date, read/write), see whether a **File** object represents a file or a directory, and delete a file. This program shows some of the other methods available with the **File** class (see the HTML documentation from *java.sun.com* for the full set):

```
//: c12:MakeDirectories.java
// Demonstrates the use of the File class to
// create directories and manipulate files.
// {Args: MakeDirectoriesTest}
import com.bruceeckel.simpletest.*;
import java.io.*;

public class MakeDirectories {
  private static Test monitor = new Test();
  private static void usage() {
    System.err.println(
      "Usage:MakeDirectories path1 ...\n" +
      "Creates each path\n" +
      "Usage:MakeDirectories -d path1 ...\n" +
      "Deletes each path\n" +
      "Usage:MakeDirectories -r path1 path2\n" +
      "Renames from path1 to path2");
    System.exit(1);
  }
  private static void fileData(File f) {
    System.out.println(
```

```
      "Absolute path: " + f.getAbsolutePath() +
      "\n Can read: " + f.canRead() +
      "\n Can write: " + f.canWrite() +
      "\n getName: " + f.getName() +
      "\n getParent: " + f.getParent() +
      "\n getPath: " + f.getPath() +
      "\n length: " + f.length() +
      "\n lastModified: " + f.lastModified());
    if(f.isFile())
      System.out.println("It's a file");
    else if(f.isDirectory())
      System.out.println("It's a directory");
  }
  public static void main(String[] args) {
    if(args.length < 1) usage();
    if(args[0].equals("-r")) {
      if(args.length != 3) usage();
      File
        old = new File(args[1]),
        rname = new File(args[2]);
      old.renameTo(rname);
      fileData(old);
      fileData(rname);
      return; // Exit main
    }
    int count = 0;
    boolean del = false;
    if(args[0].equals("-d")) {
      count++;
      del = true;
    }
    count--;
    while(++count < args.length) {
      File f = new File(args[count]);
      if(f.exists()) {
        System.out.println(f + " exists");
        if(del) {
          System.out.println("deleting..." + f);
          f.delete();
        }
      }
      else { // Doesn't exist
        if(!del) {
          f.mkdirs();
```

```
          System.out.println("created " + f);
        }
      }
      fileData(f);
    }
    if(args.length == 1 &&
       args[0].equals("MakeDirectoriesTest"))
      monitor.expect(new String[] {
        "%% (MakeDirectoriesTest exists"+
          "|created MakeDirectoriesTest)",
        "%% Absolute path: "
          + "\\S+MakeDirectoriesTest",
        "%%  Can read: (true|false)",
        "%%  Can write: (true|false)",
        " getName: MakeDirectoriesTest",
        " getParent: null",
        " getPath: MakeDirectoriesTest",
        "%%  length: \\d+",
        "%%  lastModified: \\d+",
        "It's a directory"
      });
  }
} ///:~
```

In **fileData( )** you can see various file investigation methods used to display information about the file or directory path.

The first method that's exercised by **main( )** is **renameTo( )**, which allows you to rename (or move) a file to an entirely new path represented by the argument, which is another **File** object. This also works with directories of any length.

If you experiment with the preceding program, you'll find that you can make a directory path of any complexity, because **mkdirs( )** will do all the work for you.

Input and output

I/O libraries often use the abstraction of a *stream*, which represents any data source or sink as an object capable of producing or receiving pieces of data. The stream hides the details of what happens to the data inside the actual I/O device.

The Java library classes for I/O are divided by input and output, as you can see by looking at the class hierarchy in the JDK documentation. By inheritance, everything derived from the **InputStream** or **Reader** classes have basic methods called **read( )** for reading a single byte or array of bytes. Likewise, everything derived from **OutputStream** or **Writer** classes have basic methods called **write( )** for writing a single byte or array of bytes. However, you won't generally use these methods; they exist so that other classes can use them—these other classes provide a more useful interface. Thus, you'll rarely create your stream object by using a single class, but instead will layer multiple objects together to provide your desired functionality. The fact that you create more than one object to create a single resulting stream is the primary reason that Java's stream library is confusing.

It's helpful to categorize the classes by their functionality. In Java 1.0, the library designers started by deciding that all classes that had anything to do with input would be inherited from **InputStream**, and all classes that were associated with output would be inherited from **OutputStream**.

Types of **InputStream**

InputStream's job is to represent classes that produce input from different sources. These sources can be:

1. An array of bytes.
2. A **String** object.
3. A file.
4. A "pipe," which works like a physical pipe: You put things in at one end and they come out the other.
5. A sequence of other streams, so you can collect them together into a single stream.
6. Other sources, such as an Internet connection. (This is covered in *Thinking in Enterprise Java*.)

Each of these has an associated subclass of **InputStream**. In addition, the **FilterInputStream** is also a type of **InputStream**, to provide a base class for "decorator" classes that attach attributes or useful interfaces to input streams. This is discussed later.

Table 12-1. Types of InputStream

Class	Function	Constructor Arguments
		How to use it
ByteArray-InputStream	Allows a buffer in memory to be used as an **InputStream**.	The buffer from which to extract the bytes.
		As a source of data: Connect it to a **FilterInputStream** object to provide a useful interface.
StringBuffer-InputStream	Converts a **String** into an **InputStream**.	A **String**. The underlying implementation actually uses a **StringBuffer**.
		As a source of data: Connect it to a **FilterInputStream** object to provide a useful interface.
File-InputStream	For reading information from a file.	A **String** representing the file name, or a **File** or **FileDescriptor** object.
		As a source of data: Connect it to a **FilterInputStream** object to provide a useful interface.
Piped-InputStream	Produces the data that's being written to the associated **PipedOutput-Stream**. Implements the "piping" concept.	**PipedOutputStream**
		As a source of data in multithreading: Connect it to a **FilterInputStream** object to provide a useful interface.
Sequence-InputStream	Converts two or more **InputStream** objects into a single	Two **InputStream** objects or an **Enumeration** for a container of **InputStream** objects.

Class	Function	Constructor Arguments
		How to use it
	InputStream.	As a source of data: Connect it to a **FilterInputStream** object to provide a useful interface.
Filter-InputStream	Abstract class that is an interface for decorators that provide useful functionality to the other **InputStream** classes. See Table 12-3.	See Table 12-3.
		See Table 12-3.

Types of **OutputStream**

This category includes the classes that decide where your output will go: an array of bytes (no **String**, however; presumably, you can create one using the array of bytes), a file, or a "pipe."

In addition, the **FilterOutputStream** provides a base class for "decorator" classes that attach attributes or useful interfaces to output streams. This is discussed later.

Table 12-2. Types of OutputStream

Class	Function	Constructor Arguments
		How to use it
ByteArray-OutputStream	Creates a buffer in memory. All the data that you send to the stream is placed in this buffer.	Optional initial size of the buffer.
		To designate the destination of your data: Connect it to a **FilterOutputStream** object to provide a useful interface.

Class	Function	Constructor Arguments How to use it
File-OutputStream	For sending information to a file.	A String representing the file name, or a **File** or **FileDescriptor** object. To designate the destination of your data: Connect it to a **FilterOutputStream** object to provide a useful interface.
Piped-OutputStream	Any information you write to this automatically ends up as input for the associated **PipedInput-Stream**. Implements the "piping" concept.	**PipedInputStream** To designate the destination of your data for multithreading: Connect it to a **FilterOutputStream** object to provide a useful interface.
Filter-OutputStream	Abstract class that is an interface for decorators that provide useful functionality to the other **OutputStream** classes. See Table 12-4.	See Table 12-4. See Table 12-4.

Adding attributes and useful interfaces

The use of layered objects to dynamically and transparently add responsibilities to individual objects is referred to as the *Decorator* pattern. (Patterns[1] are the subject of *Thinking in Patterns (with Java)* at

[1] *Design Patterns*, Erich Gamma *et al.*, Addison-Wesley 1995.

www.BruceEckel.com.) The decorator pattern specifies that all objects that wrap around your initial object have the same interface. This makes the basic use of the decorators transparent—you send the same message to an object whether it has been decorated or not. This is the reason for the existence of the "filter" classes in the Java I/O library: The abstract "filter" class is the base class for all the decorators. (A decorator must have the same interface as the object it decorates, but the decorator can also extend the interface, which occurs in several of the "filter" classes).

Decorators are often used when simple subclassing results in a large number of classes in order to satisfy every possible combination that is needed—so many classes that it becomes impractical. The Java I/O library requires many different combinations of features, and this is the justification for using the decorator pattern.[2] There is a drawback to the decorator pattern, however. Decorators give you much more flexibility while you're writing a program (since you can easily mix and match attributes), but they add complexity to your code. The reason that the Java I/O library is awkward to use is that you must create many classes—the "core" I/O type plus all the decorators—in order to get the single I/O object that you want.

The classes that provide the decorator interface to control a particular **InputStream** or **OutputStream** are the **FilterInputStream** and **FilterOutputStream**, which don't have very intuitive names. **FilterInputStream** and **FilterOutputStream** are derived from the base classes of the I/O library, **InputStream** and **OutputStream**, which is the key requirement of the decorator (so that it provides the common interface to all the objects that are being decorated).

Reading from an **InputStream** with **FilterInputStream**

The **FilterInputStream** classes accomplish two significantly different things. **DataInputStream** allows you to read different types of primitive data as well as **String** objects. (All the methods start with "read," such as **readByte( )**, **readFloat( )**, etc.) This, along with its companion **DataOutputStream**, allows you to move primitive data from one place to

---

[2] It's not clear that this was a good design decision, especially compared to the simplicity of I/O libraries in other languages. But it's the justification for the decision.

another via a stream. These "places" are determined by the classes in Table 12-1.

The remaining classes modify the way an **InputStream** behaves internally: whether it's buffered or unbuffered, if it keeps track of the lines it's reading (allowing you to ask for line numbers or set the line number), and whether you can push back a single character. The last two classes look a lot like support for building a compiler (that is, they were probably added to support the construction of the Java compiler), so you probably won't use them in general programming.

You'll need to buffer your input almost every time, regardless of the I/O device you're connecting to, so it would have made more sense for the I/O library to make a special case (or simply a method call) for unbuffered input rather than buffered input.

Table 12-3. Types of FilterInputStream

Class	Function	Constructor Arguments How to use it
Data-InputStream	Used in concert with **DataOutputStream**, so you can read primitives (**int**, **char**, **long**, etc.) from a stream in a portable fashion.	**InputStream** Contains a full interface to allow you to read primitive types.
Buffered-InputStream	Use this to prevent a physical read every time you want more data. You're saying "Use a buffer."	**InputStream**, with optional buffer size. This doesn't provide an interface *per se*, just a requirement that a buffer be used. Attach an interface object.
LineNumber-InputStream	Keeps track of line numbers in the input stream; you can call	**InputStream**

	getLineNumber( ) and **setLineNumber(int)**.	This just adds line numbering, so you'll probably attach an interface object.
Pushback-InputStream	Has a one byte push-back buffer so that you can push back the last character read.	**InputStream**
		Generally used in the scanner for a compiler and probably included because the Java compiler needed it. You probably won't use this.

Writing to an **OutputStream** with **FilterOutputStream**

The complement to **DataInputStream** is **DataOutputStream**, which formats each of the primitive types and **String** objects onto a stream in such a way that any **DataInputStream**, on any machine, can read them. All the methods start with "write," such as **writeByte( )**, **writeFloat( )**, etc.

The original intent of **PrintStream** was to print all of the primitive data types and **String** objects in a viewable format. This is different from **DataOutputStream**, whose goal is to put data elements on a stream in a way that **DataInputStream** can portably reconstruct them.

The two important methods in **PrintStream** are **print( )** and **println( )**, which are overloaded to print all the various types. The difference between **print( )** and **println( )** is that the latter adds a newline when it's done.

PrintStream can be problematic because it traps all **IOException**s (You must explicitly test the error status with **checkError( )**, which returns **true** if an error has occurred). Also, **PrintStream** doesn't internationalize properly and doesn't handle line breaks in a platform-independent way (these problems are solved with **PrintWriter**, described later).

BufferedOutputStream is a modifier and tells the stream to use buffering so you don't get a physical write every time you write to the stream. You'll probably always want to use this when doing output.

Table 12-4. Types of FilterOutputStream

Class	Function	Constructor Arguments How to use it
Data-OutputStream	Used in concert with **DataInputStream** so you can write primitives (int, char, long, etc.) to a stream in a portable fashion.	**OutputStream** Contains full interface to allow you to write primitive types.
PrintStream	For producing formatted output. While **DataOutputStream** handles the *storage* of data, **PrintStream** handles *display*.	**OutputStream**, with optional **boolean** indicating that the buffer is flushed with every newline. Should be the "final" wrapping for your **OutputStream** object. You'll probably use this a lot.
Buffered-OutputStream	Use this to prevent a physical write every time you send a piece of data. You're saying "Use a buffer." You can call **flush( )** to flush the buffer.	**OutputStream**, with optional buffer size. This doesn't provide an interface *per se*, just a requirement that a buffer is used. Attach an interface object.

Readers & Writers

Java 1.1 made some significant modifications to the fundamental I/O stream library. When you see the **Reader** and **Writer** classes, your first thought (like mine) might be that these were meant to replace the **InputStream** and **OutputStream** classes. But that's not the case. Although some aspects of the original streams library are deprecated (if you use them you will receive a warning from the compiler), the **InputStream** and **OutputStream** classes still provide valuable functionality in the form of **byte**-oriented I/O, whereas the **Reader** and **Writer** classes provide Unicode-compliant, character-based I/O. In addition:

1. Java 1.1 added new classes into the **InputStream** and **OutputStream** hierarchy, so it's obvious those hierarchies weren't being replaced.

2. There are times when you must use classes from the "byte" hierarchy *in combination* with classes in the "character" hierarchy. To accomplish this, there are "adapter" classes: **InputStreamReader** converts an **InputStream** to a **Reader** and **OutputStreamWriter** converts an **OutputStream** to a **Writer**.

The most important reason for the **Reader** and **Writer** hierarchies is for internationalization. The old I/O stream hierarchy supports only 8-bit byte streams and doesn't handle the 16-bit Unicode characters well. Since Unicode is used for internationalization (and Java's native **char** is 16-bit Unicode), the **Reader** and **Writer** hierarchies were added to support Unicode in all I/O operations. In addition, the new libraries are designed for faster operations than the old.

As is the practice in this book, I will attempt to provide an overview of the classes, but assume that you will use the JDK documentation to determine all the details, such as the exhaustive list of methods.

Sources and sinks of data

Almost all of the original Java I/O stream classes have corresponding **Reader** and **Writer** classes to provide native Unicode manipulation. However, there are some places where the **byte**-oriented **InputStream**s and **OutputStream**s are the correct solution; in particular, the **java.util.zip** libraries are **byte**-oriented rather than **char**-oriented. So the most sensible approach to take is to *try* to use the **Reader** and **Writer** classes whenever you can, and you'll discover the situations when you have to use the **byte**-oriented libraries, because your code won't compile.

Here is a table that shows the correspondence between the sources and sinks of information (that is, where the data physically comes from or goes to) in the two hierarchies.

Sources & Sinks:	**Corresponding Java 1.1 class**

Java 1.0 class	
InputStream	**Reader** adapter: **InputStreamReader**
OutputStream	**Writer** adapter: **OutputStreamWriter**
FileInputStream	**FileReader**
FileOutputStream	**FileWriter**
StringBufferInputStream	**StringReader**
(no corresponding class)	**StringWriter**
ByteArrayInputStream	**CharArrayReader**
ByteArrayOutputStream	**CharArrayWriter**
PipedInputStream	**PipedReader**
PipedOutputStream	**PipedWriter**

In general, you'll find that the interfaces for the two different hierarchies are similar if not identical.

Modifying stream behavior

For **InputStream**s and **OutputStream**s, streams were adapted for particular needs using "decorator" subclasses of **FilterInputStream** and **FilterOutputStream.** The **Reader** and **Writer** class hierarchies continue the use of this idea—but not exactly.

In the following table, the correspondence is a rougher approximation than in the previous table. The difference is because of the class organization; although **BufferedOutputStream** is a subclass of **FilterOutputStream**, **BufferedWriter** is *not* a subclass of **FilterWriter** (which, even though it is **abstract**, has no subclasses and so appears to have been put in either as a placeholder or simply so you wouldn't wonder where it was). However, the interfaces to the classes are quite a close match.

Filters: Java 1.0 class	Corresponding Java 1.1 class
FilterInputStream	**FilterReader**
FilterOutputStream	**FilterWriter** (abstract class with no

Filters: Java 1.0 class	Corresponding Java 1.1 class
	subclasses)
BufferedInputStream	**BufferedReader** (also has **readLine( )**)
BufferedOutputStream	**BufferedWriter**
DataInputStream	Use **DataInputStream** (except when you need to use **readLine( )**, when you should use a **BufferedReader**)
PrintStream	**PrintWriter**
LineNumberInputStream (deprecated)	**LineNumberReader**
StreamTokenizer	**StreamTokenizer** (use constructor that takes a **Reader** instead)
PushBackInputStream	**PushBackReader**

There's one direction that's quite clear: Whenever you want to use **readLine( )**, you shouldn't do it with a **DataInputStream** (this is met with a deprecation message at compile time), but instead use a **BufferedReader**. Other than this, **DataInputStream** is still a "preferred" member of the I/O library.

To make the transition to using a **PrintWriter** easier, it has constructors that take any **OutputStream** object as well as **Writer** objects. However, **PrintWriter** has no more support for formatting than **PrintStream** does; the interfaces are virtually the same.

The **PrintWriter** constructor also has an option to perform automatic flushing, which happens after every **println( )** if the constructor flag is set.

Unchanged Classes

Some classes were left unchanged between Java 1.0 and Java 1.1:

Java 1.0 classes without corresponding Java 1.1 classes
DataOutputStream

Java 1.0 classes without corresponding Java 1.1 classes
File
RandomAccessFile
SequenceInputStream

DataOutputStream, in particular, is used without change, so for storing and retrieving data in a transportable format, you use the **InputStream** and **OutputStream** hierarchies.

Off by itself: RandomAccessFile

RandomAccessFile is used for files containing records of known size so that you can move from one record to another using **seek( )**, then read or change the records. The records don't have to be the same size; you just have to be able to determine how big they are and where they are placed in the file.

At first it's a little bit hard to believe that **RandomAccessFile** is not part of the **InputStream** or **OutputStream** hierarchy. However, it has no association with those hierarchies other than that it happens to implement the **DataInput** and **DataOutput** interfaces (which are also implemented by **DataInputStream** and **DataOutputStream**). It doesn't even use any of the functionality of the existing **InputStream** or **OutputStream** classes; it's a completely separate class, written from scratch, with all of its own (mostly native) methods. The reason for this may be that **RandomAccessFile** has essentially different behavior than the other I/O types, since you can move forward and backward within a file. In any event, it stands alone, as a direct descendant of **Object**.

Essentially, a **RandomAccessFile** works like a **DataInputStream** pasted together with a **DataOutputStream**, along with the methods **getFilePointer( )** to find out where you are in the file, **seek( )** to move to a new point in the file, and **length( )** to determine the maximum size of the file. In addition, the constructors require a second argument (identical to **fopen( )** in C) indicating whether you are just randomly reading (**"r"**) or reading and writing (**"rw"**). There's no support for write-only files, which could suggest that **RandomAccessFile** might have worked well if it were inherited from **DataInputStream**.

The seeking methods are available only in **RandomAccessFile**, which works for files only. **BufferedInputStream** does allow you to **mark( )** a position (whose value is held in a single internal variable) and **reset( )** to that position, but this is limited and not very useful.

Most, if not all, of the **RandomAccessFile** functionality is superceded in JDK 1.4 with the **nio** *memory-mapped files*, which will be described later in this chapter.

Typical uses of I/O streams

Although you can combine the I/O stream classes in many different ways, you'll probably just use a few combinations. The following example can be used as a basic reference; it shows the creation and use of typical I/O configurations. Note that each configuration begins with a commented number and title that corresponds to the heading for the appropriate explanation that follows in the text.

```
//: c12:IOStreamDemo.java
// Typical I/O stream configurations.
// {RunByHand}
// {Clean: IODemo.out,Data.txt,rtest.dat}
import com.bruceeckel.simpletest.*;
import java.io.*;

public class IOStreamDemo {
  private static Test monitor = new Test();
  // Throw exceptions to console:
  public static void main(String[] args)
  throws IOException {
    // 1. Reading input by lines:
    BufferedReader in = new BufferedReader(
      new FileReader("IOStreamDemo.java"));
    String s, s2 = new String();
    while((s = in.readLine())!= null)
      s2 += s + "\n";
    in.close();

    // 1b. Reading standard input:
    BufferedReader stdin = new BufferedReader(
      new InputStreamReader(System.in));
    System.out.print("Enter a line:");
    System.out.println(stdin.readLine());
```

```
    // 2. Input from memory
    StringReader in2 = new StringReader(s2);
    int c;
    while((c = in2.read()) != -1)
      System.out.print((char)c);

    // 3. Formatted memory input
    try {
      DataInputStream in3 = new DataInputStream(
        new ByteArrayInputStream(s2.getBytes()));
      while(true)
        System.out.print((char)in3.readByte());
    } catch(EOFException e) {
      System.err.println("End of stream");
    }

    // 4. File output
    try {
      BufferedReader in4 = new BufferedReader(
        new StringReader(s2));
      PrintWriter out1 = new PrintWriter(
        new BufferedWriter(new FileWriter("IODemo.out")));
      int lineCount = 1;
      while((s = in4.readLine()) != null )
        out1.println(lineCount++ + ": " + s);
      out1.close();
    } catch(EOFException e) {
      System.err.println("End of stream");
    }

    // 5. Storing & recovering data
    try {
      DataOutputStream out2 = new DataOutputStream(
        new BufferedOutputStream(
          new FileOutputStream("Data.txt")));
      out2.writeDouble(3.14159);
      out2.writeUTF("That was pi");
      out2.writeDouble(1.41413);
      out2.writeUTF("Square root of 2");
      out2.close();
      DataInputStream in5 = new DataInputStream(
        new BufferedInputStream(
          new FileInputStream("Data.txt")));
```

```
      // Must use DataInputStream for data:
      System.out.println(in5.readDouble());
      // Only readUTF() will recover the
      // Java-UTF String properly:
      System.out.println(in5.readUTF());
      // Read the following double and String:
      System.out.println(in5.readDouble());
      System.out.println(in5.readUTF());
    } catch(EOFException e) {
      throw new RuntimeException(e);
    }

    // 6. Reading/writing random access files
    RandomAccessFile rf =
      new RandomAccessFile("rtest.dat", "rw");
    for(int i = 0; i < 10; i++)
      rf.writeDouble(i*1.414);
    rf.close();
    rf = new RandomAccessFile("rtest.dat", "rw");
    rf.seek(5*8);
    rf.writeDouble(47.0001);
    rf.close();
    rf = new RandomAccessFile("rtest.dat", "r");
    for(int i = 0; i < 10; i++)
      System.out.println("Value " + i + ": " +
        rf.readDouble());
    rf.close();
    monitor.expect("IOStreamDemo.out");
  }
} ///:~
```

Here are the descriptions for the numbered sections of the program:

Input streams

Parts 1 through 4 demonstrate the creation and use of input streams. Part 4 also shows the simple use of an output stream.

1. Buffered input file

To open a file for character input, you use a **FileInputReader** with a **String** or a **File** object as the file name. For speed, you'll want that file to be buffered so you give the resulting reference to the constructor for a **BufferedReader**. Since **BufferedReader** also provides the **readLine( )** method, this is your final object and the interface you read from. When you reach the end of the file, **readLine( )** returns **null** so that is used to break out of the **while** loop.

The **String s2** is used to accumulate the entire contents of the file (including newlines that must be added since **readLine( )** strips them off). **s2** is then used in the later portions of this program. Finally, **close( )** is called to close the file. Technically, **close( )** will be called when **finalize( )** runs, and this is supposed to happen (whether or not garbage collection occurs) as the program exits. However, this has been inconsistently implemented, so the only safe approach is to explicitly call **close( )** for files.

Section 1b shows how you can wrap **System.in** for reading console input. **System.in** is an **InputStream**, and **BufferedReader** needs a **Reader** argument, so **InputStreamReader** is brought in to perform the adaptation.

2. Input from memory

This section takes the **String s2** that now contains the entire contents of the file and uses it to create a **StringReader**. Then **read( )** is used to read each character one at a time and send it out to the console. Note that **read( )** returns the next byte as an **int** and thus it must be cast to a **char** to print properly.

3. Formatted memory input

To read "formatted" data, you use a **DataInputStream**, which is a **byte**-oriented I/O class (rather than **char**-oriented). Thus you must use all **InputStream** classes rather than **Reader** classes. Of course, you can read anything (such as a file) as bytes using **InputStream** classes, but here a **String** is used. To convert the **String** to an array of bytes, which is what is appropriate for a **ByteArrayInputStream**, **String** has a **getBytes( )** method to do the job. At that point, you have an appropriate **InputStream** to hand to **DataInputStream**.

If you read the characters from a **DataInputStream** one byte at a time using **readByte( )**, any byte value is a legitimate result, so the return value cannot be used to detect the end of input. Instead, you can use the **available( )** method to find out how many more characters are available. Here's an example that shows how to read a file one byte at a time:

```
//: c12:TestEOF.java
// Testing for end of file while reading a byte at a time.
import java.io.*;
```

```java
public class TestEOF {
  // Throw exceptions to console:
  public static void main(String[] args)
  throws IOException {
    DataInputStream in = new DataInputStream(
      new BufferedInputStream(
        new FileInputStream("TestEOF.java")));
    while(in.available() != 0)
      System.out.print((char)in.readByte());
  }
} ///:~
```

Note that **available( )** works differently depending on what sort of medium you're reading from; it's literally "the number of bytes that can be read *without blocking*." With a file, this means the whole file, but with a different kind of stream this might not be true, so use it thoughtfully.

You could also detect the end of input in cases like these by catching an exception. However, the use of exceptions for control flow is considered a misuse of that feature.

4. File output

This example also shows how to write data to a file. First, a **FileWriter** is created to connect to the file. You'll virtually always want to buffer the output by wrapping it in a **BufferedWriter** (try removing this wrapping to see the impact on the performance—buffering tends to dramatically increase performance of I/O operations). Then for the formatting it's turned into a **PrintWriter**. The data file created this way is readable as an ordinary text file.

As the lines are written to the file, line numbers are added. Note that **LineNumberInputStream** is *not* used, because it's a silly class and you don't need it. As shown here, it's trivial to keep track of your own line numbers.

When the input stream is exhausted, **readLine( )** returns **null**. You'll see an explicit **close( )** for **out1**, because if you don't call **close( )** for all your output files, you might discover that the buffers don't get flushed, so they're incomplete.

Output streams

The two primary kinds of output streams are separated by the way they write data; one writes it for human consumption, and the other writes it to be reacquired by a **DataInputStream**. The **RandomAccessFile** stands alone, although its data format is compatible with the **DataInputStream** and **DataOutputStream**.

5. Storing and recovering data

A **PrintWriter** formats data so that it's readable by a human. However, to output data for recovery by another stream, you use a **DataOutputStream** to write the data and a **DataInputStream** to recover the data. Of course, these streams could be anything, but here a file is used, buffered for both reading and writing. **DataOutputStream** and **DataInputStream** are **byte**-oriented and thus require the **InputStream**s and **OutputStream**s.

If you use a **DataOutputStream** to write the data, then Java guarantees that you can accurately recover the data using a **DataInputStream**—regardless of what different platforms write and read the data. This is incredibly valuable, as anyone knows who has spent time worrying about platform-specific data issues. That problem vanishes if you have Java on both platforms.[3]

When using a **DataOutputStream**, the only reliable way to write a **String** so that it can be recovered by a **DataInputStream** is to use UTF-8 encoding, accomplished in section 5 of the example using **writeUTF( )** and **readUTF( )**. UTF-8 is a variation on Unicode, which stores all characters in two bytes. If you're working with ASCII or mostly ASCII characters (which occupy only seven bits), this is a tremendous waste of space and/or bandwidth, so UTF-8 encodes ASCII characters in a single byte, and non-ASCII characters in two or three bytes. In addition, the length of the string is stored in the first two bytes. However, **writeUTF( )** and **readUTF( )** use a special variation of UTF-8 for Java (which is completely described in the JDK documentation for those methods) , so if you read a string written with

---

3 XML is another way to solve the problem of moving data across different computing platforms, and does not depend on having Java on all platforms. JDK 1.4 contains XML tools in **javax.xml.*** libraries. These are covered in *Thinking in Enterprise Java*, at *www.MindView.net.*

writeUTF( ) using a non-Java program, you must write special code in order to read the string properly.

With **writeUTF( )** and **readUTF( )**, you can intermingle **String**s and other types of data using a **DataOutputStream** with the knowledge that the **String**s will be properly stored as Unicode, and will be easily recoverable with a **DataInputStream**.

The **writeDouble( )** stores the **double** number to the stream and the complementary **readDouble( )** recovers it (there are similar methods for reading and writing the other types). But for any of the reading methods to work correctly, you must know the exact placement of the data item in the stream, since it would be equally possible to read the stored **double** as a simple sequence of bytes, or as a **char**, etc. So you must either have a fixed format for the data in the file, or extra information must be stored in the file that you parse to determine where the data is located. Note that object serialization (described later in this chapter) may be an easier way to store and retrieve complex data structures.

6. Reading and writing random access files

As previously noted, the **RandomAccessFile** is almost totally isolated from the rest of the I/O hierarchy, save for the fact that it implements the **DataInput** and **DataOutput** interfaces. So you cannot combine it with any of the aspects of the **InputStream** and **OutputStream** subclasses. Even though it might make sense to treat a **ByteArrayInputStream** as a random-access element, you can use **RandomAccessFile** only to open a file. You must assume a **RandomAccessFile** is properly buffered since you cannot add that.

The one option you have is in the second constructor argument: you can open a **RandomAccessFile** to read (**"r"**) or read and write (**"rw"**).

Using a **RandomAccessFile** is like using a combined **DataInputStream** and **DataOutputStream** (because it implements the equivalent interfaces). In addition, you can see that **seek( )** is used to move about in the file and change one of the values.

With the advent of new I/O in JDK 1.4, you may want to consider using memory-mapped files instead of **RandomAccessFile**.

Piped streams

The **PipedInputStream**, **PipedOutputStream**, **PipedReader** and **PipedWriter** have been mentioned only briefly in this chapter. This is not to suggest that they aren't useful, but their value is not apparent until you begin to understand multithreading, since the piped streams are used to communicate between threads. This is covered along with an example in Chapter 13.

File reading & writing utilities

A very common programming task is to read a file into memory, modify it, and then write it out again. One of the problems with the Java I/O library is that it requires you to write quite a bit of code in order to perform these common operations—there are no basic helper function to do them for you. What's worse, the decorators make it rather hard to remember how to open files. Thus, it makes sense to add helper classes to your library that will easily perform these basic tasks for you. Here's one that contains **static** methods to read and write text files as a single string. In addition, you can create a **TextFile** class that holds the lines of the file in an **ArrayList** (so you have all the **ArrayList** functionality available while manipulating the file contents):

```
//: com:bruceeckel:util:TextFile.java
// Static functions for reading and writing text files as
// a single string, and treating a file as an ArrayList.
// {Clean: test.txt test2.txt}
package com.bruceeckel.util;
import java.io.*;
import java.util.*;

public class TextFile extends ArrayList {
  // Tools to read and write files as single strings:
  public static String
  read(String fileName) throws IOException {
    StringBuffer sb = new StringBuffer();
    BufferedReader in =
      new BufferedReader(new FileReader(fileName));
    String s;
    while((s = in.readLine()) != null) {
      sb.append(s);
      sb.append("\n");
    }
```

```
    in.close();
    return sb.toString();
  }
  public static void
  write(String fileName, String text) throws IOException {
    PrintWriter out = new PrintWriter(
      new BufferedWriter(new FileWriter(fileName)));
    out.print(text);
    out.close();
  }
  public TextFile(String fileName) throws IOException {
    super(Arrays.asList(read(fileName).split("\n")));
  }
  public void write(String fileName) throws IOException {
    PrintWriter out = new PrintWriter(
      new BufferedWriter(new FileWriter(fileName)));
    for(int i = 0; i < size(); i++)
      out.println(get(i));
    out.close();
  }
  // Simple test:
  public static void main(String[] args) throws Exception {
    String file = read("TextFile.java");
    write("test.txt", file);
    TextFile text = new TextFile("test.txt");
    text.write("test2.txt");
  }
} ///:~
```

All methods simply pass **IOExceptions** out to the caller. **read( )** appends each line to a **StringBuffer** (for efficiency) followed by a newline, because that is stripped out during reading. Then it returns a **String** containing the whole file. **Write( )** opens and writes the text to the file. Both methods remember to **close( )** the file when they are done.

The constructor uses the **read( )** method to turn the file into a **String**, then uses **String.split( )** to divide the result into lines along newline boundaries (if you use this class a lot, you may want to rewrite this constructor to improve efficiency). Alas, there is no corresponding "join" method, so the non-**static write( )** method must write the lines out by hand.

In **main( )**, a basic test is performed to ensure that the methods work. Although this is a small amount of code, using it can save a lot of time and make your life easier, as you'll see in some of the examples later in this chapter.

Standard I/O

The term *standard I/O* refers to the Unix concept (which is reproduced in some form in Windows and many other operating systems) of a single stream of information that is used by a program. All the program's input can come from *standard input*, all its output can go to *standard output*, and all of its error messages can be sent to *standard error*. The value of standard I/O is that programs can easily be chained together, and one program's standard output can become the standard input for another program. This is a powerful tool.

Reading from standard input

Following the standard I/O model, Java has **System.in**, **System.out,** and **System.err**. Throughout this book, you've seen how to write to standard output using **System.out,** which is already prewrapped as a **PrintStream** object. **System.err** is likewise a **PrintStream**, but **System.in** is a raw **InputStream** with no wrapping. This means that although you can use **System.out** and **System.err** right away, **System.in** must be wrapped before you can read from it.

Typically, you'll want to read input a line at a time using **readLine( )**, so you'll want to wrap **System.in** in a **BufferedReader**. To do this, you must convert **System.in** to a **Reader** using **InputStreamReader**. Here's an example that simply echoes each line that you type in:

```
//: c12:Echo.java
// How to read from standard input.
// {RunByHand}
import java.io.*;

public class Echo {
  public static void main(String[] args)
  throws IOException {
    BufferedReader in = new BufferedReader(
      new InputStreamReader(System.in));
    String s;
    while((s = in.readLine()) != null && s.length() != 0)
      System.out.println(s);
```

```
    // An empty line or Ctrl-Z terminates the program
  }
} ///:~
```

The reason for the exception specification is that **readLine( )** can throw an **IOException**. Note that **System.in** should usually be buffered, as with most streams.

Changing **System.out** to a **PrintWriter**

System.out is a **PrintStream**, which is an **OutputStream**. **PrintWriter** has a constructor that takes an **OutputStream** as an argument. Thus, if you want, you can convert **System.out** into a **PrintWriter** using that constructor:

```
//: c12:ChangeSystemOut.java
// Turn System.out into a PrintWriter.
import com.bruceeckel.simpletest.*;
import java.io.*;

public class ChangeSystemOut {
  private static Test monitor = new Test();
  public static void main(String[] args) {
    PrintWriter out = new PrintWriter(System.out, true);
    out.println("Hello, world");
    monitor.expect(new String[] {
      "Hello, world"
    });
  }
} ///:~
```

It's important to use the two-argument version of the **PrintWriter** constructor and to set the second argument to **true** in order to enable automatic flushing; otherwise, you may not see the output.

Redirecting standard I/O

The Java **System** class allows you to redirect the standard input, output, and error I/O streams using simple static method calls:

setIn(InputStream)
setOut(PrintStream)
setErr(PrintStream)

Redirecting output is especially useful if you suddenly start creating a large amount of output on your screen, and it's scrolling past faster than you can read it.[4] Redirecting input is valuable for a command-line program in which you want to test a particular user-input sequence repeatedly. Here's a simple example that shows the use of these methods:

```
//: c12:Redirecting.java
// Demonstrates standard I/O redirection.
// {Clean: test.out}
import java.io.*;

public class Redirecting {
  // Throw exceptions to console:
  public static void main(String[] args)
  throws IOException {
    PrintStream console = System.out;
    BufferedInputStream in = new BufferedInputStream(
      new FileInputStream("Redirecting.java"));
    PrintStream out = new PrintStream(
      new BufferedOutputStream(
        new FileOutputStream("test.out")));
    System.setIn(in);
    System.setOut(out);
    System.setErr(out);
    BufferedReader br = new BufferedReader(
      new InputStreamReader(System.in));
    String s;
    while((s = br.readLine()) != null)
      System.out.println(s);
    out.close(); // Remember this!
    System.setOut(console);
  }
} ///:~
```

This program attaches standard input to a file and redirects standard output and standard error to another file.

---

[4] Chapter 13 shows an even more convenient solution for this: a GUI program with a scrolling text area.

I/O redirection manipulates streams of bytes, not streams of characters, thus **InputStream**s and **OutputStream**s are used rather than **Reader**s and **Writer**s.

New I/O

The Java "new" I/O library, introduced in JDK 1.4 in the **java.nio.*** packages, has one goal: speed. In fact, the "old" I/O packages have been reimplemented using **nio** in order to take advantage of this speed increase, so you will benefit even if you don't explicitly write code with **nio**. The speed increase occurs in both file I/O, which is explored here,[5] and in network I/O, which is covered in *Thinking in Enterprise Java*.

The speed comes from using structures that are closer to the operating system's way of performing I/O: *channels* and *buffers*. You could think of it as a coal mine; the channel is the mine containing the seam of coal (the data), and the buffer is the cart that you send into the mine. The cart comes back full of coal, and you get the coal from the cart. That is, you don't interact directly with the channel; you interact with the buffer and send the buffer into the channel. The channel either pulls data from the buffer, or puts data into the buffer.

The only kind of buffer that communicates directly with a channel is a **ByteBuffer**—that is, a buffer that holds raw bytes. If you look at the JDK documentation for **java.nio.ByteBuffer**, you'll see that it's fairly basic: You create one by telling it how much storage to allocate, and there are a selection of methods to put and get data, in either raw byte form or as primitive data types. But there's no way to put or get an object, or even a **String**. It's fairly low-level, precisely because this makes a more efficient mapping with most operating systems.

Three of the classes in the "old" I/O have been modified so that they produce a **FileChannel**: **FileInputStream**, **FileOutputStream**, and, for both reading and writing, **RandomAccessFile**. Notice that these are the byte manipulation streams, in keeping with the low-level nature of **nio**. The **Reader** and **Writer** character-mode classes do not produce channels, but

[5] Chintan Thakker contributed to this section.

the class **java.nio.channels.Channels** has utility methods to produce **Readers** and **Writers** from channels.

Here's a simple example that exercises all three types of stream to produce channels that are writeable, read/writeable, and readable:

```
//: c12:GetChannel.java
// Getting channels from streams
// {Clean: data.txt}
import java.io.*;
import java.nio.*;
import java.nio.channels.*;

public class GetChannel {
  private static final int BSIZE = 1024;
  public static void main(String[] args) throws Exception {
    // Write a file:
    FileChannel fc =
      new FileOutputStream("data.txt").getChannel();
    fc.write(ByteBuffer.wrap("Some text ".getBytes()));
    fc.close();
    // Add to the end of the file:
    fc =
      new RandomAccessFile("data.txt", "rw").getChannel();
    fc.position(fc.size()); // Move to the end
    fc.write(ByteBuffer.wrap("Some more".getBytes()));
    fc.close();
    // Read the file:
    fc = new FileInputStream("data.txt").getChannel();
    ByteBuffer buff = ByteBuffer.allocate(BSIZE);
    fc.read(buff);
    buff.flip();
    while(buff.hasRemaining())
      System.out.print((char)buff.get());
  }
} ///:~
```

For any of the stream classes shown here, **getChannel( )** will produce a **FileChannel**. A channel is fairly basic: You can hand it a **ByteBuffer** for reading or writing, and you can lock regions of the file for exclusive access (this will be described later).

One way to put bytes into a **ByteBuffer** is to stuff them in directly using one of the "put" methods, to put one or more bytes, or values of primitive types.

However, as seen here, you can also "wrap" an existing **byte** array in a **ByteBuffer** using the **wrap( )** method. When you do this, the underlying array is not copied, but instead is used as the storage for the generated **ByteBuffer**. We say that the **ByteBuffer** is "backed by" the array.

The **data.txt** file is reopened using a **RandomAccessFile**. Notice that you can move the **FileChannel** around in the file; here, it is moved to the end so that additional writes will be appended.

For read-only access, you must explicitly allocate a **ByteBuffer** using the **static allocate( )** method. The goal of **nio** is to rapidly move large amounts of data, so the size of the **ByteBuffer** should be significant—in fact, the 1K used here is probably quite a bit smaller than you'd normally want to use (you'll have to experiment with your working application to find the best size).

It's also possible to go for even more speed by using **allocateDirect( )** instead of **allocate( )** to produce a "direct" buffer that may have an even higher coupling with the operating system. However, the overhead in such an allocation is greater, and the actual implementation varies from one operating system to another, so again, you must experiment with your working application to discover whether direct buffers will buy you any advantage in speed.

Once you call **read( )** to tell the **FileChannel** to store bytes into the **ByteBuffer**, you must call **flip( )** on the buffer to tell it to get ready to have its bytes extracted (yes, this seems a bit crude, but remember that it's very low-level and is done for maximum speed). And if we were to use the buffer for further **read( )** operations, we'd also have to call **clear( )** to prepare it for each **read( )**. You can see this in a simple file copying program:

```
//: c12:ChannelCopy.java
// Copying a file using channels and buffers
// {Args: ChannelCopy.java test.txt}
// {Clean: test.txt}
import java.io.*;
import java.nio.*;
import java.nio.channels.*;

public class ChannelCopy {
  private static final int BSIZE = 1024;
  public static void main(String[] args) throws Exception {
```

```
    if(args.length != 2) {
      System.out.println("arguments: sourcefile destfile");
      System.exit(1);
    }
    FileChannel
      in = new FileInputStream(args[0]).getChannel(),
      out = new FileOutputStream(args[1]).getChannel();
    ByteBuffer buffer = ByteBuffer.allocate(BSIZE);
    while(in.read(buffer) != -1) {
      buffer.flip(); // Prepare for writing
      out.write(buffer);
      buffer.clear();  // Prepare for reading
    }
  }
} ///:~
```

You can see that one **FileChannel** is opened for reading, and one for writing. A **ByteBuffer** is allocated, and when **FileChannel.read( )** returns **-1** (a holdover, no doubt, from Unix and C), it means that you've reached the end of the input. After each **read( )**, which puts data into the buffer, **flip( )** prepares the buffer so that its information can be extracted by the **write( )**. After the **write( )**, the information is still in the buffer, and **clear( )** resets all the internal pointers so that it's ready to accept data during another **read( )**.

The preceding program is not the ideal way to handle this kind of operation, however. Special methods **transferTo( )** and **transferFrom( )** allow you to connect one channel directly to another:

```
//: c12:TransferTo.java
// Using transferTo() between channels
// {Args: TransferTo.java TransferTo.txt}
// {Clean: TransferTo.txt}
import java.io.*;
import java.nio.*;
import java.nio.channels.*;

public class TransferTo {
  public static void main(String[] args) throws Exception {
    if(args.length != 2) {
      System.out.println("arguments: sourcefile destfile");
      System.exit(1);
    }
    FileChannel
      in = new FileInputStream(args[0]).getChannel(),
```

```
      out = new FileOutputStream(args[1]).getChannel();
    in.transferTo(0, in.size(), out);
    // Or:
    // out.transferFrom(in, 0, in.size());
  }
} ///:~
```

You won't do this kind of thing very often, but it's good to know about.

Converting data

If you look back at **GetChannel.java**, you'll notice that, to print the information in the file, we are pulling the data out one **byte** at a time and casting each **byte** to a **char**. This seems a bit primitive—if you look at the **java.nio.CharBuffer** class, you'll see that it has a **toString( )** method that says: "Returns a string containing the characters in this buffer." Since a **ByteBuffer** can be viewed as a **CharBuffer** with the **asCharBuffer( )** method, why not use that? As you can see from the first line in the **expect( )** statement below, this doesn't work out:

```
//: c12:BufferToText.java
// Converting text to and from ByteBuffers
// {Clean: data2.txt}
import java.io.*;
import java.nio.*;
import java.nio.channels.*;
import java.nio.charset.*;
import com.bruceeckel.simpletest.*;

public class BufferToText {
  private static Test monitor = new Test();
  private static final int BSIZE = 1024;
  public static void main(String[] args) throws Exception {
    FileChannel fc =
      new FileOutputStream("data2.txt").getChannel();
    fc.write(ByteBuffer.wrap("Some text".getBytes()));
    fc.close();
    fc = new FileInputStream("data2.txt").getChannel();
    ByteBuffer buff = ByteBuffer.allocate(BSIZE);
    fc.read(buff);
    buff.flip();
    // Doesn't work:
    System.out.println(buff.asCharBuffer());
    // Decode using this system's default Charset:
```

```
    buff.rewind();
    String encoding = System.getProperty("file.encoding");
    System.out.println("Decoded using " + encoding + ": "
      + Charset.forName(encoding).decode(buff));
    // Or, we could encode with something that will print:
    fc = new FileOutputStream("data2.txt").getChannel();
    fc.write(ByteBuffer.wrap(
      "Some text".getBytes("UTF-16BE")));
    fc.close();
    // Now try reading again:
    fc = new FileInputStream("data2.txt").getChannel();
    buff.clear();
    fc.read(buff);
    buff.flip();
    System.out.println(buff.asCharBuffer());
    // Use a CharBuffer to write through:
    fc = new FileOutputStream("data2.txt").getChannel();
    buff = ByteBuffer.allocate(24); // More than needed
    buff.asCharBuffer().put("Some text");
    fc.write(buff);
    fc.close();
    // Read and display:
    fc = new FileInputStream("data2.txt").getChannel();
    buff.clear();
    fc.read(buff);
    buff.flip();
    System.out.println(buff.asCharBuffer());
    monitor.expect(new String[] {
      "????",
      "%% Decoded using [A-Za-z0-9_\\-]+: Some text",
      "Some text",
      "Some text\0\0\0"
    });
  }
} ///:~
```

The buffer contains plain bytes, and to turn these into characters we must either *encode* them as we put them in (so that they will be meaningful when they come out) or *decode* them as they come out of the buffer. This can be accomplished using the **java.nio.charset.Charset** class, which provides tools for encoding into many different types of character sets:

```
//: c12:AvailableCharSets.java
// Displays Charsets and aliases
```

```
import java.nio.charset.*;
import java.util.*;
import com.bruceeckel.simpletest.*;

public class AvailableCharSets {
  private static Test monitor = new Test();
  public static void main(String[] args) {
    Map charSets = Charset.availableCharsets();
    Iterator it = charSets.keySet().iterator();
    while(it.hasNext()) {
      String csName = (String)it.next();
      System.out.print(csName);
      Iterator aliases = ((Charset)charSets.get(csName))
        .aliases().iterator();
      if(aliases.hasNext())
        System.out.print(": ");
      while(aliases.hasNext()) {
        System.out.print(aliases.next());
        if(aliases.hasNext())
          System.out.print(", ");
      }
      System.out.println();
    }
    monitor.expect(new String[] {
      "Big5: csBig5",
      "Big5-HKSCS: big5-hkscs, Big5_HKSCS, big5hkscs",
      "EUC-CN",
      "EUC-JP: eucjis, x-eucjp, csEUCPkdFmtjapanese, " +
      "eucjp, Extended_UNIX_Code_Packed_Format_for" +
      "_Japanese, x-euc-jp, euc_jp",
      "euc-jp-linux: euc_jp_linux",
      "EUC-KR: ksc5601, 5601, ksc5601_1987, ksc_5601, " +
      "ksc5601-1987, euc_kr, ks_c_5601-1987, " +
      "euckr, csEUCKR",
      "EUC-TW: cns11643, euc_tw, euctw",
      "GB18030: gb18030-2000",
      "GBK: GBK",
      "ISCII91: iscii, ST_SEV_358-88, iso-ir-153, " +
      "csISO153GOST1976874",
      "ISO-2022-CN-CNS: ISO2022CN_CNS",
      "ISO-2022-CN-GB: ISO2022CN_GB",
      "ISO-2022-KR: ISO2022KR, csISO2022KR",
      "ISO-8859-1: iso-ir-100, 8859_1, ISO_8859-1, " +
      "ISO8859_1, 819, csISOLatin1, IBM-819, " +
```

```
        "ISO_8859-1:1987, latin1, cp819, ISO8859-1, " +
        "IBM819, ISO_8859_1, l1",
        "ISO-8859-13",
        "ISO-8859-15: 8859_15, csISOlatin9, IBM923, cp923," +
        " 923, L9, IBM-923, ISO8859-15, LATIN9, " +
        "ISO_8859-15, LATIN0, csISOlatin0, " +
        "ISO8859_15_FDIS, ISO-8859-15",
        "ISO-8859-2", "ISO-8859-3", "ISO-8859-4",
        "ISO-8859-5", "ISO-8859-6", "ISO-8859-7",
        "ISO-8859-8", "ISO-8859-9",
        "JIS0201: X0201, JIS_X0201, csHalfWidthKatakana",
        "JIS0208: JIS_C6626-1983, csISO87JISX0208, x0208, " +
        "JIS_X0208-1983, iso-ir-87",
        "JIS0212: jis_x0212-1990, x0212, iso-ir-159, " +
        "csISO159JISC02121990",
        "Johab: ms1361, ksc5601_1992, ksc5601-1992",
        "KOI8-R",
        "Shift_JIS: shift-jis, x-sjis, ms_kanji, " +
        "shift_jis, csShiftJIS, sjis, pck",
        "TIS-620",
        "US-ASCII: IBM367, ISO646-US, ANSI_X3.4-1986, " +
        "cp367, ASCII, iso_646.irv:1983, 646, us, iso-ir-6,"+
        " csASCII, ANSI_X3.4-1968, ISO_646.irv:1991",
        "UTF-16: UTF_16",
        "UTF-16BE: X-UTF-16BE, UTF_16BE, ISO-10646-UCS-2",
        "UTF-16LE: UTF_16LE, X-UTF-16LE",
        "UTF-8: UTF8", "windows-1250", "windows-1251",
        "windows-1252: cp1252",
        "windows-1253", "windows-1254", "windows-1255",
        "windows-1256", "windows-1257", "windows-1258",
        "windows-936: ms936, ms_936",
        "windows-949: ms_949, ms949", "windows-950: ms950",
    });
  }
} ///:~
```

So, returning to **BufferToText.java**, if you **rewind( )** the buffer (to go back to the beginning of the data) and then use that platform's default character set to **decode( )** the data, the resulting **CharBuffer** will print to the console just fine. To discover the default character set, use **System.getProperty("file.encoding")**, which produces the string that names the character set. Passing this to **Charset.forName( )** produces the **Charset** object that can be used to decode the string.

Another alternative is to **encode( )** using a character set that will result in something printable when the file is read, as you see in the third part of **BufferToText.java**. Here, UTF-16BE is used to write the text into the file, and when it is read, all you have to do is convert it to a **CharBuffer**, and it produces the expected text.

Finally, you see what happens if you *write* to the **ByteBuffer** through a **CharBuffer** (you'll learn more about this later). Note that 24 bytes are allocated for the **ByteBuffer**. Since each **char** requires two bytes, this is enough for 12 **char**s, but "Some text" only has 9. The remaining zero bytes still appear in the representation of the **CharBuffer** produced by its **toString( )**, as you can see in the output.

Fetching primitives

Although a **ByteBuffer** only holds bytes, it contains methods to produce each of the different types of primitive values from the bytes it contains. This example shows the insertion and extraction of various values using these methods:

```
//: c12:GetData.java
// Getting different representations from a ByteBuffer
import java.nio.*;
import com.bruceeckel.simpletest.*;

public class GetData {
  private static Test monitor = new Test();
  private static final int BSIZE = 1024;
  public static void main(String[] args) {
    ByteBuffer bb = ByteBuffer.allocate(BSIZE);
    // Allocation automatically zeroes the ByteBuffer:
    int i = 0;
    while(i++ < bb.limit())
      if(bb.get() != 0)
        System.out.println("nonzero");
    System.out.println("i = " + i);
    bb.rewind();
    // Store and read a char array:
    bb.asCharBuffer().put("Howdy!");
    char c;
    while((c = bb.getChar()) != 0)
      System.out.print(c + " ");
    System.out.println();
```

```
    bb.rewind();
    // Store and read a short:
    bb.asShortBuffer().put((short)471142);
    System.out.println(bb.getShort());
    bb.rewind();
    // Store and read an int:
    bb.asIntBuffer().put(99471142);
    System.out.println(bb.getInt());
    bb.rewind();
    // Store and read a long:
    bb.asLongBuffer().put(99471142);
    System.out.println(bb.getLong());
    bb.rewind();
    // Store and read a float:
    bb.asFloatBuffer().put(99471142);
    System.out.println(bb.getFloat());
    bb.rewind();
    // Store and read a double:
    bb.asDoubleBuffer().put(99471142);
    System.out.println(bb.getDouble());
    bb.rewind();
    monitor.expect(new String[] {
      "i = 1025",
      "H o w d y ! ",
      "12390", // Truncation changes the value
      "99471142",
      "99471142",
      "9.9471144E7",
      "9.9471142E7"
    });
  }
} ///:~
```

After a **ByteBuffer** is allocated, its values are checked to see whether buffer allocation automatically zeroes the contents—and it does. All 1,024 values are checked (up to the **limit( )** of the buffer), and all are zero.

The easiest way to insert primitive values into a **ByteBuffer** is to get the appropriate "view" on that buffer using **asCharBuffer( )**, **asShortBuffer( )**, etc., and then to use that view's **put( )** method. You can see this is the process used for each of the primitive data types. The only one of these that is a little odd is the **put( )** for the **ShortBuffer**, which requires a cast (note that the cast truncates and changes the resulting value). All the other view buffers do not require casting in their **put( )** methods.

View buffers

A "view buffer" allows you to look at an underlying **ByteBuffer** through the window of a particular primitive type. The **ByteBuffer** is still the actual storage that's "backing" the view, so any changes you make to the view are reflected in modifications to the data in the **ByteBuffer**. As seen in the previous example, this allows you to conveniently insert primitive types into a **ByteBuffer**. A view also allows you to read primitive values from a **ByteBuffer**, either one at a time (as **ByteBuffer** allows) or in batches (into arrays). Here's an example that manipulates **int**s in a **ByteBuffer** via an **IntBuffer**:

```
//: c12:IntBufferDemo.java
// Manipulating ints in a ByteBuffer with an IntBuffer
import java.nio.*;
import com.bruceeckel.simpletest.*;
import com.bruceeckel.util.*;

public class IntBufferDemo {
  private static Test monitor = new Test();
  private static final int BSIZE = 1024;
  public static void main(String[] args) {
    ByteBuffer bb = ByteBuffer.allocate(BSIZE);
    IntBuffer ib = bb.asIntBuffer();
    // Store an array of int:
    ib.put(new int[] { 11, 42, 47, 99, 143, 811, 1016 });
    // Absolute location read and write:
    System.out.println(ib.get(3));
    ib.put(3, 1811);
    ib.rewind();
    while(ib.hasRemaining()) {
      int i = ib.get();
      if(i == 0) break; // Else we'll get the entire buffer
      System.out.println(i);
    }
    monitor.expect(new String[] {
      "99",
      "11",
      "42",
      "47",
      "1811",
      "143",
      "811",
```

```
      "1016"
    });
  }
} ///:~
```

The overloaded **put( )** method is first used to store an array of **int**. The following **get( )** and **put( )** method calls directly access an **int** location in the underlying **ByteBuffer**. Note that these absolute location accesses are available for primitive types by talking directly to a **ByteBuffer**, as well.

Once the underlying **ByteBuffer** is filled with **int**s or some other primitive type via a view buffer, then that **ByteBuffer** can be written directly to a channel. You can just as easily read from a channel and use a view buffer to convert everything to a particular type of primitive. Here's an example that interprets the same sequence of bytes as **short**, **int**, **float**, **long**, and **double** by producing different view buffers on the same **ByteBuffer**:

```
//: c12:ViewBuffers.java
import java.nio.*;
import com.bruceeckel.simpletest.*;

public class ViewBuffers {
  private static Test monitor = new Test();
  public static void main(String[] args) {
    ByteBuffer bb = ByteBuffer.wrap(
      new byte[]{ 0, 0, 0, 0, 0, 0, 0, 'a' });
    bb.rewind();
    System.out.println("Byte Buffer");
    while(bb.hasRemaining())
      System.out.println(bb.position()+ " -> " + bb.get());
    CharBuffer cb =
      ((ByteBuffer)bb.rewind()).asCharBuffer();
    System.out.println("Char Buffer");
    while(cb.hasRemaining())
      System.out.println(cb.position()+ " -> " + cb.get());
    FloatBuffer fb =
      ((ByteBuffer)bb.rewind()).asFloatBuffer();
    System.out.println("Float Buffer");
    while(fb.hasRemaining())
      System.out.println(fb.position()+ " -> " + fb.get());
    IntBuffer ib =
      ((ByteBuffer)bb.rewind()).asIntBuffer();
    System.out.println("Int Buffer");
    while(ib.hasRemaining())
```

```
      System.out.println(ib.position()+ " -> " + ib.get());
    LongBuffer lb =
      ((ByteBuffer)bb.rewind()).asLongBuffer();
    System.out.println("Long Buffer");
    while(lb.hasRemaining())
      System.out.println(lb.position()+ " -> " + lb.get());
    ShortBuffer sb =
      ((ByteBuffer)bb.rewind()).asShortBuffer();
    System.out.println("Short Buffer");
    while(sb.hasRemaining())
      System.out.println(sb.position()+ " -> " + sb.get());
    DoubleBuffer db =
      ((ByteBuffer)bb.rewind()).asDoubleBuffer();
    System.out.println("Double Buffer");
    while(db.hasRemaining())
      System.out.println(db.position()+ " -> " + db.get());
    monitor.expect(new String[] {
      "Byte Buffer",
      "0 -> 0",
      "1 -> 0",
      "2 -> 0",
      "3 -> 0",
      "4 -> 0",
      "5 -> 0",
      "6 -> 0",
      "7 -> 97",
      "Char Buffer",
      "0 -> \0",
      "1 -> \0",
      "2 -> \0",
      "3 -> a",
      "Float Buffer",
      "0 -> 0.0",
      "1 -> 1.36E-43",
      "Int Buffer",
      "0 -> 0",
      "1 -> 97",
      "Long Buffer",
      "0 -> 97",
      "Short Buffer",
      "0 -> 0",
      "1 -> 0",
      "2 -> 0",
      "3 -> 97",
```

```
      "Double Buffer",
      "0 -> 4.8E-322"
    });
  }
} ///:~
```

The **ByteBuffer** is produced by "wrapping" an eight-byte array, which is then displayed via view buffers of all the different primitive types. You can see in the following diagram the way the data appears differently when read from the different types of buffers:

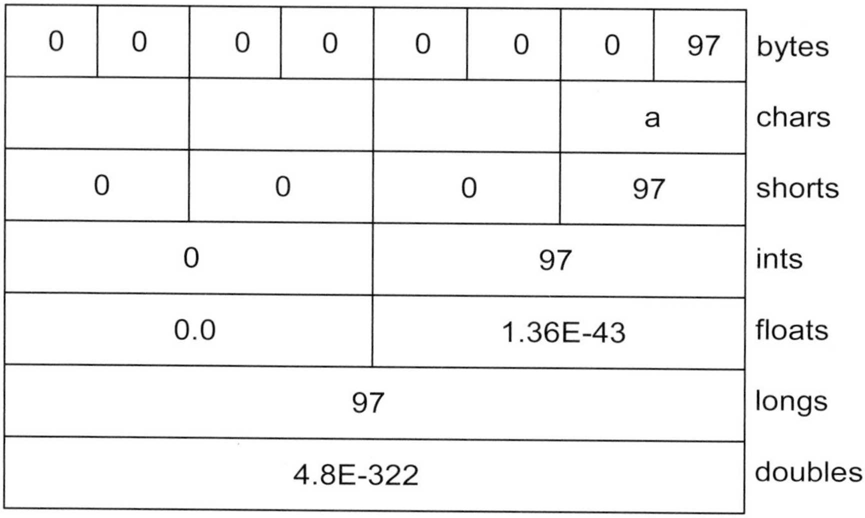

<table>
<tr><td>0</td><td>0</td><td>0</td><td>0</td><td>0</td><td>0</td><td>0</td><td>97</td><td>bytes</td></tr>
<tr><td colspan="2"></td><td colspan="2"></td><td colspan="2"></td><td colspan="2">a</td><td>chars</td></tr>
<tr><td colspan="2">0</td><td colspan="2">0</td><td colspan="2">0</td><td colspan="2">97</td><td>shorts</td></tr>
<tr><td colspan="4">0</td><td colspan="4">97</td><td>ints</td></tr>
<tr><td colspan="4">0.0</td><td colspan="4">1.36E-43</td><td>floats</td></tr>
<tr><td colspan="8">97</td><td>longs</td></tr>
<tr><td colspan="8">4.8E-322</td><td>doubles</td></tr>
</table>

This corresponds to the output from the program.

Endians

Different machines may use different byte-ordering approaches to store data. "Big endian" places the most significant byte in the lowest memory address, and "little endian" places the most significant byte in the highest memory address. When storing a quantity that is greater than one byte, like **int**, **float**, etc., you may need to consider the byte ordering. A **ByteBuffer** stores data in big endian form, and data sent over a network always uses big endian order. You can change the endian-ness of a **ByteBuffer** using **order( )** with an argument of **ByteOrder.BIG_ENDIAN** or **ByteOrder.LITTLE_ENDIAN**.

Consider a **ByteBuffer** containing the following two bytes:

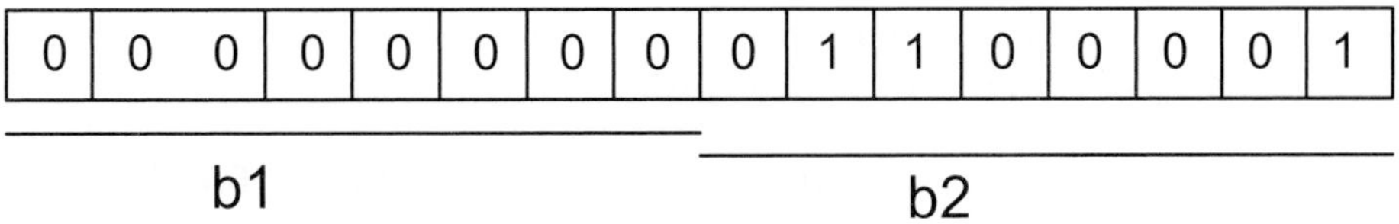

0	0	0	0	0	0	0	0	0	1	1	0	0	0	0	1

b1 b2

If you read the data as a **short** (**ByteBuffer.asShortBuffer( )**), you will get the number 97 (00000000 01100001), but if you change to little endian, you will get the number 24832 (01100001 00000000).

Here's an example that shows how byte ordering is changed in characters depending on the endian setting:

```
//: c12:Endians.java
// Endian differences and data storage.
import java.nio.*;
import com.bruceeckel.simpletest.*;
import com.bruceeckel.util.*;

public class Endians {
  private static Test monitor = new Test();
  public static void main(String[] args) {
    ByteBuffer bb = ByteBuffer.wrap(new byte[12]);
    bb.asCharBuffer().put("abcdef");
    System.out.println(Arrays2.toString(bb.array()));
    bb.rewind();
    bb.order(ByteOrder.BIG_ENDIAN);
    bb.asCharBuffer().put("abcdef");
    System.out.println(Arrays2.toString(bb.array()));
    bb.rewind();
    bb.order(ByteOrder.LITTLE_ENDIAN);
    bb.asCharBuffer().put("abcdef");
    System.out.println(Arrays2.toString(bb.array()));
    monitor.expect(new String[]{
      "[0, 97, 0, 98, 0, 99, 0, 100, 0, 101, 0, 102]",
      "[0, 97, 0, 98, 0, 99, 0, 100, 0, 101, 0, 102]",
      "[97, 0, 98, 0, 99, 0, 100, 0, 101, 0, 102, 0]"
    });
  }
} ///:~
```

The **ByteBuffer** is given enough space to hold all the bytes in **charArray** as an external buffer so that that **array( )** method can be called to display the underlying bytes. The **array( )** method is "optional," and you can only call it on a buffer that is backed by an array; otherwise, you'll get an **UnsupportedOperationException**.

charArray is inserted into the **ByteBuffer** via a **CharBuffer** view. When the underlying bytes are displayed, you can see that the default ordering is the same as the subsequent big endian order, whereas the little endian order swaps the bytes.

Data manipulation with buffers

The diagram here illustrates the relationships between the **nio** classes, so that you can see how to move and convert data. For example, if you wish to write a **byte** array to a file, then you wrap the byte array using the **ByteBuffer.wrap( )** method, open a channel on the **FileOutputStream** using the **getChannel( )** method, and then write data into **FileChannel** from this **ByteBuffer**.

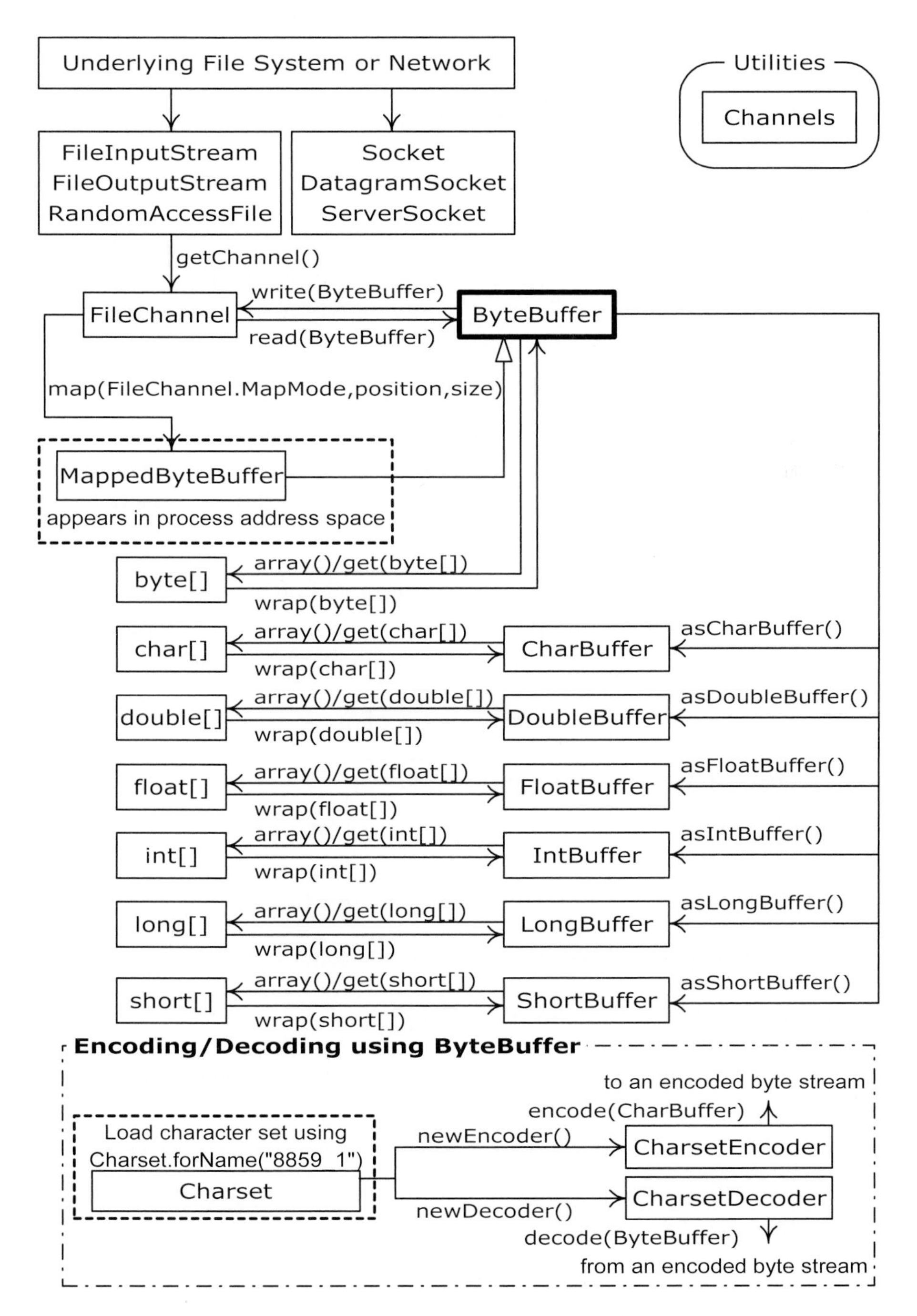

Note that **ByteBuffer** is the only way to move data in and out of channels, and that you can only create a standalone primitive-typed buffer, or get one from a **ByteBuffer** using an "as" method. That is, you cannot convert a primitive-typed buffer *to* a **ByteBuffer**. However, since you are able to move primitive data into and out of a **ByteBuffer** via a view buffer, this is not really a restriction.

Buffer details

A **Buffer** consists of data and four indexes to access and manipulate this data efficiently: *mark, position, limit* and *capacity*. There are methods to set and reset these indexes and to query their value.

capacity( )	Returns the buffer's *capacity*
clear( )	Clears the buffer, sets the *position* to zero, and *limit* to *capacity*. You call this method to overwrite an existing buffer.
flip( )	Sets *limit* to *position* and *position* to zero. This method is used to prepare the buffer for a read after data has been written into it.
limit( )	Returns the value of *limit*.
limit(int lim)	Sets the value of *limit*.
mark( )	Sets *mark* at *position*.
position( )	Returns the value of *position*.
position(int pos)	Sets the value of *position*.
remaining( )	Returns (*limit - position*).
hasRemaining( )	Returns **true** if there are any elements between *position* and *limit*.

Methods that insert and extract data from the buffer update these indexes to reflect the changes.

This example uses a very simple algorithm (swapping adjacent characters) to scramble and unscramble characters in a **CharBuffer**:

```
//: c12:UsingBuffers.java
```

```
import java.nio.*;
import com.bruceeckel.simpletest.*;

public class UsingBuffers {
  private static Test monitor = new Test();
  private static void symmetricScramble(CharBuffer buffer){
    while(buffer.hasRemaining()) {
      buffer.mark();
      char c1 = buffer.get();
      char c2 = buffer.get();
      buffer.reset();
      buffer.put(c2).put(c1);
    }
  }
  public static void main(String[] args) {
    char[] data = "UsingBuffers".toCharArray();
    ByteBuffer bb = ByteBuffer.allocate(data.length * 2);
    CharBuffer cb = bb.asCharBuffer();
    cb.put(data);
    System.out.println(cb.rewind());
    symmetricScramble(cb);
    System.out.println(cb.rewind());
    symmetricScramble(cb);
    System.out.println(cb.rewind());
    monitor.expect(new String[] {
      "UsingBuffers",
      "sUniBgfuefsr",
      "UsingBuffers"
    });
  }
} ///:~
```

Although you could produce a **CharBuffer** directly by calling **wrap( )** with a **char** array, an underlying **ByteBuffer** is allocated instead, and a **CharBuffer** is produced as a view on the **ByteBuffer**. This emphasizes that fact that the goal is always to manipulate a **ByteBuffer**, since that is what interacts with a channel.

Here's what the buffer looks like after the **put( )**:

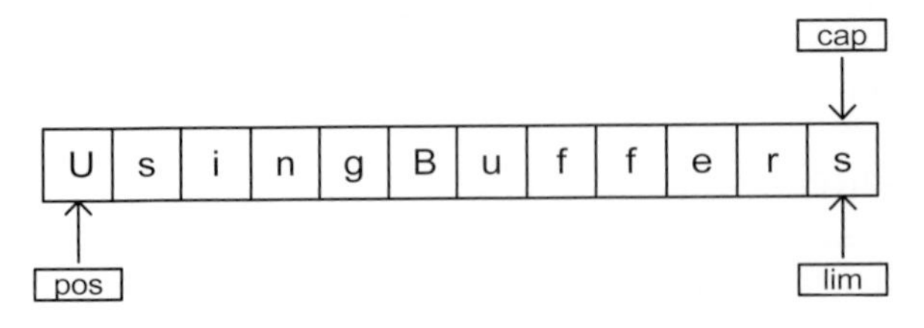

The *position* points to the first element in the buffer, and the *capacity* and *limit* point to the last element.

In **symmetricScramble( )**, the while loop iterates until *position* is equivalent to *limit*. The *position* of the buffer changes when a relative **get( )** or **put( )** function is called on it. You can also call absolute **get( )** and **put( )** methods that include an index argument, which is the location where the **get( )** or **put( )** takes place. These methods do not modify the value of the buffer's *position*.

When the control enters the while loop, the value of *mark* is set using **mark( )** call. The state of the buffer then:

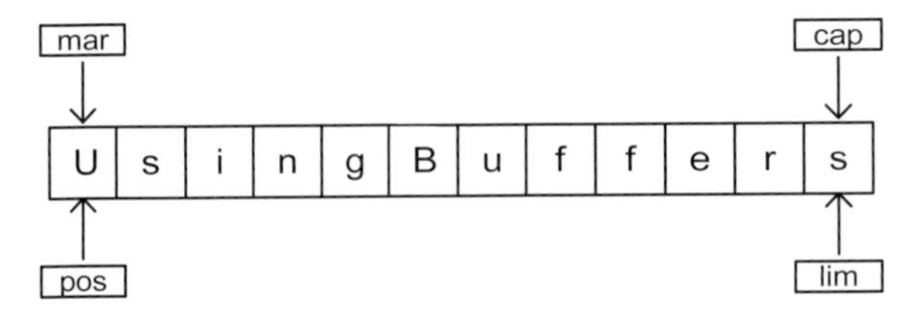

The two relative **get( )** calls save the value of the first two characters in variables **c1** and **c2**. After these two calls, the buffer looks like this:

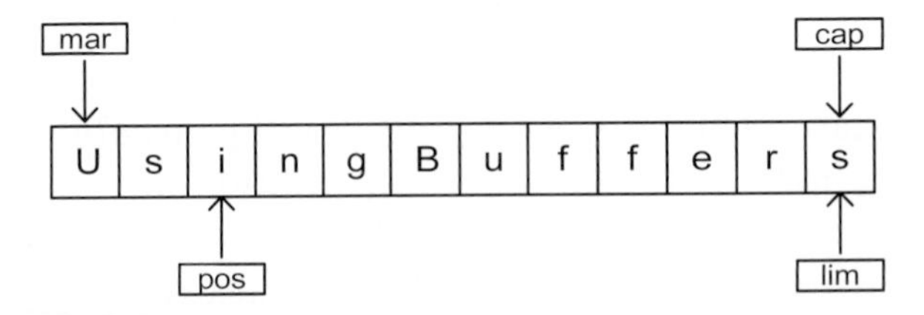

To perform the swap, we need to write **c2** at *position* = 0 and **c1** at *position* = 1. We can either use the absolute put method to achieve this, or set the value of *position* to *mark*, which is what **reset( )** does:

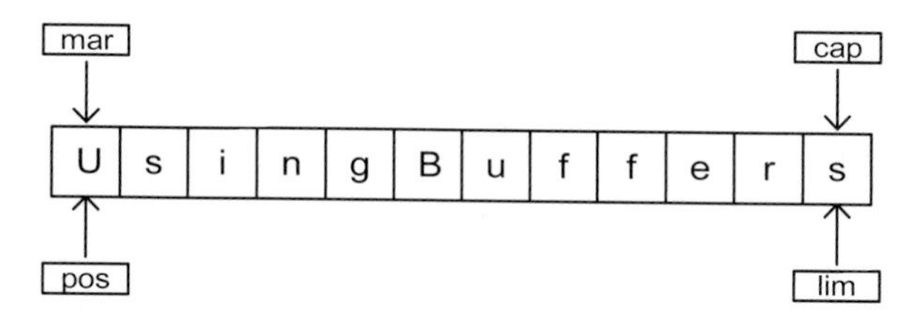

The two **put( )** methods write **c2** and then **c1**:

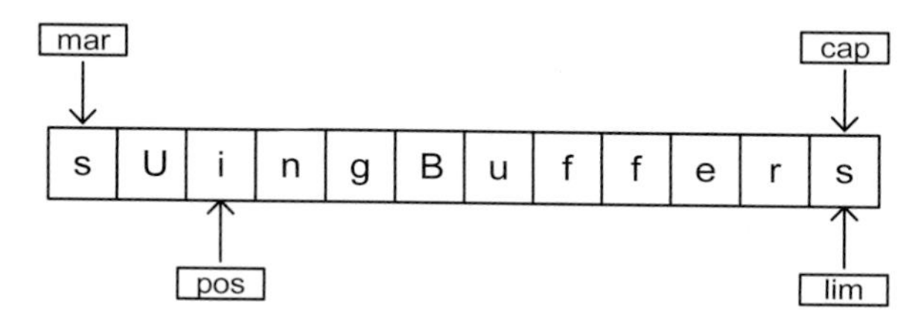

During the next iteration of the loop, *mark* is set to the current value of *position*:

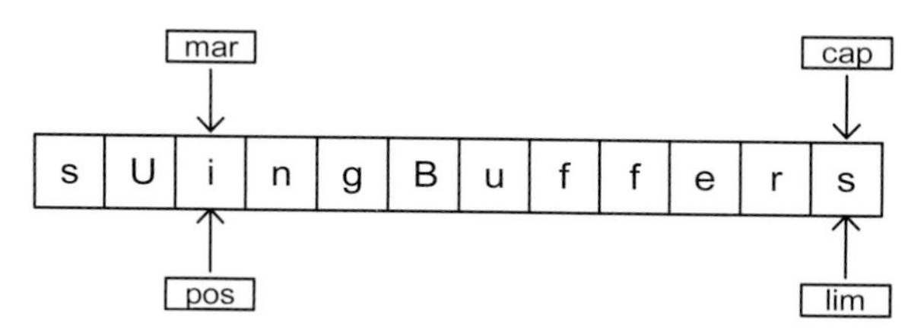

The process continues until the entire buffer is traversed. At the end of the **while** loop, *position* is at the end of the buffer. If you print the buffer, only the characters between the *position* and *limit* are printed. Thus, if you want to show the entire contents of the buffer you must set *position* to the start of the buffer using **rewind( )**. Here is the state of buffer after the **rewind( )** call (the value of *mark* becomes undefined):

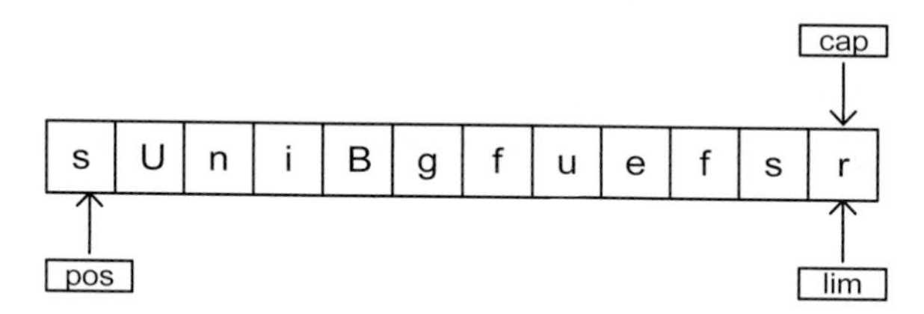

When the function **symmetricScramble( )** is called again, the **CharBuffer** undergoes the same process and is restored to its original state.

Memory-mapped files

Memory-mapped files allow you to create and modify files that are too big to bring into memory. With a memory-mapped file, you can pretend that the entire file is in memory and that you can access it by simply treating it as a very large array. This approach greatly simplifies the code you write in order to modify the file. Here's a small example:

```
//: c12:LargeMappedFiles.java
// Creating a very large file using mapping.
// {RunByHand}
// {Clean: test.dat}
import java.io.*;
import java.nio.*;
import java.nio.channels.*;

public class LargeMappedFiles {
  static int length = 0x8FFFFFF; // 128 Mb
  public static void main(String[] args) throws Exception {
    MappedByteBuffer out =
      new RandomAccessFile("test.dat", "rw").getChannel()
      .map(FileChannel.MapMode.READ_WRITE, 0, length);
    for(int i = 0; i < length; i++)
      out.put((byte)'x');
    System.out.println("Finished writing");
    for(int i = length/2; i < length/2 + 6; i++)
      System.out.print((char)out.get(i));
  }
} ///:~
```

To do both writing and reading, we start with a **RandomAccessFile**, get a channel for that file, and then call **map( )** to produce a **MappedByteBuffer**, which is a particular kind of direct buffer. Note that you must specify the starting point and the length of the region that you want to map in the file; this means that you have the option to map smaller regions of a large file.

MappedByteBuffer is inherited from **ByteBuffer**, so it has all of **ByteBuffer**'s methods. Only the very simple uses of **put( )** and **get( )** are shown here, but you can also use things like **asCharBuffer( )**, etc.

The file created with the preceding program is 128 MB long, which is probably larger than the space your OS will allow. The file appears to be accessible all at once because only portions of it are brought into memory, and other parts are swapped out. This way a very large file (up to 2 GB) can easily be modified. Note that the file-mapping facilities of the underlying operating system are used to maximize performance.

Performance

Although the performance of "old" stream I/O has been improved by implementing it with **nio**, mapped file access tends to be dramatically faster. This program does a simple performance comparison:

```
//: c12:MappedIO.java
// {Clean: temp.tmp}
import java.io.*;
import java.nio.*;
import java.nio.channels.*;

public class MappedIO {
  private static int numOfInts = 4000000;
  private static int numOfUbuffInts = 200000;
  private abstract static class Tester {
    private String name;
    public Tester(String name) { this.name = name; }
    public long runTest() {
      System.out.print(name + ": ");
      try {
        long startTime = System.currentTimeMillis();
        test();
        long endTime = System.currentTimeMillis();
        return (endTime - startTime);
      } catch (IOException e) {
        throw new RuntimeException(e);
      }
    }
    public abstract void test() throws IOException;
  }
  private static Tester[] tests = {
    new Tester("Stream Write") {
      public void test() throws IOException {
        DataOutputStream dos = new DataOutputStream(
          new BufferedOutputStream(
            new FileOutputStream(new File("temp.tmp"))));
        for(int i = 0; i < numOfInts; i++)
          dos.writeInt(i);
```

```
        dos.close();
      }
    },
    new Tester("Mapped Write") {
      public void test() throws IOException {
        FileChannel fc =
          new RandomAccessFile("temp.tmp", "rw")
          .getChannel();
        IntBuffer ib = fc.map(
          FileChannel.MapMode.READ_WRITE, 0, fc.size())
          .asIntBuffer();
        for(int i = 0; i < numOfInts; i++)
          ib.put(i);
        fc.close();
      }
    },
    new Tester("Stream Read") {
      public void test() throws IOException {
        DataInputStream dis = new DataInputStream(
          new BufferedInputStream(
            new FileInputStream("temp.tmp")));
        for(int i = 0; i < numOfInts; i++)
          dis.readInt();
        dis.close();
      }
    },
    new Tester("Mapped Read") {
      public void test() throws IOException {
        FileChannel fc = new FileInputStream(
          new File("temp.tmp")).getChannel();
        IntBuffer ib = fc.map(
          FileChannel.MapMode.READ_ONLY, 0, fc.size())
          .asIntBuffer();
        while(ib.hasRemaining())
          ib.get();
        fc.close();
      }
    },
    new Tester("Stream Read/Write") {
      public void test() throws IOException {
        RandomAccessFile raf = new RandomAccessFile(
          new File("temp.tmp"), "rw");
        raf.writeInt(1);
        for(int i = 0; i < numOfUbuffInts; i++) {
```

```
          raf.seek(raf.length() - 4);
          raf.writeInt(raf.readInt());
        }
        raf.close();
      }
    },
    new Tester("Mapped Read/Write") {
      public void test() throws IOException {
        FileChannel fc = new RandomAccessFile(
          new File("temp.tmp"), "rw").getChannel();
        IntBuffer ib = fc.map(
          FileChannel.MapMode.READ_WRITE, 0, fc.size())
          .asIntBuffer();
        ib.put(0);
        for(int i = 1; i < numOfUbuffInts; i++)
          ib.put(ib.get(i - 1));
        fc.close();
      }
    }
  };
  public static void main(String[] args) {
    for(int i = 0; i < tests.length; i++)
      System.out.println(tests[i].runTest());
  }
} ///:~
```

As seen in earlier examples in this book, **runTest( )** is the *Template Method* that provides the testing framework for various implementations of **test( )** defined in anonymous inner subclasses. Each of these subclasses perform one kind of test, so the **test( )** methods also give you a prototype for performing the various I/O activities.

Although a mapped write would seem to use a **FileOutputStream**, all output in file mapping must use a **RandomAccessFile**, just as read/write does in the preceding code.

Here's the output from one run:

```
Stream Write: 1719
Mapped Write: 359
Stream Read: 750
Mapped Read: 125
Stream Read/Write: 5188
Mapped Read/Write: 16
```

Note that the **test( )** methods include the time for initialization of the various I/O objects, so even though the setup for mapped files can be expensive, the overall gain compared to stream I/O is significant.

File locking

File locking, introduced in JDK 1.4, allows you to synchronize access to a file as a shared resource. However, the two threads that contend for the same file may be in different JVMs, or one may be a Java thread and the other some native thread in the operating system. The file locks are visible to other operating system processes because Java file locking maps directly to the native operating system locking facility.

Here is a simple example of file locking.

```
//: c12:FileLocking.java
// {Clean: file.txt}
import java.io.FileOutputStream;
import java.nio.channels.*;

public class FileLocking {
  public static void main(String[] args) throws Exception {
    FileOutputStream fos= new FileOutputStream("file.txt");
    FileLock fl = fos.getChannel().tryLock();
    if(fl != null) {
      System.out.println("Locked File");
      Thread.sleep(100);
      fl.release();
      System.out.println("Released Lock");
    }
    fos.close();
  }
} ///:~
```

You get a **FileLock** on the entire file by calling either **tryLock( )** or **lock( )** on a **FileChannel**. (**SocketChannel**, **DatagramChannel**, and **ServerSocketChannel** do not need locking since they are inherently single-process entities; you don't generally share a network socket between two processes.) **tryLock( )** is non-blocking. It tries to grab the lock, but if it cannot (when some other process already holds the same lock and it is not shared), it simply returns from the method call. **lock( )** blocks until the lock is acquired, or the thread that invoked **lock( )** is interrupted, or the channel on which the **lock( )** method is called is closed. A lock is released using **FileLock.release( )**.

It is also possible to lock a part of the file by using

```
tryLock(long position, long size, boolean shared)
```

or

```
lock(long position, long size, boolean shared)
```

which locks the region **(size - position)**. The third argument specifies whether this lock is shared.

Although the zero-argument locking methods adapt to changes in the size of a file, locks with a fixed size do not change if the file size changes. If a lock is acquired for a region from **position** to **position+size** and the file increases beyond **position+size**, then the section beyond **position+size** is not locked. The zero-argument locking methods lock the entire file, even if it grows.

Support for exclusive or shared locks must be provided by the underlying operating system. If the operating system does not support shared locks and a request is made for one, an exclusive lock is used instead. The type of lock (shared or exclusive) can be queried using **FileLock.isShared( )**.

Locking portions of a mapped file

As mentioned earlier, file mapping is typically used for very large files. One thing that you may need to do with such a large file is to lock portions of it so that other processes may modify unlocked parts of the file. This is something that happens, for example, with a database, so that it can be available to many users at once.

Here's an example that has two threads, each of which locks a distinct portion of a file:

```
//: c12:LockingMappedFiles.java
// Locking portions of a mapped file.
// {RunByHand}
// {Clean: test.dat}
import java.io.*;
import java.nio.*;
import java.nio.channels.*;
```

```java
public class LockingMappedFiles {
  static final int LENGTH = 0x8FFFFFF; // 128 Mb
  static FileChannel fc;
  public static void main(String[] args) throws Exception {
    fc =
      new RandomAccessFile("test.dat", "rw").getChannel();
    MappedByteBuffer out =
      fc.map(FileChannel.MapMode.READ_WRITE, 0, LENGTH);
    for(int i = 0; i < LENGTH; i++)
      out.put((byte)'x');
    new LockAndModify(out, 0, 0 + LENGTH/3);
    new LockAndModify(out, LENGTH/2, LENGTH/2 + LENGTH/4);
  }
  private static class LockAndModify extends Thread {
    private ByteBuffer buff;
    private int start, end;
    LockAndModify(ByteBuffer mbb, int start, int end) {
      this.start = start;
      this.end = end;
      mbb.limit(end);
      mbb.position(start);
      buff = mbb.slice();
      start();
    }
    public void run() {
      try {
        // Exclusive lock with no overlap:
        FileLock fl = fc.lock(start, end, false);
        System.out.println("Locked: "+ start +" to "+ end);
        // Perform modification:
        while(buff.position() < buff.limit() - 1)
          buff.put((byte)(buff.get() + 1));
        fl.release();
        System.out.println("Released: "+start+" to "+ end);
      } catch(IOException e) {
        throw new RuntimeException(e);
      }
    }
  }
} ///:~
```

The **LockAndModify** thread class sets up the buffer region and creates a **slice( )** to be modified, and in **run( )**, the lock is acquired on the file channel (you can't acquire a lock on the buffer—only the channel). The call to **lock( )**

is very similar to acquiring a threading lock on an object—you now have a "critical section" with exclusive access to that portion of the file.

The locks are automatically released when the JVM exits, or the channel on which it was acquired is closed, but you can also explicitly call **release( )** on the **FileLock** object, as shown here.

Compression

The Java I/O library contains classes to support reading and writing streams in a compressed format. These are wrapped around existing I/O classes to provide compression functionality.

These classes are not derived from the **Reader** and **Writer** classes, but instead are part of the **InputStream** and **OutputStream** hierarchies. This is because the compression library works with bytes, not characters. However, you might sometimes be forced to mix the two types of streams. (Remember that you can use **InputStreamReader** and **OutputStreamWriter** to provide easy conversion between one type and another.)

Compression class	Function
CheckedInputStream	**GetCheckSum( )** produces checksum for any **InputStream** (not just decompression).
CheckedOutputStream	**GetCheckSum( )** produces checksum for any **OutputStream** (not just compression).
DeflaterOutputStream	Base class for compression classes.
ZipOutputStream	A **DeflaterOutputStream** that compresses data into the Zip file format.
GZIPOutputStream	A **DeflaterOutputStream** that compresses data into the GZIP file format.
InflaterInputStream	Base class for decompression classes.
ZipInputStream	An **InflaterInputStream** that decompresses data that has been stored in the Zip file format.
GZIPInputStream	An **InflaterInputStream** that decompresses data that has been stored in

Compression class	Function
	the GZIP file format.

Although there are many compression algorithms, Zip and GZIP are possibly the most commonly used. Thus you can easily manipulate your compressed data with the many tools available for reading and writing these formats.

Simple compression with GZIP

The GZIP interface is simple and thus is probably more appropriate when you have a single stream of data that you want to compress (rather than a container of dissimilar pieces of data). Here's an example that compresses a single file:

```
//: c12:GZIPcompress.java
// {Args: GZIPcompress.java}
// {Clean: test.gz}
import com.bruceeckel.simpletest.*;
import java.io.*;
import java.util.zip.*;

public class GZIPcompress {
  private static Test monitor = new Test();
  // Throw exceptions to console:
  public static void main(String[] args)
  throws IOException {
    if(args.length == 0) {
      System.out.println(
        "Usage: \nGZIPcompress file\n" +
        "\tUses GZIP compression to compress " +
        "the file to test.gz");
      System.exit(1);
    }
    BufferedReader in = new BufferedReader(
      new FileReader(args[0]));
    BufferedOutputStream out = new BufferedOutputStream(
      new GZIPOutputStream(
        new FileOutputStream("test.gz")));
    System.out.println("Writing file");
    int c;
    while((c = in.read()) != -1)
      out.write(c);
    in.close();
```

```
    out.close();
    System.out.println("Reading file");
    BufferedReader in2 = new BufferedReader(
      new InputStreamReader(new GZIPInputStream(
        new FileInputStream("test.gz"))));
    String s;
    while((s = in2.readLine()) != null)
      System.out.println(s);
    monitor.expect(new String[] {
      "Writing file",
      "Reading file"
    }, args[0]);
  }
} ///:~
```

The use of the compression classes is straightforward; you simply wrap your output stream in a **GZIPOutputStream** or **ZipOutputStream**, and your input stream in a **GZIPInputStream** or **ZipInputStream**. All else is ordinary I/O reading and writing. This is an example of mixing the **char**-oriented streams with the **byte**-oriented streams; **in** uses the **Reader** classes, whereas **GZIPOutputStream**'s constructor can accept only an **OutputStream** object, not a **Writer** object. When the file is opened, the **GZIPInputStream** is converted to a **Reader**.

Multifile storage with Zip

The library that supports the Zip format is much more extensive. With it you can easily store multiple files, and there's even a separate class to make the process of reading a Zip file easy. The library uses the standard Zip format so that it works seamlessly with all the tools currently downloadable on the Internet. The following example has the same form as the previous example, but it handles as many command-line arguments as you want. In addition, it shows the use of the **Checksum** classes to calculate and verify the checksum for the file. There are two **Checksum** types: **Adler32** (which is faster) and **CRC32** (which is slower but slightly more accurate).

```
//: c12:ZipCompress.java
// Uses Zip compression to compress any
// number of files given on the command line.
// {Args: ZipCompress.java}
// {Clean: test.zip}
import com.bruceeckel.simpletest.*;
import java.io.*;
```

```
import java.util.*;
import java.util.zip.*;

public class ZipCompress {
  private static Test monitor = new Test();
  // Throw exceptions to console:
  public static void main(String[] args)
  throws IOException {
    FileOutputStream f = new FileOutputStream("test.zip");
    CheckedOutputStream csum =
      new CheckedOutputStream(f, new Adler32());
     ZipOutputStream zos = new ZipOutputStream(csum);
     BufferedOutputStream out =
      new BufferedOutputStream(zos);
    zos.setComment("A test of Java Zipping");
    // No corresponding getComment(), though.
    for(int i = 0; i < args.length; i++) {
      System.out.println("Writing file " + args[i]);
      BufferedReader in =
        new BufferedReader(new FileReader(args[i]));
      zos.putNextEntry(new ZipEntry(args[i]));
      int c;
      while((c = in.read()) != -1)
        out.write(c);
      in.close();
    }
    out.close();
    // Checksum valid only after the file has been closed!
    System.out.println("Checksum: " +
      csum.getChecksum().getValue());
    // Now extract the files:
    System.out.println("Reading file");
    FileInputStream fi = new FileInputStream("test.zip");
    CheckedInputStream csumi =
      new CheckedInputStream(fi, new Adler32());
    ZipInputStream in2 = new ZipInputStream(csumi);
    BufferedInputStream bis = new BufferedInputStream(in2);
    ZipEntry ze;
    while((ze = in2.getNextEntry()) != null) {
      System.out.println("Reading file " + ze);
      int x;
      while((x = bis.read()) != -1)
        System.out.write(x);
    }
```

```
    if(args.length == 1)
      monitor.expect(new String[] {
        "Writing file " + args[0],
        "%% Checksum: \\d+",
        "Reading file",
        "Reading file " + args[0]}, args[0]);
    System.out.println("Checksum: " +
      csumi.getChecksum().getValue());
    bis.close();
    // Alternative way to open and read zip files:
    ZipFile zf = new ZipFile("test.zip");
    Enumeration e = zf.entries();
    while(e.hasMoreElements()) {
      ZipEntry ze2 = (ZipEntry)e.nextElement();
      System.out.println("File: " + ze2);
      // ... and extract the data as before
    }
    if(args.length == 1)
      monitor.expect(new String[] {
        "%% Checksum: \\d+",
        "File: " + args[0]
      });
  }
} ///:~
```

For each file to add to the archive, you must call **putNextEntry( )** and pass it a **ZipEntry** object. The **ZipEntry** object contains an extensive interface that allows you to get and set all the data available on that particular entry in your Zip file: name, compressed and uncompressed sizes, date, CRC checksum, extra field data, comment, compression method, and whether it's a directory entry. However, even though the Zip format has a way to set a password, this is not supported in Java's Zip library. And although **CheckedInputStream** and **CheckedOutputStream** support both **Adler32** and **CRC32** checksums, the **ZipEntry** class supports only an interface for CRC. This is a restriction of the underlying Zip format, but it might limit you from using the faster **Adler32**.

To extract files, **ZipInputStream** has a **getNextEntry( )** method that returns the next **ZipEntry** if there is one. As a more succinct alternative, you can read the file using a **ZipFile** object, which has a method **entries( )** to return an **Enumeration** to the **ZipEntries**.

In order to read the checksum, you must somehow have access to the associated **Checksum** object. Here, a reference to the **CheckedOutputStream** and **CheckedInputStream** objects is retained, but you could also just hold onto a reference to the **Checksum** object.

A baffling method in Zip streams is **setComment( )**. As shown in **ZipCompress.java**, you can set a comment when you're writing a file, but there's no way to recover the comment in the **ZipInputStream**. Comments appear to be supported fully on an entry-by-entry basis only via **ZipEntry**.

Of course, you are not limited to files when using the **GZIP** or **Zip** libraries—you can compress anything, including data to be sent through a network connection.

Java ARchives (JARs)

The Zip format is also used in the JAR (Java ARchive) file format, which is a way to collect a group of files into a single compressed file, just like Zip. However, like everything else in Java, JAR files are cross-platform, so you don't need to worry about platform issues. You can also include audio and image files as well as class files.

JAR files are particularly helpful when you deal with the Internet. Before JAR files, your Web browser would have to make repeated requests of a Web server in order to download all of the files that make up an applet. In addition, each of these files was uncompressed. By combining all of the files for a particular applet into a single JAR file, only one server request is necessary and the transfer is faster because of compression. And each entry in a JAR file can be digitally signed for security (see Chapter 14 for an example of signing).

A JAR file consists of a single file containing a collection of zipped files along with a "manifest" that describes them. (You can create your own manifest file; otherwise, the **jar** program will do it for you.) You can find out more about JAR manifests in the JDK documentation.

The **jar** utility that comes with Sun's JDK automatically compresses the files of your choice. You invoke it on the command line:

```
jar [options] destination [manifest] inputfile(s)
```

The options are simply a collection of letters (no hyphen or any other indicator is necessary). Unix/Linux users will note the similarity to the **tar** options. These are:

c	Creates a new or empty archive.
t	Lists the table of contents.
x	Extracts all files.
x file	Extracts the named file.
f	Says: "I'm going to give you the name of the file." If you don't use this, **jar** assumes that its input will come from standard input, or, if it is creating a file, its output will go to standard output.
m	Says that the first argument will be the name of the user-created manifest file.
v	Generates verbose output describing what **jar** is doing.
0	Only store the files; doesn't compress the files (use to create a JAR file that you can put in your classpath).
M	Don't automatically create a manifest file.

If a subdirectory is included in the files to be put into the JAR file, that subdirectory is automatically added, including all of its subdirectories, etc. Path information is also preserved.

Here are some typical ways to invoke **jar**:

```
jar cf myJarFile.jar *.class
```

This creates a JAR file called **myJarFile.jar** that contains all of the class files in the current directory, along with an automatically generated manifest file.

```
jar cmf myJarFile.jar myManifestFile.mf *.class
```

Like the previous example, but adding a user-created manifest file called **myManifestFile.mf**.

```
jar tf myJarFile.jar
```

Produces a table of contents of the files in **myJarFile.jar**.

```
jar tvf myJarFile.jar
```

Adds the "verbose" flag to give more detailed information about the files in **myJarFile.jar**.

```
jar cvf myApp.jar audio classes image
```

Assuming **audio**, **classes,** and **image** are subdirectories, this combines all of the subdirectories into the file **myApp.jar**. The "verbose" flag is also included to give extra feedback while the **jar** program is working.

If you create a JAR file using the **o** (zero) option, that file can be placed in your CLASSPATH:

```
CLASSPATH="lib1.jar;lib2.jar;"
```

Then Java can search **lib1.jar** and **lib2.jar** for class files.

The **jar** tool isn't as useful as a **zip** utility. For example, you can't add or update files to an existing JAR file; you can create JAR files only from scratch. Also, you can't move files into a JAR file, erasing them as they are moved. However, a JAR file created on one platform will be transparently readable by the **jar** tool on any other platform (a problem that sometimes plagues **zip** utilities).

As you will see in Chapter 14, JAR files are also used to package JavaBeans.

Object serialization

Java's *object serialization* allows you to take any object that implements the **Serializable** interface and turn it into a sequence of bytes that can later be fully restored to regenerate the original object. This is even true across a network, which means that the serialization mechanism automatically compensates for differences in operating systems. That is, you can create an object on a Windows machine, serialize it, and send it across the network to a Unix machine, where it will be correctly reconstructed. You don't have to worry about the data representations on the different machines, the byte ordering, or any other details.

By itself, object serialization is interesting because it allows you to implement *lightweight persistence*. Remember that persistence means that an object's lifetime is not determined by whether a program is executing; the object lives *in between* invocations of the program. By taking a serializable object and writing it to disk, then restoring that object when the program is reinvoked, you're able to produce the effect of persistence. The reason it's called "lightweight" is that you can't simply define an object using some kind of "persistent" keyword and let the system take care of the details (although this might happen in the future). Instead, you must explicitly serialize and deserialize the objects in your program. If you need a more serious persistence mechanism, consider *Java Data Objects* (JDO) or a tool like Hibernate (*http://hibernate.sourceforge.net*). For details, see *Thinking in Enterprise Java*, downloadable from *www.BruceEckel.com.*

Object serialization was added to the language to support two major features. Java's *Remote Method Invocation* (RMI) allows objects that live on other machines to behave as if they live on your machine. When sending messages to remote objects, object serialization is necessary to transport the arguments and return values. RMI is discussed in *Thinking in Enterprise Java.*

Object serialization is also necessary for JavaBeans, described in Chapter 14. When a Bean is used, its state information is generally configured at design time. This state information must be stored and later recovered when the program is started; object serialization performs this task.

Serializing an object is quite simple as long as the object implements the **Serializable** interface (this is a tagging interface and has no methods). When serialization was added to the language, many standard library classes were changed to make them serializable, including all of the wrappers for the primitive types, all of the container classes, and many others. Even **Class** objects can be serialized.

To serialize an object, you create some sort of **OutputStream** object and then wrap it inside an **ObjectOutputStream** object. At this point you need only call **writeObject( )**, and your object is serialized and sent to the **OutputStream**. To reverse the process, you wrap an **InputStream** inside an **ObjectInputStream** and call **readObject( )**. What comes back is, as usual, a reference to an upcast **Object**, so you must downcast to set things straight.

A particularly clever aspect of object serialization is that it not only saves an image of your object, but it also follows all the references contained in your object and saves *those* objects, and follows all the references in each of those objects, etc. This is sometimes referred to as the "web of objects" that a single object can be connected to, and it includes arrays of references to objects as well as member objects. If you had to maintain your own object serialization scheme, maintaining the code to follow all these links would be a bit mind-boggling. However, Java object serialization seems to pull it off flawlessly, no doubt using an optimized algorithm that traverses the web of objects. The following example tests the serialization mechanism by making a "worm" of linked objects, each of which has a link to the next segment in the worm as well as an array of references to objects of a different class, **Data**:

```
//: c12:Worm.java
// Demonstrates object serialization.
// {Clean: worm.out}
import java.io.*;
import java.util.*;

class Data implements Serializable {
  private int n;
  public Data(int n) { this.n = n; }
  public String toString() { return Integer.toString(n); }
}

public class Worm implements Serializable {
  private static Random rand = new Random();
  private Data[] d = {
    new Data(rand.nextInt(10)),
    new Data(rand.nextInt(10)),
    new Data(rand.nextInt(10))
  };
  private Worm next;
  private char c;
  // Value of i == number of segments
  public Worm(int i, char x) {
    System.out.println("Worm constructor: " + i);
    c = x;
    if(--i > 0)
      next = new Worm(i, (char)(x + 1));
  }
  public Worm() {
    System.out.println("Default constructor");
  }
  public String toString() {
    String s = ":" + c + "(";
    for(int i = 0; i < d.length; i++)
      s += d[i];
    s += ")";
    if(next != null)
      s += next;
```

```
    return s;
  }
  // Throw exceptions to console:
  public static void main(String[] args)
  throws ClassNotFoundException, IOException {
    Worm w = new Worm(6, 'a');
    System.out.println("w = " + w);
    ObjectOutputStream out = new ObjectOutputStream(
      new FileOutputStream("worm.out"));
    out.writeObject("Worm storage\n");
    out.writeObject(w);
    out.close(); // Also flushes output
    ObjectInputStream in = new ObjectInputStream(
      new FileInputStream("worm.out"));
    String s = (String)in.readObject();
    Worm w2 = (Worm)in.readObject();
    System.out.println(s + "w2 = " + w2);
    ByteArrayOutputStream bout =
      new ByteArrayOutputStream();
    ObjectOutputStream out2 = new ObjectOutputStream(bout);
    out2.writeObject("Worm storage\n");
    out2.writeObject(w);
    out2.flush();
    ObjectInputStream in2 = new ObjectInputStream(
      new ByteArrayInputStream(bout.toByteArray()));
    s = (String)in2.readObject();
    Worm w3 = (Worm)in2.readObject();
    System.out.println(s + "w3 = " + w3);
  }
} ///:~
```

To make things interesting, the array of **Data** objects inside **Worm** are initialized with random numbers. (This way you don't suspect the compiler of keeping some kind of meta-information.) Each **Worm** segment is labeled with a **char** that's automatically generated in the process of recursively generating the linked list of **Worm**s. When you create a **Worm**, you tell the constructor how long you want it to be. To make the **next** reference, it calls the **Worm** constructor with a length of one less, etc. The final **next** reference is left as **null**, indicating the end of the **Worm**.

The point of all this was to make something reasonably complex that couldn't easily be serialized. The act of serializing, however, is quite simple. Once the **ObjectOutputStream** is created from some other stream, **writeObject( )** serializes the object. Notice the call to **writeObject( )** for a **String**, as well.

You can also write all the primitive data types using the same methods as **DataOutputStream** (they share the same interface).

There are two separate code sections that look similar. The first writes and reads a file and the second, for variety, writes and reads a **ByteArray**. You can read and write an object using serialization to any **DataInputStream** or **DataOutputStream** including, as you can see in *Thinking in Enterprise Java*, a network. The output from one run was:

```
Worm constructor: 6
Worm constructor: 5
Worm constructor: 4
Worm constructor: 3
Worm constructor: 2
Worm constructor: 1
w = :a(414):b(276):c(773):d(870):e(210):f(279)
Worm storage
w2 = :a(414):b(276):c(773):d(870):e(210):f(279)
Worm storage
w3 = :a(414):b(276):c(773):d(870):e(210):f(279)
```

You can see that the deserialized object really does contain all of the links that were in the original object.

Note that no constructor, not even the default constructor, is called in the process of deserializing a **Serializable** object. The entire object is restored by recovering data from the **InputStream**.

Object serialization is **byte**-oriented, and thus uses the **InputStream** and **OutputStream** hierarchies.

Finding the class

You might wonder what's necessary for an object to be recovered from its serialized state. For example, suppose you serialize an object and send it as a file or through a network to another machine. Could a program on the other machine reconstruct the object using only the contents of the file?

The best way to answer this question is (as usual) by performing an experiment. The following file goes in the subdirectory for this chapter:

```
//: c12:Alien.java
// A serializable class.
import java.io.*;
```

```
public class Alien implements Serializable {} ///:~
```

The file that creates and serializes an **Alien** object goes in the same directory:

```
//: c12:FreezeAlien.java
// Create a serialized output file.
// {Clean: X.file}
import java.io.*;

public class FreezeAlien {
  // Throw exceptions to console:
  public static void main(String[] args) throws Exception {
    ObjectOutput out = new ObjectOutputStream(
      new FileOutputStream("X.file"));
    Alien zorcon = new Alien();
    out.writeObject(zorcon);
  }
} ///:~
```

Rather than catching and handling exceptions, this program takes the quick-and-dirty approach of passing the exceptions out of **main( )**, so they'll be reported on the console.

Once the program is compiled and run, it produces a file called **X.file** in the **c12** directory. The following code is in a subdirectory called **xfiles**:

```
//: c12:xfiles:ThawAlien.java
// Try to recover a serialized file without the
// class of object that's stored in that file.
// {ThrowsException}
import java.io.*;

public class ThawAlien {
  public static void main(String[] args) throws Exception {
    ObjectInputStream in = new ObjectInputStream(
      new FileInputStream(new File("..", "X.file")));
    Object mystery = in.readObject();
    System.out.println(mystery.getClass());
  }
} ///:~
```

Even opening the file and reading in the object **mystery** requires the **Class** object for **Alien**; the JVM cannot find **Alien.class** (unless it happens to be in the Classpath, which it shouldn't be in this example). You'll get a **ClassNotFoundException.** (Once again, all evidence of alien life vanishes before proof of its existence can be verified!) The JVM must be able to find the associated **.class** file.

Controlling serialization

As you can see, the default serialization mechanism is trivial to use. But what if you have special needs? Perhaps you have special security issues and you don't want to serialize portions of your object, or perhaps it just doesn't make sense for one subobject to be serialized if that part needs to be created anew when the object is recovered.

You can control the process of serialization by implementing the **Externalizable** interface instead of the **Serializable** interface. The **Externalizable** interface extends the **Serializable** interface and adds two methods, **writeExternal( )** and **readExternal( ),** that are automatically called for your object during serialization and deserialization so that you can perform your special operations.

The following example shows simple implementations of the **Externalizable** interface methods. Note that **Blip1** and **Blip2** are nearly identical except for a subtle difference (see if you can discover it by looking at the code):

```
//: c12:Blips.java
// Simple use of Externalizable & a pitfall.
// {Clean: Blips.out}
import com.bruceeckel.simpletest.*;
import java.io.*;
import java.util.*;

class Blip1 implements Externalizable {
  public Blip1() {
    System.out.println("Blip1 Constructor");
  }
  public void writeExternal(ObjectOutput out)
      throws IOException {
    System.out.println("Blip1.writeExternal");
  }
  public void readExternal(ObjectInput in)
     throws IOException, ClassNotFoundException {
    System.out.println("Blip1.readExternal");
  }
}
```

```
class Blip2 implements Externalizable {
  Blip2() {
    System.out.println("Blip2 Constructor");
  }
  public void writeExternal(ObjectOutput out)
      throws IOException {
    System.out.println("Blip2.writeExternal");
  }
  public void readExternal(ObjectInput in)
     throws IOException, ClassNotFoundException {
    System.out.println("Blip2.readExternal");
  }
}

public class Blips {
  private static Test monitor = new Test();
  // Throw exceptions to console:
  public static void main(String[] args)
  throws IOException, ClassNotFoundException {
    System.out.println("Constructing objects:");
    Blip1 b1 = new Blip1();
    Blip2 b2 = new Blip2();
    ObjectOutputStream o = new ObjectOutputStream(
      new FileOutputStream("Blips.out"));
    System.out.println("Saving objects:");
    o.writeObject(b1);
    o.writeObject(b2);
    o.close();
    // Now get them back:
    ObjectInputStream in = new ObjectInputStream(
      new FileInputStream("Blips.out"));
    System.out.println("Recovering b1:");
    b1 = (Blip1)in.readObject();
    // OOPS! Throws an exception:
//! System.out.println("Recovering b2:");
//! b2 = (Blip2)in.readObject();
    monitor.expect(new String[] {
      "Constructing objects:",
      "Blip1 Constructor",
      "Blip2 Constructor",
      "Saving objects:",
      "Blip1.writeExternal",
      "Blip2.writeExternal",
```

```
      "Recovering b1:",
      "Blip1 Constructor",
      "Blip1.readExternal"
    });
  }
} ///:~
```

The reason that the **Blip2** object is not recovered is that trying to do so causes an exception. Can you see the difference between **Blip1** and **Blip2**? The constructor for **Blip1** is **public**, while the constructor for **Blip2** is not, and that causes the exception upon recovery. Try making **Blip2**'s constructor **public** and removing the **//!** comments to see the correct results.

When **b1** is recovered, the **Blip1** default constructor is called. This is different from recovering a **Serializable** object, in which the object is constructed entirely from its stored bits, with no constructor calls. With an **Externalizable** object, all the normal default construction behavior occurs (including the initializations at the point of field definition), and *then* **readExternal( )** is called. You need to be aware of this—in particular, the fact that all the default construction always takes place—to produce the correct behavior in your **Externalizable** objects.

Here's an example that shows what you must do to fully store and retrieve an **Externalizable** object:

```
//: c12:Blip3.java
// Reconstructing an externalizable object.
import com.bruceeckel.simpletest.*;
import java.io.*;
import java.util.*;

public class Blip3 implements Externalizable {
  private static Test monitor = new Test();
  private int i;
  private String s; // No initialization
  public Blip3() {
    System.out.println("Blip3 Constructor");
    // s, i not initialized
  }
  public Blip3(String x, int a) {
    System.out.println("Blip3(String x, int a)");
    s = x;
    i = a;
    // s & i initialized only in nondefault constructor.
```

```
  }
  public String toString() { return s + i; }
  public void writeExternal(ObjectOutput out)
  throws IOException {
    System.out.println("Blip3.writeExternal");
    // You must do this:
    out.writeObject(s);
    out.writeInt(i);
  }
  public void readExternal(ObjectInput in)
  throws IOException, ClassNotFoundException {
    System.out.println("Blip3.readExternal");
    // You must do this:
    s = (String)in.readObject();
    i = in.readInt();
  }
  public static void main(String[] args)
  throws IOException, ClassNotFoundException {
    System.out.println("Constructing objects:");
    Blip3 b3 = new Blip3("A String ", 47);
    System.out.println(b3);
    ObjectOutputStream o = new ObjectOutputStream(
      new FileOutputStream("Blip3.out"));
    System.out.println("Saving object:");
    o.writeObject(b3);
    o.close();
    // Now get it back:
    ObjectInputStream in = new ObjectInputStream(
      new FileInputStream("Blip3.out"));
    System.out.println("Recovering b3:");
    b3 = (Blip3)in.readObject();
    System.out.println(b3);
    monitor.expect(new String[] {
      "Constructing objects:",
      "Blip3(String x, int a)",
      "A String 47",
      "Saving object:",
      "Blip3.writeExternal",
      "Recovering b3:",
      "Blip3 Constructor",
      "Blip3.readExternal",
      "A String 47"
    });
  }
```

```
} ///:~
```

The fields **s** and **i** are initialized only in the second constructor, but not in the default constructor. This means that if you don't initialize **s** and **i** in **readExternal( )**, **s** will be **null** and **i** will be zero (since the storage for the object gets wiped to zero in the first step of object creation). If you comment out the two lines of code following the phrases "You must do this" and run the program, you'll see that when the object is recovered, **s** is **null** and **i** is zero.

If you are inheriting from an **Externalizable** object, you'll typically call the base-class versions of **writeExternal( )** and **readExternal( )** to provide proper storage and retrieval of the base-class components.

So to make things work correctly you must not only write the important data from the object during the **writeExternal( )** method (there is no default behavior that writes any of the member objects for an **Externalizable** object), but you must also recover that data in the **readExternal( )** method. This can be a bit confusing at first because the default construction behavior for an **Externalizable** object can make it seem like some kind of storage and retrieval takes place automatically. It does not.

The transient keyword

When you're controlling serialization, there might be a particular subobject that you don't want Java's serialization mechanism to automatically save and restore. This is commonly the case if that subobject represents sensitive information that you don't want to serialize, such as a password. Even if that information is **private** in the object, once it has been serialized, it's possible for someone to access it by reading a file or intercepting a network transmission.

One way to prevent sensitive parts of your object from being serialized is to implement your class as **Externalizable**, as shown previously. Then nothing is automatically serialized, and you can explicitly serialize only the necessary parts inside **writeExternal( )**.

If you're working with a **Serializable** object, however, all serialization happens automatically. To control this, you can turn off serialization on a field-by-field basis using the **transient** keyword, which says "Don't bother saving or restoring this—I'll take care of it."

For example, consider a **Login** object that keeps information about a particular login session. Suppose that, once you verify the login, you want to store the data, but without the password. The easiest way to do this is by implementing **Serializable** and marking the **password** field as **transient**. Here's what it looks like:

```
//: c12:Logon.java
// Demonstrates the "transient" keyword.
// {Clean: Logon.out}
import java.io.*;
import java.util.*;

public class Logon implements Serializable {
  private Date date = new Date();
  private String username;
  private transient String password;
  public Logon(String name, String pwd) {
    username = name;
    password = pwd;
  }
  public String toString() {
    String pwd = (password == null) ? "(n/a)" : password;
    return "logon info: \n   username: " + username +
      "\n   date: " + date + "\n   password: " + pwd;
  }
  public static void main(String[] args) throws Exception {
    Logon a = new Logon("Hulk", "myLittlePony");
    System.out.println( "logon a = " + a);
    ObjectOutputStream o = new ObjectOutputStream(
      new FileOutputStream("Logon.out"));
    o.writeObject(a);
    o.close();
    Thread.sleep(1000); // Delay for 1 second
    // Now get them back:
    ObjectInputStream in = new ObjectInputStream(
      new FileInputStream("Logon.out"));
    System.out.println("Recovering object at "+new Date());
    a = (Logon)in.readObject();
    System.out.println("logon a = " + a);
  }
} ///:~
```

You can see that the **date** and **username** fields are ordinary (not **transient**), and thus are automatically serialized. However, the **password** is **transient**, so it is not stored to disk; also, the serialization mechanism makes no attempt to recover it. The output is:

```
logon a = logon info:
   username: Hulk
   date: Mon Oct 21 12:10:13 MDT 2002
   password: myLittlePony
Recovering object at Mon Oct 21 12:10:14 MDT 2002
logon a = logon info:
   username: Hulk
   date: Mon Oct 21 12:10:13 MDT 2002
   password: (n/a)
```

When the object is recovered, the **password** field is **null**. Note that **toString( )** must check for a **null** value of **password**, because if you try to assemble a **String** object using the overloaded '+' operator, and that operator encounters a **null** reference, you'll get a **NullPointerException.** (Newer versions of Java might contain code to avoid this problem.)

You can also see that the **date** field is stored to and recovered from disk and not generated anew.

Since **Externalizable** objects do not store any of their fields by default, the **transient** keyword is for use with **Serializable** objects only.

An alternative to **Externalizable**

If you're not keen on implementing the **Externalizable** interface, there's another approach. You can implement the **Serializable** interface and *add* (notice I say "add" and not "override" or "implement") methods called **writeObject( )** and **readObject( )** that will automatically be called when the object is serialized and deserialized, respectively. That is, if you provide these two methods, they will be used instead of the default serialization.

The methods must have these exact signatures:

```
private void writeObject(ObjectOutputStream stream)
throws IOException;

private void readObject(ObjectInputStream stream)
throws IOException, ClassNotFoundException
```

From a design standpoint, things get really weird here. First of all, you might think that because these methods are not part of a base class or the **Serializable** interface, they ought to be defined in their own interface(s). But notice that they are defined as **private**, which means they are to be called only by other members of this class. However, you don't actually call them from other members of this class, but instead the **writeObject( )** and **readObject( )** methods of the **ObjectOutputStream** and **ObjectInputStream** objects call your object's **writeObject( )** and **readObject( )** methods. (Notice my tremendous restraint in not launching into a long diatribe about using the same method names here. In a word: confusing.) You might wonder how the **ObjectOutputStream** and **ObjectInputStream** objects have access to **private** methods of your class. We can only assume that this is part of the serialization magic.

In any event, anything defined in an **interface** is automatically **public** so if **writeObject( )** and **readObject( )** must be **private**, then they can't be part of an **interface**. Since you must follow the signatures exactly, the effect is the same as if you're implementing an **interface**.

It would appear that when you call **ObjectOutputStream.writeObject( )**, the **Serializable** object that you pass it to is interrogated (using reflection, no doubt) to see if it implements its own **writeObject( )**. If so, the normal serialization process is skipped and the **writeObject( )** is called. The same sort of situation exists for **readObject( )**.

There's one other twist. Inside your **writeObject( )**, you can choose to perform the default **writeObject( )** action by calling **defaultWriteObject( )**. Likewise, inside **readObject( )** you can call **defaultReadObject( )**. Here is a simple example that demonstrates how you can control the storage and retrieval of a **Serializable** object:

```
//: c12:SerialCtl.java
// Controlling serialization by adding your own
// writeObject() and readObject() methods.
import com.bruceeckel.simpletest.*;
import java.io.*;

public class SerialCtl implements Serializable {
  private static Test monitor = new Test();
  private String a;
  private transient String b;
  public SerialCtl(String aa, String bb) {
    a = "Not Transient: " + aa;
    b = "Transient: " + bb;
  }
  public String toString() { return a + "\n" + b; }
  private void writeObject(ObjectOutputStream stream)
  throws IOException {
```

```
    stream.defaultWriteObject();
    stream.writeObject(b);
  }
  private void readObject(ObjectInputStream stream)
  throws IOException, ClassNotFoundException {
    stream.defaultReadObject();
    b = (String)stream.readObject();
  }
  public static void main(String[] args)
  throws IOException, ClassNotFoundException {
    SerialCtl sc = new SerialCtl("Test1", "Test2");
    System.out.println("Before:\n" + sc);
    ByteArrayOutputStream buf= new ByteArrayOutputStream();
    ObjectOutputStream o = new ObjectOutputStream(buf);
    o.writeObject(sc);
    // Now get it back:
    ObjectInputStream in = new ObjectInputStream(
      new ByteArrayInputStream(buf.toByteArray()));
    SerialCtl sc2 = (SerialCtl)in.readObject();
    System.out.println("After:\n" + sc2);
    monitor.expect(new String[] {
     "Before:",
     "Not Transient: Test1",
     "Transient: Test2",
     "After:",
     "Not Transient: Test1",
     "Transient: Test2"
    });
  }
} ///:~
```

In this example, one **String** field is ordinary and the other is **transient**, to prove that the non-**transient** field is saved by the **defaultWriteObject( )** method and the **transient** field is saved and restored explicitly. The fields are initialized inside the constructor rather than at the point of definition to prove that they are not being initialized by some automatic mechanism during deserialization.

If you are going to use the default mechanism to write the non-**transient** parts of your object, you must call **defaultWriteObject( )** as the first operation in **writeObject( )**, and **defaultReadObject( )** as the first operation in **readObject( )**. These are strange method calls. It would appear, for example, that you are calling **defaultWriteObject( )** for an **ObjectOutputStream** and passing it no arguments, and yet it somehow turns around and knows the reference to your object and how to write all the non-**transient** parts. Spooky.

The storage and retrieval of the **transient** objects uses more familiar code. And yet, think about what happens here. In **main( )**, a **SerialCtl** object is created, and then it's serialized to an **ObjectOutputStream.** (Notice in this case that a buffer is used instead of a file—it's all the same to the **ObjectOutputStream**.) The serialization occurs in the line:

```
o.writeObject(sc);
```

The **writeObject( )** method must be examining **sc** to see if it has its own **writeObject( )** method. (Not by checking the interface—there isn't one—or the class type, but by actually hunting for the method using reflection.) If it does, it uses that. A similar approach holds true for **readObject( )**. Perhaps this was the only practical way that they could solve the problem, but it's certainly strange.

Versioning

It's possible that you might want to change the version of a serializable class (objects of the original class might be stored in a database, for example). This is supported, but you'll probably do it only in special cases, and it requires an extra depth of understanding that we will not attempt to achieve here. The JDK documents downloadable from *java.sun.com* cover this topic quite thoroughly.

You will also notice in the JDK documentation many comments that begin with:

> ***Warning:*** *Serialized objects of this class will not be compatible with future Swing releases. The current serialization support is appropriate for short term storage or RMI between applications ...*

This is because the versioning mechanism is too simple to work reliably in all situations, especially with JavaBeans. They're working on a correction for the design, and that's what the warning is about.

Using persistence

It's quite appealing to use serialization technology to store some of the state of your program so that you can easily restore the program to the current state later. But before you can do this, some questions must be answered.

What happens if you serialize two objects that both have a reference to a third object? When you restore those two objects from their serialized state, do you get only one occurrence of the third object? What if you serialize your two objects to separate files and deserialize them in different parts of your code?

Here's an example that shows the problem:

```
//: c12:MyWorld.java
import java.io.*;
import java.util.*;

class House implements Serializable {}

class Animal implements Serializable {
  private String name;
  private House preferredHouse;
  Animal(String nm, House h) {
    name = nm;
    preferredHouse = h;
  }
  public String toString() {
    return name + "[" + super.toString() +
      "], " + preferredHouse + "\n";
  }
}

public class MyWorld {
  public static void main(String[] args)
  throws IOException, ClassNotFoundException {
    House house = new House();
    List animals = new ArrayList();
    animals.add(new Animal("Bosco the dog", house));
    animals.add(new Animal("Ralph the hamster", house));
    animals.add(new Animal("Fronk the cat", house));
    System.out.println("animals: " + animals);
    ByteArrayOutputStream buf1 =
      new ByteArrayOutputStream();
    ObjectOutputStream o1 = new ObjectOutputStream(buf1);
    o1.writeObject(animals);
    o1.writeObject(animals); // Write a 2nd set
    // Write to a different stream:
    ByteArrayOutputStream buf2 =
      new ByteArrayOutputStream();
    ObjectOutputStream o2 = new ObjectOutputStream(buf2);
```

```
    o2.writeObject(animals);
    // Now get them back:
    ObjectInputStream in1 = new ObjectInputStream(
      new ByteArrayInputStream(buf1.toByteArray()));
    ObjectInputStream in2 = new ObjectInputStream(
      new ByteArrayInputStream(buf2.toByteArray()));
    List
      animals1 = (List)in1.readObject(),
      animals2 = (List)in1.readObject(),
      animals3 = (List)in2.readObject();
    System.out.println("animals1: " + animals1);
    System.out.println("animals2: " + animals2);
    System.out.println("animals3: " + animals3);
  }
} ///:~
```

One thing that's interesting here is that it's possible to use object serialization to and from a byte array as a way of doing a "deep copy" of any object that's **Serializable.** (A deep copy means that you're duplicating the entire web of objects, rather than just the basic object and its references.) Object copying is covered in depth in Appendix A.

Animal objects contain fields of type **House**. In **main( )**, a **List** of these **Animal**s is created and it is serialized twice to one stream and then again to a separate stream. When these are deserialized and printed, you see the following results for one run (the objects will be in different memory locations each run):

```
animals: [Bosco the dog[Animal@1cde100], House@16f0472
, Ralph the hamster[Animal@18d107f], House@16f0472
, Fronk the cat[Animal@360be0], House@16f0472
]
animals1: [Bosco the dog[Animal@e86da0], House@1754ad2
, Ralph the hamster[Animal@1833955], House@1754ad2
, Fronk the cat[Animal@291aff], House@1754ad2
]
animals2: [Bosco the dog[Animal@e86da0], House@1754ad2
, Ralph the hamster[Animal@1833955], House@1754ad2
, Fronk the cat[Animal@291aff], House@1754ad2
]
animals3: [Bosco the dog[Animal@ab95e6], House@fe64b9
, Ralph the hamster[Animal@186db54], House@fe64b9
, Fronk the cat[Animal@a97b0b], House@fe64b9
]
```

Of course you expect that the deserialized objects have different addresses from their originals. But notice that in **animals1** and **animals2**, the same addresses appear, including the references to the **House** object that both share. On the other hand, when **animals3** is recovered, the system has no way of knowing that the objects in this other stream are aliases of the objects in the first stream, so it makes a completely different web of objects.

As long as you're serializing everything to a single stream, you'll be able to recover the same web of objects that you wrote, with no accidental duplication of objects. Of course, you can change the state of your objects in between the time you write the first and the last, but that's your responsibility; the objects will be written in whatever state they are in (and with whatever connections they have to other objects) at the time you serialize them.

The safest thing to do if you want to save the state of a system is to serialize as an "atomic" operation. If you serialize some things, do some other work, and serialize some more, etc., then you will not be storing the system safely. Instead, put all the objects that comprise the state of your system in a single container and simply write that container out in one operation. Then you can restore it with a single method call as well.

The following example is an imaginary computer-aided design (CAD) system that demonstrates the approach. In addition, it throws in the issue of **static** fields; if you look at the JDK documentation you'll see that **Class** is **Serializable**, so it should be easy to store the **static** fields by simply serializing the **Class** object. That seems like a sensible approach, anyway.

```
//: c12:CADState.java
// Saving and restoring the state of a pretend CAD system.
// {Clean: CADState.out}
//package c12;
import java.io.*;
import java.util.*;

abstract class Shape implements Serializable {
  public static final int RED = 1, BLUE = 2, GREEN = 3;
  private int xPos, yPos, dimension;
  private static Random r = new Random();
  private static int counter = 0;
  public abstract void setColor(int newColor);
  public abstract int getColor();
```

```
  public Shape(int xVal, int yVal, int dim) {
    xPos = xVal;
    yPos = yVal;
    dimension = dim;
  }
  public String toString() {
    return getClass() +
      "color[" + getColor() + "] xPos[" + xPos +
      "] yPos[" + yPos + "] dim[" + dimension + "]\n";
  }
  public static Shape randomFactory() {
    int xVal = r.nextInt(100);
    int yVal = r.nextInt(100);
    int dim = r.nextInt(100);
    switch(counter++ % 3) {
      default:
      case 0: return new Circle(xVal, yVal, dim);
      case 1: return new Square(xVal, yVal, dim);
      case 2: return new Line(xVal, yVal, dim);
    }
  }
}

class Circle extends Shape {
  private static int color = RED;
  public Circle(int xVal, int yVal, int dim) {
    super(xVal, yVal, dim);
  }
  public void setColor(int newColor) { color = newColor; }
  public int getColor() { return color; }
}

class Square extends Shape {
  private static int color;
  public Square(int xVal, int yVal, int dim) {
    super(xVal, yVal, dim);
    color = RED;
  }
  public void setColor(int newColor) { color = newColor; }
  public int getColor() { return color; }
}

class Line extends Shape {
  private static int color = RED;
```

```
  public static void
  serializeStaticState(ObjectOutputStream os)
  throws IOException { os.writeInt(color); }
  public static void
  deserializeStaticState(ObjectInputStream os)
  throws IOException { color = os.readInt(); }
  public Line(int xVal, int yVal, int dim) {
    super(xVal, yVal, dim);
  }
  public void setColor(int newColor) { color = newColor; }
  public int getColor() { return color; }
}

public class CADState {
  public static void main(String[] args) throws Exception {
    List shapeTypes, shapes;
    if(args.length == 0) {
      shapeTypes = new ArrayList();
      shapes = new ArrayList();
      // Add references to the class objects:
      shapeTypes.add(Circle.class);
      shapeTypes.add(Square.class);
      shapeTypes.add(Line.class);
      // Make some shapes:
      for(int i = 0; i < 10; i++)
        shapes.add(Shape.randomFactory());
      // Set all the static colors to GREEN:
      for(int i = 0; i < 10; i++)
        ((Shape)shapes.get(i)).setColor(Shape.GREEN);
      // Save the state vector:
      ObjectOutputStream out = new ObjectOutputStream(
        new FileOutputStream("CADState.out"));
      out.writeObject(shapeTypes);
      Line.serializeStaticState(out);
      out.writeObject(shapes);
    } else { // There's a command-line argument
      ObjectInputStream in = new ObjectInputStream(
        new FileInputStream(args[0]));
      // Read in the same order they were written:
      shapeTypes = (List)in.readObject();
      Line.deserializeStaticState(in);
      shapes = (List)in.readObject();
    }
    // Display the shapes:
```

```
      System.out.println(shapes);
   }
} ///:~
```

The **Shape** class **implements Serializable**, so anything that is inherited from **Shape** is automatically **Serializable** as well. Each **Shape** contains data, and each derived **Shape** class contains a **static** field that determines the color of all of those types of **Shape**s. (Placing a **static** field in the base class would result in only one field, since **static** fields are not duplicated in derived classes.) Methods in the base class can be overridden to set the color for the various types (**static** methods are not dynamically bound, so these are normal methods). The **randomFactory( )** method creates a different **Shape** each time you call it, using random values for the **Shape** data.

Circle and **Square** are straightforward extensions of **Shape**; the only difference is that **Circle** initializes **color** at the point of definition and **Square** initializes it in the constructor. We'll leave the discussion of **Line** for later.

In **main( )**, one **ArrayList** is used to hold the **Class** objects and the other to hold the shapes. If you don't provide a command-line argument, the **shapeTypes ArrayList** is created and the **Class** objects are added, and then the **shapes ArrayList** is created and **Shape** objects are added. Next, all the **static color** values are set to **GREEN**, and everything is serialized to the file **CADState.out**.

If you provide a command-line argument (presumably **CADState.out**), that file is opened and used to restore the state of the program. In both situations, the resulting **ArrayList** of **Shape**s is printed. The results from one run are:

```
$ java CADState
[class Circlecolor[3] xPos[71] yPos[82] dim[44]
, class Squarecolor[3] xPos[98] yPos[21] dim[49]
, class Linecolor[3] xPos[16] yPos[80] dim[37]
, class Circlecolor[3] xPos[51] yPos[74] dim[7]
, class Squarecolor[3] xPos[7] yPos[78] dim[98]
, class Linecolor[3] xPos[38] yPos[79] dim[93]
, class Circlecolor[3] xPos[84] yPos[12] dim[62]
, class Squarecolor[3] xPos[16] yPos[51] dim[94]
, class Linecolor[3] xPos[51] yPos[0] dim[73]
, class Circlecolor[3] xPos[47] yPos[6] dim[49]
]
```

```
$ java CADState CADState.out
[class Circlecolor[1] xPos[71] yPos[82] dim[44]
, class Squarecolor[0] xPos[98] yPos[21] dim[49]
, class Linecolor[3] xPos[16] yPos[80] dim[37]
, class Circlecolor[1] xPos[51] yPos[74] dim[7]
, class Squarecolor[0] xPos[7] yPos[78] dim[98]
, class Linecolor[3] xPos[38] yPos[79] dim[93]
, class Circlecolor[1] xPos[84] yPos[12] dim[62]
, class Squarecolor[0] xPos[16] yPos[51] dim[94]
, class Linecolor[3] xPos[51] yPos[0] dim[73]
, class Circlecolor[1] xPos[47] yPos[6] dim[49]
]
```

You can see that the values of **xPos**, **yPos,** and **dim** were all stored and recovered successfully, but there's something wrong with the retrieval of the **static** information. It's all "3" going in, but it doesn't come out that way. **Circle**s have a value of 1 (**RED**, which is the definition), and **Square**s have a value of 0 (remember, they are initialized in the constructor). It's as if the **static**s didn't get serialized at all! That's right—even though class **Class** is **Serializable**, it doesn't do what you expect. So if you want to serialize **statics**, you must do it yourself.

This is what the **serializeStaticState( )** and **deserializeStaticState( ) static** methods in **Line** are for. You can see that they are explicitly called as part of the storage and retrieval process. (Note that the order of writing to the serialize file and reading back from it must be maintained.) Thus to make **CADState.java** run correctly, you must:

1. Add a **serializeStaticState( )** and **deserializeStaticState( )** to the shapes.

2. Remove the **ArrayList shapeTypes** and all code related to it.

3. Add calls to the new serialize and deserialize static methods in the shapes.

Another issue you might have to think about is security, since serialization also saves **private** data. If you have a security issue, those fields should be marked as **transient**. But then you have to design a secure way to store that information so that when you do a restore you can reset those **private** variables.

Preferences

JDK 1.4 introduced the *Preferences* API, which is much closer to persistence than object serialization because it automatically stores and retrieves your information. However, its use is restricted to small and limited data sets—you can only hold primitives and **Strings**, and the length of each stored **String** can't be longer than 8K (not tiny, but you don't want to build anything serious with it, either). As the name suggests, the Preferences API is designed to store and retrieve user preferences and program-configuration settings.

Preferences are key-value sets (like **Maps**) stored in a hierarchy of nodes. Although the node hierarchy can be used to create complicated structures, it's typical to create a single node named after your class and store the information there. Here's a simple example:

```
//: c12:PreferencesDemo.java
import java.util.prefs.*;
import java.util.*;

public class PreferencesDemo {
  public static void main(String[] args) throws Exception {
    Preferences prefs = Preferences
      .userNodeForPackage(PreferencesDemo.class);
    prefs.put("Location", "Oz");
    prefs.put("Footwear", "Ruby Slippers");
    prefs.putInt("Companions", 4);
    prefs.putBoolean("Are there witches?", true);
    int usageCount = prefs.getInt("UsageCount", 0);
    usageCount++;
    prefs.putInt("UsageCount", usageCount);
    Iterator it = Arrays.asList(prefs.keys()).iterator();
    while(it.hasNext()) {
      String key = it.next().toString();
      System.out.println(key + ": "+ prefs.get(key, null));
    }
    // You must always provide a default value:
    System.out.println(
      "How many companions does Dorothy have? " +
      prefs.getInt("Companions", 0));
  }
} ///:~
```

Here, **userNodeForPackage( )** is used, but you could also choose **systemNodeForPackage( )**; the choice is somewhat arbitrary, but the idea is that "user" is for individual user preferences, and "system" is for general installation configuration. Since **main( )** is **static**, **PreferencesDemo.class** is used to identify the node, but inside a non-static method, you'll usually use **getClass( )**. You don't need to use the current class as the node identifier, but that's the usual practice.

Once you create the node, it's available for either loading or reading data. This example loads the node with various types of items and then gets the **keys( )**. These come back as a **String[]**, which you might not expect if you're used to **keys( )** in the collections library. Here, they're converted to a **List** that is used to produce an **Iterator** for printing the keys and values. Notice the second argument to **get( )**. This is the default value that is produced if there isn't any entry for that key value. While iterating through a set of keys, you always know there's an entry, so using **null** as the default is safe, but normally you'll be fetching a named key, as in:

```
prefs.getInt("Companions", 0));
```

In the normal case, you'll want to provide a reasonable default value. In fact, a typical idiom is seen in the lines:

```
int usageCount = prefs.getInt("UsageCount", 0);
usageCount++;
prefs.putInt("UsageCount", usageCount);
```

This way, the first time you run the program, the **UsageCount** will be zero, but on subsequent invocations it will be nonzero.

When you run **PreferencesDemo.java** you'll see that the **UsageCount** does indeed increment every time you run the program, but where is the data stored? There's no local file that appears after the program is run the first time. The Preferences API uses appropriate system resources to accomplish its task, and these will vary depending on the OS. In Windows, the registry is used (since it's already a hierarchy of nodes with key-value pairs). But the whole point is that the information is magically stored for you so that you don't have to worry about how it works from one system to another.

There's more to the Preferences API than shown here. Consult the JDK documentation, which is fairly understandable, for further details.

Regular expressions

To finish this chapter, we'll look at *regular expressions*, which were added in JDK 1.4 but have been integral to standard Unix utilities like sed and awk, and languages like Python and Perl (some would argue that they are predominant reason for Perl's success). Technically, these are string manipulation tools (previously delegated to the **String**, **StringBuffer**, and **StringTokenizer** classes in Java), but they are typically used in conjunction with I/O, so it's not too far-fetched to include them here.[6]

Regular expressions are powerful and flexible text-processing tools. They allow you to specify, programmatically, complex patterns of text that can be discovered in an input string. Once you discover these patterns, you can then react to them any way you want. Although the syntax of regular expressions can be intimidating at first, they provide a compact and dynamic language that can be employed to solve all sorts of string processing, matching and selection, editing, and verification problems in a completely general way.

Creating regular expressions

You can begin learning regular expressions with a useful subset of the possible constructs. A complete list of constructs for building regular expressions can be found in the javadocs for the **Pattern** class for package **java.util.regex**.

Characters	
B	The specific character **B**
\xhh	Character with hex value **oxhh**
\uhhhh	The Unicode character with hex representation **oxhhhh**
\t	Tab
\n	Newline
\r	Carriage return
\f	Form feed

[6] A chapter dedicated to strings will have to wait until the 4th edition. Mike Shea contributed to this section.

\e	Escape

The power of regular expressions begins to appear when defining character classes. Here are some typical ways to create character classes, and some predefined classes:

Character Classes	
.	Represents any character
[abc]	Any of the characters **a**, **b**, or **c** (same as **a|b|c**)
[^abc]	Any character except **a**, **b**, and **c** (negation)
[a-zA-Z]	Any character **a** through **z** or **A** through **Z** (range)
[abc[hij]]	Any of **a**,**b**,**c**,**h**,**i**,**j** (same as **a|b|c|h|i|j**) (union)
[a-z&&[hij]]	Either **h**, **i**, or **j** (intersection)
\s	A whitespace character (space, tab, newline, formfeed, carriage return)
\S	A non-whitespace character (**[^\s]**)
\d	A numeric digit **[0-9]**
\D	A non-digit **[^0-9]**
\w	A word character **[a-zA-Z_0-9]**
\W	A non-word character **[^\w]**

If you have any experience with regular expressions in other languages, you'll immediately notice a difference in the way backslashes are handled. In other languages, "\\" means "I want to insert a plain old (literal) backslash in the regular expression. Don't give it any special meaning." In Java, "\\" means "I'm inserting a regular expression backslash, so the following character has special meaning." For example, if you want to indicate one or more word characters, your regular expression string will be "**\\w+**". If you want to insert a literal backslash, you say "\\\\". However, things like newlines and tabs just use a single backslash: "\n\t".

What's shown here is only a sampling; you'll want to have the **java.util.regex.Pattern** JDK documentation page bookmarked or on your "Start" menu so you can easily access all the possible regular expression patterns.

Logical Operators	
XY	X followed by Y
X|Y	X or Y
(X)	A *capturing group*. You can refer to the *i^th^* captured group later in the expression with \i

Boundary Matchers	
^	Beginning of a line
$	End of a line
\b	Word boundary
\B	Non-word boundary
\G	End of the previous match

As an example, each of the following represent valid regular expressions, and all will successfully match the character sequence "Rudolph":

```
Rudolph
[rR]udolph
[rR][aeiou][a-z]ol.*
R.*
```

Quantifiers

A *quantifier* describes the way that a pattern absorbs input text:

- *Greedy*: Quantifiers are greedy unless otherwise altered. A greedy expression finds as many possible matches for the pattern as possible. A typical cause of problems is to assume that your pattern will only match the first possible group of characters, when it's actually greedy and will keep going.

- *Reluctant*: Specified with a question mark, this quantifier matches the minimum necessary number of characters to satisfy the pattern. Also called *lazy*, *minimal matching*, *non-greedy*, or *ungreedy*.

- *Possessive*: Currently only available in Java (not in other languages), and it is more advanced, so you probably won't use it right away. As a regular expression is applied to a string, it generates many states so that it can backtrack if the match fails. Possessive quantifiers do not keep those intermediate states, and thus prevent backtracking. They can be used to prevent a regular expression from running away and also to make it execute more efficiently.

Greedy	Reluctant	Possessive	Matches
X?	X??	X?+	X, one or none
X*	X*?	X*+	X, zero or more
X+	X+?	X++	X, one or more
X{n}	X{n}?	X{n}+	X, exactly n times
X{n,}	X{n,}?	X{n,}+	X, at least n times
X{n,m}	X{n,m}?	X{n,m}+	X, at least n but not more than m times

You should be very aware that the expression 'X' will often need to be surrounded in parentheses for it to work the way you desire. For example:

```
abc+
```

Might seem like it would match the sequence 'abc' one or more times, and if you apply it to the input string 'abcabcabc', you will in fact get three matches. However, the expression *actually* says "match 'ab' followed by one or more occurrences of 'c'." To match the entire string 'abc' one or more times, you must say:

```
(abc)+
```

You can easily be fooled when using regular expressions; it's a new language, on top of Java.

CharSequence

JDK 1.4 defines a new interface called **CharSequence**, which establishes a definition of a character sequence abstracted from the **String** or **StringBuffer** classes:

```
interface CharSequence {
  charAt(int i);
```

```
  length();
  subSequence(int start, int end);
  toString();
}
```

The **String**, **StringBuffer**, and **CharBuffer** classes have been modified to implement this new **CharSequence** interface. Many regular expression operations take **CharSequence** arguments.

Pattern and Matcher

As a first example, the following class can be used to test regular expressions against an input string. The first argument is the input string to match against, followed by one or more regular expressions to be applied to the input. Under Unix/Linux, the regular expressions must be quoted on the command line.

This program can be useful in testing regular expressions as you construct them to see that they produce your intended matching behavior.

```
//: c12:TestRegularExpression.java
// Allows you to easly try out regular expressions.
// {Args: abcabcabcdefabc "abc+" "(abc)+" "(abc){2,}" }
import java.util.regex.*;

public class TestRegularExpression {
  public static void main(String[] args) {
    if(args.length < 2) {
      System.out.println("Usage:\n" +
        "java TestRegularExpression " +
        "characterSequence regularExpression+");
      System.exit(0);
    }
    System.out.println("Input: \"" + args[0] + "\"");
    for(int i = 1; i < args.length; i++) {
      System.out.println(
        "Regular expression: \"" + args[i] + "\"");
      Pattern p = Pattern.compile(args[i]);
      Matcher m = p.matcher(args[0]);
      while(m.find()) {
        System.out.println("Match \"" + m.group() +
          "\" at positions " +
          m.start() + "-" + (m.end() - 1));
      }
```

```
    }
  }
} ///:~
```

Regular expressions are implemented in Java through the **Pattern** and **Matcher** classes in the package **java.util.regex**. A **Pattern** object represents a compiled version of a regular expression. The static **compile( )** method compiles a regular expression string into a **Pattern** object. As seen in the preceding example, you can use the **matcher( )** method and the input string to produce a **Matcher** object from the compiled **Pattern** object. **Pattern** also has a

```
static boolean matches(String regex, CharSequence input)
```

for quickly discerning if **regex** can be found in **input**, and a **split( )** method that produces an array of **String** that has been broken around matches of the **regex**.

A **Matcher** object is generated by calling **Pattern.matcher( )** with the input string as an argument. The **Matcher** object is then used to access the results, using methods to evaluate the success or failure of different types of matches:

```
boolean matches()
boolean lookingAt()
boolean find()
boolean find(int start)
```

The **matches( )** method is successful if the pattern matches the entire input string, while **lookingAt( )** is successful if the input string, starting at the beginning, is a match to the pattern.

find( )

Matcher.find( ) can be used to discover multiple pattern matches in the **CharSequence** to which it is applied. For example:

```
//: c12:FindDemo.java
import java.util.regex.*;
import com.bruceeckel.simpletest.*;
import java.util.*;

public class FindDemo {
  private static Test monitor = new Test();
  public static void main(String[] args) {
```

```
    Matcher m = Pattern.compile("\\w+")
      .matcher("Evening is full of the linnet's wings");
    while(m.find())
      System.out.println(m.group());
    int i = 0;
    while(m.find(i)) {
      System.out.print(m.group() + " ");
      i++;
    }
    monitor.expect(new String[] {
      "Evening",
      "is",
      "full",
      "of",
      "the",
      "linnet",
      "s",
      "wings",
      "Evening vening ening ning ing ng g is is s full " +
      "full ull ll l of of f the the he e linnet linnet " +
      "innet nnet net et t s s wings wings ings ngs gs s "
    });
  }
} ///:~
```

The pattern "**w+**" indicates "one or more word characters," so it will simply split up the input into words. **find( )** is like an iterator, moving forward through the input string. However, the second version of **find( )** can be given an integer argument that tells it the character position for the beginning of the search—this version resets the search position to the value of the argument, as you can see from the output.

Groups

Groups are regular expressions set off by parentheses that can be called up later with their group number. Group zero indicates the whole expression match, group one is the first parenthesized group, etc. Thus in

```
A(B(C))D
```

there are three groups: Group 0 is **ABCD**, group 1 is **BC**, and group 2 is **C**.

The **Matcher** object has methods to give you information about groups:

public int groupCount( ) returns the number of groups in this matcher's pattern. Group zero is not included in this count.

public String group( ) returns group zero (the entire match) from the previous match operation (**find( )**, for example).

public String group(int i) returns the given group number during the previous match operation. If the match was successful, but the group specified failed to match any part of the input string, then null is returned.

public int start(int group) returns the start index of the group found in the previous match operation.

public int end(int group) returns the index of the last character, plus one, of the group found in the previous match operation.

Here's an example of regular expression groups:

```
//: c12:Groups.java
import java.util.regex.*;
import com.bruceeckel.simpletest.*;

public class Groups {
  private static Test monitor = new Test();
  static public final String poem =
    "Twas brillig, and the slithy toves\n" +
    "Did gyre and gimble in the wabe.\n" +
    "All mimsy were the borogoves,\n" +
    "And the mome raths outgrabe.\n\n" +
    "Beware the Jabberwock, my son,\n" +
    "The jaws that bite, the claws that catch.\n" +
    "Beware the Jubjub bird, and shun\n" +
    "The frumious Bandersnatch.";
  public static void main(String[] args) {
    Matcher m =
      Pattern.compile("(?m)(\\S+)\\s+((\\S+)\\s+(\\S+))$")
        .matcher(poem);
    while(m.find()) {
      for(int j = 0; j <= m.groupCount(); j++)
        System.out.print("[" + m.group(j) + "]");
      System.out.println();
    }
    monitor.expect(new String[]{
      "[the slithy toves]" +
```

```
      "[the][slithy toves][slithy][toves]",
      "[in the wabe.][in][the wabe.][the][wabe.]",
      "[were the borogoves,]" +
      "[were][the borogoves,][the][borogoves,]",
      "[mome raths outgrabe.]" +
      "[mome][raths outgrabe.][raths][outgrabe.]",
      "[Jabberwock, my son,]" +
      "[Jabberwock,][my son,][my][son,]",
      "[claws that catch.]" +
      "[claws][that catch.][that][catch.]",
      "[bird, and shun][bird,][and shun][and][shun]",
      "[The frumious Bandersnatch.][The]" +
      "[frumious Bandersnatch.][frumious][Bandersnatch.]"
    });
  }
} ///:~
```

The poem is the first part of Lewis Carroll's "Jabberwocky," from *Through the Looking Glass*. You can see that the regular expression pattern has a number of parenthesized groups, consisting of any number of non-whitespace characters ('**\S+**') followed by any number of whitespace characters ('**\s+**'). The goal is to capture the last three words on each line; the end of a line is delimited by '**$**'. However, the normal behavior is to match '**$**' with the end of the entire input sequence, so we must explicitly tell the regular expression to pay attention to newlines within the input. This is accomplished with the '**(?m)**' pattern flag at the beginning of the sequence (pattern flags will be shown shortly).

start( ) and end( )

Following a successful matching operation, **start( )** returns the start index of the previous match, and **end( )** returns the index of the last character matched, plus one. Invoking either **start( )** or **end( )** following an unsuccessful matching operation (or prior to a matching operation being attempted) produces an **IllegalStateException**. The following program also demonstrates **matches( )** and **lookingAt( )**:

```
//: c12:StartEnd.java
import java.util.regex.*;
import com.bruceeckel.simpletest.*;

public class StartEnd {
  private static Test monitor = new Test();
  public static void main(String[] args) {
```

```
    String[] input = new String[] {
      "Java has regular expressions in 1.4",
      "regular expressions now expressing in Java",
      "Java represses oracular expressions"
    };
    Pattern
      p1 = Pattern.compile("re\\w*"),
      p2 = Pattern.compile("Java.*");
    for(int i = 0; i < input.length; i++) {
      System.out.println("input " + i + ": " + input[i]);
      Matcher
        m1 = p1.matcher(input[i]),
        m2 = p2.matcher(input[i]);
      while(m1.find())
        System.out.println("m1.find() '" + m1.group() +
          "' start = "+ m1.start() + " end = " + m1.end());
      while(m2.find())
        System.out.println("m2.find() '" + m2.group() +
          "' start = "+ m2.start() + " end = " + m2.end());
      if(m1.lookingAt()) // No reset() necessary
        System.out.println("m1.lookingAt() start = "
          + m1.start() + " end = " + m1.end());
      if(m2.lookingAt())
        System.out.println("m2.lookingAt() start = "
          + m2.start() + " end = " + m2.end());
      if(m1.matches()) // No reset() necessary
        System.out.println("m1.matches() start = "
          + m1.start() + " end = " + m1.end());
      if(m2.matches())
        System.out.println("m2.matches() start = "
          + m2.start() + " end = " + m2.end());
    }
    monitor.expect(new String[] {
      "input 0: Java has regular expressions in 1.4",
      "m1.find() 'regular' start = 9 end = 16",
      "m1.find() 'ressions' start = 20 end = 28",
      "m2.find() 'Java has regular expressions in 1.4'" +
      " start = 0 end = 35",
      "m2.lookingAt() start = 0 end = 35",
      "m2.matches() start = 0 end = 35",
      "input 1: regular expressions now " +
      "expressing in Java",
      "m1.find() 'regular' start = 0 end = 7",
      "m1.find() 'ressions' start = 11 end = 19",
```

```
      "m1.find() 'ressing' start = 27 end = 34",
      "m2.find() 'Java' start = 38 end = 42",
      "m1.lookingAt() start = 0 end = 7",
      "input 2: Java represses oracular expressions",
      "m1.find() 'represses' start = 5 end = 14",
      "m1.find() 'ressions' start = 27 end = 35",
      "m2.find() 'Java represses oracular expressions' " +
      "start = 0 end = 35",
      "m2.lookingAt() start = 0 end = 35",
      "m2.matches() start = 0 end = 35"
    });
  }
} ///:~
```

Notice that **find( )** will locate the regular expression anywhere in the input, but **lookingAt( )** and **matches( )** only succeed if the regular expression starts matching at the very beginning of the input. While **matches( )** only succeeds if the *entire* input matches the regular expression, **lookingAt( )**[7] succeeds if only the first part of the input matches.

Pattern flags

An alternative **compile( )** method accepts flags that affect the behavior of regular expression matching:

```
Pattern Pattern.compile(String regex, int flag)
```

where **flag** is drawn from among the following **Pattern** class constants:

Compile Flag	Effect
Pattern.CANON_EQ	Two characters will be considered to match if, and only if, their full canonical decompositions match. The expression "a\u030A", for example, will match the string "?" when this flag is specified. By default, matching does not take canonical equivalence into

[7] I have no idea how they came up with this method name, or what it's supposed to refer to. But it's reassuring to know that whoever comes up with nonintuitive method names is still employed at Sun. And that their apparent policy of not reviewing code designs is still in place. Sorry for the sarcasm, but this kind of thing gets tiresome after a few years.

	account.
Pattern.CASE_INSENSITIVE (?i)	By default, case-insensitive matching assumes that only characters in the US-ASCII character set are being matched. This flag allows your pattern to match without regard to case (upper or lower). Unicode-aware case-insensitive matching can be enabled by specifying the **UNICODE_CASE** flag in conjunction with this flag.
Pattern.COMMENTS (?x)	In this mode, whitespace is ignored, and embedded comments starting with # are ignored until the end of a line. Unix lines mode can also be enabled via the embedded flag expression.
Pattern.DOTALL (?s)	In dotall mode, the expression '**.**' matches any character, including a line terminator. By default, the '**.**' expression does not match line terminators.
Pattern.MULTILINE (?m)	In multiline mode, the expressions '^' and '**$**' match the beginning and ending of a line, respectively. '^' also matches the beginning of the input string, and '**$**' also matches the end of the input string. By default, these expressions only match at the beginning and the end of the entire input string.
Pattern.UNICODE_CASE (?u)	When this flag is specified, case-insensitive matching, when enabled by the **CASE_INSENSITIVE** flag, is done in a manner consistent with the Unicode Standard. By default, case-insensitive matching assumes that only characters in the US-ASCII character

	set are being matched.
Pattern.UNIX_LINES (?d)	In this mode, only the '**\n**' line terminator is recognized in the behavior of '**.**', '**^**', and '**$**'.

Particularly useful among these flags are **Pattern.CASE_INSENSITIVE**, **Pattern.MULTILINE**, and **Pattern.COMMENTS** (which is helpful for clarity and/or documentation). Note that the behavior of most of the flags can also be obtained by inserting the parenthesized characters, shown in the table beneath the flags, into your regular expression preceding the place where you want the mode to take effect.

You can combine the effect of these and other flags through an "OR" ('|') operation:

```
//: c12:ReFlags.java
import java.util.regex.*;
import com.bruceeckel.simpletest.*;

public class ReFlags {
  private static Test monitor = new Test();
  public static void main(String[] args) {
    Pattern p =  Pattern.compile("^java",
      Pattern.CASE_INSENSITIVE | Pattern.MULTILINE);
    Matcher m = p.matcher(
      "java has regex\nJava has regex\n" +
      "JAVA has pretty good regular expressions\n" +
      "Regular expressions are in Java");
    while(m.find())
      System.out.println(m.group());
    monitor.expect(new String[] {
      "java",
      "Java",
      "JAVA"
    });
  }
} ///:~
```

This creates a pattern that will match lines starting with "java," "Java," "JAVA," etc., and attempt a match for each line within a multiline set (matches starting at the beginning of the character sequence and following each line terminator within the character sequence). Note that the **group( )** method only produces the matched portion.

split( )

Splitting divides an input string into an array of **String** objects, delimited by the regular expression.

```
String[] split(CharSequence charseq)
String[] split(CharSequence charseq, int limit)
```

This is a quick and handy way of breaking up input text over a common boundary:

```
//: c12:SplitDemo.java
import java.util.regex.*;
import com.bruceeckel.simpletest.*;
import java.util.*;

public class SplitDemo {
  private static Test monitor = new Test();
  public static void main(String[] args) {
    String input =
      "This!!unusual use!!of exclamation!!points";
    System.out.println(Arrays.asList(
      Pattern.compile("!!").split(input)));
    // Only do the first three:
    System.out.println(Arrays.asList(
      Pattern.compile("!!").split(input, 3)));
    System.out.println(Arrays.asList(
      "Aha! String has a split() built in!".split(" ")));
    monitor.expect(new String[] {
      "[This, unusual use, of exclamation, points]",
      "[This, unusual use, of exclamation!!points]",
      "[Aha!, String, has, a, split(), built, in!]"
    });
  }
} ///:~
```

The second form of **split( )** limits the number of splits that occur.

Notice that regular expressions are so valuable that some operations have also been added to the **String** class, including **split( )** (shown here), **matches( )**, **replaceFirst( )**, and **replaceAll( )**. These behave like their **Pattern** and **Matcher** counterparts.

Replace operations

Regular expressions become especially useful when you begin replacing text. Here are the available methods:

replaceFirst(String replacement) replaces the first matching part of the input string with **replacement**.

replaceAll(String replacement) replaces every matching part of the input string with **replacement**.

appendReplacement(StringBuffer sbuf, String replacement) performs step-by-step replacements into **sbuf**, rather than replacing only the first one or all of them, as in **replaceFirst( )** and **replaceAll( )**, respectively. This is a *very* important method, because it allows you to call methods and perform other processing in order to produce **replacement** (**replaceFirst( )** and **replaceAll( )** are only able to put in fixed strings). With this method, you can programmatically pick apart the groups and create powerful replacements.

appendTail(StringBuffer sbuf, String replacement) is invoked after one or more invocations of the **appendReplacement( )** method in order to copy the remainder of the input string.

Here's an example that shows the use of all the replace operations. In addition, the block of commented text at the beginning is extracted and processed with regular expressions for use as input in the rest of the example:

```
//: c12:TheReplacements.java
import java.util.regex.*;
import java.io.*;
import com.bruceeckel.util.*;
import com.bruceeckel.simpletest.*;

/*! Here's a block of text to use as input to
    the regular expression matcher. Note that we'll
    first extract the block of text by looking for
    the special delimiters, then process the
    extracted block. !*/

public class TheReplacements {
  private static Test monitor = new Test();
  public static void main(String[] args) throws Exception {
```

```java
    String s = TextFile.read("TheReplacements.java");
    // Match the specially-commented block of text above:
    Matcher mInput =
      Pattern.compile("/\\*!(.*)!\\*/", Pattern.DOTALL)
        .matcher(s);
    if(mInput.find())
      s = mInput.group(1); // Captured by parentheses
    // Replace two or more spaces with a single space:
    s = s.replaceAll(" {2,}", " ");
    // Replace one or more spaces at the beginning of each
    // line with no spaces. Must enable MULTILINE mode:
    s = s.replaceAll("(?m)^ +", "");
    System.out.println(s);
    s = s.replaceFirst("[aeiou]", "(VOWEL1)");
    StringBuffer sbuf = new StringBuffer();
    Pattern p = Pattern.compile("[aeiou]");
    Matcher m = p.matcher(s);
    // Process the find information as you
    // perform the replacements:
    while(m.find())
      m.appendReplacement(sbuf, m.group().toUpperCase());
    // Put in the remainder of the text:
    m.appendTail(sbuf);
    System.out.println(sbuf);
    monitor.expect(new String[]{
      "Here's a block of text to use as input to",
      "the regular expression matcher. Note that we'll",
      "first extract the block of text by looking for",
      "the special delimiters, then process the",
      "extracted block. ",
      "H(VOWEL1)rE's A blOck Of tExt tO UsE As InpUt tO",
      "thE rEgUlAr ExprEssIOn mAtchEr. NOtE thAt wE'll",
      "fIrst ExtrAct thE blOck Of tExt by lOOkIng fOr",
      "thE spEcIAl dElImItErs, thEn prOcEss thE",
      "ExtrActEd blOck. "
    });
  }
} ///:~
```

The file is opened and read using the **TextFile.read( )** method introduced earlier in this chapter. **mInput** is created to match all the text (notice the grouping parentheses) between '**/*!**' and '**!*/**'. Then, more than two spaces are reduced to a single space, and any space at the beginning of each line is removed (in order to do this on all lines and not just the beginning of the input, multiline mode must be enabled). These two replacements are performed with the equivalent (but more convenient, in this case) **replaceAll( )** that's part of **String**. Note that since each replacement is only used once in the program, there's no extra cost to doing it this way rather than precompiling it as a **Pattern**.

replaceFirst( ) only performs the first replacement that it finds. In addition, the replacement strings in **replaceFirst( )** and **replaceAll( )** are just literals, so if you want to perform some processing on each replacement they don't help. In that case, you need to use **appendReplacement( )**, which allows you to write any amount of code in the process of performing the replacement. In the preceding example, a **group( )** is selected and processed—in this situation, setting the vowel found by the regular expression to upper case—as the resulting **sbuf** is being built. Normally, you would step through and perform all the replacements and then call **appendTail( )**, but if you wanted to simulate **replaceFirst( )** (or "replace n"), you would just do the replacement one time and then call **appendTail( )** to put the rest into **sbuf**.

appendReplacement( ) also allows you to refer to captured groups directly in the replacement string by saying "$g" where 'g' is the group number. However, this is for simpler processing and wouldn't give you the desired results in the preceding program.

reset( )

An existing **Matcher** object can be applied to a new character sequence Using the **reset( )** methods:

```
//: c12:Resetting.java
import java.util.regex.*;
import java.io.*;
import com.bruceeckel.simpletest.*;

public class Resetting {
  private static Test monitor = new Test();
  public static void main(String[] args) throws Exception {
    Matcher m = Pattern.compile("[frb][aiu][gx]")
      .matcher("fix the rug with bags");
    while(m.find())
      System.out.println(m.group());
    m.reset("fix the rig with rags");
```

```
      while(m.find())
        System.out.println(m.group());
      monitor.expect(new String[]{
        "fix",
        "rug",
        "bag",
        "fix",
        "rig",
        "rag"
      });
    }
  } ///:~
```

reset( ) without any arguments sets the **Matcher** to the beginning of the current sequence.

Regular expressions and Java I/O

Most of the examples so far have shown regular expressions applied to static strings. The following example shows one way to apply regular expressions to search for matches in a file. Inspired by Unix's *grep*, **JGrep.java** takes two arguments: a filename and the regular expression that you want to match. The output shows each line where a match occurs and the match position(s) within the line.

```
//: c12:JGrep.java
// A very simple version of the "grep" program.
// {Args: JGrep.java "\\b[Ssct]\\w+"}
import java.io.*;
import java.util.regex.*;
import java.util.*;
import com.bruceeckel.util.*;

public class JGrep {
  public static void main(String[] args) throws Exception {
    if(args.length < 2) {
      System.out.println("Usage: java JGrep file regex");
      System.exit(0);
    }
    Pattern p = Pattern.compile(args[1]);
    // Iterate through the lines of the input file:
    ListIterator it = new TextFile(args[0]).listIterator();
    while(it.hasNext()) {
      Matcher m = p.matcher((String)it.next());
```

```
      while(m.find())
        System.out.println(it.nextIndex() + ": " +
          m.group() + ": " + m.start());
    }
  }
} ///:~
```

The file is opened as a **TextFile** object (these were introduced earlier in this chapter). Since a **TextFile** contains the lines of the file in an **ArrayList**, from that array a **ListIterator** is produced. The result is an iterator that will allow you to move through the lines of the file (forward and backward).

Each input line is used to produce a **Matcher**, and the result is scanned with **find( )**. Note that the **ListIterator.nextIndex( )** keeps track of the line numbers.

The test arguments open the **JGrep.java** file to read as input, and search for words starting with **[Ssct]**.

Is StringTokenizer needed?

The new capabilities provided with regular expressions might prompt you to wonder whether the original **StringTokenizer** class is still necessary. Before JDK 1.4, the way to split a string into parts was to "tokenize" it with **StringTokenizer**. But now it's much easier and more succinct to do the same thing with regular expressions:

```
//: c12:ReplacingStringTokenizer.java
import java.util.regex.*;
import com.bruceeckel.simpletest.*;
import java.util.*;

public class ReplacingStringTokenizer {
  private static Test monitor = new Test();
  public static void main(String[] args) {
    String input = "But I'm not dead yet! I feel happy!";
    StringTokenizer stoke = new StringTokenizer(input);
    while(stoke.hasMoreElements())
      System.out.println(stoke.nextToken());
    System.out.println(Arrays.asList(input.split(" ")));
    monitor.expect(new String[] {
      "But",
      "I'm",
      "not",
```

```
      "dead",
      "yet!",
      "I",
      "feel",
      "happy!",
      "[But, I'm, not, dead, yet!, I, feel, happy!]"
    });
  }
} ///:~
```

With regular expressions, you can also split a string into parts using more complex patterns—something that's much more difficult with **StringTokenizer**. It seems safe to say that regular expressions replace any tokenizing classes in earlier versions of Java.

You can learn much more about regular expressions in *Mastering Regular Expressions, 2nd Edition*, by Jeffrey E. F. Friedl (O'Reilly, 2002).

Summary

The Java I/O stream library does satisfy the basic requirements: you can perform reading and writing with the console, a file, a block of memory, or even across the Internet. With inheritance, you can create new types of input and output objects. And you can even add a simple extensibility to the kinds of objects a stream will accept by redefining the **toString( )** method that's automatically called when you pass an object to a method that's expecting a **String** (Java's limited "automatic type conversion").

There are questions left unanswered by the documentation and design of the I/O stream library. For example, it would have been nice if you could say that you want an exception thrown if you try to overwrite a file when opening it for output—some programming systems allow you to specify that you want to open an output file, but only if it doesn't already exist. In Java, it appears that you are supposed to use a **File** object to determine whether a file exists, because if you open it as a **FileOutputStream** or **FileWriter**, it will always get overwritten.

The I/O stream library brings up mixed feelings; it does much of the job and it's portable. But if you don't already understand the decorator pattern, the design is not intuitive, so there's extra overhead in learning and teaching it. It's also incomplete; for example, I shouldn't have to write utilities like

TextFile, and there's no support for the kind of output formatting that virtually every other language's I/O package supports.

However, once you *do* understand the decorator pattern and begin using the library in situations that require its flexibility, you can begin to benefit from this design, at which point its cost in extra lines of code may not bother you as much.

If you do not find what you're looking for in this chapter (which has only been an introduction and is not meant to be comprehensive), you can find in-depth coverage in *Java I/O*, by Elliotte Rusty Harold (O'Reilly, 1999).

Exercises

Solutions to selected exercises can be found in the electronic document *The Thinking in Java Annotated Solution Guide*, available for a small fee from *www.BruceEckel.com*.

1. Open a text file so that you can read the file one line at a time. Read each line as a **String** and place that **String** object into a **LinkedList**. Print all of the lines in the **LinkedList** in reverse order.

2. Modify Exercise 1 so that the name of the file you read is provided as a command-line argument.

3. Modify Exercise 2 to also open a text file so you can write text into it. Write the lines in the **ArrayList**, along with line numbers (do not attempt to use the "LineNumber" classes), out to the file.

4. Modify Exercise 2 to force all the lines in the **ArrayList** to uppercase and send the results to **System.out**.

5. Modify Exercise 2 to take additional command-line arguments of words to find in the file. Print all lines in which any of the words match.

6. Modify **DirList.java** so that the **FilenameFilter** actually opens each file and accepts the file based on whether any of the trailing arguments on the command line exist in that file.

7. Modify **DirList.java** to produce all the file names in the current directory *and subdirectories* that satisfy the given regular expression. Hint: use recursion to traverse the subdirectories.

8. Create a class called **SortedDirList** with a constructor that takes file path information and builds a sorted directory list from the files at that path. Create two overloaded **list( )** methods that will either produce the whole list or a subset of the list based on an argument. Add a **size( )** method that takes a file name and produces the size of that file.

9. Modify **WordCount.java** so that it produces an alphabetic sort instead, using the tool from Chapter 11.

10. Modify **WordCount.java** so that it uses a class containing a **String** and a count value to store each different word, and a **Set** of these objects to maintain the list of words.

11. Modify **IOStreamDemo.java** so that it uses **LineNumberReader** to keep track of the line count. Note that it's much easier to just keep track programmatically.

12. Starting with section 4 of **IOStreamDemo.java**, write a program that compares the performance of writing to a file when using buffered and unbuffered I/O.

13. Modify section 5 of **IOStreamDemo.java** to eliminate the spaces in the line produced by the first call to **in5.readUTF( )**.

14. Repair the program **CADState.java** as described in the text.

15. In **Blips.java**, copy the file and rename it to **BlipCheck.java** and rename the class **Blip2** to **BlipCheck** (making it **public** and removing the public scope from the class **Blips** in the process). Remove the **//!** marks in the file and execute the program including the offending lines. Next, comment out the default constructor for **BlipCheck**. Run it and explain why it works. Note that after compiling, you must execute the program with "**java Blips**" because the **main( )** method is still in class **Blips**.

16. In **Blip3.java**, comment out the two lines after the phrases "You must do this:" and run the program. Explain the result and why it differs from when the two lines are in the program.

17. (Intermediate) In Chapter 8, locate the **GreenhouseController.java** example, which consists of four files.

GreenhouseController contains a hard-coded set of events. Change the program so that it reads the events and their relative times from a text file. (Challenging: use a design patterns *factory method* to build the events—see *Thinking in Patterns (with Java)* at *www.BruceEckel.com.*)

18. Create and test a utility method to print the contents of a **CharBuffer** up to the point where the characters are no longer printable.

19. Experiment with changing the **ByteBuffer.allocate( )** statements in the examples in this chapter to **ByteBuffer.allocateDirect( )**. Demonstrate performance differences, but also notice whether the startup time of the programs noticeably changes.

20. For the phrase "Java now has regular expressions" evaluate whether the following expressions will find a match:

```
^Java
\Breg.*
n.w\s+h(a|i)s
s?
s*
s+
s{4}
s{1.}
s{0,3}
```

21. Apply the regular expression

```
(?i)((^[aeiou])|(\s+[aeiou]))\w+?[aeiou]\b
```

to

```
"Arline ate eight apples and one orange while
Anita hadn't any"
```

22. Modify **JGrep.java** to accept flags as arguments (e.g., **Pattern.CASE_INSENSITIVE**, **Pattern.MULTILINE**).

23. Modify **JGrep.java** to use Java **nio** memory-mapped files.

24. Modify **JGrep.java** to accept a directory name or a file name as argument (if a directory is provided, search should include all files in the directory). Hint: you can generate a list of filenames with:

```
String[] filenames = new File(".").list();
```

13: Concurrency

Objects provide a way to divide a program into independent sections. Often, you also need to turn a program into separate, independently running subtasks.

Each of these independent subtasks is called a *thread*, and you program as if each thread runs by itself and has the CPU to itself. Some underlying mechanism is actually dividing up the CPU time for you, but in general, you don't have to think about it, which makes programming with multiple threads a much easier task.

A *process* is a self-contained running program with its own address space. A *multitasking* operating system is capable of running more than one process (program) at a time, while making it look like each one is chugging along on its own, by periodically switching the CPU from one task to another. A thread is a single sequential flow of control within a process. A single process can thus have multiple concurrently executing threads.

There are many possible uses for multithreading, but in general, you'll have some part of your program tied to a particular event or resource, and you don't want that to hold up the rest of your program. So, you create a thread associated with that event or resource and let it run independently of the main program.

Concurrent programming is like stepping into an entirely new world and learning a new programming language, or at least a new set of language concepts. With the appearance of thread support in most microcomputer operating systems, extensions for threads have also been appearing in programming languages or libraries. In all cases, thread programming:

1. Seems mysterious and requires a shift in the way you think about programming
2. Looks similar to thread support in other languages, so when you understand threads, you understand a common tongue

And although support for threads can make Java a more complicated language, this isn't entirely the fault of Java—threads are tricky.

Understanding concurrent programming is on the same order of difficulty as understanding polymorphism. If you apply some effort, you can fathom the basic mechanism, but it generally takes deep study and understanding in order to develop a true grasp of the subject. The goal of this chapter is to give you a solid foundation in the basics of concurrency so that you can understand the concepts and write reasonable multithreaded programs. Be aware that you can easily become overconfident, so if you are writing anything complex, you will need to study dedicated books on the topic.

Motivation

One of the most compelling reasons for concurrency is to produce a responsive user interface. Consider a program that performs some CPU-intensive operation and thus ends up ignoring user input and being unresponsive. The basic problem is that the program needs to continue performing its operations, and at the same time it needs to return control to the user interface so that the program can respond to the user. If you have a "quit" button, you don't want to be forced to poll it in every piece of code you write in your program, and yet you want the quit button to be responsive, as if you *were* checking it regularly.

A conventional method cannot continue performing its operations and at the same time return control to the rest of the program. In fact, this sounds like an impossible thing to accomplish, as if the CPU must be in two places at once, but this is precisely the illusion that concurrency provides.

Concurrency can also be used to optimize throughput. For example, you might be able to do important work while you're stuck waiting for input to arrive on an I/O port. Without threading, the only reasonable solution is to poll the I/O port, which is awkward and can be difficult.

If you have a multiprocessor machine, multiple threads may be distributed across multiple processors, which can dramatically improve throughput. This is often the case with powerful multiprocessor web servers, which can distribute large numbers of user requests across CPUs in a program that allocates one thread per request.

One thing to keep in mind is that a program with many threads must be able to run on a single-CPU machine. Therefore, it must also be possible to write the same program without using any threads. However, multithreading provides a very important organizational benefit, so that the design of your program can be greatly simplified. Some types of problems, such as simulation—a video game, for example—are very difficult to solve without support for concurrency.

The threading model is a programming convenience to simplify juggling several operations at the same time within a single program. With threads, the CPU will pop around and give each thread some of its time. Each thread has the consciousness of constantly having the CPU to itself, but the CPU's time is actually sliced between all the threads. The exception to this is if your program is running on multiple CPUs, but one of the great things about threading is that you are abstracted away from this layer, so your code does not need to know whether it is actually running on a single CPU or many. Thus, threads are a way to create transparently scalable programs—if a program is running too slowly, it can easily be made faster by adding CPUs to your computer. Multitasking and multithreading tend to be the most reasonable ways to utilize multiprocessor systems.

Threading can reduce computing efficiency somewhat in single-CPU machines, but the net improvement in program design, resource balancing, and user convenience is often quite valuable. In general, threads enable you to create a more loosely-coupled design; otherwise, parts of your code would be forced to pay explicit attention to tasks that would normally be handled by threads.

Basic threads

The simplest way to create a thread is to inherit from **java.lang.Thread**, which has all the wiring necessary to create and run threads. The most important method for **Thread** is **run( )**, which you must override to make the thread do your bidding. Thus, **run( )** is the code that will be executed "simultaneously" with the other threads in a program.

The following example creates five threads, each with a unique identification number generated with a **static** variable. The **Thread**'s **run( )** method is overridden to count down each time it passes through its loop and to return when the count is zero (at the point when **run( )** returns, the thread is terminated by the threading mechanism).

```java
//: c13:SimpleThread.java
// Very simple Threading example.
import com.bruceeckel.simpletest.*;

public class SimpleThread extends Thread {
  private static Test monitor = new Test();
  private int countDown = 5;
  private static int threadCount = 0;
  public SimpleThread() {
    super("" + ++threadCount); // Store the thread name
    start();
  }
  public String toString() {
    return "#" + getName() + ": " + countDown;
  }
  public void run() {
    while(true) {
      System.out.println(this);
      if(--countDown == 0) return;
    }
  }
  public static void main(String[] args) {
    for(int i = 0; i < 5; i++)
      new SimpleThread();
    monitor.expect(new String[] {
      "#1: 5",
      "#2: 5",
      "#3: 5",
      "#5: 5",
      "#1: 4",
      "#4: 5",
      "#2: 4",
      "#3: 4",
      "#5: 4",
      "#1: 3",
      "#4: 4",
      "#2: 3",
      "#3: 3",
      "#5: 3",
      "#1: 2",
      "#4: 3",
      "#2: 2",
      "#3: 2",
      "#5: 2",
```

```
      "#1: 1",
      "#4: 2",
      "#2: 1",
      "#3: 1",
      "#5: 1",
      "#4: 1"
    }, Test.IGNORE_ORDER + Test.WAIT);
  }
} ///:~
```

The thread objects are given specific names by calling the appropriate **Thread** constructor. This name is retrieved in **toString( )** using **getName( )**.

A **Thread** object's **run( )** method virtually always has some kind of loop that continues until the thread is no longer necessary, so you must establish the condition on which to break out of this loop (or, as in the preceding program, simply **return** from **run( )**). Often, **run( )** is cast in the form of an infinite loop, which means that, barring some factor that causes **run( )** to terminate, it will continue forever (later in the chapter you'll see how to safely signal a thread to stop).

In **main( )** you can see a number of threads being created and run. The **start( )** method in the **Thread** class performs special initialization for the thread and then calls **run( )**. So the steps are: the constructor is called to build the object, it calls **start( )** to configure the thread, and the thread execution mechanism calls **run( )**. If you don't call **start( )** (which you don't have to do in the constructor, as you will see in subsequent examples), the thread will never be started.

The output for one run of this program will be different from that of another, because the thread scheduling mechanism is not deterministic. In fact, you may see dramatic differences in the output of this simple program between one version of the JDK and the next. For example, a previous JDK didn't time-slice very often, so thread 1 might loop to extinction first, then thread 2 would go through all of its loops, etc. This was virtually the same as calling a routine that would do all the loops at once, except that starting up all those threads is more expensive. In JDK 1.4 you get something like the output from **SimpleThread.java**, which indicates better time-slicing behavior by the scheduler—each thread seems to be getting regular service. Generally, these kinds of JDK behavioral changes have not been mentioned by Sun, so you cannot plan on any consistent threading behavior. The best approach is to be as conservative as possible while writing threading code.

When **main( )** creates the **Thread** objects, it isn't capturing the references for any of them. With an ordinary object, this would make it fair game for garbage collection, but not with a **Thread**. Each **Thread** "registers" itself so there is actually a reference to it someplace, and the garbage collector can't clean it up until the thread exits its **run( )** and dies.

Yielding

If you know that you've accomplished what you need to in your **run( )** method, you can give a hint to the thread scheduling mechanism that you've done enough and that some other thread might as well have the CPU. This hint (and it *is* a hint—there's no guarantee your implementation will listen to it) takes the form of the **yield( )** method.

We can modify the preceding example by yielding after each loop:

```
//: c13:YieldingThread.java
// Suggesting when to switch threads with yield().
import com.bruceeckel.simpletest.*;

public class YieldingThread extends Thread {
  private static Test monitor = new Test();
  private int countDown = 5;
  private static int threadCount = 0;
  public YieldingThread() {
    super("" + ++threadCount);
    start();
  }
  public String toString() {
    return "#" + getName() + ": " + countDown;
  }
  public void run() {
    while(true) {
      System.out.println(this);
      if(--countDown == 0) return;
      yield();
    }
  }
  public static void main(String[] args) {
    for(int i = 0; i < 5; i++)
      new YieldingThread();
```

```
    monitor.expect(new String[] {
      "#1: 5",
      "#2: 5",
      "#4: 5",
      "#5: 5",
      "#3: 5",
      "#1: 4",
      "#2: 4",
      "#4: 4",
      "#5: 4",
      "#3: 4",
      "#1: 3",
      "#2: 3",
      "#4: 3",
      "#5: 3",
      "#3: 3",
      "#1: 2",
      "#2: 2",
      "#4: 2",
      "#5: 2",
      "#3: 2",
      "#1: 1",
      "#2: 1",
      "#4: 1",
      "#5: 1",
      "#3: 1"
    }, Test.IGNORE_ORDER + Test.WAIT);
  }
} ///:~
```

By using **yield( )**, the output is evened up quite a bit. But note that if the output string is longer, you will see output that is roughly the same as it was in **SimpleThread.java** (try it—change **toString( )** to put out longer and longer strings to see what happens). Since the scheduling mechanism is *preemptive*, it decides to interrupt a thread and switch to another whenever it wants, so if I/O (which is executed via the **main( )** thread) takes too long, it is interrupted before **run( )** has a chance to **yield( )**. In general, **yield( )** is useful only in rare situations, and you can't rely on it to do any serious tuning of your application.

Sleeping

Another way you can control the behavior of your threads is by calling **sleep( )** to cease execution for a given number of milliseconds. In the preceding example, if you replace the call to **yield( )** with a call to **sleep( )**, you get the following:

```
//: c13:SleepingThread.java
// Calling sleep() to wait for awhile.
import com.bruceeckel.simpletest.*;

public class SleepingThread extends Thread {
  private static Test monitor = new Test();
  private int countDown = 5;
  private static int threadCount = 0;
  public SleepingThread() {
    super("" + ++threadCount);
    start();
  }
  public String toString() {
    return "#" + getName() + ": " + countDown;
  }
  public void run() {
    while(true) {
      System.out.println(this);
      if(--countDown == 0) return;
      try {
        sleep(100);
      } catch (InterruptedException e) {
        throw new RuntimeException(e);
      }
    }
  }
  public static void
  main(String[] args) throws InterruptedException {
    for(int i = 0; i < 5; i++)
      new SleepingThread().join();
    monitor.expect(new String[] {
      "#1: 5",
      "#1: 4",
      "#1: 3",
      "#1: 2",
      "#1: 1",
      "#2: 5",
      "#2: 4",
      "#2: 3",
      "#2: 2",
      "#2: 1",
```

```
        "#3: 5",
        "#3: 4",
        "#3: 3",
        "#3: 2",
        "#3: 1",
        "#4: 5",
        "#4: 4",
        "#4: 3",
        "#4: 2",
        "#4: 1",
        "#5: 5",
        "#5: 4",
        "#5: 3",
        "#5: 2",
        "#5: 1"
    });
  }
} ///:~
```

When you call **sleep( )**, it must be placed inside a **try** block because it's possible for **sleep( )** to be interrupted before it times out. This happens if someone else has a reference to the thread and they call **interrupt( )** on the thread (**interrupt( )** also affects the thread if **wait( )** or **join( )** has been called for it, so those calls must be in a similar **try** block—you'll learn about those methods later). Usually, if you're going to break out of a suspended thread using **interrupt( )** you will use **wait( )** rather than **sleep( )**, so that ending up inside the **catch** clause is unlikely. Here, we follow the maxim "don't catch an exception unless you know what to do with it" by re-throwing it as a **RuntimeException**.

You'll notice that the output is deterministic—each thread counts down before the next one starts. This is because **join( )** (which you'll learn about shortly) is used on each thread, so that **main( )** waits for the thread to complete before continuing. If you did not use **join( )**, you'd see that the threads tend to run in any order, which means that **sleep( )** is also not a way for you to control the order of thread execution. It just stops the execution of the thread for awhile. The only guarantee that you have is that the thread will sleep at least 100 milliseconds, but it may take longer before the thread resumes execution, because the thread scheduler still has to get back to it after the sleep interval expires.

If you must control the order of execution of threads, your best bet is not to use threads at all, but instead to write your own cooperative routines that hand control to each other in a specified order.

Priority

The *priority* of a thread tells the scheduler how important this thread is. Although the order that the CPU attends to an existing set of threads is indeterminate, if there are a number of threads blocked and waiting to be run, the scheduler will lean toward the one with the highest priority first. However, this doesn't mean that threads with lower priority aren't run (that is, you can't get deadlocked because of priorities). Lower priority threads just tend to run less often.

Here's **SimpleThread.java** modified so that the priority levels are demonstrated. The priorities are adjusting by using **Thread**'s **setPriority( )** method.

```
//: c13:SimplePriorities.java
// Shows the use of thread priorities.
import com.bruceeckel.simpletest.*;

public class SimplePriorities extends Thread {
  private static Test monitor = new Test();
  private int countDown = 5;
  private volatile double d = 0; // No optimization
  public SimplePriorities(int priority) {
    setPriority(priority);
    start();
  }
  public String toString() {
    return super.toString() + ": " + countDown;
  }
  public void run() {
    while(true) {
      // An expensive, interruptable operation:
      for(int i = 1; i < 100000; i++)
        d = d + (Math.PI + Math.E) / (double)i;
      System.out.println(this);
      if(--countDown == 0) return;
    }
  }
  public static void main(String[] args) {
```

```
      new SimplePriorities(Thread.MAX_PRIORITY);
      for(int i = 0; i < 5; i++)
        new SimplePriorities(Thread.MIN_PRIORITY);
      monitor.expect(new String[] {
        "Thread[Thread-1,10,main]: 5",
        "Thread[Thread-1,10,main]: 4",
        "Thread[Thread-1,10,main]: 3",
        "Thread[Thread-1,10,main]: 2",
        "Thread[Thread-1,10,main]: 1",
        "Thread[Thread-2,1,main]: 5",
        "Thread[Thread-2,1,main]: 4",
        "Thread[Thread-2,1,main]: 3",
        "Thread[Thread-2,1,main]: 2",
        "Thread[Thread-2,1,main]: 1",
        "Thread[Thread-3,1,main]: 5",
        "Thread[Thread-4,1,main]: 5",
        "Thread[Thread-5,1,main]: 5",
        "Thread[Thread-6,1,main]: 5",
        "Thread[Thread-3,1,main]: 4",
        "Thread[Thread-4,1,main]: 4",
        "Thread[Thread-5,1,main]: 4",
        "Thread[Thread-6,1,main]: 4",
        "Thread[Thread-3,1,main]: 3",
        "Thread[Thread-4,1,main]: 3",
        "Thread[Thread-5,1,main]: 3",
        "Thread[Thread-6,1,main]: 3",
        "Thread[Thread-3,1,main]: 2",
        "Thread[Thread-4,1,main]: 2",
        "Thread[Thread-5,1,main]: 2",
        "Thread[Thread-6,1,main]: 2",
        "Thread[Thread-4,1,main]: 1",
        "Thread[Thread-3,1,main]: 1",
        "Thread[Thread-6,1,main]: 1",
        "Thread[Thread-5,1,main]: 1"
      }, Test.IGNORE_ORDER + Test.WAIT);
  }
} ///:~
```

In this version, **toString( )** is overridden to use **Thread.toString( )**, which prints the thread name (which you can set yourself via the constructor; here it's automatically generated as **Thread-1**, **Thread-2**, etc.), the priority level, and the "thread group" that the thread belongs to. Because the threads are self-identifying, there is no **threadNumber** in this example. The overridden **toString( )** also shows the countdown value of the thread.

You can see that the priority level of thread 1 is at the highest level, and all the rest of the threads are at the lowest level.

Inside **run( )**, 100,000 repetitions of a rather expensive floating-point calculation have been added, involving **double** addition and division. The variable **d** has been made **volatile** to ensure that no optimization is performed. Without this calculation, you don't see the effect of setting the priority levels (try it: comment out the **for** loop containing the **double** calculations). With the calculation, you see that thread 1 is given a higher preference by the thread scheduler (at least, this was the behavior on my Windows 2000 machine). Even though printing to the console is also an expensive behavior, you won't see the priority levels that way, because console printing doesn't get interrupted (otherwise, the console display would get garbled during threading), whereas the math calculation can be interrupted. The calculation takes long enough that the thread scheduling mechanism jumps in and changes threads, and pays attention to the priorities so that thread 1 gets preference.

You can also read the priority of an existing thread with **getPriority( )** and change it at any time (not just in the constructor, as in **SimplePriorities.java**) with **setPriority( )**.

Although the JDK has 10 priority levels, this doesn't map well to many operating systems. For example, Windows 2000 has 7 priority levels that are not fixed, so the mapping is indeterminate (although Sun's Solaris has 2^{31} levels). The only portable approach is to stick to **MAX_PRIORITY**, **NORM_PRIORITY**, and **MIN_PRIORITY** when you're adjusting priority levels.

Daemon threads

A "daemon" thread is one that is supposed to provide a general service in the background as long as the program is running, but is not part of the essence of the program. Thus, when all of the non-daemon threads complete, the program is terminated. Conversely, if there are any non-daemon threads still running, the program doesn't terminate. There is, for instance, a non-daemon thread that runs **main( )**.

```
//: c13:SimpleDaemons.java
// Daemon threads don't prevent the program from ending.

public class SimpleDaemons extends Thread {
```

```
  public SimpleDaemons() {
    setDaemon(true); // Must be called before start()
    start();
  }
  public void run() {
    while(true) {
      try {
        sleep(100);
      } catch (InterruptedException e) {
        throw new RuntimeException(e);
      }
      System.out.println(this);
    }
  }
  public static void main(String[] args) {
    for(int i = 0; i < 10; i++)
      new SimpleDaemons();
  }
} ///:~
```

You must set the thread to be a daemon by calling **setDaemon( )** before it is started. In **run( )**, the thread is put to sleep for a little bit. Once the threads are all started, the program terminates immediately, before any threads can print themselves, because there are no non-daemon threads (other than **main( )**) holding the program open. Thus, the program terminates without printing any output.

You can find out if a thread is a daemon by calling **isDaemon( )**. If a thread is a daemon, then any threads it creates will automatically be daemons, as the following example demonstrates:

```
//: c13:Daemons.java
// Daemon threads spawn other daemon threads.
import java.io.*;
import com.bruceeckel.simpletest.*;

class Daemon extends Thread {
  private Thread[] t = new Thread[10];
  public Daemon() {
    setDaemon(true);
    start();
  }
  public void run() {
    for(int i = 0; i < t.length; i++)
```

```
      t[i] = new DaemonSpawn(i);
    for(int i = 0; i < t.length; i++)
      System.out.println("t[" + i + "].isDaemon() = "
        + t[i].isDaemon());
    while(true)
      yield();
  }
}

class DaemonSpawn extends Thread {
  public DaemonSpawn(int i) {
    start();
    System.out.println("DaemonSpawn " + i + " started");
  }
  public void run() {
    while(true)
      yield();
  }
}

public class Daemons {
  private static Test monitor = new Test();
  public static void main(String[] args) throws Exception {
    Thread d = new Daemon();
    System.out.println("d.isDaemon() = " + d.isDaemon());
    // Allow the daemon threads to
    // finish their startup processes:
    Thread.sleep(1000);
    monitor.expect(new String[] {
      "d.isDaemon() = true",
      "DaemonSpawn 0 started",
      "DaemonSpawn 1 started",
      "DaemonSpawn 2 started",
      "DaemonSpawn 3 started",
      "DaemonSpawn 4 started",
      "DaemonSpawn 5 started",
      "DaemonSpawn 6 started",
      "DaemonSpawn 7 started",
      "DaemonSpawn 8 started",
      "DaemonSpawn 9 started",
      "t[0].isDaemon() = true",
      "t[1].isDaemon() = true",
      "t[2].isDaemon() = true",
      "t[3].isDaemon() = true",
```

```
      "t[4].isDaemon() = true",
      "t[5].isDaemon() = true",
      "t[6].isDaemon() = true",
      "t[7].isDaemon() = true",
      "t[8].isDaemon() = true",
      "t[9].isDaemon() = true"
    }, Test.IGNORE_ORDER + Test.WAIT);
  }
} ///:~
```

The **Daemon** thread sets its daemon flag to "true" and then spawns a bunch of other threads—which *do not* set themselves to daemon mode—to show that they are daemons anyway. Then it goes into an infinite loop that calls **yield( )** to give up control to the other processes.

There's nothing to keep the program from terminating once **main( )** finishes its job, since there are nothing but daemon threads running. So that you can see the results of starting all the daemon threads, the **main( )** thread is put to sleep for a second. Without this, you see only some of the results from the creation of the daemon threads. (Try **sleep( )** calls of various lengths to see this behavior.)

Joining a thread

One thread may call **join( )** on another thread to wait for the second thread to complete before proceeding. If a thread calls **t.join( )** on another thread **t**, then the calling thread is suspended until the target thread **t** finishes (when **t.isAlive( )** is **false**).

You may also call **join( )** with a timeout argument (in either milliseconds or milliseconds and nanoseconds) so that if the target thread doesn't finish in that period of time, the call to **join( )** returns anyway.

The call to **join( )** may be aborted by calling **interrupt( )** on the calling thread, so a **try-catch** clause is required.

All of these operations are shown in the following example:

```
//: c13:Joining.java
// Understanding join().
import com.bruceeckel.simpletest.*;

class Sleeper extends Thread {
  private int duration;
```

```java
  public Sleeper(String name, int sleepTime) {
    super(name);
    duration = sleepTime;
    start();
  }
  public void run() {
    try {
      sleep(duration);
    } catch (InterruptedException e) {
      System.out.println(getName() + " was interrupted. " +
        "isInterrupted(): " + isInterrupted());
      return;
    }
    System.out.println(getName() + " has awakened");
  }
}

class Joiner extends Thread {
  private Sleeper sleeper;
  public Joiner(String name, Sleeper sleeper) {
    super(name);
    this.sleeper = sleeper;
    start();
  }
  public void run() {
   try {
      sleeper.join();
    } catch (InterruptedException e) {
      throw new RuntimeException(e);
    }
    System.out.println(getName() + " join completed");
  }
}

public class Joining {
  private static Test monitor = new Test();
  public static void main(String[] args) {
    Sleeper
      sleepy = new Sleeper("Sleepy", 1500),
      grumpy = new Sleeper("Grumpy", 1500);
    Joiner
      dopey = new Joiner("Dopey", sleepy),
      doc = new Joiner("Doc", grumpy);
    grumpy.interrupt();
```

```
    monitor.expect(new String[] {
      "Grumpy was interrupted. isInterrupted(): false",
      "Doc join completed",
      "Sleepy has awakened",
      "Dopey join completed"
    }, Test.AT_LEAST + Test.WAIT);
  }
} ///:~
```

A **Sleeper** is a type of **Thread** that goes to sleep for a time specified in its constructor. In **run( )**, the call to **sleep( )** may terminate when the time expires, but it may also be interrupted. Inside the **catch** clause, the interruption is reported, along with the value of **isInterrupted( )**. When another thread calls **interrupt( )** on this thread, a flag is set to indicate that the thread has been interrupted. However, this flag is cleared when the exception is caught, so the result will always be false inside the **catch** clause. The flag is used for other situations where a thread may examine its interrupted state apart from the exception.

A **Joiner** is a thread that waits for a **Sleeper** to wake up by calling **join( )** on the **Sleeper** object. In **main( )**, each **Sleeper** has a **Joiner**, and you can see in the output that if the **Sleeper** is either interrupted or if it ends normally, the **Joiner** completes in conjunction with the **Sleeper**.

Coding variations

In the simple examples that you've seen so far, the thread objects are all inherited from **Thread**. This makes sense because the objects are clearly only being created *as* threads and have no other behavior. However, your class may already be inheriting from another class, in which case you can't also inherit from **Thread** (Java doesn't support multiple inheritance). In this case, you can use the alternative approach of implementing the **Runnable** interface. **Runnable** specifies only that there be a **run( )** method implemented, and **Thread** also implements **Runnable**.

This example demonstrates the basics:

```
//: c13:RunnableThread.java
// SimpleThread using the Runnable interface.

public class RunnableThread implements Runnable {
  private int countDown = 5;
  public String toString() {
```

```
    return "#" + Thread.currentThread().getName() +
      ": " + countDown;
  }
  public void run() {
    while(true) {
      System.out.println(this);
      if(--countDown == 0) return;
    }
  }
  public static void main(String[] args) {
    for(int i = 1; i <= 5; i++)
      new Thread(new RunnableThread(), "" + i).start();
    // Output is like SimpleThread.java
  }
} ///:~
```

The only thing required by a **Runnable** class is a **run( )** method, but if you want to do anything else to the **Thread** object (such as **getName( )** in **toString( )**) you must explicitly get a reference to it by calling **Thread.currentThread( )**. This particular **Thread** constructor takes a **Runnable** and a name for the thread.

When something has a **Runnable** interface, it simply means that it has a **run( )** method, but there's nothing special about that—it doesn't produce any innate threading abilities, like those of a class inherited from **Thread**. So to produce a thread from a **Runnable** object, you must create a separate **Thread** object as shown in this example, handing the **Runnable** object to the special **Thread** constructor. You can then call **start( )** for that thread, which performs the usual initialization and then calls **run( )**.

The convenient aspect about the **Runnable interface** is that everything belongs to the same class; that is, **Runnable** allows a mixin in combination with a base class and other interfaces. If you need to access something, you simply do it without going through a separate object. However, inner classes have this same easy access to all the parts of an outer class, so member access is not a compelling reason to use **Runnable** as a mixin rather than an inner subclass of **Thread**.

When you use **Runnable**, you're generally saying that you want to create a *process* in a piece of code—implemented in the **run( )** method—rather than an object representing that process. This is a matter of some debate, depending on whether you feel that it makes more sense to represent a thread as an object or as a completely different entity, a process.[1] If you choose to think of it as a process, then you are freed from the object-oriented imperative that "everything is an object." This also means that there's no reason to make your whole class **Runnable** if you only want to start a process to drive some part of your program. Because of this, it often makes more sense to hide your threading code inside your class by using an inner class, as shown here:

```
//: c13:ThreadVariations.java
// Creating threads with inner classes.
import com.bruceeckel.simpletest.*;

// Using a named inner class:
class InnerThread1 {
  private int countDown = 5;
  private Inner inner;
  private class Inner extends Thread {
    Inner(String name) {
      super(name);
      start();
    }
    public void run() {
      while(true) {
        System.out.println(this);
        if(--countDown == 0) return;
        try {
          sleep(10);
        } catch (InterruptedException e) {
          throw new RuntimeException(e);
        }
      }
    }
    public String toString() {
      return getName() + ": " + countDown;
    }
  }
```

[1] **Runnable** was in Java 1.0, while inner classes were not introduced until Java 1.1, which may partially account for the existence of **Runnable**. Also, traditional multithreading architectures focused on a function to be run rather than an object. My preference is always to inherit from **Thread** if I can; it seems cleaner and more flexible to me.

```
  public InnerThread1(String name) {
    inner = new Inner(name);
  }
}

// Using an anonymous inner class:
class InnerThread2 {
  private int countDown = 5;
  private Thread t;
  public InnerThread2(String name) {
    t = new Thread(name) {
      public void run() {
        while(true) {
          System.out.println(this);
          if(--countDown == 0) return;
          try {
            sleep(10);
          } catch (InterruptedException e) {
            throw new RuntimeException(e);
          }
        }
      }
      public String toString() {
        return getName() + ": " + countDown;
      }
    };
    t.start();
  }
}

// Using a named Runnable implementation:
class InnerRunnable1 {
  private int countDown = 5;
  private Inner inner;
  private class Inner implements Runnable {
    Thread t;
    Inner(String name) {
      t = new Thread(this, name);
      t.start();
    }
    public void run() {
      while(true) {
        System.out.println(this);
        if(--countDown == 0) return;
```

```java
        try {
          Thread.sleep(10);
        } catch (InterruptedException e) {
          throw new RuntimeException(e);
        }
      }
    }
    public String toString() {
      return t.getName() + ": " + countDown;
    }
  }
  public InnerRunnable1(String name) {
    inner = new Inner(name);
  }
}

// Using an anonymous Runnable implementation:
class InnerRunnable2 {
  private int countDown = 5;
  private Thread t;
  public InnerRunnable2(String name) {
    t = new Thread(new Runnable() {
      public void run() {
        while(true) {
          System.out.println(this);
          if(--countDown == 0) return;
          try {
            Thread.sleep(10);
          } catch (InterruptedException e) {
            throw new RuntimeException(e);
          }
        }
      }
      public String toString() {
        return Thread.currentThread().getName() +
          ": " + countDown;
      }
    }, name);
    t.start();
  }
}

// A separate method to run some code as a thread:
class ThreadMethod {
```

```
  private int countDown = 5;
  private Thread t;
  private String name;
  public ThreadMethod(String name) { this.name = name; }
  public void runThread() {
    if(t == null) {
      t = new Thread(name) {
        public void run() {
          while(true) {
            System.out.println(this);
            if(--countDown == 0) return;
            try {
              sleep(10);
            } catch (InterruptedException e) {
              throw new RuntimeException(e);
            }
          }
        }
        public String toString() {
          return getName() + ": " + countDown;
        }
      };
      t.start();
    }
  }
}

public class ThreadVariations {
  private static Test monitor = new Test();
  public static void main(String[] args) {
    new InnerThread1("InnerThread1");
    new InnerThread2("InnerThread2");
    new InnerRunnable1("InnerRunnable1");
    new InnerRunnable2("InnerRunnable2");
    new ThreadMethod("ThreadMethod").runThread();
    monitor.expect(new String[] {
      "InnerThread1: 5",
      "InnerThread2: 5",
      "InnerThread2: 4",
      "InnerRunnable1: 5",
      "InnerThread1: 4",
      "InnerRunnable2: 5",
      "ThreadMethod: 5",
      "InnerRunnable1: 4",
```

```
      "InnerThread2: 3",
      "InnerRunnable2: 4",
      "ThreadMethod: 4",
      "InnerThread1: 3",
      "InnerRunnable1: 3",
      "ThreadMethod: 3",
      "InnerThread1: 2",
      "InnerThread2: 2",
      "InnerRunnable2: 3",
      "InnerThread2: 1",
      "InnerRunnable2: 2",
      "InnerRunnable1: 2",
      "ThreadMethod: 2",
      "InnerThread1: 1",
      "InnerRunnable1: 1",
      "InnerRunnable2: 1",
      "ThreadMethod: 1"
    }, Test.IGNORE_ORDER + Test.WAIT);
  }
} ///:~
```

InnerThread1 creates a named inner class that extends **Thread**, and makes an instance of this inner class inside the constructor. This makes sense if the inner class has special capabilities (new methods) that you need to access in other methods. However, most of the time the reason for creating a thread is only to use the **Thread** capabilities, so it's not necessary to create a named inner class. **InnerThread2** shows the alternative: An anonymous inner subclass of **Thread** is created inside the constructor and is upcast to a **Thread** reference **t**. If other methods of the class need to access **t**, they can do so through the **Thread** interface, and they don't need to know the exact type of the object.

The third and fourth classes in the example repeat the first two classes, but they use the **Runnable** interface rather than the **Thread** class. This is just to show that **Runnable** doesn't buy you anything more in this situation, but is in fact slightly more complicated to code (and to read the code). As a result, my inclination is to use **Thread** unless I'm somehow compelled to use **Runnable**.

The **ThreadMethod** class shows the creation of a thread inside a method. You call the method when you're ready to run the thread, and the method returns after the thread begins. If the thread is only performing an auxiliary operation rather than being fundamental to the class, this is probably a more useful/appropriate approach than starting a thread inside the constructor of the class.

Creating responsive user interfaces

As stated earlier, one of the motivations for using threading is to create a responsive user interface. Although we won't get to *graphical* user interfaces until Chapter 14, you can see a simple example of a console-based user interface. The following example has two versions: one that gets stuck in a calculation and thus can never read console input, and a second that puts the calculation inside a thread and thus can be performing the calculation *and* listening for console input.

```
//: c13:ResponsiveUI.java
// User interface responsiveness.
import com.bruceeckel.simpletest.*;

class UnresponsiveUI {
  private volatile double d = 1;
  public UnresponsiveUI() throws Exception {
    while(d > 0)
      d = d + (Math.PI + Math.E) / d;
    System.in.read(); // Never gets here
  }
}

public class ResponsiveUI extends Thread {
  private static Test monitor = new Test();
  private static volatile double d = 1;
  public ResponsiveUI() {
    setDaemon(true);
    start();
  }
  public void run() {
    while(true) {
      d = d + (Math.PI + Math.E) / d;
    }
  }
  public static void main(String[] args) throws Exception {
    //! new UnresponsiveUI(); // Must kill this process
    new ResponsiveUI();
    Thread.sleep(300);
    System.in.read(); // 'monitor' provides input
    System.out.println(d); // Shows progress
```

```
    }
} ///:~
```

UnresponsiveUI performs a calculation inside an infinite **while** loop, so it can obviously never reach the console input line (the compiler is fooled into believing that the input line is reachable by the **while** conditional). If you run the program with the line that creates an **UnresponsiveUI** uncommented, you'll have to kill the process to get out.

To make the program responsive, putting the calculation inside a **run( )** method allows it to be preempted, and when you press the Enter key you'll see that the calculation has indeed been running in the background while waiting for your user input (for testing purposes, the console input line is automatically provided to **System.in.read( )** by the **com.bruceeckel.simpletest.Test** object, which is explained in Chapter 15).

Sharing limited resources

You can think of a single-threaded program as one lonely entity moving around through your problem space and doing one thing at a time. Because there's only one entity, you never have to think about the problem of two entities trying to use the same resource at the same time, problems like two people trying to park in the same space, walk through a door at the same time, or even talk at the same time.

With multithreading, things aren't lonely anymore, but you now have the possibility of two or more threads trying to use the same limited resource at once. Colliding over a resource must be prevented, or else you'll have two threads trying to access the same bank account at the same time, print to the same printer, adjust the same valve, and so on.

Improperly accessing resources

Consider the following example in which the class "guarantees" that it will always deliver an even number when you call **getValue( )**. However, there's a second thread named "Watcher" that is constantly calling **getValue( )** and checking to see if this value is truly even. This seems like a needless activity, since it appears obvious by looking at the code that the value will indeed be even. But that's where the surprise comes in. Here's the first version of the program:

```java
//: c13:AlwaysEven.java
// Demonstrating thread collision over resources by
// reading an object in an unstable intermediate state.

public class AlwaysEven {
  private int i;
  public void next() { i++; i++; }
  public int getValue() { return i; }
  public static void main(String[] args) {
    final AlwaysEven ae = new AlwaysEven();
    new Thread("Watcher") {
      public void run() {
        while(true) {
          int val = ae.getValue();
          if(val % 2 != 0) {
            System.out.println(val);
            System.exit(0);
          }
        }
      }
    }.start();
    while(true)
      ae.next();
  }
} ///:~
```

In **main( )**, an **AlwaysEven** object is created—it must be **final** because it is accessed inside the anonymous inner class defined as a **Thread**. If the value read by the thread is not even, it prints it out (as proof that it has caught the object in an unstable state) and then exits the program.

This example shows a fundamental problem with using threads. You never know when a thread might be run. Imagine sitting at a table with a fork, about to spear the last piece of food on your plate, and as your fork reaches for it, the food suddenly vanishes (because your thread was suspended and another thread came in and stole the food). That's the problem that you're dealing with when writing concurrent programs.

Sometimes you don't care if a resource is being accessed at the same time you're trying to use it (the food is on some other plate). But for multithreading to work, you need some way to prevent two threads from accessing the same resource, at least during critical periods.

Preventing this kind of collision is simply a matter of putting a lock on a resource when one thread is using it. The first thread that accesses a resource locks it, and then the other threads cannot access that resource until it is unlocked, at which time another thread locks and uses it, etc. If the front seat of the car is the limited resource, the child who shouts "Dibs!" asserts the lock.

A resource testing framework

Before going on, let's try to simplify things a bit by creating a little framework for performing tests on these types of threading examples. We can accomplish this by separating out the common code that might appear across multiple examples. First, note that the "watcher" thread is actually watching for a violated invariant in a particular object. That is, the object is supposed to preserve rules about its internal state, and if you can see the object from outside in an invalid intermediate state, then the invariant has been violated from the standpoint of the client (this is not to say that the object can never exist in the invalid intermediate state, just that it should not be visible by the client in such a state). Thus, we want to be able to detect that the invariant is violated, and also know what the violation value is. To get both of these values from one method call, we combine them in a tagging interface that exists only to provide a meaningful name in the code:

```
//: c13:InvariantState.java
// Messenger carrying invariant data
public interface InvariantState {} ///:~
```

In this scheme, the information about success or failure is encoded in the class name and type to make the result more readable. The class indicating success is:

```
//: c13:InvariantOK.java
// Indicates that the invariant test succeeded
public class InvariantOK implements InvariantState {} ///:~
```

To indicate failure, the **InvariantFailure** object will carry an object with information about what caused the failure, typically so that it can be displayed:

```
//: c13:InvariantFailure.java
// Indicates that the invariant test failed

public class InvariantFailure implements InvariantState {
```

```
  public Object value;
  public InvariantFailure(Object value) {
    this.value = value;
  }
} ///:~
```

Now we can define an interface that must be implemented by any class that wishes to have its invariance tested:

```
//: c13:Invariant.java
public interface Invariant {
  InvariantState invariant();
} ///:~
```

Before creating the generic "watcher" thread, note that some of the examples in this chapter will not behave as expected on all platforms. Many of the examples here attempt to show violations of single-threaded behavior when multiple threads are present, and this may not always happen.[2] Alternatively, an example may attempt to show that the violation does *not* occur by attempting (and failing) to demonstrate the violation. In these cases, we'll need a way to stop the program after a few seconds. The following class does this by subclassing the standard library **Timer** class:

```
//: c13:Timeout.java
// Set a time limit on the execution of a program
import java.util.*;

public class Timeout extends Timer {
  public Timeout(int delay, final String msg) {
    super(true); // Daemon thread
    schedule(new TimerTask() {
      public void run() {
        System.out.println(msg);
        System.exit(0);
      }
    }, delay);
  }
```

[2] Some examples were developed on a dual-processor Win2K machine that would immediately show collisions. However, the same example run on single-processor machines might run for extended periods without demonstrating a collision—this is the kind of scary behavior that makes multithreading difficult. You can imagine developing on a single-processor machine and thinking that your code is thread safe, then discovering breakages as soon as it's moved to a multiprocessor machine.

```
} ///:~
```

The delay is in milliseconds, and the message will be printed if the timeout expires. Note that by calling **super(true)**, this is created as a daemon thread so that if your program completes in some other way, this thread will not prevent it from exiting. The **Timer.schedule( )** method is given a **TimerTask** subclass (created here as an anonymous inner class) whose **run( )** is executed after the second **schedule( )** argument **delay** (in milliseconds) runs out. Using **Timer** is generally simpler and clearer than writing the code directly with an explicit **sleep( )**. In addition, **Timer** is designed to scale to large numbers of concurrently scheduled tasks (in the thousands), so it can be a very useful tool.

Now we can use the **Invariant** interface and the **Timeout** class in the **InvariantWatcher** thread:

```
//: c13:InvariantWatcher.java
// Repeatedly checks to ensure invariant is not violated

public class InvariantWatcher extends Thread {
  private Invariant invariant;
  public InvariantWatcher(Invariant invariant) {
    this.invariant = invariant;
    setDaemon(true);
    start();
  }
  // Stop everything after awhile:
  public
  InvariantWatcher(Invariant invariant, final int timeOut){
    this(invariant);
    new Timeout(timeOut,
      "Timed out without violating invariant");
  }
  public void run() {
    while(true) {
      InvariantState state = invariant.invariant();
      if(state instanceof InvariantFailure) {
        System.out.println("Invariant violated: "
          + ((InvariantFailure)state).value);
        System.exit(0);
      }
    }
  }
} ///:~
```

The constructor captures a reference to the **Invariant** object to be tested, and starts the thread. The second constructor calls the first constructor, then creates a **Timeout** that stops everything after a desired delay—this is used in situations where the program may not exit by violating an invariant. In **run( )**, the current **InvariantState** is captured and tested, and if it fails, the **value** is printed. Note that we cannot throw an exception inside this thread, because that would only terminate the thread, not the program.

Now **AlwaysEven.java** can be rewritten using the framework:

```
//: c13:EvenGenerator.java
// AlwaysEven.java using the invariance tester

public class EvenGenerator implements Invariant {
  private int i;
  public void next() { i++; i++; }
  public int getValue() { return i; }
  public InvariantState invariant() {
    int val = i; // Capture it in case it changes
    if(val % 2 == 0)
      return new InvariantOK();
    else
      return new InvariantFailure(new Integer(val));
  }
  public static void main(String[] args) {
    EvenGenerator gen = new EvenGenerator();
    new InvariantWatcher(gen);
    while(true)
      gen.next();
  }
} ///:~
```

When defining the **invariant( )** method, you must capture all the values of interest into local variables. This way, you can return the actual value you have tested, not one that may have been changed (by another thread) in the meantime.

In this case, the problem is not that the object goes through a state that violates invariance, but that methods can be called by threads while the object is in that intermediate unstable state.

Colliding over resources

The worst thing that happens with **EvenGenerator** is that a client thread might see it in an unstable intermediate state. The object's internal consistency is maintained, however, and it eventually becomes visible in a good state. But if two threads are actually modifying an object, the contention over shared resources is much worse, because the object can be put into an incorrect state.

Consider the simple concept of a *semaphore*, which is a flag object used for communication between threads. If the semaphore's value is zero, then whatever it is monitoring is available, but if the value is nonzero, then the monitored entity is unavailable, and the thread must wait for it. When it's available, the thread increments the semaphore and then goes ahead and uses the monitored entity. Because incrementing and decrementing are *atomic* operations (that is, they cannot be interrupted), the semaphore keeps two threads from using the same entity at the same time.

If the semaphore is going to properly guard the entity that it is monitoring, then it must never get into an unstable state. Here's a simple version of the semaphore idea:

```
//: c13:Semaphore.java
// A simple threading flag

public class Semaphore implements Invariant {
  private volatile int semaphore = 0;
  public boolean available() { return semaphore == 0; }
  public void acquire() { ++semaphore; }
  public void release() { --semaphore; }
  public InvariantState invariant() {
    int val = semaphore;
    if(val == 0 || val == 1)
      return new InvariantOK();
    else
      return new InvariantFailure(new Integer(val));
  }
} ///:~
```

The core part of the class is straightforward, consisting of **available( )**, **acquire( )**, and **release( )**. Since a thread should check for availability before acquiring, the value of **semaphore** should never be other than one or zero, and this is tested by **invariant( )**.

But look what happens when **Semaphore** is tested for thread consistency:

```
//: c13:SemaphoreTester.java
// Colliding over shared resources

public class SemaphoreTester extends Thread {
  private volatile Semaphore semaphore;
  public SemaphoreTester(Semaphore semaphore) {
    this.semaphore = semaphore;
    setDaemon(true);
    start();
  }
  public void run() {
    while(true)
      if(semaphore.available()) {
        yield(); // Makes it fail faster
        semaphore.acquire();
        yield();
        semaphore.release();
        yield();
      }
  }
  public static void main(String[] args) throws Exception {
    Semaphore sem = new Semaphore();
    new SemaphoreTester(sem);
    new SemaphoreTester(sem);
    new InvariantWatcher(sem).join();
  }
} ///:~
```

The **SemaphoreTester** creates a thread that continuously tests to see if a **Semaphore** object is available, and if so acquires and releases it. Note that the **semaphore** field is **volatile** to make sure that the compiler doesn't optimize away any reads of that value.

In **main( )**, two **SemaphoreTester** threads are created, and you'll see that in short order the invariant is violated. This happens because one thread might get a **true** result from calling **available( )**, but by the time that thread calls **acquire( )**, the other thread may have already called **acquire( )** and incremented the **semaphore** field. The **InvariantWatcher** may see the field with too high a value, or possibly see it after both threads have called **release( )** and decremented it to a negative value. Note that **InvariantWatcher join( )**s with the main thread to keep the program running until there is a failure.

On my machine, I discovered that the inclusion of **yield( )** caused failure to occur much faster, but this will vary with operating systems and JVM implementations. You should experiment with taking the **yield( )** statements out; the failure might take a very long time to occur, which demonstrates how difficult it can be to detect a flaw in your program when you're writing multithreaded code.

This class emphasizes the risk of concurrent programming: If a class this simple can produce problems, you can never trust any assumptions about concurrency.

Resolving shared resource contention

To solve the problem of thread collision, virtually all multithreading schemes *serialize access to shared resources*. This means that only one thread at a time is allowed to access the shared resource. This is ordinarily accomplished by putting a locked clause around a piece of code so that only one thread at a time may pass through that piece of code. Because this locked clause produces *mutual exclusion*, a common name for such a mechanism is *mutex*.

Consider the bathroom in your house; multiple people (threads) may each want to have exclusive use of the bathroom (the shared resource). To access the bathroom, a person knocks on the door to see if it's available. If so, they enter and lock the door. Any other thread that wants to use the bathroom is "blocked" from using it, so that thread waits at the door until the bathroom is available.

The analogy breaks down a bit when the bathroom is released and it comes time to give access to another thread. There isn't actually a line of people and we don't know for sure who gets the bathroom next, because the thread scheduler isn't deterministic that way. Instead, it's as if there is a group of blocked threads milling about in front of the bathroom, and when the thread that has locked the bathroom unlocks it and emerges, the one that happens to be nearest the door at the moment goes in. As noted earlier, suggestions can be made to the thread scheduler via **yield( )** and **setPriority( )**, but these suggestions may not have much of an effect depending on your platform and JVM implementation.

Java has built-in support to prevent collisions over resources in the form of the **synchronized** keyword. This works much like the **Semaphore** class was supposed to: When a thread wishes to execute a piece of code guarded by the **synchronized** keyword, it checks to see if the semaphore is available, then acquires it, executes the code, and releases it. However, **synchronized** is built into the language, so it's guaranteed to always work, unlike the **Semaphore** class.

The shared resource is typically just a piece of memory in the form of an object, but may also be a file, I/O port, or something like a printer. To control access to a shared resource, you first put it inside an object. Then any method that accesses that resource can be made **synchronized**. This means that if a thread is inside one of the **synchronized** methods, all other threads are blocked from entering any of the **synchronized** methods of the class until the first thread returns from its call.

Since you typically make the data elements of a class **private** and access that memory only through methods, you can prevent collisions by making methods **synchronized**. Here is how you declare **synchronized** methods:

```
synchronized void f() { /* ... */ }
synchronized void g(){ /* ... */ }
```

Each object contains a single lock (also referred to as a *monitor*) that is automatically part of the object (you don't have to write any special code). When you call any **synchronized** method, that object is locked and no other **synchronized** method of that object can be called until the first one finishes and releases the lock. In the preceding example, if **f( )** is called for an object, **g( )** cannot be called for the same object until **f( )** is completed and releases the lock. Thus, there is a single lock that is shared by all the **synchronized** methods of a particular object, and this lock prevents common memory from being written by more than one thread at a time.

One thread may acquire an object's lock multiple times. This happens if one method calls a second method on the same object, which in turn calls another method on the same object, etc. The JVM keeps track of the number of times the object has been locked. If the object is unlocked, it has a count of zero. As a thread acquires the lock for the first time, the count goes to one. Each time the thread acquires a lock on the same object, the count is incremented. Naturally, multiple lock acquisition is only allowed for the thread that acquired the lock in the first place. Each time the thread leaves a **synchronized** method, the count is decremented, until the count goes to zero, releasing the lock entirely for use by other threads.

There's also a single lock per class (as part of the **Class** object for the class), so that **synchronized static** methods can lock each other out from simultaneous access of **static** data on a class-wide basis.

Synchronizing the **EvenGenerator**

By adding **synchronized** to **EvenGenerator.java**, we can prevent the undesirable thread access:

```
//: c13:SynchronizedEvenGenerator.java
// Using "synchronized" to prevent thread collisions

public
class SynchronizedEvenGenerator implements Invariant {
  private int i;
  public synchronized void next() { i++; i++; }
  public synchronized int getValue() { return i; }
  // Not synchronized so it can run at
  // any time and thus be a genuine test:
  public InvariantState invariant() {
    int val = getValue();
    if(val % 2 == 0)
      return new InvariantOK();
    else
      return new InvariantFailure(new Integer(val));
  }
  public static void main(String[] args) {
    SynchronizedEvenGenerator gen =
      new SynchronizedEvenGenerator();
    new InvariantWatcher(gen, 4000); // 4-second timeout
    while(true)
      gen.next();
  }
} ///:~
```

You'll notice that both **next( )** and **getValue( )** are **synchronized**. If you synchronize only one of the methods, then the other is free to ignore the object lock and can be called with impunity. This is an important point: Every method that accesses a critical shared resource must be **synchronized** or it won't work right. On the other hand, **InvariantState** is *not* **synchronized** because it is doing the testing, and we want it to be called at any time so that it produces a true test of the object.

Atomic operations

A common piece of lore often repeated in Java threading discussions is that "atomic operations do not need to be synchronized." An *atomic operation* is one that cannot be interrupted by the thread scheduler; if the operation begins, then it will run to completion before the possibility of a *context switch* (switching execution to another thread).

The atomic operations commonly mentioned in this lore include simple assignment and returning a value when the variable in question is a primitive type that is *not* a **long** or a **double**. The latter types are excluded because they are larger than the rest of the types, and the JVM is thus not required to perform reads and assignments as single atomic operations (a JVM may choose to do so anyway, but there's no guarantee). However, you do get atomicity if you use the **volatile** keyword with **long** or **double**.

If you were to blindly apply the idea of atomicity to **SynchronizedEvenGenerator.java**, you would notice that

```
  public synchronized int getValue() { return i; }
```

fits the description. But try removing **synchronized**, and the test will fail, because even though **return i** is indeed an atomic operation, removing **synchronized** allows the value to be read while the object is in an unstable intermediate state. You must genuinely understand what you're doing before you try to apply optimizations like this. There are no easily-applicable rules that work.

As a second example, consider something even simpler: a class that produces serial numbers.[3] Each time **nextSerialNumber( )** is called, it must return a unique value to the caller:

```
//: c13:SerialNumberGenerator.java

public class SerialNumberGenerator {
  private static volatile int serialNumber = 0;
  public static int nextSerialNumber() {
    return serialNumber++;
  }
} ///:~
```

---

[3] Inspired by Joshua Bloch's *Effective Java*, Addison-Wesley 2001, page 190.

SerialNumberGenerator is about as simple a class as you can imagine, and if you're coming from C++ or some other low-level background, you would expect the increment to be an atomic operation, because increment is usually implemented as a microprocessor instruction. However, in the JVM an increment is *not* atomic and involves both a read and a write, so there's room for threading problems even in such a simple operation.

The **serialNumber** field is **volatile** because it is possible for each thread to have a local stack and maintain copies of some variables there. If you define a variable as **volatile**, it tells the compiler not to do any optimizations that would remove reads and writes that keep the field in exact synchronization with the local data in the threads.

To test this, we need a set that doesn't run out of memory, in case it takes a long time to detect a problem. The **CircularSet** shown here reuses the memory used to store **int**s, with the assumption that by the time you wrap around, the possibility of a collision with the overwritten values is minimal. The **add( )** and **contains( )** methods are **synchronized** to prevent thread collisions:

```
//: c13:SerialNumberChecker.java
// Operations that may seem safe are not,
// when threads are present.

// Reuses storage so we don't run out of memory:
class CircularSet {
  private int[] array;
  private int len;
  private int index = 0;
  public CircularSet(int size) {
    array = new int[size];
    len = size;
    // Initialize to a value not produced
    // by the SerialNumberGenerator:
    for(int i = 0; i < size; i++)
      array[i] = -1;
  }
  public synchronized void add(int i) {
    array[index] = i;
    // Wrap index and write over old elements:
    index = ++index % len;
  }
  public synchronized boolean contains(int val) {
```

```
    for(int i = 0; i < len; i++)
      if(array[i] == val) return true;
    return false;
  }
}

public class SerialNumberChecker {
  private static CircularSet serials =
    new CircularSet(1000);
  static class SerialChecker extends Thread {
    SerialChecker() { start(); }
    public void run() {
      while(true) {
        int serial =
          SerialNumberGenerator.nextSerialNumber();
        if(serials.contains(serial)) {
          System.out.println("Duplicate: " + serial);
          System.exit(0);
        }
        serials.add(serial);
      }
    }
  }
  public static void main(String[] args) {
    for(int i = 0; i < 10; i++)
      new SerialChecker();
    // Stop after 4 seconds:
    new Timeout(4000, "No duplicates detected");
  }
} ///:~
```

SerialNumberChecker contains a **static CircularSet** that contains all the serial numbers that have been extracted, and a nested **Thread** that gets serial numbers and ensures that they are unique. By creating multiple threads to contend over serial numbers, you'll discover that the threads get a duplicate serial number reasonably soon (note that this program may not indicate a collision on your machine, but it has successfully detected collisions on a multiprocessor machine). To solve the problem, add the **synchronized** keyword to **nextSerialNumber( )**.

The atomic operations that are supposed to be safe are reading and assignment of primitives. However, as seen in **EvenGenerator.java**, it's still easily possible to use an atomic operation that accesses your object while it's in an unstable intermediate state, so you cannot make any assumptions.

On top of this, the atomic operations are not guaranteed to work with **long** and **double** (although some JVM implementations do guarantee atomicity for **long** and **double** operations, you won't be writing portable code if you depend on this).

It's safest to use the following guidelines:

1. If you need to synchronize one method in a class, synchronize all of them. It's often difficult to tell for sure if a method will be negatively affected if you leave synchronization out.

2. Be extremely careful when removing synchronization from methods. The typical reason to do this is for performance, but in JDK 1.3 and 1.4 the overhead of **synchronized** has been greatly reduced. In addition, you should only do this after using a profiler to determine that **synchronized** is indeed the bottleneck.

Fixing **Semaphore**

Now consider **Semaphore.java**. It would seem that we should be able to repair this by **synchronizing** the three class methods, like this:

```
//: c13:SynchronizedSemaphore.java
// Colliding over shared resources

public class SynchronizedSemaphore extends Semaphore {
  private volatile int semaphore = 0;
  public synchronized boolean available() {
    return semaphore == 0;
  }
  public synchronized void acquire() { ++semaphore; }
  public synchronized void release() { --semaphore; }
  public InvariantState invariant() {
    int val = semaphore;
    if(val == 0 || val == 1)
      return new InvariantOK();
    else
      return new InvariantFailure(new Integer(val));
  }
  public static void main(String[] args) throws Exception {
    SynchronizedSemaphore sem =new SynchronizedSemaphore();
    new SemaphoreTester(sem);
    new SemaphoreTester(sem);
    new InvariantWatcher(sem).join();
```

```
  }
} ///:~
```

This looks rather odd at first—**SynchronizedSemaphore** is inherited from **Semaphore**, and yet all the overridden methods are **synchronized**, but the base-class versions aren't. Java doesn't allow you to change the method signature during overriding, and yet doesn't complain about this. That's because the **synchronized** keyword is not part of the method signature, so you can add it in and it doesn't limit overriding.

The reason for inheriting from **Semaphore** is to reuse the **SemaphoreTester** class. When you run the program you'll see that it still causes an **InvariantFailure**.

Why does this fail? By the time a thread detects that the **Semaphore** is available because **available( )** returns **true**, it has released the lock on the object. Another thread can dash in and increment the **semaphore** value before the first thread does. The first thread still assumes the **Semaphore** object is available and so goes ahead and blindly enters the **acquire( )** method, putting the object into an unstable state. This is just one more lesson about rule zero of concurrent programming: Never make any assumptions.

The only solution to this problem is to make the test for availability and the acquisition a single atomic operation—which is exactly what the **synchronized** keyword provides in conjunction with the lock on an object. That is, Java's lock and **synchronized** keyword is a built-in semaphore mechanism, so you don't need to create your own.

Critical sections

Sometimes, you only want to prevent multiple thread access to part of the code inside a method instead of the entire method. The section of code you want to isolate this way is called a *critical section* and is also created using the **synchronized** keyword. Here, **synchronized** is used to specify the object whose lock is being used to synchronize the enclosed code:

```
synchronized(syncObject) {
  // This code can be accessed
  // by only one thread at a time
}
```

This is also called a *synchronized block*; before it can be entered, the lock must be acquired on **syncObject**. If some other thread already has this lock, then the critical section cannot be entered until the lock is given up.

The following example compares both approaches to synchronization by showing how the time available for other threads to access an object is significantly increased by using a synchronized block instead of synchronizing an entire method. In addition, it shows how an unprotected class can be used in a multithreaded situation if it is controlled and protected by another class:

```
//: c13:CriticalSection.java
// Synchronizing blocks instead of entire methods. Also
// demonstrates protection of a non-thread-safe class
// with a thread-safe one.
import java.util.*;

class Pair { // Not thread-safe
  private int x, y;
  public Pair(int x, int y) {
    this.x = x;
    this.y = y;
  }
  public Pair() { this(0, 0); }
  public int getX() { return x; }
  public int getY() { return y; }
  public void incrementX() { x++; }
  public void incrementY() { y++; }
  public String toString() {
    return "x: " + x + ", y: " + y;
  }
  public class PairValuesNotEqualException
  extends RuntimeException {
    public PairValuesNotEqualException() {
      super("Pair values not equal: " + Pair.this);
    }
  }
  // Arbitrary invariant -- both variables must be equal:
  public void checkState() {
    if(x != y)
      throw new PairValuesNotEqualException();
  }
}
```

```
// Protect a Pair inside a thread-safe class:
abstract class PairManager {
  protected Pair p = new Pair();
  private List storage = new ArrayList();
  public synchronized Pair getPair() {
    // Make a copy to keep the original safe:
    return new Pair(p.getX(), p.getY());
  }
  protected void store() { storage.add(getPair()); }
  // A "template method":
  public abstract void doTask();
}

// Synchronize the entire method:
class PairManager1 extends PairManager {
  public synchronized void doTask() {
    p.incrementX();
    p.incrementY();
    store();
  }
}

// Use a critical section:
class PairManager2 extends PairManager {
  public void doTask() {
    synchronized(this) {
      p.incrementX();
      p.incrementY();
    }
    store();
  }
}

class PairManipulator extends Thread {
  private PairManager pm;
  private int checkCounter = 0;
  private class PairChecker extends Thread {
    PairChecker() { start(); }
    public void run() {
      while(true) {
        checkCounter++;
        pm.getPair().checkState();
      }
    }
```

```java
  }
  public PairManipulator(PairManager pm) {
    this.pm = pm;
    start();
    new PairChecker();
  }
  public void run() {
    while(true) {
      pm.doTask();
    }
  }
  public String toString() {
    return "Pair: " + pm.getPair() +
      " checkCounter = " + checkCounter;
  }
}

public class CriticalSection {
  public static void main(String[] args) {
    // Test the two different approaches:
    final PairManipulator
      pm1 = new PairManipulator(new PairManager1()),
      pm2 = new PairManipulator(new PairManager2());
    new Timer(true).schedule(new TimerTask() {
      public void run() {
        System.out.println("pm1: " + pm1);
        System.out.println("pm2: " + pm2);
        System.exit(0);
      }
    }, 500); // run() after 500 milliseconds
  }
} ///:~
```

As noted, **Pair** is not thread-safe because its invariant (admittedly arbitrary) requires that both variables maintain the same values. In addition, as seen earlier in this chapter, the increment operations are not thread-safe, and because none of the methods are **synchronized**, you can't trust a **Pair** object to stay uncorrupted in a threaded program.

The **PairManager** class holds a **Pair** object and controls all access to it. Note that the only **public** methods are **getPair( )**, which is **synchronized**, and the **abstract doTask( )**. Synchronization for this method will be handled when it is implemented.

The structure of **PairManager**, where some of the functionality is implemented in the base class with one or more **abstract** methods defined in derived classes, is called a *Template Method* in *Design Patterns* parlance.[4] Design patterns allow you to encapsulate change in your code; here, the part that is changing is the template method **doTask( )**. In **PairManager1** the entire **doTask( )** is **synchronized**, but in **PairManager2** only part of **doTask( )** is **synchronized** by using a **synchronized** block. Note that the **synchronized** keyword is not part of the method signature and thus may be added during overriding.

PairManager2 is observing, in effect, that **store( )** is a **protected** method and thus is not available to the general client, but only to subclasses. Thus, it doesn't necessarily need to be guarded inside a **synchronized** method, and is instead placed outside of the **synchronized** block.

A **synchronized** block must be given an object to synchronize upon, and usually the most sensible object to use is just the current object that the method is being called for: **synchronized(this)**, which is the approach taken in **PairManager2**. That way, when the lock is acquired for the synchronized block, other synchronized methods in the object cannot be called. So the effect is that of simply reducing the scope of synchronization.

Sometimes this isn't what you want, in which case you can create a separate object and synchronize on that. The following example demonstrates that two threads can enter an object when the methods in that object synchronize on different locks:

```
//: c13:SyncObject.java
// Synchronizing on another object
import com.bruceeckel.simpletest.*;

class DualSynch {
  private Object syncObject = new Object();
  public synchronized void f() {
    System.out.println("Inside f()");
    // Doesn't release lock:
    try {
      Thread.sleep(500);
    } catch(InterruptedException e) {
```

4 See *Design Patterns*, by Gamma et. al., Addison-Wesley 1995.

```
        throw new RuntimeException(e);
      }
      System.out.println("Leaving f()");
    }
    public void g() {
      synchronized(syncObject) {
        System.out.println("Inside g()");
        try {
          Thread.sleep(500);
        } catch(InterruptedException e) {
          throw new RuntimeException(e);
        }
        System.out.println("Leaving g()");
      }
    }
  }

  public class SyncObject {
    private static Test monitor = new Test();
    public static void main(String[] args) {
      final DualSynch ds = new DualSynch();
      new Thread() {
        public void run() {
          ds.f();
        }
      }.start();
      ds.g();
      monitor.expect(new String[] {
        "Inside g()",
        "Inside f()",
        "Leaving g()",
        "Leaving f()"
      }, Test.WAIT + Test.IGNORE_ORDER);
    }
  } ///:~
```

The **DualSync** method **f( )** synchronizes on **this** (by synchronizing the entire method) and **g( )** has a synchronized block that synchronizes on **syncObject**. Thus, the two synchronizations are independent. This is demonstrated in **main( )** by creating a **Thread** that calls **f( )**. The **main( )** thread is used to call **g( )**. You can see from the output that both methods are running at the same time, so neither one is blocked by the synchronization of the other.

Returning to **CriticalSection.java**, **PairManipulator** is created to test the two different types of **PairManager** by running **doTask( )** in one thread and an instance of the inner class **PairChecker** in the other. To trace how often it is able to run the test, **PairChecker** increments **checkCounter** every time it is successful. In **main( )**, two **PairManipulator** objects are created and allowed to run for awhile. When the **Timer** runs out, it executes its **run( )** method, that displays the results of each **PairManipulator** and exits. When you run the program, you should see something like this:

```
pm1: Pair: x: 58892, y: 58892 checkCounter = 44974
pm2: Pair: x: 73153, y: 73153 checkCounter = 100535
```

Although you will probably see a lot of variation from one run to the next, in general you will see that **PairManager1.doTask( )** does not allow the **PairChecker** nearly as much access as **PairManager2.doTask( )**, which has the synchronized block and thus provides more unlocked time. This is typically the reason that you want to use a synchronized block instead of synchronizing the whole method: to allow other threads more access (as long as it is safe to do so).

Of course, all synchronization depends on programmer diligence: Every piece of code that can access a shared resource must be wrapped in an appropriate synchronized block.

Thread states

A thread can be in any one of four states:

1. *New*: The thread object has been created, but it hasn't been started yet, so it cannot run.

2. *Runnable*: This means that a thread *can* be run when the time-slicing mechanism has CPU cycles available for the thread. Thus, the thread might or might not be running at any moment, but there's nothing to prevent it from being run if the scheduler can arrange it; it's not dead or blocked.

3. *Dead*: The normal way for a thread to die is by returning from its **run( )** method. Before it was deprecated in Java 2, you could also call **stop( )**, but this could easily put your program into an unstable state. There's also a **destroy( )** method (which has never been implemented, and probably never will be, so it's effectively

deprecated). You'll learn about an alternative way to code a **stop( )** equivalent later in the chapter.

4. *Blocked*: The thread could be run, but there's something that prevents it. While a thread is in the blocked state, the scheduler will simply skip over it and not give it any CPU time. Until a thread reenters the runnable state, it won't perform any operations.

Becoming blocked

When a thread is blocked, there's some reason that it cannot continue running. A thread can become blocked for the following reasons:

1. You've put the thread to sleep by calling **sleep(milliseconds),** in which case it will not be run for the specified time.

2. You've suspended the execution of the thread with **wait( )**. It will not become runnable again until the thread gets the **notify( )** or **notifyAll( )** message. We'll examine these in the next section.

3. The thread is waiting for some I/O to complete.

4. The thread is trying to call a **synchronized** method on another object, and that object's lock is not available.

In old code, you may also see **suspend( )** and **resume( )** used to block and unblock threads, but these are deprecated in Java 2 (because they are deadlock-prone), and so will not be examined in this book.

Cooperation between threads

After understanding that threads can collide with each other, and how you keep them from colliding, the next step is to learn how to make threads cooperate with each other. The key to doing this is by handshaking between threads, which is safely implemented using the **Object** methods **wait( )** and **notify( )**.

Wait and notify

It's important to understand that **sleep( )** *does not* release the lock when it is called. On the other hand, the method **wait( )** does release the lock, which means that other **synchronized** methods in the thread object can be called during a **wait( )**. When a thread enters a call to **wait( )** inside a method, that thread's execution is suspended, and the lock on that object is released.

There are two forms of **wait( )**. The first takes an argument in milliseconds that has the same meaning as in **sleep( )**: "Pause for this period of time." The difference is that in **wait( )**:

1. The object lock is released during the **wait( )**.
2. You can come out of the **wait( )** due to a **notify( )** or **notifyAll( )**, or by letting the clock run out.

The second form of **wait( )** takes no arguments; this version is more commonly used. This **wait( )** continues indefinitely until the thread receives a **notify( )** or **notifyAll( )**.

One fairly unique aspect of **wait( )**, **notify( )**, and **notifyAll( )** is that these methods are part of the base class **Object** and not part of **Thread**, as is **sleep( )**. Although this seems a bit strange at first—to have something that's exclusively for threading as part of the universal base class—it's essential because they manipulate the lock that's also part of every object. As a result, you can put a **wait( )** inside any **synchronized** method, regardless of whether that class extends **Thread** or implements **Runnable**. In fact, the *only* place you can call **wait( )**, **notify( )**, or **notifyAll( )** is within a **synchronized** method or block (**sleep( )** can be called within non-**synchronized** methods since it doesn't manipulate the lock). If you call any of these within a method that's not **synchronized,** the program will compile, but when you run it, you'll get an **IllegalMonitorStateException** with the somewhat nonintuitive message "current thread not owner." This message means that the thread calling **wait( )**, **notify( )**, or **notifyAll( )** must "own" (acquire) the lock for the object before it can call any of these methods.

You can ask another object to perform an operation that manipulates its own lock. To do this, you must first capture that object's lock. For example, if you want to **notify( )** an object **x**, you must do so inside a **synchronized** block that acquires the lock for **x**:

```
synchronized(x) {
  x.notify();
}
```

Typically, **wait( )** is used when you're waiting for some condition that is under the control of forces outside of the current method to change (typically, this condition will be changed by another thread). You don't want to idly wait while testing the condition inside your thread; this is called a "busy wait" and it's a very bad use of CPU cycles. So **wait( )** allows you to put the thread to sleep while waiting for the world to change, and only when a **notify( )** or **notifyAll( )** occurs does the thread wake up and check for changes. Thus, **wait( )** provides a way to synchronize activities between threads.

As an example, consider a restaurant that has one chef and one waitperson. The waitperson must wait for the chef to prepare a meal. When the chef has a meal ready, the chef notifies the waitperson, who then gets the meal and goes back to waiting. This is an excellent example of thread cooperation: The chef represents the *producer*, and the waitperson represents the *consumer*. Here is the story modeled in code:

```
//: c13:Restaurant.java
// The producer-consumer approach to thread cooperation.
import com.bruceeckel.simpletest.*;

class Order {
  private static int i = 0;
  private int count = i++;
  public Order() {
    if(count == 10) {
      System.out.println("Out of food, closing");
      System.exit(0);
    }
  }
  public String toString() { return "Order " + count; }
}

class WaitPerson extends Thread {
  private Restaurant restaurant;
  public WaitPerson(Restaurant r) {
    restaurant = r;
    start();
  }
  public void run() {
    while(true) {
      while(restaurant.order == null)
        synchronized(this) {
          try {
```

```
            wait();
          } catch(InterruptedException e) {
            throw new RuntimeException(e);
          }
        }
      System.out.println(
        "Waitperson got " + restaurant.order);
      restaurant.order = null;
    }
  }
}

class Chef extends Thread {
  private Restaurant restaurant;
  private WaitPerson waitPerson;
  public Chef(Restaurant r, WaitPerson w) {
    restaurant = r;
    waitPerson = w;
    start();
  }
  public void run() {
    while(true) {
      if(restaurant.order == null) {
        restaurant.order = new Order();
        System.out.print("Order up! ");
        synchronized(waitPerson) {
          waitPerson.notify();
        }
      }
      try {
        sleep(100);
      } catch(InterruptedException e) {
        throw new RuntimeException(e);
      }
    }
  }
}

public class Restaurant {
  private static Test monitor = new Test();
  Order order; // Package access
  public static void main(String[] args) {
    Restaurant restaurant = new Restaurant();
    WaitPerson waitPerson = new WaitPerson(restaurant);
```

```
    Chef chef = new Chef(restaurant, waitPerson);
    monitor.expect(new String[] {
      "Order up! Waitperson got Order 0",
      "Order up! Waitperson got Order 1",
      "Order up! Waitperson got Order 2",
      "Order up! Waitperson got Order 3",
      "Order up! Waitperson got Order 4",
      "Order up! Waitperson got Order 5",
      "Order up! Waitperson got Order 6",
      "Order up! Waitperson got Order 7",
      "Order up! Waitperson got Order 8",
      "Order up! Waitperson got Order 9",
      "Out of food, closing"
    }, Test.WAIT);
  }
} ///:~
```

Order is a simple self-counting class, but notice that it also includes a way to terminate the program; on order 10, **System.exit( )** is called.

A **WaitPerson** must know what **Restaurant** they are working for because they must fetch the order from the restaurant's "order window," **restaurant.order**. In **run( )**, the **WaitPerson** goes into **wait( )** mode, stopping that thread until it is woken up with a **notify( )** from the **Chef**. Since this is a very simple program, we know that only one thread will be waiting on the **WaitPerson**'s lock: the **WaitPerson** thread itself. For this reason it's safe to call **notify( )**. In more complex situations, multiple threads may be waiting on a particular object lock, so you don't know which thread should be awakened. The solutions is to call **notifyAll( )**, which wakes up all the threads waiting on that lock. Each thread must then decide whether the notification is relevant.

Notice that the **wait( )** is wrapped in a **while( )** statement that is testing for the same thing that is being waited for. This seems a bit strange at first—if you're waiting for an order, once you wake up the order must be available, right? The problem is that in a multithreading application, some other thread might swoop in and grab the order while the **WaitPerson** is waking up. The only safe approach is to *always* use the following idiom for a **wait( )**:

```
while(conditionIsNotMet)
  wait( );
```

This guarantees that the condition will be met before you get out of the wait loop, and if you have either been notified of something that doesn't concern the condition (as can happen with **notifyAll( )**), or the condition changes before you get fully out of the wait loop, you are guaranteed to go back into waiting.

A **Chef** object must know what restaurant he or she is working for (so the **Order**s can be placed in **restaurant.order**) and the **WaitPerson** who is picking up the meals, so that **WaitPerson** can be notified when an order is ready. In this simplified example, the **Chef** is generating the **Order** objects, then notifying the **WaitPerson** that an order is ready.

Observe that the call to **notify( )** must first capture the lock on **waitPerson**. The call to **wait( )** in **WaitPerson.run( )** automatically releases the lock, so this is possible. Because the lock must be owned in order to call **notify( )**, it's guaranteed that two threads trying to call **notify( )** on one object won't step on each other's toes.

The preceding example has only a single spot for one thread to store an object so that another thread can later use that object. However, in a typical producer-consumer implementation, you use a first-in, first-out queue in order to store the objects being produced and consumed. See the exercises at the end of the chapter to learn more about this.

Using Pipes for I/O between threads

It's often useful for threads to communicate with each other by using I/O. Threading libraries may provide support for inter-thread I/O in the form of *pipes*. These exist in the Java I/O library as the classes **PipedWriter** (which allows a thread to write into a pipe) and **PipedReader** (which allows a different thread to read from the same pipe). This can be thought of as a variation of the producer-consumer problem, where the pipe is the canned solution.

Here's a simple example in which two threads use a pipe to communicate:

```
//: c13:PipedIO.java
// Using pipes for inter-thread I/O
import java.io.*;
import java.util.*;

class Sender extends Thread {
```

```java
  private Random rand = new Random();
  private PipedWriter out = new PipedWriter();
  public PipedWriter getPipedWriter() { return out; }
  public void run() {
    while(true) {
      for(char c = 'A'; c <= 'z'; c++) {
        try {
          out.write(c);
          sleep(rand.nextInt(500));
        } catch(Exception e) {
          throw new RuntimeException(e);
        }
      }
    }
  }
}

class Receiver extends Thread {
  private PipedReader in;
  public Receiver(Sender sender) throws IOException {
    in = new PipedReader(sender.getPipedWriter());
  }
  public void run() {
    try {
      while(true) {
        // Blocks until characters are there:
        System.out.println("Read: " + (char)in.read());
      }
    } catch(IOException e) {
      throw new RuntimeException(e);
    }
  }
}

public class PipedIO {
  public static void main(String[] args) throws Exception {
    Sender sender = new Sender();
    Receiver receiver = new Receiver(sender);
    sender.start();
    receiver.start();
    new Timeout(4000, "Terminated");
  }
} ///:~
```

Sender and **Receiver** represent threads that are performing some tasks and need to communicate with each other. **Sender** creates a **PipedWriter**, which is a standalone object, but inside **Receiver** the creation of **PipedReader** must be associated with a **PipedWriter** in the constructor. The **Sender** puts data into the **Writer** and sleeps for a random amount of time. However, **Receiver** has no **sleep( )** or **wait( )**. But when it does a **read( )**, it automatically blocks when there is no more data. You get the effect of a producer-consumer, but no **wait( )** loop is necessary.

Notice that the **sender** and **receiver** are started in **main( )**, *after* the objects are completely constructed. If you don't start completely constructed objects, the pipe can produce inconsistent behavior on different platforms.

More sophisticated cooperation

Only the most basic cooperation approach (producer-consumer, usually implemented with **wait( )** and **notify( )/notifyAll( )**) has been introduced in this section. This will solve most kinds of thread cooperation problems, but there are numerous more sophisticated approaches that are described in more advanced texts (in particular, *Lea*, noted at the end of this chapter).

Deadlock

Because threads can become blocked *and* because objects can have **synchronized** methods that prevent threads from accessing that object until the synchronization lock is released, it's possible for one thread to get stuck waiting for another thread, which in turn waits for another thread, etc., until the chain leads back to a thread waiting on the first one. You get a continuous loop of threads waiting on each other, and no one can move. This is called *deadlock*.

If you try running a program and it deadlocks right away, you immediately know you have a problem and you can track it down. The real problem is when your program seems to be working fine but has the hidden potential to deadlock. In this case you may get no indication that deadlocking is a possibility, so it will be latent in your program until it unexpectedly happens to a customer (and you probably won't be able to easily reproduce it). Thus, preventing deadlock by careful program design is a critical part of developing concurrent programs.

Let's look at the classic demonstration of deadlock, invented by Dijkstra: the *dining philosophers* problem. The basic description specifies five philosophers (but the example shown here will allow any number). These philosophers spend part of their time thinking and part of their time eating. While they are thinking, they don't need any shared resources, but when they are eating, they sit at a table with a limited number of utensils. In the original problem description, the utensils are forks, and two forks are required to get spaghetti from a bowl in the middle of the table, but it seems to make more sense to say that the utensils are chopsticks; clearly, each philosopher will require two chopsticks in order to eat.

A difficulty is introduced into the problem: As philosophers, they have very little money, so they can only afford five chopsticks. These are spaced around the table between them. When a philosopher wants to eat, he or she must get the chopstick to the left and the one to the right. If the philosopher on either side is using the desired chopstick, then our philosopher must wait.

Note that the reason this problem is interesting is because it demonstrates that a program can appear to run correctly but actually be deadlock prone. To show this, the command-line arguments allow you to adjust the number of philosophers and a factor to affect the amount of time each philosopher spends thinking. If you have lots of philosophers and/or they spend a lot of time thinking, you may never see the deadlock even though it remains a possibility. The default command-line arguments tend to make it deadlock fairly quickly:

```
//: c13:DiningPhilosophers.java
// Demonstrates how deadlock can be hidden in a program.
// {Args: 5 0 deadlock 4}
import java.util.*;

class Chopstick {
  private static int counter = 0;
  private int number = counter++;
  public String toString() {
    return "Chopstick " + number;
  }
}

class Philosopher extends Thread {
  private static Random rand = new Random();
  private static int counter = 0;
```

```java
  private int number = counter++;
  private Chopstick leftChopstick;
  private Chopstick rightChopstick;
  static int ponder = 0; // Package access
  public Philosopher(Chopstick left, Chopstick right) {
    leftChopstick = left;
    rightChopstick = right;
    start();
  }
  public void think() {
    System.out.println(this + " thinking");
    if(ponder > 0)
      try {
        sleep(rand.nextInt(ponder));
      } catch(InterruptedException e) {
        throw new RuntimeException(e);
      }
  }
  public void eat() {
    synchronized(leftChopstick) {
      System.out.println(this + " has "
        + this.leftChopstick + " Waiting for "
        + this.rightChopstick);
      synchronized(rightChopstick) {
        System.out.println(this + " eating");
      }
    }
  }
  public String toString() {
    return "Philosopher " + number;
  }
  public void run() {
    while(true) {
      think();
      eat();
    }
  }
}

public class DiningPhilosophers {
  public static void main(String[] args) {
    if(args.length < 3) {
      System.err.println("usage:\n" +
        "java DiningPhilosophers numberOfPhilosophers " +
```

```
        "ponderFactor deadlock timeout\n" +
        "A nonzero ponderFactor will generate a random " +
        "sleep time during think().\n" +
        "If deadlock is not the string " +
        "'deadlock', the program will not deadlock.\n" +
        "A nonzero timeout will stop the program after " +
        "that number of seconds.");
      System.exit(1);
    }
    Philosopher[] philosopher =
      new Philosopher[Integer.parseInt(args[0])];
    Philosopher.ponder = Integer.parseInt(args[1]);
    Chopstick
      left = new Chopstick(),
      right = new Chopstick(),
      first = left;
    int i = 0;
    while(i < philosopher.length - 1) {
      philosopher[i++] =
        new Philosopher(left, right);
      left = right;
      right = new Chopstick();
    }
    if(args[2].equals("deadlock"))
      philosopher[i] = new Philosopher(left, first);
    else // Swapping values prevents deadlock:
      philosopher[i] = new Philosopher(first, left);
    // Optionally break out of program:
    if(args.length >= 4) {
      int delay = Integer.parseInt(args[3]);
      if(delay != 0)
        new Timeout(delay * 1000, "Timed out");
    }
  }
} ///:~
```

Both **Chopstick** and **Philosopher** use an auto-incremented **static counter** to give each element an identification number. Each **Philosopher** is given a reference to a left and right **Chopstick** object; these are the utensils that must be picked up before that **Philosopher** can eat.

The **static** field **ponder** indicates whether the philosophers will spend any time thinking. If the value is nonzero, then it will be used to randomly generate a sleep time inside **think( )**. This way, you can show that if your threads (philosophers) are spending more time on other tasks (thinking) then they have a much lower probability of requiring the shared resources (chopsticks) and thus you can convince yourself that the program is deadlock free, even though it isn't.

Inside **eat( )**, a **Philosopher** acquires the left chopstick by synchronizing on it. If the chopstick is unavailable, then the philosopher blocks while waiting. When the left chopstick is acquired, the right one is acquired the same way. After eating, the right chopstick is released, then the left.

In **run( )**, each **Philosopher** just thinks and eats continuously.

The **main( )** method requires at least three arguments and prints a usage message if these are not present. The third argument can be the string "deadlock," in which case the deadlocking version of the program is used. Any other string will cause the non-deadlocking version to be used. The last (optional) argument is a timeout factor, which will abort the program after that number of seconds (whether it's deadlocked or not). The timeout is necessary for the program to be run automatically as part of the book code testing process.

After the array of **Philosopher** is created and the ponder value is set, two **Chopstick** objects are created, and the first one is also stored in the **first** variable for use later. Every reference in the array except the last one is initialized by creating a new **Philosopher** object and handing it the **left** and **right** chopsticks. After each initialization, the left chopstick is moved to the right and the right is given a new **Chopstick** object to be used for the next **Philosopher**.

In the deadlocking version, the last **Philosopher** is given the left chopstick and the **first** chopstick that was stored earlier. That's because the last **Philosopher** is sitting right next to the very first one, and they both share that first chopstick. With this arrangement, it's possible at some point for all the philosophers to be trying to eat and waiting on the philosopher next to them to put down their chopstick, and the program will deadlock.

Try experimenting with different command-line values to see how the program behaves, and in particular to see all the ways that the program can appear to be executing without deadlock.

To repair the problem, you must understand that deadlock can occur if four conditions are simultaneously met:

1. Mutual exclusion: At least one resource used by the threads must not be shareable. In this case, a chopstick can be used by only one philosopher at a time.

2. At least one process must be holding a resource and waiting to acquire a resource currently held by another process. That is, for deadlock to occur, a philosopher must be holding one chopstick and waiting for the other one.

3. A resource cannot be preemptively taken away from a process. All processes must only release resources as a normal event. Our philosophers are polite and they don't grab chopsticks from other philosophers.

4. A circular wait must happen, whereby a process waits on a resource held by another process, which in turn is waiting on a resource held by another process, and so on, until one of the processes is waiting on a resource held by the first process, thus gridlocking everything. In this example, the circular wait happens because each philosopher tries to get the left chopstick first and then the right. In the preceding example, the deadlock is broken by swapping the initialization order in the constructor for the last philosopher, causing that last philosopher to actually get the right chopstick first, then the left.

Because all of these conditions must be met in order to cause deadlock, you only need to stop one of them from occurring in order to prevent deadlock. In this program, the easiest way to prevent deadlock is to break condition four. This condition happens because each philosopher is trying to pick up their chopsticks in a particular sequence: first left, then right. Because of that, it's possible to get into a situation where each of them is holding their left chopstick and waiting to get the right one, causing the circular wait condition. However, if the last philosopher is initialized to try to get the right chopstick first and then the left, then that philosopher will never prevent the philosopher on the immediate left from picking up his or her right chopstick, so the circular wait is prevented. This is only one solution to the problem, but you could also solve it by preventing one of the other conditions (see more advanced threading books for more details).

There is no Java language support to help prevent deadlock; it's up to you to avoid it by careful design. These are not comforting words to the person who's trying to debug a deadlocking program.

The proper way to stop

One change that was introduced in Java 2 to reduce the possibility of deadlock is the deprecation of the **Thread** class's **stop( )**, **suspend( )**, and **resume( )** methods.

The reason that the **stop( )** method is deprecated is because it doesn't release the locks that the thread has acquired, and if the objects are in an inconsistent state ("damaged"), other threads can view and modify them in that state. The resulting problems can be subtle and difficult to detect. Instead of using **stop( )**, you should use a flag to tell the thread when to terminate itself by exiting its **run( )** method. Here's a simple example:

```
//: c13:Stopping.java
// The safe way to stop a thread.
import java.util.*;

class CanStop extends Thread {
  // Must be volatile:
  private volatile boolean stop = false;
  private int counter = 0;
  public void run() {
    while(!stop && counter < 10000) {
      System.out.println(counter++);
    }
    if(stop)
      System.out.println("Detected stop");
  }
  public void requestStop() { stop = true; }
}

public class Stopping {
  public static void main(String[] args) {
    final CanStop stoppable = new CanStop();
    stoppable.start();
    new Timer(true).schedule(new TimerTask() {
      public void run() {
        System.out.println("Requesting stop");
        stoppable.requestStop();
      }
    }, 500); // run() after 500 milliseconds
  }
} ///:~
```

The flag **stop** must be **volatile** so that the **run( )** method is sure to see it (otherwise the value may be cached locally). The "job" of this thread is to print out 10,000 numbers, so it is finished whenever **counter >= 10000** *or* someone requests a stop. Note that **requestStop( )** is not **synchronized** because **stop** is both **boolean** (changing it to **true** is an atomic operation) and **volatile**.

In **main( )**, a **CanStop** object is started, then a **Timer** is set up to call **requestStop( )** after one half second. The constructor for **Timer** is passed the argument **true** to make it a daemon thread so that it doesn't prevent the program from terminating.

Interrupting a blocked thread

There are times when a thread blocks—such as when it is waiting for input—and it cannot poll a flag as it does in the previous example. In these cases, you can use the **Thread.interrupt( )** method to break out of the blocked code:

```
//: c13:Interrupt.java
// Using interrupt() to break out of a blocked thread.
import java.util.*;

class Blocked extends Thread {
  public Blocked() {
    System.out.println("Starting Blocked");
    start();
  }
  public void run() {
    try {
      synchronized(this) {
        wait(); // Blocks
      }
    } catch(InterruptedException e) {
      System.out.println("Interrupted");
    }
    System.out.println("Exiting run()");
  }
}

public class Interrupt {
  static Blocked blocked = new Blocked();
  public static void main(String[] args) {
    new Timer(true).schedule(new TimerTask() {
```

```
      public void run() {
        System.out.println("Preparing to interrupt");
        blocked.interrupt();
        blocked = null; // to release it
      }
    }, 2000); // run() after 2000 milliseconds
  }
} ///:~
```

The **wait( )** inside **Blocked.run( )** produces the blocked thread. When the **Timer** runs out, the object's **interrupt( )** method is called. Then the **blocked** reference is set to **null** so the garbage collector will clean it up (not necessary here, but important in a long-running program).

Thread groups

A *thread group* holds a collection of threads. The value of thread groups can be summed up by a quote from Joshua Bloch,[5] the software architect at Sun who fixed and greatly improved the Java collections library in JDK 1.2:

> *"Thread groups are best viewed as an unsuccessful experiment, and you may simply ignore their existence."*

If you've spent time and energy trying to figure out the value of thread groups (as I have), you may wonder why there was not some more official announcement from Sun on the topic, sooner than this (the same question could be asked about any number of other changes that have happened to Java over the years). The Nobel Laureate economist Joseph Stiglitz has a philosophy of life that would seem to apply here.[6] It's called *The Theory of Escalating Commitment*:

> *"The cost of continuing mistakes is borne by others, while the cost of admitting mistakes is borne by yourself."*

There is one tiny remaining use for thread groups. If a thread in the group throws an uncaught exception, **ThreadGroup.uncaughtException( )** is

---

5 *Effective Java*, by Joshua Bloch, Addison-Wesley 2001, page 211.

6 And in a number of other places throughout the experience of Java. Well, why stop there?—I've consulted on more than a few projects where this has applied.

invoked, which prints a stack trace to the standard error stream. If you want to modify this behavior, you must override this method.

Summary

It is vital to learn when to use concurrency and when to avoid it. The main reasons to use it are: to manage a number of tasks whose intermingling will make more efficient use of the computer (including the ability to transparently distribute the tasks across multiple CPUs), allow better code organization, or be more convenient for the user. The classic example of resource balancing is to use the CPU during I/O waits. The classic example of user convenience is to monitor a "stop" button during long downloads.

An additional advantage to threads is that they provide "light" execution context switches (on the order of 100 instructions) rather than "heavy" process context switches (thousands of instructions). Since all threads in a given process share the same memory space, a light context switch changes only program execution and local variables. A process change –the heavy context switch—must exchange the full memory space.

The main drawbacks to multithreading are:

1. Slowdown occurs while waiting for shared resources.
2. Additional CPU overhead is required to manage threads.
3. Unrewarded complexity arises from poor design decisions.
4. Opportunities are created for pathologies such as starving, racing, deadlock, and livelock.
5. Inconsistenciesoccur across platforms. For instance, while developing some of the examples for this book, I discovered race conditions that quickly appeared on some computers but that wouldn't appear on others. If you developed a program on the latter, you might get badly surprised when you distribute it.

One of the biggest difficulties with threads occurs because more than one thread might be sharing a resource—such as the memory in an object—and you must make sure that multiple threads don't try to read and change that resource at the same time. This requires judicious use of the **synchronized** keyword, which is an essential tool, but must be understood thoroughly because it can quietly introduce deadlock situations.

In addition, there's a certain art to the application of threads. Java is designed to allow you to create as many objects as you need to solve your problem—at least in theory. (Creating millions of objects for an engineering finite-element analysis, for example, might not be practical in Java.) However, it seems that there is an upper bound to the number of threads you'll want to create, because at some number, threads seem to become balky. This critical point can be hard to detect, and will often depend on the OS and JVM; it could be less than a hundred or in the thousands. As you often create only a handful of threads to solve a problem, this is typically not much of a limit; yet in a more general design it becomes a constraint.

A significant nonintuitive issue in threading is that, because of thread scheduling, you can typically make your applications run *faster* by inserting calls to **yield( )** or even **sleep( )** inside **run( )**'s main loop. This definitely makes it feel like an art, in particular when the longer delays seem to speed up performance. The reason this happens is that shorter delays can cause the end-of-**sleep( )** scheduler interrupt to happen before the running thread is ready to go to sleep, forcing the scheduler to stop it and restart it later so it can finish what it was doing and then go to sleep. The extra context switches can end up slowing things down, and the use of **yield( )** or **sleep( )** may prevent the extra switches. It takes extra thought to realize how messy things can get.

For more advanced discussions of threading, see *Concurrent Programming in Java*, 2nd Edition, by Doug Lea, Addison-Wesley, 2000.

Exercises

Solutions to selected exercises can be found in the electronic document *The Thinking in Java Annotated Solution Guide*, available for a small fee from *www.BruceEckel.com*.

1. Inherit a class from **Thread** and override the **run( )** method. Inside **run( )**, print a message, and then call **sleep( )**. Repeat this three times, then return from **run( )**. Put a start-up message in the constructor and override **finalize( )** to print a shut-down message. Make a separate thread class that calls **System.gc( )** and **System.runFinalization( )** inside **run( )**, printing a message as it does so. Make several thread objects of both types and run them to see what happens.

2. Experiment with different sleep times in **Daemons.java** to see what happens.

3. In Chapter 8, locate the **GreenhouseController.java** example, which consists of four files. In **Event.java**, the class **Event** is based on watching the time. Change **Event** so that it is a **Thread**, and change the rest of the design so that it works with this new **Thread**-based **Event**.

4. Modify the previous exercise so that the **java.util.Timer** class is used to run the system.

5. Modify **SimpleThread.java** so that all the threads are daemon threads and verify that the program ends as soon as **main( )** is able to exit.

6. Demonstrate that **java.util.Timer** scales to large numbers by creating a program that generates many **Timer** objects that perform some simple task when the timeout completes (if you want to get fancy, you can jump forward to the "Windows and Applets" chapter and use the **Timer** objects to draw pixels on the screen, but printing to the console is sufficient).

7. Demonstrate that a **synchronized** method in a class can call a second **synchronized** method in the same class, which can then call a third **synchronized** method in the same class. Create a separate **Thread** object that invokes the first **synchronized** method.

8. Create two **Thread** subclasses, one with a **run( )** that starts up and then calls **wait( )**. The other class's **run( )** should capture the reference of the first **Thread** object. Its **run( )** should call **notifyAll( )** for the first thread after some number of seconds have passed so that first thread can print a message.

9. Create an example of a "busy wait." One thread sleeps for awhile and then sets a flag to **true**. The second thread watches that flag inside a while loop (this is the "busy wait") and when the flag becomes **true**, sets it back to false and reports the change to the console. Note how much wasted time the program spends inside the "busy wait" and create a second version of the program that uses **wait( )** instead of the "busy wait."

10. Modify **Restaurant.java** to use **notifyAll( )** and observe any difference in behavior.

11. Modify **Restaurant.java** so that there are multiple **WaitPerson**s, and indicate which one gets each **Order**. Note that you must use **notifyAll( )** instead of **notify( )** in this case.

12. Modify **Restaurant.java** so that multiple **WaitPerson**s generate order requests to multiple **Chef**s, who produce orders and notify the **WaitPerson** who generated the request. You'll need to use queues for both incoming order requests and outgoing orders.

13. Modify the previous exercise to add **Customer** objects that are also threads. The **Customer**s will place order requests with **WaitPerson**s, who give the requests to the **Chef**s, who fulfill the orders and notify the appropriate **WaitPerson**, who gives it to the appropriate **Customer**.

14. Modify **PipedIO.java** so that **Sender** reads and sends lines from a text file.

15. Change **DiningPhilosophers.java** so that the philosophers just pick the next available chopstick (when a philosopher is done with their chopsticks, they drop them into a bin. When a philosopher wants to eat, they take the next two available chopsticks from the bin). Does this eliminate the possibility of deadlock? Can you re-introduce deadlock by simply reducing the number of available chopsticks?

16. Inherit a class from **java.util.Timer** and implement the **requestStop( )** method as in **Stopping.java**.

17. Modify **SimpleThread.java** so that all threads receive an **interrupt( )** before they are completed.

18. Solve a single producer, single consumer problem using **wait( )** and **notify( )**. The producer must not overflow the receiver's buffer, which can happen if the producer is faster than the consumer. If the consumer is faster than the producer, then it must not read the same data more than once. Do not assume anything about the relative speeds of the producer or consumer.

14: Creating Windows & Applets

A fundamental design guideline is "make simple things easy, and difficult things possible."[1]

The original design goal of the graphical user interface (GUI) library in Java 1.0 was to allow the programmer to build a GUI that looks good on all platforms. That goal was not achieved. Instead, the Java 1.0 *Abstract Window Toolkit* (AWT) produced a GUI that looked equally mediocre on all systems. In addition, it was restrictive; you could use only four fonts and you couldn't access any of the more sophisticated GUI elements that exist in your operating system. The Java 1.0 AWT programming model is also awkward and non-object-oriented. A student in one of my seminars (who had been at Sun during the creation of Java) explained why: The original AWT had been conceptualized, designed, and implemented in a month. Certainly a marvel of productivity, and also an object lesson in why design is important.

The situation improved with the Java 1.1 AWT event model, which takes a much clearer, object-oriented approach, along with the addition of JavaBeans, a component programming model that is oriented toward the easy creation of visual programming environments. Java 2 (JDK 1.2) finished the transformation away from the old Java 1.0 AWT by essentially replacing everything with the *Java Foundation Classes* (JFC), the GUI portion of which is called "Swing." These are a rich set of easy-to-use, easy-to-understand JavaBeans that can be dragged and dropped (as well as hand programmed) to create a GUI that you can (finally) be satisfied with. The "revision 3" rule of

---

[1] A variation on this is called "the principle of least astonishment," which essentially says: "don't surprise the user."

the software industry (a product isn't good until revision 3) seems to hold true with programming languages as well.

This chapter does not cover anything but the modern Java 2 Swing library and makes the reasonable assumption that Swing is the final destination GUI library for Java.[2] If for some reason you need to use the original "old" AWT (because you're supporting old code or you have browser limitations), you can find that introduction in the first edition of this book, downloadable at *www.BruceEckel.com* (also included on the CD ROM bound with this book) Note that some AWT components remain in Java, and in some situations you must use them.

Early in this chapter, you'll see how things are different when you want to create an applet versus a regular application using Swing, and how to create programs that are both applets and applications so they can be run either inside a browser or from the command line. Almost all the GUI examples in this book will be executable as both applets and applications.

Please be aware that this is not a comprehensive glossary of either all the Swing components or all the methods for the described classes. What you see here is intended to be simple. The Swing library is vast, and the goal of this chapter is only to get you started with the essentials and comfortable with the concepts. If you need to do more, then Swing can probably give you what you want if you're willing to do the research.

I assume here that you have downloaded and installed the JDK library documents in HTML format from *java.sun.com* and will browse the **javax.swing** classes in that documentation to see the full details and methods of the Swing library. Because of the simplicity of the Swing design, this will often be enough information to solve your problem. There are numerous (rather thick) books dedicated solely to Swing, and you'll want to go to those if you need more depth, or if you want to modify the default Swing behavior.

As you learn about Swing, you'll discover:

[2] Note that IBM created a new open-source GUI library for their Eclipse editor (*www.Eclipse.org*), which you may want to consider as an alternative to Swing.

1. Swing is a much better programming model than you've probably seen in other languages and development environments. JavaBeans (which will be introduced toward the end of this chapter) is the framework for that library.

2. "GUI builders" (visual programming environments) are a *de rigueur* aspect of a complete Java development environment. JavaBeans and Swing allow the GUI builder to write code for you as you place components onto forms using graphical tools. This not only rapidly speeds development during GUI building, but it allows for greater experimentation and thus the ability to try out more designs and presumably come up with a better one.

3. The simplicity and well-designed nature of Swing means that even if you do use a GUI builder rather than coding by hand, the resulting code will still be comprehensible; this solves a big problem with GUI builders from the past, which could easily generate unreadable code.

Swing contains all the components that you expect to see in a modern UI: everything from buttons that contain pictures to trees and tables. It's a big library, but it's designed to have appropriate complexity for the task at hand; if something is simple, you don't have to write much code, but as you try to do more complex things, your code becomes proportionally more complex. This means an easy entry point, but you've got the power if you need it.

Much of what you'll like about Swing could be called "orthogonality of use." That is, once you pick up the general ideas about the library, you can apply them everywhere. Primarily because of the standard naming conventions, much of the time that I was writing these examples I could guess at the method names and get it right the first time without looking anything up. This is certainly the hallmark of a good library design. In addition, you can generally plug components into other components and things will work correctly.

For speed, all the components are "lightweight," and Swing is written entirely in Java for portability.

Keyboard navigation is automatic; you can run a Swing application without using the mouse, and this doesn't require any extra programming. Scrolling support is effortless; you simply wrap your component in a **JScrollPane** as you add it to your form. Features such as tool tips typically require a single line of code to use.

Swing also supports a rather radical feature called "pluggable look and feel," which means that the appearance of the UI can be dynamically changed to suit the expectations of users working under different platforms and operating systems. It's even possible (albeit difficult) to invent your own look and feel.

The basic applet

Java has the ability to create *applets*, which are little programs that run inside a Web browser. Because they must be safe, applets are limited in what they can accomplish. However, applets are a powerful tool that support client-side programming, a major issue for the Web.

Applet restrictions

Programming within an applet is so restrictive that it's often referred to as being "inside the sandbox," since you always have someone—that is, the Java run-time security system—watching over you.

However, you can also step outside the sandbox and write regular applications rather than applets, in which case you can access the other features of your OS. We've been writing regular applications all along in this book, but they've been *console applications* without any graphical components. Swing can be used to build GUI interfaces for regular applications.

You can generally answer the question of what an applet is able to do by looking at what it is *supposed* to do: extend the functionality of a Web page in a browser. Since, as a Net surfer, you never really know if a Web page is from a friendly place or not, you want any code that it runs to be safe. So the biggest restrictions you'll notice are probably:

1. *An applet can't touch the local disk.* This means writing *or* reading, since you wouldn't want an applet to read and transmit private information over the Internet without your permission. Writing is prevented, of course, since that would be an open invitation to a virus. Java offers *digital signing* for applets. Many applet restrictions are relaxed when you choose to allow *signed applets* (those signed by a

trusted source) to have access to your machine. You'll see an example later in this chapter, as well as an example of *Java Web Start*, a way to safely send applications to a client over the Internet.

2. *Applets can take longer to display,* since you must download the whole thing every time, including a separate server hit for each different class. Your browser can cache the applet, but there are no guarantees. Because of this, you should always package your applets in a JAR (Java ARchive) file that combines all the applet components (including other **.class** files as well as images and sounds) together into a single compressed file that can be downloaded in a single server transaction. "Digital signing" is available for each individual entry in the JAR file.

Applet advantages

If you can live within the restrictions, applets have definite advantages, especially when building client/server or other networked applications:

1. *There is no installation issue.* An applet has true platform independence (including the ability to easily play audio files, etc.), so you don't need to make any changes in your code for different platforms, nor does anyone have to perform any installation "tweaking." In fact, installation is automatic every time the user loads a Web page that contains applets, so updates happen silently and automatically. In traditional client/server systems, building and installing a new version of the client software is often a nightmare.

2. *You don't have to worry about bad code causing damage to someone's system,* because of the security built into the core Java language and applet structure. This, along with the previous point, makes Java useful for so-called *intranet* client/server applications that live only within a company or restricted arena of operation where the user environment (Web browser and add-ins) can be specified and/or controlled.

Because applets are automatically integrated with HTML, you have a built-in platform-independent documentation system to support the applet. It's an interesting twist, since we're used to having the documentation part of the program rather than vice versa.

Application frameworks

Libraries are often grouped according to their functionality. Some libraries, for example, are used as is, off the shelf. The standard Java library **String** and **ArrayList** classes are examples of these. Other libraries are designed specifically as building blocks to create other classes. A certain category of library is the *application framework*, whose goal is to help you build applications by providing a class or set of classes that produces the basic behavior that you need in every application of a particular type. Then, to customize the behavior to your own needs, you inherit from the application class and override the methods of interest. The application framework's default control mechanism will call your overridden methods at the appropriate time. An application framework is a good example of "separating the things that change from the things that stay the same," since it attempts to localize all the unique parts of a program in the overridden methods.[3]

Applets are built using an application framework. You inherit from class **JApplet** and override the appropriate methods. There are a few methods that control the creation and execution of an applet on a Web page:

Method	Operation
init( )	Automatically called to perform first-time initialization of the applet, including component layout. You'll always override this method.
start( )	Called every time the applet moves into sight on the Web browser to allow the applet to start up its normal operations (especially those that are shut off by **stop( )**). Also called after **init( )**.
stop( )	Called every time the applet moves out of sight on the Web browser to allow the applet to shut off expensive operations. Also called right before **destroy( )**.
destroy( )	Called when the applet is being unloaded from the page to perform final release of resources when the applet is no longer used

With this information you are ready to create a simple applet:

---

3 Application frameworks are an example of the design pattern called the *Template Method*.

```java
//: c14:Applet1.java
// Very simple applet.
import javax.swing.*;
import java.awt.*;

public class Applet1 extends JApplet {
  public void init() {
    getContentPane().add(new JLabel("Applet!"));
  }
} ///:~
```

Note that applets are not required to have a **main( )**. That's all wired into the application framework; you put any startup code in **init( )**.

In this program, the only activity is putting a text label on the applet, via the **JLabel** class (the old AWT appropriated the name **Label** as well as other names of components, so you will often see a leading "**J**" used with Swing components). The constructor for this class takes a **String** and uses it to create the label. In the preceding program this label is placed on the form.

The **init( )** method is responsible for putting all the components on the form using the **add( )** method. You might think that you ought to be able to simply call **add( )** by itself, and in fact that's the way it used to be in the old AWT. However, Swing requires that you add all components to the "content pane" of a form, so you must call **getContentPane( )** as part of the **add( )** process.

Running applets inside a Web browser

To run this program you must place it inside a Web page and view that page inside your Java-enabled Web browser. To place an applet inside a Web page, you put a special tag inside the HTML source for that Web page[4] to tell the page how to load and run the applet.

This process used to be very simple, when Java itself was simple and everyone was on the same bandwagon and incorporated the same Java support inside their Web browsers. Then you might have been able to get away with a very simple bit of HTML inside your Web page, like this:

---

[4] It is assumed that the reader is familiar with the basics of HTML. It's not too hard to figure out, and there are lots of books and resources.

```
<applet code=Applet1 width=100 height=50>
</applet>
```

Then along came the browser and language wars, and we (programmers and end users alike) lost. After awhile, Sun realized that we could no longer expect browsers to support the correct flavor of Java, and the only solution was to provide some kind of add-on that would conform to a browser's extension mechanism. By using the extension mechanism (which a browser vendor cannot disable—in an attempt to gain competitive advantage—without breaking all the third-party extensions), Sun guarantees that Java cannot be shut out of the Web browser by an antagonistic vendor.

With Internet Explorer, the extension mechanism is the ActiveX control, and with Netscape, it is the plug-in. In your HTML code, you must provide tags to support both, but you can automatically generate the necessary tags with the **HTMLconverter** tool that comes with the JDK download. Here's what the simplest resulting HTML page looks like for **Applet1** after running **HTMLconverter** on the preceding applet tag:

```
<!--"CONVERTED_APPLET"-->
<!-- HTML CONVERTER -->
<OBJECT
    classid = "clsid:CAFEEFAC-0014-0001-0000-ABCDEFFEDCBA"
    codebase =
"http://java.sun.com/products/plugin/autodl/jinstall-1_4_1-
windows-i586.cab#Version=1,4,1,0"
    WIDTH = 100 HEIGHT = 50 >
    <PARAM NAME = CODE VALUE = Applet1 >
    <PARAM NAME = "type" VALUE = "application/x-java-
applet;jpi-version=1.4.1">
    <PARAM NAME = "scriptable" VALUE = "false">
    <COMMENT>
      <EMBED
          type = "application/x-java-applet;jpi-
version=1.4.1"
          CODE = Applet1
          WIDTH = 100
          HEIGHT = 50
          scriptable = false
          pluginspage =
"http://java.sun.com/products/plugin/index.html#download">
          <NOEMBED>
          </NOEMBED>
      </EMBED>
```

```
    </COMMENT>
</OBJECT>
<!--
<APPLET CODE = Applet1 WIDTH = 100 HEIGHT = 50>
</APPLET>
-->
<!--"END_CONVERTED_APPLET"-->
```

Some of these lines were too long and had to be wrapped to fit on the page. The code in this book's source code (downloadable from *www.BruceEckel.com*) will work without having to worry about correcting line wraps.

The **code** value gives the name of the **.class** file where the applet resides. The **width** and **height** specify the initial size of the applet (in pixels, as before). There are other items you can place within the applet tag: a place to find other **.class** files on the Internet (**codebase**), alignment information (**align**), a special identifier that makes it possible for applets to communicate with each other (**name**), and applet parameters to provide information that the applet can retrieve. Parameters are in the form:

```
<param name="identifier" value = "information">
```

and there can be as many as you want.

The source code package for this book (freely downloadable at *www.BruceEckel.com*) provides an HTML page for each of the applets in this book, and thus many examples of the applet tag, all driven from the **index.html** file corresponding to this chapter's source code. You can find a full and current description of the details of placing applets in Web pages at *java.sun.com*.

Using *Appletviewer*

Sun's JDK contains a tool called the *Appletviewer* that picks the **<applet>** tags out of the HTML file and runs the applets without displaying the surrounding HTML text. Because the Appletviewer ignores everything but APPLET tags, you can put those tags in the Java source file as comments:

```
// <applet code=MyApplet width=200 height=100></applet>
```

This way, you can run "**appletviewer MyApplet.java**" and you don't need to create tiny HTML files to run tests. For example, you can add the commented HTML tags to **Applet1.java**:

```
//: c14:Applet1b.java
// Embedding the applet tag for Appletviewer.
// <applet code=Applet1b width=100 height=50></applet>
import javax.swing.*;
import java.awt.*;

public class Applet1b extends JApplet {
  public void init() {
    getContentPane().add(new JLabel("Applet!"));
  }
} ///:~
```

Now you can invoke the applet with the command

```
appletviewer Applet1b.java
```

In this book, this form will be used for easy testing of applets. Shortly, you'll see another coding approach that will allow you to execute applets from the command line without the Appletviewer.

Testing applets

You can perform a simple test without any network connection by starting up your Web browser and opening the HTML file containing the applet tag. As the HTML file is loaded, the browser will discover the applet tag and go hunt for the **.class** file specified by the **code** value. Of course, it looks at the CLASSPATH to find out where to hunt, and if your **.class** file isn't in the CLASSPATH, then it will give an error message on the status line of the browser to the effect that it couldn't find that **.class** file.

When you want to try this out on your Web site, things are a little more complicated. First of all, you must *have* a Web site, which for most people means a third-party Internet Service Provider (ISP) at a remote location. Since the applet is just a file or set of files, the ISP does not have to provide any special support for Java. You must also have a way to move the HTML files and the **.class** files from your site to the correct directory on the ISP machine. This is typically done with a File Transfer Protocol (FTP) program, of which there are many different types available for free or as shareware. So it would seem that all you need to do is move the files to the ISP machine with FTP, then connect to the site and HTML file using your browser; if the applet comes up and works, then everything checks out, right?

Here's where you can get fooled. If the browser on the client machine cannot locate the **.class** file on the server, it will hunt through the CLASSPATH on your *local* machine. Thus, the applet might not be loading properly from the server, but to you it looks fine during your testing process because the browser finds it on your machine. When someone else connects, however, his or her browser can't find it. So when you're testing, make sure you erase the relevant **.class** files (or **.jar** file) on your local machine to verify that they exist in the proper location on the server.

One of the most insidious places where this happened to me is when I innocently placed an applet inside a **package**. After uploading the HTML file and applet, it turned out that the server path to the applet was confused because of the package name. However, my browser found it in the local CLASSPATH. So I was the only one who could properly load the applet. It's important to specify the full class name including the package in the CODE parameter of your applet tag. In many published applet examples, the applet is not put inside a package, but it's generally best to use packages in production code.

Running applets from the command line

There are times when you'd like to make a windowed program do something else other than sit on a Web page. Perhaps you'd also like it to do some of the things a "regular" application can do, but still have the vaunted instant portability provided by Java. In previous chapters in this book we've made command-line applications, but in some operating environments (the Macintosh, for example) there isn't a command line. So for any number of reasons, you'd like to build a windowed, non-applet program using Java. This is certainly a reasonable desire.

The Swing library allows you to make an application that preserves the look and feel of the underlying operating environment. If you want to build windowed applications, it makes sense to do so[5] only if you can use the latest version of Java and associated tools so you can deliver applications that won't

---

[5] In my opinion. And after you learn about Swing, you won't want to waste your time on the pre-Swing stuff.

confound your users. If for some reason you're forced to use an older version of Java, think hard before committing to building a significant windowed application.

Often you'll want to be able to create a class that can be invoked as either a window or an applet. This is especially convenient when you're testing the applets, since it's typically much faster and easier to run the resulting applet-application from the command line than it is to start up a Web browser or the Appletviewer.

To create an applet that can be run from the console command line, you simply add a **main( )** to your applet that builds an instance of the applet inside a **Jframe**.[6] As a simple example, let's look at **Applet1b.java** modified to work as both an application and an applet:

```
//: c14:Applet1c.java
// An application and an applet.
// <applet code=Applet1c width=100 height=50></applet>
import javax.swing.*;
import java.awt.*;

public class Applet1c extends JApplet {
  public void init() {
    getContentPane().add(new JLabel("Applet!"));
  }
  // A main() for the application:
  public static void main(String[] args) {
    JApplet applet = new Applet1c();
    JFrame frame = new JFrame("Applet1c");
    // To close the application:
    frame.setDefaultCloseOperation(JFrame.EXIT_ON_CLOSE);
    frame.getContentPane().add(applet);
    frame.setSize(100,50);
    applet.init();
    applet.start();
    frame.setVisible(true);
  }
} ///:~
```

[6] As described earlier, "Frame" was already taken by the AWT, so Swing uses JFrame.

main( ) is the only element added to the applet, and the rest of the applet is untouched. The applet is created and added to a **JFrame** so that it can be displayed.

You can see that in **main( )**, the applet is explicitly initialized and started because in this case the browser isn't available to do it for you. Of course, this doesn't provide the full behavior of the browser, which also calls **stop( )** and **destroy( )**, but for most situations it's acceptable. If it's a problem, you can force the calls yourself.[7]

Notice the last line:

```
frame.setVisible(true);
```

Without this, you won't see anything on the screen.

A display framework

Although the code that turns programs into both applets and applications produces valuable results, if used everywhere it becomes distracting and wastes paper. Instead, the following display framework will be used for the Swing examples in the rest of this book:

```
//: com:bruceeckel:swing:Console.java
// Tool for running Swing demos from the
// console, both applets and JFrames.
package com.bruceeckel.swing;
import javax.swing.*;
import java.awt.event.*;

public class Console {
  // Create a title string from the class name:
  public static String title(Object o) {
    String t = o.getClass().toString();
    // Remove the word "class":
    if(t.indexOf("class") != -1)
      t = t.substring(6);
    return t;
```

[7] This will make sense after you've read further in this chapter. First, make the reference **JApplet** a **static** member of the class (instead of a local variable of **main( )**), and then call **applet.stop( )** and **applet.destroy( )** inside **WindowAdapter.windowClosing( )** before you call **System.exit( )**.

```
  }
  public static void
  run(JFrame frame, int width, int height) {
    frame.setDefaultCloseOperation(JFrame.EXIT_ON_CLOSE);
    frame.setSize(width, height);
    frame.setVisible(true);
  }
  public static void
  run(JApplet applet, int width, int height) {
    JFrame frame = new JFrame(title(applet));
    frame.setDefaultCloseOperation(JFrame.EXIT_ON_CLOSE);
    frame.getContentPane().add(applet);
    frame.setSize(width, height);
    applet.init();
    applet.start();
    frame.setVisible(true);
  }
  public static void
  run(JPanel panel, int width, int height) {
    JFrame frame = new JFrame(title(panel));
    frame.setDefaultCloseOperation(JFrame.EXIT_ON_CLOSE);
    frame.getContentPane().add(panel);
    frame.setSize(width, height);
    frame.setVisible(true);
  }
} ///:~
```

This is a tool you may want to use yourself, so it's placed in the library **com.bruceeckel.swing**. The **Console** class consists entirely of **static** methods. The first is used to extract the class name (using RTTI) from any object and to remove the word "class," which is typically prepended by **getClass( )**. This uses the **String** methods **indexOf( )** to determine whether the word "class" is there, and **substring( )** to produce the new string without "class" or the trailing space. This name is used to label the window that is displayed by the **run( )** methods.

setDefaultCloseOperation( ) causes a **JFrame** to exit a program when that **JFrame** is closed. The default behavior is to do nothing, so if you don't call **setDefaultCloseOperation( )** or write the equivalent code for your **JFrame**, the application won't close.

The **run( )** method is overloaded to work with **JApplet**s, **JPanel**s, and **JFrame**s. Note that only if it's a **JApplet** are **init( )** and **start( )** called.

Now any applet can be run from the console by creating a **main( )** containing a line like this:

```
Console.run(new MyClass(), 500, 300);
```

in which the last two arguments are the display width and height. Here's **Applet1c.java** modified to use **Console**:

```
//: c14:Applet1d.java
// Console runs applets from the command line.
// <applet code=Applet1d width=100 height=50></applet>
import javax.swing.*;
import java.awt.*;
import com.bruceeckel.swing.*;

public class Applet1d extends JApplet {
  public void init() {
    getContentPane().add(new JLabel("Applet!"));
  }
  public static void main(String[] args) {
    Console.run(new Applet1d(), 100, 50);
  }
} ///:~
```

This allows the elimination of repeated code while providing the greatest flexibility in running the examples.

Making a button

Making a button is quite simple: you just call the **JButton** constructor with the label you want on the button. You'll see later that you can do fancier things, like putting graphic images on buttons.

Usually, you'll want to create a field for the button inside your class so that you can refer to it later.

The **JButton** is a component—its own little window—that will automatically get repainted as part of an update. This means that you don't explicitly paint a button or any other kind of control; you simply place them on the form and let them automatically take care of painting themselves. So to place a button on a form, you do it inside **init( )**:

```
//: c14:Button1.java
// Putting buttons on an applet.
```

```
// <applet code=Button1 width=200 height=50></applet>
import javax.swing.*;
import java.awt.*;
import com.bruceeckel.swing.*;

public class Button1 extends JApplet {
  private JButton
    b1 = new JButton("Button 1"),
    b2 = new JButton("Button 2");
  public void init() {
    Container cp = getContentPane();
    cp.setLayout(new FlowLayout());
    cp.add(b1);
    cp.add(b2);
  }
  public static void main(String[] args) {
    Console.run(new Button1(), 200, 50);
  }
} ///:~
```

Something new has been added here: Before any elements are placed on the content pane, it is given a new "layout manager," of type **FlowLayout**. The layout manager is the way that the pane implicitly decides where to place the control on the form. The normal behavior of an applet is to use the **BorderLayout**, but that won't work here because (as you will learn later in this chapter when controlling the layout of a form is examined in more detail) it defaults to covering each control entirely with every new one that is added. However, **FlowLayout** causes the controls to flow evenly onto the form, left to right and top to bottom.

Capturing an event

You'll notice that if you compile and run the preceding applet, nothing happens when you press the buttons. This is where you must step in and write some code to determine what will happen. The basis of event-driven programming, which comprises a lot of what a GUI is about, is tying events to code that responds to those events.

The way that this is accomplished in Swing is by cleanly separating the interface (the graphical components) and the implementation (the code that you want to run when an event happens to a component). Each Swing component can report all the events that might happen to it, and it can report each kind of event individually. So if you're not interested in, for example, whether the mouse is being moved over your button, you don't register your interest in that event. It's a very straightforward and elegant way to handle event-driven programming, and once you understand the basic concepts, you can easily use Swing components that you haven't seen before—in fact, this model extends to anything that can be classified as a JavaBean (discussed later in the chapter).

At first, we will just focus on the main event of interest for the components being used. In the case of a **JButton**, this "event of interest" is that the button is pressed. To register your interest in when a button is pressed, you call the **JButton**'s **addActionListener( )** method. This method expects an argument that is an object that implements the **ActionListener** interface, which contains a single method called **actionPerformed( )**. So all you have to do to attach code to a **JButton** is to implement the **ActionListener** interface in a class, and register an object of that class with the **JButton** via **addActionListener( )**. The method will be called when the button is pressed (this is normally referred to as a *callback*).

But what should the result of pressing that button be? We'd like to see something change on the screen, so a new Swing component will be introduced: the **JTextField**. This is a place where text can be typed, or in this case, inserted by the program. Although there are a number of ways to create a **JTextField**, the simplest is just to tell the constructor how wide you want that field to be. Once the **JTextField** is placed on the form, you can modify its contents by using the **setText( )** method (there are many other methods in **JTextField**, but you must look these up in the HTML documentation for the JDK from *java.sun.com*). Here is what it looks like:

```
//: c14:Button2.java
// Responding to button presses.
// <applet code=Button2 width=200 height=75></applet>
import javax.swing.*;
import java.awt.event.*;
import java.awt.*;
import com.bruceeckel.swing.*;

public class Button2 extends JApplet {
  private JButton
    b1 = new JButton("Button 1"),
    b2 = new JButton("Button 2");
  private JTextField txt = new JTextField(10);
  class ButtonListener implements ActionListener {
```

```
    public void actionPerformed(ActionEvent e) {
      String name = ((JButton)e.getSource()).getText();
      txt.setText(name);
    }
  }
  private ButtonListener bl = new ButtonListener();
  public void init() {
    b1.addActionListener(bl);
    b2.addActionListener(bl);
    Container cp = getContentPane();
    cp.setLayout(new FlowLayout());
    cp.add(b1);
    cp.add(b2);
    cp.add(txt);
  }
  public static void main(String[] args) {
    Console.run(new Button2(), 200, 75);
  }
} ///:~
```

Creating a **JTextField** and placing it on the canvas takes the same steps as for **Jbutton**s or for any Swing component. The difference in the preceding program is in the creation of the aforementioned **ActionListener** class **ButtonListener**. The argument to **actionPerformed( )** is of type **ActionEvent**, which contains all the information about the event and where it came from. In this case, I wanted to describe the button that was pressed; **getSource( )** produces the object where the event originated, and I assumed (using a cast) that the object is a **JButton**. **getText( )** returns the text that's on the button, and this is placed in the **JTextField** to prove that the code was actually called when the button was pressed.

In **init( )**, **addActionListener( )** is used to register the **ButtonListener** object with both the buttons.

It is often more convenient to code the **ActionListener** as an anonymous inner class, especially since you tend to use only a single instance of each listener class. **Button2.java** can be modified to use an anonymous inner class as follows:

```
//: c14:Button2b.java
// Using anonymous inner classes.
// <applet code=Button2b width=200 height=75></applet>
import javax.swing.*;
import java.awt.event.*;
```

```
import java.awt.*;
import com.bruceeckel.swing.*;

public class Button2b extends JApplet {
  private JButton
    b1 = new JButton("Button 1"),
    b2 = new JButton("Button 2");
  private JTextField txt = new JTextField(10);
  private ActionListener bl = new ActionListener() {
    public void actionPerformed(ActionEvent e) {
      String name = ((JButton)e.getSource()).getText();
      txt.setText(name);
    }
  };
  public void init() {
    b1.addActionListener(bl);
    b2.addActionListener(bl);
    Container cp = getContentPane();
    cp.setLayout(new FlowLayout());
    cp.add(b1);
    cp.add(b2);
    cp.add(txt);
  }
  public static void main(String[] args) {
    Console.run(new Button2b(), 200, 75);
  }
} ///:~
```

The approach of using an anonymous inner class will be preferred (when possible) for the examples in this book.

Text areas

A **JTextArea** is like a **JTextField** except that it can have multiple lines and has more functionality. A particularly useful method is **append( )**; with this you can easily pour output into the **JTextArea**, thus making a Swing program an improvement (since you can scroll backward) over what has been accomplished thus far using command-line programs that print to standard output. As an example, the following program fills a **JTextArea** with the output from the **geography** generator in Chapter 11:

```
//: c14:TextArea.java
// Using the JTextArea control.
import javax.swing.*;
```

```java
import java.awt.event.*;
import java.awt.*;
import java.util.*;
import com.bruceeckel.swing.*;
import com.bruceeckel.util.*;

public class TextArea extends JFrame {
  private JButton
    b = new JButton("Add Data"),
    c = new JButton("Clear Data");
  private JTextArea t = new JTextArea(20, 40);
  private Map m = new HashMap();
  public TextArea() {
    // Use up all the data:
    Collections2.fill(m, Collections2.geography,
      CountryCapitals.pairs.length);
    b.addActionListener(new ActionListener() {
      public void actionPerformed(ActionEvent e) {
        Iterator it = m.entrySet().iterator();
        while(it.hasNext()) {
          Map.Entry me = (Map.Entry)(it.next());
          t.append(me.getKey() + ": "+ me.getValue()+"\n");
        }
      }
    });
    c.addActionListener(new ActionListener() {
      public void actionPerformed(ActionEvent e) {
        t.setText("");
      }
    });
    Container cp = getContentPane();
    cp.setLayout(new FlowLayout());
    cp.add(new JScrollPane(t));
    cp.add(b);
    cp.add(c);
  }
  public static void main(String[] args) {
    Console.run(new TextArea(), 475, 425);
  }
} ///:~
```

This is a **JFrame** rather than a **JApplet** because it reads from the local disk, and therefore cannot be run as an applet in an HTML page.

In **init( )**, the **Map** is filled with all the countries and their capitals. Note that for both buttons, the **ActionListener** is created and added without defining an intermediate variable, since you never need to refer to that listener again during the program. The "Add Data" button formats and appends all the data, and the "Clear Data" button uses **setText( )** to remove all the text from the **JTextArea**.

As the **JTextArea** is added to the applet, it is wrapped in a **JScrollPane** to control scrolling when too much text is placed on the screen. That's all you must do in order to produce full scrolling capabilities. Having tried to figure out how to do the equivalent in some other GUI programming environments, I am very impressed with the simplicity and good design of components like **JScrollPane**.

Controlling layout

The way that you place components on a form in Java is probably different from any other GUI system you've used. First, it's all code; there are no "resources" that control placement of components. Second, the way components are placed on a form is controlled not by absolute positioning but by a "layout manager" that decides how the components lie based on the order that you **add( )** them. The size, shape, and placement of components will be remarkably different from one layout manager to another. In addition, the layout managers adapt to the dimensions of your applet or application window, so if the window dimension is changed, the size, shape, and placement of the components can change in response.

JApplet, **JFrame JWindow**, and **JDialog** can all produce a **Container** with **getContentPane( )** that can contain and display **Component**s. In **Container,** there's a method called **setLayout( )** that allows you to choose a different layout manager. Other classes, such as **JPanel**, contain and display components directly, so you also set the layout manager directly, without using the content pane.

In this section we'll explore the various layout managers by placing buttons in them (since that's the simplest thing to do). There won't be any capturing of button events because these examples are just intended to show how the buttons are laid out.

BorderLayout

Applets use a default layout scheme: the **BorderLayout** (a number of the previous examples have changed the layout manager to **FlowLayout**). Without any other instruction, this takes whatever you **add( )** to it and places it in the center, stretching the object all the way out to the edges.

However, there's more to the **BorderLayout**. This layout manager has the concept of four border regions and a center area. When you add something to a panel that's using a **BorderLayout**, you can use the overloaded **add( )** method that takes a constant value as its first argument. This value can be any of the following:

BorderLayout. NORTH	Top
BorderLayout. SOUTH	Bottom
BorderLayout. EAST	Right
BorderLayout. WEST	Left
BorderLayout.CENTER	Fill the middle, up to the other components or to the edges

If you don't specify an area to place the object, it defaults to **CENTER**.

Here's a simple example. The default layout is used, since **JApplet** defaults to **BorderLayout**:

```
//: c14:BorderLayout1.java
// Demonstrates BorderLayout.
//<applet code=BorderLayout1 width=300 height=250></applet>
import javax.swing.*;
import java.awt.*;
import com.bruceeckel.swing.*;

public class BorderLayout1 extends JApplet {
  public void init() {
    Container cp = getContentPane();
    cp.add(BorderLayout.NORTH, new JButton("North"));
    cp.add(BorderLayout.SOUTH, new JButton("South"));
    cp.add(BorderLayout.EAST, new JButton("East"));
    cp.add(BorderLayout.WEST, new JButton("West"));
    cp.add(BorderLayout.CENTER, new JButton("Center"));
  }
  public static void main(String[] args) {
```

```
    Console.run(new BorderLayout1(), 300, 250);
  }
} ///:~
```

For every placement but **CENTER**, the element that you add is compressed to fit in the smallest amount of space along one dimension while it is stretched to the maximum along the other dimension. **CENTER**, however, spreads out in both dimensions to occupy the middle.

FlowLayout

This simply "flows" the components onto the form, from left to right until the top space is full, then moves down a row and continues flowing.

Here's an example that sets the layout manager to **FlowLayout** and then places buttons on the form. You'll notice that with **FlowLayout**, the components take on their "natural" size. A **JButton**, for example, will be the size of its string.

```
//: c14:FlowLayout1.java
// Demonstrates FlowLayout.
// <applet code=FlowLayout1 width=300 height=250></applet>
import javax.swing.*;
import java.awt.*;
import com.bruceeckel.swing.*;

public class FlowLayout1 extends JApplet {
  public void init() {
    Container cp = getContentPane();
    cp.setLayout(new FlowLayout());
    for(int i = 0; i < 20; i++)
      cp.add(new JButton("Button " + i));
  }
  public static void main(String[] args) {
    Console.run(new FlowLayout1(), 300, 250);
  }
} ///:~
```

All components will be compacted to their smallest size in a **FlowLayout**, so you might get a little bit of surprising behavior. For example, because a **JLabel** will be the size of its string, attempting to right-justify its text yields an unchanged display when using **FlowLayout**.

GridLayout

A **GridLayout** allows you to build a table of components, and as you add them, they are placed left-to-right and top-to-bottom in the grid. In the constructor you specify the number of rows and columns that you need, and these are laid out in equal proportions.

```
//: c14:GridLayout1.java
// Demonstrates GridLayout.
// <applet code=GridLayout1 width=300 height=250></applet>
import javax.swing.*;
import java.awt.*;
import com.bruceeckel.swing.*;

public class GridLayout1 extends JApplet {
  public void init() {
    Container cp = getContentPane();
    cp.setLayout(new GridLayout(7,3));
    for(int i = 0; i < 20; i++)
      cp.add(new JButton("Button " + i));
  }
  public static void main(String[] args) {
    Console.run(new GridLayout1(), 300, 250);
  }
} ///:~
```

In this case there are 21 slots but only 20 buttons. The last slot is left empty because no "balancing" goes on with a **GridLayout**.

GridBagLayout

The **GridBagLayout** provides you with tremendous control in deciding exactly how the regions of your window will lay themselves out and reformat themselves when the window is resized. However, it's also the most complicated layout manager, and is quite difficult to understand. It is intended primarily for automatic code generation by a GUI builder (GUI builders might use **GridBagLayout** instead of absolute placement). If your design is so complicated that you feel you need to use **GridBagLayout**, then you should be using a GUI builder tool to generate that design. If you feel you must know the intricate details, I'll refer you to *Core Java 2, Volume 1*, by Horstmann & Cornell (Prentice Hall, 2001), or a dedicated Swing book as a starting point.

Absolute positioning

It is also possible to set the absolute position of the graphical components in this way:

1. Set a **null** layout manager for your **Container**: **setLayout(null)**.

2. Call **setBounds( )** or **reshape( )** (depending on the language version) for each component, passing a bounding rectangle in pixel coordinates. You can do this in the constructor or in **paint( )**, depending on what you want to achieve.

Some GUI builders use this approach extensively, but this is usually not the best way to generate code.

BoxLayout

Because people had so much trouble understanding and working with **GridBagLayout**, Swing also includes **BoxLayout**, which gives you many of the benefits of **GridBagLayout** without the complexity, so you can often use it when you need to do hand-coded layouts (again, if your design becomes too complex, use a GUI builder that generates layouts for you). **BoxLayout** allows you to control the placement of components either vertically or horizontally, and to control the space between the components using something called “struts and glue.” First, let’s see how to use the **BoxLayout** directly, in the same way that the other layout managers have been demonstrated:

```
//: c14:BoxLayout1.java
// Vertical and horizontal BoxLayouts.
// <applet code=BoxLayout1 width=450 height=200></applet>
import javax.swing.*;
import java.awt.*;
import com.bruceeckel.swing.*;

public class BoxLayout1 extends JApplet {
  public void init() {
    JPanel jpv = new JPanel();
    jpv.setLayout(new BoxLayout(jpv, BoxLayout.Y_AXIS));
    for(int i = 0; i < 5; i++)
      jpv.add(new JButton("jpv " + i));
    JPanel jph = new JPanel();
    jph.setLayout(new BoxLayout(jph, BoxLayout.X_AXIS));
```

```
    for(int i = 0; i < 5; i++)
      jph.add(new JButton("jph " + i));
    Container cp = getContentPane();
    cp.add(BorderLayout.EAST, jpv);
    cp.add(BorderLayout.SOUTH, jph);
  }
  public static void main(String[] args) {
    Console.run(new BoxLayout1(), 450, 200);
  }
} ///:~
```

The constructor for **BoxLayout** is a bit different than the other layout managers—you provide the **Container** that is to be controlled by the **BoxLayout** as the first argument, and the direction of the layout as the second argument.

To simplify matters, there's a special container called **Box** that uses **BoxLayout** as its native manager. The following example lays out components horizontally and vertically using **Box**, which has two **static** methods to create boxes with vertical and horizontal alignment:

```
//: c14:Box1.java
// Vertical and horizontal BoxLayouts.
// <applet code=Box1 width=450 height=200></applet>
import javax.swing.*;
import java.awt.*;
import com.bruceeckel.swing.*;

public class Box1 extends JApplet {
  public void init() {
    Box bv = Box.createVerticalBox();
    for(int i = 0; i < 5; i++)
      bv.add(new JButton("bv " + i));
    Box bh = Box.createHorizontalBox();
    for(int i = 0; i < 5; i++)
      bh.add(new JButton("bh " + i));
    Container cp = getContentPane();
    cp.add(BorderLayout.EAST, bv);
    cp.add(BorderLayout.SOUTH, bh);
  }
  public static void main(String[] args) {
    Console.run(new Box1(), 450, 200);
  }
} ///:~
```

Once you have a **Box**, you pass it as a second argument when adding components to the content pane.

Struts add space, measured in pixels, between components. To use a strut, you simply add it between the addition of the components that you want spaced apart:

```
//: c14:Box2.java
// Adding struts.
// <applet code=Box2 width=450 height=300></applet>
import javax.swing.*;
import java.awt.*;
import com.bruceeckel.swing.*;

public class Box2 extends JApplet {
  public void init() {
    Box bv = Box.createVerticalBox();
    for(int i = 0; i < 5; i++) {
      bv.add(new JButton("bv " + i));
      bv.add(Box.createVerticalStrut(i * 10));
    }
    Box bh = Box.createHorizontalBox();
    for(int i = 0; i < 5; i++) {
      bh.add(new JButton("bh " + i));
      bh.add(Box.createHorizontalStrut(i * 10));
    }
    Container cp = getContentPane();
    cp.add(BorderLayout.EAST, bv);
    cp.add(BorderLayout.SOUTH, bh);
  }
  public static void main(String[] args) {
    Console.run(new Box2(), 450, 300);
  }
} ///:~
```

Struts separate components by a fixed amount, but glue is the opposite; it separates components by as much as possible. Thus it's more of a "spring" than "glue" (and the design on which this was based was called "springs and struts," so the choice of the term is a bit mysterious).

```
//: c14:Box3.java
// Using Glue.
// <applet code=Box3 width=450 height=300></applet>
import javax.swing.*;
```

```
import java.awt.*;
import com.bruceeckel.swing.*;

public class Box3 extends JApplet {
  public void init() {
    Box bv = Box.createVerticalBox();
    bv.add(new JLabel("Hello"));
    bv.add(Box.createVerticalGlue());
    bv.add(new JLabel("Applet"));
    bv.add(Box.createVerticalGlue());
    bv.add(new JLabel("World"));
    Box bh = Box.createHorizontalBox();
    bh.add(new JLabel("Hello"));
    bh.add(Box.createHorizontalGlue());
    bh.add(new JLabel("Applet"));
    bh.add(Box.createHorizontalGlue());
    bh.add(new JLabel("World"));
    bv.add(Box.createVerticalGlue());
    bv.add(bh);
    bv.add(Box.createVerticalGlue());
    getContentPane().add(bv);
  }
  public static void main(String[] args) {
    Console.run(new Box3(), 450, 300);
  }
} ///:~
```

A strut works in one direction, but a rigid area fixes the spacing between components in both directions:

```
//: c14:Box4.java
// Rigid areas are like pairs of struts.
// <applet code=Box4 width=450 height=300></applet>
import javax.swing.*;
import java.awt.*;
import com.bruceeckel.swing.*;

public class Box4 extends JApplet {
  public void init() {
    Box bv = Box.createVerticalBox();
    bv.add(new JButton("Top"));
    bv.add(Box.createRigidArea(new Dimension(120, 90)));
    bv.add(new JButton("Bottom"));
    Box bh = Box.createHorizontalBox();
    bh.add(new JButton("Left"));
```

```
    bh.add(Box.createRigidArea(new Dimension(160, 80)));
    bh.add(new JButton("Right"));
    bv.add(bh);
    getContentPane().add(bv);
  }
  public static void main(String[] args) {
    Console.run(new Box4(), 450, 300);
  }
} ///:~
```

You should be aware that rigid areas are a bit controversial. Since they use absolute values, some people feel that they cause more trouble than they are worth.

The best approach?

Swing is powerful; it can get a lot done with a few lines of code. The examples shown in this book are reasonably simple, and for learning purposes it makes sense to write them by hand. You can actually accomplish quite a bit by combining simple layouts. At some point, however, it stops making sense to hand-code GUI forms; it becomes too complicated and is not a good use of your programming time. The Java and Swing designers oriented the language and libraries to support GUI building tools, which have been created for the express purpose of making your programming experience easier. As long as you understand what's going on with layouts and how to deal with the events (described next), it's not particularly important that you actually know the details of how to lay out components by hand; let the appropriate tool do that for you (Java is, after all, designed to increase programmer productivity).

The Swing event model

In the Swing event model, a component can initiate ("fire") an event. Each type of event is represented by a distinct class. When an event is fired, it is received by one or more "listeners," which act on that event. Thus, the source of an event and the place where the event is handled can be separate. Since you typically use Swing components as they are, but need to write code that is called when the components receive an event, this is an excellent example of the separation of interface and implementation.

Each event listener is an object of a class that implements a particular type of listener interface. So as a programmer, all you do is create a listener object and register it with the component that's firing the event. This registration is performed by calling an **addXXXListener( )** method in the event-firing component, in which "**XXX**" represents the type of event listened for. You can easily know what types of events can be handled by noticing the names of the "addListener" methods, and if you try to listen for the wrong events, you'll discover your mistake at compile time. You'll see later in the chapter that JavaBeans also use the names of the "addListener" methods to determine what events a Bean can handle.

All of your event logic, then, will go inside a listener class. When you create a listener class, the sole restriction is that it must implement the appropriate interface. You can create a global listener class, but this is a situation in which inner classes tend to be quite useful, not only because they provide a logical grouping of your listener classes inside the UI or business logic classes they are serving, but also because (as you shall see later) an inner-class object keeps a reference to its parent object, which provides a nice way to call across class and subsystem boundaries.

All the examples so far in this chapter have been using the Swing event model, but the remainder of this section will fill out the details of that model.

Event and listener types

All Swing components include **addXXXListener( )** and **removeXXXListener( )** methods so that the appropriate types of listeners can be added and removed from each component. You'll notice that the "**XXX**" in each case also represents the argument for the method, for example, **addMyListener(MyListener m)**. The following table includes the basic associated events, listeners, and methods, along with the basic components that support those particular events by providing the **addXXXListener( )** and **removeXXXListener( )** methods. You should keep in mind that the event model is designed to be extensible, so you may encounter other events and listener types that are not covered in this table.

Event, listener interface and add- and remove-methods	Components supporting this event
ActionEvent **ActionListener** **addActionListener( )** **removeActionListener( )**	**JButton, JList, JTextField, JMenuItem** and its derivatives including **JCheckBoxMenuItem, JMenu,** and **JpopupMenu**
AdjustmentEvent **AdjustmentListener**	**JScrollbar** and anything you create that

Event, listener interface and add- and remove-methods	Components supporting this event
addAdjustmentListener( ) **removeAdjustmentListener( )**	implements the **Adjustable interface**
ComponentEvent **ComponentListener** **addComponentListener( )** **removeComponentListener( )**	***Component** and its derivatives, including **JButton, JCheckBox, JComboBox, Container, JPanel, JApplet, JScrollPane, Window, JDialog, JFileDialog, JFrame, JLabel, JList, JScrollbar, JTextArea**, and **JTextField**
ContainerEvent **ContainerListener** **addContainerListener( )** **removeContainerListener( )**	**Container** and its derivatives, including **JPanel, JApplet, JScrollPane, Window, JDialog, JFileDialog,** and **JFrame**
FocusEvent **FocusListener** **addFocusListener( )** **removeFocusListener( )**	**Component** and **derivatives***
KeyEvent **KeyListener** **addKeyListener( )** **removeKeyListener( )**	**Component** and **derivatives***
MouseEvent (for both clicks and motion) **MouseListener** **addMouseListener( )** **removeMouseListener( )**	**Component** and **derivatives***
MouseEvent[8] (for both clicks and motion) **MouseMotionListener** **addMouseMotionListener( )** **removeMouseMotionListener( )**	**Component** and **derivatives***
WindowEvent **WindowListener** **addWindowListener( )** **removeWindowListener( )**	**Window** and its derivatives, including **JDialog, JFileDialog, and JFrame**

[8] There is no **MouseMotionEvent** even though it seems like there ought to be. Clicking and motion is combined into **MouseEvent**, so this second appearance of **MouseEvent** in the table is not an error.

Event, listener interface and add- and remove-methods	Components supporting this event
ItemEvent **ItemListener** **addItemListener( )** **removeItemListener( )**	**JCheckBox,** **JCheckBoxMenuItem,** **JComboBox, JList,** and anything that implements the **ItemSelectable interface**
TextEvent **TextListener** **addTextListener( )** **removeTextListener( )**	Anything derived from **JTextComponent,** including **JTextArea** and **JTextField**

You can see that each type of component supports only certain types of events. It turns out to be rather difficult to look up all the events supported by each component. A simpler approach is to modify the **ShowMethods.java** program from Chapter 10 so that it displays all the event listeners supported by any Swing component that you enter.

Chapter 10 introduced *reflection* and used that feature to look up methods for a particular class—either the entire list of methods or a subset of those whose names match a keyword that you provide. The magic of reflection is that it can automatically show you *all* the methods for a class without forcing you to walk up the inheritance hierarchy, examining the base classes at each level. Thus, it provides a valuable timesaving tool for programming; because the names of most Java methods are made nicely verbose and descriptive, you can search for the method names that contain a particular word of interest. When you find what you think you're looking for, check the JDK documentation.

However, by Chapter 10 you hadn't seen Swing, so the tool in that chapter was developed as a command-line application. Here is the more useful GUI version, specialized to look for the "addListener" methods in Swing components:

```
//: c14:ShowAddListeners.java
// Display the "addXXXListener" methods of any Swing class.
// <applet code=ShowAddListeners
// width=500 height=400></applet>
import javax.swing.*;
import javax.swing.event.*;
import java.awt.*;
import java.awt.event.*;
```

```
import java.lang.reflect.*;
import java.util.regex.*;
import com.bruceeckel.swing.*;

public class ShowAddListeners extends JApplet {
  private JTextField name = new JTextField(25);
  private JTextArea results = new JTextArea(40, 65);
  private static Pattern addListener =
    Pattern.compile("(add\\w+?Listener\\(.*?\\))");
  private static Pattern qualifier =
    Pattern.compile("\\w+\\.");
  class NameL implements ActionListener {
    public void actionPerformed(ActionEvent e) {
      String nm = name.getText().trim();
      if(nm.length() == 0) {
        results.setText("No match");
        return;
      }
      Class klass;
      try {
        klass = Class.forName("javax.swing." + nm);
      } catch(ClassNotFoundException ex) {
        results.setText("No match");
        return;
      }
      Method[] methods = klass.getMethods();
      results.setText("");
      for(int i = 0; i < methods.length; i++) {
        Matcher matcher =
          addListener.matcher(methods[i].toString());
        if(matcher.find())
          results.append(qualifier.matcher(
            matcher.group(1)).replaceAll("") + "\n");
      }
    }
  }
  public void init() {
    NameL nameListener = new NameL();
    name.addActionListener(nameListener);
    JPanel top = new JPanel();
    top.add(new JLabel("Swing class name (press ENTER):"));
    top.add(name);
    Container cp = getContentPane();
    cp.add(BorderLayout.NORTH, top);
```

```
    cp.add(new JScrollPane(results));
    // Initial data and test:
    name.setText("JTextArea");
    nameListener.actionPerformed(
      new ActionEvent("", 0 ,""));
  }
  public static void main(String[] args) {
    Console.run(new ShowAddListeners(), 500,400);
  }
} ///:~
```

You enter the Swing class name that you want to look up in the **name JTextField**. The results are extracted using regular expressions, and displayed in a **JTextArea**.

You'll notice that there are no buttons or other components to indicate that you want the search to begin. That's because the **JTextField** is monitored by an **ActionListener**. Whenever you make a change and press ENTER, the list is immediately updated. If the text field isn't empty, it is used inside **Class.forName( )** to try to look up the class. If the name is incorrect, **Class.forName( )** will fail, which means that it throws an exception. This is trapped, and the **JTextArea** is set to "No match." But if you type in a correct name (capitalization counts), **Class.forName( )** is successful, and **getMethods( )** will return an array of **Method** objects.

Two regular expressions are used here. The first, **addListener**, looks for "add" followed by any word characters, followed by "Listener" and the argument list in parentheses. Notice that this whole regular expression is surrounded by non-escaped parentheses, which means it will be accessible as a regular expression "group" when it matches. Inside **NameL.ActionPerformed( )**, a **Matcher** is created by passing each **Method** object to the **Pattern.matcher( )** method. When **find( )** is called for this **Matcher** object, it returns **true** only if a match occurs, and in that case you can select the first matching parenthesized group by calling **group(1)**. This string still contains qualifiers, so to strip them off the **qualifier Pattern** object is used just as it was in **c09:ShowMethods.java**.

At the end of **init( )**, an initial value is placed in **name** and the action event is run to provide a test with initial data.

This program is a convenient way to investigate the capabilities of a Swing component. Once you know which events a particular component supports, you don't need to look anything up to react to that event. You simply:

1. Take the name of the event class and remove the word "**Event**." Add the word "**Listener**" to what remains. This is the listener interface you must implement in your inner class.

2. Implement the interface above and write out the methods for the events you want to capture. For example, you might be looking for mouse movements, so you write code for the **mouseMoved( )** method of the **MouseMotionListener** interface. (You must implement the other methods, of course, but there's often a shortcut for this, which you'll see soon.)

3. Create an object of the listener class in Step 2. Register it with your component with the method produced by prefixing "**add**" to your listener name. For example, **addMouseMotionListener( )**.

Here are some of the listener interfaces:

Listener interface w/ adapter	Methods in interface
ActionListener	actionPerformed(ActionEvent)
AdjustmentListener	adjustmentValueChanged(AdjustmentEvent)
ComponentListener ComponentAdapter	componentHidden(ComponentEvent) componentShown(ComponentEvent) componentMoved(ComponentEvent) componentResized(ComponentEvent)
ContainerListener ContainerAdapter	componentAdded(ContainerEvent) componentRemoved(ContainerEvent)
FocusListener FocusAdapter	focusGained(FocusEvent) focusLost(FocusEvent)
KeyListener KeyAdapter	keyPressed(KeyEvent) keyReleased(KeyEvent) keyTyped(KeyEvent)
MouseListener MouseAdapter	mouseClicked(MouseEvent) mouseEntered(MouseEvent) mouseExited(MouseEvent) mousePressed(MouseEvent)

Listener interface w/ adapter	Methods in interface
	mouseReleased(MouseEvent)
MouseMotionListener **MouseMotionAdapter**	**mouseDragged(MouseEvent)** **mouseMoved(MouseEvent)**
WindowListener **WindowAdapter**	**windowOpened(WindowEvent)** **windowClosing(WindowEvent)** **windowClosed(WindowEvent)** **windowActivated(WindowEvent)** **windowDeactivated(WindowEvent)** **windowIconified(WindowEvent)** **windowDeiconified(WindowEvent)**
ItemListener	**itemStateChanged(ItemEvent)**

This is not an exhaustive listing, partly because the event model allows you to create your own event types and associated listeners. Thus, you'll regularly come across libraries that have invented their own events, and the knowledge gained in this chapter will allow you to figure out how to use these events.

Using listener adapters for simplicity

In the table above, you can see that some listener interfaces have only one method. These are trivial to implement, because you'll implement them only when you want to write that particular method. However, the listener interfaces that have multiple methods can be less pleasant to use. For example, if you want to capture a mouse click (that isn't already captured for you, for example, by a button), then you need to write a method for **mouseClicked( )**. But since **MouseListener** is an **interface**, you must implement all of the other methods even if they don't do anything. This can be annoying.

To solve the problem, some (but not all) of the listener interfaces that have more than one method are provided with *adapters*, the names of which you can see in the table above. Each adapter provides default empty methods for each of the interface methods. Then all you need to do is inherit from the adapter and override only the methods you need to change. For example, the typical **MouseListener** you'll use looks like this:

```
class MyMouseListener extends MouseAdapter {
  public void mouseClicked(MouseEvent e) {
    // Respond to mouse click...
```

```
    }
  }
```

The whole point of the adapters is to make the creation of listener classes easy.

There is a downside to adapters, however, in the form of a pitfall. Suppose you write a **MouseAdapter** like the previous one:

```
class MyMouseListener extends MouseAdapter {
  public void MouseClicked(MouseEvent e) {
    // Respond to mouse click...
  }
}
```

This doesn't work, but it will drive you crazy trying to figure out why, since everything will compile and run fine—except that your method won't be called for a mouse click. Can you see the problem? It's in the name of the method: **MouseClicked( )** instead of **mouseClicked ( )**. A simple slip in capitalization results in the addition of a completely new method. However, this is not the method that's called when the window is closing, so you don't get the desired results. Despite the inconvenience, an **interface** will guarantee that the methods are properly implemented.

Tracking multiple events

To prove to yourself that these events are in fact being fired, and as an interesting experiment, it's worth creating an applet that tracks extra behavior in a **JButton** (in addition to whether it has been pressed). This example also shows you how to inherit your own button object because that's what is used as the target of all the events of interest. To do so, you can just inherit from **Jbutton**.[9]

The **MyButton** class is an inner class of **TrackEvent**, so **MyButton** can reach into the parent window and manipulate its text fields, which is what's necessary to be able to write the status information into the fields of the parent. Of course, this is a limited solution, since **MyButton** can be used only in conjunction with **TrackEvent**. This kind of code is sometimes called "highly coupled":

---

[9] In Java 1.0/1.1 you could *not* usefully inherit from the button object. This was only one of numerous fundamental design flaws.

```java
//: c14:TrackEvent.java
// Show events as they happen.
// <applet code=TrackEvent width=700 height=500></applet>
import javax.swing.*;
import java.awt.*;
import java.awt.event.*;
import java.util.*;
import com.bruceeckel.swing.*;

public class TrackEvent extends JApplet {
  private HashMap h = new HashMap();
  private String[] event = {
    "focusGained", "focusLost", "keyPressed",
    "keyReleased", "keyTyped", "mouseClicked",
    "mouseEntered", "mouseExited", "mousePressed",
    "mouseReleased", "mouseDragged", "mouseMoved"
  };
  private MyButton
    b1 = new MyButton(Color.BLUE, "test1"),
    b2 = new MyButton(Color.RED, "test2");
  class MyButton extends JButton {
    void report(String field, String msg) {
      ((JTextField)h.get(field)).setText(msg);
    }
    FocusListener fl = new FocusListener() {
      public void focusGained(FocusEvent e) {
        report("focusGained", e.paramString());
      }
      public void focusLost(FocusEvent e) {
        report("focusLost", e.paramString());
      }
    };
    KeyListener kl = new KeyListener() {
      public void keyPressed(KeyEvent e) {
        report("keyPressed", e.paramString());
      }
      public void keyReleased(KeyEvent e) {
        report("keyReleased", e.paramString());
      }
      public void keyTyped(KeyEvent e) {
        report("keyTyped", e.paramString());
      }
    };
    MouseListener ml = new MouseListener() {
```

```
      public void mouseClicked(MouseEvent e) {
        report("mouseClicked", e.paramString());
      }
      public void mouseEntered(MouseEvent e) {
        report("mouseEntered", e.paramString());
      }
      public void mouseExited(MouseEvent e) {
        report("mouseExited", e.paramString());
      }
      public void mousePressed(MouseEvent e) {
        report("mousePressed", e.paramString());
      }
      public void mouseReleased(MouseEvent e) {
        report("mouseReleased", e.paramString());
      }
    };
    MouseMotionListener mml = new MouseMotionListener() {
      public void mouseDragged(MouseEvent e) {
        report("mouseDragged", e.paramString());
      }
      public void mouseMoved(MouseEvent e) {
        report("mouseMoved", e.paramString());
      }
    };
    public MyButton(Color color, String label) {
      super(label);
      setBackground(color);
      addFocusListener(fl);
      addKeyListener(kl);
      addMouseListener(ml);
      addMouseMotionListener(mml);
    }
  }
  public void init() {
    Container c = getContentPane();
    c.setLayout(new GridLayout(event.length + 1, 2));
    for(int i = 0; i < event.length; i++) {
      JTextField t = new JTextField();
      t.setEditable(false);
      c.add(new JLabel(event[i], JLabel.RIGHT));
      c.add(t);
      h.put(event[i], t);
    }
    c.add(b1);
```

```
    c.add(b2);
  }
  public static void main(String[] args) {
    Console.run(new TrackEvent(), 700, 500);
  }
} ///:~
```

In the **MyButton** constructor, the button's color is set with a call to **SetBackground( )**. The listeners are all installed with simple method calls.

The **TrackEvent** class contains a **HashMap** to hold the strings representing the type of event and **JTextField**s where information about that event is held. Of course, these could have been created statically rather than putting them in a **HashMap**, but I think you'll agree that it's a lot easier to use and change. In particular, if you need to add or remove a new type of event in **TrackEvent**, you simply add or remove a string in the **event** array—everything else happens automatically.

When **report( )** is called, it is given the name of the event and the parameter string from the event. It uses the **HashMap h** in the outer class to look up the actual **JTextField** associated with that event name and then places the parameter string into that field.

This example is fun to play with because you can really see what's going on with the events in your program.

A catalog of Swing components

Now that you understand layout managers and the event model, you're ready to see how Swing components can be used. This section is a non-exhaustive tour of the Swing components and features that you'll probably use most of the time. Each example is intended to be reasonably small so that you can easily lift the code and use it in your own programs.

Keep in mind:

1. You can easily see what each of these examples looks like while running by viewing the HTML pages in the downloadable source code for this chapter (*www.BruceEckel.com*).

2. The JDK documentation from *java.sun.com* contains all of the Swing classes and methods (only a few are shown here).

3. Because of the naming convention used for Swing events, it's fairly easy to guess how to write and install a handler for a particular type of event. Use the lookup program **ShowAddListeners.java** from earlier in this chapter to aid in your investigation of a particular component.

4. When things start to get complicated you should graduate to a GUI builder.

Buttons

Swing includes a number of different types of buttons. All buttons, check boxes, radio buttons, and even menu items are inherited from **AbstractButton** (which, since menu items are included, would probably have been better named "AbstractSelector" or something equally general). You'll see the use of menu items shortly, but the following example shows the various types of buttons available:

```
//: c14:Buttons.java
// Various Swing buttons.
// <applet code=Buttons width=350 height=100></applet>
import javax.swing.*;
import java.awt.*;
import java.awt.event.*;
import javax.swing.plaf.basic.*;
import javax.swing.border.*;
import com.bruceeckel.swing.*;

public class Buttons extends JApplet {
  private JButton jb = new JButton("JButton");
  private BasicArrowButton
    up = new BasicArrowButton(BasicArrowButton.NORTH),
    down = new BasicArrowButton(BasicArrowButton.SOUTH),
    right = new BasicArrowButton(BasicArrowButton.EAST),
    left = new BasicArrowButton(BasicArrowButton.WEST);
  public void init() {
    Container cp = getContentPane();
    cp.setLayout(new FlowLayout());
    cp.add(jb);
    cp.add(new JToggleButton("JToggleButton"));
    cp.add(new JCheckBox("JCheckBox"));
    cp.add(new JRadioButton("JRadioButton"));
    JPanel jp = new JPanel();
```

```
    jp.setBorder(new TitledBorder("Directions"));
    jp.add(up);
    jp.add(down);
    jp.add(left);
    jp.add(right);
    cp.add(jp);
  }
  public static void main(String[] args) {
    Console.run(new Buttons(), 350, 100);
  }
} ///:~
```

This begins with the **BasicArrowButton** from **javax.swing.plaf.basic**, then continues with the various specific types of buttons. When you run the example, you'll see that the toggle button holds its last position, in or out. But the check boxes and radio buttons behave identically to each other, just clicking on or off (they are inherited from **JToggleButton**).

Button groups

If you want radio buttons to behave in an "exclusive or" fashion, you must add them to a "button group." But, as the following example demonstrates, any **AbstractButton** can be added to a **ButtonGroup**.

To avoid repeating a lot of code, this example uses reflection to generate the groups of different types of buttons. This is seen in **makeBPanel( )**, which creates a button group and a **JPanel**. The second argument to **makeBPanel( )** is an array of **String**. For each **String**, a button of the class represented by the first argument is added to the **JPanel**:

```
//: c14:ButtonGroups.java
// Uses reflection to create groups
// of different types of AbstractButton.
// <applet code=ButtonGroups width=500 height=300></applet>
import javax.swing.*;
import java.awt.*;
import java.awt.event.*;
import javax.swing.border.*;
import java.lang.reflect.*;
import com.bruceeckel.swing.*;

public class ButtonGroups extends JApplet {
  private static String[] ids = {
    "June", "Ward", "Beaver",
```

```java
      "Wally", "Eddie", "Lumpy",
    };
    static JPanel makeBPanel(Class klass, String[] ids) {
      ButtonGroup bg = new ButtonGroup();
      JPanel jp = new JPanel();
      String title = klass.getName();
      title = title.substring(title.lastIndexOf('.') + 1);
      jp.setBorder(new TitledBorder(title));
      for(int i = 0; i < ids.length; i++) {
        AbstractButton ab = new JButton("failed");
        try {
          // Get the dynamic constructor method
          // that takes a String argument:
          Constructor ctor =
            klass.getConstructor(new Class[]{String.class});
          // Create a new object:
          ab = (AbstractButton)
            ctor.newInstance(new Object[] { ids[i] });
        } catch(Exception ex) {
          System.err.println("can't create " + klass);
        }
        bg.add(ab);
        jp.add(ab);
      }
      return jp;
    }
    public void init() {
      Container cp = getContentPane();
      cp.setLayout(new FlowLayout());
      cp.add(makeBPanel(JButton.class, ids));
      cp.add(makeBPanel(JToggleButton.class, ids));
      cp.add(makeBPanel(JCheckBox.class, ids));
      cp.add(makeBPanel(JRadioButton.class, ids));
    }
    public static void main(String[] args) {
      Console.run(new ButtonGroups(), 500, 300);
    }
  } ///:~
```

The title for the border is taken from the name of the class, stripping off all the path information. The **AbstractButton** is initialized to a **JButton** that has the label "Failed," so if you ignore the exception message, you'll still see the problem on screen. The **getConstructor( )** method produces a **Constructor** object that takes the array of arguments of the types in the

Class array passed to **getConstructor( )**. Then all you do is call **newInstance( )**, passing it an array of **Object** containing your actual arguments—in this case, just the **String** from the **ids** array.

This adds a little complexity to what is a simple process. To get "exclusive or" behavior with buttons, you create a button group and add each button for which you want that behavior to the group. When you run the program, you'll see that all the buttons except **JButton** exhibit this "exclusive or" behavior.

Icons

You can use an **Icon** inside a **JLabel** or anything that inherits from **AbstractButton** (including **JButton**, **JCheckBox**, **JRadioButton,** and the different kinds of **JMenuItem**). Using **Icon**s with **JLabel**s is quite straightforward (you'll see an example later). The following example explores all the additional ways you can use **Icon**s with buttons and their descendants.

You can use any **gif** files you want, but the ones used in this example are part of this book's code distribution, available at *www.BruceEckel.com*. To open a file and bring in the image, simply create an **ImageIcon** and hand it the file name. From then on, you can use the resulting **Icon** in your program.

```
//: c14:Faces.java
// Icon behavior in Jbuttons.
// <applet code=Faces width=400 height=100></applet>
import javax.swing.*;
import java.awt.*;
import java.awt.event.*;
import java.io.*;
import com.bruceeckel.swing.*;

public class Faces extends JApplet {
  private static Icon[] faces;
  private JButton jb, jb2 = new JButton("Disable");
  private boolean mad = false;
  public void init() {
    faces = new Icon[] {
      new ImageIcon(getClass().getResource("Face0.gif")),
      new ImageIcon(getClass().getResource("Face1.gif")),
      new ImageIcon(getClass().getResource("Face2.gif")),
      new ImageIcon(getClass().getResource("Face3.gif")),
      new ImageIcon(getClass().getResource("Face4.gif")),
```

```
    };
    jb = new JButton("JButton", faces[3]);
    Container cp = getContentPane();
    cp.setLayout(new FlowLayout());
    jb.addActionListener(new ActionListener() {
      public void actionPerformed(ActionEvent e) {
        if(mad) {
          jb.setIcon(faces[3]);
          mad = false;
        } else {
          jb.setIcon(faces[0]);
          mad = true;
        }
        jb.setVerticalAlignment(JButton.TOP);
        jb.setHorizontalAlignment(JButton.LEFT);
      }
    });
    jb.setRolloverEnabled(true);
    jb.setRolloverIcon(faces[1]);
    jb.setPressedIcon(faces[2]);
    jb.setDisabledIcon(faces[4]);
    jb.setToolTipText("Yow!");
    cp.add(jb);
    jb2.addActionListener(new ActionListener() {
      public void actionPerformed(ActionEvent e) {
        if(jb.isEnabled()) {
          jb.setEnabled(false);
          jb2.setText("Enable");
        } else {
          jb.setEnabled(true);
          jb2.setText("Disable");
        }
      }
    });
    cp.add(jb2);
  }
  public static void main(String[] args) {
    Console.run(new Faces(), 400, 200);
  }
} ///:~
```

An **Icon** can be used as an argument for many different Swing component constructors, but you can also use **setIcon( )** to add or change an **Icon**. This example also shows how a **JButton** (or any **AbstractButton**) can set the various different sorts of icons that appear when things happen to that button: when it's pressed, disabled, or "rolled over" (the mouse moves over it without clicking). You'll see that this gives the button a nice animated feel.

Tool tips

The previous example added a "tool tip" to the button. Almost all of the classes that you'll be using to create your user interfaces are derived from **JComponent**, which contains a method called **setToolTipText(String)**. So, for virtually anything you place on your form, all you need to do is say (for an object **jc** of any **JComponent**-derived class):

```
jc.setToolTipText("My tip");
```

and when the mouse stays over that **JComponent** for a predetermined period of time, a tiny box containing your text will pop up next to the mouse.

Text fields

This example shows the extra behavior that **JTextField**s are capable of:

```
//: c14:TextFields.java
// Text fields and Java events.
// <applet code=TextFields width=375 height=125></applet>
import javax.swing.*;
import javax.swing.event.*;
import javax.swing.text.*;
import java.awt.*;
import java.awt.event.*;
import com.bruceeckel.swing.*;

public class TextFields extends JApplet {
  private JButton
    b1 = new JButton("Get Text"),
    b2 = new JButton("Set Text");
  private JTextField
    t1 = new JTextField(30),
    t2 = new JTextField(30),
    t3 = new JTextField(30);
  private String s = new String();
  private UpperCaseDocument ucd = new UpperCaseDocument();
  public void init() {
    t1.setDocument(ucd);
    ucd.addDocumentListener(new T1());
```

```
    b1.addActionListener(new B1());
    b2.addActionListener(new B2());
    DocumentListener dl = new T1();
    t1.addActionListener(new T1A());
    Container cp = getContentPane();
    cp.setLayout(new FlowLayout());
    cp.add(b1);
    cp.add(b2);
    cp.add(t1);
    cp.add(t2);
    cp.add(t3);
  }
  class T1 implements DocumentListener {
    public void changedUpdate(DocumentEvent e) {}
    public void insertUpdate(DocumentEvent e) {
      t2.setText(t1.getText());
      t3.setText("Text: "+ t1.getText());
    }
    public void removeUpdate(DocumentEvent e) {
      t2.setText(t1.getText());
    }
  }
  class T1A implements ActionListener {
    private int count = 0;
    public void actionPerformed(ActionEvent e) {
      t3.setText("t1 Action Event " + count++);
    }
  }
  class B1 implements ActionListener {
    public void actionPerformed(ActionEvent e) {
      if(t1.getSelectedText() == null)
        s = t1.getText();
      else
        s = t1.getSelectedText();
      t1.setEditable(true);
    }
  }
  class B2 implements ActionListener {
    public void actionPerformed(ActionEvent e) {
      ucd.setUpperCase(false);
      t1.setText("Inserted by Button 2: " + s);
      ucd.setUpperCase(true);
      t1.setEditable(false);
    }
```

```
  }
  public static void main(String[] args) {
    Console.run(new TextFields(), 375, 125);
  }
}

class UpperCaseDocument extends PlainDocument {
  private boolean upperCase = true;
  public void setUpperCase(boolean flag) {
    upperCase = flag;
  }
  public void
  insertString(int offset, String str, AttributeSet attSet)
  throws BadLocationException {
    if(upperCase) str = str.toUpperCase();
    super.insertString(offset, str, attSet);
  }
} ///:~
```

The **JTextField t3** is included as a place to report when the action listener for the **JTextField t1** is fired. You'll see that the action listener for a **JTextField** is fired only when you press the "enter" key.

The **JTextField t1** has several listeners attached to it. The **T1** listener is a **DocumentListener** that responds to any change in the "document" (the contents of the **JTextField**, in this case). It automatically copies all text from **t1** into **t2**. In addition, **t1**'s document is set to a derived class of **PlainDocument**, called **UpperCaseDocument**, which forces all characters to uppercase. It automatically detects backspaces and performs the deletion, adjusting the caret and handling everything as you would expect.

Borders

JComponent contains a method called **setBorder( )**, which allows you to place various interesting borders on any visible component. The following example demonstrates a number of the different borders that are available, using a method called **showBorder( )** that creates a **JPanel** and puts on the border in each case. Also, it uses RTTI to find the name of the border that you're using (stripping off all the path information), then puts that name in a **JLabel** in the middle of the panel:

```
//: c14:Borders.java
```

```java
// Different Swing borders.
// <applet code=Borders width=500 height=300></applet>
import javax.swing.*;
import java.awt.*;
import java.awt.event.*;
import javax.swing.border.*;
import com.bruceeckel.swing.*;

public class Borders extends JApplet {
  static JPanel showBorder(Border b) {
    JPanel jp = new JPanel();
    jp.setLayout(new BorderLayout());
    String nm = b.getClass().toString();
    nm = nm.substring(nm.lastIndexOf('.') + 1);
    jp.add(new JLabel(nm, JLabel.CENTER),
      BorderLayout.CENTER);
    jp.setBorder(b);
    return jp;
  }
  public void init() {
    Container cp = getContentPane();
    cp.setLayout(new GridLayout(2,4));
    cp.add(showBorder(new TitledBorder("Title")));
    cp.add(showBorder(new EtchedBorder()));
    cp.add(showBorder(new LineBorder(Color.BLUE)));
    cp.add(showBorder(
      new MatteBorder(5,5,30,30,Color.GREEN)));
    cp.add(showBorder(
      new BevelBorder(BevelBorder.RAISED)));
    cp.add(showBorder(
      new SoftBevelBorder(BevelBorder.LOWERED)));
    cp.add(showBorder(new CompoundBorder(
      new EtchedBorder(),
      new LineBorder(Color.RED))));
  }
  public static void main(String[] args) {
    Console.run(new Borders(), 500, 300);
  }
} ///:~
```

You can also create your own borders and put them inside buttons, labels, etc.—anything derived from **JComponent**.

JScrollPanes

Most of the time you'll just want to let a **JScrollPane** do its job, but you can also control which scroll bars are allowed—vertical, horizontal, both, or neither:

```
//: c14:JScrollPanes.java
// Controlling the scrollbars in a JScrollPane.
// <applet code=JScrollPanes width=300 height=725></applet>
import javax.swing.*;
import java.awt.*;
import java.awt.event.*;
import javax.swing.border.*;
import com.bruceeckel.swing.*;

public class JScrollPanes extends JApplet {
  private JButton
    b1 = new JButton("Text Area 1"),
    b2 = new JButton("Text Area 2"),
    b3 = new JButton("Replace Text"),
    b4 = new JButton("Insert Text");
  private JTextArea
    t1 = new JTextArea("t1", 1, 20),
    t2 = new JTextArea("t2", 4, 20),
    t3 = new JTextArea("t3", 1, 20),
    t4 = new JTextArea("t4", 10, 10),
    t5 = new JTextArea("t5", 4, 20),
    t6 = new JTextArea("t6", 10, 10);
  private JScrollPane
    sp3 = new JScrollPane(t3,
      JScrollPane.VERTICAL_SCROLLBAR_NEVER,
      JScrollPane.HORIZONTAL_SCROLLBAR_NEVER),
    sp4 = new JScrollPane(t4,
      JScrollPane.VERTICAL_SCROLLBAR_ALWAYS,
      JScrollPane.HORIZONTAL_SCROLLBAR_NEVER),
    sp5 = new JScrollPane(t5,
      JScrollPane.VERTICAL_SCROLLBAR_NEVER,
      JScrollPane.HORIZONTAL_SCROLLBAR_ALWAYS),
    sp6 = new JScrollPane(t6,
      JScrollPane.VERTICAL_SCROLLBAR_ALWAYS,
      JScrollPane.HORIZONTAL_SCROLLBAR_ALWAYS);
  class B1L implements ActionListener {
    public void actionPerformed(ActionEvent e) {
      t5.append(t1.getText() + "\n");
```

```
    }
  }
  class B2L implements ActionListener {
    public void actionPerformed(ActionEvent e) {
      t2.setText("Inserted by Button 2");
      t2.append(": " + t1.getText());
      t5.append(t2.getText() + "\n");
    }
  }
  class B3L implements ActionListener {
    public void actionPerformed(ActionEvent e) {
      String s = " Replacement ";
      t2.replaceRange(s, 3, 3 + s.length());
    }
  }
  class B4L implements ActionListener {
    public void actionPerformed(ActionEvent e) {
      t2.insert(" Inserted ", 10);
    }
  }
  public void init() {
    Container cp = getContentPane();
    cp.setLayout(new FlowLayout());
    // Create Borders for components:
    Border brd = BorderFactory.createMatteBorder(
      1, 1, 1, 1, Color.BLACK);
    t1.setBorder(brd);
    t2.setBorder(brd);
    sp3.setBorder(brd);
    sp4.setBorder(brd);
    sp5.setBorder(brd);
    sp6.setBorder(brd);
    // Initialize listeners and add components:
    b1.addActionListener(new B1L());
    cp.add(b1);
    cp.add(t1);
    b2.addActionListener(new B2L());
    cp.add(b2);
    cp.add(t2);
    b3.addActionListener(new B3L());
    cp.add(b3);
    b4.addActionListener(new B4L());
    cp.add(b4);
    cp.add(sp3);
```

```
    cp.add(sp4);
    cp.add(sp5);
    cp.add(sp6);
  }
  public static void main(String[] args) {
    Console.run(new JScrollPanes(), 300, 725);
  }
} ///:~
```

Using different arguments in the **JScrollPane** constructor controls the scrollbars that are available. This example also dresses things up a bit using borders.

A mini-editor

The **JTextPane** control provides a great deal of support for editing, without much effort. The following example makes very simple use of this component, ignoring the bulk of the functionality of the class:

```
//: c14:TextPane.java
// The JTextPane control is a little editor.
import javax.swing.*;
import java.awt.*;
import java.awt.event.*;
import com.bruceeckel.swing.*;
import com.bruceeckel.util.*;

public class TextPane extends JFrame {
  private JButton b = new JButton("Add Text");
  private JTextPane tp = new JTextPane();
  private static Generator sg =
    new Arrays2.RandStringGenerator(7);
  public TextPane() {
    b.addActionListener(new ActionListener() {
      public void actionPerformed(ActionEvent e) {
        for(int i = 1; i < 10; i++)
          tp.setText(tp.getText() + sg.next() + "\n");
      }
    });
    Container cp = getContentPane();
    cp.add(new JScrollPane(tp));
    cp.add(BorderLayout.SOUTH, b);
  }
  public static void main(String[] args) {
```

```
    Console.run(new TextPane(), 475, 425);
  }
} ///:~
```

The button just adds randomly generated text. The intent of the **JTextPane** is to allow text to be edited in place, so you will see that there is no **append( )** method. In this case (admittedly, a poor use of the capabilities of **JTextPane**), the text must be captured, modified, and placed back into the pane using **setText( )**.

As mentioned before, the default layout behavior of an applet is to use the **BorderLayout**. If you add something to the pane without specifying any details, it just fills the center of the pane out to the edges. However, if you specify one of the surrounding regions (NORTH, SOUTH, EAST, or WEST) as is done here, the component will fit itself into that region; in this case, the button will nest down at the bottom of the screen.

Notice the built-in features of **JTextPane**, such as automatic line wrapping. There are lots of other features that you can look up using the JDK documentation.

Check boxes

A check box provides a way to make a single on/off choice. It consists of a tiny box and a label. The box typically holds a little "x" (or some other indication that it is set) or is empty, depending on whether that item was selected.

You'll normally create a **JCheckBox** using a constructor that takes the label as an argument. You can get and set the state, and also get and set the label if you want to read or change it after the **JCheckBox** has been created.

Whenever a **JCheckBox** is set or cleared, an event occurs, which you can capture the same way you do a button: by using an **ActionListener**. The following example uses a **JTextArea** to enumerate all the check boxes that have been checked:

```
//: c14:CheckBoxes.java
// Using JCheckBoxes.
// <applet code=CheckBoxes width=200 height=200></applet>
import javax.swing.*;
import java.awt.event.*;
import java.awt.*;
import com.bruceeckel.swing.*;
```

```java
public class CheckBoxes extends JApplet {
  private JTextArea t = new JTextArea(6, 15);
  private JCheckBox
    cb1 = new JCheckBox("Check Box 1"),
    cb2 = new JCheckBox("Check Box 2"),
    cb3 = new JCheckBox("Check Box 3");
  public void init() {
    cb1.addActionListener(new ActionListener() {
      public void actionPerformed(ActionEvent e) {
        trace("1", cb1);
      }
    });
    cb2.addActionListener(new ActionListener() {
      public void actionPerformed(ActionEvent e) {
        trace("2", cb2);
      }
    });
    cb3.addActionListener(new ActionListener() {
      public void actionPerformed(ActionEvent e) {
        trace("3", cb3);
      }
    });
    Container cp = getContentPane();
    cp.setLayout(new FlowLayout());
    cp.add(new JScrollPane(t));
    cp.add(cb1);
    cp.add(cb2);
    cp.add(cb3);
  }
  private void trace(String b, JCheckBox cb) {
    if(cb.isSelected())
      t.append("Box " + b + " Set\n");
    else
      t.append("Box " + b + " Cleared\n");
  }
  public static void main(String[] args) {
    Console.run(new CheckBoxes(), 200, 200);
  }
} ///:~
```

The **trace( )** method sends the name of the selected **JCheckBox** and its current state to the **JTextArea** using **append( )**, so you'll see a cumulative list of the checkboxes that were selected and what their state is.

Radio buttons

The concept of a radio button in GUI programming comes from pre-electronic car radios with mechanical buttons; when you push one in, any other button that was pressed pops out. Thus, it allows you to force a single choice among many.

All you need to do to set up an associated group of **JRadioButton**s is to add them to a **ButtonGroup** (you can have any number of **ButtonGroup**s on a form). One of the buttons can optionally have its starting state set to **true** (using the second argument in the constructor). If you try to set more than one radio button to **true**, then only the final one set will be **true**.

Here's a simple example of the use of radio buttons. Note that you capture radio button events like all others:

```
//: c14:RadioButtons.java
// Using JRadioButtons.
// <applet code=RadioButtons width=200 height=100></applet>
import javax.swing.*;
import java.awt.event.*;
import java.awt.*;
import com.bruceeckel.swing.*;

public class RadioButtons extends JApplet {
  private JTextField t = new JTextField(15);
  private ButtonGroup g = new ButtonGroup();
  private JRadioButton
    rb1 = new JRadioButton("one", false),
    rb2 = new JRadioButton("two", false),
    rb3 = new JRadioButton("three", false);
  private ActionListener al = new ActionListener() {
    public void actionPerformed(ActionEvent e) {
      t.setText("Radio button " +
        ((JRadioButton)e.getSource()).getText());
    }
  };
  public void init() {
    rb1.addActionListener(al);
    rb2.addActionListener(al);
    rb3.addActionListener(al);
    g.add(rb1); g.add(rb2); g.add(rb3);
    t.setEditable(false);
    Container cp = getContentPane();
```

```
    cp.setLayout(new FlowLayout());
    cp.add(t);
    cp.add(rb1);
    cp.add(rb2);
    cp.add(rb3);
  }
  public static void main(String[] args) {
    Console.run(new RadioButtons(), 200, 100);
  }
} ///:~
```

To display the state, a text field is used. This field is set to non-editable because it's used only to display data, not to collect it. Thus it is an alternative to using a **JLabel**.

Combo boxes (drop-down lists)

Like a group of radio buttons, a drop-down list is a way to force the user to select only one element from a group of possibilities. However, it's a more compact way to accomplish this, and it's easier to change the elements of the list without surprising the user. (You can change radio buttons dynamically, but that tends to be visibly jarring).

By default, **JComboBox** box is not like the combo box in Windows, which lets you select from a list *or* type in your own selection. To produce this behavior you must call **setEditable( )**. With a **JComboBox** box, you choose one and only one element from the list. In the following example, the **JComboBox** box starts with a certain number of entries, and then new entries are added to the box when a button is pressed.

```
//: c14:ComboBoxes.java
// Using drop-down lists.
// <applet code=ComboBoxes width=200 height=125></applet>
import javax.swing.*;
import java.awt.event.*;
import java.awt.*;
import com.bruceeckel.swing.*;

public class ComboBoxes extends JApplet {
  private String[] description = {
    "Ebullient", "Obtuse", "Recalcitrant", "Brilliant",
    "Somnescent", "Timorous", "Florid", "Putrescent"
  };
  private JTextField t = new JTextField(15);
```

```
  private JComboBox c = new JComboBox();
  private JButton b = new JButton("Add items");
  private int count = 0;
  public void init() {
    for(int i = 0; i < 4; i++)
      c.addItem(description[count++]);
    t.setEditable(false);
    b.addActionListener(new ActionListener() {
      public void actionPerformed(ActionEvent e) {
        if(count < description.length)
          c.addItem(description[count++]);
      }
    });
    c.addActionListener(new ActionListener() {
      public void actionPerformed(ActionEvent e) {
        t.setText("index: "+ c.getSelectedIndex() + "   " +
         ((JComboBox)e.getSource()).getSelectedItem());
      }
    });
    Container cp = getContentPane();
    cp.setLayout(new FlowLayout());
    cp.add(t);
    cp.add(c);
    cp.add(b);
  }
  public static void main(String[] args) {
    Console.run(new ComboBoxes(), 200, 125);
  }
} ///:~
```

The **JTextField** displays the "selected index," which is the sequence number of the currently selected element, as well as the text of the selected item in the combo box.

List boxes

List boxes are significantly different from **JComboBox** boxes, and not just in appearance. While a **JComboBox** box drops down when you activate it, a **JList** occupies some fixed number of lines on a screen all the time and doesn't change. If you want to see the items in a list, you simply call **getSelectedValues( ),** which produces an array of **String** of the items that have been selected.

A **JList** allows multiple selection; if you control-click on more than one item (holding down the "control" key while performing additional mouse clicks), the original item stays highlighted and you can select as many as you want. If you select an item, then shift-click on another item, all the items in the span between the two are selected. To remove an item from a group, you can control-click it.

```
//: c14:List.java
// <applet code=List width=250 height=375></applet>
import javax.swing.*;
import javax.swing.event.*;
import java.awt.*;
import java.awt.event.*;
import javax.swing.border.*;
import com.bruceeckel.swing.*;

public class List extends JApplet {
  private String[] flavors = {
    "Chocolate", "Strawberry", "Vanilla Fudge Swirl",
    "Mint Chip", "Mocha Almond Fudge", "Rum Raisin",
    "Praline Cream", "Mud Pie"
  };
  private DefaultListModel lItems=new DefaultListModel();
  private JList lst = new JList(lItems);
  private JTextArea t =
    new JTextArea(flavors.length, 20);
  private JButton b = new JButton("Add Item");
  private ActionListener bl = new ActionListener() {
    public void actionPerformed(ActionEvent e) {
      if(count < flavors.length) {
        lItems.add(0, flavors[count++]);
      } else {
        // Disable, since there are no more
        // flavors left to be added to the List
        b.setEnabled(false);
      }
    }
  };
  private ListSelectionListener ll =
    new ListSelectionListener() {
      public void valueChanged(ListSelectionEvent e) {
        if(e.getValueIsAdjusting()) return;
        t.setText("");
        Object[] items=lst.getSelectedValues();
```

```
      for(int i = 0; i < items.length; i++)
        t.append(items[i] + "\n");
    }
  };
  private int count = 0;
  public void init() {
    Container cp = getContentPane();
    t.setEditable(false);
    cp.setLayout(new FlowLayout());
    // Create Borders for components:
    Border brd = BorderFactory.createMatteBorder(
      1, 1, 2, 2, Color.BLACK);
    lst.setBorder(brd);
    t.setBorder(brd);
    // Add the first four items to the List
    for(int i = 0; i < 4; i++)
      lItems.addElement(flavors[count++]);
    // Add items to the Content Pane for Display
    cp.add(t);
    cp.add(lst);
    cp.add(b);
    // Register event listeners
    lst.addListSelectionListener(ll);
    b.addActionListener(bl);
  }
  public static void main(String[] args) {
    Console.run(new List(), 250, 375);
  }
} ///:~
```

You can see that borders have also been added to the lists.

If you just want to put an array of **Strings** into a **JList**, there's a much simpler solution; you pass the array to the **JList** constructor, and it builds the list automatically. The only reason for using the "list model" in the preceding example is so that the list could be manipulated during the execution of the program.

JLists do not automatically provide direct support for scrolling. Of course, all you need to do is wrap the **JList** in a **JScrollPane**, and the details are automatically managed for you.

Tabbed panes

The **JTabbedPane** allows you to create a "tabbed dialog," which has file-folder tabs running across one edge, and all you have to do is press a tab to bring forward a different dialog.

```
//: c14:TabbedPane1.java
// Demonstrates the Tabbed Pane.
// <applet code=TabbedPane1 width=350 height=200></applet>
import javax.swing.*;
import javax.swing.event.*;
import java.awt.*;
import com.bruceeckel.swing.*;

public class TabbedPane1 extends JApplet {
  private String[] flavors = {
    "Chocolate", "Strawberry", "Vanilla Fudge Swirl",
    "Mint Chip", "Mocha Almond Fudge", "Rum Raisin",
    "Praline Cream", "Mud Pie"
  };
  private JTabbedPane tabs = new JTabbedPane();
  private JTextField txt = new JTextField(20);
  public void init() {
    for(int i = 0; i < flavors.length; i++)
      tabs.addTab(flavors[i],
        new JButton("Tabbed pane " + i));
    tabs.addChangeListener(new ChangeListener() {
      public void stateChanged(ChangeEvent e) {
        txt.setText("Tab selected: " +
          tabs.getSelectedIndex());
      }
    });
    Container cp = getContentPane();
    cp.add(BorderLayout.SOUTH, txt);
    cp.add(tabs);
  }
  public static void main(String[] args) {
    Console.run(new TabbedPane1(), 350, 200);
  }
} ///:~
```

In Java, the use of some sort of "tabbed panel" mechanism is quite important, because in applet programming the use of pop-up dialogs is discouraged by automatically adding a little warning to any dialog that pops up out of an applet.

When you run the program, you'll see that the **JTabbedPane** automatically stacks the tabs if there are too many of them to fit on one row. You can see this by resizing the window when you run the program from the console command line.

Message boxes

Windowing environments commonly contain a standard set of message boxes that allow you to quickly post information to the user or to capture information from the user. In Swing, these message boxes are contained in **JOptionPane**. You have many different possibilities (some quite sophisticated), but the ones you'll most commonly use are probably the message dialog and confirmation dialog, invoked using the **static JOptionPane.showMessageDialog( )** and **JOptionPane.showConfirmDialog( )**. The following example shows a subset of the message boxes available with **JOptionPane**:

```
//: c14:MessageBoxes.java
// Demonstrates JoptionPane.
// <applet code=MessageBoxes width=200 height=150></applet>
import javax.swing.*;
import java.awt.event.*;
import java.awt.*;
import com.bruceeckel.swing.*;

public class MessageBoxes extends JApplet {
  private JButton[] b = {
    new JButton("Alert"), new JButton("Yes/No"),
    new JButton("Color"), new JButton("Input"),
    new JButton("3 Vals")
  };
  private JTextField txt = new JTextField(15);
  private ActionListener al = new ActionListener() {
    public void actionPerformed(ActionEvent e) {
      String id = ((JButton)e.getSource()).getText();
      if(id.equals("Alert"))
        JOptionPane.showMessageDialog(null,
          "There's a bug on you!", "Hey!",
          JOptionPane.ERROR_MESSAGE);
      else if(id.equals("Yes/No"))
```

```
        JOptionPane.showConfirmDialog(null,
          "or no", "choose yes",
          JOptionPane.YES_NO_OPTION);
      else if(id.equals("Color")) {
        Object[] options = { "Red", "Green" };
        int sel = JOptionPane.showOptionDialog(
          null, "Choose a Color!", "Warning",
          JOptionPane.DEFAULT_OPTION,
          JOptionPane.WARNING_MESSAGE, null,
          options, options[0]);
        if(sel != JOptionPane.CLOSED_OPTION)
          txt.setText("Color Selected: " + options[sel]);
      } else if(id.equals("Input")) {
        String val = JOptionPane.showInputDialog(
            "How many fingers do you see?");
        txt.setText(val);
      } else if(id.equals("3 Vals")) {
        Object[] selections = {"First", "Second", "Third"};
        Object val = JOptionPane.showInputDialog(
          null, "Choose one", "Input",
          JOptionPane.INFORMATION_MESSAGE,
          null, selections, selections[0]);
        if(val != null)
          txt.setText(val.toString());
      }
    }
  };
  public void init() {
    Container cp = getContentPane();
    cp.setLayout(new FlowLayout());
    for(int i = 0; i < b.length; i++) {
      b[i].addActionListener(al);
      cp.add(b[i]);
    }
    cp.add(txt);
  }
  public static void main(String[] args) {
    Console.run(new MessageBoxes(), 200, 200);
  }
} ///:~
```

To be able to write a single **ActionListener**, I've used the somewhat risky approach of checking the **String** labels on the buttons. The problem with this is that it's easy to get the label a little bit wrong, typically in capitalization, and this bug can be hard to spot.

Note that **showOptionDialog( )** and **showInputDialog( )** provide return objects that contain the value entered by the user.

Menus

Each component capable of holding a menu, including **JApplet**, **JFrame**, **JDialog**, and their descendants, has a **setJMenuBar( )** method that accepts a **JMenuBar** (you can have only one **JMenuBar** on a particular component). You add **JMenu**s to the **JMenuBar**, and **JMenuItem**s to the **JMenu**s. Each **JMenuItem** can have an **ActionListener** attached to it, to be fired when that menu item is selected.

Unlike a system that uses resources, with Java and Swing you must hand assemble all the menus in source code. Here is a very simple menu example:

```
//: c14:SimpleMenus.java
// <applet code=SimpleMenus width=200 height=75></applet>
import javax.swing.*;
import java.awt.event.*;
import java.awt.*;
import com.bruceeckel.swing.*;

public class SimpleMenus extends JApplet {
  private JTextField t = new JTextField(15);
  private ActionListener al = new ActionListener() {
    public void actionPerformed(ActionEvent e) {
      t.setText(((JMenuItem)e.getSource()).getText());
    }
  };
  private JMenu[] menus = {
    new JMenu("Winken"), new JMenu("Blinken"),
    new JMenu("Nod")
  };
  private JMenuItem[] items = {
    new JMenuItem("Fee"), new JMenuItem("Fi"),
    new JMenuItem("Fo"),  new JMenuItem("Zip"),
    new JMenuItem("Zap"), new JMenuItem("Zot"),
    new JMenuItem("Olly"), new JMenuItem("Oxen"),
    new JMenuItem("Free")
  };
  public void init() {
```

```
    for(int i = 0; i < items.length; i++) {
      items[i].addActionListener(al);
      menus[i % 3].add(items[i]);
    }
    JMenuBar mb = new JMenuBar();
    for(int i = 0; i < menus.length; i++)
      mb.add(menus[i]);
    setJMenuBar(mb);
    Container cp = getContentPane();
    cp.setLayout(new FlowLayout());
    cp.add(t);
  }
  public static void main(String[] args) {
    Console.run(new SimpleMenus(), 200, 75);
  }
} ///:~
```

The use of the modulus operator in "**i%3**" distributes the menu items among the three **JMenus**. Each **JMenuItem** must have an **ActionListener** attached to it; here, the same **ActionListener** is used everywhere, but you'll usually need an individual one for each **JMenuItem**.

JMenuItem inherits **AbstractButton**, so it has some button-like behaviors. By itself, it provides an item that can be placed on a drop-down menu. There are also three types inherited from **JMenuItem**: **JMenu** to hold other **JMenuItems** (so you can have cascading menus); **JCheckBoxMenuItem**, which produces a checkmark to indicate whether that menu item is selected; and **JRadioButtonMenuItem**, which contains a radio button.

As a more sophisticated example, here are the ice cream flavors again, used to create menus. This example also shows cascading menus, keyboard mnemonics, **JCheckBoxMenuItems**, and the way you can dynamically change menus:

```
//: c14:Menus.java
// Submenus, checkbox menu items, swapping menus,
// mnemonics (shortcuts) and action commands.
// <applet code=Menus width=300 height=100></applet>
import javax.swing.*;
import java.awt.*;
import java.awt.event.*;
import com.bruceeckel.swing.*;
```

```
public class Menus extends JApplet {
  private String[] flavors = {
    "Chocolate", "Strawberry", "Vanilla Fudge Swirl",
    "Mint Chip", "Mocha Almond Fudge", "Rum Raisin",
    "Praline Cream", "Mud Pie"
  };
  private JTextField t = new JTextField("No flavor", 30);
  private JMenuBar mb1 = new JMenuBar();
  private JMenu
    f = new JMenu("File"),
    m = new JMenu("Flavors"),
    s = new JMenu("Safety");
  // Alternative approach:
  private JCheckBoxMenuItem[] safety = {
    new JCheckBoxMenuItem("Guard"),
    new JCheckBoxMenuItem("Hide")
  };
  private JMenuItem[] file = { new JMenuItem("Open") };
  // A second menu bar to swap to:
  private JMenuBar mb2 = new JMenuBar();
  private JMenu fooBar = new JMenu("fooBar");
  private JMenuItem[] other = {
    // Adding a menu shortcut (mnemonic) is very
    // simple, but only JMenuItems can have them
    // in their constructors:
    new JMenuItem("Foo", KeyEvent.VK_F),
    new JMenuItem("Bar", KeyEvent.VK_A),
    // No shortcut:
    new JMenuItem("Baz"),
  };
  private JButton b = new JButton("Swap Menus");
  class BL implements ActionListener {
    public void actionPerformed(ActionEvent e) {
      JMenuBar m = getJMenuBar();
      setJMenuBar(m == mb1 ? mb2 : mb1);
      validate(); // Refresh the frame
    }
  }
  class ML implements ActionListener {
    public void actionPerformed(ActionEvent e) {
      JMenuItem target = (JMenuItem)e.getSource();
      String actionCommand = target.getActionCommand();
      if(actionCommand.equals("Open")) {
        String s = t.getText();
```

```
      boolean chosen = false;
      for(int i = 0; i < flavors.length; i++)
        if(s.equals(flavors[i])) chosen = true;
      if(!chosen)
        t.setText("Choose a flavor first!");
      else
        t.setText("Opening " + s + ". Mmm, mm!");
    }
  }
}
class FL implements ActionListener {
  public void actionPerformed(ActionEvent e) {
    JMenuItem target = (JMenuItem)e.getSource();
    t.setText(target.getText());
  }
}
// Alternatively, you can create a different
// class for each different MenuItem. Then you
// Don't have to figure out which one it is:
class FooL implements ActionListener {
  public void actionPerformed(ActionEvent e) {
    t.setText("Foo selected");
  }
}
class BarL implements ActionListener {
  public void actionPerformed(ActionEvent e) {
    t.setText("Bar selected");
  }
}
class BazL implements ActionListener {
  public void actionPerformed(ActionEvent e) {
    t.setText("Baz selected");
  }
}
class CMIL implements ItemListener {
  public void itemStateChanged(ItemEvent e) {
    JCheckBoxMenuItem target =
      (JCheckBoxMenuItem)e.getSource();
    String actionCommand = target.getActionCommand();
    if(actionCommand.equals("Guard"))
      t.setText("Guard the Ice Cream! " +
        "Guarding is " + target.getState());
    else if(actionCommand.equals("Hide"))
      t.setText("Hide the Ice Cream! " +
```

```
        "Is it hidden? " + target.getState());
    }
  }
  public void init() {
    ML ml = new ML();
    CMIL cmil = new CMIL();
    safety[0].setActionCommand("Guard");
    safety[0].setMnemonic(KeyEvent.VK_G);
    safety[0].addItemListener(cmil);
    safety[1].setActionCommand("Hide");
    safety[1].setMnemonic(KeyEvent.VK_H);
    safety[1].addItemListener(cmil);
    other[0].addActionListener(new FooL());
    other[1].addActionListener(new BarL());
    other[2].addActionListener(new BazL());
    FL fl = new FL();
    for(int i = 0; i < flavors.length; i++) {
      JMenuItem mi = new JMenuItem(flavors[i]);
      mi.addActionListener(fl);
      m.add(mi);
      // Add separators at intervals:
      if((i + 1) % 3 == 0)
        m.addSeparator();
    }
    for(int i = 0; i < safety.length; i++)
      s.add(safety[i]);
    s.setMnemonic(KeyEvent.VK_A);
    f.add(s);
    f.setMnemonic(KeyEvent.VK_F);
    for(int i = 0; i < file.length; i++) {
      file[i].addActionListener(fl);
      f.add(file[i]);
    }
    mb1.add(f);
    mb1.add(m);
    setJMenuBar(mb1);
    t.setEditable(false);
    Container cp = getContentPane();
    cp.add(t, BorderLayout.CENTER);
    // Set up the system for swapping menus:
    b.addActionListener(new BL());
    b.setMnemonic(KeyEvent.VK_S);
    cp.add(b, BorderLayout.NORTH);
    for(int i = 0; i < other.length; i++)
```

```
      fooBar.add(other[i]);
    fooBar.setMnemonic(KeyEvent.VK_B);
    mb2.add(fooBar);
  }
  public static void main(String[] args) {
    Console.run(new Menus(), 300, 100);
  }
} ///:~
```

In this program I placed the menu items into arrays and then stepped through each array calling **add( )** for each **JMenuItem**. This makes adding or subtracting a menu item somewhat less tedious.

This program creates not one but two **JMenuBar**s to demonstrate that menu bars can be actively swapped while the program is running. You can see how a **JMenuBar** is made up of **JMenus**, and each **JMenu** is made up of **JMenuItems**, **JCheckBoxMenuItem**s, or even other **JMenu**s (which produce submenus). When a **JMenuBar** is assembled, it can be installed into the current program with the **setJMenuBar( )** method. Note that when the button is pressed, it checks to see which menu is currently installed by calling **getJMenuBar( )**, then it puts the other menu bar in its place.

When testing for "Open," notice that spelling and capitalization are critical, but Java signals no error if there is no match with "Open." This kind of string comparison is a source of programming errors.

The checking and unchecking of the menu items is taken care of automatically. The code handling the **JCheckBoxMenuItem**s shows two different ways to determine what was checked: string matching (which, as mentioned above, isn't a very safe approach although you'll see it used) and matching on the event target object. As shown, the **getState( )** method can be used to reveal the state. You can also change the state of a **JCheckBoxMenuItem** with **setState( )**.

The events for menus are a bit inconsistent and can lead to confusion: **JMenuItem**s use **ActionListener**s, but **JCheckBoxMenuItem**s use **ItemListener**s. The **JMenu** objects can also support **ActionListener**s, but that's not usually helpful. In general, you'll attach listeners to each **JMenuItem**, **JCheckBoxMenuItem**, or **JRadioButtonMenuItem**, but the example shows **ItemListener**s and **ActionListener**s attached to the various menu components.

Swing supports mnemonics, or "keyboard shortcuts," so you can select anything derived from **AbstractButton** (button, menu item, etc.) by using the keyboard instead of the mouse. These are quite simple; for **JmenuItem**,you can use the overloaded constructor that takes as a second argument the identifier for the key. However, most **AbstractButton**s do not have constructors like this, so the more general way to solve the problem is to use the **setMnemonic( )** method. The preceding example adds mnemonics to the button and some of the menu items; shortcut indicators automatically appear on the components.

You can also see the use of **setActionCommand( )**. This seems a bit strange because in each case, the "action command" is exactly the same as the label on the menu component. Why not just use the label instead of this alternative string? The problem is internationalization. If you retarget this program to another language, you want to change only the label in the menu, and not change the code (which would no doubt introduce new errors). So to make this easy for code that checks the text string associated with a menu component, the "action command" can be immutable, but the menu label can change. All the code works with the "action command," so it's unaffected by changes to the menu labels. Note that in this program, not all the menu components are examined for their action commands, so those that aren't do not have their action command set.

The bulk of the work happens in the listeners. **BL** performs the **JMenuBar** swapping. In **ML**, the "figure out who rang" approach is taken by getting the source of the **ActionEvent** and casting it to a **JMenuItem**, then getting the action command string to pass it through a cascaded **if** statement.

The **FL** listener is simple even though it's handling all the different flavors in the flavor menu. This approach is useful if you have enough simplicity in your logic, but in general, you'll want to take the approach used with **FooL**, **BarL**, and **BazL**, in which each is attached to only a single menu component, so no extra detection logic is necessary, and you know exactly who called the listener. Even with the profusion of classes generated this way, the code inside tends to be smaller, and the process is more foolproof.

You can see that menu code quickly gets long-winded and messy. This is another case where the use of a GUI builder is the appropriate solution. A good tool will also handle the maintenance of the menus.

Pop-up menus

The most straightforward way to implement a **JPopupMenu** is to create an inner class that extends **MouseAdapter**, then add an object of that inner class to each component that you want to produce pop-up behavior:

```
//: c14:Popup.java
// Creating popup menus with Swing.
// <applet code=Popup width=300 height=200></applet>
import javax.swing.*;
import java.awt.*;
import java.awt.event.*;
import com.bruceeckel.swing.*;

public class Popup extends JApplet {
  private JPopupMenu popup = new JPopupMenu();
  private JTextField t = new JTextField(10);
  public void init() {
    Container cp = getContentPane();
    cp.setLayout(new FlowLayout());
    cp.add(t);
    ActionListener al = new ActionListener() {
      public void actionPerformed(ActionEvent e) {
        t.setText(((JMenuItem)e.getSource()).getText());
      }
    };
    JMenuItem m = new JMenuItem("Hither");
    m.addActionListener(al);
    popup.add(m);
    m = new JMenuItem("Yon");
    m.addActionListener(al);
    popup.add(m);
    m = new JMenuItem("Afar");
    m.addActionListener(al);
    popup.add(m);
    popup.addSeparator();
    m = new JMenuItem("Stay Here");
    m.addActionListener(al);
    popup.add(m);
    PopupListener pl = new PopupListener();
    addMouseListener(pl);
    t.addMouseListener(pl);
  }
  class PopupListener extends MouseAdapter {
```

```
    public void mousePressed(MouseEvent e) {
      maybeShowPopup(e);
    }
    public void mouseReleased(MouseEvent e) {
      maybeShowPopup(e);
    }
    private void maybeShowPopup(MouseEvent e) {
      if(e.isPopupTrigger())
        popup.show(((JApplet)e.getComponent())
          .getContentPane(), e.getX(), e.getY());
    }
  }
  public static void main(String[] args) {
    Console.run(new Popup(), 300, 200);
  }
} ///:~
```

The same **ActionListener** is added to each **JMenuItem**, so that it fetches the text from the menu label and inserts it into the **JTextField**.

Drawing

In a good GUI framework, drawing should be reasonably easy—and it is, in the Swing library. The problem with any drawing example is that the calculations that determine where things go are typically a lot more complicated that the calls to the drawing routines, and these calculations are often mixed together with the drawing calls, so it can seem that the interface is more complicated than it actually is.

For simplicity, consider the problem of representing data on the screen—here, the data will be provided by the built-in **Math.sin( )** method, that produces a mathematical sine function. To make things a little more interesting, and to further demonstrate how easy it is to use Swing components, a slider will be placed at the bottom of the form to dynamically control the number of sine wave cycles that are displayed. In addition, if you resize the window, you'll see that the sine wave refits itself to the new window size.

Although any **JComponent** may be painted and thus used as a canvas, if you just want a straightforward drawing surface, you will typically inherit from a **JPanel**. The only method you need to override is **paintComponent( )**, which is called whenever that component must be repainted (you normally don't need to worry about this, because the decision is managed by Swing).

When it is called, Swing passes a **Graphics** object to the method, and you can then use this object to draw or paint on the surface.

In the following example, all the intelligence concerning painting is in the **SineDraw** class; the **SineWave** class simply configures the program and the slider control. Inside **SineDraw**, the **setCycles( )** method provides a hook to allow another object—the slider control, in this case—to control the number of cycles.

```
//: c14:SineWave.java
// Drawing with Swing, using a JSlider.
// <applet code=SineWave width=700 height=400></applet>
import javax.swing.*;
import javax.swing.event.*;
import java.awt.*;
import com.bruceeckel.swing.*;

class SineDraw extends JPanel {
  private static final int SCALEFACTOR = 200;
  private int cycles;
  private int points;
  private double[] sines;
  private int[] pts;
  public SineDraw() { setCycles(5); }
  public void setCycles(int newCycles) {
    cycles = newCycles;
    points = SCALEFACTOR * cycles * 2;
    sines = new double[points];
    for(int i = 0; i < points; i++) {
      double radians = (Math.PI/SCALEFACTOR) * i;
      sines[i] = Math.sin(radians);
    }
    repaint();
  }
  public void paintComponent(Graphics g) {
    super.paintComponent(g);
    int maxWidth = getWidth();
    double hstep = (double)maxWidth/(double)points;
    int maxHeight = getHeight();
    pts = new int[points];
    for(int i = 0; i < points; i++)
      pts[i] =
        (int)(sines[i] * maxHeight/2 * .95 + maxHeight/2);
    g.setColor(Color.RED);
```

```
    for(int i = 1; i < points; i++) {
      int x1 = (int)((i - 1) * hstep);
      int x2 = (int)(i * hstep);
      int y1 = pts[i-1];
      int y2 = pts[i];
      g.drawLine(x1, y1, x2, y2);
    }
  }
}

public class SineWave extends JApplet {
  private SineDraw sines = new SineDraw();
  private JSlider adjustCycles = new JSlider(1, 30, 5);
  public void init() {
    Container cp = getContentPane();
    cp.add(sines);
    adjustCycles.addChangeListener(new ChangeListener() {
      public void stateChanged(ChangeEvent e) {
        sines.setCycles(
          ((JSlider)e.getSource()).getValue());
      }
    });
    cp.add(BorderLayout.SOUTH, adjustCycles);
  }
  public static void main(String[] args) {
    Console.run(new SineWave(), 700, 400);
  }
} ///:~
```

All of the fields and arrays are used in the calculation of the sine wave points; **cycles** indicates the number of complete sine waves desired, **points** contains the total number of points that will be graphed, **sines** contains the sine function values, and **pts** contains the y-coordinates of the points that will be drawn on the **JPanel**. The **setCycles( )** method creates the arrays according to the number of points needed and fills the **sines** array with numbers. By calling **repaint( )**, **setCycles( )** forces **paintComponent( )** to be called so the rest of the calculation and redraw will take place.

The first thing you must do when you override **paintComponent( )** is to call the base-class version of the method. Then you are free to do whatever you like; normally, this means using the **Graphics** methods that you can find in the documentation for **java.awt.Graphics** (in the JDK documentation from *java.sun.com*) to draw and paint pixels onto the **JPanel**. Here, you can see that almost all the code is involved in performing the calculations; the only two method calls that actually manipulate the screen are **setColor( )** and **drawLine( )**. You will probably have a similar experience when creating your own program that displays graphical data; you'll spend most of your time figuring out what it is you want to draw, but the actual drawing process will be quite simple.

When I created this program, the bulk of my time was spent in getting the sine wave to display. Once I did that, I thought it would be nice to be able to dynamically change the number of cycles. My programming experiences when trying to do such things in other languages made me a bit reluctant to try this, but it turned out to be the easiest part of the project. I created a **JSlider** (the arguments are the left-most value of the **JSlider**, the right-most value, and the starting value, respectively, but there are other constructors as well) and dropped it into the **JApplet**. Then I looked at the JDK documentation and noticed that the only listener was the **addChangeListener**, which was triggered whenever the slider was changed enough for it to produce a different value. The only method for this was the obviously named **stateChanged( )**, which provided a **ChangeEvent** object so that I could look backward to the source of the change and find the new value. By calling the **sines** object's **setCycles( )**, the new value was incorporated and the **JPanel** redrawn.

In general, you will find that most of your Swing problems can be solved by following a similar process, and you'll find that it's generally quite simple, even if you haven't used a particular component before.

If your problem is more complex, there are other more sophisticated alternatives for drawing, including third-party JavaBeans components and the Java 2D API. These solutions are beyond the scope of this book, but you should look them up if your drawing code becomes too onerous.

Dialog Boxes

A dialog box is a window that pops up out of another window. Its purpose is to deal with some specific issue without cluttering the original window with those details. Dialog boxes are heavily used in windowed programming environments, but less frequently used in applets.

To create a dialog box, you inherit from **JDialog**, which is just another kind of **Window**, like a **JFrame**. A **JDialog** has a layout manager (which defaults to **BorderLayout**), and you add event listeners to deal with events. One significant difference when the dialog window is closed is that you don't want to shut down the application. Instead, you release the resources used by the dialog's window by calling **dispose( )**. Here's a very simple example:

```
//: c14:Dialogs.java
// Creating and using Dialog Boxes.
// <applet code=Dialogs width=125 height=75></applet>
import javax.swing.*;
import java.awt.event.*;
import java.awt.*;
import com.bruceeckel.swing.*;

class MyDialog extends JDialog {
  public MyDialog(JFrame parent) {
    super(parent, "My dialog", true);
    Container cp = getContentPane();
    cp.setLayout(new FlowLayout());
    cp.add(new JLabel("Here is my dialog"));
    JButton ok = new JButton("OK");
    ok.addActionListener(new ActionListener() {
      public void actionPerformed(ActionEvent e) {
        dispose(); // Closes the dialog
      }
    });
    cp.add(ok);
    setSize(150,125);
  }
}

public class Dialogs extends JApplet {
  private JButton b1 = new JButton("Dialog Box");
  private MyDialog dlg = new MyDialog(null);
  public void init() {
    b1.addActionListener(new ActionListener() {
      public void actionPerformed(ActionEvent e) {
        dlg.show();
      }
    });
    getContentPane().add(b1);
  }
  public static void main(String[] args) {
    Console.run(new Dialogs(), 125, 75);
  }
```

```
} ///:~
```

Once the **JDialog** is created, the **show( )** method must be called to display and activate it. For the dialog to close, it must call **dispose( )**.

You'll see that anything that pops up out of an applet, including dialog boxes, is "untrusted." That is, you get a warning in the window that's been popped up. This is because, in concept, it would be possible to fool users into thinking that they're dealing with a regular native application and to get them to type in their credit card number, which then goes across the Web. An applet is always attached to a Web page and visible within your Web browser, while a dialog box is detached—so theoretically, it's possible. As a result, it is not so common to see an applet that uses a dialog box.

The following example is more complex; the dialog box is made up of a grid (using **GridLayout**) of a special kind of button that is defined here as class **ToeButton**. This button draws a frame around itself and, depending on its state, a blank, an "x," or an "o" in the middle. It starts out blank, and then depending on whose turn it is, changes to an "x" or an "o." However, it will also flip back and forth between "x" and "o" when you click on the button. (This makes the tic-tac-toe concept only slightly more annoying than it already is.) In addition, the dialog box can be set up for any number of rows and columns by changing numbers in the main application window.

```
//: c14:TicTacToe.java
// Dialog boxes and creating your own components.
// <applet code=TicTacToe width=200 height=100></applet>
import javax.swing.*;
import java.awt.*;
import java.awt.event.*;
import com.bruceeckel.swing.*;

public class TicTacToe extends JApplet {
  private JTextField
    rows = new JTextField("3"),
    cols = new JTextField("3");
  private static final int BLANK = 0, XX = 1, OO = 2;
  class ToeDialog extends JDialog {
    private int turn = XX; // Start with x's turn
    ToeDialog(int cellsWide, int cellsHigh) {
      setTitle("The game itself");
      Container cp = getContentPane();
      cp.setLayout(new GridLayout(cellsWide, cellsHigh));
```

```
      for(int i = 0; i < cellsWide * cellsHigh; i++)
        cp.add(new ToeButton());
      setSize(cellsWide * 50, cellsHigh * 50);
      setDefaultCloseOperation(DISPOSE_ON_CLOSE);
    }
    class ToeButton extends JPanel {
      private int state = BLANK;
      public ToeButton() { addMouseListener(new ML()); }
      public void paintComponent(Graphics g) {
        super.paintComponent(g);
        int
          x1 = 0, y1 = 0,
          x2 = getSize().width - 1,
          y2 = getSize().height - 1;
        g.drawRect(x1, y1, x2, y2);
        x1 = x2/4;
        y1 = y2/4;
        int wide = x2/2, high = y2/2;
        if(state == XX) {
          g.drawLine(x1, y1, x1 + wide, y1 + high);
          g.drawLine(x1, y1 + high, x1 + wide, y1);
        }
        if(state == OO)
          g.drawOval(x1, y1, x1 + wide/2, y1 + high/2);
      }
      class ML extends MouseAdapter {
        public void mousePressed(MouseEvent e) {
          if(state == BLANK) {
            state = turn;
            turn = (turn == XX ? OO : XX);
          }
          else
            state = (state == XX ? OO : XX);
          repaint();
        }
      }
    }
  }
  class BL implements ActionListener {
    public void actionPerformed(ActionEvent e) {
      JDialog d = new ToeDialog(
        Integer.parseInt(rows.getText()),
        Integer.parseInt(cols.getText()));
      d.setVisible(true);
```

```
    }
  }
  public void init() {
    JPanel p = new JPanel();
    p.setLayout(new GridLayout(2,2));
    p.add(new JLabel("Rows", JLabel.CENTER));
    p.add(rows);
    p.add(new JLabel("Columns", JLabel.CENTER));
    p.add(cols);
    Container cp = getContentPane();
    cp.add(p, BorderLayout.NORTH);
    JButton b = new JButton("go");
    b.addActionListener(new BL());
    cp.add(b, BorderLayout.SOUTH);
  }
  public static void main(String[] args) {
    Console.run(new TicTacToe(), 200, 100);
  }
} ///:~
```

Because **static**s can only be at the outer level of the class, inner classes cannot have **static** data or nested classes.

The **paintComponent( )** method draws the square around the panel and the "x" or the "o." This is full of tedious calculations, but it's straightforward.

A mouse click is captured by the **MouseListener**, which first checks to see if the panel has anything written on it. If not, the parent window is queried to find out whose turn it is, which establishes the state of the **ToeButton**. Via the inner class mechanism, the **ToeButton** then reaches back into the parent and changes the turn. If the button is already displaying an "x" or an "o," then that is flopped. You can see in these calculations the convenient use of the ternary if-else described in Chapter 3. After a state change, the **ToeButton** is repainted.

The constructor for **ToeDialog** is quite simple; It adds into a **GridLayout** as many buttons as you request, then resizes it for 50 pixels on a side for each button.

TicTacToe sets up the whole application by creating the **JTextField**s (for inputting the rows and columns of the button grid) and the "go" button with its **ActionListener**. When the button is pressed, the data in the

JTextFields must be fetched, and, since they are in **String** form, turned into **int**s using the **static Integer.parseInt( )** method.

File dialogs

Some operating systems have a number of special built-in dialog boxes to handle the selection of things such as fonts, colors, printers, and the like. Virtually all graphical operating systems support the opening and saving of files, so Java's **JFileChooser** encapsulates these for easy use.

The following application exercises two forms of **JFileChooser** dialogs, one for opening and one for saving. Most of the code should by now be familiar, and all the interesting activities happen in the action listeners for the two different button clicks:

```
//: c14:FileChooserTest.java
// Demonstration of File dialog boxes.
import javax.swing.*;
import java.awt.*;
import java.awt.event.*;
import com.bruceeckel.swing.*;

public class FileChooserTest extends JFrame {
  private JTextField
    filename = new JTextField(),
    dir = new JTextField();
  private JButton
    open = new JButton("Open"),
    save = new JButton("Save");
  public FileChooserTest() {
    JPanel p = new JPanel();
    open.addActionListener(new OpenL());
    p.add(open);
    save.addActionListener(new SaveL());
    p.add(save);
    Container cp = getContentPane();
    cp.add(p, BorderLayout.SOUTH);
    dir.setEditable(false);
    filename.setEditable(false);
    p = new JPanel();
    p.setLayout(new GridLayout(2,1));
    p.add(filename);
    p.add(dir);
    cp.add(p, BorderLayout.NORTH);
```

```
    }
    class OpenL implements ActionListener {
      public void actionPerformed(ActionEvent e) {
        JFileChooser c = new JFileChooser();
        // Demonstrate "Open" dialog:
        int rVal = c.showOpenDialog(FileChooserTest.this);
        if(rVal == JFileChooser.APPROVE_OPTION) {
          filename.setText(c.getSelectedFile().getName());
          dir.setText(c.getCurrentDirectory().toString());
        }
        if(rVal == JFileChooser.CANCEL_OPTION) {
          filename.setText("You pressed cancel");
          dir.setText("");
        }
      }
    }
    class SaveL implements ActionListener {
      public void actionPerformed(ActionEvent e) {
        JFileChooser c = new JFileChooser();
        // Demonstrate "Save" dialog:
        int rVal = c.showSaveDialog(FileChooserTest.this);
        if(rVal == JFileChooser.APPROVE_OPTION) {
          filename.setText(c.getSelectedFile().getName());
          dir.setText(c.getCurrentDirectory().toString());
        }
        if(rVal == JFileChooser.CANCEL_OPTION) {
          filename.setText("You pressed cancel");
          dir.setText("");
        }
      }
    }
    public static void main(String[] args) {
      Console.run(new FileChooserTest(), 250, 110);
    }
  } ///:~
```

Note that there are many variations you can apply to **JFileChooser**, including filters to narrow the file names that you will allow.

For an "open file" dialog, you call **showOpenDialog( )**, and for a "save file" dialog, you call **showSaveDialog( )**. These commands don't return until the dialog is closed. The **JFileChooser** object still exists, so you can read data from it. The methods **getSelectedFile( )** and **getCurrentDirectory( )** are two ways you can interrogate the results of the operation. If these return **null**, it means the user canceled out of the dialog.

HTML on Swing components

Any component that can take text can also take HTML text, which it will reformat according to HTML rules. This means you can very easily add fancy text to a Swing component. For example:

```
//: c14:HTMLButton.java
// Putting HTML text on Swing components.
// <applet code=HTMLButton width=250 height=500></applet>
import javax.swing.*;
import java.awt.event.*;
import java.awt.*;
import com.bruceeckel.swing.*;

public class HTMLButton extends JApplet {
  private JButton b = new JButton(
    "<html><b><font size=+2>" +
    "<center>Hello!<br><i>Press me now!");
  public void init() {
    b.addActionListener(new ActionListener() {
      public void actionPerformed(ActionEvent e) {
        getContentPane().add(new JLabel("<html>" +
          "<i><font size=+4>Kapow!"));
        // Force a re-layout to include the new label:
        validate();
      }
    });
    Container cp = getContentPane();
    cp.setLayout(new FlowLayout());
    cp.add(b);
  }
  public static void main(String[] args) {
    Console.run(new HTMLButton(), 200, 500);
  }
} ///:~
```

You must start the text with "<html>," and then you can use normal HTML tags. Note that you are not forced to include the normal closing tags.

The **ActionListener** adds a new **JLabel** to the form, which also contains HTML text. However, this label is not added during **init( )**, so you must call the container's **validate( )** method in order to force a re-layout of the components (and thus the display of the new label).

You can also use HTML text for **JTabbedPane**, **JMenuItem**, **JToolTip**, **JradioButton**, and **JCheckBox**.

Sliders and progress bars

A slider (which has already been used in **SineWave.java**) allows the user to input data by moving a point back and forth, which is intuitive in some situations (volume controls, for example). A progress bar displays data in a relative fashion from "full" to "empty" so the user gets a perspective. My favorite example for these is to simply hook the slider to the progress bar so when you move the slider, the progress bar changes accordingly:

```
//: c14:Progress.java
// Using progress bars and sliders.
// <applet code=Progress width=300 height=200></applet>
import javax.swing.*;
import java.awt.*;
import java.awt.event.*;
import javax.swing.event.*;
import javax.swing.border.*;
import com.bruceeckel.swing.*;

public class Progress extends JApplet {
  private JProgressBar pb = new JProgressBar();
  private JSlider sb =
    new JSlider(JSlider.HORIZONTAL, 0, 100, 60);
  public void init() {
    Container cp = getContentPane();
    cp.setLayout(new GridLayout(2,1));
    cp.add(pb);
    sb.setValue(0);
    sb.setPaintTicks(true);
    sb.setMajorTickSpacing(20);
    sb.setMinorTickSpacing(5);
    sb.setBorder(new TitledBorder("Slide Me"));
    pb.setModel(sb.getModel()); // Share model
    cp.add(sb);
  }
  public static void main(String[] args) {
    Console.run(new Progress(), 300, 200);
  }
```

```
} ///:~
```

The key to hooking the two components together is in sharing their model, in the line:

```
pb.setModel(sb.getModel());
```

Of course, you could also control the two using a listener, but this is more straightforward for simple situations.

The **JProgressBar** is fairly straightforward, but the **JSlider** has a lot of options, such as the orientation and major and minor tick marks. Notice how straightforward it is to add a titled border.

Trees

Using a **JTree** can be as simple as saying:

```
add(new JTree(new Object[] {"this", "that", "other"}));
```

This displays a primitive tree. The API for trees is vast, however—certainly one of the largest in Swing. It appears that you can do just about anything with trees, but more sophisticated tasks might require quite a bit of research and experimentation.

Fortunately, there is a middle ground provided in the library: the "default" tree components, which generally do what you need. So most of the time you can use these components, and only in special cases will you need to delve in and understand trees more deeply.

The following example uses the "default" tree components to display a tree in an applet. When you press the button, a new subtree is added under the currently selected node (if no node is selected, the root node is used):

```
//: c14:Trees.java
// Simple Swing tree. Trees can be vastly more complex.
// <applet code=Trees width=250 height=250></applet>
import javax.swing.*;
import java.awt.*;
import java.awt.event.*;
import javax.swing.tree.*;
import com.bruceeckel.swing.*;

// Takes an array of Strings and makes the first
// element a node and the rest leaves:
```

```
class Branch {
  private DefaultMutableTreeNode r;
  public Branch(String[] data) {
    r = new DefaultMutableTreeNode(data[0]);
    for(int i = 1; i < data.length; i++)
      r.add(new DefaultMutableTreeNode(data[i]));
  }
  public DefaultMutableTreeNode node() { return r; }
}

public class Trees extends JApplet {
  private String[][] data = {
    { "Colors", "Red", "Blue", "Green" },
    { "Flavors", "Tart", "Sweet", "Bland" },
    { "Length", "Short", "Medium", "Long" },
    { "Volume", "High", "Medium", "Low" },
    { "Temperature", "High", "Medium", "Low" },
    { "Intensity", "High", "Medium", "Low" },
  };
  private static int i = 0;
  private DefaultMutableTreeNode root, child, chosen;
  private JTree tree;
  private DefaultTreeModel model;
  public void init() {
    Container cp = getContentPane();
    root = new DefaultMutableTreeNode("root");
    tree = new JTree(root);
    // Add it and make it take care of scrolling:
    cp.add(new JScrollPane(tree), BorderLayout.CENTER);
    // Capture the tree's model:
    model =(DefaultTreeModel)tree.getModel();
    JButton test = new JButton("Press me");
    test.addActionListener(new ActionListener() {
      public void actionPerformed(ActionEvent e) {
        if(i < data.length) {
          child = new Branch(data[i++]).node();
          // What's the last one you clicked?
          chosen = (DefaultMutableTreeNode)
            tree.getLastSelectedPathComponent();
          if(chosen == null)
            chosen = root;
          // The model will create the appropriate event.
          // In response, the tree will update itself:
          model.insertNodeInto(child, chosen, 0);
```

```
          // Puts the new node on the chosen node.
        }
      }
    });
    // Change the button's colors:
    test.setBackground(Color.BLUE);
    test.setForeground(Color.WHITE);
    JPanel p = new JPanel();
    p.add(test);
    cp.add(p, BorderLayout.SOUTH);
  }
  public static void main(String[] args) {
    Console.run(new Trees(), 250, 250);
  }
} ///:~
```

The first class, **Branch**, is a tool to take an array of **String** and build a **DefaultMutableTreeNode** with the first **String** as the root and the rest of the **String**s in the array as leaves. Then **node( )** can be called to produce the root of this "branch."

The **Trees** class contains a two-dimensional array of **String**s, from which **Branch**es can be made, and a **static int i** to count through this array. The **DefaultMutableTreeNode** objects hold the nodes, but the physical representation on screen is controlled by the **JTree** and its associated model, the **DefaultTreeModel**. Note that when the **JTree** is added to the applet, it is wrapped in a **JScrollPane**—this is all it takes to provide automatic scrolling.

The **JTree** is controlled through its *model*. When you make a change to the model, the model generates an event that causes the **JTree** to perform any necessary updates to the visible representation of the tree. In **init( )**, the model is captured by calling **getModel( )**. When the button is pressed, a new "branch" is created. Then the currently selected component is found (or the root is used if nothing is selected) and the model's **insertNodeInto( )** method does all the work of changing the tree and causing it to be updated.

An example like the preceding one may give you what you need in a tree. However, trees have the power to do just about anything you can imagine—everywhere you see the word "default" in the preceding example, you can substitute your own class to get different behavior. But beware: Almost all of these classes have a large interface, so you could spend a lot of time struggling to understand the intricacies of trees. Despite this, it's a good design, and the alternatives are usually much worse.

Tables

Like trees, tables in Swing are vast and powerful. They are primarily intended to be the popular "grid" interface to databases via Java Database Connectivity (JDBC, discussed in *Thinking in Enterprise Java*), and thus they have a tremendous amount of flexibility, which you pay for in complexity. There's easily enough here to allow the creation of a full-blown spreadsheet application and could probably justify an entire book. However, it is also possible to create a relatively simple **JTable** if you understand the basics.

The **JTable** controls how the data is displayed, but the **TableModel** controls the data itself. So to create a **JTable**, you'll typically create a **TableModel** first. You can fully implement the **TableModel** interface, but it's simpler to inherit from the helper class **AbstractTableModel**:

```
//: c14:JTableDemo.java
// Simple demonstration of JTable.
// <applet code=Table width=350 height=200></applet>
import javax.swing.*;
import java.awt.*;
import java.awt.event.*;
import javax.swing.table.*;
import javax.swing.event.*;
import com.bruceeckel.swing.*;

public class JTableDemo extends JApplet {
  private JTextArea txt = new JTextArea(4, 20);
  // The TableModel controls all the data:
  class DataModel extends AbstractTableModel {
    Object[][] data = {
      {"one", "two", "three", "four"},
      {"five", "six", "seven", "eight"},
      {"nine", "ten", "eleven", "twelve"},
    };
    // Prints data when table changes:
    class TML implements TableModelListener {
      public void tableChanged(TableModelEvent e) {
        txt.setText(""); // Clear it
        for(int i = 0; i < data.length; i++) {
          for(int j = 0; j < data[0].length; j++)
```

```
          txt.append(data[i][j] + " ");
        txt.append("\n");
      }
    }
  }
  public DataModel() { addTableModelListener(new TML());}
  public int getColumnCount() { return data[0].length; }
  public int getRowCount() { return data.length; }
  public Object getValueAt(int row, int col) {
    return data[row][col];
  }
  public void setValueAt(Object val, int row, int col) {
    data[row][col] = val;
    // Indicate the change has happened:
    fireTableDataChanged();
  }
  public boolean isCellEditable(int row, int col) {
    return true;
  }
 }
 public void init() {
  Container cp = getContentPane();
  JTable table = new JTable(new DataModel());
  cp.add(new JScrollPane(table));
  cp.add(BorderLayout.SOUTH, txt);
 }
 public static void main(String[] args) {
  Console.run(new JTableDemo(), 350, 200);
 }
} ///:~
```

DataModel contains an array of data, but you could also get the data from some other source such as a database. The constructor adds a **TableModelListener** that prints the array every time the table is changed. The rest of the methods follow the Beans naming convention (using "get" and "set" methods, which will be described later in this chapter) and are used by **JTable** when it wants to present the information in **DataModel**. **AbstractTableModel** provides default methods for **setValueAt( )** and **isCellEditable( )** that prevent changes to the data, so if you want to be able to edit the data, you must override these methods.

Once you have a **TableModel**, you only need to hand it to the **JTable** constructor. All the details of displaying, editing, and updating will be taken care of for you. This example also puts the **JTable** in a **JScrollPane**.

Selecting Look & Feel

"Pluggable Look & Feel" allows your program to emulate the look and feel of various operating environments. You can even do all sorts of fancy things, like dynamically changing the look and feel while the program is executing. However, you generally just want to do one of two things: either select the "cross platform" look and feel (which is Swing's "metal"), or select the look and feel for the system you are currently on so your Java program looks like it was created specifically for that system (this is almost certainly the best choice in most cases, to avoid confounding the user). The code to select either of these behaviors is quite simple, but you must execute it *before* you create any visual components, because the components will be made based on the current look and feel, and will not be changed just because you happen to change the look and feel midway during the program (that process is more complicated and uncommon, and is relegated to Swing-specific books).

Actually, if you want to use the cross-platform ("metal") look and feel that is characteristic of Swing programs, you don't have to do anything—it's the default. But if you want instead to use the current operating environment's look and feel, you just insert the following code, typically at the beginning of your **main( )**, but at least before any components are added:

```
try {
  UIManager.setLookAndFeel(UIManager.
    getSystemLookAndFeelClassName());
} catch(Exception e) {
  throw new RuntimeException(e);
}
```

You don't need anything in the **catch** clause because the **UIManager** will default to the cross-platform look and feel if your attempts to set up any of the alternatives fail. However, during debugging the exception can be quite useful, so you may at least want see some results via the catch clause.

Here is a program that takes a command-line argument to select a look and feel, and shows how several different components look under the chosen look and feel:

```
//: c14:LookAndFeel.java
// Selecting different looks & feels.
import javax.swing.*;
import java.awt.*;
import java.awt.event.*;
```

```
import java.util.*;
import com.bruceeckel.swing.*;

public class LookAndFeel extends JFrame {
  private String[] choices = {
    "eeny","meeny","Minnie","Mickey","Moe","Larry","Curly"
  };
  private Component[] samples = {
    new JButton("JButton"),
    new JTextField("JTextField"),
    new JLabel("JLabel"),
    new JCheckBox("JCheckBox"),
    new JRadioButton("Radio"),
    new JComboBox(choices),
    new JList(choices),
  };
  public LookAndFeel() {
    super("Look And Feel");
    Container cp = getContentPane();
    cp.setLayout(new FlowLayout());
    for(int i = 0; i < samples.length; i++)
      cp.add(samples[i]);
  }
  private static void usageError() {
    System.out.println(
      "Usage:LookAndFeel [cross|system|motif]");
    System.exit(1);
  }
  public static void main(String[] args) {
    if(args.length == 0) usageError();
    if(args[0].equals("cross")) {
      try {
        UIManager.setLookAndFeel(UIManager.
          getCrossPlatformLookAndFeelClassName());
      } catch(Exception e) {
        e.printStackTrace();
      }
    } else if(args[0].equals("system")) {
      try {
        UIManager.setLookAndFeel(UIManager.
          getSystemLookAndFeelClassName());
      } catch(Exception e) {
        e.printStackTrace();
      }
```

```
    } else if(args[0].equals("motif")) {
      try {
        UIManager.setLookAndFeel("com.sun.java."+
          "swing.plaf.motif.MotifLookAndFeel");
      } catch(Exception e) {
        e.printStackTrace();
      }
    } else usageError();
    // Note the look & feel must be set before
    // any components are created.
    Console.run(new LookAndFeel(), 300, 200);
  }
} ///:~
```

You can see that one option is to explicitly specify a string for a look and feel, as seen with **MotifLookAndFeel**. However, that one and the default "metal" look and feel are the only ones that can legally be used on any platform; even though there are strings for Windows and Macintosh look and feels, those can only be used on their respective platforms (these are produced when you call **getSystemLookAndFeelClassName( )** and you're on that particular platform).

It is also possible to create a custom look and feel package, for example, if you are building a framework for a company that wants a distinctive appearance. This is a big job and is far beyond the scope of this book (in fact, you'll discover it is beyond the scope of many dedicated Swing books!).

The clipboard

The JFC supports limited operations with the system clipboard (in the **java.awt.datatransfer** package). You can copy **String** objects to the clipboard as text, and you can paste text from the clipboard into **String** objects. Of course, the clipboard is designed to hold any type of data, but how this data is represented on the clipboard is up to the program doing the cutting and pasting. The Java clipboard API provides for extensibility through the concept of a "flavor." When data comes off the clipboard, it has an associated set of flavors that it can be converted to (for example, a graph might be represented as a string of numbers or as an image), and you can see if that particular clipboard data supports the flavor you're interested in.

The following program is a simple demonstration of cut, copy, and paste with **String** data in a **JTextArea**. One thing you'll notice is that the keyboard sequences you normally use for cutting, copying, and pasting also work. But if you look at any **JTextField** or **JTextArea** in any other program, you'll find that they also automatically support the clipboard key sequences. This example simply adds programmatic control of the clipboard, and you could use these techniques if you want to capture clipboard text into something other than a **JTextComponent**.

```
//: c14:CutAndPaste.java
// Using the clipboard.
import javax.swing.*;
import java.awt.*;
import java.awt.event.*;
import java.awt.datatransfer.*;
import com.bruceeckel.swing.*;

public class CutAndPaste extends JFrame  {
  private JMenuBar mb = new JMenuBar();
  private JMenu edit = new JMenu("Edit");
  private JMenuItem
    cut = new JMenuItem("Cut"),
    copy = new JMenuItem("Copy"),
    paste = new JMenuItem("Paste");
  private JTextArea text = new JTextArea(20, 20);
  private Clipboard clipbd =
    getToolkit().getSystemClipboard();
  public CutAndPaste()  {
    cut.addActionListener(new CutL());
    copy.addActionListener(new CopyL());
    paste.addActionListener(new PasteL());
    edit.add(cut);
    edit.add(copy);
    edit.add(paste);
    mb.add(edit);
    setJMenuBar(mb);
    getContentPane().add(text);
  }
  class CopyL implements ActionListener {
    public void actionPerformed(ActionEvent e) {
      String selection = text.getSelectedText();
      if(selection == null)
        return;
      StringSelection clipString =
        new StringSelection(selection);
      clipbd.setContents(clipString,clipString);
```

```
    }
  }
  class CutL implements ActionListener {
    public void actionPerformed(ActionEvent e) {
      String selection = text.getSelectedText();
      if(selection == null)
        return;
      StringSelection clipString =
        new StringSelection(selection);
      clipbd.setContents(clipString, clipString);
      text.replaceRange("", text.getSelectionStart(),
        text.getSelectionEnd());
    }
  }
  class PasteL implements ActionListener {
    public void actionPerformed(ActionEvent e) {
      Transferable clipData =
        clipbd.getContents(CutAndPaste.this);
      try {
        String clipString = (String)clipData.
          getTransferData(DataFlavor.stringFlavor);
        text.replaceRange(clipString,
          text.getSelectionStart(),text.getSelectionEnd());
      } catch(Exception ex) {
        System.err.println("Not String flavor");
      }
    }
  }
  public static void main(String[] args) {
    Console.run(new CutAndPaste(), 300, 200);
  }
} ///:~
```

The creation and addition of the menu and **JTextArea** should by now seem a pedestrian activity. What's different is the creation of the **Clipboard** field **clipbd**, which is done through the **Toolkit**.

All the action takes place in the listeners. The **CopyL** and **CutL** listeners are the same except for the last line of **CutL**, which erases the line that's been copied. The special two lines are the creation of a **StringSelection** object from the **String** and the call to **setContents( )** with this **StringSelection**. That's all there is to putting a **String** on the clipboard.

In **PasteL,** data is pulled off the clipboard using **getContents( )**. What comes back is a fairly anonymous **Transferable** object, and you don't really know what it contains. One way to find out is to call **getTransferDataFlavors( )**, which returns an array of **DataFlavor** objects indicating which flavors are supported by this particular object. You can also ask it directly with **isDataFlavorSupported( )**, passing in the flavor you're interested in. Here, however, the bold approach is taken: **getTransferData( )** is called, assuming that the contents supports the **String** flavor, and if it doesn't, the problem is sorted out in the exception handler.

In the future you can expect more data flavors to be supported.

Packaging an applet into a JAR file

An important use of the JAR utility is to optimize applet loading. In Java 1.0, people tended to try to cram all their code into a single applet class so the client would need only a single server hit to download the applet code. Not only did this result in messy, hard-to-read (and maintain) programs, but the **.class** file was still uncompressed so downloading wasn't as fast as it could have been.

JAR files solve the problem by compressing all of your **.class** files into a single file that is downloaded by the browser. Now you can create the right design without worrying about how many **.class** files it will generate, and the user will get a much faster download time.

Consider **TicTacToe.java**. It looks like a single class, but in fact it contains five inner classes, so that's six in all. Once you've compiled the program, you package it into a JAR file with the line:

```
jar cf TicTacToe.jar *.class
```

This assumes that the only **.class** files in the current directory are the ones from **TicTacToe.java** (otherwise, you'll get extra baggage).

Now you can create an HTML page with the new **archive** tag to indicate the name of the JAR file. Here is the basic applet tag:

```
<head><title>TicTacToe Example Applet
</title></head>
<body>
<applet code=TicTacToe.class
```

```
        archive=TicTacToe.jar
        width=200 height=100>
</applet>
</body>
```

You'll need to run this file through the **HTMLconverter** application that comes with the JDK in order to get it to work.

Signing applets

Because of the sandbox security model, unsigned applets are prevented from performing certain tasks on the client, like writing to a file or connecting to a local network.[10] A signed applet verifies to the user that the person who claims to have created the applet actually did, and that the contents of the JAR file have not been tampered with since that file left the server. Without this minimum guarantee, the applet will not be allowed to do anything that could damage a person's machine or violate their privacy. This is a restriction that is vital for the safe use of applets through the Internet, but which also makes applets relatively powerless.

Since the release of the Java Plugin, the process of signing applets has become simpler and more standardized, and applets have become a more viable means of deploying your application. Signing an applet has become a reasonably straightforward process and uses standard Java tools.

Prior to the plugin, you had to sign a **.jar** file with the Netscape tools for a Netscape client, a **.cab** file with the Microsoft tools for an Internet Explorer client, and create an applet tag in the HTML file for both platforms. The user would then have to install a certificate on the browser so that the applet would be trusted.

The plugin not only provides a standard approach to applet signing and deployment, but it also provides the end user with a better experience by making certificate installation automatic.

Consider an applet that wants to have access to the client's file system and read and write some files. This is very similar to **FileChooserTest.java**, but because this is an applet, it will only be able to open the Swing

---

[10] This section and the next were created by Jeremy Meyer.

JFileChooser dialog if it is running from a signed JAR file. Otherwise, the **showOpenDialog( )** method will throw a **SecurityException**.

```
//: c14:signedapplet:FileAccessApplet.java
// Demonstration of File dialog boxes.
package c14.signedapplet;
import javax.swing.*;
import java.awt.*;
import java.awt.event.*;
import java.io.*;
import com.bruceeckel.swing.*;

public class FileAccessApplet extends JApplet {
  private JTextField
    filename = new JTextField(),
    dir = new JTextField();
  private JButton
    open = new JButton("Open"),
    save = new JButton("Save");
  private JEditorPane ep = new JEditorPane();
  private JScrollPane jsp = new JScrollPane();
  private File file;
  public void init() {
    JPanel p = new JPanel();
    open.addActionListener(new OpenL());
    p.add(open);
    save.addActionListener(new SaveL());
    p.add(save);
    Container cp = getContentPane();
    jsp.getViewport().add(ep);
    cp.add(jsp, BorderLayout.CENTER);
    cp.add(p, BorderLayout.SOUTH);
    dir.setEditable(false);
    save.setEnabled(false);
    ep.setContentType("text/html");
    filename.setEditable(false);
    p = new JPanel();
    p.setLayout(new GridLayout(2, 1));
    p.add(filename);
    p.add(dir);
    cp.add(p, BorderLayout.NORTH);
  }
  class OpenL implements ActionListener {
    public void actionPerformed(ActionEvent e) {
```

```
      JFileChooser c = new JFileChooser();
      c.setFileFilter(new TextFileFilter());
      // Demonstrate "Open" dialog:
      int rVal = c.showOpenDialog(FileAccessApplet.this);
      if(rVal == JFileChooser.APPROVE_OPTION) {
        file = c.getSelectedFile();
        filename.setText(file.getName());
        dir.setText(c.getCurrentDirectory().toString());
        try {
          System.out.println("Url is " + file.toURL());
          ep.setPage(file.toURL());
          // ep.repaint();
        } catch (IOException ioe) {
          throw new RuntimeException(ioe);
        }
      }
      if(rVal == JFileChooser.CANCEL_OPTION) {
        filename.setText("You pressed cancel");
        dir.setText("");
      } else {
        save.setEnabled(true);
      }
    }
  }
  class SaveL implements ActionListener {
    public void actionPerformed(ActionEvent e) {
      JFileChooser c = new JFileChooser(file);
      c.setSelectedFile(file);
      // Demonstrate "Save" dialog:
      int rVal = c.showSaveDialog(FileAccessApplet.this);
      if(rVal == JFileChooser.APPROVE_OPTION) {
        filename.setText(c.getSelectedFile().getName());
        dir.setText(c.getCurrentDirectory().toString());
        try {
          FileWriter fw = new FileWriter(file);
          ep.write(fw);
        } catch (IOException ioe) {
          throw new RuntimeException(ioe);
        }
      }
      if(rVal == JFileChooser.CANCEL_OPTION) {
        filename.setText("You pressed cancel");
        dir.setText("");
      }
```

```
    }
  }
  public class TextFileFilter extends
    javax.swing.filechooser.FileFilter {
    public boolean accept(File f) {
      return f.getName().endsWith(".txt")
        || f.isDirectory();
    }
    public String getDescription() {
      return "Text Files (*.txt)";
    }
  }
  public static void main(String[] args) {
    Console.run(new FileAccessApplet(), 500, 500);
  }
} ///:~
```

It appears to be an ordinary applet. However, as it stands, it would not be allowed to open and close files on a client's system. To make this run as a signed applet, you need to put it into a JAR file (see the section on the **jar** utility, earlier in this chapter) and sign the JAR file.

Once you have a JAR file, you will need a certificate or a key to sign it with. If you were a large corporation, you would apply to a signing authority like Verisign or Thawte, and they would issue you a certificate. This is used to sign code and thus identify to a user that you are indeed the provider of the code they are downloading, and that the code that has been deployed hasn't been modified since you signed it. Essentially, the digital signature is a load of bits, and the signing authority vouches for you when someone downloads that signature.

A certificate from a signing authority costs money and requires regular renewal. In our case we can just make a little self-signed one. This needs to be stored in a file somewhere (it is usually called the *keychain*). If you type:

```
keytool -list
```

then it will try to access the default file. If there is no file, then you need to create one, or specify an existing one. You might try to search for a file called "cacerts," and then try

```
keytool -list -file <path/filename>
```

The default location is usually

```
{java.home}/lib/security/cacerts
```

where the **java.home** property points to the JRE home.

You can also easily make a self-signed certificate for testing purposes using the **keytool**. If you have your Java "bin" directory in your executable path, you can type:

```
keytool -genkey -alias <keyname> -keystore <url>
```

where **keyname** is the alias name that you want to give the key, say "mykeyname," and **url** is the location of the file that stores your keys, usually the **cacerts** file as described above.

You will now be prompted for the password. Unless you have changed the default, this will be "changeit" (a hint to do just that). Next you will be asked for your name, the organizational unit, the organization, city, state, and country. This information is stored in the certificate. Lastly, you will be asked for a password for that key. If you are really security conscious, you can give it a separate password, but the default password is the same as the keystore itself, and is usually adequate. The above information can be specified on the command line from within a build tool such as Ant.

If you invoke the **keytool** utility with no parameters at the command prompt, it will give you a list of its numerous options. You might like to use the **–valid** option, for example, which enables you to specify how many days the key will be valid for.

To confirm that your key is now in the **cacerts** file, type:

```
keytool -list -keystore <url>
```

and enter the password as before. Your key may be hidden among the other keys already in your certificate files.

Your new certificate is self-signed and thus not actually trusted by a signing authority. If you use this certificate to sign a JAR file, the end user will get a warning, and a strong recommendation *not* to use your software. You and your users will have to tolerate this until you are prepared to pay for a trusted certificate for commercial purposes.

To sign your JAR file, use the standard Java **jarsigner** tool as follows:

```
jarsigner -keystore <url> <jarfile> <keyname>
```

where **url** is the location of your cacerts file, **jarfile** is the name of your JAR file, and **keyname** is the alias that you gave to your key. You will again be prompted for the password.

You now have a JAR file that can be identified as being signed with your key, and that can guarantee it has not been tampered with (i.e., no files have been changed, added, or removed) since you signed it.

All you have to do now is make sure that the applet tag in your HTML file has an "archive" element, which specifies the name of your JAR file.

The applet tag is somewhat more complicated for the plugin, but if you create a simple tag like:

```
<APPLET
  CODE=package.AppletSubclass.class
  ARCHIVE = myjar.jar
  WIDTH=300
  HEIGHT=200>
</APPLET>
```

and run the **HTMLConverter** tool on it (this is packaged with the freely downloadable JDK), it will create the correct applet tag for you.

Now, when your applet is downloaded by a client, they will be informed that a signed applet is being loaded, and given the option of trusting the signer. As previously mentioned, your test certificate doesn't have a very high degree of trust, and the user will get a warning to this effect. If they opt to trust your applet, it will have full access to their system and behave as if it were an ordinary application.

The source code for this book, downloadable from **www.BruceEckel.com,** contains complete working configuration files and an Ant build script to properly compile and build this project.

JNLP and Java Web Start

Signed applets are powerful and can effectively take the place of an application, but they must run inside a Web browser. This requires the extra overhead of the browser running on the client machine, and also means that the user interface of the applet is limited and often visually confusing. The Web browser has its own set of menus and toolbars, which will appear above the applet.

The *Java Network Launch Protocol* (JNLP) solves the problem without sacrificing the advantages of applets. With a JNLP application, you can download and install a standalone Java application onto the client's machine. This can be run from the command prompt, a desktop icon, or the application manager that is installed with your JNLP implementation. The application can even be run from the Web site from which it was originally downloaded.

A JNLP application can dynamically download resources from the Internet at run time, and the version can be automatically checked (if the user is connected to the Internet) . This means that it has all of the advantages of an applet together with the advantages of standalone applications.

Like applets, JNLP applications need to be treated with some caution by the client's system. A JNLP application is Web-based and easy to download, so it might be malevolent. Because of this, JNLP applications are subject to the same sandbox security restrictions as applets. Like applets, they can be deployed in signed JAR files, giving the user the option to trust the signer. Unlike applets, if they are deployed in an unsigned JAR file, they can still request access to certain resources of the client's system by means of services in the JNLP API (the user must approve the requests during program execution).

Because JNLP describes a protocol, not an implementation, you will need an implementation in order to use it. Java Web Start, or JAWS, is Sun's freely-available official reference implementation. All you need to do is download and install it, and if you are using it for development, make sure that the JAR files are in your classpath. If you are deploying your JNLP application from a Web server, you have to ensure that your server recognizes the MIME type application/x-java-jnlp-file. If you are using a recent version of the Tomcat server (*http://jakarta.apache.org/tomcat*) this will already be configured. Consult the user guide for your particular server.

Creating a JNLP application is not difficult. You create a standard application that is archived in a JAR file, and then you provide a launch file, which is a simple XML file that gives the client all the information it needs to download and install your application. If you choose not to sign your JAR file, then you must make use of the services supplied by the JNLP API for each type of resource you want access to on the users machine.

Here is a variation of the example using the **JFileChooser** dialog, but this time using the JNLP services to open it, so that the class can be deployed as a JNLP application in an unsigned JAR file.

```
//: c14:jnlp:JnlpFileChooser.java
// Opening files on a local machine with JNLP.
// {Depends: javaws.jar}
package c14.jnlp;
import javax.swing.*;
import java.awt.*;
import java.awt.event.*;
import java.io.*;
import javax.jnlp.*;

public class JnlpFileChooser extends JFrame {
  private JTextField filename = new JTextField();
  private JButton
    open = new JButton("Open"),
    save = new JButton("Save");
  private JEditorPane ep = new JEditorPane();
  private JScrollPane jsp = new JScrollPane();
  private FileContents fileContents;
  public JnlpFileChooser() {
    JPanel p = new JPanel();
    open.addActionListener(new OpenL());
    p.add(open);
    save.addActionListener(new SaveL());
    p.add(save);
    Container cp = getContentPane();
    jsp.getViewport().add(ep);
    cp.add(jsp, BorderLayout.CENTER);
    cp.add(p, BorderLayout.SOUTH);
    filename.setEditable(false);
    p = new JPanel();
    p.setLayout(new GridLayout(2,1));
    p.add(filename);
    cp.add(p, BorderLayout.NORTH);
    ep.setContentType("text");
    save.setEnabled(false);
  }
  class OpenL implements ActionListener {
    public void actionPerformed(ActionEvent e) {
      FileOpenService fs = null;
      try {
```

```
        fs = (FileOpenService)ServiceManager.lookup(
          "javax.jnlp.FileOpenService");
      } catch(UnavailableServiceException use) {
        throw new RuntimeException(use);
      }
      if(fs != null) {
        try {
          fileContents = fs.openFileDialog(".",
            new String[]{"txt", "*"});
          if(fileContents == null)
            return;
          filename.setText(fileContents.getName());
          ep.read(fileContents.getInputStream(), null);
        } catch (Exception exc) {
          throw new RuntimeException (exc);
        }
        save.setEnabled(true);
      }
    }
  }
  class SaveL implements ActionListener {
    public void actionPerformed(ActionEvent e) {
      FileSaveService fs = null;
      try {
        fs = (FileSaveService)ServiceManager.lookup(
          "javax.jnlp.FileSaveService");
      } catch(UnavailableServiceException use) {
        throw new RuntimeException(use);
      }
      if(fs != null) {
        try {
          fileContents = fs.saveFileDialog(".",
            new String[]{"txt"},
            new ByteArrayInputStream(
              ep.getText().getBytes()),
            fileContents.getName());
          if(fileContents == null)
            return;
          filename.setText(fileContents.getName());
        } catch (Exception exc) {
          throw new RuntimeException (exc);
        }
      }
    }
```

```
  }
  public static void main(String[] args) {
    JnlpFileChooser fc = new JnlpFileChooser();
    fc.setSize(400, 300);
    fc.setVisible(true);
  }
} ///:~
```

Note that the **FileOpenService** and the **FileCloseService** classes are imported from the **javax.jnlp** package and that nowhere in the code is the **JFileChooser** dialog box referred to directly. The two services used here must be requested using the **ServiceManager.lookup( )** method, and the resources on the client system can only be accessed via the objects returned from this method. In this case, the files on the client's file system are being written to and read from using the **FileContent** interface, provided by the JNLP. Any attempt to access the resources directly by using, say, a **File** or a **FileReader** object would cause a **SecurityException** to be thrown in the same way that it would if you tried to use them from an unsigned applet. If you want to use these classes and not be restricted to the JNLP service interfaces, you must sign the JAR file (see the previous section on signing JAR files).

Now that we have a runnable class that makes use of the JNLP services, all that is needed is for the class to be put into a JAR file and a launch file to be written. Here is an appropriate launch file for the preceding example.

```
<?xml version="1.0" encoding="UTF-8"?>
<jnlp spec = "1.0+"
  codebase="file://C:\TIJ3code\c14\jnlp"
  href="filechooser.jnlp">
    <information>
      <title>FileChooser demo application</title>
      <vendor>Mindview Inc.</vendor>
      <description>
        Jnlp File choose Application
      </description>
      <description kind="short">
        A demonstration of opening, reading and
        writing a text file
      </description>
      <icon href="images/tijicon.gif"/>
      <offline-allowed/>
    </information>
```

```
    <resources>
      <j2se version="1.3+"/>
      <jar href="jnlpfilechooser.jar" download="eager"/>
    </resources>
    <application-desc
      main-class="c14.jnlp.JnlpFileChooser"/>
</jnlp>
```

This launch file needs to be saved as a **.jnlp** file, in this case, **filechooser.jnlp,** in the same directory as the JAR file.

As you can see, it is an XML file with one **<jnlp>** tag. This has a few subelements, which are mostly self-explanatory.

The **spec** attribute of the **jnlp** element tells the client system what version of the JNLP the application can be run with. The **codebase** attribute points to the directory where this launch file and the resources can be found. Typically, it would be an HTTP URL pointing to a Web server, but in this case it points to a directory on the local machine, which is a good means of testing the application. The **href** attribute must specify the name of this file.

The **information** tag has various subelements that provide information about the application. These are used by the Java Web Start administrative console or equivalent, which installs the JNLP application and allows the user to run it from the command line, make short cuts and so on.

The **resources** tag serves a similar purpose as the applet tag in an HTML file. The **j2se** subelement specifies the version of the j2se that is needed to run the application, and the **jar** subelement specifies the JAR file in which the class is archived. The **jar** element has an attribute **download**, which can have the values "eager" or "lazy" that tell the JNLP implementation whether or not the entire archive needs to be downloaded before the application can be run.

The **application-desc** attribute tells the JNLP implementation which class is the executable class, or entry point, to the JAR file.

Another useful subelement of the **jnlp** tag is the **security** tag, not shown here. Here's what a security tag looks like:

```
<security>
   <all-permissions/>
<security/>
```

You use the security tag when your application is deployed in a signed JAR file. It is not needed in the preceding example because the local resources are all accessed via the JNLP services.

There are a few other tags available, the details of which can be found in the specification *http://java.sun.com/products/javawebstart/download-spec.html.*

Now that the **.jnlp** is written, you will need to add a hypertext link to it in an HTML page. This will be its download page. You might have a complex layout with a detailed introduction to your application, but as long as you have something like:

```
<a href="filechooser.jnlp">click here</a>
```

in your HTML file, then you will be able to initiate the installation of the JNLP application by clicking on the link. Once you have downloaded the application once, you will be able to configure it by using the administrative console. If you are using Java Web Start on Windows, then you will be prompted to make a short cut to your application the second time you use it. This behavior is configurable.

The source code for this book, downloadable from **www.BruceEckel.com,** contains complete working configuration files and an Ant build script to properly compile and build this project.

Only two of the JNLP services are covered here, but there are seven services in the current release. Each is designed for a specific task such as printing, or cutting, and pasting to the clipboard. An in-depth discussion of these services is beyond the scope of this chapter.

Programming techniques

Because GUI programming in Java has been an evolving technology with some very significant changes between Java 1.0/1.1 and the Swing library in Java 2, there have been some old programming idioms that have seeped through to examples that you might see given for Swing. In addition, Swing allows you to program in more and better ways than were allowed by the old models. In this section, some of these issues will be demonstrated by introducing and examining some programming idioms.

Binding events dynamically

One of the benefits of the Swing event model is flexibility. You can add and remove event behavior with single method calls. The following example demonstrates this:

```
//: c14:DynamicEvents.java
// You can change event behavior dynamically.
// Also shows multiple actions for an event.
// <applet code=DynamicEvents
// width=250 height=400></applet>
import javax.swing.*;
import java.awt.*;
import java.awt.event.*;
import java.util.*;
import com.bruceeckel.swing.*;

public class DynamicEvents extends JApplet {
  private java.util.List list = new ArrayList();
  private int i = 0;
  private JButton
    b1 = new JButton("Button1"),
    b2 = new JButton("Button2");
  private JTextArea txt = new JTextArea();
  class B implements ActionListener {
    public void actionPerformed(ActionEvent e) {
      txt.append("A button was pressed\n");
    }
  }
  class CountListener implements ActionListener {
    private int index;
    public CountListener(int i) { index = i; }
    public void actionPerformed(ActionEvent e) {
      txt.append("Counted Listener " + index + "\n");
    }
  }
  class B1 implements ActionListener {
    public void actionPerformed(ActionEvent e) {
      txt.append("Button 1 pressed\n");
      ActionListener a = new CountListener(i++);
      list.add(a);
      b2.addActionListener(a);
    }
  }
```

```
  class B2 implements ActionListener {
    public void actionPerformed(ActionEvent e) {
      txt.append("Button2 pressed\n");
      int end = list.size() - 1;
      if(end >= 0) {
        b2.removeActionListener(
          (ActionListener)list.get(end));
        list.remove(end);
      }
    }
  }
  public void init() {
    Container cp = getContentPane();
    b1.addActionListener(new B());
    b1.addActionListener(new B1());
    b2.addActionListener(new B());
    b2.addActionListener(new B2());
    JPanel p = new JPanel();
    p.add(b1);
    p.add(b2);
    cp.add(BorderLayout.NORTH, p);
    cp.add(new JScrollPane(txt));
  }
  public static void main(String[] args) {
    Console.run(new DynamicEvents(), 250, 400);
  }
} ///:~
```

The new twists in this example are:

1. There is more than one listener attached to each **Button**. Usually, components handle events as *multicast*, meaning that you can register many listeners for a single event. In the special components in which an event is handled as *unicast*, you'll get a **TooManyListenersException**.

2. During the execution of the program, listeners are dynamically added and removed from the **Button b2**. Adding is accomplished in the way you've seen before, but each component also has a **removeXXXListener( )** method to remove each type of listener.

This kind of flexibility provides much greater power in your programming.

You should notice that event listeners are not guaranteed to be called in the order they are added (although most implementations do in fact work that way).

Separating business logic from UI logic

In general, you'll want to design your classes so that each one does "only one thing." This is particularly important when user-interface code is concerned, since it's easy to tie up "what you're doing" with "how you're displaying it." This kind of coupling prevents code reuse. It's much more desirable to separate your "business logic" from the GUI. This way, not only can you reuse the business logic more easily, but it's also easier to reuse the GUI.

Another issue is *multitiered* systems, where the "business objects" reside on a completely separate machine. This central location of the business rules allows changes to be instantly effective for all new transactions, and is thus a compelling way to set up a system. However, these business objects can be used in many different applications and so should not be tied to any particular mode of display. They should just perform the business operations and nothing more.[11]

The following example shows how easy it is to separate the business logic from the GUI code:

```
//: c14:Separation.java
// Separating GUI logic and business objects.
// <applet code=Separation width=250 height=150></applet>
import javax.swing.*;
import java.awt.*;
import javax.swing.event.*;
import java.awt.event.*;
import java.applet.*;
import com.bruceeckel.swing.*;

class BusinessLogic {
  private int modifier;
  public BusinessLogic(int mod) { modifier = mod; }
```

[11] This concept is more fully explored in *Thinking in Enterprise Java*, at *www.BruceEckel.com*.

```
  public void setModifier(int mod) { modifier = mod; }
  public int getModifier() { return modifier; }
  // Some business operations:
  public int calculation1(int arg){ return arg * modifier;}
  public int calculation2(int arg){ return arg + modifier;}
}

public class Separation extends JApplet {
  private JTextField
    t = new JTextField(15),
    mod = new JTextField(15);
  private JButton
    calc1 = new JButton("Calculation 1"),
    calc2 = new JButton("Calculation 2");
  private BusinessLogic bl = new BusinessLogic(2);
  public static int getValue(JTextField tf) {
    try {
      return Integer.parseInt(tf.getText());
    } catch(NumberFormatException e) {
      return 0;
    }
  }
  class Calc1L implements ActionListener {
    public void actionPerformed(ActionEvent e) {
      t.setText(Integer.toString(
        bl.calculation1(getValue(t))));
    }
  }
  class Calc2L implements ActionListener {
    public void actionPerformed(ActionEvent e) {
      t.setText(Integer.toString(
        bl.calculation2(getValue(t))));
    }
  }
  // If you want something to happen whenever
  // a JTextField changes, add this listener:
  class ModL implements DocumentListener {
    public void changedUpdate(DocumentEvent e) {}
    public void insertUpdate(DocumentEvent e) {
      bl.setModifier(getValue(mod));
    }
    public void removeUpdate(DocumentEvent e) {
      bl.setModifier(getValue(mod));
    }
```

```
  }
  public void init() {
    Container cp = getContentPane();
    cp.setLayout(new FlowLayout());
    cp.add(t);
    calc1.addActionListener(new Calc1L());
    calc2.addActionListener(new Calc2L());
    JPanel p1 = new JPanel();
    p1.add(calc1);
    p1.add(calc2);
    cp.add(p1);
    mod.getDocument().addDocumentListener(new ModL());
    JPanel p2 = new JPanel();
    p2.add(new JLabel("Modifier:"));
    p2.add(mod);
    cp.add(p2);
  }
  public static void main(String[] args) {
    Console.run(new Separation(), 250, 100);
  }
} ///:~
```

You can see that **BusinessLogic** is a straightforward class that performs its operations without even a hint that it might be used in a GUI environment. It just does its job.

Separation keeps track of all the UI details, and it talks to **BusinessLogic** only through its **public** interface. All the operations are centered around getting information back and forth through the UI and the **BusinessLogic** object. So **Separation**, in turn, just does its job. Since **Separation** knows only that it's talking to a **BusinessLogic** object (that is, it isn't highly coupled), it could be massaged into talking to other types of objects without much trouble.

Thinking in terms of separating UI from business logic also makes life easier when you're adapting legacy code to work with Java.

A canonical form

Inner classes, the Swing event model, and the fact that the old AWT event model is still supported, along with new library features that rely on old-style programming, has added a new element of confusion to the code design process. Now there are even more different ways for people to write unpleasant code.

Except in extenuating circumstances, you can always use the simplest and clearest approach: Listener classes (typically written as inner classes) to solve your event-handling needs. This is the form used in most of the examples in this chapter.

By following this model you should be able to reduce the statements in your programs that say "I wonder what caused this event." Each piece of code is concerned with *doing*, not type checking. This is the best way to write your code; not only is it easier to conceptualize, but it's much easier to read and maintain.

Concurrency & Swing

It is easy to forget that you are using threads when you program with Swing. The fact that you don't have to explicitly create a **Thread** object means that threading issues can catch you by surprise. Typically, when you write a Swing program, or any GUI application with a windowed display, the majority of the application is event driven, and nothing really happens until the user generates and event by clicking on a GUI component with the mouse, or striking a key.

Just remember that there is a Swing event dispatching thread, which is always there, handling all the Swing events in turn. This needs to be considered if you want to guarantee that your application won't suffer from deadlocking or race conditions.

This section looks at a couple of issues worth noting when working with threads under Swing.

Runnable revisited

In Chapter 13, I suggested that you think carefully before making a class as an implementation of **Runnable**. Of course, if you must inherit from a class *and* you want to add threading behavior to the class, **Runnable** is the correct solution. The following example exploits this by making a **Runnable JPanel** class that paints different colors on itself. This application is set up to take values from the command line to determine how big the grid of colors is and how long to **sleep( )** between color changes. By playing with these values, you'll discover some interesting and possibly inexplicable features of threads:

```
//: c14:ColorBoxes.java
// Using the Runnable interface.
// <applet code=ColorBoxes width=500 height=400>
// <param name=grid value="12">
// <param name=pause value="50"></applet>
import javax.swing.*;
import java.awt.*;
import java.awt.event.*;
import java.util.*;
import com.bruceeckel.swing.*;

class CBox extends JPanel implements Runnable {
  private Thread t;
  private int pause;
  private static final Color[] colors = {
    Color.BLACK, Color.BLUE, Color.CYAN,
    Color.DARK_GRAY, Color.GRAY, Color.GREEN,
    Color.LIGHT_GRAY, Color.MAGENTA,
    Color.ORANGE, Color.PINK, Color.RED,
    Color.WHITE, Color.YELLOW
  };
  private static Random rand = new Random();
  private static final Color newColor() {
    return colors[rand.nextInt(colors.length)];
  }
  private Color cColor = newColor();
  public void paintComponent(Graphics  g) {
    super.paintComponent(g);
    g.setColor(cColor);
    Dimension s = getSize();
    g.fillRect(0, 0, s.width, s.height);
  }
  public CBox(int pause) {
    this.pause = pause;
    t = new Thread(this);
    t.start();
  }
  public void run() {
    while(true) {
      cColor = newColor();
      repaint();
```

```
        try {
          t.sleep(pause);
        } catch(InterruptedException e) {
          throw new RuntimeException(e);
        }
      }
    }
  }

public class ColorBoxes extends JApplet {
  private boolean isApplet = true;
  private int grid = 12;
  private int pause = 50;
  public void init() {
    // Get parameters from Web page:
    if(isApplet) {
      String gsize = getParameter("grid");
      if(gsize != null)
        grid = Integer.parseInt(gsize);
      String pse = getParameter("pause");
      if(pse != null)
        pause = Integer.parseInt(pse);
    }
    Container cp = getContentPane();
    cp.setLayout(new GridLayout(grid, grid));
    for(int i = 0; i < grid * grid; i++)
      cp.add(new CBox(pause));
  }
  public static void main(String[] args) {
    ColorBoxes applet = new ColorBoxes();
    applet.isApplet = false;
    if(args.length > 0)
      applet.grid = Integer.parseInt(args[0]);
    if(args.length > 1)
      applet.pause = Integer.parseInt(args[1]);
    Console.run(applet, 500, 400);
  }
} ///:~
```

ColorBoxes is the usual applet/application with an **init( )** that sets up the GUI. This configures a **GridLayout** so that it has **grid** cells in each dimension. Then it adds the appropriate number of **CBox** objects to fill the grid, passing the **pause** value to each one. In **main( )** you can see how

pause and **grid** have default values that can be changed if you pass in command-line arguments, or by using applet parameters.

CBox is where all the work takes place. This is inherited from **JPanel** and it implements the **Runnable** interface so that each **JPanel** can also be a **Thread**. Remember that when you implement **Runnable**, you don't make a **Thread** object, just a class that has a **run( )** method. Thus, you must explicitly create a **Thread** object and hand the **Runnable** object to the constructor, then call **start( )** (this happens in the constructor). In **CBox** this thread is called **t**.

Notice the array **colors**, which is an enumeration of all the colors in class **Color**. This is used in **newColor( )** to produce a randomly selected color. The current cell color is **cColor**.

paintComponent( ) is quite simple; it just sets the color to **cColor** and fills the entire **JPanel** with that color.

In **run( )**, you see the infinite loop that sets the **cColor** to a new random color and then calls **repaint( )** to show it. Then the thread goes to **sleep( )** for the amount of time specified on the command line.

Precisely because this design is flexible and threading is tied to each **JPanel** element, you can experiment by making as many threads as you want. (In reality, there is a restriction imposed by the number of threads your JVM can comfortably handle.)

This program also makes an interesting benchmark, since it can and has shown dramatic performance and behavioral differences between one JVM threading implementation and another.

Managing concurrency

When you make changes to any Swing component properties from the **main** method of your class or in a separate thread, be aware that the event dispatching thread might be vying for the same resources. [12]

The following program shows how you can get an unexpected result by not paying attention to the event dispatching thread:

---

[12] This section was created by Jeremy Meyer.

```java
//: c14:EventThreadFrame.java
// Race Conditions using Swing Components.
import javax.swing.*;
import java.awt.*;
import java.awt.event.*;
import com.bruceeckel.swing.Console;

public class EventThreadFrame extends JFrame {
  private JTextField statusField =
    new JTextField("Initial Value");
  public EventThreadFrame() {
    Container cp = getContentPane();
    cp.add(statusField, BorderLayout.NORTH);
    addWindowListener(new WindowAdapter() {
      public void windowOpened(WindowEvent e) {
        try { // Simulate initialization overhead
          Thread.sleep(2000);
        } catch (InterruptedException ex) {
          throw new RuntimeException(ex);
        }
        statusField.setText("Initialization complete");
      }
    });
  }
  public static void main (String[] args) {
    EventThreadFrame etf = new EventThreadFrame();
    Console.run(etf, 150, 60);
    etf.statusField.setText("Application ready");
    System.out.println("Done");
  }
} ///:~
```

It is easy to see what is supposed to happen. In the **main** method, a new **EventThreadFrame** class is created and run using the **Console.run( )** method. After the frame has been created and run, the value of the text field is set to "Application ready," and then, just before exiting **main( )**, "Done" is sent to the console.

When the frame is created, the text field is constructed with the value "Initial Value" in the constructor of the frame, and an event listener is added that listens for the opening of the window. This event will be received by the **JFrame** as soon as the **setVisible(true)** method has been called (by **Console.run( )**) and is the right place to do any initialization that affects the view of the window. In this example, a call to **sleep( )** simulates some initialization code that might take a couple of seconds. After this is done, the value of the text box is set to "Initialization complete."

You would expect that the text field would display "Initial Value" followed by "Initialization complete" and then "Application Ready." Next the word "Done" should appear on the command prompt. What really happens is that the **setText( )** method on the **TextField** is called by the main thread *before* the **EventThreadFrame** has had a chance to process its events. This means that the string "Application ready" might actually appear before "Initialization complete." In reality, things might not even appear in this order. Depending on the speed of your system, the Swing event dispatching thread may already be busy handling the **windowOpened** event, so you won't see the text field value until after that event, but by then the text will have been changed to "Initialization Complete." Since the text field was set to this value last, the message "Application ready" is lost. To makes things worse, the word "Done" appears on the command prompt before anything else happens at all!

This undesirable and somewhat unpredictable effect is caused by the simple fact that there are two threads that need some sort of synchronization. It shows that you can sometimes get into trouble with threads and Swing. To solve this problem, you must ensure that Swing component properties are only ever updated by the event dispatch thread.

This is easier than it sounds, using one of Swing's two mechanisms, **SwingUtilities.invokeLater( )** and **SwingUtilities.invokeandWait( )**. They do most of the work, which means that you don't have to do too much complicated synchronization or thread programming.

They both take runnable objects as parameters and drive the **run( )** with the Swing event processing thread, after it has processed any pending events in the queue.

```
//: c14:InvokeLaterFrame.java
// Eliminating race Conditions using Swing Components.
import javax.swing.*;
import java.awt.*;
import java.awt.event.*;
import com.bruceeckel.swing.Console;

public class InvokeLaterFrame extends JFrame {
  private JTextField statusField =
```

```
    new JTextField("Initial Value");
  public InvokeLaterFrame() {
    Container cp = getContentPane();
    cp.add(statusField, BorderLayout.NORTH);
    addWindowListener(new WindowAdapter() {
      public void windowOpened(WindowEvent e) {
        try { // Simulate initialization overhead
          Thread.sleep(2000);
        } catch (InterruptedException ex) {
           throw new RuntimeException(ex);
        }
        statusField.setText("Initialization complete");
      }
    });
  }
  public static void main(String[] args) {
    final InvokeLaterFrame ilf = new InvokeLaterFrame();
    Console.run(ilf, 150, 60);
    // Use invokeAndWait() to synchronize output to prompt:
    // SwingUtilities.invokeAndWait(new Runnable() {
    SwingUtilities.invokeLater(new Runnable() {
      public void run() {
        ilf.statusField.setText("Application ready");
      }
    });
    System.out.println("Done");
  }
} ///:~
```

A **Runnable** anonymous inner class is passed to **SwingUtilities.invokeLater( )**, which calls the **setText( )** method of the text field. This queues the runnable object as an event so that it is the event dispatching thread that calls the **setText( )** method after first processing any pending events. This means that the **windowOpening** event will be processed before the text field displays "Application ready," which is the intended result.

invokeLater( ) is asynchronous, so it returns right away. This can be useful because it doesn't block, so your code runs smoothly. However, it doesn't solve the problem with the "Done" string, which is still printed to the command prompt before anything else happens.

The solution to this problem is to use **invokeAndWait( )** instead of **invokeLater( )** to set the text field value to "Application Ready." This method is synchronous, which means that it will block until the event has been processed before returning. The **System.out.println("Done")** statement will only be reached after the text field value has been set, so it will be the last statement to be executed. This gives us completely predictable and correct behavior.

Using **invokeAndWait( )** provides one of the necessary conditions for deadlock, so make sure that you are careful about controlling shared resources if you are using **invokeAndWait( )**, especially if you are calling it from more than one thread.

You will probably use **invokeLater( )** more often than **invokeAndWait( )**, but remember that if you set the properties of a Swing component any time after initialization, it should be done using one of these methods.

Visual programming and JavaBeans

So far in this book you've seen how valuable Java is for creating reusable pieces of code. The "most reusable" unit of code has been the class, since it comprises a cohesive unit of characteristics (fields) and behaviors (methods) that can be reused either directly via composition or through inheritance.

Inheritance and polymorphism are essential parts of object-oriented programming, but in the majority of cases when you're putting together an application, what you really want is components that do exactly what you need. You'd like to drop these parts into your design like the chips an electronic engineer puts on a circuit board. It seems, too, that there should be some way to accelerate this "modular assembly" style of programming.

"Visual programming" first became successful—*very* successful—with Microsoft's Visual BASIC (VB), followed by a second-generation design in Borland's Delphi (the primary inspiration for the JavaBeans design). With these programming tools the components are represented visually, which makes sense since they usually display some kind of visual component such as a button or a text field. The visual representation, in fact, is often exactly the way the component will look in the running program. So part of the process of visual programming involves dragging a component from a palette and dropping it onto your form. The application builder tool writes code as you do this, and that code will cause the component to be created in the running program.

Simply dropping the component onto a form is usually not enough to complete the program. Often, you must change the characteristics of a component, such as its color, the text that's on it, the database it's connected to, etc. Characteristics that can be modified at design time are referred to as *properties*. You can manipulate the properties of your component inside the application builder tool, and when you create the program, this configuration data is saved so that it can be rejuvenated when the program is started.

By now you're probably used to the idea that an object is more than characteristics; it's also a set of behaviors. At design time, the behaviors of a visual component are partially represented by *events*, meaning "Here's something that can happen to the component." Ordinarily, you decide what you want to happen when an event occurs by tying code to that event.

Here's the critical part: The application builder tool uses reflection to dynamically interrogate the component and find out which properties and events the component supports. Once it knows what they are, it can display the properties and allow you to change them (saving the state when you build the program), and also display the events. In general, you do something like double-clicking on an event, and the application builder tool creates a code body and ties it to that particular event. All you have to do at that point is write the code that executes when the event occurs.

All this adds up to a lot of work that's done for you by the application builder tool. As a result, you can focus on what the program looks like and what it is supposed to do, and rely on the application builder tool to manage the connection details for you. The reason that visual programming tools have been so successful is that they dramatically speed up the process of building an application—certainly the user interface, but often other portions of the application as well.

What is a JavaBean?

After the dust settles, then, a component is really just a block of code, typically embodied in a class. The key issue is the ability for the application builder tool to discover the properties and events for that component. To create a VB component, the programmer had to write a fairly complicated piece of code following certain conventions to expose the properties and events. Delphi was a second-generation visual programming tool, and the language was actively designed around visual programming, so it was much easier to create a visual component. However, Java has brought the creation of visual components to its most advanced state with JavaBeans, because a Bean is just a class. You don't have to write any extra code or use special language extensions in order to make something a Bean. The only thing you need to do, in fact, is slightly modify the way that you name your methods. It is the method name that tells the application builder tool whether this is a property, an event, or just an ordinary method.

In the JDK documentation, this naming convention is mistakenly termed a "design pattern." This is unfortunate, since design patterns (see *Thinking in Patterns (with Java)* at *www.BruceEckel.com*) are challenging enough without this sort of confusion. It's not a design pattern, it's just a naming convention and it's fairly simple:

1. For a property named **xxx**, you typically create two methods: **getXxx( )** and **setXxx( )**. Note that the first letter after "get" or "set" is automatically lower-cased to produce the property name. The type produced by the "get" method is the same as the type of the argument to the "set" method. The name of the property and the type for the "get" and "set" are not related.

2. For a **boolean** property, you can use the "get" and "set" approach above, but you can also use "is" instead of "get."

3. Ordinary methods of the Bean don't conform to the above naming convention, but they're **public**.

4. For events, you use the Swing "listener" approach. It's exactly the same as you've been seeing: **addBounceListener(BounceListener)** and **removeBounceListener(BounceListener)** to handle a **BounceEvent**. Most of the time, the built-in events and listeners will satisfy your needs, but you can also create your own events and listener interfaces.

Point 1 answers a question about something you might have noticed when looking at older code versus newer code: A number of method names have had small, apparently meaningless name changes. Now you can see that most of those changes had to do with adapting to the "get" and "set" naming conventions in order to make that particular component into a JavaBean.

We can use these guidelines to create a simple Bean:

```
//: frogbean:Frog.java
// A trivial JavaBean.
package frogbean;
import java.awt.*;
import java.awt.event.*;

class Spots {}

public class Frog {
  private int jumps;
  private Color color;
  private Spots spots;
  private boolean jmpr;
  public int getJumps() { return jumps; }
  public void setJumps(int newJumps) {
    jumps = newJumps;
  }
  public Color getColor() { return color; }
  public void setColor(Color newColor) {
    color = newColor;
  }
  public Spots getSpots() { return spots; }
  public void setSpots(Spots newSpots) {
    spots = newSpots;
  }
  public boolean isJumper() { return jmpr; }
  public void setJumper(boolean j) { jmpr = j; }
  public void addActionListener(ActionListener l) {
    //...
  }
  public void removeActionListener(ActionListener l) {
    // ...
  }
  public void addKeyListener(KeyListener l) {
    // ...
  }
  public void removeKeyListener(KeyListener l) {
    // ...
  }
  // An "ordinary" public method:
```

```
  public void croak() {
    System.out.println("Ribbet!");
  }
} ///:~
```

First, you can see that it's just a class. Usually, all your fields will be **private** and accessible only through methods. Following the naming convention, the properties are **jumps**, **color**, **spots**, and **jumper** (notice the case change of the first letter in the property name). Although the name of the internal identifier is the same as the name of the property in the first three cases, in **jumper** you can see that the property name does not force you to use any particular identifier for internal variables (or, indeed, to even *have* any internal variables for that property).

The events this Bean handles are **ActionEvent** and **KeyEvent**, based on the naming of the "add" and "remove" methods for the associated listener. Finally, you can see that the ordinary method **croak( )** is still part of the Bean simply because it's a **public** method, not because it conforms to any naming scheme.

Extracting **BeanInfo** with the **Introspector**

One of the most critical parts of the JavaBean scheme occurs when you drag a Bean off a palette and plop it onto a form. The application builder tool must be able to create the Bean (which it can do if there's a default constructor) and then, without access to the Bean's source code, extract all the necessary information to create the property sheet and event handlers.

Part of the solution is already evident from Chapter 10: Java *reflection* discovers all the methods of an unknown class. This is perfect for solving the JavaBean problem without requiring you to use any extra language keywords like those required in other visual programming languages. In fact, one of the prime reasons that reflection was added to Java was to support JavaBeans (although reflection also supports object serialization and remote method invocation). So you might expect that the creator of the application builder tool would have to reflect each Bean and hunt through its methods to find the properties and events for that Bean.

This is certainly possible, but the Java designers wanted to provide a standard tool, not only to make Beans simpler to use, but also to provide a standard gateway to the creation of more complex Beans. This tool is the **Introspector** class, and the most important method in this class is **static getBeanInfo( )**. You pass a **Class** reference to this method, and it fully interrogates that class and returns a **BeanInfo** object that you can then dissect to find properties, methods, and events.

Usually, you won't care about any of this; you'll probably get most of your Beans off the shelf from vendors, and you don't need to know all the magic that's going on underneath. You'll simply drag your Beans onto your form, then configure their properties and write handlers for the events you're interested in. However, it's an interesting and educational exercise to use the **Introspector** to display information about a Bean, so here's a tool that does it:

```
//: c14:BeanDumper.java
// Introspecting a Bean.
import java.beans.*;
import java.lang.reflect.*;
import javax.swing.*;
import java.awt.*;
import java.awt.event.*;
import com.bruceeckel.swing.*;

public class BeanDumper extends JFrame {
  private JTextField query = new JTextField(20);
  private JTextArea results = new JTextArea();
  public void print(String s) { results.append(s + "\n"); }
  public void dump(Class bean) {
    results.setText("");
    BeanInfo bi = null;
    try {
      bi = Introspector.getBeanInfo(bean, Object.class);
    } catch(IntrospectionException e) {
      print("Couldn't introspect " +  bean.getName());
      return;
    }
    PropertyDescriptor[] properties =
      bi.getPropertyDescriptors();
    for(int i = 0; i < properties.length; i++) {
      Class p = properties[i].getPropertyType();
      if(p == null) continue;
      print("Property type:\n  " + p.getName() +
        "Property name:\n  " + properties[i].getName());
```

```
      Method readMethod = properties[i].getReadMethod();
      if(readMethod != null)
        print("Read method:\n  " + readMethod);
      Method writeMethod = properties[i].getWriteMethod();
      if(writeMethod != null)
        print("Write method:\n  " + writeMethod);
      print("====================");
    }
    print("Public methods:");
    MethodDescriptor[] methods = bi.getMethodDescriptors();
    for(int i = 0; i < methods.length; i++)
      print(methods[i].getMethod().toString());
    print("======================");
    print("Event support:");
    EventSetDescriptor[] events =
      bi.getEventSetDescriptors();
    for(int i = 0; i < events.length; i++) {
      print("Listener type:\n  " +
        events[i].getListenerType().getName());
      Method[] lm =  events[i].getListenerMethods();
      for(int j = 0; j < lm.length; j++)
        print("Listener method:\n  " + lm[j].getName());
      MethodDescriptor[] lmd =
        events[i].getListenerMethodDescriptors();
      for(int j = 0; j < lmd.length; j++)
        print("Method descriptor:\n  "
          + lmd[j].getMethod());
      Method addListener= events[i].getAddListenerMethod();
      print("Add Listener Method:\n  " + addListener);
      Method removeListener =
        events[i].getRemoveListenerMethod();
      print("Remove Listener Method:\n  "+ removeListener);
      print("====================");
    }
  }
  class Dumper implements ActionListener {
    public void actionPerformed(ActionEvent e) {
      String name = query.getText();
      Class c = null;
      try {
        c = Class.forName(name);
      } catch(ClassNotFoundException ex) {
        results.setText("Couldn't find " + name);
        return;
```

```
      }
      dump(c);
    }
  }
  public BeanDumper() {
    Container cp = getContentPane();
    JPanel p = new JPanel();
    p.setLayout(new FlowLayout());
    p.add(new JLabel("Qualified bean name:"));
    p.add(query);
    cp.add(BorderLayout.NORTH, p);
    cp.add(new JScrollPane(results));
    Dumper dmpr = new Dumper();
    query.addActionListener(dmpr);
    query.setText("frogbean.Frog");
    // Force evaluation
    dmpr.actionPerformed(new ActionEvent(dmpr, 0, ""));
  }
  public static void main(String[] args) {
    Console.run(new BeanDumper(), 600, 500);
  }
} ///:~
```

BeanDumper.dump( ) is the method that does all the work. First it tries to create a **BeanInfo** object, and if successful, calls the methods of **BeanInfo** that produce information about properties, methods, and events. In **Introspector.getBeanInfo( )**, you'll see there is a second argument. This tells the **Introspector** where to stop in the inheritance hierarchy. Here, it stops before it parses all the methods from **Object**, since we're not interested in seeing those.

For properties, **getPropertyDescriptors( )** returns an array of **PropertyDescriptors**. For each **PropertyDescriptor**, you can call **getPropertyType( )** to find the class of object that is passed in and out via the property methods. Then, for each property, you can get its pseudonym (extracted from the method names) with **getName( )**, the method for reading with **getReadMethod( )**, and the method for writing with **getWriteMethod( )**. These last two methods return a **Method** object that can actually be used to invoke the corresponding method on the object (this is part of reflection).

For the **public** methods (including the property methods), **getMethodDescriptors( )** returns an array of **MethodDescriptor**s. For each one, you can get the associated **Method** object and print its name.

For the events, **getEventSetDescriptors( )** returns an array of (what else?) **EventSetDescriptor**s. Each of these can be queried to find out the class of the listener, the methods of that listener class, and the add- and remove-listener methods. The **BeanDumper** program prints out all of this information.

Upon startup, the program forces the evaluation of **frogbean.Frog**. The output, after removing extra details that are unnecessary here, is:

```
class name: Frog
Property type:
  Color
Property name:
  color
Read method:
  public Color getColor()
Write method:
  public void setColor(Color)
====================
Property type:
  Spots
Property name:
  spots
Read method:
  public Spots getSpots()
Write method:
  public void setSpots(Spots)
====================
Property type:
  boolean
Property name:
  jumper
Read method:
  public boolean isJumper()
Write method:
  public void setJumper(boolean)
====================
Property type:
  int
Property name:
```

```
  jumps
Read method:
  public int getJumps()
Write method:
  public void setJumps(int)
====================
Public methods:
public void setJumps(int)
public void croak()
public void removeActionListener(ActionListener)
public void addActionListener(ActionListener)
public int getJumps()
public void setColor(Color)
public void setSpots(Spots)
public void setJumper(boolean)
public boolean isJumper()
public void addKeyListener(KeyListener)
public Color getColor()
public void removeKeyListener(KeyListener)
public Spots getSpots()
======================
Event support:
Listener type:
  KeyListener
Listener method:
  keyTyped
Listener method:
  keyPressed
Listener method:
  keyReleased
Method descriptor:
  public void keyTyped(KeyEvent)
Method descriptor:
  public void keyPressed(KeyEvent)
Method descriptor:
  public void keyReleased(KeyEvent)
Add Listener Method:
  public void addKeyListener(KeyListener)
Remove Listener Method:
  public void removeKeyListener(KeyListener)
====================
Listener type:
  ActionListener
Listener method:
```

```
  actionPerformed
Method descriptor:
  public void actionPerformed(ActionEvent)
Add Listener Method:
  public void addActionListener(ActionListener)
Remove Listener Method:
  public void removeActionListener(ActionListener)
====================
```

This reveals most of what the **Introspector** sees as it produces a **BeanInfo** object from your Bean. You can see that the type of the property and its name are independent. Notice the lowercasing of the property name. (The only time this doesn't occur is when the property name begins with more than one capital letter in a row.) And remember that the method names you're seeing here (such as the read and write methods) are actually produced from a **Method** object that can be used to invoke the associated method on the object.

The **public** method list includes the methods that are not associated with a property or event, such as **croak( )**, as well as those that are. These are all the methods that you can call programmatically for a Bean, and the application builder tool can choose to list all of these while you're making method calls, to ease your task.

Finally, you can see that the events are fully parsed out into the listener, its methods, and the add- and remove-listener methods. Basically, once you have the **BeanInfo**, you can find out everything of importance for the Bean. You can also call the methods for that Bean, even though you don't have any other information except the object (again, a feature of reflection).

A more sophisticated Bean

This next example is slightly more sophisticated, albeit frivolous. It's a **JPanel** that draws a little circle around the mouse whenever the mouse is moved. When you press the mouse, the word "Bang!" appears in the middle of the screen, and an action listener is fired.

The properties you can change are the size of the circle as well as the color, size, and text of the word that is displayed when you press the mouse. A **BangBean** also has its own **addActionListener( )** and **removeActionListener( )**, so you can attach your own listener that will be fired when the user clicks on the **BangBean**. You should be able to recognize the property and event support:

```
//: bangbean:BangBean.java
// A graphical Bean.
package bangbean;
import javax.swing.*;
import java.awt.*;
import java.awt.event.*;
import java.io.*;
import java.util.*;
import com.bruceeckel.swing.*;

public class
BangBean extends JPanel implements Serializable {
  private int xm, ym;
  private int cSize = 20; // Circle size
  private String text = "Bang!";
  private int fontSize = 48;
  private Color tColor = Color.RED;
  private ActionListener actionListener;
  public BangBean() {
    addMouseListener(new ML());
    addMouseMotionListener(new MML());
  }
  public int getCircleSize() { return cSize; }
  public void setCircleSize(int newSize) {
    cSize = newSize;
  }
  public String getBangText() { return text; }
  public void setBangText(String newText) {
    text = newText;
  }
  public int getFontSize() { return fontSize; }
  public void setFontSize(int newSize) {
    fontSize = newSize;
  }
  public Color getTextColor() { return tColor; }
  public void setTextColor(Color newColor) {
    tColor = newColor;
  }
  public void paintComponent(Graphics g) {
    super.paintComponent(g);
    g.setColor(Color.BLACK);
```

```
    g.drawOval(xm - cSize/2, ym - cSize/2, cSize, cSize);
  }
  // This is a unicast listener, which is
  // the simplest form of listener management:
  public void addActionListener(ActionListener l)
  throws TooManyListenersException {
    if(actionListener != null)
      throw new TooManyListenersException();
    actionListener = l;
  }
  public void removeActionListener(ActionListener l) {
    actionListener = null;
  }
  class ML extends MouseAdapter {
    public void mousePressed(MouseEvent e) {
      Graphics g = getGraphics();
      g.setColor(tColor);
      g.setFont(
        new Font("TimesRoman", Font.BOLD, fontSize));
      int width = g.getFontMetrics().stringWidth(text);
      g.drawString(text, (getSize().width - width) /2,
        getSize().height/2);
      g.dispose();
      // Call the listener's method:
      if(actionListener != null)
        actionListener.actionPerformed(
          new ActionEvent(BangBean.this,
            ActionEvent.ACTION_PERFORMED, null));
    }
  }
  class MML extends MouseMotionAdapter {
    public void mouseMoved(MouseEvent e) {
      xm = e.getX();
      ym = e.getY();
      repaint();
    }
  }
  public Dimension getPreferredSize() {
    return new Dimension(200, 200);
  }
} ///:~
```

The first thing you'll notice is that **BangBean** implements the **Serializable** interface. This means that the application builder tool can "pickle" all the information for the **BangBean** by using serialization after the program designer has adjusted the values of the properties. When the Bean is created as part of the running application, these "pickled" properties are restored so that you get exactly what you designed.

You can see that all the fields are **private**, which is what you'll usually do with a Bean—allow access only through methods, usually using the "property" scheme.

When you look at the signature for **addActionListener( )**, you'll see that it can throw a **TooManyListenersException**. This indicates that it is *unicast*, which means it notifies only one listener when the event occurs. Ordinarily, you'll use *multicast* events so that many listeners can be notified of an event. However, that runs into threading issues, so it will be revisited under the heading "JavaBeans and synchronization" later in this chapter. In the meantime, a unicast event sidesteps the problem.

When you click the mouse, the text is put in the middle of the **BangBean**, and if the **actionListener** field is not **null**, its **actionPerformed( )** is called, creating a new **ActionEvent** object in the process. Whenever the mouse is moved, its new coordinates are captured and the canvas is repainted (erasing any text that's on the canvas, as you'll see).

Here is the **BangBeanTest** class to test the Bean:

```
//: c14:BangBeanTest.java
import bangbean.*;
import javax.swing.*;
import java.awt.*;
import java.awt.event.*;
import java.util.*;
import com.bruceeckel.swing.*;

public class BangBeanTest extends JFrame {
  private JTextField txt = new JTextField(20);
  // During testing, report actions:
  class BBL implements ActionListener {
    private int count = 0;
    public void actionPerformed(ActionEvent e) {
      txt.setText("BangBean action "+ count++);
    }
  }
  public BangBeanTest() {
```

```
    BangBean bb = new BangBean();
    try {
      bb.addActionListener(new BBL());
    } catch(TooManyListenersException e) {
      txt.setText("Too many listeners");
    }
    Container cp = getContentPane();
    cp.add(bb);
    cp.add(BorderLayout.SOUTH, txt);
  }
  public static void main(String[] args) {
    Console.run(new BangBeanTest(), 400, 500);
  }
} ///:~
```

When a Bean is in a development environment, this class will not be used, but it's helpful to provide a rapid testing method for each of your Beans. **BangBeanTest** places a **BangBean** within the applet, attaching a simple **ActionListener** to the **BangBean** to print an event count to the **JTextField** whenever an **ActionEvent** occurs. Usually, of course, the application builder tool would create most of the code that uses the Bean.

When you run the **BangBean** through **BeanDumper** or put the **BangBean** inside a Bean-enabled development environment, you'll notice that there are many more properties and actions than are evident from the preceding code. That's because **BangBean** is inherited from **JPanel**, and **JPanel** is also Bean, so you're seeing its properties and events as well.

JavaBeans and synchronization

Whenever you create a Bean, you must assume that it will run in a multithreaded environment. This means that:

1. Whenever possible, all the **public** methods of a Bean should be **synchronized**. Of course, this incurs the **synchronized** run-time overhead (which has been significantly reduced in recent versions of the JDK). If that's a problem, methods that will not cause problems in critical sections can be left un-**synchronized**, but keep in mind that this is not always obvious. Methods that qualify tend to be small (such as **getCircleSize( )** in the following example) and/or "atomic," that is, the method call executes in such a short amount of code that the object cannot be changed during execution. Making such methods un-**synchronized** might not have a significant effect on the execution

speed of your program. You might as well make all **public** methods of a Bean **synchronized** and remove the **synchronized** keyword only when you know for sure that it's necessary and that it makes a difference.

2. When firing a multicast event to a bunch of listeners interested in that event, you must assume that listeners might be added or removed while moving through the list.

The first point is fairly easy to deal with, but the second point requires a little more thought. The previous version of **BangBean.java** ducked out of the multithreading question by ignoring the **synchronized** keyword and making the event unicast. Here is a modified version that works in a multithreaded environment and uses multicasting for events:

```
//: c14:BangBean2.java
// You should write your Beans this way so they
// can run in a multithreaded environment.
import javax.swing.*;
import java.awt.*;
import java.awt.event.*;
import java.util.*;
import java.io.*;
import com.bruceeckel.swing.*;

public class BangBean2 extends JPanel
implements Serializable {
  private int xm, ym;
  private int cSize = 20; // Circle size
  private String text = "Bang!";
  private int fontSize = 48;
  private Color tColor = Color.RED;
  private ArrayList actionListeners = new ArrayList();
  public BangBean2() {
    addMouseListener(new ML());
    addMouseMotionListener(new MM());
  }
  public synchronized int getCircleSize() { return cSize; }
  public synchronized void setCircleSize(int newSize) {
    cSize = newSize;
  }
  public synchronized String getBangText() { return text; }
  public synchronized void setBangText(String newText) {
    text = newText;
```

```
  }
  public synchronized int getFontSize(){ return fontSize; }
  public synchronized void setFontSize(int newSize) {
    fontSize = newSize;
  }
  public synchronized Color getTextColor(){ return tColor;}
  public synchronized void setTextColor(Color newColor) {
    tColor = newColor;
  }
  public void paintComponent(Graphics g) {
    super.paintComponent(g);
    g.setColor(Color.BLACK);
    g.drawOval(xm - cSize/2, ym - cSize/2, cSize, cSize);
  }
  // This is a multicast listener, which is more typically
  // used than the unicast approach taken in BangBean.java:
  public synchronized void
  addActionListener(ActionListener l) {
    actionListeners.add(l);
  }
  public synchronized void
  removeActionListener(ActionListener l) {
    actionListeners.remove(l);
  }
  // Notice this isn't synchronized:
  public void notifyListeners() {
    ActionEvent a = new ActionEvent(BangBean2.this,
      ActionEvent.ACTION_PERFORMED, null);
    ArrayList lv = null;
    // Make a shallow copy of the List in case
    // someone adds a listener while we're
    // calling listeners:
    synchronized(this) {
      lv = (ArrayList)actionListeners.clone();
    }
    // Call all the listener methods:
    for(int i = 0; i < lv.size(); i++)
      ((ActionListener)lv.get(i)).actionPerformed(a);
  }
  class ML extends MouseAdapter {
    public void mousePressed(MouseEvent e) {
      Graphics g = getGraphics();
      g.setColor(tColor);
      g.setFont(
```

```
        new Font("TimesRoman", Font.BOLD, fontSize));
      int width = g.getFontMetrics().stringWidth(text);
      g.drawString(text, (getSize().width - width) /2,
        getSize().height/2);
      g.dispose();
      notifyListeners();
    }
  }
  class MM extends MouseMotionAdapter {
    public void mouseMoved(MouseEvent e) {
      xm = e.getX();
      ym = e.getY();
      repaint();
    }
  }
  public static void main(String[] args) {
    BangBean2 bb = new BangBean2();
    bb.addActionListener(new ActionListener() {
      public void actionPerformed(ActionEvent e) {
        System.out.println("ActionEvent" + e);
      }
    });
    bb.addActionListener(new ActionListener() {
      public void actionPerformed(ActionEvent e) {
        System.out.println("BangBean2 action");
      }
    });
    bb.addActionListener(new ActionListener() {
      public void actionPerformed(ActionEvent e) {
        System.out.println("More action");
      }
    });
    Console.run(bb, 300, 300);
  }
} ///:~
```

Adding **synchronized** to the methods is an easy change. However, notice in **addActionListener( )** and **removeActionListener( )** that the **ActionListener**s are now added to and removed from an **ArrayList**, so you can have as many as you want.

You can see that the method **notifyListeners( )** is *not* **synchronized**. It can be called from more than one thread at a time. It's also possible for **addActionListener( )** or **removeActionListener( )** to be called in the middle of a call to **notifyListeners( )**, which is a problem because it traverses the **ArrayList actionListeners**. To alleviate the problem, the **ArrayList** is cloned inside a **synchronized** clause, and the clone is traversed (see Appendix A for details of cloning). This way, the original **ArrayList** can be manipulated without impact on **notifyListeners( )**.

The **paintComponent( )** method is also not **synchronized**. Deciding whether to synchronize overridden methods is not as clear as when you're just adding your own methods. In this example, it turns out that **paintComponent( )** seems to work OK whether it's **synchronized** or not. But the issues you must consider are:

1. Does the method modify the state of "critical" variables within the object? To discover whether the variables are "critical," you must determine whether they will be read or set by other threads in the program. (In this case, the reading or setting is virtually always accomplished via **synchronized** methods, so you can just examine those.) In the case of **paintComponent( )**, no modification takes place.

2. Does the method depend on the state of these "critical" variables? If a **synchronized** method modifies a variable that your method uses, then you might very well want to make your method **synchronized** as well. Based on this, you might observe that **cSize** is changed by **synchronized** methods, and therefore **paintComponent( )** should be **synchronized**. Here, however, you can ask "What's the worst thing that will happen if **cSize** is changed during a **paintComponent( )**?" When you see that it's nothing too bad, and a transient effect at that, you can decide to leave **paintComponent( )** un-**synchronized** to prevent the extra overhead from the **synchronized** method call.

3. A third clue is to notice whether the base-class version of **paintComponent( )** is **synchronized**, which it isn't. This isn't an airtight argument, just a clue. In this case, for example, a field that *is* changed via **synchronized** methods (that is **cSize**) has been mixed into the **paintComponent( )** formula and might have changed the situation. Notice, however, that **synchronized** doesn't inherit; that is, if a method is **synchronized** in the base class, then it *is not* automatically **synchronized** in the derived class overridden version.

4. **paint( )** and **paintComponent( )** are methods that must be as fast as possible. Anything that takes processing overhead out of these methods is highly recommended, so if you think you need to synchronize these methods it may be an indicator of bad design.

The test code in **main( )** has been modified from that seen in **BangBeanTest** to demonstrate the multicast ability of **BangBean2** by adding extra listeners.

Packaging a Bean

Before you can bring a JavaBean into a Bean-enabled visual builder tool, it must be put into the standard Bean container, which is a JAR file that includes all the Bean classes as well as a "manifest" file that says "This is a Bean." A manifest file is simply a text file that follows a particular form. For the **BangBean**, the manifest file looks like this:

```
Manifest-Version: 1.0

Name: bangbean/BangBean.class
Java-Bean: True
```

The first line indicates the version of the manifest scheme, which until further notice from Sun is 1.0. The second line (empty lines are ignored) names the **BangBean.class** file, and the third says "It's a Bean." Without the third line, the program builder tool will not recognize the class as a Bean.

The only tricky part is that you must make sure that you get the proper path in the "Name:" field. If you look back at **BangBean.java**, you'll see it's in **package bangbean** (and thus in a subdirectory called "bangbean" that's off of the classpath), and the name in the manifest file must include this package information. In addition, you must place the manifest file in the directory *above* the root of your package path, which in this case means placing the file in the directory above the "bangbean" subdirectory. Then you must invoke **jar** from the same directory as the manifest file, as follows:

```
jar cfm BangBean.jar BangBean.mf bangbean
```

This assumes that you want the resulting JAR file to be named **BangBean.jar**, and that you've put the manifest in a file called **BangBean.mf**.

You might wonder "What about all the other classes that were generated when I compiled **BangBean.java**?" Well, they all ended up inside the **bangbean** subdirectory, and you'll see that the last argument for the above **jar** command line is the **bangbean** subdirectory. When you give **jar** the name of a subdirectory, it packages that entire subdirectory into the JAR file (including, in this case, the original **BangBean.java** source-code file—you might not choose to include the source with your own Beans). In addition, if you turn around and unpack the JAR file you've just created, you'll discover that your manifest file isn't inside, but that **jar** has created its own manifest file (based partly on yours) called **MANIFEST.MF** and placed it inside the subdirectory **META-INF** (for "meta-information"). If you open this manifest file, you'll also notice that digital signature information has been added by **jar** for each file, of the form:

```
Digest-Algorithms: SHA MD5
SHA-Digest: pDpEAG9NaeCx8aFtqPI4udSX/O0=
MD5-Digest: O4NcS1hE3Smnzlp2hj6qeg==
```

In general, you don't need to worry about any of this, and if you make changes, you can just modify your original manifest file and reinvoke **jar** to create a new JAR file for your Bean. You can also add other Beans to the JAR file simply by adding their information to your manifest.

One thing to notice is that you'll probably want to put each Bean in its own subdirectory, since when you create a JAR file you hand the **jar** utility the name of a subdirectory, and it puts everything in that subdirectory into the JAR file. You can see that both **Frog** and **BangBean** are in their own subdirectories.

Once you have your Bean properly inside a JAR file, you can bring it into a Beans-enabled program-builder environment. The way you do this varies from one tool to the next, but Sun provides a freely available test bed for JavaBeans in their "Bean Builder." (Download from *java.sun.com/beans*.) You place a Bean into the Bean Builder by simply copying the JAR file into the correct subdirectory.

More complex Bean support

You can see how remarkably simple it is to make a Bean, but you aren't limited to what you've seen here. The JavaBeans architecture provides a simple point of entry but can also scale to more complex situations. These situations are beyond the scope of this book, but they will be briefly introduced here. You can find more details at *java.sun.com/beans*.

One place where you can add sophistication is with properties. The examples you've seen here have shown only single properties, but it's also possible to represent multiple properties in an array. This is called an *indexed property*. You simply provide the appropriate methods (again following a naming convention for the method names), and the **Introspector** recognizes an indexed property so that your application builder tool can respond appropriately.

Properties can be *bound*, which means that they will notify other objects via a **PropertyChangeEvent**. The other objects can then choose to change themselves based on the change to the Bean.

Properties can be *constrained*, which means that other objects can veto a change to that property if it is unacceptable. The other objects are notified by using a **PropertyChangeEvent**, and they can throw a **PropertyVetoException** to prevent the change from happening and to restore the old values.

You can also change the way your Bean is represented at design time:

1. You can provide a custom property sheet for your particular Bean. The ordinary property sheet will be used for all other Beans, but yours is automatically invoked when your Bean is selected.

2. You can create a custom editor for a particular property, so the ordinary property sheet is used, but when your special property is being edited, your editor will automatically be invoked.

3. You can provide a custom **BeanInfo** class for your Bean that produces information different from the default created by the **Introspector**.

4. It's also possible to turn "expert" mode on and off in all **FeatureDescriptor**s to distinguish between basic features and more complicated ones.

More to Beans

There are a number of books about JavaBeans; for example, *JavaBeans* by Elliotte Rusty Harold (IDG, 1998).

Summary

Of all the libraries in Java, the GUI library has seen the most dramatic changes from Java 1.0 to Java 2. The Java 1.0 AWT was roundly criticized as being one of the worst designs seen, and while it would allow you to create portable programs, the resulting GUI was "equally mediocre on all platforms." It was also limiting, awkward, and unpleasant to use compared with the native application development tools available on a particular platform.

When Java 1.1 introduced the new event model and JavaBeans, the stage was set—now it was possible to create GUI components that could be easily dragged and dropped inside visual application builder tools. In addition, the design of the event model and JavaBeans clearly shows strong consideration for ease of programming and maintainable code (something that was not evident in the 1.0 AWT). But it wasn't until the JFC/Swing classes appeared that the job was finished. With the Swing components, cross-platform GUI programming can be a civilized experience.

Actually, the only thing that's missing is the application builder tool, and this is where the real revolution lies. Microsoft's Visual BASIC and Visual C++ require Microsoft's application builder tools, as does Borland's Delphi and C++ Builder. If you want the application builder tool to get better, you have to cross your fingers and hope the vendor will give you what you want. But Java is an open environment, so not only does it allow for competing application builder environments, it encourages them. And for these tools to be taken seriously, they must support JavaBeans. This means a leveled playing field; if a better application builder tool comes along, you're not tied to the one you've been using. You can pick up and move to the new one and increase your productivity. This kind of competitive environment for GUI application builder tools has not been seen before, and the resulting marketplace can generate only positive results for the productivity of the programmer.

This chapter was meant only to give you an introduction to the power of Swing and to get you started so you could see how relatively simple it is to feel your way through the libraries. What you've seen so far will probably suffice for a good portion of your UI design needs. However, there's a lot more to Swing; it's intended to be a fully powered UI design tool kit. There's probably a way to accomplish just about everything you can imagine.

If you don't see what you need here, delve into the JDK documentation from Sun and search the Web, and if that's not enough, then find a dedicated Swing book. A good place to start is *The JFC Swing Tutorial*, by Walrath & Campione (Addison Wesley, 1999).

Exercises

Solutions to selected exercises can be found in the electronic document *The Thinking in Java Annotated Solution Guide*, available for a small fee from *www.BruceEckel.com.*

1. Create an applet/application using the **Console** class as shown in this chapter. Include a text field and three buttons. When you press each button, make some different text appear in the text field.

2. Add a check box to the applet created in Exercise 1, capture the event, and insert different text into the text field.

3. Create an applet/application using **Console**. In the JDK documentation from *java.sun.com*, find the **JPasswordField** and add this to the program. If the user types in the correct password, use **Joptionpane** to provide a success message to the user.

4. Create an applet/application using **Console**, and add all the Swing components that have an **addActionListener( )** method. (Look these up in the JDK documentation from *java.sun.com*. Hint: use the index.) Capture their events and display an appropriate message for each inside a text field.

5. Create an applet/application using **Console**, with a **JButton** and a **JTextField**. Write and attach the appropriate listener so that if the button has the focus, characters typed into it will appear in the **JTextField**.

6. Create an applet/application using **Console**. Add to the main frame all the components described in this chapter, including menus and a dialog box.

7. Modify **TextFields.java** so that the characters in **t2** retain the original case that they were typed in, instead of automatically being forced to upper case.

8. Locate and download one or more of the free GUI builder development environments available on the Internet, or buy a commercial product. Discover what is necessary to add **BangBean** to this environment and to use it.

9. Add **Frog.class** to the manifest file as shown in this chapter and run **jar** to create a JAR file containing both **Frog** and **BangBean**. Now either download and install the Bean Builder from Sun, or use your own Beans-enabled program builder tool and add the JAR file to your environment so you can test the two Beans.

10. Create your own JavaBean called **Valve** that contains two properties: a **boolean** called "on" and an **int** called "level." Create a manifest file, use **jar** to package your Bean, then load it into the Bean Builder or into a Beans-enabled program builder tool so that you can test it.

11. Modify **MessageBoxes.java** so that it has an individual **ActionListener** for each button (instead of matching the button text).

12. Monitor a new type of event in **TrackEvent.java** by adding the new event handling code. You'll need to discover on your own the type of event that you want to monitor.

13. Inherit a new type of button from **JButton**. Each time you press this button, it should change its color to a randomly selected value. See **ColorBoxes.java** for an example of how to generate a random color value.

14. Modify **TextPane.java** to use a **JTextArea** instead of a **JTextPane**.

15. Modify **Menus.java** to use radio buttons instead of check boxes on the menus.

16. Simplify **List.java** by passing the array to the constructor and eliminating the dynamic addition of elements to the list.

17. Modify **SineWave.java** to turn **SineDraw** into a JavaBean by adding "getter" and "setter" methods.

18. Remember the "sketching box" toy with two knobs, one that controls the vertical movement of the drawing point, and one that controls the horizontal movement? Create one of those, using **SineWave.java** to get you started. Instead of knobs, use sliders. Add a button that will erase the entire sketch.

19. Starting with **SineWave.java**, create a program (an applet/application using the **Console** class) that draws an animated sine wave that appears to scroll past the viewing window like an oscilloscope, driving the animation with a **Thread**. The speed of the animation should be controlled with a **java.swing.JSlider** control.

20. Modify Exercise 19 so that multiple sine wave panels are created within the application. The number of sine wave panels should be controlled by HTML tags or command-line parameters.

21. Modify Exercise 19 so that the **java.swing.Timer** class is used to drive the animation. Note the difference between this and **java.util.Timer**.

22. Create an "asymptotic progress indicator" that gets slower and slower as it approaches the finish point. Add random erratic behavior so it will periodically look like it's starting to speed up.

23. Modify **Progress.java** so that it does not share models, but instead uses a listener to connect the slider and progress bar.

24. Follow the instructions in the section titled "Packaging an applet into a JAR file" to place **TicTacToe.java** into a JAR file. Create an HTML page with the simple version of the applet tag along with the archive specification to use the JAR file. Run **HTMLconverter** on file to produce a working HTML file.

25. Create an applet/application using **Console**. This should have three sliders, one each for the red, green, and blue values in **java.awt.Color**. The rest of the form should be a **JPanel** that displays the color determined by the three sliders. Also include non-editable text fields that show the current RGB values.

26. In the JDK documentation for **javax.swing**, look up the **JColorChooser**. Write a program with a button that brings up the color chooser as a dialog.

27. Almost every Swing component is derived from **Component**, which has a **setCursor( )** method. Look this up in the JDK documentation. Create an applet and change the cursor to one of the stock cursors in the **Cursor** class.

28. Starting with **ShowAddListeners.java**, create a program with the full functionality of **c10:ShowMethods.java**.

29. Turn **c12:TestRegularExpression.java** into an interactive Swing program that allows you to put an input string in one **TextArea** and a regular expression in a **TextField**. The results should be displayed in a second **TextArea**.

30. Modify **InvokeLaterFrame.java** to use **invokeAndWait( )**.

15: Discovering Problems

Before C was tamed into ANSI C, we had a little joke: "My code compiles, so it should run!" (Ha ha!)

This was funny only if you understood C, because at that time the C compiler would accept just about anything; C was truly a "portable assembly language" created to see if it was possible to develop a portable operating system (Unix) that could be moved from one machine architecture to another without rewriting it from scratch in the new machine's assembly language. So C was actually created as a side-effect of building Unix and not as a general-purpose programming language.

Because C was targeted at programmers who wrote operating systems in assembly language, it was implicitly assumed that those programmers knew what they were doing and didn't need safety nets. For example, assembly-language programmers didn't need the compiler to check argument types and usage, and if they decided to use a data type in a different way than it was originally intended, they certainly must have good reason to do so, and the compiler didn't get in the way. Thus, getting your pre-ANSI C program to compile was only the first step in the long process of developing a bug-free program.

The development of ANSI C along with stronger rules about what the compiler would accept came after lots of people used C for projects other than writing operating systems, and after the appearance of C++, which greatly improved your chances of having a program run decently once it compiled. Much of this improvement came through *strong static type checking*: "strong" because the compiler prevented you from abusing the type, "static" because ANSI C and C++ perform type checking at compile time.

To many people (myself included), the improvement was so dramatic that it appeared that strong static type checking was the answer to a large portion of our problems. Indeed, one of the motivations for Java was that C++'s type checking wasn't strong *enough* (primarily because C++ had to be backward-compatible with C, and so was chained to its limitations). Thus Java has gone even further to take advantage of the benefits of type checking, and since Java has language-checking mechanisms that exist at run time (C++ doesn't; what's left at run time is basically assembly language—very fast, but with no self-awareness), it isn't restricted to only static type checking.[1]

It seems, however, that language-checking mechanisms can take us only so far in our quest to develop a correctly-working program. C++ gave us programs that worked a lot sooner than C programs, but often still had problems such as memory leaks and subtle, buried bugs. Java went a long way toward solving those problems, yet it's still quite possible to write a Java program containing nasty bugs. In addition (despite the amazing performance claims always touted by the flaks at Sun), all the safety nets in Java added additional overhead, so sometimes we run into the challenge of getting our Java programs to run fast enough for a particular need (although it's usually more important to have a working program than one that runs at a particular speed).

This chapter presents tools to solve the problems that the compiler doesn't. In a sense, we are admitting that the compiler can take us only so far in the creation of robust programs, so we are moving beyond the compiler and creating a build system and code that know more about what a program is and isn't supposed to do.

One of the biggest steps forward is the incorporation of *automated unit testing*. This means writing tests and incorporating those tests into a build system that compiles your code and runs the tests every single time, as if the tests were part of the compilation process (you'll soon start relying upon

---

[1] It is primarily oriented to static checking, however. There is an alternative system, called *latent typing* or *dynamic typing* or *weak typing*, in which the type of an object is still enforced, but it is enforced at run time, when the type is used, rather than at compile time. Writing code in such a language—Python (http://www.python.org) is an excellent example—gives the programmer much more flexibility and requires far less verbiage to satisfy the compiler, and yet still guarantees that objects are used properly. However, to a programmer convinced that strong, static type checking is the only sensible solution, latent typing is anathema and serious flame wars have resulted from comparisons between the two approaches. As someone who is always in pursuit of greater productivity, I have found the value of latent typing to be very compelling. In addition, the ability to think about the issues of latent typing help you, I believe, to solve problems that are difficult to think about in strong, statically typed languages.

them as if they are). For this book, a custom testing system was developed to ensure the correctness of the program output (and to display the output directly in the code listing), but the defacto standard **JUnit** testing system will also be used when appropriate. To make sure that testing is automatic, tests are run as part of the build process using Ant, an open-source tool that has also become a defacto standard in Java development, and CVS, another open-source tool that maintains a repository containing all your source code for a particular project.

JDK 1.4 introduced an *assertion* mechanism to aid in the verification of code at run time. One of the more compelling uses of assertions is *Design by Contract* (DBC), a formalized way to describe the correctness of a class. In conjunction with automated testing, DBC can be a powerful tool.

Sometimes unit testing isn't enough, and you need to track down problems in a program that runs, but doesn't run right. In JDK 1.4, the *logging API* was introduced to allow you to easily report information about your program. This is a significant improvement over adding and removing **println( )** statements in order to track down a problem, and this section will go into enough detail to give you a thorough grounding in this API. This chapter also provides an introduction to debugging, showing the information a typical debugger can provide to aid you in the discovery of subtle problems. Finally, you'll learn about profiling and how to discover the bottlenecks that cause your program to run too slowly.

Unit Testing

A recent realization in programming practice is the dramatic value of unit testing. This is the process of building integrated tests into all the code that you create and running those tests every time you do a build. That way, the build process can check for more than just syntax errors, since you teach it how to check for semantic errors as well. C-style programming languages, and C++ in particular, have typically valued performance over programming safety. The reason that developing programs in Java is so much faster than in C++ (roughly twice as fast, by most accounts) is because of Java's safety net: features like garbage collection and improved type checking. By integrating unit testing into your build process, you can extend this safety net, resulting in faster development. You can also be bolder in the changes that you make, more easily refactor your code when you discover design or implementation flaws, and in general produce a better product, more quickly.

The effect of unit testing on development is so significant that it is used throughout this book, not only to validate the code in the book, but also to display the expected output. My own experience with unit testing began when I realized that, to guarantee the correctness of code in a book, every program in that book must be automatically extracted and organized into a source tree, along with an appropriate build system. The build system used in this book is *Ant* (described later in this chapter), and after you install it, you can just type **ant** to build all the code for the book. The effect of the automatic extraction and compilation process on the code quality of the book was so immediate and dramatic that it soon became (in my mind) a requisite for any programming book—how can you trust code that you didn't compile? I also discovered that if I wanted to make sweeping changes, I could do so using search-and-replace throughout the book or just by bashing the code around. I knew that if I introduced a flaw, the code extractor and the build system would flush it out.

As programs became more complex, however, I also found that there was a serious hole in my system. Being able to successfully compile programs is clearly an important first step, and for a published book it seems a fairly revolutionary one; usually because of the pressures of publishing, it's quite typical to randomly open a programming book and discover a coding flaw. However, I kept getting messages from readers reporting semantic problems in my code. These problems could be discovered only by running the code. Naturally, I understood this and took some early faltering steps toward implementing a system that would perform automatic execution tests, but I had succumbed to publishing schedules, all the while knowing that there was definitely something wrong with my process and that it would come back to bite me in the form of embarrassing bug reports (in the open source world,[2] embarrassment is one of the prime motivating factors towards increasing the quality of one's code!).

The other problem was that I lacked a structure for the testing system. Eventually, I started hearing about unit testing and JUnit, which provided a basis for a testing structure. I found the initial versions of JUnit to be intolerable because they required the programmer to write too much code to create even the simplest test suite. More recent versions have significantly

---

[2] Although the electronic version of this book is freely available, it is not open source.

reduced this required code by using reflection, so they are much more satisfactory.

I needed to solve another problem, however, and that was to validate the output of a program and to show the validated output in the book. I had gotten regular complaints that I didn't show enough program output in the book. My attitude was that the reader should be running the programs while reading the book, and many readers did just that and benefited from it. A hidden reason for that attitude, however, was that I didn't have a way to test that the output shown in the book was correct. From experience, I knew that over time, something would happen so that the output was no longer correct (or, I wouldn't get it right in the first place). The simple testing framework shown here not only captures the console output of the program—and most programs in this book produce console output—but it also compares it to the expected output that is printed in the book as part of the source-code listing, so readers can see what the output will be and also know that this output has been verified by the build process, and that they can verify it themselves.

I wanted to see if the test system could be even easier and simpler to use, applying the Extreme Programming principle of "do the simplest thing that could possibly work" as a starting point, and then evolving the system as usage demands. (In addition, I wanted to try to reduce the amount of test code in an attempt to fit more functionality in less code for screen presentations.) The result[3] is the simple testing framework described next.

A Simple Testing Framework

The primary goal of this framework[4] is to verify the output of the examples in the book. You have already seen lines such as

```
private static Test monitor = new Test();
```

at the beginning of most classes that contain a **main( )** method. The task of the **monitor** object is to intercept and save a copy of standard output and standard error into a text file. This file is then used to verify the output of an

---

[3] The first try, anyway. I find that the process of building something for the first time eventually produces insights and new ideas.

[4] Inspired by Python's **doctest** module.

example program by comparing the contents of the file to the expected output.

We start by defining the exceptions that will be thrown by this test system. The general-purpose exception for the library is the base class for the others. Note that it extends **RuntimeException** so that checked exceptions are not involved:

```
//: com:bruceeckel:simpletest:SimpleTestException.java
package com.bruceeckel.simpletest;

public class SimpleTestException extends RuntimeException {
  public SimpleTestException(String msg) {
    super(msg);
  }
} ///:~
```

A basic test is to verify that the number of lines sent to the console by the program is the same as the expected number of lines:

```
//: com:bruceeckel:simpletest:NumOfLinesException.java
package com.bruceeckel.simpletest;

public class NumOfLinesException
extends SimpleTestException {
  public NumOfLinesException(int exp, int out) {
    super("Number of lines of output and "
      + "expected output did not match.\n" +
      "expected: <" + exp + ">\n" +
      "output:   <" + out + "> lines)");
  }
} ///:~
```

Or, the number of lines might be correct, but one or more lines might not match:

```
//: com:bruceeckel:simpletest:LineMismatchException.java
package com.bruceeckel.simpletest;
import java.io.PrintStream;

public class LineMismatchException
  extends SimpleTestException {
  public LineMismatchException(
    int lineNum, String expected, String output) {
    super("line " + lineNum +
```

```
      " of output did not match expected output\n" +
      "expected: <" + expected + ">\n" +
      "output:   <" + output + ">");
  }
} ///:~
```

This test system works by intercepting the console output using the **TestStream** class to replace the standard console output and console error:

```
//: com:bruceeckel:simpletest:TestStream.java
// Simple utility for testing program output. Intercepts
// System.out to print both to the console and a buffer.
package com.bruceeckel.simpletest;
import java.io.*;
import java.util.*;
import java.util.regex.*;

public class TestStream extends PrintStream {
  protected int numOfLines;
  private PrintStream
    console = System.out,
    err = System.err,
    fout;
  // To store lines sent to System.out or err
  private InputStream stdin;
  private String className;
  public TestStream(String className) {
    super(System.out, true); // Autoflush
    System.setOut(this);
    System.setErr(this);
    stdin = System.in; // Save to restore in dispose()
    // Replace the default version with one that
    // automatically produces input on demand:
    System.setIn(new BufferedInputStream(new InputStream(){
      char[] input = ("test\n").toCharArray();
      int index = 0;
      public int read() {
        return
          (int)input[index = (index + 1) % input.length];
      }
    }));
    this.className = className;
    openOutputFile();
  }
  // public PrintStream getConsole() { return console; }
```

```
  public void dispose() {
    System.setOut(console);
    System.setErr(err);
    System.setIn(stdin);
  }
  // This will write over an old Output.txt file:
  public void openOutputFile() {
    try {
      fout = new PrintStream(new FileOutputStream(
        new File(className + "Output.txt")));
    } catch (FileNotFoundException e) {
      throw new RuntimeException(e);
    }
  }
  // Override all possible print/println methods to send
  // intercepted console output to both the console and
  // the Output.txt file:
  public void print(boolean x) {
    console.print(x);
    fout.print(x);
  }
  public void println(boolean x) {
    numOfLines++;
    console.println(x);
    fout.println(x);
  }
  public void print(char x) {
    console.print(x);
    fout.print(x);
  }
  public void println(char x) {
    numOfLines++;
    console.println(x);
    fout.println(x);
  }
  public void print(int x) {
    console.print(x);
    fout.print(x);
  }
  public void println(int x) {
    numOfLines++;
    console.println(x);
    fout.println(x);
  }
```

```
    public void print(long x) {
      console.print(x);
      fout.print(x);
    }
    public void println(long x) {
      numOfLines++;
      console.println(x);
      fout.println(x);
    }
    public void print(float x) {
      console.print(x);
      fout.print(x);
    }
    public void println(float x) {
      numOfLines++;
      console.println(x);
      fout.println(x);
    }
    public void print(double x) {
      console.print(x);
      fout.print(x);
    }
    public void println(double x) {
      numOfLines++;
      console.println(x);
      fout.println(x);
    }
    public void print(char[] x) {
      console.print(x);
      fout.print(x);
    }
    public void println(char[] x) {
      numOfLines++;
      console.println(x);
      fout.println(x);
    }
    public void print(String x) {
      console.print(x);
      fout.print(x);
    }
    public void println(String x) {
      numOfLines++;
      console.println(x);
      fout.println(x);
```

```
  }
  public void print(Object x) {
    console.print(x);
    fout.print(x);
  }
  public void println(Object x) {
    numOfLines++;
    console.println(x);
    fout.println(x);
  }
  public void println() {
    if(false) console.print("println");
    numOfLines++;
    console.println();
    fout.println();
  }
  public void
  write(byte[] buffer, int offset, int length) {
    console.write(buffer, offset, length);
    fout.write(buffer, offset, length);
  }
  public void write(int b) {
    console.write(b);
    fout.write(b);
  }
} ///:~
```

The constructor for **TestStream**, after calling the constructor for the base class, first saves references to standard output and standard error, and then redirects both streams to the **TestStream** object. The static methods **setOut( )** and **setErr( )** both take a **PrintStream** argument. **System.out** and **System.err** references are unplugged from their normal object and instead are plugged into the **TestStream** object, so **TestStream** must also be a **PrintStream** (or equivalently, something inherited from **PrintStream**). The original standard output **PrintStream** reference is captured in the console reference inside **TestStream**, and every time console output is intercepted, it is sent to the original console as well as to an output file. The **dispose( )** method is used to set standard I/O references back to their original objects when **TestStream** is finished with them.

For automatic testing of examples that require user input from the console, the constructor redirects calls to standard input. The current standard input is stored in a reference so that **dispose( )** can restore it to its original state.

Using **System.setIn( )**, an anonymous inner class is set to handle any requests for input by the program under test. The **read( )** method of this inner class produces the letters "test" followed by a newline.

TestStream overrides a variety of **PrintStream print( )** and **println( )** methods for each type. Each of these methods writes both to the "standard" output and to an output file. The **expect( )** method can then be used to test whether output produced by a program matches the expected output provided as argument to **expect( )**.

These tools are used in the **Test** class:

```
//: com:bruceeckel:simpletest:Test.java
// Simple utility for testing program output. Intercepts
// System.out to print both to the console and a buffer.
package com.bruceeckel.simpletest;
import java.io.*;
import java.util.*;
import java.util.regex.*;

public class Test {
  // Bit-shifted so they can be added together:
  public static final int
    EXACT = 1 << 0, // Lines must match exactly
    AT_LEAST = 1 << 1, // Must be at least these lines
    IGNORE_ORDER = 1 << 2, // Ignore line order
    WAIT = 1 << 3; // Delay until all lines are output
  private String className;
  private TestStream testStream;
  public Test() {
    // Discover the name of the class this
    // object was created within:
    className =
      new Throwable().getStackTrace()[1].getClassName();
    testStream = new TestStream(className);
  }
  public static List fileToList(String fname) {
    ArrayList list = new ArrayList();
    try {
      BufferedReader in =
        new BufferedReader(new FileReader(fname));
      try {
        String line;
        while((line = in.readLine()) != null) {
```

```
          if(fname.endsWith(".txt"))
            list.add(line);
          else
            list.add(new TestExpression(line));
        }
      } finally {
        in.close();
      }
    } catch (IOException e) {
      throw new RuntimeException(e);
    }
    return list;
  }
  public static List arrayToList(Object[] array) {
    List l = new ArrayList();
    for(int i = 0; i < array.length; i++) {
      if(array[i] instanceof TestExpression) {
        TestExpression re = (TestExpression)array[i];
        for(int j = 0; j < re.getNumber(); j++)
          l.add(re);
      } else {
        l.add(new TestExpression(array[i].toString()));
      }
    }
    return l;
  }
  public void expect(Object[] exp, int flags) {
    if((flags & WAIT) != 0)
      while(testStream.numOfLines < exp.length) {
        try {
          Thread.sleep(1000);
        } catch (InterruptedException e) {
          throw new RuntimeException(e);
        }
      }
      List output = fileToList(className + "Output.txt");
      if((flags & IGNORE_ORDER) == IGNORE_ORDER)
        OutputVerifier.verifyIgnoreOrder(output, exp);
      else if((flags & AT_LEAST) == AT_LEAST)
        OutputVerifier.verifyAtLeast(output,
          arrayToList(exp));
      else
        OutputVerifier.verify(output, arrayToList(exp));
    // Clean up the output file - see c06:Detergent.java
```

```
    testStream.openOutputFile();
  }
  public void expect(Object[] expected) {
    expect(expected, EXACT);
  }
  public void expect(Object[] expectFirst,
    String fname, int flags) {
    List expected = fileToList(fname);
    for(int i = 0; i < expectFirst.length; i++)
      expected.add(i, expectFirst[i]);
    expect(expected.toArray(), flags);
  }
  public void expect(Object[] expectFirst, String fname) {
    expect(expectFirst, fname, EXACT);
  }
  public void expect(String fname) {
    expect(new Object[] {}, fname, EXACT);
  }
} ///:~
```

There are several overloaded versions of **expect( )** provided for convenience (so the client programmer can, for example, provide the name of the file containing the expected output instead of an array of expected output lines). These overloaded methods all call the main **expect( )** method, which takes as arguments an array of **Objects** containing expected output lines and an **int** containing various flags. Flags are implemented using bit shifting, with each bit corresponding to a particular flag as defined at the beginning of **Test.java**.

The **expect( )** method first inspects the **flags** argument to see if it should delay processing to allow a slow program to catch up. It then calls a **static** method **fileToList( )**, which converts the contents of the output file produced by a program into a **List**. The **fileToList( )** method also wraps each **String** object in an **OutputLine** object; the reason for this will become clear. Finally, the **expect( )** method calls the appropriate **verify( )** method based on the flags argument.

There are three verifiers: **verify( )**, **verifyIgnoreOrder( )**, and **verifyAtLeast( )**, corresponding to **EXACT**, **IGNORE_ORDER**, and **AT_LEAST** modes, respectively:

```
//: com:bruceeckel:simpletest:OutputVerifier.java
package com.bruceeckel.simpletest;
```

```java
import java.util.*;
import java.io.PrintStream;

public class OutputVerifier {
  private static void verifyLength(
    int output, int expected, int compare) {
    if((compare == Test.EXACT && expected != output)
      || (compare == Test.AT_LEAST && output < expected))
      throw new NumOfLinesException(expected, output);
  }
  public static void verify(List output, List expected) {
    verifyLength(output.size(),expected.size(),Test.EXACT);
    if(!expected.equals(output)) {
      //find the line of mismatch
      ListIterator it1 = expected.listIterator();
      ListIterator it2 = output.listIterator();
      while(it1.hasNext()
        && it2.hasNext()
        && it1.next().equals(it2.next()));
      throw new LineMismatchException(
        it1.nextIndex(), it1.previous().toString(),
        it2.previous().toString());
    }
  }
  public static void
  verifyIgnoreOrder(List output, Object[] expected) {
    verifyLength(expected.length,output.size(),Test.EXACT);
    if(!(expected instanceof String[]))
      throw new RuntimeException(
        "IGNORE_ORDER only works with String objects");
    String[] out = new String[output.size()];
    Iterator it = output.iterator();
    for(int i = 0; i < out.length; i++)
      out[i] = it.next().toString();
    Arrays.sort(out);
    Arrays.sort(expected);
    int i =0;
    if(!Arrays.equals(expected, out)) {
      while(expected[i].equals(out[i])) {i++;}
      throw new SimpleTestException(
        ((String) out[i]).compareTo(expected[i]) < 0
          ? "output: <" + out[i] + ">"
          : "expected: <" + expected[i] + ">");
    }
```

```
  }
  public static void
  verifyAtLeast(List output, List expected) {
    verifyLength(output.size(), expected.size(),
      Test.AT_LEAST);
    if(!output.containsAll(expected)) {
      ListIterator it = expected.listIterator();
      while(output.contains(it.next())) {}
      throw new SimpleTestException(
        "expected: <" + it.previous().toString() + ">");
    }
  }
} ///:~
```

The "verify" methods test whether the output produced by a program matches the expected output as specified by the particular mode. If this is not the case, the "verify" methods raise an exception that aborts the build process.

Each of the "verify" methods uses **verifyLength( )** to test the number of lines of output. **EXACT** mode requires that both output and expected output arrays be the same size, and that each output line is equal to the corresponding line in the expected output array. **IGNORE_ORDER** still requires that both arrays be the same size, but the actual order of appearance of the lines is disregarded (the two output arrays must be permutations of one another). **IGNORE_ORDER** mode is used to test threading examples where, due to non-deterministic scheduling of threads by the JVM, it is possible that the sequence of output lines produced by a program cannot be predicted. **AT_LEAST** mode does not require the two arrays to be the same size, but each line of expected output must be contained in the actual output produced by a program, regardless of order. This feature is particularly useful for testing program examples that contain output lines that may or may not be printed, as is the case with most of the examples dealing with garbage collection. Notice that the three modes are canonical; that is, if a test passes in **IGNORE_ORDER** mode, then it will also pass in **AT_LEAST** mode, and if it passes in **EXACT** mode, it will also pass in the other two modes.

Notice how simple the implementation of the "verify" methods is. **verify( )**, for example, simply calls the **equals( )** method provided by the **List** class, and **verifyAtLeast( )** calls **List.containsAll( )**. Remember that the two output **List**s can contain both **OutputLine** or **RegularExpression** objects. The reason for wrapping the simple **String** object in **OutputLines** should now become clear; this approach allows us to override the **equals( )** method, which is necessary in order to take advantage of the Java **Collections** API.

Objects in the **expect( )** array can be either **Strings** or **TestExpressions**, which can encapsulate a regular expression (described in Chapter 12), which is useful for testing examples that produce random output. The **TestExpression** class encapsulates a **String** representing a particular regular expression.

```
//: com:bruceeckel:simpletest:TestExpression.java
// Regular expression for testing program output lines
package com.bruceeckel.simpletest;
import java.util.regex.*;

public class TestExpression implements Comparable {
  private Pattern p;
  private String expression;
  private boolean isRegEx;
  // Default to only one instance of this expression:
  private int duplicates = 1;
  public TestExpression(String s) {
    this.expression = s;
    if(expression.startsWith("%% ")) {
      this.isRegEx = true;
      expression = expression.substring(3);
      this.p = Pattern.compile(expression);
    }
  }
  // For duplicate instances:
  public TestExpression(String s, int duplicates) {
    this(s);
    this.duplicates = duplicates;
  }
  public String toString() {
    if(isRegEx) return p.pattern();
    return expression;
  }
  public boolean equals(Object obj) {
    if(this == obj) return true;
    if(isRegEx) return (compareTo(obj) == 0);
    return expression.equals(obj.toString());
  }
  public int compareTo(Object obj) {
    if((isRegEx) && (p.matcher(obj.toString()).matches()))
```

```
      return 0;
    return
      expression.compareTo(obj.toString());
  }
  public int getNumber() {  return duplicates; }
  public String getExpression() { return expression;}
  public boolean isRegEx() { return isRegEx; }
} ///:~
```

TestExpression can distinguish regular expression patterns from **String** literals. The second constructor allows multiple identical expression lines to be wrapped in a single object for convenience.

This test system has been reasonably useful, and the exercise of creating it and putting it into use has been invaluable. However, in the end I'm not that pleased with it and have ideas that will probably be implemented in the next edition of the book (or possibly sooner).

JUnit

Although the testing framework just described allows you to verify program output simply and easily, in some cases you may want to perform more extensive functionality testing on a program. *JUnit*, available at *www.junit.org*, is a quickly emerging standard for writing repeatable tests for Java programs, and provides both simple and complex testing.

The original JUnit was presumably based on JDK 1.0 and thus could not make use of Java's reflection facilities. As a result, writing unit tests with the old JUnit was a rather busy and wordy activity, and I found the design to be unpleasant. Because of this, I wrote my own unit testing framework for Java,[5] going to the other extreme and "doing the simplest thing that could possibly work."[6] Since then, JUnit has been modified and uses reflection to greatly simplify the process of writing unit test code. Although you still have the option of writing code the "old" way with test suites and all the other complex

---

[5] Originally placed in *Thinking in Patterns (with Java)* at www.BruceEckel.com. However, with the addition of the reflection approach in JUnit, my framework doesn't make much sense anymore and will probably be removed.

[6] A key phrase from Extreme Programming (XP). Ironically, one of the JUnit authors (Kent Beck) is also the author of *Extreme Programming Explained* (Addison-Wesley 2000) and a main proponent of XP.

details, I believe that in the great majority of cases you can follow the simple approach shown here (and make your life more pleasant).

In the simplest approach to using JUnit, you put all your tests in a subclass of **TestCase**. Each test must be **public**, take no arguments, return **void**, and have a method name beginning with the word "test." Junit's reflection will identify these methods as individual tests and set up and run them one at a time, taking measures to avoid side effects between the tests.

Traditionally, the **setUp( )** method creates and initializes a common set of objects that will be used in all the tests; however, you can also just put all such initialization in the constructor for the test class. JUnit creates an object for each test to ensure there will be no side effects between test runs. However, all the objects for all the tests are created at once (rather than creating the object right before the test), so the only difference between using **setUp( )** and the constructor is that **setUp( )** is called directly before the test. In most situations this will not be an issue, and you can use the constructor approach for simplicity.

If you need to perform any cleanup after each test (if you modify any statics that need to be restored, open files that need to be closed, open network connections, etc.), you write a **tearDown( )** method. This is also optional.

The following example uses this simple approach to create JUnit tests that exercise the standard Java **ArrayList** class. To trace how JUnit creates and cleans up its test objects, **CountedList** is inherited from **ArrayList** and tracking information is added:

```
//: c15:JUnitDemo.java
// Simple use of JUnit to test ArrayList
// {Depends: junit.jar}
import java.util.*;
import junit.framework.*;

// So we can see the list objects being created,
// and keep track of when they are cleaned up:
class CountedList extends ArrayList {
  private static int counter = 0;
  private int id = counter++;
  public CountedList() {
    System.out.println("CountedList #" + id);
  }
  public int getId() { return id; }
```

```
}

public class JUnitDemo extends TestCase {
  private static com.bruceeckel.simpletest.Test monitor =
    new com.bruceeckel.simpletest.Test();
  private CountedList list = new CountedList();
  // You can use the constructor instead of setUp():
  public JUnitDemo(String name) {
    super(name);
    for(int i = 0; i < 3; i++)
      list.add("" + i);
  }
  // Thus, setUp() is optional, but is run right
  // before the test:
  protected void setUp() {
    System.out.println("Set up for " + list.getId());
  }
  // tearDown() is also optional, and is called after
  // each test. setUp() and tearDown() can be either
  // protected or public:
  public void tearDown() {
    System.out.println("Tearing down " + list.getId());
  }
  // All tests have method names beginning with "test":
  public void testInsert() {
    System.out.println("Running testInsert()");
    assertEquals(list.size(), 3);
    list.add(1, "Insert");
    assertEquals(list.size(), 4);
    assertEquals(list.get(1), "Insert");
  }
  public void testReplace() {
    System.out.println("Running testReplace()");
    assertEquals(list.size(), 3);
    list.set(1, "Replace");
    assertEquals(list.size(), 3);
    assertEquals(list.get(1), "Replace");
  }
  // A "helper" method to reduce code duplication. As long
  // as the name doesn't start with "test," it will not
  // be automatically executed by JUnit.
  private void compare(ArrayList lst, String[] strs) {
    Object[] array = lst.toArray();
    assertTrue("Arrays not the same length",
```

```
      array.length == strs.length);
    for(int i = 0; i < array.length; i++)
      assertEquals(strs[i], (String)array[i]);
  }
  public void testOrder() {
    System.out.println("Running testOrder()");
    compare(list, new String[] { "0", "1", "2" });
  }
  public void testRemove() {
    System.out.println("Running testRemove()");
    assertEquals(list.size(), 3);
    list.remove(1);
    assertEquals(list.size(), 2);
    compare(list, new String[] { "0", "2" });
  }
  public void testAddAll() {
    System.out.println("Running testAddAll()");
    list.addAll(Arrays.asList(new Object[] {
      "An", "African", "Swallow"}));
    assertEquals(list.size(), 6);
    compare(list, new String[] { "0", "1", "2",
       "An", "African", "Swallow" });
  }
  public static void main(String[] args) {
    // Invoke JUnit on the class:
    junit.textui.TestRunner.run(JUnitDemo.class);
    monitor.expect(new String[] {
      "CountedList #0",
      "CountedList #1",
      "CountedList #2",
      "CountedList #3",
      "CountedList #4",
      // '.' indicates the beginning of each test:
      ".Set up for 0",
      "Running testInsert()",
      "Tearing down 0",
      ".Set up for 1",
      "Running testReplace()",
      "Tearing down 1",
      ".Set up for 2",
      "Running testOrder()",
      "Tearing down 2",
      ".Set up for 3",
      "Running testRemove()",
```

```
        "Tearing down 3",
        ".Set up for 4",
        "Running testAddAll()",
        "Tearing down 4",
        "",
        "%% Time: .*",
        "",
        "OK (5 tests)",
        "",
      });
  }
} ///:~
```

To set up unit testing, you must only **import junit.framework.*** and extend **TestCase**, as **JUnitDemo** does. In addition, you must create a constructor that takes a **String** argument and passes it to its **super** constructor.

For each test, a new **JUnitDemo** object will be created, and thus all the non-**static** members will also be created. This means a new **CountedList** object (**list**) will be created and initialized for each test, since it is a field of **JUnitDemo**. In addition, the constructor will be called for each test, so **list** will be initialized with the strings "0", "1", and "2" before each test is run.

To observe the behavior of **setUp( )** and **tearDown( )**, these methods are created to display information about the test that's being initialized or cleaned up. Note that the base-class methods are **protected**, so the overridden methods may be either **protected** or **public**.

testInsert( ) and **testReplace( )** demonstrate typical test methods, since they follow the required signature and naming convention. JUnit discovers these methods using reflection and runs each one as a test. Inside the methods, you perform any desired operations and use JUnit assertion methods (which all start with the name "assert") to verify the correctness of your tests (the full range of "assert" statements can be found in the JUnit javadocs for **junit.framework.Assert**). If the assertion fails, the expression and values that caused the failure will be displayed. This is usually enough, but you can also use the overloaded version of each JUnit assertion statement and include a **String** that will be printed if the assertion fails.

The assertion statements are not required; you can also just run the test without assertions and consider it a success if no exceptions are thrown.

The **compare( )** method is an example of a "helper" method that is not executed by JUnit but instead is used by other tests in the class. As long as the method name doesn't begin with "test," JUnit doesn't run it or expect it to have a particular signature. Here, **compare( )** is **private** to emphasize that it is only used within the test class, but it could also be public. The remaining test methods eliminate duplicate code by refactoring it into the **compare( )** method.

To execute the JUnit tests, the static method **TestRunner.run( )** is invoked in **main( )**. This method is handed the class that contains the collection of tests, and it automatically sets up and runs all the tests. From the **expect( )** output, you can see that all the objects needed to run all the tests are created first, in a batch—this is where the construction happens.[7] Before each test, the **setUp( )** method is called. Then the test is run, followed by the **tearDown( )** method. JUnit demarcates each test with a '**.**'.

Although you can probably survive easily by only using the simplest approach to JUnit as shown in the preceding example, JUnit was originally designed with a plethora of complicated structures. If you are curious, you can easily learn more about them, because the JUnit download from *www.JUnit.org* comes with documentation and tutorials.

Improving reliability with assertions

Assertions, which you've seen used in earlier examples in this book, were added to the JDK 1.4 version of Java in order to aid programmers in improving the reliability of their programs. Properly used, assertions can add to program robustness by verifying that certain conditions are satisfied during the execution of your program. For example, suppose you have a numerical field in an object that represents the month on the Julian calendar. You know that this value must always be in the range 1-12, and an assertion can be used to check this and report an error if it somehow falls outside of that range. If you're inside a method, you can check the validity of an argument with an assertion. These are important tests to make sure that your

---

7 Bill Venners and I have discussed this at some length, and we haven't been able to figure out why it is done this way rather than creating each object right before the test is run. It is likely that it is simply an artifact of the way JUnit was originally implemented.

program is correct, but they cannot be performed by compile-time checking, and they do not fall into the purview of unit testing. In this section, we'll look at the mechanics of the assertion mechanism, and the way that you can use assertions to partially implement the *design by contract* concept.

Assertion syntax

Since you can simulate the effect of assertions using other programming constructs, it can be argued that the whole point of adding assertions to Java is that they are easy to write. Assertion statements come in two forms:

```
assert boolean-expression;
assert boolean-expression: information-expression;
```

Both of these statements say "I assert that the boolean-expression will produce a **true** value." If this is not the case, the assertion will produce an **AssertionError** exception. This is a **Throwable** subclass, and as such doesn't require an exception specification.

Unfortunately, the first form of assertion does *not* produce any information containing the boolean-expression in the exception produced by a failed assertion (in contrast with most other languages' assertion mechanisms). Here's an example showing the use of the first form:

```
//: c15:Assert1.java
// Non-informative style of assert
// Compile with: javac -source 1.4 Assert1.java
// {JVMArgs: -ea} // Must run with -ea
// {ThrowsException}

public class Assert1 {
  public static void main(String[] args) {
    assert false;
  }
} ///:~
```

Assertions are turned off in JDK 1.4 by default (this is annoying, but the designers managed to convince themselves it was a good idea). To prevent compile-time errors, you must compile with the flag:

```
-source 1.4
```

If you don't use this flag, you'll get a chatty message saying that **assert** is a keyword in JDK 1.4 and cannot be used as an identifier anymore.

If you just run the program the way you normally do, without any special assertion flags, nothing will happen. You must enable assertions when you run the program. The easiest way to do this is with the **-ea** flag, but you can also spell it out: **-enableassertions**. This will run the program and execute any assertion statements, so you'll get:

```
Exception in thread "main" java.lang.AssertionError
        at Assert1.main(Assert1.java:8)
```

You can see that the output doesn't contain much in the way of useful information. On the other hand, if you use the information-expression, you'll produce a helpful message when the assertion fails.

To use the second form, you provide an information-expression that will be displayed as part of the exception stack trace. This information-expression can produce any data type at all. However, the most useful information-expression will typically be a string with text that is useful to the programmer. Here's an example:

```
//: c15:Assert2.java
// Assert with an informative message
// {JVMArgs: -ea}
// {ThrowsException}

public class Assert2 {
  public static void main(String[] args) {
    assert false: "Here's a message saying what happened";
  }
} ///:~
```

Now the output is:

```
Exception in thread "main" java.lang.AssertionError: Here's
a message saying what happened
        at Assert2.main(Assert2.java:6)
```

Although what you see here is just a simple **String** object, the information-expression can produce any kind of object, so you will typically construct a more complex string containing, for example, the value(s) of objects that were involved with the failed assertion.

Because the only way to see useful information from a failed assertion is to use the information-expression, that is the form that is always used in this book, and the first form will be considered to be a poor choice.

You can also decide to turn assertions on and off based on class name or package name (that is, you can enable or disable assertions in an entire package). You can find the details in the JDK 1.4 documentation on assertions. This can be useful if you have a large project instrumented with assertions and you want to turn some of them off. However, logging or debugging (both described later in this chapter) are probably better tools for capturing that kind of information. This book will just turn on all assertions when necessary, so we will ignore the fine-grained control of assertions.

There's one other way you can control assertions: programmatically, by hooking into the **ClassLoader** object. JDK 1.4 added several new methods to **ClassLoader** that allow the dynamic enabling and disabling of assertions, including **setDefaultAssertionStatus( )**, which sets the assertion status for all the classes loaded afterward. So you might think you could almost silently turn on all assertions like this:

```
//: c15:LoaderAssertions.java
// Using the class loader to enable assertions
// Compile with: javac -source 1.4 LoaderAssertions.java
// {ThrowsException}

public class LoaderAssertions {
  public static void main(String[] args) {
    ClassLoader.getSystemClassLoader()
      .setDefaultAssertionStatus(true);
    new Loaded().go();
  }
}

class Loaded {
  public void go() {
    assert false: "Loaded.go()";
  }
} ///:~
```

Although this does eliminate the need to use the **-ea** flag on the command line when the Java program is run, it's not a complete solution because you must still compile everything with the **-source 1.4** flag. It may be just as straightforward to enable assertions using command-line arguments; when delivering a standalone product, you probably have to set up an execution script for the user to start the program anyway, in order to configure other startup parameters.

It does make sense, however, to decide that you want to *require* assertions to be enabled when the program is run. You can accomplish this with the following **static** clause, placed in the main class of your system:

```
static {
  boolean assertionsEnabled = false;
  // Note intentional side effect of assignment:
  assert assertionsEnabled = true;
  if (!assertionsEnabled)
    throw new RuntimeException("Assertions disabled");
}
```

If assertions are enabled, then the **assert** statement will be executed and **assertionsEnabled** will be set to **true**. The assertion will never fail, because the return value of the assignment is the assigned value. If assertions are not enabled, the **assert** statement will not be executed and **assertionsEnabled** will remain **false**, resulting in the exception.

Using Assertions for *Design by Contract*

Design by Contract (DBC) is a concept developed by Bertrand Meyer, creator of the Eiffel programming language, to help in the creation of robust programs by guaranteeing that objects follow certain rules that cannot be verified by compile-time type checking.[8] These rules are determined by the nature of the problem that is being solved, which is outside the scope of what the compiler can know about and test.

Although assertions do not directly implement DBC (as does the Eiffel language), they can be used to create an informal style of DBC programming.

The fundamental idea of DBC is that a clearly-specified contract exists between the supplier of a service and the consumer or client of that service. In object-oriented programming, services are usually supplied by objects, and the boundary of the object—the division between the supplier and consumer—is the interface of the object's class. When clients call a particular public method, they are expecting certain behavior from that call: a state change in the object, and a predictable return value. Meyer's thesis is that:

---

[8] Design by contract is described in detail in Chapter 11 of *Object-Oriented Software Construction, 2nd Edition,* by Bertrand Meyer, Prentice Hall 1997.

1. This behavior can be clearly specified, as if it were a contract.

2. This behavior can be guaranteed by implementing certain run-time checks, which he calls *preconditions*, *postconditions* and *invariants*.

Whether or not you agree that point 1 is always true, it does appear to be true for enough situations to make DBC an interesting approach. (I believe that, like any solution, there are boundaries to its usefulness. But if you know these boundaries, you know when to try to apply it.) In particular, a very valuable part of the design process is the expression of the DBC constraints for a particular class; if you are unable to specify the constraints, you probably don't know enough about what you're trying to build.

Check instructions

Before going into in-depth DBC facilities, consider the simplest use for assertions, which Meyer calls the *check instruction*. A check instruction expresses your conviction that a particular property will be satisfied at this point in your code. The idea of the check instruction is to express non-obvious conclusions in code, not only to verify the test, but also as documentation to future readers of the code.

For example, in a chemistry process, you may be titrating one clear liquid into another, and when you reach a certain point, everything turns blue. This is not obvious from the color of the two liquids; it is part of a complex reaction. A useful check instruction at the completion of the titration process would assert that the resulting liquid is blue.

Another example is the **Thread.holdsLock( )** method introduced in JDK 1.4. This is used for complex threading situations (such as iterating through a collection in a thread-safe way) where you must rely on the client programmer or another class in your system using the library properly, rather than on the **synchronized** keyword alone. To ensure that the code is properly following the dictates of your library design, you can assert that the current thread does indeed hold the lock:

```
assert Thread.holdsLock(this); // lock-status assertion
```

Check instructions are a valuable addition to your code. Since assertions can be disabled, check instructions should be used whenever you have non-obvious knowledge about the state of your object or program.

Preconditions

A precondition is a test to make sure that the client (the code calling this method) has fulfilled its part of the contract. This almost always means checking the arguments at the very beginning of a method call (before you do anything else in that method) to make sure that those arguments are appropriate for use in the method. Since you never know what a client is going to hand you, precondition checks are always a good idea.

Postconditions

A postcondition test checks the results of what you did in the method. This code is placed at the end of the method call, before the **return** statement, if there is one. For long, complex methods where the result of the calculations should be verified before returning them (that is, in situations where for some reason you cannot always trust the results), postcondition checks are essential, but any time you can describe constraints on the result of the method, it's wise to express those constraints in code as a postcondition. In Java these are coded as assertions, but the assertion statements will vary from one method to another.

Invariants

An invariant gives guarantees about the state of the object that will be maintained between method calls. However, it doesn't restrain a method from temporarily diverging from those guarantees during the execution of the method. It just says that the state information of the object will always obey these rules:

1. Upon entry to the method.

2. Before leaving the method.

In addition, the invariant is a guarantee about the state of the object after construction.

According to the this description, an effective invariant would be defined as a method, probably named **invariant( )**, which would be invoked after construction, and at the beginning and end of each method. The method could be invoked as:

```
assert invariant();
```

This way, if you chose to disable assertions for performance reasons, there would be no overhead at all.

Relaxing DBC

Although he emphasizes the importance of being able to express preconditions, postconditions, and invariants, and the value of using these during development, Meyer admits that it is not always practical to include all DBC code in a shipping product. You may relax DBC checking based on the amount of trust you can place in the code at a particular point. Here is the order of relaxation, from safest to least safe:

1. The invariant check at the beginning of each method may be disabled first, since the invariant check at the end of each method will guarantee that the object's state will be valid at the beginning of every method call. That is, you can generally trust that the state of the object will not change between method calls. This one is such a safe assumption that you might choose to write code with invariant checks only at the end.

2. The postcondition check may be disabled next, if you have reasonable unit testing that verifies that your methods are returning appropriate values. Since the invariant check is watching the state of the object, the postcondition check is only validating the results of the calculation during the method, and therefore may be discarded in favor of unit testing. The unit testing will not be as safe as a run-time postcondition check, but it may be enough, especially if you have enough confidence in the code.

3. The invariant check at the end of a method call may be disabled if you have enough certainty that the method body does not put the object into an invalid state. It may be possible to verify this with white-box unit testing (that is, unit tests that have access to private fields, so they may validate the object state). Thus, although it may not be quite as robust as calls to **invariant( )**, it is possible to "migrate" the invariant checking from run-time tests to build-time tests (via unit testing), just as with postconditions.

4. Finally, as a last resort you may disable precondition checks. This is the least safe and least advisable thing to do, because although you know and have control over your own code, you have no control over what arguments the client may pass to a method. However, in a

situation where (a) performance is desperately needed and profiling has pointed at precondition checks as a bottleneck and (b) you have some kind of reasonable assurance that the client will not violate preconditions (as in the case where you've written the client code yourself) it may be acceptable to disable precondition checks.

You shouldn't remove the code that performs the checks described here as you disable the checks. If a bug is discovered, you'll want to easily turn on the checks so that you can rapidly discover the problem.

Example: DBC + white-box unit testing

The following example demonstrates the potency of combining concepts from Design by Contract with unit testing. It shows a small first-in, first-out (FIFO) queue class that is implemented as a "circular" array—that is, an array used in a circular fashion. When the end of the array is reached, the class wraps back around to the beginning.

We can make a number of contractual definitions for this queue:

1. Precondition (for a **put( )**): Null elements are not allowed to be added to the queue.
2. Precondition (for a **put( )**): It is illegal to put elements into a full queue.
3. Precondition (for a **get( )**): It is illegal to try to get elements from an empty queue.
4. Postcondition (for a **get( )**): Null elements cannot be produced from the array.
5. Invariant: The region in the array that contains objects cannot contain any null elements.
6. Invariant: The region in the array that doesn't contain objects must have only null values.

Here is one way you could implement these rules, using explicit method calls for each type of DBC element:

```
//: c15:Queue.java
// Demonstration of Design by Contract (DBC) combined
// with white-box unit testing.
```

```java
// {Depends: junit.jar}
import junit.framework.*;
import java.util.*;

public class Queue {
  private Object[] data;
  private int
    in = 0, // Next available storage space
    out = 0; // Next gettable object
  // Has it wrapped around the circular queue?
  private boolean wrapped = false;
  public static class
  QueueException extends RuntimeException {
    public QueueException(String why) { super(why); }
  }
  public Queue(int size) {
    data = new Object[size];
    assert invariant(); // Must be true after construction
  }
  public boolean empty() {
    return !wrapped && in == out;
  }
  public boolean full() {
    return wrapped && in == out;
  }
  public void put(Object item) {
    precondition(item != null, "put() null item");
    precondition(!full(), "put() into full Queue");
    assert invariant();
    data[in++] = item;
    if(in >= data.length) {
      in = 0;
      wrapped = true;
    }
    assert invariant();
  }
  public Object get() {
    precondition(!empty(), "get() from empty Queue");
    assert invariant();
    Object returnVal = data[out];
    data[out] = null;
    out++;
    if(out >= data.length) {
      out = 0;
```

```
      wrapped = false;
    }
    assert postcondition(
      returnVal != null, "Null item in Queue");
    assert invariant();
    return returnVal;
  }
  // Design-by-contract support methods:
  private static void
  precondition(boolean cond, String msg) {
    if(!cond) throw new QueueException(msg);
  }
  private static boolean
  postcondition(boolean cond, String msg) {
    if(!cond) throw new QueueException(msg);
    return true;
  }
  private boolean invariant() {
    // Guarantee that no null values are in the
    // region of 'data' that holds objects:
    for(int i = out; i != in; i = (i + 1) % data.length)
      if(data[i] == null)
        throw new QueueException("null in queue");
    // Guarantee that only null values are outside the
    // region of 'data' that holds objects:
    if(full()) return true;
    for(int i = in; i != out; i = (i + 1) % data.length)
      if(data[i] != null)
        throw new QueueException(
          "non-null outside of queue range: " + dump());
    return true;
  }
  private String dump() {
    return "in = " + in +
      ", out = " + out +
      ", full() = " + full() +
      ", empty() = " + empty() +
      ", queue = " + Arrays.asList(data);
  }
  // JUnit testing.
  // As an inner class, this has access to privates:
  public static class WhiteBoxTest extends TestCase {
    private Queue queue = new Queue(10);
    private int i = 0;
```

```
  public WhiteBoxTest(String name) {
    super(name);
    while(i < 5) // Preload with some data
      queue.put("" + i++);
  }
  // Support methods:
  private void showFullness() {
    assertTrue(queue.full());
    assertFalse(queue.empty());
    // Dump is private, white-box testing allows access:
    System.out.println(queue.dump());
  }
  private void showEmptiness() {
    assertFalse(queue.full());
    assertTrue(queue.empty());
    System.out.println(queue.dump());
  }
  public void testFull() {
    System.out.println("testFull");
    System.out.println(queue.dump());
    System.out.println(queue.get());
    System.out.println(queue.get());
    while(!queue.full())
      queue.put("" + i++);
    String msg = "";
    try {
      queue.put("");
    } catch(QueueException e) {
      msg = e.getMessage();
      System.out.println(msg);
    }
    assertEquals(msg, "put() into full Queue");
    showFullness();
  }
  public void testEmpty() {
    System.out.println("testEmpty");
    while(!queue.empty())
      System.out.println(queue.get());
    String msg = "";
    try {
      queue.get();
    } catch(QueueException e) {
      msg = e.getMessage();
      System.out.println(msg);
```

```
      }
      assertEquals(msg, "get() from empty Queue");
      showEmptiness();
    }
    public void testNullPut() {
      System.out.println("testNullPut");
      String msg = "";
      try {
        queue.put(null);
      } catch(QueueException e) {
        msg = e.getMessage();
        System.out.println(msg);
      }
      assertEquals(msg, "put() null item");
    }
    public void testCircularity() {
      System.out.println("testCircularity");
      while(!queue.full())
        queue.put("" + i++);
      showFullness();
      // White-box testing accesses private field:
      assertTrue(queue.wrapped);
      while(!queue.empty())
        System.out.println(queue.get());
      showEmptiness();
      while(!queue.full())
        queue.put("" + i++);
      showFullness();
      while(!queue.empty())
        System.out.println(queue.get());
      showEmptiness();
    }
  }
  public static void main(String[] args) {
    junit.textui.TestRunner.run(Queue.WhiteBoxTest.class);
  }
} ///:~
```

The **in** counter indicates the place in the array where the next object will go into, and the **out** counter indicates where the next object will come from. The **wrapped** flag shows that **in** has gone "around the circle" and is now coming up from behind **out**. When **in** and **out** coincide, the queue is empty (if **wrapped** is false) or full (if **wrapped** is true).

You can see that the **put( )** and **get( )** methods call the methods **precondition( )**, **postcondition( )**, and **invariant( )**, which are **private** methods defined further down in the class. **precondition( )** and **postcondition( )** are helper methods designed to clarify the code. Note that **precondition( )** returns **void**, because it is not used with **assert**. As previously noted, you'll generally want to keep preconditions in your code; however, by wrapping them in a **precondition( )** method call, you have better options if you are reduced to the dire move of turning them off.

postcondition( ) and **invariant( )** return a Boolean value so that they can be used in **assert** statements. Then, if assertions are disabled for performance reasons, there will be no method calls at all.

invariant( ) performs internal validity checks on the object. You can see that this is an expensive operation to do at both the beginning and ending of every method call, as Meyer suggests. However, it's very valuable to have this clearly represented in code, and it helped me get the implementation to be correct. In addition, if you make any changes to the implementation, the **invariant( )** will ensure that you haven't broken the code. But you can see that it would be fairly trivial to move the invariant tests from the method calls into the unit test code. If your unit tests are reasonably thorough, you can have a reasonable level of confidence that the invariants will be respected.

Notice that the **dump( )** helper method returns a string containing all the data rather than printing the data directly. This approach allows many more options as to how the information can be used.

The **TestCase** subclass **WhiteBoxTest** is created as an inner class so that it has access to the **private** elements of **Queue** and is thus able to validate the underlying implementation, not just the behavior of the class as in a white-box test. The constructor adds some data so that the **Queue** is partially full for each test. The support methods **showFullness( )** and **showEmptiness( )** are meant to be called to verify that the **Queue** is full or empty, respectively. Each of the four test methods ensures that a different aspect of the **Queue** operation functions correctly.

Note that by combining DBC with unit testing, you not only get the best of both worlds, but you also have a migration path—you can move DBC tests to unit tests rather than simply disabling them, so you still have some level of testing.

Building with Ant

I began my career writing assembly-language programs that controlled real-time devices. These programs usually fit into a single file, so when I was introduced to the **make** utility, I wasn't too excited, because the most complex thing I had ever needed to do was run an assembler or a C compiler on a few files of code. Back then, building a project wasn't the difficult part of my task, and it wasn't too cumbersome to run everything by hand.

Time passed, and two events occurred. First, I started to create more complex projects comprising many more files. Keeping track of which files needed compilation became more than I was able (or wanted) to think about. Second, because of this complexity I began to realize that no matter how simple the build process might be, if you do something more than a couple of times, you begin to get sloppy, and parts of the process start to fall through the cracks.

Automate everything

I came to realize that for a system to be built in a robust and reliable fashion, I needed to automate *everything* that goes into the build process. This requires some concentration up front, just like writing a program requires concentration, but the payoff is that you solve the problems *once*, and you rely on your build configuration to take care of the details from then on. It's a variation of the fundamental programming principle of *abstraction*: We raise ourselves up from the grinding details by hiding those details inside a process and giving that process a name. For many years, the name of that process was **make**.

The **make** utility appeared along with C as a tool to create the Unix operating system. **make**'s primary function is to compare the date of two files and to perform some operation that will bring those two files up-to-date with each other. The relationships between all the files in your projects and the rules necessary to bring them up-to-date (the rule is usually running the C/C++ compiler on a source file) are contained in a *makefile*. The programmer creates a makefile containing the description of how to build the system. When you want to bring the system up-to-date, you simply type **make** at the command line. To this day, installing Unix/Linux programs consists of unpacking them and typing **make** commands.

Problems with **make**

The concept of **make** is clearly a good idea, and this idea proliferated to produce many versions of **make**. C and C++ compiler vendors typically included their own variation of **make** along with their compiler—these variations often took liberties with what people considered to be the standard makefile rules, so the resulting makefiles wouldn't run with each other. The problem was finally solved (as has often been the case) by a **make** that was, and still is, superior to all the other **make**s, and is also free, so there's no resistance to using it: GNU **make**.[9] This tool has a significantly better feature set than the other versions of **make** and is available on all platforms.

In the previous two editions of *Thinking in Java*, I used makefiles to build all the code in the book's source-code tree. I automatically generated these makefiles—one in each directory, and a master makefile in the root directory that would call the rest—using a tool that I originally wrote in C++ (in about 2 weeks) for *Thinking in C++*, and later rewrote in Python (in about half a day) called **MakeBuilder.py**.[10] It worked for both Windows and Linux/Unix, but I had to write extra code to make this happen, and I never tried it on the Macintosh. Therein lies the first problem with **make**: You *can* get it to work on multiple platforms, but it's not inherently cross-platform. So for a language that's supposed to be "write once, run anywhere" (that is, Java), you can spend a lot of effort getting the same behavior in the build system if you use **make**.

The rest of the problems with **make** can probably be summarized by saying that it is like a lot of tools developed for Unix; the person creating the tool couldn't resist the temptation to create their own language syntax, and as a result, Unix is filled with tools that are all remarkably different, and equally incomprehensible. That is to say, the **make** syntax is quite difficult to

---

[9] Except by the occasional company which, for reasons beyond comprehension, is still convinced that closed-source tools are somehow better or have superior tech support. The only situations where I've seen this to be true are when tools have a very small user base, but even then it would be safer to hire consultants to modify open-source tools, and thus leverage prior work and guarantee that the work you pay for won't become unavailable to you (and also make it more likely that you'll find other consultants already up to speed on the program).

[10] This is not available on the web site because it's too customized to be generally useful.

understand in its entirety—I've been learning it for years—and has lots of annoying things like its insistence on tabs instead of spaces.[11]

All that said, note that I still find GNU **make** indispensable for many of the projects I create.

Ant: the defacto standard

All of these issues with **make** irritated a Java programmer named James Duncan Davidson enough to cause him to create Ant as an open-source tool that migrated to the Apache project at *http://jakarta.apache.org/ant*. This site contains the full download including the Ant executable and documentation. Ant has grown and improved until it is now generally accepted as the defacto standard build tool for Java projects.

To make Ant cross-platform, the format for the project description files is XML (covered in *Thinking in Enterprise Java*). Instead of a makefile, you create a buildfile, which is named by default **build.xml** (this allows you to just say '**ant**' on the command line. If you name your buildfile something else, you have to specify that name with a command-line flag).

The only rigid requirement for your buildfile is that it be a valid XML file. Ant compensates for platform-specific issues like end-of-line characters and directory path separators. You can use tabs or spaces in the buildfile as you prefer. In addition, the syntax and tag names used in buildfiles result in readable, understandable (and thus, maintainable) code.

On top of all this, Ant is designed to be extensible, with a standard interface that allows you to write your own tasks if the ones that come with Ant aren't enough (however, they usually are, and the arsenal is regularly expanding).

Unlike **make**, the learning curve for Ant is reasonably gentle. You don't need to know much in order to create a buildfile that compiles Java code in a directory. Here's a very basic **build.xml** file, for example, from Chapter 2 of this book:

```
<?xml version="1.0"?>
```

[11] Other tools are under development, that attempt to repair the problems with **make** without making Ant's compromises. See, for example, *www.a-a-p.org* or search the Web for "bjam."

```
<project name="Thinking in Java (c02)"
  default="c02.run" basedir=".">
  <!-- build all classes in this directory -->
  <target name="c02.build">
    <javac
      srcdir="${basedir}"
      classpath="${basedir}/.."
      source="1.4"
    />
  </target>

  <!-- run all classes in this directory -->
  <target name="c02.run" depends="c02.build">
    <antcall target="HelloDate.run"/>
  </target>

  <target name="HelloDate.run">
    <java
      taskname="HelloDate"
      classname="HelloDate"
      classpath="${basedir};${basedir}/.."
      fork="true"
      failonerror="true"
    />
  </target>

  <!-- delete all class files -->
  <target name="clean">
    <delete>
      <fileset dir="${basedir}" includes="**/*.class"/>
      <fileset dir="${basedir}" includes="**/*Output.txt"/>
    </delete>
    <echo message="clean successful"/>
  </target>

</project>
```

The first line states that this file conforms to version 1.0 of XML. XML looks a lot like HTML (notice the comment syntax is identical), except that you can make up your own tag names and the format must strictly conform to XML rules. For example, an opening tag like **<project** must either end within the tag at its closing angle brace with a slash (/>) or have a matching closing tag like you see at the end of the file (**</project>**). Within a tag you can have *attributes*, but the attribute values must be surrounded in quotes. XML allows free formatting, but indentation like you see here is typical.

Each buildfile can manage a single project described by its **<project>** tag. The project has an optional **name** attribute that is used when displaying information about the build. The **default** attribute is required and refers to the *target* that is built when you just type **ant** at the command line without giving a specific target name. The directory reference **basedir** can be used in other places in the buildfile.

A target has *dependencies* and *tasks*. The dependencies say "which other targets must be built before this target can be built?" You'll notice that the **default** target to build is **c02.run**, and the **c02.run target** says that it in turn depends on **c02.build**. Thus, the **c02.build** target must be executed before **c02.run** can be executed. Partitioning the buildfile this way not only makes it easier to understand, but it also allows you to choose what you want to do via the Ant command line; if you say '**ant c02.build**,' then it will only compile the code, but if you say '**ant c02.run**' (or, because of the default target, just '**ant**'), then it will first make sure things have been built, and then run the examples.

So, for the project to be successful, targets **c02.build** and **c02.run** must first succeed, in that order. The **c02.build** target contains a single *task*, which is a command that actually does the work of bringing things up-to-date. This task runs the **javac** compiler on all the Java files in this current base directory; notice the **${}** syntax used to produce the value of a previously-defined variable, and that the orientation of slashes in directory paths is not important, since Ant compensates depending on the operating system you run it on. The **classpath** attribute gives a directory list to *add* to Ant's classpath, and **source** specifies the compiler to use (this is actually only noticed by JDK 1.4 and beyond). Note that the Java compiler is responsible for sorting out the dependencies between the classes themselves, so you don't have to explicitly state inter-file dependencies like you must with **make** and C/C++ (this saves a lot of effort).

To run the programs in the directory (which, in this case, is only the single program **HelloDate**), this buildfile uses a task named **antcall**. This task does a recursive invocation of Ant on another target, which in this case just uses **java** to execute the program. Note that the **java** task has a **taskname** attribute; this attribute is actually available for all tasks, and is used when Ant outputs logging information.

As you might expect, the **java** tag also has options to establish the class name to be executed, and the classpath. In addition, the

```
fork="true"
failonerror="true"
```

attributes tell Ant to fork off a new process to run this program, and to fail the Ant build if the program fails. You can look up all the different tasks and their attributes in the documentation that comes with the Ant download.

The last target is one that's typically found in every buildfile; it allows you to say **ant clean** and delete all the files that have been created in order to perform this build. Whenever you create a buildfile, you should be careful to include a **clean** target, because you're the person who typically knows the most about what can be deleted and what should be preserved.

The **clean** target introduces some new syntax. You can delete single items with the one-line version of this task, like this:

```
<delete file="${basedir}/HelloDate.class"/>
```

The multiline version of the task allows you to specify a *fileset*, which is a more complex description of a set of files and may specify files to include and exclude by using wildcards. In this example, the filesets to delete include all files in this directory and all subdirectories that have a **.class** extension, and all files in the current subdirectory that end with **Output.txt**.

The buildfile shown here is fairly simple; within this book's source code tree (which is downloadable from www.BruceEckel.com) you'll find more complex buildfiles. Also, Ant is capable of doing much more that what we use for this book. For the full details of its capabilities, see the documentation that comes with the Ant installation.

Ant extensions

Ant comes with an extension API so that you can create your own tasks by writing them in Java. You can find full details in the official Ant documentation and in the published books on Ant.

As an alternative, you can simply write a Java program and call it from Ant; this way, you don't have to learn the extension API. For example, to compile the code in this book, we need to verify that the version of Java that the user is running is JDK 1.4 or greater, so we created the following program:

```java
//: com:bruceeckel:tools:CheckVersion.java
// {RunByHand}
package com.bruceeckel.tools;

public class CheckVersion {
  public static void main(String[] args) {
    String version = System.getProperty("java.version");
    char minor = version.charAt(2);
    char point = version.charAt(4);
    if(minor < '4' || point < '1')
      throw new RuntimeException("JDK 1.4.1 or higher " +
        "is required to run the examples in this book.");
    System.out.println("JDK version "+ version + " found");
  }
} ///:~
```

This simply uses **System.getProperty( )** to discover the Java version, and throws an exception if it isn't at least 1.4. When Ant sees the exception, it will halt. Now you can include the following in any buildfile where you want to check the version number:

```xml
    <java
      taskname="CheckVersion"
      classname="com.bruceeckel.tools.CheckVersion"
      classpath="${basedir}"
      fork="true"
      failonerror="true"
    />
```

If you use this approach to adding tools, you can write them and test them quickly, and if it's justified, you can invest the extra effort and write an Ant extension.

Version control with CVS

A *revision control system* is a class of tool that has been developed over many years to help manage large team programming projects. It has also turned out to be fundamental to the success of virtually all open-source projects, because open-source teams are almost always distributed globally via the Internet. So even if there are only two people working on a project, they benefit from using a revision control system.

The defacto standard revision control system for open-source projects is called Concurrent Versions System (CVS), available at *www.cvshome.org*.

Because it is open-source and so many people know how to use it, CVS is also a common choice for closed projects. Some projects even use CVS as a way to distribute the system. CVS has the usual benefits of a popular open-source project: the code has been thoroughly reviewed, it's available for your review and modification, and flaws are rapidly corrected.

CVS keeps your code in a repository on a server. This server may be on a local area network, but it is typically available on the Internet so that people on the team can get updates without being at a particular location. To connect to CVS, you must have an assigned user name and password, so there's a reasonable level of security; for more security, you can use the **ssh** protocol (although these are Linux tools, they are readily available in Windows using Cygwin—see *www.cygwin.com*). Some graphical development environments (like the free Eclipse editor; see *www.eclipse.org*) provide excellent integration with CVS.

Once the repository is initialized by your system administrator, team members may get a copy of the code tree by checking it out. For example, once your machine is logged into the appropriate CVS server (details of which are omitted here), you can perform the initial checkout with a command like this:

```
cvs -z5 co TIJ3
```

This will connect with the CVS server and negotiate the checkout ('**co**') of the code repository called **TIJ3**. The '**-z5**' argument tells the CVS programs at both ends to communicate using a gzip compression level of 5 in order to speed up the transfer over the network.

Once this command is completed, you'll have a copy of the code repository on your local machine. In addition, you'll see that each directory in the repository has an additional subdirectory named CVS. This is where all the CVS information about the files in that directory are stored.

Now that you have your own copy of the CVS repository, you can make changes to the files in order to develop the project. Typically, these changes include corrections and feature additions along with test code and modified buildfiles necessary to compile and run the tests. You'll find that it's very unpopular to check in code that doesn't successfully run all its tests, because then everyone else on the team will get the broken code (and thus fail their builds).

When you've made your improvements and you're ready to check them in, you must go through a two-step process that is the crux of CVS code synchronization. First, you update your local repository to synchronize it with the main CVS repository by moving into the root of your local code repository and running this command:

```
cvs update -dP
```

At this point, you aren't required to log in because the CVS subdirectory keeps the login information for the remote repository, and the remote repository keeps signature information about your machine as a double check to verify your identity.

The '**-dP**' flag is optional; '**-d**' tells CVS to create any new directories on your local machine that might have been added to the main repository, and '**-P**' tells CVS to prune off any directories on your local machine that have been emptied on the main repository. Neither of these things happens by default.

The main activity of **update**, however, is quite interesting. You should actually run **update** on a regular basis, not just before you do a checkin, because it synchronizes your local repository with the main repository. If it finds any files in the main repository that are newer than files on your local repository, it brings the changes onto your local machine. However, it doesn't just copy the files, but instead does a line-by-line comparison of the files and patches the changes from the main repository into your local version. If you've made some changes to a file and someone else has made changes to the same file, CVS will patch the changes together as long as the changes don't happen to the same lines of code (CVS matches the *contents* of the lines, and not just the line numbers, so even if line numbers change, it will be able to synchronize properly). Thus, you can be working on the same file as someone else, and when you do an **update**, any changes the other person has committed to the main repository will be merged with your changes.

Of course, it's possible that two people might make changes to the same lines of the same file. This is an accident due to lack of communication; normally you'll tell each other what you're working on so as not to tread on each other's code (also, if files are so big that it makes sense for two different people to work on different parts of the same file, you might consider breaking up the big files into smaller files for easier project management). If this happens, CVS simply notes the collision and forces you to resolve it by fixing the lines of code that collide.

Note that no files from your machine are moved into the main repository during an **update**. The **update** brings only changed files from the main repository onto your machine and patches in any modifications you've made. So how do your modifications get into the main repository? This is the second step: the **commit**.

When you type

```
cvs commit
```

CVS will start up your default editor and ask you to write a description of your modification. This description will be entered into the repository so that others will know what's been changed. After that, your modified files will be placed into the main repository so they are available to everyone else the next time they do an **update**.

CVS has other capabilities, but checking out, updating, and committing are what you'll be doing most of the time. For detailed information about CVS, books are available, and the main CVS Web site has full documentation: *www.cvshome.org*. In addition, you can search on the Internet using Google or other search engines; there are some very nice condensed introductions to CVS that can get you started without bogging you down with too many details (the "Gentoo Linux CVS Tutorial" by Daniel Robbins (*www.gentoo.org/doc/cvs-tutorial.html*) is particularly straightforward).

Daily builds

By incorporating compilation and testing into your buildfiles, you can follow the practice of performing *daily builds*, advocated by the Extreme Programming folks and others. Regardless of the number of features that you currently have implemented, you always keep your system in a state in which it can be successfully built, so that if someone performs a checkout and runs Ant, the buildfile will perform all the compilations and run all the tests without failing.

This is a powerful technique. It means that you always have, as a baseline, a system that compiles and passes all its tests. At any time, you can always see what the true state of the development process is by examining the features that are actually implemented in the running system. One of the timesavers of this approach is that no one has to waste time coming up with a report explaining what is going on with the system; everybody can see for themselves by checking out a current build and running the program.

Running builds daily, or more often, also ensures that if someone (accidentally, we presume) checks in changes that cause tests to fail, you'll know about it in short order, before those bugs have a chance to propagate further problems in the system. Ant even has a task that will send email, because many teams set up their buildfile as a **cron**[12] job to automatically run daily, or even several times a day, and send email if it fails. There is also an open-source tool that automatically performs builds and provides a Web page to show the project status; see *http://cruisecontrol.sourceforge.net*.

Logging

Logging is the process of reporting information about a running program. In a debugged program, this information can be ordinary status data that describes the progress of the program (for example, if you have an installation program, you may log the steps taken during installation, the directories where you stored files, startup values for the program, etc.).

Logging is also very useful during debugging. Without logging, you might try to decipher the behavior of a program by inserting **println( )** statements. Many examples in this book use that very technique, and in the absence of a debugger (a topic that will be introduced shortly), it's about all you have. However, once you decide the program is working properly, you'll probably take the **println( )** statements out. Then if you run into more bugs, you may need to put them back in. It's much nicer if you can put in some kind of output statements, which will only be used when necessary.

Prior to the availability of the logging API in JDK 1.4, programmers would often use a technique that relies on the fact that the Java compiler will optimize away code that will never be called. If **debug** is a **static final boolean** and you say:

```
if(debug) {
  System.out.println("Debug info");
}
```

then when **debug** is **false**, the compiler will completely remove the code within the braces (thus the code doesn't cause any run-time overhead at all

---

[12] **Cron** is a program that was developed under Unix to run programs at specified times. However, it is also available in free versions under Windows, and as a Windows NT/2000 service: http://www.kalab.com/freeware/cron/cron.htm.

when it isn't used). Using this technique, you can place trace code throughout your program and easily turn it on and off. One drawback to the technique, however, is that you must recompile your code in order to turn your trace statements on and off, whereas it's generally more convenient to be able to turn on the trace without recompiling the program by using a configuration file that you can change to modify the logging properties.

The logging API in JDK 1.4 provides a more sophisticated facility to report information about your program with almost the same efficiency of the technique in the preceding example. For very simple informational logging, you can do something like this:

```
//: c15:InfoLogging.java
import com.bruceeckel.simpletest.*;
import java.util.logging.*;
import java.io.*;

public class InfoLogging {
  private static Test monitor = new Test();
  private static Logger logger =
    Logger.getLogger("InfoLogging");
  public static void main(String[] args) {
    logger.info("Logging an INFO-level message");
    monitor.expect(new String[] {
      "%% .* InfoLogging main",
      "INFO: Logging an INFO-level message"
    });
  }
} ///:~
```

The output during one run is:

```
Jul 7, 2002 6:59:46 PM InfoLogging main
INFO: Logging an INFO-level message
```

Notice that the logging system has detected the class name and method name from which the log message originated. It's not guaranteed that these names will be correct, so you shouldn't rely on their accuracy. If you want to ensure that the proper class name and method are printed, you can use a more complex method to log the message, like this:

```
//: c15:InfoLogging2.java
// Guaranteeing proper class and method names
import com.bruceeckel.simpletest.*;
```

```
import java.util.logging.*;
import java.io.*;

public class InfoLogging2 {
  private static Test monitor = new Test();
  private static Logger logger =
    Logger.getLogger("InfoLogging2");
  public static void main(String[] args) {
    logger.logp(Level.INFO, "InfoLogging2", "main",
      "Logging an INFO-level message");
    monitor.expect(new String[] {
      "%% .* InfoLogging2 main",
      "INFO: Logging an INFO-level message"
    });
  }
} ///:~
```

The **logp( )** method takes arguments of the logging level (you'll learn about this next), the class name and method name, and the logging string. You can see that it's much simpler to just rely on the automatic approach if the class and method names reported during logging are not critical.

Logging Levels

The logging API provides multiple levels of reporting and the ability to change to a different level during program execution. Thus, you can dynamically set the logging level to any of the following states:

Level	Effect	Numeric Value
OFF	No logging messages are reported.	**Integer.MAX_VALUE**
SEVERE	Only logging messages with the level SEVERE are reported.	1000
WARNING	Logging messages with levels of WARNING and SEVERE are reported.	900
INFO	Logging messages with	800

	levels of INFO and above are reported.	
CONFIG	Logging messages with levels of CONFIG and above are reported.	700
FINE	Logging messages with levels of FINE and above are reported.	500
FINER	Logging messages with levels of FINER and above are reported.	400
FINEST	Logging messages with levels of FINEST and above are reported.	300
ALL	All logging messages are reported.	**Integer.MIN_VALUE**

You can even inherit from **java.util.Logging.Level** (which has **protected** constructors) and define your own level. This could, for example, have a value of less than 300, so the level is less than FINEST. Then logging messages at your new level would not appear when the level is FINEST.

You can see the effect of trying out the different levels of logging in the following example:

```
//: c15:LoggingLevels.java
import com.bruceeckel.simpletest.*;
import java.util.logging.Level;
import java.util.logging.Logger;
import java.util.logging.Handler;
import java.util.logging.LogManager;

public class LoggingLevels {
  private static Test monitor = new Test();
  private static Logger
    lgr = Logger.getLogger("com"),
    lgr2 = Logger.getLogger("com.bruceeckel"),
```

```java
    util = Logger.getLogger("com.bruceeckel.util"),
    test = Logger.getLogger("com.bruceeckel.test"),
    rand = Logger.getLogger("random");
  private static void logMessages() {
    lgr.info("com : info");
    lgr2.info("com.bruceeckel : info");
    util.info("util : info");
    test.severe("test : severe");
    rand.info("random : info");
  }
  public static void main(String[] args) {
    lgr.setLevel(Level.SEVERE);
    System.out.println("com level: SEVERE");
    logMessages();
    util.setLevel(Level.FINEST);
    test.setLevel(Level.FINEST);
    rand.setLevel(Level.FINEST);
    System.out.println("individual loggers set to FINEST");
    logMessages();
    lgr.setLevel(Level.SEVERE);
    System.out.println("com level: SEVERE");
    logMessages();
    monitor.expect("LoggingLevels.out");
  }
} ///:~
```

The first few lines of **main( )** are necessary because the default level of logging messages that will be reported is **INFO** and greater (more severe). If you do not change this, then the messages of level **CONFIG** and below will not be reported (try taking out the lines to see this happen).

You can have multiple logger objects in your program, and these loggers are organized into a hierarchical tree, which can be programmatically associated with the package namespace. Child loggers keep track of their immediate parent and by default pass the logging records up to the parent.

The "root" logger object is always created by default, and is the base of the tree of logger objects. You get a reference to the root logger by calling the static method **Logger.getLogger("")**. Notice that it takes an empty string rather than no arguments.

Each **Logger** object can have one or more **Handler** objects associated with it. Each **Handler** object provides a *strategy*[13] for publishing the logging information, which is contained in **LogRecord** objects. To create a new type of **Handler**, you simply inherit from the **Handler** class and override the **publish( )** method (along with **flush( )** and **close( )**, to deal with any streams you may use in the **Handler**).

The root logger always has one associated handler by default, which sends output to the console. In order to access the handlers, you call **getHandlers( )** on the **Logger** object. In the preceding example, we know that there's only one handler so we don't technically need to iterate through the list, but it's safer to do so in general because someone else may have added other handlers to the root logger. The default level of each handler is **INFO**, so in order to see all the messages, we set the level to **ALL** (which is the same as **FINEST**).

The **levels** array allows easy testing of all the **Level** values. The **logger** is set to each value and all the different logging levels are attempted. In the output you can see that only messages at the currently selected logging level, and those messages that are more severe, are reported.

LogRecords

A **LogRecord** is an example of a *Messenger* object,[14] whose job is simply to carry information from one place to another. All the methods in the **LogRecord** are getters and setters. Here's an example that dumps all the information stored in a **LogRecord** using the getter methods:

```
//: c15:PrintableLogRecord.java
// Override LogRecord toString()
import com.bruceeckel.simpletest.*;
import java.util.ResourceBundle;
import java.util.logging.*;

public class PrintableLogRecord extends LogRecord {
```

---

[13] A pluggable algorithm. Strategies allow you to easily change one part of a solution while leaving the rest unchanged. They are often used (as in this case) as ways to allow the client programmer to provide a portion of the code needed to solve a particular problem. For more details, see *Thinking in Patterns (with Java)* at *www.BruceEckel.com*.

[14] A term coined by Bill Venners. This may or may not be a design pattern.

```
  private static Test monitor = new Test();
  public PrintableLogRecord(Level level, String str) {
    super(level, str);
  }
  public String toString() {
    String result = "Level<" + getLevel() + ">\n"
      + "LoggerName<" + getLoggerName() + ">\n"
      + "Message<" + getMessage() + ">\n"
      + "CurrentMillis<" + getMillis() + ">\n"
      + "Params";
    Object[] objParams = getParameters();
    if(objParams == null)
      result += "<null>\n";
    else
      for(int i = 0; i < objParams.length; i++)
        result += "  Param # <" + i + " value " +
          objParams[i].toString() + ">\n";
    result += "ResourceBundle<" + getResourceBundle()
      + ">\nResourceBundleName<" + getResourceBundleName()
      + ">\nSequenceNumber<" + getSequenceNumber()
      + ">\nSourceClassName<" + getSourceClassName()
      + ">\nSourceMethodName<" + getSourceMethodName()
      + ">\nThread Id<" + getThreadID()
      + ">\nThrown<" + getThrown() + ">";
    return result;
  }
  public static void main(String[] args) {
    PrintableLogRecord logRecord = new PrintableLogRecord(
      Level.FINEST, "Simple Log Record");
    System.out.println(logRecord);
    monitor.expect(new String[] {
      "Level<FINEST>",
      "LoggerName<null>",
      "Message<Simple Log Record>",
      "%% CurrentMillis<.+>",
      "Params<null>",
      "ResourceBundle<null>",
      "ResourceBundleName<null>",
      "SequenceNumber<0>",
      "SourceClassName<null>",
      "SourceMethodName<null>",
      "Thread Id<10>",
      "Thrown<null>"
    });
```

```
  }
} ///:~
```

PrintableLogRecord is a simple extension of **LogRecord** that overrides **toString( )** to call all the getter methods available in **LogRecord**.

Handlers

As noted previously, you can easily create your own handler by inheriting from **Handler** and defining **publish( )** to perform your desired operations. However, there are predefined handlers that will probably satisfy your needs without doing any extra work:

StreamHandler	Writes formatted records to an **OutputStream**
ConsoleHandler	Writes formatted records to **System.err**
FileHandler	Writes formatted log records either to a single file, or to a set of rotating log files
SocketHandler	Writes formatted log records to remote TCP ports
MemoryHandler	Buffers log records in memory

For example, you often want to store logging output to a file. The **FileHandler** makes this easy:

```
//: c15:LogToFile.java
// {Clean: LogToFile.xml,LogToFile.xml.lck}
import com.bruceeckel.simpletest.*;
import java.util.logging.*;

public class LogToFile {
  private static Test monitor = new Test();
  private static Logger logger =
    Logger.getLogger("LogToFile");
  public static void main(String[] args) throws Exception {
    logger.addHandler(new FileHandler("LogToFile.xml"));
    logger.info("A message logged to the file");
    monitor.expect(new String[] {
      "%% .* LogToFile main",
      "INFO: A message logged to the file"
    });
  }
} ///:~
```

When you run this program, you'll notice two things. First, even though we're sending output to a file, you'll still see console output. That's because each message is converted to a **LogRecord**, which is first used by the local **logger** object, which passes it to its own handlers. At this point the **LogRecord** is passed to the parent object, which has its own handlers. This process continues until the root logger is reached. The root logger comes with a default **ConsoleHandler**, so the message appears on the screen as well as appearing in the log file (you can turn off this behavior by calling **setUseParentHandlers(false)**).

The second thing you'll notice is that the contents of the log file is in XML format, which will look something like this:

```
<?xml version="1.0" standalone="no"?>
<!DOCTYPE log SYSTEM "logger.dtd">
<log>
<record>
  <date>2002-07-08T12:18:17</date>
  <millis>1026152297750</millis>
  <sequence>0</sequence>
  <logger>LogToFile</logger>
  <level>INFO</level>
  <class>LogToFile</class>
  <method>main</method>
  <thread>10</thread>
  <message>A message logged to the file</message>
</record>
</log>
```

The default output format for a **FileHandler** is XML. If you want to change the format, you must attach a different **Formatter** object to the handler. Here, a **SimpleFormatter** is used for the file in order to output as plain text format:

```
//: c15:LogToFile2.java
// {Clean: LogToFile2.txt,LogToFile2.txt.lck}
import com.bruceeckel.simpletest.*;
import java.util.logging.*;

public class LogToFile2 {
  private static Test monitor = new Test();
  private static Logger logger =
    Logger.getLogger("LogToFile2");
  public static void main(String[] args) throws Exception {
```

```
    FileHandler logFile= new FileHandler("LogToFile2.txt");
    logFile.setFormatter(new SimpleFormatter());
    logger.addHandler(logFile);
    logger.info("A message logged to the file");
    monitor.expect(new String[] {
      "%% .* LogToFile2 main",
      "INFO: A message logged to the file"
    });
  }
} ///:~
```

The **LogToFile2.txt** file will look like this:

```
Jul 8, 2002 12:35:17 PM LogToFile2 main
INFO: A message logged to the file
```

Multiple Handlers

You can register multiple handlers with each **Logger** object. When a logging request comes to the **Logger**, it notifies all the handlers that have been registered with it,[15] as long as the logging level for the **Logger** is greater than or equal to that of the logging request. Each handler, in turn, has its own logging level; if the level of the **LogRecord** is greater than or equal to the level of the handler, then that handler publishes the record.

Here's an example that adds a **FileHandler** and a **ConsoleHandler** to the **Logger** object:

```
//: c15:MultipleHandlers.java
// {Clean: MultipleHandlers.xml,MultipleHandlers.xml.lck}
import com.bruceeckel.simpletest.*;
import java.util.logging.*;

public class MultipleHandlers {
  private static Test monitor = new Test();
  private static Logger logger =
    Logger.getLogger("MultipleHandlers");
  public static void main(String[] args) throws Exception {
    FileHandler logFile =
      new FileHandler("MultipleHandlers.xml");
    logger.addHandler(logFile);
    logger.addHandler(new ConsoleHandler());
```

[15] This is the *Observer* design pattern (ibid).

```
    logger.warning("Output to multiple handlers");
    monitor.expect(new String[] {
      "%% .* MultipleHandlers main",
      "WARNING: Output to multiple handlers",
      "%% .* MultipleHandlers main",
      "WARNING: Output to multiple handlers"
    });
  }
} ///:~
```

When you run the program, you'll notice that the console output occurs twice; that's because the root logger's default behavior is still enabled. If you want to turn this off, make a call to **setUseParentHandlers(false)**:

```
//: c15:MultipleHandlers2.java
// {Clean: MultipleHandlers2.xml,MultipleHandlers2.xml.lck}
import com.bruceeckel.simpletest.*;
import java.util.logging.*;

public class MultipleHandlers2 {
  private static Test monitor = new Test();
  private static Logger logger =
    Logger.getLogger("MultipleHandlers2");
  public static void main(String[] args) throws Exception {
    FileHandler logFile =
      new FileHandler("MultipleHandlers2.xml");
    logger.addHandler(logFile);
    logger.addHandler(new ConsoleHandler());
    logger.setUseParentHandlers(false);
    logger.warning("Output to multiple handlers");
    monitor.expect(new String[] {
      "%% .* MultipleHandlers2 main",
      "WARNING: Output to multiple handlers"
    });
  }
} ///:~
```

Now you'll see only one console message.

Writing your own Handlers

You can easily write custom handlers by inheriting from the **Handler** class. To do this, you must not only implement the **publish( )** method (which performs the actual reporting), but also **flush( )** and **close( )**, which ensure that the stream used for reporting is properly cleaned up. Here's an example that stores information from the **LogRecord** into another object (a **List** of **String**). At the end of the program, the object is printed to the console:

```
//: c15:CustomHandler.java
// How to write custom handler
import com.bruceeckel.simpletest.*;
import java.util.logging.*;
import java.util.*;

public class CustomHandler {
  private static Test monitor = new Test();
  private static Logger logger =
    Logger.getLogger("CustomHandler");
  private static List strHolder = new ArrayList();
  public static void main(String[] args) {
    logger.addHandler(new Handler() {
      public void publish(LogRecord logRecord) {
        strHolder.add(logRecord.getLevel() + ":");
        strHolder.add(logRecord.getSourceClassName()+":");
        strHolder.add(logRecord.getSourceMethodName()+":");
        strHolder.add("<" + logRecord.getMessage() + ">");
        strHolder.add("\n");
      }
      public void flush() {}
      public void close() {}
    });
    logger.warning("Logging Warning");
    logger.info("Logging Info");
    System.out.print(strHolder);
    monitor.expect(new String[] {
      "%% .* CustomHandler main",
      "WARNING: Logging Warning",
      "%% .* CustomHandler main",
      "INFO: Logging Info",
      "[WARNING:, CustomHandler:, main:, " +
      "<Logging Warning>, ",
      ", INFO:, CustomHandler:, main:, <Logging Info>, ",
      "]"
    });
  }
} ///:~
```

The console output comes from the root logger. When the **ArrayList** is printed, you can see that only selected information has been captured into the object.

Filters

When you write the code to send a logging message to a **Logger** object, you often decide, at the time you're writing the code, what level the logging message should be (the logging API certainly allows you to devise more complex systems wherein the level of the message can be determined dynamically, but this is less common in practice). The **Logger** object has a level that can be set so that it can decide what level of message to accept; all others will be ignored. This can be thought of as a basic filtering functionality, and it's often all you need.

Sometimes, however, you need more sophisticated filtering so that you can decide whether to accept or reject a message based on something more than just the current level. To accomplish this you can write custom **Filter** objects. **Filter** is an **interface** that has a single method, **boolean isLoggable(LogRecord record)**, which decides whether or not this particular **LogRecord** is interesting enough to report.

Once you create a **Filter**, you register it with either a **Logger** or a **Handler** by using the **setFilter( )** method. For example, suppose you'd like to only log reports about **Ducks**:

```
//: c15:SimpleFilter.java
import com.bruceeckel.simpletest.*;
import java.util.logging.*;

public class SimpleFilter {
  private static Test monitor = new Test();
  private static Logger logger =
    Logger.getLogger("SimpleFilter");
  static class Duck {};
  static class Wombat {};
  static void sendLogMessages() {
    logger.log(Level.WARNING,
      "A duck in the house!", new Duck());
    logger.log(Level.WARNING,
      "A Wombat at large!", new Wombat());
  }
  public static void main(String[] args) {
```

```
    sendLogMessages();
    logger.setFilter(new Filter() {
      public boolean isLoggable(LogRecord record) {
        Object[] params = record.getParameters();
        if(params == null)
          return true; // No parameters
        if(record.getParameters()[0] instanceof Duck)
          return true;  // Only log Ducks
        return false;
      }
    });
    logger.info("After setting filter..");
    sendLogMessages();
    monitor.expect(new String[] {
      "%% .* SimpleFilter sendLogMessages",
      "WARNING: A duck in the house!",
      "%% .* SimpleFilter sendLogMessages",
      "WARNING: A Wombat at large!",
      "%% .* SimpleFilter main",
      "INFO: After setting filter..",
      "%% .* SimpleFilter sendLogMessages",
      "WARNING: A duck in the house!"
    });
  }
} ///:~
```

Before setting the **Filter**, messages about **Duck**s and **Wombat**s are reported. The **Filter** is created as an anonymous inner class that looks at the **LogRecord** parameter to see if a **Duck** was passed as an extra argument to the **log( )** method. If so, it returns **true** to indicate that the message should be processed.

Notice that the signature of **getParameters( )** says that it will return an **Object[]**. However, if no additional arguments have been passed to the **log( )** method, **getParameters( )** will return **null** (in violation of its signature—this is a bad programming practice). So instead of assuming that an array is returned (as promised) and checking to see if it is of zero length, we must check for **null**. If you don't do this correctly, then the call to **logger.info( )** will cause an exception to be thrown.

Formatters

A **Formatter** is a way to insert a formatting operation into a **Handler**'s processing steps. If you register a **Formatter** object with a **Handler**, then before the **LogRecord** is published by the **Handler**, it is first sent to the **Formatter**. After formatting, the **LogRecord** is returned to the **Handler**, which then publishes it.

To write a custom **Formatter**, extend the **Formatter** class and override **format(LogRecord record)**. Then, register the **Formatter** with the **Handler** by using the **setFormatter( )** call, as seen here:

```
//: c15:SimpleFormatterExample.java
import com.bruceeckel.simpletest.*;
import java.util.logging.*;
import java.util.*;

public class SimpleFormatterExample {
  private static Test monitor = new Test();
  private static Logger logger =
    Logger.getLogger("SimpleFormatterExample");
  private static void logMessages() {
    logger.info("Line One");
    logger.info("Line Two");
  }
  public static void main(String[] args) {
    logger.setUseParentHandlers(false);
    Handler conHdlr = new ConsoleHandler();
    conHdlr.setFormatter(new Formatter() {
      public String format(LogRecord record) {
        return record.getLevel()  + "  :  "
          + record.getSourceClassName()  + " -:- "
          + record.getSourceMethodName()  + " -:- "
          + record.getMessage() + "\n";
      }
    });
    logger.addHandler(conHdlr);
    logMessages();
    monitor.expect(new String[] {
      "INFO  :  SimpleFormatterExample -:- logMessages "
        + "-:- Line One",
      "INFO  :  SimpleFormatterExample -:- logMessages "
        + "-:- Line Two"
    });
```

```
  }
} ///:~
```

Remember that a logger like **myLogger** has a default handler that it gets from the parent logger (the root logger, in this case). Here, we are turning off the default handler by calling **setUseParentHandlers(false)**, and then adding in a console handler to use instead. The new **Formatter** is created as an anonymous inner class in the **setFormatter( )** statement. The overridden **format( )** statement simply extracts some of the information from the **LogRecord** and formats it into a string.

Example: Sending email to report log messages

You can actually have one of your logging handlers send you an email so that you can be automatically notified of important problems. The following example uses the JavaMail API to develop a mail user agent to send an email.

The JavaMail API is a set of classes that interface to the underlying mailing protocol (IMAP, POP, SMTP). You can devise a notification mechanism on some exceptional condition in the running code by registering an additional **Handler** to send an email.

```
//: c15:EmailLogger.java
// {RunByHand} Must be connected to the Internet
// {Depends: mail.jar,activation.jar}
import java.util.logging.*;
import java.io.*;
import java.util.Properties;
import javax.mail.*;
import javax.mail.internet.*;

public class EmailLogger {
  private static Logger logger =
    Logger.getLogger("EmailLogger");
  public static void main(String[] args) throws Exception {
    logger.setUseParentHandlers(false);
    Handler conHdlr = new ConsoleHandler();
    conHdlr.setFormatter(new Formatter() {
      public String format(LogRecord record) {
        return record.getLevel() + "  :  "
          + record.getSourceClassName() + ":"
          + record.getSourceMethodName() + ":"
```

```
          + record.getMessage() + "\n";
      }
    });
    logger.addHandler(conHdlr);
    logger.addHandler(
      new FileHandler("EmailLoggerOutput.xml"));
    logger.addHandler(new MailingHandler());
    logger.log(Level.INFO,
      "Testing Multiple Handlers", "SendMailTrue");
  }
}

// A handler that sends mail messages
class MailingHandler extends Handler {
  public void publish(LogRecord record) {
    Object[] params = record.getParameters();
    if(params == null) return;
    // Send mail only if the parameter is true
    if(params[0].equals("SendMailTrue")) {
      new MailInfo("bruce@theunixman.com",
        new String[] { "bruce@theunixman.com" },
        "smtp.theunixman.com", "Test Subject",
        "Test Content").sendMail();
    }
  }
  public void close() {}
  public void flush() {}
}

class MailInfo {
  private String fromAddr;
  private String[] toAddr;
  private String serverAddr;
  private String subject;
  private String message;
  public MailInfo(String from, String[] to,
    String server, String subject, String message) {
    fromAddr = from;
    toAddr = to;
    serverAddr = server;
    this.subject = subject;
    this.message = message;
  }
  public void sendMail() {
```

```
    try {
      Properties prop = new Properties();
      prop.put("mail.smtp.host", serverAddr);
      Session session =
        Session.getDefaultInstance(prop, null);
      session.setDebug(true);
      // Create a message
      Message mimeMsg = new MimeMessage(session);
      // Set the from and to address
      Address addressFrom = new InternetAddress(fromAddr);
      mimeMsg.setFrom(addressFrom);
      Address[] to = new InternetAddress[toAddr.length];
      for(int i = 0; i < toAddr.length; i++)
        to[i] = new InternetAddress(toAddr[i]);
      mimeMsg.setRecipients(Message.RecipientType.TO,to);
      mimeMsg.setSubject(subject);
      mimeMsg.setText(message);
      Transport.send(mimeMsg);
    } catch (Exception e) {
      throw new RuntimeException(e);
    }
  }
} ///:~
```

MailingHandler is one of the **Handler**s registered with the logger. To send an email, the **MailingHandler** uses the **MailInfo** object. When a logging message is sent with an additional parameter of "**SendMailTrue**," the **MailingHandler** sends an email.

The **MailInfo** object contains the necessary state information, such as the *to* address, *from* address, and the subject information required to send an email. This state information is provided to the **MailInfo** object through the constructor when it is instantiated.

To send an email you must first establish a **Session** with the *Simple Mail Transfer Protocol* (SMTP) server. This is done by passing the address of the server inside a **Properties** object, in a property named **mail.smtp.host**. You establish a session by calling **Session.getDefaultInstance( )**, passing it the **Properties** object as the first argument. The second argument is an instance of **Authenticator** that may be used for authenticating the user. Passing a **null** value for the **Authenticator** argument specifies no authentication. If the debugging flag in the **Properties** object is set, information regarding the communication between the **SMTP** server and the program will be printed.

MimeMessage is an abstraction of an Internet email message that extends the class **Message**. It constructs a message that complies with the MIME (Multipurpose Internet Mail Extensions) format. A **MimeMessage** is constructed by passing it an instance of **Session**. You may set the *from* and *to* addresses by creating an instance of **InternetAddress** class (a subclass of **Address**). You send the message using the static call **Transport.send( )** from the abstract class **Transport**. An implementation of **Transport** uses a specific protocol (generally SMTP) to communicate with the server to send the message.

Controlling Logging Levels through Namespaces

Although not mandatory, it's advisable to give a logger the name of the class in which it is used. This allows you to manipulate the logging level of groups of loggers that reside in the same package hierarchy, at the granularity of the directory package structure. For example, you can modify all the logging levels of all the packages in **com**, or just the ones in **com.bruceeckel**, or just the ones in **com.bruceeckel.util**, as shown in the following example:

```
//: c15:LoggingLevelManipulation.java
import com.bruceeckel.simpletest.*;
import java.util.logging.Level;
import java.util.logging.Logger;
import java.util.logging.Handler;
import java.util.logging.LogManager;

public class LoggingLevelManipulation {
  private static Test monitor = new Test();
  private static Logger
    lgr = Logger.getLogger("com"),
    lgr2 = Logger.getLogger("com.bruceeckel"),
    util = Logger.getLogger("com.bruceeckel.util"),
    test = Logger.getLogger("com.bruceeckel.test"),
    rand = Logger.getLogger("random");
  static void printLogMessages(Logger logger) {
    logger.finest(logger.getName() + " Finest");
    logger.finer(logger.getName() + " Finer");
    logger.fine(logger.getName() + " Fine");
```

```
    logger.config(logger.getName() + " Config");
    logger.info(logger.getName() + " Info");
    logger.warning(logger.getName() + " Warning");
    logger.severe(logger.getName() + " Severe");
  }
  static void logMessages() {
    printLogMessages(lgr);
    printLogMessages(lgr2);
    printLogMessages(util);
    printLogMessages(test);
    printLogMessages(rand);
  }
  static void printLevels() {
    System.out.println(" -- printing levels -- "
      + lgr.getName() + " : " + lgr.getLevel()
      + " " + lgr2.getName() + " : " + lgr2.getLevel()
      + " " + util.getName() + " : " + util.getLevel()
      + " " + test.getName() + " : " + test.getLevel()
      + " " + rand.getName() + " : " + rand.getLevel());
  }
  public static void main(String[] args) {
    printLevels();
    lgr.setLevel(Level.SEVERE);
    printLevels();
    System.out.println("com level: SEVERE");
    logMessages();
    util.setLevel(Level.FINEST);
    test.setLevel(Level.FINEST);
    rand.setLevel(Level.FINEST);
    printLevels();
    System.out.println(
      "individual loggers set to FINEST");
    logMessages();
    lgr.setLevel(Level.FINEST);
    printLevels();
    System.out.println("com level: FINEST");
    logMessages();
    monitor.expect("LoggingLevelManipulation.out");
  }
} ///:~
```

As you can see in this code, if you pass **getLogger( )** a string representing a namespace, the resulting **Logger** will control the severity levels of that namespace; that is, all the packages within that namespace will be affected by changes to the severity level of the logger.

Each **Logger** keeps a track of its existing ancestor **Logger.** If a child logger already has a logging level set, then that level is used instead of the parent's logging level. Changing the logging level of the parent does not affect the logging level of the child once the child has its own logging level.

Although the level of individual loggers is set to **FINEST**, only messages with a logging level equal to or more severe than **INFO** are printed because we are using the **ConsoleHandler** of the root logger, which is at **INFO**.

Because it isn't in the same namespace, the logging level of **random** remains unaffected when the logging level of the logger **com** or **com.bruceeckel** is changed.

Logging Practices for Large Projects

At first glance, the Java logging API can seem rather over-engineered for most programming problems. The extra features and abilities don't come in handy until you start building larger projects. In this section we'll look at these features and recommended ways to use them. If you're only using logging on smaller projects, you probably won't need to use these features.

Configuration files

The following file shows how you can configure loggers in a project by using a properties file:

```
//:! c15:log.prop
#### Configuration File ####
# Global Params
# Handlers installed for the root logger
handlers= java.util.logging.ConsoleHandler
java.util.logging.FileHandler
# Level for root logger—is used by any logger
# that does not have its level set
.level= FINEST
# Initialization class—the public default constructor
# of this class is called by the Logging framework
config = ConfigureLogging

# Configure FileHandler
# Logging file name - %u specifies unique
```

```
java.util.logging.FileHandler.pattern = java%g.log
# Write 100000 bytes before rotating this file
java.util.logging.FileHandler.limit = 100000
# Number of rotating files to be used
java.util.logging.FileHandler.count = 3
# Formatter to be used with this FileHandler
java.util.logging.FileHandler.formatter =
java.util.logging.SimpleFormatter

# Configure ConsoleHandler
java.util.logging.ConsoleHandler.level = FINEST
java.util.logging.ConsoleHandler.formatter =
java.util.logging.SimpleFormatter

# Set Logger Levels #
com.level=SEVERE
com.bruceeckel.level = FINEST
com.bruceeckel.util.level = INFO
com.bruceeckel.test.level = FINER
random.level= SEVERE
///:~
```

The configuration file allows you to associate handlers with the root logger. The property handlers specify the comma-separated list of handlers you wish to register with the root logger. Here, we register the **FileHandler** and the **ConsoleHandler** with the root logger. The **.level** property species the default level for the logger. This level is used by all the loggers that are children of the root logger and do not have their own level specified. Note that, without a properties file, the default logging level of the root logger is INFO. This is because, in absence of a custom configuration file, the virtual machine uses the configuration from the JAVA_HOME\jre\lib\logging.properties file.

Rotating log files

The preceding configuration file generates *rotating log files*, which are used to prevent any log file from becoming too large. By setting the **FileHandler.limit** value, you give the maximum number of bytes allowed in one log file before the next one begins to fill. **FileHandler.count** determines the number of rotating log files to use; the configuration file shown here specifies three files. If all three files are filled to their maximum, then the first file begins to fill again, overwriting the old contents.

Alternatively, all the output can be put in a single file by giving a **FileHandler.count** value of one. (**FileHandler** parameters are explained in detail in the JDK documentation).

In order for the following program to use the preceding configuration file, you must specify the parameter **java.util.logging.config.file** on the command line:

```
java -Djava.util.logging.config.file=log.prop
ConfigureLogging
```

The configuration file can only modify the root logger. If you want to add filters and handlers for other loggers, you must write the code to do it inside a Java file, as noted in the constructor:

```
//: c15:ConfigureLogging.java
// {JVMArgs: -Djava.util.logging.config.file=log.prop}
// {Clean: java0.log,java0.log.lck}
import com.bruceeckel.simpletest.*;
import java.util.logging.*;

public class ConfigureLogging {
  private static Test monitor = new Test();
  static Logger lgr = Logger.getLogger("com"),
    lgr2 = Logger.getLogger("com.bruceeckel"),
    util = Logger.getLogger("com.bruceeckel.util"),
    test = Logger.getLogger("com.bruceeckel.test"),
    rand = Logger.getLogger("random");
  public ConfigureLogging() {
    /* Set Additional formatters, Filters and Handlers for
       the loggers here. You cannot specify the Handlers
       for loggers except the root logger from the
       configuration file. */
  }
  public static void main(String[] args) {
    sendLogMessages(lgr);
    sendLogMessages(lgr2);
    sendLogMessages(util);
    sendLogMessages(test);
    sendLogMessages(rand);
    monitor.expect("ConfigureLogging.out");
  }
  private static void sendLogMessages(Logger logger) {
    System.out.println(" Logger Name : "
```

```
        + logger.getName() + " Level: " + logger.getLevel());
    logger.finest("Finest");
    logger.finer("Finer");
    logger.fine("Fine");
    logger.config("Config");
    logger.info("Info");
    logger.warning("Warning");
    logger.severe("Severe");
  }
} ///:~
```

The configuration will result in the output being sent to the files named **java0.log**, **java1.log**, and **java2.log** in the directory from which this program is executed.

Suggested practices

Although it's not mandatory, you should generally consider using a logger for each class, following the standard of setting the logger name to be the same as the fully qualified name of the class. As shown earlier, this allows for finer-grained control of logging because of the ability to turn logging on and off based on namespaces.

If you don't set the logging level for individual classes in that package, then the individual classes default to the logging level set for the package (assuming that you name the loggers according to their package and class).

If you control the logging level in a configuration file instead of changing it dynamically in your code, then you can modify logging levels without recompiling your code. Recompilation is not always an option when the system is deployed; often, only the class files are shipped to the destination environment.

Sometimes there is a requirement to execute some code to perform initialization activities such as adding **Handler**s, **Filter**s, and **Formatter**s to loggers. This can be achieved by setting the **config** property in the properties file. You can have multiple classes whose initialization can be done using the **config** property. These classes should be specified using space-delimited values like this:

```
config = ConfigureLogging1 ConfigureLogging2 Bar Baz
```

Classes specified in this fashion will have their default constructors invoked.

Summary

Although this has been a fairly thorough introduction to the logging API, it doesn't include everything. For instance, we haven't talked about the **LogManager** or details of the various built-in handlers, such as **MemoryHandler**, **FileHandler**, **ConsoleHandler**, etc. You should go to the JDK documentation for further details.

Debugging

Although judicious use of **System.out** statements or logging information can produce valuable insight into the behavior of a program,[16] for difficult problems this approach becomes cumbersome and time-consuming. In addition, you may need to peek more deeply into the program than print statements will allow. For this, you need a *debugger*.

In addition to more quickly and easily displaying information that you could produce with print statements, a debugger will also set *breakpoints* and then stop the program when it reaches those breakpoints. A debugger can also display the state of the program at any instant, view the values of variables that you're interested in, step through the program line-by-line, connect to a remotely running program, and more. Especially when you start building larger systems (where bugs can easily become buried), it pays to become familiar with debuggers.

Debugging with JDB

The *Java Debugger* (JDB) is a command-line debugger that ships with the JDK. JDB is at least conceptually a descendant of the Gnu Debugger (GDB, which was inspired by the original Unix DB), in terms of the instructions for debugging and its command-line interface. JDB is useful for learning about debugging and performing simpler debugging tasks, and it's helpful to know that it's always available wherever the JDK is installed. However, for larger projects you'll probably want to use a graphical debugger, described later.

Suppose you've written the following program:

---

[16] I learned C++ primarily by printing information, since at the time I was learning there were no debuggers available.

```java
//: c15:SimpleDebugging.java
// {ThrowsException}
public class SimpleDebugging {
  private static void foo1() {
    System.out.println("In foo1");
    foo2();
  }
  private static void foo2() {
    System.out.println("In foo2");
    foo3();
  }
  private static void foo3() {
    System.out.println("In foo3");
    int j = 1;
    j--;
    int i = 5 / j;
  }
  public static void main(String[] args) {
    foo1();
  }
} ///:~
```

If you look at **foo3( )**, the problem is obvious; you're dividing by zero. But suppose this code is buried in a large program (as is implied here by the sequence of calls) and you don't know where to start looking for the problem. As it turns out, the exception that will be thrown will give enough information for you to locate the problem (this is just one of the great things about exceptions). But let's just suppose that the problem is more difficult than that, and that you need to drill into it more deeply and get more information than what an exception provides.

To run JDB, you must tell the compiler to generate debugging information by compiling **SimpleDebugging.java** with the **–g** flag. Then you start debugging the program with the command line:

```
jdb SimpleDebugging
```

This brings up JDB and gives you a command prompt. You can view the list of available JDB commands by typing '?' at the prompt.

Here's an interactive debugging trace that shows how to chase down a problem:

```
Initializing jdb ...
```

```
> catch Exception
```

The > indicates that JDB is waiting for a command, and the commands typed in by the user are shown in bold. The command **catch Exception** causes a breakpoint to be set at any point where an exception is thrown (however, the debugger will stop anyway, even if you don't explicitly give this comment—exceptions appear to be default breakpoints in JDB).

```
Deferring exception catch Exception.
It will be set after the class is loaded.
> run
```

Now the program will run until the next breakpoint, which in this case is where the exception occurs. Here's the result of the **run** command:

```
run SimpleDebugging
>
VM Started: In foo1
In foo2
In foo3
Exception occurred: java.lang.ArithmeticException
(uncaught)"thread=main", SimpleDebugging.foo3(), line=18
bci=15
18          int i = 5 / j;
```

The program runs until line 18, where the exception generated, but JDB does not exit when it hits the exception. The debugger also displays the line of code that caused the exception. You can list the point where the execution stopped in the program source by the **list** command as shown here:

```
main[1] list
14        private static void foo3() {
15          System.out.println("In foo3");
16          int j = 1;
17          j--;
18 =>       int i = 5 / j;
19        }
20
21        public static void main(String[] args) {
22          foo1();
23        }
```

The pointer ("=>") in this listing shows the current point from where the execution will resume. You *could* resume the execution by the **cont** (continue) command. But doing that will make JDB exit at the exception, printing the stack trace.

The **locals** command dumps the value of all the local variables:

```
main[1] locals
Method arguments:
Local variables:
j = 0
```

You can see that the value of **j=0** is what caused the exception.

The **wherei** command prints the stack frames pushed in the method stack of the current thread:

```
main[1] wherei
[1] SimpleDebugging.foo3 (SimpleDebugging.java:18), pc = 15
[2] SimpleDebugging.foo2 (SimpleDebugging.java:11), pc = 8
[3] SimpleDebugging.foo1 (SimpleDebugging.java:6), pc = 8
[4] SimpleDebugging.main (SimpleDebugging.java:22), pc = 0
```

Each line after the **wherei** command represents a method call and the point where the call will return (which is shown by the value of the program counter **pc**). Here the calling sequence was **main( ), foo1( ), foo2( )**, and **foo3( )**. You can pop the stack frame pushed when the call was made to **foo3( )** with the **pop** command:

```
main[1] pop
main[1] wherei
[1] SimpleDebugging.foo2 (SimpleDebugging.java:11), pc = 8
[2] SimpleDebugging.foo1 (SimpleDebugging.java:6), pc = 8
[3] SimpleDebugging.main (SimpleDebugging.java:22), pc = 0
```

You can make the JDB step through the call to **foo3( )** again with the **reenter** command:

```
main[1] reenter
>
Step completed: "thread=main", SimpleDebugging.foo3(),
line=15 bci=0
15          System.out.println("In foo3");
```

The **list** command shows us that the execution begins at the start of **foo3( )**:

```
main[1] list
11          foo3();
```

```
12      }
13
14      private static void foo3() {
15 =>     System.out.println("In foo3");
16        int j = 1;
17        j--;
18        int i = 5 / j;
19      }
20
```

JDB also allows you to modify the value of the local variables. The divide by zero that was caused by executing this piece of code the last time can be avoided by changing the value of **j**. You can do this directly in the debugger, so you can continue debugging the program without going back and changing the source file. Before you set the value of **j**, you will have to execute through line 25 since that is where **j** is declared.

```
main[1] step
> In foo3

Step completed: "thread=main", SimpleDebugging.foo3(),
line=16 bci=8
16        int j = 1;

main[1] step
>
Step completed: "thread=main", SimpleDebugging.foo3(),
line=17 bci=10
17        j--;

main[1] list
13
14      private static void foo3() {
15        System.out.println("In foo3");
16        int j = 1;
17 =>     j--;
18        int i = 5 / j;
19      }
20
21      public static void main(String[] args) {
22        foo1();
```

At this point, **j** is defined and you can set its value so that the exception can be avoided.

```
main[1] set j=6
 j=6 = 6
main[1] next
>
Step completed: "thread=main", SimpleDebugging.foo3(),
line=18 bci=13
18          int i = 5 / j;
main[1] next
>
Step completed: "thread=main", SimpleDebugging.foo3(),
line=19 bci=17
19        }
main[1] next
>
Step completed: "thread=main", SimpleDebugging.foo2(),
line=12 bci=11
12        }
main[1] list
8
9        private static void foo2() {
10          System.out.println("In foo2");
11          foo3();
12 =>     }
13
14        private static void foo3() {
15          System.out.println("In foo3");
16          int j = 1;
17          j--;
main[1] next
>
Step completed: "thread=main", SimpleDebugging.foo1(),
line=7 bci=11
7        }
main[1] list
3     public class SimpleDebugging {
4        private static void foo1() {
5          System.out.println("In foo1");
6          foo2();
7 =>     }
8
9        private static void foo2() {
10          System.out.println("In foo2");
11          foo3();
12        }
```

```
main[1] next
>
Step completed: "thread=main", SimpleDebugging.main(),
line=23 bci=3
23      }

main[1] list
19      }
20
21      public static void main(String[] args) {
22        foo1();
23 =>   }
24    } ///:~
main[1] next
>
The application exited
```

next executes a line at a time. You can see that the exception is avoided and we can continue stepping through the program. **list** is used to show the position in the program from where execution will proceed.

Graphical debuggers

Using a command-line debugger like JDB can be inconvenient. You must use explicit commands to do things like looking at the state of the variables (locals, dump), listing the point of execution in the source code (list), finding out the threads in the system(threads), setting breakpoints (stop in, stop at), etc. A graphical debugger allows you to do all these things with a few clicks and also view the latest details of program being debugged without using explicit commands.

Thus, although you may want to get started by experimenting with JDB, you'll probably find it much more productive to learn to use a graphical debugger in order to quickly track down your bugs. During the development of this edition of this book, we began using IBM's *Eclipse* editor and development environment, which contains a very good graphical debugger for Java. Eclipse is well designed and implemented, and you can download it for free from *www.Eclipse.org* (this is a free tool, not a demo or shareware—thanks to IBM for investing the money, time, and effort to make this available to everyone).

Other free development tools have graphical debuggers as well, such as Sun's *Netbeans* and the free version of Borland's *JBuilder*.

Profiling and optimizing

"We should forget about small efficiencies, say about 97% of the time: Premature optimization is the root of all evil."—Donald Knuth

Although you should always keep this quote in mind, especially when you discover yourself on the slippery slope of premature optimization, sometimes you *do* need to determine where your program is spending all its time, to see if you can improve the performance of those sections.

A profiler gathers information that allows you to see which parts of the program consume memory and which methods consume maximum time. Some profilers even allow you to disable the garbage collector to help determine patterns of memory allocation.

A profiler can also be a useful tool in detecting threading deadlock in your program.

Tracking memory consumption

Here is the kind of data a profiler can show for memory usage:

- Number of object allocations for a specific type.
- Places where the object allocations are taking place.
- Methods involved in allocation of instances of this class.
- Loitering objects: objects that are allocated, not used, and not garbage collected. These keep increasing the size of the JVM heap and represent memory leaks, which can cause an out-of-memory error or excessive overhead on the garbage collector.
- Excessive allocation of temporary objects that increase the work of the garbage collector and thus reduce the performance of the application.
- Failure to release instances added to a collection and not removed (this is a special case of loitering objects).

Tracking CPU usage

Profilers also keep track of how much time the CPU spends in various parts of your code. They can tell you:

- The number of times a method was invoked.
- The percentage of CPU time utilized by each method. If this method calls other methods, the profiler can tell you the amount of time spent in these other methods.
- Total absolute time spent by each method, including the time it waits for I/O, locks, etc. This time depends on the available resources of the system.

This way you can decide which sections of your code need optimizing.

Coverage testing

Coverage testing shows the lines of code that were not executed during the test. This can draw your attention to code that is not used and might therefore be a candidate for removal or refactoring.

To get coverage testing information for **SimpleDebugging.java**, you use the command:

```
java -Xrunjcov:type=M SimpleDebugging
```

As an experiment, try putting lines of code that will not be executed into **SimpleDebugging.java** (you'll have to be somewhat clever about this since the compiler can detect unreachable lines of code).

JVM Profiling Interface

The *profiler agent* communicates the events it is interested in to the JVM. The JVM profiling interface supports the following events:

- Enter and exit a method
- Allocate, move, and free an object
- Create and delete a heap arena
- Begin and end a garbage collection cycle
- Allocate and free a JNI global reference
- Allocate and free a JNI weak global reference

- Load and unload a compiled method
- Start and end a thread
- Class file data ready for instrumentation
- Load and unload a class
- For a Java monitor under contention: Wait To Enter , entered, and exit
- For a raw monitor under contention: Wait To Enter, entered, and exit
- For an uncontended Java monitor: Wait and waited
- Monitor Dump
- Heap Dump
- Object Dump
- Request to dump or reset profiling data
- JVM initialization and shutdown

While profiling, the JVM sends these events to the profiler agent, which then transfers the desired information to the *profiler front end*, which can be a process running on another machine, if desired.

Using HPROF

The example in this section shows how you can run the profiler that ships with the JDK. Although the information from this profiler is in the somewhat crude form of text files rather than the graphical representation that most commercial profilers produce, it still provides valuable help in determining the characteristics of your program.

You run the profiler by passing an extra argument to the JVM when you invoke the program. This argument must be a single string, without any spaces after the commas, like this (although it should be on a single line, it has wrapped in the book):

```
java -
Xrunhprof:heap=sites,cpu=samples,depth=10,monitor=y,thread=
y,doe=y ListPerformance
```

- The **heap=sites** tells the profiler to write information about memory utilization on the heap, indicating where it was allocated.
- **cpu=samples** tells the profiler to do statistical sampling to determine CPU use.

* **depth=10** indicates the depth of the trace for threads.
* **thread=y** tells the profiler to identify the threads in the stack traces.
* **doe=y** tells the profiler to produce dump of profiling data on exit.

The following listing contains only a portion of the file produced by HPROF. The output file is created in the current directory and is named **java.hprof.txt**.

The beginning of **java.hprof.txt** describes the details of the remaining sections in the file. The data produced by the profiler is in different sections; for example, TRACE represents a trace section in the file. You will see many TRACE sections, each numbered so that they can be referenced later.

The SITES section shows memory allocation sites. The section has several rows, sorted by the number of bytes that are allocated and are being referenced—the live bytes. The memory is listed in bytes. The column *self* represents the percentage of memory taken up by this site, the next column, *accum*, represents the cumulative memory percentage. The *live bytes* and *live objects* columns represent the number of live bytes at this site and the number of objects that were created that consumes these bytes. The *allocated bytes and objects* represent the total number of objects and bytes that are instantiated, including the ones being used and the ones not being used. The difference in the number of bytes listed in allocated and live represent the bytes that can be garbage collected. The *trace* column actually references a TRACE in the file. The first row references trace 668 as shown below. The *name* represents the class whose instance was created.

```
SITES BEGIN (ordered by live bytes) Thu Jul 18 11:23:06 2002
          percent          live       alloc'ed  stack class
 rank   self  accum     bytes objs   bytes objs trace name
    1 59.10% 59.10%   573488    3  573488    3   668 java.lang.Object
    2  7.41% 66.50%    71880  543   72624  559     1 [C
    3  7.39% 73.89%    71728    3   82000   10   649 java.lang.Object
    4  5.14% 79.03%    49896  232   49896  232     1 [B
    5  2.53% 81.57%    24592  310   24592  310     1 [S

TRACE 668: (thread=1)
    java.util.Vector.ensureCapacityHelper(Vector.java:222)
    java.util.Vector.insertElementAt(Vector.java:564)
    java.util.Vector.add(Vector.java:779)
    java.util.AbstractList$ListItr.add(AbstractList.java:495)
    ListPerformance$3.test(ListPerformance.java:40)
```

```
    ListPerformance.test(ListPerformance.java:63)
    ListPerformance.main(ListPerformance.java:93)
```

This trace shows the method call sequence that allocates the memory. If you go through the trace as indicated by the line numbers, you will find that an object allocation takes place on line number 222 of **Vector.java**:

```
elementData = new Object[newCapacity];
```

This helps you discover parts of the program that use up significant amounts of memory (59.10 %, in this case).

Note the **[C** in SITE 1 represents the primitive type **char**. This is the internal representation of the JVM for the primitive types.

Thread performance

The CPU SAMPLES section shows the CPU utilization. Here is part of a trace from this section.

```
SITES END
CPU SAMPLES BEGIN (total = 514) Thu Jul 18 11:23:06 2002
rank   self  accum   count trace method
   1 28.21% 28.21%     145   662 java.util.AbstractList.iterator
   2 12.06% 40.27%      62   589 java.util.AbstractList.iterator
   3 10.12% 50.39%      52   632 java.util.LinkedList.listIterator
   4  7.00% 57.39%      36   231 java.io.FileInputStream.open
   5  5.64% 63.04%      29   605 ListPerformance$4.test
   6  3.70% 66.73%      19   636 java.util.LinkedList.addBefore
```

The organization of this listing is similar to the organization of the SITES listings. The rows are sorted by CPU utilization. The row on the top has the maximum CPU utilization, as indicated in the *self* column. The *accum* column lists the cumulative CPU utilization. The *count* field specifies the number of times this trace was active. The next two columns specify the trace number and the method that took this time.

Consider the first row of the CPU SAMPLES section. 28.12% of total CPU time was utilized in the method **java.util.AbstractList.iterator( )**, and it was called 145 times. The details of this call can be seen by looking at trace number 662:

```
TRACE 662: (thread=1)
    java.util.AbstractList.iterator(AbstractList.java:332)
    ListPerformance$2.test(ListPerformance.java:28)
```

```
    ListPerformance.test(ListPerformance.java:63)
    ListPerformance.main(ListPerformance.java:93)
```

You can infer that iterating through a list takes a significant amount of time.

For large projects it is often more helpful to have the information represented in graphical form. A number of profilers produce graphical displays, but coverage of these is beyond the scope of this book.

Optimization guidelines

- Avoid sacrificing code readability for performance.
- Performance should not be considered in isolation. Weigh the amount of effort required versus the advantage gained.
- Performance can be a concern in big projects but is often not an issue for small projects.
- Getting a program to work should have a higher priority than delving into the performance of the program. Once you have a working program you can use the profiler to make it more efficient. Performance should be considered during the initial design/development process only if it is determined to be a critical factor.
- Do not make assumptions about where the bottlenecks are. Run a profiler to get the data.
- Whenever possible try to explicitly discard an instance by setting it to null. This can sometimes be a useful hint to the garbage collector.
- The size of the program matters. Performance optimization is generally valuable only when the size of the project is large, it runs for a long time and speed is an issue.
- **static final** variables can be optimized by the JVM to improve program speed. Program constants should thus be declared as **static** and **final**.

Doclets

Although it might be a bit surprising to think of a tool that was developed for documentation support as something that helps you track down problems in your programs, *doclets* can be surprisingly useful. Because a doclet hooks into the javadoc parser, it has information available to that parser. With this, you can programmatically examine the class names, field names, and method signatures in your code and flag potential problems.

The process of producing the JDK documentation from the Java source files involves the parsing of the source file and the formatting of this parsed file by using the *standard doclet*. You can write a custom doclet to customize the formatting of your javadoc comments. However, doclets allow you to do far more than just formatting the comment because a doclet has available much of the information about the source file that's being parsed.

You can extract information about all the members of the class: fields, constructors, methods, and the comments associated with each of the members (alas, the method code body is not available). Details about the members are encapsulated inside special objects, which contain information about the properties of the member (private, static, final etc.). This information can be helpful in detecting poorly written code, such as member variables that should be private but are public, method parameters without comments, and identifiers that do not follow naming conventions.

Javadoc may not catch all compilation errors. It will spot syntax errors, such as an unmatched brace, but it may not catch semantic errors. The safest approach is to run the Java compiler on your code before attempting to use a doclet-based tool.

The parsing mechanism provided by javadoc parses the entire source file and stores it in memory in an object of class **RootDoc**. The entry point for the doclet submitted to javadoc is **start(RootDoc doc)**. It is comparable to a normal Java program's **main(String[] args)**. You may traverse through the **RootDoc** object and extract the necessary information. The following example shows how to write a simple doclet; it just prints out all the members of each class that was parsed:

```
//: c15:PrintMembersDoclet.java
// Doclet that prints out all members of the class.
import com.sun.javadoc.*;
```

```java
public class PrintMembersDoclet {
  public static boolean start(RootDoc root) {
    ClassDoc[] classes = root.classes();
    processClasses(classes);
    return true;
  }
  private static void processClasses(ClassDoc[] classes) {
    for(int i = 0; i < classes.length; i++) {
      processOneClass(classes[i]);
    }
  }
  private static void processOneClass(ClassDoc cls) {
    FieldDoc[] fd = cls.fields();
    for(int i = 0; i < fd.length; i++)
      processDocElement(fd[i]);
    ConstructorDoc[] cons = cls.constructors();
    for(int i = 0; i < cons.length; i++)
      processDocElement(cons[i]);
    MethodDoc[] md = cls.methods();
    for(int i = 0; i < md.length; i++)
      processDocElement(md[i]);
  }
  private static void processDocElement(Doc dc) {
    MemberDoc md = (MemberDoc)dc;
    System.out.print(md.modifiers());
    System.out.print(" " + md.name());
    if(md.isMethod())
      System.out.println("()");
    else if(md.isConstructor())
      System.out.println();
  }
} ///:~
```

You can use the doclet to print the members like this:

```
javadoc -doclet PrintMembersDoclet -private PrintMembersDoclet.java
```

This invokes javadoc on the last argument in the command, which means it will parse the **PrintMembersDoclet.java** file. The **-doclet** option tells javadoc to use the custom doclet **PrintMembersDoclet**. The **-private** tag instructs javadoc to also print **private** members (the default is to print only **protected** and **public** members).

RootDoc contains a collection of **ClassDoc** that holds all the information about the class. Classes such as **MethodDoc**, **FieldDoc**, and **ConstructorDoc** contain information regarding methods, fields, and constructors, respectively. The method **processOneClass( )** extracts the list of these members and prints them.

You can also create *taglets*, which allow you to implement custom javadoc tags. The JDK documentation presents an example that implements a **@todo** tag, which displays its text in yellow in the resulting Javadoc output. Search for "taglet" in the JDK documentation for more details.

Summary

This chapter introduced what I've come to realize may be the most essential issue in programming, superceding language syntax and design issues: *How do you make sure your code is correct, and keep it that way?*

Recent experience has shown that the most useful and practical tool to date is unit testing, which, as shown in this chapter, may be combined very effectively with Design by Contract. There are other types of tests as well, such as conformance testing to verify that your use cases/user stories have all been implemented. But for some reason, we have in the past relegated testing to be done later by someone else. Extreme Programming insists that the unit tests be written before the code; you create the test framework for the class, and then the class itself (on one or two occasions I've successfully done this, but I'm generally pleased if testing appears somewhere during the initial coding process). There remains resistance to testing, usually by those who haven't tried it and believe they can write good code without testing. But the more experience I have, the more I repeat to myself:

> *If it's not tested, it's broken.*

This a worthwhile mantra, especially when you're thinking about cutting corners. The more of your own bugs you discover, the more attached you grow to the security of built-in tests.

Build systems (in particular, Ant) and revision control (CVS) were also introduced in this chapter because they provide structure for your project and its tests. To me, the primary goal of Extreme Programming is *velocity*—the ability to rapidly move your project forward (but in a reliable fashion), and to quickly refactor it when you realize that it can be improved. Velocity requires a support structure to give you confidence that things won't fall through the cracks when you start making big changes to your project. This includes a reliable repository, which allows you to roll back to any previous version, and an automatic build system that, once configured, guarantees that the project can be compiled and tested in a single step.

Once you have reason to believe that your program is healthy, logging provides a way to monitor its pulse, and even (as shown in this chapter) to automatically email you if something starts to go wrong. When it does, debugging and profiling help you track down bugs and performance issues.

Perhaps it's the nature of computer programming to want a single, clear, concrete answer. After all, we work with ones and zeros, which do not have fuzzy boundaries (they actually do, but the electronic engineers have gone to great lengths to give us the model we want). When it comes to solutions, it's great to believe that there's one answer. But I've found that there are boundaries to any technique, and understanding where those boundaries are is far more powerful than any single approach can be, because it allows you to use a method where its greatest strength lies, and to combine it with other approaches where it isn't so strong. For example, in this chapter Design by Contract was presented in combination with white-box unit testing, and as I was creating the example, I discovered that the two working in concert were much more useful than either one alone.

I have found this idea to be true in more than just the issue of discovering problems, but also in building systems in the first place. For example, using a single programming language or tool to solve your problem is attractive from the standpoint of consistency, but I've often found that I can solve certain problems much more quickly and effectively by using the Python programming language instead of Java, to the general benefit of the project. You may also discover that Ant works in some places, and in others, make is more useful. Or, if your clients are on Windows platforms, it may be sensible to make the radical decision of using Delphi or Visual BASIC to develop client-side programs more rapidly than you could in Java. The important thing is to keep an open mind and remember that you are trying to achieve results, not necessarily use a certain tool or technique. This can be difficult, but if you remember that the project failure rate is quite high and your chances of success are proportionally low, you could be a little more open to solutions that might be more productive. One of my favorite phrases from Extreme Programming (and one I find that I violate often for usually silly reasons) is "do the simplest thing that could possibly work." Most of the time, the simplest and most expedient approach, if you can discover it, is the best one.

Exercises

1. Create a class containing a **static** clause that throws an exception if assertions are not enabled. Demonstrate that this test works correctly.

2. Modify the preceding exercise to use the approach in **LoaderAssertions.java** to turn on assertions instead of throwing an exception. Demonstrate that this works correctly.

3. In **LoggingLevels.java**, comment out the code that sets the severity level of the root logger handlers and verify that messages of level **CONFIG** and below are not reported.

4. Inherit from **java.util.Logging.Level** and define your own level with a value less than FINEST. Modify **LoggingLevels.java** to use your new level and show that messages at your level will not appear when the logging level is FINEST.

5. Associate a **FileHandler** with the root logger.

6. Modify the **FileHandler** so that it formats output to a simple text file.

7. Modify **MultipleHandlers.java** so that it generates output in plain text format instead of XML.

8. Modify **LoggingLevels.java** to set different logging levels for the handlers associated with the root logger.

9. Write a simple program that sets the root logger logging level based on a command-line argument.

10. Write an example using Formatters and Handlers to output a log file as HTML.

11. Write an example using Handlers and Filters to log messages with any severity level over INFO in one file and any severity level

including and below INFO in other file. The files should be written in simple text.

12. Modify **log.prop** to add an additional initialization class that initializes a custom **Formatter** for the logger **com**.

13. Run JDB on **SimpleDebugging.java**, but do not give the command **catch Exception**. Show that it still catches the exception.

14. Add an uninitialized reference to **SimpleDebugging.java** (you'll have to do it in a way that the compiler doesn't catch the error!) and use JDB to track down the problem.

15. Perform the experiment described in the "Coverage Testing" section.

16. Create a doclet that displays identifiers that might not follow the Java naming convention by checking how capital letters are used for those identifiers.

16: Analysis and Design

The object-oriented paradigm is a new and different way of thinking about programming.

Many people have trouble at first knowing how to approach an OOP project. Now that you understand the concept of an object, and as you learn to think more in an object-oriented style, you can begin to create "good" designs that take advantage of all the benefits that OOP has to offer. This chapter introduces the ideas of analysis, design, and some ways to approach the problems of developing good object-oriented programs in a reasonable amount of time.

Methodology

A *methodology* (sometimes simply called a *method*) is a set of processes and heuristics used to break down the complexity of a programming problem. Many OOP methodologies have been formulated since the dawn of object-oriented programming. This section will give you a feel for what you're trying to accomplish when using a methodology.

Especially in OOP, methodology is a field of many experiments, so it is important to understand what problem the methodology is trying to solve before you consider adopting one. This is particularly true with Java, in which the programming language is intended to reduce the complexity (compared to C) involved in expressing a program. This may in fact alleviate the need for ever-more-complex methodologies. Instead, simple methodologies may suffice in Java for a much larger class of problems than you could handle using simple methodologies with procedural languages.

It's also important to realize that the term "methodology" is often too grand and promises too much. Whatever you do now when you design and write a program is a methodology. It may be your own methodology, and you may not be conscious of doing it, but it is a process you go through as you create. If it is an effective process, it may need only a small tune-up to work with Java. If you are not satisfied with your productivity and the way your programs turn out, you may want to consider adopting a formal methodology, or choosing pieces from among the many formal methodologies.

While you're going through the development process, the most important issue is this: Don't get lost. It's easy to do. Most of the analysis and design methodologies are intended to solve the largest of problems. Remember that most projects don't fit into that category, so you can usually have successful analysis and design with a relatively small subset of what a methodology recommends.[1] But some sort of process, no matter how small or limited, will generally get you on your way in a much better fashion than simply beginning to code.

It's also easy to get stuck, to fall into "analysis paralysis," where you feel like you can't move forward because you haven't nailed down every little detail at the current stage. Remember, no matter how much analysis you do, there are some things about a system that won't reveal themselves until design time, and more things that won't reveal themselves until you're coding, or not even until a program is up and running. Because of this, it's crucial to move fairly quickly through analysis and design, and to implement a test of the proposed system.

This point is worth emphasizing. Because of the history we've had with procedural languages, it is commendable that a team will want to proceed carefully and understand every minute detail before moving to design and implementation. Certainly, when creating a Database Management System (*DBMS*), it pays to understand a customer's needs thoroughly. But a DBMS is in a class of problems that is very well-posed and well-understood; in many such programs, the database structure *is* the problem to be tackled. The class of programming problem discussed in this chapter is of the "wild-card" (my term) variety, in which the solution isn't simply re-forming a well-known solution, but instead involves one or more "wild-card factors"—elements for which there is no well-understood previous solution, and for which research

---

[1] An excellent example of this is *UML Distilled*, 2nd edition, by Martin Fowler (Addison-Wesley 2000), which reduces the sometimes-overwhelming UML process to a manageable subset.

is necessary.[2] Attempting to thoroughly analyze a wild-card problem before moving into design and implementation results in analysis paralysis because you don't have enough information to solve this kind of problem during the analysis phase. Solving such a problem requires iteration through the whole cycle, and that requires risk-taking behavior (which makes sense, because you're trying to do something new and the potential rewards are higher). It may seem like the risk is compounded by "rushing" into a preliminary implementation, but it can instead reduce the risk in a wild-card project because you're finding out early whether a particular approach to the problem is viable. Product development is risk management.

It's often proposed that you "build one to throw away." With OOP, you may still throw *part* of it away, but because code is encapsulated into classes, during the first pass you will inevitably produce some useful class designs and develop some worthwhile ideas about the system design that do not need to be thrown away. Thus, the first rapid pass at a problem not only produces critical information for the next analysis, design, and implementation pass, it also creates a code foundation.

That said, if you're looking at a methodology that contains tremendous detail and suggests many steps and documents, it's still difficult to know when to stop. Keep in mind what you're trying to discover:

5. What are the objects? (How do you partition your project into its component parts?)

6. What are their interfaces? (What messages do you need to send to each object?)

If you come up with nothing more than the objects and their interfaces, then you can write a program. For various reasons you might need more descriptions and documents than this, but you can't get away with any less.

The process can be undertaken in five phases, and a Phase 0 that is just the initial commitment to using some kind of structure.

---

[2] My rule of thumb for estimating such projects: If there's more than one wild card, don't even try to plan how long it's going to take or how much it will cost until you've created a working prototype. There are too many degrees of freedom.

Phase 0: Make a plan

You must first decide what steps you're going to have in your process. It sounds simple (in fact, *all* of this sounds simple), and yet people often don't make this decision before they start coding. If your plan is "let's jump in and start coding," fine. (Sometimes that's appropriate when you have a well-understood problem.) At least agree that this is the plan.

You might also decide at this phase that some additional process structure is necessary, but not the whole nine yards. Understandably, some programmers like to work in "vacation mode," in which no structure is imposed on the process of developing their work; "It will be done when it's done." This can be appealing for a while, but I've found that having a few milestones along the way helps to focus and galvanize your efforts around those milestones instead of being stuck with the single goal of "finish the project." In addition, it divides the project into more bite-sized pieces and makes it seem less threatening (plus the milestones offer more opportunities for celebration).

When I began to study story structure (so that I will someday write a novel) I was initially resistant to the idea of structure, feeling that I wrote best when I simply let it flow onto the page. But I later realized that when I write about computers the structure is clear enough to me that I don't have to think about it very much. I still structure my work, albeit only semi-consciously in my head. Even if you think that your plan is to just start coding, you still somehow go through the subsequent phases while asking and answering certain questions.

The mission statement

Any system you build, no matter how complicated, has a fundamental purpose—the business that it's in, the basic need that it satisfies. If you can look past the user interface, the hardware- or system-specific details, the coding algorithms and the efficiency problems, you will eventually find the core of its being—simple and straightforward. Like the so-called *high concept* from a Hollywood movie, you can describe it in one or two sentences. This pure description is the starting point.

The high concept is quite important because it sets the tone for your project; it's a mission statement. You won't necessarily get it right the first time (you may be in a later phase of the project before it becomes completely clear), but keep trying until it feels right. For example, in an air-traffic control system you may start out with a high concept focused on the system that you're building: "The tower program keeps track of the aircraft." But consider what happens when you shrink the system to a very small airfield; perhaps there's only a human controller, or none at all. A more useful model won't concern the solution you're creating as much as it describes the problem: "Aircraft arrive, unload, service and reload, then depart."

Phase 1: What are we making?

In the previous generation of program design (called *procedural design*), this is called "creating the *requirements analysis* and *system specification*." These, of course, were places to get lost; documents with intimidating names that could become big projects in their own right. Their intention was good, however. The requirements analysis says "Make a list of the guidelines we will use to know when the job is done and the customer is satisfied."[3] The system specification says "Here's a description of *what* the program will do (not *how*) to satisfy the requirements." The requirements analysis is really a contract between you and the customer (even if the customer works within your company, or is some other object or system). The system specification is a top-level exploration into the problem and in some sense a discovery of whether it can be done and how long it will take. Since both of these will require consensus among people (and because they will usually change over time), I think it's best to keep them as bare as possible—ideally, to lists and basic diagrams—to save time (this is in line with Extreme Programming, which advocates very minimal documentation, albeit for small- to medium-sized projects). You might have other constraints that require you to expand them into bigger documents, but by keeping the initial document small and concise, it can be created in a few sessions of group brainstorming with a leader who dynamically creates the description. This not only solicits input from everyone, it also fosters initial buy-in and agreement by everyone on the team. Perhaps most importantly, it can kick off a project with a lot of enthusiasm.

It's necessary to stay focused on the heart of what you're trying to accomplish in this phase: Determine what the system is supposed to do. The most valuable tool for this is a collection of what are called "use cases," or in

---

3 An excellent resource for requirements analysis is *Exploring Requirements: Quality Before Design*, by Gause & Weinberg (Dorset House 1989).

Extreme Programming, "user stories." Use cases identify key features in the system that will reveal some of the fundamental classes you'll be using. These are essentially descriptive answers to questions like:[4]

- "Who will use this system?"
- "What can those actors do with the system?"
- "How does *this* actor do *that* with this system?"
- "How else might this work if someone else were doing this, or if the same actor had a different objective?" (to reveal variations)
- "What problems might happen while doing this with the system?" (to reveal exceptions)

If you are designing a bank auto-teller, for example, the use case for a particular aspect of the functionality of the system is able to describe what the auto-teller does in every possible situation. Each of these "situations" is referred to as a *scenario*, and a use case can be considered a collection of scenarios. You can think of a scenario as a question that starts with: "What does the system do if...?" For example, "What does the auto-teller do if a customer has just deposited a check within the last 24 hours, and there's not enough in the account without the check having cleared to provide a desired withdrawal?"

Use case diagrams are intentionally simple to prevent you from getting bogged down in system implementation details prematurely:

[4] Thanks for help from James H Jarrett.

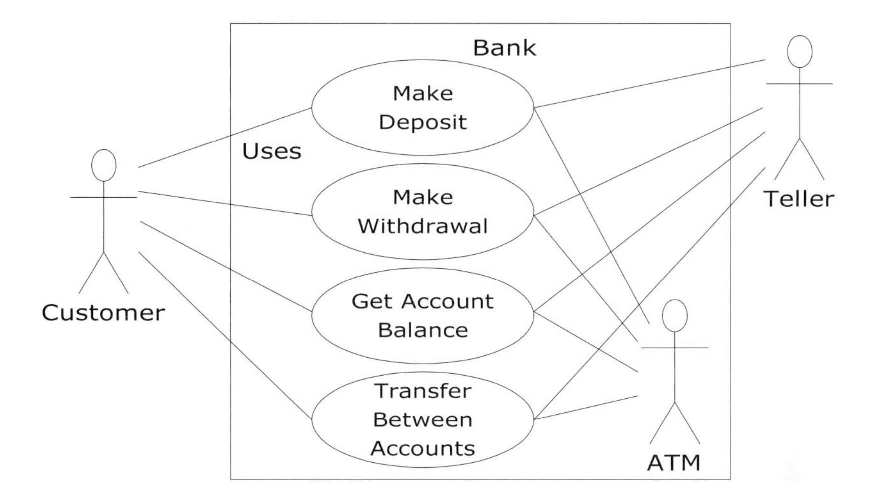

Each stick person represents an "actor," which is typically a human or some other kind of free agent. (These can even be other computer systems, as is the case with "ATM.") The box represents the boundary of your system. The ellipses represent the use cases, which are descriptions of valuable work that can be performed with the system. The lines between the actors and the use cases represent the interactions.

It doesn't matter how the system is actually implemented, as long as it looks like this to the user.

A use case does not need to be terribly complex, even if the underlying system is complex. It is only intended to show the system as it appears to the user. For example:

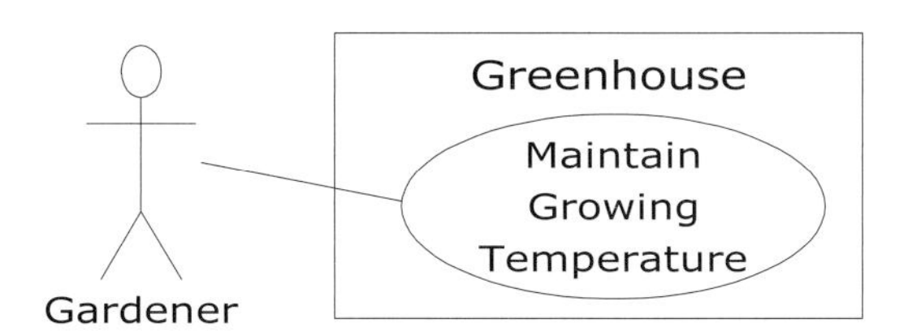

The use cases produce the requirements specifications by determining all the interactions that the user may have with the system. You try to discover a full set of use cases for your system, and once you've done that you have the core of what the system is supposed to do. The nice thing about focusing on use cases is that they always bring you back to the essentials and keep you from drifting off into issues that aren't critical for getting the job done. That is, if you have a full set of use cases, you can describe your system and move on to the next phase. You probably won't get it all figured out perfectly on the first try, but that's OK. Everything will reveal itself in time, and if you demand a perfect system specification at this point you'll get stuck.

If you do get stuck, you can kick-start this phase by using a rough approximation tool: Describe the system in a few paragraphs and then look for nouns and verbs. The nouns can suggest actors, context of the use case (e.g., "lobby"), or artifacts manipulated in the use case. Verbs can suggest interactions between actors and use cases, and specify steps within the use case. You'll also discover that nouns and verbs produce objects and messages during the design phase (and note that use cases describe interactions between subsystems, so the "noun and verb" technique can be used only as a brainstorming tool because it does not generate use cases).[5]

The boundary between a use case and an actor can point out the existence of a user interface, but it does not define such a user interface. For a process of defining and creating user interfaces, see *Software for Use* by Larry Constantine and Lucy Lockwood, (Addison-Wesley Longman, 1999) or go to *www.ForUse.com.*

Although it's a black art, at this point some kind of basic scheduling is important. You now have an overview of what you're building, so you'll probably be able to get some idea of how long it will take. A lot of factors come into play here. If you estimate a long schedule then the company might decide not to build it (and thus use their resources on something more reasonable—that's a *good* thing). Or a manager might have already decided how long the project should take and will try to influence your estimate. But it's best to have an honest schedule from the beginning and deal with the tough decisions early. There have been a lot of attempts to come up with accurate scheduling techniques (much like techniques to predict the stock market), but probably the best approach is to rely on your experience and intuition. Get a gut feeling for how long it will really take, then double that and add 10 percent. Your gut feeling is probably correct; you *can* get something working in that time. The "doubling" will turn that into something

---

[5] More information on use cases can be found in *Use Case Driven Object Modeling with UML* by Rosenberg (Addison-Wesley 1999) . A good overview of user stories is found in *Planning Extreme Programming*, by Beck & Fowler (Addison-Wesley 2001).

decent, and the 10 percent will deal with the final polishing and details.[6] However you want to explain it, and regardless of the moans and manipulations that happen when you reveal such a schedule, it just seems to work out that way.[7]

Phase 2: How will we build it?

In this phase you must come up with a design that describes what the classes look like and how they will interact. An excellent technique in determining classes and interactions is the *Class-Responsibility-Collaboration* (CRC) card. Part of the value of this tool is that it's so low-tech: You start out with a set of blank 3 x 5 cards, and you write on them. Each card represents a single class, and on the card you write:

7. The name of the class. It's important that this name capture the essence of what the class does, so that it makes sense at a glance.

8. The "responsibilities" of the class: what it should do. This can typically be summarized by just stating the names of the methods (since those names should be descriptive in a good design), but it does not preclude other notes. If you need to seed the process, look at the problem from a lazy programmer's standpoint: What objects would you like to magically appear to solve your problem?

9. The "collaborations" of the class: What other classes does it interact with? "Interact" is an intentionally broad term; it could mean aggregation or simply that some other object exists that will perform services for an object of the class. Collaborations should also consider the audience for this class. For example, if you create a class **Firecracker**, who is going to observe it, a **Chemist** or a **Spectator**? The former will want to know what chemicals go into the construction,

---

[6] My personal take on this has changed lately. Doubling and adding 10 percent will give you a reasonably accurate estimate (assuming there are not too many wild-card factors), but you still have to work quite diligently to finish in that time. If you want time to really make it elegant and to enjoy yourself in the process, the correct multiplier is more like three or four times, I believe. See *PeopleWare*, by DeMarco & Lister (Dorset House 1999) for studies of the effect of schedule estimates on productivity and a debunking of "Parkinson's Law."

[7] *Planning Extreme Programming* (ibid.) has some valuable insights on planning and time estimation.

and the latter will respond to the colors and shapes released when it explodes.

You may feel that the cards should be bigger because of all the information you'd like to get on them. However, they are intentionally small, not only to keep your classes small but also to keep you from getting into too much detail too early. If you can't fit all you need to know about a class on a small card, then the class is too complex (either you're getting too detailed, or you should create more than one class). The ideal class should be understood at a glance. The idea of CRC cards is to assist you in coming up with a first cut of the design so that you can get the big picture and then refine your design.

One of the great benefits of CRC cards is in communication. It's best done in real time, in a group, without computers. Each person takes responsibility for several classes (which at first have no names or other information). You run a live simulation by solving one scenario at a time, deciding which messages are sent to the various objects to satisfy each scenario. As you go through this process, you discover the classes that you need along with their responsibilities and collaborations, and you fill out the cards as you do this. When you've moved through all the use cases, you should have a fairly complete first cut of your design.

Before I began using CRC cards, the most successful consulting experiences I had when coming up with an initial design involved standing in front of a team—who hadn't built an OOP project before—and drawing objects on a whiteboard. We talked about how the objects should communicate with each other, and erased some of them and replaced them with other objects. Effectively, I was managing all the "CRC cards" on the whiteboard. The team (who knew what the project was supposed to do) actually created the design; they "owned" the design rather than having it given to them. All I was doing was guiding the process by asking the right questions, trying out the assumptions, and taking the feedback from the team to modify those assumptions. The true beauty of the process was that the team learned how to do object-oriented design not by reviewing abstract examples, but by working on the one design that was most interesting to them at that moment: theirs.

Once you've come up with a set of CRC cards, you may want to create a more formal description of your design using UML.[8] You don't need to use UML,

---

[8] For starters, I recommend the aforementioned *UML Distilled*, 2nd edition.

but it can be helpful, especially if you want to put up a diagram on the wall for everyone to ponder, which is a good idea (there is a plethora of UML diagramming tools available). An alternative to UML is a textual description of the objects and their interfaces, or, depending on your programming language, the code itself.[9]

UML also provides an additional diagramming notation for describing the dynamic model of your system. This is helpful in situations in which the state transitions of a system or subsystem are dominant enough that they need their own diagrams (such as in a control system). You may also need to describe the data structures, for systems or subsystems in which data is a dominant factor (such as a database).

You'll know you're done with Phase 2 when you have described the objects and their interfaces. Well, most of them—there are usually a few that slip through the cracks and don't make themselves known until Phase 3. But that's OK. What's important is that you eventually discover all of your objects. It's nice to discover them early in the process, but OOP provides enough structure so that it's not so bad if you discover them later. In fact, the design of an object tends to happen in five stages, throughout the process of program development.

Five stages of object design

The design life of an object is not limited to the time when you're writing the program. Instead, the design of an object appears over a sequence of stages. It's helpful to have this perspective because you stop expecting perfection right away; instead, you realize that the understanding of what an object does and what it should look like happens over time. This view also applies to the design of various types of programs; the pattern for a particular type of program emerges through struggling again and again with that problem (which is chronicled in the book *Thinking in Patterns (with Java)* at *www.BruceEckel.com*). Objects, too, have their patterns that emerge through understanding, use, and reuse.

1. Object discovery. This stage occurs during the initial analysis of a program. Objects may be discovered by looking for external factors and boundaries, duplication of elements in the system, and the smallest

---

[9] Python (www.Python.org) is often used as "executable pseudocode."

conceptual units. Some objects are obvious if you already have a set of class libraries. Commonality between classes suggesting base classes and inheritance may appear right away, or later in the design process.

2. Object assembly. As you're building an object you'll discover the need for new members that didn't appear during discovery. The internal needs of the object may require other classes to support it.

3. System construction. Once again, more requirements for an object may appear at this later stage. As you learn, you evolve your objects. The need for communication and interconnection with other objects in the system may change the needs of your classes or require new classes. For example, you may discover the need for facilitator or helper classes, such as a linked list, that contain little or no state information and simply help other classes function.

4. System extension. As you add new features to a system you may discover that your previous design doesn't support easy system extension. With this new information, you can restructure parts of the system, possibly adding new classes or class hierarchies. This is also a good time to consider taking features *out* of a project.

5. Object reuse. This is the real stress test for a class. If someone tries to reuse the class in an entirely new situation, they'll probably discover some shortcomings. As you change it to adapt to more new programs, the general principles of the class will become clearer, until you have a truly reusable type. However, don't expect most objects from a system design to be reusable—it is perfectly acceptable for the bulk of your objects to be system-specific. Reusable types tend to be less common, and they must solve more general problems in order to be reusable.

Guidelines for object development

These stages suggest some guidelines when thinking about developing your classes:

1. Let a specific problem generate a class, then let the class grow and mature during the solution of other problems.

2. Remember, discovering the classes you need (and their interfaces) is the majority of the system design. If you already had those classes, this would be an easy project.

3. Don't force yourself to know everything at the beginning. Learn as you go. This will happen anyway.

4. Start programming. Get something working so you can prove or disprove your design. Don't fear that you'll end up with procedural-style spaghetti code—classes partition the problem and help control anarchy and entropy. Bad classes do not break good classes.

5. Always keep it simple. Little clean objects with obvious utility are better than big complicated interfaces. When decision points come up, use an Ockham's Razor[10] approach: Consider the choices and select the one that is simplest, because simple classes are almost always best. Start small and simple, and you can expand the class interface when you understand it better. It's easy to add methods, but as time goes on, it's difficult to remove methods from a class.

Phase 3: Build the core

This is the initial conversion from the rough design into a compiling and executing body of code that can be tested, and especially that will prove or disprove your architecture. This is not a one-pass process, but rather the beginning of a series of steps that will iteratively build the system, as you'll see in Phase 4.

Your goal is to find the core of your system architecture that needs to be implemented in order to generate a running system, no matter how incomplete that system is in this initial pass. You're creating a framework that you can build on with further iterations. You're also performing the first of many system integrations and tests, and giving the stakeholders feedback about what their system will look like and how it is progressing. Ideally, you are exposing some of the critical risks. You'll probably discover changes and improvements that can be made to your original architecture—things you would not have learned without implementing the system.

Part of building the system is the reality check that you get from testing against your requirements analysis and system specification (in whatever form they exist). Make sure that your tests verify the requirements and use

---

[10] "What can be done with fewer ... is done in vain with more ... the mind should not multiply things without necessity." William of Ockham, 1290-1349.

cases. When the core of the system is stable, you're ready to move on and add more functionality.

Phase 4: Iterate the use cases

Once the core framework is running, each feature set you add is a small project in itself. You add a feature set during an *iteration*, a reasonably short period of development.

How big is an iteration? Ideally, each iteration lasts one to three weeks (this can vary based on the implementation language). At the end of that period, you have an integrated, tested system with more functionality than it had before. But what's particularly interesting is the basis for the iteration: a single use case. Each use case is a package of related functionality that you build into the system all at once, during one iteration. Not only does this give you a better idea of what the scope of a use case should be, but it also gives more validation to the idea of a use case, since the concept isn't discarded after analysis and design, but instead it is a fundamental unit of development throughout the software-building process.

You stop iterating when you achieve target functionality or an external deadline arrives and the customer can be satisfied with the current version. (Remember, software is a subscription business.) Because the process is iterative, you have many opportunities to ship a product rather than having a single endpoint; open-source projects work exclusively in an iterative, high-feedback environment, which is precisely what makes them successful.

An iterative development process is valuable for many reasons. You can reveal and resolve critical risks early, the customers have ample opportunity to change their minds, programmer satisfaction is higher, and the project can be steered with more precision. But an additional important benefit is the feedback to the stakeholders, who can see by the current state of the product exactly where everything lies. This may reduce or eliminate the need for mind-numbing status meetings and increase the confidence and support from the stakeholders.

Phase 5: Evolution

This is the point in the development cycle that has traditionally been called "maintenance," a catch-all term that can mean everything from "getting it to work the way it was really supposed to in the first place" to "adding features that the customer forgot to mention" to the more traditional "fixing the bugs that show up" and "adding new features as the need arises." So many misconceptions have been applied to the term "maintenance" that it has taken on a slightly deceiving quality, partly because it suggests that you've actually built a pristine program and all you need to do is change parts, oil it, and keep it from rusting. Perhaps there's a better term to describe what's going on.

I'll use the term *evolution*.[11] That is, "You won't get it right the first time, so give yourself the latitude to learn and to go back and make changes." You might need to make a lot of changes as you learn and understand the problem more deeply. The elegance you'll produce if you evolve until you get it right will pay off, both in the short and the long term. Evolution is where your program goes from good to great, and where those issues that you didn't really understand in the first pass become clear. It's also where your classes can evolve from single-project usage to reusable resources.

What it means to "get it right" isn't just that the program works according to the requirements and the use cases. It also means that the internal structure of the code makes sense to you, and feels like it fits together well, with no awkward syntax, oversized objects, or ungainly exposed bits of code. In addition, you must have some sense that the program structure will survive the changes that it will inevitably go through during its lifetime, and that those changes can be made easily and cleanly. This is no small feat. You must not only understand what you're building, but also how the program will evolve (what I call the *vector of change*). Fortunately, object-oriented programming languages are particularly adept at supporting this kind of continuing modification—the boundaries created by the objects are what tend to keep the structure from breaking down. They also allow you to make changes—ones that would seem drastic in a procedural program—without causing earthquakes throughout your code. In fact, support for evolution might be the most important benefit of OOP.

With evolution, you create something that at least approximates what you think you're building, and then you kick the tires, compare it to your requirements, and see where it falls short. Then you can go back and fix it by

---

[11] At least one aspect of evolution is covered in Martin Fowler's book *Refactoring: Improving the Design of Existing Code* (Addison-Wesley 1999), which uses Java examples exclusively.

redesigning and reimplementing the portions of the program that didn't work right.[12] You might actually need to solve the problem, or an aspect of the problem, several times before you hit on the right solution. (A study of *Design Patterns* is usually helpful here. You can find information in *Thinking in Patterns (with Java)* at *www.BruceEckel.com.*)

Evolution also occurs when you build a system, see that it matches your requirements, and then discover it wasn't actually what you wanted. When you see the system in operation, you may find that you really wanted to solve a different problem. If you think this kind of evolution is going to happen, then you owe it to yourself to build your first version as quickly as possible so you can find out if it is indeed what you want.

Perhaps the most important thing to remember is that by default—by definition, really—if you modify a class, its super- and subclasses will still function. You need not fear modification (especially if you have a built-in set of unit tests to verify the correctness of your modifications). Modification won't necessarily break the program, and any change in the outcome will be limited to subclasses and/or specific collaborators of the class you change.

Plans pay off

Of course you wouldn't build a house without a lot of carefully drawn plans. If you build a deck or a dog house your plans won't be so elaborate, but you'll probably still start with some kind of sketches to guide you on your way. Software development has gone to extremes. For a long time, people didn't have much structure in their development, but then big projects began failing. In reaction, we ended up with methodologies that had an intimidating amount of structure and detail, primarily intended for those big projects. These methodologies were too scary to use—it looked like you'd spend all your time writing documents and no time programming. (This was often the case.) I hope that what I've shown you here suggests a middle path—a sliding scale. Use an approach that fits your needs (and your personality). No matter

---

[12] This is something like "rapid prototyping," in which you were supposed to build a quick-and-dirty version so that you could learn about the system, and then throw away your prototype and build it right. The trouble with rapid prototyping is that people didn't throw away the prototype, but instead built upon it. Combined with the lack of structure in procedural programming, this often leads to messy systems that are expensive to maintain.

how minimal you choose to make it, *some* kind of plan will make a big improvement in your project, as opposed to no plan at all. Remember that, by most estimates, over 50 percent of projects fail (some estimates go up to 70 percent!).

By following a plan—preferably one that is simple and brief—and coming up with design structure before coding, you'll discover that things fall together far more easily than if you dive in and start hacking. You'll also realize a great deal of satisfaction. It's my experience that coming up with an elegant solution is deeply satisfying at an entirely different level; it feels closer to art than technology. And elegance always pays off; it's not a frivolous pursuit. Not only does it give you a program that's easier to build and debug, but it's also easier to understand and maintain, and that's where the financial value lies.

Extreme Programming

I have studied analysis and design techniques, on and off, since I was in graduate school. The concept of *Extreme Programming* (XP) is the most radical, and delightful, that I've seen. You can find it chronicled in *Extreme Programming Explained* by Kent Beck (Addison-Wesley, 2000) and on the Web at *www.xprogramming.com*. Addison-Wesley also seems to come out with a new book in the XP series every month or two; the goal seems to be to convince everyone to convert using sheer weight of books (generally, however, these books are small and pleasant to read).

XP is both a philosophy about programming work and a set of guidelines to do it. Some of these guidelines are reflected in other recent methodologies, but the two most important and distinct contributions, in my opinion, are "write tests first" and "pair programming." Although he argues strongly for the whole process, Beck points out that if you adopt only these two practices you'll greatly improve your productivity and reliability.

Write tests first

Testing has traditionally been relegated to the last part of a project, after you've "gotten everything working, but just to be sure." It has implicitly had a low priority, and people who specialize in it have not been given a lot of status and have often even been cordoned off in a basement, away from the "real programmers." Test teams have responded in kind, going so far as to wear black clothing and cackling with glee whenever they break something (to be honest, I've had this feeling myself when breaking compilers).

XP completely revolutionizes the concept of testing by giving it equal (or even greater) priority than the code. In fact, you write the tests *before* you write the code that will be tested, and the tests stay with the code forever. The tests must be executed successfully every time you do a build of the project (which is often, sometimes more than once a day).

Writing tests first has two extremely important effects.

First, it forces a clear definition of the interface of a class. I've often suggested that people "imagine the perfect class to solve a particular problem" as a tool when trying to design the system. The XP testing strategy goes further than that—it specifies exactly what the class must look like, to the consumer of that class, and exactly how the class must behave. In no uncertain terms. You can write all the prose, or create all the diagrams you want, describing how a class should behave and what it looks like, but nothing is as real as a set of tests. The former is a wish list, but the tests are a contract that is enforced by the compiler and the test framework. It's hard to imagine a more concrete description of a class than the tests.

While creating the tests, you are forced to completely think out the class and will often discover needed functionality that might be missed during the thought experiments of UML diagrams, CRC cards, use cases, etc.

The second important effect of writing the tests first comes from running the tests every time you do a build of your software. This activity gives you the other half of the testing that's performed by the compiler. If you look at the evolution of programming languages from this perspective, you'll see that the real improvements in the technology have actually revolved around testing. Assembly language checked only for syntax, but C imposed some semantic restrictions, and these prevented you from making certain types of mistakes. OOP languages impose even more semantic restrictions, which if you think about it are actually forms of testing. "Is this data type being used properly?" and "Is this method being called properly?" are the kinds of tests that are being performed by the compiler or run-time system. We've seen the results of having these tests built into the language: People have been able to write more complex systems, and get them to work, with much less time and effort. I've puzzled over why this is, but now I realize it's the tests: You do something wrong, and the safety net of the built-in tests tells you there's a problem and points you to where it is.

But the built-in testing afforded by the design of the language can only go so far. At some point, *you* must step in and add the rest of the tests that produce a full suite (in cooperation with the compiler and run-time system) that verifies all of your program. And, just like having a compiler watching over your shoulder, wouldn't you want these tests helping you right from the beginning? That's why you write them first, and run them automatically with every build of your system. Your tests become an extension of the safety net provided by the language.

One of the things that I've discovered about the use of more and more powerful programming languages is that I am emboldened to try more brazen experiments, because I know that the language will keep me from wasting my time chasing bugs. The XP test scheme does the same thing for your entire project. Because you know your tests will always catch any problems that you introduce (and you regularly add any new tests as you think of them), you can make big changes when you need to without worrying that you'll throw the whole project into complete disarray. This is incredibly powerful.

In this third edition of this book, I realized that testing was so important that it must also be applied to the examples in the book itself. With the help of the Crested Butte Summer 2002 Interns, we developed the testing system that you will see used throughout this book. The code and description is in Chapter 15. This system has increased the robustness of the code examples in this book immeasurably.

Pair programming

Pair programming goes against the rugged individualism that we've been indoctrinated into from the beginning, through school (where we succeed or fail on our own, and working with our neighbors is considered "cheating"), and media, especially Hollywood movies in which the hero is usually fighting against mindless conformity.[13] Programmers, too, are considered paragons of individuality—"cowboy coders," as Larry Constantine likes to say. And yet XP, which is itself battling against conventional thinking, says that code should be

---

[13] Although this may be a more American perspective, the stories of Hollywood reach everywhere.

written with two people per workstation. And that this should be done in an area with a group of workstations, without the barriers that the facilities-design people are so fond of. In fact, Beck says that the first task of converting to XP is to arrive with screwdrivers and Allen wrenches and take apart everything that gets in the way.[14] (This will require a manager who can deflect the ire of the facilities department.)

The value of pair programming is that one person is actually doing the coding while the other is thinking about it. The thinker keeps the big picture in mind—not only the picture of the problem at hand, but the guidelines of XP. If two people are working, it's less likely that one of them will get away with saying, "I don't want to write the tests first," for example. And if the coder gets stuck, they can swap places. If both of them get stuck, their musings may be overheard by someone else in the work area who can contribute. Working in pairs keeps things flowing and on track. Probably more important, it makes programming a lot more social and fun.

I've begun using pair programming during the exercise periods in some of my seminars, and it seems to significantly improve everyone's experience.

Strategies for transition

If you buy into OOP, your next question is probably, "How can I get my manager/colleagues/department/peers to start using objects?" Think about how you—one independent programmer—would go about learning to use a new language and a new programming paradigm. You've done it before. First comes education and examples; then comes a trial project to give you a feel for the basics without doing anything too confusing. Then comes a "real world" project that actually does something useful. Throughout your first projects you continue your education by reading, asking questions of experts, and trading hints with friends. This is the approach many experienced programmers suggest for the switch to Java. Switching an entire company will of course introduce certain group dynamics, but it will help at each step to remember how one person would do it.

---

[14] Including (especially) the PA system. I once worked in a company that insisted on broadcasting every phone call that arrived for every executive, and it constantly interrupted our productivity (but the managers couldn't begin to conceive of stifling such an important service as the PA). Finally, when no one was looking I started snipping speaker wires.

libraries that solve your problem rather than trying to build those libraries yourself. These are hard-money costs that must be factored into a realistic proposal. In addition, there are the hidden costs in loss of productivity while learning a new language and possibly a new programming environment. Training and mentoring can certainly minimize these, but team members must overcome their own struggles to understand the new technology. During this process they will make more mistakes (this is a feature, because acknowledged mistakes are the fastest path to learning) and be less productive. Even then, with some types of programming problems, the right classes, and the right development environment, it's possible to be more productive while you're learning Java (even considering that you're making more mistakes and writing fewer lines of code per day) than if you'd stayed with C.

Performance issues

A common question is, "Doesn't OOP automatically make my programs a lot bigger and slower?" The answer is, "It depends." The extra safety features in Java have traditionally extracted a performance penalty over a language like C++. Technologies such as "hotspot" and compilation technologies have improved the speed significantly in most cases, and efforts continue toward higher performance.

When your focus is on rapid prototyping, you can throw together components as fast as possible while ignoring efficiency issues. If you're using any third-party libraries, these are usually already optimized by their vendors; in any case it's not an issue while you're in rapid-development mode. When you have a system that you like, if it's small and fast enough, then you're done. If not, you begin tuning with a profiler, looking first for speedups that can be done by rewriting small portions of code. If that doesn't help, you look for modifications that can be made in the underlying implementation so no code that uses a particular class needs to be changed. Only if nothing else solves the problem do you need to change the design. If performance is so critical in that portion of the design, it must be part of the primary design criteria. You have the benefit of finding this out early using rapid development.

Chapter 15 introduces *profilers*, which can help you discover bottlenecks in your system so you can optimize that portion of your code (with the hotspot technologies, Sun no longer recommends using native methods for performance optimization). Optimization tools are also available.

Common design errors

When starting your team into OOP and Java, programmers will typically go through a series of common design errors. This often happens due to insufficient feedback from experts during the design and implementation of early projects, because no experts have been developed within the company, and because there may be resistance to retaining consultants. It's easy to feel that you understand OOP too early in the cycle and go off on a bad tangent. Something that's obvious to someone experienced with the language may be a subject of great internal debate for a novice. Much of this trauma can be skipped by using an experienced outside expert for training and mentoring.

Summary

This chapter was only intended to give you concepts of OOP methodologies, and the kinds of issues you will encounter when moving your own company to OOP and Java. More about Object design can be learned at the MindView seminar "Designing Objects and Systems" (see "Seminars" at *www.MindView.net*).

A: Passing & Returning Objects

By now you should be reasonably comfortable with the idea that when you're "passing" an object, you're actually passing a reference.

In many programming languages you can use that language's "regular" way to pass objects around, and most of the time everything works fine. But it always seems that there comes a point at which you must do something irregular, and suddenly things get a bit more complicated (or in the case of C++, quite complicated). Java is no exception, and it's important that you understand exactly what's happening as you pass objects around and manipulate them. This appendix will provide that insight.

Another way to pose the question of this appendix, if you're coming from a programming language so equipped, is "Does Java have pointers?" Some have claimed that pointers are hard and dangerous and therefore bad, and since Java is all goodness and light and will lift your earthly programming burdens, it cannot possibly contain such things. However, it's more accurate to say that Java has pointers; indeed, every object identifier in Java (except for primitives) is one of these pointers, but their use is restricted and guarded not only by the compiler but by the run-time system. Or to put it another way, Java has pointers, but no pointer arithmetic. These are what I've been calling "references," and you can think of them as "safety pointers," not unlike the safety scissors of elementary school—they aren't sharp, so you cannot hurt yourself without great effort, but they can sometimes be slow and tedious.

Passing references around

When you pass a reference into a method, you're still pointing to the same object. A simple experiment demonstrates this:

```
//: appendixa:PassReferences.java
// Passing references around.
import com.bruceeckel.simpletest.*;

public class PassReferences {
  private static Test monitor = new Test();
  public static void f(PassReferences h) {
    System.out.println("h inside f(): " + h);
  }
  public static void main(String[] args) {
    PassReferences p = new PassReferences();
    System.out.println("p inside main(): " + p);
    f(p);
    monitor.expect(new String[] {
      "%% p inside main\\(\\): PassReferences@[a-z0-9]+",
      "%% h inside f\\(\\): PassReferences@[a-z0-9]+"
    });
  }
} ///:~
```

The method **toString( )** is automatically invoked in the print statements, and **PassReferences** inherits directly from **Object** with no redefinition of **toString( )**. Thus, **Object**'s version of **toString( )** is used, which prints out the class of the object followed by the address where that object is located (not the reference, but the actual object storage). The output looks like this:

```
p inside main(): PassReferences@ad3ba4
h inside f(): PassReferences@ad3ba4
```

You can see that both **p** and **h** refer to the same object. This is far more efficient than duplicating a new **PassReferences** object just so that you can send an argument to a method. But it brings up an important issue.

Aliasing

Aliasing means that more than one reference is tied to the same object, as in the preceding example. The problem with aliasing occurs when someone *writes* to that object. If the owners of the other references aren't expecting that object to change, they'll be surprised. This can be demonstrated with a simple example:

```
//: appendixa:Alias1.java
// Aliasing two references to one object.
import com.bruceeckel.simpletest.*;

public class Alias1 {
  private static Test monitor = new Test();
  private int i;
  public Alias1(int ii) { i = ii; }
  public static void main(String[] args) {
    Alias1 x = new Alias1(7);
    Alias1 y = x; // Assign the reference
    System.out.println("x: " + x.i);
    System.out.println("y: " + y.i);
    System.out.println("Incrementing x");
    x.i++;
    System.out.println("x: " + x.i);
    System.out.println("y: " + y.i);
    monitor.expect(new String[] {
      "x: 7",
      "y: 7",
      "Incrementing x",
      "x: 8",
      "y: 8"
    });
  }
} ///:~
```

In the line:

```
Alias1 y = x; // Assign the reference
```

a new **Alias1** reference is created, but instead of being assigned to a fresh object created with **new**, it's assigned to an existing reference. So the contents of reference **x**, which is the address of the object **x** is pointing to, is assigned to **y**, and thus both **x** and **y** are attached to the same object. So when **x**'s **i** is incremented in the statement:

```
x.i++;
```

y's **i** will be affected as well. This can be seen in the output:

```
x: 7
```

```
y: 7
Incrementing x
x: 8
y: 8
```

One good solution in this case is simply not to do it; don't consciously alias more than one reference to an object at the same scope. Your code will be much easier to understand and debug. However, when you're passing a reference in as an argument—which is the way Java is supposed to work—you automatically alias, because the local reference that's created can modify the "outside object" (the object that was created outside the scope of the method). Here's an example:

```
//: appendixa:Alias2.java
// Method calls implicitly alias their arguments.
import com.bruceeckel.simpletest.*;

public class Alias2 {
  private static Test monitor = new Test();
  private int i;
  public Alias2(int ii) { i = ii; }
  public static void f(Alias2 reference) { reference.i++; }
  public static void main(String[] args) {
    Alias2 x = new Alias2(7);
    System.out.println("x: " + x.i);
    System.out.println("Calling f(x)");
    f(x);
    System.out.println("x: " + x.i);
    monitor.expect(new String[] {
      "x: 7",
      "Calling f(x)",
      "x: 8"
    });
  }
} ///:~
```

The method is changing its argument, the outside object. When this kind of situation arises, you must decide whether it makes sense, whether the user expects it, and whether it's going to cause problems.

In general, you call a method in order to produce a return value and/or a change of state in the object *that the method is called for*. It's much less common to call a method in order to manipulate its arguments; this is referred to as "calling a method for its *side effects*." Thus, when you create a method that modifies its arguments, the user must be clearly instructed and warned about the use of that method and its potential surprises. Because of the confusion and pitfalls, it's much better to avoid changing the argument.

If you need to modify an argument during a method call and you don't intend to modify the outside argument, then you should protect that argument by making a copy inside your method. That's the subject of much of this appendix.

Making local copies

To review: All argument passing in Java is performed by passing references. That is, when you pass "an object," you're really passing only a reference to an object that lives outside the method, so if you perform any modifications with that reference, you modify the outside object. In addition:

- Aliasing happens automatically during argument passing.
- There are no local objects, only local references.
- References have scopes, objects do not.
- Object lifetime is never an issue in Java.
- There is no language support (e.g., "const") to prevent objects from being modified and stop the negative effects of aliasing. You can't simply use the **final** keyword in the argument list; that simply prevents you from rebinding the reference to a different object.

If you're only reading information from an object and not modifying it, passing a reference is the most efficient form of argument passing. This is nice; the default way of doing things is also the most efficient. However, sometimes it's necessary to be able to treat the object as if it were "local" so that changes you make affect only a local copy and do not modify the outside object. Many programming languages support the ability to automatically make a local copy of the outside object, inside the method.[1] Java does not, but it allows you to produce this effect.

---

[1] In C, which generally handles small bits of data, the default is pass by value. C++ had to follow this form, but with objects pass by value isn't usually the most efficient way. In addition, coding classes to support pass by value in C++ is a big headache.

Pass by value

This brings up the terminology issue, which always seems good for an argument. The term is "pass by value," and the meaning depends on how you perceive the operation of the program. The general meaning is that you get a local copy of whatever you're passing, but the real question is how you think about what you're passing. When it comes to the meaning of "pass by value," there are two fairly distinct camps:

1. Java passes everything by value. When you're passing primitives into a method, you get a distinct copy of the primitive. When you're passing a reference into a method, you get a copy of the reference. Ergo, everything is pass by value. Of course, the assumption is that you're always thinking (and caring) that references are being passed, but it seems like the Java design has gone a long way toward allowing you to ignore (most of the time) that you're working with a reference. That is, it seems to allow you to think of the reference as "the object," since it implicitly dereferences it whenever you make a method call.

2. Java passes primitives by value (no argument there), but objects are passed by reference. This is the world view that the reference is an alias for the object, so you *don't* think about passing references, but instead say "I'm passing the object." Since you don't get a local copy of the object when you pass it into a method, objects are clearly not passed by value. There appears to be some support for this view within Sun, since at one time, one of the "reserved but not implemented" keywords was **byvalue** (This will probably never be implemented).

Having given both camps a good airing, and after saying "It depends on how you think of a reference," I will attempt to sidestep the issue. In the end, it isn't *that* important—what is important is that you understand that passing a reference allows the caller's object to be changed unexpectedly.

Cloning objects

The most likely reason for making a local copy of an object is if you're going to modify that object and you don't want to modify the caller's object. If you decide that you want to make a local copy, one approach is to use the **clone( )** method to perform the operation. This is a method that's defined as **protected** in the base class **Object**, and that you must override as **public** in any derived classes that you want to clone. For example, the standard library class **ArrayList** overrides **clone( )**, so we can call **clone( )** for **ArrayList**:

```
//: appendixa:Cloning.java
// The clone() operation works for only a few
// items in the standard Java library.
import com.bruceeckel.simpletest.*;
import java.util.*;

class Int {
  private int i;
  public Int(int ii) { i = ii; }
  public void increment() { i++; }
  public String toString() { return Integer.toString(i); }
}

public class Cloning {
  private static Test monitor = new Test();
  public static void main(String[] args) {
    ArrayList v = new ArrayList();
    for(int i = 0; i < 10; i++ )
      v.add(new Int(i));
    System.out.println("v: " + v);
    ArrayList v2 = (ArrayList)v.clone();
    // Increment all v2's elements:
    for(Iterator e = v2.iterator();
        e.hasNext(); )
      ((Int)e.next()).increment();
    // See if it changed v's elements:
    System.out.println("v: " + v);
    monitor.expect(new String[] {
      "v: [0, 1, 2, 3, 4, 5, 6, 7, 8, 9]",
      "v: [1, 2, 3, 4, 5, 6, 7, 8, 9, 10]"
    });
  }
} ///:~
```

The **clone( )** method produces an **Object**, which must then be recast to the proper type. This example shows how **ArrayList**'s **clone( )** method *does not* automatically try to clone each of the objects that the **ArrayList** contains—the old **ArrayList** and the cloned **ArrayList** are aliased to the same objects. This is often called a *shallow copy,* since it's copying only the "surface" portion of an object. The actual object consists of this "surface," plus all the objects that the references are pointing to, plus all the objects *those* objects are pointing to, etc. This is often referred to as the "web of objects." Copying the entire mess is called a *deep copy*.

You can see the effect of the shallow copy in the output, where the actions performed on **v2** affect **v**:

```
v: [0, 1, 2, 3, 4, 5, 6, 7, 8, 9]
v: [1, 2, 3, 4, 5, 6, 7, 8, 9, 10]
```

Not trying to **clone( )** the objects contained in the **ArrayList** is probably a fair assumption, because there's no guarantee that those objects *are* cloneable.[2]

Adding cloneability to a class

Even though the clone method is defined in the base-of-all-classes **Object**, cloning is *not* automatically available in every class.[3] This would seem to be counterintuitive to the idea that base-class methods are always available in derived classes. Cloning in Java does indeed go against this idea; if you want it to exist for a class, you must specifically add code to make cloning work.

Using a trick with **protected**

To prevent default cloneability in every class you create, the **clone( )** method is **protected** in the base class **Object**. Not only does this mean that it's not available by default to the client programmer who is simply using the class (not subclassing it), but it also means that you cannot call **clone( )** via a

---

[2] This is not the dictionary spelling of the word, but it's what is used in the Java library, so I've used it here, too, in some hopes of reducing confusion.

[3] You can apparently create a simple counter-example to this statement, like this:

```
public class Cloneit implements Cloneable {
  public static void main (String[] args)
  throws CloneNotSupportedException {
    Cloneit a = new Cloneit();
    Cloneit b = (Cloneit)a.clone();
  }
}
```

However, this only works because **main( )** is a method of **Cloneit** and thus has permission to call the **protected** base-class method **clone( )**. If you call it from a different class, it won't compile.

reference to the base class. (Although that might seem to be useful in some situations, such as to polymorphically clone a bunch of **Objects**.) It is, in effect, a way to give you, at compile time, the information that your object is not cloneable—and oddly enough, most classes in the standard Java library are not cloneable. Thus, if you say:

```
Integer x = new Integer(1);
x = x.clone();
```

You will get, at compile time, an error message that says **clone( )** is not accessible (since **Integer** doesn't override it and it defaults to the **protected** version).

If, however, you're in a method of a class *derived* from **Object** (as all classes are), then you have permission to call **Object.clone( )** because it's **protected** and you're an inheritor. The base class **clone( )** has useful functionality; it performs the actual bitwise duplication *of the derived-class object*, thus acting as the common cloning operation. However, you then need to make *your* clone operation **public** for it to be accessible. So, two key issues when you clone are:

- Call **super.clone( )**
- Make your clone **public**

You'll probably want to override **clone( )** in any further derived classes; otherwise, your (now **public**) **clone( )** will be used, and that might not do the right thing (although, since **Object.clone( )** makes a copy of the actual object, it might). The **protected** trick works only once: the first time you inherit from a class that has no cloneability and you want to make a class that's cloneable. In any classes inherited from your class, the **clone( )** method is available since it's not possible in Java to reduce the access of a method during derivation. That is, once a class is cloneable, everything derived from it is cloneable unless you use provided mechanisms (described later) to "turn off" cloning.

Implementing the **Cloneable** interface

There's one more thing you need to do to complete the cloneability of an object: implement the **Cloneable interface**. This **interface** is a bit strange, because it's empty!

```
interface Cloneable {}
```

The reason for implementing this empty **interface** is obviously not because you are going to upcast to **Cloneable** and call one of its methods. The use of **interface** in this way is called a *tagging interface* because it acts as a kind of flag, wired into the type of the class.

There are two reasons for the existence of the **Cloneable interface**. First, you might have an upcast reference to a base type and not know whether it's possible to clone that object. In this case, you can use the **instanceof** keyword (described in Chapter 10) to find out whether the reference is connected to an object that can be cloned:

```
if(myReference instanceof Cloneable) // ...
```

The second reason is that mixed into this design for cloneability was the thought that maybe you didn't want all types of objects to be cloneable. So **Object.clone( )** verifies that a class implements the **Cloneable** interface. If not, it throws a **CloneNotSupportedException** exception. So in general, you're forced to **implement Cloneable** as part of support for cloning.

Successful cloning

Once you understand the details of implementing the **clone( )** method, you're able to create classes that can be easily duplicated to provide a local copy:

```
//: appendixa:LocalCopy.java
// Creating local copies with clone().
import com.bruceeckel.simpletest.*;
import java.util.*;

class MyObject implements Cloneable {
  private int n;
  public MyObject(int n) { this.n = n; }
  public Object clone() {
    Object o = null;
    try {
      o = super.clone();
    } catch(CloneNotSupportedException e) {
      System.err.println("MyObject can't clone");
    }
    return o;
  }
  public int getValue() { return n; }
  public void setValue(int n) { this.n = n; }
```

```
  public void increment() { n++; }
  public String toString() { return Integer.toString(n); }
}

public class LocalCopy {
  private static Test monitor = new Test();
  public static MyObject g(MyObject v) {
    // Passing a reference, modifies outside object:
    v.increment();
    return v;
  }
  public static MyObject f(MyObject v) {
    v = (MyObject)v.clone(); // Local copy
    v.increment();
    return v;
  }
  public static void main(String[] args) {
    MyObject a = new MyObject(11);
    MyObject b = g(a);
    // Reference equivalence, not object equivalence:
    System.out.println("a == b: " + (a == b) +
      "\na = " + a + "\nb = " + b);
    MyObject c = new MyObject(47);
    MyObject d = f(c);
    System.out.println("c == d: " + (c == d) +
      "\nc = " + c + "\nd = " + d);
    monitor.expect(new String[] {
      "a == b: true",
      "a = 12",
      "b = 12",
      "c == d: false",
      "c = 47",
      "d = 48"
    });
  }
} ///:~
```

First of all, for **clone( )** to be accessible, you must make it **public**. Second, for the initial part of your **clone( )** operation, you should call the base-class version of **clone( )**. The **clone( )** that's being called here is the one that's predefined inside **Object**, and you can call it because it's **protected** and thereby accessible in derived classes.

Object.clone( ) figures out how big the object is, creates enough memory for a new one, and copies all the bits from the old to the new. This is called a *bitwise copy,* and is typically what you'd expect a **clone( )** method to do. But before **Object.clone( )** performs its operations, it first checks to see if a class is **Cloneable**—that is, whether it implements the **Cloneable** interface. If it doesn't, **Object.clone( )** throws a **CloneNotSupportedException** to indicate that you can't clone it. Thus, you've got to surround your call to **super.clone( )** with a **try** block to catch an exception that should never happen (because you've implemented the **Cloneable** interface).

In **LocalCopy**, the two methods **g( )** and **f( )** demonstrate the difference between the two approaches for argument passing. The **g( )** method shows passing by reference in which it modifies the outside object and returns a reference to that outside object, whereas **f( )** clones the argument, thereby decoupling it and leaving the original object alone. It can then proceed to do whatever it wants—even return a reference to this new object without any ill effects to the original. Notice the somewhat curious-looking statement:

```
v = (MyObject)v.clone();
```

This is where the local copy is created. To prevent confusion by such a statement, remember that this rather strange coding idiom is perfectly feasible in Java because every object identifier is actually a reference. So the reference **v** is used to **clone( )** a copy of what it refers to, and this returns a reference to the base type **Object** (because it's defined that way in **Object.clone( )**) that must then be cast to the proper type.

In **main( )**, the difference between the effects of the two different argument-passing approaches is tested. It's important to notice that the equivalence tests in Java do not look inside the objects being compared to see if their values are the same. The **==** and **!=** operators are simply comparing the *references.* If the addresses inside the references are the same, the references are pointing to the same object and are therefore "equal." So what the operators are really testing is whether the references are aliased to the same object!

The effect of **Object.clone( )**

What actually happens when **Object.clone( )** is called that makes it so essential to call **super.clone( )** when you override **clone( )** in your class? The **clone( )** method in the root class is responsible for creating the correct amount of storage and making the bitwise copy of the bits from the original object into the new object's storage. That is, it doesn't just make storage and copy an **Object**; it actually figures out the size of the *real* object (not just the base-class object, but the derived object) that's being copied and duplicates that. Since all this is happening from the code in the **clone( )** method defined in the root class (that has no idea what's being inherited from it), you can guess that the process involves RTTI to determine the actual object that's being cloned. This way, the **clone( )** method can create the proper amount of storage and do the correct bitwise copy for that type.

Whatever you do, the first part of the cloning process should normally be a call to **super.clone( )**. This establishes the groundwork for the cloning operation by making an exact duplicate. At this point you can perform other operations necessary to complete the cloning.

To know for sure what those other operations are, you need to understand exactly what **Object.clone( )** buys you. In particular, does it automatically clone the destination of all the references? The following example tests this:

```
//: appendixa:Snake.java
// Tests cloning to see if destination
// of references are also cloned.
import com.bruceeckel.simpletest.*;

public class Snake implements Cloneable {
  private static Test monitor = new Test();
  private Snake next;
  private char c;
  // Value of i == number of segments
  public Snake(int i, char x) {
    c = x;
    if(--i > 0)
      next = new Snake(i, (char)(x + 1));
  }
  public void increment() {
    c++;
    if(next != null)
      next.increment();
  }
  public String toString() {
    String s = ":" + c;
    if(next != null)
      s += next.toString();
```

```java
    return s;
  }
  public Object clone() {
    Object o = null;
    try {
      o = super.clone();
    } catch(CloneNotSupportedException e) {
      System.err.println("Snake can't clone");
    }
    return o;
  }
  public static void main(String[] args) {
    Snake s = new Snake(5, 'a');
    System.out.println("s = " + s);
    Snake s2 = (Snake)s.clone();
    System.out.println("s2 = " + s2);
    s.increment();
    System.out.println("after s.increment, s2 = " + s2);
    monitor.expect(new String[] {
      "s = :a:b:c:d:e",
      "s2 = :a:b:c:d:e",
      "after s.increment, s2 = :a:c:d:e:f"
    });
  }
} ///:~
```

A **Snake** is made up of a bunch of segments, each of type **Snake**. Thus, it's a singly linked list. The segments are created recursively, decrementing the first constructor argument for each segment until zero is reached. To give each segment a unique tag, the second argument, a **char**, is incremented for each recursive constructor call.

The **increment( )** method recursively increments each tag so you can see the change, and the **toString( )** recursively prints each tag. From the output, you can see that only the first segment is duplicated by **Object.clone( )**, therefore it does a shallow copy. If you want the whole snake to be duplicated—a deep copy—you must perform the additional operations inside your overridden **clone( )**.

You'll typically call **super.clone( )** in any class derived from a cloneable class to make sure that all of the base-class operations (including **Object.clone( )**) take place. This is followed by an explicit call to **clone( )** for every reference in your object; otherwise those references will be aliased to those of the original object. It's analogous to the way constructors are called: base-class constructor first, then the next-derived constructor, and so on, to the most-derived constructor. The difference is that **clone( )** is not a constructor, so there's nothing to make it happen automatically. You must make sure to do it yourself.

Cloning a composed object

There's a problem you'll encounter when trying to deep copy a composed object. You must assume that the **clone( )** method in the member objects will in turn perform a deep copy on *their* references, and so on. This is quite a commitment. It effectively means that for a deep copy to work, you must either control all of the code in all of the classes, or at least have enough knowledge about all of the classes involved in the deep copy to know that they are performing their own deep copy correctly.

This example shows what you must do to accomplish a deep copy when dealing with a composed object:

```
//: appendixa:DeepCopy.java
// Cloning a composed object.
// {Depends: junit.jar}
import junit.framework.*;

class DepthReading implements Cloneable {
  private double depth;
  public DepthReading(double depth) { this.depth = depth; }
  public Object clone() {
    Object o = null;
    try {
      o = super.clone();
    } catch(CloneNotSupportedException e) {
      e.printStackTrace();
    }
    return o;
  }
  public double getDepth() { return depth; }
  public void setDepth(double depth){ this.depth = depth; }
  public String toString() { return String.valueOf(depth);}
}

class TemperatureReading implements Cloneable {
  private long time;
```

```
  private double temperature;
  public TemperatureReading(double temperature) {
    time = System.currentTimeMillis();
    this.temperature = temperature;
  }
  public Object clone() {
    Object o = null;
    try {
      o = super.clone();
    } catch(CloneNotSupportedException e) {
      e.printStackTrace();
    }
    return o;
  }
  public double getTemperature() { return temperature; }
  public void setTemperature(double temperature) {
    this.temperature = temperature;
  }
  public String toString() {
    return String.valueOf(temperature);
  }
}

class OceanReading implements Cloneable {
  private DepthReading depth;
  private TemperatureReading temperature;
  public OceanReading(double tdata, double ddata) {
    temperature = new TemperatureReading(tdata);
    depth = new DepthReading(ddata);
  }
  public Object clone() {
    OceanReading o = null;
    try {
      o = (OceanReading)super.clone();
    } catch(CloneNotSupportedException e) {
      e.printStackTrace();
    }
    // Must clone references:
    o.depth = (DepthReading)o.depth.clone();
    o.temperature =
      (TemperatureReading)o.temperature.clone();
    return o; // Upcasts back to Object
  }
  public TemperatureReading getTemperatureReading() {
```

```
    return temperature;
  }
  public void setTemperatureReading(TemperatureReading tr){
    temperature = tr;
  }
  public DepthReading getDepthReading() { return depth; }
  public void setDepthReading(DepthReading dr) {
    this.depth = dr;
  }
  public String toString() {
    return "temperature: " + temperature +
      ", depth: " + depth;
  }
}

public class DeepCopy extends TestCase {
  public DeepCopy(String name) { super(name); }
  public void testClone() {
    OceanReading reading = new OceanReading(33.9, 100.5);
    // Now clone it:
    OceanReading clone = (OceanReading)reading.clone();
    TemperatureReading tr = clone.getTemperatureReading();
    tr.setTemperature(tr.getTemperature() + 1);
    clone.setTemperatureReading(tr);
    DepthReading dr = clone.getDepthReading();
    dr.setDepth(dr.getDepth() + 1);
    clone.setDepthReading(dr);
    assertEquals(reading.toString(),
      "temperature: 33.9, depth: 100.5");
    assertEquals(clone.toString(),
      "temperature: 34.9, depth: 101.5");
  }
  public static void main(String[] args) {
    junit.textui.TestRunner.run(DeepCopy.class);
  }
} ///:~
```

DepthReading and **TemperatureReading** are quite similar; they both contain only primitives. Therefore, the **clone( )** method can be quite simple: it calls **super.clone( )** and returns the result. Note that the **clone( )** code for both classes is identical.

OceanReading is composed of **DepthReading** and **TemperatureReading** objects and so, to produce a deep copy, its **clone( )**

must clone the references inside **OceanReading**. To accomplish this, the result of **super.clone( )** must be cast to an **OceanReading** object (so you can access the **depth** and **temperature** references).

A deep copy with **ArrayList**

Let's revisit **Cloning.java** from earlier in this appendix. This time the **Int2** class is cloneable, so the **ArrayList** can be deep copied:

```
//: appendixa:AddingClone.java
// You must go through a few gyrations
// to add cloning to your own class.
import com.bruceeckel.simpletest.*;
import java.util.*;

class Int2 implements Cloneable {
  private int i;
  public Int2(int ii) { i = ii; }
  public void increment() { i++; }
  public String toString() { return Integer.toString(i); }
  public Object clone() {
    Object o = null;
    try {
      o = super.clone();
    } catch(CloneNotSupportedException e) {
      System.err.println("Int2 can't clone");
    }
    return o;
  }
}

// Inheritance doesn't remove cloneability:
class Int3 extends Int2 {
  private int j; // Automatically duplicated
  public Int3(int i) { super(i); }
}

public class AddingClone {
  private static Test monitor = new Test();
  public static void main(String[] args) {
    Int2 x = new Int2(10);
    Int2 x2 = (Int2)x.clone();
    x2.increment();
    System.out.println("x = " + x + ", x2 = " + x2);
```

```
    // Anything inherited is also cloneable:
    Int3 x3 = new Int3(7);
    x3 = (Int3)x3.clone();
    ArrayList v = new ArrayList();
    for(int i = 0; i < 10; i++ )
      v.add(new Int2(i));
    System.out.println("v: " + v);
    ArrayList v2 = (ArrayList)v.clone();
    // Now clone each element:
    for(int i = 0; i < v.size(); i++)
      v2.set(i, ((Int2)v2.get(i)).clone());
    // Increment all v2's elements:
    for(Iterator e = v2.iterator(); e.hasNext(); )
      ((Int2)e.next()).increment();
    System.out.println("v2: " + v2);
    // See if it changed v's elements:
    System.out.println("v: " + v);
    monitor.expect(new String[] {
      "x = 10, x2 = 11",
      "v: [0, 1, 2, 3, 4, 5, 6, 7, 8, 9]",
      "v2: [1, 2, 3, 4, 5, 6, 7, 8, 9, 10]",
      "v: [0, 1, 2, 3, 4, 5, 6, 7, 8, 9]"
    });
  }
} ///:~
```

Int3 is inherited from **Int2**, and a new primitive member, **int j**, is added. You might think that you'd need to override **clone( )** again to make sure **j** is copied, but that's not the case. When **Int2**'s **clone( )** is called as **Int3**'s **clone( )**, it calls **Object.clone( ),** which determines that it's working with an **Int3** and duplicates all the bits in the **Int3**. As long as you don't add references that need to be cloned, the one call to **Object.clone( )** performs all of the necessary duplication regardless of how far down in the hierarchy **clone( )** is defined.

You can see what's necessary in order to do a deep copy of an **ArrayList**: After the **ArrayList** is cloned, you have to step through and clone each one of the objects pointed to by the **ArrayList**. You'd have to do something similar to this to do a deep copy of a **HashMap**.

The remainder of the example shows that the cloning did happen by showing that, once an object is cloned, you can change it, and the original object is left untouched.

Deep copy via serialization

When you consider Java's object serialization (introduced in Chapter 12), you might observe that an object that's serialized and then deserialized is, in effect, cloned.

So why not use serialization to perform deep copying? Here's an example that compares the two approaches by timing them:

```
//: appendixa:Compete.java
import java.io.*;

class Thing1 implements Serializable {}
class Thing2 implements Serializable {
  Thing1 o1 = new Thing1();
}

class Thing3 implements Cloneable {
  public Object clone() {
    Object o = null;
    try {
      o = super.clone();
    } catch(CloneNotSupportedException e) {
      System.err.println("Thing3 can't clone");
    }
    return o;
  }
}

class Thing4 implements Cloneable {
  private Thing3 o3 = new Thing3();
  public Object clone() {
    Thing4 o = null;
    try {
      o = (Thing4)super.clone();
    } catch(CloneNotSupportedException e) {
      System.err.println("Thing4 can't clone");
    }
    // Clone the field, too:
    o.o3 = (Thing3)o3.clone();
    return o;
  }
}
```

```java
public class Compete {
  public static final int SIZE = 25000;
  public static void main(String[] args) throws Exception {
    Thing2[] a = new Thing2[SIZE];
    for(int i = 0; i < a.length; i++)
      a[i] = new Thing2();
    Thing4[] b = new Thing4[SIZE];
    for(int i = 0; i < b.length; i++)
      b[i] = new Thing4();
    long t1 = System.currentTimeMillis();
    ByteArrayOutputStream buf= new ByteArrayOutputStream();
    ObjectOutputStream o = new ObjectOutputStream(buf);
    for(int i = 0; i < a.length; i++)
      o.writeObject(a[i]);
    // Now get copies:
    ObjectInputStream in = new ObjectInputStream(
        new ByteArrayInputStream(buf.toByteArray()));
    Thing2[] c = new Thing2[SIZE];
    for(int i = 0; i < c.length; i++)
      c[i] = (Thing2)in.readObject();
    long t2 = System.currentTimeMillis();
    System.out.println("Duplication via serialization: " +
      (t2 - t1) + " Milliseconds");
    // Now try cloning:
    t1 = System.currentTimeMillis();
    Thing4[] d = new Thing4[SIZE];
    for(int i = 0; i < d.length; i++)
      d[i] = (Thing4)b[i].clone();
    t2 = System.currentTimeMillis();
    System.out.println("Duplication via cloning: " +
      (t2 - t1) + " Milliseconds");
  }
} ///:~
```

Thing2 and **Thing4** contain member objects so that there's some deep copying going on. It's interesting to notice that while **Serializable** classes are easy to set up, there's much more work going on to duplicate them. Cloning involves a lot of work to set up the class, but the actual duplication of objects is relatively simple. The results are interesting. Here is the output from three different runs:

```
Duplication via serialization: 547 Milliseconds
Duplication via cloning: 110 Milliseconds
```

```
Duplication via serialization: 547 Milliseconds
Duplication via cloning: 109 Milliseconds

Duplication via serialization: 547 Milliseconds
Duplication via cloning: 125 Milliseconds
```

In earlier versions of the JDK, the time required for serialization was much longer than that of cloning (roughly 15 times slower), and the serialization time tended to vary a lot. More recent versions of the JDK have sped up serialization and apparently made the time more consistent, as well. Here, it's approximately four times slower, which brings it into the realm of reasonability for use as a cloning alternative.

Adding cloneability farther down a hierarchy

If you create a new class, its base class defaults to **Object**, which defaults to noncloneability (as you'll see in the next section). As long as you don't explicitly add cloneability, you won't get it. But you can add it in at any layer and it will then be cloneable from that layer downward, like this:

```
//: appendixa:HorrorFlick.java
// You can insert Cloneability at any level of inheritance.
package appendixa;
import java.util.*;

class Person {}
class Hero extends Person {}
class Scientist extends Person implements Cloneable {
  public Object clone() {
    try {
      return super.clone();
    } catch(CloneNotSupportedException e) {
      // This should never happen: It's Cloneable already!
      throw new RuntimeException(e);
    }
  }
}
class MadScientist extends Scientist {}

public class HorrorFlick {
  public static void main(String[] args) {
    Person p = new Person();
```

```
    Hero h = new Hero();
    Scientist s = new Scientist();
    MadScientist m = new MadScientist();
    //! p = (Person)p.clone(); // Compile error
    //! h = (Hero)h.clone(); // Compile error
    s = (Scientist)s.clone();
    m = (MadScientist)m.clone();
  }
} ///:~
```

Before cloneability was added in the hierarchy, the compiler stopped you from trying to clone things. When cloneability is added in **Scientist**, then **Scientist** and all its descendants are cloneable.

Why this strange design?

If all this seems to be a strange scheme, that's because it is. You might wonder why it worked out this way. What is the meaning behind this design?

Originally, Java was designed as a language to control hardware boxes, and definitely not with the Internet in mind. In a general-purpose language like this, it makes sense that the programmer be able to clone any object. Thus, **clone( )** was placed in the root class **Object**, *but* it was a **public** method so you could always clone any object. This seemed to be the most flexible approach, and after all, what could it hurt?

Well, when Java was seen as the ultimate Internet programming language, things changed. Suddenly, there are security issues, and of course, these issues are dealt with using objects, and you don't necessarily want anyone to be able to clone your security objects. So what you're seeing is a lot of patches applied on the original simple and straightforward scheme: **clone( )** is now **protected** in **Object**. You must override it *and* **implement Cloneable** *and* deal with the exceptions.

It's worth noting that you must implement the **Cloneable** interface *only* if you're going to call **Object**'s **clone( )** method, since that method checks at run time to make sure that your class implements **Cloneable**. But for consistency (and since **Cloneable** is empty anyway), you should implement it.

Controlling cloneability

You might suggest that, to remove cloneability, the **clone( )** method should simply be made **private**, but this won't work, because you cannot take a base-class method and make it less accessible in a derived class. And yet, it's necessary to be able to control whether an object can be cloned. There are a number of attitudes you can take to this for your classes:

1. Indifference. You don't do anything about cloning, which means that your class can't be cloned, but a class that inherits from you can add cloning if it wants. This works only if the default **Object.clone( )** will do something reasonable with all the fields in your class.

2. Support **clone( )**. Follow the standard practice of implementing **Cloneable** and overriding **clone( )**. In the overridden **clone( )**, you call **super.clone( )** and catch all exceptions (so your overridden **clone( )** doesn't throw any exceptions).

3. Support cloning conditionally. If your class holds references to other objects that might or might not be cloneable (a container class, for example), your **clone( )** can try to clone all of the objects for which you have references, and if they throw exceptions, just pass those exceptions out to the programmer. For example, consider a special sort of **ArrayList** that tries to clone all the objects it holds. When you write such an **ArrayList**, you don't know what sort of objects the client programmer might put into your **ArrayList**, so you don't know whether they can be cloned.

4. Don't implement **Cloneable** but override **clone( )** as **protected**, producing the correct copying behavior for any fields. This way, anyone inheriting from this class can override **clone( )** and call **super.clone( )** to produce the correct copying behavior. Note that your implementation can and should invoke **super.clone( )** even though that method expects a **Cloneable** object (it will throw an exception otherwise), because no one will directly invoke it on an object of your type. It will get invoked only through a derived class, which, if it is to work successfully, implements **Cloneable**.

5. Try to prevent cloning by not implementing **Cloneable** and overriding **clone( )** to throw an exception. This is successful only if

any class derived from this calls **super.clone( )** in its redefinition of **clone( )**. Otherwise, a programmer may be able to get around it.

6. Prevent cloning by making your class **final**. If **clone( )** has not been overridden by any of your ancestor classes, then it can't be. If it has, then override it again and throw **CloneNotSupportedException**. Making the class **final** is the only way to guarantee that cloning is prevented. In addition, when dealing with security objects or other situations in which you want to control the number of objects created, you should make all constructors **private** and provide one or more special methods for creating objects. That way, these methods can restrict the number of objects created and the conditions in which they're created. (A particular case of this is the *singleton* pattern shown in *Thinking in Patterns (with Java)* at *www.BruceEckel.com.*)

Here's an example that shows the various ways cloning can be implemented and then, later in the hierarchy, "turned off":

```
//: appendixa:CheckCloneable.java
// Checking to see if a reference can be cloned.
import com.bruceeckel.simpletest.*;

// Can't clone this because it doesn't override clone():
class Ordinary {}

// Overrides clone, but doesn't implement Cloneable:
class WrongClone extends Ordinary {
  public Object clone() throws CloneNotSupportedException {
    return super.clone(); // Throws exception
  }
}

// Does all the right things for cloning:
class IsCloneable extends Ordinary implements Cloneable {
  public Object clone() throws CloneNotSupportedException {
    return super.clone();
  }
}

// Turn off cloning by throwing the exception:
class NoMore extends IsCloneable {
  public Object clone() throws CloneNotSupportedException {
    throw new CloneNotSupportedException();
```

```java
  }
}

class TryMore extends NoMore {
  public Object clone() throws CloneNotSupportedException {
    // Calls NoMore.clone(), throws exception:
    return super.clone();
  }
}

class BackOn extends NoMore {
  private BackOn duplicate(BackOn b) {
    // Somehow make a copy of b and return that copy.
    // This is a dummy copy, just to make the point:
    return new BackOn();
  }
  public Object clone() {
    // Doesn't call NoMore.clone():
    return duplicate(this);
  }
}

// You can't inherit from this, so you can't override
// the clone method as you can in BackOn:
final class ReallyNoMore extends NoMore {}

public class CheckCloneable {
  private static Test monitor = new Test();
  public static Ordinary tryToClone(Ordinary ord) {
    String id = ord.getClass().getName();
    System.out.println("Attempting " + id);
    Ordinary x = null;
    if(ord instanceof Cloneable) {
      try {
        x = (Ordinary)((IsCloneable)ord).clone();
        System.out.println("Cloned " + id);
      } catch(CloneNotSupportedException e) {
        System.err.println("Could not clone " + id);
      }
    } else {
      System.out.println("Doesn't implement Cloneable");
    }
    return x;
  }
```

```
  public static void main(String[] args) {
    // Upcasting:
    Ordinary[] ord = {
      new IsCloneable(),
      new WrongClone(),
      new NoMore(),
      new TryMore(),
      new BackOn(),
      new ReallyNoMore(),
    };
    Ordinary x = new Ordinary();
    // This won't compile; clone() is protected in Object:
    //! x = (Ordinary)x.clone();
    // Checks first to see if a class implements Cloneable:
    for(int i = 0; i < ord.length; i++)
      tryToClone(ord[i]);
    monitor.expect(new String[] {
      "Attempting IsCloneable",
      "Cloned IsCloneable",
      "Attempting WrongClone",
      "Doesn't implement Cloneable",
      "Attempting NoMore",
      "Could not clone NoMore",
      "Attempting TryMore",
      "Could not clone TryMore",
      "Attempting BackOn",
      "Cloned BackOn",
      "Attempting ReallyNoMore",
      "Could not clone ReallyNoMore"
    });
  }
} ///:~
```

The first class, **Ordinary**, represents the kinds of classes we've seen throughout this book: no support for cloning, but as it turns out, no prevention of cloning either. But if you have a reference to an **Ordinary** object that might have been upcast from a more derived class, you can't tell if it can be cloned or not.

The class **WrongClone** shows an incorrect way to implement cloning. It does override **Object.clone( )** and makes that method **public**, but it doesn't implement **Cloneable**, so when **super.clone( )** is called (which results in a call to **Object.clone( )**), **CloneNotSupportedException** is thrown, so the cloning doesn't work.

IsCloneable performs all the right actions for cloning; **clone( )** is overridden and **Cloneable** is implemented. However, this **clone( )** method and several others that follow in this example *do not* catch **CloneNotSupportedException,** but instead pass it through to the caller, who must then put a try-catch block around it. In your own **clone( )** methods you will typically catch **CloneNotSupportedException** *inside* **clone( )** rather than passing it through. As you'll see, in this example it's more informative to pass the exceptions through.

Class **NoMore** attempts to "turn off" cloning in the way that the Java designers intended: in the derived class **clone( )**, you throw **CloneNotSupportedException**. The **clone( )** method in class **TryMore** properly calls **super.clone( )**, and this resolves to **NoMore.clone( ),** which throws an exception and prevents cloning.

But what if the programmer doesn't follow the "proper" path of calling **super.clone( )** inside the overridden **clone( )** method? In **BackOn**, you can see how this can happen. This class uses a separate method **duplicate( )** to make a copy of the current object and calls this method inside **clone( )** *instead* of calling **super.clone( )**. The exception is never thrown and the new class is cloneable. You can't rely on throwing an exception to prevent making a cloneable class. The only sure-fire solution is shown in **ReallyNoMore**, which is **final** and thus cannot be inherited. That means if **clone( )** throws an exception in the **final** class, it cannot be modified with inheritance, and the prevention of cloning is assured. (You cannot explicitly call **Object.clone( )** from a class that has an arbitrary level of inheritance; you are limited to calling **super.clone( )**, which has access to only the direct base class.) Thus, if you make any objects that involve security issues, you'll want to make those classes **final**.

The first method you see in class **CheckCloneable** is **tryToClone( )**, which takes any **Ordinary** object and checks to see whether it's cloneable with **instanceof**. If so, it casts the object to an **IsCloneable**, calls **clone( )**, and casts the result back to **Ordinary**, catching any exceptions that are thrown. Notice the use of run-time type identification (RTTI; see Chapter 10) to print the class name so you can see what's happening.

In **main( )**, different types of **Ordinary** objects are created and upcast to **Ordinary** in the array definition. The first two lines of code after that create a plain **Ordinary** object and try to clone it. However, this code will not compile because **clone( )** is a **protected** method in **Object**. The remainder of the code steps through the array and tries to clone each object, reporting the success or failure of each.

So to summarize, if you want a class to be cloneable:

1. Implement the **Cloneable** interface.
2. Override **clone( )**.
3. Call **super.clone( )** inside your **clone( )**.
4. Capture exceptions inside your **clone( )**.

This will produce the most convenient effects.

The copy constructor

Cloning can seem to be a complicated process to set up. It might seem like there should be an alternative. One approach is to use serialization, as shown earlier. Another approach that might occur to you (especially if you're a C++ programmer) is to make a special constructor whose job it is to duplicate an object. In C++, this is called the *copy constructor*. At first, this seems like the obvious solution, but in fact it doesn't work. Here's an example:

```
//: appendixa:CopyConstructor.java
// A constructor for copying an object of the same
// type, as an attempt to create a local copy.
import com.bruceeckel.simpletest.*;
import java.lang.reflect.*;

class FruitQualities {
  private int weight;
  private int color;
  private int firmness;
  private int ripeness;
  private int smell;
  // etc.
  public FruitQualities() { // Default constructor
    // Do something meaningful...
  }
  // Other constructors:
  // ...
  // Copy constructor:
  public FruitQualities(FruitQualities f) {
    weight = f.weight;
```

```
    color = f.color;
    firmness = f.firmness;
    ripeness = f.ripeness;
    smell = f.smell;
    // etc.
  }
}

class Seed {
  // Members...
  public Seed() { /* Default constructor */ }
  public Seed(Seed s) { /* Copy constructor */ }
}

class Fruit {
  private FruitQualities fq;
  private int seeds;
  private Seed[] s;
  public Fruit(FruitQualities q, int seedCount) {
    fq = q;
    seeds = seedCount;
    s = new Seed[seeds];
    for(int i = 0; i < seeds; i++)
      s[i] = new Seed();
  }
  // Other constructors:
  // ...
  // Copy constructor:
  public Fruit(Fruit f) {
    fq = new FruitQualities(f.fq);
    seeds = f.seeds;
    s = new Seed[seeds];
    // Call all Seed copy-constructors:
    for(int i = 0; i < seeds; i++)
      s[i] = new Seed(f.s[i]);
    // Other copy-construction activities...
  }
  // To allow derived constructors (or other
  // methods) to put in different qualities:
  protected void addQualities(FruitQualities q) {
    fq = q;
  }
  protected FruitQualities getQualities() {
    return fq;
```

```
    }
  }

  class Tomato extends Fruit {
    public Tomato() {
      super(new FruitQualities(), 100);
    }
    public Tomato(Tomato t) { // Copy-constructor
      super(t); // Upcast for base copy-constructor
      // Other copy-construction activities...
    }
  }

  class ZebraQualities extends FruitQualities {
    private int stripedness;
    public ZebraQualities() { // Default constructor
      super();
      // do something meaningful...
    }
    public ZebraQualities(ZebraQualities z) {
      super(z);
      stripedness = z.stripedness;
    }
  }

  class GreenZebra extends Tomato {
    public GreenZebra() {
      addQualities(new ZebraQualities());
    }
    public GreenZebra(GreenZebra g) {
      super(g); // Calls Tomato(Tomato)
      // Restore the right qualities:
      addQualities(new ZebraQualities());
    }
    public void evaluate() {
      ZebraQualities zq = (ZebraQualities)getQualities();
      // Do something with the qualities
      // ...
    }
  }

  public class CopyConstructor {
    private static Test monitor = new Test();
    public static void ripen(Tomato t) {
```

```
    // Use the "copy constructor":
    t = new Tomato(t);
    System.out.println("In ripen, t is a " +
      t.getClass().getName());
  }
  public static void slice(Fruit f) {
    f = new Fruit(f); // Hmmm... will this work?
    System.out.println("In slice, f is a " +
      f.getClass().getName());
  }
  public static void ripen2(Tomato t) {
    try {
      Class c = t.getClass();
      // Use the "copy constructor":
      Constructor ct = c.getConstructor(new Class[] { c });
      Object obj = ct.newInstance(new Object[] { t });
      System.out.println("In ripen2, t is a " +
        obj.getClass().getName());
    }
    catch(Exception e) { System.out.println(e); }
  }
  public static void slice2(Fruit f) {
    try {
      Class c = f.getClass();
      Constructor ct = c.getConstructor(new Class[] { c });
      Object obj = ct.newInstance(new Object[] { f });
      System.out.println("In slice2, f is a " +
        obj.getClass().getName());
    }
    catch(Exception e) { System.out.println(e); }
  }
  public static void main(String[] args) {
    Tomato tomato = new Tomato();
    ripen(tomato); // OK
    slice(tomato); // OOPS!
    ripen2(tomato); // OK
    slice2(tomato); // OK
    GreenZebra g = new GreenZebra();
    ripen(g); // OOPS!
    slice(g); // OOPS!
    ripen2(g); // OK
    slice2(g); // OK
    g.evaluate();
    monitor.expect(new String[] {
```

```
      "In ripen, t is a Tomato",
      "In slice, f is a Fruit",
      "In ripen2, t is a Tomato",
      "In slice2, f is a Tomato",
      "In ripen, t is a Tomato",
      "In slice, f is a Fruit",
      "In ripen2, t is a GreenZebra",
      "In slice2, f is a GreenZebra"
    });
  }
} ///:~
```

This seems a bit strange at first. Sure, fruit has qualities, but why not just put fields representing those qualities directly into the **Fruit** class? There are two potential reasons.

The first is that you might want to easily insert or change the qualities. Note that **Fruit** has a **protected addQualities( )** method to allow derived classes to do this. (You might think the logical thing to do is to have a **protected** constructor in **Fruit** that takes a **FruitQualities** argument, but constructors don't inherit, so it wouldn't be available in second or greater level classes.) By making the fruit qualities into a separate class and using composition, you have greater flexibility, including the ability to change the qualities midway through the lifetime of a particular **Fruit** object.

The second reason for making **FruitQualities** a separate object is in case you want to add new qualities or to change the behavior via inheritance and polymorphism. Note that for **GreenZebra** (which *really is* a type of tomato—I've grown them and they're fabulous), the constructor calls **addQualities( )** and passes it a **ZebraQualities** object, which is derived from **FruitQualities**, so it can be attached to the **FruitQualities** reference in the base class. Of course, when **GreenZebra** uses the **FruitQualities**, it must downcast it to the correct type (as seen in **evaluate( )**), but it always knows that type is **ZebraQualities**.

You'll also see that there's a **Seed** class, and that **Fruit** (which by definition carries its own seeds)[4] contains an array of **Seed**s.

---

[4] Except for the poor avocado, which has been reclassified to simply "fat."

Finally, notice that each class has a copy constructor, and that each copy constructor must take care to call the copy constructors for the base class and member objects to produce a deep copy. The copy constructor is tested inside the class **CopyConstructor**. The method **ripen( )** takes a **Tomato** argument and performs copy-construction on it in order to duplicate the object:

```
t = new Tomato(t);
```

while **slice( )** takes a more generic **Fruit** object and also duplicates it:

```
f = new Fruit(f);
```

These are tested with different kinds of **Fruit** in **main( )**. From the output, you can see the problem. After the copy-construction that happens to the **Tomato** inside **slice( )**, the result is no longer a **Tomato** object, but just a **Fruit**. It has lost all of its tomato-ness. Furthermore, when you take a **GreenZebra**, both **ripen( )** and **slice( )** turn it into a **Tomato** and a **Fruit**, respectively. Thus, unfortunately, the copy constructor scheme is no good to us in Java when attempting to make a local copy of an object.

Why does it work in C++ and not Java?

The copy constructor is a fundamental part of C++, since it automatically makes a local copy of an object. Yet the preceding example proves that it does not work for Java. Why? In Java, everything that we manipulate is a reference, but in C++, you can have reference-like entities and you can *also* pass around the objects directly. That's what the C++ copy constructor is for: when you want to take an object and pass it in by value, thus duplicating the object. So it works fine in C++, but you should keep in mind that this scheme fails in Java, so don't use it.

Read-only classes

Although the local copy produced by **clone( )** gives the desired results in the appropriate cases, it is an example of forcing the programmer (the author of the method) to be responsible for preventing the ill effects of aliasing. What if you're making a library that's so general purpose and commonly used that you cannot make the assumption that it will always be cloned in the proper places? Or more likely, what if you *want* to allow aliasing for efficiency—to prevent the needless duplication of objects—but you don't want the negative side effects of aliasing?

One solution is to create *immutable objects* that belong to read-only classes. You can define a class such that no methods in the class cause changes to the internal state of the object. In such a class, aliasing has no impact since you can read only the internal state, so if many pieces of code are reading the same object, there's no problem.

As a simple example of immutable objects, Java's standard library contains "wrapper" classes for all the primitive types. You might have already discovered that, if you want to store an **int** inside a container such as an **ArrayList** (which takes only **Object references**), you can wrap your **int** inside the standard library **Integer** class:

```
//: appendixa:ImmutableInteger.java
// The Integer class cannot be changed.
import java.util.*;

public class ImmutableInteger {
  public static void main(String[] args) {
    List v = new ArrayList();
    for(int i = 0; i < 10; i++)
      v.add(new Integer(i));
    // But how do you change the int inside the Integer?
  }
} ///:~
```

The **Integer** class (as well as all the primitive "wrapper" classes) implements immutability in a simple fashion: It has no methods that allow you to change the object.

If you do need an object that holds a primitive type that can be modified, you must create it yourself. Fortunately, this is trivial. The following class uses the JavaBeans naming conventions:

```
//: appendixa:MutableInteger.java
// A changeable wrapper class.
import com.bruceeckel.simpletest.*;
import java.util.*;

class IntValue {
  private int n;
  public IntValue(int x) { n = x; }
  public int getValue() { return n; }
  public void setValue(int n) { this.n = n; }
  public void increment() { n++; }
```

```java
  public String toString() { return Integer.toString(n); }
}

public class MutableInteger {
  private static Test monitor = new Test();
  public static void main(String[] args) {
    List v = new ArrayList();
    for(int i = 0; i < 10; i++)
      v.add(new IntValue(i));
    System.out.println(v);
    for(int i = 0; i < v.size(); i++)
      ((IntValue)v.get(i)).increment();
    System.out.println(v);
    monitor.expect(new String[] {
      "[0, 1, 2, 3, 4, 5, 6, 7, 8, 9]",
      "[1, 2, 3, 4, 5, 6, 7, 8, 9, 10]"
    });
  }
} ///:~
```

IntValue can be even simpler if privacy is not an issue, the default initialization to zero is adequate (then you don't need the constructor), and you don't care about printing it out (then you don't need the **toString( )**):

```java
class IntValue { int n; }
```

Fetching the element out and casting it is a bit awkward, but that's a feature of **ArrayList,** not of **IntValue**.

Creating read-only classes

It's possible to create your own read-only class. Here's an example:

```java
//: appendixa:Immutable1.java
// Objects that cannot be modified are immune to aliasing.
import com.bruceeckel.simpletest.*;

public class Immutable1 {
  private static Test monitor = new Test();
  private int data;
  public Immutable1(int initVal) {
    data = initVal;
  }
  public int read() { return data; }
  public boolean nonzero() { return data != 0; }
```

```
  public Immutable1 multiply(int multiplier) {
    return new Immutable1(data * multiplier);
  }
  public static void f(Immutable1 i1) {
    Immutable1 quad = i1.multiply(4);
    System.out.println("i1 = " + i1.read());
    System.out.println("quad = " + quad.read());
  }
  public static void main(String[] args) {
    Immutable1 x = new Immutable1(47);
    System.out.println("x = " + x.read());
    f(x);
    System.out.println("x = " + x.read());
    monitor.expect(new String[] {
      "x = 47",
      "i1 = 47",
      "quad = 188",
      "x = 47"
    });
  }
} ///:~
```

All data is **private**, and you'll see that none of the **public** methods modify that data. Indeed, the method that does appear to modify an object is **multiply( )**, but this creates a new **Immutable1** object and leaves the original one untouched.

The method **f( )** takes an **Immutable1** object and performs various operations on it, and the output of **main( )** demonstrates that there is no change to **x**. Thus, **x**'s object could be aliased many times without harm, because the **Immutable1** class is designed to guarantee that objects cannot be changed.

The drawback to immutability

Creating an immutable class seems at first to provide an elegant solution. However, whenever you do need a modified object of that new type, you must suffer the overhead of a new object creation, as well as potentially causing more frequent garbage collections. For some classes this is not a problem, but for others (such as the **String** class) it is prohibitively expensive.

The solution is to create a companion class that *can* be modified. Then, when you're doing a lot of modifications, you can switch to using the modifiable companion class and switch back to the immutable class when you're done.

The preceding example can be modified to show this:

```
//: appendixa:Immutable2.java
// A companion class to modify immutable objects.
import com.bruceeckel.simpletest.*;

class Mutable {
  private int data;
  public Mutable(int initVal) { data = initVal; }
  public Mutable add(int x) {
    data += x;
    return this;
  }
  public Mutable multiply(int x) {
    data *= x;
    return this;
  }
  public Immutable2 makeImmutable2() {
    return new Immutable2(data);
  }
}

public class Immutable2 {
  private static Test monitor = new Test();
  private int data;
  public Immutable2(int initVal) { data = initVal; }
  public int read() { return data; }
  public boolean nonzero() { return data != 0; }
  public Immutable2 add(int x) {
    return new Immutable2(data + x);
  }
  public Immutable2 multiply(int x) {
    return new Immutable2(data * x);
  }
  public Mutable makeMutable() {
    return new Mutable(data);
  }
  public static Immutable2 modify1(Immutable2 y) {
    Immutable2 val = y.add(12);
    val = val.multiply(3);
```

```
    val = val.add(11);
    val = val.multiply(2);
    return val;
  }
  // This produces the same result:
  public static Immutable2 modify2(Immutable2 y) {
    Mutable m = y.makeMutable();
    m.add(12).multiply(3).add(11).multiply(2);
    return m.makeImmutable2();
  }
  public static void main(String[] args) {
    Immutable2 i2 = new Immutable2(47);
    Immutable2 r1 = modify1(i2);
    Immutable2 r2 = modify2(i2);
    System.out.println("i2 = " + i2.read());
    System.out.println("r1 = " + r1.read());
    System.out.println("r2 = " + r2.read());
    monitor.expect(new String[] {
      "i2 = 47",
      "r1 = 376",
      "r2 = 376"
    });
  }
} ///:~
```

Immutable2 contains methods that, as before, preserve the immutability of the objects by producing new objects whenever a modification is desired. These are the **add( )** and **multiply( )** methods. The companion class is called **Mutable**, and it also has **add( )** and **multiply( )** methods, but these modify the **Mutable** object rather than making a new one. In addition, **Mutable** has a method to use its data to produce an **Immutable2** object and vice versa.

The two static methods **modify1( )** and **modify2( )** show two different approaches to producing the same result. In **modify1( )**, everything is done within the **Immutable2** class and you can see that four new **Immutable2** objects are created in the process. (And each time **val** is reassigned, the previous object becomes garbage.)

In the method **modify2( )**, you can see that the first action is to take the **Immutable2 y** and produce a **Mutable** from it. (This is just like calling **clone( )** as you saw earlier, but this time a different type of object is created.) Then the **Mutable** object is used to perform a lot of change operations *without* requiring the creation of many new objects. Finally, it's turned back into an **Immutable2**. Here, two new objects are created (the **Mutable** and the result **Immutable2**) instead of four.

This approach makes sense, then, when:

1. You need immutable objects and

2. You often need to make a lot of modifications or

3. It's expensive to create new immutable objects.

Immutable **Strings**

Consider the following code:

```
//: appendixa:Stringer.java
import com.bruceeckel.simpletest.*;

public class Stringer {
  private static Test monitor = new Test();
  public static String upcase(String s) {
    return s.toUpperCase();
  }
  public static void main(String[] args) {
    String q = new String("howdy");
    System.out.println(q); // howdy
    String qq = upcase(q);
    System.out.println(qq); // HOWDY
    System.out.println(q); // howdy
    monitor.expect(new String[] {
      "howdy",
      "HOWDY",
      "howdy"
    });
  }
} ///:~
```

When **q** is passed in to **upcase( )** it's actually a copy of the reference to **q**. The object this reference is connected to stays put in a single physical location. The references are copied as they are passed around.

Looking at the definition for **upcase( )**, you can see that the reference that's passed in has the name **s**, and it exists for only as long as the body of **upcase( )** is being executed. When **upcase( )** completes, the local reference

s vanishes. **upcase( )** returns the result, which is the original string with all the characters set to uppercase. Of course, it actually returns a reference to the result. But it turns out that the reference that it returns is for a new object, and the original **q** is left alone. How does this happen?

Implicit constants

If you say:

```
String s = "asdf";
String x = Stringer.upcase(s);
```

do you really want the **upcase( )** method to *change* the argument? In general, you don't, because an argument usually looks to the reader of the code as a piece of information provided to the method, not something to be modified. This is an important guarantee, since it makes code easier to write and understand.

In C++, the availability of this guarantee was important enough to put in a special keyword, **const**, to allow the programmer to ensure that a reference (pointer or reference in C++) could not be used to modify the original object. But then the C++ programmer was required to be diligent and remember to use **const** everywhere. It can be confusing and easy to forget.

Overloading '+' and the **StringBuffer**

Objects of the **String** class are designed to be immutable, using the companion-class technique shown previously. If you examine the JDK documentation for the **String** class (which is summarized a little later in this appendix), you'll see that every method in the class that appears to modify a **String** really creates and returns a brand new **String** object containing the modification. The original **String** is left untouched. Thus, there's no feature in Java like C++'s **const** to make the compiler support the immutability of your objects. If you want it, you have to wire it in yourself, like **String** does.

Since **String** objects are immutable, you can alias to a particular **String** as many times as you want. Because it's read-only, there's no possibility that one reference will change something that will affect the other references. So a read-only object solves the aliasing problem nicely.

It also seems possible to handle all the cases in which you need a modified object by creating a brand new version of the object with the modifications, as **String** does. However, for some operations this isn't efficient. A case in point is the operator '+' that has been overloaded for **String** objects. Overloading means that it has been given an extra meaning when used with a particular class. (The '+' and '+=' for **String** are the only operators that are overloaded in Java, and Java does not allow the programmer to overload any others).[5]

When used with **String** objects, the '+' allows you to concatenate **String**s together:

```
String s = "abc" + foo + "def" + Integer.toString(47);
```

You could imagine how this *might* work. The **String** "abc" could have a method **append( )** that creates a new **String** object containing "abc" concatenated with the contents of **foo**. The new **String** object would then create another new **String** that added "def," and so on.

This would certainly work, but it requires the creation of a lot of **String** objects just to put together this new **String**, and then you have a bunch of the intermediate **String** objects that need to be garbage-collected. I suspect that the Java designers tried this approach first (which is a lesson in software design—you don't really know anything about a system until you try it out in code and get something working). I also suspect they discovered that it delivered unacceptable performance.

The solution is a mutable companion class similar to the one shown previously. For **String**, this companion class is called **StringBuffer**, and the compiler automatically creates a **StringBuffer** to evaluate certain expressions, in particular when the overloaded operators '+' and '+=' are used with **String** objects. This example shows what happens:

```
//: appendixa:ImmutableStrings.java
// Demonstrating StringBuffer.
import com.bruceeckel.simpletest.*;

public class ImmutableStrings {
  private static Test monitor = new Test();
```

---

[5] C++ allows the programmer to overload operators at will. Because this can often be a complicated process (see Chapter 10 of *Thinking in C++, 2nd edition*, Prentice Hall, 2000), the Java designers deemed it a "bad" feature that shouldn't be included in Java. It wasn't so bad that they didn't end up doing it themselves, and ironically enough, operator overloading would be much easier to use in Java than in C++. This can be seen in Python (see www.Python.org) which has garbage collection and straightforward operator overloading.

```
  public static void main(String[] args) {
    String foo = "foo";
    String s = "abc" + foo + "def" + Integer.toString(47);
    System.out.println(s);
    // The "equivalent" using StringBuffer:
    StringBuffer sb =
      new StringBuffer("abc"); // Creates String!
    sb.append(foo);
    sb.append("def"); // Creates String!
    sb.append(Integer.toString(47));
    System.out.println(sb);
    monitor.expect(new String[] {
      "abcfoodef47",
      "abcfoodef47"
    });
  }
} ///:~
```

In the creation of **String s**, the compiler is doing the rough equivalent of the subsequent code that uses **sb**: a **StringBuffer** is created, and **append( )** is used to add new characters directly into the **StringBuffer** object (rather than making new copies each time). While this is more efficient, it's worth noting that each time you create a quoted character string such as **"abc"** and **"def"**, the compiler turns those into **String** objects. So there can be more objects created than you expect, despite the efficiency afforded through **StringBuffer**.

The **String** and **StringBuffer** classes

Here is an overview of the methods available for both **String** and **StringBuffer** so you can get a feel for the way they interact. These tables don't contain every single method, but rather the ones that are important to this discussion. Methods that are overloaded are summarized in a single row.

First, the **String** class:

Method	**Arguments, Overloading**	**Use**
Constructor	Overloaded: default, **String**, **StringBuffer**, **char** arrays, **byte**	Creating **String** objects.

Method	Arguments, Overloading	Use
	arrays.	
length( )		Number of characters in the **String**.
charAt( )	**int** Index	The char at a location in the **String**.
getChars( ), getBytes( )	The beginning and end from which to copy, the array to copy into, an index into the destination array.	Copy **char**s or **byte**s into an external array.
toCharArray( )		Produces a **char[]** containing the characters in the **String**.
equals( ), equals-IgnoreCase( )	A **String** to compare with.	An equality check on the contents of the two **Strings**.
compareTo( )	A **String** to compare with.	Result is negative, zero, or positive depending on the lexicographical ordering of the **String** and the argument. Uppercase and lowercase are not equal!
regionMatches( )	Offset into this **String**, the other **String** and its offset and length to compare. Overload adds "ignore case."	**boolean** result indicates whether the region matches.
startsWith( )	**String** that it might start with. Overload adds offset into argument.	**boolean** result indicates whether the **String** starts with the argument.
endsWith( )	**String** that might be a suffix of this **String**.	**boolean** result indicates whether the argument is a suffix.
indexOf( ), lastIndexOf( )	Overloaded: **char**, **char** and starting index, **String**, **String**,	Returns -1 if the argument is not found within this **String**,

Method	Arguments, Overloading	Use
	and starting index.	otherwise returns the index where the argument starts. **lastIndexOf( )** searches backward from end.
substring( )	Overloaded: starting index, starting index, and ending index.	Returns a new **String** object containing the specified character set.
concat( )	The **String** to concatenate.	Returns a new **String** object containing the original **String**'s characters followed by the characters in the argument.
replace( )	The old character to search for, the new character to replace it with.	Returns a new **String** object with the replacements made. Uses the old **String** if no match is found.
toLowerCase( ) **toUpperCase( )**		Returns a new **String** object with the case of all letters changed. Uses the old **String** if no changes need to be made.
trim( )		Returns a new **String** object with the white space removed from each end. Uses the old **String** if no changes need to be made.
valueOf( )	Overloaded: **Object**, **char[]**, **char[]** and offset and count, **boolean**, **char**, **int**, **long**, **float**, **double**.	Returns a **String** containing a character representation of the argument.
intern( )		Produces one and only one **String** reference per unique character sequence.

You can see that every **String** method carefully returns a new **String** object when it's necessary to change the contents. Also notice that if the contents don't need changing, the method will just return a reference to the original **String**. This saves storage and overhead.

Here's the **StringBuffer** class:

Method	Arguments, overloading	Use
Constructor	Overloaded: default, length of buffer to create, **String** to create from.	Create a new **StringBuffer** object.
toString( )		Creates a **String** from this **StringBuffer**.
length( )		Number of characters in the **StringBuffer**.
capacity( )		Returns current number of spaces allocated.
ensure-Capacity( )	Integer indicating desired capacity.	Makes the **StringBuffer** hold at least the desired number of spaces.
setLength( )	Integer indicating new length of character string in buffer.	Truncates or expands the previous character string. If expanding, pads with nulls.
charAt( )	Integer indicating the location of the desired element.	Returns the **char** at that location in the buffer.
setCharAt( )	Integer indicating the location of the desired element and the new **char** value for the element.	Modifies the value at that location.
getChars( )	The beginning and end from which to copy, the array to copy into, an index into the destination array.	Copy **char**s into an external array. There is no **getBytes( )** as in **String**.
append( )	Overloaded: **Object**, **String**, **char[]**, **char[]** with offset	The argument is converted to a string

Method	Arguments, overloading	Use
	and length, **boolean**, **char**, **int**, **long**, **float**, **double**.	and appended to the end of the current buffer, increasing the buffer if necessary.
insert( )	Overloaded, each with a first argument of the offset at which to start inserting: **Object**, **String**, **char[]**, **boolean**, **char**, **int**, **long**, **float**, **double**.	The second argument is converted to a string and inserted into the current buffer beginning at the offset. The buffer is increased if necessary.
reverse( )		The order of the characters in the buffer is reversed.

The most commonly used method is **append( )**, which is used by the compiler when evaluating **String** expressions that contain the '+' and '+=' operators. The **insert( )** method has a similar form, and both methods perform significant manipulations to the buffer instead of creating new objects.

Strings are special

By now you've seen that the **String** class is not just another class in Java. There are a lot of special cases in **String**, not the least of which is that it's a built-in class and fundamental to Java. Then there's the fact that a quoted character string is converted to a **String** by the compiler and the special overloaded operators '+' and '+='. In this appendix you've seen the remaining special case: the carefully-built immutability using the companion **StringBuffer** and some extra magic in the compiler.

Summary

Because all object identifiers are references in Java, and because every object is created on the heap and garbage collected only when it is no longer used, the flavor of object manipulation changes, especially when passing and returning objects. For example, in C or C++, if you wanted to initialize some piece of storage in a method, you'd probably request that the user pass the address of that piece of storage into the method. Otherwise, you'd have to worry about who was responsible for destroying that storage. Thus, the interface and understanding of such methods is more complicated. But in Java, you never have to worry about responsibility or whether an object will still exist when it is needed, since that is always taken care of for you. You can create an object at the point that it is needed (and no sooner) and never worry about the mechanics of passing around responsibility for that object; you simply pass the reference. Sometimes the simplification that this provides is unnoticed. Other times it is staggering.

The downside to all this underlying magic is twofold:

1. You always take the efficiency hit for the extra memory management (although this can be quite small), and there's always a slight amount of uncertainty about the time something can take to run (since the garbage collector can be forced into action whenever you get low on memory). For most applications, the benefits outweigh the drawbacks, and the hotspot technologies in particular have sped things up to the point where it's not much of an issue.

2. Aliasing: Sometimes you can accidentally end up with two references to the same object, which is a problem only if both references are assumed to point to a *distinct* object. This is where you need to pay a little closer attention and, when necessary, **clone( )** or otherwise duplicate an object to prevent the other reference from being surprised by an unexpected change. Alternatively, you can support aliasing for efficiency by creating immutable objects whose operations can return a new object of the same type or some different type, but never change the original object so that anyone aliased to that object sees no change.

Some people say that cloning in Java is a botched design that shouldn't be used, so they implement their own version of cloning[6] and never call the **Object.clone( )** method, thus eliminating the need to implement **Cloneable** and catch the **CloneNotSupportedException**. This is certainly a reasonable approach, and since **clone( )** is supported so rarely within the standard Java library, it is apparently a safe one as well.

---

[6] Doug Lea, who was helpful in resolving this issue, suggested this to me, saying that he simply creates a function called **duplicate( )** for each class.

Exercises

Solutions to selected exercises can be found in the electronic document *The Thinking in Java Annotated Solution Guide*, available for a small fee from *www.BruceEckel.com.*

1. Demonstrate a second level of aliasing. Create a method that takes a reference to an object but doesn't modify that reference's object. However, the method calls a second method, passing it the reference, and this second method does modify the object.

2. Create a class **MyString** containing a **String** object that you initialize in the constructor using the constructor's argument. Add a **toString( )** method and a method **concatenate( )** that appends a **String** object to your internal string. Implement **clone( )** in **MyString**. Create two **static** methods that each take a **MyString x** reference as an argument and call **x.concatenate("test")**, but in the second method call **clone( )** first. Test the two methods and show the different effects.

3. Create a class called **Battery** containing an **int** that is a battery number (as a unique identifier). Make it cloneable and give it a **toString( )** method. Now create a class called **Toy** that contains an array of **Battery** and a **toString( )** that prints out all the batteries. Write a **clone( )** for **Toy** that automatically clones all of its **Battery** objects. Test this by cloning **Toy** and printing the result.

4. Change **CheckCloneable.java** so that all of the **clone( )** methods catch the **CloneNotSupportedException** rather than passing it to the caller.

5. Using the mutable-companion-class technique, make an immutable class containing an **int**, a **double**, and an array of **char**.

6. Modify **Compete.java** to add more member objects to classes **Thing2** and **Thing4** and see if you can determine how the timings vary with complexity—whether it's a simple linear relationship or if it seems more complicated.

7. Starting with **Snake.java**, create a deep-copy version of the snake.

8. Implement the **Collection** interface in a class called **CloningCollection** by using a **private ArrayList** to provide the

container functionality. Override the **clone( )** method so that **CloningCollection** performs a "conditional deep copy"; it attempts to **clone( )** all the elements it contains, but if it cannot it leaves the reference(s) aliased.

B: Java Programming Guidelines

This appendix contains suggestions to help guide you in performing low-level program design and in writing code.

Naturally, these are guidelines and not rules. The idea is to use them as inspirations and to remember that there are occasional situations where they should be bent or broken.

Design

1. **Elegance always pays off**. In the short term it might seem like it takes much longer to come up with a truly graceful solution to a problem, but when it works the first time and easily adapts to new situations instead of requiring hours, days, or months of struggle, you'll see the rewards (even if no one can measure them). Not only does it give you a program that's easier to build and debug, but it's also easier to understand and maintain, and that's where the financial value lies. This point can take some experience to understand, because it can appear that you're not being productive while you're making a piece of code elegant. Resist the urge to hurry; it will only slow you down.

2. **First make it work, then make it fast**. This is true even if you are certain that a piece of code is really important and that it will be a principal bottleneck in your system. Don't do it. Get the system going first with as simple a design as possible. Then if it isn't going fast enough, profile it. You'll almost always discover that "your" bottleneck isn't the problem. Save your time for the really important stuff.

3. **Remember the "divide and conquer" principle**. If the problem you're looking at is too confusing, try to imagine what the basic operation of the program would be, given the existence of a magic "piece" that handles the hard parts. That "piece" is an object—write the code that uses the object, then look at the object and encapsulate *its* hard parts into other objects, etc.

4. **Separate the class creator from the class user (*client programmer*)**. The class user is the "customer" and doesn't need or want to know what's going on behind the scenes of the class. The class creator must be the expert in class design and write the class so that it can be used by the most novice programmer possible, yet still work robustly in the application. Think of the class as a *service provider* for other classes. Library use will be easy only if it's transparent.

5. **When you create a class, attempt to make your names so clear that comments are unnecessary**. Your goal should be to make the client programmer's interface conceptually simple. To this end, use method overloading when appropriate to create an intuitive, easy-to-use interface.

6. **Your analysis and design must produce, at minimum, the classes in your system, their public interfaces, and their relationships to other classes, especially base classes**. If your design methodology produces more than that, ask yourself if all the pieces produced by that methodology have value over the lifetime of the program. If they do not, maintaining them will cost you. Members of development teams tend not to maintain anything that does not contribute to their productivity; this is a fact of life that many design methods don't account for.

7. **Automate everything**. Write the test code first (before you write the class), and keep it with the class. Automate the running of your tests through a build tool—you'll probably want to use Ant, the defacto standard Java build tool. This way, any changes can be automatically verified by running the test code, and you'll immediately discover errors. Because you know that you have the safety net of your test framework, you will be bolder about making sweeping changes when you discover the need. Remember that the greatest improvements in languages come from the built-in testing provided by type checking, exception handling, etc., but those features take you only so far. You

must go the rest of the way in creating a robust system by filling in the tests that verify features that are specific to your class or program.

8. **Write the test code first (before you write the class) in order to verify that your class design is complete**. If you can't write test code, you don't know what your class looks like. In addition, the act of writing the test code will often flush out additional features or constraints that you need in the class—these features or constraints don't always appear during analysis and design. Tests also provide example code showing how your class can be used.

9. **All software design problems can be simplified by introducing an extra level of conceptual indirection**. This fundamental rule of software engineering[1] is the basis of abstraction, the primary feature of object-oriented programming. In OOP, we could also say this as: "If your code is too complicated, make more objects."

10. **An indirection should have a meaning** (in concert with guideline 9). This meaning can be something as simple as "putting commonly used code in a single method." If you add levels of indirection (abstraction, encapsulation, etc.) that don't have meaning, it can be as bad as not having adequate indirection.

11. **Make classes as atomic as possible**. Give each class a single, clear purpose—a cohesive service that it provides to other classes. If your classes or your system design grows too complicated, break complex classes into simpler ones. The most obvious indicator of this is sheer size; if a class is big, chances are it's doing too much and should be broken up.
    Clues to suggest redesign of a class are:
    1) A complicated switch statement: consider using polymorphism.
    2) A large number of methods that cover broadly different types of operations: consider using several classes.
    3) A large number of member variables that concern broadly different characteristics: consider using several classes.
    4) Other suggestions can be found in *Refactoring: Improving the Design of Existing Code* by Martin Fowler (Addison-Wesley 1999).

---

[1] Explained to me by Andrew Koenig.

12. **Watch for long argument lists**. Method calls then become difficult to write, read, and maintain. Instead, try to move the method to a class where it is (more) appropriate, and/or pass objects in as arguments.

13. **Don't repeat yourself**. If a piece of code is recurring in many methods in derived classes, put that code into a single method in the base class and call it from the derived-class methods. Not only do you save code space, but you provide for easy propagation of changes. Sometimes the discovery of this common code will add valuable functionality to your interface. A simpler version of this guideline also occurs without inheritance: If a class has methods that repeat code, factor that code into a common method and call it from the other methods.

14. **Watch for *switch* statements or chained *if-else* clauses**. This is typically an indicator of *type-check coding*, which means that you are choosing what code to execute based on some kind of type information (the exact type may not be obvious at first). You can usually replace this kind of code with inheritance and polymorphism; a polymorphic method call will perform the type checking for you and allow for more reliable and easier extensibility.

15. **From a design standpoint, look for and separate things that change from things that stay the same**. That is, search for the elements in a system that you might want to change without forcing a redesign, then encapsulate those elements in classes. You can learn much more about this concept in *Thinking in Patterns (with Java)* at *www.BruceEckel.com.*

16. **Don't extend fundamental functionality by subclassing**. If an interface element is essential to a class it should be in the base class, not added during derivation. If you're adding methods by inheriting, perhaps you should rethink the design.

17. **Less is more**. Start with a minimal interface to a class, as small and simple as you need to solve the problem at hand, but don't try to anticipate all the ways that your class *might* be used. As the class is used, you'll discover ways you must expand the interface. However, once a class is in use, you cannot shrink the interface without breaking client code. If you need to add more methods, that's fine; it won't break code. But even if new methods replace the functionality of old

ones, leave the existing interface alone (you can combine the functionality in the underlying implementation if you want). If you need to expand the interface of an existing method by adding more arguments, create an overloaded method with the new arguments; this way, you won't disturb any calls to the existing method.

18. **Read your classes aloud to make sure they're logical**. Refer to the relationship between a base class and derived class as "is-a" and member objects as "has-a."

19. **When deciding between inheritance and composition, ask if you need to upcast to the base type**. If not, prefer composition (member objects) to inheritance. This can eliminate the perceived need for multiple base types. If you inherit, users will think they are supposed to upcast.

20. **Use fields for variation in value, and method overriding for variation in behavior**. That is, if you find a class that uses state variables along with methods that switch behavior based on those variables, you should probably redesign it to express the differences in behavior within subclasses and overridden methods.

21. **Watch for overloading**. A method should not conditionally execute code based on the value of an argument. In this case, you should create two or more overloaded methods instead.

22. **Use exception hierarchies**—preferably derived from specific appropriate classes in the standard Java exception hierarchy. The person catching the exceptions can then write handlers for the specific types of exceptions, followed by handlers for the base type. If you add new derived exceptions, existing client code will still catch the exception through the base type.

23. **Sometimes simple aggregation does the job**. A "passenger comfort system" on an airline consists of disconnected elements: seat, air conditioning, video, etc., and yet you need to create many of these in a plane. Do you make private members and build a whole new interface? No—in this case, the components are also part of the public interface, so you should create public member objects. Those objects have their own private implementations, which are still safe. Be aware

that simple aggregation is not a solution to be used often, but it does happen.

24. **Consider the perspective of the client programmer and the person maintaining the code**. Design your class to be as obvious as possible to use. Anticipate the kind of changes that will be made, and design your class so that those changes will be easy.

25. **Watch out for "giant object syndrome."** This is often an affliction of procedural programmers who are new to OOP and who end up writing a procedural program and sticking it inside one or two giant objects. With the exception of application frameworks, objects represent concepts in your application, not the application itself.

26. **If you must do something ugly, at least localize the ugliness inside a class**.

27. **If you must do something nonportable, make an abstraction for that service and localize it within a class**. This extra level of indirection prevents the nonportability from being distributed throughout your program. (This idiom is embodied in the *Bridge* Pattern, among others).

28. **Objects should not simply hold some data**. They should also have well-defined behaviors. (Occasionally, "data objects" are appropriate, but only when used expressly to package and transport a group of items when a generalized container is innappropriate.)

29. **Choose composition first when creating new classes from existing classes**. You should only use inheritance if it is required by your design. If you use inheritance where composition will work, your designs will become needlessly complicated.

30. **Use inheritance and method overriding to express differences in behavior, and fields to express variations in state**. An extreme example of what not to do is to inherit different classes to represent colors instead of using a "color" field.

31. **Watch out for *variance***. Two semantically different objects may have identical actions, or responsibilities, and there is a natural temptation to try to make one a subclass of the other just to benefit from inheritance. This is called variance, but there's no real

justification to force a superclass/subclass relationship where it doesn't exist. A better solution is to create a general base class that produces an interface for both as derived classes; it requires a bit more space, but you still benefit from inheritance and will probably make an important discovery about the design.

32. **Watch out for *limitation* during inheritance**. The clearest designs add new capabilities to inherited ones. A suspicious design removes old capabilities during inheritance without adding new ones. But rules are made to be broken, and if you are working from an old class library, it may be more efficient to restrict an existing class in its subclass than it would be to restructure the hierarchy so your new class fits in where it should, above the old class.

33. **Use design patterns to eliminate "naked functionality."** That is, if only one object of your class should be created, don't bolt ahead to the application and write a comment "Make only one of these." Wrap it in a singleton. If you have a lot of messy code in your main program that creates your objects, look for a creational pattern like a factory method in which you can encapsulate that creation. Eliminating "naked functionality" will not only make your code much easier to understand and maintain, but it will also make it more bulletproof against the well-intentioned maintainers that come after you.

34. **Watch out for "analysis paralysis."** Remember that you must usually move forward in a project before you know everything, and that often the best and fastest way to learn about some of your unknown factors is to go to the next step rather than trying to figure it out in your head. You can't know the solution until you *have* the solution. Java has built-in firewalls; let them work for you. Your mistakes in a class or set of classes won't destroy the integrity of the whole system.

35. **When you think you've got a good analysis, design, or implementation, do a walkthrough**. Bring someone in from outside your group—this doesn't have to be a consultant, but can be someone from another group within your company. Reviewing your work with a fresh pair of eyes can reveal problems at a stage when it's much easier to fix them, and more than pays for the time and money "lost" to the walkthrough process.

Implementation

36. **In general, follow the Sun coding conventions**. These are available at *java.sun.com/docs/codeconv/index.html* (the code in this book follows these conventions as much as I was able). These are used for what constitutes arguably the largest body of code that the largest number of Java programmers will be exposed to. If you doggedly stick to the coding style you've always used, you will make it harder for your reader. Whatever coding conventions you decide on, ensure that they are consistent throughout the project. There is a free tool to automatically reformat Java code at *http://jalopy.sourceforge.net*. You can find a free style checker at *http://jcsc.sourceforge.net*.

37. **Whatever coding style you use, it really does make a difference if your team (and even better, your company) standardizes on it**. This means to the point that everyone considers it fair game to fix someone else's coding style if it doesn't conform. The value of standardization is that it takes less brain cycles to parse the code, so that you can focus more on what the code means.

38. **Follow standard capitalization rules**. Capitalize the first letter of class names. The first letter of fields, methods, and objects (references) should be lowercase. All identifiers should run their words together, and capitalize the first letter of all intermediate words. For example:
    ThisIsAClassName
    thisIsAMethodOrFieldName
    Capitalize *all* the letters (and use underscore word separators) of **static final** primitive identifiers that have constant initializers in their definitions. This indicates that they are compile-time constants. **Packages are a special case**—they are all lowercase letters, even for intermediate words. The domain extension (com, org, net, edu, etc.) should also be lowercase. (This was a change between Java 1.1 and Java 2.)

39. **Don't create your own "decorated" private field names**. This is usually seen in the form of prepended underscores and characters. Hungarian notation is the worst example of this, where you attach extra characters that indicate data type, use, location, etc., as if you

were writing assembly language and the compiler provided no extra assistance at all. These notations are confusing, difficult to read, and unpleasant to enforce and maintain. Let classes and packages do the name scoping for you. If you feel that you must decorate your names to prevent confusion, your code is probably too confusing anyway and should be simplified.

40. **Follow a "canonical form"** when creating a class for general-purpose use. Include definitions for **equals( )**, **hashCode( )**, **toString( )**, **clone( )** (implement **Cloneable**, or choose some other object copying approach, like serialization), and implement **Comparable** and **Serializable**.

41. **Use the JavaBeans "get," "set," and "is" naming conventions** for methods that read and change **private** fields, even if you don't think you're making a JavaBean at the time. Not only does it make it easy to use your class as a Bean, but it's a standard way to name these kinds of methods, so it will be more easily understood by the reader.

42. **For each class you create, include JUnit tests for that class** (see *www.junit.org*, and examples in Chapter 15). You don't need to remove the test code to use the class in a project, and if you make any changes, you can easily rerun the tests. This code also provides examples of how to use your class.

43. **Sometimes you need to inherit in order to access *protected* members of the base class**. This can lead to a perceived need for multiple base types. If you don't need to upcast, first derive a new class to perform the protected access. Then make that new class a member object inside any class that needs to use it, rather than inheriting.

44. **Avoid the use of *final* methods for efficiency purposes**. Use **final** only when the program is running, but not fast enough, and your profiler has shown you that a method invocation is the bottleneck.

45. **If two classes are associated with each other in some functional way (such as containers and iterators), try to make one an inner class of the other**. This not only emphasizes the association between the classes, but it allows the class name to be reused within a single package by nesting it within another class. The Java containers library does this by defining an inner **Iterator** class

inside each container class, thereby providing the containers with a common interface. The other reason you'll want to use an inner class is as part of the **private** implementation. Here, the inner class is beneficial for implementation hiding rather than the class association and prevention of namespace pollution noted above.

46. **Anytime you notice classes that appear to have high coupling with each other, consider the coding and maintenance improvements you might get by using inner classes**. The use of inner classes will not uncouple the classes, but rather make the coupling explicit and more convenient.

47. **Don't fall prey to premature optimization**. This way lies madness. In particular, don't worry about writing (or avoiding) native methods, making some methods **final**, or tweaking code to be efficient when you are first constructing the system. Your primary goal should be to prove the design. Even if the design requires a certain efficiency, *first make it work, then make it fast*.

48. **Keep scopes as small as possible so the visibility and lifetime of your objects are as small as possible**. This reduces the chance of using an object in the wrong context and hiding a difficult-to-find bug. For example, suppose you have a container and a piece of code that iterates through it. If you copy that code to use with a new container, you may accidentally end up using the size of the old container as the upper bound of the new one. If, however, the old container is out of scope, the error will be caught at compile time.

49. **Use the containers in the standard Java library**. Become proficient with their use and you'll greatly increase your productivity. Prefer **ArrayList** for sequences, **HashSet** for sets, **HashMap** for associative arrays, and **LinkedList** for stacks (rather than **Stack**, although you may want to create an adapter to give a stack interface) and queues (which may also warrant an adapter, as shown in this book). When you use the first three, you should upcast to **List**, **Set**, and **Map**, respectively, so that you can easily change to a different implementation if necessary.

50. **For a program to be robust, each component must be robust**. Use all the tools provided by Java—access control, exceptions, type checking, synchronization, and so on—in each class you create. That

way you can safely move to the next level of abstraction when building your system.

51. **Prefer compile-time errors to run-time errors**. Try to handle an error as close to the point of its occurrence as possible. Catch any exceptions in the nearest handler that has enough information to deal with them. Do what you can with the exception at the current level; if that doesn't solve the problem, rethrow the exception.

52. **Watch for long method definitions**. Methods should be brief, functional units that describe and implement a discrete part of a class interface. A method that is long and complicated is difficult and expensive to maintain, and is probably trying to do too much all by itself. If you see such a method, it indicates that, at the least, it should be broken up into multiple methods. It may also suggest the creation of a new class. Small methods will also foster reuse within your class. (Sometimes methods must be large, but they should still do just one thing.)

53. **Keep things as "*private* as possible**." Once you publicize an aspect of your library (a method, a class, a field), you can never take it out. If you do, you'll wreck somebody's existing code, forcing them to rewrite and redesign. If you publicize only what you must, you can change everything else with impunity, and since designs tend to evolve, this is an important freedom. In this way, implementation changes will have minimal impact on derived classes. Privacy is especially important when dealing with multithreading—only **private** fields can be protected against un-**synchronized** use.
Classes with package access should still have **private** fields, but it usually makes sense to give the methods of package access rather than making them **public**.

54. **Use comments liberally, and use the *javadoc* comment-documentation syntax to produce your program documentation**. However, the comments should add geniune meaning to the code; comments that only reiterate what the code is clearly expressing are annoying. Note that the typical verbose detail of Java class and method names reduce the need for some comments.

55. **Avoid using "magic numbers"**—which are numbers hard-wired into code. These are a nightmare if you need to change them, since you

never know if "100" means "the array size" or "something else entirely." Instead, create a constant with a descriptive name and use the constant identifier throughout your program. This makes the program easier to understand and much easier to maintain.

56. **When creating constructors, consider exceptions**. In the best case, the constructor won't do anything that throws an exception. In the next-best scenario, the class will be composed and inherited from robust classes only, so they will need no cleanup if an exception is thrown. Otherwise, you must clean up composed classes inside a **finally** clause. If a constructor must fail, the appropriate action is to throw an exception, so the caller doesn't continue blindly, thinking that the object was created correctly.

57. **Inside constructors, do only what is necessary to set the object into the proper state**. Actively avoid calling other methods (except for **final** methods), because those methods can be overridden by someone else to produce unexpected results during construction. (See Chapter 7 for details.) Smaller, simpler constructors are less likely to throw exceptions or cause problems.

58. **If your class requires any cleanup when the client programmer is finished with the object, place the cleanup code in a single, well-defined method**, with a name like **dispose( )** that clearly suggests its purpose. In addition, place a **boolean** flag in the class to indicate whether **dispose( )** has been called so that **finalize( )** can check for "the termination condition" (see Chapter 4).

59. **The responsibility of *finalize( )* can only be to verify "the termination condition" of an object for debugging**. (See Chapter 4.) In special cases, it might be needed to release memory that would not otherwise be released by the garbage collector. Since the garbage collector might not get called for your object, you cannot use **finalize( )** to perform necessary cleanup. For that you must create your own **dispose( )** method. In the **finalize( )** method for the class, check to make sure that the object has been cleaned up and throw a class derived from **RuntimeException** if it hasn't, to indicate a programming error. Before relying on such a scheme, ensure that **finalize( )** works on your system. (You might need to call **System.gc( )** to ensure this behavior.)

60. **If an object must be cleaned up (other than by garbage collection) within a particular scope, use the following idiom:** initialize the object and, if successful, immediately enter a **try** block with a **finally** clause that performs the cleanup.

61. **When overriding *finalize( )* during inheritance, remember to call *super.finalize( )*.** (This is not necessary if **Object** is your immediate superclass.) You should call **super.finalize( )** as the *final* act of your overridden **finalize( )** rather than the first, to ensure that base-class components are still valid if you need them.

62. **When you are creating a fixed-size container of objects, transfer them to an array**, especially if you're returning this container from a method. This way you get the benefit of the array's compile-time type checking, and the recipient of the array might not need to cast the objects in the array in order to use them. Note that the base-class of the containers library, **java.util.Collection**, has two **toArray( )** methods to accomplish this.

63. **Choose *interfaces* over *abstract* classes.** If you know something is going to be a base class, your first choice should be to make it an **interface**, and only if you're forced to have method definitions or member variables should you change it to an **abstract** class. An **interface** talks about what the client wants to do, while a class tends to focus on (or allow) implementation details.

64. **To avoid a highly frustrating experience, make sure that there is only one unpackaged class of each name anywhere in your classpath**. Otherwise, the compiler can find the identically-named other class first, and report error messages that make no sense. If you suspect that you are having a classpath problem, try looking for **.class** files with the same names at each of the starting points in your classpath. Ideally, put all your classes within packages.

65. **Watch out for accidental overloading.** If you attempt to override a base-class method and you don't quite get the spelling right, you'll end up adding a new method rather than overriding an existing method. However, this is perfectly legal, so you won't get any error message from the compiler or run-time system; your code simply won't work correctly.

66. **Watch out for premature optimization**. First make it work, then make it fast—but only if you must, and only if it's proven that there is a performance bottleneck in a particular section of your code. Unless you have used a profiler to discover a bottleneck, you will probably be wasting your time. The hidden extra cost of performance tweaks is that your code becomes less understandable and maintainable.

67. **Remember that code is read much more than it is written**. Clean designs make for easy-to-understand programs, but comments, detailed explanations, tests, and examples are invaluable. They will help both you and everyone who comes after you. If nothing else, the frustration of trying to ferret out useful information from the JDK documentation should convince you.

C: Supplements

There are several supplements to this book, including the seminar-on-CD packaged in the back and other items, seminars, and services available through the MindView web site.

This appendix describes these supplements so that you can decide if they will be helpful to you.

Foundations for Java seminar-on-CD

The CD that is bound in the back of this book is intended to provide foundation material to prepare you to learn Java from this book or from the *Thinking in Java* seminar. The bulk of the 400+ Megabytes of the CD is a full multimedia course called *Foundations for Java*. This includes the *Thinking in C* seminar, which gives you an introduction to the C syntax, operators and functions that Java syntax is based upon. In addition, it includes the first seven lectures from the 2nd edition of the *Hands-On Java* seminar-on-CD that I created and present. Although historically the entire *Hands-On Java* CD is only available for sale separately (this is also the case with the 3rd edition of the *Hands-On Java* CD), I decided to include the first seven lectures from the 2nd edition because the concepts in these lectures have not changed substantially due to the 3rd edition of the book, so it will not only provide you (along with *Thinking in C*) with a foundation for this book and the *Thinking in Java* seminar, but in addition I hope it will give you a taste for the quality and value of the *Hands-On Java CD*, 3rd edition.

The CD is described in more detail in this book's Introduction.

Thinking in Java seminar

My company MindView, Inc. provides five-day, hands-on, public and in-house training seminars based on the material in this book. Formerly called the *Hands-On Java* seminar, this is our main introductory seminar that provides the foundation for our more advanced seminars. Selected material from each chapter represents a lesson, which is followed by a monitored exercise period so that each student receives personal attention. You can find schedule and location information, testimonials, and details at *www.MindView.net.*

Hands-On Java seminar-on-CD 3rd edition

The Hands-On Java CD, 3rd edition, contains an extended version of the material from the *Thinking in Java* seminar and is based on this book. It provides at least some of the experience of the live seminar without the travel and expense. There is an audio lecture and slides corresponding to every chapter in the book. I created the seminar (more recently, with input from Andrea Provaglio, who teaches most of the live versions of the seminar) and I narrate the material on the CD. The *Hands-On Java CD* 3rd edition is for sale at *www.MindView.net.*

Designing Objects & Systems seminar

This seminar has evolved from the popular *Objects & Patterns* seminar that Bill Venners and I have given together for the past several years. The material in that seminar grew beyond its bounds, so we've split it into two seminars: this one, and the *Thinking in Patterns* seminar described later in this appendix.

An important part of good object-oriented design is well-designed objects. A major part of the seminar (distributed throughout the week) is the *Object Design Workshop*, which focuses on guidelines and idioms that help you create well-designed objects. Each of these will be explained and justified, and then discussed by the attendees. This discussion is an integral part of the workshop, aimed at facilitating a conversation about design among peers that can help everyone to learn from each other's experiences and perspectives. The Object Design Workshop will give you a specific set of practical guidelines and concrete idioms that you can draw upon in your future object designs.

The other portion of this seminar will focus on the process of developing and building a system, primarily focusing on so-called "Agile Methods" or "Lightweight Methodologies," especially Extreme Programming (XP). We will introduce methodologies in general, small tools like the "index-card" planning techniques described in *Planning Extreme Programming* (Beck and Fowler, 2002), CRC cards for object design, pair programming, iteration planning, unit testing, automated building, source-code control, and similar topics. The course will include an XP project that will be developed throughout the week.

Visit *www.MindView.net* for schedule and location information, testimonials, and details.

Thinking in Enterprise Java

This is the book that has been spawned from some of the more advanced chapters formerly in *Thinking in Java*. This book isn't a second volume of *Thinking in Java*, but rather focused coverage of the more advanced topic of enterprise programming. It is currently available (in some form) as a free download from *www.BruceEckel.com*. Because it is a separate book, it can expand to fit the necessary topics. The goal, like *Thinking in Java*, is to produce a very understandable introduction to the basics of the enterprise programming technologies so that the reader is prepared for more advanced coverage of those topics.

The list of topics will include, but is not limited to:

- Introduction to Enterprise Programming
- Network Programming with Sockets and Channels
- Remote Method Invocation (RMI)
- Connecting to Databases
- Naming and directory services
- Servlets
- Java Server Pages
- Tags, JSP Fragments and Expression Language
- Automating the creation of user interfaces
- Enterprise Java Beans
- XML
- Web Services
- Automated Testing

You can find the current state of *Thinking in Enterprise Java* at *www.BruceEckel.com*.

The J2EE seminar

This seminar introduces you to the practical development of real-world, Web-enabled, distributed applications with Java. It covers J2EE and its key technologies: Enterprise JavaBeans, Servlets, Java ServerPages, and the basic architectural patterns used to combine these technologies into maintainable applications.

You'll come out of this course with a comprehensive understanding of the J2EE architecture, of the problems it is designed to solve, how to select the most appropriate tools, and how to code your solutions.

Visit *www.MindView.net* for schedule and location information, testimonials, and details.

Thinking in Patterns (with Java)

One of the most important steps forward in object-oriented design is the "Design Patterns" movement, chronicled in *Design Patterns*, by Gamma, Helm, Johnson & Vlissides (Addison-Wesley 1995). That book shows 23 different solutions to particular classes of problems, primarily written in C++. The Design Patterns book is a source of what has now become an essential, almost mandatory, vocabulary for OOP programmers. *Thinking in Patterns* introduces the basic concepts of design patterns along with examples in Java. The book is not intended to be a simple translation of *Design Patterns*, but rather a new perspective with a Java mindset. It is not limited to the traditional 23 patterns, but also includes other ideas and problem-solving techniques as appropriate.

This book began as the last chapter in *Thinking in Java, 1st Edition*, and as ideas continued to develop it became clear that it needed to be its own book. At the time of this writing it is still in development, but the material has been worked and reworked through numerous presentations of the *Objects & Patterns* seminar (which has now been split into *Designing Objects & Systems* and the *Thinking in Patterns* seminars).

Thinking in Patterns seminar

This seminar has evolved from the *Objects & Patterns* seminar that Bill Venners and I have given for the past several years. That seminar grew too full, so we've split it into two seminars: this one, and the *Designing Objects & Systems* seminar described earlier in this appendix.

The seminar strongly follows the material and presentation in the *Thinking in Patterns* book, so the best way to find out what's in the seminar is to download the book from *www.MindView.net.*

Much of the presentation is an example of the design evolution process, starting with an initial solution and moving through the logic and process of evolving the solution to more appropriate designs. The last project shown (a trash recycling simulation) has evolved over time, and you can look at that evolution as a prototype for the way your own design can start as an adequate solution to a particular problem and evolve into a flexible approach to a class of problems.

- Dramatically increase the flexibility of your designs.
- Build in extensibility and reusability.
- Create denser communications about designs using the language of patterns.

Following each lecture there will be a set of patterns exercises for you to solve, where you are guided to write code to apply particular patterns to the solution of programming problems.

Visit *www.MindView.net* for schedule and location information, testimonials, and details.

Design consulting and reviews

My company also provides consulting, mentoring, design reviews and implementation reviews to help guide your project through its development cycle—especially your company's first Java project. Visit *www.MindView.net* for availability and details.

D: Resources

Software

The JDK from *java.sun.com*. Even if you choose to use a third-party development environment, it's always a good idea to have the JDK on hand in case you come up against what might be a compiler error. The JDK is the touchstone, and if there is a bug in it, chances are it will be well known.

The JDK documentation from *java.sun.com*, in HTML. I have never found a reference book on the standard Java libraries that wasn't out of date or missing information. Although the HTML documentation from Sun is shot-through with small bugs and is sometimes unusably terse, all the classes and methods are at least *there*. People are sometimes uncomfortable at first using an online resource rather than a printed book, but it's worth your while to get over this and open the HTML docs first so you can at least get the big picture. If you can't figure it out at that point, then reach for the printed books.

Books

Thinking in Java, 2nd Edition. Available as fully-indexed, color-syntax-highlighted HTML on the CD ROM bound in with this book, or as a free download from *www.BruceEckel.com*. Includes material that didn't make it into the third edition; see the table of contents in that book for details.

Thinking in Java, 1st Edition. Available as fully-indexed, color-syntax-highlighted HTML on the CD ROM bound in with this book, or as a free download from *www.BruceEckel.com*. Includes older material and material that was not considered interesting enough to carry through to the second edition.

Just Java 2, 5th edition by Peter van der Linden (Prentice Hall, 2002). Not only useful but fun. He often takes a similar approach as I do, and doggedly follows a problem through to discover the complete details, so he often has answers you won't find elsewhere.

Core Java 2, Volume I—Fundamentals (Prentice-Hall, 1999) and Volume II—Advanced Features (2000), by Horstmann & Cornell.. Huge, comprehensive, and the first place I go when I'm hunting for answers. The book I recommend when you've completed *Thinking in Java* and need to cast a bigger net.

The Java Class Libraries: An Annotated Reference, by Patrick Chan and Rosanna Lee (Addison-Wesley, 1997). Although sadly out of date, this is what the JDK reference *should* have been: enough description to make it usable. One of the technical reviewers for *Thinking in Java* said, "If I had only one Java book, this would be it (well, in addition to yours, of course)." I'm not as thrilled with it as he is. It's big, it's expensive, and the quality of the examples doesn't satisfy me. *But* it's a place to look when you're stuck and it seems to have more depth (and sheer size) than most alternatives.

Java Network Programming, 2nd Edition, by Elliotte Rusty Harold (O'Reilly, 2000). I didn't begin to understand Java networking until I found this book. I also find his Web site, Café au Lait, to be a stimulating, opinionated, and up-to-date perspective on Java developments, unencumbered by allegiances to any vendors. His regular updates keep up with fast-changing news about Java. See *www.cafeaulait.org*.

Design Patterns, by Gamma, Helm, Johnson and Vlissides (Addison-Wesley, 1995). The seminal book that started the patterns movement in programming.

Practical Algorithms for Programmers, by Binstock & Rex (Addison-Wesley, 1995). The algorithms are in C, so they're fairly easy to translate into Java. Each algorithm is thoroughly explained.

Analysis & design

Extreme Programming Explained, by Kent Beck (Addison-Wesley, 2000). I *love* this book. Yes, I tend to take a radical approach to things but I've always felt that there could be a much different, much better program development process, and I think XP comes pretty darn close. The only book that has had a similar impact on me was *PeopleWare* (described later), which talks primarily about the environment and dealing with corporate culture. *Extreme Programming Explained* talks about programming and turns most things, even recent "findings," on their ear. They even go so far as to say that pictures are OK as long as you don't spend too much time on them and are willing to throw them away. (You'll notice that this book does *not* have the "UML stamp of approval" on its cover.) I could see deciding to work for a company based solely on whether they used XP. Small book, small chapters, effortless to read, exciting to think about. You start imagining yourself working in such an atmosphere, and it brings visions of a whole new world.

UML Distilled, 2nd Edition, by Martin Fowler (Addison-Wesley, 2000). When you first encounter UML, it is daunting because there are so many diagrams and details. According to Fowler, most of this stuff is unnecessary, so he cuts through to the essentials. For most projects, you only need to know a few diagramming tools, and Fowler's goal is to come up with a good design rather than worry about all the artifacts of getting there. A nice, thin, readable book; the first one you should get if you need to understand UML.

The Unified Software Development Process, by Ivar Jacobsen, Grady Booch, and James Rumbaugh (Addison-Wesley, 1999). I went in fully prepared to dislike this book. It seemed to have all the makings of a boring college text. I was pleasantly surprised—although there are a few parts that have explanations that seem as if those concepts aren't clear to the authors. The bulk of the book is not only clear, but enjoyable. And best of all, the process makes a lot of practical sense. It's not Extreme Programming (and does not have their clarity about testing), but it's also part of the UML juggernaut; even if you can't get XP adopted, most people have climbed aboard the "UML is good" bandwagon (regardless of their *actual* level of experience with it), so you can probably get it adopted. I think this book should be the flagship of UML, and the one you can read after Fowler's *UML Distilled* when you want more detail.

Before you choose any method, it's helpful to gain perspective from those who are not trying to sell one. It's easy to adopt a method without really understanding what you want out of it or what it will do for you. Others are using it, which seems a compelling reason. However, humans have a strange little psychological quirk: If they want to believe something will solve their problems, they'll try it. (This is experimentation, which is good.) But if it doesn't solve their problems, they may redouble their efforts and begin to announce loudly what a great thing they've discovered. (This is denial, which is not good.) The assumption here may be that if you can get other people in the same boat, you won't be lonely, even if it's going nowhere (or sinking).

This is not to suggest that all methodologies go nowhere, but that you should be armed to the teeth with mental tools that help you stay in experimentation mode ("It's not working; let's try something else") and out of denial mode ("No, that's not really a problem. Everything's wonderful, we don't need to change"). I think the following books, read *before* you choose a method, will provide you with these tools.

Software Creativity, by Robert Glass (Prentice Hall, 1995). This is the best book I've seen that discusses *perspective* on the whole methodology issue. It's a collection of short essays and papers that Glass has written and sometimes acquired (P.J. Plauger is one contributor), reflecting his many years of thinking and study on the subject. They're entertaining and only long enough to say what's necessary; he doesn't ramble and bore you. He's not just blowing smoke, either; there are hundreds of references to other papers and studies. All programmers and managers should read this book before wading into the methodology mire.

Software Runaways: Monumental Software Disasters, by Robert Glass (Prentice Hall, 1997). The great thing about this book is that it brings to the forefront what we don't talk about: the number of projects that not only fail, but fail spectacularly. I find that most of us still think "that can't happen to me" (or "that can't happen *again*"), and I think this puts us at a disadvantage. By keeping in mind that things can always go wrong, you're in a much better position to make them go right.

Peopleware, 2nd Edition, by Tom Demarco and Timothy Lister (Dorset House, 1999). You *must* read this book. It's not only fun, but it rocks your world and destroys your assumptions. Although they have backgrounds in software development, this book is about projects and teams in general. But the focus is on the *people* and their needs, rather than the technology and its needs. They talk about creating an environment where people will be happy and productive, rather than deciding what rules those people should follow to be adequate components of a machine. This latter attitude, I think, is the biggest contributor to programmers smiling and nodding when XYZ method is adopted and then quietly doing whatever they've always done.

Secrets of Consulting: A Guide to Giving & Getting Advice Successfully, by Gerald M. Weinberg (Dorset House, 1985). A superb book, one of my all-time favorites. It's perfect if you are trying to be a consultant *or* if you're working with consultants and trying to do a better job. Short chapters, filled with stories and anecdotes that teach you how to get to the core of the issue with minimal struggle. Also see *More Secrets of Consulting*, published in 2002, or most any other Weinberg book.

Complexity, by M. Mitchell Waldrop (Simon & Schuster, 1992). This chronicles the coming together in Santa Fe, New Mexico of a group of scientists from different disciplines, to discuss real problems that their individual disciplines couldn't solve (the stock market in economics, the initial formation of life in biology, why people do what they do in sociology, etc.). By crossing physics, economics, chemistry, math, computer science, sociology, and others, a multidisciplinary approach to these problems is developing. But more important, a different way of *thinking* about these ultra-complex problems is emerging: away from mathematical determinism and the illusion that you can write an equation that predicts all behavior, and toward first *observing* and looking for a pattern and trying to emulate that pattern by any means possible. (The book chronicles, for example, the emergence of genetic algorithms.) This kind of thinking, I believe, is useful as we observe ways to manage more and more complex software projects.

Python

Learning Python, by Mark Lutz and David Ascher (O'Reilly, 1999). A nice programmer's introduction to my favorite language, an excellent companion to Java. The book includes an introduction to Jython, which allows you to combine Java and Python in a single program (the Jython interpreter is compiled to pure Java bytecodes, so there is nothing special you need to add to accomplish this). This language union promises great possibilities.

My own list of books

Listed in order of publication. Not all of these are currently available.

Computer Interfacing with Pascal & C, (Self-published via the Eisys imprint, 1988. Only available via *www.BruceEckel.com*). An introduction to electronics from back when CP/M was still king and DOS was an upstart. I used high-level languages and often the parallel port of the computer to drive various electronic projects. Adapted from my columns in the first and best magazine I wrote for, *Micro Cornucopia*. (To paraphrase Larry O'Brien, long-time editor of *Software Development Magazine*: The best computer magazine ever published—they even had plans for building a robot in a flower pot!) Alas, Micro C became lost long before the Internet appeared. Creating this book was an extremely satisfying publishing experience.

Using C++, (Osborne/McGraw-Hill, 1989). One of the first books out on C++. This is out of print and replaced by its second edition, the renamed *C++ Inside & Out*.

C++ Inside & Out, (Osborne/McGraw-Hill, 1993). As noted, actually the second edition of **Using C++**. The C++ in this book is reasonably accurate, but it's circa 1992 and *Thinking in C++* is intended to replace it. You can find out more about this book and download the source code at *www.BruceEckel.com.*

Thinking in C++, 1st Edition, (Prentice Hall, 1995).

Thinking in C++, 2nd Edition, Volume 1, (Prentice Hall, 2000). Downloadable from *www.BruceEckel.com.*

Thinking in C++, 2nd Edition, Volume 2, Coauthored with Chuck Allison (Prentice Hall, 2003). Downloadable from *www.BruceEckel.com.*

Thinking in C#, By Larry O'Brien and Bruce Eckel. This is Larry's translation of *Thinking in Java* into C#, with some help from me (Prentice Hall, 2003).

Black Belt C++: the Master's Collection, Bruce Eckel, editor (M&T Books, 1994). Out of print. A collection of chapters by various C++ luminaries based on their presentations in the C++ track at the Software Development Conference, which I chaired. The cover on this book stimulated me to gain control over all future cover designs.

Thinking in Java, 1st Edition, (Prentice Hall, 1998). The first edition of this book won the *Software Development Magazine* Productivity Award, the *Java Developer's Journal* Editor's Choice Award, and the *JavaWorld Reader's Choice Award for best book.* On the CD ROM in the back of this book, and downloadable from *www.BruceEckel.com.*

Thinking in Java, 2nd Edition, (Prentice Hall, 2000). This edition won the *JavaWorld Editor's Choice Award for best book.* On the CD ROM in the back of this book, and downloadable from *www.BruceEckel.com.*

Index

Please note that some names will be duplicated in capitalized form. Following Java style, the capitalized names refer to Java classes, while lowercase names refer to a general concept.

!

&

.

@

[

^

|

+

<

=

>

A

B

C

D

E

F

G

H

I

J

K

L

M

N

O

P

Q

R

S

T

U

V

W

X

Y

Z

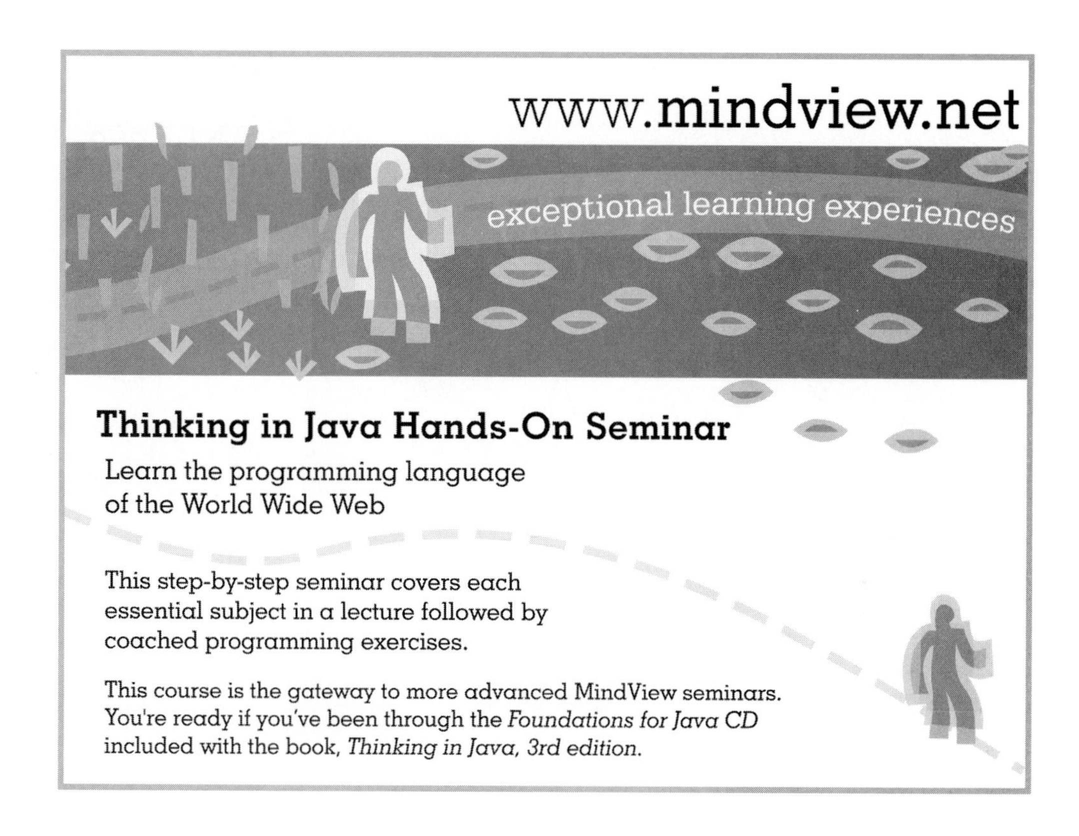

www.mindview.net
exceptional learning experiences
Thinking in Java Hands-On Seminar
Learn the programming language
of the World Wide Web
This step-by-step seminar covers each
essential subject in a lecture followed by
coached programming exercises.
This course is the gateway to more advanced MindView seminars.
You're ready if you've been through the Foundations for Java CD
included with the book, Thinking in Java, 3rd edition.

Bruce Eckel's
Hands On Java
Seminar
Book
Links
Help

LICENSE AGREEMENT FOR MindView, Inc.'s
Foundations for Java CD ROM
by Bruce Eckel and Chuck Allison
This CD is provided together with the book "Thinking in Java, 3rd edition."

READ THIS AGREEMENT BEFORE USING THIS "Foundations for Java" (Hereafter called "CD"). BY USING THE CD YOU AGREE TO BE BOUND BY THE TERMS AND CONDITIONS OF THIS AGREEMENT. IF YOU DO NOT AGREE TO THE TERMS AND CONDITIONS OF THIS AGREEMENT, IMMEDIATELY RETURN THE UNUSED CD FOR A FULL REFUND OF MONIES PAID, IF ANY.

SOFTWARE REQUIREMENTS
The purpose of this CD is to provide the Content, not the associated software necessary to view the Content. The Content of this CD is in HTML for viewing with a Web Browser (it has been tested with Microsoft Internet Explorer 6 and Mozilla; see *www.Mozilla.org*) and an MP3 player such as the free RealPlayer from *www.Real.com*. It is your responsibility to correctly install the appropriate software for your system.

The text, images, and other media included on this CD ("Content") and their compilation are licensed to you subject to the terms and conditions of this Agreement by MindView, Inc., having a place of business at 5343 Valle Vista, La Mesa, CA 91941. Your rights to use other programs and materials included on the CD are also governed by separate agreements distributed with those programs and materials on the CD (the "Other Agreements"). In the event of any inconsistency between this Agreement and the Other Agreements, this Agreement shall govern. By using this CD, you agree to be bound by the terms and conditions of this Agreement. MindView, Inc. owns title to the Content and to all intellectual property rights therein, except insofar as it contains materials that are proprietary to third-party suppliers. All rights in the Content except those expressly granted to you in this Agreement are reserved to MindView, Inc. and such suppliers as their respective interests may appear.

1. LIMITED LICENSE
MindView, Inc. grants you a limited, nonexclusive, nontransferable license to use the Content on a single dedicated computer (excluding network servers). This Agreement and your rights hereunder shall automatically terminate if you fail to comply with any provisions of this Agreement or any of the Other Agreements. Upon such termination, you agree to destroy the CD and all

copies of the CD, whether lawful or not, that are in your possession or under your control.

2. ADDITIONAL RESTRICTIONS

a. You shall not (and shall not permit other persons or entities to) directly or indirectly, by electronic or other means, reproduce (except for archival purposes as permitted by law), publish, distribute, rent, lease, sell, sublicense, assign, or otherwise transfer the Content or any part thereof.

b. You shall not (and shall not permit other persons or entities to) use the Content or any part thereof for any commercial purpose or merge, modify, create derivative works of, or translate the Content.

c. You shall not (and shall not permit other persons or entities to) obscure MindView's or its suppliers copyright, trademark, or other proprietary notices or legends from any portion of the Content or any related materials.

3. PERMISSIONS

a. Except as noted in the Contents of the CD, you must treat this software just like a book. However, you may copy it onto a computer to be used and you may make archival copies of the software for the sole purpose of backing up the software and protecting your investment from loss. By saying, "just like a book," MindView, Inc. means, for example, that this software may be used by any number of people and may be freely moved from one computer location to another, so long as there is no possibility of its being used at one location or on one computer while it is being used at another. Just as a book cannot be read by two different people in two different places at the same time, neither can the software be used by two different people in two different places at the same time.

b. You may show or demonstrate the un-modified Content in a live presentation, live seminar, or live performance as long as you attribute all material of the Content to MindView, Inc.

c. Other permissions and grants of rights for use of the CD must be obtained directly from MindView, Inc. at http://www.MindView.net. (Bulk copies of the CD may also be purchased at this site.)

4. DISCLAIMER OF WARRANTY

The Content and CD are provided "AS IS" without warranty of any kind, either express or implied, including, without limitation, any warranty of merchantability and fitness for a particular purpose. The entire risk as to the results and performance of the CD and Content is assumed by you. MindView, Inc. and its suppliers assume no responsibility for defects in the CD, the accuracy of the Content, or omissions in the CD or the Content. MindView, Inc. and its suppliers do not warrant, guarantee, or make any representations regarding the use, or the results of the use, of the product in terms of correctness, accuracy, reliability, currentness, or otherwise, or that the Content will meet your needs, or that operation of the CD will be uninterrupted or error-free, or that any defects in the CD or Content will be corrected. MindView, Inc. and its suppliers shall not be liable for any loss, damages, or costs arising from the use of the CD or the interpretation of the Content. Some states do not allow exclusion or limitation of implied warranties or limitation of liability for incidental or consequential damages, so all of the above limitations or exclusions may not apply to you.

In no event shall MindView, Inc. or its suppliers' total liability to you for all damages, losses, and causes of action (whether in contract, tort, or otherwise) exceed the amount paid by you for the CD.
MindView, Inc., and Prentice Hall, Inc. specifically disclaim the implied warrantees of merchantability and fitness for a particular purpose. No oral or written information or advice given by MindView, Inc., Prentice Hall, Inc., their dealers, distributors, agents or employees shall create a warrantee. You may have other rights, which vary from state to state.

IN NO EVENT SHALL MINDVIEW, INC., BRUCE ECKEL, CHUCK ALLISON, PRENTICE HALL, NOR ANYONE ELSE WHO HAS BEEN INVOLVED IN THE CREATION, PRODUCTION OR DELIVERY OF THE PRODUCT BE LIABLE TO ANY PARTY UNDER ANY LEGAL THEORY FOR DIRECT, INDIRECT, SPECIAL, INCIDENTAL, OR CONSEQUENTIAL DAMAGES, INCLUDING LOST PROFITS, BUSINESS INTERRUPTION, LOSS OF BUSINESS INFORMATION, OR ANY OTHER PECUNIARY LOSS, OR FOR PERSONAL INJURIES, ARISING OUT OF THE USE OF THIS CD AND ITS CONTENT, OR ARISING OUT OF THE INABILITY TO USE ANY RESULTING PROGRAM, EVEN IF MINDVIEW, INC., OR ITS PUBLISHER HAS BEEN ADVISED OF THE POSSIBILITY OF SUCH DAMAGE. MINDVIEW, INC. SPECIFICALLY DISCLAIMS ANY WARRANTIES, INCLUDING, BUT NOT LIMITED TO, THE IMPLIED WARRANTIES OF MERCHANTABILITY AND FITNESS FOR A PARTICULAR PURPOSE. THE SOURCE CODE AND DOCUMENTATION PROVIDED HEREUNDER IS ON AN "AS IS" BASIS, WITHOUT ANY ACCOMPANYING SERVICES FROM MINDVIEW, INC., AND MINDVIEW, INC. HAS NO OBLIGATIONS TO PROVIDE MAINTENANCE, SUPPORT, UPDATES, ENHANCEMENTS, OR MODIFICATIONS.

This CD is provided as a supplement to the book "Thinking in Java 3rd edition." The sole responsibility of Prentice Hall will be to provide a replacement CD in the event that the one that came with the book is defective. This replacement warrantee shall be in effect for a period of sixty days from the purchase date. MindView, Inc. does not bear any additional responsibility for the CD.

NO TECHNICAL SUPPORT IS PROVIDED WITH THIS CD ROM

Foundations for Java

Multimedia Seminar-on-CD ROM

WARNING: BEFORE OPENING THE DISC PACKAGE, CAREFULLY READ THE TERMS AND CONDITIONS OF THE LICENSE AGREEMENT & WARANTEE LIMITATION ON THE PREVIOUS PAGES.

The CD ROM packaged with this book is a multimedia seminar consisting of synchronized slides and audio lectures. The goal of this seminar is to introduce you to the fundamentals necessary for you to move on to Java. The CD also contains a link to the source code for this book, a link to the HTML version of this book, and the 1st and 2nd editions of this book in HTML form.

This CD ROM will work with most computers that have a sound system, including Windows, Linux, and Mac OS/9 and OS/10. However, you must:

1. Install a web browser on your machine, if you don't already have one. Tested browsers include Mozilla (*www.Mozilla.org*) and the most recent version of Microsoft's Internet Explorer.
2. Install an MP3 sound player on your machine. The slides are designed to work either with the free RealPlayer from *www.Real.com* or with another MP3 player (newer machines come with MP3 players pre-installed).
3. At this point you should be able to play the lectures on the CD. Using the the most recent version of Internet Explorer or the Mozilla Web browser, open the file **Install.html** that you'll find on the CD. This will introduce you to the CD and provide further instructions about the use of the CD. Note that on Windows machines and some Linux machines, the CD should auto-run when you insert it in your CD player.